THE *Virgin* ENCYCLOPE

COUNTRY MUSIC

WIGAN & !
CC

COLIN LARKIN

IN ASSC

Dedicated To Johnny Cash

First published in Great Britain in 1998 by
VIRGIN BOOKS
an imprint of Virgin Publishing Ltd
332 Ladbroke Grove, London W10 5AH

A catalogue record for this book is available from the British Library

ISBN 0 7535 0236 4

Written, edited and produced by
MUZE UK Ltd
to whom all editorial enquiries should be sent
Iron Bridge House, 3 Bridge Approach, Chalk Farm, London NW1 8BD

Editor In Chief: Colin Larkin
Production Editor: Susan Pipe
Editorial and Research Assistant: Nic Oliver
Copy Editor: Sarah Lavelle
Typographic Design Consultant: Roger Kohn
Special thanks to Trev Huxley, Anthony Patterson, Paul Zullo
and all the Klugettes at Muze Inc.,
and to Rob Shreeve of Virgin Publishing.
Typeset by Old John Robertson Studios
Printed and bound in Great Britain by Butler & Tanner Ltd, Frome and London

INTRODUCTION

This new edition proudly bears the Virgin banner. *The Virgin Encyclopedia Of Country Music* is one in the major series of books taken from the *Encyclopedia Of Popular Music*. Other titles already available are:

The Virgin Encyclopedia Of Sixties Music
The Virgin Encyclopedia Of Seventies Music
The Virgin Encyclopedia Of Eighties Music
The Virgin Encyclopedia Of Popular Music
The Virgin Encyclopedia Of Indie & New Wave
The Virgin Encyclopedia Of The Blues
The Virgin Encyclopedia Of R&B And Soul
in preparation
The Virgin Encyclopedia Of Reggae
The Virgin Encyclopedia Of Fifties Music

It is no longer necessary to feel coy about liking Country music in the UK. The stigma attached to the genre has been transformed over the past three decades. Those early converts were, like me, probably first hooked by the likes of The Flying Burrito Brothers or albums such as *Sweetheart Of The Rode*o or Gram Parsons' *GP*. Although I was familiar with Hank Williams often being played on the BBC and Slim Whitman being mobbed when he played London in the early 50s, I just didn't get it. Having often travelled to the USA, particularly over the past few years, I now understand the power and importance it commands. It is the biggest-grossing area of popular music in the USA thanks to that bit of land in between San Francisco and New York. Major country artists are front page news and the songwriting hives in Nashville and Austin make the former glories of Tin Pan Alley and the Brill Building look positively pedestrian. As I write, Shania Twain has just entered the UK pop chart at number 10, a significant breakthrough, when you consider her album, *The Woman In Me* is fast approaching 10 million units in the USA alone. Garth Brooks, has overtaken Elvis Presley as the biggest selling artist in the history of popular music. None of this is news to the serious followers of the genre, they have known it for years. In the UK, magazines such as *Country Music People* flourish, seemingly unaffected by the world suddenly waking up to music that they have been quietly pioneering for many years. They gave us a pretty bad review for the previous edition; this was particularly disappointing as our main contributors are contributors to that magazine. We almost had the extra assistance of Tony Byworth, but all the work he did in making amendments and corrections were left on an aeroplane between the USA and UK. Somebody somewhere has a copy of *The Who's Who Of Country Music*, heavily corrected edition. We in turn have listened and acted. For example, I hope Jim Marshall is happy with our revised Jimmie Rodgers entry (written by Hugh T. Wilson) and our special Everly Brothers entry created for this book. Our pillar of salt for ol' timey stuff is the aforementioned Mr Wilson and my special thanks go to him and Spencer Leigh for their continuing efforts. The other new entries were written by myself and the brilliantly adaptable Alex Ogg. Missing in action: John Philibert, please phone home!

ENTRY STYLE

Albums, EPs (extended play 45s), newspapers, magazines, television programmes, films and stage musicals are referred to in italics. All song titles appear in single quotes. We spell rock 'n' roll like this. There are two main reasons for spelling rock 'n' roll with 'n' as opposed to 'n'. First, historical precedent: when the term was first coined in the 50s, the popular spelling was 'n'. Second, the 'n' is not simply an abbreviation of 'and' (in which case 'n' would apply) but a phonetic representation of n as a sound. ~~~ ~~~ ~~ as inverted commas rather than as apostrophes. The further reading section at the end of each entry has been expanded to give the reader a much wider choice of available books. These are not necessarily recommended titles but we have attempted to leave out any publication that has little or no merit.

We have also started to add videos at the ends of the entries. Again, this is an area that is expanding faster than we can easily cope with, but there are many items in the videography and further items in the filmography, which is another new section we have decided to include. Release dates in keeping with albums attempt to show the release date in the country of origin. We have also tried to include both US and UK titles where applicable.

ALBUM RATING

Due to many requests from our readers we have now decided to rate all albums. All new releases are reviewed either by myself or by our team of contributors. We also take into consideration the review ratings of the leading music journals and critics' opinions.

Our system is slightly different to most 5 Star ratings

in that we rate according to the artist in question's work. Therefore, a 4 Star album from Waylon Jennings may have the overall edge over a 4 Star album by Rusty Draper. Sorry Rusty.

Our ratings are carefully made, and consequently you will find we are very sparing with 5 Star and 1 Star albums.

Outstanding in every way. A classic and therefore strongly recommended. No comprehensive record collection should be without this album.

Excellent. A high standard album from this artist and therefore highly recommended.

Good. By the artist's usual standards and therefore recommended.

Disappointing. Flawed or lacking in some way.

Poor. An album to avoid unless you are a completist.

PLAGIARISM

In maintaining the largest text database of popular music in the world we are naturally protective of its content. We license to approved licensees only. It is both flattering and irritating to see our work reproduced without credit. Time and time again over the past few years I have read an obituary, when suddenly: hang on, I wrote that line. Secondly, it has come to our notice that other companies attempting to produce their own rock or pop encyclopedias use our material as a core. Flattering this might also be, but highly illegal. We have therefore dropped a few more textual 'depth charges' in addition to the original ones. Be warned.

ACKNOWLEDGEMENTS

Our in-house editorial team is lean and efficient. Our Database is now a fully grown child and needs only regular food, attention and love. Thanks to the MUZE UK team and their efficiency while the cat's away: Susan Pipe, Nic Oliver and Sarah Lavelle and the cotton pickin' Roger Kohn's parrot. Our outside contributors are further reduced in number, as we now write and amend all our existing text. However, we could not function without the continuing efforts and dedication of Big John Martland, Alex Ogg, Brian Hogg. Both Hugh T. Wilson and Spencer Leigh continue to supply their specialist knowledge and experience.

Other past contributors' work may appear in this volume and I acknowledge once again; Simon Adams, David Ades, Mike Atherton, Gavin Badderley, Alan Balfour, Michael Barnett, Steve Barrow, John Bauldie, Lol Bell-Brown, Johnny Black, Chris Blackford, Pamela Boniface, Keith Briggs, Michael Ian Burgess, Paul M. Brown, Tony Burke, John Child, Linton Chiswick, Rick Christian, Alan Clayson, Tom Collier, Paul Cross, Bill Dahl, Norman Darwen, Roy Davenport, Peter Doggett, Kevin Eden, John Eley, Lars Fahlin, John Fordham, Per Gardin, Ian Garlinge, Mike Gavin, Andy Hamilton, Harry Hawk, Mark Hodkinson, Mike Hughes, Arthur Jackson, Mark Jones, Max Jones, Simon Jones, Ian Kenyon, Dave Laing, Steve Lake, Paul Lewis, Graham Lock, John Masouri, Bernd Matheja, Chris May, Dave McAleer, Ian McCann, David McDonald, York Membery, Toru Mitsui, Greg Moffitt, Nick Morgan, Michael Newman, Pete Nickols, Lyndon Noon, Zbigniew Nowara, James Nye, Ken Orton, Ian Peel, Dave Penny, Alan Plater, Barry Ralph, John Reed, Emma Rees, Lionel Robinson, Johnny Rogan, Alan Rowett, Jean Scrivener, Roy Sheridan, Dave Sissons, Neil Slaven, Chris Smith, Steve Smith, Mitch Solomons, Christopher Spencer, Jon Staines, Mike Stephenson, Sam Sutherland, Jeff Tamarkin, Ray Templeton, Liz Thompson, Gerard Tierney, John Tobler, Adrian T'Vell, Pete Wadeson, Frank Warren, Ben Watson, Pete Watson, Simon Williams, Val Wilmer, Dave Wilson and Barry Witherden.

Record company press offices are often bombarded with my requests for biogs and review copies. Theirs is a thankless task, but thanks anyway, especially to Alan Robinson of Demon, Sue and Dave Williams at Frontier, Mal Smith at Delta, Richard Wooton and his colleagues at the Manor House and Pat Naylor and Nicola Powell at Ryko/Hannibal.

Thanks for the enthusiasm and co-operation of all our new colleagues at Virgin Publishing under the guidance of the delagatory Rob Shreeve, in particular to sex-siren Roz Scott who is so efficient.

To our owners at Muze Inc., who feed the smooth running of the UK operation and are the business partners I always knew I wanted but never knew where to find. To all colleagues at the office on 304 Hudson Street in New York. In particular to the committed Tony Patterson, the absolutely dressed Paul Zullo, Steve 'Numbers' Figard, Marc 'Guitar' Miller, Mike Nevins, Uri's brother, Gary Geller, all other Klugettes and the graciously modest Trev Huxley. And lastly to Dave and Sabra for some 'real country living' at Cherry Plain and my invaluable tin lids, who get better the older they get: you don't miss your water till your wells run dry.

Colin Larkin, March 1998

ACKLES, STEPHEN

b. Norway. The 90s Norwegian country singer Stephen Ackles plays a powerful brand of rock 'n' roll country that shows how strongly he has been influenced by Jerry Lee Lewis. Lewis's fiddle player, Kenneth Lovelace, plays on *If This Ain't Music*, which was produced by Narvel Felts. Felts joins Ackles for 'Remember' in which they recall their favourite acts. *If This Ain't Music* was voted the Best Country Album Of The Year in a Norwegian poll. Following this, he was invited to make an album in Nashville, again supported by Lovelace, but also using the instrumental talents of James Burton and Glen D. Hardin, and singing duets with Waylon Jennings and Linda Gail Lewis.
● ALBUMS: *If This Ain't Music* (Fox 1991)★★, *Hey You!* (Columbia 1992)★★★.

ACUFF, ROY

b. Roy Claxton Acuff, 15 September 1903, Maynardsville, Tennessee, USA, d. 23 November 1992. The third of five children born to Neill and Ida Acuff, Roy learned to play the harmonica and Jew's harp as a child and was involved with music from an early age. His father played the fiddle, his mother the piano and guitar and Roy sang with his siblings. School did not appeal to him in the early years and although he showed some interest in poetry and verse and excelled at sports, he was frequently in trouble. In 1919, the family moved to Knoxville suburb, Fountain City, and he attended Central High School. After leaving school he developed a reputation as a fighter which caused his parents concern and sometimes landed him in court. Roy auditioned unsuccessfully for a stage show in Chicago and did a few jobs locally in Knoxville. In 1929, the family moved to the Knoxville suburb of Arlington and he played semi-professional baseball. He seemed set to join the New York Yankees but during the summer of 1929 he suffered severe sunstroke and collapsed. He also had a nervous breakdown that resulted in him being bedridden for most of 1930. During these long months, he learned to play his father's fiddle and listened to the records of early country artists.

In 1931, he began to appear on the streets, where he first learned to play the yo-yo that he later featured in his stage show. Realizing that a baseball career was impossible, he turned to country music, later stating: 'Everything was dark, until I found the fiddle. If it had not come along I don't know what I would have become.' In 1932, he toured with Dr Hauer's Medicine Show, where he played fiddle and took part in skits that were designed to encourage the watchers to buy Mocoton Tonic, 'the cure for everything'. Encouraged by his success, he began to play with other musicians in the Knoxville area. He also appeared with his brother Claude (always called 'Spot') and Red Jones as the Three Rolling Stones. In 1934, he appeared on radio with Jess Easterday, Clell Summey and Bob Wright as the Tennessee Crackerjacks on WROL Knoxville before moving to WNOX, where six days a week they presented *Mid-Day Merry-Go-Round*. In 1935, they became Roy Acuff and the Crazy Tennesseans and the same year he began to sing a song called 'The Great Speckled Bird', which he had first heard sung by Charles Swain and his group, the Black Shirts. (The title came from the Bible and although several people later claimed ownership of the song, the original six verses were written by Reverend Guy Smith and set to a traditional English melody very similar to 'I'm Thinking Tonight Of My Blue Eyes'.) He made his first recordings in Chicago for ARC Records in October 1936, under the direction of William Calloway, who it seems, had been looking for someone to record that song. They recorded 20 sides in all and Acuff later commented, 'He wanted "The Bird", he didn't want me.' Two songs, 'When Lulu's Gone' and 'Doin' It The Old Fashioned Way', were self-penned numbers of a somewhat risqué nature and were released as being by the Bang Boys, when Acuff refused to let the company use his name on them.

Further recordings were made in 1937, after which Acuff stopped recording because he felt that Calloway and ARC were not treating him well. Acuff made a somewhat inauspicious debut on the *Grand Ole Opry* in October 1937, playing two fiddle tunes and attempting a crooning version of 'The Bird'. A return visit in February 1938, although hardly sensational, created such interest among listeners that WSM offered him radio spots and concert appearances with the Delmore Brothers. He again sang 'The Bird', and Clell Summey made history by playing a dobro on the *Opry* for the first time. Harry Stone, the WSM manager, suggested that the name Crazy Tennesseans was not complimentary to the state, and that since they came from the Smoky Mountains they should use that name. Accordingly, when they appeared a week later it was as Roy Acuff and The Smoky Mountain Boys. In 1938, ARC became part of Columbia and Acuff was persuaded by Art Satherley to sign a recording contract with that company. A single release of the Carter Family song 'Wabash Cannonball' became one of the most popular records of the year and won him a gold disc. In 1939 he toured the USA while various changes occurred in his band. He recorded in Dallas in April 1940 and the following month travelled to Hollywood, where he appeared with his band in the Republic Pictures film *Grand Ole Opry*. During the making of the film he was suffering from appendicitis and had to be strapped up during filming. On completion he underwent surgery in Nashville and only missed one *Opry* show. His band's popularity grew, with many members establishing their own reputation, especially Pete Kirby who, as Bashful Brother Oswald, provided excellent dobro playing and harmony vocals. It was estimated that Acuff earned more than $200,000 in 1942.

He became great friends with Fred Rose, who at the time had a daily piano programme on WSM, and in 1943, the two men founded the Acuff-Rose Publication Company to provide protection for songwriters and performers. Acuff-Rose was the first country music publishing house in the States and played a major part in the development of Nashville becoming Music City USA. In later years, when asked if he and Fred Rose had ever imagined that their creation would turn out to be such a tremendous success, Acuff replied: 'Not at all. I only thought possibly it might do good. But I never had any idea it would turn out like this, grow this big. At the time Fred and I were like two blind pigs scratching for an acorn.' Rose, who wrote the Sophie Tucker hit 'Red Hot Mama', initially did not like country music but changed his mind after standing in the wings of the *Opry* one night and watching Acuff sing 'Don't Make Me Go To Bed And I'll Be Good'.

After twice declining the invitation, in 1944 and 1946, Acuff was finally persuaded to run for state governor in 1948. He stood as a Republican and although he failed to be elected, he polled more votes than any previous Republican candidate in Tennessee. He later said, 'I could have won, if I had run as a Democrat, been a puppet and made campaign promises.' He took defeat with no regrets, saying, 'As a Governor I would have been just another politician. As a singer I can be Roy Acuff.' He made further film appearances in *Hi Neighbor* (1942), *O' My Darling Clementine* (1943) (not to be confused with the later Henry Fonda film *Oh My Darling Clementine*), *Cowboy Canteen* (1944), *Sing Neighbor Sing* (1944), *Night Train To Memphis* (1946), *Smoky Mountain Melody* (1948) and *Home In San Antone* (1948). Acuff resisted any further attempts to lure him back into films. He reckoned: 'Give me radio every time, if you get scared you can hang on the mike. In the movies there's nothing to hold you up.'

In 1949, he was featured in the *Opry*'s first overseas tour when he visited Europe with other major stars, including Hank Williams. He had great success with recordings of such songs as 'Wreck On The Highway' and 'Fireball Mail', and enjoyed US country and pop chart success in 1944 with 'The Prodigal Son' and 'I'll Forgive You But I Can't Forget'. Other Top 10 country hits in the 40s included 'Jole Blon' and 'Waltz Of The Wind'. During World War II, he had success with his recording of 'Cowards Over Pearl Harbour' and his fame was such that Japanese troops are reported to have yelled 'To hell with Roosevelt! To hell with Babe Ruth! To hell with Roy Acuff!' before making suicidal charges on the Pacific island of Okinawa. In 1947, he founded the Dunbar Cave Resort, a country music park near Clarksville, Tennessee, which quickly proved to be an astute investment and with his wife's business ability and the Acuff-Rose interest, he soon acquired a considerable fortune. He maintained a very active schedule during the 50s and 60s, with concert appearances in the States, *Opry* shows and 18 overseas tours. He played at Burtonwood, England, during a 1951 European tour and in 1953, toured Japan and Korea. A private tour of Australia in 1959, drew a review from a Sydney critic that stated: 'First there was Mr. Acuff - a clear cut case of strangulation of the tonsils.' He parted from Columbia in 1952 and recorded for MGM, Decca and Capitol and although his records sold, he had few chart successes. He and Fred Rose formed Hickory records and Acuff had a Top 10 country chart hit in 1958 with 'Once More'. In 1962, the Country Music Association, grateful for his services to the music over the years, elected him the first living member of the Country Music Hall Of Fame. The plaque described him as the 'King Of Country Music'. In July 1965, he was seriously injured in a car crash, but he soon recovered and was back at the *Opry*. He cancelled his personal concerts for the year but in 1966 and 1967, he played in Vietnam and other

Far East venues. Acuff cut back severely on his touring in the early 70s but still maintained a prominent role at the *Opry*. He was one of the many stars to record with the Nitty Gritty Dirt Band in 1972, when they recorded their triple album *Will The Circle Be Unbroken*, and continued to record in his own right, including the re-recording of some of his earlier numbers for different labels. In 1971, accompanied by Charlie Collins on guitar, he recorded 20 tunes playing the fiddle for an instrumental album that remains unreleased.

Acuff became involved with the *Opry*land complex and figured prominently in the opening night ceremonies for the new *Opry* in 1974. He not only sang the 'Wabash Cannonball', but also endeavoured to teach President Nixon how to play with a yo-yo. The same year, at the age of 70, he claimed the record of being the oldest person to make the US country charts. The simplicity of his songs with their tuneful melodies had been the secret of his success over the years. His recordings were never aimed at the charts; in the main they were either of a religious nature, about mother and/or home or train songs. They appealed to ordinary people and this is what led to his very considerable record sales over his long career. He had recorded duets with several artists including Kitty Wells ('Goodbye, Mr. Brown'), June Stearns ('Before I Met You'), Bill Anderson ('I Wonder If God Likes Country Music') and Boxcar Willie ('Fireball Mail'). His last country chart hit was 'Old Time Sunshine Song', a modest number 97 in 1974.

In 1992, Acuff's health began to deteriorate, but whenever possible he maintained appearances on the *Opry*, even though he frequently had to resort to having a chair in the wings. At 6 am on 23 November 1992, he died of congestive heart failure. He had left instructions that he did not wish his funeral to become a showbusiness event, as had happened with some other stars; in accordance with his wishes only the family and a few close friends were present when he was buried at 10 am that same day.

● ALBUMS: *Songs Of The Smoky Mountains* (Columbia 1949)★★★, *Old Time Barn Dance* (Columbia 1949)★★★★, *Songs Of The Saddle* (Columbia 1950)★★★, *Songs Of The Smoky Mountains* (Capitol 1955)★★★, *Favorite Hymns* (MGM 1958)★★★, *The Great Speckled Bird* (Harmony 1958)★★★★, *That Glory Bound Train* (Harmony 1961)★★★, *Once More* (Hickory 1961)★★★, *Hymn Time* (MGM 1962)★★★, *Star Of The Grand Ole Opry* (Hickory 1963)★★★, *The World Is His Stage* (Hickory 1963)★★★, *Sings American Folk Songs* (Hickory 1963)★★★, with the Jordanaires *Handclapping Gospel Songs* (Hickory 1963)★★★★, *Roy Acuff & His Smoky Mountain Boys* (1963)★★★★, *The King Of Country Music* (Hickory 1963)★★★, *Roy Acuff: Star Of The Grand Ole Opry* (Hickory 1963)★★★, *The Great Roy Acuff* (Capitol 1964)★★★, *Country Music Hall Of Fame* (Hickory 1964)★★★, *Great Train Songs* (Hickory 1965)★★★★, *The Great Roy Acuff* (Harmony 1965)★★★, *Roy Acuff (How Beautiful Heaven Must Be)* (Metro/MGM 1965)★★★, *The Voice Of Country Music* (Capitol 1965)★★★, *Sings Hank Williams* (Hickory 1966)★★★, *Waiting For My Call To Glory* (Harmony 1966)★★★, *Sings Famous Opry Favorites* (Hickory 1967)★★★, *Living Legend* (Hickory 1968)★★★, *Roy Acuff Country* (1969)★★★, *Treasury Of Country Hits* (Hickory 1969)★★★, *Roy Acuff Time* (Hickory 1970)★★★, *I Saw The*

Light (Hickory 1970)★★★, *Night Train To Memphis* (Harmony 1970)★★★, *Who Is Roy Acuff* (Hickory 1973)★★★, *Back In The Country* (Hickory 1974)★★★, *Smoky Mountain Memories* (1975)★★★★, *That's Country* (1975)★★★, *Sings Hank Williams* (Hickory 1980)★★★★, *Back In The Country* (1981)★★★.
● COMPILATIONS: *All Time Greatest Hits* (Hickory 1962)★★★★, *Greatest Hits* (Columbia 1970)★★★, *Greatest Hits Volume 1* (Elektra 1978)★★★★, *Greatest Hits Volume 2* (Elektra 1979)★★★★, *Columbia Historic Edition* (Columbia 1985)★★★, *Steamboat Whistle Blues 1936-1939* (Rounder 1985)★★★★, *Best Of Roy Acuff* (Curb 1991)★★★, *The Essential Roy Acuff 1936-49* (Columbia/Legacy 1992)★★★★, *The King Of Country Music* 2-CD set (1993)★★★★.
● FURTHER READING: *King Of Country Music: The Life Story Of Roy Acuff*, A.C Dunkleberger. *Roy Acuff The Smoky Mountain Boy*, Elizabeth Schlappi.

ACUFF, ROY, JNR.
b. Roy Neill Acuff, 25 July 1943, Nashville, Tennessee, USA. The son of Roy Acuff, at times during his childhood, Roy Jnr. saw little of his father owing to his touring commitments. Initially showing little interest in music, he began to work in the offices at Acuff-Rose but in 1963, unbeknown to his father, he learned to sing and play the guitar. In 1965, he was given the opportunity to record for Columbia by Wesley Rose and a month later his father introduced him on the *Grand Ole Opry*. He played various venues in the USA and even toured US military bases in Germany. Occasionally he appeared with his father and in the early 70s, he sang backing vocals on some of his recordings. However, audiences made him nervous and he never enjoyed performing. He was much happier working behind the scenes and by the mid-70s, he had retired as a performer to become an executive of Acuff-Rose. During his brief recording career, he wrote and recorded several of his own songs including 'Back Down To Atlanta' and 'Street Singer'.
● ALBUMS: *Roy Acuff Jnr* (Hickory 1970)★★★, *California Lady* (1974)★★★.

ADKINS, TRACE
b. 13 January 1962, Sarepta, Louisiana, USA. Before entering the entertainment world and the Nashville music community, Trace Adkins was employed as an oil-rigger. What some critics have labelled his 'blue-collar authenticity' was first conveyed to audiences on the honky-tonk circuit on his evenings off work. This eventually led him to Nashville and a meeting with Scott Hendricks of Capitol Records Nashville. Adkins became Hendricks' first signing. Hendricks also served as co-producer of Adkins' 1996 debut album, *Dreamin' Out Loud*. This was promoted by the release of three successful singles - 'There's A Girl In Texas', 'Every Light In The House' and '(This Ain't) No Thinking Thing'. By February 1997 the album had reached the *Billboard* Top 100, despite strong competition from an emerging new generation of Nashville singer-songwriters. His profile was increased by singing the national anthem at Dallas Cowboys and Texas Rangers matches. He also received considerable attention from the press when he took the unusual step of proposing to his girlfriend from the stage of the *Grand Ole Opry* in 1996.
● ALBUMS: *Dreamin' Out Loud* (Capitol Nashville 1996)★★★★, *Big Time* (Capitol 1997)★★★.

ADKINS, WENDEL
Wendel Adkins was born in Kentucky, USA, c. 1950 and raised in Fremont, Ohio. During his teens, he played organ in a rock band, but he preferred to sing country music. He went to Nashville but poor management stifled his talent and his ambition. Adkins moved to Las Vegas and, because he was tall, good-looking and entertaining, he attracted a following in the casino hotels. His country act included impersonations of Willie Nelson and Johnny Cash, and he sounded like Waylon Jennings without trying. Ironically, it was Willie Nelson who discovered him and suggested that he move from Las Vegas to Texas. He became associated with 'outlaw country' and he opened shows for both Nelson and David Allan Coe. His first album, *Sundowners*, was released on Motown's Hitsville label in 1977 and included a tribute to Nelson, 'Willie Didn't Win'. His second album was recorded live at one of Nelson's clubs, Whiskey River, and included the prophetic 'Luckenbach Ain't Never Gonna Be The Same', a reference to the Texas town where the outlaws spent some time. During a residency at Gilley's, he recorded a live album but although he was recording through the 80s, he never became a national country star. His outspoken language on 'Rodeo Cowboys', the opening track of *If That Ain't Country*, may have lost him support.
● ALBUMS: *Sundowners* (Hitsville 1977)★★★, *Live At Whiskey River* (1982)★★★, *Live At Gilley's* (1983)★★, *Cowboy Singer* (1984)★★, *If That Ain't Country* (Sundown 1985)★★, *I Can't Let You Be A Memory* (Sundown 1987)★★.

AKINS, RHETT
b. 23 October 1969, Valdosta, Georgia, USA. Although his mother played piano and his grandfather led the church choir, Akins was more interested in becoming a football quarterback. He gave up his studies at the University of Georgia after a year and getting married, he worked for his father's oil and gas distribution company. He played guitar in his spare time and after performing at a family gathering, determined to become a country singer in the vein of Randy Travis. He went to Nashville and obtained a management contract with Reba McEntire's husband, Narvel Blackstock. Paraded as a Hat Act, he had Top 40 country hits with 'What They're Talkin' About' and 'I Brake For Brunettes'. He made the Top 3 with 'That Ain't My Truck', but after further success with 'She Said Yes' and 'Don't Get Me Started', his own career braked for brunettes. *Somebody New*, which features a song called 'Somebody Knew', includes several of his own compositions and, although an improvement on *A Thousand Memories*, found limited appeal with the US record-buyers. In early 1997, 'Every Cowboy's Dream' was struggling to make the US country Top 50.
● ALBUMS: *A Thousand Memories* (Decca 1995)★★, *Somebody New* (Decca 1996)★★★.

ALABAMA
One of the biggest US country rock acts of the 80s, the band's origins can be traced back to Fort Payne, Alabama. They were originally formed in 1969 as Wild Country by cousins Jeff Cook (b. 27 August 1949, Fort Payne, Alabama, USA; vocals, guitar), Randy Owen (b. 13 December 1949, Fort Payne, Alabama, USA; vocals, guitar) and Teddy Gentry (b. 22 January 1952, Fort Payne, Alabama, USA; bass, vocals). Their original drummer was the only non-relation and was

soon rejected. After several misfires at the start of their career their big breakthrough came with a residency at a club in Myrtle Beach, South Carolina, in 1973. Soon afterwards they turned professional. They recorded for several small labels in the 70s before they changed their name to Alabama in 1977. Their career blossomed with a sequence of hits in the country charts which followed the success of 'I Want To Be With You'. At this point they sought out a full-time drummer to fill out their sound and recruited Mark Herndon (b. 11 May 1955, Springfield, Massachusetts, USA). After 'My Home's In Alabama' reached the US Top 20 they signed to RCA Records in 1980 and found immediate success. A rich vein of country hits followed with 'Tennessee River' and 'Feels So Right'. Later singles such as 'Love In The First Degree' also acquired crossover pop success. Of their five platinum albums during the 80s, the most successful was *40 Hour Week* which reached number 10 in the US chart. In 1986 they worked with Lionel Richie, but their recent work has seen them return almost exclusively to the C&W charts. Despite an increasingly formulaic sound, they remain a major live attraction, although their commercial profile has suffered from the rival attractions of younger bands. However, their environmental anthem, 'Pass It On Down' in 1990, confirmed that they were still capable of surprising their audience. In 1995 the group celebrated its 15th anniversary, in which time it could lay claim to many outstanding achievements, including sales of over 50 million albums, and the Academy Of Country Music's Artist Of The Decade Award for their work in the 80s. Singer Randy Owen described their enduring appeal thus: 'What you see is what you get with Alabama. We're basically a blue-collar working band. We work really hard at what we do, and we work for our fans and listen to them.' By 1995 they had amassed 40 number 1s, equalling Conway Twitty's remarkable feat.
● ALBUMS: *Wild Country* (LSI 1977)★★★, *Deuces Wild* (LSI 1978)★★★, *My Home's In Alabama* (RCA 1980)★★★, *Feels So Right* (RCA 1981)★★★, *Mountain Music* (RCA 1982)★★★, *The Closer You Get* (RCA 1983)★★★, *Roll On* (RCA 1984)★★★, *Alabama Christmas* (RCA 1985)★★, *40 Hour Week* (RCA 1985)★★★, *The Touch* (RCA 1986)★★★, *Just Us* (RCA 1987)★★★, *Alabama Live* (RCA 1988)★★, *Southern Star* (RCA 1989)★★★, *Pass It On Down* (RCA 1990)★★★, *American Pride* (RCA 1992)★★★, *Gonna Have A Party . . . Live* (RCA 1993)★★, *Cheap Seats* (RCA 1993)★★★, *In Pictures* (RCA 1995)★★★, *Alabama Christmas Volume II* (RCA 1996)★★, *Dancin' On The Boulevard* (RCA 1997)★★★.
● COMPILATIONS: *Wild Country* (LSI 1981)★★★, *Greatest Hits* (RCA 1986)★★★★, *Greatest Hits, Volume 2* (RCA 1991)★★★, *Greatest Hits, Volume 3* (RCA 1994)★★★, *Super Hits* (RCA 1996)★★★.

ALAN, BUDDY

b. Alvis Alan Owens, 22 May 1948, Tempe, Arizona, USA. The son of Buck Owens and Bonnie Owens, he followed his parents into country music as an accomplished rhythm guitarist and vocalist. After starting in the business as Buddy Alan Owens, he decided that he did not wish to seek a successful career because of his family name and dropped the Owens. However, bearing a strong facial resemblance to his father, sounding very similar (though slightly lower) and performing the same type of material, it was almost impossible for him to escape comparison. He worked as a disc

jockey on his father's radio stations in Bakersfield and Phoenix, as well as touring as a member of his band, the Buckeroos. Like Buck, he also became a regular on the popular *Hee-Haw* television show. He also worked as a session guitarist for Capitol, for whom he recorded. Between 1968 and 1975, he had 23 *Billboard* country chart hits. Only two made the Top 20, both being duets. His first chart entry, 'Let The World Keep On A Turnin'', recorded with Buck and the Buckeroos, peaked at number 10 and in 1970, 'Cowboy Convention', recorded with the Buckeroos' lead guitarist and vocalist Don Rich, made number 19. He also had minor duet hits with Rich (with whom he also recorded an album) on 'I'm On The Road To Memphis' and with his father on 'Too Old To Cut The Mustard', both in 1971. His second album, on which he wrote six of the songs, was critically acclaimed, but *Chains* received a lukewarm reception, and by the late 70s, his solo career had ended.
● ALBUMS: *Wild, Free And 21* (Capitol 1970)★★★, *A Whole Lot Of Something* (Capitol 1970)★★★, with Don Rich *We're Real Good Friends* (Capitol 1971)★★, *The Best Of Buddy Alan* (Capitol 1972)★★★, with Buck Owens *Too Old To Cut The Mustard* (Capitol 1972)★★★, *Chains/Another Saturday Night* (Capitol 1975)★★.

ALBERT, CHRISTINE

b. 1955, Rome, New York State, USA. The 90s country singer Christine Albert has a mixed Swiss and French family background. For a while, she worked in her brother Rick's soul band, Honky De Luxe, but at the age of 19 formed her own band, Ozone Express. She subsequently became a backing vocalist with Elia's Turquoise Trail Band. In 1982 she moved to Austin, marrying a local musician, Ernie 'Sky' Gammage, and developed a solo act. In 1988 she signed an eight-album contract with Columbia but, by 1990, the label had lost interest and agreed to release her. She produced *You Are Gold*, which included her version of 'She's In Love With The Boy'. Unfortunately for Albert, Trisha Yearwood picked up on the song and made it a US country hit. *Texafrance* included her versions of 'La Vie En Rose' and 'Hymne A L'Amour'. She sang the title track on *Pastures Of Plenty*, a tribute album to Woody Guthrie, and she sang harmony vocals on Jerry Jeff Walker's version of 'Navajo Rug'. *The High Road* and *Underneath The Lone Star Sky* were lacklustre in comparison to her earlier work.
● ALBUMS: *Across The Miles* (Gambini 1985)★★★, *You Are Gold* (Gambini 1990)★★★, *Texafrance* (Gambini 1992)★★★, *The High Road* (Gambini 1993)★★, *Underneath The Lone Star Sky* (Dos 1995)★★.

ALEXANDER, DANIELE

b. 2 December 1954, Fort Worth, Texas, USA. Alexander learned piano as a child and started singing for a living in her late teens. Initially she sang jazz numbers but after including rock and country in her repertoire, she moved to Las Vegas and worked in casinos. Tiring of that town and the lifestyle, she sang with bands in various cities, including Los Angeles, before finally arriving in Nashville in 1986. She worked as a songwriter but when nobody recorded her songs she took to singing them herself. Crediting K.T. Oslin as an inspiration, she was eventually signed by Mercury Records and gained her first *Billboard* country chart Top 20 hit with 'She's There' in 1989. Sadly, only two minor hits have fol-

lowed and although once described as 'a breezy Texas Ms, who's stretching the boundaries of country music', she has seemingly so far failed to confirm that writer's prediction.
● ALBUMS: *First Move* (Mercury 1989)★★, *I Dream In Color* (Mercury 1991)★★.

ALGER, PAT

b. 1947, New York City, USA. The 90s country singer and songwriter Pat Alger grew up in Georgia and had two uncles who played bluegrass and taught him the rudiments of country music. He was also inspired by James Taylor and Jimmy Webb. In 1980 he wrote his first hit song with 'First Time Love' by Livingston Taylor as well as 'City Lights', a duet by Livingston and his brother James. He worked as a graphic designer and wrote songs in the evening such as 'Once In A Very Blue Moon' (Nanci Griffith) and 'Goin' Gone' (Kathy Mattea). After befriending Don Everly, he opened for his Dead Cowboy Band and then the Everly Brothers when they re-formed. He has made three albums and although he has a pleasant voice, it lacks range and his songs sound better sung by others. He co-wrote a country standard, 'Lone Star State Of Mind' for Nanci Griffith, which was an answer to Billy Joel's 'New York State Of Mind'. However, his greatest successes have been with Garth Brooks as he has written four of his number 1 country singles - 'Unanswered Prayers', 'The Thunder Rolls', 'What's She's Doing Now' and 'That Summer'. Other successful songs include 'Eighteen Inches Of Rain' (Ian Tyson), 'She Came From Fort Worth' (Kathy Mattea), 'Small Town Saturday Night' (Hal Ketchum) and 'True Love' (Don Williams). Trisha Yearwood said, 'I loved "Like We Never Had A Broken Heart" from the first time I heard it because it is about real life. Pat Alger writes from the heart, and I believe every word.' Alger also has good business sense as he owns at least half the publishing on all his hit songs. Pat Alger has taken over from Harlan Howard as Nashville's premier songwriter. However, unlike Howard, relatively few of his songs are known outside of country music circles. He often attends Garth Brooks concerts and has said of them: 'It's great to hear about 10,000 people singing "Unanswered Prayers" - what could be more fun than that?'
● ALBUMS: *True Love And Other Short Stories* (Sugar Hill 1991)★★★, *Seeds* (Sugar Hill 1993)★★★, *Notes And Grace Notes* (Liberty 1995)★★★.

ALLAN, GARY

b. California, USA. Although Allan is grouped with the New Country acts, he is more in keeping with the traditions of George Jones and Merle Haggard than most. He was brought up on the surfing coastline, but his father loved country music and they played together in a country band. Allan formed his own trucking company and used his savings to finance a demo. He signed with Decca 'because they didn't want to change anything'. His debut album included a new Garth Brooks song, 'From Where I'm Standing', but the key cut is 'Her Man', which had been recorded by Waylon Jennings. 'Her Man' (the subject of which was 'an S.O.B. right down to the letter') was a Top 10 country single early in 1997. The video presents Allan as a man who changes his shirt several times while doing the housework, but his black felt hat never leaves his head.
● ALBUMS: *Used Heart For Sale* (MCA 1996)★★★.

ALLAN, JOHNNIE

b. John Allan Guillot, 10 March 1938, Rayne, Louisiana, USA. Allan was raised in a sharecropping family, speaking both English and French. His great-uncle, Joe Falcon, made one of the first Cajun records, 'Allons A Lafayette'. From the age of 13, he was playing rhythm guitar and steel guitar in local bands. In 1958 and as part of the Krazy Kats, Allan had regional hits with 'Lonely Days, Lonely Nights' and 'Angel Of Love'. Allan, who qualified as a teacher, divided his time between music and teaching in Lafayette. 'South To Louisiana', a regional version of Johnny Horton's 'North To Alaska', was a successful solo single. Allan also made a single, 'Somewhere On Skid Row', with 'Promised Land' on the b-side, for Jin Records of Ville Patte, Louisiana. In 1972 Charlie Gillett, looking for releases for his new UK label Oval, delighted in the fast and furious Cajun treatment of Chuck Berry's song, and so 'Promised Land' became a UK single. Sadly, another cover version by Elvis Presley put paid to its chances. Allan is revered by the UK rock 'n' roll fraternity and has made successful appearances in the UK.
● ALBUMS: *Another Man's Woman* (Jin 1979)★★★, *Dedicated To You* (Jin 1979)★★★, *South To Louisiana* (Jin 1979)★★★, *Johnnie Allan And The Krazy Kats 1959-1960s* (Krazy Kat 1985)★★★★, *From Louisiana To The Promised Land* (1993)★★★.
● COMPILATIONS: *Johnnie Allan Sings* (70s)★★★★, *Johnnie Allan's Greatest Hits* (Jin 1979)★★★, *Singles* (Jin 1979)★★★, *Portrait Of Johnnie Allan* (Jin 1979)★★★, *Good Timin' Man* (Flyright 1980)★★★.

ALLANSON, SUSIE

b. 17 March 1952, Minneapolis, Minnesota, USA. Susie Allanson's grandmother taught her to play piano and she began singing in churches and at rodeos. In 1970, she successfully auditioned for a role in a twelve-month touring production of *Hair*. She then spent 18 months touring with the original company of *Jesus Christ Superstar*, sang on the show's album and appeared in the film version. In 1974, she moved to Los Angeles, where she did studio work and sang backing vocals on the recordings of various artists. She joined ABC Records the following year, after meeting producer Ray Ruff, who produced her debut album in 1976. She married Ruff and when ABC folded, she recorded her debut chart hit, 'Don't Keep Me Hangin' On', on his own Oak label. She then joined Warner Brothers, where she recorded her second album, which, through her husband's production and promotion, produced three country hits including Top 10 placings for 'Maybe Baby' (a 1958 Buddy Holly pop hit) and the title track, 'We Belong Together'. In 1979, recording on the Elektra/Curb label, she registered further Top 10 hits with her version of the Bee Gees' 1968 pop hit 'Words' and 'Two Steps Forward And Three Steps Back'. The same year she was named by *Billboard* as the year's Most Promising Female Country Artist. She and Ruff divorced in 1980 and she moved to United Artists (recording on their Liberty label), where she registered six mostly minor hits, the biggest being 'Dance The Two Step'.
● ALBUMS: *Susie Allanson* (ABC 1976)★★★, *We Belong Together* (Warners/Curb 1978)★★★, *Heart To Heart* (Elektra 1979)★★, *Susie* (United Artists 1980)★★.

ALLEN BROTHERS

Austin Allen (b. 7 February 1901, Sewanee, near Chattanooga, Tennessee, USA, d. 1959, Williamstown, South Carolina, USA; banjo, guitar, vocals) and his brother Lee Allen (b. 1 June 1906, Sewanee, near Chattanooga, Tennessee, USA, d. 80s, Lebanon, Tennessee, USA; guitar, piano, kazoo, vocals). Affectionately known as the Chattanooga Boys, the brothers established a reputation as one of the most popular brother duet acts of the 20s and early 30s. In 1923, they began touring in the Tennessee-West Virginia area, often playing at remote settlements or mining camps. They carefully collected new songs on their travels with the result that they developed a wider repertoire than most of their fellow acts. They are especially remembered for singing some blues numbers so proficiently that their recordings were wrongly categorized in the 'Race' instead of 'Hillbilly' series by Columbia Records, for whom they first recorded in 1927. A dispute over this saw them leave the label. Between 1928 and 1932, they recorded for Victor Records and are remembered for songs of topical interest such as 'Price Of Cotton Blues' and 'Jake Walk Blues'. However, of all their recorded output, their Columbia recording of 'A New Salty Dog Blues' is probably the best known. In the early 30s, they also appeared in a stage presentation of *The Bushwacker*. In 1934, they made their final recordings on the ARC label. During their career Austin usually sang lead vocals, with Lee occasionally adding tenor harmonies. However, Lee is perhaps best remembered for his outstanding ability to make a child's toy kazoo sound convincingly like a trumpet. After leaving the music business, both became involved in the construction industry. With the renewed interest in old-time music in the 70s, many of their recordings have reappeared on compilation albums on various labels. Lee was even persuaded to make personal appearances at a few venues, until his death at his home during the 80s.

● COMPILATIONS: *Country Ragtime - The Allen Brothers* (Bear Family 1973)★★★★, *The Chattanooga Boys* (Old Timey 1988)★★★★, *Are You Feeling It Too?* (Smithsonian/Folkways 1994)★★★★.

ALLEN, DEBORAH

b. Deborah Lynn Thurgood, 30 September 1953, Memphis, Tennessee, USA. A singer-songwriter, whose songs have proved major successes for other artists, including 'Don't Worry 'Bout Me Baby' (Janie Fricke) and 'Can I See You Tonight?' (Tanya Tucker), Allen's own first US country chart success came in 1979 when she was working as a session singer. Thanks to the miracles of modern recording techniques and the thoughtfulness of RCA producer Bud Logan, she was chosen to superimpose her vocals over recordings made years earlier by Jim Reeves, a star then dead for almost 15 years. These so-called 'duets' produced three Top 10 US country hits, 'Don't Let Me Cross Over', 'Oh, How I Miss You Tonight' and 'Take Me In Your Arms And Hold Me'. Between 1980 and 1984, she had eight solo country singles including 'Baby I Lied' (a US country number 4 and US pop number 26) and 'I've Been Wrong Before' (a country number 2). She married songwriter Rafe Van Hoy, co-wrote songs with him and sang on the soundtrack of *The River Rat*. After a long absence from the charts, which suggested that perhaps her solo singing career was over, she reappeared in

December 1992. The reappearance, however, hardly matched the gentle vocals associated with the Reeves recordings. She joined the Giant label in 1992 and her debut album on the label contained 10 contemporary offerings either self-penned or written by Allen with others. She shared production with husband Van Hoy. 'Rock Me (In The Cradle Of Love)', the first single from the album, accompanied by a raunchy video, made the US country Top 30. A follow-up single, 'If You're Not Gonna Love Me', managed only a Top 50 placing and the year ended sadly for her when she and Rafe Van Hoy parted. Next year's *All That I Am* was another strong collection.

● ALBUMS: with Jim Reeves *Don't Let Me Cross Over* (RCA Victor 1979)★★, *Trouble In Paradise* (Capitol 1980)★★★, *Cheat The Night* mini-album (RCA 1983)★★, *Let Me Be The First* (RCA 1984)★★, *Delta Dreamland* (Giant 1993)★★★, *All That I Am* (Giant 1994)★★★.
● VIDEOS: *Break These Chains* (Scene Three 1994).

ALLEN, JULES VERNE

b. 1 April 1883, Waxahachie, Ellis County, Texas, USA, d. 1945. Allen has strong claims to the title of the original singing cowboy. By the time he was 10, he was working as a ranch boy and over the years progressed to be a horse-wrangler, a rough-string rider and finally a top ranch-hand, who also did occasional police work. During earlier years he had played the guitar and sung for the entertainment of his fellow cowboys and, after a period in the army, decided to try for a singing career. Around 1920, he became a western folk singer and sang of trail drives, round-ups and rodeos using many of the traditional ballads collected by such authorities as John Lomax, as well as songs he had written from personal experience. Sometimes appearing as Longhorn Luke, he soon became popular on several radio stations, including WFAA Dallas (where he first broadcast), WOAI San Antonio and WFI and KNX Los Angeles. Between April 1928 and April 1929, he recorded a total of 24 songs for Victor, all but four being of a cowboy nature and including such western classics as 'Home On The Range', 'The Chisholm Trail' and 'Little Joe The Wrangler'. His version of 'The Sante Fe Trail' was the first ever recorded. During the 30s, he continued with radio work, appearances at rodeos and other western events and was also a part-time police officer in the El Paso area. He never recorded again and little is known of his latter years except that he died in 1945.

● ALBUMS: *Jules Allen, The Texas Cowboy* (1973)★★★.
● FURTHER READING: *Cowboy Lore*, Jules Verne Allen.

ALLEN, RED

b. Harley Allen, 12 February 1930, Hazard, Perry County, Kentucky, USA, d. 3 April 1993, Dayton, Ohio, USA. Greatly influenced in his early years by Charlie Monroe, whom he regularly heard on WNOX Knoxville, he developed a great love for bluegrass music. During his career, Allen, an outstanding vocalist and competent rhythm guitarist (he also played banjo and mandolin), established himself as one of the leading exponents of the genre. After service with the US Marine Corps in the late 40s, he began to play with various musicians, including banjoist Noah Crase (with whom he made his first recordings for a minor label in 1953), around Dayton, Ohio. Between 1954 and 1958, he worked with the Osborne Brothers, the act being very popular on the WWVA

Wheeling Jamboree and also for some MGM recordings, especially 'Once More' which, in 1958, reached number 13 in the US country charts. In 1960, he relocated to the Washington area where, in partnership with Frank Wakefield, he formed his noted bluegrass band, the Kentuckians. During the next few years, he made many fine recordings for several major labels, including his version of 'Beautiful Brown Eyes'. In 1967, when Lester Flatt was hospitalized by a heart attack, Allen moved to Nashville to deputize for him. The following year, he relocated to Lexington, where he formed the Kentucky Mountain Boys with J.D. Crowe. By 1970, he had returned to Dayton, where he worked with a band consisting of four of his sons. They became very popular on WWVA *Jamboree* and also recorded for Lemco and King Bluegrass. (His sons have also recorded less traditional bluegrass music as the Allen Brothers but they should not be confused with the old-time country act of the same name.) In the late 70s, Allen recorded an album on Folkways Records as his tribute to the memory of Lester Flatt and he even had two albums released in Japan. In the late 80s, failing health limited his contributions, but he continued to make appearances at various festivals until he finally lost his battle with cancer on 3 April 1993.

● ALBUMS: with the Osborne Brothers *Country Pickin' & Hillside Singin'* (MGM 1959)★★★, *Red Allen, Frank Wakefield & The Kentuckians* (Folkways 1964)★★★, *The Solid Bluegrass Sound Of The Kentuckians* (Melodeon 1966)★★★, *Bluegrass Country* (County 1966)★★★, *Bluegrass Country Volume 2* (County 1967)★★★, with J.D. Crowe And The Kentucky Mountain Boys *Bluegrass Holiday* (Lemco 1969)★★★, *My Old Kentucky Home* (King Bluegrass 1973)★★★, *Allengrass* (Lemco 1973)★★★, *Red Allen Favorites* (King Bluegrass 1975)★★★, *Red Allen & Frank Wakefield* (Red Clay 1976)★★★, *Live And Let Live* (Folkways 1979)★★★, *In Memory Of The Man* (Folkways 1980)★★★, *Family & Friends* (Folkways 1982)★★★, *The Red Allen Tradition* (Folkways 1983)★★★.

● COMPILATIONS: with Osborne Brothers *The Osborne Brothers & Red Allen* (Rounder 1977)★★★, *Classic Recordings 1954-69* reissue of 45s (Collector Classics 1984)★★★, *Bluegrass Special - 1960s Radio Shows* (Storyville)★★★.

ALLEN, REX

b. Rex Elvie Allen, 31 December 1922, Willcox, Arizona, USA. Country singer Allen was no imitation cowboy - his family were homesteaders: a mountain lion was killed close to his home, his brother died from a rattlesnake bite, and the family lost everything in the drought of 1934. As Allen had ridden on the farm, he thought he could transfer to rodeos, but a fall from a Brahman bull directed his thoughts towards music. In 1945, he hosted *The National Barn Dance* for a radio station in Chicago and was able to afford an operation to correct his congenital squint. His first local hit was 'Take It Back And Change It For A Boy', and his early recordings found him yodelling, although he subsequently kept his tone and pitch the same. Country singer Red Foley was not interested when he was asked to replace the popular singing cowboy, Roy Rogers, at Republic Studios, but he recommended the good-looking, well-spoken Allen instead. Republic named him 'The Arizona Cowboy', which was also his name in the 19 films in which he starred between 1950 and 1954. The last, *The Phantom Stallion*, marked the end of

the B-movie western. His son, country singer Rex Allen Jnr., said: 'He wanted to be the opposite of Roy Rogers. He rode a black horse, he didn't wear fringed shirts and he had his guns back-to-front. If he'd got involved in a real gunfight, he'd have been dead.' Allen's weather-beaten sidekick was Slim Pickens, who was featured in *Dr. Strangelove* and *Pat Garrett And Billy The Kid*. Pickens also made an album of narrations, *Slim Pickens* (1977), which included the outlandish 'The Fireman Cowboy', which they had written together. Although Allen had a million-selling single, 'Crying In The Chapel' (later a hit for Elvis Presley), in 1953, he did not record regularly and, in 1962, when he returned to the US charts, it was with a song he disliked: 'Don't Go Near The Indians'. His own suggestion, a new Willie Nelson song, 'Night Life', was vetoed. Allen's clear diction earned him the opportunity to narrate documentaries for Walt Disney, and in 1973, his voice was heard in the Hanna-Barbera feature cartoon *Charlotte's Web*. He returned to Arizona and still makes a living doing voice-overs on commercials. He occasionally joins his son on stage.

● ALBUMS: *Under Western Skies* (Decca 1956)★★★, *Mister Cowboy* (Decca 1959)★★★, *Rex Allen Sings* (Hacienda 1960)★★★, *Rex Allen Sings 16 Favourites* (Buena Vista 1961)★★★, *Faith Of A Man* (Mercury 1962)★★★, *Rex Allen Sings Melodies Of The Plains* (Design 1962)★★★, *Rex Allen Sings And Tells Tales* (Mercury 1962)★★★, *Rex Allen* (Wing 1964)★★★, *Rex Allen Sings Western Ballads* (Hilltop 1965)★★★, *The Smooth Country Sound Of Rex Allen* (Decca 1968)★★★, *The Touch Of God's Hand* (Decca 1970)★★★, *Favorite Songs* (Disneyland 1970)★★★, *Golden Songs Of The Golden West* (Vocalion 1970)★★★.

● COMPILATIONS: *Boney Kneed, Hairy Legged Cowboy Songs* (Bear Family 1984)★★★, *Under Western Skies* (Stetson 1985)★★★, *Rex Allen, The Hawaiian Cowboy* (Bear Family 1986)★★★, *Voice Of The West* (Bear Family 1986)★★★, *Mister Cowboy* (Stetson 1987)★★★, *Very Best Of Rex Allen* (Warners 1994)★★★.

● FURTHER READING: *My Life-Sunrise To Sunset: The Arizona Cowboy Rex Allen*, Paula Simpson with Snuff Garrett.

● FILMS: *Under Mexicali Stars* (1950), *Arizona Cowboy* (1950), *The Phantom Stallion* (1953), *The Old Overland Trail* (1953).

ALLEN, REX, JNR.

b. Rex Elvie Allen Jnr., 23 August 1947, Chicago, Illinois, USA. Rex Jnr. spent school holidays touring with his father, the cowboy actor Rex Allen. He wrangled horses, played rodeo clown and sang 'That Little Boy Of Mine' with him. He recorded for several labels before having success with Warner Brothers in the US country charts with 'The Great Mail Robbery' in 1973, a tribute to his heritage, 'Can You Hear Those Pioneers?', and his first Top 10 country record, 'Two Less Lonely People'. When he was invited to star in a modern-day western, he recorded an album, *Singing Cowboy*, including 'Last Of The Silver Screen Cowboys' with his father and Roy Rogers, but the film was never made. He often revived pop hits such as 'Crying In The Rain', 'Cat's In The Cradle' and 'The Air That I Breathe', but he is no longer a regular in the country charts.

● ALBUMS: *Another Goodbye Song* (1974)★★★★, *Riding High* (1976)★★★, *Rex* (Warners 1977)★★★ *Brand New* (1978)★★, *Me And My Broken Heart* (1979)★★★, *Oklahoma*

Rose (1980)★★★, *Cat's In The Cradle* (1981)★★★, *Country Cowboy* (1982)★★★, *Singing Cowboy* (1982)★★, *On The Move* (1985)★★★, *Live At Gilley's* (Westwood One 1985)★★.

ALLEN, ROSALIE

b. Julie Marlene Bedra, 27 June 1924, Old Forge, Pennsylvania, USA. Born of Polish immigrant stock, as a child Allen was taught to play guitar and yodel, and moved to New York in her mid-teens where she found work on Denver Darling's *Swing Billies* radio programme. Between 1946 and 1953 she recorded for RCA, having country chart successes in 1946 with her version of the Patsy Montana yodelling classic 'I Want To Be A Cowboy's Sweetheart' and 'Guitar Polka'. She also popularized 'He Taught Me How To Yodel', a female version of the Kenny Roberts novelty number 'She Taught Me To Yodel', a song that in 1962 became one of Frank Ifield's most popular stage numbers after being released as the b-side of his recording of 'Lovesick Blues'. She later joined Zeke Manners' show where she recorded duets with Elton Britt, including US country chart Top 10 hits with 'Beyond The Sunset' and 'Quicksilver' in 1950. In the early 50s she had her own television show, later opened a large record store in New Jersey and became New York's first hillbilly yodelling disc jockey on WOV. She eventually retired from the music business and moved to Alabama.

● ALBUMS: *Rosalie Allen Sings Country & Western* (Waldorf Music Hall 1954)★★★, with Britt *Starring Rosalie Allen & Elton Britt* (Waldorf Music Hall 1957)★★★, *Songs Of The Golden West* (Grand Award 1957)★★★, with Tex Fletcher *Rodeo* (Grand Award 1959)★★★, *Rosalie Allen* (RCA Victor 1961)★★★.

● COMPILATIONS: *Queen Of The Yodellers* (Cattle 1983)★★★★, *The Cowboy's Sweetheart* (Cowgirlboy 1990)★★★.

ALLEN, TERRY

b. 7 May 1943, Wichita, Kansas, USA. A sculptor, multimedia artist and songwriter, the gravel-voiced Allen remained an enigmatic figure during the 70s and 80s. Despite his living in California for many years, Allen is more often associated with the new country movement in Texas. Many listeners first became aware of him when his 'New Delhi Freight Train' was covered by Little Feat on *Time Loves A Hero*. Allen had already recorded *Juarez* (which Little Feat's Lowell George was at one point going to produce), utilizing the talents of Peter Kaukonen and Greg Douglas; four of its songs were covered by Peter Rowan. Two of the album's finest songs surfaced several years later on Allen's *Bloodlines*. In the interim, he and his Panhandle Mystery Band produced the double *Lubbock (On Everything)* and *Smokin' The Dummy*, the latter containing a tribute to George. Allen next worked on the soundtrack to a German film, *Amerasia*, with a Thai group, and was said to be at work on a screenplay himself. His sardonic wit and strong feeling for his roots have led Allen to produce many memorable songs. The concept album *Human Remains* featured backing from David Byrne, Joe Ely and Lucinda Williams.

● ALBUMS: *Juarez* (Fate 1975)★★★, *Lubbock (On Everything)* (Fate 1979)★★★★, *Smokin' The Dummy* (Fate 1980)★★★, *Bloodlines* (Fate 1983)★★★, *Amerasia* film soundtrack (Fete 1990)★★★, *Human Remains* (Sugar Hill 1996)★★★.

ALVIN, DAVE

The country guitarist Dave Alvin (b. 1955, Los Angeles, California, USA) had a successful career with his brother Phil in the Blasters, whose best-known song, 'Marie Marie', was a UK hit for Shakin' Stevens. On leaving the band, he worked with the punk band X and scored the film *Border Radio*. His solo albums are typical of his career, being a mixture of rockabilly, blues, country and rock 'n' roll. He has recorded with Rosie Flores and Jo-El Sonnier and is renowned as a fine songwriter, sometimes writing with Chris Gaffney and Tom Russell. He and Russell co-produced a tribute album to Merle Haggard, *Tulare Dust* (HighTone 1994). *Interstate City*, recorded at the Continental Club in Austin, Texas, is a powerful live album.

● ALBUMS: *Romeo's Escape* UK title *Every Night About This Time* (Epic 1987)★★★, *Border Radio* film soundtrack (Capitol 1987)★★, *Blue Blvd* (Hightone 1991)★★★, *Museum Of Heart* (Hightone 1993)★★★, *King Of California* (Hightone 1994)★★★, with the Guilty Men *Interstate City* (Hightone 1996)★★★★.

ANDERSON, BILL

b. James William Anderson III, 1 November 1937, Columbia, South Carolina, USA. Country performer Anderson learned the guitar when he was aged 12 and formed his own school band. He graduated in journalism from the University of Georgia, becoming a sports writer and also working for a radio station, an experience that influenced his song 'Country DJ'. In 1958 Ray Price won a gold disc when he recorded Anderson's 'City Lights'. Anderson's first hit as an artist was with 'That's What It's Like To Be Lonesome' in 1959. He followed this with 'The Tips Of My Fingers' (1960), a country success for Roy Clark and Eddy Arnold and a UK pop hit for Des O'Connor, and 'Po' Folks' (1961), which inspired the Po' Boys, the name of his band. His frontman, Jimmy Gateley, wrote Sonny James's country hit 'The Minute You're Gone', a UK success for Cliff Richard. Anderson had his first US country number 1 in 1962 with 'Mama Sang A Sad Song' and the following year he reached number 8 in the US pop charts with his half-spoken 'Still', which was successfully covered in the UK by both Karl Denver and Ken Dodd. Dodd also had success with '8 x 10' and always closed his stage show with 'Happiness'. Anderson also wrote several other successful songs including 'Once A Day' (the 1964 US country number 1 for Connie Smith, which launched her career), 'Happy Birthday To Me' (Hank Locklin), 'I Missed Me' (Jim Reeves), 'I've Enjoyed As Much Of This As I Can Stand' (Porter Wagoner), 'Five Little Fingers' (Frankie McBride), 'It Comes And Goes' (Burl Ives) and 'My Whole World Is Falling Down' (Brenda Lee). Anderson also wrote 'Face To The Wall' with Faron Young and 'When Two Worlds Collide' with Roger Miller, which they wrote by coming up with alternate lines on a car trip. Following his narration on 'Golden Guitar', which was written by Curtis Leach, he was nicknamed 'Whispering Bill' by the disc jockey Don Bowman, who also recorded a parody of 'Still'. Anderson says of his intimate and effusive style, 'I accepted a long time ago that a lot of people weren't going to like me. I'm glad some do.' During the Vietnam War, he recorded the patriotic 'Where Have All My Heroes Gone?' and says, 'There's a lot of me in my songs but that's not to say that they've got to be factual. Sometimes it's hard to make the truth rhyme.' For many years he worked and recorded with Jan Howard and they had a US country number 1 with 'For Loving You'. In 1972 her place was taken by Mary Lou Turner. He has also recorded with Roy Acuff ('I Wonder If God Loves Country Music') and, curiously, with David Allan Coe ('Get A Little Dirt On Your Hands'). In the late 70s he established country disco with 'I Can't Wait Any Longer' and 'Double S', thus paving the way for T.G. Sheppard. During the 80s he was featured in US soap operas and hosted game shows, but his new career was set back in 1984 when he and his wife were involved in a car crash with a hit-and-run driver. Both recovered and Anderson has returned to working country venues. He published his autobiography in 1989, and a book of anecdotes in 1993.

● ALBUMS: *Bill Anderson Sings Country Heart Songs* (Decca 1962)★★★, *Still* (Decca 1963)★★★★, *Sings* (Decca 1964)★★★, *The Bill Anderson Showcase* (Decca 1964)★★★, with the Jordanaires *From This Pen* (Decca 1965)★★★★, *Bright Lights And Country Music* (Decca 1965)★★★, *Bill Anderson Presents The Po' Boys* (1966)★★, *I Love You Drops* (Decca 1966)★★★, with the Jordanaires *Get While The Gettin's Good* (Decca 1967)★★★★, *The Po' Boys Pick Again* (1967)★★, *I Can Do Nothing Alone* (Decca 1967)★★★, with Jan Howard *For Loving You* (Decca 1967)★★★, *Wild Weekend* (Decca 1968)★★★, *Happy State Of Mind* (Decca 1968)★★★, *Bill Anderson's Country Style* (1969)★★, *My Life/But You Know I Love You* (1970)★★★, *Christmas* (1970)★★, *Love Is A Sometimes Thing* (1971)★★★★, with Howard *If It's All The Same To You* (1971)★★★, *Where Have All Our Heroes Gone?* (1971)★★, *Always Remember* (MCA 1971)★★★, as Bill Anderson's Po' Boys *That Casual Country Feelin'* (1971)★★★, *Bill Anderson Sings For All The Lonely Women In The World* (MCA 1972)★★, with Howard *Bill And Jan (Or Jan And Bill)* (MCA 1972)★★★, *Just Plain Bill* (MCA 1972)★★, with Howard *Singing His Praise* (MCA 1972)★★, *Don't She Look Good* (MCA 1973)★★★, *Bill* (MCA 1973)★★★, *The Rich Sound Of Bill Anderson's Po' Boys* (1973)★★★, *Can I Come Home To You?* (MCA 1974)★★★, *Every Time I Turn The Radio On* (MCA 1974)★★★, with Mary Lou Turner *Sometimes* (MCA 1975)★★, *Gentle On My Mind* (MCA 1975)★★★, *Live From London* (MCA 1975)★★, *Peanuts And Diamonds And Other Jewels* (MCA 1976)★★★, *Scorpio* (MCA 1976)★★★, with Turner *Billy Boy And Mary Lou* (MCA 1977)★★★, *Love And Other Sad Stories* (1978)★★★, *Ladies Choice* (1978)★★, *Whispering Bill Anderson* (1979)★★★, *On The Road With Bill Anderson* (1980)★★, *Nashville Mirrors* (1980)★★, *Bill Anderson Hosts Backstage At The Grand Ole Opry* (1982)★★, *Southern Fried* (1983)★★★, *Yesterday Today And Tomorrow* (1984)★★★, *Bill Anderson Presents The Po' Folks Band* (1984)★★, *A Place In The Country* (1986)★★★, *Yesteryear* (1990)★★★, *Country Music Heaven* (1993)★★★.

● COMPILATIONS: *The Bill Anderson Story* (Decca 1969)★★★★, *Greatest Hits* (MCA 1971)★★★, *Bill Anderson's Greatest Hits* (Varese Vintage 1996)★★★★.

● FURTHER READING: *Whispering Bill*, Bill Anderson. *I Hope You're Living As High On The Hog As The Pig You Turned Out To Be*, Bill Anderson.

ANDERSON, JOHN

b. 12 December 1955, Apopka, Florida, USA. As an adolescent, Anderson was playing the songs of British beat groups in his school band, but he then became enthused with country music. He joined his sister, Donna, in Nashville in 1972 and they played together in clubs and bars. In 1974 he began recording for the Ace Of Hearts label but none of his singles ('Swoop Down Sweet Jesus', 'Losing Again', 'A Heartbreak Ago') made any impression. He signed with Warner Brothers Records in 1977 and his first single was 'I Got A Feelin' (Somebody's Stealin')'. Although Anderson had several country hits ('My Pledge Of Love', 'Low Dog Blues', 'Your Lying Blue Eyes' and a perfect country theme, 'She Just Started Liking Cheating Songs'), he was not allowed to make an album until he was established. Some regard Anderson as continuing the tradition of Lefty Frizzell and George Jones, and he was delighted when his song, 'The Girl At The End Of The Bar', was covered by Jones. His revival of a poignant ballad, 'I Just Came Home To Count The Memories', originally a US country hit for Cal Smith, was given an identical arrangement to Elvis Costello's 'Good Year For The Roses'. As well as honky tonk ballads, he recorded the cheerful Billy Joe Shaver song, 'I'm Just An Old Chunk Of Coal (But I'm Gonna Be A Diamond Someday)', and his own up-tempo 'Chicken Truck'. In 1982 he had his first US country number 1 with a song recommended to him by his sister, 'Wild And Blue'. Anderson and his frequent co-writer, Lionel Delmore, the son of Alton Delmore, wrote 'Swingin'', which sold 1.4 million and became the biggest-selling country single in Warners' history. Anderson, who plays lead guitar in his road band, named his instrument after the character in 'Swingin'', Charlotte. Anderson was one of country music's first video stars, but he fell out with both his record label and his management. He fared relatively poorly on MCA, although there was a spirited duet with Waylon Jennings, 'Somewhere Between Ragged And Right'. Mark Knopfler wrote and played guitar on a 1991 release, 'When It Comes To You'. That song appeared on *Seminole Wind*, a triumphant comeback album which restored Anderson to the top rank of his profession, spawning a succession of hit singles. Its title track, a lament for the loss of traditional Indian lands, was reminiscent of Robbie Robertson's best work with the Band in its portrayal of history and American landscape. Since that time Anderson has become a little unfashionable as he has not embraced contemporary rock. From time to time he has country hits, such as 'Money In The Bank' and 'Straight Tequila Night', but he is no longer a major contender. He still makes quality albums even though there is no element of surprise from one to the next, steady being the key word.

● ALBUMS: *John Anderson* (Warners 1980)★★, *John Anderson 2* (Warners 1981)★★★, *I Just Came Home To Count The Memories* (Warners 1981)★★★, *Wild And Blue* (Warners 1982)★★★, *All The People Are Talking* (Warners 1983)★★★, *Eye Of The Hurricane* (Warners 1984)★★★, *Tokyo, Oklahoma* (Warners 1985)★★, *Countryfied* (Warners 1986)★★★, *Blue Skies Again* (MCA 1987)★★★, *10* (MCA 1988)★★, *Too Tough To Tame* (MCA 1990)★★, *Seminole Wind* (RCA 1992)★★★★, *Solid Ground* (BNA 1993)★★★★, *Country Till I Die* (1994)★★★, *Christmas Time* (BNA 1994)★★, *Paradise* (BNA 1996)★★★, *Takin' The Country Back* (Mercury 1997)★★★.

● COMPILATIONS: *Greatest Hits* (Warners 1984)★★★★, *Greatest Hits, Volume 2* (Warners 1990)★★★, *Greatest Hits* (BNA 1996)★★★★.

● VIDEOS: *Country 'Til I Die* (1994).

ANDERSON, LIZ

b. Elizabeth Jane Haaby, 13 March 1930, Pine Creek, near Roseau, Minnesota, USA. Anderson married country songwriter Casey Anderson in 1946, but worked as a secretary before turning to songwriting herself. She wrote 'Pick Of The Week' (Roy Drusky, 1964), '(My Friends Are Gonna Be) Strangers' (Merle Haggard, 1965), 'Guess My Eyes Were Bigger Than My Heart' (Conway Twitty, 1966), 'Just Between The Two Of Us' (Merle Haggard and Bonnie Owens, 1966) and 'I'm A Lonesome Fugitive' (Merle Haggard, 1967), which was written with her husband and established Haggard's rebellious image. She recorded on RCA from 1964-70, and had country hits with 'Mama Spank', 'Tiny Tears', 'Husband Hunting' and, in 1972, she recorded a country version of 'I'll Never Fall In Love Again' for Epic. 'The Game Of Triangles' was sung with Bobby Bare and Norma Jean. She wrote Lynn Anderson's (her daughter) first country hit, 'Ride, Ride, Ride' in 1966, and they later made the US country charts with a duet, 'Mother May I'. Lynn recorded *Songs My Mother Wrote* and is still placing her mother's songs with contemporary artists. Liz and Casey remain in the music business and host a country show on cable television in Nashville.

● ALBUMS: *Liz Anderson Sings* (RCA Victor 1967)★★★, with Bobby Bare and Norma Jean *The Game Of Triangles* (RCA Victor 1967)★★, *Cookin' Up Hits* (RCA Victor 1967)★★★, *Favourites* (RCA Victor 1968)★★★, *Like A Merry-Go-Round* (RCA Victor 1968)★★, *If The Creek Don't Rise* (RCA Victor 1969)★★, *The Liz Anderson Style* (RCA Victor 1969)★★, *Husband Hunting* (RCA Victor 1970)★★★.

ANDERSON, LYNN

b. Lynn Rene Anderson, 26 September 1947, Grand Forks, North Dakota, USA. Anderson, the daughter of country songwriters Casey and Liz Anderson, was raised in California. She started performing at the age of six, but her first successes were in horse shows. Her quarter horses amassed 700 trophies and she won major awards as a rider at shows all over California. In 1966, recording for the small Chart label, she had a US country entry with a song written by her mother, 'Ride, Ride, Ride', and then made the Top 10 with 'If I Kiss You, Will You Go Away?' and 'That's A No No'. She secured a residency on *The Lawrence Welk Show*, and in 1968 married songwriter Glenn Sutton, who then produced her records. The combination of her stunning blonde hair and the catchy Joe South song 'Rose Garden' ('I beg your pardon, I never promised you a rose garden') helped her to number 3 on both the US and UK pop charts. It also topped the US country charts for five weeks. The album of the same name also went gold. Anderson regards 'Rose Garden' as perfect timing, 'We were coming out of the Vietnam war, and a lot of people were trying to recover. The song's message was that you can make something out of nothing.' Although she did not repeat her pop success, she had US country number 1s with 'You're My Man', 'How Can I Unlove You?', 'Keep Me In Mind' and 'What A Man My Man Is'. She also scored with 'Top Of The World' and 'Wrap Your Love All Around Your Man'. Sutton and Anderson divorced in the mid-70s after she was promised more than a rose garden by Louisiana oilman Harold Stream III. During this marriage, she concentrated on horse-riding and fund-raising activities, but, upon their separation in 1982, she returned to country music. She

had further country hits with 'You're Welcome To Tonight', a duet with Gary Morris, 'Fools For Each Other' with Ed Bruce, and 'Under The Boardwalk' with harmonies from Billy Joe Royal, but she is no longer recording albums prolifically.

● ALBUMS: *Ride, Ride, Ride* (Chart 1967)★★★, *Big Girls Don't Cry* (Chart 1968)★★, *Promises, Promises* (Chart 1968)★★★, *Songs That Made Country Girls Famous* (Chart 1969)★★★★, *At Home With Lynn Anderson* (Chart 1969)★★★, *With Love From Lynn* (Chart 1969)★★★, *I'm Alright* (Chart 1970)★★★, *No Love At All* (Chart 1970)★★★, *Stay There 'Til I Get There* (1970)★★★, *Uptown Country Girl* (Chart 1970)★★★, *Rose Garden* (Columbia 1970)★★★★, *Songs My Mother Wrote* (Columbia 1970)★★★★, *Lynn Anderson With Strings* (Columbia 1971)★★★, *A Woman Lives For Love* (Columbia 1971)★★★★, *How Can I Unlove You?* (Columbia 1971)★★★, *You're My Man* (Columbia 1971)★★★★, *The Christmas Album* (Columbia 1971)★★★, *Cry* (Columbia 1972)★★★, *Listen To A Country Song* (Columbia 1972)★★★, *Keep Me In Mind* (Columbia 1973)★★★, *Top Of The World* (Columbia 1973)★★★, *Singing My Song* (Columbia 1973)★★★, *What A Man My Man Is* (Columbia 1974)★★★, *Smile For Me* (Columbia 1974)★★★, *I've Never Loved Anyone More* (Columbia 1975)★★★, *All The King's Horses* (Columbia 1976)★★★, *Wrap Your Arms Around Your Man* (Columbia 1977)★★★, *I Love What Love Is Doing To Me* reissued in UK as *Angel In Your Arms* (Columbia 1977)★★★, *From The Inside* (Columbia 1978)★★, *Outlaw Is Just A State Of Mind* (Columbia 1979)★★, *Even Cowgirls Get The Blues* (Columbia 1981)★★★, *Lynn Anderson Is Back* (Permian 1983)★★★, *What She Does Best* (Mercury 1988)★★, *Cowboy's Sweetheart* (Laserlight 1992)★★.

● COMPILATIONS: *Greatest Hits* (Chart 1970)★★★★, *Best Of Lynn Anderson* (K-Tel 1982)★★★, *Greatest Hits* (Columbia 1992)★★★★.

ANGLIN, JACK

b. 13 March 1916, Columbia, Williamson County, Tennessee, USA, d. 7 March 1963, Madison, Wisconsin, USA. The youngest of seven children, he learned to play guitar as a child and at an early age was singing in a trio with his brothers, Jim and Van (aka Red). Jim wrote some songs and the three began to appear at local venues and radio as the Anglin Brothers. They briefly located in Athens, Alabama, where they became friendly with and influenced by the Delmore Brothers. Around 1930, they moved to Nashville. Jack worked at a local hosiery mill and here became acquainted with his future wife, Louise, and through her, her brother Johnnie Wright. At the time Wright, his wife Muriel (Kitty Wells) and Louise were regulars on WSIX as Johnnie Wright And The Harmony Girls. The two men became friends and when, in 1939, the Anglin Brothers disbanded, Jack was soon performing with Wright as Johnnie Wright And The Happy Roving Cowboys with Jack Anglin. In 1940, they became Johnnie And Jack, who enjoyed much success as a vocal duo until Jack Anglin's career came to an end in 1963. Driving alone to attend a memorial service for Patsy Cline not far from his home, he rounded a bend on New Due West Avenue in Madison at high speed, crashed and was instantly killed. No other vehicle was involved.

● COMPILATIONS: as the Anglin Brothers *The South's Favorite Trio (Early Harmony)* (Old Homestead 1979)★★★.

AREA CODE 615

After Bob Dylan's album *Nashville Skyline* in 1969, it became fashionable to record in Nashville. Hence, New York record producer Elliot Mazer went to Nashville and took four noted sessionmen into a studio to record some instrumentals - Kenneth Buttrey (drums), David Briggs (keyboards), Mac Gayden (guitar) and Norbert Putnam (bass). Mazer felt that the sessions needed more of a country feel so he then added Charlie McCoy (b. 28 March 1941; harmonica), Wayne Moss (guitar), Ken Lauber (piano), Weldon Myrick (steel guitar), Buddy Spicher (fiddle) and Bobby Thompson (banjo). These leading session musicians began recording in their own right following interest generated by *Nashville Skyline*, on which McCoy and Buttery appeared. Area Code 615 was never intended as a permanent vehicle. The sessions came alive when Spicher and Thompson developed a bluegrass arrangement of 'Hey Jude', and the concept of recording familiar tunes, with the lead instruments playing country and the rhythm section playing rock 'n' roll, was born. They named themselves Area Code 615 after the telephone code number for Nashville. McCoy and Buttrey alone developed 'Stone Fox Chase', which became the theme for BBC Television's rock programme *The Old Grey Whistle Test*. The musicians returned to individual session work, although Moss, Gayden, Buttrey, and occasionally McCoy worked as Barefoot Jerry.
● ALBUMS: *Area Code 615* (Polydor 1969)★★★, *Trip In The Country* (Polydor 1970)★★★.

ARKIE THE ARKANSAS WOODCHOPPER

b. Luther William Ossenbrink, 21 September 1915, Knobnoster, Missouri, USA, d. 23 June 1981. He played guitar and fiddle and acted as the caller at local square dances as a boy before making his radio debut on KMBC, Kansas City, in 1928. The nickname was drawn from real life; he had actually worked with an axe felling trees and splitting rails, and later took an axe on stage with him as a gimmick. His act, which consisted of humour and recitations (frequently drawn from his own country boy upbringing), plus a mixture of popular ballads, mountain music and cowboy songs soon endeared him to the listeners. In 1929, he was hired by WLS Chicago as a regular for their *National Barn Dance*. He stayed with the show until it was dropped by WLS in 1960, a stay only beaten by one other artist, contralto Grace Wilson. When the programme restarted on WGN in 1960, Arkie joined the cast and remained with it until it finally ended in 1970, when he retired to his native Missouri. He recorded a few sides for ARC and Columbia Records but achieved little fame as a recording artist. He was, however, always very popular as a square dance caller, which led to the publication of a book of his calls in 1940 and the following year, he recorded some for an album release. He regularly toured with the *National Barn Dance* shows and on several occasions worked with Lulu Belle.
● ALBUMS: *Arkie & His Square Dance Band - Swing Your Partner* (Columbia 1950)★★★.

ARMSTRONG, BILLY

b. William Russell Armstrong, 18 March 1930, Streator, Illinois, USA. Educated in California, after the family relocated in 1935, Armstrong was encouraged to play violin as a child by his piano-playing mother, although at school, he was made to play sousaphone. In 1943, influenced by former Texas Playboy Joe Holley, he played professionally with the Dude Ranch Cowboys, in Costa Mesa. In 1947, he formed his own band, the Westerners, which began a career that has seen Armstrong play with numerous bands all over the USA and abroad and win countless awards as one of country music's outstanding fiddle players. In 1949, his idol, Holley, left Tommy Duncan's band and Armstrong, although totally inexperienced on the electrified fiddle required by Duncan, replaced him and toured the south-west. He next returned to Los Angeles and joined Hi Busse And The Frontiersmen. In 1951, Armstrong formed his Westernaires and before disbanding in 1957, they played residencies in Long Beach and broadcast on KXLA Pasadena. In 1958, he played with Hank Thompson until, tired of travelling, he joined Cliffie Stone's Hometown Jamboree, before joining Tex Williams' band, the Western Caravan. In 1963, he left to rejoin Hi Busse And The Frontiersmen on their tours with several film and television stars, including the cast of *Bonanza*. In 1963, he rejected the opportunity to join the Sons Of The Pioneers but when asked again in October 1966, he accepted. He sang lead and in trios and varied his own fiddle playing to match the style of Karl Farr. He remained a Pioneer for six years, during which time they toured extensively, even to the Orient, but he never recorded with them. In 1972, he reluctantly left the group to pursue a solo career and later that year toured with the Chaparrel Brothers. He made his first solo recording in 1959, and in 1965 recorded a much respected version of the 'Orange Blossom Special'. During the 70s, he recorded albums for Hillside and toured extensively. He was named by the Academy of Country Music as Fiddle Player Of The Year for 13 successive years from 1965-77.
● ALBUMS: *Billy Don't Sell Your Fiddle* (Hillside 1972)★★★, *The World's Greatest Fiddle Player* (Hillside 1976)★★★.
● COMPILATIONS: *The Best Of Billy Armstrong* (Hillside 1975)★★★.

ARNOLD, EDDY

b. Richard Edward Arnold, 15 May 1918, on a farm near Madisonville, Chester County, Tennessee, USA. Arnold's father and mother played fiddle and guitar, respectively, and he learned guitar as a child. His father died on Eddy's 11th birthday and he left school to work on the farm. By the end of the year the bank foreclosed, and the farm was sold but the family stayed as sharecroppers. Deciding that such a thing would not happen to him again he turned his thoughts to music and began playing at local dances. In 1936, working with a fiddle-playing friend, Speedy McNatt, he made his debut on local radio WTJS Jackson and during the next few years played various venues including Memphis, Louisville and St. Louis. Between 1940 and 1943 he was a member of Pee Wee King's Golden West Cowboys, appearing with them on the *Grand Ole Opry* and touring with the *Opry*'s travelling *Camel Caravan Show*. Late in 1943, as 'The Tennessee Plowboy', he launched his solo career, playing six days a week on WSM. Signed by RCA Records he made his country chart debut in 1945 with 'Each Minute Seems A Million Years' and soon replaced Roy Acuff as country music's most popular and prolific singer. Between 1945 and 1955 he had 21 number 1 singles among his 68 US country chart hits. Sentimental ballads, incorporating the plaintive steel guitar work of Little Roy Wiggins, were the norm and many, such as the million-sellers 'I'll Hold You In My Heart Till I Can Hold You In My Arms', 'Anytime', 'Bouquet Of Roses' and 'Just A Little Lovin' Will Go A Long Way', also became Top 30 US pop chart hits. Perhaps his best-remembered recording from this decade is 'Cattle Call'. During the late 40s he varied his image: although still retaining the nickname he became a country crooner wearing a tuxedo and bow tie. Colonel Tom Parker became his manager and was so successful with his promotion that Arnold was soon a nationally known star. Some of Parker's publicity stunts were unique for their time, such as the occasion when he travelled to a disc jockey convention in Nashville astride an elephant, bearing a cloth saying 'Never Forget Eddy Arnold'. Arnold began his solo *Opry* career as host of the *Ralston Purina* segment in 1946 but in 1948, due to Parker's unacceptable demands on the WSM management for shares of gate receipts, he left, being replaced on the *Opry* roster by another country crooner, George Morgan. In 1948, with the exception of Jimmy Wakely's recording of 'One Has My Heart', Arnold's recordings held the number 1 position in the country charts for the whole year. Arnold eventually tired of Parker's management and apparently sacked him; he has said it was because 'I am a very conservative man', but few believed that was the sole reason.

During the 50s, he appeared on all major radio and television shows and became the first country singer to host his own network television show, *Eddy Arnold Time*. He also became one of the first country singers to play at Carnegie Hall and later appeared in concerts with major symphony orchestras. It is impossible to categorize his new style as either country or pure pop. Many of his early fans objected to it but the television and cabaret performances won him countless new fans from the wider audience and he easily maintained his popularity and chart successes. After 1954, his nickname no longer appeared on the records and he moved to MGM in 1972, but returned to RCA four years later. Between 1956 and 1983 he took his tally of US country chart hits to 145, and his number 1 singles to 28 (and 92 of the entries had made the Top 10!). Again, many recordings achieved crossover success, including 'Tennessee Stud', 'What's He Doing In My World' and his biggest US pop hit 'Make The World Go Away', which reached number 6 in 1965 and the next year repeated the feat in the UK pop charts. Several of his albums have also achieved Top 10 status in the US album charts. He appeared in several films, including starring roles in *Feudin' Rhythm* and *Hoedown*, and he even received a mention in *Jailhouse Rock*. He was elected to the Country Music Hall Of Fame in 1966 and by the 80s he had semi-retired to his home near Nashville. RCA have assessed that his record sales are in excess of 85 million.

● ALBUMS: *Anytime* (RCA 1952)★★★★, *All-Time Hits From The Hills* (RCA 1952)★★★★, *All Time Favorites* (RCA 1953)★★★★, *An American Institution (10th Anniversary Album)* (RCA 1954)★★★, *Chapel On The Hill* (RCA 1954)★★★, *Wanderin' With Eddy Arnold* (RCA 1955)★★★, *Anytime* (RCA 1955)★★★★, *A Dozen Hits* (RCA 1956)★★★, *A Little On The Lonely Side* (RCA 1956)★★★, *When They Were Young* (RCA 1957)★★★, *My Darling, My Darling* (RCA 1957)★★★, *Praise Him, Praise Him (Fanny Crosby Hymns)* (RCA 1958)★★, *Have Guitar, Will Travel* (reissued as *Eddy Arnold Goes Travelin'*) (RCA 1959)★★★, *Eddy Arnold* (RCA 1959)★★★★, *Thereby Hangs A Tale* (RCA 1959)★★★, *Eddy Arnold Sings Them Again* (RCA 1960)★★★, *More Eddy Arnold* (RCA 1960)★★★★, *You Gotta Have Love* (RCA 1960)★★★, *Christmas With Eddy Arnold* (RCA 1961)★★, *Let's Make Memories Tonight* (RCA 1961)★★★, *One More Time* (RCA 1962)★★★★, *Our Man Down South* (RCA 1963)★★★, *Country Songs I Love To Sing* (RCA 1963)★★★, *Faithfully Yours* (RCA 1963)★★★, *Cattle Call* (RCA 1963)★★★★, *Pop Hits From The Country Side* (RCA 1964)★★★, *Eddy's Songs* (RCA 1964)★★★, with Needmore Creek Singers *Folk Song Book* (RCA 1964)★★★, *Sometimes I'm Happy, Sometimes I'm Blue* (RCA 1964)★★★, *The Easy Way* (RCA 1965)★★★, *I'm Throwing Rice (At The Girl I Love)* (RCA 1965)★★★, *My World* (RCA 1965)★★★, *Somebody Liked Me* (RCA 1966)★★★, *I Want To Go With You* (RCA 1966)★★★, *The Last Word In Lonesome* (RCA 1966)★★★, *Lonely Again* (RCA 1967)★★★, *Turn The World Around* (RCA 1967)★★★, *The Everloving World Of Eddy Arnold* (RCA 1968)★★★★, *Romantic World Of Eddy Arnold* (RCA 1968)★★★★, *Walkin' In Love Land* (RCA 1968)★★★, *Songs Of The Young World* (RCA 1969)★★★, *The Warmth Of Eddy Arnold* (RCA 1969)★★★, *The Glory Of Love* (RCA 1969)★★★, *This Is Eddy Arnold* (RCA 1970)★★★★, *Standing Alone* (RCA 1970)★★★, *Love And Guitars* (RCA 1970)★★★, *Then You Can Tell Me Goodbye* (RCA 1971)★★★, *Welcome To My World* (RCA 1971)★★★, *Loving Her Was Easier* (RCA 1971)★★★, *Portrait Of My Woman* (RCA 1971)★★★, *Chained To A Memory* (MGM 1972)★★★, *Eddy Arnold (Sings For Housewives & Other Lovers)* (MGM 1972)★★, *Lonely People* (MGM 1972)★★★, *I Love How You Love Me* (MGM 1973)★★★, *The World Of Eddy Arnold* (MGM 1973)★★★★, *Christmas Greetings From Nashville* (MGM 1973)★★★, *So Many Ways/If The Whole World Stopped Lovin'* (MGM 1973)★★★, *Eddy Arnold Sings Love Songs* (MGM 1974)★★★, *I Wish That I Had Loved You Better* (MGM 1974)★★★, *Misty Blue* (MGM 1974)★★★, *She's Got Everything I Need* (MGM 1974)★★★, *The Wonderful World Of Eddy Arnold* (MGM 1975)★★★★, *Eddy* (MGM 1976)★★★, *Eddy Arnold's World Of Hits* (MGM 1976)★★★★, *I Need You All The Time* (RCA 1977)★★★, *Somebody Loves You* (RCA 1979)★★★, *A Legend And His Lady* (RCA 1980)★★★, *Man For All Seasons* (RCA 1981)★★★, *Country Music - Eddy Arnold* (RCA 1981)★★★, *Don't Give Up On Me* (RCA 1982)★★★, *Close Enough To Love* (RCA 1983)★★★, *Anytime* (RCA 1988)★★★, *Christmas With Eddy Arnold* (RCA 1990)★★, *Hand-Holdin' Songs* (RCA 1990)★★★, *You Don't Miss A Thing* (RCA 1991)★★★, *Last Of The Love Song Singers: Then & Now* (RCA 1993)★★★.

● COMPILATIONS: *The Best Of Eddy Arnold* (RCA 1967)★★★, *Living Legend* (K-Tel 1974)★★★, *Country Gold* (RCA 1975)★★★, *Pure Gold-Eddy Arnold* (RCA1975)★★★, *Eddy Arnold's Best* (RCA 1979)★★★, *20 Of The Best* (RCA 1982)★★★, *Eddy Arnold - A Legendary Performer* (RCA 1983)★★★, *Collector's Series* (RCA 1987)★★★, *All Time Favourites* (RCA 1987)★★★★, *Best Of Eddy Arnold* (Curb 1990)★★★, *The Essential Eddy Arnold* (RCA 1996)★★★★.

● FURTHER READING: *It's A Long Way From Chester County*, Eddy Arnold. *Eddy Arnold: I'll Hold You In My Heart*, Don Cusic. *Eddy Arnold: Pioneer Of The Nashville Sound*, Michael Streissguth. *Eddy Arnold Discography (1944-1996)*, Michael D. Freda.

ARTHUR, CHARLINE

b. Charline Highsmith, 2 September 1929, Henrietta, Texas, USA, d. 27 November 1987, Pocatello, Idaho, USA. The second of a Pentecostal preacher's 12 children, she grew up in Paris, Texas, and first sang locally with her sister Dottie. By 1945, inspired by Ernest Tubb, she sang on KPLT and married Jack Arthur, who later played bass on her recordings. In the late 40s, she played Texas clubs and made her first recordings for Bullet, including 'I've Got The Boogie Blues'. After relocating to KERB Kermit, she was heard by 'Colonel' Tom Parker, which led to a songwriting contract with Hill & Range and her recording for RCA/Victor Records. Between February 1953 and May 1956, she recorded 28 tracks, although none charted. She toured with major artists, including Elvis Presley, who was impressed with her bouncy style, and she appeared on major shows, including the *Ozark Jubilee* and the *Louisiana Hayride*. She also played the *Grand Ole Opry* who vetted her material, some being considered too racy. She left RCA, probably through her inability to work with Chet Atkins, but she also had a reputation for unpredictability. In 1957, she and Jack Arthur separated and her career slumped on to hard times. In the 60s, financially embarrassed, she sang in small clubs and in a trio with sisters Dottie and Betty Sue, before spending five years resident at a Chubbuck, Idaho nightclub. Between 1965 and 1978, constantly struggling to make a living, she was active on the west coast, where she also recorded two sides each for Rustic, Wytra and Republic. In 1978, a major problem with arthritis saw her retire to Idaho, where she lived on a small disability pension until dying in her sleep at her home in Idaho in November 1987. In the early 50s, she was an important female contributor when that sex had few major performers, but her unpredictability and bold, blues-tinged vocals did not cater to the establishment. She was the first female country singer ever to wear trousers on stage, which suited her very mobile stage presentation. She always maintained that she was 'shaking that thing on stage long before Elvis even thought about it'. Writer Bob Allen summarized her approach when he stated: 'She had the misfortune of being stylistically slightly ahead of and out of step with her times. Her unique presence was indeed a far cry from the prim proper image and style that the conservative music industry demanded of female country singers in that era'. In 1986, German Bear Family Records issued an album containing 16 of her RCA recordings. They included the 1955 recording of 'Kiss The Baby Goodnight', which, in those days, was considered to be somewhat infamous or suggestive in certain quarters.
● COMPILATIONS: *Welcome To The Club* (Bear Family 1986)★★★★.

ASHLEY, CLARENCE TOM

b. Clarence Earl McCurry, 29 September 1895, Bristol, Tennessee, USA, d. 2 June 1967. After the family relocated to Mountain City, in eastern Tennessee, he was raised by his grandfather, Enoch Ashley, and legally assumed his grandfather's surname. He learned banjo and guitar as a child and developed a repertoire of traditional and mountain songs. In 1911, he began singing with medicine shows and with few breaks, he continued to play the show circuits until the mid-40s. He worked, at different times, with several other artists including Roy Acuff, Tex Isley, Lester Flatt and Charlie Monroe. Between 1928 and 1933, he made some solo recordings but the majority, usually playing guitar and singing some vocals, were made as a member of a band. He recorded with the Carolina Tar Heels (including Garley Foster and Dock Boggs), the Hayward County Ramblers, Byrd Moore And His Hot Shots, the Blue Ridge Mountain Entertainers (including Gwen Foster, no relation to Garley) and in 1933, he and Gwen Foster (harmonica) recorded numerous tracks for ARC. In 1929 and 1930, he made solo recordings with his banjo, including his noted versions of 'The Coo Coo Bird' and 'The House Carpenter'. In 1960, at a fiddle convention in Galax, Virginia, folk historian Ralph Rinzler persuaded Ashley to come out of retirement and again play his banjo, and in 1961 and 1962, Ashley, along with Doc Watson, Clint Howard and Fred Price, recorded (in New York) and made concert appearances. Ashley proved a hit with the 60s folk revival audiences and he played at New York's Carnegie Hall and at major folk festivals, including Newport. Greatly surprised but delighted with the interest in his old-time music, he continued to perform until his death in June 1967. Ashley claimed to have written the noted bluegrass standard 'My Home's Across The Blue Ridge Mountains', which he first recorded in 1929. Examples of his early recordings may also be found on compilations by various labels including Folkways, County and Rounder Records.
● COMPILATIONS: with Doc Watson *Old Time Music at Clarence Ashley's Volume 1* (Folkways 1961)★★★, with Watson *Old Time Music At Clarence Ashley's Volume 2* (Folkways 1963)★★★, *Clarence Ashley & Tex Isley* (Folkways 1966)★★★, with Gwen Foster *Ashley & Foster* (Yazoo)★★★.

ASHWORTH, ERNIE

b. Ernest Bert Ashworth, 15 December 1928, Huntsville, Alabama, USA. In his youth, the country singer-songwriter longed to be a star on the *Grand Ole Opry*. His first job was in the civil service, but he moved into radio in Huntsville in the late 40s and played in a local band, the Tune Twisters. Ashworth moved to Nashville in 1950 where he worked in radio and television. In 1955, as Billy Worth, he made his first recordings for MGM but he grew disillusioned and returned to Huntsville in 1957 where he worked in a missile factory. In 1960 Wesley Rose became his manager and he secured a contract with US Decca Records. His first release, 'Each Moment Spent With You', reached number 4 in the US country charts. In 1962, after further country hits with 'You Can't Pick A Rose In December' and 'Forever Gone', he moved to Hickory Records and found success with 'Everybody But Me'. In 1963 his recording of John D. Loudermilk's 'Talk Back Trembling Lips' topped the US country charts, although it was a pop hit for Johnny Tillotson. In March 1964 Ashworth became a member of the *Opry* and remains a regular performer, now known as Ernie rather than Ernest. He was featured in the 1965 film *The Farmer's Other Daughter*, and other successes included 'I Love To Dance With Annie' and 'The D.J. Cried'. Ashworth still tours occasionally.
● ALBUMS: *Talk Back Trembling Lips* (Hickory 1963)★★★, *Hits Of Today And Tomorrow* (Hickory 1964)★★.
● COMPILATIONS: *The Best Of Ernie Ashworth* (Hickory 1968)★★★, *Ernest Ashworth Sings His Greatest Hits* (Starday 1976)★★.

ASLEEP AT THE WHEEL

Ray Benson (b. 16 March 1951, Philadelphia, Pennsylvania, USA; guitar, vocals), Christine O'Connell (b. 21 March 1953, Williamsport, Maryland, USA; vocals), Lucky Oceans (b. Reuben Gosfield, 22 April 1951, Philadelphia, Pennsylvania, USA; steel guitar), Floyd Domino (piano) and Leroy Preston (rhythm guitar, drums) formed the core of this protean western swing-styled unit. Although initially based in West Virginia, the group later moved to Austin, Texas, where they found a more receptive audience in the wake of their infectious debut album. They had a US Top 10 single in 1973 with 'The Letter That Johnny Walker Read' and won a Grammy for their version of Count Basie's 'One O'Clock Jump'. However, despite an undoubted live appeal and an appearance in the rock film *Roadie*, the group's anachronistic style has hampered a more widespread success. The Bob Wills tribute album featured several guest artists, including Willie Nelson, Chet Atkins, Merle Haggard and Dolly Parton.
● ALBUMS: *Comin' Right At Ya* (Sunset 1973)★★★, *Asleep At The Wheel* (Epic 1974)★★★, *Texas Gold* (Capitol 1975)★★★★, *Wheelin' And Dealin'* (Capitol 1975)★★★, with various artists *Texas Country* (1976)★★, *The Wheel* (Capitol 1977)★★★★, *Collision Course* (Capitol 1978)★★★, *Served Live* (Capitol 1979)★★★, *Framed* (MCA 1980)★★★, *Asleep At The Wheel* (MCA/Dot 1985)★★, *Jumpin' At The Woodside* (Edsel 1986)★★★, *Ten* (Epic 1987)★★★, *Western Standard Time* (Epic 1988)★★★, *Keepin' Me Up Nights* (Arista 1990)★★★, *Tribute To The Music Of Bob Wills And The Texas Playboys* (Liberty 1993)★★★, *The Wheel Keeps On Rollin'* (Capitol Nashville 1995)★★★, *Back To The Future Now - Live At Arizona Charlie's, Las Vegas* (Epic 1997)★★★, *Merry Texas Christmas, Y'All* (High Street Records 1997)★★★.
● COMPILATIONS: *The Very Best Of Asleep At The Wheel* (See For Miles 1987)★★★, *Greatest Hits - Live & Kickin'* (Arista 1991)★★★, *Best Of* (CEMA 1992)★★★, *The Swinging Best Of Asleep At The Wheel* (Epic 1992)★★★.

ASTON, JOHN

b. 1 July 1942, Oldbury, near Birmingham, Warwickshire, England. He gained his first musical inspiration from his parents who both sang old-time music hall hits and popular songs of the day. He obtained his first guitar in 1957, at the height of the skiffle craze and subsequently played in a skiffle group but maintains that, when it was his turn to sing, he always sang a country song. In 1966, primarily because of the greater opportunity to become involved in country music in the area than he found in Birmingham, he relocated to Doncaster, Yorkshire. He played with several different groups for experience until March 1971, when he decided to embark on a solo career. He made his first recordings in 1973, 'The Old Lamplighter' and the self-penned 'I Haven't Changed A Bit'. A television appearance singing the former attracted attention and led to work around the British country club circuit. Since then, apart from his albums, he has recorded two EPs, *Waylon & Willie* (Bird's Nest 1978) and with Julie Allison *Together* (Future Earth 1984), and three cassette-only releases *Memories* (1988), *The Old Lamplighter* (1989), *Evergreen* (1992), and worked on recording sessions with other artists. He has toured the UK with visiting American artists including Red Sovine (1975) and Mac Wiseman (1976). During his long associations with the British country music scene, he has to date received 20

awards, including the Radio & Record Mirror award for 'Top Solo Performer In Great Britain', which was presented to him by Jim Reeves' widow, Mary Reeves Davis. He has written several of his own songs, including his popular ballad 'Room Of Shadows', which was written late one night while driving home down the motorway from a show. He has a vast knowledge of songs, even those from music hall days, and in concert, on occasions, he enjoys himself by inviting his audience to try to request a song that he does not know - since his repertoire is in excess of 1,500 songs and goes back to the 20s, he is rarely beaten.
● ALBUMS: *Just An Old Fashioned Locket* (Westwood 1974)★★★, *Riverboat Queen* (Look 1977)★★★, *You Take The Blame For The Roses* (Happy Face 1980)★★★.

ATCHER, BOB

b. James Robert Atcher, 11 May 1914, Hardin County, Kentucky, USA. Atcher was the son of a tobacco farmer and square dance fiddler. The family moved to the Red River Valley of North Dakota in 1918 and here Atcher developed his love for cowboy songs. In 1926 the family returned to Kentucky and Atcher was soon performing on local radio. By 1931, he had a repertoire of hundreds of songs and his shows were heard over a wide area. Bob Atcher And His Kentucky Mountain Minstrels included his brother Francis, and Loeta Applegate who was the first of several vocalists to be given the name of 'Bonnie Blue Eyes'. Atcher recorded for US Columbia Records from 1937-58. In 1939, his comic 'crying' version of the Carter Family's 'I'm Thinking Tonight Of My Blue Eyes', was successful. Atcher appeared in westerns, wore cowboy outfits and often appeared with his horse, Golden Storm. He recorded many western songs and his version of 'You Are My Sunshine' was recorded before that of Jimmie Davis. He was a featured performer on WLS's *National Barn Dance* for many years from 1948. His country hits include 'I Must Have Been Wrong', 'Signed, Sealed And Delivered', 'Tennessee Border' and 'Why Don't You Haul Off And Love Me?'. He also wrote 'Don't Rob Another Man's Castle' and 'Money, Marbles And Chalk'. In 1959 he became the Mayor of Schaumburg, Illinois, and concentrated on politics for the next 16 years. In the mid-70s, he started performing with his family, often featuring gospel music.
● ALBUMS: *Bob Atcher's Early American Folk Songs* 10-inch (Columbia 1953)★★★, *Songs Of The Saddle* (Columbia 1954)★★★, *Bob Atcher's Early American Folk Songs* 12-inch (Columbia 1955)★★★, *The Dean Of Cowboy Singers* (Columbia 1964)★★★.

ATKINS, BOBBY

b. Bobby Lee Atkins, 22 May 1933, High Shoals, North Carolina, USA. Atkins' mother first taught him to play guitar but, in his early teens, after seeing Don Reno, he changed to banjo, which has become his main instrument. His interest in bluegrass music grew and in the early 50s, he played with several bluegrass bands. Later in the decade, he played with the bands of both Bill and Charlie Monroe. In 1956, he and Joe Stone formed the Dixie Mountaineers and worked various radio stations and were regulars on WRVA's *New Dominican Barn Dance*. They eventually disbanded and Atkins returned to play with Bill Monroe until in the early 60s, he formed his band the Countrymen and with this unit he continued to play into the 90s. Obviously there have been many changes of personnel and among noted band members are Frank Poindexter, Slim Martin and Tony Rice. In more recent times the band has become more of a family unit. Several of his sons are talented bluegrass musicians, and his daughter Torey often sings lead vocals. Atkins, over the years, has recorded for various labels and his friendship with Jim Eanes, with whom he often worked, led to them recording two albums together.

● ALBUMS: *Country 'N' Grass* (Colony 1974)★★★, *Back Home In Gold Hill* (Heritage 1976)★★★, *A Tribute To Charlie Monroe* (Old Homestead 1977)★★★, *Bluegrass With A Country Flavor* (Old Homestead 1978)★★★★, with Frank Poindexter, Tony Rice *1968 Sessions* (Old Homestead 1980)★★, *Enough To Keep Me Dreaming On* (Old Homestead 1981)★★★, featuring Torey Atkins *Sounds Of Starlight Lounge* (Old Homestead 1981)★★★, *Ole Time Sundays* (Rich-R-Tone 1983)★★★, *Back In The Good Ole Days* (Cattle 1984)★★★, *Good Times Can't Last* (Webco 1985)★★, *A Song For You* (Old Homestead 1986), *I've Lived A Lot In My Time* (Old Homestead 1986)★★, *Jim Eanes & Bobby Atkins & The Countrymen* (Old Homestead 1986)★★★, *Songs For Mama* (Old Homestead 1988)★★★, *Songs & Tunes Of The 50's* (Old Homestead 1988)★★★, *Feelings Of A Country Man* (Old Homestead 1989)★★★, *Dirty Rich* (Stokes 1991)★★, with Jim Eanes *Heart Of The South* (Rural Rhythm 1991)★★★, with Margie Lynn *Crimes Of The Heart* (Richway 1994)★★★.

ATKINS, CHET

b. Chester Burton Atkins, 20 June 1924, Luttrell, Tennessee, USA. Atkins is one of the most influential and prolific guitarists of the 20th century, as well as an important producer and an RCA Records executive. The son of a music teacher and brother of guitarist Jim Atkins (who played with Les Paul), Atkins began as a fiddler in the early 40s, with the Dixieland Swingers in Knoxville, Tennessee. He also played with artists including Bill Carlisle and Shorty Thompson. He moved to Cincinnati, Ohio, in 1946 and his first recording session took place that year, for Jim Bullet. In 1947 Atkins was signed to RCA, recording 16 tracks on 11 August, including a number of vocals. Atkins first performed at the *Grand Ole Opry* in Nashville in 1948, working with a band that included satirists Homer And Jethro. He toured with Maybelle Carter in 1949 and recorded as an accompanist with the Carter Family the following year. At that time he made a decision to concentrate on session work, encouraged and often hired by music publisher Fred Rose. During this period, Atkins recorded largely with MGM Records artists, such as Red Sovine and the Louvin Brothers, and most notably on 24 of Hank Williams' tracks for the label. He also recorded on several of the Everly Brothers' Cadence Records hits later in the 50s. In 1952 RCA executive Steve Sholes, who had signed Atkins for session work, gave him authority to build up the label's roster, and Atkins began a second career as a talent scout. By the mid-50s he was recording his own albums and producing 30 artists a year for RCA. Atkins' first album, *Chet Atkins' Gallopin' Guitar*, was issued in 1953, his discography eventually comprising over 100 albums under his own name. Among the other artists with whom he worked at RCA were Elvis Presley, Jim Reeves, Don Gibson, Charley Pride, Waylon Jennings, Hank Snow, Jerry Reed and Perry Como. He is generally regarded as the chief archi-

tect of the 'Nashville Sound'. His trademark guitar was a Grestch, which was later manufactured as the 'Chet Atkins Country Gentleman'. George Harrison endorsed this instrument, and this led to a huge increase in sales for the company during the 60s. During this decade Chet recorded the first of a series of guitar duet albums, including works with Snow, Reed, Merle Travis, Les Paul and Doc Watson. Atkins was named an RCA vice-president in 1968 and remained in that position until 1979. In the early 80s he left RCA for Columbia Records and continued to record for that company into the 90s. He has won several Grammy awards and was elected to the Country Music Hall of Fame in 1973. In the 90s he collaborated with Suzy Bogguss and Mark Knopfler and went full circle in 1996 with a true solo work, *Almost Alone*, which contained tributes to the aforementioned artists.

● ALBUMS: *Chet Atkins' Gallopin' Guitar* (RCA Victor 1953)★★★, *Stringin' Along With Chet Atkins* (RCA Victor 1953)★★★, *A Session With Chet Atkins* (RCA Victor 1954)★★★, *Chet Atkins In Three Dimensions* (RCA Victor 1956)★★★, *Finger Style Guitar* (RCA Victor 1956)★★, *Hi Fi In Focus* (RCA Victor 1957)★★, *Mister Guitar* (RCA Victor 1959)★★★, *Chet Atkins In Hollywood* (RCA Victor 1959)★★, *Teensville* (RCA Victor 1959)★★★, *Hum And Strum Along* (RCA Victor 1959)★★, *Chet Atkins' Workshop* (RCA Victor 1960)★★, *The Other Chet Atkins* (RCA Victor 1960)★★★, *Teensville* (RCA Victor 1960)★★, *Down Home* (RCA Victor 1961)★★★, *The Most Popular Guitar* (RCA Victor 1961)★★★, *Christmas With Chet Atkins* (RCA Victor 1961)★★, *Caribbean Guitar* (RCA Victor 1962)★★, *Back Home Hymns* (RCA Victor 1962)★★, *Our Man In Nashville* (RCA Victor 1963)★★★, *Travelin'* (RCA Victor 1963)★★★, *Teen Scene* (RCA Victor 1963)★★★, with Hank Snow *Reminiscing* (RCA Victor 1964)★★★, *Chet Atkins Picks On The Beatles* (RCA Victor 1965)★★, *Play Guitar With Chet Atkins* (RCA Victor 1966)★★★, *It's A Guitar World* (RCA Victor 1967)★★★, *Chet Atkins Picks The Best* (RCA Victor 1967)★★, *Class Guitar* (RCA Victor 1967)★★★, *Solo Flights* (RCA Victor 1968)★★, with Jerry Reed *Me And Jerry* (RCA Victor 1970)★★, with Hank Snow *C.B. Atkins & C.E. Snow By Special Request* (RCA Victor 1970)★★★, with Floyd Cramer and Boots Randolph *Chet, Floyd And Boots* (RCA 1971)★★★, with Reed *Me And Chet* (RCA Victor 1972)★★, with Merle Travis *The Atkins-Travis Traveling Show* (RCA Victor 1975)★★★, with Les Paul *Chester And Lester* (RCA Victor 1976)★★★, with Floyd Cramer and Danny Davis *Chet, Floyd And Danny* (RCA Victor 1977)★★★★, *A Legendary Performer* (RCA Victor 1977)★★★, *Me And My Guitar* (RCA Victor 1977)★★★, with Les Paul *Guitar Monsters* (RCA Victor 1978)★★★, *The First Nashville Guitar Quartet* (RCA Victor 1979)★★, *The Best Of Chet On The Road...Live* (RCA Victor 1980)★★, with Doc Watson *Reflections* (RCA Victor 1980)★★★, with Lenny Breau *Standard Brands* (1981)★★, *Work It Out With Chet Atkins* (Columbia 1983)★★, *Stay Tuned* (Columbia 1985)★★, *Street Dreams* (Columbia 1986)★★★, *Sails* (Columbia 1987)★★★, *Chet Atkins, C.G.P.* (Columbia 1988)★★★, with Mark Knopfler *Neck & Neck* (Columbia 1990)★★★, with Jerry Reed *Sneakin' Around* (Columbia 1992)★★★, *Read My Licks* (Columbia 1994)★★★★, *Almost Alone* (Columbia 1996)★★★, with Timmy Emmanuel *The Day Finger Pickers Took Over The World* (Columbia 1997)★★★.

● COMPILATIONS: *The Best Of Chet Atkins* (RCA Victor 1963)★★★★, *The Best Of Chet Atkins And Friends* (RCA 1976)★★★, *Solid Gold Guitar* (RCA 1982)★★★, *Guitar Pickin' Man* (1983)★★★, *Collector's Series* (RCA 1985)★★★, *Tennessee Guitar Man* (Pair 1986)★★, *Guitar For All Seasons* (Pair 1986)★★★, *20 Of The Best* (RCA 1986)★★★★, *The Best Of Chet Atkins & Friends* (RCA 1987)★★★, *The Best Of Chet Atkins & Friends, Volume 2* (RCA 1987)★★★, *Country Gems* (Pair 1990)★★★, *The RCA Years* 2-CD box set (RCA 1992)★★★★, *The Collection* (1993)★★★, *The Early Years 1945-54* 4-CD box set (1993)★★★, *The Essential Chet Atkins* (RCA 1996)★★★★.
● VIDEOS: *Chet Atkins & Friends* (MMG Video 1991).
● FURTHER READING: *Country Gentleman*, Chet Atkins with Bill Neeley.

AULDRIDGE, MIKE

b. 30 December 1938, Washington DC, USA. This highly respected US dobro player has performed on a number of bluegrass and country albums, mostly with the Seldom Scene. Auldridge is the nephew of Ellsworth T. Cozzens, the Hawaiian steel guitarist who played on several Jimmie Rodgers records. Having started playing guitar at the age of 12, Auldridge progressed to banjo within a short space of time, and was almost 20 when he played dobro for the first time. In 1969, Auldridge joined Emerson and Waldron, but with Bill Emerson leaving to join the Country Gentlemen, Auldridge continued performing with Cliff Waldron, from Jolo, West Virginia. The act grew to become the New Shades Of Grass, a six-piece outfit. Waldron planned to tour extensively, not a popular move in the eyes of Auldridge, who left with group member Ben Eldridge (banjo). With John Duffey (mandolin), Tom Gray (bass) and John Starling (guitar, vocals), they formed the Seldom Scene. The name came from the fact that they only played once a week and continued their day jobs in the meantime. They have made a number of fine bluegrass recordings and Auldridge continues to do session work for other artists.
● ALBUMS: *Blues And Bluegrass* (Takoma 1974)★★★★, *Dobro* (Takoma 1974)★★★, *Mike Auldridge* (Flying Fish 1976)★★★, *Mike Auldridge And Old Dog* (Flying Fish 1978)★★★, with Jeff Newman *Slidin' Smoke* (Flying Fish 1979)★★★★, *Eight String Swing* (Sugar Hill 1988)★★★, *Treasures Untold* (Sugar Hill 1989)★★★, as Auldridge, Reid And Coleman *High Time* (Sugar Hill 1989)★★★.

AUTRY, GENE

b. Orvin Gene Autry, 29 September 1907, near Tioga, Texas, USA. The eldest of four children of Delbert Autry, a poor tenant farmer, who moved his family many times over the years, before eventually arriving at Ravia, Oklahoma. His grandfather, a Baptist minister, taught him to sing when he was a child so that he could perform in his church choir and at other local events. Autry also learned to ride at an early age and worked the fields with his father. He grew up listening to cowboy songs and received his first guitar at the age of 12 (initially he studied the saxophone but chose the guitar so that he could sing as well). He graduated from school in 1924 and found work as a telegraph operator for the Frisco Railroad in Chelsea, Oklahoma. He used to take his guitar to work and one night his singing was heard by the famous entertainer Will Rogers, who stopped to send a

telegram. He suggested that Autry should look for a job in radio. After trying unsuccessfully to find work in New York, he returned to Oklahoma and began to appear on KVOO Tulsa as The Oklahoma Yodeling Cowboy. After hearing recordings of Jimmie Rodgers, he became something of a Rodgers clone as he tried to further his career. In 1929, he made his first RCA Victor recordings, 'My Dreaming Of You' and 'My Alabama Home', on which he was accompanied by Jimmy Long (a fellow telegrapher) and Frankie and Johnny Marvin. Further recordings followed for ARC Records under the direction of Art Satherley, some being released on various labels for chain store sales. It was because of releases on Conqueror for Sears that Autry found himself given the opportunity to join WLS in Chicago. In 1931, he became a featured artist on the *National Barn Dance*, as well as having his own *Conqueror Record Time*. Before long, Gene Autry 'Roundup' guitars and songbooks were being sold by Sears. Interestingly, WLS portrayed him as a singing cowboy even though, at this time, few of his songs were of that genre. Between 1931 and 1934, he was a hillbilly singer, who still at times sounded like Rodgers. In fact, most experts later rated him the best of the Rodgers impersonators. He began to include his own songs and such numbers as 'The Gangster's Warning' and 'My Old Pal Of Yesterday' became very popular.

Late in 1931, he recorded 'That Silver Haired Daddy Of Mine' as a duet with Jimmy Long, with whom he had co-written the song. The song eventually became Autry's first million-selling record. By 1934, he was well known as a radio and recording personality. Having for some time been portrayed as a singing cowboy by the publicity departments of his record companies, he now took his first steps to make the publicity come true. He was given a small part in the Ken Maynard film *In Old Santa Fe*, and soon afterwards starred in a strange 12-episode western/science fiction serial called *The Phantom Empire*. In 1935, Republic Pictures signed him to a contract and *Tumbling Tumbleweeds* became his first starring western film. His previous singing cowboy image was now reality. He sang eight songs in the film including the title track, 'That Silver Haired Daddy' and 'Ridin' Down The Canyon'. Further films followed in quick succession and by 1940 Autry ranked fourth among all Hollywood money-making stars at the box office. In January 1940, Gene Autry's *Melody Ranch* radio show, sponsored by the Wrigley Gum Company, first appeared on CBS and soon became a national institution, running until 1956. Helped out by such artists as Pat Buttram, Johnny Bond and the Cass County Boys, Autry regularly righted wrongs, sang his hits and as a result of the programme, built himself a new home in the San Fernando Valley called Melody Ranch.

Quite apart from the radio shows and films, he toured extensively with his stage show. It featured roping, Indian dancers, comedy, music, fancy riding from Autry, and smart horse tricks by Champion. By 1941, he was respected and famous all over the USA The little town of Berwyn, Oklahoma, even changed its name to Gene Autry, Oklahoma. His songs such as 'Be Honest With Me', 'Back In The Saddle Again' (which became his signature tune), 'You're The Only Star In My Blue Heaven', 'Goodbye, Little Darlin' Goodbye' (later recorded by Johnny Cash) and many more, became tremendously popular. In 1942, his income took a severe cut when he enlisted in the Air Force, being sworn in live on a *Melody Ranch* programme. He spent some time working on recruitment but then became a pilot in Air Ferry Command and saw service in the Far East, India and North Africa. During this period, he co-wrote with Fred Rose his classic song 'At Mail Call Today'. After his release from the services, he resumed his acting and recording career. Between 1944 and 1951, he registered 25 successive Top 10 country hits, including 'Here Comes Santa Claus' (later recorded by Elvis Presley), 'Rudolph, The Red-Nosed Reindeer', 'Peter Cottontail' and 'Frosty The Snow Man', which each sold one million copies. He also had Top 20 US pop chart success with 'Buttons And Bows'. He left Republic in 1947 and formed his own Flying A Productions, which produced his later films for release by Columbia. When he made his last B-movie western, *Last Of The Pony Riders*, in 1953, he had 89 feature films to his credit. Contrary to pre-vailing belief, there never was a feud between Autry and his replacement at Republic, Roy Rogers - it was purely the invention of Republic's publicity department.

During the 50s, he became very successful in business and purchased many radio and television stations. Between 1950 and 1956, he produced 91 episodes of *The Gene Autry Show* for CBS-TV. His company also produced many other televi-sion series, including *The Range Rider, The Adventures Of Champion* and *Annie Oakley*. His business interest became even more involved during the 60s, when apart from owning various radio and television companies, he became the owner of the California Angels major league baseball team. *Melody Ranch* reappeared as a television programme in the 60s and ran for seven years on Autry's KTLA station. It was syndicated to stations across the country and although Autry did not appear as a regular, he did make guest appearances. In 1986, Nashville Network decided to screen his Republic and Columbia B-movie westerns under the title of *Melody Ranch Theatre* with Autry himself doing opening and closing announcements. During his long career, Autry had three horses to fill the role of Champion. The original died in 1947. Champion III, who appeared in the Gene Autry television series and also as the star of the *Adventures Of Champion* television series, died in 1991 at the age of 42. There was also a personal appearance Champion and a pony known as Little Champ. During his career he regularly sported a custom-made C.F. Martin guitar, with beautiful ornamental pearl inlay, together with his name.

Autry was elected to the Country Music Hall Of Fame in 1969 for his songwriting abilities as well as his singing and acting. In 1980, he was inducted into the Cowboy Hall Of Fame Of Great Westerners. At the time of his induction, he was described as 'one of the most famous men, not only in America but in the world'. Autry sold the final 10 acres of his Melody Ranch film set in 1991. The ranch, in Placerita Canyon, California, which was used for the making of such classic westerns as *High Noon* and the television series *Gunsmoke* is scheduled to become a historical feature. His last US country chart entry was 'Old Soldiers Never Die' in 1971. Judging by the popularity of his old films and his recordings, it is probably true to say that neither do old cow-boys.

● ALBUMS: *Western Classics* (Columbia 1949)★★★, *Western Classics Vol. 2* (Columbia 1949)★★★, *Easter Favorites* (Columbia 1949)★★, *Champion* (Columbia 1950)★★★, *Merry Christmas with Gene Autry* (Columbia 1950)★★, *The Story Of The Nativity* (Columbia 1955)★★, *Little Johnny Pilgrim & Guffy The Goofy Gobbler* (Columbia 1955)★, *Rusty The Rocking Horse & Bucky, The Bucking Bronco* (Columbia 1955)★, *Sings Peter Cottontail* (Columbia 1955)★, *Stampede* (Columbia 1955)★★★, *Gene Autry & Champion Western Adventures* (Columbia 1955)★★, *At The Rodeo* (Columbia 1958)★★★, *Christmas With Gene Autry* (Challenge 1958)★★, with Rosemary Clooney and Art Carney *Christmas Favorites* (Harmony 1964)★★★★, *Great Western Hits* (Harmony 1965)★★★, *Melody Ranch* (Melody Ranch 1965)★★★, with Clooney, Art Carney *Sings Peter Cottontail (First Easter Record For Children)* (Harmony 1965)★, *Back In The Saddle Again* (Harmony 1966)★★★, *Gene Autry Sings* (Harmony 1966)★★★, *Rudolph The Red-Nosed Reindeer* (Grand Prix 1968)★, *Live From Madison Square Garden* (Republic 1968)★★, *Christmas Time* (1974)★★★, *Melody Ranch - A Radio Adventure* (Radiola 1975)★★, *Cowboy Hall Of Fame* (1976)★★★, *Murray Hill Record Theatre Presents Gene Autry's Melody Ranch* (1977)★★★, *50th Anniversary Album* (Republic 1978)★★★, *Songs Of Faith* (1978)★★, *Christmas Classics* (Starday 1978)★★, *Sounds Like Jimmie Rodgers* (1985)★★★.

● COMPILATIONS: *Greatest Hits* (Columbia 1961)★★★, *Golden Hits* (RCA Victor 1962)★★★★, *Country Music Hall Of Fame* (Columbia 1970)★★★, *Back In The Saddle Again* (Sony 1977)★★★, *22 All Time Favorites* (GRT 1977)★★★, *Columbia Historic Edition* (Columbia 1982)★★★, *Golden Hits* (Good Music 1985)★★★, *Christmas Favorites* (Columbia 1989)★★★, *Greatest Hits* (Sony 1992)★★★★, *The Essential 1933-46* (Columbia/Legacy 1992)★★★★, *South Of The Border* (Castle 1994)★★★, *Portrait Of An Artist* (Sound Exchange 1995)★★★★, *Blues Singer 1929-1931: Booger Rooger Saturday* (1996)★★★, *Sing, Cowboy, Sing! The Gene Autry Collection* 3-CD box set (Rhino 1997)★★★★.

● FURTHER READING: *Back In The Saddle Again*, Gene Autry with Mickey Herskowitz. *The Gene Autry Book*, David Rothel.

AXTON, HOYT

b. 25 March 1938, Duncan, Oklahoma, USA. The son of Mae Axton (who wrote 'Heartbreak Hotel'), Hoyt began as a folk-singer on the west coast. In 1962, he signed for Horizon Records for his first album, *The Balladeer*, which featured future Byrds leader Jim McGuinn on guitar. As the 60s unfolded, Axton expanded his repertoire to include blues and country, while also establishing himself as a songwriter of considerable talent. His first hit as a composer was the Kingston Trio's 'Greenback Dollar' and later in the decade he wrote Steppenwolf's famous drug song, 'The Pusher'. The victim of cocaine addiction for many years, he still managed to record prolifically, though it was as a composer that he enjoyed commercial success. Two major hits in the 70s, courtesy of Three Dog Night ('Joy To The World') and Ringo Starr ('No No Song') supplemented his income, while also maintaining his standing as a recording artist. Having over-come his drug dependency at the end of the decade, he had major acting roles in the films *The Black Stallion* (1979) and *Gremlins* (1984), formed his own record label Jeremiah, and continued touring on a regional basis. In 1991 he made an attempt to re-enter the recording market with the critically acclaimed *Spin Of The Wheel*. His rejuvenated career suf-fered a blow in 1995 when he had a heart attack.

● ALBUMS: *The Balladeer* (Horizon 1962)★★★, *Thunder 'n' Lightnin'* (Horizon 1963)★★★★, *Saturday's Child* (Horizon 1963)★★★, *Hoyt Axton Explodes* (Vee Jay 1964)★★★, *Greenback Dollar* (Vee Jay 1965)★★★★, *Hoyt Axton Sings Bessie Smith* (Exodus 1965)★★, *My Griffin Is Gone* (Columbia 1969)★★, *Joy To The World* (Capitol 1971)★★, *Country Anthem* (1971)★★★, *Less Than A Song* (1973)★★, *Life Machine* (A&M 1974)★★★, *Southbound* (A&M 1975)★★, *Fearless* (A&M 1976)★★★, *Road Songs* (A&M 1977)★★★, *Snowblind Friend* (MCA 1977)★★★, *Free Sailin'* (MCA 1978)★★★, *A Rusty Old Halo* (Young Blood 1979)★★, *Where Did The Money Go* (Young Blood 1980)★★★, *Everybody's Going On The Road* (Young Blood 1982)★★, *Spin Of The Wheel* (1991)★★.
● COMPILATIONS: *The Best Of Hoyt Axton* (Vee Jay 1964)★★★★.

AXTON, MAE BOREN

b. Mae Boren, 14 September 1914, Bardwell, Texas, USA, d. 9 April 1997, Hendersonville, Tennessee, USA. Axton's contribution to popular music was dwarfed by a singular piece of work. As co-composer of one of Elvis Presley's definitive works - 'Heartbreak Hotel' - she was able to live the rest of her life in financial security. Raised in Oklahoma, many of Axton's siblings were politicians, including her brother David, a state senator. She attended the University of Oklahoma and gained a degree in journalism, and began work for *Life* magazine as a reporter. After marrying schoolteacher John Axton, she moved to Jacksonville, Florida, and herself began a teaching career. However, she also began working as a songwriter with local musicians Glen Reeves and Tommy Durden. It was while working for Hank Snow, that she first saw Presley performing in May 1955. Axton and Durden composed 'Heartbreak Hotel' within an hour, based on a story Durden had read in the *Miami Herald* about a hotel suicide. Axton played a demo of the song to Presley at a radio convention in Nashville. Presley agreed to record the song, on the condition that he would be credited as co-composer and receive a third of the royalties. It duly became his first single for RCA Records, and his first US chart-topper, playing a significant part in launching the singer as a global phenomenon. Despite this, Presley never used any other Axton composition (though he did record 'Never Been To Spain', written by her son, Hoyt Axton). 'Heartbreak Hotel' was her only hit composition, although she did write material for other artists, including Patsy Cline ('Pick Me Up On Your Way Down'), Wanda Jackson ('Honey Bop') and Hank Snow ('What Do I Know Today'). She also wrote the sleevenotes to the Elvis tribute album *The King Is Gone*, by Ronnie McDowell. Her son Hoyt eventually became a successful solo artist, and later a film actor. Mae Axton continued to work in publicity and radio, and in 1973, published her memoir, *Country Singers As I Know 'Em*. Hoyt also recorded for the record label his mother started in 1992, DPJ Records.
● FURTHER READING: *Country Singers As I Know 'Em*, Mae Boren Axton.

BAD LIVERS

A startling bluegrass trio from Austin, Texas, USA, the Bad Livers' career has done much to deflate criticisms about that particular musical strand being obsolete. The group was formed in late 1990 by Mark Rubin (double bass, tuba), Danny Barnes (banjo, guitar) and Ralph White III (fiddle, accordion). With their influences spanning Cajun, heavy metal, punk and gospel, Rubin and Barnes started out in the Dallas bluegrass band Killbilly. After recruiting White they became first the Danny Barnes Trio, then Bad Livers. Early performances at the Saxon club in Austin found Paul Leary of the Butthole Surfers in the audience. Liking what he heard, Leary insisted on producing the group's debut album, and also secured them a recording contract with his label, Touch & Go Records (via the subsidiary outlet Quarterstick). This kinetic collection of songs included a cover version of a Butthole Surfers track, as well as Reno And Smiley's 'I Know You're Married'. They then travelled to the UK for a month's tour, confounding audiences and contributing to an album by the Rockingbirds. *The Golden Years* EP featured cover versions of Motörhead and Johnny Cash songs, although the group's members were keen to point out that they saw both as legitimate musical reference points, and maintained that they had not been included for novelty value. *Horses In Mines*, a humorous and bizarre collection of songs featuring a guest appearance by bluesman Steve James, was mastered at the Beatles' Abbey Road Studios. Rubin then spent several months collaborating with Santiago Jiminez Jnr., before work on a third Bad Livers album, *Hogs On The Highway*, commenced. However, its release was delayed because of a move to a new label, Sugar Hill Records. Although Ralph White III contributed to the record, he had left the group by the time of its release because of the band's demanding touring schedule. His replacement was Bob Grant (mandolin, guitar).
● ALBUMS: *Delusions Of Banjer* (Quarterstick 1992)★★★, *Horses In The Mines* (Quarterstick 1994)★★★, *Hogs On The Highway* (Sugar Hill 1997)★★★.

BAILES BROTHERS

Homer Bailes, a carpenter and preacher, and his wife Nannie rented a small farm in Kanawha County, near Charleston, West Virginia, USA, and in the face of abject poverty, they struggled to raise their four sons. They were Kyle (b. 7 May 1915, d. 3 March 1996), John (b. 24 June 1918, d. January 1990, Swainsboro, Georgia, USA), Walter Butler (b. 17 January 1920) and Homer (b. 8 May 1922). After her husband's death in 1925, Nannie took in washing to supplement the income and Kyle's schooling was stopped as he found work to bring in some money. The boys had a guitar, which their mother managed to buy from a mail-order catalogue. Nannie had children by a previous marriage and in the early 30s, their half-brother, Jennings Thomas, who worked as a rodeo rider and musician, arrived home and created sufficient interest for he and Kyle to sing together on local radio. A few years later, after crop failure, the family moved to Charleston, where Johnny found work to keep his two siblings at school but soon looked for a musical career. The boys sang together locally and appeared in churches as the Hymn Singers. Johnny worked for a time with a medicine show but he soon joined with Kyle and Walter on a regular radio programme on WCHS. In 1937, Johnny Bailes and his close friend Red Sovine appeared as Smiley and Red the Singing Sailors and also became members of Jim Pike's Carolina Tar Heels. For a short time, in 1938, they played on WWVA Wheeling but returned to Charleston when Sovine married. In 1939, Johnny formed a group known as the Happy Valley Folks, which included Skeets Williamson, his sister LaVerne (who became famous as Molly O'Day) and Little Jimmy Dickens, who was billed as the Singing Midget. They played regularly on WJLS Beckley and proved very popular. Walter and Kyle Bailes were playing with their group at WCHS and at WPAR but also soon moved to Beckley. Early in 1941, both groups disbanded and Johnny and Walter appeared on WCHS as a duo, although on occasions they were joined by their brothers. They moved to WSAZ Huntington, where their popularity grew as a result of their radio show, *Tri-State Jamboree*, so called because of the station's powerful transmissions that covered parts of Kentucky and Ohio as well as West Virginia. In 1943, their friendship with Roy Acuff led to their becoming members of the *Grand Ole Opry*. (Johnny and Walter became the first West Virginians to star on the *Opry*). Kyle worked at various stations and after Homer's military service, both eventually joined their brothers in Nashville. Late in 1946, they recorded for King and about the same time, they left the *Opry* and moved to KWKH Shreveport. When the *Louisiana Hayride* commenced in 1948, they soon became firm favourites and had so many requests to play outside venues that a second group was formed, which contained Jimmie Osborne and Claude King. Their band, the West Virginia Home Folks, contained several noted instrumentalists, including steel guitarist Shot Jackson and mandolinist Clyde Baum. The four brothers recorded for Columbia in April 1947 and in July, Walter left to become a minister. Soon after Kyle also withdrew from playing but acted as manager and his place was taken by Tillman Franks. Johnny and Homer had some disagreement and parted late in 1949, which led to them performing on different stations. After this the family continued to be involved with country and gospel music. In August 1952, Walter and Johnny reunited at KCRT, Baytown, Texas, for a religious show in which Walter preached and Johnny sang.

They also recorded together for King Records in 1953 and continued to work together until 1956, when Johnny became a disc jockey in Georgia. During the 60s, Walter was in Birmingham and continued his work as an evangelist and sometimes sang with his wife. She had worked throughout the 50s with Homer, then joined Walter in 1962 and together they performed with bluegrass gospel groups on occasions collaborating with Johnny. Walter made many solo recordings and duets with Kyle, and in 1967 recorded an album with Homer. Late in 1972, Johnny and Homer recorded an album for Starday. By the mid-70s, Kyle was involved with an air-conditioning business, Johnny was the general manager of three radio stations owned by Webb Pierce. Homer, having entered the ministry, was the pastor of a church in Roanoke. Walter (sometimes referred to as the Chaplain of Music Row) continued to work as a gospel singer and evangelist and appeared and recorded with Frankie and Dorothy Jo Hope as the Walter Bailes Singers. The Bailes later promoted recordings on their own White Dove label. In the early 80s, Homer recorded two albums and in 1982, Kyle and Walter did a tour of Holland. Quite apart from their own recordings many other artists have also recorded songs written by the brothers. These include such noted country numbers as 'Give Mother My Crown' (Carl And Pearl Butler and Flatt And Scruggs), 'The Pale Horse And His Rider' (Hank Williams and Roy Acuff), 'Dust On The Bible' (Blue Sky Boys and Johnnie And Jack and Kitty Wells), 'Whiskey Is The Devil' (Webb Pierce), 'Oh, So Many Years' (Everly Brothers and George Hamilton IV) and 'Will The Angels Have A Sweetheart' (Bill Clifton). Johnny Bailes died in January 1990 at Swainsboro, Georgia, USA. Kyle Bailes died in March 1996.

● ALBUMS: as the Bailes Brothers (various combinations) *The Avenue Of Prayer* (1959)★★★, *Gospel Reunion* (Starday 1973), *I've Got My One Way Ticket* (1976)★★★★, *Johnny And Homer* (1977)★★★★, *Johnny And Homer Volume 2* (1977)★★, *Johnny And Walter* (1978)★★★, *Yesterday And Today* (White Dove 1983)★★.
Solo albums: Homer Bailes *Golden Treasures* (c.80s)★★, *Tenderly He Watched* (c.80s)★★★. Walter Bailes *Bluegrass Gospel* (c.80s)★★★, *It Takes A Lot Of Living To Learn* (c.80s)★★★.

BAILEY BROTHERS

Charlie Bailey (b. 9 February 1916, Klondyke, Happy Valley, Tennessee, USA; mandolin, guitar, vocals) and Danny Bailey (b. 1 December 1919, Klondyke, Happy Valley, Tennessee, USA; guitar, vocals). This mandolin-guitar duo were one of the few brother acts to successfully link the old-time close harmony singing, popular when their career commenced, with the later harmony styles of bluegrass music. Charlie's career began around 1936 but by 1940, the brothers were regulars on Knoxville radio stations. Between 1941 and 1946, when military service halted Charlie's career, Danny worked with the Happy Valley Boys and, in 1944, moved with them to WSM Nashville and played the *Grand Ole Opry*. When Charlie returned, the brothers relaunched their career, even briefly adding steel guitar, but soon tired of both it and Nashville and returned to WNOX Knoxville. Now fully adapted to bluegrass music, they formed a new version of the Happy Valley Boys, which initially included L.E. White (fiddle), Wiley Birchfield (banjo), Jake Tullock (bass) and on occasions Carl Butler (rhythm guitar). They recorded eight sides for Rich-R-Tone, including the first recorded version of 'The Sweetest Gift'. In 1949, they relocated to WPTF Raleigh, North Carolina (where fiddler 'Tater' Tate and banjoist Hoke Jenkins joined), and recorded for their own Canary label. In 1952, they worked on WDBJ Roanoke, Virginia, before moving to WWVA's *Wheeling Jamboree*, where Don McHan became their banjo player. In 1954, health problems saw Danny return south to Knoxville, where he worked on radio and television until the early 80s. Charlie continued to work at various stations including, in 1955, with the Osborne Brothers at WWVA, with whom he also recorded a gospel album. The brothers briefly worked together again in 1957, before Charlie toured Canada prior to retiring to run a pest control business in Wilmington, Delaware, in 1960. In 1970, the brothers were persuaded to appear at the Smithsonian Folk Festival and to record for Rounder Records. After that they made occasional appearances at some old-time reunion events, and at the 1992 Knoxville World's Fair.

● ALBUMS: *Early Days Of Bluegrass Volume 6, The Bailey Brothers - Have You Forgotten?* (Rounder 1974)★★★★, *Take Me Back To Happy Valley* (Rounder 1975)★★★, *Just As The Sun Went Down* (Rounder 1980)★★★, *Early Duet Stylings* (Old Homestead 1981)★★★. Charlie Bailey with the Osborne Brothers: *Everlasting Joy (Early Bluegrass Gospel)* (Old Homestead 1976)★★★.

BAILEY, DEFORD
b. 1899, Carthage, Smith County, Tennessee, USA, d. 2 July 1982. Bailey suffered from infantile paralysis and although he recovered, he was left with a deformed back and only grew to 4 feet 10 inches. He learned guitar, fiddle, banjo and harmonica from his father and uncle, who were both noted musicians, and by the age of 14, was making a living from playing the harmonica. He moved to Nashville and, in 1925, he met Dr. Humphrey Bate, a respected harmonica player, who brought him to the attention of the *Grand Ole Opry*. Quite apart from being the *Opry*'s first black artist, Bailey was also its first solo star, although he only received $5 a performance. It was, however, difficult for him to play his self-termed 'black hillbilly' music to white audiences in the south. He recorded for the US labels, Columbia, Brunswick and Victor during 1927-28 but did not record after that date. His best-known work is 'Pan American Blues', which is remembered for its train imitations, and he always appeared smartly dressed in a three-piece suit, matching hat and highly polished shoes. Bailey was dismissed by the *Opry* in 1941, allegedly for refusing to learn new tunes. Bailey, however, maintained that the real reason was racial prejudice. He never forgave the *Opry* for this and was forced to shine shoes for a living. He made a brief television appearance on a blues show in the 60s but he invariably rejected offers he received. There was no other black performer at the *Opry* until Charley Pride. In April 1982, Bailey made his last appearance at the *Opry*, playing 'Pan American Blues' on an old-timers show.

● ALBUMS: *Harmonica Showcase* (Matchbox 1985)★★★.

● FURTHER READING: *Deford Bailey - A Black Star In Early Country Music*, David C. Morton and Charles K. Wolfe.

BAILEY, JUDY
b. 6 January 1955, Winchester, Kentucky, USA. Little seems known of her childhood except that she was the eleventh of twelve children. She emerged on the country music scene in 1981, when 'Following A Feeling', a duet cut and the title track of a Moe Bandy, Columbia Records album, became a Top 10 US country hit. She followed it the same year with two Top 60 solo hits 'Slow Country Dancing' and 'The Best Bedroom In Town'. After two further minor hits, 'Tender Loving Lies' (1983) and 'There's A Lot Of Good About Goodbye' (1985), she seemed to disappear from the scene. She had no further chart success, but in 1995, she reap-

peared with a release on the Irish Hawk label. The album drew favourable reviews and her songwriting and vocal ability has received praise from Melba Montgomery and Bandy. She is a fine singer of honky tonk songs; some critics have, in fact, compared her style to Montgomery's. Top songwriter Whitey Shafer, with whom she has co-written, has also praised her songwriting ability.

● ALBUMS: *I've Never Seen It Rain* (Hawk 1995)★★★.

BAILEY, RAZZY
b. Erastus Michael Bailey, 14 February 1939, Five Points, Alabama, USA. Bailey grew up on a small farm and his parents encouraged him to learn the guitar for their Saturday night singalongs. He recorded his first record at the age of 10, formed his first band when he was 15 and spent nearly 20 years playing honky tonks in Georgia and Alabama. Among his singles were 'Stolen Moments', which was produced by Freddy Weller, and 'I Hate Hate', but commercial success eluded him (he also released albums with the bands Daily Bread and the Aquarians). He recorded his own song, '9,999,999 Tears', with Freddy Weller and Billy Joe Royal on back-up vocals and production by Joe South. In 1976, Dickie Lee covered the song and made both the US country and pop charts. Bailey then started recording for the same label and in 1978 registered his first country Top 10 hit with 'What Time Do You Have To Be Back To Heaven?'. In 1980, he topped the US country charts with a cheating song, 'Loving Up A Storm', and then, most unusually, he had three double-sided number 1s, 'I Keep Coming Back'/'True Life Country Music', 'Friends'/ 'Anywhere There's A Jukebox' and 'Midnight Hauler'/'Scratch My Back (And Whisper In My Ear)'. His last US country number 1 was with 'She Left Love All Over Me' in 1982. Bailey's records combine R&B with country music and his version of Wilson Pickett's 'In The Midnight Hour' was a country hit. From 1987 onwards he issued records through his own Sounds Of America label. His 1993 release coincided with the suicide of his wife.

● ALBUMS: *Razzy Bailey* (RCA 1980)★★★, *Makin' Friends* (RCA 1981)★★★, *Feelin' Right* (RCA 1982)★★★, *A Little More Razzy* (RCA 1982)★★★, *In The Midnight Hour* (RCA 1984)★★★, *A Little Razzle Dazzle* (RCA 1984)★★★, *Arrival* (RCA 1985)★★, *Cut From A Different Stone* (1985)★★, *Still Going Strong* (Sundown 1987)★★, *Razzy Bailey: Fragile, Handle With Care* (SOA 1993)★★★.

● COMPILATIONS: *Greatest Hits* (RCA 1983)★★★.

BAILLIE AND THE BOYS
Michael Bonagura and Alan LeBoeuf merged their talents in the early 70s in a band called London Fog, and in 1973 they met Kathie Baillie, who was to marry Bonagura. They provided backing vocals for several pop acts including the Ramones and Talking Heads. In 1977, Alan LeBoeuf spent two years portraying Paul McCartney in the Broadway show *Beatlemania*. In the 80s, they worked with country performer Ed Bruce, and soon they were signed in their own right to make their own close harmony albums for RCA Records. They had US Top 10 country singles with 'Oh Heart', 'Wilder Days' and 'Long Shot'. LeBoeuf left in 1989 leaving them effectively Baillie And The Boy. They returned after a long silence with 1996's *Loving' Every Minute*, featuring new member Roger McVay.

● ALBUMS: *Baillie And The Boys* (RCA 1987)★★★, *Turn*

The Tide (RCA 1989)★★★, *The Lights Of Home* (RCA 1990)★★, *Lovin' Every Minute* (Intersound 1996)★★★.
● COMPILATIONS: *The Best Of Baillie And The Boys* (RCA 1991)★★★.

BAKER, CARROLL

b. 4 March 1949, Bridgewater, Nova Scotia, Canada. Baker spent much of her childhood in the small fishing village of Port Medway, Nova Scotia. She was greatly influenced by her father, a well-known, old-time country fiddler, but did not share his dislike of rock 'n' roll. When she was 16 years old, the family moved away from Toronto and she built up a reputation singing in local clubs. In 1970, she had a Canadian hit with her first record, 'Memories Of Home'. After several other successes, RCA Records, impressed that she was outselling their American country stars, guaranteed her worldwide distribution. Although Baker only ever had minor successes in the US country charts, she is known for her full-scale assault on Conway Twitty's 'I've Never Been This Far Before' and a maudlin narrative in which she assumed a child's voice, 'Portrait In The Window'. Her version of 'Me And Bobby McGee' successfully merged Kris Kristofferson and Janis Joplin's approaches. After a few years she realized that her main audience was in Canada. In 1985, she was among the featured artists on the Canadian charity single 'Tears Are Not Enough', by Northern Lights, and in 1988 she recorded a passionate duet with Jack Scott, 'The Best Of Love'.
● ALBUMS: *Carroll Baker* (RCA 1976)★★★, *Sweet Sensation* (RCA 1977)★★★, *If It Wasn't For You* (RCA 1978)★★★, *I'd Go Thru It All Over Again* (RCA 1979)★★★, *Hollywood Love* (RCA 1980)★★★, *All For The Love Of A Song* (RCA 1981)★★, *A Step In The Right Direction* (1985)★★, *Heartbreak To Happiness* (Tembo 1986)★★★, *At Home In The Country* (Tembo 1988)★★★.
● COMPILATIONS: *20 Country Classics* (RCA 1985)★★★★.

BAKER, KENNY

b. 26 June 1926, Jenkins, Kentucky, USA. His father and grandfather were both noted Kentucky fiddlers and he first played at the age of eight. Prior to joining the navy in 1942, he changed to guitar but returned to the fiddle during his naval service where he played publicly on occasions. After completing his military service, he worked in the mines but played fiddle at local dances. Influenced in his early career by jazz violinist Stéphane Grappelli, he really played little country music until 1953, when he joined Don Gibson's band at WNOX Knoxville. Late in 1957, Bill Monroe persuaded him to turn to bluegrass music and he made his first recordings with Monroe in December that year. During the 50s, lack of work saw him employed in the mines for periods before rejoining Monroe in the late 60s. He worked with him more or less continually through to the late 80s, appearing on most of Monroe's noted recordings, as well as recording solo albums and with James Monroe on his noted tribute album to Charlie Monroe. He toured and recorded with Josh Graves and worked with other musicians but began to spend more time on his farm. In the 90s, he made some special appearances and recorded with other fiddle players including Bobby Hicks. In 1982, noted historian Charles K. Wolfe wrote 'a former coal miner and part time hog breeder from Jenkins, Kentucky, Baker is without doubt the most influential fiddler playing today; his style - a sophisticated mixture of Texas, modern country and Kentucky styles is adaptable to everything from western swing to polkas.'
● ALBUMS: with Joe Greene *High Country* (County 1968)★★★★, *Portrait Of A Bluegrass Fiddler* (County 1969)★★★, *A Baker's Dozen* (County 1971)★★★, *Kenny Baker Country* (County 1972)★★★, with Josh Graves *Something Different* (Puritan 1972)★★, with Graves *Bucktime* (Puritan 1973)★★, *Dry & Dusty* (County 1973)★★★, *Grassy Fiddle Blues* (County 1975)★★★★, *Plays Bill Monroe* (County 1976)★★★★, with Sam Bush *Frost On The Pumpkin* (County 1977)★★★, with the Osborne Brothers *Farmyard Swing* (County 1979)★★★, with Bobby Hicks *Darkness On The Delta* (County 1980)★★★, with Howdy Forrester *Red Apple Rag* (County 1983)★★★, *Highlights* (County 1984)★★★★, with Graves *Flying South* (Ridge Runner 1986)★★★, *Carpetbagger* (Amber 1988)★★★, with Graves *Bluegrass Instrumentals* Swiss release (Montana 1988)★★, with Blaine Sprouse *Indian Springs* (Rounder 1989)★★★, with Graves *The Puritan Sessions* (Rebel 1989)★★.
● COMPILATIONS: *Master Fiddler* (County 1980s)★★★★.

BALFA BROTHERS

The Balfa family name is legendary in Cajun music. They grew up in abject poverty in Bayou Grand Louis, near Big Mamou, Louisiana, USA, where their father, from whom they gained their musical interest, worked as a sharecropper. The music offered a means of escape and relief and in the mid-40s, brothers Will (b. *c*.1920, d. 6 February 1979; fiddle), Harry (b. 1931; accordion) and Dewey (b. 20 March 1927, d. 17 June 1992; fiddle, harmonica, accordion, guitar and sundry other minor instruments) began to play for local dances. In 1951, they made their first recording on home recording equipment, but during the 50s Dewey frequently played and recorded with Nathan Abshire. He also appeared at the Newport Folk Festival in 1964, playing guitar with Gladius Thibodeaux (accordion) and Louis Lejeune (fiddle). In 1967, Dewey was joined by Will, Rodney (b. 1934, d. 6 February 1979; guitar, harmonica, vocals), daughter Nelda and Hadley Fontenot (an accordion-playing local farmer) and the unit toured extensively both in the USA and Europe as the Balfa Brothers (incidentally, Will always preferred to spell his name as Bolfa). In the late 60s, they recorded for Swallow and their recording of 'Drunkard's Sorrow Waltz' was a bestselling Cajun single in 1967. In 1968, they appeared in Mexico City at music festivals run in conjunction with the Olympic Games. They played music for and appeared in the 1972 film on Cajun life, *Spend It All*. Dewey also formed his nightclub orchestra, which comprised himself and Rodney (fiddle, guitar, vocals), Nathan Menard (accordion), Ervin 'Dick' Richard (fiddle), J.W. Pelsia (steel guitar), Austin Broussard (drums) and Rodney's son, Tony (bass guitar). In the mid-70s, they made further recordings (with Nathan Abshire) for Swallow and Sonet Records and appeared in a documentary on Cajuns. On 6 February 1979, Will and Rodney were killed in a car accident. Dewey continued to perform and record as the Balfa Brothers with other musicians, including Tony, his daughter Christine (triangle), Tony, Ally Young (accordion), Dick Richard, Mark Savoy (b. 1940; accordion), Robert Jardell (accordion) and Peter Schwartz (bass, fiddle, piano) (Schwartz, who first played with the group in his early teens, was Tracy

Schwartz's son). Many of the Swallow and other recordings made by the Balfa Brothers have been reissued in the UK by Ace Records. Dewey Balfa later ran a furniture business but remained active in music until his death on 17 June 1992. After his death his daughters, Christine and Nelda, continued the family tradition by playing and recording with other Cajun musicians, including Mike Chapman, Dick Powell and Kevin Wimmer, as Balfa Toujours.

● ALBUMS: *Balfa Brothers Play Traditional Cajun Music* (Swallow 1965)★★★★, *Balfa Brothers Play More Cajun Music* (Swallow 1968)★★★, *The Cajuns* (Sonet 1972)★★★, with Nathan Abshire *The Good Times Are Killing Me* (Swallow 1975)★★★, *Cajun Fiddle Tunes By Dewey Balfa* (Folkways 70s)★★★, *Dewey Balfa & Tracy Schwartz Traditional Cajun Fiddle Volumes 1 & 2* (Folkways 70s)★★★, *J'ai Vu Le Loup, Le Renard Et La Belette* (Cezame/Rounder 1975)★★★, *The New York Concerts* (Swallow 1980)★★, *Dewey Balfa, Marc Savoy, D.L. Menard: Under The Green Oak Tree* (Arhoolie 1982)★★★, *The New York Concerts Plus* (Ace 1991)★★★.

● COMPILATIONS: *The Balfa Brothers Play Traditional Cajun Music Volumes 1 & 2* (Ace 1991)★★★★, *Dewey Balfa & Friends* (Ace 1991)★★★★. As Balfa Toujours *New Cajun Tradition* (Ace 1995)★★★.

BALHAM ALLIGATORS

The group centres around singer, accordionist and pianist Geraint Watkins, who first came to London with the Welsh combo Red Beans And Rice. He has played with many of the biggest names in UK rock music including a stint in Mickey Jupp's Cable Lawyers and Willie And The Poor Boys with Bill Wyman and Paul Rodgers. He formed the goodtime Balham Alligators in 1986 and the music mixes rock 'n' roll, cajun, country, and R&B with 'a whole lotta alcohol'. Other members include Gary Richard (guitar), Robin McKidd (fiddle), Bobby Irwin, who replaced Kiernan O'Connor (drums), and Paul Riley (bass). Their jazz-slanted arrangement of 'Johnny B. Goode' is particularly enjoyable and features Bill Kirchen on trombone.

● ALBUMS: *Gateway To The South* (Proper 1996)★★★, *A Po' Boy 'N' Make It Snappy* originally issued as *Cajun Dance Party* (Proper 1997)★★★.

BALL, DAVID

b. 3 May 1959, Rock Hill, South Carolina, USA. Country singer-songwriter David Ball was born into a musical family headed by his Baptist preacher father. Later he moved with his family to Spartanburg, South Carolina. There he was able to persuade his parents to buy him a guitar - a Stella. Having written his first song in seventh grade, he played it in a school talent show with a band he had formed, the Strangers. Afterwards, he played bass in various local youth groups and also the school orchestra. Together with friends he played various bluegrass and country festivals in the Carolinas. By the time Ball left high school he was a proficient stand-up bass player, readily able to adapt to classical, country, bluegrass and swing. He was also a member of Uncle Walt's Band, a trio headed by Walter Hyatt who relocated to Austin, Texas, in the mid-70s, in an attempt to make a mainstream breakthrough. He subsequently graduated to a solo career, moving to Nashville where he was signed to a publishing contract. Three singles for RCA Records in the late 80s failed to provide a solo breakthrough, however, and a projected

album was shelved. The experience did at least serve to introduce him to producer Blake Chancey, son of legendary country producer Ron Chancey. In the spring of 1993 Chancey rang Warner Brothers Records' A&R director Doug Grau on Ball's behalf. A new recording contract followed. *Thinkin' Problem* retained Chancey's services and duly attracted a rapturous reception in the country music press, with its hard-edged realism and taut, emotive delivery. The title track, 'Look What Followed Me Home' and 'When The Thought Of You Catches Up With Me' were the best examples of this material, which placed him firmly within the Hank Williams tradition of resigned but evocative country balladeers. The follow-up, *Starlite Lounge*, was also well-received.

● ALBUMS: *Thinkin' Problem* (Warners 1994)★★★★, *Starlite Lounge* (Warners 1996)★★★.

BALL, MARCIA

b. 20 March 1949, Orange, Texas, USA. Born into a musical family, Ball took piano lessons throughout her childhood until she was 14. Her formative years were spent in Vinton, Louisiana, and while at Louisiana State University she played in a blues-rock band, Gum. She also took particular interest in the styles of Fats Domino and Professor Longhair. Moving to Austin in the early 70s, she joined the progressive country group Freda And The Firedogs, along with guitarist John X. Reed. She went solo in 1974 and had a country single released the following year. Her subsequent solo albums combine R&B standards with original songs that combine elements of blues and country swing. She wrote the title song for *Dreams Come True*, a project that began in 1985 and took five years to bring to fruition with the help of producer Dr. John. Constant touring may have been a factor in the subsequent four-year hiatus before *Blue House* was finally issued in 1994. *Let Me Play With Your Poodle* included songs by Randy Newman and Tampa Red alongside Ball originals.

● ALBUMS: *Circuit Queen* (Capitol 1978)★★★, *Soulful Dress* (Rounder 1983)★★★, *Hot Tamale Baby* (Rounder 1985)★★★, *Gatorhythms* (Rounder 1989)★★★, with Lou Ann Barton, Angela Strehli *Dreams Come True* (Antone's 1990)★★★, *Blue House* (Rounder 1994)★★★, *Let Me Play With Your Poodle* (Rounder 1997)★★★.

BANDY, MOE

b. Marion Bandy, 12 February 1944, Meridian, Mississippi, USA. Bandy was nicknamed Moe by his father when a child in the home-town of the legendary Jimmie Rodgers, so it is perhaps not surprising that Bandy grew up to be a country singer. He later stated: 'My grandfather worked on the railroads with Jimmie Rodgers. He was the boss of the railway yard in Meridian and Jimmie Rodgers worked for him. He said that he played his guitar all the time between work.' The Bandy family moved to San Antonio, Texas, when Moe was six years old and he was educated there, graduating in 1962. His mother played piano and sang; Bandy was taught to play the guitar by his father but made little use of the ability until he was in his teens. His father's wish that he also play the fiddle never quite materialized. He made some appearances with his father's country band, the Mission City Playboys, but generally during his high school days, he showed little interest in music but a great deal in rodeos. He tried bronco-busting and bull-riding and by the time he was 16, he was competing in rodeos all over Texas. In 1962, tired of the bruises and fractured bones, he began to pursue a career in country music. He assembled a band that he called Moe And The Mavericks and found work playing small beer parlours, honky tonks and clubs over a wide area around San Antonio, Texas. When he was young he tried to sound like Hank Williams and George Jones - 'I even had my hair cut short like his'. Although work was plentiful the pay was poor and during the day he worked for his father as a sheet metal worker. This was to last for the next 12 years, during which time he made a few recordings for various small labels. In 1964, he had his first single, 'Lonely Lady', on the Satin label but it made little impression. He did manage to get his band a residency on a local television programme called *Country Corner* and in this capacity, he provided backing for several touring stars. In 1973, he went solo when record producer Ray Baker, who had listened to Bandy's demos the previous year, suggested he come to Nashville. Bandy managed to obtain a loan and recorded a song called 'I Just Started Hatin' Cheatin' Songs Today'. Initially released on Footprint Records with a limited pressing of 500 copies, it soon came to the attention of the Atlanta-based GRC label. In March 1974, it entered the US country charts, eventually peaking at number 17. Other hits followed, including 'It Was Always So Easy To Find An Unhappy Woman (Till I Started Looking For Mine)' and 'Don't Anyone Make Love At Home Anymore'. In 1975, a song written by his friend Lefty Frizzell and Whitey Shaffer gave him a number 7 country hit, firmly establishing his reputation. 'Bandy The Rodeo Clown' was to become not only one of his own favourites but also one of his most popular recordings. (Shaffer was greatly amused by the way Bandy pronounced woman as 'wah-man' and began to send him songs with 'wah-man' in them.) Bandy sang in a simple style that extracted the utmost from his songs of lost love, sadness and life. Although by no means a Hank Williams sound-alike, he showed a very distinct influence in his method of putting across his honky tonk songs. He met with immediate success at Columbia with Paul Craft's 'Hank Williams, You Wrote My Life' and quickly added further hits, including 'Here I Am Drunk Again'. Between 1977 and 1979, he was a country chart regular with singles such as 'I'm Sorry For You, My Friend' (the song Williams had written for their mutual friend Lefty Frizzell), 'Cowboys Ain't Supposed To Cry', 'That's What Makes The Juke Box Play' and a duet with Janie Fricke, 'It's A Cheatin' Situation'. In 1979, he achieved his first solo number 1 with 'I Cheated Me Right Out Of You'. Also during 1979, as a result of touring together in Europe, Bandy joined forces with Joe Stampley and a single release of 'Just Good Ol' Boys' became a number 1 country hit, leading to a continuation of the partnership over the following years. It was not too surprising that they proved a successful double act. Between 1979 and 1985, their further hits included 'Holding The Bag', 'Tell Ol' I Ain't Here' and 'Hey Joe (Hey Moe)'. In 1984, they ran into copyright problems with their parody of pop singer Boy George called 'Where's The Dress', when they used the introduction of Culture Club's hit 'Karma Chameleon'. Referring to the matter later, Bandy said, 'He didn't appreciate what we'd done and naturally he sued us. We paid him money, but I didn't like the way he spent it.' In addition to their single successes, Moe and Joe recorded several albums together.

During the 80s, Bandy maintained a steady line of solo successes including 'Yesterday Once More', 'Rodeo Romeo', 'She's Not Really Cheatin' (She's Just Gettin' Even)' and 'Till I'm Too Old To Die Young'. He also registered duet successes with Judy Bailey ('Following The Feeling') and Becky Hobbs ('Let's Get Over Them Together'). Over the years he maintained a touring schedule estimated to average between 250 and 300 days a year and he also made numerous network television shows. In later years he cut back considerably on his schedules. He was never a regular *Grand Ole Opry* member but has made guest appearances from time to time. Bandy summed up his music when he said, 'I really think my songs are about life. There's cheating, drinking and divorcing going on everywhere and that's what hardcore country music is all about.' He added: 'If I'd done all the things I sing about, I'd be dead.' Critics reviewing some of his later recordings wrote that it was strange that, at a time when more artists were actually recording his type of music, some of his recordings were spoiled by string and/or choir arrangements and advised that an immediate return to his roots was necessary. Bandy opened his popular Americana Theatre in Branson, Missouri in 1991.

● ALBUMS: *I Just Started Hatin' Cheatin' Songs Today* (GRC 1974)★★★, *It Was Always So Easy (To Find An Unhappy Woman)* (GRC 1975)★★★, *Bandy The Rodeo Clown* (GRC 1975)★★★, *Hank Williams, You Wrote My Life* (Columbia 1976)★★★, *Here I Am Drunk Again* (Columbia 1976)★★★, *I'm Sorry For You, My Friend* (Columbia 1977)★★★, *Cowboys Ain't Supposed To Cry* (Columbia 1977)★★★, *Love Is What Life's All About* (Columbia 1978)★★★, *Soft Lights And Hard Country Music* (Columbia 1978)★★★★, *It's A Cheating Situation* (Columbia 1979)★★★★, *One Of A Kind* (Columbia 1979)★★★, with Joe Stampley *Just Good Ol' Boys* (Columbia 1979)★★★, *The Champ* (Columbia 1980)★★★, *Following The Feeling* (Columbia 1980)★★★, *Rodeo Romeo* (Columbia 1981)★★★, with Stampley *Hey Moe!, Hey Joe!* (Columbia 1981)★★, *She's Not Really Cheatin' (She's Just Gettin' Even)* (Columbia 1982)★★, *20 Great Songs Of The American Cowboy* (Columbia 1982)★★, *Devoted To Your Memory* (Columbia 1983)★★, *I Still Love You The Same Ol' Way* (Columbia 1983)★★, *Sings The Songs Of Hank Williams* (Columbia 1983)★★, *Motel Matches* (Columbia 1984)★★, with Stampley *The Good Ole Boys Alive And Well* (Columbia 1984)★★, with Stampley *Live From Bad Bob's In Memphis* (Columbia 1985)★★, *Keeping It Country* (Curb 1986)★★★, *You Haven't Heard The Last Of Me* (Curb 1987)★★★, *No Regrets* (Curb 1988)★★★, *Many Mansions* (Curb 1989)★★, *Live In Branson, MO, USA* (Curb 1993)★★★.

● COMPILATIONS: *The Best Of Moe Bandy, Volume 1* (Columbia 1977)★★★, with Stampley *Greatest Hits* (Columbia 1982)★★★, *Greatest Hits* (Curb 1992)★★★, *Honky Tonk Amnesia: The Hard Country Sound Of Mo Bandy* (Razor & Tie 1996)★★★★.

BANNON, R.C.

b. Daniel Shipley, 2 May 1945, Dallas, Texas, USA. Bannon sang in a church choir when young, and then worked numerous clubs in Texas in rock and soul bands. In 1968, while working as a disc jockey for a radio station in Seattle, he took the name R.C. Bannon, based on the product RC Cola. In 1973 Bannon opened for Marty Robbins but the solo records he subsequently made for Capitol were unsuc-

cessful. He moved to Nashville in 1976 and secured a publishing contract with Warner Brothers Music. He wrote the US country hits 'Only One Love In My Life' (a number 1 for Ronnie Milsap) and 'Women Get Lonely' (Charly McClain). His *R.C.Bannon Arrives* had sleeve-notes by Robbins, and he had a US country chart entry with 'Somebody's Gonna Do It Tonight'. He married Louise Mandrell in February 1979 and their duets include 'Reunited', 'We Love Each Other' and 'Where There's Smoke, There's Fire'. He worked on arrangements for the US television series *Barbara Mandrell And The Mandrell Sisters*, and wrote Barbara's 1983 US country number 1, 'One Of A Kind Pair Of Fools'.
● ALBUMS: *R.C. Bannon Arrives* (1978)★★, with Louise Mandrell *Inseparable* (1979)★★★, with Mandrell *Love Won't Let Us Go* (1980)★★★, with Mandrell *Me And My R.C.* (1982)★★★, with Mandrell *(You're My) Superwoman, (You're My) Incredible Man* (1982)★★.

BARBER, GLENN
b. Martin Glenn Barber, 2 February 1935, Hollis, Oklahoma, USA. The Barber family moved to Pasadena, Texas, and from an early age Glenn showed an interest in country music. He first learned guitar but later became equally proficient on banjo, mandolin, steel guitar, dobro, bass and drums. He began to write songs and gained his first US *Billboard* country chart successes on the Sims and Starday labels in 1964. In 1968, he joined Hickory and immediately had a minor hit with his own song 'Don't Worry 'Bout The Mule'. This was followed by 'Kissed By The Rain, Warmed By The Sun' and 'She Cheats On Me', the latter also being recorded by Roy Orbison. During the 70s, he mustered 16 minor hits including his own version of 'Yes Ma'am, He Found Me In A Honky Tonk', a song later recorded by Leona Williams, and a version of Mickey Newbury's ballad 'Poison Red Berries'. In 1979, he had a minor hit with the optimistically titled 'Everyone Wants To Disco'. When five years later it became an album track, he had discovered that everybody did not, in fact, want to disco, and the song had been renamed 'Don't Take My Country Away'. In spite of his multi-instrumental talents and songwriting abilities, Barber has had no chart hits since 1980. Although busily recording in the early 80s, he now seems to have drifted from the music scene and has turned his attentions to being a portrait painter and screenwriter.
● ALBUMS: *A New Star* (Hickory 1970)★★★, *Glenn Barber* (Hickory 1974)★★★, *First Love Feelings* (Tudor 1983)★★, *Saturday's Heroes Are Gone* (Tudor 1984)★★★.
● COMPILATIONS: *The Best Of Glenn Barber* (Hickory 1972)★★★.

BARE, BOBBY
b. Robert Joseph Bare, 7 April 1935, Ironton, Ohio, USA. Bare was raised on a farm, his mother died when he was five, and his sister was adopted. As an adolescent, he dreamed of being Hank Williams: 'then Hank died and I didn't want to be like him no more'. Nevertheless, he started songwriting and secured an early morning radio spot, and later worked on television in Charleston, West Virginia. He moved to California and impressed Capitol Records, recording for them in 1955. After receiving his draft notice in 1958, he wrote a parody of Elvis Presley going into the army, 'All American Boy'. Returning to Ohio to join the army, he met his friend Bill Parsons and joined his recording session. He contributed 'All American Boy' with the intention that Parsons would learn it later. Parsons' name was put on the tape-box because Bare was still under contract to Capitol. The label's owner liked 'All American Boy' and released it under Parsons' name. The single climbed to number 2 on the US charts and made number 22 in the UK. The song resembles Shel Silverstein's, which was later recorded by Bare, but most of Bare's early songs were straight country, being recorded by such contemporary stars as Wynn Stewart and Ferlin Husky. Bare resumed his own career on leaving the army, but the singles ('Lynchin' Party', 'Sailor Man', 'Lorena') made little impact. He wrote twist songs for Chubby Checker's film *Teenage Millionaire*, but Nashville songwriter Harlan Howard persuaded Chet Atkins to record him for RCA Victor. A ballad, 'Shame On Me', made number 23 on the US pop charts and crossed over to the country market. Bare was travelling to Nashville to record the follow-up when he heard Billy Grammar's 'I Wanna Go Home'. He admired the story of the country boy going to the city ('By day I make the cars/By night I make the bars') so much that he recorded the song as 'Detroit City'. Bare's record made number 16 on the US charts and won a Grammy.

He had his biggest US hit (number 10) with '500 Miles Away From Home'. His fourth pop hit (number 33) came with 'Miller's Cave'. Bare appeared in the 1964 film *A Distant Trumpet*, but he disliked being stuck in the Arizona desert and was determined to move to Nashville, join the *Grand Ole Opry* and become a full-time country singer. He recorded prolifically, including an album of standards with Skeeter Davis, which featured a successful single, 'A Dear John Letter'. In 1966, Bare returned to his favourite theme (a country boy uneasy in the city) with the Tompall Glaser and Harlan Howard song 'Streets Of Baltimore', which was arranged by Ray Stevens. It was followed by Tom T. Hall's 'Margie's At The Lincoln Park Inn'. 'It's a great cheating song,' says Bare, 'because you don't know if the guy is going to go back or not.' By this time, Bare was recording consistently strong material including an album about nostalgia, *A Bird Named Yesterday*, mostly written by Jack Clement. In 1970 Bare moved to Mercury and found success with two early Kris Kristofferson compositions, 'Come Sundown' and 'Please Don't Tell Me How The Story Ends'. Producer Jerry Kennedy's pared-down arrangements were ideal for his half-singing, half-talking style. Chet Atkins invited him back to RCA, where he signed on condition that he could produce his own records. He subsequently recruited songwriter Shel Silverstein to compose an album. The concept was simply one of stories, but *Lullabys, Legends And Lies*, released as a double album in the USA and a single album in the UK with no loss in music, has become a classic country album. It included the Cajun 'Marie Laveau', based on fact, which is his only US country number 1 and a concert favourite where Bare, arm outstretched, fist clenched, punches out the words. He had a US country hit with another track, 'Daddy What If', featuring his five-year-old son, Bobby Bare Jnr. 'The Winner', a witty song about the price of winning, had another 20 verses, which Bare omitted but which were subsequently published in *Playboy*. Another Silverstein-Bare collaboration, *Hard Time Hungrys*, dealt with social issues and included a sombre song about unemployment, 'Daddy's Been Around The House Too Long'. The success of his good-natured, family album *Singin' In The Kitchen*, was marred by the death of his daughter, Cari, in 1976. Bare, never one to stand still, took chances by recording such strange, controversial material as 'Dropkick Me Jesus (Through The Goalposts Of Life)' and the expletive-driven 'Redneck Hippie Romance'. He returned to the mainstream with the superb *Bare* in 1978, which included laid-back ballads ('Too Many Nights Alone', 'Childhood Hero') and the hilarious 'Greasy Grit Gravy' with Waylon Jennings, Willie Nelson and Dr. Hook. His album, *Sleeper Wherever I Fall*, cost $100,000 to make, but Bare was lost in the varied arrangements and reverted to albums with small studio audiences. In 1979, Bare helped to establish Rosanne Cash's career by singing with her on 'No Memories Hangin' Round'. Bare's singles for Columbia included 'The Jogger', 'Tequila Sheila', 'Gotta Get Rid Of This Band', 'When Hippies Get Older' and 'Numbers', inspired by the Dudley Moore film *10*. Bare has become more laconic and droopy-eyed with age but he continues to entertain audiences around the world. 'I like everything I record. I'm afraid that if I recorded something that I didn't like, it might be a big hit and I'd be stuck with it every night for the rest of my life. That's a real nightmare.'

● ALBUMS: *Detroit City And Other Hits* (RCA Victor 1963)★★★, *500 Miles Away From Home* (RCA Victor 1963)★★★★, *The Travelling Bare* (RCA Victor 1964)★★★, *Tender Years* (RCA Victor 1965)★★★, with Skeeter Davis *Tunes For Two* (RCA Victor 1965)★★★, *Constant Sorrow* (RCA Victor 1965)★★★, *Talk Me Some Sense* (RCA Victor 1966)★★★, *Streets Of Baltimore* (RCA Victor 1966)★★★,*This I Believe* (RCA Victor 1966)★★★, with Norma Jean, Liz Anderson *The Game Of Triangles* (RCA Victor 1967)★★★, *A Bird Named Yesterday* (RCA Victor 1967)★★★, with the Hillsiders *The English Countryside* (RCA Victor 1967)★★★, *Folsom Prison Blues* (RCA Victor 1968)★★★, *Lincoln Park Inn* (RCA Victor 1969)★★★, with Davis *Your Husband, My Wife* aka *More Tunes For Two* (Mercury 1970)★★★, *This Is Bare Country* (Mercury 1970)★★★★, *Where Have All The Seasons Gone?* (Mercury 1971)★★★, *The Real Thing* (Mercury 1971)★★★, *I Need Some Good News Bad* (Mercury 1971)★★★, *I'm A Long Way From Home* (Mercury 1971)★★★, *What Am I Gonna Do?* (Mercury 1972)★★★, *Memphis, Tennessee* (RCA Victor 1973)★★★, *I Hate Goodbyes/Ride Me Down Easy* (RCA 1973)★★★, *Lullabys, Legends And Lies* (RCA 1974)★★★★, as Bobby Bare And Family *Singin' In The Kitchen* (RCA 1974)★★★, *Hard Time Hungrys* (RCA 1975)★★★, *Cowboys And Daddys* (RCA 1975)★★★, *The Winner And Other Losers* (RCA 1976)★★★, *Me And McDill* (RCA 1977)★★★, *Bare* (Columbia 1978)★★★, *Sleeper Wherever I Fall* (Columbia 1978)★★★, *Down And Dirty* (Columbia 1980)★★★, *Drunk And Crazy* (Columbia 1980)★★★, *As Is* (Columbia 1981)★★★, *Ain't Got Nothin' To Lose* (Columbia 1982)★★★, *Drinkin' From The Bottle, Singin' From The Heart* (Columbia 1983)★★★.

● COMPILATIONS: *The Best Of Bobby Bare* (RCA Victor 1966)★★★, *This Is Bobby Bare 1963-1969* (RCA 1970)★★★, *Greatest Hits* (RCA 1981)★★, *Encore* (Columbia 1982)★★★, *Biggest Hits* (Columbia 1984)★★★, *Bobby Bare-The Mercury Years, 1970-72* 3-CD box set (Bear Family 1987)★★★★, *The Best Of Bobby Bare* (Razor & Tie 1994)★★★★, *The All American Boy* 4-CD box set covering RCA material from 1962-1970 (Bear Family 1994)★★★★, *The Essential Bobby Bare* (RCA 1997)★★★.

BARFIELD, JOHNNY

b. John Alexander Barfield, 3 March 1909, Tifton, Georgia, USA, d. 16 January 1974. The son of a cotton farmer, he learned guitar and first sang around the Columbus area with his brother, Coot. They recorded for Columbia Records but in the early 30s, after becoming friendly with fiddler Bert Lane, he joined the Skillet Lickers at WCKY Covington, Kentucky. In 1936, he played on WGST Atlanta but in the late 30s, back in Columbus, he played WRLB and at dancehalls with his band, as well as often appearing with his great friend, Rex Griffin. Between 1939 and 1941, he recorded for Bluebird Records and 'Boogie Woogie', his best-known number, has seemingly given him the distinction of being the first artist to use that phrase on a recording. In 1942, he enlisted for the army and finished the war in a German prison camp. After release, he returned to Columbus and relaunched his singing career. He played local residencies and toured with several major artists, including Bill Monroe and Rex Griffin. He actually declined the chance to join the *Grand Ole Opry* in Nashville, as he wanted to stay in his local area. Around 1958, he made further recordings for his own JB label but his main recording success was in Australia, where his Bluebird tracks had proved so popular that reissues were released in the 80s. Barfield remained active in the Columbus area, although forgotten in many others, almost until his death on 16 January 1974.

BARLOW, JACK

b. Jack Butcher, Muscatine, Iowa, USA. Barlow grew up on a farm and although learning to play guitar, he had no thoughts of a musical career, until he became a disc jockey on his local radio station. He later worked on WQUA Moline and WIRE Indianapolis and then, after visits to Nashville, he decided to seek a recording career. He became a writer for Tree Publishing and made his first recordings on the Dial label. In 1965, his self-penned 'I Love Country' reached number 21 on the Cash Box charts. In 1968, after two years with Epic, he moved to Dot Records, where his first single, 'Baby Ain't That Love', reached number 40 in the *Billboard* country charts. He relocated to Nashville and played the *Grand Ole Opry*. In 1971/2, he achieved a Top 30 hit with his version of Donovan's 'Catch The Wind' and Top 60 success with 'They Call The Wind Maria'. In all, he only registered eight *Billboard* country chart hits, the last, 'The Man On Page 602' (which refers to a revealing photo in the Sears catalogue), being issued on the Antique label under the name of Zoot Fenster in 1975. His deep and very distinctive voice has seen him, in later years, achieved acclaim for his work on commercials and voice-overs.

● ALBUMS: *Baby Ain't That Love* (Dot 1969)★★★, *Son Of The South* (Dot 1969)★★★, *Catch The Wind* (Dot 1970)★★★, *I Live The Songs I Sing* (Antique 1975)★★★.

BARNES, BENNY

b. Benjamin M. Barnes Jnr., 1934, Beaumont, Texas, USA, d. 1985. At the age of 15, he, like his father and grandfather before him, was working in the Texas oilfields. He learned to play guitar and developed a love for country music and actually played guitar on an early George Jones Starday recording. In 1956, after an oilfield injury, he began singing locally and joined Starday himself. The following year, he scored a number 2 country hit with 'Poor Man's Riches'. This led to him making appearances on the *Grand Old Opry* and becoming a regular on the *Louisiana Hayride*, but he found a follow-up hit hard to find. In 1959, he recorded 'Gold Records In The Snow', a tribute to Buddy Holly, the Big Bopper and Richie Valens. In 1960, he gave up singing and relocated to Beaumont, where he opened a bar, The Blue Lantern. He gained a number 22 hit in 1961, when Mercury Records decided to release his earlier recording of 'Yearning'. He ran his bar for several years, during which time he wrote a song called 'Bar With No Beer' which, to anybody except probably Barnes and his family, was literally nothing but a very slight variation of Australian Gordon Parson's 'Pub With No Beer' (a major hit, in 1959, for Slim Dusty). However, in the USA, Barnes' 1965 recording achieved some success. In 1970, he moved to California but returned to Beaumont the following year and built his Benny Barnes Melody Ranch where, with his band the Ranch Hands, he proved a popular entertainer. He made various other recordings, namely for Hallway (1962-65), Musicor (1965-68), Kapp (1968), Mega (1972), Starday (1973) and Playboy (1976). Only 'I've Got Some Getting Over You To Do' on Playboy made the charts - a very modest number 94, in 1977.

● COMPILATIONS: *The Rocking Honky Tonk Man* (Country Classics Library)★★★, *Heading For A Heartbreak* (Brylen 1982)★★★, *Country Classics Hayride Style* (Cowgirl Boy 1992)★★★.

BASHFUL BROTHER OSWALD
(see Kirby, Pete)

BASHFUL HARMONICA JOE
b. Joseph Troyan, 25 March 1913, Pleasant City, Ohio, USA. Troyan learned to play harmonica as a child and he also possessed a natural ability to imitate birds, animals and humans. In 1929, his mother relocated with her eight children to Cleveland, where Joe made his debut on local radio. He acquired his nickname of Bashful due to a severe attack of stage fright early in his career. The audience thought his heavy swallowing and hiding behind the curtains was all part of the act and laughed so he decided to adopt it ever after. He worked for over a year on Lum And Abner's *Friday Night Sociable* before Bradley Kincaid made him a regular on his show. In 1936, he began to work with Pie Plant Pete, whom he had first met in Cleveland in 1935. They worked stations in Cleveland, Boston and Rochester, before their career was interrupted by World War II (Pete served briefly in the Quartermaster Corps but was discharged owing to his age and they resumed their partnership in Cleveland). In 1942, Joe joined the US Air Force and spent most of his time entertaining his fellow servicemen. After the war, they relaunched their partnership, working at Cleveland, Rochester and Detroit. In 1947, they recorded 20 sides for Process Records of Buffalo, New York, which were released as ten singles. After they ended their partnership, Joe worked solo for a time but eventually retired to live in Cleveland. In 1989, Cattle Records of Germany issued an album containing all their Process recordings.

● COMPILATIONS: *The Oldtime Country Music Collection Of Pie Plant Pete And Bashful Harmonica Joe* (Cattle 1989)★★★.

BATE, DR. HUMPHREY, (AND THE POSSUM HUNTERS)
b. 1875, Sumner County, near Nashville, Tennessee, USA, d. 1936, Nashville, Tennessee, USA. He learned to play harmonica as a boy but followed his father's profession when he graduated from Vanderbilt Medical School. He served in the Medical Corps during the 1898 Spanish-American War, before taking over his father's long-established practice at Castalian Springs, near Gallatin, Tennessee. His keen interest in music, particularly light classics and the marches of Souza, saw him form his first string band in the early 1900s and by 1919 his Castalian String Band was popular in the area. When, in 1925, Nashville's first two radio stations began broadcasts, Bate seemingly became the first old-time musician to play anything resembling country music. He played initially on WDAD and then led the first string band to play on WSM, on 25 October; George D. Hay would later name Bate's band the Possum Hunters. Bate's daughter, Alcyone (b. 1912, Nashville, Tennessee, USA, d. 14 October 1982, Nashville, Tennessee, USA), first sang with his band as a four-year-old and by 1926, at the age of 13, she was the regular pianist who could also play ukulele. She is reckoned to be the first woman to both appear on and sing on the *Grand Ole Opry*. Bate, who was fondly known as the 'Dean of the Opry', remained an active *Opry* artist for 11 years. He discovered Deford Bailey and it was his recommendation to WSM that led to Bailey becoming the *Opry*'s first black star. In March 1928, Bate and his band recorded for Brunswick in Atlanta. The session (the only one of his career) saw 10 Brunswick and two Vocalion sides released. In 1936, he suffered severe heart problems but pleaded successfully with Hay 'to let me die in harness' and remained on the *Opry* until the end. Being a doctor, he recognized the seriousness of his final attack, saying to his wife, 'Ethel, this one's going to take me away from here', and was apparently taking his own pulse when it stopped. The Possum Hunters inevitably saw some personnel changes but usual players were Bate (harmonica), Oscar Stone (fiddle), Walter Ligget (banjo), Oscar Albright (bass), Staley Walton (guitar), Burt Hutcherson (guitar) and from 1931, Humphrey 'Buster' Bate Jnr. (harmonica, guitar, Jew's harp). After Bate's death, Stone (b. *c*.1881, Obion County, Tennessee, USA) led the band until his own death in 1949. Alcyone Bate also had her own programme on WSM; during the 30s she sang with Jack Shook's band, led a vocal group, the Dixie Dons, worked as a staff composer and arranger for WSM and even made a few solo recordings, of which a version of 'Silver Threads Among The Gold' is highly rated. After Stone's death, she and Walton kept the Possum Hunters going into the 50s but eventually the band folded and for a time, they played with the Crook Brothers. After Walton's death, Alcyone Bate Beasley basically retired after a career lasting over 40 years. She died in Nashville's Memorial Hospital on 14 October 1982, following a stroke. A few of Bate's recordings have appeared on County and Rounder compilation albums, being perhaps the only examples left of an early day artist who seemingly appeared on the *Opry* before any other country act.

BAXTER, ANDREW AND JIM
b. Calhoun, Georgia, USA. A father and son duo, playing violin and guitar, respectively, the Baxters recorded at four sessions between 1927 and 1929. Their records offer a rare

example of an older, more rural, black music tradition in Georgia. While some were blues, notably the gentle and melancholy 'KC Railroad Blues', others such as 'Georgia Stomp' were country dance tunes, similar in many ways to some of the white traditional music recorded around the same time. The latter even included spoken dance calls of the type more usually associated with white country music. Emphasizing this connection, Andrew, the father (who is said to have been half-Cherokee Indian), made one record with the white old-time group the Georgia Yellow Hammers, at the 1927 session.

● COMPILATIONS: *The East Coast States, Vol. 2* (1968)★★★.

BAYOU SECO

Rejuvenating the classical American music traditions of Cajun, country and Tex-Mex, Bayou Seco comprise Ken Keppeler (b. Los Angeles, California, USA; accordion), Jeannie McLerie (b. 1942, New Jersey, USA; fiddle) and Frannie Leopold (b. New York, USA; guitar). The latter pair also record as the Delta Sisters. McLerie grew up listening to old-time music on West Virginian radio station WWVA Wheeling, and was particularly influenced by the Carter Family. In the 50s she taught James Taylor how to fingerpick the guitar, before moving to Paris for her final year of college in 1962. There she dropped out of studies at the Sorbonne and formed a street singing duo with Sandy Darlington. They moved to London in 1964, remaining there for three years and performing together as Sandy And Jeannie. Leopold too grew up in the left-field folk tradition, taking her main influences from the likes of Lead Belly, the Almanac Singers and the Weavers. After moving to Mendocino County she began to busk, meeting McLerie in 1974. Keppeler's father was an old-time singer who played harmonica, and his uncle was also a reputed singer (Vincente Guereca). In the late 50s he learned the mandolin and began to play in bluegrass bands, before joining the army during the Vietnam war. His first permanent band was the Hogwood String Band who toured Germany in the mid-70s. Returning to Louisiana in 1978 he met McLerie, temporarily playing together in Beausoleil and forming a romantic attachment. Though they enjoyed the musical climate of Louisiana they were forced to relocate their home to New Mexico owing to McLerie's medical condition (an allergy to mould and mildew). They continued their quest to explore musical folklore, learning Spanish colonial dance tunes as part of the Cleofes Ortiz Band. Bayou Seco originated when the duo were joined by Leopold, with the Delta Sisters also growing out of this arrangement. Their work is expressly directed to rekindling interest in forgotten traditionalists such as Ortiz and Dennis McGhee.

● ALBUMS: including *Following In The Tuneprints* (Ubik 1994)★★★.

BEAR FAMILY RECORDS

This Bremen-based German record label was launched in 1975 by Richard Weize, a dedicated record collector. Initially, in the early 70s, with a partner and a limited budget, Weize had formed Folk Variety Records but when the partner decided politics, rather than records, offered a more interesting career, Weize continued on his own. His lifelong interest in bears saw him incorporate the bear logo and a change of name to Bear Family. The first releases were reis-

sues of the Folk Variety albums, but after the success achieved in 1978 by an album of previously unissued recordings of Johnny Cash (BF 15016), he came to the conclusion that there must be a lot of material gathering dust in the vaults of major record companies. He set about not only finding it, but actually releasing it under licence from the original owners. He has sometimes upset people but very often, he has found material that the majors had either overlooked or were simply too busy to bother about. There have also been releases of material by relatively unknown artists that would not otherwise have been heard. Gradually, the issues started to include boxed sets of specific artists' work, and when changing times saw vinyl give way to compact discs, Bear Family were very quick to update to that format. Their valued issues include a 16-CD set of Jim Reeves, which arguably contains everything the artist ever recorded including demos, and six boxed sets containing all the studio and Thesaurus recordings of Hank Snow. There have been many other sets containing recordings by artists such as Lefty Frizzell, Bill Monroe, Flatt And Scruggs, and others. Great care has always been taken in remastering recordings, the packaging is to an exceptional standard and all releases are accompanied by informative booklets giving biographical and recording data. Many of these sets and booklets provide the most detailed information available and the Bear Family catalogue is a most impressive one.

BEAUSOLEIL

Widely considered to be the pre-eminent Cajun band of the 80s and 90s, BeauSoleil (the capitalized 'S' having been added in the 90s) have amassed a huge discography during that time which features some of the most exciting music extant within the traditional music realm. Rather than contemplate retirement, if anything, their output seems to have increased and intensified during recent years. They were almost entirely responsible for the Cajun music boom of the late 80s when their music was featured extensively in *The Big Easy*. Formed in 1975 by fiddler, vocalist and songwriter Michael Doucet (who had formerly piloted a Cajun group entitled Coteau which he revived in the mid-90s), the regular group additionally comprises brother David Doucet (guitar, vocals), Tommy Alesi (drums), Al Tharp (bass), Billy Ware (percussion) and Jimmy Breaux (accordion). Other prominent members over the years include guitarist Bessyl Duhon (of Riff Raffs fame), while guest collaborators have included artists of the calibre of Richard Thompson, Keith Richards, the Grateful Dead and Augie Meyers. Despite their already vast recorded legacy, BeauSoleil remain predominantly a live attraction, the group having rarely left the road for any extended period during their 25 years together. 1989's *Bayou Cadillac* and *Cajun Conja*, a collaboration with Thompson that was nominated for a Grammy, are but two stand-out albums in a distinguished recording career. Despite their genre popularity, they have too often had to rely on the recommendations or lip-service of others to gain media prominence. For example, they received a major boost in 1991 when Mary-Chapin Carpenter mentioned the group in the lyrics to her hit 'Down At The Twist And Shout'. The video for the award-winning song prominently featured BeauSoleil themselves. In 1997, the group joined Carpenter for a reprise of the song at the Super Bowl, in New Orleans.

● ALBUMS: *The Spirit Of Cajun Music* (Swallow 1977)★★★,

Zydeco Gris Gris (Rounder 1980)★★★, *Parlez-Nous A Boire* (Arhoolie 1981)★★★, *Bayou Boogie* (Rounder 1986)★★★, *Allons A Lafayette* (Arhoolie 1986)★★★, *Hot Chili Mama* (Arhoolie 1988)★★★★, *Live From The Left Coast* (Rounder 1989)★★★, *Bayou Cadillac* (Rounder 1989)★★★★, *Déjà Vu* (Swallow 1990)★★★, *Cajun Conja* (Rhino 1991)★★★★, *L'Echo* (Rhino 1995)★★★, *L'Amour Ou La Folie* (Rhino 1997)★★★.
● COMPILATIONS: *Their Swallow Recordings* (Ace 1992)★★★★, *Vintage Beausoleil* (Music Of The World 1995)★★★★.

BECKETT, BARRY

b. 1944, Birmingham, Alabama, USA. Beckett was a young club pianist in Pensacola in Florida when he was asked to move to Muscle Shoals, Alabama, by 'Papa' Don Schroder with one of his acts, James And Bobby Purify. Beckett quickly became established as a pianist at the Fame studios in Muscle Shoals and he played on many R&B recordings. Paul Simon featured Beckett on the exhilarating 'Kodachrome', the bluesy 'One Man's Ceiling Is Another Man's Floor' and later the Simon And Garfunkel reunion track, 'My Little Town'. In 1987 Beckett produced Eddy Raven and he added a blues feel to Raven's repertoire and had several US country number 1 records with him in the late 80s - 'Joe Knows How To Live', 'Bayou Boys', 'I'm Gonna Get You' and 'In A Letter To You'. He was ideally suited to the powerhouse rave-ups of Hank Williams Jnr., producing his defiant 'Born To Boogie' and a revival of 'Mind Your Own Business', which included guest appearances by Willie Nelson, Reba McEntire and Tom Petty. Both records were US country number 1s. At the start of 1996, he was enjoying US country hits with Kenny Chesney and Neal McCoy.

BEGLEY, PHILOMENA

b. 1946, Pomeroy, County Tyrone, Northern Ireland. Begley is the fourth child in a family of eight. Her father played accordion and her mother sang and, like many Irish performers, Philomena grew up with a love of country music. She worked in a hat factory and began singing part-time with the Old Cross Ceili Band, which, owing to the late 60s country boom in Ireland, became Country Flavour. In 1971 Philomena Begley and Country Flavour made the Irish Top 10 with 'Here Today, Gone Tomorrow', to be followed by 'Never Again'. In 1972 she formed her own band, the Ramblin' Men and had an Irish hit with 'Rambling Man'. Her subsequent Irish chart successes include 'Wait A Little Longer Please, Jesus', 'Blanket On The Ground' (number 5, while Billie Jo Spears reached number 11) and duets with Ray Lynam, 'You're The One I Can't Live Without' and 'My Elusive Dreams'. Begley has appeared on Nashville's *Grand Ole Opry* and has recorded at Porter Wagoner's studios. She is a favourite at London's Wembley Country Music Festivals and regularly tours the UK, both in her own right and as a support act to American performers. Despite her popularity as the Queen of Irish Country, Begley has no pretensions to stardom, happily living on the family farm with her husband and three children.
● ALBUMS: with Ray Lynam *The Two Of Us* (Release 1973)★★★, *Meet The Queen Of Country Music* (Release 1974)★★★★, with Lynam *Together Again* (Release 1976)★★★, *Philomena Begley Introduces Her Ramblin' Men*

(Topspin 1976)★★★, with Lynam *The Best Of Ray And Phil* (1976)★★★, *Queen Of The Silver Dollar* (Topspin 1976)★★★★, *Irish Country Queen* (Topspin 1977)★★★, *Nashville Country* (Shannon 1978)★★★, *Truckin' Queen* (Topspin 1978)★★★, with Lynam *We Love To Sing* (1979)★★★, *Fireside Country* (1980)★★, *Philomena's Country* (1980)★★★, *Philomena* (Ritz 1984)★★★★, *Truck Drivin' Woman* (Ritz 1984)★★★, *You're In My Heart* (Ritz 1984)★★★, with Lynam *Simply Divine* (Ritz 1985)★★, *More About Love* (Ritz 1987)★★★, *Silver Anniversary Album* (Ritz 1988)★★★, *Reflections* (K-Tel 1990)★★★, with Mick Flavin *In Harmony* (Ritz 1991)★★★, *Country Queen for 30 Years* (1992)★★★.
● COMPILATIONS: *Best Of* (Ritz 1984)★★★★.
● VIDEOS: *Live In Concert* (Ritz 1991)

BELEW, CARL

b. 21 April 1931, Salina, Oklahoma, USA, d. 31 October 1990. Belew left school at 15 and became a plumber, but he was intent on becoming a musician. Marvin Rainwater arranged a recording session for Four Star Records in 1955 and then, in 1958, he wrote Johnnie And Jack's hit single 'Stop The World (And Let Me Off)'. He also recorded rockabilly ('Cool Gator Shoes' and 'Folding Money') but eventually found success with his self-penned 'Lonely Street', a maudlin country ballad with a lyrical nod to 'Heartbreak Hotel'. It made the US Top 10 for Andy Williams and was subsequently recorded by Gene Vincent and Rex Allen Jnr. Another country hit, 'Am I That Easy To Forget?', was a 1960 US pop entry for Debbie Reynolds but he did not have UK success until Engelbert Humperdinck recorded it in 1968. The song, now a country standard, has also been recorded by Jim Reeves, Don Gibson, Leon Russell and, once again, Gene Vincent. Although Belew did not compose 'Crystal Chandelier' or 'Hello Out There', he garnered success with both songs. He did, however, write Eddy Arnold's US country number 1, 'What's He Doing In My World?'. Belew returned to the country charts in the 70s with 'All I Need Is You', a duet with Betty Jean Robinson, but ill health dogged his later years.
● ALBUMS: *Carl Belew* (Decca 1960)★★★, *Carl Belew* (Wrangler 1962)★★, *Hello Out There* (RCA Victor 1964)★★★, *Am I That Easy To Forget?* (RCA Victor 1965)★★★, *Another Lonely Night* (1965)★★★, *Country Songs* (Vocalion 1966)★★★, *Lonely Street* (Vocalion 1967)★★★, *Twelve Shades Of Belew* (RCA Victor 1968)★★★★, with Betty Jean Robinson *When My Baby Sings His Song* (Decca 1972)★★★, *Singing My Song* (1974)★★★.

BELL, DELIA, AND BILL GRANT

Bell (b. Delia Nowell, 16 April c.30s, Bonham, Texas, USA; guitar, vocals) and Grant (b. Billy Joe Grant, 9 May c.1930, Hugo, Oklahoma, USA; mandolin, vocals) have established a reputation as one of bluegrass music's finest harmony duos. Grant grew up on the family ranch greatly influenced by the music of Bill Monroe and the Stanley Brothers. Bell's family relocated to Hugo, Oklahoma, when she was a small child and she first sang there in the church choir. She married Bobby Bell, a close friend of Bill Grant, and in the late 50s, she and Grant, with matching musical tastes, began singing together. They sang on local radio and television and, in 1969, they formed the Kiamichi Mountain Boys, which featured the Bonham family, and played various bluegrass venues in their area. In 1971, Grant launched his Kiamichi label and they recorded a series of albums featuring standards and new material written by Grant. In 1978, Bell recorded a solo album for County and the following year, they toured the UK, where they recorded an album released on the Kama label. Emmylou Harris was so impressed with Bell's recording of 'Roses In The Snow' that she became a great fan of the singer and subsequently recorded the song herself, as the title track of an album. She also helped Bell to gain a recording contract with Warner Brothers Records. The Kiamichi Mountain Boys disbanded in 1980 due to disagreements over travelling, but Grant and Bell continued to appear as a duo, while Bell also made solo recordings. In 1983, she registered minor *Billboard* country chart hits with 'Flame In My Heart' and 'Coyote Song'. During the 80s, with backing from the Johnson Mountain Boys, the duo recorded albums for Rebel and Rounder Records, before moving to Old Homestead who also reissued some of their earlier Kiamichi albums. Several of Grant's songs have become popular, including 'My Kiamichi Mountain Home'.

● ALBUMS: *My Kiamichi Mountain Home* (Kiamichi 1972)★★★, *Kiamichi Country* (Kiamichi 1974, reissued by Old Homestead 1986)★★★★, *There Is A Fountain* (Kiamichi 1975)★★★ *14 Memories* (Kiamichi 1976)★★★, *The Last Christmas Tree* (Kiamichi 1977)★★, *My Pathway Leads To Oklahoma* (Kiamichi 1978)★★★, *The Blues Mountain Style* (Kiamichi 1979, reissued by Old Homestead 1986)★★★★, *In England* (Kama 1979)★★, *The Man In The Middle* (Kiamichi 1980, reissued by Old Homestead 1986)★★★, *Bill Grant & Delia Bell* (Rebel 1980)★★, *Rollin'* (Rebel 1981)★, *The Cheer Of The Home Fires* (Rounder 1984)★★★, *A Few Dollars More* (Rounder 1986)★★★, *Following A Feeling* (Rounder 1988)★★★, *Dreaming Of The Times* (Old Homestead 1992)★★★.

Solo: Delia Bell *Bluer Than Midnight* (County 1978)★★★, *Delia Bell* (Warners 1983)★★.

BELLAMY BROTHERS

Howard (b. 2 February 1946, Darby, Florida, USA) and David (b. 16 September 1950, Darby, Florida, USA). The Bellamy Brothers became one of the top country acts of the 80s after beginning their career in pop and soul. The brothers' father played bluegrass music but David Bellamy's first professional job was as keyboardist with the soul band the Accidents in the mid-60s, backing artists including Percy Sledge. The brothers formed the band Jericho in 1968, but disbanded three years later. They then began writing songs for other artists, and David's 'Spiders And Snakes' was a Top 3 pop hit for Jim Stafford in 1973-74. The Bellamy Brothers signed to Warner Brothers Records the following year and in 1976 reached the top of the US charts and the UK Top 10 with 'Let Your Love Flow'. Although they continued to release albums and singles for the next few years, their days as a pop act were over. In 1979 the ambiguously and suggestively titled 'If I Said You Had A Beautiful Body (Would You Hold It Against Me)?' became the first of 10 country chart singles for the group. This became their biggest hit in the UK where it reached the Top 3. By the late 80s, having transferred to Curb Records, the brothers still recorded Top 10 country singles on a regular basis, and enjoyed a strong following. To date in their long and successful career (including 12 country number 1s) they remain an enigma;

often their material is lightweight and their stage act is strangely static. 'Kids Of The Baby Boom Time' trivializes Kennedy's assassination, while 'Jesus Is Coming' features the line: 'Jesus is coming and boy is he pissed.' In 1995 they updated 'Old Hippie' with 'Old Hippie (The Sequel)': it is to be hoped that they are not planning to update all their novelty hits.

● ALBUMS: *Let Your Love Flow* (Warners 1976)★★★★, *Plain And Fancy* (Warners 1977)★★★, *Beautiful Friends* (Warners 1978)★★, *The Two And Only* (Warners 1979)★★★, *You Can Get Crazy* (Warners 1980)★★★, *Sons Of The Sun* (Warners 1980)★★, *When We Were Boys* (Elektra 1982)★★, *Strong Weakness* (1983)★★, *Restless* (MCA 1984)★★, *Howard And David* (MCA 1986)★★, *Country Rap* (MCA 1987)★★, *Crazy From The Heart* (1987)★★, *Rebels Without A Clue* (MCA 1988)★★, *Rolling Thunder* (Atlantic 1991)★★, *Rip Off The Knob* (Bellamy Brothers 1993)★★, *Heartbreak Overload* (Intersound 1994)★★, *Sons Of Beaches* (Bellamy Brothers 1995)★★, *The Bellamy Brothers Dancin'* (Bellamy Brothers 1996)★★, *A Tropical Christmas* (Bellamy Brothers 1996)★★, *Over The Line* (Bellamy Brothers 1997)★★★.

● COMPILATIONS: *The Bellamy Brothers' Greatest Hits* (MCA 1982)★★★, *Bellamy Brothers' Greatest Hits Vol. 2* (MCA 1986)★★, *Bellamy Brothers' Greatest Hits Vol. 3* (MCA 1989)★★, *Best Of The Best* (Intersound 1992)★★★, *Let Your Love Flow: Twenty Years Of Hits* (Bellamy Brothers/Intersound 1997)★★★.

● VIDEOS: *Best Of The Best* (Start Video 1994).

BENNETT, PINTO

b. 20 May 1948, Mountain Home, Idaho, USA. Bennett grew up on a ranch and became immersed in the music of Hank Williams and Lefty Frizzell. From the 60s, he has been fusing honky tonk with more contemporary sounds and, although he is hardly a singer, he has developed a hard-rocking country style. In 1983, he tried his luck in Nashville without success. His *Pure Quill* album was highly acclaimed but Bennett - a huge, tattooed man with a handlebar moustache - is an unlikely star.

● ALBUMS: *Famous Motel Cowboy Songs* (P.T. Music 1988)★★★, *Big In Winnemucca* (P.T. Music 1988)★★★, *Pure Quill* (P.T. Music 1989)★★★, *Ravages Of Time* (1992)★★.

BERG, MATRACA

b. 3 February 1964, Nashville, Tennessee, USA. The song 'Appalachian Rain', on 90s country singer Berg's first album, is about an unmarried mother moving away to have her baby, and she explained, 'It is what happened to my mom; and in the song I tried to deal with how she must have felt, and what I wished had happened to my father.' Berg is one of the few country singers to have been born in Nashville and her mother, Icee Berg, who died when Matraca was 20, was a songwriter and backing vocalist. Matraca Berg and Bobby Braddock wrote a US country number 1 for T.G. Sheppard and Karen Brooks, 'Faking Love', and she followed it with another chart-topper, 'The Last One To Know' for Reba McEntire. Her songs, usually for female artists, include 'Eat At Joe's', 'Diamonds And Tears', 'Hey Cinderella', 'Give Me Some Wheels' (all recorded by Suzy Bogguss), 'Walk On' (Linda Ronstadt), 'Wrong Side Of Memphis', 'Everybody Knows' (Trisha Yearwood), 'Black Water Bayou' (Tanya Tucker), 'Wild Angels', 'Cryin' On The Shoulder Of The

Road' (Martina McBride), 'You Can Feel Bad' (Patty Loveless), 'Strawberry Wine', 'We Danced Anyway' (Deana Carter) and 'Calico Plains' (Pam Tillis). Her album, *Lying To The Moon*, included some minor country hits but the title track has the makings of a country standard, having also been recorded by Trisha Yearwood. Strangely, Berg moved to RCA's pop division for her second album, which was much more melancholy. She is arguably the most prolifically successful country songwriter of the decade and her own recording career tends to become buried beneath the success of others. In 1997 she won the CMA Song Of The Year Award for 'Strawberry Wine', co-written with Gary Harrison for Deana Carter. She released a debut album for her new label Rising Tide the same year.
● ALBUMS: *Lyin' To The Moon* (RCA 1990)★★★, *Bittersweet Surrender* (RCA 1991)★★★, *The Speed Of Grace* (RCA 1993)★★★, *Sunday Morning To Saturday Night* (Rising Tide 1997)★★★.

BERLINE, BYRON

b. 6 July 1944, Caldwell, Kansas, USA. The masterful newgrass fiddle player has been a much sought-after sessionman in addition to his spells with a number of prestigious country/rock groups, notably the Dillards, Dillard And Clark Expedition, the Flying Burrito Brothers and his own highly respected Country Gazette. His father Luke was also a bluegrass fiddler and Byron started playing at the age of five. Later on he studied music at the University Of Oklahoma and it was there that he formed his first band. He joined the Dillards in 1967 after a spell with Bill Monroe and followed Doug Dillard when he teamed up with Gene Clark in 1968. Over the years he has appeared on albums by the Rolling Stones ('Honky Tonk Woman', and 'Country Honk from *Let It Bleed*), Dan Baird and Vince Gill in addition to his ongoing work with Dan Crary and John Hickman (as BCH and California).
● ALBUMS: with Dan Crary, John Hickman *Progressive Bluegrass* (1975)★★★, *Live At McCabes* (Takoma 1978)★★★, *Byron Berline & The L.A. Fiddle Band* (Sugar Hill 1980)★★★★, *Outrageous* (Flying Fish 1980)★★★, *Night Run* (Sugar Hill 1984)★★★, with Crary, Hickman *B-C-H* (Sugar Hill 1986)★★★, with Crary, Hickman *Double Trouble* (Sugar Hill 1986)★★★, with Crary, Hickman and Steve Spurgin *Now They Are Four* (Sugar Hill 1989)★★★, *Fiddle And A Song* (Sugar Hill 1995)★★★, *Jumpin' The Strings* (Sugar Hill 1996)★★★.

BERRY, JOHN

b. 14 September, 1959, Aiken, South Carolina, USA. The 90s country singer John Berry grew up appreciating soul music and the singer-songwriters of the early 70s. In 1981 both his legs were crushed in a motorcycle accident, but he recovered fully and decided to devote his time to music. He performed in Midwest clubs until settling in Athens, Georgia, in 1985. He self-financed six albums that he sold at concerts, the sixth of which sold over 10,000 copies. By that time, he was graduating from southern soul into new country. His powerful voice can be heard to good effect on his first album for Liberty Records, *John Berry*, and the ballad 'Your Love Amazes Me' shot Berry to country music stardom. Further drama with his health ensued when in 1994 he had a delicate operation to remove a cyst in his brain. Recalling the

earlier appalling road accident, Berry fully recovered, reinforcing the artist's remarkable thirst for life. That same turbulent year he topped the US country charts with 'Your Love Amazes Me'. Berry's vocal inflections still retain strong elements of white soul music, in keeping with the styles of Kenny Loggins and Michael McDonald. His wife, Robin, adds backing vocals on a number of tracks. Berry excels at power ballads such as 'What Are We Fighting For', 'There's No Cross That Love Won't Bear', 'I Never Lost You' and 'If I Had Any Pride Left At All' (all from the excellent *Standing On The Edge*). He has said, perhaps with a touch of foreknowledge, 'If you have a big hit, you have to sing it for the rest of your life, and it would be awful if you hated the song.' *Faces* was a rather formulaic follow-up.
● ALBUMS: *Things Are Not The Same* (Patriot 1986)★★★, *Saddle The Wind* (Patriot 1990)★★★, *John Berry* (Liberty 1993)★★★, *Standing On The Edge* (Patriot 1995)★★★★, *Faithfully* (Capitol 1996)★★★, *Faces* (Capitol 1996)★★.

BEST, TONY

Tony Best is a UK country performer who became a promoter (Tony Best Promotions, Tony Best Leisure) and manager (the Haley Sisters, Dave Sheriff). He has his own record label, organizes extensive charity work and keeps his hand in as a performer at his club in Shrewsbury.

BIG SLIM, THE LONE COWBOY

b. Harry C. McAuliffe, 9 May, possibly near Bluefield, Mercer County, West Virginia, USA, d. 13 October 1966, New York, USA. The year of his birth remains obscure, due to what has been politely described as 'his own capacity for contradictory statements'. (He gave it at differing times as 1899, 1903, 1904 and 1905.) He also claimed that he was born on a 750-acre farm but on other occasions said it was Bluefield, and there have even been claims that he was born in Pennsylvania. He may well have, as he always claimed, worked both as a cowboy and on the railroad, before gaining radio work in Pittsburgh in 1929. He certainly had considerable skill with horses, which he later used to great effect in his stage act. It has also been alleged that he worked on the border radio station at Eagle Pass, Texas. On 17 December 1936, in New York, as Big Slim Aliff and with only his own guitar, he recorded four sides for Decca Records, including the first recording of 'Footprints In The Snow', a song that is now a country standard. In 1937, he joined WWVA, first as a member of Doc Williams' band but he soon became one of the *Wheeling Jamboree*'s most loved stars. Although, on occasions, he made some appearances on other stations, he spent almost all of his career at WWVA. He possessed a strong deep voice and his renditions of western songs, such as 'Strawberry Roan' and 'Patanio, The Pride Of The Plains', endeared him to radio listeners and live audiences alike. Along with his horse, Golden Flash, Slim's skill with a bullwhip was part of his stage act. He copyrighted some songs including 'On The Sunny Side Of The Mountain', although some of his claims for authorship have been disputed. In the late 40s, he made recordings for Dixie and Page and some years later, he had three albums released by the Canadian Arc label. Surrounded by what was no doubt his own carefully spun mixture of fact and fiction, he was an important contributor to country music, not only by his personal input but certainly for the fact that both Hank Snow and

Hawkshaw Hawkins owed a great deal to Big Slim for his help in the early parts of their careers. Snow relates a considerable amount of information about their association in his autobiography. Big Slim died in 1966 and is buried at Wheeling, West Virginia.

● ALBUMS: *Big Slim, The Lone Cowboy* (Arc 1960)★★★, *Big Slim's Old Favorites* (Arc 1961)★★★, *On Tour With Big Slim, The Lone Cowboy* (Arc 1962)★★.

● COMPILATIONS: *Sunny Side Of The Mountain* (Old Homestead 1986)★★★.

BIG TOM AND THE MAINLINERS

b. Thomas McBride, 18 September, Moy, Drumakill, Castleblayney, County Monaghan, Eire. A stalwart of Irish country music, McBride grew up on the family farm and achieved some success as a footballer, before relocating to work in England in the early 60s. While employed in London's building industry, he bought his first guitar and began singing in local pubs before the death of his younger brother saw him return home to work the family farm. In 1965, he and six other local youths formed the Mainliners and began playing local venues. In May 1966, McBride (who also plays saxophone) appeared on RTE's *Showband Show* singing 'Gentle Mother' and his career was launched. Released on a single, the song quickly became one of the biggest-selling records of all time in Ireland. From that point until 1978, Big Tom And The Mainliners were a household name. They toured extensively both in Eire and the UK. They recorded numerous albums and registered major hits with such songs as 'Old Log Cabin For Sale', 'Broken Marriage Vows', 'The Sunset Years Of Life' and 'Back To Castleblayney'. Many were surprised when, in the late 70s, he left the Mainliners to front his own band, the Travellers, and John Glenn became lead singer with the Mainliners. The change had little, if any, effect on his popularity and he continued to be one of Ireland's most popular entertainers. His records, including a series called *King Of Country Music*, sold in prodigious numbers and, in 1980, while playing a London venue, he was presented with a Gold Award for sales in excess of a million on the Denver label. This did not take into consideration the fact that some of his bestselling albums were recorded on the Emerald label, prior to him joining Denver. In 1980, singer Susan McCann launched her career, when her recording of 'Big Tom Is Still The King' topped the Irish pop charts and for over a month outsold any other record in Ireland. Big Tom recorded 14 original songs written by John McCawley (his business partner in Denver records) in Nashville for *Blue Wing*. On 30 June 1989, by popular demand, Big Tom And The Mainliners were reunited at a special show at The Oasis, Carrickmacross (Ireland's biggest nightclub), where more than 4,000 people showed that they had not been forgotten. After a major tour of Ireland and the UK, Big Tom remains a popular performer.

● ALBUMS: *A Little Bit Of Country And Irish* (Emerald 1969)★★★, *Ashes Of Love* (Emerald 1970)★★★, *From Ireland Big Tom* (Emerald 1970)★★★, *All Time Hits* (Emerald 1971)★★, *The Sunset Years Of Life* (Emerald 1972)★★★, *I'll Settle For Old Ireland* (Emerald 1973)★★★ *Big Tom And The Mainliners* (Emerald 70s)★★★, *Smoke Along The Track* (Denver 1975)★★★, *When The Roses Bloom Again* (Denver 70s)★★★, *Requests* (Denver 1970)★★★, *The*

Heart Of Country Music (Denver 1970)★★★, *Hits By The Dozen* (Denver 70s)★★, *Souvenirs* (Denver 70s)★★★, *Blue Wings* (Denver 1980)★★★, *Teardrops In The Snow* (Denver 80s)★★★, *Around Ireland With Big Tom* (Denver 80s)★★★, *Big Tom And The Mainliners - Today* (90s)★★★, *Greatest Hits* (MM 90s)★★★. Albums with the Travellers: *Introducing Tom And The Travellers*, *Travel On* (Denver 1977)★★★, *I Would Like To See You Again*, *Live At The Irish Festival*, *Songs Of Home And Faraway* (Denver c.80s)★★★.

● COMPILATIONS: *King of Country Music Vols 1 to 7* (Denver 70s, reissued Warners 1988)★★★★.

BINKLEY BROTHERS

Amos Binkley (b. 1895, Cheatham County, Tennessee, USA; banjo) and his brother Gale Binkley (b. 1896, Cheatham County, Tennessee, USA; fiddle). Although important as one of the early acts in country music, the brothers basically performed as part-time musicians, running their watchmaking and jewellery shop in Nashville for their living. Along with their friend guitarist Tom Andrews, as the Binkley Brothers String Orchestra, they made their debut on the *Grand Ole Opry*, on 30 October 1926. George D. Hay, with his penchant for colourful nicknames for the performers, soon renamed their act the Binkley Brothers Dixie Clodhoppers, and they retained that name until they finally left the *Opry* in August 1939. On 28 September 1928, with vocalist Jack Jackson, since neither brother had any claim to vocal ability, they and Paul Warmack And The Gully Jumpers were the first artists to actually record in Nashville. Seemingly, a recording equipment fault saw them re-record the numbers on 2 October 1928. Six of their Victor recordings were released and two, 'I'll Rise When The Rooster Crows' and 'Give Me Back My Fifteen Cents', issued on Victor V-40048, became local hits. Some of their recordings have been reissued by County on compilation albums. (Jackson, often referred to as The Strolling Yodeler, later made solo recordings for Columbia Records.) At a time when similar *Opry* bands were renowned for their loudness, the Dixie Clodhoppers were noted for having what one writer described as 'a delicate, restrained sound for an old time string band perhaps because the brothers were watch repairmen by trade'. After they left the *Opry*, they retired and nothing seems known of their later years.

BLACK, CLINT

b. 4 February 1962, Long Branch, New Jersey, USA. Black was born in New Jersey when his father was working there, but the family soon headed back to their home of Houston, Texas. Black was playing the harmonica at the age of 13 and the guitar at 15. He spent several years playing country music in Houston clubs, and his career took off when he met local musician Hayden Nicholas. They wrote 'Straight From The Factory' as soon as they met and have since been a songwriting partnership. Their demos impressed Bill Ham, the manager of ZZ Top, who quickly secured a contract with RCA Records. Most unusually, Black reached number 1 on the US country chart with his first record, 'A Better Man', which he had written about his own broken romance. The title track from his album *Killin' Time* was also a number 1 record. The album was a multi-million-seller and his second album, *Put Yourself In My Shoes*, is not far behind. It includes another number 1 single, 'Loving Blind'. In both vocal and songwriting ability, the obvious comparison is with Merle Haggard, and one that Black is happy to acknowledge. Managerial disputes halted his recording career after the release of *Put Yourself In My Shoes*, but Black's superstar status was affirmed in 1992 with the belated appearance of *The Hard Way*, which spawned a number 1 single ('We Tell Ourselves'), and showed heartening signs that Black was unwilling to rest on his artistic laurels. In 1991, apart from a US country number 1 with 'Loving Blind', Black surprisingly duetted with Roy Rogers and the two reached the charts with 'Hold On Partner'. Black has also recorded 'No Time To Kill' with Wynonna and started to write with Merle Haggard, recording their witty composition 'Untanglin' My Mind'. Black sang 'A Run Of Bad Luck' on the *Maverick* soundtrack album and has had further hits with 'We Tell Ourselves', 'Burn One Down' and 'Life Gets Away'. In 1995 he recorded a Christmas album with a difference, eschewing traditional material in favour of his own songs. *Nothing But The Taillights* saw Black supported by high quality guest musicians including Alison Krauss, Mark Knopfler and Chet Atkins.

● ALBUMS: *Killin' Time* (RCA 1989)★★★, *Put Yourself In My Shoes* (RCA 1990)★★★★, *The Hard Way* (RCA 1992)★★★★, *No Time To Kill* (RCA 1993)★★★, *One Emotion* (RCA 1994)★★★★, *Looking For Christmas* (RCA 1995)★★, *Nothing But The Taillights* (RCA 1997)★★★.
● COMPILATIONS: *Clint Black* (RCA 1993)★★, *The Greatest Hits* (RCA 1996)★★★★.
● VIDEOS: *Summer's Comin'* (RCA 1995).
● FURTHER READING: *A Better Man*, R.D. Brown.

BLACK, JEANNE

b. Gloria Jeanne Black, 25 October 1937, Pomona, California, USA. Between 1951 and 1955, she attended Chaffey High School, Ontario, California, and in 1956, she began her singing career as a vocalist with Cliffie Stone's band on the *Hometown Jamboree* television show, while still a student at Chaffey College. In 1958, while appearing on the *Jamboree*, she also worked solo in Las Vegas and Lake Tahoe venues. She first recorded for Verve Records but in 1960, after singing with Billy Strange's orchestra the previous year, she secured a recording contract with Capitol Records. Her debut single, 'He'll Have To Stay', the 'answer' song to the Jim Reeves hit 'He'll Have To Go', became a Top 10 hit on both US country and pop charts. Some further singles were issued and in 1962, she also recorded as Jeanne And Janie with her sister. She had no further record success and unfortunately, she has to be described as one of the one-hit-wonders of country music, even though she can proudly claim to be one of the few singers to have had a hit with an 'answer' song in both country and pop charts.
● ALBUMS: *A Little Bit Lonely* (Capitol 1960)★★.

BLACKHAWK

When Henry Paul, the lead singer of the southern rock band the Outlaws, moved to Nashville, Tennessee, USA, the rest of the band elected not to join him. He formed the 90s country band Blackhawk with Van Stephenson and Dave Robbins, who were both session musicians and songwriters. The duo had written Willie Nelson's 1983 US country hit 'All My Life' and several singles for Restless Heart. Stephenson had also made the solo albums *Suspicious Heart* and *Righteous Anger*,

and had enjoyed a US Top 40 hit with 'Modern Day Delilah' in 1984. Blackhawk took their name from the Stutz Blackhawk, an American pre-war sports car, and their single, 'Goodbye Says It All', was heavily promoted on CMT. Following the success of their first album, they developed into a touring band. Heavily influenced by Restless Heart, their records are as much middle-of-the-road rock as country.
● ALBUMS: *Blackhawk* (Arista 1994)★★★, *Strong Enough* (Arista 1995)★★★, *Blackhawk 3: Love And Gravity* (Arista 1997)★★.
● VIDEOS: *Almost A Memory Now* (Arista 1996).

BLAKE, NORMAN

b. 10 March 1938, Chattanooga, Tennessee, USA. Norman Blake is a singer-songwriter and talented multi-instrumentalist. He plays dobro, mandolin, mandola, fiddle and viola, but is especially respected for his flat-picking acoustic guitar playing. When he was a baby, the family moved to Sulphur Springs, Georgia, and he grew up in an area where old-time traditional and country music was very popular. He later wrote the songs for his debut album from his childhood memories of life at Sulphur Springs. Blake first played guitar at the age of 11 and, far more interested in playing music than attending school, he quit Trenton High School at 16 to play mandolin in a group called the Dixieland Drifters, who appeared on radio in Knoxville and Chattanooga, as well as on television in Rome, Georgia. He played traditional Appalachian music and recorded an album of old folk tunes with Walter Forbes. In 1960, he toured with June Carter and played dobro and mandolin with Hylo Brown on the WWVA Wheeling Jamboree, West Virginia, before moving to Nashville. He did military service from 1961 to 1962, during which time he recorded *12 Shades Of Bluegrass* with Bob Johnson And The Lonesome Travellers for Parkway Records. After completing his military service, he returned to Nashville and in 1963, played on the first of many recordings with Johnny Cash. He later appeared on Cash's network show, but by 1969, he had become a very popular session musician. He played on Bob Dylan's album *Nashville Skyline* and toured with Kris Kristofferson and Joan Baez. He also played on Baez's popular recording of 'The Night They Drove Old Dixie Down'. In 1971, returning more to his bluegrass roots, he played with a group led by John Hartford, which included fiddler Vassar Clements. He and Clements also played on the Nitty Gritty Dirt Band's album *Will The Circle Be Unbroken*. Since then Blake has appeared with various groups and recorded both old-time country, newgrass, bluegrass and even jazz-grass on countless albums with other progressive bluegrass musicians, including Jethro Burns, Sam Bush, Alan Munde, Mark O'Connor, Red Rector, Tony Rice, Tut Taylor and Doc Watson. He has also recorded several albums with his wife, Nancy, another talented instrumentalist, who is equally at home with cello, mandolin, guitar, bass, fiddle and accordion.
● ALBUMS: *Back Home In Sulphur Springs* (Rounder 1972)★★★, *Blackberry Blossom* (Flying Fish 1974)★★★, *The Fields Of November* (Flying Fish 1974)★★★★, with Jethro Burns, Sam Bush, Vassar Clements *Norman Blake-Super Jam Session* (Flying Fish 1975, issued in UK Sonet 1976)★★★, *Old & New* (Flying Fish 1975)★★★, with Nancy Blake *Live At McCabe's* (Takoma 1976)★★, *Whiskey Before Breakfast*

(Rounder 1976)★★★, *Norman Blake And Red Rector* (County 1976)★★★, *Directions* (Takoma 1978)★★★, *The Rising Fawn String Ensemble* (Rounder 1979)★★★, *Full Moon On The Farm* (Rounder 1981)★★★, *Original Underground Music* (Rounder 1982)★★★, *Nashville Blues* (Rounder 1984)★★★, *Lighthouse On The Shore* (Rounder 1985)★★★, *Slow Train Through Georgia* (Rounder 1987)★★★, with Tony Rice *Blake And Rice* (Rounder 1987)★★★★, with Jethro Burns *Norman Blake & Jethro Burns* (Flying Fish 1988)★★★, with Rice *Norman Blake And Tony Rice 2* (Rounder 1990)★★★, with Nancy Blake *Just Gimme Somethin' I'm Used To* (Shanachie 1992)★★★, with Nancy Blake *While Passing Along This Way* (Shanachie 1995)★★★, with Nancy Blake *The Hobo's Last Ride* (Shanachie 1996)★★★.
Nancy Blake: *Grand Junction* (Rounder 1986)★★★.
● COMPILATIONS: with Nancy Blake *Natasha's Waltz* (Rounder 1987)★★★★, with Nancy Blake *The Norman & Nancy Blake Compact Disc* (Rounder 1988)★★★★, *Blind Dog* (Rounder 1988)★★★★.
● VIDEOS: *My Dear Old Southern Home* (Shanachie 1995).

BLANCHARD, JACK, AND MISTY MORGAN

b. 8 May 1942 and 23 May 1945, respectively, both in Buffalo, New York, USA, but moved to Ohio when still children. Blanchard learned to play the saxophone and keyboards and found work with a small band; Morgan learned piano and organ as a child and initially worked clubs in the Cincinnati area. Their paths eventually crossed in the mid-60s when they met in Florida and soon afterwards, they married. They moved to Nashville, where Blanchard worked in song-writing, record production and as a newspaper cartoonist, and in 1969 achieved a minor US country hit with 'Big Black Bird', one of Blanchard's songs. In 1970, his novelty song 'Tennessee Birdwalk' reached number 1 in the US country and number 23 in the US pop charts. This was followed by further country and pop chart success with 'Humphrey The Camel' and country success with the Fortunes' 'You've Got Your Troubles'. From 1971-75, they had 11 more country hits on Mega or Epic, including 'Somewhere In Virginia In The Rain' and 'The Legendary Chicken Fairy'. There were no further chart hits after 1975. Nothing further was heard of the duo until 1993 when they suddenly reappeared with *Back In Harmony* on the Playback label. The album drew poor comments from reviewers, who appeared to know nothing of what the couple had achieved, or where they had been, during the years that their names had been missing from the charts. Their singing career has presumably now ended.
● ALBUMS: *Birds Of A Feather* (Wayside 1970)★★★, *Two Sides Of Jack & Misty* (Mega 1972)★★★, *Back In Harmony* (Playback 1993)★★.

BLINKHORN, SMILIN' BILLY

b. 28 December 1914, Nanimo, near Vancouver, British Columbia, Canada. The son of a miner, Blinkhorn had the ambition to be a singer and was playing guitar and singing cowboy songs on local radio at the age of 13. Encouraged by the recordings of Carson Robison and Jimmie Rodgers, he later formed the BC Rangers. Throughout the 30s, his singing and yodelling on CJOR Vancouver and his appearances, with his horse Silver, at countless venues for his show's sponsors Dad's Cookies, gained him a considerable

reputation throughout the Province. In 1938, his sponsors opened a branch in Australia and, finding himself unable to get a recording contract in Canada at that time, Blinkhorn took up their suggestion to try his luck in Australia, where the competition was less fierce. He was soon performing regularly on both Australian radio and at personal appearances. Using only his own guitar for accompaniment, he made his first six recordings for Regal-Zonophone on 27 October 1939 and a second six in July 1940. When World War II interrupted his career, he saw military service in New Guinea and the Philippines, where his ability to speak Japanese saw him employed as an interpreter. In 1947, this time with a backing group, he made further recordings, including his noted version of 'Sunny Queensland'. He continued to perform for a few years, before seemingly losing interest. After marrying, he settled in Sydney, later working for the University of New South Wales. During the early 50s, he made his final recordings for Fidelity, including several square dance records, whereon he demonstrated his talent as a caller, no doubt learned as a boy in his native Canada. Arterial disease, in 1974, led to him losing a leg, but he recovered and was soon back to his normal happy self.

BLUE BOYS

The Blue Boys were Jim Reeves' road band and at differing times had various personnel. Initially, Reeves called his band the Wagon Masters, but to avoid confusion in Nashville with Porter Wagoner, he renamed it in 1958, after his hit 'Blue Boy'. The band initially comprised Billy Harlan (bass), Royce Morgan (guitar), Jimmy Day (steel guitar) and Pee Wee Kershaw (drums). Until shortly before the new name, Leo Jackson was Reeves' lead guitarist but at the time of the formation, he was doing military service and Morgan was deputizing. About a year later, Reeves changed the band and after permutations that saw appearances from James Kirkland, Henry Strzelecki, Mel Rogers, Bobby Dyson and Roy Aldridge, he ended with a line-up that featured Leo Jackson (lead guitar), Dean Manuel (piano), Bud Logan (bass, vocals) and Jimmy Orr (drums). After Manuel died with Reeves in the plane crash on 31 July 1964, Bunky Keels played piano and the group continued to perform until disbanding in 1968. They recorded four albums for RCA/Victor Records in the late 60s and enjoyed hits with 'My Cup Runneth Over' (1967) and 'I'm Not Ready Yet' (1968), as The Blue Boys featuring Bud Logan. In 1973-74, Logan achieved further chart successes duetting with Wilma Burgess on 'Wake Me Into Love' and 'The Best Day Of The Rest Of My Life' recorded on Mary Reeves' Shannon label. Jackson and Keels both later worked as session musicians and Logan became a successful record producer.
● ALBUMS: *We Remember Jim Reeves* (RCA Victor 1965)★★★, *Sounds Of Jim Reeves* (RCA Victor 1966)★★, *The Blue Boys In Person* (RCA Victor 1967)★★, *Hit After Hit* (RCA Victor 1967)★★★.

BLUE SKY BOYS

The Blue Sky Boys were Bill Bolick (b. 28 October 1917) and his brother Earl (b. 16 November 1919, both near Hickory, North Carolina, USA). The fourth and fifth of six children of religious parents, they learned many hymns and gospel songs as youngsters, but no other member of the family played an instrument. Bill first learned banjo and guitar

from a neighbour and passed on both his knowledge and the instruments to Earl. He was given a mandolin but, preferring the guitar, he showed no interest in it. Bill taught himself to play and adopted it as his main instrument and appeared as vocalist with a local group on WWNC Asheville in 1935. Soon afterwards, the brothers joined fiddler Homer Sherrill and appeared on radio as the Good Coffee Boys. Before long, they moved to WGST Atlanta, where they became the Blue Ridge Hillbillies. They first recorded for RCA Victor on 16 June 1936, where, for the first time, they became the Blue Sky Boys. They recorded 10 vocal duets with mandolin and guitar accompaniment, including their popular 'Sunny Side Of Life'. Further regular recordings followed and by the end of 1940, they had made almost 100 RCA recordings. Their quiet gentle harmonies, with Earl's melodic baritone and Bill's harmony tenor, also saw them much in demand for personal appearances, in spite of competition from other harmony groups, such as the Monroe Brothers and the Delmore Brothers. They popularized their versions of old songs such as 'Mary Of The Wild Moor' and 'The Knoxville Girl' and their records sold well. In 1938, they even had a British release on Regal Zonophone, although the label saw fit to bill them as The Alabama Barnstormers. Their career was suspended from 1941 to early 1946, when both saw military service overseas during World War II. They re-formed at WGST; their harmonies were even better but they found ideas had changed, and when they recorded in September 1946, they were reinforced by fiddle and bass. In May 1947, they recorded their classic 'Kentucky'. They accepted that modern acts were appearing but, believing that they were solely old-time artists, they resisted any attempts to change their style or their basic repertoire. They still toured but did not record again until 1949, when they made their version of the Louvin Brothers' 'Alabama'. After arguments with the label over which songs to record and their firm rejection of the suggestion that they use an electric guitar on the session, they made their final recordings for RCA in Nashville, in March 1950. In 1951, with differing ideas and tired of the attempts to modernize them, they not only retired but separated, with Earl moving to Georgia and Bill to North Carolina. In 1962, Starday unsuccessfully tried to persuade them to make a comeback and released an album taken from earlier radio transcriptions. In 1963, Bill did persuade Earl to join him and they recorded two albums, *Together Again* and *Precious Moments*, for Starday Records. The former saw them with other musical backing, but the latter featured them with only a fiddle to complement their own mandolin and guitar. They made a few appearances at folk festivals and in 1965, Capitol recorded them singing their old-time songs in concert at the UCLA Folk Festival in Los Angeles; the resultant album became a collector's item. Soon afterwards, they retired again, but in 1975 they recorded in Nashville once more. The Blue Sky Boys were one of the finest of all the duet harmony groups and were a model for several later acts, including Jim And Jesse (McReynolds) and the Everly Brothers.
● ALBUMS: *The Original & Great Blue Sky Boys* (Camden 1963)★★★, *Together Again* (Starday 1963)★★★, *Precious Moments* (Starday 1963)★★★★, *Presenting The Blue Sky Boys* (Capitol 1966)★★★, *The Sunny Side Of Life* (1974)★★★, *The Blue Sky Boys* 1963 recording (Bluebird 1976)★★.
● COMPILATIONS: *A Treasury Of Rare Song Gems From The Past* (Starday 1962)★★★, *Bluegrass Mountain Music* (Camden 1974)★★★, *On Radio (Volumes 1 And 2)* 1946/7 recordings (Copper Creek 1993)★★★★.

BLUEGRASS ALBUM BAND

This band was basically assembled for a one-off recording project rather than for live performances. However, there have been occasions at festivals where the members have played sets. Initially organized in 1981, their first two albums featured Tony Rice (b. 1950, Los Angeles, California, USA; guitar), J.D. Crowe (b. August 1937, Lexington, Kentucky, USA; banjo, vocals), Doyle Lawson (b. 20 April 1944, Fordtown, Tennessee, USA; mandolin, guitar, vocals), Bobby Hicks (fiddle) and Todd Phillips (bass, mandolin). The combination was then joined by Jerry Douglas (dobro), and for their 1989 album, Vasser Clements replaced Bobby Hicks and Mark Shatz played bass in lieu of Todd Phillips. In the 70s, Rice and Douglas had previously played with Crowe as members of the New South. The various members are all top bluegrass musicians in their own right and when not recording for this unit, they either front their own groups or play in various other bands. They have all also recorded with other combinations of musicians.
● ALBUMS: *The Bluegrass Album* (Rounder 1981)★★★★, *The Bluegrass Album Volume II* (Rounder 1982)★★★, *The Bluegrass Album Volume III: California Connection* (Rounder 1983)★★★, *The Bluegrass Album Volume IV* (Rounder 1984)★★★, *The Bluegrass Album Band Volume V: Sweet Sunny South* (Rounder 1989)★★★.
● COMPILATIONS: *The Bluegrass Compact Disc* (Rounder)★★★★.

BOGGS, DOCK

b. Moran Lee Boggs, 7 February 1898, Norton, Virginia, USA, d. 1971. Boggs was known for his unusual banjo style which he learned from a black musician in Virginia. The technique involved a lower tuning of the banjo. Despite Boggs' interest in music, his devoutly religious wife frowned on him showing any real interest in music, so he continued playing as a hobby. Boggs had recorded briefly for Brunswick Records in 1927. He spent more than 40 years as a miner and turned again to music once he had retired. At the same time, there was growing demand for him to play at festivals and clubs. Boggs was 'discovered' by Mike Seeger on a field-collecting expedition at a time when Boggs had not played the banjo for some 25 years. He recorded mainly traditional and sentimental songs such as 'Pretty Polly' and 'Loving Nancy'. Between 1963 and 1966, Boggs recorded two albums for Folkways and one for Asch.
● COMPILATIONS: *Dock Boggs: Legendary Singer And Banjo Player* (1965)★★★, *Dock Boggs: Vol. 2, Songs Of The Cumberland* (1965)★★★, *Excerpts From Interviews With Dock Boggs, Legendary Banjo Player And Singer* (1965)★★★, *The Legendary Dock Boggs* (1965)★★★, *Dock Boggs Vol. 3* (1970)★★★, *Dock Boggs, Vols. 1/2 & Vols. 3/4* (c.1980)★★★.
● FURTHER READING: *Invisible Republic: Bob Dylan's Basement Tapes*, Greil Marcus.

BOGGS, NOEL

b. Noel Edwin Boggs, 14 November 1917, Oklahoma City, Oklahoma, USA, d. 31 August 1974. Boggs was attracted to the steel guitar as a way of making a living at the time of the

Depression and practised as a child. He made his radio debut in the mid-30s, on local stations in Oklahoma City and toured as a member of Hank Penny's Radio Cowboys. He gained further experience working as a staff musician on stations in New Orleans and Birmingham, before returning to WKY Oklahoma City in 1937. He recorded with Wiley And Gene and, influenced by Leon McAuliffe, he fronted his own band in a local dancehall for three years. In the early 40s, he played with Jimmy Wakely and in 1944, when McAuliffe left Bob Wills, Boggs took his place. He played on some of Wills' Tiffany Transcriptions and Columbia recordings, including 'New Spanish Two Step' and 'Texas Playboy Rag'. Between 1947 and 1954, he was a member of Spade Cooley's band. In 1955, he suffered the first of several heart attacks and he was inactive until 1956. He later formed his Noel Boggs Quintet (one member being fiddler Billy Armstrong). He continued to perform although he never really recovered from the first heart attack. During his career he appeared in several films, including with Bob Wills, and worked on radio with singing cowboys Gene Autry, Roy Rogers, Rex Allen and the Sons Of The Pioneers. It is estimated that he played on well over 2,000 recordings and apart from appearances on Wills' recordings, he is featured on some Spade Cooley albums released on the Club of Spade label and with Jimmy Wakely. He often helped other musicians, especially fellow steel guitarist Speedy West, at a time when he was a youngster struggling to succeed in the music business. He made numerous tours including ones to Alaska and the Orient and he owned property on Redondo Beach, California. He was a practical joker, who once wired up six of Spade Cooley's musicians' chairs and put a live lobster in the piano where he concealed the ends of the wires. The lobster, in its efforts to escape, shorted out the wiring and the startled musicians failed to share Boggs' laughter. His strange sense of humour is further witnessed by the story that he returned home from one tour in a hearse and every time the vehicle stopped, he would sit up in the coffin and look around. He also left instructions that he wanted only good steel guitar and not organ music at his funeral. His family solved that problem by playing some of his own recordings, when he was buried at Granada Hills, California.

● ALBUMS: with Hank Penny *Tobacco State Swing* (Rambler 60s)★★★. With Noel Boggs Quintet *Magic Steel* (Shasta 1960)★★, *Hollywood & Vine* (Shasta 60s)★★★, *Noel Boggs With Friends* (Shasta 60s)★★★, *Western Swing* (Repeat 1965)★★★★, *Any Time* (Repeat 1968)★★★.

BOGGUSS, SUZY

b. Suzy Kay Bogguss, 30 December 1956, Aledo, Illinois, USA. Bogguss grew up in a farming family that loved music but had diverse tastes: Bogguss's father favoured country music, her mother big bands, and her brothers and sister the 60s hits. She gained a degree in art, but sang in clubs and coffee-houses to earn extra money. She included country songs in her repertoire such as 'I Want To Be A Cowboy's Sweetheart' and 'Night Rider's Lament'. After five years of touring in a van, she secured a residency at a restaurant in Nashville. A tape she made in 1986 to sell at Dolly Parton's Dollywood impressed Capitol Records. Both 'I Don't Want To Set The World On Fire' and Merle Haggard's 'Somewhere Between' did reasonably well on the US country charts and her first album had an appealing mixture of old and new

songs. Bogguss sang 'Happy Trails' with Michael Martin Murphey on his *Cowboy Songs* (1990), and she and Lee Greenwood had a US country hit with the duet 'Hopelessly Yours'. Her strategy paid off when she won the Horizon Award for the most promising artist at the 1992 CMA Awards ceremony. *Something Up My Sleeve* built upon her success and contained some excellent radio-friendly songs that were able to cross over to mainstream appeal. 'Hey Cinderella', for example, falls comfortably into both pop and country genres, while the sparkling Matraca Berg and Gary Harrison song 'Diamonds And Tears' is pure country rock. Her admiration for Chet Atkins led to him being jointly billed for *Simpatico*, and sharing centrestage on the video for the engaging 'One More For The Road'. *Give Me Some Wheels* broke a three year hiatus, and was an accomplished set whose title-track was co-written with Matricia Berg and Gary Harrison.

● ALBUMS: *Somewhere Between* (Liberty 1988)★★, *Moment Of Truth* (Liberty 1990)★★, *Aces* (Liberty 1991)★★, *Voices In The Wind* (Liberty 1992)★★★, *Something Up My Sleeve* (Liberty 1993)★★★★, with Chet Atkins *Simpatico* (Liberty 1994)★★★, *Give Me Some Wheels* (Capitol 1996)★★★★.
● COMPILATIONS: *Greatest Hits* (Liberty 1994)★★★★.
● VIDEOS: *Hey, Cinderella* (1993).

BONAMY, JAMES

b. Florida, USA. Contemporary country singer James Bonamy gravitated to the honky tonk scene through the auspices of his father, a fan of Johnny Paycheck and Merle Haggard. However, when he began to attend high school he invested much of his time in sports, at which he achieved great proficiency, while his listening tastes changed to those of Bon Jovi *et al*. Despite this, he maintained in an interview with *Country Music People*: 'The songs are laid out the same, and what they're saying is pretty close, too.' However, as he surmised, 'It's country music I was raised on, so that's the music I came back to.' His first steps into the music industry also came while at college. In his first year at the University of Alabama in Birmingham, he gained a spot on local radio. However, it was not until he left academia and took a job at an Orlando gift store back in his home state that he began to take his musical ambitions more seriously. There he sat in with numerous house bands, before relocating to Nashville and a job at the Opryland Theme Park as a summer singer. After months of auditions he finally secured a recording contract with Epic Records. His debut album, *What I Live To Do*, immediately spawned the Top 30 country hit 'She's Got A Mind Of Her Own'. However, Bonamy's career had still not taken off by the time he released the follow-up *Roots And Wings*, a rather unimaginative and lacklustre collection.
● ALBUMS: *What I Live To Do* (Epic 1996)★★★, *Roots And Wings* (Epic 1997)★★★.

BOND, EDDIE

b. Edward James Bond, 1 July 1933, Memphis, Tennessee, USA. Bond first sang on local Memphis radio and television in 1955 and released his first single, 'Double Duty Lovin''/'Talking Off The Wall', on Ekko that year. He worked with Elvis Presley and Johnny Horton on Shreveport's *Louisiana Hayride* and in 1957/8, he recorded six tracks in Memphis for Sam Phillips at Sun Records. In the late 50s, he recorded rockabilly songs for Diplomat and Mercury

Records, in later years claiming that his producers had changed his style to rockabilly, and insisted that, influenced by the sound of Carl Smith, he was always a country boy at heart. On 29 January 1962, he returned to the Sun studios and with session men including steel guitarist John Hughey, he first recorded 14 gospel tracks, followed by a further 16 others, which varied from rockabilly to country numbers such as 'Back Street Affair'. Eleven of the gospel tracks found release on Phillips Records but only three of the others, which included 'Rockin' Daddy', were issued at the time. He continued to appear on various programmes including the *Grand Ole Opry* and the *Big D Jamboree* and in 1966, he was a regular on the televised *Country Shindig*. He recorded for numerous minor labels, including his own Tab, Millionaire and Diplomat and, in 1974, having been involved with law enforcement for some time, he even ran for the post of local Sheriff. In the late 80s, an astute business man and local Memphis personality, he also owned and ran a local radio station.

● ALBUMS: *Sings The Greatest Country Gospel Hits* (Phillips 1962)★★, *Favorite Country Hits From Down Home* (Millionaire 1967)★★★, *My Choice Is Eddie Bond* (MCCR 1969)★★★, *Sings The Legend Of Buford Pusser* (Enterprise 1973)★★, *Sings Carl Smith* (Balser 1984)★★★, *Caution - Eddie Bond Music Is Contagious* (Tab 1976)★★★, *Tennessee Legend Maker* (Hitsound 1986)★★★.

● COMPILATIONS: *Early Days* (Sunjay 1988)★★, *Rockin' Daddy* (Stomper Time 1993)★★★.

● FURTHER READING: *The Eddie Bond Story*, Adam Komorowski and Dact Grint.

BOND, JOHNNY

b. Cyrus Whitfield Bond, 1 June 1915, Enville, Oklahoma, USA, d. 29 June 1978, Burbank, California, USA. Born into a poor farming family, Bond taught himself to play ukelele and guitar and played at local dances In 1934 he moved to Oklahoma and worked on radio, appearing as Cyrus Whitfield, Johnny Whitfield and then Johnny Bond. In 1937, he worked with Jimmy Wakely and Scotty Harrel as the Singing Cowboy Trio and then the Bell Boys. They appeared with Roy Rogers in the film *Saga Of Death Valley*, and then became regulars on Gene Autry's radio series *Melody Ranch* as the Jimmy Wakely Trio. Bond wrote the standard 'Cimarron' in 1938 and toured, performed and made films with Autry after his own trio had broken up. He subsequently did the same for Tex Ritter by forming the Red River Valley Boys to back him. He also appeared in the western *Duel In The Sun*, alongside Gregory Peck. During his 17 years with the US Columbia label, he wrote and recorded classics such as 'I Wonder Where You Are Tonight', 'Your Old Love Letters' and 'I'll Step Aside'. His novelty, 'Hot Rod Lincoln', for Autry's Republic label was subsequently revived by Commander Cody And His Lost Planet Airmen. With Starday Records, he had a hit with the humorous 'Ten Little Bottles' and its sequel, 'The Morning After'. Their success prompted Bond to record numerous other songs about drinking. He wrote scripts for, and performed in, a revamped *Melody Ranch* from 1964-70. In failing health, he wrote *The Tex Ritter Story*, and an unpublished biography of Gene Autry.

● ALBUMS: *That Wild, Wicked But Wonderful West* (Starday 1961)★★★, *Live It Up & Laugh It Up* (Starday 1962)★★, *The Songs That Made Him Famous* (Starday 1963)★★★, *Johnny Bond's Best* (Harmony 1964)★★, *Hot Rod Lincoln* (Starday 1964)★★★, *Bottled In Bond* (Harmony 1965)★★★, *Famous Hot Rodders I Have Known* (Starday 1965)★★★, *Ten Little Bottles* (Starday 1965)★★★, *Bottles Up* (Starday 1966)★★★, *The Branded Stock Of Johnny Bond* (Starday 1966)★★, *The Man Who Comes Around* (Starday 1966)★★★, *Little Ole Wine Drinker Me* (Starday 1967)★★, *Ten Nights In A Barroom* (Starday 1967)★★★, *Drink Up And Go Home* (Starday 1968)★★★, with Merle Travis *Great Songs Of The Delmore Brothers* (Capitol 1969)★★★, *Something Old, New, Patriotic And Blue* (Starday 1970)★★, *Three Sheets In The Wind* (Starday 1971)★★★, *Here Come The Elephants* (Starday 1971)★★★, *Sick, Sober And Sorry* (Starday 1971)★★, *How I Love Them Old Songs* (1974)★★★, with the Willis Brothers *The Singing Cowboy Rides Again* (1977)★★★, *The Return Of The Singing Cowboy* (1977)★★★.

● COMPILATIONS: *The Best Of Johnny Bond* (Starday 1969)★★★★.

● FURTHER READING: *Reflections*, Johnny Bond. *The Tex Ritter Story*, Johnny Bond.

BONNIE LOU

b. Sally Carson, 27 November 1924, Bloomington, Illinois, USA. The exact location of her birth has variously been given as Talawanda, Lawndale and Bloomington. Although there seems little known about her, she was a popular artist on KMBC Kansas City but her break came when she was signed to WLW radio (and WLW-TV) Cincinnati, where she featured on the *Midwestern Hayride* for over 20 years. She recorded for King Records registering Top 10 US country chart hits in 1953 including 'Seven Lonely Days' and 'Tennessee Wig Walk' and in 1955, a Top 20 pop hit with 'Daddy-O', which featured clarinet and accordion and was based around a new teenage phrase. She later recorded some rock 'n' roll numbers, before disappearing from the music scene in the mid-70s.

● ALBUMS: *Bonnie Lou Sings* (King 1958)★★★, *Daddy-O* (King 1958)★★★.

BOONE, CLAUDE

b. 18 February 1916, near Asheville, Yancey County, North Carolina, USA. Although usually remembered for his song-writing abilities, Boone has performed as a singer and is also a talented guitarist. In the mid-30s, he played in Cliff Carlisle's band at WWNC Asheville and recorded with him for Bluebird and Decca Records. On 3 June 1938, working with Leon Scott as the Elk Mountain Boys, he recorded ten Decca tracks in Charlotte, including such tearjerkers as 'Don't Dig Mother's Grave Before She Is Dead' and 'I'm Just A Drunkard's Child'. He played WCHS Charleston with Carlisle for a time but returned to Asheville in 1939, to join Carl Story, with whom he became associated for almost 30 years. He served in the US Navy during World War II but returned to work, mainly at Knoxville, with Story's Rambling Mountaineers on his discharge. He played guitar or bass on countless Starday, Mercury, Columbia, and other recordings with the band, as well as singing harmony and some lead vocals. At a time when all bands were expected to have a comedian, Boone created a character called Homeless Homer to fill the void. He recorded for Mercury as a solo artist in 1949, with musical backing provided by Jethro

Burns, Homer Haynes (Homer And Jethro) and Anita Carter. In the mid-60s, although continuing to make some appearances with Carl Story, Boone became a staff musician at WBIR-TV Knoxville and appeared on the daily *Cas Walker Show* until the programme ended in 1983. Boone then decided he should concentrate on his fishing and basically retired. His numerous songs include 'You Can't Judge A Book By Its Cover', 'Have You Come To Say Goodbye', 'Heaven's My Home', 'Why Don't You Haul Off And Get Religion' and 'Wedding Bells'. However, it appears that he actually bought the latter, which was recorded for King Records in 1947 by Bill Carlisle, from Arthur Q. Smith (James Arthur Pritchett) for $25. In view of the fact that it became a smash hit for Hank Williams and Margaret Whiting and Jimmy Wakely, it proved a very smart purchase and he later stated that he built his retirement home with the royalties. 'Don't Dig Mother's Grave Before She Is Dead' was later reissued by MCA Japan on *Old Timey Music* (VIM 4013).

BOONE, DEBBY

b. Deborah Anne Boone, 22 September 1956, Hackensack, New Jersey, USA. Debby Boone is the third daughter of pop/country singer Pat Boone and wife Shirley, and also the grand-daughter of country star Red Foley. She worked with the Boones family group from 1969, joining her three sisters Cherry, Lindy and Laury in the quartet. In 1977 she went solo, achieving a 10 week stay at number 1 in the US pop charts and sales in excess of four million with her Warner Brothers Records/Curb recording of the title song (a gentle ballad) from the film *You Light Up My Life*. She won a Grammy for Best New Artist and the song also won an Oscar for Best Original Song. The album of the same name eventually went platinum with sales of two million copies. The same song also gave her a debut in the US country charts, where it peaked at number 4. The following year, she had Top 40 country hits with 'God Knows' and 'Baby I'm Yours', and in 1979 a number 11 hit with her version of 'My Heart Has A Mind Of Its Own' - a 1960 pop number 1 for Connie Francis. Her biggest country hit came in 1980, a number 1 success with 'Are You On The Road To Loving Me Again'. She then married Gabriel Ferrer, the son of actor José Ferrer and singer Rosemary Clooney. In the early 80s, after a few more minor hits, she decided to pursue an acting career. She stated at the time that she felt that it was dishonest for her to seek further success as a country singer when it was not really her first choice of music. Instead she returned to the devotional Christian music which had been such a major factor in her upbringing, releasing a series of albums for CCM/Benson Records.
● ALBUMS: *You Light Up My Life* (Warners 1977)★★★★, *Midstream* (Warners 1978)★★★, *Love Has No Reason* (Warners 1980)★★★, *Friends For Life* (Benson 1987)★★★, *Reflections* (Benson 1988)★★.
● FURTHER READING: *Debby Boone*, Patricia Eldred.

BOONE, LARRY

b. 7 June 1956, Cooper City, Florida, USA. Larry Boone sang around local honky tonks and clubs to finance his way through college and gained a degree in education. In 1981, he moved to Nashville where, while working to establish himself as a songwriter, he busked on Music Row. On some

occasions, his educational qualification gained him work as a supply teacher in schools. He joined MTM as a writer and, in 1985, Marie Osmond's version of his song 'Until I Fall In Love Again' charted. Other artists began to record his songs and his own singing also began to attract attention. In 1986, his traditional honky tonk style, similar to Moe Bandy, saw him signed to a singles-only contract with Mercury Records. By 1987, he had registered only five minor hits (the highest being 'Roses In December', a number 44), but the sales had been good enough for Mercury to have a rethink and consequently release an album in 1988. 'Don't Give Candy To A Stranger' (a clever twist, with Candy actually being the little girl involved in the ex-wife's remarriage), a Top 10 hit in 1988, has so far proved his biggest hit. However, his name has been kept to the fore by some further chart entries of his own and by the recordings of other artists including John Conlee ('American Faces'), Ronnie Milsap and Shurfire ('Roll The Dice'), Don Williams ('Old Coyote Town'), George Jones ('King Of The Mountain') and he also co-wrote Kathy Mattea's 1989 number 1, 'Burnin' Old Memories'. He then made his film debut playing a drug addict/drunk country singer, opposite Catherine Bach, in *Music City Blues*. After three successful albums, he left Mercury and moved to the Columbia label in 1991, but his first two albums failed to gain the critical acclaim of the Mercury releases. He has also failed, in the early 90s, to find another major hit following the Columbia move. In 1991, 'To Be With You' proved his best. It remained charted for 20 weeks but in spite of the long stay, it reached no higher than number 34.
● ALBUMS: *Larry Boone* (Mercury 1987)★★★, *Swingin' Doors, Sawdust Floors* (Mercury 1988)★★★, *Down That River Road* (Mercury 1990)★★★, *One Way To Go* (Columbia 1991)★★, *Get In Line* (Columbia 1993)★★.

BOWEN, JIMMY

b. 30 November 1937, Santa Rita, New Mexico, USA. From an early age Bowen was a star athlete who earned a scholarship to Texas State University. While there he formed the Serenaders with Buddy Knox (guitar, vocals) and Don Lanier (lead guitar) in 1955, sharing vocal duties with Knox and playing bass himself. Later they changed their name to the Rhythm Orchids with the addition of young drummer Don Mills, and became a rockabilly troupe. They recorded a session at Norman Petty's studios in Clovis, New Mexico, with Dave 'Dicky Do' Alldred (then of the Norman Petty Trio and later of Dicky Do And The Don'ts) sitting in on drums. On the two tracks recorded, 'Party Doll' and 'I'm Sticking With You', a session player was drafted in to play bass as Bowen was no virtuoso. The songs were originally put out back-to-back on the Blue Moon label then reissued on Triple D, both of which were small local labels. The Roulette label heard the record via Petty, and released the two sides separately. 'Party Doll' was credited to Buddy Knox And The Rhythm Orchids, and 'I'm Sticking With You' to Jimmy Bowen And The Rhythm Orchids; both sold a million and charted high in the USA ('Party Doll' number 1, 'I'm Sticking With You' number 14). Knox went into the US Army for a time and Bowen took a job at Roulette Records as a performer and producer. Other Bowen singles included 'Warm Up To Me Baby', 'Cross Over' and 'By The Light Of The Silvery Moon'. Later he moved to Crest where he also moved into management. This was followed by a spell at Chancellor in 1962 then on to Frank Sinatra's Reprise label in 1963. During this time he helped to oversee the musical careers of Sinatra, Dean Martin, and Frank's daughter Nancy Sinatra, whom he also dated. In 1969 he formed his own Amos label, before moving to Nashville in 1977 where he joined MCA Records and undertook production for a variety of artists. Soon afterwards, he became Warner Brothers' Nashville executive, before becoming the Nashville President of Capitol Records. His greatest accomplishments have come in the past decade where he has been able to guide the careers of Reba McEntire and Garth Brooks, clearly the man has a midas touch.

● ALBUMS: *Jimmy Bowen* (Roulette 1957)★★★.
● COMPILATIONS: with Buddy Knox *The Complete Roulette Recordings* (Sequel 1996)★★★★.

BOWERS, BRYAN

b. Bryan Benson Bowers, 18 August 1940, Yorktown, Virginia, USA. Although also a singer, songwriter, guitarist, dulcimer and mandocello player, it is as an expert on the autoharp, with his unique five-fingered picking rather than the more common strumming style, for which Bowers is most respected. He quit college in the late 60s and learned to play guitar before eventually turning to his favourite instrument. Relocating to Seattle in 1971, he sang and played on the streets or in bars before moving to Washington DC, where he eventually gained a residency at a local club. A chance meeting with the Dillards led to his appearance with that group, at a major bluegrass festival, which did much to promote his solo career. He was offered a contract by Flying Fish in 1977 and continued to record for that label into the 90s. The readers of *Frets* magazine voted him the winner of the publication's Stringed Instrument, Open Category for five successive years, which led to him becoming a member of the magazine's *First Gallery Of The Greats*. He remains a popular artist at various festivals and other venues.

● ALBUMS: *The View From Home* (Flying Fish 1977)★★★★, with Sam Bush And Seldom Scene *Home, Home On The Road* (Flying Fish 1981)★★★, *By Heart* (Flying Fish 1985)★★★, *For You* (Flying Fish 1991)★★★.

BOWES, MARGIE

b. 18 March 1941, Roxboro, North Carolina, USA. Bowes learned guitar and was singing on the *Virginia Barn Dance* on WDVA, Danville and on television in Roanoke, Virginia, in her early teens. In 1958, she won a talent competition organized by the Pet Milk Company, which led to her recording for Hickory and soon afterwards appearing on the *Grand Ole Opry*. In 1959, 'Poor Old Heartsick Me' became her first country chart hit, peaking at number 10 and charting for 16 weeks. She followed it with a number 15 with her version of Phil Everly's 'My Love And Little Me'. She moved to Mercury Records in 1961 but only managed a single hit with the strangely titled 'Little Miss Belong To No One' and by 1964, she had joined Decca Records. Two more chart entries followed with 'Our Things' (number 33) and 'Understand Your Gal' (number 26), the 'answer' song to Johnny Cash's 'Understand Your Man'. She achieved no further chart entries and in 1969, her final Decca single, 'Go Woman Go', seemed prophetically correct, in spite of the b-side being 'I Have What It Takes'. During her career, she appeared on ABC's networked *Jubilee, USA* and in the film *Golden Guitar*.

She was for a time married to Doyle Wilburn of the Wilburn Brothers.

● ALBUMS: *15 Country Greats* (Hickory 1960)★★★, *Country Boys, Country Girls* (Mercury 1962)★★, *Margie Bowes Sings* (Decca 1967)★★, *Today's Country Sound* (Decca 1969)★★.

BOWMAN, DON

b. 26 August 1937, Lubbock, Texas, USA. Bowman fulfilled a childhood ambition by becoming a disc jockey, working initially at Lubbock and Littlefield, at times with Waylon Jennings. The two men became friends and later wrote many songs together including 'Just To Satisfy You' and 'Anita You're Dreaming', which became hits for Jennings. Bowman's guitar playing (supposedly limited to three chords) led him to boast that he was the world's worst, which added to the comedy image he conveyed in establishing himself in the USA. He browbeat Chet Atkins into signing him to RCA in 1963 and he soon had US country chart success with 'Chit [sic] Atkins, Make Me A Star'. Further successes include 'Giddyup Do-Nut', 'Folsom Prison Blues #2', 'For Loving You' (a duet with Skeeter Davis) and finally in 1969 his version of a song co-written with Jennings called 'Poor Ole Ugly Gladys Jones', which featured guest appearances by Jennings, Willie Nelson and Bobby Bare. He was voted CMA Comedian of the Year in 1967 and appeared in the films *Hillbillies In A Haunted House* and *Hillbillies In Las Vegas*. His 1970 album *Whispering Country* was a tribute to Bill Anderson.

● ALBUMS: *Our Man In Trouble* (RCA Victor 1964)★★★, *Fresh From The Funny Farm* (RCA Victor 1965)★★, *Funny Way To Make An Album* (RCA Victor 1966)★★, *From Mexico With Laughs* (RCA Victor 1967)★★, *Recorded Almost Live* (RCA Victor 1967), with Skeeter Davis *Funny Folk Flops* (RCA Victor 1968)★★, *Still Fighting Mental Health* (Lone Star 1969)★★★★, *Support Your Local Prison* (1969)★★★, *Whispering Country* (1970)★★★, *The All New Don Bowman* (1972)★★★, *Willon And Waylee* (1979)★★★.
● FILMS: *Hillbillies In A Haunted House* (1967), *Hillbillies In Las Vegas* (1968).

BOXCAR WILLIE

b. Lecil Travis Martin, 1 September 1931, Sterratt, Dallas, Texas, USA. Boxcar Willie sings 'Daddy Was A Railroad Man' with pride and conviction, as his father was a farmer and section hand on the railway, who sympathized with the hobos. Boxcar Willie's own love of trains is reflected in 'I Love The Sound Of A Whistle'. As a youngster, he ran away to ride the rails but he was always brought back to school. He developed an early love of country music and has recorded many songs associated with Jimmie Rodgers, Hank Williams and Lefty Frizzell, as well as writing several tributes - 'Hank, You Still Make Me Cry', 'Hank And The Hobo' and 'Lefty Left Us Lonely'. Boxcar's first performances were as a straight country singer. He wrote a song called 'Boxcar Willie' and thereafter adopted that name. Although Marty Martin's first album was released in the late 50s, it was not until 1975 that he decided to create Boxcar Willie. The cover of the first Boxcar Willie album shows him in battered hat, striped bib overalls, crumpled jacket and worn-out shoes. It included 'The Lord Made A Hobo Out Of Me'. Boxcar's noted 'Train Medley' is an express featuring seven songs and seven train-whistles in four minutes. His jokey name and love of train whistles led to wide public recognition, although he has been mocked by country star David Allan Coe. Boxcar Willie's duets have been diverse: he has recorded with Roy Acuff ('Fireball Mail', 'Streamline Cannonball'), Willie Nelson ('Song Of Songs', 'Boxcar's My Home') and Hank Williams Jnr. ('Ramblin' In My Shoes'). Boxcar Willie's single of 'Good Hearted Woman' was recorded partly in English, partly in German, with European country star Gunter Gabriel. In 1981, at the age of 50, he won the Music City News award for Most Promising Male Vocalist. In 1982, he finally found success on the US country charts via a revival of Johnny Cash's 'Bad News', this time complete with train whistle, and he was made a member of the *Grand Ole Opry*. Among his subsequent entries were 'Country Music Nightmare', 'Not On The Bottom' and a duet of 'We Made Memories' with Penny DeHaven. In 1985 he recorded some tracks with Willie Nelson. He acted as a hobo in a jail scene in the film about Patsy Cline, *Sweet Dreams*. Boxcar Willie is the World Ambassador for the Hobo Foundation and he owns a travelling railway museum. While never a serious contender for country stardom in the USA, his persona and his belief in old-fashioned values have allowed him to retain vast popularity in Europe. He has apparently composed several hundred original songs, but is best known for versions of country classics such as 'Wabash Cannonball', 'Wreck Of The Old 97' and 'Kaw-Liga'. He was reported to be suffering from leukaemia in 1996.

● ALBUMS: *Marty Martin Sings Country Music And Stuff Like That* (AHMC 1958/1976)★★★, *Boxcar Willie* (MCA 1976)★★★★, *Daddy Was A Railroad Man* (1978)★★★★, *Boxcar Willie Sings Hank Williams And Jimmie Rodgers* (1976)★★★★, *Take Me Home* (Mainstreet 1980)★★★, *King Of The Road* (Mainstreet 1981)★★★, *Good Ol' Country Songs* (Mainstreet 1982)★★★, *Last Train To Heaven* (Mainstreet 1982)★★★, *Not The Man I Used To Be* (Mainstreet 1983)★★★, *Live In Concert* (Hallmark 1984)★★, *Falling In Love* (1988)★★★, *Jesus Makes House Calls* (1988)★★, *Best Loved Favourites* (Vanguard 1989)★★★, *Best Loved Favourites, Vol. 2* (Vanguard 1990)★★★, *The Spirit Of America* (1991)★★★, *Truck Driving Favourites* (1991)★★★, *Rockabilly* (K-Tel 1993)★★★.

● COMPILATIONS: *20 Great Hits* (Big R 1981)★★★, *Best Of Boxcar, Volume 1* (Mainstreet 1982)★★★★, *The Boxcar Willie Collection* (Castle 1987)★★★★, *Best Of Boxcar Willie* (Hallmark 1988)★★★.

● VIDEOS: *Boxcar Willie Sings Country* (BBC Video 1988).

● FILMS: *Sweet Dreams* (1985).

BOY HOWDY

Boy Howdy are a 90s country band from California, USA, very much in the mould of Little Texas. Most of their songs are written by Jeff Steele (b. 27 August 1961, Burbank, California, USA; vocals, bass) and the band's producer Chris Farren, although their albums also include cover versions such as the Kinks' 'You Really Got Me' and Stephen Stills' 'Love The One You're With'. Their most successful record, the ballad 'She'd Give Anything', reached number 4 on the US country charts. They made an appearance in George Strait's film *Pure Country*. In 1992 their drummer Hugh Wright (b. 18 December 1951, Keokuk, Iowa, USA) was hit by a car while trying to help the victim of another accident and he spent five months in a coma. Wright was professionally trained and has a degree in music gained from the University Of Iowa School Of Music. The three remaining members - Steele and brothers Cary (b. 15 March 1956, Stockton, California, USA; guitar, mandolin, harmony vocals) and Larry Parks (b. 3 June 1959, Stockton, California, USA; guitar, fiddle, harmony vocals) - decided to keep the band going so that Wright would have something to which he could return. The brothers' father is Ray Parks, a noted bluegrass fiddler who formed the duo Vern And Ray, which included Herb Pederson (who also sang on Boy Howdy's debut single). Says Larry Parks: 'Our name's like a celebration of country music. In the old western movies, you'd see somebody riding off on a horse and they'd say, "Boy howdy, did you see that guy shoot that gun?"'

● ALBUMS: *Welcome To Howdywood* (Curb 1992)★★★, *She'd Give Anything* mini-album (Curb 1994)★★★, *Born That Way* (Curb 1995)★★★.

BOYD, BILL AND JIM

Bill Boyd (b. 29 September 1910, Fannin County, Texas, USA, d. 7 December 1977, Dallas, Texas, USA; vocals, guitar) and brother Jim (b. 28 September 1914, both on a ranch in Fannin County, Texas, USA; bass) first appeared on radio together in Greenville in 1926, before they moved to Dallas in 1929 and formed a band called Alexander's Daybreakers. In February 1932, Bill played guitar for Jimmie Rodgers' Dallas recordings of 'Roll Along Kentucky Moon' and 'Hobo's Meditation'. Shortly after this, with Jim, Art Davis and Walter Kirkes, he formed the Cowboy Ramblers. Primarily a recording band, with members also playing in other groups at times, they first recorded for Bluebird in 1934, drawing their music from country, jazz and pop. Their most successful recording was a version of an old German instrumental march 'Under The Double Eagle', in which Boyd's guitar lead was complemented by Davis's blue-sounding fiddle. The Cowboys increased later to a 10-piece western swing band, appeared in films, recorded extensively for Bluebird and were immensely popular in the Dallas area. Boyd, who should not be confused with cowboy actor William Boyd, hosted his own show on WRR Dallas for many years. He retired from the music business soon after making his last recordings in February 1950 and died in 1977. Jim appeared mainly with his brother as a member of the Cowboy Ramblers, although he was also a member of the Light Crust Doughboys (1938-39) and Men Of The West (1949-51). After his brother's death he continued to work in the Dallas area.

● ALBUMS: with Jim Boyd *Bill Boyd's Cowboy Ramblers* (RCA Bluebird)★★★★, with Jim Boyd *Bill Boyd With His Cowboy Ramblers 1943-47* (RCA Bluebird)★★★.

BOYS FROM INDIANA

An excellent bluegrass band which, when formed in 1973, comprised Aubrey Holt (b. Aubrey Lee Holt, 15 August 1938, Milan, Indiana, USA; guitar, bass, vocals), Jerry Holt (b. Jerry Ray Holt, 15 August 1941, Cincinnati, Ohio, USA; bass, vocals), Harley Gabbard (b. Harley Royce Gabbard, 31 December 1935, West Harrison, Indiana, USA; dobro, banjo, fiddle, guitar, vocals), Paul Mullins (b. 24 September 1936, Frenchburg, Kentucky, USA; fiddle, guitar, mandolin, bass, disc jockey) and Noel Crase (banjo). As teenagers, Aubrey Holt and Gabbard (his uncle) had previously formed a band, which recorded for Starday before breaking up. This time, however, the band quickly became popular on the bluegrass circuit and soon began recording, often using excellent material written by Holt. Their first album was a gospel one recorded for Jewel, before they joined King Bluegrass. They quickly had considerable success with 'Atlanta Is Burning', a Holt song about the Civil War. Holt's writing became so prolific that, in the late 70s, he contributed half of the numbers on three further albums. In the late 70s, personnel changes saw Crase and Mullins leave (he later fronted Traditional Grass), being replaced by Rodney Case (banjo) and Billy Thomas (fiddle). The band became even more a family unit when Tommy Holt (b. 17 July 1949, Hamilton, Ohio, USA; mandolin, bass, guitar, vocals) joined his brothers and uncle on completion of military service. They continued to be a top bluegrass unit throughout the 80s and into the 90s. Their stage shows are particularly popular for their inclusion of specific topics such as their tributes to the pioneers of bluegrass and to the American soldier. Other classic Holt songs included 'Play Hank's Song Once Again' and 'The Grand Ole Opry Show'. In the 80s, they released a series of albums on their own Old Heritage label but later recorded for Atteiram and Rebel. In 1989, they played at the White House at the request of President Bush and over the years they have made popular appearances on the *Grand Ole Opry*. Other musicians who have played with the band include Jeff Murray (banjo), Glen Duncan and Steve Williams (fiddle) and Frank Godbey (mandolin). Aubrey Holt continues to write the majority of their numbers and can still write classics, such as 'Big Silver Moon Over Dallas' and 'Will Heaven Be Like Kentucky', which appear on *Touchin' Home*.

● ALBUMS: *We Missed You In Church Last Sunday* (Jewel 1973)★★, *Atlanta Is Burning* (King Bluegrass 1974)★★★, *Bluegrass Music Is Out Of Sight* (King Bluegrass 1975)★★★, *One More Bluegrass Show* (King Bluegrass 1976)★★★, *Memories And Dreams* (King Bluegrass 1977)★★★, *An American Heritage - A Tribute To The Pioneers Of Bluegrass Music* (Old Heritage 1980)★★★, *Show Me My Home* (Old Heritage 1981)★★★, *Did You Forget God Today* (Old Heritage 1982)★★★, *Showtime* (Old Heritage 1984)★★★, *Life On The Road* (Atteiram 1985)★★, *Guide This Silver Eagle* (Old Heritage 1988)★★★, with Chubby Wise *Live At Gilley's* (Old Heritage 1988)★★, *Touchin' Home* (Rebel 1992)★★★★.

● COMPILATIONS: *Best Of The Boys From Indiana* (Rebel 1981)★★★★.

BR5-49

Regarded by many as the most exciting country rock-inspired band in Nashville since Jason And The Scorchers, BR5-49 arrived in 1996 with a provocative manifesto. As guitarist and singer Chuck Mead (b. 22 December 1960, Nevada, Montana, USA) told the press: 'I don't want it to be seen as some kind of planned competition to stamp out new country. But that'd be nice, because it sucks.' Mead had formerly played as a child in the Family Tree, a gospel hillbilly group made up of relatives, then Kansas roots rock group the Homestead Grays (one EP, *Big Hits*, and a CD, *El Supremo*, in 1991). The group additionally comprises Gary Bennett (b. 9 October 1964, Las Vegas, Nevada, USA; acoustic guitar, joint lead vocals), Shaw Wilson (drums), Smilin' Jay McDowell (b. 11 June 1969, Bedford, Indiana, USA; slap bass) and Donnie Herron (dobro, mandolin, fiddle). Since its formation in

1994 the group has built a widespread reputation for its uninhibited, ferocious, good-time honky tonk. As well as cover versions of standards by Hank Williams, Bob Wills, Carl Perkins and Faron Young, group originals such as '18 Wheels And A Crowbar', 'Do Something Even If It's Wrong' and 'Me And Opie Down By The Duck Pond', when combined with the group's exhaustive four-hour live sets, place them firmly in the 50s tradition of hillbilly music. Taking their name from the phone number used for Junior Samples' used car lot in the comedy television show *Hee Haw*, the group made their debut with a typically enthralling live set for Arista Records in 1996. This was quickly followed later in the year by the group's full-length debut. Among the treats on display here was 'Little Ramona (Gone Hillbilly Nuts)', Bennett's evocative account, with reference to the Ramones, of former hardcore punk friends now turned on to 50s hillbilly records. The record also included cover versions of two staples of that period, 'I Ain't Never' and 'Crazy Arms'.

● ALBUMS: *Live At Robert's* mini-album (Arista 1996)★★★, *The Number To Call Is ... BR5-49* (Arista 1996)★★★★.

BRADDOCK, BOBBY

b. Robert Valentine Braddock, 5 August 1940, Auburndale, Florida, USA. Braddock has become one of country music's best-known songwriters, but started his career playing piano in local Florida bars before moving to Nashville, where, between 1964 and 1966, he played keyboards in Marty Robbins' band. After Robbins' recording of 'While You're Dancing' gave him his first songwriting chart entry, he replaced Roger Miller as a staff writer with Tree Publishing and also played as a session musician. In 1967, recording for MGM Records, he gained a minor hit with 'I Know How To Do It'. The same year, his songs 'Ruthless' and 'You Can't Have Your Kate And Edith Too', became Top 10 hits for the Statler Brothers. He co-wrote, with Curly Putman, Tammy Wynette's 1968 number 1, 'D-I-V-O-R-C-E', which confirmed his reputation as a top songwriter. From that time, through to the 80s, songs written by Braddock either alone or in co-operation with other writers such as Putman, Sonny Throckmorton and Rafe Van Hoy, have rarely been out of the charts, and the list of Top 20 hits is considerable. The hits include 'Something To Brag About', 'Did You Ever' (both Charlie Louvin and Melba Montgomery 1970, 1971), 'Nothing Ever Hurts Me' and 'Her Name Is...' (both George Jones 1973, 1976), 'I Believe The South Is Going To Rise Again' (Tanya Tucker 1975), 'Golden Ring' (co-written with Rafe Van Hoy; George Jones and Tammy Wynette 1976), 'Peanuts And Diamonds' (Bill Anderson 1976), 'Thinking Of A Rendezvous' (Johnny Duncan 1976), 'Come On In' (Jerry Lee Lewis 1978), 'Womanhood' and 'They Call It Making Love' (both Tammy Wynette 1978, 1979), 'Hard Times' (Lacy J. Dalton 1980), and many others. In 1971, 'Did You Ever' was a UK number 2 pop hit for Nancy Sinatra And Lee Hazlewood. There is little doubt that one of the greatest country songs of all times is 'He Stopped Loving Her Today', which he co-wrote with Putman. George Jones's number 1 recording of the song received a Grammy award as Best Country Male Vocal of the year in 1980 and the song received the CMA award as Country Song Of The Year in both 1980 and 1981. His own recordings failed to compare but he achieved minor hits with 'The Girls In Country

Music' (1969), 'Between The Lines' (1979) and 'Nag, Nag, Nag' (1980). The latter demonstrated his sense of humour, which often surfaced in his songs, including such epics as 'I Lobster But Never Flounder', and a nightmare for disc jockeys called 'Dolly Parton's Hits'. He also released an RCA mini-album in 1983, called *Hardpore Cornography*. Braddock was elected to the Nashville Songwriters' Hall Of Fame in 1981, and although the hits are fewer now, and his honky-tonk and crying in the beer-type songs are losing out to new country, he remains active.

● ALBUMS: *Between The Lines* (Elektra 1979)★★★, *Love Bomb* (Elektra 1980)★★★.

BRADLEY, OWEN

b. 21 October 1915, Westmoreland, Tennessee, USA, d. 7 January 1998. Bradley learned to play piano, guitar, harmonica and vibes, and as a young man worked as a musician and arranger. He played in the famous dance band of Ted Weems, but between 1940 and 1958 he was the musical director and leader of the studio orchestra at WSM radio in Nashville. In 1947, he was also hired by Paul Cohen to work with him on record production for Decca in Nashville. Bradley's own recording career started on the Bullet label but in 1949, a Decca recording with his quintet of the Delmore Brothers' 'Blues Stay Away From Me', became a Top 20 US country and pop hit - albeit his only chart entry. He enjoyed record production and in 1952, he and his brother Harold (b. 2 January 1926, Nashville, Tennessee, USA; he worked with Ernest Tubb and Eddy Arnold, and later became a leading Nashville session musician) built their own recording studio (one of the first in Nashville), where initially they produced short documentary films. However, they also began to record singers such as Ernest Tubb and Kitty Wells. By 1956, they had moved to larger premises and had their famed Quonset hut studio on 16th Avenue South, Nashville. It was only a surplus army building but it contained superb recording equipment and facilities. It was here that Buddy Holly and Gene Vincent recorded some of their earliest sessions, although in the latter's case production was by Ken Nelson. Bradley also recorded several of the new country artists of the time, including Johnny Cash and Marty Robbins. The immediate area surrounding the old Quonset hut eventually became known as Music Row. It was here that, over the years, the recording industry of Nashville developed. When, in 1962, Columbia persuaded Bradley to sell the studios, they carefully built their new complex over and around the hut, so as not to destroy the excellent acoustics of the building. His contract with Columbia prohibited him from opening another studio in the immediate area of Nashville for five years, but in 1965, he found an old barn about 20 miles away and restored it to the standards of the hut. It became known as Bradley's Barn and proved an extremely popular venue for Nashville musicians, as well as rock acts such as the Beau Brummels, who issued an LP entitled *Bradley's Barn*. Bradley and Chet Atkins were two of the leading record producers, who were mainly responsible for developing what came to be known as the Nashville Sound. Bradley (like Atkins) lessened the use of steel guitars and fiddles and instead gave his recordings a more pop-orientated treatment with the use of strings and backing vocals. He did, in fact, record both pop and country artists. He also appeared as a musician, not only on some of his Decca recording sessions but he actually played with Chet Atkins on Elvis Presley's first RCA sessions. Between 1958 and 1968, he was the country A&R director for Decca and was then promoted to be the label's vice-president in Nashville. During his years involved with record production, he worked with many major stars including Patsy Cline, Red Foley, Brenda Lee and Loretta Lynn. He proved popular with both the artists and with the management, and as a reward for his services to the industry, he was elected to the Country Music Hall Of Fame in 1974. After retiring from MCA, he continued to work as a record producer - notably on k.d. lang's *Shadowland*, which reunited him with Brenda Lee and Loretta Lynn. He died in January 1998.

● ALBUMS: *Christmas Time* (Coral 1955)★★, *Strauss Waltzes* (Coral 1955)★★, *Lazy River* (1956)★★★, *Singin' In The Rain* (Coral 1956)★★★, *Cherished Hymns* (Coral 1956)★★, *Bandstand Hop* (Decca 1958)★★★, *Big Guitar* (Decca 1959)★★★, *Paradise Island* (Decca 1960)★★★. By Harold Bradley *Bossa Nova Goes To Nashville* (Columbia 1963)★★, *Misty Guitar* (Columbia 1963)★★★, *Guitar For Lovers Only* (Columbia 1965)★★.

BRADY, PAT

b. Robert Ellsworth O'Brady, 31 December 1914, Toledo, Ohio, USA, d. 27 February 1972, Colorado Springs, Colorado, USA. An important member of the Sons Of The Pioneers and a successful film actor. His parents, who were vaudeville performers, separated when Robert was 12 years old and he moved to California with his father. He was inspired by western films, and from an early age had a natural flair for comedy, no doubt inherited from his father, who had regularly played the clown's role in vaudeville. Brady was also interested in pop and jazz music and by 1935, having learned to play stand-up bass, he was playing in a local band. In October 1937, although not at the time appreciating their music, he was invited to play bass for the Sons Of the Pioneers. Since the group already had one Bob (Bob Nolan), he became Pat. A naturally funny man, he also began to sing a comedy song or two, and generally imparted some humour into the Pioneers' act. He first appeared in films with Charles Starrett in 1937. In 1943, he was drafted and served with the US Army in Europe during World War II, but returned to the Pioneers early in 1946 and remained a regular group member until 1949, when his friend Roy Rogers featured him first in B-movie westerns and then later in his popular long-running television series. He returned to the Pioneers, to replace Shug Fisher, in 1959, and played with them until 1967. He then retired and made his home in Colorado Springs.

BRADY, PHIL, AND THE RANCHERS

b. 4 March 1939, Liverpool, England. Like many adolescents raised in the south of Liverpool, Brady learned about country music from the seamen returning from the USA. Encouraged by Hank Walters' Black Cat club, he formed his own band, the Ranchers, in 1962, including Frank Peters on steel guitar, and they built a reputation in the north-west despite the fierce competition from beat music. They were featured on Decca's 1965 album, *Liverpool Goes Country*, and Brady recorded the first single ('An American Sailor At The Cavern') for the Cavern Club's own label. Because the

Cavern went into liquidation, most copies went to the official receiver, and it is the UK's most collectable British country single. Phil Brady And The Ranchers became nationally popular through the BBC programme *Country Meets Folk*. He went to Nashville in 1968, played *Grand Ole Opry*, and recorded *Songs Of Nashville* on his return. They toured the UK with Buck Owens and Slim Whitman, and their instrumental, *A Little Bit Country*, was recorded at Joe Brown's studio with Brown on fiddle. The tear-jerking 'Little Rosa' is his most requested number, and other popular singles include 'The Exeter Bypass' and 'Let The Whole World Sing It With Me'. Brady now works solo.

● ALBUMS: *Brady Country* (1968)★★, *Songs Of Nashville* (1969)★★★, *No. 1 In The Country* (1970)★★★, with Jed Ford *On The Country Stage, Live From Gunton Hall* (1972)★★, as the Ranchers *A Little Bit Country* (1973)★★★★ reissued in 1974 as *'Me And Bobbie McGee' And Other Favourites, Liverpool Sounds* (1977)★★★★.

● COMPILATIONS: *Some Old Favourites* (80s)★★★.

BRANDT, PAUL

b. Paul Rennee Belobersycky, 21 July 1972, Calgary, Alberta, Canada. Before entering the music world, Paul Brandt, whose parents are both involved in the medical profession, worked as a paediatric nurse. During those years he continued to sing and play the guitar, however, having first sung in church. He began entering talent competitions while in high school but also concentrated on his career in medicine. The change came when he won the $1,000 first prize at the 1992 Calgary Stampede. The following year, he won the category for best original Canadian country song for 'Calm Before The Storm', in a contest sponsored by the Canadian performing rights society, SOCAN. He was subsequently signed to Warner Brothers Records in 1995 by Paige Levy. Brandt made his debut for the label with the single 'My Heart Has A History', which made a strong impression on *Billboard*'s Hot Country Singles & Tracks chart, and paved the way for the release of his debut album. On both, he accredited his maturity as a songwriter to some of the experiences he had endured in his former career: 'I think a lot of the emotions that I had to deal with working in a hospital come through in my songwriting and it seems to connect with people. When I look down at an audience and see them smile or wipe away a tear and know for three minutes I get to hold their heart right in my hand, it's an incredible feeling.' *Calm Before The Storm* was co-produced by Josh Leo, and he co-wrote several of the songs. The follow-up album has weaker material and fails to create a distinctive identity for the singer.

● ALBUMS: *Calm Before The Storm* (Reprise 1996)★★★, *Outside The Frame* (Reprise 1997)★★.

BRANNEN, JOHN

The 90s country singer John Brannen was raised by his mother in Charleston, South Carolina, USA. He became interested in travelling and playing music and, combining the two, he sailed the Caribbean for a year, pulling into ports and playing in local clubs. Back in Charleston, he joined Wheat Ridge and became converted to country music through Waylon Jennings' records. He signed recording contracts with Capitol Records and then Apache, but when they did not work out, he spent a year as a labourer. The song-writer and producer David Malloy signed Brannen to Mercury Records and produced his first album. He has a wide-ranging voice, capable of Roy Orbison's heights, but he has yet to achieve a US country hit.

● ALBUMS: *John Brannen* (Mercury 1995)★★★.

BRASFIELD, ROD

b. Rodney Leon Brasfield, 2 August 1910, Smithville, near Tupelo, Mississippi, USA, d. 12 September 1958, Nashville, Tennessee, USA. In 1926, Brasfield left home and joined his brother Lawrence 'Boob' Brasfield, who was working with a touring tent show. Here he played bit parts and ran errands for the other members. After a while the brothers left the show and became a comedy act with Bisbee's Comedians, a more prestigious touring show. Rod acted as the straight man for his brother until one day when Lawrence was late, Rod found himself playing the main comedy act. He proved so successful that he never did anything but comedy again. He worked with the show until World War II, when he was called up for service in the US Army Air Corps. In 1943, owing to a back injury suffered when he was a child, he was given a medical discharge and immediately rejoined Bisbee. He was auditioned for the *Grand Ole Opry* and made his debut there in July 1944. In 1948, he replaced comedian Whitey Ford (Duke Of Paducah) on the NBC-networked *Prince Albert Show*. Here his cross-patter and rapport with Minnie Pearl saw them both become major stars of the *Opry*. The two comedians toured with the *Opry* roadshows and visited Europe with Hank Williams, Marty Robbins and Little Jimmy Dickens. In 1955, Brasfield was a television regular appearing on the *Ozark Jubilee* as well as the sponsored *Opry* shows and worked with Red Foley, who acted as straight man for the two comedians. In 1956, he was hired by director Elia Kazan to play a serious role in his film *A Face In The Crowd*. He played opposite Andy Griffiths and his performance drew praise from the critics. It is generally accepted that on stage Brasfield never had a serious moment in his life, but behind the scenes he suffered from a drink problem. Few serious interviews were obtained as he greatly disliked being questioned, and on occasions when he had to talk to the media, the answers were invariably of a humorous nature. Brasfield continued to work with Minnie Pearl and to play the *Opry* right up to his death. He suffered a heart attack in September 1958, in his caravan home in Nashville, and was dead on arrival at hospital. Rod Brasfield was inducted in 1987 into the Country Music Hall Of Fame in Nashville.

BRENNAN, WALTER

b. 25 July 1894, Lynn, Massachusetts, USA, d. 21 September 1974. A character actor who specialized in playing the classic ol' timer and 'toothless old men', especially in westerns, Brennan appeared in dozens of films from 1924 onwards. Notable among these were *The Adventures Of Tom Sawyer*, *To Have And Have Not*, and *Rio Bravo*. He went on to play Grandpa in *The Real McCoys* television series, which was a forerunner of *The Beverly Hillbillies*. He hit the pop charts with three spoken word singles - 'Dutchman's Gold' (1960), 'Old Rivers' and 'Mama Sang Me A Song' (1962). He was still acting during his 70s in *The Love Bug Rides Again*, but died in 1974.

● ALBUMS: *Dutchman's Gold* (Dot 1960)★★★, *World Of*

Miracles (Everste 1960)★★★, *The President* (Everest 1960)★★★, *By The Fireside* (RPC 1962), *Old Rivers* (Liberty 1962)★★★, *Twas The Night Before Christmas Back Home* (Liberty 1962)★★, *Mama Sang A Song* (Liberty 1963)★★★★, *Talkin' From The Heart* (Liberty 1964)★★★, *Gunfight At The OK Corral* (Liberty 1964)★★★.

BRESH, THOM

b. 1948, Hollywood, California, USA. Bresh's father was a photographer who worked at the Corriganville movie ranch, so Thom grew up among singing cowboys and western swing musicians. As the movie ranch was open to the public at weekends, Bresh was performing country songs on stage from the age of three. He made his movie debut when only seven years old and became 'Hollywood's youngest stuntman'. He also appeared in television's *Gunsmoke* and *Cheyenne*. In 1963 Bresh made the US Hot 100 with 'Pink Dominoes' as part of the Crescents. Then he joined Hank Penny's western swing band, playing in Las Vegas and Nevada. A solo single, 'D.B. Cooper, Where Are You?', about the first skyjacker, did well until the radio stations decided the song was glorifying a criminal. In 1976, Bresh had his first US country hits with 'Home Made Love' and 'Sad Country Love Song'.
● ALBUMS: *Homemade Love* (Farr 1976)★★, *Kicked Back* (ABC 1977)★★★, *Portrait* (ABC 1978)★★★.

BRITT, ELTON

b. James Britt Baker, 17 June 1913 (but over the years various other dates have been given), near Marshall, Arkansas, USA, d. 23 June 1972. Britt's father was a champion fiddle player and his mother a noted singer. He learned to sing and play guitar and was performing in public by the age of 12. After hearing recordings by Riley Puckett and Jimmie Rodgers, he became interested in yodelling and soon became proficient at the art. In 1929, he joined the Beverly Hillbillies, and appeared with them on KMPC Hollywood. When the group split in 1933, Britt moved with Zeke Manners to New York, where (under various aliases) the pair recorded for ARC. Britt entered and won a yodelling competition organized by cowboy star Tom Mix, in spite of the challenge of leading exponents from Switzerland and Bavaria. The win saw Britt become known as the unofficial world yodelling champion. He made his first solo recordings for RCA Victor in 1937, but it was in 1942 that he enjoyed major success with his million-selling recording of 'There's A Star Spangled Banner Waving Somewhere'. In 1944, his recording of this patriotic war song saw Britt become the first country artist to be awarded an official Gold Disc. In 1946, he registered six Top 10 country hits including his smash hit 'Someday You'll Want Me To Want You' (a number 2 that charted for 18 weeks) and 'Detour', and achieved US Top 20 pop chart success with 'Wave To Me My Lady'. Further success came with his popular 1948 recording of 'Chime Bells'. A yodelling classic, though generally attributed now to Britt and Bob Miller, it originated from the English vaudeville song 'Happy And Free Yodel', written and recorded years earlier by Harry Torrani. In 1949, Britt had a hit with George Morgan's song 'Candy Kisses' and also made several successful recordings with RCA's female yodelling star Rosalie Allen, including 'Beyond The Sunset' and 'Quicksilver'. In 1951, Britt toured Korea entertaining American troops and

contracted a form of Asian fever, which for a time prevented him making appearances and had a lasting effect on his career. During the late 50s and 60s, he made some television appearances and guested on the *Grand Ole Opry*. He made few recordings but did have some success with his yodelling version of 'The Skater's Waltz'. He was reunited with Zeke Manners when, in 1959, he recorded an album with Manners' band. Britt spent 22 years with RCA, later recording for Decca, ABC-Paramount and Ampar and apart from his own recordings, appeared as a guitarist on other artists' recordings. He also formed his own El-Tone Music publishing company. During his career he held the unique distinction for a country artist of having long-running radio series on three major networks, namely NBC, CBS and Mutual. He also appeared in several B-movie western films including *Laramie*, *The Last Doggie* and *The Prodigal Son*.
● ALBUMS: *Elton Britt Yodel Songs* 10-inch album (RCA Victor 1954)★★★★, *Yodel Songs* (RCA Victor 1956)★★★ *Rosalie Allen & Elton Britt* (Waldorf 1957)★★★★, *The Wandering Cowboy* (ABC-Paramount 1959)★★★, *Beyond The Sunset* (ABC-Paramount 1960)★★★, *I Heard A Forest Praying* (ABC-Paramount 1960), *The Singing Hills* (ABC-Paramount 1965)★★★, *Something For Everyone* (ABC-Parmount 1966)★★, *Starring Elton Britt & Rosalie Allen* (Grand Award 1966)★★★★, *When Evening Shadows Fall* (RCA Victor 1968)★★★, *The Jimmie Rodgers Blues* (Camden 1969)★★★, *I Left My Heart In San Francisco* (1979)★★.
● COMPILATIONS: *The Best Of Elton Britt* (RCA Victor 1963)★★★, *Sixteen Great Country Performances* (ABC-Paramount 1971)★★★.

BRITTON, MARSHA

b. Oak Cliffs, Texas, USA. The 90s country singer Marsha Britton graduated from the University of North Texas with a degree in music. She was a featured vocalist at Billy Bob's honky tonk in Fort Worth and then moved to Nashville. Like Benny Berry, she records for Mike Headrick, a producer and songwriter based in South Pittsburgh, Tennessee. Her records include duets with Benny Berry.
● ALBUMS: *Good Times And Hard Times* (Hawk 1992)★★★, *Bad News Boy* (Hawk 1994)★★★, *Hayride* (Hawk 1995)★★★.

BROOKS AND DUNN

Kix Brooks (b. Leon Eric Brooks, 12 May 1955, Shreveport, Louisiana, USA) and Ronnie Gene Dunn (b. 1 June 1953, Coleman, Texas, USA). As an adolescent, Brooks lived close to Johnny Horton and sang with Horton's daughter. He moved to Nashville and found success as a songwriter, co-writing a US country number 1 by John Conlee ('I'm Only In It For The Love') in 1983, and then the Nitty Gritty Dirt Band's 'Modern Day Romance' and Highway 101's 'Who's Lonely Now'. Having limited success with 'There's A Telephone Ringing', he wanted to succeed as a solo performer but his Capitol Records debut album, *Kix Brooks*, in 1989, made little impression, all songs being written by Brooks with 11 other writers. Although Ronnie Dunn planned to be a Baptist minister, he could not reconcile it with his love of honky tonks, and eventually he was leading the house band at Duke's Country, a successful club in Tulsa. He had minor US country chart entries with 'It's Written All Over Your Face' and 'She Put The Sad In All His

Songs'. After winning a talent contest in 1989, he moved to Nashville and Arista's vice-president, Tim DuBois, suggested that he should try to write some songs with Brooks. They came up with 'Brand New Man' and, as they sounded good together and became friends, they formed the duo Brooks And Dunn. Their high-energy, debut album sold three million copies and yielded four chart-topping country singles; one of them, the line-dancing 'Boot Scootin' Boogie', was also a US pop hit. The song also appears in a dance version on their second album and as Brooks says, 'We added a synthesiser and pumped this hillbilly record full of steroids.' 'Rock My World (Little Country Girl)', with its Rolling Stones-styled intro, boasted eight international versions and a video. Their stage act features a manic performance by Brooks, complete with duckwalks and wild leaps. Not surprisingly, they have won CMA Vocal Duo Of The Year awards and with their success, they have been able to design and model western shirts for Panhandle Slim. *Borderline* debuted at number 1 on the *Billboard* country chart in May 1996 and was followed by a number 1 single, 'My Maria'. They culminated the year with a CMA award for Entertainer Of the Year and once more Duo Of The Year. Whether they will have the longevity of the Bellamy Brothers remains to be seen, but to date, they rock harder, write sharper novelty songs and have considerably more stage personality. They are the most popular duo in country music since the heyday of the Everly Brothers. In 1997 they picked up a further CMA award for Best Vocal Duo.

● ALBUMS: *Brand New Man* (Arista 1991)★★★★, *Hard Workin' Man* (Arista 1993)★★★★, *Waitin' On Sundown* (Arista 1994)★★★★, *Borderline* (Arista 1996)★★★★. Solo: Kix Brooks *Kix Brooks* (Capitol 1993)★★★.

● COMPILATIONS: *The Greatest Hits Collection* (Arista 1997)★★★★.

● VIDEOS: *That Ain't No Way To Go* (DNA 1994).

BROOKS, GARTH

b. Troyal Garth Brooks, 7 February 1962, Yukon, Oklahoma, USA. Brooks' mother, country singer Colleen Carroll, appeared on *Ozark Mountain Jubilee* and recorded for Capitol Records. Brooks won an athletic scholarship in Oklahoma and entertained in clubs at night. He preferred music and was soon playing full-time. While having a club residency, he learned over 350 songs. Working as a bouncer in Stillwater, he broke up a fight and hence met his future wife, Sandy. When he first married, he reminisced about his high school sweetheart and wondered if he had made a mistake. A few years later, he met her, realized that they had both changed, and wrote the song 'Unanswered Prayers'. Brooks signed with Capitol Records and was assigned to producer Allen Reynolds, known for his work with Don Williams. His first album, *Garth Brooks*, had an old-time, western swing and country feel and included a revival of a Jim Reeves success ('I Know One'), a western saga ('Cowboy Bill') and several new love songs ('The Dance', 'If Tomorrow Never Comes' and his own 'Not Counting You'). Brooks' second album, *No Fences*, was even better, including his concert-stopping 'Friends In Low Places', and a revival of the Fleetwoods' 'Mr. Blue', both written by Dwayne Blackwell. The album sold ten million copies in the USA and Brooks has won numerous awards. *Ropin' The Wind* sold four million copies in its first month of release and topped both the

US pop and country charts (nine million sales by mid-1993). His version of Billy Joel's 'Shameless' was a US country number 1, as were his recordings of 'The Thunder Rolls', 'Two Of A Kind' and 'Working On A Full House'. Brooks chooses his songs carefully but he has yet to find the right duet song for himself and his mother. He says, 'My mother has told me to take care of myself. In that way, I'll be around in 10 or 15 years and I can pay back the people who have invested time in me.' Brooks' survival as a commercial force seems in no doubt, but during 1992 rumours began to circulate that he was planning to quit the music business to concentrate on raising a family (his first daughter, named Taylor in honour of James Taylor, was born that spring). In the event, Brooks cancelled his touring engagements for the summer, but re-emerged before the end of the year with a Christmas record, *Beyond The Season*, and another album, *The Chase*. Within four months, that album had sold five million copies. Critics noted that Brooks was moving subtly away from the honky-tonk style of his debut towards a 70s-orientated soft rock sound. Brooks reached the UK pop chart in 1994 with 'The Red Strokes', one of the few US country singers to do so; this further reinforced the view that he was not just a US phenomenon. *Fresh Horses* was his first album to have simultaneous worldwide release, and a further international hit came with the sugar-drenched 'She's Every Woman'. In 1995 he was distracted by having his former managers sueing each other. He took over his own business affairs with the help of his wife Sandy. His worldwide album sales reached 60 million in 1996, making him the all-time biggest-selling solo artist in the world. Brooks has changed the whole perception of country music, making it fashionable. He is still ambitious and he is determined to initiate One World Flag when, one day of the year, the world flag would be flown in every country as a symbol of unity. Brooks was named Entertainer Of The Year at the 1997 Country Music Awards. At the end of the year he released *Sevens*, which predictably debuted at number 1 in the *Billboard* Pop and Country charts with pre-orders of more than five million units.

● ALBUMS: *Garth Brooks* (Liberty 1989)★★★★, *No Fences* (Liberty 1990)★★★★, *Ropin' The Wind* (Liberty 1991)★★★, *The Chase* (Liberty 1992)★★★★, *Beyond The Season* (Liberty 1992)★★, *In Pieces* (Liberty 1993)★★★★, *Fresh Horses* (Capitol Nashville 1995)★★★, *Seven* (Capitol Nashville 1997)★★★.

● COMPILATIONS: *The Hits* (Liberty 1994)★★★★.

● VIDEOS: *Garth Brooks* (1991), *This Is Garth Brooks* (1992), *The Video Collection Vol. II* (Capitol 1996).

● FURTHER READING: *Garth Brooks: Platinum Cowboy*, Edward Morris. *One Of A Kind, Workin' On A Full House*, Rick Mitchell.

BROOKS, KAREN

b. 29 April 1954, Dallas, Texas, USA. Brooks learned to play guitar at the age of 17 and worked on a ranch at Denton, before starting her musical career in Austin, Texas. Singing around the clubs, she worked with Jerry Jeff Walker, Townes Van Zandt and Gary P. Nunn (to whom she was once married). After meeting Rodney Crowell and Rosanne Cash, she moved to Los Angeles and worked with Emmylou Harris, sang backing vocals and demos and worked on songwriting. In the late 70s, she wrote 'Couldn't Do Nothin' Right', which became a Top 15 hit for Rosanne Cash in 1980. Around 1980, she moved to Nashville and in 1982, gained further success as a songwriter when Emmylou Harris had a Top 10 hit with 'Tennessee Rose'. The same year, recording for Warner Brothers, she made her own debut in the *Billboard* country charts with 'New Way Out'. She received some praise for her debut album with its mixture of easy listening, contemporary country, pop and rock but the follow-up disappointed. In 1983, 'Faking Love', a duet with T.G. Sheppard, went to number 1. However, she failed to repeat such a high placing and by 1985 had only achieved six more modest chart entries, the last being 'I Will Dance With You', a duet with her old friend Johnny Cash - a modest number 45. She continued to write and formed her own publishing house, Babblin' Brooks Music. By the time she recorded an album containing a mixture of solo and duet recordings with singer-songwriter Randy Sharp, the man who had written her first chart hit, she had moved to the Mercury label.

● ALBUMS: *Walk On* (Warner 1982)★★, *Hearts Of Fire* (Warner 1984)★★★, *I Will Dance With You* (Warner 1985)★★, with Randy Sharp *That's Another Story* (Mercury 1992)★★★.

BROTHER PHELPS

Ricky Lee Phelps (b. Richard Lee Phelps, 8 October 1953, Edmonton, Kentucky, USA) sang and Doug Phelps (b. 16 February 1960, Edmonton, Kentucky, USA) played bass for the Kentucky Headhunters before forming the 90s country band Brother Phelps. They held a nationwide competition to find the name of the band, they finally chose Brother Phelps as a tribute to their late father, a preacher who was known to his congregation by this name. Their debut *Let Go* was surprisingly soft in its approach, while their version of J.J. Cale's 'Any Way The Wind Blows' was first class. 'Were You Really Living' is an admonition to the listener to live life to the full.

● ALBUMS: *Let Go* (Asylum 1993)★★★, *Any Way The Wind Blows* (Asylum 1995)★★★.

BROUSSARD, VAN

b. 29 March 1937, Prairieville, Louisiana, USA. The name of Broussard is well known in Louisiana since many artists of that name are noted for their contributions to Cajun and its connected forms of music. Van Broussard is something of a legend in the Bayou country of Louisiana as a performer of swamp-pop music. He fronted his own Cajun band and for a great many years mainly performed in the Baton Rouge area. He was also a regular performer at Cal's Club, Prairieville, where he often sang with his sister Grace (b. *c.*1943, Prairieville, Louisiana, USA). Grace also found fame in the 60s, as one half of the Dale And Grace duo that made several popular recordings, the best-known, undoubtedly, being their 1963 pop smash 'I'm Leaving It Up To You', which had the distinction of being the first ever national swamp-pop number 1 (Dale was Dale Houston, a country pianist/singer from Ferriday, Louisiana). Van Broussard never actually achieved a major hit but in the late 70s, while recording on the Bayou Boogie label, he had two very popular local successes with 'Lord, I Need Somebody Bad' and 'Feed The Flame'. An album release for that label was hailed as one of the best releases of classic swamp-pop for many years. His voice has been likened to Bobby Charles and his

material actually ranged from classic swamp-pop to New Orleans R&B. He and Grace both appeared with Johnny Allen when he organized the major *South Louisiana Music All-Star Show* in September 1981. In 1992, the CSP label released a CD that contained recordings made by Broussard in the 50s and 60s.

● ALBUMS: *Van Broussard* (Bayou Boogie 70s)★★★.

● COMPILATIONS: *Bayou Boogie Fever* (CSP 1992)★★★.

BROWN, DERWOOD

b. Melvin Derwood Brown, 29 September 1915, Stephenville, Texas, USA, d. 24 December 1978, Fort Worth, Texas, USA. The family relocated in 1918 and he grew up in Fort Worth. A talented guitarist, who at the age of 12 was playing professionally with elder brother Milton Brown. During his career, he was known as a robust guitarist who so regularly broke strings that younger brother Roy Lee Brown had to be in attendance to replace them, while Derwood used a spare instrument. He played with his brother in the Aladdin Laddies, the Light Crust Doughboys and in the Musical Brownies. When Milton died in 1936, Derwood (also a competent vocalist) took over the band but he never possessed his brother's organizing skills. However, for a time, they had a programme on KTAT and played dancehalls. They recorded 14 tracks in Dallas for Decca in February 1937, with Jimmie Davis providing the vocal on 'High Geared Daddy' and 'Honky Tonk Blues'. Although the band was still playing fine music, some members acutely felt the absence of Milton, and the Musical Brownies disbanded. Ocie Stockard and Cliff Bruner went on to form their own bands. Derwood formed a new band and for a time worked out of Houston or Tyler. He then joined Bill Boyd in Dallas, before returning to Fort Worth. Here he re-formed a band called the Musical Brownies with Stockard and Wanna Coffman. He worked on army camp construction during the war, but in 1946, he and Roy Lee (banjo) formed a band that played on KDNT Denton and for weekly dance nights at a club. This marked the end of Derwood's regular work with a band. He then moved to Colorado to work in the oilfields.

BROWN, GREG

b. Iowa, USA. Greg Brown's traditional folk songwriting is infused with a distinctive Midwestern sensibility. Growing up in a family obsessed by music, he began to play the pump organ when he was six, before picking up the guitar a few years later (he was taught by his mother). A series of concerts followed at local church venues, where his father was a preacher. Eventually he abandoned his classical aspirations after an accident when he was aged 18. Working at a meat-packing plant, a co-worker accidentally cut off half of his left thumb, making classical playing an impossibility. At college in Iowa City, he encountered a folk-singer from New York called Eric Andersen. Brown won a contest to open at his Iowan concert date, and travelled to New York to meet the singer a few weeks after the show. He failed to find him. Instead he found a job at Gerde's Folk City as the resident singer. However, after three or four years in New York he tired of the hand-to-mouth existence and concentrated on other matters. Inevitably, however, he found himself back in a band and a demo tape was recorded and sent to the manager who had originally formed the Platters. He needed songs for his coterie of artists and Brown was recruited for the task. At this point he also had a composition recorded by Willie Nelson, and further recognition followed with regular slots on the *Prairie Home Companion* radio programme. Brown has gone on to record a succession of albums for his own Red House Records, based in Minneapolis, which have gradually increased his profile. The vast majority of his songs combine humour with empathy for his character studies, with the focus of his subject matter primarily on domestic concerns. He is also capable of addressing larger themes, with 'America Will Eat You' on 1989's *One Big Town* expressing his real concerns about the collapse of the American dream. He has also recorded an album of William Blake poems (*Songs Of Innocence And Experience*) and a children's collection. His critical breakthrough came in 1994 with *The Poet Game*, on which his signature vocal style (world-weary enough to see him compared with Tom Waits) animated a collection of startling songs that included the memorable 'Brand New '64 Dodge'.

● ALBUMS: *In The Dark With You* (Red House 1985)★★★, *Songs Of Innocence And Experience* (Red House 1986)★★★, *One More Goodnight Kiss* (Red House 1986)★★, *One Big Town* (Red House 1989)★★★, *The Poet Game* (Red House 1994)★★★, *The Live One* (Red House 1995)★★, *Bath Tub Blues* (Red House 1995)★★★.

BROWN, HYLO

b. Frank Brown, 20 April 1922, River, Kentucky, USA. Brown began his long and distinguished career on WCMI Ashland, Kentucky, in 1939. Over the years he has played with many of the top names including Bradley Kincaid and Bill Monroe and appeared at country music's most important venues. He acquired the nickname of 'Hylo' from his ability to sing in both tenor and bass voices and is also a fine guitarist. The full credit that he deserves has eluded him, perhaps because he was born a few years too early. He possessed the ability to sing both bluegrass and ordinary country material equally well, but the general opinion in his day was that one should sing either one or the other. Consequently, he was never afforded the opportunity to demonstrate his full potential. It was not until years later that Ricky Skaggs convinced both record companies and the public that it was possible to sing both genres equally well. Between 1954 and 1960, Brown recorded for Capitol, being especially remembered for the versions of his self-penned 'Lost To A Stranger' and the Vagabonds' 'When It's Lamp Lighting Time In The Valley'. In the early 60s, he recorded several albums for Starday and in the late 60s, a whole series for Rural Rhythm. Other albums have appeared and some 1960 Capitol recordings, with an overdub by the Jordanaires, were released for the first time by Bear Family in 1992.

● ALBUMS: *Hylo Brown* (Capitol 1959)★★★★, *Bluegrass Balladeer* (Starday 1962)★★★★, *Bluegrass Goes To College* (Starday 1962)★★★, *Sing Me A Bluegrass Song* (Starday 1963)★★★, *Sings Bluegrass With A Five-String Banjo* (Starday 1963)★★★, *Meets The Lonesome Pine Fiddlers* (Starday 1963)★★★, *Hylo Brown* (1967)★★★, *Legends & Tall Tales* (Rural Rhythms 1967)★★★, *Sings Country Gospel Songs* (Rural Rhythms 1967)★★, *Folk Songs Of America* (Rural Rhythms 1967)★★★, *America's Favorite Balladeer* (Rural Rhythms 1968)★★, *Sings The Blues* (Rural Rhythms 1968)★★★, *With The Blue Ridge Mountain Boys* (Rural Rhythms 1968)★★★, *Sings His Bluegrass Hits* (1973)★★,

Original Radio Recordings (1976)★★★★, *A Tribute To My Heroes* (1977)★★★ *Early Bluegrass* (1983)★★★.

● COMPILATIONS: *Hylo Brown & His Timberliners Vol. 1* (1973)★★★★, *Hylo Brown & The Timberliners 1954-60* (Bear Family 1992)★★★★.

BROWN, JIM ED

b. Jim Edward Brown, 1 April 1934, Sparkman, Arkansas, USA. From the early 50s to 1967, Brown sang with sisters Maxine and Bonnie as the Browns but had solo successes in 1965 with 'I Heard From A Memory Last Night' and 'I'm Just A Country Boy', after his sisters had persuaded Chet Atkins to record him solo. When the trio disbanded in 1967, he pursued a solo career. He appeared on the *Grand Ole Opry* and other top radio and television shows, actually hosting the Nashville Network *You Can Be A Star* Show and toured extensively. Between 1967 and 1981, recording for RCA, he registered a total of 46 US country chart entries. These included Top 10 hits with 'Pop A Top' (1967), 'Morning' (1970), 'Southern Loving' (1973) and 'It's That Time Of Night' (1974). In 1976, he began a successful association with Helen Cornelius. 'I Don't Want To Have To Marry You' was a country number 1 and the follow-up, 'Saying Hello, Saying I Love You, Saying Goodbye', a number 2. In 1977, they were voted Vocal Duo Of The Year by the Country Music Association. Further duet successes followed, including 'If The World Ran Out Of Love Tonight' (1978), 'Lying In Love With You' (1979) and 'Morning Comes Too Early' (1980). Some of his recordings were probably too pop-country for the traditionalists, but in 1979, they had a Top 10 country hit with their version of the Barbra Streisand/Neil Diamond number 1 pop hit 'You Don't Bring Me Flowers'. Their partnership ended in the early 80s, their last chart entry being 'Don't Bother To Knock'. Brown is still active in the music business but rarely records; he opened the Jim Ed Brown Theater in Nashville, Tennessee in the late 80s.

● ALBUMS: *Alone With You* (RCA 1966)★★★, *Just Jim* (RCA 1967)★★★★, *Gems By Jim* (RCA 1967)★★★, *Bottle Bottle* (RCA 1968)★★★, *Country's Best On Record* (RCA 1968)★★, *Jim Ed Sings The Browns* (RCA 1968)★★★ *Remember Me* (RCA 1969)★★★, *This Is My Beat* (RCA 1969)★★, *Just For You* (RCA 1970)★★★, *Going Up The Country* (RCA 1971)★★★, *Gentle On My Mind* (RCA 1971)★★, *Morning* (RCA 1971)★★★, *Angel's Sunday* (RCA 1971)★★★, *She's Leaving* (RCA 1971)★★★, *Brown Is Blue* (RCA 1972)★★★, *Country Cream* (RCA 1972)★★★, *Evening* (RCA 1972)★★, *Barrooms & Pop-A-Tops* (RCA 1973)★★★, *Hey Good Looking* (RCA 1973)★★★, *It's That Time Of Night* (RCA 1974)★★. With Helen Cornelius I *Don't Want To Have To Marry You* (RCA 1976)★★★, *Born Believer* (RCA 1977)★★★, *I'll Never Be Free* (RCA 1978)★★★, *You Don't Bring Me Flowers* (RCA 1979)★★, *One Man One Woman* (RCA 1980)★★.

● COMPILATIONS: *Greatest Hits* (RCA 1992)★★★★, *Essential Series* (RCA 1996)★★★★

BROWN, JUNIOR

b. Arizona, USA. The 90s country singer Junior Brown dropped out of high school in 1969 and then played the Texas clubs for many years, writing 'Too Many Nights In A Roadhouse' for Alvin Crow. He pioneered the guit-steel, a double-neck electric and steel guitar lap-top, which is featured to good effect on the 10-minute 'Guit-Steel Blues'. He cites his influences as Jimi Hendrix, Ernest Tubb and the Ventures, and the opening cut on *12 Shades Of Brown* is 'My Baby Don't Dance To Nothing But Ernest Tubb'. He does an uncanny, deadpan Tubb impersonation on the comic 'My Wife Thinks You're Dead'. His 'Sugarfoot Rag' contains licks from Jimi Hendrix's 'The Wind Cries Mary'. Brown's wife Tanya Rae plays rhythm guitar and his road band includes Steve Holley of Wings. *Semi-Crazy* was another strong and defiantly uncommercial set.

● ALBUMS: *12 Shades Of Brown* (Curb 1989)★★★, *Guit With It* (Curb 1993)★★★★, *Junior High* mini-album (Curb 1995)★★★, *Semi-Crazy* (Curb 1996)★★★.

BROWN, MARTY

b. 25 July 1965, Owensboro, Kentucky, USA. The 90s country singer Marty Brown is a hillbilly and proud of it, saying, 'I went to New York City once and I felt I ought to have a passport.' On record he sounds like Hank Williams, while Buddy Holly and the Everly Brothers are also strong influences. Marty Brown arrived in Nashville with a demo tape and accosted Barry Beckett with the words: 'I know you, I've seen you in a video.' He visited a succession of shopping malls for a promotional tour, driving to each of them in a 1969 Cadillac. The third album, *Cryin', Lovin', Leavin'*, features guest appearances from Melba Montgomery and Joy Lynn White, but, despite being a good writer, he has still to have a substantial country hit. He was signed to the Californian Hightone label in 1996, releasing the highly accessible *Here's To The Honky Tonks*.

● ALBUMS: *High And Dry* (MCA 1991)★★★, *Wild Kentucky Skies* (MCA 1993)★★★, *Cryin', Lovin', Leavin'* (MCA 1994)★★★★, *Here's To The Honky Tonks* (Hightone 1996)★★★.

BROWN, MILTON

b. William Milton Brown, 8 September 1903, Stephenville, Texas, USA, d. 18 April 1936, Fort Worth, Texas, USA. In 1918, the family moved to Fort Worth where, after completing his education and nursing a strong desire to be an entertainer, Brown worked as a salesman with the Lowe Cigar company. He did not play an instrument but he hoped for the chance to work with a band as a vocalist. By 1927, with guitar backing provided by his 12-year-old brother Derwood Brown, he was regularly singing at local house dances. Late in 1929, he was made redundant and thought seriously about making a living from music. The two Brown brothers soon joined with fiddler Bob Wills and guitarist Herman Arnspiger (then performing together as the Wills Fiddle Band) and together they played dances. In 1930, they were sponsored by the Aladdin Lamp company and with the addition of Clifton 'Sleepy' Johnson (guitar), they began to play on WBAP as the Aladdin Laddies. Milton was an astute organizer and when the Aladdin show ended, he found work for the group playing for dances at the Crystal Springs entertainment centre in downtown Fort Worth. They soon came to the notice of W. Lee O'Daniel, the sales manager of Burrus Mill And Elevator Company. Late in 1930, O'Daniel, seeking to increase sales of the company's Light Crust Flour, employed the band. Performing as the Light Crust Doughboys, first on KFJZ before moving them to the more powerful WBAP, they soon became a popular act with O'Daniel (who wrote several songs including 'Beautiful

Texas' and 'Put Me In Your Pocket') acting as their announcer. In 1932, as the Fort Worth Doughboys, they recorded for RCA-Victor. The recordings of 'Nancy Jane' and 'Sunbonnet Sue' represent the first recorded example of Brown's singing and Wills' fiddle playing. Although neither realized it at the time, it was probably the first example of what eventually became known as western swing music. Differences of opinion with O'Daniel saw first Brown and then Wills leave the Doughboys to pursue their own careers and become competitive rivals for the musical audiences. In September 1932, Milton Brown formed his Musical Brownies consisting of brother Derwood (guitar and harmony vocals), Jesse Ashlock and Cecil Brower (fiddles), Ocie Stockard (banjo), Wanna Coffman (bass) and Fred 'Papa' Calhoun (piano) and began to establish himself in the area, including regular broadcasting on KTAT. The band made its first RCA recordings on Bluebird, in San Antonio, on 4 April 1934, by which time Ashlock had joined Wills. After a further session in August, they next recorded for Decca in Chicago in January 1935 - a two-day session that produced over 30 recordings. By this time, Milton had added the steel guitar of Bob Dunn and had finally arrived at the sound that he had been seeking from the start (Dunn is now regarded as the instrument's pioneer and finest player of western swing music). The numbers varied from the 'St. Louis Blues' and 'Chinatown, My Chinatown' to 'In The Shade of the Old Apple Tree' and included a dazzling instrumental of Dunn's own composition, 'Taking Off'. Brower left for a short time and was replaced by Cliff Bruner, but when Brower returned, Brown also kept Bruner, thus giving the band their strong twin-fiddle lead. By this time, the popularity of the Musical Brownies ensured a spot on WBAP and regular bookings at dancehalls all over the state. In March 1936, a three-day session produced 49 more recordings, which proved to be the last that Milton Brown would make. In the early hours of 13 April 1936, Brown, accompanied by 16-year-old Katherine Prehoditch, was driving home from a show, when for some unknown reason, he crashed. Brown did not drink but it seems possible that he fell asleep. The girl died instantly and Brown, after initially showing signs of recovery to the extent that he sang to Bruner when he visited him in hospital, died of what the death certificate described as 'pneumonia, traumatic' on 18 April 1936, in the Methodist Hospital, Fort Worth. Milton Brown's career was brief; he played no instrument and although a great vocalist, he never had a hit record. Through persevering in his aim to create a genre of music, he has become accepted as a founder of western swing music. After Milton's death, Derwood fronted the band for a time to fulfil bookings but early in 1938, his Musical Brownies disbanded.

● ALBUMS: *Dance-O-Rama* 10-inch album (Decca 1955)★★★★, *Dance-O-Rama Vol. 1* (Decca 1955)★★★, *Pioneer Western Swing Band 1935-36* (MCA 1973)★★★★, *Taking Off* (String 1977)★★★, *Milton Brown And His Brownies* (MCA 1983)★★★, *Easy Ridin' Papa* (Charly 1987)★★.

● COMPILATIONS: *Complete Recordings Of The Father Of Western Swing: 1932-1937* 5-CD box set (Texas Rose 1996)★★★★.

● FURTHER READING: *Milton Brown And The Founding Of Western Swing*, Cary Ginell with Roy Lee Brown.

BROWN, ROY LEE

b. 27 February 1921, Fort Worth, Texas, USA. The younger brother of Milton and Derwood Brown, he learned banjo and when permitted by school requirements toured around with his elder brothers, usually working behind the scenes, including regularly restringing Derwood's guitar. In 1946, after naval service, he played with Derwood, both on KDNT and at clubs. When Derwood left, Roy Lee fronted the band until he returned to Fort Worth. He gained a full-time job with the Fire Department but also formed a new band that worked several local venues, had a daily show on KCNC and recorded four songs as Roy Lee Brown And His Musical Brownies. The various jobs began to clash, and in the early 50s he gave up the band and worked for the Fire Department until he retired in 1982. Subsequently, he decided to start playing Milton's western swing music again and in 1989, with a new edition of the Musical Brownies, he recorded for the Priority label. In 1991 he made further recordings fronting a band that included Leon Rausch, one of Bob Wills' old Texas Playboys.

● ALBUMS: *Western Swing Heritage* cassette only (Priory 1989)★★★, *Western Swing Heritage II* cassette only (Brownie 1991)★★.

BROWN, T. GRAHAM

b. Anthony Graham Brown, 30 October 1954, Arabi, Georgia, USA. As much a southern R&B singer as a country singer-songwriter, Brown was at school in Athens, Georgia, with members of the B-52's. He earned extra cash singing cover versions in lounge bars, until he saw a television documentary on David Allen Coe, after which he formed Rio Diamond, an 'outlaw' band, in 1976. By 1979, he was fronting T. Graham Brown's Rack Of Spam, a white soul band, singing Otis Redding material. In 1982, he moved to Nashville, where he worked as a demo singer, recording songs for publishers who wanted famous artists to record their copyrighted material. A song he demoed as '1962' was later recorded by Randy Travis as '1982', but more lucrative was the use of his voice on jingles for products such as Budweiser beer and McDonald hamburgers. Signed to a major label in 1985, he was known as T. Graham Brown to avoid confusion with Nashville producer Tony Brown. His first album *I Tell It Like It Used To Be*, included two US country number 1 singles, 'Hell Or High Water' and 'Don't Go To Strangers', and he returned to the top again in 1988 with 'Darlene'.

● ALBUMS: *I Tell It Like It Used To Be* (Capitol 1986)★★★, *Brilliant Conversationalist* (Capitol 1987)★★★, *Come As You Were* (1988)★★★, *Bumper To Bumper* (Capitol 1990)★★★, *You Can't Take It With You* (1991)★★★.
● COMPILATIONS: *The Best Of T. Graham Brown* (Liberty 1992)★★★★.

BROWN, TONY

In 1974, the pianist Tony Brown replaced Glen D. Hardin in Elvis Presley's touring band and remained with him until his death. He says, 'When we cut "Way Down", he put his hands over mine on the piano.' Brown moved into country music through being on the road with Rodney Crowell and he subsequently produced Crowell's *Diamonds And Dirt*, which included five number 1 country singles. He had sustained success with Steve Wariner, producing several number 1 sin-

gles, and then with Vince Gill. He is one of the most popular producers in Nashville and has enjoyed success with Tracy Byrd, Reba McEntire, Mark Chesnutt, George Strait and Wynonna.

BROWNE, JANN

b. 14 March 1954, Anderson, Indiana, USA. Browne was a featured vocalist with Asleep At The Wheel between 1981 and 1983. She then developed a solo career in California and married songwriter Roger Stebner in 1985. Despite guest musicians such as Duane Eddy, Emmylou Harris, Albert Lee and Wanda Jackson, her albums failed to sell. She has had minor US country hits with 'You Ain't Down Home' and 'Tell Me Why'. Her good looks have ensured regular CMT plays and she has success in her sights: 'It took Rodney Crowell and Vince Gill a long time to break through, so that gives me some hope.' Her third album, *Count Me In*, was counted out by American record companies and eventually released by an Australian label Massive Country.

● ALBUMS: *Tell Me Why* (Curb 1990)★★★, *It Only Hurts When I Laugh* (Capitol 1991)★★★, *Count Me In* (Massive Country 1995)★★★.

BROWNS

Ella Maxine Brown (b. 27 April 1932, Sampti, Louisiana, USA), Jim Edward Brown (b. 1 April 1934, Sparkman, Arkansas, USA) and Bonnie Brown (b. 31 July 1937, Sparkman, Arkansas, USA). In 1953, greatly influenced by WSM broadcasts of the *Grand Ole Opry*, Maxine and her brother began singing as a duo. They first featured on *Barnyard Hayride* on KLRA Little Rock, before being signed to the *Louisiana Hayride* on KWKH Shreveport. They recorded some duet tracks for Fabor and in 1954 registered a Top 10 US country hit with their own song, 'Looking Back To See' (Jim Reeves actually played rhythm guitar on the recording). In 1955, after being joined by sister Bonnie, they became a featured act on Red Foley's *Ozark Jubilee* and their recording of 'Here Today And Gone Tomorrow' became their first country hit as a trio. In 1956, with help from Jim Reeves, they moved to RCA, where they immediately had a US country number 2 hit with their recording of the Louvin's 'I Take The Chance'. The following year they had major success with 'I Heard The Bluebirds Sing', but it was in 1959 that they enjoyed their biggest hit with their million-selling recording of 'The Three Bells'. Based on a song called 'While The Angelus Was Ringing' and sometimes known as 'The Jimmy Brown Song' or 'Les Trois Cloches', the song was popularized in Europe by both Les Compagnons de la Chanson and Edith Piaf. The Browns' recording topped both the US country and pop charts and even reached number 6 on the UK pop charts. Between 1959 and 1967, 12 further hits followed including 'Scarlet Ribbons', 'The Old Lamplighter', 'Then I'll Stop Loving You' and 'I'd Just Be Fool Enough'. In the early 60s, they appeared on all major television shows and toured extensively including trips to Europe and Japan, as well as running their own club in Pine Bluff, Arkansas. They joined the *Grand Ole Opry* in 1963, but in 1967, with Maxine and Bonnie wishing to spend more time with their families, they disbanded. In 1968, Maxine had a minor hit as a solo artist on the Chart label with 'Sugar Cane County', while Jim Ed continued his career as a solo artist with RCA. The Browns reunited in 1996 for the gospel set, *Family Bible*.

● ALBUMS: *Jim Edward, Maxine & Bonnie Brown* (RCA Victor 1957)★★★, *Sweet Sounds By The Browns* (RCA Victor 1959)★★★, *Town & Country* (RCA Victor 1960)★★★, *The Browns Sing Their Hits* (RCA Victor 1960)★★★★, *Our Favorite Folk Songs* (RCA Victor 1961)★★★, *Songs From The Little Brown Church Hymnal* (RCA Victor 1961)★★★, *Grand Ole Opry Favorites* (RCA Victor 1964)★★★, *This Young Land* (RCA Victor 1964)★★★, *Three Shades Of Brown* (RCA Victor 1965)★★★, *I Heard The Bluebirds Sing* (Camden 1965)★★★, *Our Kind Of Country* (RCA Victor 1966)★★★, *The Browns Sing The Big Ones From The Country* (RCA Victor 1967)★★★, *The Old Country Church* (RCA Victor 1967)★★★★, *A Harvest Of Country Songs* (Camden 1968)★★★, *Family Bible* (Step One 1996)★★★.
Solo: Maxine Brown *Sugar Cane County* (Chart 1969)★★.
● COMPILATIONS: *Best Of The Browns* (RCA Victor 1966)★★★★, *Rockin' Rollin' Browns* (Bear Family 1984)★★★, *20 Of The Best* (RCA 1985)★★★★, *Looking Back To See* (Bear Family 1986)★★★, *Three Bells* 8-CD box set (Bear Family 1993)★★★★.

BRUCE, ED

b. William Edwin Bruce, 29 December 1939, Keiser, Arkansas, USA. His family moved to Memphis and Bruce was to spend many years promoting tourism as 'the Tennessean'. He loved the early Sun records of Carl Perkins and, after graduating in 1957, was given the money to make a demo and so impressed Sun's engineer, Jack Clement, that he was signed to the label. His singles, 'Rock Boppin' Baby' and 'Sweet Woman', under the name of Edwin Bruce are collector's items, but they are also included, along with previously unreleased Sun tracks, on the 1986 Bear Family collection. He had his first financial success when he wrote 'Save Your Kisses', the b-side of Tommy Roe's chart-topping 'Sheila'. He also wrote 'See The Big Man Cry', a solo hit for Charlie Louvin, and 'Northeast Arkansas Mississippi County Bootlegger' for Kenny Price. Bruce had a minor country hit with the Monkees' 'Last Train To Clarksville' and found himself a country star with 'The Last Cowboy Song' and 'You're The Best Break This Old Heart Ever Had', his only number 1. Bruce regards himself primarily as a songwriter and 'Mammas, Don't Let Your Babies Grow Up To Be Cowboys', for Waylon Jennings and Willie Nelson, became the anthem of outlaw country. Nelson added a final chorus to his 1980 version of 'The Last Cowboy Song'. Other songs include 'The Man That Turned My Mama On' (Tanya Tucker), 'Workingman's Prayer' (Arthur Prysock, Tex Ritter), 'Restless' (Crystal Gayle) and 'Too Much Love Between Us' (Kitty Wells). Many songs were co-written with his former wife and manager, Patsy. Bruce starred as Tom Guthrie alongside James Garner in the US television series *Maverick* and recorded 'Theme From Bret Maverick'.
● ALBUMS: *If I Could Just Go Home* (RCA 1968)★★★, *Shades Of Ed Bruce* (Monument 1969)★★★★, *Ed Bruce* (United Artists 1976)★★, *The Tennessean* (Epic 1977)★★★, *Cowboys And Dreamers* (Epic 1978)★★★, *Ed Bruce* (MCA 1980)★★★, *One To One* (MCA 1981)★★★, *Last Train To Clarksville* (RCA International 1982), *I Write It Down* (MCA 1982)★★, *You're Not Leavin' Here Tonight* (MCA 1983)★★★ *Tell 'Em I've Gone Crazy* (MCA 1984)★★★, *Homecoming* (RCA 1984)★★★, *Night Things* (RCA 1986)★★.
● COMPILATIONS: *Rockin' And Boppin' Baby* (Bear Family

1986)★★★★, *Greatest Hits* (MCA 1986)★★★★, *The Best Of Ed Bruce* (Varèse Sarabande 1995)★★★★, *Puzzles* (Bear Family 1995)★★★.

BRUMLEY, ALBERT

b. Albert Edward Brumley, 29 October 1905, Spiro, Indian Territory, Oklahoma, USA, d. 15 November 1977. Brumley is remembered as one of the greatest gospel songwriters of all time, although many of his hundreds of songs have also been recorded by country singers including Roy Acuff, Red Foley, Webb Pierce, Louvin Brothers, Jim Reeves and Elvis Presley. He learned to play organ as a boy and at 19 studied at the Hartford Musical Institute at Hartford, Arkansas. He sang in a quartet but his shyness of solo work prevented him becoming a singer. He turned to writing and in 1931, after he married Goldie Edith Schell, she persuaded him to send some of his songs to the Hartford Music Company for publication. 'I'll Fly Away' appeared in their book *The Wonderful Message* and they soon asked Brumley for more songs. Soon all the major gospel acts were singing his songs. He became one of the few writers to have whole albums of work recorded by groups such as the Chuck Wagon Gang, Smitty Gatlin Trio and the Statesmen. His popular songs include 'Jesus Hold My Hand', 'I'll Meet You In The Morning', 'Little Pine Log Cabin', 'If We Never Meet Again', 'Turn Your Radio On', 'He Set Me Free' and 'Nobody Answered Me'. He established his own publishing company and, in 1948, he also bought Hartford Music Company. Albert Brumley was one of the first inductees of the Nashville Songwriters' Hall Of Fame when it opened in 1970, and in 1972, he also became a member of the Gospel Music Hall Of Fame. He died at his home in November 1977 but three of his six children, Bill, Bob and Betty, run Albert E Brumley & Sons Publishing Company. His son Al is a country and gospel singer with several albums to his credit, Tom is a noted steel guitarist and Jackson works as a publisher/manager.
● ALBUMS: *Al Brumley Sings Al Brumley* (American Artists 1965)★★★.

BRUNER, CLIFF

b. Clifton Lafayette Bruner, 25 April 1915, Texas City, Texas, USA. Bruner learned to play fiddle as a child, later boasting: 'I could play fiddle before I could talk'. While still at school, he played at local dances and later gained a great deal of experience touring with Doc Scott's medicine show. Bruner became a jazz and swing music fiddler (as opposed to the more usual country breakdown fiddlers) and, playing both fiddle and mandolin, he worked with several bands. He joined Milton Brown's Musical Brownies in Fort Worth and played on many of Brown's recordings. Bruner and fellow fiddler Cecil Brower gave the band the strong twin fiddle lead that was an instantly recognizable part of Brown's music. After Brown's death in 1936, he moved to Houston, where he formed his own band, the Texas Wanderers. This outfit, which at times included the electric mandolinist Leo Raley, fiddler J.R. Chatwell, guitarist and vocalist Dickie McBride and country boogie pianist Moon Mullican, became one of the most popular and successful bands to work both the Texas Gulf Coast and from Houston (also broadcasting regularly on KXYZ) and Beaumont to the Cajun area of Louisiana. Bruner recorded several sessions for Decca Records between 1937 and 1941. On 13 September 1938, with McBride taking the vocal, the band recorded the first version of 'It Makes No Difference Now' - a song that has since become a country standard. On 26 August 1939, Bruner achieved another first, when the band recorded the first truck driving song, 'Truck Driver's Blues', with vocals by Bruner and Mullican. In the 50s, Bruner dissolved the band and worked in insurance until his retirement. In 1994, he was still playing on weekend events with local musicians in Houston and according to reports, still amazing younger musicians with his fiddling skills.

● ALBUMS: *Then And Now* (Delta 1981)★★★, *Cliff Bruner's Texas Wanderers* (Texas Rose 1983)★★★★.

BRYANT, BOUDLEAUX

b. Diadorius Boudleaux Bryant, 13 February 1920, Shellman, Georgia, USA, d. 30 June 1987. With his wife Felice Bryant, he formed one of the greatest songwriting teams in country music and pop history. From a musical family, Boudleaux learned classical violin and piano from the age of five. During the early 30s his father organized a family band with Boudleaux and his four sisters and brothers, playing at county fairs in the Midwest. In 1937 Boudleaux moved to Atlanta, playing with the Atlanta Symphony Orchestra as well as jazz and country music groups. For several years he went on the road, playing in radio station bands in Detroit and Memphis before joining Hank Penny's Radio Cowboys, who performed over the airwaves of WSB Atlanta. In 1945 he met and married Felice Scaduto and the pair began composing together. The earliest recordings of Bryant songs included the Three Sons with 'Give Me Some Sugar, Sugar Baby, And I'll Be Your Sweetie Pie', but the first break came when they sent 'Country Boy' to Nashville publisher Fred Rose of Acuff-Rose. When this became a hit for Jimmy Dickens, the duo moved to Nashville as staff writers for Acuff-Rose. Among their numerous successes in the 50s were 'Have A Good Time' (a pop success for Tony Bennett in 1952), 'Hey Joe' (recorded by Carl Smith and Frankie Laine in 1953) and the Eddy Arnold hits 'I've Been Thinking' and 'The Richest Man' (1955). In 1957, Rose's son Wesley Rose commissioned the Bryants to switch to teenage material for the Everly Brothers. Beginning with 'Bye Bye Love', they supplied a stream of songs that were melodramatic vignettes of teen life. Several of them were composed by Boudleaux alone. These included the wistful 'All I Have To Do Is Dream', the tough and vengeful 'Bird Dog', 'Devoted To You' and 'Like Strangers'. At this time he wrote what has become his most recorded song, 'Love Hurts'. This sorrowful, almost self-pitying ballad has been a favourite with the country rock fraternity, through notable versions by Roy Orbison and Gram Parsons. There have also been less orthodox rock treatments by Jim Capaldi and Nazareth. From the early 60s, the Bryants returned to the country sphere, composing the country standard 'Rocky Top' as well as providing occasional hits for artists such as Sonny James ('Baltimore') and Roy Clark ('Come Live With Me'). Shortly before Boudleaux's death in June 1987, the Bryants were inducted into the Songwriters' Hall Of Fame.

● ALBUMS: *Boudleaux Bryant's Best Sellers* (Monument 1963)★★★, *All I Have To Do Is Dream* aka *A Touch Of Bryant* (CMH 1979)★★, *Surfin' On A New Wave* (1979)★★.

BRYANT, FELICE

b. Felice Scaduto, 7 August 1925, Milwaukee, Wisconsin, USA. The lyricist of some of the Everly Brothers' biggest hits, Felice Bryant was a member of one of the most famous husband-and-wife songwriting teams in pop and country music. Recordings of their 750 published songs have sold over 300 million copies in versions by over 400 artists as diverse as Bob Dylan and Lawrence Welk. Of Italian extraction, Felice was already writing lyrics when she met Boudleaux Bryant while working as an elevator attendant in a Milwaukee hotel. A violinist with Hank Penny's band, Boudleaux had composed instrumental pieces and after their marriage in 1945 the duo began to write together. The success of 'Country Boy' for Jimmy Dickens led them to Nashville where they were the first full-time songwriters and pluggers. During the 50s, the Bryants' country hits were often covered by pop artists such as Al Martino, Frankie Laine and Tony Bennett. Then, in 1957, they switched to composing teenage pop material for the Everly Brothers. Felice and Boudleaux proved to have a sharp eye for the details of teen life and among the hits they supplied to the close-harmony duo were 'Bye Bye Love', 'Wake Up Little Susie', 'Problems', 'Poor Jenny' and 'Take A Message To Mary'. They also composed 'Raining In My Heart' (for Buddy Holly) and the witty 'Let's Think About Livin'' (Bob Luman). After the rock 'n' roll era had subsided, the Bryants returned to the country scene, composing prolifically throughout the 60s and 70s in bluegrass and American Indian folk material. Their most enduring song from this period has been 'Rocky Top', a hymn of praise to the state of Tennessee. First recorded by the Osborne Brothers in 1969, it was adopted as a theme song by the University of Tennessee. In the late 70s, Felice and Boudleaux recorded their own compositions for the first time.

● ALBUMS: *A Touch Of Bryant* (CMH 1979)★★, *Surfin' On A New Wave* (1979)★★.

BRYANT, HOYT 'SLIM'

b. Thomas Hoyt Bryant, 7 December 1908, Atlanta, Georgia, USA. Both of Bryant's parents were musicians who sang, and with their encouragement, he soon began to play guitar. After completing his education, he worked in the electrical business and was a promising semi-professional baseball pitcher. In the late 20s, after guitar tuition from professional tutor Perry Bechtel, Bryant began to play local dances and shows with other musicians. A friendship with Clayton McMichen, a talented fiddle-playing member of the Skillet Lickers, led to the two playing on WSB Atlanta as the Georgia Wildcats. They later moved to WCKY Covington, where they worked with Riley Puckett as the Skillet Lickers. During the 30s, Bryant played on many stations and was featured on WRVA Richmond's *Old Dominion Barn Dance* and the *National Barn Dance* on WLS Chicago. He also worked on the latter with Jack Dunigan as Slim And Jack. In the late 30s, after McMichen left to pursue a solo career, Slim Bryant And His Wildcats continued as a popular act on many stations. In 1940, with a reputation as one of America's finest guitarists, he moved to KDKA Pittsburgh as a staff member. He remained there for 19 years appearing on radio, and later easily adapted to television, working with his band on KDKA-TV for 10 years. Between 1929 and 1959, he made recordings on several labels. The first were for OKeh as a member of McMichen's Harmony Boys and then for Columbia and Crown with McMichen's Georgia Wildcats. Early in August 1932, he played on nine of Jimmie Rodgers' RCA-Victor recordings and during the session, Rodgers recorded Bryant's song 'Mother, The Queen Of My Heart'. Rodgers was so impressed with Bryant's playing that he asked him to play on four more recordings in New York, which included Rodgers' very popular 'Miss The Mississippi And You'. Gene Autry recorded Bryant's song 'If You'll Let Me Be Your Sweetheart' in 1933. In 1937 and 1939, Bryant recorded for Decca, including 'I Wonder Who's Kissing Her Now' and his own song 'Yum Yum Blues' (later recorded by Red Foley). During the late 40s, recording as Slim Bryant And His Wildcats, he recorded for Majestic and MGM and also made 289 NBC Thesaurus Transcriptions, which were on the US radio networks. After receiving many requests from aspiring guitarists, Bryant built a small studio in Pittsburgh and gave guitar lessons. Some other recorded examples of Bryant's work appear on compilation albums of old-time bands.

BRYANT, JIMMY

b. 5 March 1925, Moultrie, Georgia, USA, d. 22 September 1980, Moultrie, Georgia, USA. Bryant grew up on the road, playing fiddle or guitar behind his fiddle-playing father. In 1941, he joined the army and was wounded on active service. Finding little work for a fiddle player, he began paying more attention to the guitar, playing country but becoming more interested in the fast jazz styles of Tony Mottola, a fellow soldier. When discharged, he used his release pay to buy an electric guitar and amplifier and began to play with a small group in Moultrie. In 1948, he moved to Los Angeles, where he found radio work, soon becoming the lead guitarist with Cliffie Stone's band on the Hometown Jamboree. He was also soon in great demand as a session guitarist. During the time he spent with Capitol Records, he recorded with country artists such as Roy Rogers, Tennessee Ernie Ford and Tex Williams, and many non-country stars including Bing Crosby, Kay Starr and Stan Kenton, and in later years, he even recorded with the Monkees. Bryant once estimated that between 1955 and 1956, he recorded with 124 different artists. Steel guitarist Speedy West, who had previously played western swing with Spade Cooley and Hank Penny was also a member of Stone's band. West was a dazzling and versatile musician whose playing was the perfect match for Bryant's extraordinary, rapid guitarwork, prompting Stone to dub them 'the Flaming Guitars'. They subsequently appeared together on many recordings, and in 1954, they recorded an album together that has become rated as a classic. In 1967, Bryant recorded a guitar tutor album, complete with instruction book, although it is doubtful that any purchaser came even remotely near the tutor's brilliance. In 1973 he recorded with the legendary steel guitarist Noel Boggs. He moved to Nashville in the mid-70s, working for Hohner Guitars, and in 1976 he was reunited with West, although the recordings they made were never released. In 1979 Bryant, a heavy smoker, was found to have lung cancer and he returned to Los Angeles, even playing at a benefit concert organized for him. Soon afterwards, his health worsening, he moved back to Moultrie, where he died in September 1980. Legendary jazz guitarist Barney Kessel once said, 'of all the guitar players I have known, Jimmy

Bryant is the fastest and the cleanest, and has more technique than any other'. Bryant, who was an inspiration for England's guitar great Albert Lee, owned the first Fender Broadcaster guitar, which carried his name and the serial number 1.
● ALBUMS: with Speedy West *Two Guitars Country Style* 10-inch album (Capitol 1954)★★★, *Country Cabin Jazz* (Capitol 1960)★★★, *Bryant's Back In Town* (Imperial 1966)★★★, *Laughing Guitar, Crying Guitar* (Imperial 1966)★★★, *We Are Young* (Imperial 1966)★★★, *The Fastest Guitar In The Country* (Imperial 1967)★★, *Play Country Guitar With Jimmy Bryant* (Dolton 1967)★★.
● COMPILATIONS: *Guitar Take-Off* (See For Miles 1989)★★★, with West *Flamin' Guitars* 4-CD box set (Bear Family 1997)★★★★.

BUCHANAN, COLIN

b. 1964, Dublin, Eire. Buchanan's family emigrated to Australia in 1970 and settled in Peakhurst, a southern suburb of Sydney. In the mid-80s Buchanan worked in an outback Christian community and then undertook rural labouring jobs. He was discovered by the Flying Emus and signed to ABC Country, a division of EMI Records. He received acclaim as an outstanding singer-songwriter for *Galahs In The Gidgee* and his stature has increased with subsequent albums. *Hard Times* is about the problems experienced by Australian farmers and *The Measure Of A Man* paints portraits of Australian life. Buchanan has also written for Australian country stars Tania and Lee Kernaghan.
● ALBUMS: all Australian releases *Galahs In The Gidgee* (ABC Country 1990)★★★★, *Hard Times* (ABC Country 1992)★★★, *I Want My Mummy* (ABC Country 1993)★★, *The Measure Of A Man* (ABC Country 1994)★★★★, with Greg Champion *Aussie Christmas With Bucko And Champs* (ABC Country 1995)★★★.

BUCKNER, RICHARD

b. 1964, Fresno, California, USA. An earnest country singer-songwriter in the tradition of Guy Clark or Townes Van Zandt, Buckner first began playing music during his college years in Chico, California. He was a member of several punk and alternative groups during the 80s, before electing to concentrate on his own songs by the turn of the decade - at which time he spent several months playing acoustic sets as a busker in Atlanta. Buckner made his debut for the Texas independent Dejadisc Records in 1994 with *Bloomed*. Its release was supported by tours along America's west coast and acclaimed performances at acoustic clubs around his San Francisco Bay Area base. As well as cementing his live popularity, the album alerted the media to his existence, the press categorizing him in the alternative country tradition of artists such as Vic Chesnutt. As a consequence he was offered a major label contract with MCA Records. *Devotion + Doubt* was his major label debut in 1997, and featured Joey Burns and John Convertino of Giant Sand. The album's evocative, earthy tones were masterminded by producer J.D. Foster. Buckner explained its title thus: 'The title of the album is a little bit ironic, but it's also very appropriate. See, my whole theory of life is based in doubt. For me, music is always about 2 per cent devotion and 98 per cent doubt.'
● ALBUMS: *Bloomed* (Dejadisc 1994)★★, *Devotion + Doubt* (MCA 1997)★★★.

BUFFALO CLUB

A US trio working in the country rock idiom, Buffalo Club's close harmonies were initially compared to those of Restless Heart - unsurprisingly, given that the group includes their long-standing drummer John Dittrich. The other members are vocalist Ron Hemby, formerly a member of the Christian vocal group the Imperials, and Charlie Kelley, a guitarist who had formerly worked with Doug Stone and Tom Wopat. Hemby had originally met Dittrich when he invited him to consider writing for Restless Heart. When that group disbanded, they decided to put their collaboration on a permanent footing. The group was finalized when they recruited Kelley and signed with manager Dan Goodman. He played a tape to Rising Tide Records president Ken Levitan to secure the group a recording contract. However, Rising Tide were unimpressed by their original choice of name, Johnny Ringo, and persuaded the group to change to Buffalo Club. The group's self-titled debut album followed in March 1997. Produced by Barry Beckett and promoted by the successful single 'If She Don't Love You', critical reaction saw the group compared to the 70s country rock sound of the Eagles.
● ALBUMS: *Buffalo Club* (Rising Tide 1997)★★★.

BUFFALO GALS

The band comprised Susie Monick (b. 1952; banjo), Carol Siegel (mandolin, dulcimer), Martha Trachtenberg (guitar, vocals), Sue Raines (fiddle) and Nancy Josephson (bass). They started when three undergraduates at Syracuse University - Monick, Siegel and guitarist Debby Gabriel - formed an old-time bluegrass trio. Gabriel left to concentrate on art and Trachtenberg and Josephson were recruited. By 1974 Raines was in the line-up and the group was playing clubs and festivals. The band moved to Nashville in 1976 and Siegel and Raines were replaced by Lainie Lyle and Kristin Wilkinson, respectively. Monick released a solo album, *Melting Pot*, and the band folded in 1979. In the 90s, Monick played mandolin and accordion for Richard Dobson's band State Of The Heart.

BUFFETT, JIMMY

b. 25 December 1946, Pascogoula, Mississippi, USA, but raised in Mobile, Alabama. Country rock singer Buffett describes his songs as '90 per cent autobiographical', a statement attested to by his narratives of wine, women and song. He is 'the son of the son of a sailor', and he describes his grandfather's life in 'The Captain And The Kid'. His father was a naval architect, who often took Buffett on sailing trips. Buffett studied journalism at the University of Southern California, and described those years and his urge to perform in 'Migration'. Working as the Nashville correspondent for *Billboard* magazine, he built up the contacts that led to his first albums on Barnaby Records. The albums were not well produced and the best song was one he re-recorded, 'In The Shelter'. On a train journey, he and Jerry Jeff Walker wrote the poignant 'Railroad Lady', which has been recorded by Lefty Frizzell and Merle Haggard. Buffett settled in Key West and although initially involved in smuggling, he changed his ways when offered $25,000 to make an album for ABC Records. He went to Nashville, recorded *A White Sport Coat And A Pink Crustacean* for $10,000 and bought a boat with the remainder. The album included several story-songs about misdemeanours ('The Great Filling Station Holdup',

'Peanut Butter Conspiracy'), together with the lazy feel of 'He Went To Paris', which was recorded by Waylon Jennings. His humorous 'Why Don't We Get Drunk And Screw?' was written under the pseudonym of Marvin Gardens, who made imaginary appearances at Buffett's one-man concerts. *Living And Dying In 3/4 Time* included his US Top 30 hit 'Come Monday'. Its ban in the UK by the BBC because of a reference to Hush Puppies shoes led to a shrewd Jonathan King cover version, referring to tennis shoes instead. Buffett's 1974 album, *A1A*, was named after the access road to the beach in Florida, and he commented, 'I never planned to make a whole series of albums about Key West. It was a natural process.' Buffett wrote the music for a film about cattle rustlers, *Rancho Deluxe*, scripted by Buffett's brother-in-law Tom McGuane. McGuane described Buffett's music as lying 'at the curious hinterland where Hank Williams and Xavier Cugat meet', and Buffett was the first person to consistently bring Caribbean rhythms to Nashville (David Allan Coe, who recorded an attack on him called 'Jimmy Buffett', nevertheless copied his style).

In 1975, Buffett formed the Coral Reefer Band and their first album together, *Havana Daydreaming*, included a song about the boredom of touring: 'This Hotel Room'. His next album, arguably his best, *Changes In Latitudes, Changes In Attitudes*, included the million-selling single 'Margaritaville'. A bitter verse about 'old men in tank tops' was initially omitted, but was included on Buffett's irrepressible concert album, *You Had To Be There*. Buffett reached the US Top 10 with *Son Of A Son Of A Sailor*, which included 'Cheeseburger In Paradise', a US pop hit, and 'Livingston Saturday Night', which was featured in the film *FM*. Buffett continued to record prolifically, moving over to contemporary rock sounds, but his songs began to lack sparkle. The best tracks on two of his albums were remakes of standards, 'Stars Fell On Alabama' and 'On A Slow Boat To China'. His *Hot Water* album included guest appearances by Rita Coolidge, the Neville Brothers, James Taylor and Steve Winwood, but it failed to restore him to the charts. Buffett is a major concert attraction, especially in Florida where he addresses his fans as 'Parrotheads'. Indeed, the magnificent 72-track, 4-CD box set *Boats Beaches, Bars And Ballads*, includes the Parrothead Handbook. *Fruitcakes* included two hilarious tracks, 'Everybody's Got A Cousin In Miama' and 'Fruitcakes' itself. The excessive length of both tracks (over seven minutes each) indicated that Buffett was ignoring potential radio and video play and merely playing for his fans. His songs continue to reflect his Key West lifestyle and to quote 'He Went To Paris': 'Some of it's tragic and some of it's magic, but I had a good life all the way.'
● ALBUMS: *Down To Earth* (Barnaby 1970)★★, *A White Sport Coat And A Pink Crustacean* (ABC 1973)★★★, *Living And Dying In 3/4 Time* (ABC 1974)★★, *A1A* (ABC 1974)★★★, *Rancho DeLuxe* film soundtrack (United Artists 1975)★★★, *Havana Daydreaming* (ABC 1976)★★★, *High Cumberland Jubilee* recorded 1972 (Barnaby 1976)★★★, *Changes In Latitudes, Changes In Attitudes* (ABC 1977)★★★, *Son Of A Son Of A Sailor* (ABC 1978)★★★, *You Had To Be There* (ABC 1978)★★★, *Volcano* (MCA 1979)★★★, *Coconut Telegraph* (MCA 1981)★★, *Somewhere Over China* (MCA 1982)★★, *Fast Times At Ridgemont High* (Full Moon/Asylum 1982)★★, *One Particular Harbour* (MCA 1983)★★, *Riddles In The Sand* (MCA 1984)★★, *Last Mango*

In Paris (MCA 1985)★★, *Floridays* (MCA 1986)★★, *Hot Water* (MCA 1988)★★, *Off To See The Lizard* (MCA 1989)★★, *Always* film soundtrack (MCA 1990)★★, *Live Feeding Frenzy* (MCA 1990)★★, *Before The Beach* reissue of Barnaby material (Margaritaville/MCA 1993)★★, *Fruitcakes* (MCA 1994)★★★★, *Barometer Soup* (Margaritaville 1995)★★★★, *Banana Wind* (Margaritaville 1996)★★★★, *Christmas Island* (Margaritaville 1996)★★★.
● COMPILATIONS: *Songs You Know By Heart - Greatest Hits* box set (MCA 1985)★★★★, *Boats Beaches, Bars And Ballads* 4-CD box set (MCA 1992)★★★★, *All The Great Hits* (Prism Leisure 1994)★★★.
● FURTHER READING: *The Jimmy Buffett Scrapbook*, Mark Humphrey with Harris Lewine. *The Man From Margaritaville Revisited*, Steve Eng.

BURGESS, SONNY

b. Albert Burgess, 28 May 1931, Newport, Arkansas, USA. As a child Burgess earned the name 'Sonny' as a result of his father also being called Albert. Inspired by the *Grand Ole Opry* show transmitted over WSM's airwaves, he set about learning to play a catalogue-purchased guitar. He joined his first country band while at high school, eventually moving from the role of supporting guitarist to lead the band. After graduation, Burgess joined the backing band of local singer Fred Waner (later a successful solo singer as Freddie Hart), along with Johnny Ray Hubbard (bass) and Gerald Jackson (drums) who had been with his high school group. Military service in Germany then intervened, but Burgess still found an opportunity to perform, eventually forming a band that successfully auditioned for the overseas forces' version of the *Grand Ole Opry*. Returning to Arkansas after his discharge in 1953, he found work at a box factory but also formed a new group, the Moonlighters, with Hubbard, Kern Kennedy and Russ Smith. After their first handful of performances at local venues the young mandolin player Joe Lewis also joined. Although their original sound was up-tempo country, the rise of Elvis Presley in the mid-50s soon led them to incorporate many of his best-known songs into their set. In 1955 the Moonlighters supported Presley at Newport's Silver Moon club. Jack Nance then joined the group in time for its name change to the Pacers. Finally, in May 1956, Burgess decided it was time to record the band, journeying to Sun Studios in Memphis to audition for Sam Phillips. 'Red Headed Woman'/'We Wanna Boogie' duly became their first single release for Sun Records, selling a respectable 90,000 copies, its popularity spreading outside of the local community. Their first major tour of the Midwest followed, before the Pacers took an engagement as Roy Orbison's backing band. Their second single, 'Restless'/'Ain't Got A Thing', followed in January 1957. Shortly afterwards, they slimmed to a trio when Lewis left to join Conway Twitty and Smith departed for Jerry Lee Lewis's band. Further singles, including 'One Broken Heart' and 'Ain't Gonna Do It', followed, as did touring engagements with Orbison. The Pacers continued to release singles, including 'My Bucket's Got A Hole In It', but were unable to secure that elusive hit. The line-up also shifted again. The 1958 model of the band saw Burgess supported by J.C. Caughron (guitar), Bobby Crafford (drums) and Kern Kennedy on piano. Further recording sessions took place, resulting in the release of several singles including 'Oh Mama!', 'What'cha

Gonna Do' and 'One Night'. Burgess later cited the recording of the latter song as the main inspiration behind Presley's version - certainly the similarities between their respective interpretations are remarkable. However, by the end of 1957 the Pacers were out of contract with Sun, and the group had to content itself with touring commitments. A final single, 'Sadie's Back In Town', was released on Sam Phillips' Phillips International, after which the Pacers broke up. Burgess remained in the music business with a new, but largely unrecorded group, Kings IV, until 1970, at which time he returned home to Newport. Between 1974 and 1986 he stayed away from the music business, preferring to work as a travelling salesman. Renewed interest in the 90s led to Rounder Records signing him and in 1996 a remarkably fresh-sounding Burgess was heard on *Sonny Burgess* (subtitled *has still got it*). An excellent choice of tracks included 'Bigger Than Elvis' and Bruce Springsteen's 'Tiger Rose'. His vital contributions to both the development of rockabilly and the Sun Records' story offers a testimony to his status denied him in simple chart placings. It would appear that recognition is coming 40 years too late.
● ALBUMS: *We Wanna Boogie* (Rounder 1990)★★★, with Dave Alvin *Tennessee Border* (Hightone 1992)★★★, *Sonny Burgess* (Rounder 1996)★★★.
● COMPILATIONS: *The Classic Recordings 1956-1959* (Bear Family 1991)★★★, *The Arkansas Wild Man* 1956-1960 recordings (Charly 1995)★★★★.

BURGESS, WILMA

b. Wilma Charlene Burgess, 11 June 1939, Orlando, Florida, USA. After high school, Burgess attended Stetson University, Orlando, to study for a degree in physical education and had no thoughts of a career in music. She was initially only interested in pop music but a visit to an Eddy Arnold concert changed her mind. After graduation in 1960, she was persuaded by a friend to go to Nashville to sing some demos of his songs. Owen Bradley was impressed with her voice and promptly signed her to Decca. Between 1965 and 1969, primarily specializing in big ballads, she had Top 20 US country chart hits with 'Baby', 'Don't Touch Me', 'Misty Blue' and 'Tear Time'. In 1973, she left Decca and joined Shannon (owned by Jim Reeves Enterprises), where she managed some minor hits, including a Top 20 duet with Bud Logan (one time leader of Reeves' band, the Blue Boys) on 'Wake Me Into Love'. Her last chart hit was in 1975. She recorded for RCA Records until 1978 but little has been heard of her in recent years.
● ALBUMS: *Don't Touch Me* (Decca 1966)★★★, *Wilma Burgess Sings Misty Blue* (Decca 1967)★★★, *Tear Time* (Decca 1967)★★★, *Tender Loving Country Sound* (Decca 1968)★★, *Parting Is Such Sweet Sorrow* (Decca 1969)★★★, with Bud Logan *Walk Me Into Love* (Shannon 1974)★★.

BURNETTE, BILLY

b. 8 May 1953, Memphis, Tennessee, USA. Burnette was the son of country rock artist Dorsey Burnette, the nephew of rock singer Johnny Burnette, and the cousin of Rocky Burnette. With his family background and frequent visitors such as Elvis Presley and Gene Vincent dropping in to his home, Burnette was drawn to a musical career at a young age, and recorded his first single at the age of seven. He continued to do so until the age of 17, when he began performing as a session guitarist and songwriter in Nashville. He worked on the road with Brenda Lee and Roger Miller and had his songs recorded by Conway Twitty and Loretta Lynn, Charlie Rich, Glen Campbell and the Everly Brothers. Burnette recorded his first album under his own name in 1972, deliberately avoiding the rockabilly and 50s influences of his upbringing. He finally paid tribute to his heritage on a self-titled album in 1980. *Try Me* included collaborations with two members of Fleetwood Mac, Mick Fleetwood and Christine McVie. That led to an offer to tour with another band Fleetwood put together in 1984, Mick Fleetwood's Zoo, and ultimately to a regular spot with Fleetwood Mac in 1987, as one of two musicians to replace the departing Lindsey Buckingham. He was featured on the highly successful *Tango In The Night* and *Behind The Mask* as well as the forgettable *Time* in 1995.

● ALBUMS: *Billy Burnette* (1972)★★★, *Billy Burnette* ii (1979)★★, *Between Friends* (1979)★★, *Billy Burnette* iii (1980)★★, *Gimme You* (1981)★★, *Try Me* (1985)★★, *Coming Home* (1993)★★.

BURNETTE, DORSEY

b. 28 December 1932, Memphis, Tennessee, USA, d. 19 August 1979. He was a member of a classic 50s rock 'n' roll act, had his own hit soloist act in the 60s and became a country singer in the 70s. He helped to form the highly respected Johnny Burnette Trio with younger brother Johnny in 1953. After appearing in the film *Rock, Rock, Rock* in 1956, Dorsey left the trio. He recorded with Johnny as The Texans (on Infinity and Jox) and wrote major hits for Ricky Nelson, including 'It's Late' and 'Waitin' In School'. As a soloist, he recorded for Abbott, Cee-Jan, and then Era, where he had his two biggest solo hits, 'Tall Oak Tree' and 'Hey Little One', in 1960, both classics of their kind and both showcasing his deep, rich, country-style voice. He then recorded without luck on Lama, Dot, Imperial, Reprise, Mel-O-Day, Condor, Liberty, Merri, Happy Tiger, Music Factory, Smash (where he re-recorded 'Tall Oak Tree'), Mercury and Hickory. In the 70s he had 15 Top 100 country hits (none making the Top 20) on Capitol, Melodyland, Calliope and Elektra, with whom he had only recently signed when he died of a heart attack in August 1979. His son Billy Burnette is also a recording artist.

● ALBUMS: *Tall Oak Tree* (Era 1960)★★, *Dorsey Burnette Sings* (Dot 1963)★★, *Dorsey Burnette's Greatest Hits* (Era 1969)★★★, *Things I Treasure* (Calliope 70s)★★.

● COMPILATIONS: *Great Shakin' Fever* (Bear Family 1992)★★★.

BURNETTE, LEGENDARY HANK C.

b. Sven Ake Hogberg, Sweden. Burnette is a multi-instrumentalist who plays and sings all parts on his records, which he also engineers, arranges and produces. He recreates the echo-laden rockabilly records of the late 50s and alternates between his own compositions and familiar titles ('Peggy Sue', 'Boppin' The Blues', 'Red Cadillac And A Black Moustache'). His own wild instrumental, 'Spinning Rock Boogie', closely based on 'A Wonderful Time Up There', was a UK Top 30 hit in 1976.

● ALBUMS: *Don't Mess With My Ducktail* (1976)★★★, *Rockabilly Gasseroonie* (1977)★★, *Hot Licks And Fancy Tricks* (1979)★★, *I've Got Rock* (1983)★★★.

BURNETTE, SMILEY

b. Lester Alvin Burnette, 18 March 1911, Summum, Illinois, USA, d. 16 February 1967, Encino, California, USA. Although making his name as the cowboy star's 'sidekick', Burnette was a talented musician, who played over 50 musical instruments, ranging from harmonica to organ, proficiently (he could also play basic tunes on 50 more, some being of his own invention). He had his own band at Astoria High School, and in the early 30s, he performed a one-man vaudeville act and worked on the WDZ Tuscola radio station. In 1933, he played accordion on WLS Chicago's *National Barn Dance* with Gene Autry and moved to Hollywood with Autry the following year. He first appeared with Autry in *In Old Santa Fe*, which starred Ken Maynard, before appearing with Autry in the *Phantom Empire* series. He went on (with his horse, Nellie) to appear in over 80 B-movie westerns with Autry (as Frog Millhouse), seven with Roy Rogers (including Rogers' first starring role) and over 50 with Charles Starrett. After *Last Of The Pony Riders*, in 1953 (Autry's last B-movie western), he retired to concentrate on songwriting. Many of over 400 songs that he wrote during his career were used in films, including the cowboy standard 'Ridin' Down The Canyon', which Autry first popularized in the 1934 film *Tumbling Tumbleweeds*. He made four recordings for Decca, in Los Angeles, in December 1938 and later recorded for ARA, Bullet and his own Rancho Records label, as well as publishing songbooks of cowboy songs. Burnette's comic and musical abilities saw him become the first B-movie western 'sidekick' to actually be voted onto the annual list of Top 10 cowboy stars. First elected to the list in 1940, he held the distinction of being voted in for 12 consecutive years. It is reported that in his later years, he donated most of his earnings to charities helping children. In 1964, he appeared on television, being particularly successful as the engineer in the comedy series *Petticoat Junction*. He died of leukaemia in February 1967.

BURNIN' DAYLIGHT

A trio of Marc Beeson, Sonny LeMaire and Kurt Howell, Burnin' Daylight are a Nashville, Tennessee, USA-based country act who have jokingly referred to themselves as 'the oldest baby act in the business'. Prior to forming the group, all three members could boast of extensive previous experience. LeMaire was formerly a member of Exile, writing many of that group's hits, including 'Give Me One More Chance'. He spent a total of 16 years with the group, which finally dissolved in 1993. Howell had spent a period of seven years as a member of Southern Pacific before going solo - amassing three alternative country radio hits in the process. Beeson, the group's lead singer, had made his name as a songwriter - his material having been performed by Restless Heart, Martina McBride, Peter Cetera, Linda Davis and Steve Wariner. He, too, enjoyed a brief solo career - though after just one single for BNA Records his projected solo debut was pulled from the schedules. After forming the trio, their original choice of name, the Loose Cannons, had to be abandoned when it was discovered that there was another group with a similar name. At that time the group also included Trey Bruce and Rob Crosby. However, the former elected to continue his career in production, while Crosby signed a solo contract with River North Records. Initially, it was intended that the group would be a live vehicle only, but when a tape was passed to Curb Records founder Mike Curb, he invited the group to record their 'dream album'. Burnin' Daylight opened its account with the release of 'Love Worth Fighting For', a minor country radio hit, prefacing a self-titled debut album that also received encouraging reviews.

● ALBUMS: *Burnin' Daylight* (Curb 1997)★★★.

BURTON, JAMES

b. 21 August 1939, Shreveport, Louisiana, USA. One of the most distinguished of rock and country rock guitar players, Burton toured and recorded with Ricky Nelson, Elvis Presley and numerous other artists. His first recording was the highly influential 'Suzie Q', sung by Dale Hawkins in 1957. Burton also performed with country singer Bob Luman before moving to Los Angeles where he was hired to work with Nelson, then the latest teen sensation. For six years he toured and recorded with Nelson, perfecting a guitar sound known as 'chicken pickin''. This was achieved by damping the strings for staccato-sounding single-string riffs and solos. Among the best examples of this style are 'Hello Mary Lou', 'Never Be Anyone Else But You' and the more frantic, rock-abilly-flavoured 'Believe What You Say'. During the late 60s and early 70s, Burton was much in demand as a session guitarist, working with Dale Hawkins on a comeback album as well as various artists including Buffalo Springfield, Judy Collins, John Phillips, Joni Mitchell, Michael Nesmith and Longbranch Pennywhistle, a group featuring future Eagles member Glenn Frey. Burton also played dobro on albums by P.F. Sloan and John Stewart. In addition, Burton's powerful, rockabilly-influenced guitarwork made a major contribution to the harsher country sound developed at this time by Merle Haggard. Burton made two albums of his own during these years, one in collaboration with steel guitarist Ralph Mooney.

During the 70s, Burton's work took him in contrasting directions. With pianist Glen D. Hardin (a former Crickets member), he was a mainstay of Elvis Presley's touring and recording band from 1969-77, but he also played a leading role in the growing trend towards country/rock fusion. Burton's most significant performances in this respect came on the albums of Gram Parsons. After Parsons' death, Burton and Hardin toured with Emmylou Harris and backed her on several solo albums. More recently he has toured with Jerry Lee Lewis. As a session guitarist, Burton played on albums by Jesse Winchester, Ronnie Hawkins, Rodney Crowell, Phil Everly, J.J. Cale and Nicolette Larson. As a result of an accident in 1995, Burton lost the use of his hands and has been receiving treatment to enable him to play the guitar again. He had no medical insurance and faced bankruptcy after financing his own treatment. A fund has been set up to help him and benefit concerts are being held.

● ALBUMS: with Ralph Mooney *Corn Pickin' And Slick Slidin'* (Capitol 1969)★★, *The Guitar Sounds Of James Burton* (A&M 1971)★★.

BUSH, JOHNNY

b. John Bush Shinn III, 17 February 1935, Houston, Texas, USA. Bush sang and played guitar as an adolescent. He moved to San Antonio, Texas, in 1962 and was resident at the Texas Star Inn. He became a drummer and worked with Willie Nelson. Nelson, and then Bush, moved to Ray Price's band but Bush had no luck in developing a solo career. He eventually became the leader of Willie Nelson's band, the Record Men, and had solo successes with 'You Ought To Hear Me Cry' and 'What A Way To Love' in 1967. Further US country hits followed with 'Undo The Right' and Marty Robbins' classic song 'You Gave Me A Mountain', before moving to RCA and the biggest single of his career with Willie Nelson's 'Whiskey River'. He became known as the 'Country Caruso'. In 1975 Bush contracted cancer of the throat and it was thought that he may not sing again. In 1982 he and Willie Nelson reunited for a slow-paced album of vintage country songs that also included Paul Simon's 'Still Crazy After All These Years'. Bush is only able to sing for a few numbers at a time, but he still performs regularly. *Time Changes Everything*, on which Bush was backed by a thirteen piece band, was recorded at Nelson's Pedernales studio.

● ALBUMS: *Sound Of A Heartache* (Stop 1968)★★★, *Undo The Right* (Stop 1968)★★, *You Gave Me A Mountain* (Stop 1969)★★★, *Johnny Bush* (Stop 1970)★★, *Bush Country* (Stop 1972)★★★, *Here's Johnny Bush* (Starday 1972)★★★, *Texas Dance Hall Girl* (RCA Victor 1973)★★★, *Here Comes The World Again* (RCA Victor 1973)★★★, *Whiskey River/There Stands The Glass* (RCA Victor 1973)★★★, *Live From Texas* (1982)★★★, with Willie Nelson *Together Again* (1982)★★★, with Darrell McCall *Hot Texas Country* (1986)★★★, *Time Changes Everything* (1994)★★★.

● COMPILATIONS: *The Best Of Johnny Bush* (Million 1972)★★★, *Greatest Hits 1968-1972* (GH 1993)★★★★, *Greatest Hits* (RCA 1994)★★★★.

BUTLER, CARL AND PEARL

b. Carl Roberts Butler, 2 June 1927, Knoxville, Tennessee, USA, d. 4 September 1992, Franklin, Tennessee, USA. Butler was playing the guitar and singing at the age of 12 and writing songs and playing local clubs by the time he left high school. He saw military service in Europe and North Africa from 1944-46. After discharge, he formed the Lonesome Pine Boys and during the late 40s, was featured on radio stations in Knoxville and Raleigh. He made his debut on the *Grand Ole Opry* in 1948 and by the early 50s, was also appearing regularly on television in Knoxville. In 1951, his songwriting abilities received a boost when 'If Teardrops Were Pennies' became a US Top 10 country hit for Carl Smith (a feat repeated 22 years later by Porter Wagoner and Dolly Parton). He made his own recording debut with Capitol in 1951 but moved to Columbia in 1953. He had minor success with such songs as 'Angel Band', 'River Of Tears' and his own version of 'If Teardrops Were Pennies'; he also often sang gospel material. During the 50s, with his powerful voice and honky-tonk style of music, he established a considerable reputation as a solo artist and in 1961, he gained his first US country chart hit with 'Honky Tonkitis'. However, in 1962, he decided to work as a duo with his wife. He had married Pearl Dee Jones (b. 20 September 1930, Nashville, Tennessee, USA, d. 3 March 1988) when he was just beginning his career but she had previously only sung with Carl at family functions. The partnership immediately proved successful, when their recording of 'Don't Let Me Cross Over' stayed at number 1 in the US country charts for 11 weeks. During the 60s, they appeared regularly on the *Opry* and had further Top 20 hits with 'Loving Arms', 'Too Late To Try Again' and 'I'm Hanging Up The Phone'. In 1967, they appeared in the film *Second Fiddle To A Steel Guitar*. The same year, as active members of the Salvation Army, they recorded their popular *Avenue Of Prayer* gospel album as a tribute to the Bailes Brothers. Carl Butler co-wrote some songs with Earl Scruggs, including 'Crying My Heart Out Over You'. It was initially a hit for Flatt And Scruggs in 1960 but became a number 1 country hit for Ricky Skaggs in 1982. Their last chart hit was in 1969 with 'We'll Sweep Out The Ashes In The Morning', but they recorded for Columbia until 1971 and later for Chart, CMH and Pedaca. Their sound was not technically harmony singing, since Carl's vocals were always totally dominant; Pearl merely sang in the background and never took solos. However, the public interest in their style and their recording successes undoubtedly led to the later appearances of male-female harmony duos such as Wagoner-Parton, Conway Twitty-Loretta Lynn and others. Carl Butler was greatly influenced, as a boy, by Roy Acuff, and this always showed in his emotional and loud style of singing. He also became noted for his gaudy western-style Nudie costumes. They continued to tour during the 70s and 80s and made some appearances on the *Opry* and on the *Midnight Jamboree* from Ernest Tubb's Record Shop. Pearl Butler died of thyroid complications on 3 March 1988. Carl began to restrict his appearances but did briefly sing with Nancy Anne. They recorded a single but it failed and the partnership ended. Carl never recovered from the loss of Pearl and eventually drifted into obscurity. He died at his home on 4 September 1992, following a heart attack, and was buried beside Pearl in the Williamson Memorial Gardens. Fellow country stars George Jones, Carl Smith, Jack Greene, Marty Stuart and Ricky Skaggs were among the pallbearers for one of country music's greatest honky tonk singers.

● ALBUMS: as Carl Butler *Don't Let Me Cross Over* (Columbia 1963)★★★, *The Great Carl Butler Sings* (Harmony 1966)★★★, *For The First Time* (Harmony 1971)★★; as Carl And Pearl Butler *Loving Arms* (Columbia 1964)★★★, *The Old And The New* (Columbia 1965)★★★, *Avenue Of Prayer* (Columbia 1967)★★, *Our Country World* (Columbia 1968)★★★, *Honky Tonkin'* (Columbia 1969)★★★, *Watch And Play* (Harmony 1972)★★★, *Temptation Keeps Twistin' Her Arm* (Chart 1972)★★, *Honky-Tonkitis* (1980)★★★, *Country We Love* (1980)★★★.

● COMPILATIONS: *Carl And Pearl Butler's Greatest Hits* (Columbia 1970)★★★★, *Crying My Heart Out Over You* (1993)★★★.

BYRD, JERRY

b. 9 March 1920, Lima, Ohio, USA. One of country music's greatest steel guitarists, he first appeared on local radio in 1935. During the late 30s, he was featured on WLW Cincinnati's *Mid-Western Hayride* and the *Renfro Valley Barn Dance*. In 1945, after a spell in Detroit, he moved to Nashville and worked on the *Grand Ole Opry*, where he played with both Ernest Tubb and Red Foley and also recorded several songs including 'Lovesick Blues', 'Mansion On The Hill' and 'I'm So Lonesome I Could Cry' with Hank Williams. He rejoined WLW and the *Mid-Western Hayride* in 1948 but in 1951, he returned to Nashville and worked with many artists including George Morgan. He first recorded as a solo artist for Mercury in 1949 but later recorded for Decca, RCA, and Monument. He wrote and recorded 'Steeling The Blues', 'Steeling The Chimes' and 'Byrd's Boogie'. Originally attracted to the instrument by Hawaiian guitarists such as Sol Hoopi, Byrd has been the influence for many of the modern steel guitar players. He always refused to play any steel guitar fitted with pedals, which he believed took away the instrument's real identity. Between 1964 and 1968, he led the band on Bobby Lord's television show. In the early 70s, after many years of playing and working there, he tired of the Nashville scene and retired to Hawaii, where he worked as a steel guitar teacher.

● ALBUMS: *On The Shores Of Waikiki* (1951)★★★, *Nani Hawaii (with Kuanna Islanders)* (Mercury 1953)★★★, *Hawaiian Beach Party* (1954★★, *Guitar Magic* (Mercury 1954)★★★, *Byrd's Expedition* (Mercury 1954)★★★, *Hi-Fi Guitar* (Decca 1958)★★★★, *Steel Guitar Favorites* (1958)★★★, *Byrd Of Paradise* (Monument 1961)★★★, *Memories Of Maria* (Monument 1962)★★★, *Blue Hawaiian Steel Guitar* (Mercury 1963)★★★, *Man Of Steel* (Mercury 1964)★★★★, *Satin Strings Of Steel* (1965)★★★, *Admirable Byrd* (1966)★★, *Potpourri* (1966)★★, *Country Steel Guitar Greats* (Mercury 1966)★★★, *Burnin' Sands, Pearly Shells And Steel Guitars* (1967)★★★, *Polynesian Suite* (1969)★★, *Sound Hawaiian* (1977)★★.

BYRD, TRACY

b. 18 December 1966, Vidor, Texas, USA. Country singer Byrd paid $8 to sing Hank Williams' 'Your Cheatin' Heart' over a pre-recorded backing track in a shopping mall. The store manageress was so impressed by Byrd's voice that she booked him for a talent show. On that show he sang 'Weary Blues' and 'Folsom Prison Blues'. He began a residency with Mark Chestnutt, at a local club Cutters and when Chestnutt began to have some chart success, Byrd formed his own band and took over the residency. He signed with MCA Records in 1992 and had to wait a year before he fitted in with their release schedule. Byrd's first records were honky tonk in the George Strait mould, but he has gradually found his own voice, starting with a remake of Johnny Paycheck's 'Someone To Give My Love To' in 1993. His major breakthrough came with the number 1 country hit 'Holdin' Heaven'. He further established himself with 'Why Don't The Telephone Ring' the same year. *No Ordinary Man* consolidated the success and *Love Lessons* in 1995 was well received. Further hit singles came with 'Watermelon Crawl' and 'Love Lessons', as Byrd attempted (alongside the likes of fellow Beaumont singer Clay Walker) to become a giant of new country in the 90s. *Big Love* was another reliable album, but showed no signs of any musical progress.

● ALBUMS: *Tracy Byrd* (MCA 1993)★★★, *No Ordinary Man* (MCA 1994)★★★★, *Love Lessons* (MCA 1995)★★★, *Big Love* (MCA 1996)★★★.

● VIDEOS: *Keeper Of The Stars* (MCA 1995).

C

CACTUS BROTHERS

Highly arresting and energetic Nashville band the Cactus Brothers formed in the late 80s as a spin-off from rock band Walk The West, who released one album on Capitol in 1986. Former members Paul Kirby (lead vocals, guitar, harmonica), Will Golemon (guitar, banjo, backing vocals), John Golemon (bass) and Richard Ice (drums) were joined by Tramp (fiddle, mandolin, guitars, backing vocals) shortly afterwards, while Dave Kennedy took over on drums. By 1991 Walk The West were no longer a going concern, and as the Cactus Brothers this nucleus earned its first recording contract with Liberty in the summer of 1992. Prior to the signing, the group was featured in *Pure Country*, a George Strait film shot in Texas, which featured the group composition 'Crazy Heart', while Tramp and Kirby contributed on two other songs. *The Cactus Brothers* was released in May 1993, with a line-up boasting the addition of Sam Poland (pedal and lap steel guitar, dobro) and David Schnaufer (electric and acoustic dulcimers, harp). It was an excellent introduction to their rough-edged country sound, that showed the influence of bluegrass and rock. Those alerted to the group's songwriting prowess would not be surprised to learn that both Kirby and the Golemon brothers descend from noted country songwriters (Dave Kirby having penned material like 'Is Anybody Going To San Antone'). In promoting the disc the group travelled over 60,000 miles in the USA, while 1994 brought appearances in Ireland, Norway, Holland, Switzerland, and at the Cambridge Folk Festival. The group has also achieved recognition for their videos, which, despite being recorded on low budgets, have twice ('Fisher's Hornpipe', 1992, and 'Sixteen Tons', 1994) come third in the prestigious and highly competitive Worldfest poll. However, the group suffered further personnel shuffles in January 1994 when Schnaufer left to resume his solo career. A month later Poland departed to return to the world of commerce, and was replaced by Jim Fungaroli (after a short tenure by Argyle Bell). Kennedy was then replaced on drums by Rick Rowell in June. The Cactus Brothers spend a lot of time on the road, even doing some shows in Estonia. Tramp recalls: 'They threw a huge party for us and everyone ended up naked, drinking beer in the sauna. Someone had booked a stripper, so we all had to get dressed again so that she would feel like she was doing an act.'
● ALBUMS: *The Cactus Brothers* (Liberty 1993)★★★, *24 Hrs, 7 Days A Week* (Demon 1996)★★★.

CAGLE, BUDDY

b. Walter L. Cagle, 8 February 1936, Concord, North Carolina, USA. Cagle was raised in the Children's Home at Winston-Salem and when old enough, he volunteered for the US Air Force. He grew to enjoy country music but had no serious thoughts of being a singer until after his Air Force release in the late 50s. He moved to California and with some assistance from singer Wynn Stewart, he signed with Capitol Records. In 1963, he had Top 30 hits with 'Your Mother's Prayer' and his version of Stewart's 'Sing A Sad Song' - the song that a month later became Merle Haggard's first hit. After moving to Mercury Records, he had Top 40 success with 'Honky Tonkin' Again', before in 1966/7 gaining his final three chart entries with Imperial Records, 'Tonight I'm Coming Home' (number 31), 'Apologize' (number 57) and 'Longtime Travelling' (a song from the Broadway musical *A Joyful Noise*, number 75). He made appearances in Europe and occasionally worked with Hank Thompson before retiring, with many regretting that his career was so short. In the late 60s, he had Imperial album releases, the title track of one, *Mi Casa, Tu Casa*, arguably being one of the best recordings never to make the country charts.
● ALBUMS: *The Way You Like It* (Imperial 1966)★★★, *Mi Casa, Tu Casa* (Imperial 1967)★★★★, *Longtime Traveling* (Imperial 1967)★★, *Through A Crack In A Boxcar Door* (Imperial 1968)★★.

CALLAHAN BROTHERS

Walter T. (known as Joe) Callahan (b. 27 January 1910, Laurel, Madison County, North Carolina, USA, d. 10 September 1971, Asheville, North Carolina, USA; guitar) and Homer C. (known as Bill) Callahan (b. 27 March 1912, Laurel, Madison County, North Carolina, USA; banjo, guitar, mandolin, ukulele, fiddle, harmonica, bass fiddle). By the mid-20s, their musical talents saw them regularly playing local venues. In January 1934, their vocal harmonies and clever duet yodelling saw them record 14 sides for ARC (American Record Company) in New York, including 'St. Louis Blues' and 'She's My Curly Headed Baby', a song that became so associated with them that they would record it twice more. They gained regular work on WWNC Asheville and in August, they returned to New York to record 15 more sides (their sister Alma sang on four which were released as the Callahan Family). Their wide repertoire of gospel, folk and traditional country, with a marked fondness for blues numbers, saw them become very successful, at a time when brother duet acts were very popular in the USA. In 1935, they worked on the *Crazy Water Barn Dance* on WHAS Louisville and recorded 14 more sides in New York. Seven further sessions during 1936 added 23 more recordings (Shorty Hobbs played mandolin on 14 of them, the first time another musician had recorded with them). In 1936, an obvious fondness for travel saw them relocate to WWVA Wheeling, West Virginia. When Walter retired for a time in 1937, Homer moved to WLW Cincinnati, where he worked with Red Foley and the Coon Creek Girls. Walter later rejoined his brother and they made their final recordings for ARC (by now called Columbia Records) in February 1939. By 1941, after spells at Springfield and Tulsa, they had moved to Texas, where they began to include more modern material and dropped their own first names to become Bill and Joe. They formed their Blue Ridge Mountain Folk, which, at one time, included two former members of the Coon Creek Girls, Esther Koehler and Evelyn Lange, Paul Buskirk (mandolin) and Georgia Slim Rutland (fiddle). They began to use electrified instruments and throughout the 40s, they became one of the most popular bands in the south-west, with regular shows on KVOO Tulsa, KRLD Dallas and KWFT Wichita Falls. They made transcription discs which were played on Border Radio and, in April 1941, accompanied by Buskirk, they made seven recordings for Decca in Dallas. They went to Hollywood in 1945 and made appearances in several B-movie westerns including *Springtime In Texas* with Jimmy Wakely, with whom they later toured. Their clever duet yodelling also saw them include some western songs in the shows. Bill also toured (as a comedian) with Ray Whitley in 1946/7 and recorded two sides for the Cowboy label in Philadelphia. His expertise with the bass fiddle saw him do session work in the late 40s and into the early 50s. In 1951, they toured with Lefty Frizzell (whom Bill managed for a time) and made their final recordings for Columbia in October that year. By the end of the 50s, they were semi-retired. In the early 60s, they made some personal and television appearances in Dallas. Ill health finally led to Joe returning to Asheville, where he died of cancer in September 1971. Bill remained in Dallas working as a photographer and continued to make appearances at local venues.

● ALBUMS: *The Callahan Brothers Early Recordings* (Old Homestead 1974)★★★.

CAMPBELL, ARCHIE

b. 7 November 1914, Bulls Gap, Greene County, Tennessee, USA, 29 August 1987. After graduating in 1936, Campbell, a singer, guitarist and comedian, gained his first radio experience on WNOX Knoxville, where he appeared on the *Tennessee Barn Dance* and *Mid-Day Merry-Go-Round*. In 1937, he moved to WDOD Chattanooga, where he remained until he joined the US Navy in 1941. After the war, he resumed his career and in 1952 he had his own television show on WATE Knoxville. In 1958, he joined the *Grand Ole Opry* where, changing both his image and style, he became a smartly dressed, cigar-smoking performer on the 'Prince Albert' segment of the Opry. One of his gimmicks consisted of narrating stories and reversing the letters in the names, such as 'Rindercella' and 'The Bleeping Beauty'. He also performed serious numbers and had chart success with 'Trouble In Amen Corner' (which he wrote), 'The Men In My Little Girl's Life' and a duet with Lorene Mann entitled 'Dark End Of The Street'. In 1969 he moved to the syndicated *Hee-Haw* television show where he not only became a star of the series but also the chief scriptwriter. He later became the host of the popular network television interview show *Yesteryear In Nashville*. During his career he recorded for RCA, Starday, Elektra and Chart. Away from country music, he was a poet, a sculptor and painter and an excellent golfer. Campbell died of a heart attack in Knoxville on 29 August 1987.

● ALBUMS: *Bedtime Stories For Adults* (Starday 1962)★★★, *Make Friends With Archie Campbell* (Starday 1962)★★★, *The Joker Is Wild* (Starday 1963)★★, *The Cockfight & Other Tall Tales* (RCA Victor 1966)★★, *The Grand Ole Opry's Good Humor Man* (Starday 1966)★★, *Have A Laugh On Me* (RCA Victor 1966)★★, *Kids, I Love 'Em* (RCA Victor 1967)★★, *The Golden Years* (RCA Victor 1967)★★★, *The Many Talents Of Archie Campbell* (1968)★★★, with Junior Samples *Bull Session At Bull's Gap* (Chart 1968)★★, with Lorene Mann *Archie & Lorene Tell It Like It Is* (RCA Victor 1968)★★★,

Didn't He Shine (RCA Victor 1970)★★, *Archie Campbell* (1976)★★, *Live At Tupelo* (1977)★★.

● COMPILATIONS: *The Best Of Archie Campbell* (RCA Victor 1969)★★★.

CAMPBELL, GLEN

b. Glen Travis Campbell, 22 April 1936, Delight, Arkansas, USA. Campbell came from a musical family and began his career with his uncle's Dick Bills Band in 1954, before forming Glen Campbell And The Western Wranglers four years later. By the end of the 50s he had moved to Los Angeles, where he became a renowned session player and one of the finest guitarists in Hollywood. After briefly joining the Champs, he released a solo single, 'Too Late To Worry - Too Blue To Cry', which crept into the US Hot 100. Ever in demand, he took on the arduous task of replacing Brian Wilson on touring commitments with the Beach Boys. Campbell's period as a Beach Boy was short-lived and he soon returned to session work and recording, even enjoying a minor hit with Buffy Sainte-Marie's 'The Universal Soldier'. By 1967, Capitol Records were seriously promoting Campbell as an artist in his own right. The breakthrough came with an accomplished version of John Hartford's 'Gentle On My Mind', which won a Grammy award for Best Country 'n' Western Recording of 1967. Campbell's finest work was recorded during the late 60s, most notably a superb trilogy of hits written by Jim Webb. 'By The Time I Get To Phoenix', 'Wichita Lineman' and 'Galveston' were richly evocative compositions, full of yearning for towns in America that have seldom been celebrated in the annals of popular music. By this stage of his career, Campbell was actively pursuing television work and even starred with John Wayne in the film *True Grit* (1969). He recorded some duets with country singer Bobbie Gentry, including a revival of the Everly Brothers' 'All I Have To Do Is Dream', which proved a worldwide smash hit. Further hits followed, including 'Honey Come Back', 'It's Only Make Believe' and 'Dream Baby'. There was a second film appearance in *Norwood* (1970) and another duet album, this time with Anne Murray. Campbell's hit record output slowed somewhat in the early 70s, but by the mid-decade he found second wind and belatedly registered his first US number 1 single with 'Rhinestone Cowboy'. Two years later he repeated that feat with a version of Allan Touissant's 'Southern Nights'. Numerous hit compilations followed and Campbell found himself still in demand as a duettist with such artists as Rita Coolidge and Tanya Tucker. By the late 70s, he had become a C&W institution, regularly releasing albums, touring and appearing on television. In 1988, he returned to his young provider Jim Webb for the title track to *Still Within The Sound Of My Voice*. Campbell's career is most remarkable for its scope. A brilliant guitarist, star session player, temporary Beach Boy, first-class interpreter, television personality, strong vocalist, in-demand duettist and C&W idol, he has run the gamut of American music and rarely faltered.

● ALBUMS: *Too Late To Worry, Too Late To Cry* (Capitol 1963)★★★, *The Astounding 12-String Guitar Of Glen Campbell* (Capitol 1964)★★★, *The Big Bad Rock Guitar Of Glen Campbell* (Capitol 1965)★★★, *Gentle On My Mind* (Capitol 1967)★★★, *By The Time I Get To Phoenix* (Capitol 1967)★★★, *Hey, Little One* (Capitol 1968)★★★, *A New Place*

In The Sun (Capitol 1968)★★★, *Bobbie Gentry And Glen Campbell* (Capitol 1968)★★★, *Wichita Lineman* (Capitol 1968)★★★, *That Christmas Feeling* (Capitol 1968)★★, *Galveston* (Capitol 1969)★★★, *Glen Campbell - Live* (Capitol 1969)★★, *Try A Little Kindness* (Capitol 1970)★★★, *Oh Happy Day* (Capitol 1970)★★★, *Norwood* film soundtrack (Capitol 1970)★★, *The Glen Campbell Goodtime Album* (Capitol 1970)★★★, *The Last Time I Saw Her* (Capitol 1971)★★★, *Anne Murray/Glen Campbell* (Capitol 1971)★★★, *Glen Travis Campbell* (Capitol 1972)★★★, *I Knew Jesus (Before He Was A Star)* (Capitol 1973)★★★, *I Remember Hank Williams* (Capitol 1973)★★, *Reunion (The Songs Of Jimmy Webb)* (Capitol 1974)★★★, *Arkansas* (Capitol 1975)★★, *Rhinestone Cowboy* (Capitol 1975)★★, *Bloodline* (Capitol 1976)★★★, *Southern Nights* (Capitol 1977)★★★, with the Royal Philharmonic Orchestra *Live At The Royal Festival Hall* (Capitol 1978)★★★, *Basic* (Capitol 1978)★★★, *Somethin' 'Bout You Baby I Like* (Capitol 1980)★★★, *It's The World Gone Crazy* (Capitol 1981)★★★★, *Old Home Town* (Atlantic 1983)★★★, *Letter To Home* (Atlantic 1984)★★★, *Just A Matter Of Time* (Atlantic 1986)★★★, *No More Night* (Word 1988)★★★, *Still Within The Sound Of My Voice* (MCA 1988)★★★, *Walkin' In The Sun* (Capitol 1990)★★★★, *Unconditional Love* (Capitol Nashville 1991)★★★, *Somebody Like That* (Capitol 1993)★★★, *The Rhinestone Cowboy Live In Concert* (Summit 1995)★★★.
● COMPILATIONS: *Glen Campbell's Greatest Hits* (Capitol 1971)★★★, *The Best Of Glen Campbell* (Capitol 1976)★★★, *20 Classic Tracks* (MFP 1981)★★, *The Very Best Of Glen Campbell* (Capitol 1987)★★★★, *The Best Of The Early Years* (Curb 1987)★★★, *Country Boy* (MFP 1988)★★, *The Complete Glen Campbell* (Stylus 1989)★★★, *Love Songs* (MFP 1990)★★, *Greatest Country Hits* (Curb 1990)★★★, *Classics Collection* (Liberty 1990)★★★, *Essential Glen Campbell, Volumes 1-3* (Capitol 1995)★★★, *Gentle On My Mind: The Collection* (Razor & Tie 1997)★★★★.
● VIDEOS: *Live At The Dome* (80s), *Glen Campbell Live* (Channel 5 1988), *An Evening With* (Music Club Video 1989), *Glen Campbell* (Castle Music Pictures 1991).
● FURTHER READING: *The Glen Campbell Story*, Freda Kramer. *Rhinestone Cowboy: An Autobiography*, Glen Campbell with Tom Carter.
● FILMS: *The Cool Ones* (1967), *True Grit* (1969), *Norwood* (1970).

CAMPBELL, KATE

b. New Orleans, Mississippi, USA. Despite her origins in the Mississippi Delta, Campbell has crafted her reputation in the singer-songwriter field rather than the blues. Growing up in Sledge, Mississippi, her father was the pastor of the local Baptist Church. She too attended church regularly, but as she later confessed: 'I always enjoyed the singing part more than the preaching'. As a four-year-old she was given her first musical instrument, a ukulele, and two years later began piano lessons. While still in elementary school she took up the guitar and started composing her own songs. The family moved to Orlando, Florida, during her junior high school year, where she sang in a jazz ensemble. She subsequently attended Samford University in Birmingham, Alabama, studying music and history, before a master's degree from graduate school in Auburn. Her subject - Southern History - had already informed many of the songs

she had written to this point. In 1988 she moved to Nashville, teaching history while continuing to develop her songwriting. She performed regularly at clubs and writer's nights until, in 1994, she signed a publishing contract with Fame and a recording contract with Nashville's Compass Records. Her debut album, *Songs From The Levee*, was released in 1996 as a culmination of her 'efforts to merge history, memories and music'. Featuring 10 originals, guest artists included Al Perkins, Dan Dugmore and Joey Miskulin, all renowned Nashville session musicians. It prompted Guy Clark to endorse her thus: 'One of the finest singer-songwriters to emerge from Nashville.' The follow-up repeated the formula to equal effect, and included a duet with Clark on 'Bud's Sea-Mint Boat'.
● ALBUMS: *Songs From The Levee* (Compass 1996)★★★, *Moonpie Dreams* (Compass 1997)★★★.

CARGILL, HENSON

b. 5 February 1941, Oklahoma City, Oklahoma, USA. After studying law and working briefly as a deputy sheriff, Cargill moved to Nashville in 1967 to attempt a career as a country singer-songwriter. He signed to Monument Records, where his debut single became his biggest hit. With producer Fred F. Carter Jnr. he recorded 'Skip A Rope', which reached the US Top 30 as well as heading the country charts. Unusually for country music, this was a protest song, condemning parents who set a bad example for their children by evading income tax and practising racial discrimination. The song was later recorded by soul singer Joe Tex. Cargill followed this with more orthodox hits such as 'Row, Row, Row', 'None Of My Business' and 'Naked And Crying'. In the early 70s, he joined the newly formed Nashville arm of Atlantic Records, having success with 'Some Old California Memory'. He later moved back to Oklahoma and in 1980 gained his last US country chart entry with 'Silence On The Line', released by Copper Mountain.
● ALBUMS: *Skip A Rope* (Monument 1968)★★★, *None Of My Business* (Monument 1969)★★, *This Is Henson Cargill Country* (Atlantic 1974)★★★.

CARLISLES

Clifford Raymond Carlisle (b. 6 May 1904, near Mount Eden, Spencer County, Kentucky, USA, d. 2 April 1983, Lexington, Kentucky, USA) and William (Bill) Carlisle (b. 19 December 1908, Wakefield, Kentucky, USA). Born in a log cabin on a tobacco farm, Cliff Carlisle developed an early affinity for yodelling blues music and the Hawaiian guitar, which led to him becoming one of the best steel guitarists to play in country music. He is also considered a pioneer of the dobro and a fine yodeller and singer of most types of country songs, comedy and blues. During the 20s, he and singer/guitarist Wilbur Ball toured with vaudeville shows and in 1930 appeared on WHAS Louisville as the Lullaby Larkers. Mainly because of Cliff's yodelling abilities, they first recorded for Gennett Records in 1930, and, in June 1931, with Cliff playing steel guitar, they accompanied Jimmie Rodgers on two recordings in Louisville. Between 1933 and 1936 Cliff also recorded several risqué ballads, including his self-penned 'Mouse's Ear Blues', sometimes using for these a pseudonym such as Bob Clifford or Amos Greene. Bill Carlisle, who had joined his brother in the late 20s when they formed the Carlisles, also recorded as a solo artist in

1933, gaining success with his recording of 'Rattlesnake Daddy'. They toured extensively throughout the Midwest and for some years were based at Charlotte. Cliff's son Tommy first performed with them when he was three years old and later recorded as Sonny Boy Tommy, singing such songs as 'Lonely Little Orphan Child' and stayed with the group until he joined the US Army in the 40s. They signed with RCA-Victor in 1936 but during their years together recorded for most major record labels. Their song content changed during the next few years, even including gospel material in lieu of the risqué numbers. In the late 40s, recordings on King Records of 'Rainbow At Midnight' and 'Tramp On The Street' made the US country charts before Cliff nominally retired in the early 50s. Bill, who acquired the nickname of 'Jumping' or 'Boundin' Bill' from his habit of leaping around when performing, formed a new Carlisles group. He soon established a reputation for humorous songs and attained major chart success with self-penned numbers such as 'Too Old To Cut The Mustard', 'Is Zat You, Myrtle?' and a country number 1, 'No Help Wanted'. In 1952, a duet recording of the first song was also a US Top 10 country hit for Ernest Tubb and Red Foley and a US pop hit for Bing Crosby and the Andrews Sisters. In 1953, the 'Carlisles' joined the *Grand Ole Opry* and when the band finally disbanded in the mid-60s, Bill stayed on, appearing at times with his children Billy and Sheila. His 1966 Hickory recording of 'What Kinda Deal Is This?' made number 4 on the US country charts. Cliff continued to write songs and in the 60s made some concert appearances and recordings with his brother, and after a gap of 40 years, appeared with Wilbur Ball at the San Diego Folk Festival in 1971. Soon afterwards his health began to deteriorate and Cliff Carlisle died following a heart attack in April 1983. Bill continued to appear on the *Opry* and make public appearances.

● ALBUMS: by Cliff Carlisle *A Country Kind Of Songs & Hymns* (Rem 60s)★★★, *Cliff Carlisle, Volume 1* (Old Timey 1988)★★★, *Cliff Carlisle, Volume 2* (Old Timey 1988)★★; by Bill Carlisle *The Best Of Bill Carlisle* (Hickory 1966)★★★★, *Jumpin' Bill Carlisle* (Brylen 1983)★★★; the Carlisle Family *Carlisle Family Album - Old Time Great Hymns featuring Bill & Cliff Carlisle* (Old Homestead 1965)★★★; the Carlisles *On Stage With The Carlisles* (Mercury 1958)★★, *Fresh From The Country* (King 1959)★★★, *Maple On The Hill* (1964)★★, *Busy Body Boogie* (Bear Family 1985)★★★★.

CARLSON, PAULETTE

b. 11 October 1953, Northfield, Minnesota, USA. Carlson left Highway 101 in 1990 just before they recorded *Bing Bang Boom*. Having had great success with the band, she had great hopes for her solo career. She appeared as a nightclub singer in the hit film *Twins*, but the material on her debut album was not as strong as Highway 101's. She had her biggest country hit with 'I'll Start With You' in 1991, but has since failed to secure another solo single in the US country Top 50. In 1995 Carlson re-formed Highway 101.

● ALBUMS: *Love Goes On* (Capitol 1992)★★★.

CARMAN, JENKS 'TEX'

b. 14 May 1903, Hardinsburg, Breckinridge County, Kentucky, USA, d. 2 February 1968. There are probably few completely accurate facts (even his year of birth) known of this eccentric country music entertainer. He enjoyed embellishing details and at times, may well have stretched the truth. He claimed Cherokee Indian ancestry, a fact reinforced by his penchant for appearing in Indian costume, but research of the Cherokee Nation failed to find any reference to him, although one of his great-grandmothers did claim to be Cherokee. He learned to play guitar as a child and in his teens, he left the family farm to become an entertainer. He worked in Louisville, for a time as leader of the Glee Club Quartette, hoboed, busked and toured the vaudeville circuit and, in 1929, he even recorded for Gennett. After becoming friendly with Frank Plada, a noted Hawaiian guitar exponent, he changed to that instrument, which he always played as an acoustic instrument hanging around his neck. Although his playing has drawn considerable criticism, he proved popular throughout the 40s and 50s. In the late 40s, he relocated to California, recorded for Four Star and as Jenks Tex Carman, the Dixie Cowboy, he played on KXLA radio, the noted Compton *Town Hall Party* and Cliffie Stone's *Hometown Jamboree*. In the early 50s, he recorded five sessions for Capitol Records; some tracks remained unissued until a 1991 release by Bear Family Records. His most popular recordings were 'Hilo March' and 'Hillbilly Hula'. Speaking 40 years later, Capitol producer Ken Nelson still winced at the memory of recording him: 'He was so lacking in rhythm but he had this goofy sound on the guitar and he sold records.' After Capitol, he recorded for Sage and had material released on several other labels, including Old Homestead. He was always liked by his fellow artists although most commented on his vocals and guitar playing. Wesley Tuttle rated him the worst musician in the world but paid tribute to his stage presence. Johnny Western commented 'He'd come to the show half-bombed and with a bottle in his guitar case but he was a born entertainer. He'd come on with a big smile, play the Hawaiian guitar with all those flourishes and playing "drums" on it but he could never play in tune. One of the major jokes that went the rounds was that Tex beat one of his kids half to death because the kid untuned one string on Tex's guitar and wouldn't tell him which one'. Carman died at the age of 64 and there is little doubt that he was indeed a character who deserves to be remembered.

● ALBUMS: *Country Caravan* (Modern 1959)★★★, *Jenks 'Tex' Carman* (Sage 1960)★★★, *The Ole Indian* red vinyl (Sage 1962)★★★, *Early Dobro* (1962)★★★, *Jenks 'Tex' Carman Sings And Plays* (Sage 1963)★★, *Tex Carman* (Crown 60s)★★★, *Wreck Of The Old '97* (Old Homestead 1982)★★, *Hillbilly Hula* (Bear Family 1991)★★★.

CAROLINA COTTON

b. Helen Hagstrom, 20 October 1933, Cash, Arkansas, USA. Hagstrom's family relocated to San Francisco, where she received her education. She sang and yodelled and also studied dancing and gained her first professional experience with western band leader Dude Martin. He gave her the nickname of Carolina Cotton, because he reckoned that Arkansas was not so well recognized in California. She gradually progressed into film work, and in 1947, she appeared with Roy Acuff in *Sing, Neighbor, Sing*. During the late 40s, she appeared in various films with such western stars as Charles Starrett, Ken Curtis and further country music films with Roy Acuff and with Eddy Arnold in *Feudin' Rhythm* (1949) and *Hoedown* (1950). In the early 50s, she played in two Gene Autry films, and in 1952, she had so established her reputation as a leading cowgirl yodeller that she was cast as Charles Starrett's leading lady in *The Rough Tough West*. In 1946, she recorded for King, including her theme song 'Three Miles South Of Cash In Arkansas'. She later recorded for Crystal and Mastertone before joining MGM Records, where, in 1950, she also recorded four numbers with Bob Wills' Texas Playboys. These later found release on the German Bear Family label's 1985 boxed set release *Bob Wills & His Texas Playboys - Papa's Jumpin'*. Her personality and talent meant that she was always very popular on overseas tours to entertain American forces in various parts of the world, including Japan, Germany and, on several occasions, Korea. She married Bill Ates (a relative of actor Roscoe Ates) in 1955, and they had two children before they were divorced. She continued to perform as a yodelling cowgirl into the early 60s, when she finally retired. After gaining qualifications at teaching college, she taught for five years in US schools in Central America. In 1974, she relocated to teach in a school in Bakersfield, California.

CAROLINA TAR HEELS

An old-time string band, formed in 1927, that played various venues and recorded for Victor Records. The act initially consisted of Dock Walsh (b. Doctor Coble Walsh, 23 July 1901, Wilkes County, North Carolina, USA, d. 1967; banjo, guitar, vocals) and Gwen Foster (b. Gaston County, North Carolina, USA; harmonica, guitar, vocals). Walsh had first recorded solo for Columbia Records in 1925, and became friendly with Foster the following year, while busking his way through the state. In 1927, accompanied by two other musicians, they auditioned for Ralph Peer. He decided to record, as the Carolina Tar Heels, only Walsh and Foster. After three Victor sessions, Walsh and Foster parted company and Walsh was joined by his old friend Garley Foster, no relation (b. 10 January 1905, Wilkes County, North Carolina, USA, d. c.1971; harmonica, vocals, whistler). In 1928, the pair were joined by Clarence Tom Ashley. Although he was an excellent banjoist, he played guitar and sang on 17 of their recordings, including one of their best remembered, 'My Home's Across The Blue Ridge Mountains', which Ashley claimed to have written. Around June 1929, Ashley left but Walsh and Foster continued as a duo and made further recordings, some as the Pine Mountain Boys. In 1932, when the original act (consisting once again of Walsh and Gwen Foster) made its last recordings in Atlanta, it was billed as the Original Carolina Tar Heels, owing to the fact that, between 1931 and March 1934, another act called the Carolina Tarheels was resident on WSB Atlanta. It played regular programmes, including a Saturday night *Broom Dance* (the pun being that one needed a broom to sweep the floor before one had a barn dance) and played various venues around the Atlanta area. A very popular band, its leader was Claude Davis (b. Claude Dennis, 25 February 1895, Salisbury, North Carolina, USA, d. 25 May 1961; guitar, fiddle, vocals) and other members who played with the band during its existence included Hoke Rice (banjo), Clyde Keiser (guitar, harmonica), Louie Bailey (comedian), Esther Mae Davis, the Carolina Sunshine Girl and Curly Fox (fiddle). In the early 60s, the reawakened interest in folk and traditional music saw Walsh and Garley Foster, accompanied by Walsh's son, Drake, come out of

retirement to record for Folk Legacy and make some festival appearances. Some of their original recordings may also be found on various compilation issues.
● ALBUMS: *The Carolina Tar Heels* (Folk Legacy 1962)★★★, *Look Who's Coming* (GHP 70s)★★★, *Can't You Remember The Carolina Tar Heels* (Bear Family 1973)★★★★.
● COMPILATIONS: *Carolina Tar Heels - Early Recordings* (Old Homestead 1977)★★★.

CARPENTER, MARY-CHAPIN

b. 21 February 1958, Princeton, New Jersey, USA. Carpenter's father was an executive for *Life* magazine, and she spent part of her early life living in Japan. She grew up with a love of contemporary pop hits, although her mother's Woody Guthrie and Judy Collins records gave her some interest in country/folk music. She spent her time at home with her guitar, and her father encouraged her to perform at a talent night. At university, she achieved a degree in American Civilization. By 1986, she was a local star, winning five Washington Area Music Awards without having made a record, after which she signed to a major label in Nashville with guitarist/producer John Jennings. She had felt she should have a conventional job, but continued performing in bars, often having to sing current favourites; unsatisfied with this situation, she resolved to perform only in bars that would let her play original material. She had also recorded John Stewart's song 'Runaway Train' for her first album, but Columbia Records decided that it would be better suited to Rosanne Cash, who took it to the top of the US country charts. Since then, she has made steady progress up the commercial ladder, attracting cover versions of her songs by artists such as Tony Rice and Joan Baez. A notable songwriter, Carpenter has also recorded cover versions, including 'Downtown Train' by Tom Waits - more recently a hit for Rod Stewart - on *Hometown Girl*, and the stunning 'Quittin' Time', co-written by Robb Royer of Bread, from *State Of The Heart*. Although she is regarded as a new star in country music, she has more in common with the folk singers of the early 70s. In 1991 she made the US country charts with a revival of Gene Vincent's light-hearted 'Right Now'. Her 1992 hit, the raunchy and self-mocking 'I Feel Lucky', preceded the release of another excellent album, *Come On, Come On*. Carpenter's complete acceptance by a country audience was sealed when she was voted the CMA's Female Vocalist Of The Year that September. On this album, in addition to country rockers with chiming 12-string guitars ('The Hard Way' and 'Passionate Kisses'), there are beautiful folk ballads (the title track is magnificent). Two years later she was able to deliver more of the same recipe with another million-seller *Stones In The Road*. This time she answered 'Passionate Kisses' with 'Shut Up And Kiss Me' and complemented 'The Hard Way' with the equally thought-provoking 'House Of Cards'. Her lyrics continue to flow without any writer's block, but what is particularly interesting is that she, together with the likes of Trisha Yearwood, Suzy Bogguss and Kathy Mattea, has brought fresh melody to an old and sometimes predictable genre. Her productivity is impressive, particularly as she suffers from depression. 'Early on, I thought I was just moody,' she told the *Daily Telegraph*, 'but I've learnt to accept it is a part of me.' This partially accounts for her subject matter: drinking, divorce and bad love affairs - but she can rock with the best of them as demonstrated by the Grammy-winning 'Down At The Twist And Shout'. She has participated on tribute albums, notably with 'Wishing' on the Buddy Holly set *notfadeaway*, and a stunning performance of 'Grow Old With Me' on *A Tribute To John Lennon*. *A Place In The World* maintained her reputation in the country field but gained a new audience as she crossed over from country rock to mainstream rock.

● ALBUMS: *Hometown Girl* (Columbia 1987)★★, *State Of The Heart* (Columbia 1989)★★★, *Shooting Straight In The Dark* (Columbia 1990)★★★, *Come On, Come On* (Columbia 1992)★★★★, *Stones In The Road* (Columbia 1994)★★★★, *A Place In The World* (Columbia 1996)★★★.

● VIDEOS: *Shut Up And Kiss Me* (1994), *5* (1994), *My Record Company Made Me Do This!* (1995), *Jubilee: Live At The Wolf Trap* (Columbia Music Video 1995).

CARROLL, JOHNNY

b. John Lewis Carrell, 23 October 1937, Cleburne, Texas, USA, d. 18 February 1995, Godley, Texas, USA. Carroll was brought up on a farm near Fort Worth, Texas, though farming held no attraction for him. By the age of 10 he was singing country music and Carroll was an early performer of rockabilly. He flew to Nashville in 1956 and recorded 'Crazy Crazy Lovin'', 'Tryin' To Get To You', 'Rock 'n' Roll Ruby', 'Hot Rock', 'Corrine Corrina' and 'Wild Wild Women' at Owen Bradley's studio. They are among the best rockabilly recordings of the period. His records were released on Decca Records and the label misspelt his name as 'Carroll'. He toured on rock 'n' roll package shows and appeared in the film *Rock, Baby, Rock It!* In August 1957 he worked with Elvis Presley's musicians, Scotty Moore and Bill Black, and they recorded 'That's The Way I Love', which was issued on Phillips International, a sister label of Sun. He often worked with Gene Vincent and wrote 'Maybe', which Vincent recorded. Chart success eluded Carroll and he moved into club management in the 1960s, working in Dallas for Jack Ruby, the man who shot John Kennedy's assassin Lee Harvey Oswald in 1963. Carroll intervened when some rowdy customers were molesting waitresses and one of them shot him in the stomach. He spent several weeks in hospital and this was to lead to the liver failure that eventually killed him. In 1974 Carroll recorded a tribute to Gene Vincent, 'Black Leather Rebel'. In 1977 he was encouraged to return to performing by model Judy Lindsey and they worked as the Johnny And Jack Band. They had a residency at the Hilton Hotel in Forth Worth and recorded several albums. Carroll died in 1995 and at his funeral Judy Lindsey sang 'Just A Closer Walk With Thee' and 'The Lord's Prayer', but the minister refused to make any reference to his career as a rock 'n' roll singer. It was still the music of the devil.

● ALBUMS: *Texabilly* (Rollin' Rock 1974)★★★, *Screamin' Demon Heatwave* (Seville 1983)★★, with Judy Lindsey *Shades Of Vincent* (Charly 1986)★★★.

● COMPILATIONS: *Rock Baby, Rock It* (1955-1960)★★★.

CARSON, FIDDLIN' JOHN

b. 23 March 1868, on a farm in the hills of Fannin County, Georgia, USA, d. 11 December 1949, Atlanta, Georgia, USA. It is likely that his forebears arrived from Ireland around 1780; probably some were fiddle players, who brought instruments with them. It is said that Carson first began to play the fiddle when he was about 11. He also rode as a

jockey as a boy until he became too big and heavy. At one time he worked in a cotton mill, and there is little doubt that he was also occupied as a moonshiner. He regularly played the fiddle and eventually relocated to Atlanta, where he earned a living busking and playing at local functions including political rallies. Over the years he became such an expert fiddler that between 1914 and 1924 he was named Champion of Dixie on seven occasions. He became one of the first country artists to play on local radio when he appeared on WSB Atlanta in 1922. In 1923, Atlanta record store manager Polk Brockman suggested to Ralph Peer of OKeh Records that he should record some local talent. When on 19 June 1923 Carson performed 'The Little Old Log Cabin In The Lane' and 'The Old Hen Cackled And The Rooster's Going To Crow', he was the first country artist that Peer recorded. Peer was unimpressed by Carson's vocal work, describing it as 'pluperfect awful' and doubted the sales potential of the record. Initially, he pressed only 500 copies and was amazed when they quickly sold. When Carson realized how successfully his record sold he was heard to remark that he would have to quit making moonshine and start making records. Peer immediately arranged for Carson to make further recordings; between 1923 and 1931, often accompanied by the Virginia Reelers, who included his daughter Rose Lee Carson (Moonshine Kate), he recorded almost 150 tracks for OKeh. The material varied from country songs such as 'Letter Edged In Black', traditional fiddle tunes such as 'Old Joe Clark' and popular ballads such as 'Long Way To Tipperary' to the humorous 'Who Bit The Wart Off Grandma's Nose'. Carson made his final recordings (again accompanied by his daughter) for RCA Victor in Camden in February 1934. He continued to play at conventions and other functions and until a few days before his death, on 11 December 1949, he was working as a lift operator in the Capitol building in Atlanta, Georgia.

● ALBUMS: *The Old Hen Cackled And The Rooster's Going To Crow* (Rounder 1976)★★★.

● FURTHER READING: *Fiddlin' Georgia Crazy; Fiddlin' John Carson, His Real World And The World Of His Songs*, Gene Wiggins.

CARSON, JEFF

b. Tulsa, Oklahoma, USA. The 90s US country singer Jeff Carson was a struggling bass player in Branson, Missouri, before his wife persuaded him to move to Nashville. He worked there as a demo singer for three years until producer Chuck Howard heard his material, leading to a publishing deal with Curb Records. He made his debut solo album in 1995 and the singles 'Not On Your Love' and his finest song to date, 'The Car', both reached the US country chart. Curb Records have long-term faith in his ability to become a major star. His problem at the moment is not a shortage of good songs, merely the lack of any image. Duetting with Merle Haggard on 'Today I Started Loving You Again' (from 1997's *Here's The Deal*) did little to remedy the situation.

● ALBUMS: *Jeff Carson* (Curb 1995)★★★, *Here's The Deal* (Curb 1997)★★.

CARSON, KEN

b. 14 November 1914, in a buckboard between Colgate and Centrahoma, Oklahoma, USA. Carson's part-Cherokee father died when he was aged one, but he developed his musical interest from his mother who played guitar, and his fiddle-playing stepfather. After first moving to Wichita, Kansas, the Carsons finally settled in Los Angeles. A good singer, he soon became a competent guitarist but first performed, playing harmonica, in a duo with Red Barton, on the KGFJ radio station. Late in 1931, he became a regular on Stuart Hamblen's popular radio show. A year later, he became a member of the Beverly Hillbillies and formed a lasting friendship with Shug Fisher. He was later part of the Ranch Boys trio and made his film debut in 1934, singing 'The Man On The Flying Trapeze' in *It Happened One Night*. The Ranch Boys moved to join NBC in Chicago in 1936, initially for a one-year contract but stayed until they disbanded in 1941. Carson then gained his own programme on WGN, where he became known to the Sons Of The Pioneers. In April 1943, they asked him to deputize for Lloyd Perryman, who was drafted for military service. He officially joined the group in June 1943 and his fine tenor vocals became an important part of some of their Decca recordings. Perryman returned early in 1946 but Carson continued to record with the group until December 1947, although officially no longer a group member. During this time, he may be heard on some of their first RCA recordings including 'Tumbling Tumbleweeds'. After leaving the Pioneers, he worked on NBC in Los Angeles, where for a time he had his own show and was backed by the Nelson Riddle Orchestra. He then moved to CBS, where he worked occasionally with Roy Rogers And The Pioneers. Between 1948 and 1958, he was a regular on major radio shows for NBC and CBS, both in Hollywood and New York where, in the late 50s, he hosted his own television show. In the early 60s, he recorded albums for the Longines Symphonette Society.

● ALBUMS: *Treasury Of The Golden West* (LSS 1962)★★★, *Campfire Favorites* (LSS 1962)★★★.

CARSON, MARTHA LOU

b. Irene Amburgey, 19 May 1921, Neon, Kentucky, USA. She learned to sing and play guitar as a child and started her musical career singing old-time and gospel songs with her sisters Bertha and Opal (Minnie and Mattie) as part of the Sunshine Sisters, a popular local radio act (Opal was also known as Jean Chapel). In 1939, Carson met James Roberts, the mandolin-playing son of legendary fiddler Doc Roberts, at the radio station WLAP Louisville on Asa Martin's *Morning Roundup*. They married and sang as a duo playing various stations including WHIS Bluefield, the *Renfro Valley Barn Dance* and in 1940 WSB Atlanta where, using the stage name of James And Martha Carson 'The Barn Dance Sweethearts', and specializing in country gospel material, they were a very popular act for 10 years. In 1950, they moved to WNOX Knoxville's *Mid-Day Merry-Go-Round*. Between 1946 and 1950, they recorded 30 tracks, initially with just their own guitar and mandolin accompaniment but on the latter backing vocals and hand-clapping were added. Their 1947 recording of 'The Sweetest Gift' and James Roberts's self-penned 'Man Of Gallilee' are very highly rated. In 1951, they divorced and Martha Carson pursued a solo career as both a singer and songwriter. The success of her hand-clapping, bouncy gospel song 'Satisfied' saw her join the *Grand Ole Opry*, in Nashville, where she quickly became a popular star. She remained a regular until 1957 when, after remarrying, she took a supposedly agreed absence for the birth of her

first child and to fulfil some commitments in New York. When she returned to the *Opry*, she was simply told that there were no vacancies. She continued to write and record for several labels. She retired from performing for several years but eventually returned to make some personal appearances.

● ALBUMS: *Journey To The Sky* (RCA-Victor 1955)★★★, *Rock-A My Soul* (RCA-Victor 1957)★★★★, *Satisfied* (Capitol 1960)★★★ *A Talk With The Lord* (Capitol 1962)★★, *Martha Carson* (Sims 1963)★★★, *Martha Carson Sings* (Camden 1965)★★.

● COMPILATIONS: *Martha Carson's Greatest Gospel Hits* (Starday 1965)★★★, with James Roberts *James & Martha Early Gospel Greats* 1940s recordings (ACM 1972)★★★.

CARTER FAMILY

The Carter Family have become known as country music's first family and are responsible for several songs such as 'The Wildwood Flower' and 'Keep On The Sunny Side' becoming country standards. The original three members of the Carter Family were A.P. Carter (b. Alvin Pleasant Delaney Carter, 15 April 1891, Maces Springs, Scott County, Virginia, USA, d. 7 November 1960, Maces Springs), his wife Sara Carter (b. Sara Dougherty, 21 July 1898, Flat Woods, Coeburn, Wise County, Virginia, USA, d. 8 January 1979, Lodi, California, USA) and Sara's cousin, Mother Maybelle Carter (b. Maybelle Addington, 10 May 1909, Copper Creek, Nickelsville, Scott County, Virginia, USA, d. 23 October 1978, Nashville, Tennessee, USA). A.P, also known as 'Doc', Carter began to play the fiddle as a boy and learned many old-time songs from his mother. His father had been a fiddler but gave it up through religious beliefs when he married. As a young man, A.P. sang in a quartet with two uncles and his eldest sister in the local church. Initially, he worked on the railroad in Indiana but became homesick for his Clinch Mountain home in Virginia and in 1911, returned to his native area. He became interested in writing songs and found work travelling, selling fruit trees. One day on his travels, he met Sara, who (legend says) was playing the auto-harp and singing 'Engine 143', and on 18 June 1915, they married. Sara had learned to play banjo, guitar and autoharp and, as a child, was regularly singing with Madge and Maybelle Addington and other friends in her local area. They made their home in Maces Springs where A.P. worked on varying jobs, including farming and gardening and began to appear singing and playing together at local church socials and other functions. They auditioned for Brunswick Records, singing such songs as 'Log Cabin By The Sea', but when the record company suggested to A.P. that, performing as Fiddlin' Doc, he only record square dance fiddle songs, he flatly refused because he felt it was against his mother and father's strong religious beliefs. After her marriage in 1926 to A.P.'s brother Ezra J. Carter, Maybelle (Addington) joined with her relatives and the trio began to entertain locally. Like her new sister-in-law, Maybelle was equally competent on guitar, banjo and autoharp and was to become the main instrumentalist of the trio, as she developed her immediately identifiable style of picking out the melody on the bass strings and strumming a backing on the treble (Maybelle may well have been influenced by black guitarist Leslie Riddle, who often accompanied A.P. when he went on his searching-for-songs trips). Sara, often playing chords on the autoharp, usually sang lead vocals, with A.P. providing bass and Maybelle alto harmonies (Sara also yodelled on some of their recordings although this was probably more the instruction of the record company's producer than her own free choice).

The Carter Family sound was something totally new. Vocals in the early folk and hillbilly music were usually of secondary importance to the instrumental work, whereas the trio, with their simple harmonies, used their instruments to provide a musical accompaniment that never took precedent over their vocal work. In July 1927, their local newspaper reported that Ralph Peer of Victor Records was to audition local artists in Bristol, Tennessee. In spite of the fact that Sara had three children (the youngest only seven months old) and that Maybelle was seven months pregnant with her first, they travelled the 25 miles to Bristol, where on 1 August, they made their first recordings. They recorded six tracks. Peer was impressed and the records proved sufficient sellers for Victor to secure them a recording contract. Between 1928 and 1935, they recorded many tracks for Victor, including the original versions of many of their classics such as 'Keep On The Sunny Side', 'Wildwood Flower', 'I'm Thinking Tonight Of My Blue Eyes', 'Homestead On The Farm' (aka 'I Wonder How The Old Folks Are At Home'), 'Jimmie Brown The Newsboy' and 'Wabash Cannonball'.

By the end of the 20s, the Carter Family were a very well-known act. In 1931 in Louisville, Kentucky, they met and recorded with Jimmie Rodgers. It was at this session that Rodgers made his only valid duet recordings with a female vocalist when he recorded 'Why There's A Tear In My Eye' and 'The Wonderful City' with Sara Carter (the latter song also being the only sacred number that Rodgers ever recorded). Combined recordings made at this time between the two acts comprised 'Jimmie Rodgers Visits The Carter Family' and 'The Carter Family And Jimmie Rodgers In Texas'. The former consisted of duets by Sara and Maybelle on 'My Clinch Mountain Home' and 'Little Darling Pal Of Mine', with Jimmie Rodgers and A.P both joining on a quartet version of 'Hot Time In The Old Town Tonight'. The latter featured Jimmie Rodgers with a solo version of 'Yodelling Cowboy' and Sara joining in with the vocal and yodel on 'T for Texas'. Both also included some talking by the two acts. The Carter Family managed to record, even though the families at times had moved apart. In 1929, A.P. relocated to Detroit to find work and at one time, Maybelle moved to Washington DC. In 1932, Sara and A.P separated; they divorced a few years later, but the trio continued to record and perform together (later, in 1939, Sara married A.P's cousin, Coy Bayes). In 1935 they left Victor and moved to ARC, where they re-recorded some of their popular earlier songs, though often using different arrangements, as well as recording new numbers. They signed to Decca Records in 1936 and later recorded for Columbia (formerly ARC). Their previous reluctance to perform outside of Virginia, Tennessee and North Carolina ended in 1938, when they accepted the opportunity to work on the powerful Border Radio stations XERA, XEG and XENT on the Mexican/Texas border at Del Rio and San Antonio. Here the Carter's children began to make appearances with the family; first, Sara's daughter Janette and Maybelle's daughter Anita Carter, followed soon afterwards by her sisters Helen and June Carter.

Apart from their normal studio recordings, they recorded radio transcription discs at this time, which were used on various stations and helped to increase their popularity. They remained in Texas until 1941, when they relocated to WBT Charlotte, North Carolina. In 14 October 1941, after rejoining Victor, the trio made their final recordings together; in 1943, while still at WBT, Sara decided to retire and the original Carter Family broke up. During their career, they recorded almost three hundred songs, never once varying from their traditional sound. A.P. claimed to have written many of them and the arguments still persist as to just how many were his own compositions and how many were traditional numbers that he had learned as a boy or found on his many song-searching trips. Sara Carter was undeniably a vocalist of great talent and could easily have become a successful solo artist. Maybelle Carter, apart from her instrumental abilities, was also a fine vocalist. A.P, who possessed a deep bass voice, was a very nervous man who suffered with palsy for many years. Some people believe this accounted for the tremolo on his voice at times and for the fact that he was often either late with his vocal, or failed to sing at all.

The influence of the Carter Family can be seen in the work of a great many artists and their songs have been recorded by the likes of Johnny Cash, Louvin Brothers, Emmylou Harris, Mac Wiseman, Flatt And Scruggs, Bill Monroe and Stonewall Jackson. They recorded the 'Wabash Cannonball' seven years before Roy Acuff first sang it; this and many other Carter songs have become standards and have been recorded by many artists. Many of their numbers were beautifully descriptive of their native state, such as 'Mid The Green Fields Of Virginia', 'My Clinch Mountain Home' and 'My Little Home In Tennessee'. Several of Woody Guthrie's best-known songs used Carter Family tunes including 'This Land Is Your Land' ('When The World's On Fire') and 'Reuben James' ('Wildwood Flower'). He also regularly performed 'It Takes A Worried Man', which the Carters sang as 'Worried Man Blues'. Other folk artists influenced by their music include Joan Baez, who recorded many of their songs such as 'Little Darling Pal Of Mine' and 'Will The Circle Be Unbroken'. After the break-up of the original trio, Maybelle and her three daughters began to perform on the *Old Dominion Barn Dance* on WRVA Richmond. They appeared as Mother Maybelle and The Carter Sisters and were a popular act between 1943 and 1948. After spells at WNOX Knoxville and KWTO Springfield, they moved to WSM Nashville and joined the *Grand Ole Opry* in 1950, taking with them a young guitarist called Chet Atkins. During the 50s, Helen and Anita left to marry and pursue their own careers and June became a solo act. Maybelle remained a featured star of the *Opry* until 1967, when she was rejoined by Helen and Anita. In 1961, Maybelle even recorded an album of Carter Family songs with Flatt And Scruggs and in 1963, she appeared at the Newport Folk Festival. After June married singer Johnny Cash in 1968, Maybelle, Helen and Anita became regular members of the *Johnny Cash Show*. They had begun to make appearances with Cash the previous year. A.P retired to Maces Springs, where he opened a country store and lived with his daughter Gladys. Sara and her husband moved to Angel's Camp, California, where she withdrew from active participation in the music scene.

In 1952, seemingly at the request of her ex-husband, she was persuaded to record once more. Between 1952 and 1956, the A.P. Carter Family, consisting of Sara, A.P. and their son and daughter Joe and Janette, recorded almost 100 tracks for Acme Records. These included a 1956 recording made with Mrs. Jimmie Rodgers, which consisted of talk and a version of 'In The Sweet Bye And Bye'. Although these recordings never matched the work of the original trio, they did maintain traditional standards, whereas Maybelle and her daughters moved to a more modern country sound. In 1953, A.P. opened his 'Summer Park' in his beloved Clinch Mountains, near the home of Joe and Janette, and held concerts that featured such artists as the Stanley Brothers. A.P. Carter died at his home in Maces Springs on 7 November 1960. After A.P's death record companies began to release their material on album for the first time. In 1967 Sara was persuaded to appear with Maybelle at the Newport Folk Festival; the same year she and Maybelle, with Joe Carter taking his late father's bass part, recorded their classic *An Historic Reunion* album, which included their rather nostalgic 'Happiest Days Of All'. It was recorded in Nashville. The trio surprised the recording engineers by recording 12 tracks in just over four hours - an unusual event. It was the first time the two had recorded together for 25 years (in 1991, Bear Family reissued these recordings, plus a version of 'No More Goodbyes' that had not been released by Columbia, on a compact disc; it also contained a reissue of Mother Maybelle's 1966 album *A Living Legend*, and a further previously unissued recording of her instrumental 'Mama's Irish Jig'). In 1970, Sara and Maybelle were both present when the Original Carter Family became the first group ever to be elected to the Country Music Hall Of Fame And Museum. Their plaque stated that the Carter Family are 'regarded by many as the epitome of country greatness and originators of a much copied style'. Maybelle Carter, a most respected member of the country music world, continued to perform until her death in Nashville on 23 October 1978. Sara Carter died in Lodi, California, after a long illness, on 8 January 1979. The Carter Family inspired other groups to reproduce their sound, notably the Phipps Family of Kentucky, who among their many albums recorded tributes to the Carters such as *Echoes Of The Carter Family* and *Most Requested Sacred Songs Of The Carter Family*. Further afield, the Canadian Romaniuk Family also showed their ability to recapture the Carter Family sound with albums such as *Country Carter Style*.

● ALBUMS: by the Original Carter Family *The Famous Carter Family* (Harmony 1961)★★★, *The Original And Great Carter Family* (Camden 1962)★★★, *Great Original Recordings By The Carter Family* (Harmony 1962)★★★★, *The Carter Family (Original Recordings)* (Harmony 1963)★★★, *Mid The Green Fields Of Virginia* (RCA/Victor 1963)★★★, *A Collection Of Favorites (Folk Country Blues And Sacred Songs)* (Decca 1963)★★★, *Home Among The Hills* (Harmony 1965)★★★, *More Favorites By The Carter Family* (Decca 1965)★★★, *Great Sacred Songs* (Harmony 1966)★★★, *The Country Album* (Columbia 1967)★★★, *Country Sounds Of The Original Carter Family* (Harmony 1967)★★★, *Lonesome Pine Special* (Camden 1971)★★★, *More Golden Gems From The Original Carter Family* (Camden 1972)★★★, *The Carter Family On Border Radio, 1939* (JEMF 1972, reissued by Arhoolie 1996)★★★★, *My Old Cottage Home* (Camden 1973)★★, *The Happiest Days Of All* (Camden 1974)★★★,

Famous Country Music Makers UK release (RCA 1974)★★★, *The Original Carter Family From 1936 Radio Transcripts* (Old Homestead 1975)★★★, *Country's First Family* (Columbia 1976)★★★, *Legendary Performers* (1978)★★★, *The Carter Family* (Audiograph 1982)★★★, *Diamonds In The Rough* (County 1992)★★★★, *Clinch Mountain Treasures* (County 1992)★★★, *Anchored In Love - Their Complete Victor Recordings, 1927* (Rounder 1993)★★★, *My Clinch Mountain Home - Their Complete Victor Recordings, 1928-1929* (Rounder 1993)★★★, *When The Roses Bloom In Dixieland - Their Complete Victor Recordings, 1929-1930* (Rounder 1995)★★★, *Worried Man Blues - Their Complete Victor Recordings, 1930* (Rounder 1995)★★★★, *Sunshine In The Shadows - Their Complete Victor Recordings, 1931-1932* (Rounder 1996)★★★★, *Give Me Roses While I Live - Their Complete Victor Recordings, Volume 6* (Rounder 1997)★★★. By the A.P. Carter Family *All Time Favorites* (Acme 1960)★★★, *In Memory Of A.P. Carter (Keep On The Sunny Side)* (Acme 1960)★★★, *A.P. Carter's Clinch Mountain Ballads* (Pine Mountain 1970)★★★, *Their Last Recording (The Original A.P. Carter Family)* (Pine Mountain 1970)★★★. By Sara And Maybelle Carter *An Historic Reunion* (Columbia 1967)★★★, *Sara & Maybelle Carter* (Bear Family 1991)★★★. By Mother Maybelle With Anita, Helen And June *The Carter Family Album* (Liberty 1962)★★★, *Keep On The Sunny Side* (Columbia 1964)★★★, *The Carter Family Country Favorites* (Sunset 1967)★★★, *I Walk The Line* (Harmony 1970)★★★, *Travellin' Minstrel Band* (Columbia 1972)★★★, *The Carter Family - Three Generations* (Columbia 1974)★★★.

● COMPILATIONS: *Carter Family In Texas Volumes 1 - 7* (Old Homestead 1979)★★★, *20 Of The Best Of The Carter Family* (RCA International 1984)★★★★, *The Carter Family: Country Music Hall Of Fame Series* (MCA 1991)★★★★,.

● FURTHER READING: *The Carter Family*, John Atkins, Bob Coltman, Alec Davidson, Kip Lornell.

CARTER, A.P.
(see Carter Family)

CARTER, ANITA
b. Ina Anita Carter, 31 March 1933, Maces Springs, Scott County, Virginia, USA. The youngest daughter of Mother Maybelle Carter of the legendary Carter Family. She always maintains that she was singing professionally at the age of four, but did not get paid until she was six. In 1939, she and her sisters, Helen and June Carter, were appearing on Border Radio with the Carter Family. When the original Carter Family retired in 1943, she sang and played stand-up bass or rhythm guitar in the family group, Mother Maybelle and the Carter Sisters, on various radio stations, and from 1950 onwards, for many years, they were regulars on the *Grand Ole Opry*. They toured with Elvis Presley in the mid-50s, and in 1961, they began to appear regularly as part of Johnny Cash's show. She married fiddler Dale Potter in 1950 but the marriage soon ended. Although singing with her family group, she did at times also pursue a partially separate career. She made many solo recordings, the first being for RCA-Victor in 1950 and she also played bass and sang backing vocals regularly as a session musician. A year later she recorded with Hank Snow and they achieved Top 5 country hits with 'Bluebird Island' and 'Down The Trail Of Aching Hearts'. She continued to work as a session musician

and also recorded with Rita Robbins and Ruby Wright (the daughter of Kitty Wells) as Nita, Rita And Ruby. Carter married Don Davis and had a daughter, divorced Davis, then later remarried him and had a son before divorcing again in 1971. In 1962, she cut a duet album with Hank Snow and she later recorded for several major labels, including Mercury and Capitol. In 1968, 'I Got You', a duet with Waylon Jennings, reached number 4 and in 1969, a duet with Johnny Darrell, 'The Coming Of The Roads', also proved popular. She continued to travel with brother-in-law Cash during the late 70s and early 80s and was for a time married to Cash's guitarist, Bob Wootton. In 1982, she and sister Helen, with some of their children and a guest appearance from June's daughter, Carlene Carter, recorded for Audiograph. In 1988, working under the production of Jack Clements, she again recorded with her two sisters and Carlene. The resulting album proved very popular and both Clements and Hank Snow have wanted Anita to make further recordings. In recent years, although she has worked on various projects, she has suffered badly from arthritis, which has severely restricted her.

● ALBUMS: with Hank Snow *Together Again* (RCA Victor 1962)★★★, *Anita Carter Sings Folk Songs Old & New* (Mercury 1963)★★★★, *Anita Carter (Of The Carter Family)* (Mercury 1964)★★★, *So Much Love* (Capitol 1972)★★★, with Helen and other Family members *The Carter Family* (Audiograph 1982)★★★, with Carlene, Helen and June Carter *Wildwood Flower* (Mercury 1988)★★★.

● COMPILATIONS: *Folk Songs Old And New* (Bear Family 1984)★★★★, as Nita, Rita And Ruby *Rock Love* 1955-57 recordings (Bear Family 1985)★★★★, *Ring Of Fire* 60s recordings (Bear Family 1989)★★★★.

CARTER, CARLENE

b. Rebecca Carlene Smith, 26 September 1955, Nashville, Tennessee, USA. Carter is the daughter of country singers Carl Smith and June Carter and the granddaughter of Maybelle Carter of the Carter Family. She learnt piano at six years of age and guitar at 10, having lessons from Carl Perkins. Her parents divorced and, when she was 12, her mother married Johnny Cash. Carlene Carter herself first married when 16, and had a daughter Tiffany, but she and Joe Simpkins were divorced within two years. After college she joined her mother and stepfather on the road and was featured on Johnny Cash's family album *The Junkie And The Juicehead Minus Me* in 1974. Carlene then met Jack Routh, a writer for Cash's publishing company, and within three months they were married. They had a son, John Jackson Routh, but they separated in 1977. Carter brought her new boyfriend, Rodney Crowell, to the UK where she made an appealing, upbeat rock album with Graham Parker And The Rumour. Crowell's song 'Never Together But Close Sometimes' was almost a UK hit, and her song 'Easy From Now On' was recorded by Emmylou Harris. Carter had an assertive personality but she struggled with the dance tracks on her second album, *Two Sides To Every Woman*, which was made in New York. *Musical Shapes* was produced by her new husband Nick Lowe; the songs included her 'Appalachian Eyes' and a duet with Dave Edmunds, 'Baby Ride Easy'. Her 1981 album *Blue Nun* was also produced by Lowe and featured members of Rockpile and Squeeze. The album, with such titles as 'Do Me Lover' and 'Think Dirty', was an

explicit celebration of sex, but just as she seemed to be rejecting her country roots, she joined her family onstage at the Wembley Country Music Festival for 'Will The Circle Be Unbroken?'. Carter, whose marriage to Lowe broke up, was prevented from calling her next album *Gold Miner's Daughter*, and settled for *C'est Bon*. She was featured in *Too Drunk To Remember*, a short film shown at the London Film Festival, based on one of her songs. In 1985 she won acclaim for her role as one of the waitresses in the London cast of the musical *Pump Boys And Dinettes*, which starred Paul Jones and Kiki Dee. In 1990 Carter, by making an album, *I Fell In Love*, aimed to please rather than alienate country fans. Produced by Howie Epstein, the musicians included Dave Edmunds, Kiki Dee, Albert Lee, Jim Keltner, and such songs as 'Me And Wildwood Rose' celebrated her country music heritage. Carter has the potential of a fine country songwriter, and the song 'Guardian Angel' shows she has enough experiences on which to draw. Unfortunately, Carter may have discarded much of her personality in order to become a mainstream country artist. *Little Acts Of Treason* was comparatively bland, a word not previously associated with her.

● ALBUMS: *Carlene Carter* (Warners 1978)★★★, *Two Sides To Every Woman* (Warners 1979)★★, *Musical Shapes* (F-Beat 1980)★★★, *Blue Nun* (F-Beat 1981)★★, *C'est Bon* (Epic 1983)★★★, with Anita, Helen and June Carter *Wildwood Flower* (Mercury 1988)★★★, *I Fell In Love* (Reprise 1990)★★, *Musical Shapes & Blue Nun* reissue (Demon 1992)★★★, *Little Love Letters* (Giant 1993)★★★, *Little Acts Of Treason* (Giant 1995)★★★.

● COMPILATIONS: *Hindsight 20/20* (Giant 1996)★★★★.

● VIDEOS: *Open Fire* (Hendring Video 1990).

CARTER, DEANA

b. 1964, Nashville, Tennessee, USA. Something of a latecomer to country music, Carter recorded her first album at the age of 29. The daughter of Nashville alumnus Fred Carter Jr (a guitarist who played with everyone from Elvis Presley to Simon And Garfunkel to Roy Orbison), she grafted pop influences onto the country singer-songwriter tradition, earning comparisons to the crossover appeal of Dolly Parton or Tammy Wynette. Songs such as 'Turn Those Wheels Around' and 'Angel Without A Prayer' caught the attention of Willie Nelson (another artist with whom Carter's father had played), and he invited her to perform at 1994's Farm Aid. Produced by Jimmy Bowen, her debut offered polished pop and country songs in 'Are You Coming Home', 'Rita Valentine' and 'Graffiti Bridge'. The success of *Did I Shave Me Legs For This?* garnered her a CMA award in September 1997, just as the album clocked up 3 million sales.

● ALBUMS: *Did I Shave Me Legs For This?* (Capitol 1996)★★★★.

CARTER, FRED F., JNR.

b. 31 December 1933, Winnsboro, Louisiana, USA. Carter has loved country music since he was a child and learned to play the guitar. Performing with local bands, he was signed by Conway Twitty in the late 50s. Carter played on numerous Nashville sessions during the 60s, putting his ability to improvise to good effect. He made a single for Monument, 'And You Wonder Why', in 1967. He played on records by Bob Dylan, Ronnie Hawkins, Waylon Jennings and, in particular, was featured on Simon And Garfunkel's 'The Boxer'.

He ran both ABC Records' Nashville office and Nugget Records and produced *Cannons In The Rain* (John Stewart) and *American Son* (Levon Helm).

CARTER, HELEN

b. September 1927, Maces Springs, Scott County, Virginia, USA. The eldest daughter of Mother Maybelle Carter of the legendary Carter Family. At the age of eight, she was playing mandolin, piano, piano accordion and guitar and in 1939, she and sisters Anita and June were appearing on Border Radio as members of the Carter Family. When the original Carter Family retired in 1943, she sang and played rhythm guitar in the family group, Mother Maybelle and the Carter Sisters, on various radio stations and from 1950 onwards, for many years, they were regulars on the *Grand Ole Opry*. They toured with Elvis Presley in the mid-50s, and in 1961, they began to appear regularly as part of Johnny Cash's show. Although most of her career has been spent playing as a member of a group, she recorded a solo album in memory of her mother on which her son, David, played guitar and sang harmony vocals in best Carter Family tradition.
● ALBUMS: *This Is For You Mama* (Old Homestead 1979)★★★, with Anita, Carlene and June Carter *Wildwood Flower* (Mercury 1988)★★★.

CARTER, MAYBELLE

(see Carter Family)

CARTER, SARA

(see Carter Family)

CARTER, WILF

b. 18 December 1904, Port Hilford, Guysborough County, Nova Scotia, Canada, d. 5 December 1996, Scottsdale, Arizona, USA. Carter's father, a travelling Baptist minister, was born in Switzerland and his mother in Aldershot, Hampshire, England. Rejecting his mother's wish for him to be a preacher, Wilf was working on a farm with a team of oxen and ploughing at the age of 13. After hearing a vaude-ville artist called the Yodelling Fool, he was so impressed that he knew he had to seek a similar career. Soon after-wards he left home, living with tramps and hobos and working as a lumberjack and teamster before finding work as a cowboy. He learned to play the guitar and, writing most of his material, he was soon singing locally. In 1924, he joined the Canadian rodeo circuit, where he mixed com-peting with singing. Around 1926, he auditioned for a Calgary radio station and was told to 'stick to milking cows' but in 1930, after singing at the famed *Calgary Stampede*, he was offered his own radio show. He also found employment with Canadian Pacific Railways, who used him as an enter-tainer on organized trail drives through the Rocky Mountains. They also sent him as a singer on their cruise ship SS *Empress Of Britain to The West Indies*. In December 1933, RCA-Victor in Montreal, noting the success of Jimmie Rodgers and his blue yodels in the USA, decided to record Carter, who had become known as the Yodelling Cowboy. His first session produced his now classic 'Swiss Moonlight Lullaby' (written when he was a trail rider in Alberta) and a song about a real life murder hunt in 'The Capture Of Albert Johnson'. When he returned from the cruise, he found the record had been released and was proving popular. This launched a recording career that extended to the 80s and saw him record hundreds of his own songs. Many had a western influence such as 'Twilight On The Prairie'; some were event songs such as 'The Life And Death Of John Dillinger'; others were nostalgic ballads of mother and home as witnessed in 'My Little Gray Haired Mother In The West'. Several referred to his rodeo days and many naturally fea-tured his considerable talent for yodelling, including a spe-ciality speed yodel, which he always referred to as his three-in-one. He worked on CFCN Calgary in 1933 but soon moved to New York, where he played on the CBS network. It was here in 1934 that he was first introduced as Montana Slim, probably to distinguish him from the Carter Family. He said he did not mind what they called him as long as they paid him, and during his long career, he has become equally well known by both names. He was involved in a bad car crash in Montana in 1940, which kept him from touring and doing radio work for nine years, but did not prevent him recording. In 1949, accompanied by his two daughters, Sheila and Carol, he again toured. He went into semi-retire-ment in Florida in the 60s but continued to make appear-ances at special events such as the *Calgary Stampede*. He has been an influence on other artists, particularly Slim Whitman, who has sung several of Carter's songs, and had success in Britain with 'Love Knot In My Lariat'. Wilf Carter (Montana Slim) was elected to the Nashville Songwriters Association International Hall Of Fame in 1971.
● ALBUMS: *Montana Slim-Wilf Carter* i (Camden 1959)★★★, *I'm Ragged But I'm Right* (Decca 1959)★★★★, *The Dynamite Trail* (Decca 1960)★★★★, *Reminiscin' With Montana Slim* (Camden 1962)★★★, *By Request* (early 60s)★★, *Wilf Carter As Montana Slim* (Starday 1964)★★★, *32 Wonderful Years* (Camden 1965)★★★, *Let's Go Back To The Bible* (mid-60s)★★, *Nuggets Of The Golden West* (mid-60s)★★★★, *Yodelling Memories* (mid-60s)★★★ *Christmas In Canada* (mid-60s)★★, *Calgary Horseman's Hall Of Fame* (mid-60s)★★★, *Balladeer Of The Golden West* (mid-60s)★★★, *Montana Slim/Wilf Carter* ii (Starday 1966)★★★★, *God Bless Our Canada* (1967)★★, *Waitin' For The Maple Leaves To Fall* (1967)★★★, *No Letter Today* (Camden 1967)★★★, *Golden Memories* (late 60s)★★, *If It Wasn't For The Farmer* (late 60s)★★, *Old Prairie Melodies* (late 60s)★★★, *Sings Jimmie Rodgers* (1969)★★★, *How My Yodelling Days Began* (1970)★★★, *Songs Of The Rail And Range* (early 70s)★★★, *Hittin' The Track* (early 70s)★★, *Sings Songs Of Australia* (early 70s)★★, *Away Out There* (early 70s)★★★, *The Yodelling Swiss* (early 70s)★★★, *Walls Of Memory* (early 70s)★★★, *Bridle Hangin' On The Wall* (early 70s)★★★, *A Message From Home Sweet Home* (early 70s)★★, *My Heartache's Your Happiness* (1972)★★, *40th Anniversary* (1973)v, *Souvenir Album* (1974)★★★★, *There Goes My Everything* (1975)★★★, *The First Five Sessions* (mid-70s)★★★, *The Sixth & Seventh Sessions* (mid-70s)★★★, *My Old Canadian Home* (mid-70s)★★★, *Have A Nice Day* (RCA Victor 1977)★★★, *Songs I Love To Sing* (1977)★★, *Walkin' The Streets Of Calgary* (1978)★★★, *I'm Happy Today* (1979)★★, *Songs Of The Calgary Stampede* (late 70s)★★★, *My Home On The Range* (1980)★★★, *Chinook Winds* (1981)★★★, *Canadian Yodelling Cowboy* (1986)★★★, *Montana Slim* (1987)★★, *Whatever Happened To All Those Years?* (1988)★★.
● COMPILATIONS: *Montana Slim's Greatest Hits* (Camden

1974)★★★★, *50 Golden Years* (1983)★★★★*The Days Of The Yodelling Cowboys, Volume 3 Wilf Carter (Montana Slim)* (1988)★★★, *Dynamite Trail - The Decca Years, 1954-1958* (Bear Family 1990)★★★★, *A Canadian Legend* 4-CD set (Bear Family 1994)★★★★, *The Golden Years* (Collectors Choice 1996)★★★, *Wilf Carter - Montana Slim* 8-CD box set (Bear Family 1997)★★★★.
● FURTHER READING: *The Yodelling Cowboy*, Wilf Carter.

CARTWRIGHT, LIONEL

b. 10 February 1960, Gallipolis, Ohio, USA. Raised in West Virginia, Cartwright has been performing country music since he was a child. He became a pianist for the WWVA Jamboree in Wheeling, West Virginia, and graduated to a position as the show's musical director. He moved to Nashville in 1982 and recorded demos for the songwriters Felice and Boudleaux Bryant. He joined the cast of the musical situation comedy *1-40 Paradise*, becoming a veteran of over 500 episodes. Success in a television soap often leads to a recording contract, and soon he was on the US country charts with 'You're Gonna Make Her Mine' and then 'Give Me His Last Chance' in 1988. His only number 1 country single was with 'Leap Of Faith' in 1991. Cartwright is proficient on guitar, mandolin and keyboards and has written most of the songs he has recorded. He parodied the television programme *30-Something* with '30-Nothing'. The backing vocalists on *Chasin' The Sun* include Marty Brown, Alison Krauss and Ricky Skaggs.
● ALBUMS: *Lionel Cartwright* (MCA 1989)★★★, *I Watched It On The Radio* (MCA 1990)★★★, *Chasin' The Sun* (MCA 1991)★★★.

CARVER, JOHNNY

b. John David Carver, 20 November 1940, Jackson, Mississippi, USA. Carver started out in a family gospel group, formed his own band in high school and then took a band on the road around the USA. In 1965 he was the featured singer at the Palomino Club in Hollywood, which led to a contract with Imperial Records. His first country hits were 'Your Lily White Hands', 'I Still Didn't Have The Sense To Go', 'Hold Me Tight' and 'Sweet Wine'. His songs were recorded by Ferlin Husky, Connie Smith and Roy Drusky. On ABC/Dot from 1973, he covered pop hits for the country market, such as 'Tie A Yellow Ribbon Round The Old Oak Tree', 'Afternoon Delight' and 'Living Next Door To Alice'. His last chart entry was in 1981 with 'S.O.S'. On the 90s Carver has performed with his Nashville All-Star Band.
● ALBUMS: *Real Country* (Imperial 1967)★★★, *Leaving Again* (Imperial 1968)★★★★, *You're In Good Hands With Johnny Carver* (1968)★★★, *Sweet Wine/Hold Me Tight* (1969)★★★, *I Start Thinking About You* (ABC 1973)★★, *Tie A Yellow Ribbon Round The Old Oak Tree* (ABC 1973)★★, *Don't Tell That Sweet Old Lady* (ABC 1974)★★★, *Double Exposure* (ABC 1974)★★★, *Lines, Circles And Triangles* (ABC 1974)★★, *Strings* (ABC 1975)★★, *Afternoon Delight* (ABC 1976)★★★.
● COMPILATIONS: *The Best Of Johnny Carver* (ABC 1977)★★★.

CASEY, CLAUDE

b. 13 September 1912, Enoree, South Carolina, USA. Casey learned guitar as a boy. The family relocated to Danville, Virginia, in the late 20s, where, in 1931, as well as working

in textile mills, he regularly appeared on WBTM as the Carolina Hobo. He first recorded in 1937, with Tex Isley for ARC, but none of the tracks were released. In 1938, with his Pine State Playboys, which included Jimmy Rouse (fiddle) and pianist Willie Coates, he recorded two sessions for RCA/Bluebird Records and played daily shows on WFTC Kinston, North Carolina. In 1939, hard times saw the band break up, and for a time, he worked in the mills. He later toured with Fat Sanders Country Cousins, which featured a hillbilly striptease, and also worked in Florida with the Rouse Brothers before forming a new band in 1940. They recorded in Atlanta, but in 1941, he gained a solo spot at WBT Charlotte where he remained for many years. Here, he also worked with the Briarhoppers and the Tennessee Ramblers, with whom he appeared in the Dale Evans film *Swing Your Partner*. In 1949, a further film appearance saw him sing two solo numbers in *Square Dance Jubilee*. In the late 40s, he recorded for RCA/Victor Records with musicians called, for the recordings, his Sagedusters, and made his final recordings in 1953 for MGM Records. He continued to perform until 1961, when he became involved in business by founding WJES Johnston, South Carolina. He ran the station through to the mid-80s, when his son, Michael, took over. Casey came out of retirement in 1985 to sing at a Charlotte reunion concert with several of his old associates from the Tennessee Ramblers, and he has also appeared at some Western Fairs. Throughout his career, he adopted a western style of dress for himself and his musicians and his Pine State Playboys have been rated, along with Hank Penny's Radio Cowboys, as one of the leading western swing bands of the south-eastern region.
● ALBUMS: *Pine State Honky Tonk* (Old Homestead 1987)★★★.

CASH, JOHNNY

b. 26 February 1932, Kingsland, Arkansas, USA. Cash has traced his ancestry to seventeenth-century Scotland and has admitted that he fabricated the much-publicized story that he was a quarter Cherokee. Cash's father, Ray, worked on sawmills and the railway; in 1936, the family was one of 600 chosen by the Federal Government to reclaim land by the Mississippi River, known as the Dyess Colony Scheme. Much of it was swampland, and in 1937, they were evacuated when the river overflowed. Cash recalled the circumstances in his 1959 country hit 'Five Foot High And Risin''. Other songs inspired by his youth are 'Pickin' Time', 'Christmas As I Knew It' and 'Cisco Clifton's Filling Station'. Carl Perkins wrote 'Daddy Sang Bass' about Cash's family and the 'little brother' is Jack Cash, who was killed when he fell across an electric saw. Cash was posted to Germany as a radio-operator in the US Army. Many think the scar on his cheek is a knife wound but it is the result of a cyst being removed by a drunken doctor, while his hearing was permanently damaged by a German girl playfully sticking a pencil down his left ear. After his discharge, he settled in San Antonio with his bride, Vivian Liberto. One of their four children, Rosanne Cash, also became a country singer. Cash auditioned as a gospel singer with Sam Phillips of Sun Records in Memphis, who told him to return with something more commercial. Cash developed his 'boom chicka boom' sound with two friends: Luther Perkins (lead guitar) and Marshall Grant (bass). Their first record, 'Hey Porter'/'Cry,

Cry, Cry', credited to Johnny Cash And The Tennessee Two, was released in June 1955, but Cash was irritated that Phillips had called him 'Johnny', as it sounded too young. 'Cry, Cry, Cry' made number 14 on the US country charts and was followed by 'Folsom Prison Blues', which Cash wrote after seeing a film called *Inside The Walls Of Folsom Prison*. They played shows with Carl Perkins (no relation to Luther Perkins). Perkins' drummer, W.S. Holland, joined Cash in 1958 to make it the Tennessee Three. Cash encouraged Perkins to complete the writing of 'Blue Suede Shoes', while he finished 'I Walk The Line' at Perkins' insistence: 'I got the idea from a Dale Carnegie course. It taught you to keep your eyes open for something good. I made a love song out of it. It was meant to be a slow, mournful ballad but Sam had us pick up the tempo until I didn't like it at all.' 'I Walk The Line' reached number 17 on the US pop charts and was the title song for a 1970 film starring Gregory Peck. Among his other excellent Sun records are 'Home Of The Blues', which was the name of a Memphis record shop, 'Big River', 'Luther Played The Boogie', 'Give My Love To Rose' and 'There You Go', which topped the US country charts for five weeks. Producer Jack Clement added piano and vocal chorus. They achieved further pop hits with the high school tale 'Ballad Of A Teenage Queen' (number 14), 'Guess Things Happen That Way' (number 11) and 'The Ways Of A Woman In Love' (number 24). While at Sun Records, Cash wrote 'You're My Baby' and 'Rock 'N' Roll Ruby' which were recorded by Roy Orbison and Warren Smith, respectively. Despite having his photograph taken with Elvis Presley, Jerry Lee Lewis and Carl Perkins, he did not take part in the 'million dollar session' but went shopping instead.

At a disc jockeys' convention in Nashville in November 1957, Sun launched their first ever album release, *Johnny Cash With His Hot And Blue Guitar*, but Phillips was reluctant to record further LPs with Cash. This, and an unwillingness to increase his royalties, led to Cash joining Columbia Records in 1958. His cautionary tale about a gunfighter not listening to his mother, 'Don't Take Your Guns To Town', sold half a million copies and prompted a response from Charlie Rich, 'The Ballad Of Billy Joe', which was also recorded by Jerry Lee Lewis. Its b-side, 'I Still Miss Someone', is one of Cash's best compositions, and has been revived by Flatt And Scruggs, Crystal Gayle and Emmylou Harris. Cash started to take drugs to help make it through his schedule of 300 shows a year; however, his artistic integrity suffered and he regards *The Sound Of Johnny Cash* as his worst album. Nevertheless, he started on an inspiring series of concept albums about the working man (*Blood, Sweat And Tears*), cowboys (*Ballads Of The True West*) and the American Indian (*Bitter Tears*). The concepts are fascinating, the songs excellent, but the albums are bogged down with narration and self-righteousness, making Cash sound like a history teacher. His sympathy for a maligned American Indian, 'The Ballad Of Ira Hayes', led to threats from the Ku Klux Klan. Cash says, 'I didn't really care what condition I was in and it showed up on my recordings, but *Bitter Tears* was so important to me that I managed to get enough sleep to do it right.' For all his worthy causes, the drugged-up country star was a troublemaker himself, although, despite press reports, he only ever spent three days in prison. His biggest misdemeanour was starting a forest fire for which he was fined $85,000. He wrecked hotel rooms and toyed with guns. He and his drinking buddy,

country singer Carl Smith, rampaged through Smith's house and ruined his wife's Cadillac. Smith's marriage to June Carter of the Carter Family was nearing its end but at that stage, few could have predicted Carter's next marriage. In 1963, Mexican brass was added to the ominous 'Ring Of Fire', written by Carter and Merle Kilgore, which again was a pop hit. Without Cash's support, Bob Dylan would have been dropped by Columbia, and Cash had his first British hit in 1965 with Dylan's 'It Ain't Me Babe'. Their offbeat duet, 'Girl From The North Country', was included on Dylan's *Nashville Skyline*, and the rest of their sessions have been widely bootlegged. Dylan also gave Cash an unreleased song, 'Wanted Man'. Cash said, 'I don't dance, tell jokes or wear my pants too tight, but I do know about a thousand songs.' With this in mind, he has turned his roadshow into a history of country music. In the 60s it featured Carl Perkins (who also played guitar for Cash after Luther Perkins' death in a fire), the Statler Brothers and the Carter Family. The highlight of Cash's act was 'Orange Blossom Special' played with two harmonicas. One night Cash proposed to June Carter on stage; she accepted and they were married in March 1968. Their successful duets include 'Jackson' and 'If I Were A Carpenter'.

In 1968 Columbia finally agreed to record one of Cash's prison concerts, and the invigorating album *Johnny Cash At Folsom Prison* is one of the most atmospheric of all live albums. It remains, arguably, Cash's best album and a contender for the best country record of all time. Cash explains: 'Prisoners are the greatest audience that an entertainer can perform for. We bring them a ray of sunshine and they're not ashamed to show their appreciation.' He included 'Graystone Chapel', written by an inmate, Glen Sherley, which he had been given by the Prison Chaplain. Sherley subsequently recorded an album with Cash's support, but he died in 1978. The Folsom Prison concert was followed by one at San Quentin, which was filmed for a television documentary. Shortly before that concert, Shel Silverstein gave Cash a poem, 'A Boy Named Sue'. Carl Perkins put chords to it and, without any rehearsals, the humorous song was recorded, giving Cash his only Top 10 on the US pop charts and a number 4 success in the UK. Cash's popularity led to him hosting his own television series from 1969-71, but, despite notable guests such as Bob Dylan, the show was hampered by feeble jokes and middle-of-the-road arrangements. Far better was the documentary *Johnny Cash - The Man, His World, His Music*. Cash's catchphrase, 'Hello, I'm Johnny Cash', became so well known that both Elvis Presley and the Kinks' Ray Davies sometimes opened with that remark. Cash championed Kris Kristofferson, wrote the liner notes for his first album, *Kristofferson*, and recorded several of his songs. 'To Beat The Devil' celebrated Cash overcoming drugs after many years, while 'The Loving Gift' was about the birth of Cash's son John Carter Cash, who has since joined his stage show. Cash has often found strength and comfort in religion and he has recorded many spiritual albums. One of his most stirring performances is 'Were You There (When They Crucified My Lord)?' with the Carter Family. He made a documentary film and double album *The Gospel Road* with Kristofferson, Larry Gatlin and the Statler Brothers, but, as he remarked, 'My record company would rather I'd be in prison than in church.' He justified himself commercially when 'A Thing Called Love', written by Jerry Reed, made with the Evangel Temple Choir, became one of his biggest-selling UK records, reaching number 4 in 1972.

Cash is an imposing figure with his huge muscular frame, black hair, craggy face and deep bass voice. Unlike other country singers, he shuns lavish colours and in his song 'Man In Black', he explains that he wears black because of the injustice in the world. In truth, he started wearing black when he first appeared on the *Grand Ole Opry* because he felt that rhinestone suits detracted from the music. With little trouble, Cash could have been a major Hollywood star, particularly in westerns, and he acquitted himself well when the occasion arose. He made his debut in *Five Minutes To Live* in 1960 and his best role was opposite Kirk Douglas in the 1972 film *A Gunfight*, which was financed by Apache money, although religious principles prevented a scene with a naked actress. He was featured alongside Kris Kristofferson and Willie Nelson in a light-hearted remake of *Stagecoach* and starred in a television movie adaptation of his pool-hall song *The Baron*. Cash also gave a moving portrayal of a coalminer overcoming illiteracy in another television movie, *The Pride Of Jesse Hallam*. He recorded the theme for the US television series *The Rebel - Johnny Yuma* and, among the previously unissued tracks released by Bear Family Records, is his submission for a James Bond theme, 'Thunderball'. By opening his own recording studios, House Of Cash, in 1972, he became even more prolific. His family joined him on the quirky *The Junkie And The Juicehead Minus Me* and his son-in-law J.W. Routh wrote several songs and performed with him on *The Rambler*. He has always followed writers and the inclusion of Nick Lowe, former husband of Carlene Carter, and Rodney Crowell, husband of Rosanne Cash, into his family increased his awareness. His recordings include the Rolling Stones' 'No Expectations', John Prine's 'Unwed Fathers', Guy Clark's 'The Last Gunfighter Ballad' and a touching portrayal of Bruce Springsteen's 'Highway Patrolman'. He showed his humour with 'Gone Girl', 'One Piece At A Time' and 'Chicken In Black'. Cash moved to Mercury Records in 1986 and found success immediately with the whimsical 'The Night Hank Williams Came To Town'. He made an all-star album, *Water From The Wells Of Home*, with Emmylou Harris, the Everly Brothers, Paul McCartney and many others. His 60s composition 'Tennessee Flat-Top Box' became a US country number 1 for daughter Rosanne in 1988. In the same year, various UK modern folk artists recorded an album of his songs *'Til Things Are Brighter*, with proceeds going to an AIDS charity. Cash particularly enjoyed Sally Timms' waltz-time treatment of 'Cry, Cry, Cry'. On the crest of a revival, Cash has been hampered by pneumonia, heart surgery and a recurrence of drug problems. He has since returned to the stage, either touring with the Carter Family or as part of the Highwaymen with Kristofferson, Waylon Jennings and Nelson. He is still passionate about his beliefs: 'A lot of people think of country singers as right-wing, redneck bigots,' he says, 'but I don't think I'm like that.'

In all, Cash has made over 70 albums of original material, plus countless guest appearances. His music reflects his love of America (a recent compilation was called *Patriot*), his compassion, his love of life, and, what is often lacking in country music, a sense of humour. His limited range is staggeringly impressive on particular songs, especially narrative ones. Like Bo Diddley's 'shave and a haircut' rhythm, he has developed his music around his 'boom chicka boom', and instilled enough variety to stave off boredom. In a genre now dominated by new country, Cash has found it difficult to obtain record contracts of late, but this worked to his advantage with the low-key *American Recordings*, produced by Rick Rubin in 1994. Featuring just his craggy voice and simple guitar, it reaffirmed his talent for storytelling. Among the many excellent songs included Nick Lowe's 'The Beast In Me' (Lowe was a former son-in-law), Tom Waits' 'Down There By The Train' and Loudon Wainwright's 'The Man Who Couldn't Cry'. An appearance at the Glastonbury Festival in 1994 also introduced him to a new audience, this time indie and new wave rockers. In the USA during 1994 Cash became a media star and was featured on the cover on many magazines (not just music ones). It was an astonishing rebirth of interest. *Unchained* continued his renaissance, with effortless cover versions of Don Gibson's 'Sea Of Heartbreak' and the Dean Martin classic 'Memories Are Made Of This'. His continuing popularity assured, Cash states he heeded the advice he was given during his one and only singing lesson, 'Never change your voice.' More worryingly, Cash announced he was suffering from Parkinson's disease at a Flint, Michigan concert on 25 October 1997, and was hospitalized with double pneumonia soon afterwards. His gigantic contribution to country music's history is inestimable and, as he says, 'They can get all the synthesizers they want, but nothing will ever take the place of the human heart.'

● ALBUMS: *Johnny Cash With His Hot And Blue Guitar* (Sun 1957)★★★, *Johnny Cash Sings The Songs That Made Him Famous* (Sun 1958)★★★, *The Fabulous Johnny Cash* (Columbia 1958)★★★, *Hymns By Johnny Cash* (Columbia 1959)★, *Songs Of Our Soil* (Columbia 1959)★★, *Now There Was A Song* (Columbia 1960)★★, *Johnny Cash Sings Hank Williams And Other Favorite Tunes* (Sun 1960)★★★, *Ride This Train* (Columbia 1960)★★★★, *Now Here's Johnny Cash* (Sun 1961)★★★, *The Lure Of The Grand Canyon* (Columbia 1961)★★, *Hymns From The Heart* (Columbia 1962)★, *The Sound Of Johnny Cash* (Columbia 1962)★★, *All Aboard The Blue Train* (Sun 1963)★★★, *Blood, Sweat And Tears* (Columbia 1963)★★★, *The Christmas Spirit* (Columbia 1963)★★, with the Carter Family *Keep On The Sunny Side* (1964)★★★, *I Walk The Line* (Columbia 1964)★★★★, *Bitter Tears (Ballads Of The American Indian)* (Columbia 1964)★★★, *Orange Blossom Special* (Columbia 1964)★★★★, *Mean As Hell* (Columbia 1965)★★, *The Sons Of Katie Elder* film soundtrack (Columbia 1965)★★, *Johnny Cash Sings Ballads Of The True West* (Columbia 1965)★★★, *Ballads Of The True West, Volume 2* (Columbia 1965)★★★, *Everybody Loves A Nut* (Columbia 1966)★, *Happiness Is You* (Columbia 1966)★★, with June Carter *Carryin' On* (Columbia 1967)★★, *From Sea To Shining Sea* (Columbia 1967)★★, *Old Golden Throat* (Columbia 1968)★★, *Johnny Cash At Folsom Prison* (Columbia 1968)★★★★, *The Holy Land* (Columbia 1968)★, *More Of Old Golden Throat* (Columbia 1969)★★, *Johnny Cash At San Quentin* (Columbia 1969)★★★★, *Hello I'm Johnny Cash* (Columbia 1970)★★★, *The Johnny Cash Show* (Columbia 1970)★★★, with Carl Perkins *Little Fauss And Big Halsey* (Columbia 1970)★★, *The Man In Black* (Columbia 1971)★★★, with Jerry Lee Lewis *Sings Hank Williams* (Sun 1971)★★, *A Thing Called Love* (Columbia 1972)★★, with Jerry Lee Lewis *Sunday Down South* (Sun 1972)★★,

Christmas And The Cash Family (Columbia 1972)★★, *America (A 200-Year Salute In Story And Song)* (Columbia 1972)★★, *Any Old Wind That Blows* (Columbia 1973)★★, *The Gospel Road* (Columbia 1973)★★, with June Carter *Johnny Cash And His Woman* (Columbia 1973)★★, *Ragged Old Flag* (Columbia 1974)★★, *The Junkie And The Juicehead Minus Me* (Columbia 1974)★★, *Pa Osteraker* (Columbia 1974)★★ reissued as *Inside A Swedish Prison* (Bear Family 1982), *John R. Cash* (Columbia 1975)★★★, *Look At Them Beans* (Columbia 1975)★★, *The Johnny Cash Children's Album* (1975)★★, *Strawberry Cake* (Columbia 1976)★★★, *One Piece At A Time* (Columbia 1976)★★★★, *The Last Gunfighter Ballad* (Columbia 1977)★★★, *The Rambler* (Columbia 1977)★★, *Gone Girl* (Columbia 1978)★★★, *I Would Like To See You Again* (Columbia 1978)★★★, *Silver* (Columbia 1979)★★★, *A Believer Sings The Truth* (Columbia 1979)★★, *Rockabilly Blues* (Columbia 1980)★★★★, *The Baron* (Columbia 1981)★★★, with Jerry Lee Lewis, Carl Perkins *The Survivors* (Columbia 1982)★★★, *The Adventures Of Johnny Cash* (Columbia 1982)★★, *Johnny 99* (Columbia 1983)★★, *Rainbow* (Columbia 1985)★★★, with Kris Kristofferson, Waylon Jennings, Willie Nelson *Highwayman* (Columbia 1985)★★★★, with Jerry Lee Lewis, Carl Perkins, Roy Orbison *The Class Of '55* (1986)★★★, with Waylon Jennings *Heroes* (Columbia 1986)★★★, *Believe In Him* (Word 1986)★★, *Johnny Cash Is Back In Town* (Mercury 1987)★★★, *Water From The Wells Of Home* (Mercury 1988)★★★★, *Boom Chicka Boom* (Mercury 1989)★★★, with Kristofferson, Jennings and Nelson *Highwayman 2* (Columbia 1990)★★★, *The Mystery Of Life* (Mercury 1991)★★★, *Get Rhythm* (Sun 1991)★★★, *American Recordings* (American 1994)★★★★, with Kristofferson, Jennings and Nelson *The Road Goes On Forever* (Liberty 1995)★★, *Unchained* (American 1996)★★★.
● COMPILATIONS: *Johnny Cash's Greatest* (Sun 1959)★★★, *Ring Of Fire (The Best Of Johnny Cash)* (Columbia 1963)★★★, *The Original Sun Sound Of Johnny Cash* (Sun 1965)★★★, *Johnny Cash's Greatest Hits, Volume 1* (Columbia 1967)★★★, *Original Golden Hits, Volume 1* (Sun 1969)★★★, *Original Golden Hits, Volume 2* (Sun 1969)★★★, *Get Rhythm* (Sun 1969)★★★, *Story Songs Of The Trains And Rivers* (Sun 1969)★★★, *Showtime* (Sun 1969)★★★, *The Rough Cut King Of Country Music* (Sun 1970)★★★, *The Singing Story Teller* (Sun 1970)★★★, *The Legend* (Sun 1970)★★★★, *The World Of Johnny Cash* (Columbia 1970)★★★★, *Original Golden Hits, Volume 3* (Sun 1971)★★, *Johnny Cash: The Man, The World, His Music* (Sun 1971)★★★, *His Greatest Hits, Volume 2* (Columbia 1971)★★★, *Destination Victoria Station* (Bear Family 1976)★★, *Superbilly* (Sun 1977)★★, *Golden Souvenirs* (Plantation 1977)★★★, *The Unissued Johnny Cash* (Bear Family 1978)★★, *Greatest Hits, Volume 3* (Columbia 1978)★★★, *Johnny And June* (Bear Family 1980)★★, *Tall Man* (Bear Family 1980)★★★, *Encore (Greatest Hits, Volume 4)* (Columbia 1981)★★★, *Biggest Hits* (Columbia 1982)★★★, *Johnny Cash: The Sun Years* 5-LP box set (Sun 1984)★★★★, *Up Through The Years, 1955-1957* (Bear Family 1986)★★★★, *Johnny Cash - Columbia Records 1958-1986* (Columbia 1987)★★★★, *Vintage Years: 1955-1963* (Rhino 1987)★★★, *Classic Cash* (Mercury 1988)★★★, *The Sun Years* (Rhino 1990)★★★★, *I Walk The Line And Other Big Hits* (Rhino 1990)★★★, *The Man In Black: 1954-1958* 5-CD box set (Bear Family 1990)★★★★, *Come Along And Ride This Train* 4-CD box set (Bear Family 1991)★★★, *The Man In Black: 1959-*

1962 5-CD box set (Bear Family 1992)★★★★, *The Essential Johnny Cash 1955-1983* 3-CD box set (Columbia/Legacy 1992)★★★★, *Wanted Man* (Mercury 1994)★★★, *The Man In Black: The Definitive Collection* (Columbia 1994)★★★★, *Get Rhythm: The Best Of The Sun Years* (Pickwick 1995)★★★, *Ring Of Fire* (Spectrum 1995)★★★, *The Man In Black: 1963-1969 Plus* 6-CD box set (Bear Family 1996)★★★★, *All American Country* (Spectrum 1997)★★★, *Tennessee Top Cat Live 1955-1965* (Cotton Town Jubilee 1997)★★★★.
● VIDEOS: *Live In London: Johnny Cash* (BBC Video 1987), *In San Quentin* (Vestron 1987), *Riding The Rails* (Hendring Video 1990), *Johnny Cash Live!* (1993), *The Tennessee Top Cat Live 1955-1965* (Jubilee 1995), *The Man, His World, The Music* (1995).
● FURTHER READING: *Johnny Cash Discography And Recording History 1954-1969*, John L. Smith. *A Boy Named Cash*, Albert Govoni. *The Johnny Cash Story*, George Carpozi. *Johnny Cash: Winners Get Scars Too*, Christopher S. Wren. *The New Johnny Cash*, Charles Paul Conn. *Man In Black*, Johnny Cash. *The Johnny Cash Discography 1954-1984*, John L. Smith. *The Johnny Cash Record Catalogue*, John L. Smith (ed.). *Johnny Cash - The Autobiography*, Johnny Cash with Patrick Carr. *The Cash Family Scrapbook*, Cindy Cash.

CASH, JUNE CARTER

b. Valerie June Carter, 23 June 1929, Maces Springs, Scott County, Virginia, USA. The second of the three daughters of Mother Maybelle Carter of the legendary Carter Family. Her mother taught her to play autoharp (and later guitar) and in 1939, she and sisters Anita and Helen Carter were appearing on Border Radio as members of the Carter Family. When the original Carter Family retired in 1943, she sang and played rhythm guitar in the family group, Mother Maybelle and the Carter Sisters, on various radio stations, and from 1950 onwards, for many years, they were regulars on the *Grand Ole Opry*. Although not possessing the finer vocal talents of her two sisters, she did develop a flair for comedy, which she used to good effect in a character she called Aunt Polly. In 1949, she enjoyed a country and pop hit with a duet version of 'Baby It's Cold Outside' recorded with comedy duo Homer And Jethro. For a time during the 50s, she was married to singer Carl Smith, with whom she had two daughters, Rozanna and Rebecca Carlene, who as Carlene Carter went on to a successful solo career. They toured with Elvis Presley in the mid-50s, but in the early 60s, June began to work with Johnny Cash's show, soon being joined by her mother and sisters. In 1964, her recording with Cash of 'It Ain't Me Babe' made both country and pop charts and in 1967, they had a number 2 country hit with their now famous version of 'Jackson'. She married Cash on 1 March 1968 and from that point, her career has naturally run in conjunction with his as she continued to be a regular and expected member of his show. The following year they were voted Vocal Group of the Year and their son John Carter Cash was born in 1970.
● ALBUMS: *Appalachian Pride* (1975)★★★. For other albums refer to Carter Family or Johnny Cash.
● FURTHER READING: *From The Heart*, June Carter Cash.

CASH, ROSANNE

b. 24 May 1955, Memphis, Tennessee, USA. The daughter of Johnny Cash from his first marriage to Vivian Liberto, Cash lived with her mother in California after her parents divorced in 1966. Perhaps inevitably, she returned to Nashville, where she studied drama at Vanderbilt University, before relocating to Los Angeles to study 'method' acting at Lee Strasberg's Institute, after which she worked for three years on her father's roadshow. In the late 70s, she spent a year in London working for CBS Records, the same label as her father, and signed a recording contract in Germany with Ariola, resulting in her debut album, which has become a collector's item. Mainly recorded and produced in Germany with German-based musicians, it also included three tracks recorded in Nashville and was produced by Rodney Crowell. At the time, Cash was influenced by punk which she had experienced in Britain, but on her return to Nashville, she worked on demos with Crowell which gained her a contract with CBS as a neo-country act. She married Crowell in 1979, the same year her first CBS album, *Right Or Wrong*, was released. While not a huge success, the album, again produced by Crowell, included three US country hits: 'No Memories Hangin' Round' (a duet with Bobby Bare), 'Couldn't Do Nothin' Right, and 'Take Me, Take Me', while many of the backing musicians were also members of Emmylou Harris's Hot Band. *Seven Year Ache* followed in 1981, again produced by Crowell, and went gold, reaching the Top 30 of the US pop chart. It included three US country chart number 1 singles: the title track, her own composition, which reached the Top 30 of the US pop chart, 'My Baby Thinks He's A Train' (written by Leroy Preston, then of Asleep At The Wheel), and another of her own songs, 'Blue Moon With Heartache'. *Somewhere In The Stars* also reached the Top 100 of the US pop album charts, and included three US country chart singles, 'Ain't No Money', 'I Wonder' and 'It Hasn't Happened Yet', but overall the album was considerably less successful than its predecessor. Her next album, *Rhythm And Romance*, included four US country hit singles, two of which were overseen by Crowell; 'Never Be You', another number 1, was written by Tom Petty and Benmont Tench. David Malloy produced most of the album, including another country number 1 single, 'I Don't Know Why You Don't Want Me' (which Cash co-wrote with Crowell) and 'Second To No-One'. After another two years' hiatus came *King's Record Shop*, named after and featuring a sleeve picture of the store of that name in Louisville, Kentucky. This album included four US country number 1 singles: John Hiatt's 'The Way We Make A Broken Heart', her revival of her father's 1962 country hit, 'Tennessee Flat Top Box', 'If You Change Your Mind', which she co-wrote with pedal steel ace Hank DeVito, and 'Rainway Train', written by John Stewart. This album was again produced by Crowell, with whom she duetted on her fifth US country number 1 within 13 months, 'It's A Small World'. This song was included on Crowell's *Diamonds And Dirt*. Cash won a Grammy award in 1985 for Best Country Vocal Performance Female, and in 1988 won *Billboard*'s Top Single Artist Award. A wife and mother, Cash has rarely had time to work live, but this has clearly had little effect on her recording career. In 1989 came a compilation album, *Hits 1979-1989* (retitled *Retrospective 1979-1989* for UK release), and in late 1990, *Interiors*, a hauntingly introspective album which was criticized for its apparently pessimistic outlook. The video for *Interiors* shows her berating Crowell in song after song, only then to have him come on for a guest appearance. Its release was later followed by the news that her the couple's mar-

riage had broken down. The emotional fall-out was subsequently explored by Cash on 1993's bleak and compelling *The Wheel*. Three years later she demoed new material for Capitol Records who persuaded her to release the songs in their unadorned state, feeling the sparse arrangements complemented the introspective nature of the material. Cash, meanwhile, seemed more interested in promoting her collection of short stories, *Bodies Of Water*.

One of the pioneers of the 'new country' movement of the late 80s, Cash's relative unavailability - she places her family firmly before her career - may ultimately result in others taking the glory. Nevertheless, her achievements to date have ensured that the Cash family heritage in country music is far from disgraced.

● ALBUMS: *Rosanne Cash* (Ariola 1978)★★, *Right Or Wrong* (Columbia 1979)★★★, *Seven Year Ache* (Columbia 1981)★★★, *Somewhere In The Stars* (Columbia 1982)★★★, *Rhythm And Romance* (Columbia 1985)★★★, *King's Record Shop* (Columbia 1988)★★★, *Interiors* (Columbia 1990)★★★★, *The Wheel* (Columbia 1993)★★★, *10 Song Demo* (Capitol 1996)★★★★.

● COMPILATIONS: *Hits 1979-1989* (Columbia 1989)★★★★, *Retrospective* (Columbia 1995)★★★★.

● VIDEOS: *Live - The Interiors Tour* (1994).

● FURTHER READING: *Bodies Of Water*, Rosanne Cash.

CASH, TOMMY

b. 5 April 1940, Dyess, Arkansas, USA. Cash is the younger brother of Johnny Cash. He originally intended to be a basketball player. In the US armed forces in Germany, he presented AFN radio's *Stickbuddy Jamboree*. Back in the USA, he worked in radio, managed his brother's music publishing company and then recorded his first single for Musicor, 'That's Where My Baby Used To Be'. He also released 'Tobacco Road' and 'Jailbirds Can't Fly' on United Artists. Over at Epic in 1969, he had his biggest success in the US country charts with 'Six White Horses', a tribute to the Kennedys and Martin Luther King. Almost as successful were 'Rise And Shine' written by Carl Perkins, and 'One Song Away'. He also holds the highest placing (number 16) in the US country charts for a version of 'I Recall A Gypsy Woman'. He won a BMI award for his composition 'You Don't Hear', a country hit for Kitty Wells. In 1991, he released *The 25th Anniversary Album*, which featured guest appearances from Johnny Cash, Tom T. Hall, George Jones and Connie Smith. The follow-up, *Let An Old Racehorse Run*, included two duets with Jeannie C. Riley. *Solid Gold Country* was a poor collection of cover versions.

● ALBUMS: *Here Comes Tommy Cash* (United Artists 1968)★★★, *Your Lovin' Takes The Leavin' Out Of Me* (Epic 1969)★★★, *Six White Horses* (Epic 1970)★★★, *Rise And Shine* (Epic 1970)★★★, *The American Way Of Life* (Epic 1971)★★★, *Cash Country* (Epic 1971)★★★, *That Certain One* (Epic 1972)★★★, *Only A Stone* (1975)★★, *The New Spirit* (1978)★★, *The 25th Anniversary Album* (1991)★★★, *Let An Old Racehorse Run* (Playback 1995)★★, *Solid Gold Country* (Country Crazy 1996)★★.

CASS COUNTY BOYS

The Cass County Boys originated from the time, in the early 40s, when Fred Martin (accordion, vocals), a staff musician at WFAA Dallas, was told to fill in 10 minutes of airtime between programmes. With no proper schedule, he filled in with some chat and a few songs. Fellow staff musician and Texan Jerry Scroggins (guitar, baritone vocals) joined him one day for a joke and their singing attracted the attention of friend Bert Dodson (bass fiddle, tenor vocals). They took their name from the fact that Martin was born in Cass County, Texas. The listeners liked their harmony singing and they were soon playing radio spots and making local appearances. One day, during his Air Force service, Gene Autry saw them and promised to hire them as his backing group as soon as he gained his service discharge. He kept his word and they remained with him for years, during which time they appeared in many of his B-westerns and also on radio, television and live appearances, being especially popular on his *Melody Ranch* programmes. They also appeared in the *Durango Kid* series which starred Charles Starrett. They recorded for ARA, Columbia and Decca Records, as well as recording many radio transcription discs. In 1949, Dodson actually sang on Autry's second version of 'That Silver Haired Daddy Of Mine' and the following year on 'Mississippi Valley Blues'. (Jimmy Long sang on both 1931 originals.) The trio also sang on Autry's popular 1956 EP *Children's Christmas*.

● ALBUMS: *A Radio Western Adventure With Gene Autry* (Radiola 1975)★★★, *Gene Autry's Melody Ranch - 3 Radio Shows* (Golden Age 1977)★★★, *Gene Autry's Melody Ranch - Murray Hill Theatre* 4-album set (Murray Hill 1977)★★★.

CHALKER, CURLY
b. *c*.1932, Enterprise, Alabama, USA. A top steel guitarist who, in his early teens, inspired by Jerry Byrd, first played Hawaiian guitars professionally in Cincinnati nightclubs. He moved to Dallas and played western swing and country around the clubs. He worked with Lefty Frizzell and, playing a double-neck Fender steel, he made his recording debut on Frizzell's hit 'Always Late'. In 1952, after a spell with Hank Thompson (playing on Thompson's hit 'Wild Side Of Life'), he was called up for military service. After his release in 1954, he worked on the *Ozark Jubilee* for over four years in Springfield, Missouri, with Red Foley and Porter Wagoner. It was during this time that he first acquired a steel guitar with pedals. He moved to Las Vegas in 1959, where he worked various venues including the Golden Nugget and with several bands, including those of Wade Ray and Hank Penny. He also established a friendship with fellow steel player Ralph Mooney. In 1967, Chalker relocated to Nashville, where he soon established a reputation as a fine musician and worked with Carl Smith and other stars. As a session musician, he played on recordings by many country artists including Skeeter Davis, Webb Pierce, Ray Price and Tommy Overstreet. He played on Marie Osmond's hit 'Paper Roses' and in 1972 he even recorded sessions with Bill Haley. Chalker became staff steel guitarist of the *Hee Haw Show*. He recorded solo albums for Columbia, GRT (never released), Midland and later an album of Gordon Lightfoot songs for Crescendo. In 1977, he recorded a highly acclaimed album of country jazz for Flying Fish with the legendary jazz violinist Joe Venuti, Eldon Shamblin and mandolin expert Jethro Burns who for years had been one half of the comedy duo Homer And Jethro. Chalker is highly respected by his fellow musicians and, owing to his preference of using a more complex tuning than the usual E9 generally used for country tunes, he became known as 'the master of the C6'.

● ALBUMS: *Big Hits On Big Steel* (Columbia 1967)★★★, *More Ways To Play* (MD 1975)★★, *Nashville Sundown* (Sonet 1977)★★★, with Joe Venuti, Eldon Shamblin, Jethro Burns *S'Wonderful (4 Giants Of Swing)* (Flying Fish 1977)★★★.

CHAPMAN, MARSHALL
b. 7 January 1949, Spartanburg, North Carolina, USA. Chapman came from a wealthy family and spent time in France before moving to Nashville, Tennessee, in 1973. She signed with Epic Records and toured as a rock act, but found her songs had more favour with country audiences. Her composition, 'A Woman's Heart (Is A Handy Place To Be)', was covered by Crystal Gayle and by Jessi Colter. 'Somewhere South Of Macon' was considered too outspoken for country radio. She also achieved notoriety with 'Don't Get Me Pregnant'.

● ALBUMS: *Me, I'm Feeling Free* (Epic 1977)★★, *Jaded Virgin* (Epic 1978)★★★, *Marshall* (Epic 1979)★★, *Pick Up The Tempo* (Rounder 1981)★★★, *Dirty Linen* (Tall Girl 1987)★★.

CHESNEY, KENNY
b. USA. A country singer-songwriter specializing in heartfelt ballads, Kenny Chesney has earned a reputation as a genial and hard-working traditional artist. In 1994 he made his debut for Capricorn Records with a self-titled collection that established him as a competent writer, though one lacking the unique qualities needed to make a bigger impression on the marketplace. Both *All I Need To Know* and *Me And You*, his two subsequent albums for BNA Records in the mid-90s, revealed steady progression, with the title track of the latter album performing well on country radio. He accompanied its release with a major nationwide tour in support of country rock veterans Alabama, and since then, his following has continued to build. George Jones and Tracy Lawrence joined Chesney on 'From Hillbilly Heaven To Honky Tonk Hell', the best track on 1997's *I Will Stand*.

● ALBUMS: *Kenny Chesney* (Capricorn 1994)★★, *All I Need To Know* (BNA 1995)★★★, *Me And You* (BNA 1996)★★★, *I Will Stand* (BNA 1997)★★★.

CHESNUTT, MARK
b. 6 September 1963, Beaumont, Texas, USA. His father, Bob Chesnutt, was a singer who, although failing to find success in Nashville in the mid-60s, was popular in Texas; however, he quit music in favour of the used-car business, because he wanted to be with his family. It is, therefore, not surprising to find that, with strong parental encouragement, Mark followed in his father's footsteps (Bob died in 1990, just before his son achieved the success that had eluded him in his career). Impressed by George Jones (who also grew up in Beaumont), Chesnutt learned to play guitar and drums, and as a 15-year-old was singing in Texas clubs. He later formed his own band and worked all over Texas. He first recorded for Axbar and other independent labels until, in 1990, his recording of 'Too Cold At Home' gained him a contract with MCA. Written by Bobby Harden, the song (which, apparently, George Jones had turned down) became a number 3 country chart hit. Chesnutt moved to Nashville and before the year was out, he gained his first number 1 with 'Brother Jukebox'. During the next three years, he charted regularly, enjoying further number 1s with 'I'll Think Of Something',

'It Sure Is Monday' and 'Almost Goodbye'. He recorded a duet, 'Talking To Hank', with George Jones, which appeared on his second album. Since his father's death, Chesnutt has become great friends with Jones and, on occasions, worked with his idol on tours. He appears on the video *George Jones - Live In Tennessee* (Prism 1994). He was honoured with the Country Music Association's Horizon Award in 1993. In 1994, he added a further number 1 with 'I Just Wanted You To Know', and a Top 10 hit with 'She Dreams'. When the Decca label was re-formed, he was one of the biggest names to sign with it, and early in 1995 he proved his point with 'Goin' Through The Big D'. He has since released three consistently strong albums for the label, *Thank God For Believers* reuniting him with Mark Wright, producer of his first four albums.

● ALBUMS: *Too Cold At Home* (MCA 1990)★★, *Longnecks And Short Stories* (MCA 1992)★★★, *Almost Goodbye* (MCA 1993)★★★★, *What A Way To Live* (Decca 1994)★★★★, *Wings* (Decca 1995)★★★, *Thank God For Believers* (Decca 1997)★★★.

● COMPILATIONS: *Mark Chesnutt's Greatest Hits* (Decca 1996)★★★★.

● VIDEOS: *Almost Goodbye* (1993), *Gonna Get A Life* (1995).

CHIAVOLA, KATHY

b. USA. Talented country vocalist Kathy Chiavola (pronounced 'key ah vo lah') made a big splash in her adopted home of Nashville, Tennessee, USA, in early 1993 with a round of excited reviews for her debut album. She had first attempted to launch her musical career as an opera singer, switching to country with far greater success and prompting heady praise such as the following review, taken from *Folk Roots*: 'Not often one finds such poise, power or purity in a voice committed to the world of contemporary country.' The subject under discussion was Chiavola's debut album, *Labor Of Love*, which included standards such as Buddy Holly's 'Well Alright', Peter Rowan's 'A Woman In Love' and the Elvis Presley hit 'A Fool Such As I', plus the work of less-celebrated artists and songwriters. Her only self-composition was the title track, an elegant, dignified tribute to the artist's own mother. However, it was the eclecticism of the collection that attracted so many supporters, leading Robert Oermann of *The Tennessean* to write: 'She has the unusual ability to 'cry' like a country star, moan like a blues mama and maintain the clarity and purity of tone of a folk soprano, often all in the same song.' Her second album, *The Harvest*, followed in 1996. A bluegrass/acoustic project, guests included Chet Atkins, Emmylou Harris, Bela Fleck, Bill Monroe and Vince Gill. On it she was accompanied by world champion fiddle player Randy Howard, Brent Truitt on mandolin and Roy Huskey on acoustic bass.

● ALBUMS: *Labor Of Love* (My Label 1993)★★★, *The Harvest* (Demon 1996)★★★.

CHILDRE, LEW

b. 1 November 1901, Opp, Alabama, USA, d. 3 December 1961. Childre began his professional career at the age of 16 as a vaudeville performer and toured for years with various tent shows and played theatres throughout the southern states. He developed into an all-round entertainer, being a fine singer, comedian, dancer and instrumentalist. He was especially proficient on steel and Hawaiian guitars. He

played on many top radio shows before he joined the *Grand Ole Opry* in 1945. Between then and 1948, he usually worked as a comedy act with Stringbean but then pursued a solo career. He was very popular on the *Opry* and is remembered for his comedy routines, particularly his imaginary character Doctor Lew, who gave supposedly helpful advice in answer to letters written to him. He also appeared regularly on Red Foley's network television show. Childre was a visual performer, whose full talents did not really show to their best on radio or record. He made some recordings for Gennett and ARC in the 30s but few survived and it is usually his later Starday recordings such as 'Old MacDonald's Farm' and 'Shanghai Rooster' that are heard today. He was known as 'that Boy From Alabama' (even when he was almost 60) and his best-known song was 'Alabamy Bound'.

● COMPILATIONS: with Cowboy Copas, Josh Graves *Old Time Get Together With Lew Childre* (Starday 1961)★★★, *On The Air 1946 Volume 1* (Old Homestead 1980)★★★★.

CHILDS, ANDY

b. Memphis, Tennessee, USA. The 90s country singer Andy Childs was raised in Memphis but was drawn more to the country sounds of Nashville. He played in small Memphis clubs and then built up his experience in state fairs and theme parks. He regularly went to Nashville but he was determined not to be a 'hat' act. His singles, 'I Wouldn't Know' and 'Broken', were only moderately successful. He is not the same former rock journalist Andy Childs who used to write for *Zig Zag* and is now press officer at Rykodisk UK.

● ALBUMS: *Andy Childs* (RCA 1994)★★.

CHOATES, HARRY

b. 26 December 1922, Rayne, Louisiana, USA, d. 17 July 1951, Austin, Texas, USA. Choates, who has been called the Cajun Hank Williams and the Godfather of Cajun Music, is reckoned by many authorities to be the most responsible for the genre becoming part of country music. During the Depression, Choates and his mother relocated to Port Arthur, Texas, where he grew up regularly spending much of his time listening to music in local honky tonks. He had a natural talent for playing instruments and soon became proficient on accordion, guitar and steel guitar, before finally favouring the fiddle. At the age of 12, already becoming addicted to alcohol, he was playing fiddle in local barbershops. In the late 30s, he played in various Cajun bands, including that of fiddler Leo Soileau, one of the first artists to record Cajun music. It was then that he undoubtedly first learned 'Jole Blon' ('Pretty Blonde'), a song that Soileau had recorded in 1935. Choates had a reputation for never remaining in one place for long and in the early 40s, he played with various Cajun units, becoming respected for his driving fiddle playing and vocals. He sang well enough in Cajun French to endear him to Cajun audiences but actually spoke it with a strong English accent, while his spoken English carried a Cajun accent. By the mid-40s, his drinking had worsened and he became unpredictable and unreliable. In 1945, he married Helen Daenen and quickly sired two children, before he once again moved on. In 1946, Choates, accompanied by his band which played a mixture of Cajun and western swing in dancehalls, recorded his now famous version of 'Jole Blon' for the Gold Star label in Houston. It entered the *Billboard* country charts on 4 January 1947 and peaked at number 4. Although the song had originally been recorded in 1928 by Amade Breaux, because of Choates' new and exciting arrangement it has always been associated with him. Following the song's success, Choates became a legend around the clubs and dancehalls in Louisiana and Texas, although his excessive drinking meant he was sometimes unable to play and often missed shows altogether. Between 1946 and 1949, he made further recordings for Gold Star, including 'Poor Hobo', 'Port Arthur Waltz' and 'Catting Around' but he never repeated the popularity of his first hit. Selected recordings that he made for Gold Star during those years were released years later on the D label. Choates' career came to an end in jail, in Austin, on 17 July 1951. He had been arrested three days earlier, for failing to answer charges filed by his wife for desertion and child support, on a warrant issued by Jefferson County Court, which had also charged him with contempt of court. One early report gave his death as being caused by delirium tremens but some of his friends stoutly maintained that he died through police brutality, having been beaten to quieten him. Another statement said that Choates, who is reputed to have appeared agitated and nervous in jail, had never recovered consciousness after falling into a coma following an epileptic fit. A later report said that his death was caused by cirrhosis of the liver and his agitated nervous state was explained as being caused by the fact that, during the three days in jail, he had been deprived of his usual heavy intake of alcohol. He actually died 30 minutes before the Jefferson County sheriff arrived to return him to Beaumont to answer the charges. Researchers into Choates' life have failed to trace any official inquest verdict. Although Choates was a brilliant instrumentalist, he never actually owned an instrument. The fiddle that brought him fame was a cheap seven-dollar instrument that he once borrowed from a friend and 'forgot' to return. Choates was buried in Port Arthur, Texas, on 20 July 1951, his grave being unmarked until the early 80s, when local Cajuns provided a gravestone.

● ALBUMS: *Jole Blon* (D 60s)★★★, *Five-Time Lobster* (Krazy Kat 1990)★★★.
● COMPILATIONS: *The Fiddle King Of Cajun Swing* (Arhoolie 1982)★★★★.

CHUCK WAGON GANG

This Carter Family, who have apparently had no ancestral connection with the legendary Carter Family, also established themselves with their fine family harmony singing. Although many of their songs have been sung and recorded by country artists, the Chuck Wagon Gang were a country gospel group. Originally the group comprised D.P. 'Dad' Carter (b. David Parker Carter, 25 September 1889, Milltown, Kentucky, USA, d. 28 April 1963) and three of his nine children, namely Jim (b. Ernest Carter, 10 August 1910, d. 2 February 1971; guitar), Rose (b. Rosa Lola Carter, 31 December 1915) and Anna (b. Effie Carter, 15 February 1917). Members' names were changed to what were believed more suitable radio names, but it led to confusion when family members of the group became interchangeable and a younger daughter was later named Anna. In the 20s, 'Dad' Carter was a brakeman on the Rock Island Line but was later moved to Calumet, Oklahoma. In 1927, following a railroad accident, he sued for lost wages, but the railroad managed to delay proceedings long enough for his lack of finance to

force him to call off his action. He was subsequently sacked by the railroad and in the Depression, he worked as a sharecropper and picked cotton. The family relocated to Texas, where for several years the various members old enough to work eked out a living. Most played some stringed instrument and they began to sing locally. In 1935, Dad and his three offspring gained a paid spot on KFYO Lubbock, singing as the Carter Quartet, with a repertoire that included western ballads such as 'At The Rainbow's End' and popular songs such as 'My Wild Irish Rose'. After moving to Fort Worth, they acquired a weekly sponsored programme, *The Round Up*, on WBAP. At the time, the station also had a male group called the Chuck Wagon Gang singing western ballads on a programme sponsored by Bewley Flour Mills. Soon afterwards, the sponsors decided to take the Chuck Wagon Gang off-air, in order that they could undertake personal appearances around the area advertising Bewley products. Not wishing to lose the on-air advertising, the sponsors suggested to 'Dad' Carter that he should deputize and the Carter Quartet became the Chuck Wagon Gang Of The Air. The original gang soon disbanded and the Carters became the Chuck Wagon Gang permanently. They soon established themselves and in November 1936, made their first recordings in San Antonio for Columbia Records. When they found that the majority of their mail requested gospel numbers, they gradually changed to that genre. They remained at WBAP for 15 years and their popularity may be judged by the fact that, on one occasion when Bewley Mills offered a free picture of the group to anyone sending in a coupon found in a bag of flour, they received more than 100,000 replies. They made their first major tour in 1951, which saw brothers Roy (b. 1 March 1926, d. 4 August 1997) and Eddie (b. 15 November 1919) and Anna's husband, guitarist Howard Gordon, perform with the group. For years they continued to tour across the length and breadth of the USA and played to vast crowds at major venues such as the Hollywood Bowl in Los Angeles, Carnegie Hall in New York, and also on Nashville's *Grand Ole Opry*. They also appeared in films and at one time hosted a television show called *Gospel Round-Up*. Their beautiful four-part harmony singing to simple guitar accompaniment made them internationally known and for 40 years, they continued to record for Columbia. On 9 November 1969, Anna (Effie), whose husband Howard Gordon had died in 1967, married country star Jimmie Davis but continued to record with the family group until the late 70s. Throughout the 80s, various combinations of the group also recorded many sides for the Copperfield and Associated Artists labels. 'Dad' Carter stopped touring in 1955 following heart trouble and collapsed and died in a theatre in Oklahoma City, moments before he was due onstage for a special concert. Jim retired from the group and worked for an electric company in Fort Worth until he died of nephritis in 1971. After their deaths and when Rose and Anna retired, Roy Carter was mainly responsible for the running of the group. Over the years, various other members (including related ones) appeared with the Chuck Wagon Gang but the other siblings of 'Dad' Carter's original family were Clellon (b. 21 February 1913, the only family member who never sang with the group), Anna (b. 23 November 1922), Ruth Ellen (b. 3 January 1924) and Bettye (b. 15 March 1930). 'Dad' Carter was posthumously elected to the Gospel Music Association's Hall of Fame in Nashville in

April 1985 and in November 1986, the group received a gold record from SESAC (Selected Editions of Standard American Catalogues) to commemorate 50 years of recording gospel music. In 1987, past and current members of the group were presented with Lifetime Achievement Awards by SESAC. In 1988, country music fans voted them the nation's top country/gospel group in America. It is estimated that sales of their records in the USA and overseas is in excess of 30 million. Excluding various compilation albums, there have been over 70 albums of their gospel recordings issued, the majority on Columbia or connected labels.

● COMPILATIONS: *Family Tradition* (K-Tel 1973)★★★, *Looking Away From Heaven* (Columbia 1976)★★★, *Columbia Historic Edition* (Columbia 1990)★★★★.
● FURTHER READING: *The Chuck Wagon Gang, A Legend Lives On* Bob Terrell.

CHURCH, CINDY

b. Bible Hill, Nova Scotia, Canada. Church originally worked as a harmony singer in the mid-80s with Ian Tyson. Later she established her own band, a country trio named the Great Western Orchestra, which included later solo collaborator, guitarist Nathan Tinkham. Her debut solo album, *Love On The Range*, furthered her reputation as a gifted singer and interpreter. Now based in Alberta, she also worked with the vocal group Quartette, who additionally comprise Colleen Peterson and Caitlin Hanford, and who record for Denon Records. These activities confirmed her burgeoning profile within Canada's folk/country community, which resulted in the strong sales attracted by the release of her second album, 1995's *Just A Little Rain*. This saw her draw on the work of a number of established Canadian songwriters, including Sylvia Tyson ('Never Got Over You'), Shirley Eikhard ('It's Just A Little Rain'), Roy Forbes ('Still A Fool'), Laurie Thain ('Trying To Rope The Wind') and Hanford's husband Chris Whitley ('Radiates'). Three songs were written by Tinkham, who also co-produced. Her self-titled 1997 release featured only one Church original but was another highly accomplished set.
● ALBUMS: *Love On The Range* (Stony Plain 1994)★★★, *Just A Little Rain* (Stony Plain 1995)★★★, *Cindy Church* (Stony Plain 1997)★★★.

CLARK, GENE

b. 17 November 1941, Tipton, Missouri, USA, d. 24 May 1991. After playing in various teenage groups, Clark was offered a place in the sprawling New Christy Minstrels in late 1963. He stayed long enough to contribute to two albums, *Merry Christmas* and *Land Of Giants*, before returning to Los Angeles, where he teamed up with Jim (Roger) McGuinn and David Crosby in the Jet Set. This fledgling trio evolved into the Byrds. At that point Clark was the leading songwriter in the group and contributed significantly to their first two albums. Classic Clark songs from this period include 'I Feel A Whole Lot Better', 'Here Without You' and 'Set You Free This Time'. Following the release of 'Eight Miles High' in March 1966, he dramatically left the group, citing fear of flying as the major cause.
Under the auspices of producer Jim Dickson, Clark recorded a solo album, *Echoes (With The Gosdin Brothers)*, which remains one of the best 'singer-songwriter' albums of its era. However, it failed to sell, effectively placing Clark's solo

career in jeopardy. At this time Clark also recorded two albums with Doug Dillard as Dillard And Clark. At the end of 1968, following Crosby's dismissal from the Byrds, Clark was re-enlisted but left within weeks due to his long-standing aerophobia. Revitalizing his career in 1971 with *White Light*, Clark seemed a prime candidate for singer-songwriter success, but middling sales and a lack of touring forestalled his progress. A recorded reunion with the original Byrds in late 1973 temporarily refocused attention on Clark. Soon, he was back in the studio recording a solo album for Asylum Records with producer Thomas Jefferson Kaye. *No Other* was a highly acclaimed work, brilliantly fusing Clark's lyrical power with an ethereal mix of choral beauty and rich musicianship provided by some of the finest session players in Hollywood. Sales again proved disappointing, prompting Clark to record a less complex album for RSO, which was reasonably publicized but fared no better. The irresistible lure of the original Byrds brought Gene back together with two of his former colleagues in the late 70s. McGuinn, Clark And Hillman enjoyed brief success, but during the recording of their second album *City* in 1980, history repeated itself and Clark left amid some acrimony. After this he mainly recorded for small labels, occasionally touring with other ex-Byrds as well as solo. He collaborated with Carla Olson, formerly of the Textones. After years of ill health, Clark died in 1991.
● ALBUMS: *Echoes (With The Gosdin Brothers)* (Columbia 1967)★★★★ reissued as *Gene Clark With The Gosdin Brothers* (Edsel 1997), *White Light* (A&M 1971)★★★, *Roadmaster* (A&M 1972)★★★, *No Other* (Asylum 1974)★★★★, *Two Sides To Every Story* (RSO 1977)★★, *Firebyrd* (Takoma 1984)★★ reissued as *This Byrd Has Flown* (Edsel 1995), with Carla Olson *So Rebellious A Lover* (Demon 1987)★★★, with Carla Olson *Silhouetted In Light* (Demon 1992)★★★.
● COMPILATIONS: *American Dreamer 1964 - '74* (1993)★★★★.

CLARK, GUY

b. 6 November 1941, Rockport, Texas, USA. Clark has achieved considerably more fame as a songwriter than as a performer, although he is revered by his nucleus of fans internationally. Brought up in the hamlet of Monahans, Texas, Clark worked in television during the 60s, and later as a photographer - his work appeared on albums released by the Texan-based International Artists Records. He briefly performed in a folk trio with Kay K.T. Oslin, and began writing songs for a living, moving to Los Angeles, which he eventually loathed, but which inspired one of his biggest songs, 'LA Freeway', a US Top 100 hit for Jerry Jeff Walker. Clark then wrote songs such as his classic 'Desperados Waiting For A Train', which was covered by acts as diverse as Tom Rush and Mallard (the group formed by ex-members of Captain Beefheart's Magic Band) and the brilliant train song 'Texas 1947', by Johnny Cash.
His first album, *Old No. 1*, was released in 1975, and included 'Freeway', 'Desperados' and '1947', as well as several more songs of similarly high quality, such as 'Let It Roll'. Despite receiving virtually unanimous and well-deserved critical acclaim, it failed to chart on either side of the Atlantic. Clark's 1976 follow-up album, *Texas Cooking*, was no more successful, although it again contained classic songs such as 'The Last Gunfighter Ballad' and 'Virginia's Real'.

Among those who contributed to these albums simply because they enjoyed Clark's music were Emmylou Harris, Rodney Crowell, Steve Earle, Jerry Jeff Walker, Hoyt Axton and Waylon Jennings. By 1978, Clark had moved labels to Warner Brothers Records, and released *Guy Clark*, which included four songs from other writers, among them Rodney Crowell's 'Viola', 'American Dream' and Townes Van Zandt's 'Don't You Take It Too Bad', while the harmonizing friends this time included Don Everly, Gordon Payne (of the Crickets) and K.T. Oslin. A three-year gap then ensued before 1981's *The South Coast Of Texas*, which was produced by Rodney Crowell. Clark wrote two of the songs with Crowell, 'The Partner Nobody Chose' (a US country Top 40 single) and 'She's Crazy For Leavin'', while the album also included 'Heartbroke', later covered by Ricky Skaggs. *Better Days*, again produced by Crowell, included vintage classics such as 'The Randall Knife' and 'The Carpenter', as well as another US country chart single, 'Homegrown Tomatoes', and Van Zandt's amusing 'No Deal', but Clark was still unable to penetrate the commercial barriers that had long been predicted by critics and his fellow musicians. He began to work as a solo troubadour, after various unsuccessful attempts to perform live with backing musicians. At this point he developed the intimate show that he brought to Europe several times during the latter half of the 80s. This resulted in his return to recording with *Old Friends*, appearing on U2's label, Mother Records. The usual array of 'heavy friends' were on hand, including Harris, Crowell, Rosanne Cash and Vince Gill, but only two of the 10 tracks were solely written by Clark. Among the contributions were Joe Ely's 'The Indian Cowboy', and Van Zandt's 'To Live Is To Fly'. Even with the implied patronage of U2, at the time one of the biggest acts in the world, Clark enjoyed little more success than he had previously experienced.

On stage, Clark is introverted, performing his material in an unplugged, unadorned and underrated way, with the aid of constant cigarettes and mumbled introductions. Time and time again, Clark's album *Old No 1* is cited by critics and performers as a landmark work. Many musicians, including Lyle Lovett, Nanci Griffith and Emmylou Harris, have acknowledged his contribution to American music and, to quote the title of one of his more recent songs, it is 'Stuff That Works'.

● ALBUMS: *Old No. 1* (RCA 1975)★★★★, *Texas Cookin'* (RCA 1976)★★★, *Guy Clark* (Warners 1978)★★★, *The South Coast Of Texas* (Warners 1981)★★★, *Better Days* (Warners 1983)★★★, *Old Friends* (Sugar Hill 1989)★★, *Boats To Build* (Asylum 1992)★★★, *Dublin Blues* (Asylum 1995)★★★, *Keepers - A Live Recording* (Sugar Hill 1997)★★★.

● COMPILATIONS: *Best Of Guy Clark* (RCA 1982)★★★, *Craftsman* (Philo 1995)★★★, *The Essential Guy Clark* (RCA 1997)★★★★.

CLARK, ROY

b. Roy Linwood Clark, 15 April 1933, Meherrin, Virginia, USA. When he was 11, the family moved to Washington DC after his father, a competent musician who played guitar, banjo and fiddle, progressed from being a cotton picker to become a computer programmer, and augmented his pay for the government job by playing at local dances (his mother also played piano). Clark played banjo and mandolin at an early age and was playing guitar at dances with his father by the time he was 14. He won the National Banjo Championship at the ages of 16 and 17, the latter occasion resulting in an appearance at the *Grand Ole Opry*. He considered a baseball career in his late teens but at 18 became a professional boxer. Fighting as a light-heavyweight, he won 15 fights in a row before the next fight convinced him he should look elsewhere for a living. He found work in clubs and appeared on local radio and television in such shows as the *Ozark Jubilee* and *Town And Country Time*. In 1955, he joined Jimmy Dean on his Washington television show *Country Style*, and when Dean left for New York, Clark was given the show. He played instruments, joked and sang and gradually built himself a reputation, but in the early 60s, he decided to seek fame further afield and became lead guitarist and frontman for Wanda Jackson. He stayed with her for about a year and played lead guitar on her hit recording of 'Let's Have A Party'. When she gave up her band, Jim Halsey took on the role of Clark's manager and soon found him a spot on one of the most popular network television shows, *The Beverly Hillbillies*. Here he appeared in the dual role of Cousin Roy and (dressed as a woman) his mother Big Mama Halsey. He also signed for Capitol Records and released his first album, which contained both songs and instrumentals. In 1963, he was given the chance to play on the *Tonight Show* on television, owing to the fact that Jimmy Dean was hosting the programme. This led to further invitations to appear on other top television shows and his popularity rapidly grew. In later years he hosted many of the shows personally. He achieved his first chart success in 1963, when his version of Bill Anderson's 'The Tips Of My Fingers' made both the US country and pop charts. He left Capitol, joining Dot Records in 1967. During the 60s, somewhat ironically, he had country hits with pop songs, when further double chart successes included Charles Aznavour's 'Yesterday When I Was Young' and 'September Song'. During the mid-60s, he fronted the *Swingin' Country* television series and in 1969, CBS invited him to co-host their new country comedy show *Hee Haw* with Buck Owens. This programme became one of the most popular on television, so much so that when CBS dropped it in 1971 because they felt it did not create the right impression for the company, it was immediately syndicated by the show's producers and even grew in popularity. During the 70s, Clark had a great number of country chart hits, including the very humorous 'Thank God And Greyhound', 'Riders In The Sky', 'Somewhere Between Love And Tomorrow' and 'Come Live With Me', his only number 1 US country hit. He also made several popular television commercials. Clark progressed to become one of country music's biggest stars and to enable himself to keep up a punishing schedule of concert appearances, he learned to fly and piloted himself around the States. He was one of the first country artists to star in his own show on Las Vegas strip, where he still appears regularly, usually backed by an orchestra. Clark also became the first star to take his show to the Soviet Union, when in January 1976, he played to packed houses during a 21-day tour of Riga, Moscow and Leningrad. The same year, Clark also played concerts with Arthur Fiedler and the Boston Pops Orchestra. In 1977, he appeared at Carnegie Hall, New York, and in 1979, he recorded an album with blues artist Clarence 'Gatemouth' Brown. Between 1979 and 1981, he recorded for MCA but during the late 80s, he was with several labels. Although he had no major hits, a version of 'Night Life' registered country hit number 50 for him in 1986. In later years, he become involved in cattle ranching, publishing, advertising and property. During his career, he has won many CMA awards including Comedian Of The Year 1970, Entertainer Of The Year 1973, Instrumental Group Of The Year (with Buck Trent) in 1975 and 1976 and was nominated as Instrumentalist Of The Year every year from 1967 to 1980, winning in 1977, 1978 and 1980. He guested on the *Opry* many times over the years but did not become a member until 1987. He has appeared in several films and in 1986, he co-starred with Mel Tillis in a comedy western called *Uphill All The Way*, which they both also produced. Clark is a talented multi-instrumentalist and all-round entertainer, who is equally at home with various types of music.

● ALBUMS: *The Lightning Fingers Of Roy Clark* (Capitol 1962)★★★, *Roy Clark Sings The Tips Of My Fingers* (Capitol 1963)★★★★, *Happy To Be Unhappy* (Capitol 1964)★★★, *Roy Clark Guitar Spectacular* (Capitol 1965)★★★, *Roy Clark Sings Lonesome Love Ballads* (Capitol 1966)★★, *Stringin' Along With The Blues* (Capitol 1966)★★★, *Roy Clark* (Capitol 1966)★★★, *Live* (Capitol 1967)★★, *Do You Believe This Roy Clark* (Dot 1968)★★★, *In The Mood* (Dot 1968)★★★, *Urban, Suburban* (Dot 1968)★★★, *Yesterday When I Was Young* (Dot 1969)★★★, *The Everlovin' Soul Of Roy Clark* (Dot 1969)★★★, *The Other Side Of Roy Clark* (Dot 1970)★★★, *I Never Picked Cotton* (Dot 1970)★★★, *The Magnificent Sanctuary Band* (Dot 1971)★★, *The Incredible Roy Clark* (Dot 1971)★★★, *Roy Clark Country!* (Dot 1972)★★★, *Family Album* (Dot 1973)★★★, *Superpicker* (Dot 1973)★★★, *Come Live With Me* (Dot 1973)★★★, *Classic Clark* (Dot 1974)★★★, *Family And Friends* (Dot 1974)★★, *The Entertainer* (Dot 1974)★★★, *Roy Clark* (Dot 1974)★★★, *Sings Gospel* (Dot 1975)★★, with Buck Trent *A Pair Of Fives (Banjos That Is)* (Dot 1975)★★★★, *So Much To Remember* (Dot 1975)★★★, *Heart To Heart* (Dot 1975)★★★, *In Concert* (Dot 1976)★★, *Hookin' It* (Dot 1977)★★★, *My Music And Me* (Dot 1977)★★★, with Freddy Fender, Hank Thompson and Don Williams *Country Comes To Carnegie Hall* (ABC/Dot 1977)★★★★, *Labour Of Love* (Dot 1978)★★★, with Trent *Banjo Bandits* (ABC 1978)★★★★, with Clarence 'Gatemouth' Brown *Making Music* (MCA 1979)★★, *My Music* (MCA 1980)★★★, *The Last Word In Jesus Is Us* (MCA 1981)★★, *Meanwhile Back At The Country* (MCA 1981)★★★, with Grandpa Jones, Buck Owens and Kenny Price *The Hee Haw Gospel Quartet* (Songbird 1981)★★★, *Live From Austin City Limits* (Churchill 1982)★★, *Turned Loose* (Churchill 1982)★★★, with Joe Pass *Play Hank Williams* 1994 recording (Ranwood 1995).

● COMPILATIONS: *The Best Of Roy Clark* (1971)★★★★, *The ABC Collection* (Dot 1977)★★★★, *20 Golden Pieces* (Bulldog 1984)★★★, *Greatest Hits* (Varèse Sarabande 1995)★★★★.

● FURTHER READING: *My Life: In Spite Of Myself*, Roy Clark with Marc Eliot (1994).

CLARK, SANFORD

b. 1935, Tulsa, Oklahoma, USA. Clark is best recalled for his 1956 Top 10 single and only chart success, 'The Fool'. He moved to Phoenix, Arizona, during his teens and there was heard by guitarist Al Casey, who introduced the young singer to local disc jockey Lee Hazlewood and songwriter Naomi Ford. They recorded Ford's song 'The Fool', and it was released first on the small MCI label, created specifi-

cally for this record's release. After it received local attention, the national Dot Records picked up distribution and the song shot to number 7 in the USA; it also reached the country and R&B charts. Clark had one further chart single with the follow-up, 'The Cheat'. In 1960 he joined the US Air Force and although he released numerous further singles on Dot and other labels into the mid-60s, none were hits.

● ALBUMS: *Return Of The Fool* (LHI 1968)★★★.

● COMPILATIONS: *The Fool* (Ace 1983)★★★★, *Rockin' Rollin', Volume 1* and *2* (Bear Family 1986)★★★★ *Shades* (Bear Family 1994)★★★★.

CLARK, TERRI

b. 5 August 1968, Medicine Hat, Alberta, Canada. The 90s country singer Terri Clark comes from a musical family: her maternal grandparents, Ray and Betty Gauthier, were popular country performers in Canada and her mother sang folk songs. Her mother recognized her talent and encouraged her to move to Nashville in 1987. She started well by working as a house singer at Tootsie's Orchid Lounge. She married fiddler Ted Stevenson, but her career suffered one setback after another. Eventually, she was signed to Mercury Records and she wrote most of her debut album. She has had US country hits with 'Better Things To Do' and 'When Boy Meets Girl'. Clark has said, 'Pam Tillis said that a woman needs to be twice as good as the men to make it in country music, and she needs ten times the guts. There is some truth in that.' Billboard named her as one of their artists of the year in 1995 and her good looks have prompted various merchandising companies to seek her out to advertise products, the most lucrative being Wrangler jeans, which accords with Clark's sexy cowgirl image. She claims that she has been wearing cowboy hats for years, except now she is paid to do so. The 1996 follow-up, *Just The Same*, proved that she had staying power.

● ALBUMS: *Terri Clark* (Mercury 1995)★★★, *Just The Same* (Mercury 1996)★★★.

● VIDEOS: *If I Were You* (Mercury Nashville 1996).

CLARK, YODELLING SLIM

b. Raymond LeRoy Clark, 11 December 1917, Springfield, Massachusetts, USA. Although Clark grew up listening to country music, he wanted to be a professional baseball player, but an injury to his pitching arm ruined his aspirations. He was then determined to follow the style of his favourite singer, Wilf Carter (Montana Slim). (Clark's son was named Wilf Carter Clark.) He copied Carter's yodel and made his first radio broadcast in 1938. He formed the Red River Rangers, whose line-up included Kenny Roberts, who went on to solo success. Clark first recorded in 1946 and he was named the World's Champion Yodeller in 1947. He has made several albums of old-time cowboy songs and is an acknowledged authority on the subject.

● ALBUMS: *Western Songs And Dances* 10-inch album (Playhouse 1954)★★★★, *Cowboy And Yodel Songs* (Continental 1962)★★★★ *Cowboy Songs* (Masterseal 1963)★★★, *Cowboy Songs, Volume 2* (Masterseal 1964)★★★, *Yodelling Slim Clark Sings Jimmie Rodgers Songs* (Palomino 1966)★★★★, *Yodelling Slim Clark Sings And Yodels Favorite Montana Slim Songs Of The Mountains And Plains (Volumes 1 and 2)* (Palomino 1966)★★★★, *I Feel A Trip Coming On* (Palomino 1966)★★★, *Old Chestnuts* (Palomino 1967)★★★,

Wilf Carter Songs (1967)★★★, *Yodelling Slim Clark Happens Again* (1968)★★★, *Yodelling Slim Clark Sings The Ballads Of Billy Venero* (1968)★★, *Yodelling Slim Clark's 50th Anniversary Album* (Palomino 1968)★★★.

CLARKE, TERRY

b. 16 October 1947, Reading, Berkshire, England. The UK country singer Terry Clarke grew up in the rock 'n' roll era and was influenced by the Everly Brothers and Johnny Cash. One of his songs, 'Bruce Channel In This Town', tells of the rock 'n' roll star visiting Reading, and another is 'Gene Vincent Sings'. Having bought a guitar at 14, Clarke joined a local band, the Statesmen. After that he played country clubs with an American ex-serviceman, Buddy Friend. He was signed as a solo act to Chrysalis Records in 1971 but no releases were forthcoming, and he moved to Polydor for one single, 'Lady'. He then worked with the folk/blues musician Mike Cooper, playing on his album *Life And Death In Paradise*. In the 80s, he formed a band, Domino Effect (whose singles included 'La Dolce Vita' and 'Getting Serious' on Stilletto Records), and then formed a partnership with another Reading musician, G.T. Moore. By 1985, he was playing guitar and providing supporting vocals for visiting American acts including Butch Hancock. He auditioned over the phone for a memorial concert for Clarence White and Gram Parsons and, while in the USA, he recorded in Nashville. He returned to complete an album in San Marcos and Austin, employing such established session musicians as Erik Hokkanen, Freddie Krc and David Grissom. Flaco Jiminez plays on the track 'The Stars Of Austin'. *Call Up A Hurricane* is a line from a song about Buddy Holly, 'Buddy's Waiting On The Flatland Road'. That song, with two other songs relating to Holly, 'Looking For Donna' and 'Lubbock Calling', was released on a CD single. Clarke made *Shelly River* about his Irish roots - his father comes from Sligo - which led to touring in Ireland with Henry McCulloch. *Rhythm Oil* was made with Mike Messer and Jesse 'Guitar' Taylor and Clarke also wrote seven of the songs on Messer's album *Moonbeat*. He has toured with Rosie Flores and a drawing of Flores by his seven-year-old daughter, Amy, appeared on the cover of *Rockabilly Filly*. 'Amy was sent a cheque for $250, which is more than I make from my own records!'
● ALBUMS: *Call Up A Hurricane* (Minidoka 1990)★★★, *Shelly River* (Minidoka 1991)★★★, *Rhythm Oil* (Minidoka 1995)★★★, *The Heart Sings* (Transatlantic 1997)★★★★.

CLAYPOOL, PHILIP

b. Memphis, Tennessee, USA. Raised in Memphis, Claypool's traditional approach to country songwriting has won him many admirers since he made his debut for Curb Records in 1995. Claypool's mother had played organ in church, and her influence bred an increasing interest in traditional and roots music that led him through gospel, folk and blues to bluegrass and country. He was already writing his own songs during his high school and college years, after which he settled in Nashville. His debut album, *A Circus Leaving Town*, was produced by Jerry Crutchfield and included singles such as 'The Strength Of A Woman' and the title track, rated by many as the best song he had written so far. As Claypool told the press, 'the more time I spend in Nashville, the more I'm learning about the craft of writing songs. I'm

learning to tap into my experiences and develop an idea rather than waiting.'
● ALBUMS: *A Circus Leaving Town* (Curb 1995)★★★.

CLAYTON, LEE

b. 29 October 1942, Russelville, Alabama, USA. Clayton moved to Oak Ridge, Tennessee, at the age of four. His father encouraged his musical abilities and, when aged only 10, he played steel guitar on radio. Clayton's background is related in his song 'Industry'. Between 1966 and 1969 and after a short-lived marriage, he flew jet fighters in the US Air Force, an experience that is described in his song 'Old Number Nine'. Clayton moved to Nashville, determined to make his name as a songwriter. The 'outlaw' scene was in its infancy and Clayton's 'Ladies Love Outlaws' was a US country hit for Waylon Jennings and later recorded by the Everly Brothers. His 1973 album *Lee Clayton* is regarded as a classic of 'outlaw country'. Jennings and Willie Nelson have both recorded his erotic love song, 'If You Can Touch Her At All'. Clayton, however, became penniless trying to establish his own band and then followed a nomadic existence. Eventually, he developed a more strident, electric sound, employing the Irish guitarist Philip Donnolly, to record dark albums full of disillusionment. The melancholy 'A Little Cocaine' is about the downfall of a friend, and his own drug habits made him unreliable. In the 80s Clayton wrote two books and one stage play, *Little Boy Blue*, all autobiographical. He returned to recording with a fine album recorded live in Oslo, *Another Night*, but the songs were familiar. Bono of U2 was reported to have said, 'There's only one country singer who has influenced me and he's an unknown feller called Lee Clayton.' Maverick UK record company Edsel had similar faith when they reissued three Clayton albums in 1996.
● ALBUMS: *Lee Clayton* (MCA/Edsel 1973)★★★★, *Border Affair* (Capitol/Edsel 1978)★★★, *Naked Child* (Capitol/Edsel 1979)★★★, *The Dream Goes On* (Capitol 1981)★★, *Another Night* (Provogue 1990)★★★, *Spirit Of The Twilight* (Provogue 1994)★★★.

CLEMENT, JACK

b. Jack Henderson Clement, 5 April 1931, Whitehaven, Memphis, Tennessee, USA. Clement, the son of a dentist and choirmaster, began playing music professionally while in the US Marines. He moved to Washington DC in 1952 and worked with the Stoneman Family and Roy Clark, before forming a novelty country music act, Buzz And Jack, with Buzz Busby. He worked as an Arthur Murray dance instructor in Memphis in 1954 and then formed the garage-based Fernwood Records with truck-driver Slim Wallace. They leased their first recording, 'Trouble Bound' by Billy Lee Riley, to Sam Phillips at Sun Records. As a result, Phillips employed Clement as a songwriter, session musician, engineer and producer. Clement produced Jerry Lee Lewis's 'Whole Lotta Shakin' Goin' On', as well as writing 'It'll Be Me' and 'Fools Like Me'. He also helped Johnny Cash develop his distinctive sound and wrote his US pop hits 'Guess Things Happen That Way' and 'Ballad Of A Teenage Queen'. Clement played rhythm guitar on Cash's classic recording of 'Big River', as well as working with Roy Orbison, Charlie Rich and Conway Twitty. In 1959 Clement left Sun and formed the unsuccessful Summer Records ('Summer hits, Summer not, Hope you like the ones we've got.').

Clement then worked as an assistant to Chet Atkins at RCA Records, producing Del Wood and writing Jim Reeves' 'I Know One' and Bobby Bare's 'Miller's Cave'. On a whim, he decided that he wanted to make Beaumont, Texas, the music capital of the world, but the only hit he produced there was Dickey Lee's 1962 US Top 10 hit, 'Patches'. Back in Nashville, Clement produced Johnny Cash's 1963 hit 'Ring Of Fire', and wrote several comic songs for *Everybody Loves A Nut*, including 'The One On The Right Is On The Left'. Just as Sam Phillips had been looking for 'a white boy who could sound black', Clement wanted a black country star. In 1966 he found what he wanted in Charley Pride and produced his records for many years. Pride recorded Clement's songs 'Just Between You And Me' and 'Gone, On The Other Hand'. He also produced Tompall And The Glaser Brothers, Sheb Wooley and, surprisingly, Louis Armstrong. One of his wittiest songs is called '(If I Had) Johnny's Cash And Charley's Pride'. In 1972 Clement formed the JMI label, signing Don Williams, but lost his money by backing a horror film set in Nashville, *Dear Dead Delilah*, with Agnes Moorehead in her last film role. He continued producing albums including *Dreaming My Dreams* (Waylon Jennings), *Our Mother The Mountain* (Townes Van Zandt) and *Two Days In November* (Doc Watson). He wrote the title track of Johnny Cash's *Gone Girl*; and Cash's hilarious liner notes indicate Clement's eccentricities. From time to time he recorded his own records including a highly regarded single, 'Never Give A Heart A Place To Grow', and in 1978, he finally made an album - *All I Want To Do In Life* for Elektra Records. In recent years, he has taken to performing as Cowboy Jack Clement. An example of his character and his self-confidence arose when he met Paul McCartney in Nashville. He advised the former-Beatle, 'Let's do "Yesterday" and I'll show you how to cut that sucker right.' More recently, Clement assisted with the recording of five tracks in the Sun Studios that featured on U2's *Rattle And Hum*, and he continues to produce Johnny Cash.

● ALBUMS: *All I Want To Do In Life* (Elektra 1978)★★.

CLEMENTS, VASSAR

b. 25 April 1928, Kinard, South Carolina, USA. In his youth he enjoyed jazz and swing music as well as country, which might explain his versatility as a fiddle player in later years. A friend who was a telephone operator overheard Bill Monroe say he was looking for a fiddle player, and she told Clements to contact Monroe immediately. Clements played with Monroe on the *Grand Ole Opry* in 1949 and recorded with him the following year. He also played with Jim And Jesse and Faron Young. He was featured on both volumes of the Nitty Gritty Dirt Band's influential *Will The Circle Be Unbroken*. He has played on innumerable sessions including ones with Jimmy Buffett, J.J. Cale, Steve Goodman, Emmylou Harris, Linda Ronstadt, Gene Parsons and Jerry Jeff Walker. He has played on records by the Grateful Dead and worked with their leader, Jerry Garcia, in Old And In The Way. Over the years, he has performed in concert more than most session players and he has been on the road with Earl Scruggs and John Hartford. He appeared in the Robert Altman film *Nashville* (1975) and his frenzied fiddle playing is featured in several instrumental albums - *New Hillbilly Jazz* is unusual in that it also features his vocals.

● ALBUMS: *Crossing The Catskills* (Rounder 1973)★★★,

Vassar Clements (Mercury 1975)★★★, *Superbow* (Mercury 1976)★★★, with Doug Jernigan, David Bromberg *Hillbilly Jazz* (Flying Fish 1976)★★★, *The Bluegrass Sessions* (Flying Fish 1977)★★★, with Jernigan, Jesse McReynolds, Buddy Spicher *Nashville Jam* (Flying Fish 1979)★★★, *Vassar* (Flying Fish 1980)★★★, with Jernigan *More Hillbilly Jazz* (Flying Fish 1980)★★★, *Westport Drive* (Mind Dust Music 1984)★★★, with John Hartford, Dave Holland *Clements, Hartford And Holland* (Rounder 1985)★★★ *Hillbilly Jazz Rides Again* (Flying Fish 1987)★★★, with Stéphane Grappelli *Together At Last* (1987)★★★, *New Hillbilly Jazz* (1988)★★, *Grass Routes* (Rounder 1991)★★★, *Once In A While* (Flying Fish 1993)★★★.

CLEMENTS, ZEKE

b. 6 September 1911, Warrior, near Dora, Alabama, USA. He began his professional career working as a comedian in burlesque shows, but in 1928 he made his radio debut on the WLS *National Barn Dance*. He later joined the band of Otto Gray and the Oklahoma Cowboys as a guitarist and vocalist and toured for some years. In the early 30s, he joined the *Grand Ole Opry* where he changed his burlesque material to a country format. He formed his own band, the Bronco Busters, one of the first *Opry* bands to wear western cowboy dress, and which included his brother Stanley 'Curly' Clements and featured Texas Ruby Owens as their vocalist. After a few years, he moved to Hollywood for radio and film work, and in 1938 provided the voice of Bashful in Walt Disney's classic film *Snow White And The Seven Dwarfs*. He returned to the *Opry* in 1939 and during the 40s, he became a popular performer. A talented vocalist, guitarist and fiddle player, he also wrote many songs. In 1944 and 1945, his war song 'Smoke On The Water' was a number 1 country hit for both Red Foley and Bob Wills, and in 1955, Kitty Wells achieved a hit with 'There's Poison In Your Heart'. He also starred on the *Louisiana Hayride* and was popular all over the south, and although nicknamed the Alabama Cowboy, he was often classed as a country crooner. He later developed various business interests in Nashville. For a time, he moved to Florida, but returned to Nashville and into the late 80s was still making appearances on the *Opry*.

CLIFTON, BILL

b. William August Marburg, 5 April 1931, Riderwood, Maryland, USA. Clifton sang and played guitar, autoharp and fiddle. He became interested in the music of the Carter Family during the 40s, having been introduced to country music through visiting the tenant farmers on his father's estate. Clifton subsequently made his first records for the Stinson label in 1952. By 1954 he was performing with his Dixie Mountain Boys and recording for Blue Ridge. During the 50s Clifton compiled 150 old-time folk and gospel songs and had them privately printed. He was essentially able to bridge the gap between urban folk and bluegrass, reaching both sets of audiences on an international level. In 1961, Clifton recorded 22 Carter Family songs for Starday, and later came to Britain and set up tours for Bill Monroe, the New Lost City Ramblers and the Stanley Brothers. He had been playing bluegrass and old-time country music for 11 years before arriving in England in 1963. He fulfilled a 'missionary' role, as the music was new to English ears, and by 1966 he was playing regularly and hosting a BBC radio show called *Cellar Full Of Folk*. Clifton toured throughout Europe during the 60s, and recorded a programme of old-time music for Radio Moscow in 1966. By the following year, Clifton and his family travelled to the Philippines, where he joined the Peace Corps. Later, during the 70s, he went to New Zealand, and formed the Hamilton County Bluegrass Band. Along with Red Rector (d. 1991) and Don Stover, Clifton formed the First Generation with whom he toured the USA and Europe in 1978. Clifton has since toured widely, including Japan. He is as well known for his work arranging tours and appearances of bluegrass performers as he is for his recordings.

● ALBUMS: with the Dixie Mountain Boys *Mountain Folk Songs* (Starday 1959)★★★, *The Carter Family Memorial Album* (Starday 1961)★★★, *The Bluegrass Sound Of Bill Clifton And The Dixie Mountain Boys* (Starday 1961)★★★, with the Dixie Mountain Boys *Soldier, Sing Me A Song* (Starday 1963)★★★, with other artists *Bluegrass Spectacular* (1963)★★★, with the Dixie Mountain Boys *Fire On The Strings* (1963)★★★, with the Dixie Mountain Boys *Code Of The Mountains* (Starday 1964)★★★, with various artists *Greatest Country Fiddlers Of Our Time* (1964)★★★, *Wanderin'* (1965)★★★, with the Dixie Mountain Boys *Mountain Bluegrass Songs* (Nashville 1966)★★★, with the Dixie Mountain Boys *Bluegrass In The American Tradition* (Nashville 1967)★★★, *Mountain Ramblings* (1967)★★★, *Walking In My Sleep* (1969)★★★, with the Hamilton County Bluegrass Band *Two Shades Of Bluegrass* (1970)★★★, *Bill Clifton Meets The Country Gentlemen* (1971)★★★, *Happy Days* (1971)★★★, with Hedy West *Getting The Folk Out Of The Country* (County 1972)★★★, with the Dixie Mountain Boys *Blue Ridge Mountain Blues* (1973)★★★, with the Dixie Mountain Boys *Blue Ridge Mountain Bluegrass* (1974)★★★, *Going Back To Dixie* (1975)★★★, *Come By The Hills* (1975)★★★, with Paul Clayton, Johnny Clark, Carl Boehm *A Bluegrass Session 1952* (Bear Family 1975)★★★, with Red Rector *Another Happy Day* (1976)★★★, with Rector *In Europe* (1976)★★, with Rector *Are You From Dixie?* (Bear Family 1977)★★★, *Clifton And Company* (1977)★★★, *The Autoharp Centennial Celebration* (1981)★★★, *Beatle Crazy* (Bear Family 1983)★★, *Where The Rainbow Finds Its End* (1991)★★★

● COMPILATIONS: *The Early Years (1957-58)* (Rounder 1992)★★★★.

CLINE, CHARLIE

b. 6 May 1931, Baisden, West Virginia, USA. A talented musician who is equally at home on fiddle, banjo, guitar, mandolin or string bass and whose name is synonymous with the best in bluegrass music. In the late 40s, he began to play various instruments with the Lonesome Pine Fiddlers (a group founded by relatives in 1939) at WHIS Bluefield, West Virginia. He did not record with the Fiddlers in 1950 but recorded with Jimmy Martin's Sunny Mountain Boys the following year on King. After a short spell back with the Fiddlers, with some breaks, he played mainly as a member of Bill Monroe's Blue Grass Boys from 1952-55. He appeared on 38 of their Decca recordings and it seems likely that during that time, he played every instrument for Monroe, except mandolin. In 1953, he rejoined the Fiddlers for a time at WJR Detroit and made some RCA recordings with them. In 1954, he played on sessions by both the Fiddlers and the Stanley Brothers and made some appearances with the Osborne Brothers. In 1958, playing electrified lead guitar and with his wife Lee on electric bass, he played in a far more modern-sounding line-up of Lonesome Fiddlers, playing on radio and television in Pikeville. The following year, he and his wife concentrated on evangelical work and relocated to Alabama. In the mid-70s, he and Lee re-formed the Fiddlers and, alternating between fiddle and mandolin, he recorded albums (some gospel) for Atteiram and Old Homestead. Around 1980, Jimmy Martin re-formed his Sunny Mountain Boys and their old friendship saw Cline make appearances around the bluegrass circuit as a member. In 1986, he joined the Warrior River Boys and recorded with them for Rutabaga and Rounder Records. He also still appeared with his Fiddlers and made recordings at a Lonesome Pine Fiddlers reunion that included his brother, Curly Ray Cline, and the Goins Brothers.

● ALBUMS: as Charlie Cline And the Lonesome Pine Fiddlers with Lee Cline *Shalom (Peace)* (Atteiram 1977)★★★, *Bluegrass Gospel* (Shiloh 1977)★★, *Lonesome Pines* (Old Homestead 1978)★★★, *Strictly Cline* (Atteiram 1978)★★, *Why Ray Ralph* (Old Homestead 1979)★★★, *Brushy Creek Bluegrass* (Old Homestead 1981)★★★ *Sunset Is Coming* (Old Homestead 1983)★★★; as Charlie Cline And The Warrior River Boys *Fiddle Favorites* (Old Homestead 1988)★★★.

CLINE, CURLY RAY

b. 10 January 1923, Baisden, West Virginia, USA, 19 August 1997. The elder brother of Charlie Cline and, like his brother, one of the most respected of bluegrass musicians. Inspired as a boy by Fiddlin' Arthur Smith, whom he first heard on the WSM broadcasts of the *Grand Ole Opry*, he soon mastered the instrument and at the age of 15, he was a founder-member of the Lonesome Pine Fiddlers, when his cousin/brother-in-law Ezra Cline first formed the group at WHIS Bluefield, in 1938. He played fiddle and performed comedy with the group, until the original Fiddlers finally disbanded in 1963. He recorded with the Fiddlers, sang duets with his brother and even worked as a session musician on recordings by other bluegrass artists, including Jimmy Martin. When times were hard and the music failed to provide a proper living, Cline worked on occasions in the mines. In 1963, he joined the Stanley Brothers and after Carter Stanley's death in 1966, he continued to work with Ralph Stanley until 1993. He played fiddle on countless recordings by Stanley's Clinch Mountain Boys and also recorded a number of solo albums. Some featured normal fiddle music, albeit with imitations of mules and dogs added on occasion, but on later recordings his love of comedy is apparent. Among his normal straight vocals, he featured some comedy songs, including 'Smarter Than The Average Idiot', and even made fun of himself in 'Why Me Ralph'.

● ALBUMS: *Old Kentucky Fox Hunter & His Lonesome Pine Fiddle* (Melody 1969)★★★, *The Working Man* (Jalyn 1970)★★★, *Chicken Reel* (Rebel 1971)★★★, *My Little Home In West Virginia* (Rebel 1972)★★★, *They Cut Down The Old Pine Tree* (Rebel 1972)★★★, *Fishin' For Another Hit* (Rebel 1974)★★★, *Why Me Ralph* (Rebel 1975)★★★, *It's Bread And Water For Curly Ray Cline* (Rebel 1977)★★★, *Who's Gonna Mow My Grass* (Rebel 1978)★★★, *Boar Hog* (Old Homestead 1980)★★★, *The Old Kentucky Fox Hunter Plays Gospel* (Old Homestead 1982)★★, *Smarter Than The Average Idiot* (Tin Ear 1984)★★★.

CLINE, PATSY

b. Virginia Patterson Hensley, 8 September 1932, Gore, near Winchester, Virginia, USA, d. 5 March 1963, Camden, Tennessee, USA. Her father, Sam Hensley, already had two children from a previous marriage when he married Hilda, Patsy's mother - a woman many years his junior. Hilda was only 16 when Patsy was born and they grew up like sisters. At the age of four, Patsy was influenced by a film of Shirley Temple and, without tuition, learned tap-dancing and showed an interest in music that was encouraged by the piano-playing of her step-sister. In spite of financial hardships, her parents gave her a piano for her seventh birthday, which she soon learned to play by ear. Hilda could never understand her daughter's affinity with country music, since neither she nor Sam was interested in the genre. At the age of 10, Patsy was eagerly listening to broadcasts from the *Grand Ole Opry* and informing everyone that one day she too would be an *Opry* star. In the early 40s, the Hensleys relocated to Winchester, where Patsy became interested in the country show on WINC presented by Joltin' Jim McCoy. Apart from playing records, he also fronted his own band in live spots on the show. At the age of 14, Patsy contacted McCoy and told him she wanted to sing on his show. He was impressed by her voice and Virginia Hensley quickly became a regular singer with his Melody Playboys. She also became associated with pianist William 'Jumbo' Rinker with whom she sang at local venues, and she left school to work in Gaunt's Drug Store to help the family finances. In 1948, Wally Fowler, a noted *Opry* artist whose gospel show was broadcast live on WSM, appeared at the Palace Theatre in Winchester. Patsy brazenly manoeuvred herself backstage on the night and confronted Fowler. Taken aback by her approach, he sarcastically suggested that perhaps she was 'Winchester's answer to Kitty Wells', but nevertheless let her sing for him. She sang unaccompanied and impressed Fowler so much that he included her in that night's show. Having sought Hilda's permission for her to audition for WSM in Nashville, a few weeks later, Patsy went to see Jim Denny, the manager of the *Opry*. Accompanied by the legendary pianist Moon Mullican, Patsy impressed Denny who asked her to remain in Nashville so that he could arrange an *Opry* appearance. However, without money, although too embarrassed to admit it, and accompanied by the two younger children, Hilda pleaded that they must return to Winchester that day. Before they left, Roy Acuff, who had heard Patsy's singing from an adjoining studio, asked her to sing on his *Noon Time Neighbours* broadcast that day. Her hopes that she would hear from Denny, however, were not realized and Patsy returned to the drug store and singing locally. In 1952, she met Bill Peer, a disc jockey and musician, who had run bands for some years, and who was at the time touring the Tri-State Moose Lodge circuit with his band, the Melody Boys and Girls. He hired Patsy as lead vocalist and on 27 September 1952, she made her first appearance with him at the Brunswick Moose Club in Maryland. Peer did not think the name Virginia was suitable and, wrongly assuming that her second name was Patricia, he billed her as Patsy Hensley. On 27 February 1953, Patsy married Gerald Cline, whom she had met at a show only a few weeks earlier. On the night of her marriage, Patsy appeared on stage for the first time as Patsy Cline. Although Cline's name was known over a considerable area, Peer was aware that she

needed national exposure, and concentrated his efforts on seeking a recording contract for her. A demo tape attracted attention and on 30 September 1954, she signed a two-year contract with Four-Star, a Pasadena-based independent company, once owned by Gene Autry, whose president was now William A. McCall, a man not highly regarded by many in the music business. The contract stated that all Patsy Cline's recordings would remain Four-Star property - in effect, she could only record songs that McCall published and, being a non-writer herself, she was obliged to record any material he chose. Cline made her first four recordings on 1 June 1955, in Bradley's 'Quonset' hut studios in Nashville, under the production of pianist, guitarist and arranger Owen Bradley. 'A Church, A Courtroom And Then Goodbye', penned by Eddie Miller and W.S. Stevenson, was the chosen song, but it failed to reach the country charts (W.S. Stevenson was a pseudonym used by McCall, seemingly for his own songs, but it is known that, on occasions, he applied the name to songs that were written by other writers, such as Donn Hecht, who were under contract to his label). Cline made further recordings on 5 January and 22 April 1956, including the toe-tapping 'I Love You Honey' and the rockabilly 'Stop, Look And Listen'. The anticipated country chart entries did not occur and she became despondent. Her private life took a new turn in April 1956, when she met Charlie Dick, who became her second husband when her marriage to Gerald Cline ended in 1957. In an effort to secure a country hit, McCall commissioned songwriter Hecht, who suggested 'Walking After Midnight', a blues-styled number that he had initially written for Kay Starr, who had turned it down. Cline did not like the song either, claiming it was 'nothing but a little old pop song'. Under pressure from Decca (who leased her records from Four-Star), she recorded it, on 8 November 1956, in a session that also included 'A Poor Man's Roses (Or A Rich Man's Gold)' and 'The Heart You Break May Be Your Own'. On 28 January 1957, although preferring 'A Poor Man's Roses', she sang 'Walking After Midnight' on the Arthur Godfrey *Talent Scouts* show. On 11 February, Decca released the two songs in a picture sleeve on 78 rpm and it immediately entered both country and pop charts. Cline first sang 'Walking After Midnight' on the *Opry* on 16 February. The song finally peaked as a number 2 country and number 12 pop hit, while 'A Poor Man's Roses' also reached number 14 on the country chart. It was later estimated that the record sold around three-quarters of a million copies.

In July 1959, she recorded two fine gospel numbers, 'Life's Railroad To Heaven' and 'Just A Closer Walk With Thee', but although Decca released various records the follow-up chart hit did not materialize. In truth, Decca had only 11 songs, recorded between February 1958 and November 1960, from which to choose. It was possible Cline chose to record the minimum number necessary under the terms of her Four-Star contract in the hope McCall would drop her, thus enabling her to pick up a promised Decca contract. The first song she recorded under her new association with Decca, on 16 November 1960, was 'I Fall To Pieces' by Hank Cochran and Harlan Howard. It quickly became a country number 1 and also peaked at number 12 on the pop charts. In August 1961 she completed a four-day recording session that included 'True Love', 'The Wayward Wind', 'San Antonio Rose' and her now legendary version of 'Crazy'. Willie

Nelson, who had written the song, had demoed it almost as a narration. With Owen Bradley's persuasion, she produced her own stunning interpretation in one take. The recording was a number 2 country and a number 9 pop hit. In 1962, 'She's Got You' was an even bigger country hit, spending five weeks at number 1, while peaking at number 14 in the pop charts. It also became her first entry in the Top 50 UK pop charts. Meanwhile, her marriage to Charlie Dick was becoming more stormy. She had long ago discarded her cowgirl outfits for more conventional dress and she seemed indifferent to her weight problem. Her wild and promiscuous lifestyle included an enduring affair with Faron Young. Her last recording session took place on 7 February 1963, when she recorded 'He Called Me Baby', 'You Took Him Off My Hands' and 'I'll Sail My Ship Alone'. The latter, ironically, was a song written by Moon Mullican, the pianist who had played for her *Opry* audition in 1948. Cline appeared in Birmingham, Alabama, with Tex Ritter and Jerry Lee Lewis on 2 March 1963, following which she agreed with other artists to appear in a charity show in Kansas City the next day, a show staged for the widow of Jack Call, a noted disc jockey on KCMK, known as Cactus Jack, who had died in a car crash. The weather was bad on 4 March but early on the afternoon of 5 March, in spite of further adverse weather forecasts, Cline, together with country singers Cowboy Copas and Hawkshaw Hawkins, set off on the five-hundred-mile flight to Nashville in a small aircraft piloted by Randy Hughes, the son-in-law of Copas and Cline's lover and manager. Hughes first landed at Little Rock to avoid rain and sleet and then at Dyersburg to refuel, where he was warned of bad weather in the area. They encountered further bad weather and, although the exact reason for the crash is unknown, the life of Patsy Cline came to an end some fifty minutes later, when the aircraft came down in woodland about a mile off Highway 70, near Camden, Tennessee. At the time of her death, Cline's recording of 'Leaving On Your Mind' was in both country and pop charts and before the year was over, both 'Sweet Dreams' and 'Faded Love' became Top 10 country and minor pop hits. It has been suggested that Patsy Cline was not an outstanding performer of up-tempo material, but it is an undisputed fact that she could extract every possible piece of emotion from a country weepie. Her versions of 'Walking After Midnight', 'I Fall To Pieces', 'Crazy', 'She's Got You' and 'Sweet Dreams' represent five of the greatest recordings ever made in country music. Those in any doubt of her standing should consult the *Billboard* back-catalogue country chart - her *Greatest Hits* stood at number 1 for over four years.

● ALBUMS: *Patsy Cline* (Decca 1957)★★★★, *Patsy Cline Showcase* (Decca 1961)★★★★, *Sentimentally Yours* (Decca 1962)★★★★, *In Memoriam* (Everest 1963)★★★★, *Encores* (Everest 1963)★★★, *A Legend* (Everest 1963)★★★, *Reflections* (Everest 1964)★★★, *A Portait Of Patsy Cline* (Decca 1964)★★★★, *That's How A Heartache Begins* (Decca 1964)★★★, *Today, Tomorrow, Forever* (Hilltop 1964)★★★, *Gotta Lot Of Rhythm In My Soul* (Metro 1965)★★★, *Stop The World And Let Me Off* (Hilltop 1966)★★★, *The Last Sessions* (MCA 1980)★★★★, *Try Again* (Quicksilver 1982)★★★, *Sweet Dreams* film soundtrack (1985)★★★, *Live At The Opry* (MCA 1988)★★★, *Live - Volume Two* (MCA 1989)★★★, *The Birth Of A Star* (Razor & Tie 1996)★★★, *Live At The Cimarron Ballroom* recorded 1961 (MCA 1997)★★★.

● COMPILATIONS: *Patsy Cline's Golden Hits* (Everest 1962)★★★, *The Patsy Cline Story* (Decca 1963)★★★★, *Patsy Cline's Greatest Hits* (Decca 1967)★★★, *Country Great* (Vocalion 1969)★★★, *Greatest Hits* (MCA 1973)★★★★★, *Golden Greats* (MCA 1979)★★★★★, *20 Golden Greats* (Astan 1984)★★★, *20 Classic Tracks* (Starburst 1987)★★★, *12 Greatest Hits* (MCA 1988)★★★, *Dreaming* (Platinum Music 1988)★★★, *20 Golden Hits* (Deluxe 1989)★★★, *Walkin' Dreams: Her First Recordings, Volume One* (Rhino 1989)★★★★, *Hungry For Love: Her First Recordings, Volume Two* (Rhino 1989)★★★★, *Rockin' Side: Her First Recordings, Volume Three* (Rhino 1989)★★★★, *The Patsy Cline Collection* 4-CD box set (MCA 1991)★★★★★, *The Definitive* (1992)★★★, *Discovery* (Prism Leisure 1994)★★★, *Premier Collection* (Pickwick 1994)★★★, *The Patsy Cline Story* (MCA 1994)★★★★, *Thinking Of You* (Summit 1995)★★★, *Today, Tomorrow And Forever* 2-CD (Parade 1995)★★★.

● VIDEOS: *The Real Patsy Cline* (Platinum Music 1989), *Remembering Patsy* (1993).

● FURTHER READING: *Patsy Cline: Sweet Dreams*, Ellis Nassour. *Honky Tonk Angel: The Intimate Story Of Patsy Cline*, Ellis Nassour. *Patsy: The Life And Times Of Patsy Cline*, Margaret Jones. *I Fall To Pieces: The Music And The Life Of Patsy Cline*, Mark Bego.

CLINE, TAMMY

b. Marilyn Margaret Croff, 16 June 1953, Hull, Humberside, England. The teenage Croff was performing in working-men's clubs in the Hull area and gave up her job at a starch factory because the chemicals were affecting her voice. She met her husband, Rod Boulton, when she sang with a local band, the Falcons. After the birth of their daughter they became a duo and, on a whim, Rod named them Tammy And Dave Cline. Although not intentional, it was the ideal name for Marilyn Croff, whose strongest influences were Tammy Wynette and Patsy Cline. With another Hull band, Uncle Sam, Tammy Cline did well in the national Marlboro Talent Contest in 1978. When they decided to turn fully professional, Uncle Sam changed its line-up and became Southern Comfort. Success on the television talent show *Search For A Star* followed, and Tammy recorded in Nashville - one single for the UK market, 'Love Is A Puzzle', and another for the USA, 'I Don't Know How To Tell Him'. Although chart success eluded her, she was voted Britain's top female country singer for five consecutive years. Tammy Cline has built a strong following around the UK clubs and has become a seasoned broadcaster.

● ALBUMS: *Tammy Cline And The Southern Comfort Band* (President 1983)★★★, *Tammy Cline Sings The Country Greats* (Music For Pleasure 1987)★★, *Tammy Cline's Country Gospel Album* (Word 1987)★★.

CLOWER, JERRY

b. 28 September 1926, Amite County, Mississippi, USA. During the Depression, Clower's father went to Memphis to look for work but took to drink and neglected his family. His 17-year-old mother moved back to her father's farm in Liberty, Mississippi, and when she remarried, they moved to another farm. Clower worked on the farm and served on an aircraft carrier during World War II. He married in 1947 and obtained a degree in agriculture in 1951. As a salesman in Yazoo, Mississippi, he found that he sold more fertilizer if he amused his customers. He developed a club act and, dressed in gaudy suits and with a loud voice, he became known as 'The Mouth of Mississippi'. His first album, *Jerry Clower From Yazoo City*, was released on a small label and, when it sold by word of mouth in large quantities, he was signed to MCA. He joined the *Grand Ole Opry* in 1973 and established a reputation for his tales and the antics of one Marcel Ledbetter. He is also a Baptist minister and an active member of the Gideon Bible Society.

● ALBUMS: *Jerry Clower From Yazoo City, Mississippi, Talkin'* (MCA 1971)★★★, *Jerry Clower - The Mouth Of The Mississippi* (MCA 1972)★★★, *Clower Power* (MCA 1973)★★, *Country Ham* (MCA 1974)★★★, *Live In Picayune* (MCA 1975)★★, *The Ambassador Of Goodwill* (MCA 1976)★★★, *Ain't God Good* (MCA 1977)★★★, *On The Road* (MCA 1977)★★, *Live From The Stage Of The Grand Ole Opry* (MCA 1978)★★, *The Ledbetter Olympics* (MCA 1980)★★★, *More Good 'Uns* (MCA 1981)★★★, *Dogs I Have Known* (MCA 1982)★★, *Live At Cleburne, Texas* (MCA 1983)★★, *Starke Raving* (MCA 1984)★★★, *Mississippi Talkin'* (MCA 1984)★★★, *An Officer And A Ledbetter* (MCA 1985)★★★, *Runaway Truck* (MCA 1987)★★★, *Top Gum* (MCA 1987)★★★.

● COMPILATIONS: *Jerry Clower's Greatest Hits* (MCA 1979)★★★.

● FURTHER READING: *Ain't God Good*, Jerry Clower. *Let The Hammer Down*, Jerry Clower. *Life Ever Laughter*, Jerry Clower.

CMA

(see Country Music Association)

COCHRAN, HANK

b. Garland Perry Cochran, 2 August 1935, Greenville, Mississippi, USA. Fellow country songwriter Glenn Martin has said, 'His life is not as pretty as his music, yet all his songs come from his life.' Cochran lost his parents while an infant and was placed in an orphanage. He was raised in Mississippi and, after finishing school, ran away to the oilfields of New Mexico. An uncle taught him guitar chords and he developed an interest in country music. He travelled to California and started performing regularly on a radio talent show as Hank Cochran. He secured bookings in small clubs and he offered 16-year-old Eddie Cochran a job as lead guitarist. As 'brother duos' were popular they decided to work as the Cochran Brothers, although they were not related. They were signed to the Ekko label and their first single combined 'Mr. Fiddle' and a tribute to Hank Williams and Jimmie Rodgers, 'Two Blue Singin' Stars'. They also backed Al Dexter on his Ekko re-recording of 'Pistol Packin' Mama'. The Cochrans broadcast as part of Dallas's *Big D Jamboree*, but, hearing about Elvis Presley's dynamic appearance, they realized they would have to change. They recorded a rock 'n' roll single, 'Tired And Sleepy', and, after opening for Lefty Frizzell in Hawaii, they split up. Eddie turned to rock 'n' roll, while Hank, who was married, secured regular work on the *California Hayride*. In 1959, Hank moved to Nashville, signed with Pamper Music and befriended another of the company's writers, Harlan Howard. Together they wrote Patsy Cline's 'I Fall To Pieces', and Cochran also wrote 'She's Got You' for her. Cochran, like Howard, wrote a string of successful songs: 'I'd Fight The World' (Jim Reeves), 'If The Back Door Could Talk' (Ronnie Sessions), 'It's Not Love (But

It's Not Bad)' (Merle Haggard), 'I Want To Go With You' (Eddy Arnold), 'Make The World Go Away' (originally recorded by Ray Price in 1963 and then a worldwide success for Eddy Arnold in 1965), 'Tears Broke Out On Me' (Eddy Arnold), 'Which One Will It Be?' (Bobby Bare), 'Who Do I Know In Dallas?' (Gene Watson), 'Willingly' (a duet for Shirley Collie and Willie Nelson) and 'You Comb Her Hair' (with Harlan Howard for George Jones). Like Howard, he also wrote country songs for Burl Ives, including 'A Little Bitty Tear' and 'Funny Way Of Laughin''. Cochran's marriage was soon over and he then married Jeannie Seely, who recorded several of his songs including her US Top 10 country hit 'Don't Touch Me', later revived by T.G. Sheppard. Hank also had his own successes including 'Sally Was A Good Old Girl' (written by Harlan Howard), 'I'd Fight The World' and 'All Of Me Belongs To You'. Despite all his productivity, he frequently had to receive treatment for alcoholism. In 1978 he made a gruff-voiced album, *With A Little Help From My Friends*, with the assistance of Merle Haggard, Willie Nelson, Jack Greene and Jeannie Seely. Seely's tribute on the sleeve disguised the fact that they lived apart and they are now divorced. He recovered sufficiently to present the noted *Austin City Limits* television show when it started in 1979. His 1980 album, *Make The World Go Away*, is basically a collection of his greatest songs. Willie Nelson guests on the album and Cochran, in turn, was featured in Nelson's film *Honeysuckle Rose*, singing 'Make The World Go Away' with Seely. Cochran and Dean Dillon wrote George Strait's US country number 1 hits 'The Chair' (1985) and 'Ocean Front Property' (1987). He teamed up with Waylon Jennings-influenced songwriter Billy Don Burns for 1997's *Desperate Men* album.

● ALBUMS: *Hits From The Heart* (RCA Victor 1963)★★★, *Going In Training* (RCA Victor 1965)★★★, *Hits From The Heart* (RCA Victor 1966)★★★, *The Heart Of Cochran* (Monument 1968)★★★, *With A Little Help From My Friends* (1978)★★★, *Make The World Go Away* (1980)★★★★, as the Cochran Brothers *The Young Eddie Cochran* (1983)★★, with Billy Don Burns *Desperate Men* (Small Dog-A-Barkin' 1997)★★★.

COE, DAVID ALLAN

b. 6 September 1939, Akron, Ohio, USA. From the age of nine, Coe was in and out of reform schools, correction centres and prisons. According to his publicity handout, he spent time on Death Row after killing a fellow inmate who demanded oral sex. When *Rolling Stone* magazine questioned this, Coe responded with a song, 'I'd Like To Kick The Shit Out Of You'. Whatever the truth of the matter, Coe was paroled in 1967 and took his songs about prison life to Shelby Singleton who released two albums on his SSS label. Coe wrote Tanya Tucker's 1974 US country number 1, 'Would You Lay With Me (In A Field Of Stone)?'. He took to calling himself Davey Coe - the Mysterious Rhinestone Cowboy, performing in a mask, and driving a hearse. He satirized the themes of country music with hilarious additions to Steve Goodman's 'You Never Even Called Me By My Name', but has often used the clichés himself. His defiant stance and love of motorbikes, multiple tattoos and ultra-long hair made him a natural 'Nashville outlaw', which he wrote about in the self-glorifying 'Longhaired Redneck' and 'Willie, Waylon And Me' (Willie Nelson and Waylon Jennings). In 1978

Johnny Paycheck had a US country number 1 with Coe's 'Take This Job And Shove It', which inspired a film of the same title in 1981, and Coe's own successes included the witty 'Divers Do It Deeper' (1978), 'Jack Daniels If You Please' (1979), 'Now I Lay Me Down To Cheat' (1982), 'The Ride' (1983), which conjures up a meeting between Coe and Hank Williams, and 'Mona Lisa's Lost Her Smile' (1984), which reached number 2 on the US country charts, his highest position as a performer. Recordings with other performers include 'Don't Cry Darlin'' and 'This Bottle (In My Hand)' with George Jones, 'I've Already Cheated On You' with Willie Nelson, and 'Get A Little Dirt On Your Hands' with Bill Anderson. Coe's 1978 album *Human Emotions* was about his divorce - one side being 'Happy Side' and the other 'Su-i-side'. The controversial cover of *Texas Moon* shows the bare backsides of his band and crew, and he has also released two mail-order albums of explicit songs, *Nothing Sacred* and *Underground*. Coe appears incapable of separating the good from the ridiculous and his albums are erratic. At his best, he is a sensitive, intelligent writer. Similarly, his stage performances with his Tennessee Hat Band differ wildly in length and quality: sometimes it is non-stop music, sometimes it features conjuring tricks. Coe's main trick, however, is to remain successful, as country music fans grow exasperated with his over-the-top publicity. He may still be an outlaw but as Waylon Jennings remarks in 'Living Legends', that only means double-parking on Music Row.

● ALBUMS: *Penitentiary Blues* (SSS 1968)★★, *Requiem For A Harlequin* (SSS 1970)★★★, *The Mysterious Rhinestone Cowboy* (Columbia 1974)★★★, *Once Upon A Rhyme* (Columbia 1974)★★★, *Longhaired Redneck* (Columbia 1976)★★★, *D.A.C. Rides Again* (Columbia 1977)★★★, *Texas Moon* (Columbia 1977)★★★, *Tattoo* (Columbia 1977)★★★, *Family Album* (Columbia 1978)★★★, *Human Emotions* (Columbia 1978)★★★, *Nothing Sacred* (1978)★★★, *Buckstone County Prison* (Columbia 1978)★★★, *Spectrum VII* (Columbia 1979)★★, *Compass Point* (Columbia 1979)★★★, *Something To Say* (Columbia 1980)★★★, *Invictus (Means) Unconquered* (Columbia 1981)★★★, *Underground* (Columbia 1981)★★★, *Tennessee Whiskey* (Columbia 1981)★★, *Rough Rider* (Columbia 1982)★★★, *D.A.C.* (Columbia 1982)★★★, *Castles In The Sand* (Columbia 1983)★★★, *Hello In There* (Columbia 1983)★★★, *Just Divorced* (Columbia 1984)★★★, *Darlin' Darlin'* (Columbia 1985)★★★, *Unchained* (DAC 1985)★★, *Son Of The South* (Columbia 1986)★★★, *A Matter Of Life And Death* (Columbia 1987)★★★, *Crazy Daddy* (Columbia 1989)★★★, *1990 Songs For Sale* (1991)★★, *Granny's Off Her Rocker* (DAC 1994)★★, *Live, If That Ain't Country* (Columbia 1997)★★, *The Ghost Of Hank Williams* (King 1997)★★★.

● COMPILATIONS: *Greatest Hits* (Columbia 1978)★★★, *17 Greatest Hits* (Columbia 1985)★★★, *For The Record: The First 10 Years* (Columbia 1985)★★★, *Super Hits* (Columbia 1993)★★★, *Super Hits, Volume 2* (Columbia 1996)★★★.

● FURTHER READING: *Just For The Record*, David Allan Coe. *Ex-Convict*, David Allan Coe. *The Book Of David. Poems, Prose And Stories*, David Allan Coe.

● FILMS: *The Last Days Of Frank And Jesse James*.

COHEN, PAUL

b. 10 November 1908, Chicago, Illinois, USA, d. 1 April 1970. Cohen first became involved in the music industry when he worked for Columbia Records, but joined Decca in the early 30s. Initially, he worked as a salesman and a talent scout until, in 1944, he became Decca's country artists and repertory director. He is credited as being the first producer to believe that Nashville had great potential as a recording centre for country artists. It the spring of 1945, with the full support of his Decca board, he recorded Red Foley in WSM's Studio B to become the first producer to actually record a contracted artist, in Nashville, in modern times. He followed, in September that year, by recording Ernest Tubb. When, in 1946, two of WSM's engineers, Aaron Shelton and Carl Jenkins, organized a commercial studio complex called Castle Recording Company, in the old Tulane Hotel, Cohen became the first producer to record artists there. Initially, he recorded Red Foley, Red Sovine and Kitty Wells but by the time he left Decca in 1958, he had also been instrumental in helping the careers of many of the label's artists. He relocated to New York, where he formed his own Todd label and later ran both Kapp and ABC-Paramount. He was later President of the Country Music Association and, as such, performed the opening ceremony, on 31 March 1967, when the Country Music Hall Of Fame And Museum complex was officially opened. In 1970, Cohen died of cancer, but in 1976, his contribution to the genre saw him posthuously elected to membership of the Country Music Hall Of Fame. Although he always had a great eye for talent, he also proved he was human when, early in the artist's career, he was once recording Buddy Holly and remarked to Owen Bradley 'that Buddy Holly was the biggest no talent he had ever worked with'.

COLE, B.J.

b. 17 June 1946, London, England. Although initially a photographer, Cole was subsequently drawn to music, inspired by the work of guitarists Hank Marvin, Chet Atkins and Eddie Lang. 'Sleep Walk', the atmospheric instrumental by Santo And Johnny, was also a notable influence and by 1964 the artist was playing a lap steel guitar. Cole fully embraced country music in the late 60s as a member of Cochise, which in turn established him as one of the UK's leading exponents of the pedal steel guitar. On the group's demise he completed the idiosyncratic *New Hovering Dog*, before contributing to many, often contrasting, recordings as a session musician. These included 'More Questions Than Answers' (Johnny Nash), the first use of pedal steel on a reggae song, 'No Regrets' (Walker Brothers), *I Robot* (the Alan Parsons Project), plus hit singles for Andy Fairweather-Low, Deacon Blue, Paul Young and Level 42. The artist's work with David Sylvian (*Gone To Earth*) and Danny Thompson's *Dizrythmia*, meanwhile, showed him using his chosen instrument in a challenging and innovative manner. A founder-member of the Hank Wangford Band, Cole produced two of the singer's albums, *Hank Wangford* (1980) and *Hank Wangford Band Live* (1982) and, in partnership with Stuart Coleman, performed similar duties on three Shakin' Stevens releases, Hot Dog', 'Hey Mae' and 'Marie Marie'. In 1989 he recorded *Transparent Music*, an 'ambient'-styled release, which in turn provided the basis for his Transparent Music Ensemble. Cole remains an in-demand musician and in 1991 completed work with such contrasting acts as Harold Budd, John Cale and the Beautiful South. In the UK B.J. has no rival, his title as leading exponent of the pedal steel guitar cannot be chal-

lenged. Additionally he has done much to further interest in an instrument that has failed to expand beyond its own territory.
● ALBUMS: *The New Hovering Dog* (United Artists 1973)★★, *Transparent Music* (Hannibal 1989)★★, *The Heart Of The Moment* (Resurgence 1995)★★★.

COLLIE, BIF

b. 25 November 1926, Little Rock, Arkansas, USA, d. 19 February 1992, Brentwood, Tennessee, USA. One of the most respected and knowledgeable producers and DJs to have played country music, Collie spent over three decades spinning records and endearing himself to his listeners on several stations including KLEE, KNUZ and KPRC (Houston) and KFOX and KLAC (Los Angeles). He also appeared on several television programmes and worked hard in the founding of the Country Music Association and the Academy of Country Music. His wife Shirley (b. Shirley Caddell, 16 March 1931, Chillicothe, Missouri, USA) sang on various shows including the *Brush Creek Follies* and, in 1962, she scored a Top 10 hit with 'Willingly', a duet with Willie Nelson. She subsequently divorced Collie to become the second Mrs Nelson, leading Bif to state: 'If there's any man I'd like to have run off with my wife, it would be Willie Nelson'. When people asked Bif why he kept playing Nelson's records, he said, 'Hell, it's my job to play the best music and Willie is one of the best no matter whose wife he's with'. In 1972, Collie, recording for United Artists under the pseudonym of Billy Bob Bowman, had a minor hit with 'Miss Pauline'. He was elected to the Country Music Disc Jockey Hall Of Fame in 1978 and died of cancer in 1992.

COLLIE, MARK

b. George Mark Collie, 18 January 1956, Waynesboro, Tennessee, USA. Collie was one of six children and he learnt piano and guitar as he was growing up. He wanted to join the army but was prevented by his diabetes. He tried to make it as a musician in both Memphis and Nashville. In 1977 country singer Ray Pillow recorded his song 'Nighttime Masquerade', but it was not until 1982 that Collie moved to Nashville permanently. He was heard by MCA executives at the Douglas Corner Cafe, and he made his US country chart debut in 1990 with 'Something With A Ring To It'. Collie and Don Cook produced what was to be his biggest single, the rockabilly country of 'Even The Man In The Moon Is Crying'. His debut album of his own compositions showed a talent for playing with words - 'What I wouldn't give is more than she could take' and 'Where's there's smoke, you'll find my old flame'. The car-racing title track became popular and he had an audience participation number with 'Shame Shame Shame Shame'. Other fine songs have included 'It Is No Secret', 'Born To Love You' and 'Another Old Soldier', which is about his father and other war veterans. Grungy guitar was added for *Unleashed* and the album included a restrained 'Ring Of Fire' with Carlene Carter's harmony vocals. Deborah Allen joined him for 'Lonely Street' and Joy Lynn White for 'Hard Lovin' Woman'. His collie dog Amos is featured in all his videos except 'Let Her Go': 'People complained so much that we had to put him back.' He signed to Warner Brothers Records in 1995, releasing *Tennessee Plates* the same year.
● ALBUMS: *Hardin County Line* (MCA 1990)★★★, *Born And Raised In Black And White* (MCA 1991)★★★, *Mark Collie* (MCA 1993)★★★★, *Unleashed* (MCA 1994)★★★, *Tennessee Plates* (Giant 1995)★★★.
● VIDEOS: *Hard Lovin' Woman* (1994).

COLLINS KIDS

A brother and sister rockabilly act, Larry Collins (b. 4 October 1944, Tulsa, Oklahoma, USA) and Lorrie Collins (b. Lawrencine Collins, 7 May 1942, Tahlequah, Oklahoma, USA) recorded numerous singles for Columbia Records in the 50s and early 60s that are revered by fans and collectors of early rock 'n' roll but never dented the charts. The duo gained what little recognition it had through frequent television appearances. Lorrie Collins was the first of the siblings to enter showbusiness. At the age of eight she won a singing contest and two years later the family moved to Los Angeles. Guitarist Larry joined his sister's act in 1954, after having won contests on his own through his prodigious musicianship. After the pair won a talent contest together, they were hired to perform for a television programme called *Town Hall Party* on which they soon became regulars, appearing on every programme. The Collins Kids, as they became known professionally, were signed to Columbia in 1955. As Columbia at that time was not primarily a rock 'n' roll label, poor promotion doomed the Collins Kids to failure. When Lorrie married in 1959, the act temporarily split up. They reunited briefly but with the birth of Lorrie's first child in 1961, the team was effectively terminated. Larry Collins recorded a handful of solo records, which also failed to chart, and later became a country songwriter, whose credits included co-writing the Tanya Tucker hit 'Delta Dawn' and David Frizzell and Shelly West's 'You're The Reason God Made Oklahoma'. In later life, he became a professional golfer and Lorrie retired to raise her family.
● COMPILATIONS: *Introducing Larry And Lorrie* (Columbia 1958)★★★, *Rockin' Rollin' Collins Kids* (Bear Family 1983)★★★, *Rockin' Rollin' Collins Kids, Volume 2* (Bear Family 1983)★★, *Hop, Skip & Jump* 2-CD box set (Bear Family 1991)★★★★, *Rockin' On T.V.* (Krazy Kat 1993)★★★.

COLLINS, TOMMY

b. Leonard Raymond Sipes, 28 September 1930, Bethany, Oklahoma, USA. Collins reflected upon his childhood in his song about being raised on a farm, 'The Roots Of My Raising', a US country number 1 for Merle Haggard. As a young man he was an avid follower of Jimmie Rodgers and, for a while, dated singer Wanda Jackson (although, contrary to some reports, it was a lesser-known Wanda that Collins later married). On moving to Bakersfield, California, Ferlin Husky named him after a drink, Tom Collins, and, like Buck Owens, he played on his Capitol recordings of the mid-50s. Collins says he was 'singing as high as I could - Webb Pierce was in fashion' and his songs were largely light-hearted, mildly suggestive narratives about courting, such as his first records, 'You Gotta Have A License', 'You Better Not Do That' and 'I Always Get A Souvenir'. 'All Of The Monkeys Ain't In The Zoo' applied to numerous politicians and he also wrote the sensitive 'High On A Hilltop' and 'Those Old Love Letters From You'. Many songs stemmed from personal experience. Collins entered a seminary and was ordained in 1961 and, for some years, had little involvement in country music. Following a tour of Vietnam in the mid-60s, he recorded for Columbia Records, his new songs including 'If You Can't Bite, Don't Growl' and 'I Made The Prison Band'. His 20 compositions for Merle Haggard included their co-written, nostalgic 'I Wish Things Were Simple Again'. After writing 'Hello Hag', Haggard retaliated with 'Leonard', which voiced his concern for Collins' drinking. Haggard needed to be persuaded to record the touching 'Carolyn' as he felt it wasn't country music, but it was the high point of their partnership. In reality, 'Carolyn' was a coded message to Collins' wife, and he said, 'I didn't set out to mess up my life but tragedies have a habit of working for you.' Hardly recognizable as the 50s star, Collins sometimes performs rough-voiced versions of his successes around country clubs, but newer songs such as 'Tilt Me A Little Toward Tilly' still reflect his ingenuity.

● ALBUMS: *Words And Music Country Style* (Capitol 1957)★★★, *Light Of The Lord* (Capitol 1959)★★★, *This Is Tommy Collins!* (Capitol 1959)★★★, *Songs I Love To Sing* (Capitol 1961)★★★, *The Dynamic Tommy Collins* (Columbia 1966)★★★, *Let's Live A Little* (Tower 1966)★★★, *Shindig* (Tower 1968)★★★, *Tommy Collins On Tour* (Columbia 1968)★★★, *Shindig* (Tower 1968)★★★, *Tommy Collins Callin'* (Starday 1972)★★★, *Country Souvenir* (1981)★★, *Cowboys Get Lucky Some Of The Time* (1981)★★, *New Patches* (1986)★★.

● COMPILATIONS: *This Is Tommy Collins* (Stetson 1988)★★★, *Leonard* 5-CD box set (Bear Family 1992)★★★.

COLORADO

Comprising Gordon Davidson (lead guitar, lead vocals), Dado Duncan (bass), Dave Duff (steel guitar, vocals), George Jack (rhythm guitar, violin) and Sandy Mackay (drums), Colorado was formed in the 70s by these five musicians, who lived within 10 miles of each other around Sutherland, Scotland. They began by performing Scottish folk music but then reverted to country. They backed touring US acts (Melba Montgomery, Vernon Oxford) and, in particular, did much to help Boxcar Willie establish himself. On one hard-working tour, they backed Boxcar Willie and Jean Shepard as well undertaking their own spot. They were the first Scottish group to perform at the prestigious Wembley Festival. In the late 80s they changed their name to Caledonia to perform Scottish folk again, but they are now a country band once more.

● ALBUMS: *Colorado Sing Country Music* (Big R 1980)★★★, *Tennessee Inspiration* (Big R 1982)★★, *Colorado* (Trimtop 1985)★★★, *Still Burning* (Trimtop 1987)★★★, *Exclusive* (Trimtop 1988)★★, *Colorado* (Trimtop 1988)★★★.

COLTER, JESSI

b. Mirriam Johnson, 25 May 1943, Phoenix, Arizona, USA. Her mother became Sister Helen, an ordained Pentecostal minister, and Colter became the church pianist when only 11, hence her subsequent gospel album, *Mirriam*. She impressed Duane Eddy who produced her 1961 single 'Lonesome Road', and who then married her in 1963. He wrote and recorded an instrumental, 'Mirriam', while she wrote some of his album tracks as well as 'No Sign Of The Living' for Dottie West. In 1967, Eddy and his wife recorded a duet single, 'Guitar On My Mind'. After her divorce from Eddy in 1968, she married Waylon Jennings on 26 October 1969 at her mother's church. She adopted the stage name

Jessi Colter after her great-great-great uncle who was in Jesse James's notorious outlaw gang. In 1975, Jessi reached number 4 in the US pop charts with the self-penned 'I'm Not Lisa', which was followed by the huge success of *Wanted! The Outlaws* (Colter was too conscious of her appearance to ever look like an outlaw). Her best-known duets with Waylon Jennings are 'Suspicious Minds', her soothing composition 'Storms Never Last' and 'The Union Mare And The Confederate Grey' from the concept album *White Mansions*. In 1977 she worked with both husbands and Willie Nelson on a revival of 'You Are My Sunshine'. In recent times she has let her recording career slip, largely to nurse Jennings through his various problems, but she is still part of his stage show. Among her many compositions are 'You Hung The Moon (Didn't You, Waylon)?' and 'Jennifer (Fly My Little Baby)' about her daughter, while she turned John Lennon and Paul McCartney's 'Hey Jude' into a song for Jennings by singing 'Hey Dude'.

● ALBUMS: *A Country Star Is Born* (RCA 1970)★★★, *I'm Jessi Colter* (Capitol 1975)★★★, with Waylon Jennings, Willie Nelson, Tompall Glaser *Wanted! The Outlaws* (RCA 1976)★★★★, *Jessi* (Capitol 1976)★★★, *Diamond In The Rough* (Capitol 1976)★★★, *Mirriam* (Capitol 1977)★★★, with Jennings, John Dillon, Steve Cash *White Mansions* (1978)★★★, *That's The Way A Cowboy Rock 'N' Rolls* (Capitol 1978)★★★, with Jennings *Leather And Lace* (RCA 1981)★★, *Ridin' Shotgun* (Capitol 1981)★★★, with Jennings *The Pursuit Of D.B. Cooper* film soundtrack (1982)★★, *Rock 'N' Roll Lullaby* (Triad 1985)★★★, with Waylon Jennings, Willie Nelson, Tompall Glaser *Wanted! The Outlaws (1976-1996, 20th Anniversary)* (RCA 1996)★★★★.

● COMPILATIONS: *Collection* (Liberty 1995)★★★★.

COMMANDER CODY AND HIS LOST PLANET AIRMEN

Although renowned for its high-energy rock, the Detroit/Ann Arbor region also formed the focal point for this entertaining country rock band. The first of several tempestuous line-ups was formed in 1967, comprising Commander Cody (b. George Frayne IV, 19 July 1944, Boise City, Idaho, USA; piano), John Tichy (b. St. Louis, Missouri, USA; lead guitar), Steve Schwartz (guitar), Don Bolton aka the West Virginia Creeper (pedal steel), Stephen Davis (bass) and Ralph Mallory (drums). Only Frayne, Tichy and Bolton remained with the group on their move to San Francisco the following year. The line-up was completed on the Airmen's debut album, *Lost In The Ozone*, by Billy C. Farlowe (b. Decatur, Alabama, USA; vocals, harp), Andy Stein (b. 31 August 1948, New York, USA; fiddle, saxophone), Billy Kirchen (b. 29 January 1948, Ann Arbor, Michigan, USA; lead guitar), 'Buffalo' Bruce Barlow (b. 3 December 1948, Oxnard, California, USA; bass) and Lance Dickerson (b. 15 October 1948, Livonia, Michigan, USA; drums). This earthy collection covered a wealth of material, including rockabilly, western swing, country and jump R&B, a pattern sustained on several subsequent releases. Despite achieving a US Top 10 single with 'Hot Rod Lincoln' (1972), the group's allure began to fade as their albums failed to capture an undoubted in-concert prowess. Although *Live From Deep In The Heart Of Texas* and *We've Got A Live One Here* redressed the balance, what once seemed so natural became increasingly laboured as individual members grew disillusioned. John Tichy's departure proved crucial and preceded an almost total desertion in 1976. The following year Cody released his first solo album, *Midnight Man*, before convening the New Commander Cody Band. Cody And Farlowe re-formed the Lost Planet Airmen in the 90s.

● ALBUMS: *Lost In The Ozone* (Paramount 1971)★★★, *Hot Licks, Cold Steel And Trucker's Favourites* (Paramount 1972)★★★, *Country Casanova* (Paramount 1973)★★★, *Live From Deep In The Heart Of Texas* (Paramount 1974)★★★★, *Commander Cody And His Lost Planet Airmen* (Warners 1975)★★, *Tales From The Ozone* (Warners 1975)★★, *We've Got A Live One Here!* (Warners 1976)★★★, *Let's Rock* (Blind Pig 1986)★★, *Sleazy Roadside Stories* 1973 live recording (Relix 1988)★★★, *Aces High* (Relix 1990)★★; as the Commander Cody Band *Rock 'N' Roll Again* (Arista 1977)★★, *Flying Dreams* (Arista 1978)★★, *Lose It Tonight* (Line 1980)★★.

Solo: Commander Cody *Midnight Man* (Arista 1977)★★. Bill Kirchen *Tombstone Every Mile* (Edsel 1994)★★★, *Have Love, Will Travel* (Black Top 1996)★★★★.

● COMPILATIONS: *The Very Best Of Commander Cody And His Lost Planet Airmen* (See For Miles 1986)★★★, *Cody Returns From Outer Space* (Edsel 1987)★★★, *Too Much Fun - The Best Of Commander Cody* (MCA 1990)★★★, *Best Of* (Relix 1995)★★★.

COMPTON BROTHERS

The three brothers Tom (vocals, lead guitar), Bill (vocals, guitar) and Harry (vocals, 12-string guitar, drums) were all born in Desloge, Missouri, USA. Their father worked on a pipeline project, which saw the family live in a mobile home and in various locations. While in Colorado, when the boys were 12, 11 and 7, respectively, they started a professional career by winning a major talent contest in Colorado. After relocating to Missouri and adding further successes, they joined *The Ozark Jubilee*. Their career was interrupted when Tom and Bill saw military service, during which time they met bass guitarist Dave Murray. They re-formed after service and with Murray won a Columbia recording contract in 1964. In 1965, they joined the WWVA *The Wheeling Jamboree* and later opened for Roger Miller and Buck Owens. In 1966, unsuccessful on Columbia, they moved to Dot Records and gained a minor hit with their first release, 'Pickin' Up The Mail'. By 1975, they had registered only 13 country chart entries. They included a cover version of Christie's 'Yellow River' and a version of Roy Orbison's song 'Claudette'. Most had failed to reach the Top 40, the exceptions being 'Haunted House' (number 11, 1969) and their version of the Coasters' 'Charlie Brown' (number 16, 1970). They achieved no further chart success and presumably concentrated on running their own publishing company, Wepedol Music.

● ALBUMS: *On Top Of The Compton Brothers* (Dot 1968)★★★, *Haunted House/Charlie Brown* (Dot 1970)★★, *Yellow River* (Dot 1972)★★.

CONFEDERATE RAILROAD

Danny Shirley (b. Chattanooga, Tennessee, USA; lead vocals, guitar), Mark DuFresne (drums), Michael Lamb (guitar, vocals), Chris McDaniel (keyboards, vocals), Gates Nichols (steel guitar, vocals) and Wayne Secrest (bass). Drenched in the southern country rock of Charlie Daniels and Lynyrd Skynyrd, Danny Shirley formed a powerful country band,

which, for a time, worked as David Allan Coe's touring band. In 1991 Shirley recorded a solo album for Atlantic Records and then persuaded the label to release it as a group effort under the name of Confederate Railroad. The CD lists both the band members and the musicians on the record - and Danny's is the only common name! Promoting the stars-and-bars flag, Confederate Railroad developed a politically incorrect stance with their praise of 'Trashy Women', a witty song by Chris Wall, and they even dressed as 'trashy women' for the video. The sentimental side to their macho posturings came through in 'Jesus And Mama'. Their theme song, 'I Am Just A Rebel', has been covered by Joy Lynn White and they showed sensitivity on 'Daddy Never Was The Cadillac Kind'. Confederate Railroad parodied their success in 'Elvis And Andy', in a video going from polka to rap and including a narration by Craig Baguley, editor of the UK magazine *Country Music People*. Although touted as the bad boys of country music, in reality they are no more 'bad boys' than Alabama.

● ALBUMS: *Confederate Railroad* (Atlantic 1992)★★★★, *Notorious* (Atlantic 1994)★★★, *When And Where* (Atlantic 1995)★★★.

● COMPILATIONS: *Greatest Hits* (Atlantic 1996)★★★★.

● VIDEOS: *Elvis & Andy* (1994), *Notorious: The Video* (1994).

CONLEE, JOHN

b. 11 August 1946, Versailles, Kentucky, USA. Conlee's early years were filled with farm chores, but he was playing the guitar on local radio before he was 10. He describes Versailles as 'a very small town with a very large barbershop chorus' in which he sang high tenor. Like soul singer Solomon Burke, he became a licensed embalmer. In the mid-70s he set about establishing himself in Nashville. He worked as a morning disc jockey, and he was signed to MCA Records. His best-known record is his debut US country hit from 1978, his own composition, 'Rose Coloured Glasses'. Ironically, it was a number 5 record, while seven others made number 1. Conlee had his first US country number 1 with 'Lady Lay Down', then 'Backside Of Thirty', which he wrote, 'Common Man', 'I'm Only In It For The Love', 'In My Eyes', 'As Long As I'm Rockin' With You', written by 60s R&B artist Bruce Channel, and, moving to Columbia Records, 'Got My Heart Set On You', written by Dobie Gray. Another move, this time to the ill-fated 16th Avenue Records, effectively ended his chart career. He lives with his family on a farm outside of Nashville and he retains his parents' farm in Versailles as well as his embalmer's license.

● ALBUMS: *Rose Coloured Glasses* (MCA 1978)★★★★, *Forever* (MCA 1980)★★★, *Friday Night Blues* (MCA 1980)★★★★, *With Love* (MCA 1981)★★★, *Busted* (MCA 1982)★★★, *In My Eyes* (MCA 1983)★★★, *Blue Highway* (MCA 1984)★★★, *Harmony* (Columbia 1987)★★★, *American Faces* (Columbia 1987)★★, *Fellow Travellers* (16th Avenue 1989)★★.

● COMPILATIONS: *Greatest Hits* (MCA 1983)★★★, *Greatest Hits, Volume 2* (MCA 1985)★★★, *Songs For The Working Man* (MCA 1986)★★★, *20 Greatest Hits* (MCA 1987)★★★★.

CONLEY, EARL THOMAS

b. 17 October 1941, Portsmouth, Ohio, USA. Conley is the son of a railway worker but he left home at 14 when his father lost his job. His influences were the *Grand Ole Opry*,

followed by Elvis Presley and Jerry Lee Lewis, and then the Beatles. He originally planned to be a painter, but developed his love for country music while in the US Army. After his military service, Conley had a succession of manual jobs and spent his spare time either playing clubs or hawking his songs around Nashville. His first successes were as a writer - 'Smokey Mountain Memories' for Mel Street and 'This Time I've Hurt Her More (Than She Loves Me)' for Conway Twitty. He recorded for Prize, GRT and Warner Brothers Records with moderate success and as Earl Conley. He started using his full name in 1979 to avoid confusion with John Conlee. His single of 'Fire And Smoke' reached number 1 on the US country charts in 1979, a major achievement for the small Sunbird label. RCA Records then took over his contract, although he continued to be produced by Nelson Larkin. His 1982 number 1, 'Somewhere Between Right And Wrong', was issued in two formats - one for country fans, one for rock fans. In 1984, Conley became the first artist in any field to have had four number 1 hits from the same album - from *Don't Make It Easy For Me* came the title tune, which was written by Conley and his frequent partner Randy Scruggs, 'Your Love's On The Line', 'Angel In Disguise' and 'Holding Her And Loving You'. His duets include 'Too Many Times' with Anita Pointer and 'We Believe In Happy Endings' with Emmylou Harris, another country number 1 in 1988. Out of his 18 US country number 1 hits, 'Right From The Start' was as much R&B as country, and was featured in the film *Roadhouse*. Conley's gutsy, emotional love songs found favour with US country fans, but despite a break from recording, he returned to the US country charts in 1991 with 'Brotherly Love', a duet recorded with Keith Whitley shortly before the latter's death in 1989.
● ALBUMS: *Blue Pearl* (Sunbird 1980)★★, *Fire And Smoke* (RCA 1981)★★★, *Somewhere Between Right And Wrong* (RCA 1982)★★★, *Don't Make It Easy For Me* (RCA 1983)★★★, *Treadin' Water* (RCA 1984)★★★, *Too Many Times* (RCA 1986)★★★, *The Heart Of It All* (RCA 1988)★★★★, *Yours Truly* (RCA 1991)★★★.
● COMPILATIONS: *Greatest Hits* (RCA 1985)★★★★, *The Best Of Earl Thomas Conley, Volume 1* (RCA 1988)★★★, *Greatest Hits, Volume 2* (RCA 1990)★★★, *Essential* (RCA 1996)★★★★.

CONLON, BILL

b. 6 July 1957, Portaferry, Co. Down, Northern Ireland. Conlon made his reputation in British country music clubs and only on rare occasions does he include traditional Irish ballads in his set. The staple material is 'The Chair', 'If We're Not Back In Love By Monday' and as an extended tribute to his hero, a Buck Owens medley. *Woman Your Love* features steel guitar and harmony vocals from Sarah Jory. 'I Don't Have To Fall' had considerable BBC Radio 2 airplay in 1991 and Conlon has made several successful appearances at European festivals. His band is called Emerald and has backed both Suzy Bogguss and Randy Vanwarmer on UK appearances. A live video was recorded at Theatre Royal, Bury St. Edmunds, and Conlon and Emerald often work with Philomena Begley on tour dates.
● ALBUMS: *Undecided* (Etude 1985)★★★, *If We're Not Back In Love By Monday* (Etude 1987)★★★, *Woman Your Love* (Etude 1988)★★★★, *With You In Mind* (Etude 1990)★★ *The Winds Of Change* (1995)★★★

CONN, MERVYN

It would be hard to come up with a more satirical name for a promoter than UK-born Mervyn Conn: 'I don't think it matters,' he says, 'As long as the show is right and the public want to see it, the name of the promoter means nothing at all.' He learnt his trade by working for Joe Collins, the father of actress Joan and writer Jackie Collins. After promoting three short UK tours by Johnny Cash in the mid-60s, he realized the potential of country music. In 1969 he started the International Festival of Country Music at the Empire Pool, Wembley, which became an annual event and established UK careers for Slim Whitman, George Hamilton IV, Tammy Wynette and Charley Pride. Both Don Williams and Boxcar Willie were stars in the UK before they had broken through at home. In the late 80s, the Festival folded through lack of sponsorship and an unfashionable image as Conn did not feel comfortable in switching to New Country performers. Found guilty of a sexual misdemeanour, Conn stopped promoting concerts for a while. In the mid-90s he promoted tours by George Hamilton IV and a West End musical about Patsy Cline.

COOK, DON

Nashville songwriter and producer. He co-wrote 'Now I Know' with Chick Rains and Cindy Greene for Lari White. His best-known productions are with the Mavericks (*What A Crying Shame*, *Music For All Occasions*) and he also works with Wade Hayes, Brooks And Dunn, Lonestar and Tracy Lawrence.

COOLEY, SPADE

b. Donnell Clyde Cooley, 22 February 1910, Grande, Oklahoma, USA, d. 23 November 1969, Vacaville, California, USA. His grandfather and father were talented fiddlers and he was playing at dances at the age of eight. Around 1930, the family moved to Modesto, California, where Cooley played local venues. In 1934, his resemblance to Roy Rogers found him employment as a stand-in and his work soon led to him fronting his own at the Pier Ballroom, Venice. Between 1943 and 1946, he was resident at the prestigious Riverside Rancho Ballroom in Santa Monica, where he acquired the nickname of 'King Of Western Swing' (Bill C. Malone records this as the first time the music pioneered by Bob Wills and Milton Brown had been so described). In 1947, Cooley adapted to television and his programme on KTLA became one of the top west coast shows until 1958. Cooley, with his orchestra playing a mixture of country, jazz and dance music, became a national star. He appeared in many films and recorded for several labels. Among his best-remembered songs are 'Shame On You' (a self-penned US country number 1), 'Detour' and 'Cause Cause I Love You' (with vocal by Tex Williams who worked with Cooley for some years). In the early 50s, he suffered a heart attack and although he recovered, by the end of the decade things began to go tragically wrong. A drink problem worsened and his wife left him. He hoped in vain for a reconciliation. In July 1961, in a drunken rage and in front of their young daughter, he beat his wife to death. He suffered another heart attack during his trial, which saw him receive a life sentence. A sad but model prisoner, he spent hours playing his fiddle and teaching other prisoners. With parole through good behaviour due early in 1970, he was given special release to attend a benefit concert in his honour in Oakland, where on 23 November 1969, his performance was well received by a crowd of over 3,000. After he had finished playing, he stayed backstage and was talking to friends when he suddenly slumped to the floor dead - the victim of another heart attack.

● ALBUMS: *Roy Rogers Souvenir Album* 10-inch album (RCA Victor 1952)★★★★, *Sagebrush Swing* 10-inch album (Columbia 1952)★★★★, *Dance-O-Rama* 10-inch album (Decca 1955)★★★, *Fidoodlin' Spade Cooley - King Of Western Swing* (Raynote 1959)★★★, *Fidoodlin'* (Roulette 1961)★★★, *Spade Cooley* (1982)★★★.

Club Of Spades Fan Club Album Releases: *Best Of Spade Cooley Transcribed Shows*, *King Of Western Swing Volumes 1 & 2*, *Mr Music Himself Volumes 1, 2, 3* (Television Transcriptions), *Oklahoma Stomp*, *As They Were*.

● COMPILATIONS: *Rompin', Stompin', Singin', Swingin'* (Bear Family 1983)★★★★, *Swingin' The Devil's Dream* (Charly 1984)★★★, *Spadella: The Essential Spade Cooley* (Columbia/Legacy 1994)★★★★.

COOLIDGE, RITA

b. 1 May 1944, Nashville, Tennessee, USA, from mixed white and Cherokee Indian parentage. Coolidge's father was a baptist minister and she first sang radio jingles in Memphis with her sister Priscilla. Coolidge recorded briefly for local label Pepper before moving to Los Angeles in the mid-60s. There she became a highly regarded session singer, working with Eric Clapton, Stephen Stills and many others. She had a relationship with Stills and he wrote a number of songs about her including 'Cherokee', 'The Raven' and 'Sugar Babe'. In 1969-70, Coolidge toured with the Delaney And Bonnie and Leon Russell (*Mad Dogs & Englishmen*) troupes. Russell's 'Delta Lady' was supposedly inspired by Coolidge. Returning to Los Angeles, she was signed to a solo recording contract by A&M. Her debut album included the cream of LA session musicians (among them Booker T. Jones, by now her brother-in-law) and it was followed by almost annual releases during the 70s. Coolidge also made several albums with Kris Kristofferson, to whom she was married between 1973 and 1979. The quality of her work was uneven since the purity of her natural voice was not always matched by subtlety of interpretation. Her first hit singles were a revival of the Jackie Wilson hit 'Higher And Higher' and 'We're All Alone', produced by Booker T. in 1977. The following year a version of the Temptations' 'The Way You Do The Things You Do' reached the Top 20. Coolidge was less active in the 80s, although in 1983 she recorded a James Bond movie theme, 'All Time High', from *Octopussy*.

● ALBUMS: *Rita Coolidge* (A&M 1971)★★★, *Nice Feelin'* (A&M 1971)★★, *The Lady's Not For Sale* (A&M 1972)★★★, with Kris Kristofferson *Full Moon* (A&M 1973)★★★, *Fall Into Spring* (A&M 1974)★★★, with Kris Kristofferson *Breakaway* (Monument 1974)★, *It's Only Love* (A&M 1975)★★, *Anytime Anywhere* (A&M 1977)★★★★, *Love Me Again* (A&M 1978)★★★, with Kris Kristofferson *Natural Act* (A&M 1979)★★, *Satisfied* (A&M 1979)★★, *Heartbreak Radio* (A&M 1981)★★, *Never Let You Go* (A&M 1983)★★, *Inside The Fire* (A&M 1988)★★, *All Time High* (1993)★★, *Cherokee* (Permanent 1995)★★, with Walela *Walela* (Triloka 1997)★★★.

● COMPILATIONS: *Greatest Hits* (A&M 1981)★★★.

COON CREEK GIRLS

History records that they were probably the first female string band to make a name in country music. They played for years over WLS and the *Renfro Valley Barn Dance*. They were led by Lily Mae Ledford (b. c.1917, Powell County, Kentucky, USA, d. July 1985, Lexington, Kentucky, USA; banjo, fiddle, vocals) and other members were her sister Rosie Ledford (d. 24 July 1976, Florida, USA; guitar, vocals), Violet Koehler (mandolin, guitar, vocals) and Daisy Lange (bass, vocals). In 1936, they became regulars on the *WLS Barn Dance* in Chicago and made history in 1939 when, at the request of Eleanor Roosevelt, they travelled to Washington DC to play before the King and Queen of England. (Around 1938, the Amburgey Sisters, Bertha, Opal and Irene, also played in the Coon Creek Girls, Irene later attaining country fame as Martha Carson.) When Koehler and Lange left in 1939, younger sister and bassist Minnie Ledford (who was known as Black Eyed Susie) joined the group and for the next 18 years, the sisters were regulars on the *Renfro Valley Barn Dance*. They retired in 1957, although during the folk revival of the 60s, they re-formed to play at some festivals. Much of their material was traditional mountain music and they became accepted experts of the genre. Many old-time music lovers fondly remember their song 'You're A Flower That Is Blooming There For Me'. Rosie Ledford died of cancer at her Florida home in July 1976 and was buried at Berea in Kentucky. Lily Mae published her autobiography in 1980; she died in July 1985.

● ALBUMS: *Lily Mae, Rosie & Susie* (County 70s)★★★, *Early Radio Favourites* (Old Homestead 1982)★★★★.

● FURTHER READING: *Coon Creek Girl*, Lily Mae Ledford.

COOPER, STONEY, AND WILMA LEE

By the time he was 12 years old, Dale T. 'Stoney' Cooper (b. 16 October 1918, near Harman, Randolph County, West Virginia, USA, d. 22 March 1977, Nashville, Tennessee, USA) could play the fiddle and guitar, and on leaving school, he joined a band called the Green Valley Boys. In 1939, he became the fiddle player with the Leary Family, a well-known gospel group, who were featured on local radio. He soon fell in love with, and married, Wilma Lee Leary (b. 7 February 1921, Valley Head, West Virginia, USA). She had started singing with her family group at the age of five and was already a fine instrumentalist, playing banjo, guitar, piano and organ. In 1938 and 1939, the Leary Family had represented the state at the National Folk Festival and made recordings in Washington for the Library of Congress. In 1940, the couple left the group and worked on local radio in Fairmont, Harrisonburg and Wheeling. Their career was slowed by the birth of their daughter Carol Lee, but by the mid-40s, they began to appear on radio stations in other states. In 1947, they returned to West Virginia where, with their band the Clinch Mountain Clan, they became stars of the WWVA *Wheeling Jamboree*. In 1950, Harvard University named them the most authentic mountain singing group in America. Between 1954 and 1957, they were the featured artists of the CBS network Saturday night *Jamboree*, broadcast from Wheeling's Virginia Theatre. In February 1957, their popularity saw them move to Nashville, where they became regulars on the *Grand Ole Opry*. They first recorded for Rich-R-Tone in 1947, having local success with 'The Tramp On The Street' but later for US Decca, Columbia and

Hickory. They achieved Top 5 US country chart hits in 1959 with 'Come Walk With Me', 'Big Midnight Special' (co-written by Wilma Lee) and 'There's A Big Wheel'. The following year, they had Top 20 country hits with 'Johnny My Love' and Stuart Hamblen's 'This Old House' (later a 1954 US number 1 pop hit for Rosemary Clooney). Their last country chart entry came in 1961, when their version of the stark warning not to drink and drive, 'Wreck On The Highway', peaked at number 8. Between 1950 and 1970, they toured extensively in the USA as well as making overseas tours. Their *Opry* popularity also ensured that they were regularly seen on most major television programmes. In 1973, Stoney's health began to fail; he suffered a series of heart attacks and spent long periods in hospital. Finally, he suffered a heart attack on 4 February 1977, from which he died in the intensive care unit of a Nashville hospital on 22 March 1977. Wilma Lee was heartbroken and for a time she retired, but in 1979 she formed a new Clinch Mountain Clan, resumed concert and *Opry* appearances and recorded several solo albums. She even began to play the 5-string banjo again, having forsaken it years earlier for the guitar. During her career, Wilma Lee wrote many songs including 'Loving You' and 'Tomorrow I'll Be Gone', and her recordings of gospel numbers such as 'Walking My Lord Up Calvary's Hill', 'Legend Of The Dogwood Tree' and 'Thirty Pieces Of Silver' are very popular. In 1974, the Smithsonian Institution named her 'First Lady Of Bluegrass' in their series of 'Women In Country Music'. The same year, pop singer Lou Christie wrote and recorded his tribute song 'Wilma Lee and Stoney'. Wilma Lee's style and singing made her unique, and prompted one writer to comment: 'She is not the imitator, she is the original'. Their daughter, Carol Lee Cooper, followed their musical career and from an early age regularly sang with her parents. She later formed the Carol Lee Singers, who became *Opry* regulars and who have sung backing vocals on countless recordings for many artists. She married Jimmie Rodgers Snow, the son of Hank Snow and had the distinction of playing her mother in an American filmed biography on Hank Williams.
● ALBUMS: *Sacred Songs* (Harmony 1960)★★★★, *There's A Big Wheel* (Hickory 1960)★★★, *Family Favorites* (Hickory 1962)★★★, *Songs Of Inspiration* (Hickory 1963)★★★, *Sunny Side Of The Mountain* (Harmony 1966)★★★, *Sing* (Decca 1966)★★★, *Walking My Lord Up Calvary's Hill* (1974)★★, *Wilma Lee & Stoney Cooper* (Starday 1976)★★★, *Satisfied* (1976)★★★.
Solo: Wilma Lee Cooper *A Daisy A Day* (1980)★★★, *Wilma Lee Cooper* (1982)★★, *White Rose* (1984)★★.
● COMPILATIONS: *Sing The Carter Family's Greatest Hits* (1977)★★★, *Classic Early Recordings* (Starday 1976)★★★★.

COPAS, COWBOY

b. Lloyd Estel Copas, 15 July 1913, near Muskogee, Oklahoma, USA, d. 5 March 1963, Camden, Tennessee, USA. Copas was raised on a small ranch and taught himself the fiddle and guitar before he was 10 years old. When the family moved to Ohio in 1929, Copas teamed with a fiddle-playing American Indian and worked in clubs and on radio. They parted in 1940 and, after working as a solo act, Copas replaced Eddy Arnold in Pee Wee King's Golden West Cowboys, but the following year he signed for King Records, became a regular at the *Grand Ole Opry*, and formed his own band, the Oklahoma Cowboys, which at times included

Hank Garland, Little Roy Wiggins, Tommy Jackson and Junior Husky. He first made the US country charts with 'Filipino Baby' in 1946, and his 10 Top 20 records between then and 1951 include 'Tennessee Waltz', 'Candy Kisses' and his own composition, 'Signed, Sealed And Delivered'. Although Copas was equally at home with ballads and honky-tonk songs, he fell victim to changing tastes and spent most of the 50s playing small clubs as a solo act. His luck changed when he signed for Starday Records in 1959. His self-penned 'Alabam' was in the US country charts for 34 weeks, 12 of them at number 1. He followed this with three more country hits, 'Flat Top', 'Sunny Tennessee' and a re-recording of 'Signed, Sealed And Delivered'. His son-in-law, Randy Hughes, also managed Patsy Cline and all three were killed, along with Hawkshaw Hawkins, in a plane crash on 5 March 1963. A few weeks later, Copas had a posthumous country hit with a record ironically entitled 'Goodbye Kisses'.
● ALBUMS: *Cowboy Copas Sings His All Time Hits* (King 1957)★★★★, *Favorite Sacred Songs* (King 1957)★★★, *Sacred Songs By Cowboy Copas* (King 1959)★★★, *All Time Country Music Greats* (Starday 1960)★★★, *Tragic Tales Of Love And Life* (King 1960)★★★, *Broken Hearted Melodies* (King 1960)★★★, *Inspirational Songs By Cowboy Copas* (Starday 1961)★★★, *Cowboy Copas* (Starday 1961)★★★, *Songs That Made Him Famous* (Starday 1962)★★★, *Mister Country Music* (Starday 1962)★★★, *Opry Star Spotlight On Cowboy Copas* (Starday 1962)★★★, *As You Remember Cowboy Copas* (King 1963)★★★, *Country Gentleman Of Song* (King 1963)★★★, *Country Music Entertainer No. 1* (Starday 1963)★★★, *Beyond The Sunset* (Starday 1963)★★★, *The Unforgettable Cowboy Copas* (Starday 1963)★★★, *Star Of The Grand Ole Opry* (Starday 1963)★★★, *Cowboy Copas And His Friends* (Starday 1964)★★★, *Hymns* (King 1964)★★, *The Legend Lives On* (Starday 1965)★★, *Shake A Hand* (Starday 1967)★★.
● COMPILATIONS: *The Cowboy Copas Story* (Starday 1965)★★★★, *Gone But Not Forgotten* (Starday 1965)★★★, *The Best Of Cowboy Copas* (Starday 1980)★★★★, *16 Greatest Hits* (Starday 1987)★★★★, *Mister Country Music* (Official 1988)★★★★.

COPLEY, JEFF

b. Crum, West Virginia, USA. Copley was raised on country and bluegrass music in the Appalachian Mountains. He has been singing since he was five and he was discovered as a young adult at a talent showcase in Nashville. He is yet another good-looking country singer being marketed with CMT in mind and over 2,000 songs were considered for his debut. Released in late 1995, this proved not to be an evergreen. One of the better songs, 'Out Where God Is', reflected his feelings for the great outdoors.
● ALBUMS: *Evergreen* (Polydor 1995)★★★.

CORNELIUS, HELEN

b. 6 December 1941, Hannibal, Missouri, USA. Cornelius was part of a large family raised on a farm. She sang with two sisters and their father took them to local engagements. By the 70s she had moved to Nashville and was working as a songwriter, although the records she made for Columbia had no success. Her first single for RCA, 'We Still Love Songs In Missouri', in 1975, sold well and she was then teamed with country singer Jim Ed Brown from the Browns for 'I Don't

Want To Have To Marry You'. The single was banned by several radio stations but it still topped the US country charts. They had six further country Top 10 singles including 'You Don't Bring Me Flowers' and 'Saying Hello, Saying I Love You, Saying Goodbye' up to 1980. Cornelius worked as a solo performer and also teamed with Dave And Sugar in a touring version of *Annie Get Your Gun*. In 1988 she and Brown began working as a duo once more on their Reunited Tour '88.

● ALBUMS: *Helen Cornelius* (RCA 1975)★★. With Jim Ed Brown: *I Don't Want To Have To Marry You* (RCA 1976)★★★, *Born Believer* (RCA 1977)★★★, *I'll Never Be Free* (RCA 1978)★★★, *You Don't Bring Me Flowers* (RCA 1979)★★, *One Man One Woman* (RCA 1980)★★.

COSTER, STAN

b. 27 May 1930, Casino, New South Wales, Australia, d. 25 March 1997. A popular songwriter and singer, who seemingly inherited his father's desire to travel, Coster had quit school at 14 and roamed around various parts of Australia. He worked on many jobs, including fencer, slaughterman, horsebreaker, kangaroo shooter, bulldozer driver and, at one time, was a rough rider with a travelling rodeo. He began to write songs in 1956, using his experiences of life on the road to provide the stories of and inspiration for his songs. His success as a songwriter was sealed in 1962, when Slim Dusty recorded his first song 'Return Of The Stockman'. Dusty has since recorded more than 60 of Coster's songs which have also attracted the attention of other Australian stars including Buddy Williams (Dusty and Coster combined their writing talents to co-write 'By A Fire Of Gidgee Coal', now a classic Australian country song). In 1979, Coster made his first recordings and also formed his own roadshow, which toured extensively in various states. His daughter Tracy (b. 12 April 1966, Winton, Queensland, Australia) became a member of his show at the age of 13, playing bass and singing with his outfit, the Blue Gum Band. He was widely recognized as Australia's top bush ballad writer and more than 100 of his songs have been recorded. In 1977, 'Three Rivers Hotel' won him a golden guitar for Best Composition in the Australian Country Music Awards and in 1982, he picked up the first ever Song Maker Of The Year award at the prestigious Tamworth Country Music Awards.

● ALBUMS: all Australian releases *My People* (Opal 1979)★★★, *Songs From A Wanderer's Pen* (Opal 1980)★★★, *The Song Maker* (Opal 1982)★★★, *This Big Old Land* (Nulla 1983)★★★, *Travellin' On My Own Track* (Gidgee 1985)★★★.

COTE, NATHALIE

Nathalie Cote obtained songs from good writers (Randy Vanwarmer, Joe Diffie) for her debut album, but generally speaking, the album was not distinctive enough. Her line-dance version of Tammy Wynette's 'Your Good Girl's Gonna Go Bad' has been popular in clubs.

● ALBUMS: *Lonely Hearts Like Mine* (M&N 1996)★★.

COUNTRY GAZETTE

Formed in 1971, this bluegrass ensemble was rooted in several Los Angeles-based outfits. The original line-up included three ex-members of Dillard And Clark, Byron Berline (b. 6 July 1944, Caldwell, Kansas, USA; fiddle, vocals), Billy Ray Latham (banjo, vocals) and Roger Bush (bass), who were ini-

tially joined by erstwhile Dillards guitarist Herb Pedersen (b. 27 April 1944, Berkeley, California, USA). The latter was then replaced by Alan Munde. Within months of its inception, Country Gazette was absorbed into a revue combining elements of the rapidly dissolving Flying Burrito Brothers. Wertz, Bush and Berline appeared on the unit's *Last Of The Red Hot Burritos* selection, before reconvening to complete their own band's debut, *A Traitor In Our Midst*. Although the founding trio each took sabbaticals from their creation, they, plus Munde, were its nucleus. Former Kentucky Colonels member Roland White joined the band in 1975, and remained until its temporary disintegration in 1982. Munde, White, Mike Anderson (bass) and Gene Wooten (dobro) reformed the band in 1983, touring for five years before a final split in 1988. Although not as influential as other contemporaries, Country Gazette was a superior exponent of its chosen genre. White joined the Nashville Bluegrass Band.

● ALBUMS: *A Traitor In Our Midst* (United Artists 1972)★★★★, *Live In Amsterdam* (United Artists 1972)★★★, *Don't Give Up Your Day Job* (United Artists 1973)★★★★, *Bluegrass Special* (Ariola 1973)★★★, *Banjo Sandwich* (1974)★★★, *Live At McCabes'* (Antilles 1975)★★, *Out To Lunch* aka *Sunnyside Of The Mountain* (Flying Fish 1977)★★★, *What A Way To Make A Living* (Ridge Runner 1977)★★★, *All This And Money Too* (Ridge Runner 1979)★★, *American And Clean* (Flying Fish 1981)★★, *Strictly Instrumental* (Flying Fish 1981)★★★, *America's Bluegrass Band* (Flying Fish 1982)★★★.

● COMPILATIONS: *Milestones* (1975)★★★, *From The Beginning* (Sunset 1978)★★★, *Hello Operator . . . This Is Country Gazette* (Flying Fish 1991)★★★★.

COUNTRY GENTLEMEN

This bluegrass group were first established in Washington DC, USA, on 4 July 1957 and over the years have undergone many personnel changes. Founder-members included Charlie Waller (b. 19 January 1935, Jointerville, Texas, USA; guitar, vocals), John Duffey (b. 4 March 1934, Washington DC, USA; guitar, vocals), Bill Emerson (b. 22 January 1938; banjo) and Tom Morgan (bass). Emerson was replaced for a short time by Pete Kuykendall (a DJ and record collector who played as Pete Roberts), who, in turn, was replaced by Eddie Adcock (b. 17 June 1938, Scottsville, Virginia, USA; banjo, mandolin, vocals). Jim Cox (b. 3 April 1930, Vansant, Virginia, USA; bass, banjo, vocals) replaced Morgan. Other members include Tom Gray (who left in 1964), Bill Yates and Jimmy Gaudreau who replaced Duffey in 1969. Adcock and McGlothlin left in 1970. Over the years, the various line-ups became popular at various major folk and bluegrass festivals. When national interest waned somewhat in bluegrass music in the late 60s, they still managed to exist and were never afraid to use material from a wide variety of writers and genres. When interest in bluegrass revived in the 70s, they were one of the first groups to appear at major venues such as Bean Blossom, Indiana. Waller, a fine vocalist, has an uncanny ability to sound like Hank Snow when he so chooses. They have toured extensively and recorded a great many albums (including one with Ricky Skaggs); since the late 60s most of their albums have been on the Rebel label. Their only US country chart hit was with 'Bringing Mary Home' in 1965.

● ALBUMS: *Travelling Dobro Blues* (Starday 1959)★★★★,

Country Songs Old & New (Folkways 1960)★★★★, *Folk Songs & Bluegrass* (Folkways 1961)★★★★, *Bluegrass At Carnegie Hall* (Starday 1962)★★, *Folk Session Inside* (Mercury 1963)★★★, *Return Engagement* (Rebel 1963)★★★, *On The Road* (Rebel 1963)★★, *Hootenanny* (Rebel 1963)★★★, *In Concert* (Rebel 1964)★★, *Bringing Mary Home* (Rebel 1965)★★★, *Folk Hits Bluegrass Style* (Rebel 1966)★★★★, *Sunrise Vol. 2.* (1966)★★★, *Live At The Roanoke Bluegrass Festival* (Zap 1967)★★, *The Traveller* (Rebel 1968)★★★, *New Look New Sound* (Rebel 1969)★★★, *Play It Like It Is* (Rebel 1969)★★★, *Last Album* (Rebel 1970)★★★, *New Country Gentlemen In London* (Rebel 1970)★★, *One Wide River To Cross* (Rebel 1971)★★, *Sound Off* (Rebel 1971)★★★, *The Award Winning Country Gentlemen* (Rebel 1972)★★, *Going Back To The Blue Ridge Mountains* (1973)★★★, *The Country Gentlemen* (Vanguard 1973)★★★, *Remembrances & Forecasts* (Vanguard 1974)★★★, *The Early Sessions* (1974)★★★★, *Live In Japan* (Rebel 1975)★★, *Joe's Last Train* (Rebel 1976)★★★, *Calling My Children Home* (Rebel 1978)★★★, *Sit Down Young Stranger* (Sugar Hill 1980)★★★, *River Bottom* (Sugar Hill 1981)★★★, *25 Years* (Rebel 1982)★★★, *Good As Gold* (1983)★★★, *New Horizons* (1992).

● COMPILATIONS: *The Country Gentlemen, Volume 1* (Folkways)★★★★, *The Country Gentlemen, Volume 2* (Folkways)★★★★, *The Country Gentlemen, Volume 3* (Folkways)★★★, *The Country Gentlemen, Volume 4* (Folkways)★★★, *Yesterday & Today Volume 1* (Rebel 1973)★★★★, *Yesterday & Today Volume 2* (Rebel 1973) *Yesterday & Today Volume 3* (Rebel 1974)★★★, *Country Gentlemen Featuring Ricky Skaggs On Fiddle* (Vanguard 1986)★★★★, *Let The Light Shine Down* (Rebel 1991)★★★, *Sugar Hill Collection* (Sugar Hill 1995)★★★.

COUNTRY MUSIC ASSOCIATION

The Country Music Association, usually referred to as the CMA, was founded in Nashville, Tennessee, in 1958, following a DJ convention. Its aim was to give respectability to country music and to endeavour to make it more popular. It hoped to prevent the then current popularity of rock 'n' roll from being detrimental to the future of country music. Operating from small offices in downtown Nashville and through the dedication of its executive secretary, Jo Walker (later Jo Walker-Meador, the CMA's executive director who finally retired in 1991), it slowly but surely achieved its aim. Bill C. Malone later wrote of the CMA: 'It saw country music as a product to be marketed on the widest possible basis. It made no attempts to define what was or was not country music and it argued that all forms of country music would prosper if the industry as a whole was healthy.' The CMA sponsored radio stations that played an all-country format and by 1967, there were almost 350, with over 2,000 others playing some country music daily. Over the years, the CMA has continued to develop and has been the inspiration for similar organizations in other countries. In the late 60s, the CMA moved to an expensive modern complex which, apart from their offices, contained the Country Music Foundation Library and Media Center and the Country Music Hall Of Fame And Museum. Further extensions to the complex eventually saw the CMA offices move a block away, in 1990, to Music Circle South. The CMA annual Awards Show attracts visitors to Nashville from all over the world.

COUNTRY MUSIC FOUNDATION

Nashville's Country Music Foundation (CMF) houses the Country Music Library and Media Center and the Country Music Hall Of Fame And Museum. It was chartered in 1964 by the State of Tennessee as a non-profit making and tax-exempt establishment designed to educate, preserve and promote country music. It is managed by a board of trustees composed of some of the respected members of the country music industry and manned by a team that includes some of the leading historians in the music. Originally manned by a staff of three, there are now around 70 full- or part-time employees. The CMF has several specialized departments which may loosely be categorized as Reference, Research and Promotional. The Library contains over 150,000 recordings, making it probably the largest collection of recordings of a single genre of music ever assembled. It also contains thousands of copies of sheet music, songbooks, articles from countless publications, audio tapes, video tapes, scrapbooks, and hundreds upon hundreds of books. Members of the public may view these by appointment and help with research is offered. Vast numbers of telephone queries from all over the world are also handled. Research is constantly being undertaken and details of important findings are regularly released to the media. In 1985, the CMF established its own record label and has subsequently released previously unissued material, such as two top-selling albums by Hank Williams, *The First Recordings* and *Just Me And My Guitar*. Other rare releases have included live recordings on the *Grand Ole Opry* by Jim Reeves and Patsy Cline. The CMF also runs its own publications department, which from time to time reprints books as well as publishing new ones, such as their prestigious 1988 publication *Country, The Music And The Musicians*. It also publishes their quarterly *Journal Of Country Music*, which contains some of the most informative material on the genre available. The CMF receives much of its income from the Country Music Hall Of Fame And Museum.

COUNTRY MUSIC HALL OF FAME AND MUSEUM

The Country Music Hall of Fame and Museum is probably Nashville's most popular tourist attraction. Here visitors can see countless exhibits, which range from instruments and mementos of country artist, to articles of stage costumes and even larger items, including Elvis Presley's 'Solid Gold' Cadillac and Webb Pierce's famous 1962 Pontiac Bonneville, which was designed by Nudie and decorated with silver dollars and silver rifles. The Hall Of Fame, inspired by the noted Baseball Hall of Fame in Cooperstown, New York, was a project designed by the Country Music Association (CMA) to combine the presentation of the history of country music with their dedicated work in promoting it, in order to attract more interest in the genre. Among the people who worked hard to see the project come to fruition were Roy Horton (later chairman of the CMA) and Steve Sholes. The project was first considered in 1961 but it was not until 31 March 1967 that the CMA complex, which also housed the Country Music Foundation and the CMA's offices, was finally opened. During 1976, the Country Music Foundation carried out considerable expansion of the Hall of Fame building, which made more space available for the ever growing list of exhibits in both the Hall of Fame and the Museum.

The rules of election to the Hall Of Fame are fairly complicated and membership is limited. The CMA organized the rather complex voting system, which is carried out by a panel composed of some 250 people connected with the music, such as businessmen, DJs, historians or songwriters. A ballot containing numerous names and with space for further additions is sent to each member of the panel. From their resultant votes, the top five names are then put forward for a second ballot with the winner then becoming that year's inductee. However, sometimes more than one member is inducted due either to a tie, or to a rule stating that a dead member must be elected at least every third year. If, on a third year, there has been no deceased entrant, the electors receive two final lists - one of living candidates and one of deceased ones. The nominee gaining the most votes on each list is then elected at the annual October CMA Awards Show. In 1961, the first members, Jimmie Rodgers, Fred Rose and Hank Williams, were elected by a CMA committee. It was originally intended that only deceased persons would be elected but in 1962, the rule was altered and Roy Acuff became the first living entrant. In 1967, when the new building housing the Hall of Fame was opened, the CMA adopted a change of policy to name people who were involved either as performers or in a non-performing category. In its early years, there was a certain amount of criticism levelled at the Hall of Fame for the fact that it seemed to be biased in favour of Nashville and contemporary performers. Complaints also focused on the fact that the important early-day country performers were totally ignored, such as Vernon Dalhart, who, in spite of his contributions in the 20s, did not gain admission until 1981. Among the elected members at the time of writing there is the unique case of father and son (Fred and Wesley Rose) and Roy Rogers being named twice - as a member of the Sons Of the Pioneers in 1980 and as a solo artist in 1988. Some were surprised when Willie Nelson gained admission in 1993, considering his Outlaw image and stated views regarding the establishment. In 1994, Merle Haggard, deservedly, was the only person inducted. The following year, the audience applauded loudly as Mrs Roger Miller accepted the nomination on behalf of her deceased husband. The association also saw fit, in 1995, to induct Jo Walker-Meador, in the non-performer category. She had joined the CMA in 1958 and served as its Executive Director for 33 years, during which time she had been involved in all its major developments, including the founding of the Hall Of Fame. Each elected member has a plaque displayed on the wall, briefly detailing their achievements.

The elected members at the time of writing are as follows:-

1961	Jimmie Rodgers, Fred Rose, Hank Williams
1962	Roy Acuff
1963	No inductee
1964	Tex Ritter
1965	Ernest Tubb
1966	Eddy Arnold, Jim Denny, George D. Hay, Uncle Dave Macon
1967	Red Foley, Joe Frank, Jim Reeves, Steve Sholes
1968	Bob Wills
1969	Gene Autry
1970	A.P. Carter, Mother Maybelle Carter, Sara Carter, Bill Monroe
1971	Art Satherley
1972	Jimmie Davis
1973	Chet Atkins, Patsy Cline
1974	Owen Bradley, Pee Wee King
1975	Minnie Pearl
1976	Paul Cohen, Kitty Wells
1977	Merle Travis
1978	Grandpa Jones
1979	Hubert Long, Hank Snow
1980	Johnny Cash, Connie B. Gay, Sons Of The Pioneers (Roy Rogers, Bob Nolan, Tim Spencer, Lloyd Perryman, and Hugh Farr)
1981	Vernon Dalhart, Grant Turner
1982	Lefty Frizzell, Roy Horton, Marty Robbins
1983	Little Jimmie Dickens
1984	Ralph Peer, Floyd Tilman
1985	Lester Flatt & Earl Scruggs
1986	Wesley Rose, Benjamin Francis 'Whitey' Ford' (The Duke of Paducah)
1987	Rod Brasfield
1988	Roy Rogers, Loretta Lynn
1989	Jack Stapp, Cliffie Stone, Hank Thompson
1990	Tennessee Ernie Ford
1991	Felice & Boudleaux Bryant
1992	George Jones, Frances Preston
1993	Willie Nelson
1994	Merle Haggard
1995	Roger Miller, Jo Walker-Meador
1996	Ray Price, Buck Owens, Patsy Montana
1997	Brenda Lee, Harlan Howard, Cindy Walker

COUSIN EMMY

b. Cynthia May Carver, 1903, Lamb, near Glasgow, Kentucky, USA, d. 11 April 1980, Sherman Oaks, California, USA. The eighth child of a struggling sharecropper, Carver received little education but later joked, 'I ain't educated but I'm sincere'. She began her career playing five-string banjo with her cousins, Bozo and Warner Carver, on WHB Kansas City. In 1935, by then playing 15 musical instruments, Cousin Emmy was a featured act with Frankie Moore's Log Cabin Boys, on WHAS Louisville. Her stage dress was a baggy gingham dress, white stockings and ankle boots and platinum blond hair, held in place by bright coloured ribbons. In 1937, she moved to WWVA Wheeling, West Virginia, where she met Grandpa Jones and seemingly tutored him on five-string banjo. In 1938, she returned to WHAS Louisville, playing daily shows and touring with her band, Her Kin Folks. During the next few years, popular wherever she went, Cousin Emmy alternated between WHAS Louisville, WSB and WAGA Atlanta and WNOX Knoxville. In 1941, she became a sponsored act on KMOX St. Louis, whose 50,000 watt transmissions, heard as far afield as Canada and Mexico, increased her popularity. In 1943, she achieved national publicity, when she was featured in *Time* magazine. She maintained her radio popularity throughout the late 40s and into the 50s, with further appearances at Atlanta and Louisville. She eventually relocated to California, where she made a few film appearances and in the early 60s, she even worked in Disneyland. Cousin Emmy made few recordings but, in 1947, Alan Lomax persuaded her to record for Decca Records. In the late 60s, she was enticed out of retirement by the Lost City Ramblers, with whom she recorded for Folkways Records and even toured Europe. She also made television appearances with Pete Seeger and in the early 70s, appeared at some major folk festivals. In spite of her lack of education, she was astute in managing her affairs, she copyrighted her songs and carefully looked after her money, often commenting: 'I'm the first hillbilly star to own a Cadillac'. She never married, joking, 'I ain't got no time to do no courting'. Her talents ran to serious music, and being very religious, she also included hymns in her act. Among her songs is 'Ruby, Are You Mad At Your Man', now a bluegrass standard, which she first popularized (the Osborne Brothers' version reached the charts in 1970). Cousin Emmy, a very talented all-round entertainer, became a star at a time when it was hard for women to break into showbusiness, and her contribution surely merits her induction to the Country Music Hall Of Fame.

● ALBUMS: *Kentucky Mountain Ballads* (Decca 1947)★★★★, *The New Lost City Ramblers With Cousin Emmy* (Folkways 1968)★★★.

COUSIN JODY

b. James Clell Summey, 14 December 1914, Possum Hollow, near Sevierville, Tennessee, USA, d. 1976. The family relocated to Knoxville where he grew up in a musical environment, since both parents (Matty and Jim) were musicians. Other musicians regularly stayed in the home and young Jody soon learned to play several instruments. He initially favoured the guitar but by 1931, was an accomplished dobro player (a relatively new instrument in those days, having only been developed in the late 20s). By 1933, he was playing local venues with a group known as the Tennessee Crackerjacks, when they were joined by Roy Acuff. He became an important member of Acuff's band and in February 1938, when Acuff and his band played the *Grand Ole Opry*, he became the first player to feature the dobro there. He also provided the dobro backing on most of Acuff's early recordings including 'The Great Speckled Bird' and 'Wabash Cannonball'. After differences of opinion over material, Summey and two other band members left Acuff in January 1939. He returned to Knoxville but was soon back in Nashville, where he worked with Pee Wee King, Lonzo And Oscar and briefly as a comedy duo with Oral Rhodes, as Odie And Jody. He had played the comedian during his days with Acuff and finally became a solo *Opry* act in his alter ego role of the baggy-panted and toothless grinning hayseed, Cousin Jody. In this guise, he mixed rube comedy with his instrumental talents and for many years remained a very popular *Opry* regular. He died of cancer in 1976.

COWBOY LOYE

b. Loye Donald Pack, 3 June 1900, Nashville, Tennessee, USA, d. 15 March 1941. Although Loye was born in Nashville, it was a long time before it became associated with country music, and, in any event, he never actually made a single record. In the 20s, a yearning for a different lifestyle saw him leave home and hobo in several states, during which time he learned to play guitar and developed a wide repertoire of songs. He eventually settled to work, for several years, as a cowboy on a Nebraska ranch. In 1929, he sang on local radio in York, Nebraska, and after a spell at Columbus, Ohio, he arrived at WWVA Wheeling, West Virginia, in November 1933. He often performed there with another singer known as Just Plain John Oldham. He gained a reputation for being able to sell his songbooks and for the amount of mail that he received from the listeners. In 1936, he organized his Blue Bonnet troupe which, at times, had 12 members, but the following year, after a short time back in Nebraska, he relocated to WMMN Fairmont, West Virginia, where he immediately became popular and sometimes worked with the Blue Bonnett Girls (Sylvia, Lillian and Florence Curry). On 12 March 1941, troubled by stomach ulcers, he entered the Cleveland Clinic for an operation. There were complications, possibly from bleeding after stitches torn when he was partially conscious, although other reports detailed a kidney problem. Loye died on 15 March and his wife, Zeta, had his body taken back to be buried at their home in Ponca, Nebraska. His great friend, Grandpa Jones, commented, 'although he was never flashy, Cowboy Loye could sell anything'.

COWBOY, COPAS

(see Copas, Cowboy)

COX FAMILY

Willard Cox, an oilfield worker from Cotton Valley, Louisiana, USA, grew up listening to country, bluegrass and gospel music. He played the fiddle and sang with his brothers for pleasure. His wife Marie was a local country singer and their children, Evelyn (guitar), Lynn (bass), Sidney (banjo) and Suzanne (b. 1967; mandolin) inherited a love of the same music. Willard put together a demo tape in 1974 to obtain bookings. Soon they were performing far afield and Willard was able to give up his day job. In 1989 Alison Krauss heard one of their tapes and was captivated by their sound and by Sidney's songwriting. The title track of Krauss's *I've Got That Old Feeling* was written by Sidney, while Suzanne sang harmony on the album. Krauss produced their highly acclaimed albums for Rounder Records, and collaborated on 1994's Grammy-nominated *Who Holds Tomorrow* (indeed, Krauss's own vocal stylings are now very close to Suzanne Cox's). Since signing for Rounder, the Cox Family, in various combinations, have sung harmony for singers such as Randy Travis and Emmylou Harris. Both Krauss and Suzanne Cox were featured on Dolly Parton's live album *Heartsongs*. Alison Krauss has said of their singing: 'When you reach the Pearly Gates, they'll be playing the Cox Family.' The Cox Family benefited from Krauss's success by signing to a major label, Arista, with Krauss producing *Just When We're Thinking It's Over*. Further surprises were in store with the first single, the Del Shannon falsetto classic 'Runaway'.

● ALBUMS: *Quiet Storm* (Wilcox)★★★, *Everybody's Reaching Out For Someone* (Rounder 1993)★★★, with Krauss *I Know Who Holds Tomorrow* (Rounder 1994)★★★, *Beyond The City* (Rounder 1995)★★★★, *Just When We're Thinking It's Over* (Arista 1996)★★★★.

CRADDOCK, BILLY 'CRASH'

b. William Wayne Craddock, 16 June 1939, Greensboro, North Carolina, USA. As a child, he would imitate the stars of *Grand Ole Opry* and he was performing with his brothers at talent shows from the age of 10. He played American football and he says that, to avoid being tackled, he would 'crash' through the larger players, hence his nickname. Craddock has been recording since 1957, although his first single,

'Smacky Mouth', for the Sky Castle label in Greensboro, was released under the name of Billy Graddock. He then recorded 'The Millionaire' as Billy Craddock for Colonial, and went to Date for 'Ah Poor Little Baby', an underrated rock 'n' roll song which was covered for the UK market by Adam Faith. Although only 19, Craddock signed for his fourth label, but this time it was a major, Columbia. For his third single, he was billed, for the first time, as Billy 'Crash' Craddock. The a-side, the rocking 'Boom Boom Baby', was a hit in Australia, but it was the ballad b-side, 'Don't Destroy Me', which scraped into the US Top 100. He toured Australia three times and became one of the earliest rock 'n' roll stars in the country. He had no success in the UK but one of his records, 'I Want That', was covered by Johnny Kidd. Craddock subsequently recorded for Mercury, King and Chart and from such records as 'Anything That's Part Of You', it was evident that he was switching to country music. However, he had limited success and by the mid-60s, he had returned to his home-town, married, taken a day job and was singing only at weekends. In 1971 he signed for a new Nashville label, Cartwheel, and had a US Top 3 country hit with 'Knock Three Times'. He then had country hits with revivals of 'Dream Lover', 'You Better Move On', 'Ain't Nothin' Shakin'' and 'I'm Gonna Knock On Your Door'. He won awards including one from *Cashbox* as The New Find Of 1972. Moving to ABC, Craddock had several more country hits including number 1 hits with a song about suntan lotion, 'Rub It In' (also number 16 on the USA pop charts), a revival of 'Ruby Baby', and 'Broken Down In Tiny Pieces', which also featured Janie Fricke. He started his country hits for Capitol with 'I Cheated On A Good Woman's Love' in 1978, and continued with 'If I Could Write A Song As Beautiful As You', 'My Mama Never Heard Me Sing', 'I Just Had You On My Mind', 'Sea Cruise' and 'Love Busted'. In direct imitation of Elvis Presley, he wore a white jumpsuit and his forceful, live album shows he was still a rock 'n' roller at heart.

● ALBUMS: *I'm Tore Up* (King 1964)★★, *Knock Three Times* (Cartwheel 1971)★★★, *You Better Move On* (Cartwheel 1972)★★★, *Two Sides Of Crash Craddock* (Harmony 1973)★★, *Mr. Country Rock* (ABC 1973)★★★, *Rub It In* (ABC 1974)★★★, *Still Thinkin' 'Bout You* (ABC 1975)★★★, with Janie Frickie *Crash* (ABC 1976)★★★, *Easy As Pie* (ABC 1976)★★★, *Live* (ABC 1977)★★, *The First Time* (ABC 1977)★★★, *Billy 'Crash' Craddock* (Capitol 1978)★★★, *I Cheated On A Good Woman's Love* (Capitol 1978)★★, *Turning Up And Turning On* (Capitol 1978)★★★, *Laughing And Crying, Living And Dying* (Capitol 1979)★★, *Changes* (Capitol 1980)★★★, *Crash Craddock* (Capitol 1981)★★, *The New Will Never Wear Off You* (Capitol 1982)★★★, *Back On Track* (1989)★★★, *Boom Boom Baby* (Bear Family 1992)★★★.

● COMPILATIONS: *The Best Of Billy 'Crash' Craddock* (Chart 1973)★★★★, *16 Favourite Hits* (1977)★★★, *Sings His Greatest Hits* (MCA 1978)★★★, *The Best Of Billy Crash Craddock* (MCA 1986)v, *Crash's Smashes: The Hits Of Billy 'Crash' Craddock* (Razor & Tie 1996)★★★★.

CRAMER, FLOYD

b. 27 October 1933, Shreveport, Louisiana, USA, d. 31 December 1997. The style and sound of Cramer's piano-playing is arguably one of the biggest influences on post-50s country music. His delicate rock 'n' roll sound is achieved by accentuating the discord in rolling from the main note to a sharp or flat, known as 'slip note'. This is perfectly high-lighted in his first major hit, 'Last Date', in 1960. Cramer was already a vastly experienced Nashville session player, playing on countless records during the 50s. He can be heard on many Jim Reeves and Elvis Presley records, often with his long-time friend Chet Atkins, and also recorded with Patsy Cline, Roy Orbison and Kitty Lester. During the early 60s he regularly entered the US charts. Two notable hits were the superb 'On The Rebound', which still sounds fresh and lively more than 30 years later, and his sombre reading of Bob Wills' 'San Antonio Rose'. After dozens of albums Cramer was still making commercially successful recordings into the 80s, having a further hit in 1980 with the theme from the television soap opera *Dallas*. With Atkins, Cramer remained Nashville's most prolific musician until his death from cancer in December 1997.

● ALBUMS: *That Honky Tonk Piano* reissued as *Floyd Cramer Goes Honky Tonkin'* (MGM 1957)★★★, *Hello Blues* (RCA 1960)★★★, *Last Date* (RCA 1961)★★★★, *On The Rebound* (RCA 1961)★★★★, *America's Biggest Selling Pianist* (RCA 1961)★★★, *Floyd Cramer Get Organ-ized* (RCA 1962)★★, *I Remember Hank Williams* (RCA 1962)★★★, *Swing Along With Floyd Cramer* (RCA 1963)★★★, *Comin' On* (RCA 1963)★★★, *Country Piano - City Strings* (RCA 1964)★★★, *Cramer At The Console* (RCA 1964)★★★, *Hits From The Country Hall Of Fame* (RCA 1965)★★★, *The Magic Touch Of Floyd Cramer* (RCA 1965)★★★, *Class Of '65* (RCA 1965)★★★, *The Distinctive Piano Styling Of Floyd Cramer* (RCA 1966)★★★, *The Big Ones* (RCA 1966)★★★, *Class Of '66* (RCA 1966)★★★, *Here's What's Happening* (RCA 1967)★★★, *Floyd Cramer Plays The Monkees* (RCA 1967)★★★, *Class Of '67* (RCA 1967)★★★, *Floyd Cramer Plays Country Classics* (RCA 1968)★★★, *Class Of '68* (RCA 1968)★★★, *Floyd Cramer Plays MacArthur Park* (RCA 1968)★★★, *Class Of '69* (RCA 1969)★★★, *More Country Classics* (RCA 1969)★★★, *Looking For Mr. Goodbar* (RCA 1968)★★★, *The Big Ones - Volume 2* (RCA 1970)★★★, *Floyd Cramer With The Music City Pops* (RCA 1970)★★★, *Class Of '70* (RCA 1970)★★, *Sounds Of Sunday* (RCA 1971)★★, with Chet Atkins and Boots Randolph *Chet, Floyd And Boots* (RCA 1971)★★★, *Class Of '71* (RCA 1971)★★★, *Floyd Cramer Detours* (RCA 1972)★★★, *Class Of '72* (RCA 1972)★★★, *Super Country Hits Featuring Crystal Chandelier And Battle Of New Orleans* (RCA 1973)★★, *Class Of '73* (RCA 1973)★★, *The Young And The Restless* (RCA 1974)★★, *Floyd Cramer In Concert* (RCA 1974)★★, *Class Of '74 And '75* (RCA 1975)★★, *Floyd Cramer Country* (RCA 1976)★★, with Chet Atkins and Danny Davis *Chet, Floyd And Danny* (RCA Victor 1977)★★★, *Floyd Cramer And The Keyboard Kick Band* (RCA 1977)★★★, *Superhits* (RCA 1979)★★, *Dallas* (RCA 1980)★★, *The Best Of The West* (RCA 1981)★★, *Country Gold* (RCA 1988)★★, *Just Me And My Piano!* (RCA 1988)★★★, *Special Songs Of Love* (RCA 1988)★★, *Originals* (RCA 1991)★★★, *Classics* (RCA 1992)★★★.

● COMPILATIONS: *The Best Of Floyd Cramer* (RCA 1964)★★★★, *The Best Of Floyd Cramer - Volume 2* (RCA 1968)★★★, *This Is Floyd Cramer* (RCA 1970)★★★★, *Plays The Big Hits* (Camden 1973)★★★, *Best Of The Class Of* (RCA 1973)★★★, *Spotlight On Floyd Cramer* (1974)★★★, *Piano Masterpieces 1900-1975* (RCA 1975)★★, *All My Best* (RCA 1980)★★★, *Great Country Hits* (RCA 1981)★★★, *Treasury Of*

Favourites (1984)★★★, *Country Classics* (1984)★★★★, *20 Of The Best: Floyd Cramer* (RCA 1986)★★★, *Our Class Reunion* (1987)★★★, *Easy Listening Favorites* (1991)★★★, *Favorite Country Hits* (Ranwood 1995)★★★, *King Of Country Piano* (Pickwick 1995)★★★, *Collector's Series* (RCA 1995)★★★, *The Essential Floyd Cramer* (RCA 1996)★★★★.

CRARY, DAN

b. 29 September 1939, Kansas City, Kansas, USA. Crary developed a keen interest in music as a child, after his classical music-loving mother took him to see the famous violinist Fritz Kreisler. At the age of 10, he took piano lessons for a time, but soon changed to guitar. In 1957, after graduating from high school, he attended Chicago's Moody Bible Institute to study theology. In 1960, he relocated to Lawrence, Kansas, and while studying at the University of Kansas, he played guitar and sang in a trio called the Carltons. He married in 1962 and in 1965, he relocated to San Francisco to continue his theological studies at the Golden Gate Seminary, playing locally both with groups and solo to make a living. In 1967, with a degree, he moved to Louisville, working on WINN, while he continued his studies for a doctorate of philosophy at the Southern Seminary. In Louisville, greatly interested in bluegrass music, he became friendly with various musicians, and in 1968, he became a member of Bluegrass Alliance. The group initially consisted of Crary, Wayne Stewart (guitar, vocals), Buddy Spurlock (banjo), Lonnie Pierce (fiddle) and Ebo Walker (bass). They played a residency in a local bar, the Red Dog, for 18 months and achieved some acclaim playing at major bluegrass festivals. Although the group did not last long, they are remembered in bluegrass for their rather non-traditional approach to the music. In 1970, worried that he might not make a satisfactory living in music, he decided to pursue his university studies for a PhD in speech communication and left the group, being replaced by Tony Rice. Family commitments and studies limited his playing in the early 70s, but in 1974, while appearing at a Canadian festival, he became friendly with noted west coast fiddler Byron Berline. After taking a teaching post in Fullerton, California, to support the family (which by that time included two daughters), Crary and Berline formed Sundance, which included John Hickman (banjo), Jack Skinner (bass) and Allen Wald (guitar). Apart from playing together, Crary, Berline and Hickman also formed a long-lasting business partnership, BCH Productions. In 1976, Crary made his first tour of Japan, where he had become a great favourite following the release there a few years earlier of his debut, *Bluegrass Guitar*. He made the first of many highly successful tours to the UK in 1978 and 1979. Over the years, Crary managed to combine playing with BCH, his solo career and his lecturing, and also completed his PhD. Later in his career, he began to introduce the 12-string guitar into his concert appearances. His popularity continued to grow throughout the 80s and into the 90s. His instrumental genius was once summed up by noted British bluegrass authority John Atkins: 'The guy just cannot be a human being, since humans just don't play that well. He should be kept away from other musicians, as sometimes a hearing can completely shatter illusions and not serve to inspire'.
● ALBUMS: *Bluegrass Guitar* (American Heritage 1970)★★★; with the Bluegrass Alliance *The Bluegrass*

Alliance (American Heritage 1969)★★★, *Alliance Newgrass* (American Heritage 1970)★★★★; with Sundance *Byron Berline And Sundance* (MCA 1976)★★★★, *Live At McCabe's* (Takoma 1977)★★, *Lady's Fancy* (Rounder 1977)★★★, *Sweet Southern Girl* (Sugar Hill 1979)★★★; with BCH *Berline-Hickman-Crary* (Sugar Hill 1981)★★★, *Guitar* (Sugar Hill 1983)★★★, *Take A Step Over* (Sugar Hill 1989)★★★; with BCH, Steve Spurgin *Now There Are Four* (Sugar Hill 1989)★★★ *Jammed If I Do* (Sugar Hill 1994)★★.

CROCKETT, HOWARD

b. Howard Hausey, Minden, Louisiana, USA, d. 1994. Crockett wrote 'Honky Tonk Man', 'Ole Slewfoot' and 'Whispering Pines' for Johnny Horton. He recorded for several small US country labels, although the musicians included Chet Atkins, Floyd Cramer and the Jordanaires. Horton had taken the best songs, but Crockett did have some popularity with 'If You Let Me'. In 1973 he almost reached the US country Top 50 with 'Last Will And Testament (Of A Drinking Man)', and then left the business. Dwight Yoakam had success with a revival of 'Honky Tonk Man', but Crockett did not return to songwriting until his son wrote 'Daddy, Get Your Guitar Down'. He wrote a tribute to his dying wife, 'Forever And A Day', and himself died in 1994.
● ALBUMS: *My Lil's Run Off* (Best Sweden 1995)★★★.

CROOK BROTHERS

The Crook Brothers must hold the long-service record for performers on the *Grand Ole Opry*. The band first played the *Opry* in 1926, only weeks after the programme was created and remained on it until 1988. The band consisted of Herman Crook (b. 1899, d. 1988; harmonica) and Matthew Crook (b. 1896; harmonica), both born at Scottsboro, Tennessee, USA. They first played for local dances and on WDAD Nashville and when George D. Hay heard them, he invited them to play on WSM. They began regular *Opry* appearances but also played on WBAW and WLAC Nashville. Herman, who always treated his music as recreation, worked as a cigar roller for a tobacco company. The brothers recorded four instrumentals for RCA/Victor Records in 1928, which sold well but surprisingly were the only recordings by the Crook Brothers until 1962. In 1929, having already added a pianist and guitarist, the brothers were further reinforced by Lewis Crook on banjo, guitar and vocals). He was, in fact, no relation, a fact that has caused some confusion over the years. In 1931, Matthew left to work for the Nashville police department and Herman, maintaining that he could not find a good enough harmonica player, for the first time added a fiddle to the band. After Sam McGee had worked with them for a time, Floyd Etheridge started a long-time association. The group's output was increased by Lewis Crook adding more vocals and, in the 40s, a vocal trio also sang on the *Opry* with the band (it included both father and son Neal Matthews, the younger later working with the Jordanaires for many years). The band, with variation in personnel, continued to play on the *Opry*, and attempts were made in the 60s to persuade them to appear at folk festivals. Herman was still rolling cigars and had no interest in touring or in making records. They did record one side of an album for Starday in 1962. Noted historian Charles K. Wolfe organized a Rounder Records session but for some reason, Herman found a way to avoid doing it. Eventually, the deaths of so many old-time musicians saw the remaining members of the Possum Hunters and the Crook Brothers combined as one band, which continued to play on the *Opry* until Herman Crook died in 1988.

● ALBUMS: *Opry Old Timers Sam & Kirk McGee And The Crook Brothers* (Starday 1962)★★★.

CROOK, LEWIS

b. 1909, Trousdale County, Tennessee, USA, d. 12 April 1997, Castalian Springs, Tennessee, USA. One of the long-standing but unsung heroes of the *Grand Ole Opry*, country music's mecca, Crook sang and played banjo on radio and stage for over 60 years as part of that institution. He first entered mainstream music as a member of the Herman and Matthew Crook Band (no relation), which he joined in 1929 after meeting the pair at a fiddling championship. After Matthew Crook left to join the police, the core duo of Lewis and Herman Crook stayed together for the rest of their professional careers. They played a traditional string-band country music, typified by material such as 'Lost John' and 'Goin' Cross The Sea'. They oversaw the transformation of *WSM Barn Dance* (as it was originally called) into *The Grand Ole Opry*, sharing a stage with similarly inclined acts such as Dr. Humphrey Bate And The Possum Hunters. Initially they were not paid, and Lewis sought outside work as a salesman and representative of the Texas Boot Company (Herman was a tobacco twister for the American Tobacco Co.). Throughout, however, the two Crooks were fixtures at the *Opry* in each of its numerous locations (they could boast of having played at the WSM Studios, the Hillsboro Theater, the Dixie Tabernacle, the War Memorial Auditorium, the Ryman Auditorium and the *Grand Ole Opry*'s current home in Opryland). However, in the 40s the string-band acts proved less popular than rising solo stars (particularly Roy Acuff), and the Crook Brothers (as they were now known) were relegated to progressively lower ranking in the show's billing. The duo's rare recordings include efforts for Victor Records in the late 20s. They also appeared on a 1962 album with fellow *Opry* stars Sam And Kirk McGee. By the 80s, only the Crook Brothers and the Fruit Jar Drinkers remained of the original string-band pioneers who appeared regularly on the *Grand Ole Opry*. The Crook Brothers made their final appearance on 4 June 1988, six days before Herman's death.

● ALBUMS: one side each act *Opry Old Timers Sam & Kirk McGee And The Crook Brothers* (Starday 1962)★★★.

CROSBY, ROB

b. Robert Crosby Hoar, 25 April 1954, Sumter, South Carolina, USA. He came to country music through listening to 60s bands such as the Beatles and Crosby, Stills And Nash. Rob Crosby was so popular in the clubs of South Carolina that it was difficult for him to try to further his career in Nashville. In 1984, a group of Atlanta businessmen gave him $700 a month in exchange for a cut of his future songwriting royalties. He found he was particularly adept at writing songs for more mature female listeners, and 'She's A Natural' refers to the 'grey in their hair' and the 'lines on their faces'. The latter song, 'Love Will Bring Her Around' and 'Still Burnin' For You' were US country hits in 1991 and he also co-wrote Lee Greenwood's 'Holdin' A Good Hand' (number 2, 1990). Further US country chart placings came with 'Working Woman', 'She Wrote The Book' and 'In The

Blood'. Arista surprisingly dropped him from the label and his next album was on the indie label River North. *Starting Now* built on his first two releases with excellent songs such as the country rocker 'Fallin' In And Out Of Love' and the heartbreaking 'Learning As She Goes'. Chart success, however, appears to elude him.

● ALBUMS: *Solid Ground* (Arista 1991)★★★, *Another Time & Place* (Arista 1992)★★★, *Starting Now* (River North 1995)★★★.

CROSS, HUGH

b. Hugh Ballard Cross, 19 October 1904, Oliver Springs, Tennessee, USA, d. mid-60s. He played banjo at the age of eight, guitar at 10 and left home to join a travelling show at 16. His light tenor renditions of sentimental ballads saw him become popular as a Columbia recording artist in the late 20s. In 1926, he began his radio career at WNOX Knoxville and in 1927/8, he played and recorded with the Skillet Lickers, often singing duets with the legendary Riley Puckett. Their duet version of 'Red River Valley', recorded on 3 November 1927, is generally accepted as the first popular recording of a song that is now rated a country classic. In 1930, he moved to WLS Chicago working with John Lair, first as a member of the Cumberland Ridge Runners, before becoming a solo member of the station's famous *National Barn Dance*. Between 1934 and 1938, he worked with Shug Fisher at WWVA Wheeling, West Virginia, where their radio show, *Hugh And Shug's Radio Pals*, was very popular. (Fisher, at times, was also a member of the Sons Of The Pioneers.) From 1938-43, he was the Master of Ceremonies for the *Boone County Jamboree* on WLW Cincinnati. He continued to perform announcing duties and sing his sentimental ballads, often being accompanied by his wife until her death in 1945. When he retired from the music business, Cross travelled around the country working in various stores as a demonstrator. In 1943, he wrote the country standard 'Don't Make Me Go To Bed And I'll Be Good'. It was this song (about a dying child) that led songwriter Fred Rose to state that he never really understood what country music was all about until one night at the *Grand Ole Opry*, when he saw Roy Acuff, with tears streaming down his face, singing it. (Red Foley's version of the song was also very popular.) Cross died in the mid-60s but some of his recordings may still be heard, including his fine 1928 duet recordings with Riley Puckett of 'Clover Blossoms' and 'Call Me Back Pal O' Mine', which can be found on *Old Time Greats - Riley Puckett Volume 1* (Old Homestead 1978).

CROWE, J.D.

b. James Dee Crowe, 27 August 1937, Lexington, Kentucky, USA. A very talented banjoist, Crowe gained his fascination for the instrument when Flatt And Scruggs were resident on a Lexington station. He attended their daily shows and watched Scruggs intently. He did building work by day and played locally in the evenings until, in 1955, he toured with Mac Wiseman. Also touring with them were Don Reno And Red Smiley, and Crowe's playing benefited further from this association with Reno. Between 1956 and 1962, he played and recorded with Jimmy Martin's Sunny Mountain Boys. In the mid-60s, he formed his Kentucky Mountain Boys, which included Red Allen and Doyle Lawson and recorded for Lemco. In 1971, he decided to adopt an electrified sound and formed his New South, which included Tony Rice, Ricky Skaggs and Jerry Douglas. They first recorded for Starday but it was their 1975 album from Rounder Records that was later described as the most influential bluegrass record of the decade. They included traditional bluegrass numbers together with modern material but presented it in a style different to that expected of bluegrass bands. The result was that it attracted many new young musicians to the genre, although Crowe was always careful to include enough of the expected sound to maintain the traditionalists' interest. Obviously, there were changes in line-up and when, in 1979, they recorded their noted *Live In Japan*, in Tokyo, the members were Keith Whitley, Bobby Stone, Jimmy Gaudreau and Steve Bryant. In 1981, Crowe recorded the first of a series of albums listed as the Bluegrass Album Band, with Tony Rice, Doyle Lawson, Bobby Hicks and Todd Phillips. (On *Volume V*, Vassar Clements and Mark Schatz replaced Hicks and Phillips.) The New South won a Grammy award for their instrumental 'Fireball' in 1983. In 1988 Crowe decided that he was tired of the travelling and until 1991, he played only occasional shows with other bands. He continued to perform into the early 90s, but resisted any attempts to lure him back to full-time touring. Crowe, with his perfect timing and fine leadership, is acknowledged by experts of the genre as one of the most influential of bluegrass musicians and many of the genre's top artists benefited from the experience gained earlier in their career with his band. Surprisingly, for some unknown reason, he has never quite achieved the international acclaim that some of those artists have enjoyed. Crowe also loves blues music, which he has sometimes adapted to his style of banjo playing.

● ALBUMS: As J.D. Crowe With The Kentucky Mountain Boys with Red Allen *Bluegrass Holiday* (Lemco 1968)★★★, *The Model Church* (Lemco 1969, reissued on CD, Rebel 1992)★★★, *Ramblin' Boy* (Lemco 1971, reissued on CD as *Blackjack*, Rebel 1991)★★★★; as J.D. Crowe And The New South *J.D. Crowe & The New South* (Rounder 1975)★★★, *J.D. Crowe & The New South* 1973 recording (Starday 1977)★★★, *You Can Share My Blanket* (Rounder 1978)★★★★, *My Home Ain't In The Hall Of Fame* (Rounder 1980)★★★, *Somewhere Between* (Rounder 1981)★★★, *Straight Ahead* (Rounder 1986)★★★, *Live In Japan* recorded 1979 (Rounder 1987)★★; with the Bluegrass Band *The Bluegrass Album* (Rounder 1981)★★★★, *The Bluegrass Album Volume II* (Rounder 1982)★★★, *The Bluegrass Album Volume III; California Connection* (Rounder 1983)★★★, *The Bluegrass Album Volume IV* (Rounder 1985)★★★, *The Bluegrass Album Band Volume V; Sweet Sunny South* (Rounder 1989)★★★.

● COMPILATIONS: *Flashback* (Rounder 1994)★★★.

CROWELL, RODNEY

b. 7 August 1950, Houston, Texas, USA. Combining careers as a country songwriter, producer and artist, Crowell has become an influential figure in Nashville's new breed, along with Emmylou Harris, in whose Hot Band he worked for three years, Rosanne Cash, and fellow songwriters such as Guy Clark. Crowell's introduction to playing music came before he was a teenager, when he played drums in his Kentucky-born father's bar band in Houston. He dropped out of college in the early 70s to move to Nashville, where he was briefly signed as a songwriter at Jerry Reed's publishing company, and in 1973 was appearing on local 'writer's night'

with contemporaries such as Clark, John Hiatt and Richard Dobson. In 1974, a demo tape of his songs was heard by Brian Ahern, who was about to produce *Pieces Of The Sky* for Emmylou Harris, and that album eventually began with Crowell's 'Bluebird Wine'. Harris's 1975 album *Elite Hotel* included Crowell's 'Till I Gain Control Again', and her 1979 release, *Quarter Moon In A Ten Cent Town*, featured his 'I Ain't Living Long Like This' and 'Leaving Louisiana In The Broad Daylight'. During this period, Crowell also worked as a permanent member of Harris's Hot Band, playing rhythm guitar and singing harmony and duet vocals. In 1978, he also recorded his own debut album for Warner Brothers Records, *Ain't Living Long Like This*, using Ahern as producer and an all-star line-up of musicians including the entire Hot Band plus Ry Cooder, Jim Keltner and Willie Nelson. Although it included two minor US country hit singles, the album was not a commercial success.

In 1979, Crowell married Rosanne Cash, and has subsequently produced most of her albums. In 1980, he tried again on his own account with *But What Will The Neighbors Think*, which he co-produced with Craig Leon. It remained in the US album charts for 10 weeks, and included a US Top 40 single, 'Ashes By Now'; in 1981, he released the self-produced *Rodney Crowell*, which just failed to reach the Top 100 of the US album chart. In 1984, he delivered *Street Language* to Warner Brothers, who rejected it, whereupon Crowell changed four tracks and leased it to Columbia Records, for whom he continues to record. The album, released in 1986, included three US country chart singles, and established him as a country artist (although many feel that he could easily cross over to rock). *Diamonds And Dirt*, co-produced by Crowell and his erstwhile Hot Band colleague Tony Brown, was much more successful, spawning five US country number 1 singles, 'It's Such A Small World' (a duet with Rosanne Cash), 'I Couldn't Leave You If I Tried' and 'She's Crazy For Leavin''. In 1989, Crowell and Brown co-produced *Keys To The Highway*, which was largely recorded with his fine band, the Dixie Pearls, whose personnel includes Stewart Smith (lead guitar), Jim Hanson (bass), Vince Santoro (drums) and another erstwhile Hot Band colleague, Hank DeVito (pedal steel). Crowell's songs have been covered by Bob Seger, Waylon Jennings, George Jones and others, while he has also produced albums for Sissy Spacek, Guy Clark and Bobby Bare. *Life Is Messy*, followed after his marriage to Rosanne Cash had broken down. Taken by most observers as a reply to Cash's stunning *Interiors*, the album attempted - with some success - to marry melancholy themes to up-tempo songs. Subsequent albums such as *Let The Picture Paint Itself* and *Jewel Of The South* have also chronicled his personal problems. As long as life is messy it appears he will be able to write great songs.

● ALBUMS: *Ain't Living Long Like This* (Warners 1978)★★★★, *But What Will The Neighbors Think* (Warners 1980)★★★, *Rodney Crowell* (Warners 1981)★★★, *Street Language* (Columbia 1986)★★★★, *Diamonds And Dirt* (Columbia 1988)★★★★, *Keys To The Highway* (Columbia 1989)★★★★, *Life Is Messy* (Columbia 1992)★★★, *Let The Picture Paint Itself* (MCA 1994)★★★, *Soul Searchin'* (Excelsior 1994)★★★, *Jewel Of The South* (MCA 1995)★★★, *The Cicadas* (Warners 1997)★★★.

● COMPILATIONS: *The Rodney Crowell Collection* (Warners 1989)★★★★, *Greatest Hits* (Columbia 1993)★★★★.

CRYNER, BOBBIE

b. 13 September 1961, Woodland, California, USA. Cryner moved to Kansas at the age of 16. She was involved in both acting and singing, often mimicking country stars Barbara Mandrell and Dolly Parton. As a performer, she took her father's name, Bobbie, as her own. Her sister married Exile bass guitarist Sonny LeMaire, and on a trip to Nashville, she met songwriter Max D. Barnes. Barnes encouraged her to move to Nashville and she left her husband to do so. She worked in a diner, while he improved her songwriting technique. Her career had a further boost when Carl Jackson recommended her to Epic, and soon she was opening for George Strait. Her first album included Dwight Yoakam and Emmylou Harris and featured six of her own songs. Merging country, gospel and the blues, it was a fine album, being described by one critic as a cross between Vern Gosdin and Bobbie Gentry. Despite its obvious quality, it failed to sell. Alone in Nashville, Cryner started drinking heavily and she also suffered from bulimia. Fortunately, she quickly recognized the severity of her condition and, to motivate her own recovery, concentrated her efforts on working on her second album, *Girl Of Your Dreams*, which was produced by Tony Brown and Barry Beckett. In March 1996, 'You'd Think He'd Know Me Better', written by Brown and Beckett, became her first US country hit. Her mother runs her fan club and it is generally predicted that she will soon be very busy.
● ALBUMS: *Bobbie Cryner* (Epic 1993)★★★, *Girl Of Your Dreams* (MCA 1995)★★★.

CUDDY, SHAWN

b. 2 May 1963, Camross, Portlaoise, County Laois, Eire. The eldest of 11 children, he grew up in a house where country music was always playing. After leaving school, he worked as an attendant at Mountmellick Hospital. In 1981, influenced by Margo and Big Tom, he and sisters Elizabeth and Martina formed a country band. When his siblings quit, he continued as a solo artist. He financed his first single by a bank loan and found that 'Little Nell' gained sufficient airplay to become a number 1 on RTE's country chart; he subsequently launched his professional career as an entertainer. Soon afterwards he formed his own band and began to play the country club and theatre circuit in the UK and Ireland. He has toured with Foster And Allen and was support act to Johnny Cash on a UK tour. He joined Harmac Records in 1992 and enjoyed considerable success with his recording of Jerry Hanlon's 'The Calling (Home)'. His easy styling finds him equally at home with the modern country song 'Don't Close Your Eyes' or Irish standards such as 'The Village Where I Went To School', although he does not seem to record as many Irish songs as some of his compatriots. It would appear that he has now established himself as one of the most popular Irish country singers.
● ALBUMS: *The Calling Home* (Harmac 1992)★★★, *Just For You* (Harmac 1994)★★★.

CUMBERLAND RIDGE RUNNERS

One of the most important of the early groups to appear regularly on the WLS *National Barn Dance* in Chicago. The singers and musicians (mainly from Mount Vernon and Berea, Kentucky) were brought to WLS in 1930 by their leader John Lair. During the time they played WLS, members of the group included Red Foley, Karl And Harty, Hugh Cross and Slim Miller (b. Homer Miller, 1898, Lisbon, Indiana, USA, d. 1963), an accomplished fiddler by the age of 12 and also the group's comedian. Also included was Doc Hopkins (b. Howard Hopkins, 26 January 1900, Harlan County, Kentucky, USA, d. 3 January 1988, Chicago, Illinois, USA), an old-time singer, who played guitar and banjo, had recorded for Broadway, ARC and Decca and became noted as a teacher of the banjo during the 50s, and also Linda Parker (b. Covington, Kentucky, USA - but grew up in Indiana, d. August 1935), who, originally well-known on the Chicago popular music scene, was really the star of the group. Known as the Sunbonnet Girl, Parker played banjo and guitar and sang authentic folk ballads, and was mourned by many when she met an untimely death in 1935. The group presented the first sponsored half-hour programme on the *National Barn Dance* (the *Aladdin Mantle Show*) and were one of the first to feature square-dancers as part of their act. When Lair left WLS in 1937, the Ridge Runners basically folded; some followed Lair and others went on to pursue their own careers. Most members recorded as solo artists.

CUNHA, RICK

Guitarist/vocalist Cunha was a founder-member of Hearts And Flowers, a pivotal mid-60s US country/folk trio. He appeared on the group's debut album, but was replaced by Bernie Leadon for *Of Horses, Kids And Forgotten Women*. Cunha subsequently enjoyed a spell as host at the famed Los Angeles Troubador Club, before spending several years touring with guitarist Mason Williams. During the 70s the artist made several session appearances, notably on John Stewart's *The Lonesome Picker Rides Again*, before recording the exemplary *Songs*, a superior selection of country-influenced material. Cunha also enjoyed a fruitful association with Emmylou Harris, contributing to *Pieces Of The Sky* (1975), *Elite Hotel* (1976) and *Luxury Liner* (1977). A recording contract with Columbia/CBS ensued, but the label failed to release the resultant album, which latterly appeared on an independent outlet, Sierra, as *Moving Pictures*. The delay undermined the career of this impressive musician who nonetheless retains the respect of his peers.
● ALBUMS: *Songs* (GRP 1974)★★★, *Moving Pictures* (Sierra 1980)★★★.

CURLESS, DICK

b. Richard William Curless, 17 March 1932, Fort Fairfield, Maine, USA, d. 25 May 1995. Both his parents were musical and in 1948, after the family moved to Massachusetts, he was soon appearing as the Tumbleweed Kid in his own show on local radio in Ware, Massachusetts. Later he joined a band called the Trail Blazers and moved back to Maine. In 1951, he was drafted into the army, later commenting: 'They must have been hard up. I had a bad eye and heart trouble'. He was sent to Korea, purely as an entertainer, and became very popular on the AFN network as the Rice Paddy Ranger. He was discharged in 1954 and worked local clubs until ill health caused him to rest. In 1957, a win on the *Arthur Godfrey Talent Show* on network television, with his version of 'Nine Pound Hammer', led to him finding work in Hollywood and Las Vegas. In the late 50s, recurring ill heath, lack of major success and personal problems led to him returning to Maine, where he bought a lorry and worked in the logging business. He returned to Hollywood in the early

60s but decided that he was not destined for success further afield and soon went back to Maine, where he worked in local clubs. In 1965, at the request of his friend, the writer Dan Fulkerson, he recorded, at his own expense on the minor Allagash label, a song called 'A Tombstone Every Mile'. The recording attracted the attention of Capitol, who released it on their Tower label and it became a Top 5 US country hit. The song was written about a stretch of dangerous and icy road through the Maine woods and was another of the truck-driving and travelling-themed numbers that became popular following Dave Dudley's success two years earlier with 'Six Days On The Road'. During 1966 and 1967, he was a regular member of Buck Owens' *All American Show* and toured extensively in the USA, Europe and the Far East. He sang on the soundtrack of the 1968 film *Killer's Three* but the same year was again incapacitated by ill health. He also had to resort to wearing the eye patch that became his trademark. He commented, 'I couldn't see much at all since the right eye was interfering with the vision I had in the left'. Further hits followed, though only 'Six Times A Day' achieved Top 20 status. He recorded 'Big Wheel Cannonball' in 1970, which was the trucker's version of the old train song 'Wabash Cannonball', originally sung by Roy Acuff in the late 30s. He also had success with the strangely titled 'Drag 'Em Off The Interstate, Sock It To 'Em, J.P. Blues'. In 1973, 'The Last Blues Song', somewhat appropriately, provided his last country chart hit. Curless's style certainly leaned towards the blues, although someone once likened his voice to an 18-wheeler revving up. In the 70s, he devoted some attention to song publishing and a talent agency but seemingly drifted into semi-retirement in his native Maine. In 1987, he attempted a comeback as a recording artist by recording an album in Norway with Norwegian musicians. In 1989, he recorded a superb album for Allagash featuring the songs of his friend Smokey Rogers, but poor distribution prevented it achieving the success it deserved. In the early 90s, he made some tours and also played in Branson, Missouri, as part of the Country Gold show that featured other stars of his era, including Bill Anderson, Bobby Bare, George Hamilton IV, Ferlin Husky, Melba Mongomery and Leroy Van Dyke. Late in 1994, he was hospitalized and on operating, the doctors discovered that what they had for years assumed to be a medical condition created by ulcers was, in fact, caused by a rare and inoperable stomach cancer. In December 1994, he completed the aptly named *Traveling Through* for Rounder Records and, in March 1995, much against his wife's wishes, he made his final tour. Curless died on 25 May 1995. Waylon Jennings summed up things when he stated, 'He had one of the great voices of country music and he certainly knew how to use it.' In 1995, Bear Family Records released a 7-CD box set that contained all the recordings he made between 1950 and 1969, including around 50 previously unissued tracks. He will perhaps be remembered as the first international country star produced by the New England state of Maine.
● ALBUMS: *Songs Of The Open Country* (Tiffany 1958)★★★, *Singing Just For Fun* (Tiffany 1959)★★★, *I Love To Tell A Story* (Tiffany 1960)★★★, *Hymns* (Tower 1965)★★★, *A Tombstone Every Mile* (Tower 1965)★★★, with Kay Adams *A Devil Like Me Needs An Angel Like You* (Tower 1966)★★★, *Travellin' Man* (Tower 1966)★★★, *All Of Me Belongs To You/House Of Memories* (Tower 1967)★★★, *At Home With*

Dick Curless (Tower 1967)★★★, *Ramblin' Country* (Tower 1967)★★★, *The Soul Of Dick Curless* (Tower 1967)★★★, *The Long Lonesome Road* (Tower 1968)★★★, *The Wild Side Of Town* (Tower 1968)★★★, *Doggin' It* (Capitol 1970)★★★, *Hard Hard Traveling Man* (Capitol 1970)★★★, *Comin' On Country* (Capitol 1971)★★★, *Stonin' Around* (Capitol 1972)★★★, with Jerry Smith *Live At The Wheeling Truck Drivers Jamboree* (Capitol 1973)★★★, *The Last Blues Song* (Capitol 1973)★★★, *End Of The Road* (Pickwick/Hilltop 1974)★★★, *Maine Train* (Interstate 1976)★★★, *The Great Race* (Belmont 1980)★★★, *Welcome To My World* (Rocade 1987)★★★, *Close Up* (Allagash 1989)★★★, *Traveling Through* (Rounder 1995)★★★.
● COMPILATIONS: *20 Great Truck Hits* (EMI 1983)★★★★, *Dick Curless, A Tombstone Every Mile (1950-1969)*, 7-CD set (Bear Family 1995)★★★★.

CURTIS, KEN

b. Curtis Wain Gates, 2 July 1916, on a farm near Lamar, Colorado, USA, d. 28 April 1991, Fresco, California, USA. In 1935, he left home and for a time studied medicine in college, at Colorado Springs, until his desire for a musical career saw him move to Hollywood. He played saxophone at college, but wanting to be a singer, he found a post as a staff vocalist on NBC radio. In 1941, after various radio work, he was signed as a temporary replacement for Frank Sinatra with the Tommy Dorsey Orchestra with whom he recorded. On Sinatra's return, he made further recordings with the Shep Fields Band. In June 1942, he volunteered for military service but resumed his musical career in 1945. A radio appearance singing 'Tumbling Tumbleweeds' led him to a contract with Columbia Pictures where, as Ken Curtis, he made a series of musical westerns until the company also acquired Gene Autry. In 1949, Curtis and Shug Fisher toured with the Sons Of The Pioneers and others, and during this period was asked to deputize for Lloyd Perryman for a time. When Perryman returned, Curtis remained with the Pioneers as replacement for Tim Spencer who, owing to a voice problem, was becoming more the manager of the group than a singer. Curtis, Perryman and Bob Nolan provided the trio harmony on their noted 1949 recording of 'Riders In The Sky' and 'Room Full Of Roses' and he appeared with them in *Wagon Master*, which starred Ben Johnson in 1950. He left the Pioneers in 1953 but still recorded with them until September 1957. He hosted the *Lucky U Ranch Show* before, in the mid-50s, he returned to film acting. He appeared in several westerns, some directed by his father-in-law John Ford, including the John Wayne classic *The Searchers*. He later moved to television where he appeared in *Ripcord* and *Rawhide* before becoming a regular (as Monk) in *Have Gun Will Travel*. He first appeared in *Gunsmoke* (aka *Gunlaw* in the UK) in December 1962 and played various roles until, in January 1964, he played the part his father had done for real, when he replaced Denis Weaver (Chester Goode) as Marshal Matt, in which role he occasionally sang numbers that he had sung with the Pioneers. When that series ended, he continued to play character parts.

CURTIS, SONNY

b. 9 May 1937, Meadow, Texas, USA. Curtis spent his first years in extreme poverty as his family lived in a 'dugout', simply a hole in the ground with a roof on the top.

Eventually the family of seven moved to a small shack, and Sonny sang and played guitar from the age of eight. He befriended Buddy Holly in nearby Lubbock and he worked with him on many occasions, notably playing a fiery guitar on his own composition, 'Rock Around With Ollie Vee', in Nashville. He left Holly to work with Slim Whitman, just before he formed the Crickets, and his song, 'The Real Buddy Holly Story', emphasizes the inaccuracies of the film. Curtis joined the Crickets after Holly left, and they recorded several of his songs - 'More Than I Can Say' (later a hit for Bobby Vee and Leo Sayer), 'When You Ask About Love' (Matchbox) and 'I Fought The Law' (Bobby Fuller Four, the Clash). The Crickets toured as the Everly Brothers' backing group and the Everlys had a number 1 with Curtis's 'Walk Right Back'. For several years, Curtis was both a Cricket and a solo performer, and he became more comfortable with ballads than out-and-out rock 'n' roll. He wrote the theme tune for *The Mary Tyler Moore Show*, 'Love Is All Around', while his song 'The Straight Life' has been recorded by Glen Campbell, Bing Crosby and Val Doonican. Rosanne Cash recorded 'Where Will The Words Come From' and Keith Whitley had a US country number 1 with 'I'm No Stranger To The Rain'. Curtis is an exceptional entertainer, who often comes to the UK on acoustic tours. His songs also show his wry sense of humour - recent titles include 'I'm Too Sexy For You' and 'Why Did You Say I Do To Me (When You Still Meant To Do It With Him)?'. He was inducted into the Songwriters Hall Of Fame by the Nashville Songwriters Association in 1991.

● ALBUMS: *Beatle Hits, Flamenco Style* (Imperial 1964)★, *The First Of Sonny Curtis* (Viva 1968)★★★, *The Sonny Curtis Style* (Viva 1969)★★★, *Sonny Curtis* (1979)★★★, *Love Is All Around* (Elektra 1980)★★, *Rollin'* (Elektra 1981)★★★, *Spectrum* (Nightflite 1987)★★★, *Ready, Able And Willing* (1988)★★★, *No Stranger To The Rain* (Ritz 1990)★★★.

CUTRER, T. TOMMY

b. Thomas Clinton Cutrer, 29 June 1924, Osyka, Mississippi, USA. A hoped-for career as a footballer was ended during his high school days by osteomyelitis. He spent months convalescing, during which time he decided to pursue a career in radio. He did menial tasks at stations in New Orleans and Jackson before gaining an announcer's post with KARK Little Rock in 1943. He relocated to Memphis around 1945, where he worked on both WMC and WREC. He had some experience as a singer and in the late 40s, he formed his first band, the Rhythm Boys. In the early 50s, he worked on stations in Houston, before moving to KCIJ Shreveport in 1952. In 1954, while on his way to Nashville to work for WSM, he was involved in a serious accident that led to him having a leg amputated. He quickly recovered and worked on WSM as a disc jockey and also as an announcer on the *Grand Ole Opry*. Cutrer holds the distinction of being the first disc jockey ever to play a record of Johnny Cash on air and during his career, he once worked as the announcer for Cash's networked television show. In 1957, he was voted America's top disc jockey and he appeared in the 1965 film *Music City USA*. He made recordings for several labels in the 50s, including Capitol, RCA, Victor, Mercury and Dot Records. He gained no chart entries but his material varied from honky tonk to gospel. He may be heard on the 1975

Starday release *Opry Time In Tennessee* and he also recorded an amusing version of 'Temptation' with June Carter and a pleasant cut of 'Wonderful World' with Ginny Wright. In 1976, he turned his attentions to politics and stood for Congress, being beaten by Al Gore. He then successfully gained election to the State Senate, where he served until 1982.

CYRUS, BILLY RAY

b. 25 August 1961, Flatwoods, Kentucky, USA. Cyrus comes from a preaching family and made his singing debut in his father's gospel group. In 1983, he formed his own band, Sly Dog, but they lost their equipment in a fire in Los Angeles. He then worked as a car salesman but he kept visiting Nashville in the hope of finding musical success. In 1992, he turned the Marcy Brothers' 'Don't Tell My Heart' into the simple but immensely catchy 'Achy Breaky Heart'. Although the Cyrus virus proved infectious, the song's rhythms were close to Don Williams' 'Tulsa Time'. The video, in which the muscular, ponytailed Cyrus was mobbed by adoring women, also introduced a country music dance - the Achy Breaky. The song topped both the US pop and country charts and was easily the most successful country single released in the UK during 1992. Another star, Travis Tritt, derided Cyrus for turning country music into 'an asswiggling contest'. Cyrus's album, *Some Gave All*, also topped the US pop and country charts, while he had a further transatlantic hit, 'Could've Been Me', and recorded a parody of 'Achy Breaky Heart' with the Chipmunks. *Storm In The Heartland*, featuring guest appearances from the Oak Ridge Boys and Danny Shirley of Confederate Railroad, and the follow-up *Trail Of Tears* attempted to move Cyrus away from his lightweight image. Unfortunately now that line-dancing clubs are forming everywhere, it appears as though he will remain associated with the Achy Breaky. Whatever happens, his Mel Gibson looks and Chippendale body will always work to his advantage.

● ALBUMS: *Some Gave All* (Mercury 1992)★★★★, *It Won't Be The Last* (Mercury 1993)★★★, *Storm In The Heartland* (Mercury 1994)★★★, *Trail Of Tears* (Mercury 1996)★★.

● COMPILATIONS: *The Best Of Billy Ray Cyrus Cover To Cover* (Mercury 1997)★★★.

● VIDEOS: *Billy Ray Cyrus* (1992), *Live* (1992), *The Video Collection* (1993), *Storm In the Heartland* (Mercury 1994), *One On One* (Polygram 1994), *The Complete Video Collection* (Polygram Video 1997).

DAFFAN, TED

b. Theron Eugene Daffan, 21 September 1912, Beauregarde Parish, Louisiana, USA, d. 6 October 1996, Houston, Texas, USA. He was raised in Texas and graduated from high school in Houston in 1930. Late in 1931, he began to teach himself to play the Hawaiian guitar and first appeared on KTRH Houston with the Blue Islanders in 1933. During the 30s, he was a member of both the Blue Ridge Playboys (where he played with Floyd Tillman and Moon Mullican) and the Bar X Cowboys. His keen interest in electronics led to him becoming one of the first to experiment with electronically amplifying guitars and he first recorded with an amplified steel guitar in 1939. He also developed a considerable talent for songwriting and in 1939, his song 'Truck Driver's Blues' became the first of the genre of truck-driving songs. In 1940, he formed his own band, the Texans (which he retained almost to the end of the 50s), and recording for Columbia, had a hit with his song 'A Worried Mind', in the face of competition from recordings by Bob Wills and Roy Acuff. In 1943, he wrote and recorded for OKeh 'No Letter Today' and his classic, million-selling 'Born To Lose'. Released on the same single, they both became US country and pop hits in January 1944. The following year, he had further Top 5 country hits including 'Headin' Down The Wrong Highway'. Between 1944 and 1946, he was resident at Venice Pier Ballroom, Los Angeles, and in the late 40s, he was a regular on the popular *Town Hall Party* from Compton. He later returned to Texas with his band and played in various venues, including Houston, Dallas and Fort Worth. In 1958, he formed a publishing company with Hank Snow and in 1961, he founded his own company in Houston. Among his best-known country songs, apart from those previously mentioned, are 'A Woman Captured Me', 'I've Got Five Dollars And It's Saturday Night', and 'Always Alone'. Over the years, his songs have also been recorded by non-country artists such as Ray Charles ('Born To Lose' and 'No Letter Today') and in 1968, pop singer Joe Barry was credited with a million-seller for his 1961 recording of 'I'm A Fool To Care', which had previously been recorded by Les Paul and Mary Ford. Daffan was one of the first to be elected to the Nashville Songwriters Association International Hall Of Fame, when it was founded in 1970.

DAILY, PAPPY

b. Harold W. Daily, 8 February 1902, Yoakum, Texas, USA, d. 5 December 1987, Houston, Texas, USA. After lying about his age, he saw service with the US Marines in World War I. He became involved in several successful business ventures but his involvement in country music did not really start until 1953, when he and Jack Starnes formed the Starday label in Beaumont, Texas. The label launched the career of George

Jones and, by doing so, ensured its own success. When Starnes left, Daily and Don Pierce worked together, until parting amicably in 1961. Daily had also formed his own D label, in 1958, and apart from the Starday work, he successfully recorded several artists, including Eddie Noack, Claude Gray and James O'Gwynn. In 1961, he joined United Artists Records, where he continued to record George Jones, who had moved to the label with him. He produced a series of solo hits for Jones, including 'The Race Is On', and also for Melba Montgomery. His foresight in recording them as a duo produced several hits, especially a number 3 hit with 'We Must Have Been Out Of Our Minds'. In 1965, when Daily and Art Talmadge formed the Musicor label, Jones joined them and charted almost 30 hits for the label, including Top 3s with 'Walk Through This World With Me', 'When The Grass Grows Over Me' and 'I'll Share My World With You'. In 1971, the close relationship with Jones encountered problems when, for some reason regarding the way he was being handled, the singer demanded his release in order to move to Epic and record with Tammy Wynette. It has been stated that Talmadge may have been the cause of the problem but Jones departed and his relationship with Daily from that point was never more than casual. Daily continued in the business for some time but never achieved further success to match that gained early in his career. He later managed the distribution companies Big State and H.W. Daily. He died following a heart attack in 1987.

DALE, KENNY

b. 1951, Artesia, New Mexico, USA. Dale, originally a drummer, grew up in Texas and had his own band, Love Country, in Houston in early 70s. In 1977, he recorded 'Bluest Heartache Of The Year' for a small Houston label, Earthrider, but it was reissued by Capitol and reached number 11 on the US country charts. Dale had further vocal successes with 'Shame, Shame On Me', 'Red Hot Memory', 'When It's Just You And Me' and 'Moanin' The Blues', and his biggest hit was with a country revival of Gene Pitney's 'Only Love Can Break A Heart' (number 7, 1969). His final chart entry was with 'I'm Going Crazy' in 1986.
● ALBUMS: *Bluest Heartache Of The Year* (1977)★★, *Red Hot Memory* (1978)★★, *Only Love Can Break A Heart* (1979)★★★, *When It's Just You And Me* (1981)★★★.

DALHART, VERNON

b. Marion Try Slaughter, 6 April 1883, Jefferson, Texas, USA, d. 14 September 1948, Bridgeport, Connecticut, USA. Dalhart spent his early life on a ranch but in 1902, seeking a career in music, he went to New York. He took the name of Vernon Dalhart by combining the names of two Texas towns. He sang with the Century Opera Company and, in 1913-14, he performed in *HMS Pinafore* at the Hippodrome. He recorded for Edison's cylinders, his first release being 'Can't Yo' Heah Me Callin' Caroline?' in 1917. Dalhart made numerous records under different names with different styles, including vaudeville. In 1924 Victor Records were about to dispense with his services when he asked if he could record hillbilly music. He chose 'The Wreck Of The Old '97', which had first been recorded the previous year by Henry Whitter. It was backed by 'The Prisoner's Song', which he said was written by his cousin, Guy Massey. It became country music's first million-seller, eventually exceeding six million. True to character, Dalhart also recorded the song under pseudonyms for many different labels. 'The Wreck Of The Old '97' was based on fact and so Dalhart consolidated his success with several topical songs written by, and performed with, Carson Jay Robison. They included 'The Death Of Floyd Collins' and 'The John T. Scopes Trial'. In 1928, following disagreements with Robison over royalties and the choice of musicians, Dalhart pursued a solo career. The cutbacks during the Depression put paid to Dalhart's vocation although, in 1931, he recorded 'The Runaway Train' in London, which became a children's favourite. He attempted a comeback in 1939 but, despite his versatility, he could not satisfy the public. He stopped performing, although he did give singing lessons and worked as a night clerk at a hotel in Bridgeport, Connecticut. He died following a heart attack in 1948, and was elected to the Country Music Hall of Fame in 1981. As Dalhart used more than 50 pseudonyms, the full extent of his recorded career will never be known.

● COMPILATIONS: *Songs Of The Railroad (1924-1934)* (1972)★★★, *Old Time Songs* (1976)★★★, *Vernon Dalhart, 1921-1927* (70s)★★★, *Vernon Dalhart - The First Recorded Railway Songs* (Mark 56 1978)★★★★, *Vernon Dalhart - The First Singing Cowboy* (1978)★★★, *Ballads And Railroad Songs* (1980)★★★, *Vernon Dalhart, Volume 2* (1985)★★★, *Vernon Dalhart, Volume 3* (1985)★★★.

DALLAS, REX

b. 6 November 1938, Wallerawang, New South Wales, Australia. Dallas inherited a love of bush poetry through a close friendship with his grandfather, who regularly read poems to him. He first appeared on local radio, on 2LT Lithgow, at the age of 15 but a year later, he relocated to Sydney. His appearance on *Australia's Amateur Hour* led to him becoming a regular on 2SM's *On The Trail And Hall Shows* for the next three years. He later toured with Lee Gordon and made his first recordings for EMI in the early 60s, his first single being 'Bicycle Wreck'. His versatility has seen him perform material varying from country to rock 'n' roll and even light operetta. Like many Australian artists, he is a very fine yodeller, being so especially devoted to Harry Torrani that in 1975, he recorded an album of Torrani songs. Its immediate success led to a second album and 20 of the tracks found subsequent release in the UK (*Yodelling Songs Of Harry Torrani* - Westwood 1978). Although an excellent yodeller, he does not use the art on all his recordings, in fact, he is perhaps best known to many of his Australasian fans for his ability to follow in the footsteps of Buddy Williams and Slim Dusty as a leading performer of bush ballads. He has, in fact, even won awards for his self-penned bush ballads. One of these, 'Old Wallerawang', a tribute to his grandfather, won him a Gold Guitar at the Tamworth awards, as did 'His Spurs Are Rusty Now', which he co-wrote with his son Colin in 1982 ('Old Wallerawang' was also recorded by several other artists, including Rolf Harris). His albums also include selections of horse songs, war songs, mother songs and even one on the theme of coalmining. From the early 70s, he toured extensively, accompanied by his band, the Dallas Cowboys, which included his two sons, Brett (b. 16 January 1963, Sydney, New South Wales, Australia; lead guitarist) and Colin (b. 8 November 1965, Cooma, New South Wales, Australia; drums). During the 80s, his two younger

sons, Jeffrey (b. 27 August 1970, Sydney, New South Wales, Australia; bass, mandolin) and Shannan, began to make appearances on his show, Shannan being only three when he made his debut. In 1981, Dallas featured in a television documentary about his touring show. He holds the distinction of being the first artist ever to take the title from constant winners Slim Dusty or Reg Lindsay, when he was voted best male vocalist at Tamworth in 1976. He has his own venue, Gully Park, in Moonbi, New South Wales, where he regularly entertains, when not touring with his country show.

● ALBUMS: *Harry Torrani Yodelling Album* (Hadley 1975)★★★★★★, *Harry Torrani Yodelling Album Volume 2* (Hadley 1975)★★★, *In The Days When I Was Me* (Hadley 1976)★★★, *I Love The Old Bush Ballad Songs* (Hadley 1978)★★★, *Old Wallerawang* (Hadley 1979)★★★, *Here's To The Songwriter* (Hadley 1979)★★, *Yodelling Mad* (Hadley 1980)★★★, *Buckjump And Saddle Tales* (Hadley 1981)★★★, *Remembering Those Hillbilly Hits* (Hadley 1982)★★★★, *Mother's Flower Garden* (Hadley 1982)★★★, *Born To The Saddle* (Hadley 1983)★★★, *Easy Loving* (Hadley 1984)★★, *For Valour* (Hadley 1985)★★★, *Rex Dallas & Sons* (Briar 1986)★★★, *Yodels Harry Torrani Classics Volume 3* (Briar 1986)★★★, with Owen Blundell *Duelling Yodellers* (Selection 1988)★★★★, *We Dig Coal* (Sundown 1990)★★★, *Heartland* (Hadley 1994)★★★.

DALLAS, YODELIN' SLIM

(see Nevada Slim).

DALTON, LACY J.

b. Jill Byrem, 13 October 1948, Bloomsburg, Pennsylvania, USA. Her father played guitar and mandolin, but she was originally determined to be an artist. At the age of 18 she moved to Los Angeles and then settled in Santa Cruz, where she played the clubs for 12 years. She worked as a protest singer and then became the lead singer with a psychedelic band, Office, under the name of Jill Croston. A demo tape impressed record producer Billy Sherrill, who signed her to Columbia Records in Nashville in 1979. Her gravelly, bluesy voice was unusual for country singers and thus made her work distinctive. Her album *Lacy J. Dalton* is regarded by many as a classic, and she is often described by the title of one of its songs, 'Hillbilly Girl With The Blues'. Her US country hits include 'Crazy Blue Eyes', 'Tennessee Waltz', 'Hard Times' and '16th Avenue'. Her *Highway Diner* album moved her into Bruce Springsteen territory and she had a pop hit with 'Working Class Man'. By way of contrast, she was featured alongside Bobby Bare, George Jones and Earl Scruggs on her album *Blue Eyed Blues*. She recorded for Liberty Records in the late 80s and early 90s.

● ALBUMS: *Jill Croston* (Harbor 1978)★★, *Lacy J. Dalton* (Columbia 1979)★★★★, *Hard Times* (Columbia 1980)★★★, *Takin' It Easy* (Columbia 1981)★★★, *16th Avenue* (Columbia 1982)★★★, *Dream Baby* (Columbia 1983)★★★, *Can't Run Away From Your Heart* (Columbia 1985)★★, *Highway Diner* (Columbia 1986)★★, *Blue Eyed Blues* (Columbia 1987)★★, *Survivor* (Liberty 1989)★★★, *Lacy J.* (Liberty 1990)★★★, *Crazy Love* (Capitol 1991)★★★, *Chains On The Wind* (Liberty 1992)★★.

● COMPILATIONS: *Greatest Hits* (Columbia 1983)★★★, *The Best Of Lacy J. Dalton* (Liberty 1993)★★★★.

DANIEL, DALE

b. Kentucky, USA. Naomi Martin, the mother of the 90s country singer Dale Daniel, was the songwriter who wrote Ronnie Milsap's country hit 'Let's Take The Long Way Around The World' and Charley Pride's 'My Eyes Can Only See As Far As You'. Dale Daniel was raised in Nashville and she wrote her first song, 'I Give Up', when 14. In 1991 she became a member of Moe Bandy's band. She launched her solo career with *Luck Of My Own* in 1994 and sang backing vocals on Lisa Brokop's *Every Little Girl's Dream*. Lorrie Morgan has recorded a song written by Dale and her mother, 'Someone To Call Me Darlin''.
● ALBUMS: *Luck Of Our Own* (BNA 1994)★★★.

DANIEL, DAVIS

b. Robert Andrykowski, 1 March 1961, Arlington Heights, Illinois, USA. The 90s country singer Davis Daniel grew up in Nebraska and was inspired after seeing Willie Nelson in concert. He moved to Nashville in 1988 and soon signed a record contract. His first album was produced by Ron Haffkine, the former manager/producer of Dr. Hook. Daniel does not set the charts alight but has recorded some interesting country songs, including 'William And Mary' about an incompatible couple ('She's got a phone in her car and a fax in her trunk/I got a horse that knows the way home if I get drunk') and 'Tyler', a tribute to his baby son, who also features on the record. His albums are marred by their inconsistency.
● ALBUMS: *Fighting Fire With Fire* (Mercury 1991)★★★, *Davis Daniel* (Polydor 1994)★★★, *I Know A Place* (A&M 1996)★★★.

DANIELS, CHARLIE

b. 28 October 1937, Wilmington, North Carolina, USA. Daniels, who wrote 'Carolina (I Love You)' about his youth, was the son of a lumberjack and was raised with a love of bluegrass music. He borrowed a guitar when he was 15 years old and immediately learned to play basic tunes. He then acquired skills on mandolin and fiddle, but had to modify his playing when he lost the tip of his ring finger in an accident in 1955. He formed a bluegrass band, the Misty Mountain Boys, but the group changed its name to the Jaguars following the single 'Jaguar', which they recorded in 1959 (produced by Bob Johnston). Daniels says, 'for nine years we played every honky-tonk dive and low-life joint between Raleigh and Texas'. This enabled him to master a variety of musical styles, but his only national success came in 1964 when he wrote an Elvis Presley b-side 'It Hurts Me', a tender ballad that remains one of his best compositions. In 1968, he followed Bob Johnston's suggestion to accept regular session work in Nashville. He played electric bass on Bob Dylan's *Nashville Skyline* and later appeared on his albums *Self Portrait* and *New Morning*. He also worked with Marty Robbins, Hank Williams Jnr. (on *Family Tradition*) and Ringo Starr (on *Beaucoups Of Blues*), and took Lester Flatt's place alongside Earl Scruggs. He produced an album by Jerry Corbitt, who, in turn, produced one by Daniels, both of which were released in the USA by Capitol Records. The Charlie Daniels Band was formed in 1970 and they started recording for the Kama Sutra label. Although a multi-instrumentalist, Daniels was a limited vocalist, but his voice was well suited to the talking-style 'Uneasy Rider', which

reached the US Top 10 in 1973. He followed it with his anthem for southern rock, 'The South's Gonna Do It'. In 1974, Daniels had members of the Marshall Tucker Band and the Allman Brothers Band join him onstage in Nashville. It was so successful that he decided to make his so-called *Volunteer Jam* an annual event. It has led to some unlikely combinations of artists such as James Brown performing with Roy Acuff, and the stylistic mergers have included Crystal Gayle singing the blues with the Charlie Daniels Band. When he moved to Epic in 1976, there was a concerted effort to turn the band into a major concert attraction, despite the fact that at 6 feet 4 inches tall and weighing 20 stone Daniels was no teenage idol: he hid his face under an oversized cowboy hat. The albums sold well, and in 1979, when recording his *Million Miles Reflections* album, he recalled a 20s poem, 'Mountain Whippoorwill', by Stephen Vincent Benet. The band developed this into 'The Devil Went Down To Georgia', in which Johnny outplays the Devil to win a gold fiddle. Daniels overdubbed his fiddle seven times to create an atmospheric recording that topped the US country charts and reached number 3 in the US pop charts. It was also a UK Top 20 success. In 1980 the band recorded 'In America' for the hostages in Iran, and then in 1982, 'Still In Saigon', about Vietnam. The band were featured on the soundtrack for *Urban Cowboy* and also recorded the theme for Burt Reynolds' film *Stroker Ace*, which featured Tommy Crain's banjo (Daniels' band has been very loyal to the latter, with Taz DiGregorio playing keyboards from the late 60s). In 1986 Daniels appeared in the television movie *Lone Star Kid*, and published a book of short stories, but he still continues touring and playing his southern boogie. In recent years he updated 'The Devil Went Down To Georgia' with Johnny Cash, and he continues in his politically incorrect way - in simple language, he advocates both lynching and redbaiting; not a man to stand next to at the bar. His most recent recordings have been aimed at the white gospel market. *The Door* won a gospel Grammy award in 1995.
● ALBUMS: *Charlie Daniels* (Capitol 1970)★★★, *The John, Grease And Wolfman* (Kama Sutra 1972)★★★, *Honey In The Rock* reissued as *Uneasy Rider* (Kama Sutra 1973)★★★, *Way Down Yonder* reissued as *Whiskey* (Kama Sutra 1974)★★★, *Fire On The Mountain* (Kama Sutra 1974)★★★★, *Nightrider* (Kama Sutra 1975)★★★, *Teach Yourself Rock Guitar, Volume 1* (1976)★★★, *Saddletramp* (Epic 1976)★★★, *High Lonesome* (Epic 1976)★★★★, *Volunteer Jam* (Epic 1976)★★★, *Midnight Wind* (Epic 1977)★★★, *Volunteer Jam 3 & 4* (Epic 1978)★★★, *Million Mile Reflections* (Epic 1979)★★★, *Volunteer Jam VI* (Epic 1980)★★★, *Full Moon* (Epic 1980)★★★★, *Volunteer Jam VII* (Epic 1981)★★★, *Windows* (Epic 1982)★★★, *Me And The Boys* (Epic 1985)★★★, *Powder Keg* (Epic 1987)★★★, *Homesick Heroes* (Epic 1988)★★★, *Simple Man* (Epic 1989)★★★, *Renegade* (Epic 1991)★★★, *America, I Believe In You* (Epic 1993)★★★, *The Door* (Sparrow 1994)★★★★, *Same 'Ol Me* (Capitol 1995)★★★, *Steel Witness* (Sparrow 1996)★★★.
● COMPILATIONS: *The Essential Charlie Daniels* (Kama Sutra 1976)★★★, *A Decade Of Hits* (Epic 1983)★★★, *All-Time Greatest Hits* (Epic 1993)★★★, *Super Hits* (Epic 1994)★★★, *Charlie Daniels, The Roots Remain* 3-CD box set (Legacy 1996)★★★★.

DANIELS, ROLY

b. 1 May c.1945, Jabalpur, India. The country singer Roly Daniels was billed in the 60s as 'Britain's King of the Twist', during the Chubby Checker-inspired dance boom of 1962. He toured the UK with Johnny Burnette and made his first record in 1963, the dubious 'Bella Bella Marie'. Daniels worked with Jim Farley and formed the Green County Showband when he moved to Ireland in 1965. He began to record country singles - 'Throw A Little Lovin' My Way', 'Sunny Tennessee', 'My Wild Mountain Rose' and 'Hello Darlin'', which made the Irish charts - but he was not able to persuade his record label that he should also make country albums. Daniels is now a successful club act, singing middle-of-the-road country in his powerful voice. He was among the first to pick up on Charlie Landsborough's songs by recording 'I Will Love You All My Life' and 'Part Of Me'.
● ALBUMS: *Ol' What's His Name* (Star 1992)★★★, *Pure Magic* (Dawn 1994)★★★.

DARBY AND TARLETON

As a small child, Tarleton (b. John James Rimbert Tarleton, 8 May 1892, Chesterfield County, South Carolina, USA, d. 1973) learned to play banjo and harmonica, but at the age of eight he changed to guitar. He soon took to playing, using a knife blade or bottleneck to fret the strings and became very efficient in the playing of negro blues and Hawaiian music, as well as the old-time songs he learned from his mother. He left home in 1912 and travelled extensively from Texas and California to New York, working in cotton mills and oilfields and on occasions playing as a street musician in Chicago and New York, or touring with medicine shows. In 1923, he became friendly with Frank Ferera, who did much to popularize the Hawaiian guitar in America, and from him learned the use of a steel bar, in lieu of the knife blade. He finally changed to an automobile wrist-pin in the late 20s and used it until his death. In 1926, he formed a partnership with Tom Darby, a guitarist and singer from Columbus, Georgia. Early in 1927, they auditioned for Columbia and in November that year, at their second session, they recorded 'Columbus Stockade Blues' and 'Birmingham Jail'. When offered the choice of a flat fee or royalties for the recordings, they accepted a fee of $75, which proved an ill-chosen decision, since both songs went on to become country standards. Tarleton arranged 'Birmingham Jail' when he was actually in jail, as a result of an involvement in illicit moonshine. Art Satherley was quoted as saying that their version of the song was the greatest hillbilly record that he ever recorded because both, as former convicts, could feel their material so deeply. Between 1927 and 1933, Tarleton recorded about 80 songs for Columbia, Victor or ARC; some were solos and others with Darby. On their duet recordings, Darby (a fine player who picked guitar in a style often described as 'black-derived') mainly sang the lead vocal with Tarleton playing the steel guitar and adding harmony work, which at times included a yodel. During the early 30s, Tarleton toured in the south, and in 1931, when not recording with Darby, he once worked in a cotton mill in Rockingham, South Carolina, with the Dixon Brothers. The Dixons, Dorsey and Howard, learned much from Tarleton's steel and ordinary guitar-playing ability and his influence was evident when they in turn became recording artists. Ironically, Tarleton and Darby were never friends and in 1933, they parted and

Darby returned to farming. Tarleton continued to play and worked with various bands and medicine shows until the mid-40s, when he semi-retired. Around 1963, he was persuaded to return to more active participation and played at several festivals and even recorded an album. Tarleton died in 1973 and it is believed that Darby died in the late 60s. John Morthland commented that 'If any one musician could be said to have laid the groundwork for future generations of steel players from western swing right up to today's pedal steel, it would probably be Tarleton'.
● ALBUMS: *Steel Guitar Rag* (1963)★★★, *Darby And Tarleton* (Old Timey 1973)★★★.
● COMPILATIONS: *Complete Recordings* 3-CD box set (Bear Family 1995)★★★★.

DARLING, DENVER

b. 6 April 1909, Whopock, but grew up in Jewett, Illinois, USA, d. 27 April 1981, Jewett, Illinois, USA. A friend taught him some guitar chords as a boy, and in 1929, he launched his singing career, basically as a singing cowboy (although he never was one) on radio. In the 30s, he sang on radio stations at various places, including Des Moines, Wheeling, Chicago and Pittsburgh, before he settled in New York in 1937. He first played on WOR but later moved to the larger WNEW. He did daily radio shows and played local clubs and worked on occasions with Rosalie Allen. On 6/7 November 1941, he made his first recordings for Decca Records, with a band labelled his Texas Cowhands (Vaughan Horton on guitar, Slim Duncan on fiddle and Eddie Smith on string bass). On 22 December, following America's entry into World War II, he recorded 'Cowards Over Pearl Harbour'. Between February 1942 and May 1945, he made further Decca recordings, some equally patriotic, including the strangely titled 'We're Gonna Have To Slap The Dirty Little Jap And Uncle Sam's The Guy Who Can Do It', 'When Mussolini Laid His Pistol Down' and the plaintive 'Send This Purple Heart To My Sweetheart'. He also made recordings for DeLuxe which, presumably because of his Decca contract, were released under the name of Tex Grande And His Range Riders. He made some more Decca recordings and, in 1947, 12 sides for MGM Records. Between 1941 and 1947, he recorded some 80 sides but it would appear that only one album of 10 DeLuxe tracks has been issued in the USA. However, in the early 90s, a 16-track selection of various label recordings was issued by a German record label. He had married in 1931 and he and his wife Garnett (Tucker) subsequently raised three children. In the late 40s, he was suffering some throat problems and tired of city life, so retired back to his farm in Jewett, Illinois, where he remained until his death.
● ALBUMS: *Songs Of The Trail* (Audio Lab 1958)★★★★, *The Illinois Cowboy* (CowgirlBoy 1992)★★★.

DARRELL, JOHNNY

b. Eddie Ray White, 23 July 1940, Hopewell, Alabama, USA, 7 October 1997, Kennesaw, Georgia, USA. Darrell taught himself the guitar when he was 14 years old and used his talent to entertain troops while in the US army. Darrell, who worked at a Holiday Inn in Nashville in 1964, signed with United Artists as a country performer and had several hits, mostly during the mid-60s. His successes on the US country charts include 'As Long As The Wind Blows', 'The Son Of

Hickory Holler's Tramp' and a number 3, 'With Pen In Hand'. He was the first to record Kenny Rogers' hit 'Ruby, Don't Take Your Love To Town', and his version reached number 9 on the US country charts in 1967 (strangely, Rogers' version only reached number 39). He subsequently recorded for Monument, Capricorn and Gusto. He died in October 1997 having suffered a prolonged spell of diabetes.
● ALBUMS: *As Long As The Wind Blows* (United Artists 1966)★★★, *Ruby, Don't Take Your Love To Town* (United Artists 1967)★★★★, *The Son Of Hickory Holler's Tramp* (United Artists 1968)★★★, *The Country Sound Of Johnny Darrell* (United Artists 1968)★★, *With Pen In Hand* (United Artists 1968)★★, *Why You Been Gone So Long* (United Artists 1969)★★★ *California Stop Over* (United Artists 1970)★★★, *Giant Country* (United Artists 1970)★★★, *Waterglass Full Of Whisky* (1974)★★.
● COMPILATIONS: *More Country Gold* (United Artists 1970)★★★, *Greatest Hits* (Gusto 1979)★★★.

DAVE AND SUGAR

Dave Rowland (b. 26 January 1942, Anaheim, California, USA) was a pop singer and trumpeter in an army band and then became a member of the Stamps Quartet. He therefore toured with Elvis Presley and appears on his records 'My Boy' and 'Help Me'. He worked as part of the Four Guys on Charley Pride's roadshow and then formed a vocal quartet, Wild Oats. He then hit upon the concept of a group comprising a boy with one blonde and one brunette girl, and he called the group Dave and Sugar. They joined Charley Pride's roadshow in 1975. Sugar were Vicki Hackeman (b. Louisville, Kentucky, USA) and Jackie Frantz (b. Sidney, Ohio, USA). Pride co-produced their first country hits, 'Queen Of The Silver Dollar', the chart-topping 'The Door Is Always Open' and 'I'm Knee Deep In Lovin' You'. By 1979 Hackeman, who married Pride's bass guitarist, Ron Baker, and Frantz had been replaced by Melissa Dean and Sue Powell. The group topped the US country charts with 'Tear Time' and 'Golden Tears'. By 1980 the group was known as Dave Rowland and Sugar, although the group did share the lead vocals. Rowland then recorded a solo album for Warner Brothers. He released a single of his tribute to actress Natalie Wood, 'Natalie', but by 1985 he was working as Dave and Sugar again.
● ALBUMS: *Dave And Sugar* (RCA 1976)★★★, *That's The Way Love Should Be* (RCA 1977)★★★, *Tear Time* (RCA 1978)★★, *Stay With Me/Golden Tears* (RCA 1979)★★★, *New York Wine And Tennessee Shine* (RCA 1980)★★★, *Pleasure* (RCA 1981)★★★ *Dave And Sugar - 2* (MCA 1986)★★
Solo: Dave Rowland *Sugar-Free* (Warners 1982)★★.
● COMPILATIONS: *Greatest Hits: Dave And Sugar* (RCA 1982)★★★.

DAVIES, GAIL

b. 1 September 1948, Broken Bow, Oklahoma, USA. Her father was a country musician who, among other things, worked on *Louisiana Hayride* and Davies was fascinated by his jukebox filled with country music. As a performer, she went on the road with her brother Ron, whose songs have since been recorded by Helen Reddy ('Long Hard Climb') and Three Dog Night ('It Ain't Easy'). An album that they made for A&M was never released. Davies married a jazz musician and, for a while, tried to be a jazz singer. When they separated, she moved to the west coast where she worked as a session singer. As a writer, she wrote 'Bucket To The South', a US country hit for Ava Barber in 1978. Her first album, *Gail Davies*, for the Lifesong label in 1978 included her first US country hit, 'No Love Have I', alongside further successes, 'Poison Love' and 'Someone Is Looking For Someone Like You'. She moved to Warner Brothers and became a rarity - a female country performer producing her own records. She had US country hits with 'Blue Heartache', 'I'll Be There (If You Ever Want Me)' and 'Singing The Blues'. At RCA in 1984 she had further success with 'Jagged Edge Of A Broken Heart' and 'Trouble With Love'. She formed Wild Choir in 1986, releasing a self-titled album for RCA. In the late 80s she moved to Liberty Records to become country music's first female staff producer. Davies has had many run-ins with the mostly male musical establishment in Nashville, and in 1995 she promoted and released her own album *Eclectic*. The tracks are as good as her previous hit records, but she has been denied radio-play by many US stations. She will continue her one-woman crusade, no doubt, supported by her husband Rob Price, the bass player with the UK Stu Page Band. She is not to be confused with Gail Davies who toured with Gene Autry's roadshow and was featured in the television series *Annie Oakley*.
● ALBUMS: *Gail Davies* (Lifesong 1978)★★★, *The Game* (Warners 1980)★★★, *I'll Be There* (Warners 1980)★★★★, *Givin' Herself Away* (Warners 1982)★★★, *What Can I Say* (Warners 1983)★★★, *Where Is A Woman To Go* (RCA 1984)★★★★, *Pretty Words* (MCA 1989)★★★, *The Other Side Of Love* (Capitol 1990)★★★, *Eclectic* (Little Chickadee 1995)★★★.
● COMPILATIONS: *Best Of* (Liberty 1991)★★★★, *Greatest Hits* (Little Chickadee 1997)★★★★.

DAVIS, DANNY, AND THE NASHVILLE BRASS

b. George Nowlan, 29 April 1925, Randolph, Massachusetts, USA. Davis, who calls himself a 'Yankee Irishman', bought his trumpet with his earnings from a delivery round and he played in high school bands. At the age of 14 he was performing with the Massachusetts Symphony Orchestra. From the age of 17, he was guesting with some of the best swing bands including Gene Krupa and Bob Crosby and he recorded 'Trumpet Cha Cha'. By 1958 he was working as a record producer and he produced several of Connie Francis's hit singles. He also had success with Herman's Hermits and Johnny Tillotson. In 1965, he began working with Chet Atkins at RCA and he formed the Nashville Brass, which added brass to a pop-country rhythm section: it was as though Herb Alpert was recording country music. Although some country fans were reluctant to accept them, their albums sold well and they had US country hits including 'Wabash Cannonball' and 'Columbus Stockade Blues'. For six consecutive years, Danny Davis And The Nashville Brass were voted the Instrumental Band Of The Year at the Country Music Association's awards, and they also won a Grammy in 1969 for their *More Nashville Sounds* album. In 1980 a curious album was released in which Davis added the Nashville Brass to some existing Willie Nelson tracks. The versions of 'Night Life' and 'Funny How Time Slips Away' both made the US country charts.
● ALBUMS: *That Happy Nashville Sound* (RCA

1967)★★★★, *More Nashville Sounds* (RCA 1969)★★★★, *Movin' On* (RCA 1969)★★★, *You Ain't Heard Nothin' Yet* (RCA 1970)★★★, *Down Homers* (RCA 1970)★★★, *Christmas* (RCA 1970)★★, *Hank Locklin, Danny Davis & The Nashville Brass* (RCA 1970)★★★, *Nashville Brass Turns To Gold* (RCA 1971)★★, *Somethin' Else* (RCA 1971)★★★, *Super Country* (RCA 1971)★★, *Live-In Person* (RCA 1972)★★, *Turn On Some Happy* (RCA 1972)★★★, *Travelin'* (RCA 1973)★★★, *Caribbean Cruise* (RCA 1973)★★★, *In Bluegrass Country* (RCA 1974)★★★, *Latest & Greatest* (RCA 1974)★★★, *Orange Blossom Special* (RCA 1974)★★★, *Dream Country* (RCA 1975)★★★, *Country Gold* (RCA 1975)★★★, *Super Songs* (RCA 1976)★★★, *Texas* (RCA 1976)★★★, *How I Love Them Ol' Songs* (RCA 1978)★★★, *Cookin' Country* (RCA 1978)★★★, *Great Songs Of The Big Band Era* (RCA 1979)★★★★, *Danny Davis, Willie Nelson & The Nashville Brass* (1980)★★★, *Cotton Eyed Joe* (1981)★★★, *Don't You Ever Get Tired Of Hurtin' Me* (1984)★★★.

DAVIS, JIMMIE

b. James Houston Davis, 11 September 1902, on a farm at Beech Springs, near Quitman, Jackson Parish, Louisiana, USA. One of 11 children in a sharecropping family, Davis progressed through local schools and in the early 20s, he gained a BA at Louisiana's Pineville College. Here he sang in the College Glee Club and in a group known as the Tiger Four. He returned to Beech Springs, where he became the first high school graduate ever to return to the school as a teacher. After school, he worked in the fields and busked on street corners until he had raised enough money to allow him to study for his master's degree at the State University in Baton Rouge. In the late 20s, he taught history and social science at Dodd College in Shreveport, but left to become the clerk at Shreveport Court. He also began to make regular appearances on KWKH, where he came to the attention of RCA-Victor. Between 1929 and 1933, he recorded almost 70 songs for the label. The material ranged from songs that clearly showed the influence of Jimmie Rodgers and ballads, to songs of a very risqué nature which, in later years, he tended to forget that he ever recorded. (Noted author John Morthland later emphatically wrote, 'Davis launched his career as a Jimmie Rodgers imitator with the dirtiest batch of songs any one person had ever recorded in country music', and added, 'Many of his early sides were *double-entendre* songs of unbridled carnality'.) These included such tracks as 'Organ Grinder Blues', 'Tom Cat And Pussy Blues' and 'She's A Hum Dum Dinger (From Dingersville)'. He seemingly has the distinction of being only the second country singer (after Rodgers) to record with a coloured musician when, in 1932, he recorded with blues singer and steel guitarist Oscar Woods. In September 1934, he made his first recordings for Decca, the first number recorded being his now standard 'Nobody's Darling But Mine'. This became his first hit and led to his recording several answer versions to it (Frank Ifield had a UK number 4 pop hit with his version of the song in 1963). A few of the old risqué songs crept in at first, but he soon abandoned both these and the Rodgers influence to concentrate on more middle-of-the-road material. In 1938, he recorded his and Floyd Tillman's 'It Makes No Difference Now' (a major pop hit for Bing Crosby in 1941) and in 1939, he co-wrote the internationally famous 'You Are My Sunshine', with his steel guitarist

Charles Mitchell. The song has been recorded by so many artists over the years that it is reputed that its copyright is the most valuable in country music. Among the artists finding success with their recordings of it, apart from Davis himself, were Bob Atcher, Gene Autry and Bing Crosby. During the 30s, Davis made a great many recordings both as a solo artist, or with others, including Brown's Musical Brownies. In 1938, Davis was made Shreveport's Commissioner Of Public Safety and in 1942, he was promoted to State Public Service Commissioner. He had Top 5 US country chart hits in the 40s with 'Is It Too Late Now', 'There's A Chill On The Hill Tonight', 'Grievin' My Heart Out Over You' and 'Bang Bang' and in 1945, he enjoyed a country number 1 with 'There's A New Moon Over My Shoulder'. In 1944, standing as a Democrat, he was elected Governor of Louisiana, in spite of his opponents raising the subject of his early RCA recordings. During the 40s, he appeared in films, including *Strictly In The Grove* (1942) (in which he sang 'You Are My Sunshine'), *Frontier Fury* (1943) and *Louisiana* (1947). In 1948, he returned to his musical career and began to specialize more in gospel music than in straight country songs. He appeared in his last film, *Square Dance Katy*, in 1950, and during the 50s he toured, making appearances at many religious events; in 1957, he was voted the Best Male Sacred Singer. He was elected to a second term as State Governor in 1960 and again the early songs were cited by the opposition. 'Where The Old Red River Flows' gave him a Top 20 country hit in 1962 and went on to become yet another very popular and much recorded song. In 1971, he was unsuccessful in his attempt to seek a third spell as Governor and instead concentrated on his gospel music. The many songs that he had written saw him elected to the Nashville Songwriters' International Hall Of Fame in 1971 and the following year he was inducted into the Country Music Hall Of Fame. In 1973, he left Decca (by then MCA) and recorded for the Canaan label, even recording a gospel version of his classic, which he called 'Christ Is My Sunshine'. During the 70s and up to the mid-80s, he continued to make recordings of gospel music and appearances at some religious venues until a heart attack in October 1987 caused him to restrict his activities. Some of his old RCA tracks were reissued in 1988 by the German Bear Family label, no doubt without Davis's blessing.

● ALBUMS: *Near The Cross* (Decca 1955)★★★, with Anita Kerr Singers *Hymn Time* (Decca 1957)★★★, *The Door Is Always Open* (Decca 1958)★★★, *Hail Him With A Song* (Decca 1958)★★★, *You Are My Sunshine* (Decca 1959)★★★, *Someone To Care* (Decca 1960)★★★, *No One Stands Alone* (Decca 1960)★★★, *Suppertime* (Decca 1960)★★★★, with Anita Kerr Singers *Sweet Hour Of Prayer* (Decca 1961)★★★, *Someone Watching Over You* (Decca 1961)★★★, *Songs Of Faith* (Decca 1962)★★★, *How Great Thou Art* (Decca 1962)★★★, *Beyond The Shadows* (Decca 1963)★★★, *Highway To Heaven* (Decca 1964)★★★, *Sings* (Decca 1964)★★★, *It's Christmas Time Again* (Decca 1964)★★, *Still I Believe* (Decca 1965)★★★, *At The Crossing* (Decca 1965)★★★, *Gospel Hour* (Decca 1966)★★★, *My Altar* (Decca 1966)★★★, *His Marvellous Grace* (Decca 1967)★★, *Going Home For Christmas* (Decca 1967)★★, *Singing The Gospel* (Decca 1968)★★★, *Let Me Walk With Jesus* (Decca 1969)★★★, *In My Father's House* (Decca 1969)★★★, *Amazing Grace* (Decca 1969)★★★, *Country Side*

Of Jimmie Davis (Decca 1969)★★★, *Songs Of Consolation* (Decca 1970)★★★, *Old Baptizing Creek* (Decca 1971)★★★, *What A Happy Day* (Decca 1972)★★★, *Memories Coming Home* (Decca 1972)★★★, *God's Last Altar Call* (1973)★★★, with Anita Kerr Singers *No One Stands Alone* (1973)★★★, *Souvenirs Of Yesterday* (1974)★★★, *Let Me Be There* (1974)★★★, *Christ Is My Sunshine* (Canaan 1974)★★★, *Living By Faith* (Canaan 1975)★★★, *Sunshine* (Canaan 1975)★★★, *Live* (1976)★★★, *Heaven's National Anthem* (1981)★★★, *The Last Walk* (1985)★★★.
● COMPILATIONS: *Golden Hits Volume 1* (1978)★★★★, *Golden Hits Volume 2* (1979)★★★, *Greatest Hits Volume 1* (1981)★★★★, *Barnyard Stomp* (Bear Family 1984)★★★, *Sounds Like Jimmie Rodgers* (ACM 1985)★★★, *Rockin' Blues* (Bear Family 1988)★★★★, *Country Music Hall Of Fame* (MCA 1991)★★★.
● FURTHER READING: *You Are My Sunshine: The Jimmie Davis Story*, Gus Weill.

DAVIS, LINDA

b. 26 November 1962, Dodson, Texas, USA. The 90s country singer Linda Davis made her debut at the age of six at a local jamboree and recorded her first album before winning the *Louisiana Hayride* Star Search when she was 15. Guitarist Phil Baugh encouraged her to pursue a career in music and partnered her with Skip Eaton as the duo Skip And Linda. The singles they recorded together, however, were not major hits, the most successful being the strangely titled 'If You Could See Through My Eyes'. She earned better money by singing commercials and eventually signed to Liberty Records and recorded two albums of dramatic songs, very much in the style of Reba McEntire. McEntire asked her to record a duet with her, 'Does He Love You'. The duo also stormed the CMA awards show. *Shoot For The Moon* features songs about alcoholism, absent fathers and crumbling relationships, and includes a song about sexual harassment at work, 'Company Time'. In 1996 both the album *Some Things Are Meant To Be* and the title track, which was released as a single, fared well in the US country charts.
● ALBUMS: *In A Different Light* (Liberty 1991)★★★, *Linda Davis* (Liberty 1992)★★★, *Shoot For The Moon* (Arista 1994)★★★★, *Some Things Are Meant To Be* (Arista 1996)★★★.

DAVIS, MAC

b. Mac Scott Davis, 21 January 1942, Lubbock, Texas, USA. Davis grew up with a love of country music but turned to rock 'n' roll in 1955 when he saw Elvis Presley and Buddy Holly on the same show, an event referred to in his 1980 song 'Texas In My Rear View Mirror'. Davis, who was already writing songs, learned the guitar and moved to Atlanta, Georgia, where he 'majored in beer and rock 'n' roll'. Davis married when he was 20 and his son, Scotty, became the subject of several songs including 'Watching Scotty Grow', recorded by Bobby Goldsboro and Anthony Newley. In the early 60s Davis took administrative jobs with Vee Jay and Liberty Records and made several unsuccessful records, including a revival of the Drifters' 'Honey Love'; much of this early work was collected in a 1984 compilation, inaccurately called *20 Golden Songs*. A parody of Bob Dylan, 'I Protest', was produced by Joe South. Davis wrote 'The Phantom Strikes Again', which was recorded by Sam The

Sham And The Pharaohs, and, in 1967, he had his first chart success when Lou Rawls recorded 'You're Good For Me'. 'Friend, Lover, Woman, Wife' and 'Daddy's Little Man' were both recorded by O.C. Smith. Davis wrote 'Memories' and 'Nothingsville' for Elvis Presley's 1968 comeback television special, and Presley's renaissance continued with Davis's social commentary 'In The Ghetto'. Presley also recorded 'Don't Cry, Daddy', inspired by Scotty telling Davis not to be upset by television footage of the Vietnam war, 'Clean Up Your Own Back Yard', 'Charro' and 'A Little Less Conversation'. 'Something's Burning' was a hit for Kenny Rogers And The First Edition, while Gallery made the US charts with the much-recorded 'I Believe In Music'. Davis wrote the songs for the Glen Campbell film *Norwood*, including 'Everything A Man Could Ever Need'. Davis's second marriage was to 18-year-old Sarah Barg in 1971. His first album, named after Glen Campbell's description of him, *Song Painter*, was full of good material but his voice was limited and the album was bathed in strings. Davis topped the US charts in 1972 with the pleasant but inconsequential 'Baby, Don't Get Hooked On Me', its success ironically being due to the publicity created by angry feminists. Davis says, 'The record sounded arrogant but I was really saying, "don't get involved with me because I don't deserve it."' Davis also had US success with 'One Hell Of A Woman', 'Stop And Smell The Roses', 'Rock 'n' Roll (I Gave You The Best Years Of My Life)' and 'Forever Lovers'. *Rolling Stone*, disliking his pop-country hits, claimed that Davis had 'done more to set back the cause of popular music in the 70s than any other figure'. The curly-haired golfer often wrote of his love for his wife but in 1975 she left him for a short marriage to Glen Campbell. Davis's own career has included playing Las Vegas showrooms and parts in the films *North Dallas 40*, *Cheaper To Keep Her* and *The Sting II*. 'You're My Bestest Friend', an obvious nod to Don Williams' success, was a US country hit in 1981 and 'I Never Made Love (Till I Made Love To You)' was on the US country charts for six months in 1985. His witty 'It's Hard To Be Humble' has become Max Bygraves' closing number. Davis's UK success has been limited but even if he has no further hits, he is assured of work in Las Vegas showrooms. He chose to retire in 1989 but after intensive treatment for alcoholism he eventually resumed his career with a new album in 1994.
● ALBUMS: *Song Painter* (Columbia 1971)★★, *I Believe In Music* (Columbia 1972)★★, *Baby, Don't Get Hooked On Me* (Columbia 1972)★★★, *Mac Davis* (Columbia 1973)★★★, *Stop And Smell The Roses* (Columbia 1974)★★, *All The Love In The World* (Columbia 1974)★★, *Burning Thing* (Columbia 1975)★★, *Forever Lovers* (Columbia 1976)★★, *Thunder In The Afternoon* (Columbia 1977)★★★, *Fantasy* (1978)★★, *It's Hard To Be Humble* (Casablanca 1980)★★, *Texas In My Rear View Mirror* (Casablanca 1980)★★, *Midnight Crazy* (Casablanca 1981)★★, *Forty '82* (1982)★★, *Soft Talk* (Casablanca 1984)★★, *Who's Loving You?* (1984)★★, *Till I Made It With You* (MCA 1985)★★, *Will Write Songs For Food* (Columbia 1994)★★.
● COMPILATIONS: *Greatest Hits* (Columbia 1979)★★★, *Very Best & More . . .* (Casablanca 1984)★★★, *20 Golden Songs* (Astan 1984)★★★.
● FILMS: *Cheaper To Keep Her* (1980), *The Sting II* (1983).

DAVIS, SKEETER

b. Mary Frances Penick, 30 December 1931, Dry Ridge, Kentucky, USA. Penick was raised on a farm and as a child knew that she wanted to be a country singer. She acquired the nickname of 'Skeeter' (a local term for a mosquito) from her grandfather because she was always active and buzzing around like the insect. In her mid-teens, she formed a duo with schoolfriend Betty Jack Davis (b. 3 March 1932, Corbin Kentucky, USA, d. August 1953) and together they began to sing in the Lexington area. In 1949, they appeared on local radio WLAX and later were featured on radio and television in Detroit, Cincinnati, and eventually on the WWVA *Wheeling Jamboree* in West Virginia. They first recorded for Fortune in 1952 but the following year they successfully auditioned for RCA Records and their recording of 'I Forgot More Than You'll Ever Know' quickly became a number 1 US country and number 18 US pop hit. On 23 August 1953, the singers' car was involved in a collision with another vehicle, resulting in the death of Betty Jack and leaving Skeeter critically injured. It was over a year before Skeeter recovered physically and mentally from the crash, and it was only with great difficulty that she was persuaded to resume her career. Eventually she briefly teamed up with Betty Jack's sister, Georgia Davis, and returned to singing. In 1955, she went solo and for a time worked with RCA's touring Caravan Of Stars as well as with Eddy Arnold and Elvis Presley. Her recording career, under the guidance of Chet Atkins, progressed and she gained her first solo US country chart hit in 1958 with 'Lost To A Geisha Girl', the female answer to the Hank Locklin hit 'Geisha Girl'. The following year, her co-written song 'Set Him Free' became her first country Top 10 hit. She fulfilled one of her greatest ambitions in 1959, when she moved to Nashville and became a regular member of the *Grand Ole Opry*. During the 60s, she became one of RCA's most successful country artists, registering 26 US country hits, 12 of them achieving crossover US pop chart success. The most popular included another 'answer' song in 'I Can't Help You, I'm Falling Too' (the reply to Hank Locklin's 'Please Help Me I'm Falling'), and 'My Last Date'. She co-wrote the latter with Boudleaux Bryant and pianist Floyd Cramer, whose instrumental version had been a million-seller in 1960. In 1963, she achieved a million-selling record herself with 'The End Of The World', which peaked at number 2 in both the US country and pop charts. It also gave her her only UK pop chart entry, reaching number 18 in a 13-week chart life in 1963 (the song also became a UK pop hit for Sonia in 1990). Davis also had successful recordings with Bobby Bare ('A Dear John Letter') and Don Bowman (a novelty number, 'For Loving You'). Davis toured extensively in the 60s and 70s, not only throughout the USA and Canada but also to Europe and the Far East, where she is very popular. She played all the major US television network shows, including regular appearances with Duke Ellington and also appeared on a Rolling Stones tour. Her recording career slowed down in the 70s but her hits included 'I'm A Lover (Not A Fighter)', 'Bus Fare To Kentucky' and 'One Tin Soldier'. She also made the charts with Bobby Bare on 'Your Husband, My Wife' and with George Hamilton IV on 'Let's Get Together' (a US pop hit for the Youngbloods in 1969). In 1973, she had a minor hit with the Bee Gees' 'Don't Forget To Remember' and a Top 20 country and minor pop hit with 'I Can't Believe That It's All

Over'. It was to prove a slightly prophetic title, since only two more chart hits followed, the last being 'I Love Us' on Mercury in 1976 (Davis having left RCA two years earlier). She has recorded several tribute albums, including one to Buddy Holly, which featured Waylon Jennings on guitar and also one to her friend Dolly Parton. She also re-recorded 'May You Never Be Alone', a Davis Sisters success, with NRBQ in 1985. From 1960-64, she was married to well-known WSM radio and television personality Ralph Emery, but she subsequently received heavy criticism in Emery's autobiography. She later married Joey Spampinato of NRBQ. She became something of a rebel after the break-up of her second marriage. She settled in a colonial-style mansion set in several hundred acres in Brentwood, Tennessee, and surrounded herself with dogs, Siamese cats, a dove in a gilded cage and even an ocelot named Fred. Her extreme religious beliefs saw her refusing to appear in places that sold intoxicating drinks. She even stopped growing tobacco on her farm, giving the reason for both actions: 'As a Christian, I think it's harmful to my body'. In 1973, her strong criticisms of the Nashville Police Department during her act at the *Opry* caused her to be dropped from the roster. She was later reinstated and still usually sings religious or gospel songs on her regular appearances.

● ALBUMS: as the Davis Sisters: *Hits* (Fortune 1952)★★, *Jealous Love* (Fortune 1952)★★★; Skeeter Davis *I'll Sing You A Song And Harmonize Too* (RCA Victor 1960)★★, *Here's The Answer* (RCA Victor 1961)★★★, *The End Of The World* (RCA Victor 1962)★★★★, with Porter Wagoner *Porter Wagoner And Skeeter Davis Sing Duets* (RCA Victor 1962)★★, *Cloudy With Occasional Tears* (RCA Victor 1963)★★★, *I Forgot More Than You'll Ever Know* (RCA Victor 1964)★★★, *Let Me Get Close To You* reissued as *Easy To Love* (RCA Victor 1964)★★★, *Authentic Southern Style Gospel* (RCA Victor 1964)★★, *Blueberry Hill (& Other Favorites)* (RCA Victor 1965)★★★, *Sings Standards* (RCA Victor 1965)★★★, *Written By The Stars* (RCA Victor 1965)★★★, with Bobby Bare *Tunes For Two* (RCA Victor 1965)★★★, *My Heart's In The Country* (RCA Victor 1966)★★★, *Singing In The Summer Sun* (RCA Victor 1966)★★★, *Hand In Hand With Jesus* (RCA Victor 1967)★★, *What Does It Take (To Keep A Man Like You Satisfied)* (RCA Victor 1967)★★★, *Skeeter Davis Sings Buddy Holly* (RCA Victor 1967)★★, *Why So Lonely* (RCA Victor 1968)★★★, *I Love Flatt & Scruggs* (RCA Victor 1968)★★, with Don Bowman *Funny Folk Flops* (RCA Victor 1968)★★, *The Closest Thing To Love* (RCA Victor 1969)★★★, *Mary Frances* (RCA Victor 1969)★★★, *A Place In The Country* (RCA Victor 1970)★★, *It's Hard To Be A Woman* (RCA Victor 1970)★★★, with Bare *Your Husband, My Wife* reissued as *More Tunes For Two* (RCA Victor 1970)★★★, with George Hamilton IV *Down Home In The Country* (RCA Victor 1970)★★★, *Skeeter* (RCA Victor 1971)★★★, *Love Takes A Lot Of My Time* (RCA Victor 1971)★★★, *Foggy Mountain Top* (RCA Victor 1971)★★, *Sings Dolly* (RCA Victor 1972)★★★, *Bring It On Home* (RCA Victor 1972)★★★, *I Can't Believe That It's All Over* (RCA Victor 1973)★★★, *The Hillbilly Singer* (RCA Victor 1973)★★★, *He Wakes Me With A Kiss Every Morning* (RCA Victor 1974)★★★, *Heart Strings* (Tudor 1983)★★★, with NRBQ *She Sings, They Play* (Rounder 1985)★★★.

● COMPILATIONS: the Davis Sisters *Memories* 2-CD set (Bear Family 1993)★★★★, *The Best Of Skeeter Davis* (RCA Victor 1965)★★★, *The Best Of Skeeter Davis Volume 2* (RCA

Victor 1973)★★★, *20 Of The Best: Skeeter Davis* (RCA 1985)★★★, *The Essential Skeeter Davis* (RCA 1995)★★★★.
● FURTHER READING: *Bus Fare To Kentucky: The Autobiography Of Skeeter Davis*, Skeeter Davis.

DAWSON, SMOKY

b. Herbert Charles Dawson, 19 March 1913, Collingwood, near Melbourne, Victoria, Australia. The family relocated to Warrnambool when he was a baby and his mother died when he was five years old. A pioneer of Australian country music, his father was a music hall baritone, who had studied to be a chemist and then a doctor, before becoming an invalid as a result of injuries received at Gallipoli. In 1926, Dawson left school to work to help support the family and also began singing, yodelling and playing concertina and harmonica at local dances. He grew up among relatives of noted Australian bushranger Ned Kelly and during this time, he learned many of the Irish-Australian ballads that he later popularized. By 1932, playing steel guitar and dobro, he formed a duo with his brother Ted (bass, guitar). They sang and played to crowds outside Melbourne theatres and broadcast on 3JR. By 1935, they had moved to the bigger 3KZ, where they played as both the Coral Island Boys and because of the then-current interest in Hawaiian music, the South Sea Island Boys. It is claimed that Dawson featured the first electric steel guitar used in Australia. By 1937, with Peggy Brooks as lead singer and other musicians, the *Smoky Dawson Show* attracted sponsorship from Pepsodent and became the first live country show on Australian radio. Adding more hillbilly music to his repertoire, Dawson progressed to play theatre and rodeo venues. He made his first recordings for Columbia in August 1941, including his noted 'The Range In The Western Sky', which was recorded years later by noted yodeller Mary Schneider. He recorded six further songs in 1942 but in 1943, army service interrupted his recording career for two years. Initially, he joined the Medical Corps but later transferred to the Entertainment Unit and was serving in Borneo when the war ended. Back in civilian life, he took to scriptwriting and producing his radio shows. He toured in partnership with Gill Brothers Rodeo and even incorporated knife and battle-axe throwing at human targets and using a stock whip as part of his act. In 1948, he recorded six songs including his famous 'My Heart Is Where The Roper Flows Tonight'. He wrote a series of songs and stories based on his own experiences for *Inlander*, a new show broadcast by ABC. The star of the show was the noted serious singer Peter Dawson. They were not related but became great friends. Dawson always referred to Smoky as his 'illustrious nephew', while Smoky called him his 'great Uncle Snakeskin Pete'. The year 1951 was an important one for Dawson. He came to England, where BBC Television covered his act live (including knife-throwing) at the Festival of Britain. He also toured in the USA (with a kangaroo called Zip), on behalf of the Australian government and still found time to record 18 songs, including his popular versions of 'The Man From Never Never' and 'The Wild Colonial Boy'. He returned to Nashville in 1952, where he appeared with Ernest Tubb and after signing with Acuff-Rose, he recorded for the Hickory label. He worked on the promotion of the film *Kangaroo* and appeared on Broadway (with his whip and knife act) in *Kiss Me Kate*. Lew Grade wanted him to play in *Paint Your Wagon* but he was unable to take the part, being

under contract for a national radio series about life in the outback. *The Adventures Of Smoky Dawson* (accompanied by his wonder horse Flash) was sponsored by Kellogg's and became so much a national institution that it ran for 10 years, only ending in 1962, not because of public reaction but simply because the actors had had enough. Flash, who in Australia enjoyed the popularity of Roy Rogers' horse, Trigger, in the USA, died in 1982, aged 35. Between 1956 and 1974, he and Dawson appeared together at countless venues, including leading the annual Sydney Spring Festival parade. During the 50s, he recorded nine more sessions and in 1957, established the Smoky Dawson Ranch, which for over 20 years occupied most of his time, until he leased it to a company. This venue hosted country music shows and other entertainments, an amusement park and a stunt school and provided a holiday camp. He also acted as a technical advisor to films and television shows as well as supplying stock. This limited his touring, and he was 60 when he eventually recorded again in 1973. Between 1973 and 1979, he made daily appearances on Channel 9 television and resumed his touring. In 1978, he joined two other Australian pioneers of country music Tex Morton and Buddy Williams, when he became the third artist to be elected to the newly created Country Music Roll Of Renown (Australia's equivalent to Nashville's Country Music Hall of Fame). In 1978, he returned to Nashville to receive a special award for services to country music and returned the following year to star on the *All Time Greats Show* and receive a pioneer award from the American Country Music Association. He has lectured on Australian life and performed at numerous American colleges and schools. In Australia, he and Flash have been immortalized in wax in Tamworth's Gallery of Stars and in 1983, he was awarded an MBE in the New Year's Honours List. Although in his early days he sang many western songs, and throughout his career has tended to portray a cowboy image, he has maintained an undying love of his native land, and his recordings show that he has actually recorded very few songs that were not Australiana.
● ALBUMS: *Bushranger Ballads* (EMI 1961)★★★★, *The Smoky Dawson Story* (Festival 1962)★★★, *Back At The Ranch* (EMI 1973)★★★, *Smoky - Western Favourites* (Dyna House 1975)★★★, *Ya Darn Right It's Country* (RCA 1979)★★★, *Once In A Lifetime* (Sundown 1983)★★★, *Land Where I Was Born* 40s-50s recordings (EMI 1983)★★★★, *I'll Paint You A Song* (Powderworks 1984)★★★.
● FURTHER READING: *Smoky Dawson, A Life*, Smoky Dawson.

DAY, CURTIS

b. 1971, Beaumont, Texas, USA. Day was unsure which career he would follow; at one stage he wanted to be a footballer and then he studied computer technology at university. His grandmother encouraged him to form a band and became his biggest supporter, but she died before he found success. Curtis Day is yet another good-looking American country singer. He has been marketed to appeal to CMT viewers but it is doubtful whether he has the talent to sustain a long career. As a review of Curtis Day in *Country Music People* said, 'His vocal presence is non-existent, at times he sounds horribly flat, and at other times he makes some quite horrible noises. Not once does he exhibit any feeling.'
● ALBUMS: *Curtis Day* (Asylum 1996)★★.

DAY, JIMMY

b. James Clayton Day, 9 January 1934, Tuscaloosa, Alabama, USA. Day began to play guitar as a child but, in 1949, after seeing Shot Jackson playing a steel guitar on television, he was fascinated by the instrument (Jackson became his friend and greatly influenced his playing). By 1951, he was playing steel guitar for Webb Pierce on the *Louisiana Hayride* on KWKH Shreveport. He made his first recording when he played on Pierce's 1952 number 1, 'That Heart Belongs To Me'. At KWKH, he worked with Red Sovine and Hank Williams and as a session musician, he played on many of Jim Reeves' Abbott and Fabor recordings. In 1953, he played on Mitchell Torok's hit 'Caribbean'. During 1954, he worked with Lefty Frizzell and on occasions with Elvis Presley, and with his friend Floyd Cramer, he organized the KWKH staff band. He relocated to Nashville in 1955, because he said the *Hayride* had 'too much rock 'n' roll', and that year played on Ray Price's hit 'Crazy Arms'. In the early 60s, he, Shot Jackson and Buddy Emmons were responsible for the manufacture of Sho-Bud pedal steel guitars. From 1958, through to the mid-60s, he played on countless sessions and worked with Ernest Tubb, Webb Pierce, Ray Price, Jim Reeves, George Jones (he played on Jones's hit 'The Race Is On'), Willie Nelson and Ferlin Husky. Between 1966 and 1973, Day mainly worked with Willie Nelson or Little Jimmy Dickens. In the 70s, Day spent a few years playing in Texas before returning to Nashville where he played the *Grand Ole Opry* and also worked with Charlie Louvin. He finally returned to Texas in 1978, where he continued to play in various bands and with different artists, including Nelson and Johnny Bush, as well as doing session work and at one time fronting his own Texas Tunesmiths. He has appeared in Europe several times and, in 1991, he toured Korea with Skeeter Davis. He was elected to the International Steel Guitar Hall Of Fame in 1982.

● ALBUMS: *Golden Steel Guitar Hits* (Phillips 1962)★★, *Steel And Strings* (Phillips 1963)★★★, *All These Years* UK release (Checkmate 1977)★★, *Jimmy Day & His Buddies Salute Don Helms* (Texas Musik 70s)★★.
● COMPILATIONS: *Jimmy Day* (Bear Family 1992)★★★.

DEAN, BILLY

b. 2 April 1962, Quincy, Florida, USA. Dean was raised in a farming community and played in his father's part-time country band. He accumulated many influences, including James Taylor and Dan Fogelberg, and he sang 'My Way' at his graduation ceremony. He won the Wrangler Star Search competition and settled in Nashville. He was given a publishing contract by former pop star Jimmy Gilmer, and Dean had his first hits with 'Only Here For A Little While', on which he sounded like one of his heroes, Larry Gatlin, and then his own song, 'Somewhere In My Broken Heart', which had previously been an album track for Randy Travis. He was best known for 'Billy The Kid' from his second album and his duet of 'Something Up My Sleeve' with Suzy Bogguss. He helped David Gates return to record-making and they both co-wrote and recorded 'I Can't Find The Words To Say Goodbye'. After taking a year off from his career to spend time with his new baby he returned in 1996, fully recharged with his most successful album to date, *It's What I Do*.

● ALBUMS: *Young Man* (Liberty 1991)★★★, *Billy Dean* (Liberty 1992)★★★, *Fire In The Dark* (Liberty 1993)★★, *Men'll Be Boys* (Liberty 1994)★★, *It's What I Do* (Capitol 1996)★★★.
● COMPILATIONS: *Greatest Hits* (Liberty 1994)★★★.

DEAN, EDDIE

b. Edgar Dean Glosup, 9 July 1907, Posey, Texas, USA. Dean first worked with his elder brother Jimmy on the *WLS National Barn Dance* in Chicago in the early 30s, before moving to Los Angeles in 1937. He subsequently appeared in films with Ken Maynard and Gene Autry and from 1946-48, he had his own film series for which he also wrote most of the title songs. A fine guitarist and singer, he first made the US country charts in 1948 with his song 'One Has My Name, The Other Has My Heart' but he also had a Top 10 hit, in 1955, with his cleverly compiled 'I Dreamed Of A Hillbilly Heaven', which became a pop hit for Tex Ritter in 1961. In 1993 he was inducted into the Cowboy Hall Of Fame.

● ALBUMS: *Greatest Westerns* (Sage & Sand 1956)★★★, *Hi-Country* (Sage & Sand 1957)★★★★, *Sings Country & Western* (50s)★★★, *Favorites Of Eddie Dean* (King 1961)★★★, *Hillbilly Heaven* (Sage & Sand 1961)★★★, *The Golden Cowboy* (Crown 1967)★★★, *Little Green Apples* (Crown 1968)★★★, *Sings* (1960s)★★★, *Tribute To Hank Williams* (Design 1970)★★★, *Sincerely Eddie Dean* (1974)★★★, *A Cowboy Sings Country* (1980)★★.
● COMPILATIONS: *Dean Of The West* (WFC 1976)★★★, *I Dreamed Of A Hillbilly Heaven* (Castle 1981)★★★.

DEAN, JIMMY

b. Seth Ward, 10 August 1928, near Plainview, Texas, USA. Dean's mother, who was the family's only provider, ran a barber shop and as a boy, he picked cotton and worked on local farms. His mother taught him to play the piano when he was 10 years old and he taught himself guitar, accordion and harmonica as soon as he had access to the instruments. At 16, he began to study engineering but then joined the Merchant Marines for two years, after which he enlisted in the Air Force. It was during his service that Dean first became an entertainer when, with a band called the Tennessee Haymakers, he played local clubs and honky-tonks near his base. He left the service in 1948 and for the next few years tried to develop his musical career. In 1952, with a new band called the Texas Wildcats, he toured US Army bases in the Caribbean, before finding work on WARL Arlington, Virginia, and WTOP-TV Washington. He first recorded for Four Star the same year and early in 1953, he gained his first US country Top 10 hit with 'Bumming Around'. He had a show called *Town And Country Jamboree* on WMAL-TV Washington in 1955 and due to its popularity and some syndication, CBS offered him his own networked programme. The *Jimmy Dean Show* ran from 1957 until 1958 but when it lost its sponsor and a proposed New York afternoon network series failed to materialize, Dean decided to abandon television. He continued to tour, signed to Columbia and in 1961, wrote and recorded a number called 'Big Bad John'. The song became a million-seller and a number 1 record in both the US country and pop charts. It also became a UK hit, reaching number 2 in the UK pop charts the same year. The song also was voted the 'Best Country and Western Recording of 1961'. Surprisingly, it was the first song that Dean had ever written. Over the years there have been several parodies of 'Big Bad John' including those by Marvin Rainwater ('Tough Top Cat'), Des O'Connor ('Thin Chow Mein') and the Country Gentlemen ('Big Bruce'). In 1962, five further US chart hits followed, including a sequel to 'Big Bad John', all achieving crossover success. Although this time not written by the artist, 'The Cajun Queen' used the same melody, but Dean later admitted that he hated recording it. Released as the b-side of the sugary narration 'To A Sleeping Beauty', it gave the single double-sided chart success. His hits also included 'P.T.109', a song devoted to the wartime career of John F. Kennedy. Several other b-sides also proved popular with the record-buying public including the amusing 'I Won't Go Huntin' With You, Jake' and 'Please Pass The Biscuits'. From 1963-66, he hosted a new show on the ABC-TV network and was much in demand for appearances on other major shows. He had another number 1 country hit with 'The First Thing Every Morning (And The Last Thing Every Night)' in 1965 and the following year, after moving to RCA, charted with 'Stand Beside Me'. Some further hits followed, including 'A Thing Called Love', but during the 70s, his career slowed down as he concentrated on his pork sausage manufacturing business. Notable among his later hits were a duet with Dottie West on Webb Pierce's 'Slowly' and a crossover country and pop hit narrative called 'I.O.U', which he claimed was his ode of thanks to his mother. This was equally as sugary as his new version of 'To A Sleeping Beauty', both of which he made for Casino. A further recording of 'I.O.U', this time for Churchill in 1983, marked his 26th and last country chart entry. In the 80s, he still maintained some television and show appearances though it has been suggested that he preferred a string of sausages to a string of hits. Throughout his career, his easy-going, crooning style and presentation managed to bridge the gap between pop and country music more successfully than many other artists ever managed, and his television shows certainly provided a shop window for many artists as well as generating interest in country music.

● ALBUMS: *Jimmy Dean Sings His Television Favorites* (Mercury 1957)★★★, *Jimmy Dean's Hour Of Prayer* (Mercury 1957)★★, *Hymns By Jimmy Dean* (Harmony 1960)★★, *Big Bad John (& Other Fabulous Songs & Tales)* (Columbia 1961)★★★★, *Favorites Of Jimmy Dean* (King 1961)★★★, *Portrait Of Jimmy Dean* (Columbia 1962)★★★, *Everybody's Favorite* (1963)★★★, *The Songs We All Love The Best* (1964)★★★, *The First Thing Every Morning* (RCA 1965)★★★, *Jimmy Dean's Christmas Card* (RCA 1965)★★, *Golden Favorites* (1965)★★★, with Johnny Horton *Bumming Around* (Starday 1965)★★★, *Sings The Big Ones* (1966)★★★, *Most Richly Blessed (& Other Great Inspirational Songs)* (1967)★★★, *Jimmy Dean Is Here* (1967)★★★, *Mr Country Music* (1967)★★★, *Speaker Of The House* (1967)★★★, *A Thing Called Love* (1968)★★, *The Jimmy Dean Show* (1968)★★, *Country's Favorite Son* (1968)★★★, *Dean's List* (1968)★★★, *Speaker Of The House* (1968)★★★, *Gotta Travel On* (1969)★★★, with Dottie West *Country Boy & Country Girl* (RCA Victor 1970)★★★★, *The Dean Of Country Music* (1970)★★★, *These Hands* (1971)★★★, *Everybody Knows* (1971)★★★, *Jimmy Dean I.O.U.* (1976)★★★, *I.O.U. (Mom, I Love You)* (1977)★★★, *Straight From The Heart* (1982)★★★.

● COMPILATIONS: *Jimmy Dean's Greatest Hits* (Columbia 1966)★★★★, *His Top Hits* (Timeless Treasures 1986)★★★,

American Originals (Columbia 1989)★★★★, *Country Spotlight* (Dominion 1991)★★, *Big Bad John 1961-62 recordings* (Bear Family 1993)★★★★.

DeHaven, Penny

b. Charlotte DeHaven, 17 May 1948, Winchester, Virginia, USA. Having relocated to Berkeley Springs, West Virginia, in 1956, DeHaven began appearing at local venues before she had completed high school. In 1966, using the name Penny Starr, she sang on *Jamboree USA* and gained a minor US country hit in 1967 on Band Box with 'Grain Of Salt'. In 1967, with a name change to Penny DeHaven, she became one of the first female country singers to entertain the troops in Vietnam. Between 1969 and 1974, recording for Imperial or United Artists, she registered 12 further hits including a solo version of the Beatles' 'I Feel Fine' and a Top 20 duet hit with Del Reeves with 'Land Mark Tavern'. She has appeared in several films, including *Country Music Story* and *Traveling Light*. She played a dramatic role in Clint Eastwood's *Honky Tonk Man* and also sang on the soundtrack of *Bronco Billy*. She also recorded duets with Buddy Cagle and charted in 1982 with 'We Made Memories' with Boxcar Willie. Though established on the contemporary Nashville scene, she is still looking for a major hit.

● ALBUMS: *Penny DeHaven* (1972)★★, *Penny DeHaven* (1984).★★

Delmore Brothers

Alton (b. 25 December 1908, Elkmont, Limestone County, Alabama, USA, d. 9 June 1964, Huntsville, USA; guitar) and Rabon (b. 3 December 1916, also Elkmont, d. 4 December 1952, Athens, Alabama, USA; fiddle, four-string tenor guitar) were two of the many children born to Charles and Mary Delmore, who, like many others of their day, struggled to make a living from a little dirt farm. The boys developed an interest in gospel music, and by 1926 they were singing harmonies and playing instruments. In 1931, they recorded for US Columbia. Two years later they secured a regular 15-minute slot on the *Grand Ole Opry* and played ragtime guitar in a style similar to Blind Boy Fuller's. Between 1933 and 1940, they recorded over 100 tracks for RCA Victor and also accompanied Arthur Smith and Uncle Dave Macon. 'Brown's Ferry Blues' from the first session was so popular that they recorded 'Brown's Ferry Blues, Part 2'. Alton sang lead to Rabon's harmony but sometimes they switched parts in mid-song. Their constant touring took its toll as both brothers drank heavily and Alton suffered from depression. They left the *Opry* in 1938 and moved to North Carolina and then Birmingham, Alabama, but they continued touring. The Delmore Brothers recorded for US Decca during 1940/1, including 'When It's Time For The Whipoorwill To Sing'. They stopped touring as a result of petrol rationing during the war, and teamed up with Grandpa Jones and Merle Travis for radio appearances, later recording as the Brown's Ferry Four. In 1944 the Delmore Brothers recorded 'Prisoner's Farewell'/'Sweet Sweet Thing', both written by Jim Scott, one of Alton's pseudonyms, for the new King label, and then had major successes with 'Hillbilly Boogie', 'Freight Train Boogie' and, in particular, 'Blues Stay Away From Me'. Their lonesome sound, helped by Wayne Raney and Lonnie Glossom's harmonicas, created both a classic blues and a classic country record. The Delmore Brothers hit a stormy patch in Houston in the early 50s as Alton suffered a heart attack, lost his daughter and drank even more heavily; their father died; and Rabon's marriage fell apart. He moved to Detroit, while Alton stayed in Houston - managing a bar. In August 1952, with Rabon suffering from cancer, the Delmore Brothers made their final recordings for King in Cincinnati. Rabon died at his home in December 1952 and Alton, overcome by grief, moved to Huntsville and became a postman. He started teaching guitar and made his last record in 1956. In the early 60s, however, he worked with his son Lionel replacing Rabon and also wrote short stories. Alton died of liver disease in June 1964. The Delmore Brothers were elected to the Nashville Songwriters' Hall Of Fame in 1971, although, in actuality, Alton wrote 10 songs to each of Rabon's. Their close-harmony work has been copied by numerous performers, notably Johnny and Dorsey Burnette and the Everly Brothers. Ray Sawyer of Dr. Hook maintains, 'The Delmore Brothers were the first country-rockers. The licks in "Blues Stay Away From Me" are the same as those in "Ain't That A Shame".'

● ALBUMS: by the Delmore Brothers *Songs By The Delmore Brothers* (King 1958)★★★, *The Delmore Brothers' 30th Anniversary Album* (King 1962)★★★, *In Memory* (King 1964)★★★, *In Memory, Volume 2* (King 1964)★★★, *24 Great Country Songs* (King 1966)★★★; by the Brown's Ferry Four: *Sacred Songs* (King 1957)★★★, *Sacred Songs, Volume 2* (King 1958)★★★, *Wonderful Sacred Songs* (King 1965)★★★.

● COMPILATIONS: *Best Of The Delmore Brothers* (Starday 1969)★★★, *Weary Lonesome Blues* (Old Homestead 1983)★★★, *When They Let The Hammer Fall* (Bear Family 1984)★★★★, *Singing My Troubles Away* (Old Homestead 1984)★★★, *Lonesome Yodel Blues* (Old Homestead 1985)★★★, *Early Sacred Songs* (Old Homestead 1985)★★★, *Sand Mountain Blues* (County 1986)★★★, *Freight Train Boogie* (Ace 1993)★★★★.

● FURTHER READING: *Truth Is Stranger Than Publicity*, Alton Delmore.

DeMent, Iris

b. 5 January 1961, Paragould, Arkansas, USA. A singer-songwriter based in Kansas City, via California, Nashville, and originally the rural regions of Arkansas, USA, DeMent made her initial impact in 1991. Her early influences included gospel, Loretta Lynn and Johnny Cash, but she was 25 years of age before she began to write her own songs, and 30 when her debut album was released. She grew up close to the Tennessee and Missouri borders, the youngest of 14 children in a farming family. Finances eventually forced the DeMents to settle first in Long Beach, Los Angeles, when she was three, and then Anaheim. Her mother's ambition had always been to sing at the *Grand Ole Opry* in Nashville (a fact later recalled in the song 'Mama's Opry' on her debut album) and the family had its own singing sessions. Indeed, one of her sisters, Faye DeMent, recorded two country/gospel albums. Iris moved to Nashville when she was 25 and embarked on writing her own songs for the first time. She subsisted by working as a secretary and waitress while trying to secure a recording contract. Eventually Philo Records signed her. Surrounded by accomplished players such as Al Perkins and Jerry Douglas, as well as friend and producer Jimmy Rooney, her debut album, *Infamous Angel*, was an acclaimed, acoustically based country folk set, that

mixed homespun reflection with charming, accessible lyrics. A good example of her approach was 'Let The Mystery Be', a highly spiritual song that was later recorded by 10,000 Maniacs on their MTV *Unplugged* appearance. The rave notices that accompanied the album resulted in a recording contract with Warner Brothers Records, and she was subsequently invited to appear on Nanci Griffith's *Other Voices, Other Rooms*. Her other hero, Emmylou Harris, had appeared on *Infamous Angel*. DeMent subsequently appeared at the Cambridge Folk Festival in 1993, though audiences were not entirely convinced of her ability to take what remain fundamentally intimate songs into a major live arena. Her first Warners album, *My Life*, followed in 1994, and introduced a much darker approach. One song, 'Easy's Getting Harder', is explained by DeMent herself thus: 'Nothing dramatic happens in that song - her husband turns over and goes to sleep after they make love, but she's not going to divorce him for that. It's not a tragedy.' It is exactly that ability to create nuance out of the everyday pain and triumph in life that continues to attract critics. *The Way I Should* included her controversial child abuse song 'Letter To Mom', but was criticised for being over-produced.

● ALBUMS: *Infamous Angel* (Philo 1992)★★, *My Life* (Warners 1994)★★★, *The Way I Should* (Warners 1996)★★★.

Denny, Jim

b. James Rea Denny, 28 February 1911, Buffalo Valley, Tennessee, USA, d. 27 August 1963, Nashville, Tennessee, USA. In 1922, when the family ran into hard times, Denny was sent to live with an aunt in Nashville. He delivered papers and worked as a telegram boy for Western Union until, at the age of 16, he found a job in the mailroom of the National Life and Accident Insurance Company who owned WSM, the station responsible for the *Grand Ole Opry*. By sheer hard work, Denny worked his way up the company ladder to become a department head. Greatly interested in the *Opry*, he first worked there at weekends and became involved with various functions. During World War II, he looked after *Opry* concessions. By 1946, he had become the head of the WSM Artists' Service Bureau and booker for the *Opry* acts; the following year he was the *Opry*'s manager. In 1953, while still manager, he turned to music publishing. He formed Driftwood with Carl Smith and Troy Martin, Cedarwood with Webb Pierce, and his own Jim Denny Music (he later also owned three Georgia radio stations with Pierce). It was Denny who supposedly told Elvis Presley to go back to driving a truck after the singer's forgettable debut on the *Opry* in 1954, a comment that allegedly had Presley crying all the way back to Memphis. Denny could at times be blunt and not everyone appreciated his manner. By 1956, Cedarwood had become an important company and Jack DeWitt, the President of WSM, feeling Denny's outside interests were detrimental to the *Opry*, replaced him as manager with Walter D. Kilpatrick. Denny immediately set up the Jim Denny Artists Bureau, which quickly acquired not only the *Opry*'s members but other artists who, aware of Denny's abilities, were glad to have him represent them. Denny had become one of the most powerful men in Nashville and is quoted as saying his sacking from the *Opry* was the best break of his life. In the early 60s, ill health slowed him down but he continued to be an important figure in the music industry until his death, in Nashville, on 27

August 1963. His place as head of Cedarwood was taken by his son, William (b. 25 August 1935, Nashville, Tennessee, USA), who was also an important figure in the industry and the youngest President of the Country Music Association. In 1966, Denny was elected to the Country Music Hall Of Fame for being, as the plaque stated, 'a leader in the publishing, management and broadcasting fields'.

DENVER, JOHN

b. Henry John Deutschendorf Jnr., 31 December 1943, Roswell, New Mexico, USA, d. 12 October 1997, Monterey Bay, California, USA. One of America's most popular performers during the 70s, Denver's rise to fame began when he was 'discovered' in a Los Angeles nightclub. He initially joined the Back Porch Majority, a nursery group for the renowned New Christy Minstrels, but, tiring of his role there, he left for the Chad Mitchell Trio where he forged a reputation as a talented songwriter. With the departure of the last original member, the Mitchell Trio became known as Denver, Boise and Johnson, but their brief lifespan ended when John embarked on a solo career in 1969. One of his compositions, 'Leaving On A Jet Plane', provided an international hit for Peter, Paul And Mary, and this evocative song was the highlight of Denver's debut album, *Rhymes And Reasons*. Subsequent releases, *Take Me To Tomorrow* and *Whose Garden Was This*, garnered some attention, but it was not until the release of *Poems, Prayers And Promises* that the singer enjoyed popular acclaim when one of its tracks, 'Take Me Home, Country Roads', broached the US Top 3 and became a UK Top 20 hit for Olivia Newton-John in 1973. The song's undemanding homeliness established a light, almost naïve style, consolidated on the albums *Aerie* and *Rocky Mountain High*. 'I'd Rather Be A Cowboy' (1973) and 'Sunshine On My Shoulders' (1974) were both gold singles, while a third million-seller, 'Annie's Song', secured Denver's international status when it topped the UK charts that same year and subsequently became an MOR standard, as well as earning the classical flautist James Galway a UK number 3 hit in 1978. Further US chart success came in 1975 with two number 1 hits, 'Thank God I'm A Country Boy' and 'I'm Sorry'. Denver's status as an all-round entertainer was enhanced by many television spectaculars, including *Rocky Mountain Christmas*, and further gold-record awards for *An Evening With John Denver* and *Windsong*, ensuring that 1975 was the artist's most successful year to date. He continued to enjoy a high profile throughout the rest of the decade and forged a concurrent acting career with his role in the film comedy *Oh, God* with George Burns. In 1981 his songwriting talent attracted the attention of yet another classically trained artist, when opera singer Placido Domingo duetted with Denver on 'Perhaps Love'. However, although Denver became an unofficial musical ambassador with tours to Russia and China, his recording became less prolific as increasingly he devoted time to charitable work and ecological interests. Despite the attacks by music critics, who have deemed his work to be bland and saccharine, Denver's cute, simplistic approach nonetheless achieved a mass popularity that was the envy of many artists. He died in October 1997 when his private plane crashed into the Pacific Ocean.

● ALBUMS: *Rhymes & Reasons* (RCA 1969)★★★, *Take Me To Tomorrow* (RCA 1970)★★★, *Whose Garden Was This* (RCA 1970)★★★, *Poems, Prayers And Promises* (RCA 1971)★★★, *Aerie* (RCA 1971)★★★, *Rocky Mountain High* (RCA 1972)★★★★, *Farewell Andromeda* (RCA 1973)★★, *Back Home Again* (RCA 1974)★★★★, *An Evening With John Denver* (RCA 1975)★★★★, *Windsong* (RCA 1975)★★★★, *Rocky Mountain Christmas* (RCA 1975)★★, *Live In London* (RCA 1976)★★, *Spirit* (RCA 1976)★★★★, *I Want To Live* (RCA 1977)★★, *Live At The Sydney Opera House* (RCA 1978)★★, *John Denver* (RCA 1979)★★★★, with the Muppets *A Christmas Together* (RCA 1979)★★, *Autograph* (RCA 1980)★★★, *Some Days Are Diamonds* (RCA 1981)★★★, with Placido Domingo *Perhaps Love* (Columbia 1981)★★, *Seasons Of The Heart* (RCA 1982)★★★, *It's About Time* (RCA 1983)★★★, *Dreamland Express* (RCA 1985)★★, *One World* (RCA 1986)★★, *Higher Ground* (RCA 1988)★★, *Stonehaven Sunrise* (1989)★★, *The Flower That Shattered The Stone* (Windstar 1990)★★, *Earth Songs* (Music Club 1990)★★, *Different Directions* (Concord 1992)★★.

● COMPILATIONS: *The Best Of John Denver* (RCA 1974)★★★, *The Best Of John Denver Volume 2* (RCA 1977)★★★, *The John Denver Collection* (Telstar 1984)★★★, *Greatest Hits Volume 3* (RCA 1985)★★★, *The Rocky Mountain Collection* (BMG 1997)★★★★.

● VIDEOS: *A Portrait* (Telstar 1994), *The Wildlife Concert* (Sony 1995).

● FURTHER READING: *John Denver*, Leonore Fleischer. *John Denver*, David Dachs. *John Denver: Rocky Mountain Wonderboy*, James Martin. *Take Me Home: An Autobiography*, John Denver with Arthur Tobier.

DERAILERS

A US country rock band from Austin, Texas, the Derailers are led by singer, rhythm guitarist and songwriter Tom Villanueva and lead guitarist, singer and songwriter Brian Hofeldt. Villanueva once described the group's mission as one of exploring 'the moan and the mournful harmonies' that inflect the most evocative country records. With influences ranging from Buck Owens to Merle Haggard, as well as honky-tonk dance music and Texan western swing, within months of forming in the mid-90s the Derailers had been dubbed 'the next big thing in Austin' by an enthusiastic local press. The *Austin-American Statesman* went further still, analogizing the group's robust country sound as a 'boot-stompin', hair raisin' good time that leaves the audience breathlessly happy'. The group made its debut for Watermelon Records in 1996 with *Jackpot*, followed by extensive touring in the USA and a promotional trip to the UK featuring new drummer Terry Kirkendall.

● ALBUMS: *Jackpot* (Watermelon 1996)★★★.

DESERT ROSE BAND

Formed in the mid-80s, the Desert Rose Band were akin to a mini-supergroup of country rock musicians. Lead vocalist and guitarist Chris Hillman was formerly a member of the Byrds, the Flying Burrito Brothers, Manassas, the Souther, Hillman, Furay Band and McGuinn, Clark And Hillman; Herb Pedersen (vocals, guitar) was one of the most famous session players on the country scene and a former member of the Dillards and Country Gazette; Bill Bryson (vocals, bass) was another Country Gazette alumnus and had also played in the Bluegrass Cardinals, as well as working on various movie soundtracks; Jay Dee Maness was one of the world's most famous pedal-steel guitarists, and among his past credentials were appearances with Gram Parsons' International Submarine Band, the Byrds and Buck Owens' Buckaroos; John Jorgenson, who played guitar, mandolin and six-string bass was the 'wunderkind' of the outfit; while Steve Duncan had drummed behind several new country artists, including Dwight Yoakam. The group were eventually signed to the independent Curb Records by Dick Whitehouse, and their highly accomplished self-titled first album appeared in 1987. Among its delights was a highly effective reworking of 'Time Between', previously recorded by Hillman on the Byrds' *Younger Than Yesterday*. The follow-up *Running* was another strong work, particularly the title track, which dealt with the suicide of Hillman's father, a matter never previously mentioned in any interview. By the end of the 80s, the band were touring extensively and registering regular hits in the country charts. A third album, *Pages Of Life*, consolidated their position, and featured the memorable anti-drugs song, 'Darkness On The Playground'. In 1991, Jay Dee Maness left the group to be replaced by Tom Brumley, formerly of Rick Nelson's Stone Canyon Band. The departure of Maness made little difference to the Desert Rose Band's sound, but John Jorgenson's decision the following year to pursue a solo career threatened the group's momentum. He was replaced by Jeff Ross (formerly with Los Angeles cow-punk band Rank And File), who for a time brought a harsher, rock-flavoured edge to their show. It was not to last and the Desert Rose Band have now broken up.

● ALBUMS: *The Desert Rose Band* (MCA 1987)★★★, *Running* (MCA 1988)★★★★, *Pages Of Life* (MCA 1989)★★★★, *True Love* (Curb 1991)★★, *Traditional* (Curb 1993)★★, *Life Goes On* (Curb 1993)★★.

● COMPILATIONS: *A Dozen Roses: Greatest Hits* (MCA 1991)★★★★, *Greatest Hits* (Curb 1994)★★★★.

DEXTER, AL

b. Albert Poindexter, 4 May 1902, Jacksonville, Cherokee County, Texas, USA, d. 28 January 1984, Lewisville, Texas, USA. Multi-instrumentalist, singer and songwriter Dexter made his first public performances at local dances and church functions. In the early 30s, he formed several bands, the first, a rarity for a white musician in Texas, consisted of all coloured musicians, when he had problems persuading white musicians to play his music. This band proved very successful, but he is best remembered for his Texas Troopers; all his bands played smooth western swing and honky tonk behind Dexter's vocals. He made his first recordings such as 'New Jelly Roll Blues' for Vocalion in 1935, and his 1937 'Honky Tonk Blues' is the first country song to feature 'honky tonk' in the title. Dexter gained his experience in the east Texas dancehalls, and many of his songs reveal that influence in their content. In 1943, his OKeh recording of the self-penned 'Pistol Packin' Mama' became a million-selling number 1 song on both the US pop and country charts (a pop version by Bing Crosby and the Andrews Sisters also became a million-seller and later a rock 'n' roll version by Gene Vincent also proved successful). Based on an event that occurred when he owned a honky tonk in Turnertown, Texas, and played in polka time, the song made Dexter a wealthy man. During the next four years, recording on OKeh or Columbia Records, he had further number 1 country hits with 'Rosalita', 'So Long Pal', 'Too Late To Worry, Too Blue To Cry', 'I'm Losing My Mind Over You', 'Guitar

Polka' and 'Wine, Women And Song'. These, plus eight other Top 10 hits, made him one of the most popular artists of the 40s. He opened his own Bridgeport Club in Dallas in the 50s and, apart from singing there, retired from entertaining. He eventually went into the property business and also bought a motel in Lufkin. In 1971 he was elected to the Nashville Songwriters' Association International Hall Of Fame. Dexter died in January 1984.

● ALBUMS: *Songs Of The Southwest* (Columbia 1954)★★★, *Pistol Packin' Mama* (Harmony 1961)★★★, *Sings And Plays His Greatest Hits* (Capitol 1962)★★★, *The Original Pistol Packin' Mama* (Hilltop 1968)★★★.

DIAMOND RIO

Gene Johnson (b. 10 August 1949, Sugar Grove, Pennsylvania, USA; mandolin, fiddle), Jimmy Olander (b. 26 August 1961, Palos Verdes, California, USA; lead guitar, banjo), Brian Prout (b. 4 December 1955, Troy, New York, USA; drums), Marty Roe (b. 28 December 1960, Lebanon, Ohio, USA; lead vocals, guitar), Dan Truman (b. 29 August 1966, St. George, Utah, USA; keyboards) and Dana Williams (b. 22 May 1961, Dayton, Ohio, USA; bass, vocals). Lead singer Roe was named after Marty Robbins and was singing country songs from the age of three; Johnson had played with David Bromberg and J.D. Crowe And The New South; Williams is a nephew of the Osborne Brothers - making a great many interesting musical connections in Diamond Rio. They began playing as the Grizzly River Boys and by the time they were signed to Arista Records, they were the Tennessee River Boys. The band were told to change their name because it sounded too much like a gospel group. Two American truck manufacturers, Diamond T and Reo, merged as Diamond-Reo and with a little misspelling, Diamond Rio was born (so, incidentally, was REO Speedwagon). In 1991 Diamond Rio became the first group to top the US country charts with their debut single, the love ballad 'Meet In The Middle'. Their first album went platinum and yielded several more hit singles. They added a powerful rhythm section for their second album, an unusual move for country music. With singles such as 'Mirror Mirror', 'Mama, Don't Forget To Pray For Me', 'Sawmill Road' and 'In A Week Or Two', the group went from strength to strength. They developed their good humour with the very catchy 'Norma Jean Riley' ('Fool, fool, nothing you can do/Never going to see her with the likes of you.') and, more recently, 'Bubba Hyde'. They challenged and then overtook Alabama as the Top Group in the Country Music Awards. Diamond Rio is state-of-the-art 90s country, featuring high harmonies and bluegrass instruments alongside solid rock sounds. With the addition of Lee Roy Parnell and Steve Wariner, they become Jed Zepplin for a new treatment of 'Workin' Man Blues' on the Merle Haggard tribute album, *Mama's Hungry Eyes*. They also performed 'Ten Feet Away' on a tribute album to Keith Whitley. Prout's wife, Nancy, is also a drummer, playing with Wild Rose, the all-female country band. In 1997 the group were awarded a CMA Award for Vocal Group Of The Year.

● ALBUMS: *Diamond Rio* (Arista 1991)★★★, *Close To The Edge* (Arista 1992)★★★, *Love A Little Stronger* (Arista 1994)★★★, *IV* (Arista 1996)★★★.

● COMPILATIONS: *Greatest Hits* (Arista 1997)★★★★.

● VIDEOS: *Bubba Hyde* (Arista 1994).

DICKENS, HAZEL

b. Hazel Jane Dickens, 1 June 1935, Mercer County, West Virginia, USA. Dickens was the eighth of 11 children in a family that struggled hard to make a living in an area where coalmining was the sole industry. Dickens learned to play guitar and bass and developed a great interest in not only the local music but also music by more modern singers she heard on the radio, such as Ernest Tubb and Kitty Wells. Her father, as well as working for the mining industry and locally as a Baptist minister, was also a banjoist of some ability. However, in the early 50s, his apparent reluctance to let his own or any of his family's musical interests diversify from the traditional folk/bluegrass artists' music prevalent in the area, saw Dickens relocate to Baltimore. Here, she eventually met Mike Seeger and accompanied by her brothers, Robert and Arnold, they began performing locally. She later became a member of several other bands, including the Greenbriar Boys, usually playing bass and singing lead or harmony vocals. In the early 60s, she met Alice Gerrard, and the two formed a partnership that saw them write songs about various aspects of life as well as performing together at numerous folk festivals all over the south. In 1972, for a time, they joined forces with Mike Seeger, Tracy Schwartz and Lamar Greer to perform as the Strange Creek Singers. After the partnership ended amicably, writing much of her own material, she pursued a solo career that gained momentum when four of her original songs were featured in an award-winning documentary on coalmining called *Harlan County, USA*. Dickens was greatly impressed by the earlier protest and anti-Union songs of Aunt Molly Jackson and her half-sister, Sarah Ogan Gunning, and soon developed a similar reputation herself in many quarters. During the 80s, she recorded albums for Rounder Records and had some of her songs featured in films, including *Coal Mining Women* (1984) and *Matewan* (1987), even making a brief singing appearance in the latter herself. She became a leading supporter of events to benefit coalminers and union workers, and as such, she has appeared at countless festivals and protest events. By their work both together and apart, Hazel Dickens and Alice Gerrard have done much to influence countless traditional music fans as well as pioneering the role of women in bluegrass. In 1994, Hazel Dickens was the first artist to be honoured with the Merit Award for contribution to bluegrass music by the International Bluegrass Music Association.
● ALBUMS: with Alice Gerrard *Who's That Knocking & Other Bluegrass Music* (Folkways 1965)★★★, with The Strange Creek Singers *The Strange Creek Singers* (Arhoolie 1972)★★★, with Gerrard *Won't You Come And Sing For Me* (Folkways 1973)★★★, *Hard Hitting Songs For Hard Hit People* (Rounder 1981)★★★, *By The Sweat Of My Brow* (Rounder 1983)★★★★, *It's Hard To Tell The Singer From The Song* (Rounder 1987)★★★.
● COMPILATIONS: with Gerrard *Hazel & Alice* (Rounder 1973)★★★, with Gerrard *Hazel Dickens & Alice Gerrard* (Rounder 1976)★★★, *A Few Old Memories* (Rounder 1987)★★★.

DICKENS, LITTLE JIMMY

b. James Cecil Dickens, 19 December 1920, Bolt, West Virginia, USA. Dickens has summarized his early life as the youngest of 13 children in humorous country songs such as

'A-Sleeping At The Foot Of The Bed' and 'Out Behind The Barn'. He had no intention of following his father into the coalmines, and being 4 feet 11 inches tall effectively ruled it out. When he was aged 17, he played guitar and sang on local radio with Johnny Bailes And His Happy Valley Boys as 'The Singing Midget' and 'Jimmy the Kid'. Dickens then worked with T. Texas Tyler but when Tyler joined the forces, he worked in his own right, being spotted in Saginaw, Michigan, by Roy Acuff. Acuff arranged a contract with US Columbia Records in 1948 and he recorded several songs including 'Country Boy' and 'Take An Old Cold Tater And Wait'. His 1950 recording 'Hillbilly Fever' provided a foretaste of rockabilly. He toured Germany with Hank Williams and he helped to start the career of the young Marty Robbins. In 1964, Dickens claimed to be the first country artist to circle the globe on a world tour. He achieved a crossover hit in 1965 with 'May The Bird Of Paradise Fly Up Your Nose', his only US country number 1. Dressed in colourful cowboy suits, he summarized himself in 'I'm Little But I'm Loud', and June Carter described him as 'Mighty Mouse in his pyjamas'. Despite being associated with comedy material, he also recorded quavering versions of country weepies such as 'Life Turned Her That Way', 'Just When I Needed You' and 'Shopping For Dresses', and made two religious albums. He was a regular member of the *Grand Ole Opry* from 1949-57 and also from 1975 onwards. Dickens was elected to the Country Music Hall Of Fame in October 1983, and in his acceptance speech, he said, 'I want to thank Mr. Acuff for his faith in me years ago.'
● ALBUMS: *Old Country Church* (Columbia 1954)★★, *Raisin' The Dickens* (Columbia 1957)★★★, *Big Songs By Little Jimmy Dickens* (Columbia 1960)★★★, *Little Jimmy Dickens Sings Out Behind The Barn* (Columbia 1962)★★★, *Little Jimmy Dickens' Best* (Harmony 1964)★★★, *Handle With Care* (Columbia 1965)★★★, *Alone With God* (Harmony 1965)★★★, *May The Bird Of Paradise Fly Up Your Nose* (Columbia 1965)★★★★, *Ain't It Fun* (Harmony 1967)★★★, *Big Man In Country Music* (Columbia 1968)★★★, *Jimmy Dickens Sings* (Decca 1968)★★★, *Jimmy Dickens Comes Callin'* (Decca 1969)★★★, *Hymns By The Hour* (1975)★★.
● COMPILATIONS: *Little Jimmy Dickens Greatest Hits* (Columbia 1966)★★★, *Greatest Hits* (Decca 1969)★★★, *Country Music Hall Of Fame* (CMH 1984)★★, *Best Of The Best Of Jimmy Dickens* (Gusto 1988)★★★, *Straight From The Heart (1949-1955)* (Rounder 1989)★★★, *I'm Little But I'm Loud: The Little Jimmy Dickens Collection* (Razor & Tie 1996)★★★★.

DIFFIE, JOE

b. 28 December 1958, Tulsa, Oklahoma, USA. According to *Entertainment Weekly*, country singer Joe Diffie is a 'first rate interpreter of working class woes', while Tammy Wynette described him as all her favourite vocalists rolled into one. His career has taken off in the 90s by dint of his honest, earthy narratives and accomplished balladeering. He grew up listening to his father's collection of Lefty Frizzell, Johnny Cash and Merle Haggard discs, although he also loved the energy of rock 'n' roll after seeing live performances from ZZ Top and Boston. After several years working in an iron foundry in Duncan, Oklahoma, Diffie sparked a second career by playing locally with gospel, country and bluegrass groups. His break came when one of the many songs he wrote in this period, 'Love On The

Rocks', was recorded by Hank Thompson. Another composition, 'Love's Hurtin' Game', was also considered by Randy Travis, and, although this later fell through, the ensuing press gave him enough impetus to relocate to Nashville. There he found work as a staff-writer with Forest Hills Music, for whom he provided material for Doug Stone and the Forester Sisters, while becoming a much demanded session singer. 'I had to keep working at developing my own style . . . I credit my friend Lonnie Wilson for the fact that I was able to find where I fit best. Lonnie had a little studio, and sometimes I'd sing demos all day, then work on my stuff half the night.' These recordings eventually reached Epic Records, resulting in his debut album, 1990's *A Thousand Winding Roads*. His arrival was confirmed by an astonishing chart feat - his first release, 'Home', simultaneously reached number 1 in the *Billboard*, *Radio & Records* and *Gavin Report* charts. Three additional number 1 s followed; 'If You Want Me To', 'If The Devil Danced In Empty Pockets' and the first of his own compositions released as a single, 'New Way To Light Up An Old Flame'. The title of *Regular Joe* reflected his no-nonsense, unpretentious appeal, and it provided two more chart-toppers, 'Is It Cold In Here' and 'Ships That Don't Come In'. Although *Honky Tonk Attitude* also contained two sizeable hits in the title track and 'Prop Me Up (Beside The Jukebox)', it was 'John Deere Green' that truly took off, with many now citing Diffie as a modern-day George Jones, able to switch effortlessly from sentimental ballads to invigorating barn hops. Indeed, he earned a Country Music Association award for his 1993 collaboration with Jones, 'I Don't Need Your Rocking Chair', and a duet with Mary-Chapin Carpenter was nominated for a Grammy for Best Vocal Collaboration. *Third Rock From The Sun* surprisingly only saw one Diffie composition, 'The Cows Came Home' (written alongside Lee Bogan and Lonnie Wilson), on a set that reflected the improvement in Diffie's love life, but that also maintained his tradition for confessional material, such as 'That Road Not Taken', 'So Help Me Girl' and 'From Here On Out'. He joined the *Grand Ole Opry* in 1993. In the wake of the renewed Beatlemania in late 1995, Diffie enjoyed a number 1 hit in the spring of 1996 with the amusingly titled 'Bigger Than The Beatles'. 'This Is Your Brain' and 'Houston, We Have A Problem' from *Twice Upon A Time* were further examples of his quirky songwriting.

● ALBUMS: *A Thousand Winding Roads* (Epic 1990)★★★, *Regular Joe* (Epic 1991)★★★, *Honky Tonk Attitude* (Epic 1993)★★★★, *Third Rock From The Sun* (Epic 1994)★★★★, *Mr Christmas* (Epic 1995)★★, *Life's So Funny* (Epic 1995)★★★, *Twice Upon A Time* (Epic 1997)★★★.

● VIDEOS: *Third Rock From The Sun* (1994).

DILLARD AND CLARK

Refugees from the Dillards and the Byrds, respectively, Doug Dillard (b. 6 March 1937, East St. Louis, Illinois, USA) and Gene Clark (b. Harold Eugene Clark, 17 November 1941, Tipton, Missouri, USA, d. 24 May 1991) joined forces in 1968 to form one of the first country rock groups. Backed by the Expedition, featuring Bernie Leadon (banjo, guitar), Don Beck (dobro, mandolin) and David Jackson (string bass), they recorded two albums for A&M Records, which confirmed their standing among the best of the early country rock exponents. *The Fantastic Expedition Of Dillard And Clark* featured several strong compositions by Clark and Leadon

including 'The Radio Song', 'Out On The Side', 'Something's Wrong' and 'Train Leaves Here This Mornin''. Leadon later took the latter to his next group, the Eagles, who included the song on their debut album. By the time of their second album, Dillard and Clark displayed a stronger country influence with the induction of Flying Burrito Brothers drummer Jon Corneal, champion fiddle player Byron Berline and additional vocalist Donna Washburn. *Through The Morning, Through The Night* combined country standards with Clark originals and featured some sumptuous duets between Clark and Washburn that pre-empted the work of Gram Parsons and Emmylou Harris. Although the Expedition experiment showed considerable promise, the group scattered in various directions at the end of the 60s, with Clark reverting to a solo career.

● ALBUMS: *The Fantastic Expedition Of Dillard And Clark* (A&M 1968)★★★, *Through The Morning, Through The Night* (A&M 1969)★★★★.

DILLARD, DOUG AND RODNEY

Brothers Doug (b. 6 March 1937, East St. Louis, Illinois, USA; banjo) and Rodney (b. 18 May 1942, East St. Louis, Illinois, USA; guitar) were the founders of the pioneering bluegrass outfit the Dillards. In 1968, Doug left after six reasonably successful years, and joined the Gram Parsons-era Byrds for a few months, before Parsons himself departed. This association led to the formation of the ground-breaking Dillard & Clark, with ex-Byrd Gene Clark, and Bernie Leadon (later with the Eagles), Michael Clarke (another former Byrd) and fiddle champion Byron Berline. Their two albums for A&M, *The Fantastic Expedition Of Dillard & Clark* (1968) and *Through The Morning, Through The Night* (1969), produced an unusual, but highly successful, blend of bluegrass and southern soul, but internal disputes caused the group to disband soon afterwards. Doug Dillard released several disjointed solo albums in the 70s, and occasionally recorded with his brother Rodney and long-time friend John Hartford. Together, they recorded the promising *Dillard Hartford Dillard* in 1975, a bluegrass-folk hybrid that mixed some good picking with lighthearted tunes. Subsequently, Doug Dillard fronted his own band with vocalist Ginger Boatwright, and played the US festival circuit with the Dillards. Never a prolific writer, he nevertheless contributed several memorable 'character' songs to the Dillards' repertoire, such as 'Dooley' and 'Ebo Walker'. After the Dillards split in the early 80s, he spent a couple of years with country music star Earl Scruggs' band. In 1985 Flying Fish released the misleadingly titled *Rodney Dillard At Silver Dollar City*, a low-budget recording that featured Rodney on two tracks. In the early 90s, Rodney followed the excellent *Let It Fly*, by the re-formed Dillards, with his own *Let The Rough Side Drag*, a mixture of bluegrass and folk.

● ALBUMS: Doug Dillard *The Banjo Album* (Together 1969)★★★★, *Duelling Banjos* (20th Century 1973)★★★, *Douglas Flint Dillard* (20th Century 1974)★★★, *Heaven* (Flying Fish 1979)★★★, *Jackrabbit!* (Flying Fish 1980)★★★, *What's That?* (Flying Fish 1986)★★, *Heartbreak Hotel* (Flying Fish 1988)★★★. Rodney Dillard *At Silver Dollar City* (Flying Fish 1985)★★, *Let The Rough Side Drag* (1992)★★★. As Dillard Hartford Dillard *Dillard-Hartford-Dillard* (Sonet 1975)★★★, *Permanent Wave* (Flying Fish 1980)★★★.

DILLARD, MOSES

This southern-based performer is best recalled for 'My Elusive Dreams', his powerful soul-styled interpretation of a C&W favourite. Credited to 'Moses And Joshua Dillard', this irresistible single later became a northern soul favourite. The fictitious brother was, in fact, a member of Dillard's backing group, the Tex-Town Display, which included future singing star Peabo Bryson. In later years, Dillard pursued a backroom role and as featured songwriter and guitarist on Al Green's 1984 gospel album *Precious Lord*, he has since continued a career as a session musician.

DILLARDS

Brothers Rodney (b. 18 May 1942, East St. Louis, Illinois, USA; guitar, vocals) and Doug Dillard (b. 6 March 1937, East St. Louis, Illinois, USA; banjo, vocals) formed this seminal bluegrass group in Salem, Missouri, USA. Roy Dean Webb (b. 28 March 1937, Independence, Missouri, USA; mandolin, vocals) and former radio announcer Mitch Jayne (b. 7 May 1930, Hammond, Indiana, USA; bass) completed the original line-up which, having enjoyed popularity throughout their home state, travelled to Los Angeles in 1962 where they signed with the Elektra label. *Back Porch Bluegrass* and *The Dillards Live! Almost!* established the unit as one of America's leading traditional acts, although purists denigrated the band's sometimes irreverent attitude. *Pickin' & Fiddlin'*, a collaboration with violinist Byron Berline, was recorded to placate such critics. The Dillards shared management with the Byrds and, whereas their distinctive harmonies proved influential to the latter group's development, the former act then began embracing a pop-based perspective. Dewey Martin (b. 30 September 1942, Chesterville, Ontario, Canada), later of Buffalo Springfield, added drums on a folk rock demo that in turn led to a brace of singles recorded for the Capitol label. Doug Dillard was unhappy with this new direction and left to form a duo with ex-Byrd Gene Clark. Herb Peterson joined the Dillards in 1968 and, having resigned from Elektra, the reshaped quartet completed two exceptional country rock sets, *Wheatstraw Suite* and *Copperfields*. The newcomer was in turn replaced by Billy Rae Latham for *Roots And Branches*, on which the unit's transformation to full-scale electric instruments was complete. A full-time drummer, Paul York, was now featured in the line-up, but further changes were wrought when founder-member Jayne dropped out following *Tribute To The American Duck*. Rodney Dillard has since remained at the helm of a capricious act, which by the end of the 70s, returned to the traditional music circuit through the Flying Fish label. He was also reunited with his brother in Dillard-Hartford-Dillard, an occasional sideline, which also featured multi-instrumentalist John Hartford.
● ALBUMS: *Back Porch Bluegrass* (Elektra 1963)★★★, *The Dillards Live. . . Almost!* (Elektra 1964)★★★, with Byron Berline *Pickin' & Fiddlin'* (Elektra 1965)★★★, *Wheatstraw Suite* (Elektra 1968)★★★★, *Copperfields* (Elektra 1970)★★★, *Roots And Branches* (Anthem 1972)★★, *Tribute To The American Duck* (Poppy 1973)★★★, *The Dillards Versus The Incredible LA Time Machine* (Sonet 1977)★★, *Glitter-Grass From The Nashwood Hollyville Strings* (1977)★★★, *Decade Waltz* (Flying Fish 1979)★★, *Homecoming & Family Reunion* (Flying Fish 1980)★★★, *Mountain Rock* (Flying Fish 1980)★★, *Let It Fly* (Vanguard 1990)★★★.
● COMPILATIONS: *Country Tracks* (Elektra 1974)★★★, *I'll*

Fly Away (Edesl 1988)★★★, *There Is A Time (1963-1970)* (Vanguard 1991)★★★★.
● VIDEOS: *A Night In The Ozarks* (Hendring 1991).
● FURTHER READING: *Everybody On The Truck*, Lee Grant.

DILLON, DEAN

b. 26 March 1955, Lake City, Knoxville, Tennessee, USA. Dillon, a self-confessed victim of alcohol and substance abuse, started writing songs in the early 70s, when he appeared on a local television show. He subsequently moved to Nashville and eventually worked at Opryland Theme Park for four years as a member of the Mac McGahey quartet (McGahey had previously worked as Porter Wagoner's fiddle player for many years), with Barry Moore (bass) and Mark Barnett (banjo). This group made an obscure independent label album, *Rise And Shine*, primarily for sale at gigs. By the mid-70s, Dillon had been signed to a songwriting contract. His first big hit as a writer came in 1979 with 'Lying In Love With You', which he co-wrote with Gary Harrison and which was a Top 3 US country hit for Jim Ed Brown and Helen Cornelius. He enjoyed eight minor US country hits between 1979 and 1983, and continued to write hits for others such as 'Tennessee Whisky' for George Jones (Top 3 country, 1983) and 'Leave Them Boys Alone' for Hank Williams Jnr. (Top 10, 1983). In 1982 Dillon teamed up with singer-songwriter Gary Stewart (both were signed to RCA at the time), and the duo recorded two albums - one of which was titled *Brotherly Love* - and a handful of minor hit singles; Dillon later described the partnership as 'the biggest mistake either of us could ever have made'. However, by the time the duo dissolved, Dillon had written a number of hits in partnership with other Nashville writers such as Paul Overstreet, Buzz Rabin, Randy Scruggs and especially Hank Cochran and Frank Dyeas. Many of these songs became big hits for country superstar George Strait, including such country chart-toppers as 'The Chair' (1985), 'Nobody In His Right Mind Would've Left Her' and 'It Ain't Cool To Be Crazy About You' (both 1986), 'Ocean Front Property' (1987) and 'Famous Last Words Of A Fool' (1988). These successes led to a new recording contract for Dillon with Capitol Records, which resulted in two albums produced by Scruggs, *Slick Nickel* and *I've Learned To Live* , which included a duet with Tanya Tucker. By 1993, he had released another two albums, but he remains more successful as a songwriter than as an artist. In the 90s Dillon's days as a rowdy honky-tonker appear to be over and he is a contented family man. 'I had the Hank Williams syndrome,' he says, 'and I almost killed myself by drinking and taking drugs.' He still looks very distinctive in performances, with his long-flowing hair and handlebar moustache.
● ALBUMS: with Gary Stewart *Brotherly Love* (RCA 1982)★★★, with Stewart *Those Were The Days* (RCA 1983)★★, *Slick Nickel* (Capitol 1988)★★★, *I've Learned To Live* (Capitol 1989)★★★, *Out Of Your Ever Lovin' Mind* (Atlantic 1991)★★, *Hot, Country And Single* (Atlantic 1993)★★★.

DIPIERO, BOB

Bob DiPiero played in rock 'n' roll bands in Ohio and used the income to fund his university education. He moved to Nashville in the late 70s to concentrate on songwriting. His first success was with 'Forever In Your Eyes' for Reba

McEntire and he also wrote 'Little Rock' for her. He himself is either a talented Nashville songwriter or his collaborators are, as he rarely writes on his own. His songs include 'American Made' (Oak Ridge Boys), 'Cleopatra, Queen Of Denial' (Pam Tillis), '(Do You Love Me) Just Say Yes' (Highway 101), 'Sentimental Ol' You' (Charly McClain) and 'That Rock Won't Roll' (Restless Heart). DiPiero is married to Pam Tillis and is a former president of the Nashville Songwriters' Association. He is also part of a goodtime band of session men and songwriters, Billy Hill, who have been on the US country charts with 'Too Much Month At The End Of The Money' and a revival of the Four Tops' 'I Can't Help Myself'. Recent songs include 'Ancient History' (Prairie Oyster), 'Forgiveness' (Victoria Shaw), ' I Am Just A Rebel' (Confederate Railroad), 'Let Me Drive' (Greg Holland), 'Take Me As I Am' (Faith Hill), 'Take That' (Lisa Brokop), 'Wink' (Neal McCoy) and, best of all, 'Wild Love' (Joy Lynn White).

DIXON BROTHERS

Brothers Dorsey Murdock Dixon (b. 14 October 1897, Darlington, South Carolina, USA, d. April 1968, Florida, USA) and Howard Britten Dixon (b. 19 June 1903, Darlington, South Carolina, USA, d. March 1960) were two of seven Dixon children. At the age of 12, Dorsey left school and like his father, William McQuiller Dixon, he worked in the mill of the Darlington Cotton Manufacturing Company. Dorsey, who was playing the guitar at 14, later taught himself to play fiddle and when Howard also learned guitar, they began playing fiddle and guitar duets in the East Rockingham film theatre. In 1929, Dorsey wrote a poem called 'The Cleveland Schoolhouse Fire', which he based on the true story of a school fire that, in May 1923, had led to the deaths of 76 children. His mother and Howard, using the tune of 'Life's Railway To Heaven', first popularized the number by singing it at local venues. In 1932, inspired by Jimmie Tarlton (of Darby And Tarlton), the brothers began to play together at local venues and two years later appeared regularly on the *Saturday Night Jamboree* on WBT Charlotte, North Carolina. Between February 1936 and 1938, they recorded 60 songs (most were written or co-written by Dorsey) for RCA-Victor, which were released on the Bluebird or Montgomery Ward labels. Without doubt the most famous of these songs was 'I Didn't Hear Anybody Pray', which must rank as the genre's first 'don't drink and drive song'. It was later recorded as 'The Wreck On The Highway' by Roy Acuff, who subsequently attempted to claim the song as his own. Dorsey opposed Acuff's claim and after some acrimony, the matter was eventually settled amicably. They eventually gave up hopes of a full-time musical career in the early 40s but continued to play locally. Howard worked for a time with Wade Mainer, with whom he co-wrote several songs including 'Intoxicated Rat' and 'Two Little Rosebuds'. He also recorded a classic version of 'Barbara Allen' with Mainer for the Library of Congress. Dorsey continued to work in various mills until 1951, when his fading sight forced him to quit. He had married Beatrice Moody, a fellow mill worker, in 1927 and they had raised four sons before divorcing in 1953. Howard continued to work in the mills and died suddenly, while at work, in March 1960. Dorsey, who appeared at the Newport Folk Festival in 1963, died in April 1968. Old Homestead released a series of albums in the 80s, which contained most of the Dixons' recorded work.

● ALBUMS: *The Dixon Brothers, (Howard And Dorsey), Volume 1, Early Recordings & Transcriptions* (Old Homestead 1983)★★★★, *The Dixon Brothers, (Howard And Dorsey), Volume 2* (Old Homestead 1984)★★★, *The Dixon Brothers, Volume 3 - Early Sacred Songs* (Old Homestead 1986)★★★, *The Dixon Brothers, Volume 4 - Fisherman's Luck* (Old Homestead 1986)★★★.

DOBSON, RICHARD

b. 19 March 1942, Tyler, Texas, USA. Dobson planned to be a novelist and he only took up the guitar and started songwriting in 1963. He played in Texas folk clubs alongside Guy Clark and Townes Van Zandt, but a meeting with David Allan Coe's band outside a Nashville recording studio led to Coe immediately recording 'Piece Of Wood And Steel'. With the money he saved from working on shrimpers and oil rigs, Dobson was able to finance his highly rated debut, *In Texas Last December*. The album included 'Baby Ride Easy', which was recorded as a duet by Carlene Carter and Dave Edmunds. Dobson wrote regularly for the UK fanzine *Omaha Rainbow*, and his novel, *Seasons And Companions*, has been published. Nanci Griffith, who recorded his song 'The Ballad Of Robin Wintersmith', calls him 'the Hemingway of country music', but he has not been able to expand his following. His best-known song is 'Old Friends', which he wrote with Guy and Susanna Clark, and which was used as the title track of Clark's 1988 album.

● ALBUMS: *In Texas Last December* (1976)★★★, *The Big Taste* (1978)★★★, *Save The World* (1982)★★★, *True West* (1986)★★★, *State Of The Heart* (1988)★★★, *Hearts And Rivers* (1989)★★★, *Sings Townes Van Zandt - Amigos* (Brambus 1994)★★★, *Love Only Love* (Brambus 1997)★★★.

DODD, DERYL

b. *c*.1964, Texas, USA. Country singer-songwriter Deryl Dodd was 32 years old when he released his debut solo album, *One Ride In Vegas*, in October 1996. He had begun his career several years earlier on the Texas honky-tonk circuit, having first picked up a guitar while a student at Baylor University in Waco. After graduation Dodd and his band became permanent fixtures on the Dallas club scene. Eventually he moved to Nashville and became a backing musician and singer to artists including Martina McBride and Tracy Lawrence. He also worked as a songwriter, but he never felt comfortable with the process of manufacturing tunes decreed by fashion and soon returned to his own songwriting. The resultant debut album featured his own original material, though the medium was implacably that of traditional country. It positioned Deryl Dodd at the forefront of a renaissance in conservative country music values, alongside other talented newcomers such as Gary Allen.

● ALBUMS: *One Ride In Vegas* (Columbia 1996)★★★★.

DOLLAR, JOHNNY

b. John Washington Dollar Jnr., 8 March 1922, Kilgore, Texas, USA, d. 13 April 1986, Nashville, Tennessee, USA. In the 50s, he worked on radio in Dallas and Shreveport, at one time fronting a band named the Texas Sons. During the 60s, recording for Columbia, Dot, Date and Chart, he registered six minor hits and a Top 15 with 'Stop The Start Of Tears In My Heart'. His last chart entry, 'Truck Driver's Lament', was a minor hit in 1970. In the early 80s, Dollar basically quit performing to work for a record company that specialized in custom recordings. It is believed he was suffering from cancer when he committed suicide in 1986.

● ALBUMS: *Johnny Dollar* (Date 1967)★★★, *Big Rig Rolling Man* (Chart 1969)★★★, *Country Hit Parade* (Chart 1969)★★★, *My Soul Is Blue* (Isabel 1980)★★.

DOSS, TOMMY

b. Lloyd Thomas Doss, 26 September 1920, Weiser, Idaho, USA. An important member of the Sons Of The Pioneers. The Doss family relocated to LeGrande, Oregon, in 1922 where, together with his normal schooling, Doss developed an interest in the early country sounds of Jimmie Rodgers, no doubt greatly encouraged by his accordion- and organ-playing father. He began singing in public at the age of 11 and in 1939, together with his brother Beek and a friend, he formed the Sons Of Grande Ronde. This trio, with a repertoire that included some of the songs of the Sons Of The Pioneers, whom he greatly admired, proved popular on local radio. During World War II, he worked on defence work before returning to LeGrande in 1946 and forming a new trio. In 1948, for a time, he replaced Tommy Duncan with Bob Wills' Texas Playboys and appears on some of that band's Tiffany transcriptions but not on their studio recordings. He then moved to Los Angeles as vocalist with Luke Wills' band. He sang on some recordings including 'Shut Up And Drink Your Beer', until RCA's producer said he sounded too much like another of their artists, Bob Nolan. In 1949, whilst singing with Ole Rasmussen's band, he achieved a lifelong ambition, when he became a member of the Sons Of The Pioneers. Nolan had wanted to retire and he and Tim Spencer saw Doss as the ideal replacement. He toured extensively, recorded and made films with the group, until, like Nolan, he found that he could no longer handle the pressures and in 1963, he gave up full-time connections with the group. He retired to Imnaha, Oregon, where he opened a store. He continued to record with the Pioneers and was even persuaded, on occasions, to undertake short tours until December 1967. In 1972, he appeared at a special reunion concert in Los Angeles to celebrate the Pioneers' 40th anniversary. Everyone was impressed with his performance and he was persuaded to make some solo recordings. They were planned as the first of a series of albums but Doss had no intention of giving up his peaceful retirement. He returned home immediately after completing the session and the recordings remained unissued until 1987. The 11 songs included 'Rosa', a song he had sung on his last session with the Pioneers, 'The Memory' and perhaps the even more appropriately titled 'I Care No More'.

● ALBUMS: *Tommy Doss Of The Sons Of The Pioneers* (Bear Family 1987)★★★.

DOTTSY

b. Dottsy Brodt, 6 April 1954, Sequin, near San Antonio, Texas, USA. In 1966, at the age of 12, she was already singing in clubs in her local area as part of a trio. She reached the finals of a major talent competition on KBER San Antonio in 1969 and appeared on television in her own show. In 1972, she began to study special education (for teaching handicapped or subnormal children) at the University of Texas, and for some time, she managed to combine her singing with her studies, even forming her own band, Meadow Muffin. While singing at a convention in San Antonio, she came to the attention of Happy Shahan, who gave her the chance to appear at major events with Johnny Rodriguez and helped her to get a contract with RCA. Her first single, 'Storms Never Last', written by Jessi Colter, became a Top 20 US country chart hit in 1975 and was quickly followed by Susanna Clark's 'I'll Be Your San Antone Rose'. In the late 70s, she had further hits, including a Top 10 with '(After Sweet Memories) Play Born To Lose Again'. In 1979, Waylon Jennings played guitar and added harmony vocals to Dottsy's lead when she recorded his song 'Trying To Satisfy You' - the result, not surprisingly, being another Top 20 hit. When it appeared that she would go on to major stardom, she decided to cut back on her singing and concentrate on completing her college education. She had always wanted to work with autistic and mentally retarded children, and by the early 80s was fully involved in this type of work. Her last chart entry, at the time of writing, was a 1981 minor hit on Tanglewood Records with the somewhat descriptive and suitable title 'Let The Little Bird Fly'.

● ALBUMS: *The Sweetest Thing* (RCA 1976)★★★, *Trying To Satisfy You* (RCA 1979)★★.

DOUGLAS, JERRY

b. Gerald Calvin Douglas, 28 May 1956, Warren, Ohio, USA. A talented musician who plays guitar and lap steel guitar but is primarily now known as one of the finest dobro players ever to have played in any form of country music, he gained his initial attraction to the instrument at the age of eight, when his father, himself a bluegrass musician, took him to see Flatt And Scruggs. At the time, their dobro player was Josh Graves and his performance captivated the boy. In 1972, by then playing with his father's band, he was given the opportunity to play for a time with the Country Gentlemen. He later worked with J.D. Crowe And The New South and with Ricky Skaggs in Boone Creek. In 1978, his debut, *Fluxology*, was named after the nickname of 'Flux', given to him by other musicians, seemingly because of his amazing finger-picking skills. During the 80s, he worked for some years with the Whites, playing dobro on most of their popular recordings, but eventually he decided to follow a solo career and also to work as a session musician. In the latter capacity, he has played on numerous albums by countless artists, whose styles have varied widely from the Nitty Gritty Dirt Band to Hank Williams Jnr. In 1986, he was one of the first musicians signed to record on the new MCA Master Series. He appeared with fiddle virtuoso Mark O'Connor, at the 1987 Wembley Festival in London and he has toured various countries including Poland. His amazing talents have won him a great number of awards, including election to *Frets* Gallery Of Greats and a 1983 Grammy for Best Country Instrumental Performance. In the 80s, he, Mike Auldridge and Josh Graves produced *Dobro Summit*, an educational video. He also featured on several albums by Irish singer Maura O'Connell. In the 90s, he also turned to production and even made regular appearances on the American TNN television channel's *American Music Shop*. He released an excellent album with Peter Rowan in 1996.

● ALBUMS: *Fluxology* (Rounder 1978)★★★, *Tennessee Fluxedo* (Rounder 1981)★★★, *Under The Wire* (MCA Master Series 1986)★★★, *Changing Channels* (MCA Master Series 1987)★★★, *Plant Early* (MCA Master Series 1989)★★, *Slide*

Rule (Sugar Hill 1992)★★★, with Russ Barenberg, Edgar Meyer *Skip, Hop & Wobble* (Sugar Hill 1993)★★, with Peter Rowan *Yonder* (Sugar Hill 1996)★★★★.
● COMPILATIONS: *Everything Is Gonna Work Out Fine* first two albums on one CD (Rounder 1987)★★★.

DOWNING, BIG AL

b. 9 January 1940, Lenapah, Oklahoma, USA. Downing was exposed to both R&B and country music as a boy, and taught himself piano on an instrument that he found on a rubbish dump. In 1958 he took the then unusual step of joining a white group, the Rhythm Rockers, led by Bobby Brant. Changing their name to the Poe Kats, they recorded the regionally successful 'Down On The Farm' for Lelan Rogers' White Rock label in Dallas: leased to the larger Challenge label, it narrowly missed the national charts but has become an acknowledged rock 'n' roll classic (as well as one of the shortest rock 'n' roll records, at one minute 31 seconds). Later sessions up to 1964 featured Downing's thumping piano and his deep voice, with its Fats Domino overtones, on such excellent rockers as 'Yes I'm Loving You' and 'Georgia Slop'. During this period he recorded duets with Esther Phillips and played piano for Wanda Jackson, but he had to wait until 1970 for chart success when 'I'll Be Holding On' was a soul hit. The versatile Downing has since reverted to his early roots and has several big US country hits. He is a frequent visitor to rock 'n' roll festivals in Europe, where his broad grin and matching waistline are familiar sights.
● COMPILATIONS: *Rockin' 'N' Rollin'* (Schoolkids 1996)★★★★.

DRAKE, PETE

b. 8 October 1932, Atlanta, Georgia, USA, d. 29 July 1988. One of the world's leading exponents of the steel guitar, Drake arrived in Nashville in the late 50s and was quickly established as one of the city's leading session musicians. His distinctive, mellow-toned style was heard on many releases, including those by Marty Robbins and Don Gibson. Pete also recorded in his own right and while billed as Pete Drake And His Talking Steel Guitar, he secured a US Top 30 hit with a 1964 single, 'Forever'. However, it was for continued studio work that Drake maintained his popularity, and he crossed over into the wider rock fraternity in the wake of his contributions to three Bob Dylan albums, *John Wesley Harding*, *Nashville Skyline* and *Self Portrait*, and to George Harrison's *All Things Must Pass*. The artist also produced Ringo Starr's C&W collection *Beaucoups Of Blues*, and assembled the stellar cast supporting the former Beatles drummer. During the 70s Drake appeared on albums by several 'new' country acts, including Linda Hargrove, Steve Young and Tracy Nelson, as well as completing sessions for Elvis Presley. This respected musician also inaugurated his own label, Stop Records, and opened Pete's Place, a recording studio. Drake died in July 1988 aged 55.
● ALBUMS: *Talking Steel And Singing Strings Forever* (1964)★★★, *Talking Steel Singing* (1965)★★★, *Pete Drake And His Talking Steel Guitar* (1965)★★★, *The Hits I Played On* (1969)★★, *Pete Drake Plays All Time Country Favourites* (1971)★★★ *Steel Away* (1973)★★★, *The Pete Drake Show* (Stop 1973)★★, *Fabulous Steel Guitar* (mid-70s)★★★, *Amazing* (1976)★★★.

DRAPER, RUSTY

b. Farrell Draper, Kirksville, Missouri, USA. Draper entered showbusiness at the age of 12, singing and playing his guitar on radio in Tulsa, Oklahoma. For the next five years, he worked on various stations including Des Moines, Iowa and Quincy, Illinois. He then became the Master of Ceremonies and vocalist at the Mel Hertz Club in San Francisco. He eventually moved to Hermie King's Rumpus Room in the same city, where he stayed for the next seven years. In 1953, his recording of 'Gambler's Guitar' reached number 6 on both the US country and pop charts and gave him his first million-seller. A second gold record followed in 1955 for his version of 'Shifting Whispering Sands', which reached number 3 in the pop charts but surprisingly did not even make the country chart at all (a cover version by Eamonn Andrews made the UK Top 20). During the 50s, he had further US Top 40 pop hits with 'Seventeen' (1955), 'Are You Satisfied' (1955), 'In The Middle Of The House' (1956) and a US cover version of the UK skiffle hit 'Freight Train' (1957). He did, however, have modest UK pop chart success in 1960 with his version of 'Muleskinner Blues', which peaked at number 39. In 1962, he joined Monument Records and reached the US pop charts with 'Night Life' in 1963. He did not achieve further US country chart successes until the late 60s, when he had very minor hits with 'My Elusive Dreams', 'California Sunshine' and 'Buffalo Nickel'. 'Two Little Boys' gave him another minor US hit in 1970, the last for 10 years, when 'Harbour Lights', an unlikely country song, became his last chart entry. During his career, he has also undertaken several acting roles, including appearances in some television western series such as *Rawhide* and *Laramie*, and stage musicals including *Oklahoma* and *Annie Get Your Gun*.
● ALBUMS: *Hits That Sold A Million* (60s)★★★, *Sing Along* (60s)★★★, *Country Classics* (60s)★★★, *Rusty Draper Plays Guitar* (60s)★★, *Night Life* (60s)★★★, *Something Old Something New* (1969)★★.

DRIFTING COWBOYS

Country star Hank Williams had been using the name the Drifting Cowboys since the late 30s, and he employed an existing group, the Alabama Rhythm Boys, as the Drifting Cowboys in 1943. The line-up only became consistent after Hank Williams appeared at the *Grand Ole Opry* in 1949 and realized the need for a permanent band. He employed Jerry Rivers (b. 25 August 1928, Miami, Florida, USA, d. 4 October 1996, Hermitage, Tennessee, USA; fiddle), Bob McNett (b. 16 October 1925, Roaring Branch, Pennsylvania, USA; guitar), Hillous Butrum (b. 21 April 1928, Lafayette, Tennessee, USA; bass) and Don Helm (b. 28 February 1927, New Brockton, Alabama, USA; steel guitar). There were no drums, as the instrument was not favoured in country circles. In 1951, McNett and Butrum were replaced, respectively, by Sammy Pruett, who had been in the Alabama Rhythm Boys with Helms, and Howard Watts. Williams used the Drifting Cowboys on his sessions, sometimes augmenting the musicians with Chet Atkins. His simply chorded songs did not need elaborate embellishment, and the Drifting Cowboys' backings perfectly complemented the material. The group disbanded after Williams' death, and Don Helms worked with the Wilburn Brothers and formed the powerful Wil-Helm Agency. Helms and Rivers also worked in Hank Williams Jnr.'s band, the Cheatin' Hearts. Rivers wrote a biography *Hank Williams - From Life To Legend* (Denver, 1967), which was updated in 1980. In 1976 the original line-up re-formed for radio shows with compere Grant Turner and comedian the Duke of Paducah. They had a minor success with 'Rag Mop' and recorded a tribute to Hank Williams, 'If The Good Lord's Willing'. Hank Williams Jnr. and Don Helms recorded a duet, 'The Ballad Of Hank Williams', which was based on 'The Battle Of New Orleans'. In 1991 the Drifting Cowboys appeared at London's Wembley country music festival with Hank Williams' illegitimate daughter, Jett Williams.

● ALBUMS: *We Remember Hank Williams* (1969)★★★★, with Jim Owen *A Song For Us All - A Salute To Hank Williams* (Epic 1977)★★★, *The Drifting Cowboys' Tribute To Hank Williams* (Epic 1979)★★★, *Best Of Hank Williams' Original Drifting Cowboys* (Epic 1979)★★★★, *Classic Instrumentals* (1981)★★, *One More Time Around* (1982)★★★.

DRIFTWOOD, JIMMY

b. James Morris, 20 June 1907, Mountain View, Arkansas, USA. His name first came to prominence as a result of the Johnny Horton recording of Driftwood's song 'The Battle Of New Orleans' in 1959. The single made the top of both the US pop and country charts, but only reached the Top 20 in the UK. Lonnie Donegan reached number 2 in the UK with the song in the same year. Driftwood himself had recorded a version of the song the previous year for RCA Victor. With a strong musical heritage Driftwood learned to play guitar, banjo and fiddle while still young. Picking up old songs from his grandparents, and other members of his family, he later travelled around collecting and recording songs. While still performing at folk festivals, Driftwood continued to teach during the 40s. With the 50s came the growing folk boom, and he found himself reaching a wider audience. RCA signed him to record *Newly Discovered Early American Folk Songs*, which included the aforementioned 'Battle Of New Orleans'. While the song's popularity grew, Driftwood was working for the *Grand Ole Opry*, but left in order to work on a project to establish a cultural centre at his home in Mountain View. The aim was to preserve the Ozark Mountain people's heritage. Having later joined the Rackensack Folklore Society, he travelled the USA, speaking at universities to pass on the importance of such a project. The first Arkansas Folk Festival, held in 1963, was successful and, in 1973, the cultural centre was established. One performer at such events organized by the Rackensack Folklore Society was Glenn Ohrlin.

● ALBUMS: *Newly Discovered Early American Folk Songs* (RCA 1958)★★★★, *The Wilderness Road* (RCA 1959)★★★, *The Westward Movement* (RCA Victor 1959)★★★, *Tall Tales In Song* (RCA Victor 1960)★★★, *Songs Of Billy Yank And Johnny Reb* (RCA Victor 1961)★★★, *Driftwood At Sea - Sea Shanties* (RCA Victor 1962)★★, *Voice Of The People* (Monument 1963)★★, *Down In The Arkansas* (Monument 1965)★★★, *A Lesson In Folk Music* (60s)★★★.

● COMPILATIONS: *Famous Country Music Makers* (70s)★★★, *Americana* (1991)★★★.

DRUSKY, ROY

b. Roy Frank Drusky, 22 June 1930, Atlanta, Georgia, USA. Drusky showed interest only in baseball during his childhood and high school days but after attending a Cleveland Indians training camp, decided against it as a career and in 1948, joined the navy. A country band on his ship gave him an interest in music, and when next on shore leave he bought a guitar and taught himself to play. In 1950, he left the navy, enrolled at Emory University to study veterinary medicine and sought singing work to pay for the course. He formed a country band called the Southern Ranch Boys and played daily on WEAS Decatur. He later left the university and became a disc jockey on WEAS, the resident singer in a local club and appeared on WLW-A television in Atlanta. In 1953, he recorded for Starday. A year later he left his band, moved as a DJ to KEVE Minneapolis, and continued with club work, but he concentrated more on songwriting. In 1958, his song 'Alone With You' became a number 1 US country hit for Faron Young and led to Drusky becoming a member of the *Grand Ole Opry*, even though he had no hit recordings of his own at the time. He moved to Nashville, signed for Decca and between 1960 and 1962 had Top 5 country hits with his own recordings of 'Another', 'Anymore' (both self-penned), 'Three Hearts In A Tangle' (also a US pop chart hit, number 35) and 'Second Hand Rose'. He moved to Mercury in 1963 and over the next decade charted several Top 10 country hits including 'Peel Me A Nanner', 'Where The Blue And Lonely Go', 'Long Long Texas Road', 'All My Hard Times' and in 1965, achieved a country number 1 with 'Yes, Mr Peters', a duet recording with Priscilla Mitchell. In 1966, he had Top 20 success with the original version of 'If The Whole World Stopped Loving', a song that gave Val Doonican a big number 3 pop hit in Britain the next year. He moved to Capitol Records in 1974, having a minor hit with Elton John's 'Dixie Lily' and then to Scorpion Records in 1977, attaining his last chart entry that year with 'Betty's Song'.

In the mid-60s he made three appearances in country and western films, *Forty Acre Feud*, *The Golden Guitar* and *White Lightning Express* (his recording of the soundtrack title song of the latter charted in 1965). From the 60s to the early 80s, he toured extensively, played the *Opry* and became involved in production and publishing work as well as hosting his own network television programmes. His relaxed singing style has led to him being referred to as the Perry Como of country music. Many felt that, had he so wished and with the right material, he may well have been the person to assume the pop/country mantle left by Jim Reeves.

● ALBUMS: *Anymore With Roy Drusky* (Decca 1961)★★★, *It's My Way* (Decca 1962)★★★★, *All Time Country Hits* (1964)★★★, *The Pick Of The Country* (Mercury 1964)★★★★, *Songs Of The Cities* (Mercury 1964)★★★, *Yesterday's Gone* (Mercury 1964)★★★★, *Country Music All Around The World* (Mercury 1965)★★, *Roy Drusky* (Buckboard 1965)★★★, *The Great Roy Drusky Sings* (Mercury 1965)★★★, with Priscilla Mitchell *Love's Eternal Triangle* (Mercury 1965)★★★, with Mitchell *Together Again* (Mercury 1966)★★★★, *Country Song Express* (Mercury 1966)★★★, *In A New Dimension* (Mercury 1966)★★★, *If The Whole World Stopped Lovin'* (Mercury 1966)★★★, *Now Is A Lonely Time* (Mercury 1967)★★★, with Mitchell *We Belong Together* (Mercury 1968)★★★, *Jody And The Kid* (Mercury 1969)★★, *My Grass Is Green* (Mercury 1969)★★★, *Portrait Of Roy Drusky* (Mercury 1969)★★★, *All My Hard Times* (Mercury 1970)★★★, *I'll Make Amends* (Mercury 1970)★★★, *I Love The Way That You've Been Loving Me*

(Mercury 1971)★★,*Doin' Something Right* (Mercury 1972)★★★,*Good Times, Hard Times* (Mercury 1973)★★★,*Peaceful Easy Feeling* (Mercury 1974)★★★,*Night Flying* (Mercury 1976)★★★,*This Life Of Mine* (Mercury 1976)★★★,*English Gold* (1980)★★★,*Roy* (Big R 1981)★★★.
● COMPILATIONS: *Twenty Grand Country Hits* (Mercury 1969)★★★,*Country Special* (Vocalion 1970)★★★,*Golden Hits* (1979)★★★,*Songs Of Love And Life* (Mercury Nashville 1995)★★★,*All American Country Duets* (Spectrum 1997).

DUCAS, GEORGE

b. 1 August 1966, Texas City, Texas, USA. George Ducas is a Nashville singer-songwriter who eschews many of the formulaic elements that such a genre description might imply. Though clearly rooted in the country music tradition, his songs are written in a wholly different register - one that maintains the evocative narratives but plays down overt sentimentality. His debut album, which contained the singles 'Kisses Don't Lie', 'Hello Cruel World', 'Teardrops' and 'Lipstick Promises', was produced with Richard Bennett, who also helmed the 1997 follow-up. To promote it, Ducas toured major baseball stadiums, singing the national anthem at half-time. He told *Billboard* magazine in 1996 that 'It's a great time to be in country music, because the parameters of it are broader than they have ever been.' Clearly, Ducas has benefited from this situation, and he has been widely tipped both inside and outside of the Nashville singer-songwriter scene as an artist on the verge of a major breakthrough.
● ALBUMS: *George Ducas* (Liberty 1994)★★★, *Where I Stand* (Liberty 1997)★★★.

DUDLEY, DAVE

b. David Pedruska, 3 May 1928, Spencer, Wisconsin, USA. In 1950, after an arm injury had ruined a baseball career, Dudley turned to performing country music. Following successful broadcasts in Idaho, he formed the Dave Dudley Trio in 1953. In 1960, Dudley was struck by a car while packing equipment, and spent several months in hospital. He had his first US country successes, 'Maybe I Do' and 'Under The Cover Of Night', and, also in 1961, he reluctantly recorded the up-tempo 'Six Days On The Road' to please a friend. In 1963 he released it on his own Golden Wing label and it reached number 32 in the US pop charts. The song spawned a new genre of songs about truckers, usually depicting them as hard-living, hard-loving macho men. Dudley declares, 'I like my woman everywhere I go', in 'Truck Drivin' Son-Of-A-Gun'. Dudley's numerous trucking songs include 'Two Six Packs Away', 'There Ain't No Easy Run', 'One More Mile', 'The Original Travelling Man', 'Trucker's Prayer' and 'Truck Driver's Waltz', many of them being written by, and sometimes with, Tom T. Hall. In 1970, Dudley had a number 1 country hit with 'The Pool Shark' and recorded a duet with Hall, 'Day Drinkin''. He recorded for Sun Records in 1980 and had some success with 'Rolaids, Doan's Pills And Preparation H'. His comedy single, 'Where's That Truck?', with the truckers' favourite disc jockey, Charlie Douglas, did not revive his career, and it seems doubtful that he will get his trucks back on the chart highway again.
● ALBUMS: *Six Days On The Road* (Golden Ring 1963)★★★★, *Songs About The Working Man* (Mercury 1964)★★★★, *Travelling With Dave Dudley* (Mercury 1964)★★★, *Talk Of The Town* (Mercury 1964)★★★, *Rural*

Route No. 1 (Mercury 1965)★★★, *Truck Drivin' Son-Of-A-Gun* (Mercury 1965)★★★, *Free And Easy* (Mercury 1966)★★★, *There's A Star Spangled Banner Waving Somewhere* (Mercury 1966)★★★, *Lonelyville* (Mercury 1966)★★★, *My Kind Of Love* (Mercury 1967)★★★, *Dave Dudley Country* (Mercury 1967)★★★, *Oh Lonesome Me/Seven Lonely Days* (Mercury 1968)★★★, *Thanks For All The Miles* (Mercury 1968)★★★, *One More Mile* (Mercury 1969)★★★, *George And The North Woods* (Mercury 1969)★★★, *It's My Lazy Day* (Mercury 1969)★★★, *Pool Shark* (Mercury 1970)★★★, *Will The Real Dave Dudley Please Sing?* (Mercury 1971)★★★, *Listen, Betty, I'm Singing Your Song* (Mercury 1971)★★, *The Original Travelling Man* (Mercury 1972)★★★, *Keep On Truckin'* (Mercury 1973)★★, *Special Delivery* (1975)★★★, *Uncommonly Good Country* (United Artists 1975)★★★, *1776* (United Artists 1976)★★, *Chrome And Polish* (1978)★★★, *Interstate Gold* (Sun 1980)★★, with Charlie Douglas *Diesel Duets* (1980)★★, *King Of The Road* (1981)★★.
● COMPILATIONS: *20 Great Truck Hits* (EMI Sweden 1983)★★★, *Collection: Dave Dudley* (EMI 1983)★★★, *Country Best* (Bulldog 1988)★★★.

DUFF, MARY

b. Lobinstown, Co. Meath, Eire. She first sang locally at the age of 12 with her accordion-playing father. On leaving school, she worked as a school secretary and sang with a semi-professional group in the evenings around the local area, and was influenced in her early days by Patsy Cline. Duff also began to make solo appearances at various talent contests and was seen and heard at one such event by Daniel O'Donnell's manager, Sean Reilly, who signed her to his management. She toured with O'Donnell, quickly establishing a reputation as a fine singer in her own right, and soon acquired a recording contract with Ritz Records. In 1989, she won the European Gold Star Award (the country music equivalent of the *Eurovision Song Contest*) in Holland. Duff won the Most Popular British Female Vocalist award in 1990-91. She has appeared at various European venues, including Switzerland, and at several international shows such as the Wembley International Country Music Festival. She is also a very popular touring act throughout the British and Irish country scene and now has several popular videos. Duff has a vibrant, happy-go-lucky personality, which suggests that she lives up to her statement that, 'You only live once so always do what you're happiest doing'. Recent albums have varied from straight country (*Just Lovin' You*) to MOR (*Shades Of Blue*).
● ALBUMS: *Love Someone Like Me* (Ritz 1988)★★★, *Winning Ways* (Ritz 1990)★★★, *Silver And Gold* (Ritz 1992)★★★, *Just Lovin' You* (Ritz 1995)★★★, with Daniel O'Donnell *Timeless* (Ritz 1996)★★★, *Shades Of Blue* (Ritz 1997)★★.
● VIDEOS: *Live In Concert* (Ritz 1990).

DUKE OF PADUCAH

b. Benjamin Francis 'Whitey' Ford, 12 May 1901, DeSoto, Missouri, USA, d. 20 June 1986, Nashville, Tennessee, USA. Ford, in his alter ego role as the Duke Of Paducah, became something of an American institution with his homespun humour and banjo playing. He was raised in Little Rock, Arkansas, by his grandmother but ran away to join the navy at the age of 17. He served for four years, during which time he learned to play the banjo and began to develop his comedy routines. In 1924, after playing banjo for a time in dancehalls with a Dixieland band, he appeared on KTHS, Hot Springs and fronted Benny Ford And His Arkansas Travellers. He later worked the vaudeville circuit and tent, medicine and burlesque shows, before joining Otto Gray's Oklahoma Cowboys. After leaving Gray, he joined Gene Autry in Chicago and acted as MC of Autry's show for nine years. During this time, he became a member of the original cast of the WLS *National Barn Dance* and it was here that he acquired his stage name. He later had his own network show, *Plantation Party*, on WLW Cincinnati. In 1937, he worked with John Lair and Red Foley to establish the Renfro Valley Barn Dance. In the early 40s, Ford, as the Duke Of Paducah, joined the *Grand Ole Opry*, where he soon became a favourite on the *Prince Albert Show* segment. Following a disagreement with the sponsors in 1948, he was replaced on that show by Rod Brasfield but he remained an *Opry* regular, on other segments, until 1959, although he then continued to make guest appearances for many more years. In the early 60s, he acted as ringmaster for his own circus but in later years, he worked with Hank Williams Jnr.'s touring show. He appeared in various television programmes and was always popular on chat shows, where he related tales from his years in showbusiness. He played in several films, including *Country Music On Broadway*, and also delivered serious lectures at colleges. His famous closing line was: 'I'm going back to the wagon, boys, these shoes are killing me.' It was, however, not the shoes but cancer that killed the Duke of Paducah, when he lost his long battle against it in 1986.

DUNCAN, JOHNNY

b. 5 October 1938, Dublin, Texas, USA. Duncan was born on a farm into a music-loving family. His cousins were Dan (of England Dan And John Ford Coley) and Jimmy Seals (of Seals And Croft). Duncan thought of himself as a guitarist, and it was not until his late teens that he appreciated his singing voice. Shortly after his marriage in 1959, Duncan moved to Clovis, New Mexico, and recorded demos for Norman Petty, although nothing evolved. In 1964, following a stint as a disc jockey in the south-west, he went to Nashville, working as a bricklayer while trying to break into the business. He was signed to Columbia Records and had his first US country chart entry with 'Hard Luck Joe' in 1967. Minor successes followed with 'To My Sorrow', 'You're Gonna Need Me' and 'When She Touches Me'. He also reached the charts with two duets with June Stearns, 'Jackson Ain't A Very Big Town' and 'Back To Back (We're Strangers)'. He became part of Charley Pride's roadshow and wrote 'I'd Rather Lose You' for him. Chet Atkins recorded another of his compositions, 'Summer Sunday'. He had further success with 'There's Something About A Lady' and 'Baby's Smile, Woman's Kiss', and enjoyed his first US country Top 10 hit with 'Sweet Country Woman' in 1973. Duncan lost interest in country music, partly caused by his marriage breaking up, and he returned to Texas. Larry Gatlin contacted him and said, 'John, apart from Ray Price and myself, you're the best singer in Texas. Why aren't you making records?'. Gatlin produced Duncan on 'Jo And The Cowboy', and, on a hunch, he asked one of the Lea Jane Singers to sing a verse. Janie Frickie then became the 'mystery voice' on Duncan's following successes, finally sharing the billing on 'Come A Little Bit Closer'. Producer Billy

Sherrill wanted Duncan relaxed for 'Stranger' and sent him to a bar for two hours. The bar-room song, which featured Frickie, was a number 4 country hit. Duncan's forte was plain-speaking songs about sleazy affairs such as 'Thinking Of A Rendezvous', 'It Couldn't Have Been Any Better' (both US country number 1s), 'Third Rate Romance' and 'Cheatin' In The Key Of C'. Apart from his records with Frickie, he had country hits with 'She Can Put Her Shoes Under My Bed (Anytime)', 'Hello Mexico (And Adios Baby To You)' and 'Slow Dancing'. Duncan's luck faltered with an album called *The Best Is Yet To Come*. In the 80s he remarried and settled in Texas with his new wife and family and now records for minor labels. His most recent chart entry was in 1986 with 'Texas Moon'.

● ALBUMS: *Johnny One Time* (Columbia 1968)★★★, with June Stearns *Back To Back* (Columbia 1969)★★, *There's Something About A Lady* (Columbia 1971)★★★, *Sweet Country Woman* (Columbia 1973)★★★, *Come A Little Bit Closer* (Columbia 1977)★★★, *The Best Is Yet To Come* (Columbia 1978)★★★, *See You When The Sun Goes Down* (Columbia 1979)★★★, *Straight From Texas* (Columbia 1979)★★★, with Janie Frickie, Millie Kirkham And the Jordanaires *In My Dreams* (Columbia 1980)★★★, *You're On My Mind* (Columbia 1980)★★★, with Frickie *Nice 'N' Easy* (Columbia 1981)★★.

● COMPILATIONS: *The Best Of Johnny Duncan* (Columbia 1976)★★★★, *Greatest Hits* (Columbia 1989)★★★★.

DUNCAN, JOHNNY, AND THE BLUE GRASS BOYS

b. John Franklin Duncan, 7 September 1932, Oliver Springs, near Knoxville, Tennessee, USA. Duncan sang from an early age in a church choir and then, when aged 13, he joined a gospel quartet. At 16, he left Tennessee for Texas and while there, he formed a country group. Duncan was drafted into the US army in 1952 and posted in England. He married an English woman, Betty, in 1953. After his demobilization, they went to the USA. Betty returned home for Christmas 1955 and, as she fell ill and needed an operation, Duncan worked in the UK for his father-in-law. He met jazz bandleader Chris Barber, who was looking to replace Lonnie Donegan. Donegan had formed his own skiffle group, a fashion he had started with Barber's band. Barber was impressed by Duncan's nasal vocal delivery and physical resemblance to Donegan and immediately recruited him, and he joined them the following night at London's Royal Festival Hall. In 1957 Duncan left the band and called his own group the Blue Grass Boys in homage to Bill Monroe, but they were all British - Denny Wright (guitar), Jack Fallon (bass), Danny Levan (violin) and Lennie Hastings (drums). Although promoted as a skiffle artist, Duncan was a straight country performer, both in terms of arrangements and repertoire. 'Last Train To San Fernando', a Trinidad calypso he re-arranged, steamed up the UK charts, but the communication cord was pulled just before it reached the top. The b-side, 'Rock-A-Billy Baby', was equally strong. Duncan was featured on BBC Television's *6.5 Special* and hosted radio programmes for the BBC and Radio Luxembourg, but he only had two more Top 30 entries, 'Blue Blue Heartache' and 'Footprints In The Snow', which both reached number 27. Duncan subsequently worked as a country singer in UK clubs and encouraged local talent. In 1974 he emigrated to

Melbourne, Australia, where he has since worked as a country singer.

● ALBUMS: *Johnny Duncan's Tennessee Songbag* (1957)★★★, *Johnny Duncan Salutes Hank Williams* (1958)★★★, *Beyond The Sunset* (1961)★★★, *Back In Town* (1970)★★, *The World Of Country Music* (Decca 1973)★★★.

● COMPILATIONS: *Last Train To San Fernando* 4-CD box set (Bear Family 1997)★★★★.

DUNCAN, TOMMY

b. Thomas Elmer Duncan, 11 January 1911, Hillsboro, Texas, USA, d. 25 July 1967. Duncan grew up loving the music of Jimmie Rodgers and made the start of a long musical career in 1932, when he joined Bob Wills in the Light Crust Doughboys. When Wills quit in 1933 to form his own band, Duncan went with him to become one of Wills' original Texas Playboys. He stayed with Wills until 1948, when, probably tired of fronting the band in Wills' absences caused mainly by his drinking, he left to form his own band, the Western All Stars, taking with him several Texas Playboys. During his years with Wills they co-wrote several songs and Duncan's fine baritone vocals appeared on countless recordings, including the 1940 million-selling 'New San Antone Rose'. In 1949, recording for Capitol, he registered his only solo chart hit with his version of the Jimmie Rodgers song 'Gambling Polka Dot Blues'. In 1959, Wills and Duncan were reunited and in 1960-61, they recorded over 40 sides for Liberty. Although he made no further recordings with Wills, Duncan remained active until his death following an heart attack in July 1967. It is impossible to separate the careers of Duncan and Wills and most experts have maintained that in their solo work, neither one ever recaptured the greatness of their partnership.

● ALBUMS: with Bob Wills *Together Again* (Liberty 1960)★★★, with Wills *Bob Wills & Tommy Duncan* (Liberty 1961)★★★.

● COMPILATIONS: with Bob Wills *Legendary Masters - Bob Wills & Tommy Duncan* (United Artists 1971)★★★, *Texas Moon* (Bear Family 1996)★★★, *Beneath A Neon Star In A Honky Tonk* (Bear Family 1996)★★★.

DUNFORD, UNCLE ECK

b. Alex (sometimes given as Aleck) Dunford, 1878, Carroll County, West Virginia, USA, d. 1953. Dunford, who was a brilliant fiddle player and almost as good on guitar, was a very intelligent person, in an area where schooling was of secondary importance. Usually fondly referred to as Uncle Eck, he could sing and had an especially commanding speaking voice, using a drawling accent totally unlike the local dialect. He surprised many with his ability to quote Shakespeare or Burns and recite monologues and he also studied photography. In 1908, he married Callie Frost, a relative of Ernest Stoneman's future wife Hattie, and he became involved in the Stoneman Family's music. A lonely figure after his wife died in 1921, he lived in a small cabin (which still stands), a mile from Galax, at Ballard Branch. He concentrated more and more on his music and played fiddle for Stoneman's Dixie Mountaineers and also made solo Victor recordings. In 1932, when Ernest Stoneman left the Galax area, Dunford began to play with the Ward Family and made recordings with them and with the Ballard Branch Bogtrotters for the Library of Congress. He began appearing at the Galax Fiddlers Convention from the mid-30s, until his death *circa* July 1953. Sadly, in his latter years, he was regularly seen on the streets of Galax selling pencils to support himself. Examples of his work appear on many Stoneman Family albums, while he is also remembered for solo recordings such as his monologue 'My First Bicycle Ride' and his song 'Old Shoes And Leggins', the latter being issued on a Folkways Records compilation. A considerable amount of information about Uncle Eck who, apart from his instrumental and vocal talents was probably one of the genre's first comedians, may be found in Ivan M. Tribe's book *The Stoneman Family*.

DUNN, HOLLY

b. Holly Suzette Dunn, 22 August 1957, San Antonio, Texas, USA. Dunn's father was a preacher and her mother a professional artist, but they encouraged their children to sing and entertain. Dunn learned guitar and became a lead vocalist with the Freedom Folk Singers, representing Texas in the White House bicentennial celebrations. After university, she joined her brother, Chris Waters (Chris Waters Dunn), who had moved to Nashville as a songwriter (he wrote 'Sexy Eyes' for Dr. Hook). Together they wrote 'Out Of Sight, Not Out Of Mind' for Cristy Lane. Among her other songs are 'An Old Friend' (Terri Gibbs), 'Love Someone Like Me' (New Grass Revival), 'Mixed Emotions' (Bruce Murray, brother of Anne Murray) and 'That Old Devil Moon' (Marie Osmond). Dunn sang on numerous demos in Nashville. Her self-named album for the MTM label in 1986, and her own composition 'Daddy's Hands', drew considerable attention. *Across The Rio Grande*, was a traditional yet contemporary country album featuring Vince Gill and Sam Bush and it won much acclaim. However, MTM went into liquidation and Dunn moved to Warner Brothers Records. Her up-tempo 'You Really Had Me Going' was a country number 1 and other country hits include 'Only When I Love', 'Strangers Again' and 'That's What Your Love Does To Me'. Her 'greatest hits' set, *Milestones*, aroused some controversy when she issued one of its tracks, the newly recorded 'Maybe I Mean Yes' as a single. The song was accused of downplaying the trauma of date-rape, and Dunn was sufficiently upset to ask radio stations not to play the record. Her career was restored to equilibrium with the low-key, but impressive, *Getting It Dunn* in 1992. *Getting It Dunn* was her last album for Warner, and she is now signed to the independent label River North. Her debut for that label, *Life And Love And All The Stages*, was undistinguished, and she may find it difficult returning to the mainstream.

● ALBUMS: *Holly Dunn* (MTM 1986)★★★, *Cornerstone* (MTM 1987)★★★, *Across The Rio Grande* (MTM 1988)★★★, *The Blue Rose Of Texas* (Warners 1989)★★★, *Heart Full Of Love* (Warners 1990)★★★, *Getting It Dunn* (Warners 1992)★★★, *Life And Love And All The Stages* (River North 1995)★★.

● COMPILATIONS: *Milestones: Greatest Hits* (Warners 1991)★★★.

● VIDEOS: *Cowboys Are My Weakness* (1995).

DUNN, RONNIE

(see Brooks And Dunn)

DURKIN, KATHY

b. Katherine Leddy, Butlers Bridge, Co. Cavan, Eire. Her father, Eugene Leddy, was a noted dance band leader in the 50s. She learned piano accordion and enjoyed singing but did not seek a professional career. In the late 70s, she married (Andrew Durkin) and had two children. She starred in the Cavan ladies football team which won All Ireland honours in 1977. In the early 80s, she sang with a local band, Cavan, around the clubs, and an appearance on RTE television gained her a recording contract with Harmac Records. Her 1988 recording of 'Midnight To Moonlight' proved very successful. She appeared at the Wembley International Country Music Festival in 1990 and a year later, she scored a big hit in Ireland with her version of Rita MacNeill's 'Working Man'. In recent years, she has worked to consolidate her position as one of the top female vocalists not only in her native Eire but also by touring country clubs in the UK.

● ALBUMS: *Memories* (Harmac 1989)★★★, *Moonlight Reflections* (Harmac 1990)★★★, *Kathy's Favourites* (Harmac 1991)★★★, *Kathy's Gold* (Harmac 1992)★★★★.

DUSTY, SLIM

b. David Gordon Kirkpatrick, 13 June 1927, Kempsey, New South Wales, Australia. He grew up on his parents' farm on Nulla Nulla Creek. His first introduction to music came through listening to renditions by his father, who was known throughout the area as Noisy Dan, owing to his overly loud vocal performances, only matched by his old-time fiddle playing. He listened avidly to the radio, being initially attracted by the recordings he heard of such singers as Jimmie Rodgers and Wilf Carter, and later, the first recordings of Australian artists Tex Morton and Buddy Williams. He was particularly attracted to cowboy songs and wrote his first song, 'The Way The Cowboy Dies', at the age of 10. At school, he became very friendly with Edwin Haberfield who lived on the next farm. The two boys spent many hours learning to play the guitar and to sing and yodel like Rodgers and Carter. They began performing as a duo around their local area. After searching for suitable names (and quickly discarding Buddy Bluebird and Buddy Blackbird), they finally became Slim Dusty and Shorty Ranger. In the early 40s, they appeared regularly on *Request Hour* on 2KM Kempsey. In 1942, impressed by his son's talent, Noisy Dan arranged an audition with Columbia Records in Sydney and afterwards paid £25 for the boy to record two self-penned songs, 'Song For The Aussies' and 'My Final Song'. Copies were sent to radio stations but they failed to make any impact, as did further similarly made recordings the following year. However, Dusty slowly built some reputation through his radio appearances and during the war years, with Shorty Ranger, he made various trips further afield. They played with travelling tent shows, but none lasted for long and they usually arrived back home broke. When Noisy Dan died suddenly in May 1945, Dusty had to spend more time looking after the farm. In 1946, perhaps because of a growing reputation, he was invited by Regal-Zonophone to record six songs. He was offered only a £10 fee (with no royalties) but on 19 November, he made the recordings. The first was a Dusty original called 'When The Rain Tumbles Down In July'. It was released in 1947 and proved a hit for him. It has since become an Australian country standard and

is rated by some followers of Australian country as the first real bush ballad (Dusty was always saddened that Noisy Dan, who had pushed so hard for his son's success, did not live to see his initial recording breakthrough). Although a hit, because of the royalty waiver, Dusty received no financial benefit and consequently, he spent much of the next two years working on the farm. He made some appearances with Shorty Ranger, including playing the agricultural show circuit at Armidale and the touring magic show of the Great Dante, until the lack of promised wages saw them quit and head for their farms. In 1948, a visit to Sydney failed and the following year a trip to Adelaide also, owing to a polio epidemic threat there, which, naturally, did not encourage people to visit theatres. However, a further trip to Sydney eventually led to them finding employment with Tim McNamara's 2SM radio show. Here they worked with Gordon Parsons and the McKean Sisters and were employed by the Foster Family to tour with their celebrated circus. In 1951, Dusty married Joy McKean and from that point his association with Shorty Ranger ended, although their friendship continued and Dusty later recorded many of his friend's songs. Between 1948 and 1953, Dusty made almost 30 more recordings, including his sad 'Rusty It's Goodbye', and the follow-up to his initial hit called 'The Rain Still Tumbles Down'. He and his wife had worked wherever they could find employment; at times he had even been employed as a plasterer and they now had their daughter Anne (b. 4 July 1952, Sydney, New South Wales, Australia) to consider. In 1954, he decided to set up his own travelling show. At the time, they decided it was for a three-month trial period, little realizing that it would still be in operation four decades later. Apart from Slim and his wife, the show initially featured Bob McKean (Joy's brother), rope-spinner Malcolm Mason and yodeller/comedian Barry Thornton. Thornton, with his alter ego character of Mulga Dan, stayed for 19 years and is rated by many as the most influential Australian country music guitarist through his development of Dusty's bush ballad style, instigated initially by providing amplification to his acoustic guitar. The Slim Dusty Show toured extensively and further recordings were made for the next three years without incident. Things began to change when Dusty asked his friend, Gordon Parsons, for permission to record a song he had written about a pub that ran out of beer (those who knew of Parsons' fondness for beer later jokingly said that he not only wrote the song, he actually caused such an event). Parsons readily agreed and on 1 April 1957, Dusty duly recorded the song, 'A Pub With No Beer', merely to make up the number of songs scheduled for the session. After initial airplay on 2UE Sydney, it sold 30,000 copies; when other stations added it to their play-lists, it became a smash hit that stayed in the Australian charts for six months. The song went on to become a number 1 in Ireland and when, in January 1959, it entered the UK pop charts to peak at number 3, it made the name of Slim Dusty known to audiences far beyond his native land. (There has been some contention over the years regarding the actual authorship of the song. It seems that Parsons had once been given some lines of verse and from them, he had written the song. It was later found that a poem by Dan Sheahan called 'A Pub Without Beer', which contained many similarities in the wording, had been printed in a 1944 newspaper. Dusty, who later became Sheahan's friend and recorded several of his songs, has always maintained that Parsons had believed the lines that he had been given were from some anonymous work.) The next year, Dusty recorded follow-ups called 'The Answer To A Pub With No Beer' and 'The Sequel To A Pub With No Beer'. He later agreed that he was being overly optimistic when, in 1959, he recorded a number called 'The Pub Rock', which failed dismally. It was also in 1957 that Dusty recorded his now classic version of Shorty Ranger's song 'Winter Winds'. Following his success with 'The Pub' (as he calls the song), Dusty and his travelling family show joined with Frank Foster's touring extravaganza. This included everything from boxers to strippers, and for six years, Dusty toured the length and breadth of Australia singing his country music to any audience that was attracted to the show. When television began to affect the audiences at such shows, Dusty decided to aim for places not covered by television transmissions. In 1964, he made his first Round Australia Slim Dusty Tour. It lasted 10 months and covered 30,000 miles, during which time he played in halls in some of the most remote areas in Australia. Since then he has repeated the process many times. He made a very successful tour to New Zealand in 1969 and the following year, on a visit to New Guinea and the Solomon Islands, he attracted thousands of fans to the concerts. During the 70s, he cut down on the length of the tours in order to meet his recording commitments. At regular sessions, he recorded a great many of his own songs and some by noted writers such as Stan Coster. His first album, *Slim Dusty Sings*, was released in 1960 and has been followed by 87 others by the mid-90s. In 1970, he became the first Australian country music entertainer to be awarded the MBE. In 1973, Radio 2TM began the Australian Country Music Awards, and over the next 10 years, the Dusty family collected no less than 27 of them. Since 1973, he has collected 25 Golden Guitars for his songs at the Tamworth Country Music Awards. His wife Joy also won awards for her songs 'Lights On The Hill' (one of Dusty's biggest hits), 'Biggest Disappointment' and 'Indian Pacific' and in 1978, daughter Anne took the best female vocal award for her recording of 'Grievous Angel'. Dusty had some throat problems in 1974 but was soon back performing. Apart from Anne, the Dusty Family show has also included son David Kirkpatrick (b. 1958, Rockampton, Queensland, Australia), and over the years various Australian artists launched their careers as part of the show. In 1977, Dusty and country comedian Chad Morgan headed the first ever country music show to be held at the Sydney Opera House. His life story, *Walk A Country Mile*, was published in 1979 and the same year, he became only the fourth person (after Australian pioneers Tex Morton, Buddy Williams and Smoky Dawson), to be elected to the Country Music Roll Of Renown (Australia's equivalent to Nashville's Country Music Hall of Fame). In 1983, Joy and sister Heather were reunited on stage together for the first time in 25 years and also elected to the Roll of Renown. Further awards followed, and in 1984, the film *The Slim Dusty Story* was released. His appearances outside of his native Australia have been very limited. He visited the UK during a world trip in 1990 that also saw him visit the USA. In Nashville, he professed interest in the Ryman Auditorium and the Country Music Hall Of Fame but was highly critical of some other places. He is reported to have said of Twitty City, 'If you put that up in Australia, they'd throw bricks through the window'. Unlike many country singers, he had no desire to perform in Nashville, not even on the *Grand Ole Opry*, which seemingly failed to impress him. It has been stated that when he arrived back on Australian soil, he knelt down to kiss the tarmac. He accepted the brilliance of the American musicians but the Nashville sound was far removed from his bush ballads and consequently held little interest for him. At times he has fuelled controversy as with the occasion when he would not remove his hat for the Queen at an Australian Royal Variety Performance. He reputedly stated, 'I don't take my hat off for anyone', but photographs of a bareheaded Dusty do exist. In 1981, his Australian hit 'Duncan' received much airplay on BBC Radio and almost made the UK pop charts. Slim Dusty recorded an album with his daughter Anne Kirkpatrick (by then a popular artist in her own right) in 1990. In the mid-90s, he was still busily entertaining, and in 1997 released an album covering pop hits from the pre-war era. Arguably, Slim Dusty may well be Australia's most recorded artist, with sales over the years that compare favourably with those of Kylie Minogue and Jason Donovan.

● ALBUMS: *Slim Dusty Sings* (EMI 1960)★★★, *Songs For Rolling Stones* (EMI 1961)★★★, *Along The Road Of Song* (EMI 1962)★★★, *Aussie Sing Song* (EMI 1962)★★★, *Songs In The Saddle* (EMI 1963)★★★, *Another Aussie Sing Song* (EMI 1963)★★★, *Songs Of Australia* (EMI 1964)★★★, *People And Places* (EMI 1964)★★★, *Australian Bush Ballads & Old Time Songs* (EMI 1965)★★★, *The Nature Of Man* (EMI 1966)★★★, with Joy McKern *An Evening With Slim And Joy* (EMI 1966)★★, *Essentially Australian* (EMI 1967)★★★, *Songs My Father Sang To Me* (EMI 1967)★★★, *Songs From The Cattle Camps* (EMI 1968)★★★, *Sing Along With Dad* (EMI 1968)★★★, *Cattle Camp Crooner* (EMI 1969)★★★, *Slim Dusty Encores* (EMI 1969)★★★, *Sing A Happy Song* (EMI 1970)★★★, *Songs From The Land I Love* (EMI 1971)★★★, *Glory Bound Train* (EMI 1971)★★★, *Live At Wagga Wagga* (EMI 1972)★★★, *Me And My Guitar* (EMI 1972)★★★, *Foolin' Around* (EMI 1973)★★★, *Live At Tamworth* (EMI 1973)★★, *Dusty Tracks* (EMI 1973)★★★, *Tall Stories And Sad Songs* (EMI 1973)★★★, *Australiana* (EMI 1974)★★★, *Dinki Di Aussies* (EMI 1974)★★★, *Lights On The Hill* (EMI 1975)★★★, *Way Out There* (EMI 1975)★★★, *Things I See Around Me* (EMI 1976)★★★, *Give Me The Road* (EMI 1976)★★★, *Slim Dusty - This Is Your Life* (EMI 1976)★★★, *Songs From Down Under* (EMI 1976)★★★, *Just Slim And Old Friends* (EMI 1977)★★, *On The Move* (EMI 1977)★★★, *Travellin' Country Man* (EMI 1977)★★★, *To Whom It May Concern* (EMI 1978)★★★, *The Entertainer - Live At The Sidney Opera House* (EMI 1978)★★★, *Spirit Of Australia* (EMI 1979)★★★, *Slim Dusty Rarities* (EMI 1979)★★, *Rodeo Riders* (EMI 1979)★★★, *Walk A Country Mile* (EMI 1980)★★★, *The Man Who Steadies The Lead* (EMI 1980)★★★, *Slim Dusty No: 50 The Anniversary Album* (EMI 1981)★★★★, *Where Country Is* (EMI 1981)★★★, *The Slim Dusty Family Album* (EMI 1981)★★★, *Vintage Album Volume 1* (EMI 1982)★★★, *Who's Riding Old Harlequin Now* (EMI 1982)★★★, *Vintage Album Volume 2* (EMI 1983)★★★, *On The Wallaby* (EMI 1983)★★★, *I Haven't Changed A Bit* (EMI 1983)★★★, *Trucks On The Track* (EMI 1984)★★★, *The Slim Dusty Movie* double album soundtrack (EMI 1984)★★★★, *I'll Take Mine Country Style* (EMI 1985)★★★, *Vintage Album Volume 3* (EMI 1985)★★★, *Singer From Down Under* (EMI 1985)★★★, *To A Mate (Mack Cormack)*

cassette only (FA 1985)★★★, *Live Across Australia* (EMI 1986)★★★, *Stories I Wanted To Tell* (EMI 1986)★★★, *Beer Drinking Songs Of Australia* (EMI 1986)★★, *Neon City* (EMI 1987)★★★, *Slim Dusty Family* (EMI 1987)★★★, *Sings Joy McKean* (EMI 1987)★★★, *Country Livin'* (EMI 1988)★★★, *Cattlemen From The High Plains* (EMI 1988)★★★, *G'Day, G'Day* (EMI 1988)★★★, *Sings Stan Coster* cassette only (FA 1988)★★★, *King Of Kalgoorlie* (EMI 1989)★★★, *Vintage Album Volume 4* (EMI 1989)★★★, *Henry Lawson & Banjo Patterson* cassette only (TP 1989)★★★, *Travellin' Guitar* (EMI 80s)★★★, *That's The Song We're Singing* (EMI 80s)★★★, *Vintage Album Volume 5* (EMI 1990)★★★, *Live Into The 90s* (EMI 1990)★★★, with Anne Kirkpatrick *Two Singers One Song* (EMI 1990)★★★, *Coming Home* (EMI 1991)★★★, *Ringer From The Top End* (EMI 1994)★★★, *Natural High* (EMI 1994)★★★, *Country Way Of Life* (EMI 1995)★★★, *The Slim Dusty Show Live At Townsville 1956* (EMI 1996)★★★, *91 Over 50* (EMI 1997)★★★★, *A Time To Remember* (EMI 1997)★★★.
● COMPILATIONS: *The Best Of Slim Dusty* 6-album box set (Reader's Digest 1984)★★★, *Australia Is His Name* 4-album box set (EMI 1985)★★★★, *Regal Zonophone Collection* 3-CD box set (EMI 1996)★★★★.
● VIDEOS: *Into The 90s, Across Australia*.
● FURTHER READING: *Slim Dusty Around Australia*, Peter Phillips. *Slim Dusty: Walk A Country Mile*, Slim Dusty and John Japsley. *Slim Dusty: Another Day, Another Town*, Slim Dusty and Joy McKean.

DYER, BOB

Dyer, born in Tennessee, USA, arrived in Australia in the late 30s as a hillbilly singer-comedian with a travelling show. A talented musician, he played banjo-ukulele, guitar and harmonica, but his musical talent was never really featured on his recordings. His first two recordings were made for Columbia in England in 1939, but he recorded nine further sides for Regal-Zonophone in Sydney in August 1940. The material was perhaps more vaudeville than country and included 'The Martins And The Coys' and 'I Never See Maggie Alone'. He was popular on the Australian country scene for some years before he later became a radio and television personality, as well as the presenter of a quiz show that ran for over 25 years.

EANES, JIM

b. Homer Robert Eanes Jnr., 6 December 1923, Mountain Valley, Henry County, Virginia, USA, d. 21 November 1995, Martinsville, Virginia, USA. His early musical interest came from his father, a talented banjo player, who ran a local band. When only six months old, he suffered severe burns to his left hand that left the fingers twisted, but as a boy he developed a style of playing that, after an operation in 1937, enabled him to become a fine guitarist. He played in his father's band, appeared on local radio, where he acquired the name of Smilin' Jim Eanes (Homer seemed unsuitable) and in 1939, became the vocalist for Roy Hall's Blue Ridge Entertainers, until Hall's death in a car crash in 1943. Between 1945 and 1949, he worked with the Blue Mountain Boys on the *Tennessee Barn Dance* on WNOX Knoxville and recorded with them in New York. He briefly joined Lester Flatt and Earl Scruggs, when they formed their first Foggy Mountain Boys, before finally moving to Nashville to join Bill Monroe. He began to write songs during his time at Knoxville, the first being his now well-known 'Baby Blue Eyes', and when, in 1949, he won a Capitol talent competition, it was one of the first songs he recorded. Another song, co-written at the same time with Arthur Q. Smith, was 'Wedding Bells', which Eanes first sang on the *Barn Dance* in 1947. The song's ownership moved to Claude Boone, when it failed to raise interest with the listeners; he subsequently passed it on to Hank Williams, for whom it became a number 2 country hit. (Arthur Q. Smith, real name James A. Pritchett, wrote several songs which he sold to artists and Eanes assisted with some of them. Smith, who died in 1963, should not be confused with either Fiddlin' Arthur Smith or Arthur 'Guitar Boogie' Smith.) In 1951, Eanes formed his famous Shenandoah Valley Boys and recorded for Blue Ridge. He achieved considerable success with the war song 'Missing In Action' (again co-written with Arthur Q. Smith), which sold in excess of 400,000 copies and led to him signing for Decca, where he recorded his popular 'I Cried Again', 'Rose Garden Waltz' and 'Little Brown Hand' (the next year, Ernest Tubb's Decca recording of 'Missing In Action' reached number 3 in the US country charts). He moved to Starday in 1956, finding success with his own songs 'Your Old Standby' (recorded by George Jones on several occasions) and 'I Wouldn't Change You If I Could' (a number 1 US country hit for Ricky Skaggs in 1983). He also made a recording of 'The Little Old Log Cabin In The Lane', which is rated by some as the best recorded version of this old song. Throughout the 60s and 70s, Eanes was occupied with performing, recording, songwriting and work on various radio stations, including, in 1967, a spell on the *Wheeling Jamboree*. During the 70s, he was also much in demand as an MC for festivals and shows. In 1978, he suffered a severe heart attack but a year later embarked on a European tour (these tours were a regular occurrence and by 1990, he had completed nine, and during one recorded an album with a Dutch country band). He formed an outfit in 1984, underwent heart surgery in 1986, but as soon as possible was back entertaining and singing, as always, a mixture of bluegrass, gospel and country material. In the early 90s, emphysema caused Eanes major problems but, in spite of a general deterioration in his health, he continued to make some local appearances and even completed an album with his old friend Bobby Atkins. He finally died of congestive heart failure in the Blue Ridge Center, Martinsville, Virginia, on 21 November 1995, and is buried at Martinsville's Roselawn Burial Park. His fine vocals and songwriting over the years earned Jim Eanes the universal nickname of The Bluegrass Balladeer.

● ALBUMS: *Your Old Standby* (Zap 1967)★★★, *Jim Eanes With Red Smiley & The Bluegrass Cut-Ups* (Rural Rhythm 1968)★★★, *Rural Rhythm Presents Jim Eanes* (Rural Rhythm 1969)★★★, *Blue Grass Special BS2* (BS 1970)★★★, *The New World Of Bluegrass* (Folly 1973)★★★, *The Shenandoah Valley Quartet With Jim Eanes* (County 1975)★★★, *Jim Eanes* (Original 1976)★★★, *Shenandoah Valley Quartet* (Outlet 1977)★★★, *A Statesman Of Bluegrass Music* (Jessup 1977)★★★, *Where The Cool Waters Flow* (Leather 1978)★★★, *Jim Eanes & The Shenandoah Valley Boys (Early Days Of Bluegrass)* (Rounder 1979)★★★, with Smoketown Strut *Ridin' The Roads* (Racoon 1981)★★★, *Shenandoah Grass Yesterday And Today* (Webco 1983)★★★, *Bluegrass Ballads* (Rebel 1986)★★★, *Jim Eanes, Bobby Atkins And The Countrymen* (Old Homestead 1986)★★★, *Reminiscing* (Rebel 1987)★★★, *Log Cabin In The Lane* (Highland 1988)★★★, *Let Him Lead You* (Rebel 1989)★★, *50th Anniversary Album* (Rebel 1990)★★★, *Hillbilly Sounds At Its Best* (CowgirlBoy 1990)★★★, with Bobby Atkins *Heart Of The South* (Rural Rhythm 1991)★★★.

EARLE, STEVE

b. 17 January 1955, Fort Monroe, Virginia, USA. Earle's father was an air-traffic controller and the family was raised in San Antonio, Texas. Steve played an acoustic guitar from the age of 11, but he also terrorized his schoolfriends with a sawn-off shotgun. He left home many times and sang 'Help Me Make It Through The Night' and 'all that shit' in bars and coffee-houses. He befriended Townes Van Zandt, whom he describes as a 'a real bad role model'. Earle married at the age of 19 but when his wife went with her parents to Mexico, he moved to Nashville, playing for tips and deciding to stay. He took several jobs to pay his way but they often ended in arguments and violence. Johnny Lee recorded one of Earle's songs, and Elvis Presley almost recorded 'Mustang Wine'. His second marriage was based, he says, 'on a mutual interest in drug abuse'. Earle formed a back-up band in Texas, the Dukes, and was signed to CBS Records, who subsequently released *Early Tracks*. Recognition came when he and the Dukes signed to MCA and made a famed 'New Country' album, *Guitar Town*, the term being the CB handle for Nashville. The title track, with its Duane Eddy-styled guitar riff, was a potent blend of country and rock 'n' roll. 'Good Ol' Boy (Gettin' Tough)' was Earle's response to President Reagan's firing of the striking air-traffic controllers, including Earle's brother. Like Bruce Springsteen, his songs often told of the restlessness of blue-collar workers. 'Someday' is a cheerless example - 'There ain't a lot

you can do in this town/You drive down to the lake and then you turn back around.' Earle wrote 'The Rain Came Down' for the Farm Aid II benefit, and 'Nothing But A Child' was for an organization to provide for homeless children. Waylon Jennings recorded 'The Devil's Right Hand' and Janie Fricke, 'My Old Friend The Blues'. Earle saw in the 1988 New Year in a Dallas jail for punching a policeman and during that year, he married his fifth wife and released an album with a heavy metal feel, *Copperhead Road*, which included the Vietnam saga 'Johnny Come Lately', which he recorded with the Pogues. His answering machine says, 'This is Steve. I'm out shooting heroin, chasing 13-year-old girls and beating up cops. But I'm old and I tire easily so leave a message and I'll get back to you.' After a lengthy break, allegedly because Earle had to detox, he returned with a fine album in 1995. *Train A Comin'* was mellow, acoustic and emotional, and featured some exceptional playing from Peter Rowan and harmony vocals from Emmylou Harris. Some of Earle's compositions are regarded as redneck anthems, but the views are not necessarily his own: he writes from the perspective of his creation, Bubba, the archetypal redneck. Another is The Beast: 'It's that unexplainable force that causes you to be depressed. As long as The Beast is there, I know I'll always write.' In the mid-90s, fired by the acclaim for *Train A Comin'*, a cleaned-up Earle started his own label, E-Squared, and contributed to the film soundtrack of *Dead Man Walking*. Earle is determined never to return to drugs. He stated in January 1996, 'I am real, real active and that is how I stay clean. It's a matter of survival to me. My life's pretty together right now. I got my family back.'

● ALBUMS: *Guitar Town* (MCA 1986)★★★★, *Exit O* (MCA 1987)★★★, *Copperhead Road* (MCA 1988)★★★★, *The Hard Way* (MCA 1990)★★★, *Shut Up And Die Like An Aviator* (MCA 1991)★★★★, *BBC Radio 1 Live In Concert* (Windsong 1992)★★★, *Train A Comin'* (Transatlantic 1995)★★★★, *I Feel Alright* (Transatlantic 1996)★★★, *El Corazón* (Warner Bros 1997)★★★★.

● COMPILATIONS: *Early Tracks* (Epic 1987)★★★, *Essential Steve Earle* (MCA 1993)★★★★, *Angry Young Man* (Nectar 1996)★★★, *Ain't Ever Satisfied* (HIPP 1996)★★★★.

EASTER BROTHERS

A country and gospel group formed in 1953, consisting of Russell Easter (b. Russell Lee Easter, 22 April 1930, Mount Airy, North Carolina, USA; banjo, guitar, vocals), James Easter (b. James Madison Easter, 24 April 1933, Mount Airy, North Carolina, USA; guitar, mandolin, vocals) and Ed Easter (b. Edward Franklin Easter, 28 March 1934, Mount Airy, North Carolina, USA; mandolin, banjo, vocals). They grew up greatly influenced by bluegrass music, in particular that of a gospel nature. Russell Easter first formed a band in 1947, and was later joined by his siblings. In 1953, with one other musician, they began to perform as the Green Valley Quartet and regularly played stations in Mount Airy and Danville. Turning more and more to bluegrass gospel music, they built their reputation throughout the 60s, playing various radio and television programmes. In 1960, they recorded for both Commandant and King. In 1968, when they recorded an acoustic album for County, the group (by then the Easter Brothers And The Green Valley Quartet) also included Russell Jnr. (banjo, dobro, guitar). During the 70s and 80s, they recorded albums for Old Homestead, Life Line and Morningstar. James's son Jeff played harmonica with the group for a time but eventually left to work as a duo with his wife Sheri (a relative of the Lewis Family) and in more recent years, a third generation Easter, namely Russell's grandson Jason, has played bass with the group.

● ALBUMS: as the Easter Brothers *I've Been Touched* (Commandment 60s)★★★; as the Easter Brothers And The Green Valley Quartet *The Bible On The Table* (Troy 60s)★★, *Let Me Stand Lord* (Commandment 1965)★★★, *Lord I Will* (Commandment 1966)★★★, *14 Songs Of Faith* (Commandment 1967)★★★, *Bluegrass & Country Hymns* (Stark 1967)★★★, *Country Hymn Time* (Commandment 1967)★★★, *The Easter Brothers & The Green Valley Quartet* (County 1968)★★★, *From Earth To Gloryland* (Commandment 1969)★★★, *He's Everything I Need* (Commandment 1970)★★★, *Just Another Hill* (Commandment 1972)★★★, *Don't Overlook Your Blessings* (Mission 1974)★★★, *Hold On* (Old Homestead 1976)★★★, *The Easter Brothers In Nashville* (Mission 70s)★★★, *Coming Home* (Mayberry 70s)★★★, *I'm Holding To His Hand* (QCA 70s)★★★, *We're Going Home* (QCA 70s)★★★, *He's The Rock I'm Leaning On* (Rebel 1981)★★★, *I Feel Like Travelling On* (Rebel 1981)★★★, *Almost Home* (Rebel 1982)★★★, *Songs About Mama* (Life Line 1981)★★★, *The Easter Brothers* (Life Line 1983)★★★, *Hereafter* (Life Line 1984)★★, *Tribute To Reno & Smiley* (Rebel 1985)★★★.

● COMPILATIONS: *Early Sessions 1960-1961* (Rebel 1984)★★★★.

EATON, CONNIE

b. 1 March 1950, Nashville, Tennessee, USA. Her father Bob sang on the *Grand Ole Opry* and in 1950, he achieved some success with 'Second Hand Heart', before he quit the business. After some experience and success as a child actor, she was signed to Chart Records and, working with producer Cliff Williamson (whom she subsequently married), she made her first recordings in 1968. Her first *Billboard* country chart entry came in 1970, when 'Angel Of The Morning' (a 1968 Top 10 pop hit for Merrilee Rush) peaked at number 34. By 1975, she added six more minor hits, two being duet recordings with Dave Peel, namely a version of Ray Charles' 1961 pop number 1, 'Hit The Road Jack', and 'It Takes Two'. In 1975, she recorded for Dunhill and gained her highest career chart placement with 'Lonely Men, Lonely Women' (number 23). Her final chart entry came the same year on ABC when 'If I Knew Enough To Come Out Of The Rain' became a very minor hit. Perhaps that song should have told her something, since her name has been conspicuous by its absence from the country charts ever since.

● ALBUMS: with Dave Peel *Hit The Road Jack* (Chart 1970)★★★, *Something Special* (Chart 1971)★★, *Connie Eaton* (ABC/Dot 1975)★★.

EDELMAN, JUDITH

b. New York, USA. Edelman embarked on a solo career in 1996 having first made her name with the acclaimed Rocky Mountain bluegrass group Ryestraw. She began piano lessons at the age of five and continued her studies until she left for college. Attending Swarthmore College in Pennsylvania, she majored in English but continued to take voice lessons and sang with various local bands. Immediately following graduation, she moved to Africa as part of her work in third world development. It was while recuperating from illness there in a friend's house that she began to teach herself the guitar. Returning to the Bay Area at the age of 26 she linked up with Ryestraw, with whom she spent several years touring, before deciding to pursue a solo career. Her debut, *Perfect World*, featured 11 original compositions matching bluegrass influences with contemporary themes, as well as Celtic and folkloric elements. Guests including Jerry Douglas, Clive Gregson, Alison Brown and Randy Howard provided the perfect backing for Edelman's sweet vocal style.

● ALBUMS: *Perfect World* (Demon 1996)★★★.

EDENTON, RAY

b. Ray Quarles Edenton, 8 November 1926, Mineral, Virginia, USA. Renowned session guitarist Ray Edenton has long been recognized as one of Nashville's most prolific and reliable session musicians. Though his preference is for rhythm guitar, he is also equally adaptable to lead guitar, mandolin and bass. His grandfather was a fiddler, and his two brothers were also musicians; hence, he found himself playing his first amateur contests from the age of six. Following his discharge from service after World War II, he earned money from truck driving while playing occasional singer-songwriter sets in the evenings. He then became a session radio player with the Old Dominion Barn Dance and Joe Maphis's Korn Krackers. After a major scare to his health in the late 40s when he contracted tuberculosis, Edenton began his first round of engagements at the *Grand Ole Opry*, later travelling with artists including Chet Atkins, George Morgan and Minnie Pearl. His first major Nashville recording session came in March 1953, Webb Pierce cutting the country number 1 'There Stands The Grass'. Edenton's guitar-playing also appeared on Kitty Wells and Red Foley's 'One By One', another chart-topper. Much more recently he has played on pop records recorded by Foley's granddaughter, Debby Boone. As well as working as a musician, Edenton has also branched out into record production, writing and plugging. However, he is still best known for his session work, which by the mid-90s included names ranging from the Beach Boys and Henry Mancini to Andy Williams and Reba McEntire.

EDWARDS, DON

b. 20 March 1939, Boonton, New Jersey, USA. Although born in an unlikely state for cowboys, Edwards has become one of the leading exponents of cowboy and western music. He taught himself guitar at the age of 10 and grew up listening to his father's 78s of such singers as Carl T. Sprague and Gene Autry, and avidly read any books on cowboy life that he could find. He was impressed by cowboys on the silver screen, especially Tom Mix and Ken Maynard, whom he described as 'sure 'nuff cowboys without the glitz and glitter'. In 1958, he headed west to work on ranches and at rodeos in Texas and New Mexico. Between 1961 and 1964, after painful rodeo experiences, he turned to music and worked as a cowboy singer, actor, gunfighter and stuntman at the Fort Worth amusement park, Six Flags Over Texas - his desire to perform, no doubt, inherited from his father who had been a vaudeville magician. A visit to Nashville in 1965 quickly convinced him that Music City was not for him, and after a short spell in Florida, he returned to Fort Worth. His residency at the prestigious White Elephant Saloon (named by *Esquire* magazine among America's 100 best bars) and personal appearances soon established him throughout Texas and Oklahoma. He has now become an authority on all things Western, especially the songs and poems. He has presented programmes on cowboy songs and their history, not only in schools but also at Yale and Havard, the Smithsonian Institute and other important venues, as well as on network television and radio. An admirer of the work of song collector Nathan 'Jack' Thorp (1867-1940), he published his own book, *Songs Of The Cowboy*, in 1986. Edwards, the Sons Of The San Joaquin and cowboy poet Waddie Mitchell, were the first artists signed by the new Warner Western label. He now appears with those acts in The Cowboy Jubilee, a travelling show of western music and verse. Before joining Warner, he released five albums on his own label. He has toured Europe and Australasia but makes his home in Parker County, Texas, on his beloved Sevenshoux Ranch. He is a great admirer of Marty Robbins for his work in popularizing cowboy songs and Robbins' influence may be noted in Edwards' own singing. He described his dedication to promoting cowboy songs by saying, 'Usually, kids play cowboys and stuff like that, but they grow out of it. I never did. My only regret is that I was born about fifty years too late. However, I'm mighty thankful I wasn't born any later than I was'.

● ALBUMS: *Happy Cowboy* (Sevenshoux 1980)★★★, *Songs Of The Cowboy* (Sevenshoux 1986)★★★, *Guitars And Saddle Songs* (Sevenshoux 1987)★★★, *Desert Nights & Cowtown Blues* (Sevenshoux 1990)★★★, *Chant Of The Wanderer* (Sevenshoux 1992)★★★, *Songs Of The Trail* (Warner Western 1992)★★★★, *Goin' Back To Texas* (Warner Western 1993)★★★, with Waddie Mitchell *The Bard And The Balladeer* (Warner Western 1994)★★★, *West Of Yesterday* (Warner Western 1996)★★★★.

EDWARDS, JONATHAN

b. 28 July 1946, Aitkin, Minnesota, USA. After forming the bluegrass band Sugar Creek in 1965, Edwards took up songwriting. Opting for a more commercial style, he saw his own composition, 'Sunshine', featuring a mid-tempo driving beat via an acoustic guitar, move swiftly up the US Hot 100 in late 1971, and peak at number 4. His self-titled album - released in the UK on Atlantic Records - also included the ballad 'Emma' and the follow-up single 'Train Of Glory', which never charted. Edwards has been featured on a number of recordings by other notable performers, including Emmylou Harris, Jimmy Buffett, and Tom Chapin. During the gap in his own recording career, he continued performing, and also produced an album, *Rainbow Reign*, for his wife Carolina, a one-time backing singer for Edwards. While Edwards' style has always veered between folk and country, the collaboration with the Seldom Scene bluegrass band saw him succeed in reworking earlier Edwards originals, alongside more standard bluegrass material. 'We Need To Be Locked Away' from 1989's *The Natural Thing* was his biggest country hit to date.

● ALBUMS: *Jonathan Edwards* (Atco 1971)★★★★, *Honky-Tonk Stardust Cowboy* (Atco 1972)★★★, *Have A Good Time For Me* (Atco 1973)★★★, *Lucky Day* (Atco 1974)★★★, *Rockin' Chair* (Reprise 1976)★★★, *Sailboat* (Reprise 1977)★★, *Jonathan Edwards Live!* (Chronic 1982)★★★, with Seldom Scene *Blue Ridge* (Sugar Hill 1985)★★★, *Little*

Hands - Songs For And About Children (American Melody 1987)★★, *The Natural Thing* (MCA Curb 1989)★★★, *One Day Closer* (1994)★★★.

EDWARDS, STONEY

b. Frenchy Edwards, 24 December 1929, Seminole, Oklahoma, USA, d. 5 April 1997. Stoney grew up listening to country music, an upbringing described in his 1973 song 'Hank And Lefty Raised My Country Soul', and that honky tonk sound has remained with him throughout his career. He played guitar from the age of 15. He moved to California and had several manual jobs before becoming a club singer and, like Charley Pride before him, he was at first something of a novelty in Nashville - a black performer working in country music. He signed with Capitol Records in 1971 and had 15 chart singles including 'Poor Folks Stick Together', 'She's My Rock', 'Mississippi, You're On My Mind', and 'Blackbird (Hold Your Head High)'. He was dropped by Capitol in 1977 and he recorded for several smaller labels including the Music America release *No Way To Drown A Memory*. He lost a leg in a shooting accident and retired from the business, but returned in 1991 with an acclaimed new album, *Just For Old Times Sake*, which was produced and mostly written by Billy Joe Kirk and featured many top session musicians. Edwards died of stomach cancer in April 1997.

● ALBUMS: *Stoney Edwards, A Country Singer* (Capitol 1971)★★★, *Down Home In The Country* (Capitol 1972)★★★, *She's My Rock* (Capitol 1973)★★, *Mississippi, You're On My Mind* (Capitol 1975)★★★, *Blackbird* (Capitol 1976)★★, *No Way To Drown A Memory* (Music America 1981)★★, *Just For Old Time's Sake* (CMP 1991)★★★.

ELLEDGE, JIMMY

b. 8 January 1943, Nashville, Tennessee, USA. When he was 18 years old, Jimmy Elledge sent a demo tape to famed country producer Chet Atkins, who signed him to RCA Victor Records. Elledge's debut single, the country ballad 'Funny How Time Slips Away' - produced by Atkins and written by soon-to-be country superstar Willie Nelson - reached the US Top 30 in early 1962 and earned him a gold disc for selling over a million copies. He later joined the Hickory label in the mid-60s but had no further US chart success.

ELLIOTT, RAMBLIN' JACK

b. Elliott Charles Adnopoz, 1 August 1931, Brooklyn, New York, USA. The son of an eminent doctor, Elliott forsook his middle-class upbringing as a teenager to join a travelling rodeo. Embarrassed by his family name, he dubbed himself Buck Elliott, before adopting the less-mannered Jack. In 1949 he met and befriended Woody Guthrie, who in turn became his mentor and prime influence. Elliott travelled and sang with Guthrie whenever possible, before emerging as a talent in his own right. He spent a portion of the 50s in Europe, introducing America's folk heritage to a new and eager audience. By the early 60s he had resettled in New York where he became an inspirational figure to a new generation of performers, including Bob Dylan. *Jack Elliott Sings The Songs Of Woody Guthrie* was the artist's first American album. This self-explanatory set was succeeded by *Ramblin' Jack Elliott*, in which he shook off the imitator tag by embracing a diverse selection of material, including songs drawn from the American tradition, the Scottish music hall and Ray Charles. Further releases included *Jack Elliott*, which featured Dylan playing harmonica under the pseudonym Tedham Porterhouse, and *Young Brigham* in 1968, which offered songs by Tim Hardin and the Rolling Stones as well as an adventurous use of dobros, autoharps, fiddles and tablas. The singer also guested on albums by Tom Rush, Phil Ochs and Johnny Cash. In 1975 Elliott was joined by Dylan during an appearance at the New York, Greenwich Village club, The Other End, and he then became a natural choice for Dylan's nostalgic carnival tour, the Rolling Thunder Revue. Elliot later continued his erratic, but intriguing, path, and an excellent 1984 release, *Kerouac's Last Dream*, showed his power undiminished.

● ALBUMS: *Jack Elliott Sings The Songs Of Woody Guthrie* (1960)★★★, *Ramblin' Jack Elliott* (Prestige 1961)★★★, *Ramblin' Jack Elliott Sings Woody Guthrie And Jimmy Rogers* (MTR 1962)★★★, *Jack Elliott* (Prestige 1964)★★★, *Ramblin' Cowboy* (1966)★★★, *Young Brigham* (Warners 1968)★★★, *Kerouac's Last Dream* (Folk Freak 1984)★★★, *South Coast* (Red House 1995)★★★, *Me And Bobby McGee* (Rounder 1996)★★★.

● COMPILATIONS: *The Essential Ramblin' Jack Elliott* (Vanguard 1976)★★★, *Talking Dust Bowl - The Best Of Ramblin' Jack Elliott* (Big Beat 1989)★★★, *Hard Travelin'* (Big Beat 1990)★★★, *Ramblin' Jack - The Legendary Topic Masters* (Topic 1996)★★★.

ELLIS, RED

b. Marvin Thrushel Ellois, 21 December 1929, Arkadelphia, USA. Ellis learned to play both guitar and mandolin in his early teens and was twice wounded during military service in the Korean War. After his discharge, he studied sound and video engineering in Little Rock before, in 1955, he relocated to Michigan. He worked on radio stations as an engineer and from 1957, he also worked as a disc jockey presenting bluegrass gospel music. A friendship with Jimmy Williams, who had played with the Stanley Brothers, led to them recording together and forming the Huron Valley Boys, a band that consisted of fellow southern musicians who were then resident in Michigan. In 1959/60, they recorded for Starday with Ellis even supervising the engineering; these sessions formed the basis of seven EPs and later albums. He formed his own Pathway label in the mid-60s, recorded with his wife Agee, and also worked on sessions with a gospel group, the Crossmen. In 1986, Old Homestead released albums of some of his Pathway material. He returned to Arkansas in 1968, where he worked as video engineer at KATV Little Rock. In 1971, he and Williams reunited to record two albums for Jessup. After this, although he and Williams have occasionally played together at some special events, Ellis virtually retired from active performing.

● ALBUMS: with Jimmy Williams *Holy Cry From The Hills* (Starday 1961)★★★, *God Brings Bluegrass Back Together* (Jessup 1971)★★★, *Little David's Harp* covers 1971 (Jessup 1975)★★; as Red Ellis And The Huron Valley Boys *The Sacred Sound Of Bluegrass* (Starday 1962)★★★, *Old Time Religion Bluegrass Style* (Starday 1963)★★, *That Beautiful Land* (Pathway 1967)★★★, *The Soldier's Dream* 60s recordings (Old Homestead 1986)★★★, *First Fall Of Snow* (Old Homestead 1986)★★★.

ELY, JOE

b. 9 February 1948, Amarillo, Texas, USA. Singer, songwriter and guitarist Ely, latterly regarded as the link between country/rock and so-called new country, moved with his parents in 1958 to Lubbock, the major city of the flatlands of Texas, from which such luminaries as Buddy Holly, Roy Orbison and Waylon Jennings had previously emerged. Ely formed his first band at the age of 13, playing a fusion of country and R&B, before dropping out of high school and following in the footsteps of Woody Guthrie and Jack Kerouac, hopping freight trains and working at a variety of non-musical jobs (including a spell with a circus) before finding himself stranded in New York with nothing but his guitar. He joined a theatrical company from Austin, Texas (where he now lives), and travelled to Europe with his theatrical employers in the early 70s before returning to Lubbock, where he teamed up with fellow singer-songwriters Jimmie Gilmore and George 'Butch' Hancock and a couple of other local musicians (including a musical saw player!) in an informal combo known as the Flatlanders. Although they were never immensely successful, the group did some recording in Nashville for Shelby Singleton's Plantation label, but only a couple of singles were released at the time. Later, when Ely was signed to MCA Records in the late 70s, the recordings by the Flatlanders, which had achieved legendary status, were anthologized on *One Road More*, an album that was first released by European label Charly Records in 1980, but did not appear in the USA until the mid-80s (the album is also available with the title *More A Legend Than A Band*). In 1976 Ely formed his own band, whose members included Jesse Taylor (guitar), Lloyd Maines (steel drum), Gregg Wright (bass) and Steve Keeton (drums), plus auxiliary picker Ponty Bone (accordion). This basic line-up recorded three albums, *Joe Ely*, *Honky Tonk Masquerade*, and *Down On The Drag*, before Keeton was replaced by Robert Marquam and Wright by Michael Robertson for *Musta Notta Gotta Lotta*, which also featured Reese Wyhans (keyboards), among others. Although these albums were artistic successes, featuring great songs mainly written by Ely, Hancock (especially) and Gilmore, the musical tide of the times was inclined far more towards punk and new wave music than towards Texan singer-songwriters.

In 1980, the Ely Band had toured extensively as opening act for the Clash, with whom Ely became very friendly, and *Live Shots* was released that year. The album featured Taylor, Marquam, Wright, Bone and Maines and was recorded on dates with the Clash, but was no more successful than the three studio albums that preceded it. In 1984 he recorded *Hi-Res*, which featured a completely new band of little-known musicians, but was no more successful than the previous albums in commercial terms.

By 1987, Ely had assembled a new band that has largely remained with him to date: David Grissom (lead guitar), Jimmy Pettit (bass) and Davis McLarty (drums). This line-up recorded two artistically stunning albums for the US independent label HighTone, *Lord Of The Highway* and *Dig All Night*, the latter featuring for the first time a repertoire totally composed of Ely's own songs. Both albums were licensed in the UK to Demon Records; in the wake of this renewed interest, Sunstorm Records, a tiny London label launched by Pete O'Brien, the editor of *Omaha Rainbow* fanzine, licensed two albums worth of Ely's early material.

Milkshakes And Malts, a compilation of Ely's recordings of songs by Butch Hancock, appeared in 1988, and *Whatever Happened To Maria?*, which similarly compiled Ely's own self-penned songs, was released in 1989. At this point, the band had been together for three years and had achieved an incredible onstage empathy, especially between Ely and Grissom, whose R&B guitar work had moved the band's music away from country. In 1990, they recorded a powerhouse live album in Austin, *Live At Liberty Lunch*, which was sufficiently impressive for Ely's old label, MCA, to re-sign him.

Among Ely's extra-curricular activities are contributions to the soundtrack of *Roadie*, a movie starring Meat Loaf, in which he can be heard playing 'Brainlock' and 'I Had My Hopes Up High', and his participation as a member of the *ad hoc* group Buzzin Cousins, in which his colleagues are John Mellencamp, John Prine, Dwight Yoakam and James McMurtry, on the soundtrack to the Mellencamp movie *Falling From Grace*. Ely, Terry Allen and Butch Hancock have together written a stage musical about a prostitute, *Chippy*. His 1995 album *Letter To Laredo* was a return to the sound of his first MCA albums and included an update of Butch Hancock's 'She Never Spoke Spanish To Me' as 'She Finally Spoke Spanish To Me'. The key track is a fine version of Tom Russell's song about cockfighting, 'Gallao Del Cielo'. Joe Ely is one of the most completely realized artists in country music of the 90s, especially in the live situation where he excels.

● ALBUMS: *Joe Ely* (MCA 1977)★★★★, *Honky Tonk Masquerade* (MCA 1978)★★★★, *Down On The Drag* (MCA 1979)★★★★, *Live Shots* (MCA 1980)★★★, *One Road More* (Charly 1980)★★★, *Musta Notta Gotta Lotta* (SouthCoast 1981)★★★, *Hi-Res* (MCA 1984)★★★, *Lord Of The Highway* (HighTone 1987)★★★★, *Dig All Night* (HighTone 1988)★★★★, *Milkshakes And Malts* (Sunstorm 1988)★★★, *Whatever Happened To Maria* (Sunstorm 1989)★★★, *Live At Liberty Lunch* (MCA 1990)★★★, *Love And Danger* (MCA 1992)★★★, *Highways And Heartaches* (1993)★★★, *Letter To Laredo* (Transatlantic 1995)★★★★.

● COMPILATIONS: *No Bad Talk Or Loud Talk '77 - '81* (Edsel 1995)★★★★, *The Time For Travellin': The Best Of ... Vol. 2* (Edsel 1996)★★★★.

EMERSON, BILL

b. William Hundley Emerson, 22 January 1938, Washington DC, USA. Emerson first played guitar at the age of 17 but a year later, he adopted the banjo as his main instrument. In 1957, he played with Buzz Busby And The Bayou Boys, before he and Charlie Waller formed the Country Gentlemen, with whom he played until late in 1958. After spells with the Stoneman Family and Bill Harrell, he joined Jimmy Martin's Sunny Mountain Boys. In 1964, he briefly played with Red Allen, during which time he also recorded albums as Bill Emerson And The Virginia Mountaineers, before rejoining Martin in 1965. In 1967/8, Emerson and Cliff Waldron led the Lee Highway Boys, who were later renamed New Shades Of Grass. In 1970, he replaced Eddie Adcock in the Country Gentlemen and recorded several successful albums with the group. In 1972, as the group were leaving a venue, shots were fired at them from a passing car and Emerson was wounded in the arm. In 1973, he joined the US Navy Band and, based in Washington DC, mainly

played guitar, although he formed a bluegrass band, the Country Current, as an offshoot from his normal service commitments. During his service career, he still managed to play on various albums, including Webco's *Shenandoah Grass - Yesterday And Today* with Jim Eanes, and to record two duet albums with Pete Goble for the label. In 1992, he recorded with some of the vocalists with whom he had worked, including Charlie Waller and Jimmy Martin, on his noted *Reunion*. He completed his naval service in 1993 and continues to play at reunion concerts and at special festivals, but seemingly has tired of the strain and stress of travelling.

● ALBUMS: with Jimmy Martin *This World Is Not My Home* (Decca 1963)★★★, *Good 'n' Country* (Decca 1966)★★★, *Big & Country Instrumentals* (Decca 1967)★★, as Bill Emerson And His Virginia Mountaineers *Banjo Pickin' And Hot Fiddlin'* (Coronet 1963)★★★★, *Banjo Pickin And Hot Fiddlin' Volume 2* (Coronet 1964)★★★, *Country Banjo* (Design 1969)★★★, *Pickin' And Fiddlin'* (Mount Vernon 1970)★★★★; as Emerson And Waldron And Lee Highway Boys *New Shades Of Bluegrass* (Rebel 1969)★★★★, *Bluegrass Country* (Rebel 1970)★★★, *Invite You To A Bluegrass Session* (Rebel 1970)★★★; with the Country Gentlemen *One Wide River To Cross* (Rebel 1971)★★★, *Country Gentlemen Sound Off* (Rebel 1971)★★★, *The Award Winning Country Gentlemen* (Rebel 1972)★★★, *The Country Gentlemen* (Vanguard 1973)★★★; with Pete Goble *Tennessee 1949* (Webco 1987)★★★, with Pete Goble *Dixie In My Eye* (Webco 1989)★★, *Home Of The Red Fox* (Rebel 1987)★★★, *Gold Plated Banjo* (Rebel 1990)★★★, *Reunion* (Webco 1992)★★★★.

● COMPILATIONS: *Little Healthy Thing* (Charly 1980)★★, *Crazy 'Bout Automobiles* (Charly 1982)★★.

EMERY, RALPH

b. Walter Ralph Emery, 10 March 1933, McEwen, Tennessee, USA. Emery became one of America's most recognizable television celebrities due to the 11 years that he spent as the host of the networked *Nashville Now* chat show. However, he had been involved with country music for many years before 1982, when he first appeared on that show. When aged four, he went to live with his grandparents, owing to his mother's breakdown caused seemingly by his alcoholic father. He grew up a shy boy, preferring to be alone and found his greatest happiness in listening to the radio, especially the *Grand Ole Opry* broadcasts. He first worked as a cinema usher but eventually attended a special academy to learn broadcasting techniques. His first work was as a disc jockey at WTPR Paris, Tennessee, before moving to Nashville. He worked briefly at WMAK, prior to moving to WSM, where he presented an all-night show. Emery quickly established his programme by encouraging local artists to appear live and listeners to phone in. His show could be heard across almost 40 states and it ran for 15 years. In 1961, he achieved success as a recording artist when his Liberty recording of 'Hello Fool' (an answer song to Faron Young's hit 'Hello Walls') reached number 4 in the US country charts. Between 1966 and 1969, Emery also presented an afternoon show called *Sixteenth Avenue*. When he had the Byrds on his radio show in 1968, he denounced them as hippies and in-between denouncing them and playing their records, he read out truck commercials. As a result of this the Byrds developed 'Drug Store Truck Drivin' Man', with the line 'this one's for you Ralph', and further suggestions in the song of

involvement in the Ku-Klux Klan. The song appeared on their pioneering country rock album *Sweetheart Of The Rodeo* in 1968. In 1972, he relinquished his all-night show to move to television, although he began a weekly country music radio show he called *Take Five For Country Music.* His *Ralph Emery Show* soon established him as a major television host and led to his subsequent hosting of the *Nashville Now* show. Other programmes that he presented included *Pop Goes Country* (a syndicated programme, 1974-80) and *Nashville Alive* (a live country music series on WTBS television, 1981-82). At times, he added a comedy touch in his television programmes with the use of a hand puppet that he called Shotgun Red. Over the years, he has collected numerous awards, including in 1988, one by SESAC as Ambassador Of Country Music, and has made appearances in four country music films, *Country Music On Broadway* (1964), *The Road To Nashville* (1966), *Nashville* (1975) and *The Girl From Tobacco Row.* In 1990, his popularity with country music artists for his services to their music saw 70 of them appear in a television special, *Salute To Ralph Emery.* He left his early morning television programme in 1991 and worked with writer Tom Clark in producing his autobiography. This proved so popular that a follow-up volume appeared in 1993. Between 1960 and 1964, he was married to country singer Skeeter Davis but the marriage ended in acrimony. This was later reactivated by comments made by Emery in his books and also by Davis in her autobiography *Bus Fare To Kentucky.*
- ALBUMS: with Shotgun Red *Songs For Children* (RCA 1989)★★, *Christmas With Ralph & Red* (RCA 1989)★★.
- FURTHER READING: *Memories (The Autobiography Of Ralph Emery)*, Ralph Emery with Tom Carter. *More Memories*, Ralph Emery with Tom Clark.

EMILIO

b Emilio Navaira, San Antonio, Texas, USA. Having established his name as a Tejano performer, Navaira dropped his surname in the mid-90s in an attempt to concentrate on a career in country music. His existing wide commercial exposure - he had been featured in advertisements for Coca-Cola, Wrangler and Stetson hats - lent itself naturally to the transition. As he told *Billboard* magazine in 1995, 'Country and Tejano are the same style, if you think about it. A good Tejano polka has a country music beat in it, so it's pretty much the same, and Latin music is involved with the girl leaving the guy, just like country.' His Capitol Records debut, *Life Is Good*, was his first record to feature English-language lyrics, written for him by a team of Nashville writers, whereas his Latin material is largely the province of his brother Raul. The album also included two Spanish-language 'bonus tracks' - a version of Van Morrison's 'Have I Told You Lately' and a return to his first ever single, 'It's Not The End Of The World'.
- ALBUMS: *Unsung Highways* (1991)★★★, *Emilio Live* (1992)★★, *Southern Exposure* (1993)★★★, *Soundlife* (EMI Latin 1994)★★★, *Life Is Good* (Capitol Nashville 1995)★★, *It's On The House* (Capitol Nashville 1997)★★.

EMMONS, BUDDY

b. 27 January 1937, Mishawaka, Indiana, USA. A multi-instrumentalist and sometime singer, Emmons began playing the fiddle when he was 10 years old. Encouraged by his father, he switched to a lap-top steel guitar and then graduated to bigger models. However, he states, 'I wanted to be a boxer, but when I found out how easy it was to play and how hard it was to box, I changed my mind.' When only 18, he stepped in for Walter Haynes, steel guitarist with Little Jimmy Dickens, on a local date. As Haynes wanted to leave the band, Emmons took his place. In 1957, he and Shot Jackson built a steel guitar from scratch, the Sho-Bud, and Emmons subsequently gave his name to a steel guitar company. Emmons played with Ernest Tubb's Texas Troubadours (1957-62) and Ray Price's Cherokee Cowboys (1962-68), and he played on records by George Jones ('Seasons Of My Heart', 'Who Shot Sam?'), Ray Price ('Nightlife') and Faron Young ('Sweet Dreams'). He then moved to Los Angeles, played sessions for Linda Ronstadt and Henry Mancini, and became a king of the road with Roger Miller. In 1975 he returned to Nashville and established himself as a leading steel guitarist. He worked on albums by the Nashville Superpickers, and among his credits are the classic albums *G.P.* (Gram Parsons), *John Phillips - The Wolfking Of L.A.*, *Now And Then* (the Carpenters), and *Who Knows Where The Time Goes?* (Judy Collins). He has also worked on albums by Sandy Denny, Doug Dillard, Annette Funicello, Mickey Gilley, Arlo Guthrie, John Hartford, Albert Lee, Manhattan Transfer, Rick Nelson, Willie Nelson, Mickey Newbury, Ricky Skaggs and John Stewart. In 1993 Emmons was in top form as a member of the Everly Brothers' touring band.
- ALBUMS: *Steel Guitar Jazz* (Mercury 1963)★★★, with Shot Jackson *Steel Guitar And Dobro Sound* (Starday 1965)★★★, *The Black Album* (Emmons 1966)★★, *Steel Guitar* (Flying Fish 1975)★★★, *Buddy Emmons Sings Bob Wills* (Flying Fish 1976)★★, with Buddy Spicher *Buddies* (Flying Fish 1977)★★, *Live From Austin City Limits* (Flying Fish 1979)★★★, with Lenny Breau *Minors Aloud* (Flying Fish 1979)★★, *First Flight* (1984)★★★, *Christmas Sounds Of The Steel Guitar* (1987)★★, *Swingin' By Request* (Step One 1992)★★★, with Ray Pennington *It's All In The Swing* (Step One 1995)★★★.

ENDSLEY, MELVIN

b. 30 January 1934, Drasco, Arkansas, USA. In 1937 Endsley was crippled by polio, which confined him to a wheelchair for life. Between 1946 and 1947, he was sent to the Crippled Children's Hospital in Memphis, where he became interested in country music after listening to such artists as Wayne Raney and the Delmore Brothers on the radio, and he learned to play guitar. He returned to Drasco and graduated from Concord High School in 1954, undecided whether he should seek a career in radio or become a teacher. He worked on KCON Conway and soon became a regular on Wayne Raney's show on KWCB Searcy. By this time, Endsley, influenced by the songwriting of Hank Williams, had already begun to write songs himself. It was on Raney's show that he first sang a song that he had originally copyrighted as 'I've Never Felt More Like Singing The Blues'. When the song attracted local attention, Endsley quickly decided to try his luck at getting his material published. Borrowing money to finance the trip and with a friend to drive for him, he made the long, painful journey to Nashville. He hoped to interest Webb Pierce but it was actually on the prompting of Marty Robbins that Wesley Rose signed Endsley to a writing contract with Acuff-Rose Music and initially acquired six of his songs. (Robbins subsequently enjoyed major hits with 'Singing The Blues' and 'Knee Deep In The Blues'. They were also major pop hits for Guy Mitchell both in the USA and the UK.) Chet Atkins signed Endsley to RCA-Victor, for whom he recorded in 1957/8 without gaining chart success. In 1959, he recorded three singles for MGM, before joining Hickory the following year. In 1961, he ended his association with Acuff-Rose and formed his own label, Melark, which he operated from his farm at Drasco, but still failed to find that elusive hit. He recorded 'Singing The Blues' again for release as a Melark single, but RCA, whom he had contracted to undertake the production, lost his master tape. This marked the end of his career as a vocalist and he more or less retired to his farm. Endsley songs recorded by other singers include 'It Happens Every Time' (Don Gibson), 'I'd Just Be Fool Enough' (Johnny Cash, Faron Young, Jimmy C. Newman and the Browns), 'Why I'm Walking' (Stonewall Jackson) and 'I Like Your Kind Of Love' (Andy Williams). Endsley may have failed to make his mark as a vocalist but he most certainly did so as a songwriter.

● ALBUMS: *I Like Your Kind Of Love* (Bear Family 1987)★★★, *I Like Your Kind Of Love* CD release with 14 additional tracks (Bear Family 1993)★★★.

ENGLAND DAN AND JOHN FORD COLEY

Dan Seals (b. 8 February 1950, McCamey, Texas, USA) comes from a family of performing Seals. His father played bass for many country stars (Ernest Tubb, Bob Wills) and his brother, Jimmy, was part of the Champs and then Seals And Croft. His cousins include 70s country star Johnny Duncan and songwriters Chuck Seals ('Crazy Arms') and Troy Seals. Seals formed a partnership with John Ford Coley (b. 13 October 1951) and they first worked as Southwest F.O.B., the initials representing 'Freight On Board'. The ridiculous name did not last, but Jimmy, not wanting them to be called Seals And Coley, suggested England Dan And John Ford Coley. Their first albums for A&M Records sold moderately well, but they struck gold in 1976 with a move to Big Tree Records. The single 'I'd Really Love To See You Tonight' went to number 2 in the US charts and also reached the UK Top 30, although its hook owed something to James Taylor's 'Fire And Rain'. The resulting album, *Nights Are Forever*, was a big seller and the pair opted for a fuller sound that drew comparisons with the Eagles. The title track, 'Nights Are Forever Without You', was another Top 10 single. With their harmonies, acoustic-based songs and tuneful melodies, they appealed to the same market as the Eagles and, naturally, Seals And Croft. They had further US hits with 'It's Sad To Belong', 'Gone Too Far', 'We'll Never Have To Say Goodbye Again' and 'Love Is The Answer'. When the duo split, Seals, after a few setbacks, became a country star. Coley found a new partner and recorded *Kelly Leslie And John Ford Coley* in 1981.

● ALBUMS: as Southwest F.O.B. *Smell Of Incense* (A&M 1968)★★, *England Dan And John Ford Coley* (A&M 1971)★★★, *Fables* (A&M 1971)★★, *I Hear The Music* (A&M 1976)★★, *Nights Are Forever* (Big Tree 1976)★★, *Dowdy Ferry Road* (Big Tree 1977)★★★, *Some Things Don't Come Easy* (Big Tree 1978)★★, *Dr. Heckle And Mr. Jive* (Big Tree 1979)★★, *Just Tell Me If You Love Me* (1980)★★.

● COMPILATIONS: *Best Of* (Big Tree 1980)★★★, *The Very Best* (Rhino 1997)★★★.

ENGLAND, TY

b. 1963, Oklahoma, USA. The 90s country singer Ty England was first turned on to country music by his grandfather, who gave him his first guitar and taught him the basic chords. He sang with high school bands and played acoustic sets at coffee shops while at university. He befriended Garth Brooks in 1982 and they made a pact that if one of them found success, he would help the other along. Therefore, in 1988, Brooks, who had just signed with Capitol Records, asked England to be in his band. For five years England worked as a guitarist and harmony singer with Brooks. He almost signed a solo contract with Liberty Records but then decided to go with RCA. His first single, 'Should've Asked Her Faster', was a western swing number that made the US country Top 30. He is refreshingly modest about his playing and songwriting, and has said: 'More than anything else, Garth taught me that every fan is important. They are the reasons you're out there. And if those fans could know one thing about me, I'd want them to know that I'm here for the right reason - a lifelong love of music.'

● ALBUMS: *Ty England* (RCA 1995)★★★★, *Two Ways To Fall* (RCA 1996)★★★.

ENGLISH, MICHAEL

b. USA. After several years' working as a contemporary Christian performer, by the mid-90s English elected to pursue a career in the mainstream pop idiom. The fact that his ensuing album for Curb Records was entitled *Freedom* was not incidental. Indeed, English saw it as the opportunity to break free of perceived notions of what Christian writers could or should do. As he told *Billboard* magazine, it afforded him 'the freedom to sing and not worry if this is going to offend anyone. Now I don't have to worry about saying "baby" or "girl" or whatever. I don't have to worry about saying "Jesus" either. I'm free to say whatever I feel there is to say.' English signed with Curb in 1994 following his departure from Warner Alliance, Warner Brothers Records' Christian label. Ironically, that move coincided with his greatest success, English having collected more awards than any other artist at that year's Dove Awards, including one as Artist Of The Year. However, a Christian media witch hunt began when it was discovered that English was having an affair with, and had impregnated, married singer Marabeth Jordan of First Call. Since then he has distanced himself from Christian music circles, choosing to play dates with rock bands such as Foreigner. His first 'secular' release was a duet with Wynonna, 'Healing', which was included on the soundtrack to the film *Silent Fall*. However, he still produces southern gospel albums, and received a further Dove award for his work with the Martins. The first single to be released from *Freedom* was 'Your Love Amazes Me', a song previously released by John Berry.

● ALBUMS: *Freedom* (Curb 1996)★★★.

EVANS, DALE

b. Frances Octavia Smith, 31 October 1912, Uvalde, Texas, USA. Her first 15 years included major problems: a nervous breakdown at 11, married at 14 (by lying about her age) and a mother at 15 are somewhat unusual, if, arguably, self-inflicted traumas. After unsuccessfully seeking a singing career in Chicago (with a baby to look after), she moved to WHAS Louisville. After auditioning as Marion Lee, she found herself named Dale Evans by the station manager and in spite of her own reservations, the name stuck. She divorced her schoolboy husband before marrying and later divorcing the pianist from WHAS. Still harbouring aspirations towards a singing career, she returned to Chicago as a jazz singer. She toured the Midwest as vocalist with an orchestra and sang with Fats Waller. Eventually she was persuaded to try her luck in films. Her agent promoted her as being 21, and when her 13-year-old son joined her, he was quickly announced as her kid brother. After many problems, she was chosen to play the lead in a college musical called *Campus In The Clouds*. When the Japanese bombed Pearl Harbor, America's subsequent involvement in World War II saw the 'epic' shelved. She gained a few small roles but suffered by being compared to Betty Grable. Eventually, after further problems, she met up with a popular young singing cowboy, Roy Rogers. Originally, she had no intention of playing roles in B-westerns but fate decreed otherwise. In 1946, Rogers' first wife died; he eventually married Evans on 31 December 1947 and from that point her career ran in parallel with that of her husband.

EVERETTE, LEON

b. Leon Everette Baughman, 21 June 1948, Aiken, South Carolina, USA. Everette was raised in New York and had no particular interest in country music as a child. In the US Navy, he worked on an aircraft carrier in the Philippines. The servicemen passed the time by singing so he bought a guitar, learned by watching others and won a talent contest. Returning to South Carolina, he married, started a family and worked at the South Carolina Power and Gas Company. After an argument at work, Everette became a professional musician, working clubs in South Carolina and Georgia. He wanted success in Nashville and, in an extraordinary act of dedication, worked in the postal rooms of record companies while still playing in his home clubs. This involved commuting 500 miles a day! On top of this, he had to sleep and maintain a family life with his wife and three children. In 1977 the small True label gave Everette a chance - though not in the way he wanted. Within hours of Elvis Presley's death, Everette had recorded 'Goodbye King Of Rock And Roll'. Although True then wanted him to record some Elvis soundalikes, he was determined that he wanted to sing country and to be himself. After a small US country hit with 'I Love That Woman (Like The Devil Loves Sin)', a Florida businessman, Carroll Fulmer, formed a record label, Orlando, around him. He made the country charts with 'Giving Up Easy', 'Don't Feel like The Lone Ranger' and 'I Don't Want To Lose'. When Everette moved to RCA in 1980, he became more involved in the production of his own records. 'If I Keep On Going Crazy', with its distinctive harmonica, made the US country Top 20 and it was followed by the pile-driving 'Hurricane', which prompted him to change his band's name from Tender Loving Care to Hurricane. Everette himself is a hurricane on stage and is prone to leaping into the audience, occasionally injuring himself; at one memorable concert, he put his arm through a glass panel. Among other successful singles were 'I Could'a Had You', 'Midnight Rodeo' and 'Soul Searchin''. His affection for old-time country music was evident in 'Shadows Of My Mind' and he revived Stonewall Jackson's 'Don't Be Angry'. In a peculiar marketing exercise, RCA issued a six-track mini-album called *Doin' What I Feel* in 1983 and reissued it in 1984 with the same packaging but three different titles. He then moved to Mercury and recorded *Where's The Fire?*, but rejoined Orlando soon afterwards. He retired from country music in 1988.

● ALBUMS: *Goodbye King Of Rock & Roll* (True 1977)★★★, *I Don't Want To Lose* (Orlando 1980)★★★, *If I Keep On Going Crazy* (RCA 1981)★★★, *Hurricane* (RCA 1981)★★★, *Maverick* (RCA 1982)★★★★, *Doin' What I Feel* (RCA 1983/84)★★★, *Where's The Fire?* (Mercury 1985)★★★.
● COMPILATIONS: *Leon Everette's Greatest Hits* (RCA 1987)★★★.

EVERLY BROTHERS

Don Everly (b. Isaac Donald Everly, 1 February 1937, Brownie, Kentucky, USA) and Phil Everly (b. Phillip Everly, 19 January 1939, Chicago, Illinois, USA). Don and Phil's father, Ike Everly, was an accomplished guitarist, working with country music celebrities and developing his style with his neighbour, Merle Travis. Ike and his wife Margaret hosted long-running family radio shows and the Everly Brothers' 1968 album, *Roots*, includes some early work. When they became a duo, Ike approached his friend, Chet Atkins, in Nashville for contacts. Don sold some songs, one of them, 'Thou Shalt Not Steal', making the charts for Kitty Wells. Although the Everly Brothers became the leading rock 'n' roll vocal group, their records were close to country and their harmonies are derived from the Blue Sky Boys, Delmore Brothers and Louvin Brothers. They used country musicians and songwriters, notably Boudleaux and Felice Bryant and John D. Loudermilk. Their own compositions, which include 'Cathy's Clown', 'So Sad' and 'When Will I Be Loved?', have been recorded by several country artists. In 1958, they surprised their fans with what can be seen as the first 'unplugged' album, *Songs Our Daddy Taught Us*, but in retrospect it is more easy to see how old-time country music fitted into their thinking. With top-flight Nashville sessionmen, they recorded the more contemporary *The Everly Brothers Sing Great Country Hits* in 1963. Ten years later, they returned to Nashville for *Pass The Chicken And Listen*, an out-and-out country record produced by Chet Atkins. It included John Prine's 'Paradise', which is a town close to where they were raised in Kentucky. Splitting up after the album, Don Everly became a country performer, working at festivals with the Dead Cowboy Band and recording a highly rated album, *Brother Jukebox*. He also sang the Louvin Brothers' 'Everytime You Leave', with Emmylou Harris. They settled their differences in 1983 with some much publicized reunion concerts and they have been on the road ever since. Their guest appearances include joining Johnny Cash on a remake of 'Ballad Of A Teenage Queen'.

● ALBUMS: *The Everly Brothers* (Cadence 1958)★★★, *Songs Our Daddy Taught Us* (Cadence 1959)★★★, *The Everly Brothers' Best* (Cadence 1959)★★★, *It's Everly Time* (Warners 1960)★★★, *The Fabulous Style Of The Everly Brothers* (Cadence 1960)★★★★, *A Date With The Everly Brothers* (Warners 1960)★★★★, *Both Sides Of An Evening* (Warners 1961)★★★, *Folk Songs Of the Everly Brothers* (Cadence 1962)★★★, *Instant Party* (Warners 1962)★★★, *Christmas With The Everly Brothers And The Boys Town Choir* (Warners 1962)★★★, *The Everly Brothers Sing Great Country Hits* (Warners 1963)★★★, *Gone Gone Gone* (Warners

1965)★★★★, *Rock 'N' Soul* (Warners 1965)★★★, *Beat 'N' Soul* (Warners 1965)★★★, *In Our Image* (Warners 1966)★★★, *Two Yanks In England* (Warners 1966)★★★, *The Hit Sound Of The Everly Brothers* (Warners 1967)★★★, *The Everly Brothers Sing* (Warners 1967)★★★, *Roots* (Warners 1968)★★★, *The Everly Brothers Show* (Warners 1970)★★★, *End Of An Era* (Barnaby/Columbia 1971)★★★, *Stories We Could Tell* (RCA Victor 1972)★★, *Pass The Chicken And Listen* (RCA Victor 1973)★★, *The Exciting Everly Brothers* (RCA 1975)★★★, *Living Legends* (Warwick 1977)★★★, *The New Album* previously unissued Warners material (Warners 1977)★★★, *The Everly Brothers Reunion Concert* (Impression 1983)★★★★, *Nice Guys* previously unissued Warners material (Magnum Force 1984)★★, *EB84* (Mercury 1984)★★★, *In The Studio* previously unissued Cadence material (Ace 1985)★★★, *Born Yesterday* (Mercury 1986)★★★, *Some Hearts* (Mercury 1989)★★★, *Live In Paris* (Big Beat 1997)★★★.
Solo: Don Everly *Don Everly* (A&M 1971)★★, *Sunset Towers* (Ode 1974)★★, *Brother Juke Box* (Hickory 1976)★★★. Phil Everly *Star Spangled Springer* (RCA 1973)★★, *Phil's Diner (There's Nothing Too Good For My Baby)* (Pye 1974)★★, *Mystic Line* (Pye 1975)★★, *Living Alone* (Elektra 1979)★★, *Phil Everly* (Capitol 1983)★★.
● COMPILATIONS: *The Golden Hits Of The Everly Brothers* (Warners 1962)★★★★, *15 Everly Hits* (Cadence 1963)★★★, *The Very Best Of The Everly Brothers* (Warners 1964)★★★★, *The Everly Brothers' Original Greatest Hits* (Columbia 1970)★★★★, *The Most Beautiful Songs Of The Everly Brothers* (Warners 1973)★★★, *Don's And Phil's Fabulous Fifties Treasury* (Janus 1974)★★★, *Walk Right Back With The Everlys* (Warners 1975)★★★★, *The Everly Brothers Greatest Hits Collection* (Pickwick 1979)★★★, *The Sensational Everly Brothers* (Reader Digest 1979)★★, *Cathy's Clown* (Pickwick 1980)★★★, *The Very Best Of The Everly Brothers* (Marks & Spencer 1980)★★, *The Everly Brothers* (Warners 1981)★★★, *Rock 'N' Roll Forever* (Warners 1981)★★★, *Love Hurts* (K-Tel 1982)★★, *Rip It Up* (Ace 1983)★★★, *Cadence Classics (Their 20 Greatest Hits)* (Rhino 1985)★★★★, *The Best Of The Everly Brothers* (Rhino 1985)★★★, *All They Had To Do Is Dream* US only (Rhino 1985)★★★, *Great Recordings* (Ace 1986)★★★, *The Everly Brothers Collection* (Castle 1988)★★★, *The Very Best Of The Everly Brothers* (Pickwick 1988)★★★, *Hidden Gems* Warners material (Ace 1989)★★★,*The Very Best Of The Everly Brothers Volume 2* (Pickwick 1990)★★, *Perfect Harmony* box set (Knight 1990)★★★, *Classic Everly Brothers* 3-CD box set (Bear Family 1992)★★★★, *The Golden Years Of The Everly Brothers* (Warners 1993)★★★★, *Heartaches And Harmonies* 4-CD box set (Rhino 1995)★★★★★, *Walk Right Back: On Warner Bros. 1960 To 1969* 2-CD (Warners 1996)★★★★, *All I Have To Do Is Dream* (Carlton 1997)★★★.
● VIDEOS: *Rock 'N' Roll Odyssey* (MGM 1984).
● FURTHER READING: *Everly Brothers: An Illustrated Discography*, John Hosum. *The Everly Brothers: Walk Right Back*, Roger White. *Ike's Boys*, Phyllis Karpp. *The Everly Brothers: Ladies Love Outlaws*, Consuelo Dodge. *For-Everly Yours*, Peter Aarts and Martin Alberts.

EWING, SKIP

b. Donald R. Ewing, 6 March 1965, Redlands, California, USA. Because he was born into a military family, Ewing travelled extensively as a child. His father bought him a guitar when he was four years old and he became hooked on country music and, in particular, Merle Haggard. In 1984, after graduating, he moved to Nashville as a songwriter and the first track to be recorded was 'One Hell Of A Song' by George Jones. Jimmy Bowen signed him to MCA and he had US country successes with 'Your Memory Wins Again' and 'Burning A Hole In My Heart'. Five hits came from his first album and his style was likened to Randy Travis and Don McLean. Ewing continues to write songs for other artists and recent compositions have included 'You Leave Me Like This' (Lorrie Morgan), 'Who Needs You' (Lisa Brokop) and the superb ballad 'Still Under The Weather' (Shania Twain). His oddest composition is the Christmas song 'It Wasn't His Child', which has been recorded by both Sawyer Brown and Trisha Yearwood. He moved to Capitol Records in 1992, releasing two further albums to date.
● ALBUMS: *The Coast Of Colorado* (MCA 1988)★★★★, *The Will To Love* (MCA 1989)★★★, *A Healin' Fire* (MCA 1990)★★★, *Homegrown Love* (Capitol 1993)★★★, *Naturally* (Capitol 1994)★★★.
● COMPILATIONS: *Greatest Hits* (MCA 1991)★★★★.

EXILE

Formed in Berea, Kentucky, USA, in 1963 as the Exiles, the band first reached the pop charts in the late 70s before changing musical direction and becoming one of the most successful country bands of the 80s. They toured with the Dick Clark Caravan of Stars in 1965 as back-up band for artists including Brian Hyland and Tommy Roe. In the late 60s they recorded for Date Records and Columbia Records, and in the early 70s for SSS International, Date, Curb and Wooden Nickel. In 1973 they changed their name to Exile and in 1977, recording for Atco Records, they scored their first chart single. After a switch to Warner Brothers Records, Exile had a number 1 pop hit with 'Kiss You All Over', in 1978. They had two more pop chart singles before making the switch to country. After numerous personnel changes, the group's membership in 1978, when they had their first hit, was guitarist and vocalist J.P. Pennington, keyboardist Buzz Cornelison, vocalist and guitarist Les Taylor, keyboardist and vocalist Marlon Hargis, bassist and vocalist Sonny LeMaire and drummer Steve Goetzman. Exile's second, and more lucrative, career as a country group began in 1983 (by which time Cornelison had left). The first country chart single, 'High Cost Of Leaving', reached number 27, but was followed by four successive number 1 country singles in 1984: 'Woke Up In Love', 'I Don't Want To Be A Memory', 'Give Me One More Chance' and 'Crazy For Your Love'. There were six further number 1 country singles by 1987: 'She's A Miracle', 'Hang On To Your Heart', 'I Could Get Used To You', 'It'll Be Me', 'She's Too Good To Be True' and 'I Can't Get Close Enough'. Hargis was replaced by Lee Carroll in 1985 and Pennington left in 1989, replaced by Paul Martin. The group signed to Arista Records in 1989 with a noticeable decline in its level of commercial success. They were dropped by the label in 1993 and broke up afterwards, but a new version with Pennington and Taylor was on the road in 1996.
● ALBUMS: *Exile* (Wooden Nickel 1973)★★★★, *Mixed Emotions* (Epic 1978)★★★, *All There Is* (Epic 1979)★★★, *Don't Leave Me This Way* (Epic 1980)★★★, *Heart And Soul* (Epic 1981)★★★, *Exile* (Epic 1983)★★★, *Kentucky Hearts* (Epic 1984)★★, *Hang On To Your Heart* (Epic 1985)★★,

Shelter From The Night (Epic 1987)★★★, *Still Standing* (Arista 1990)★★★★, *Justice* (Arista 1991)★★★.
● COMPILATIONS: *The Best Of Exile* (Curb 1985)★★★★, *Exile's Greatest Hits* (Epic 1986)★★★, *The Complete Collection* (Curb 1991)★★★★, *Super Hits* (Epic 1993)★★★.

FAIRCHILD, BARBARA

b. 12 November 1950, Knobel, Arkansas, USA. Fairchild was raised on a farm and was entertaining at every opportunity. The family moved to St. Louis when she was 12 years old and she was soon recording for the local Norman label and working on television. In 1968 she moved to Nashville to further her career and among her early singles is 'Remember The Alimony' for Kapp Records. Her song 'This Stranger (My Little Girl)' has been recorded by Loretta Lynn, Dottie West and Liz Anderson. Fairchild was signed to Columbia in 1969 and immediately achieved her first US country hit with 'Love Is A Gentle Thing', followed by various minor entries, including 'A Girl Who'll Satisfy Her Man' and 'Love's Old Song'. Then, the novelty 'Teddy Bear Song', written by a St. Louis policeman, topped the US country charts. She never repeated that success although she had country hits with 'Kid Stuff', 'Baby Doll', 'You've Lost That Lovin' Feelin'', 'Mississippi', 'Cheatin' Is' and 'Let Me Love You Once Before You Go'. She wrote 'Tara' for one of her daughters, and her husband and songwriting partner, steel guitarist Randy Reinhard, was part of her road band. After their divorce, she married Milton Carroll, who had recorded for RCA. In the early 80s, she became a born-again Christian and left the music business for several years. In 1986 she recorded an album with production by her old friend Don Williams, but only a single was released. She joined the band Heirloom in 1989, and has also released two solo gospel albums.
● ALBUMS: *Something Special* (Columbia 1970)★★, *Love's Old Song* (Columbia 1971)★★★, *The Barbara Fairchild Way* reissued as *Love's Old Song* (Columbia 1971)★★★, *A Sweeter Love* (Columbia 1972)★★★, *Teddy Bear Song* (Columbia 1972)★★, *Kid Stuff* (Columbia 1973)★★, *Standing In Your Line* (Columbia 1974)★★★, *Love Is A Gentle Thing* (Columbia 1974)★★★, *Barbara Fairchild* (Columbia 1975)★★★, *Mississippi* (Columbia 1976)★★, *Free And Easy* (Columbia 1977)★★★, *This Is Me!* (Columbia 1978)★★★, with Billy Walker *The Answer Game* reissued as *It Takes Two* (RCA 1979)★★★, *The Biggest Hurt* (1983)★★, *The Light* (Benson 1991)★★★, *The Son In My Eyes* (Benson 90s)★★★.

FAIRCHILD, RAYMOND

b. 5 March 1939, Cherokee, North Carolina, USA. Fairchild, who is of Cherokee Indian extraction, first played guitar but in the late 50s, greatly impressed by the playing of an aunt, he decided to specialize in banjo. He first recorded for Sim around 1963 but in 1965, with his Maggie Valley Boys, he recorded several instrumental albums for Uncle Jim O'Neal's popular Rural Rhythm label. Some gained release at varying dates but by 1976, his releases and reissues were attracting a great deal of attention. He quickly built his reputation and amazed his audiences by his playing, not only in his own Maggie Valley locale but also at various major bluegrass and folk festivals. Between 1975 and 1990, he worked with Wayne and Wallace Crowe, who played guitar and bass and added vocals. The trio became very popular around the bluegrass circuit and recorded albums for Skyline and Atteiram. He then re-formed his Maggie Valley Boys, which included his son Zane on lead guitar and Wallace Crowe's son, Shane, on bass. In 1989, he recorded with Ralph Stanley, singing for the first time and in 1990, he recorded with Chubby Wise. He is noted for his deadpan expressions, even while executing his most speedy instrumental breaks and also for his humorous anecdotes, such as his hints on how to keep rattlesnakes as household pets. He continued to play into the 90s and his talents have seen him fondly dubbed The King of the Smoky Mountain Banjo Players.
● ALBUMS: with Frank Buchanan *America's Most Authentic Folk Banjo* (Sim 1963)★★★, *King Of The Smoky Mountain 5 String Banjo Players* i (Rural Rhythm 1966)★★★★, *Raymond Fairchild & The Maggie Valley Boys* (Rural Rhythm 1967)★★★, *Mama Likes Bluegrass Music* (Rural Rhythm 1968)★★★★, *Honky Tonkin Country Blues* (Rural Rhythm 1971)★★★★, *King Of The Smoky Mountain 5 String Banjo Players* ii (Rural Rhythm 1972)★★★, *Smoky Mountain Banjo* (Paradise & Atteiram 1974)★★★, *King Of The 5 String Banjo* 4-volumes (Rural Rhythm 1976)★★★★, *World's Greatest Banjo Picker* (Rural Rhythm 1976)★★★★, *The Maggie Valley Boys, Picking And Singing In Maggie Valley* (Atteiram 1978)★★★, *The Legendary Raymond Fairchild Plays Little Zane* (Skyline 1981)★★★, *Always True* (Skyline 1981)★★★, *The Gospel Way* (Skyline 1984)★★★, *The Winds Are Blowing In Maggie Valley* (Atteiram 1986)★★★, *Plays Requests* (Skyline 1986)★★★, *World Champion Banjo* (Skyline 1987)★★★, *Jesus Is Coming* (Atteiram 1988)★★, *Me And My Banjo At Home In Maggie Valley* (Atteiram 1989)★★★, *Ralph Stanley & Raymond Fairchild* (Rebel 1989)★★★, with Chubby Wise *Cherokee Tunes & Seminole Swing* (Rebel 1990)★★★.

FARGO, DONNA

b. Yvonne Vaughn, 10 November 1949, Mount Airy, North Carolina, USA. Fargo is the daughter of a tobacco farmer, and she sang in church as a child. She became a schoolteacher and was discovered by her future husband, record producer Stan Silver, singing in a club in Los Angeles. She first recorded in 1969, but her success started once she had signed with Dot Records in 1971. She won gold records for her compositions 'The Happiest Girl In The Whole USA' (number 11 US pop charts, number 1 country) and 'Funny Face' (number 5 pop, number 1 country), which was Silver's nickname for her (she called him 'fuzzy face' because of his beard). In 1973 she had country hits with more of her own songs - 'Superman', 'You Were Always There', a tribute to her late mother (both number 1), and 'Little Girl Gone' (number 2). In 1974 she topped the country charts again, this time with Marty Cooper's gospel song 'You Can't Be A Beacon (If Your Light Don't Shine)'. The packaging of the US versions of her early albums included guitar chords as well as lyrics. She moved to WEA Records and went to number 1 on the country charts with a narration, 'That Was Yesterday'. For some years she was in poor health but multiple sclerosis was not diagnosed until 1979. She has continued her career to the best of her ability and her strong beliefs led to a gospel album, *Brotherly Love*. Her duet with Billy Joe Royal, 'Members Only', was a US country hit in 1988 and she topped the US country singles chart for independent labels with a revival of the Shirelles' 'Soldier Boy', which was aimed at US forces involved in the Gulf War. Donna Fargo and her husband, Stan Silver, were declared bankrupt in 1991.

● ALBUMS: *The Happiest Girl In The Whole USA* UK title *The Country Sounds Of Donna Fargo* (Dot 1972)★★★★, *My Second Album* (Dot 1973)★★★, *All About A Feeling* (Dot 1973)★★★, *Miss Donna Fargo* (ABC 1974)★★★★, *Whatever I Say Means I Love You* (ABC 1975)★★★, *On The Move* (1976)★★★, *Shame On Me* (Warners 1977)★★★, *Fargo Country* (Warners 1977)★★★, *Dark Eyed Lady* (Warners 1978)★★★, *Just For You* (Warners 1979)★★★, *Fargo* (Warners 1980)★★★, *Brotherly Love* (Warners 1981)★★★, *Donna* (1983)★★★, *Winners* (1986)★★★★.

● COMPILATIONS: *The Best Of Donna Fargo* (MCA 1977)★★★, *Best Of Donna Fargo* (Varèse Vintage 1995)★★★★.

FARR, HUGH

b. Thomas Hubert Farr, 6 December 1903, Llano, Texas, USA, d. 17 March 1980. An important member of the Sons Of The Pioneers. His father played fiddle and his mother guitar at local venues and at the age of seven, Hugh was playing guitar with his father at such events. At nine, he was so proficient on his father's fiddle that his father took to playing guitar only. In 1925, after several moves, the Farr family relocated to Encino, California. He first worked in the construction industry but eventually became a full-time musician. Between 1929 and 1933, he and brother Karl played with Len Nash And His Country Boys on local venues and on KFOX Long Beach, where the two also acted as station staff musicians. During the time with Nash, Hugh also played on several Brunswick recordings. In 1933, the two brothers and Ira McCullough performed as the Haywire Trio and also played with Jack LeFevre And His Texas Outlaws. Soon afterwards, he became a fourth member of the Pioneer Trio (joining Leonard Slye (Roy Rogers), Bob Nolan and Tim Spencer) who, before long, became the Sons Of The Pioneers. His brilliant fiddle playing and deep bass vocals became an integral part of the group's sound. He stayed with the group until late in 1958, when he quit following differences of opinion. He formed his own Sons Of The Pioneers, an action that immediately led to controversy and he quickly disbanded and for some time, he played with Jimmy Wakely's band. In the early 60s, he again attempted to use the old name for a group he formed, until legally instructed to stop following objections by Rogers, Nolan and Spencer. He briefly formed a group he called the Country Gentlemen but after recording *Songs Of The Pioneers*, the group folded.

Farr's fiddle playing could receive no greater praise than that afforded by noted conductor Walter Winchell. When asked whom he believed was the greatest natural violinist of the century, his answer was: 'It is two musicians, the left hand of Fritz Kreisler and the right hand of that gentleman, who plays the violin with the Sons Of The Pioneers, I don't recall his name.' Hugh Farr died in March 1980 but his playing may be heard on countless recordings of the Pioneers.

● COMPILATIONS: as Farr Brothers *Texas Crapshooter* (JEMF 1978)★★★, *South In My Soul* covers 1930-1940 (Cattle 1978)★★★, *Texas Stomp 1934-1944* (Country Routes 1993)★★★★.

FARR, KARL

b. Karl Marx Farr, 25 April 1909, Rochele, Texas, USA, d. 20 September 1961. An important member of the Sons Of The Pioneers. The younger brother of Hugh Farr, he grew up in a musical environment and as a child played local venues with his brothers, Hugh and Glen. At the age of 13, he competently played guitar, mandolin, banjo and drums. After the family relocated to Encino, California, in 1925, he picked cotton and played some local venues, before joining Hugh as a member of Len Nash And His Country Boys. Between 1929 and 1933, they played with Nash at local venues and on KFOX Long Beach, where the two also worked as station staff musicians. In 1933, the two brothers and Ira McCullough performed as the Haywire Trio and also played with Jack LeFevre And His Texas Outlaws. After Hugh joined the Sons Of The Pioneers, he soon persuaded the members that the group badly needed a guitarist of Karl's ability. Karl's style of playing was unlike that of the usual Texas guitarists - he used single note runs rather than the closed chord rhythm. There is little doubt that his guitarwork was an inspiration to all members of the group and especially complemented the excellent fiddle playing of his brother. He has been classed as one of the true early guitar stylists, whose playing has been a direct influence on several later noted exponents of the instrument, including Merle Travis and Joe Maphis. In 1949, the Fender company gave him one of their earliest electric instruments, Telecast #0757, in appreciation of his contribution to guitar music. On 22 September 1961, Karl Farr appeared on stage with the group before a 4,000 crowd in West Springfield, Massachusetts. While playing his acoustic Martin on a solo of 'Up A Lazy River', he broke a string. Fellow members noted that he appeared greatly upset by it and while attempting to remove the broken string, he slumped to the floor. Tommy Doss and Dale Warren quickly carried him from the stage for medical attention. He was rushed to hospital but the doctor later reported that for all practical purposes Karl Farr was dead on arrival, the victim of a heart attack.

● COMPILATIONS: as Farr Brothers *Texas Crapshooter* (JEMF 1978)★★★, *South In My Soul* covers 1930-1940 (Cattle 1978)★★★, *Texas Stomp 1934-1944* (Country Routes 1993)★★★★.

FEATHERS, CHARLIE

b. Charles Arthur Feathers, 12 June 1932, Holly Springs, Mississippi, USA. The work of rockabilly legend Feathers becomes more elevated during each revival of interest in the genre. Feathers is now an enigmatic superstar, although in reality his influence totally overshadows his commercial success. His upbringing on a farm, being taught guitar by a cotton-picking black bluesman and leaving home to work on an oilfield, gave Feathers a wealth of material for his compositions. In the early 50s, together with Jody Chastain and Jerry Huffman, he performed as the Musical Warriors. He was an early signing to Sam Phillips' Sun Records. He recorded his first song, 'Defrost Your Heart', in 1955, and claimed to have co-written Elvis Presley's debut, 'Blue Moon Of Kentucky'. He did, however, co-write Presley's first hit, 'I Forgot To Remember To Forget'. Over the years he has continued to record for a number of labels, still unable to break through the barrier between 'cult' and 'star'. Among his early rockabilly sides was 'One Hand Loose' on King, regarded by many collectors as one of the finest examples of its kind. His highly applauded performance at London's famous Rainbow theatre in 1977 gave his career a significant boost and brought him a new audience, notably the fans who were following Dave Edmunds and his crusade for 'rockabilly'. Feathers' recent recordings have suffered from the problem of being helped out by younger musicians who are merely in awe of his work, and his best material is from the 50s. Influential but spartan, full of whoops and growls, but ultimately, irresistible country rock, Feather's 'light comedy' style has been an 'invisible influence' over many decades, from Big Bopper in the 50s to Hank Wangford in the 80s. His 1991 release contained a reworked version of his classic 'I Forgot To Remember To Forget'. He now performs with his son and daughter on guitar and vocals, respectively. A remarkable crop of unissued demos appeared in 1995 as *Tip Top Daddy* and further highlighted the originality of the man who defined country rockabilly long before Garth Brooks was born, and yet has never received widespread recognition for his contribution.

● ALBUMS: *Live In Memphis* (Barrelhouse 1979)★★★, *Charlie Feathers* (Elektra 1991)★★★.

● COMPILATIONS: *Rockabilly Mainman* (Charly 1978)★★★, *Honky Tonk Man* (1982)★★★, *Rockabilly Kings* (1984)★★★, *The Legendary 1956 Demo Session* (Zu Zazz 1986)★★, *Jungle Fever* (Kay 1987)★★★, *Wild Wild Party* (Rockstar 1987)★★★, *The Living Legend* (Redita 1988)★★★, *Rock-A-Billy* (Zu Zazz 1991)★★★, *Tip Top Daddy* (Norton 1995)★★★.

FELL, TERRY

b. 13 May 1921, Dora, Alabama, USA. Although Terry Fell's name appears only once in the *Billboard* country charts, he staked his claim to fame by being not only the writer of 'Truck Driving Man' but also the original recorder of the song. In 1930, he swapped his pet groundhog for a guitar, although it was to be three years before anyone showed him how to play it, or the mandolin that he also acquired. At 16, he hitch-hiked his way to California, spending some time with the Civilian Conservation Corps. He eventually returned home but he and his widowed mother finally relocated to the Los Angeles area. In 1943, while working for Tru-Flex tyres, he began to play bass with Merle Lindsey's Nightriders. Around 1945, he joined Billy Hughes, made his first recordings for Fargo and began to write songs for the American Music Company. In 1954, after further recordings for Memo, Courtney and 4-Star, he joined RCA/Victor Records, making his first recordings on their subsidiary 'X'

label. 'Truck Driving Man' appeared as the b-side of his first 'X' single, in April 1954. The a-side, 'Don't Drop It', became a number 4 US country chart hit (his only one) and although 'Truck Driving Man' failed to chart for Fell, it went on to become a country standard. It has since been charted by both George Hamilton IV and Red Steagall and recorded by countless other artists, including Buck Owens. He made further recordings and worked as an artist for a few years, until the lack of further hits and throat problems saw him lose interest in performing. In 1962, he relocated to Nashville, where he wrote songs and worked for several publishing companies, until he eventually retired. In 1993, Bear Family Records issued a CD containing all 24 of his RCA masters - two previously unissued. Fell also co-wrote 'You're The Reason', a US country and pop Top 12 hit for Bobby Edwards in 1961 and later successfully recorded by Daniel O'Donnell.

● COMPILATIONS: *Truck Driving Man* (Bear Family 1993)★★★, *The Original Truck Driving Man* (CowgirlBoy 1994)★★★.

FELLER, DICK

b. 2 January 1943, Bronaugh, Missouri, USA. Feller grew up with a love of both country and blues music and became a proficient rock 'n' roll guitarist. In 1966, intent on becoming a professional songwriter, he moved to Nashville and found work playing sessions or going on the road with musicians including Skeeter Davis, Warner Mack and Mel Tillis. Johnny Cash had a US number 1 country hit with Feller's 'Any Old Wind That Blows' in 1972. Jerry Reed did the same in 1973 with 'Lord Mr. Ford', a song rejected by Jimmy Dean, and recorded many more of Feller's songs: 'East Bound And Down' (for the film *Smokey And The Bandit*), 'Second-Hand Satin Lady (And A Bargain Basement Boy)' and 'The Phantom Of The Opry'. In the mid-70s Feller had his own country hits with 'Biff, The Friendly Purple Bear', 'Making The Best Of A Bad Situation', 'Uncle Hiram And His Homemade Beer' and a narrative that is even more pertinent today, 'The Credit Card Song'. His tours of UK country clubs have shown that he is not just another Feller and he can stop any show with 'Daisy Hill'.

● ALBUMS: *Dick Feller Wrote...* (United Artists 1973)★★★, *No Word On Me* (Asylum 1975)★★★★, *Some Days Are Diamonds* (Asylum 1975)★★★, *Children In Their Wishes, Ladies In Their Dreams* (Asylum 1977)★★★, *Audiograph Alive* (1984)★★★.

FELTS, NARVEL

b. Albert Narvel Felts, 11 November 1938, Keiser, Arkansas, USA. Felts obtained his first guitar when aged 13 and taught himself to play. In 1956, he won a talent contest, appeared on local radio and passed an audition as a rock 'n' roll singer for Sun Records in Memphis, although his sessions were not released at the time. In 1957, his first record for Mercury Records, 'Kiss-a-me Baby', sold 20,000 copies. He made the US charts in 1959 with '3,000 Miles' and 'Honey Love', both for Pink Records. He had sporadic success for some years ('I'm Movin' On', 'Rockin' Little Angel') and then, in 1973, he had a huge country hit for the Cinnamon label with Mentor Williams' 'Drift Away', which was followed by a string of country hits - 'When Your Good Love Was Mine', 'All In The Name Of Love', 'Raindrops'. In 1975, moving to Dot Records, he had a number 2 US country hit with 'Reconsider Me'. He recorded the most successful version of 'Funny How Time Slips Away' and issued emotional revivals of 'Lonely Teardrops' and 'My Prayer'. In 1976, he had a US country hit with a song Conway Twitty had given him 16 years earlier, 'Lonely Kind Of Love'. He continued to register minor country hits into the 80s, such as the 1987 recording of 'When A Man Loves A Woman'. Looking like a haggard Omar Sharif, he tours with his band, the Driftaways, regularly visiting the UK and including songs from all periods of his career; his drummer is his son Narvel Felts Jnr.

● ALBUMS: *Drift Away* (Cinnamon 1973)★★★, *Live* (Cinammon 1974)★★, *When Your Good Love Was Mine* (Cinammon 1974)★★, *Reconsider Me* (Dot 1975)★★★, *Narvel Felts* (Dot 1975)★★★, *Narvel The Marvel* (Dot 1976)★★★, *Doin' What I Feel* (1976)★★★, *This Time* (Hi 1976)★★★, *The Touch Of Felts* (Dot 1977)★★, *Narvel* (Dot 1977)★★★, *Inside Love* (ABC 1978)★★★, *One Run For The Roses* (1979)★★, *A Teen's Way* (Bear Family 1987)★★★, *Memphis Days* (Bear Family 1991)★★★, *Pink And Golden Days* (1991)★★★.

● COMPILATIONS: *Narvel Felts' Greatest Hits* (Dot 1976)★★★, *Drift Away: The Best Of 1973-1979* (Bear Family 1996)★★★★.

FENDER, FREDDY

b. Baldemar G. Huerta, 4 June 1937, San Benito, Texas, USA. Fender, a Mexican-American, comes from a family of migrant workers who were based in the San Benito valley. A farm worker from the age of 10, Fender says he 'worked beets in Michigan, pickles in Ohio, baled hay and picked tomatoes in Indiana. When that was over, it was cotton-picking time in Arkansas.' Fender sang and played guitar along with the blues, country and Mexican records he heard on the radio, which eventually developed into his own hybrid style. He joined the US marines in 1953, spending his time in the brig and eventually being dismissed for bad conduct. He began playing rockabilly in Texas honky tonks in the late 50s and he recorded a Spanish version of 'Don't Be Cruel' as well as his own composition, 'Wasted Days And Wasted Nights' (1958). He recalls, 'I had a gringo manager and started recording in English. Since I was playing a Fender guitar and amplifier, I changed my name to Freddy Fender.' A fight in one club left him with a broken nose and a knife wound in his neck. Starting in 1960, Fender spent three years in Angola State Prison, Louisiana, on drug offences and he recorded several tracks on a cassette recorder while in jail, later collected on an album. Upon his release, he secured a residency at a Bourbon Street club in New Orleans. Despairing of ever finding real success, he returned to San Benito in 1969 and took regular work as a mechanic. He gained a sociology degree with a view to helping ex-convicts. He returned to performing, however, and 'Before The Next Teardrop Falls', which he performed in English and Spanish, became a number 1 US pop hit in 1975. He had further US chart success with 'Wasted Days And Wasted Nights' (number 8 and dedicated to Doug Sahm), 'Secret Love' (number 20), 'You'll Lose A Good Thing' and 'Vaya Con Dios'. Fender's overwrought vocals, which even added something to 'How Much Is That Doggie In The Window?', were skilfully matched by Huey P. Meaux's arrangements featuring marimbas, accordion, harpsichord and steel guitar. His fuzzy hair and roly-poly body made him

an unlikely pop star, but his admirers included Elvis Presley. Fender succumbed to alcohol and drugs which forced his wife, in 1985, to enter him in a clinic, which apparently cured him. Fender played a corrupted mayor in the 1987 film *The Milagro Beanfield War*, directed by Robert Redford. In 1990, he formed an all-star Tex-Mex band, the Texas Tornados, with long-time friends Doug Sahm and Augie Meyers (from Sir Douglas Quintet), and accordionist Flaco Jiminez. Their eponymous debut album was a critical and commercial success, but subsequent collaborations have failed to match its stylist blend of conjunto, country and R&B. Fender was signed to Warner Brothers Records as a soloist on the back of the group's success. *The Freddy Fender Collection*, his initial offering, was a disappointing collection of remakes of his early hits. Referring back to his military service, he says, 'It has taken me 35 years to have my discharge changed from bad conduct, and this means I am now eligible for a military funeral.'

● ALBUMS: *Before The Next Teardrop Falls* (ABC 1975)★★★, *Recorded Inside Louisiana State Prison* (ABC 1975)★★★, *Since I Met You Baby* (ABC 1975)★★★, *Are You Ready For Freddy?* (ABC 1975)★★★, *Rock n' Country* (ABC 1976)★★, *If You're Ever In Texas* (ABC 1976)★★★, *If You Don't Love Me* (ABC 1977)★★★, *Merry Christmas - Feliz Navidad* (ABC 1977)★★, with Roy Clark, Hank Thompson, Don Williams *Country Comes To Carnegie Hall* (ABC/Dot 1977)★★★★, *Swamp Gold* (ABC 1978)★★★, *The Texas Balladeer* (1979)★★★, *Tex-Mex* (1979)★★★, *Together We Drifted Apart* (1980)★★★, *El Major De Freddy Fender* (1986)★★★, *Crazy Baby* (Starburst 1987)★★★, with Texas Tornados *The Freddie Fender Collection* (Warners 1991)★★, *Christmas Time In The Valley* (1991)★★, *Canciones De Mi Barrio* (Arhoolie 1994)★★★.

● COMPILATIONS: *The Best Of Freddy Fender* (Dot 1977)★★★, *20 Greatest Hits* (Astan 1984)★★★, *Best Of Freddy Fender* (MCA 1985)★★★, *Early Years 1959-1963* (Krazy Kat 1986)★★★, *Greatest Hits: Freddy Fender* (Big Country 1988)★★★, *16 Greatest Hits* (1993)★★★.

FISHER, SHUG

b. George Clinton Fisher, 26 September 1907, Spring Creek, near Chickasha, Grady County, Oklahoma, USA, d. 16 March 1984. Later a member of the Sons Of The Pioneers, by the age of 16, Fisher was playing the fiddle and had also developed a natural talent for comedy. He moved to California, where he made a living at various jobs, including fruit-picking and labouring in oilfields. He played fiddle at local dances and made his radio debut on KMS Fresno in 1927. In 1931, he worked with the Hollywood Hillbillies, where he first played bass fiddle, and the following year, he became a member of the Beverly Hillbillies. In the mid-30s, he worked with Stuart Hamblem and Roy Faulkner, before linking up with Hugh Cross. They played together in West Wheeling for almost four years, before moving to WLW Cincinnati, to host their popular *Hugh And Shugs's Radio Pals*. In 1941, Fisher returned to Los Angeles to undertake defence work and entertained locally. Late in 1943, he became a member of the Sons Of The Pioneers, when their comedian and bass player Pat Brady was drafted. He remained a member until Brady returned in 1946, but rejoined in 1949, when Brady left for film and television work with Roy Rogers. He remained a Pioneer until 1953, when he joined Ken Curtis to work in films and on radio and television. In 1955, when

Deuce Spriggens left the Pioneers, he was persuaded to return and stayed with the group until 1959 when he retired, stating it was time he 'kinda took it easy and did a lot of hunting and fishing'. However, this was soon postponed when, until 1961, he became a regular on Red Foley's *Ozark Jubilee* at Springfield, Missouri. With retirement still on hold, he returned to Hollywood, where he played many film and television character parts, including a regular role in *Ripcord* with Ken Curtis, 19 episodes of *Beverly Hillbillies* and several roles in *Gunsmoke*. Deteriorating health finally forced him into retirement and after a long illness, with old friend Ken Curtis at his side, Fisher died on 16 March 1984.

FJELLAARD, GARY

b. Sasketchewan, Canada. Fjellaard (pronounced Fell-gard) grew up on an isolated Canadian farm and learnt to play guitar through his own initiative and through listening to the radio. He worked as a Canadian lumberjack for 15 years and became a country star in his homeland, performing originally under just his surname. His first UK release was gentle folk/country, highly derivative of Gordon Lightfoot. 'Riding On The Wind' was awarded the Canadian country single of the year in 1987.
● ALBUMS: *Me And Martin* (Emerald 1978)★★★, *Ballads And Beers* (Royalty 1980)★★★, *Time And Innocence* (Savannah 1985)★★★, *No Time To Lose* (Savannah 1987)★★★★, *Heart Of A Dream* (Savannah 1989)★★★.

FLATLANDERS

The seminal US country band the Flatlanders were formed in Lubbock, Texas, USA, in 1971. The three main members were all singer-songwriters and guitarists; Joe Ely, Jimmie Dale Gilmore and Butch Hancock. Ely met Gilmore in Lubbock and, realizing they shared a love of Jimmie Rodgers, they formed a traditional country band. They were joined by Butch Hancock, Sylvester Rice (bass), Tommy Hancock (fiddle) and Steve Wesson (musical saw). Tommy Hancock owned the Cotton Club in Lubbock, where Buddy Holly had played. According to Butch Hancock, the Flatlanders played 'parties, goat roasts and the Old Town pub in Lubbock'. An independent producer, Royce Clark, recorded them in February 1972 for Plantation Records in Nashville. They released one single, 'Dallas', written by Gilmore and credited to Jimmie Dale And The Flatlanders. It featured Ely's dobro and a prominent use of Wesson's musical saw. Seventeen tracks were recorded (including five by Hancock, four by Gilmore and three by the occasional member Al Strehli), although they were not released until several years later when the three main members had become better known as solo artists. From time to time, all three have collaborated on various projects, while Steve Wesson is now a full-time carpenter.
● ALBUMS: *One More Road (1972 Recording)* (Charly 1980)★★★, *More A Legend Than A Band* (Rounder 1990)★★★.

FLATT AND SCRUGGS

Lester Flatt (b. 28 June 1914, Overton County, Tennessee, USA, d. 11 May 1979, Nashville, Tennessee, USA; guitar) and Earl Scruggs (b. 6 January 1924, Cleveland County, North Carolina, USA; banjo). These influential musicians began working together in December 1945 as members of Bill

Monroe's Bluegrass Boys. In February 1948 they left to form the Foggy Mountain Boys with Jim Shumate (fiddle), Howard Watts aka Cedric Rainwater (bass fiddle) - both ex-Bill Monroe - and, latterly, Mac Wiseman (tenor vocals, guitar). They became an established feature of Virginia's WCYB radio station and undertook recording sessions for the Mercury label before embarking on a prolonged tour of the south. Here they forged a more powerful, ebullient sound than was associated with their chosen genre and in November 1950 Flatt and Scruggs joined Columbia/CBS Records, with whom they remained throughout their career together. Three years later they signed a sponsorship agreement with Martha White Mills which engendered a regular show on Nashville's WSM and favoured slots on their patron's television shows. Josh Graves (dobro) was then added to the line-up which in turn evolved a less frenetic sound and reduced the emphasis on Scruggs' banjo playing. Appearances on the nationally syndicated *Folk Sound USA* brought the group's modern bluegrass sound to a much wider audience, while their stature was further enhanced by an appearance at the 1960 Newport Folk Festival. Flatt and Scruggs were then adopted by the college circuit where they were seen as antecedents to a new generation of acts, including the Kentucky Colonels, the Hillmen and the Dillards. The Foggy Mountain Boys performed the theme song, 'The Ballad Of Jed Clampett', to the popular *Beverly Hillbillies* television show in the early 60s while their enduring instrumental, 'Foggy Mountain Breakdown', was heavily featured in the film *Bonnie And Clyde*. Bluegrass students suggested that this version lacked the sparkle of earlier arrangements and declared that the group lacked its erstwhile vitality. By 1968 Earl Scruggs' sons, Randy and Gary, had been brought into the line-up, but the banjoist nonetheless grew dissatisfied with the constraints of a purely bluegrass setting. The partnership was dissolved the following year. While Flatt formed a new act, the Nashville Grass, his former partner added further members of his family to found the Earl Scruggs Revue. Plans for a reunion album were thwarted by Flatt's death in May 1979. The duo were inducted into the Country Music Hall Of Fame in 1985.
● ALBUMS: *Foggy Mountain Jamboree* (Columbia 1957)★★★★, *Country Music* (Mercury 1958)★★★, *Lester Flatt And Earl Scruggs* (Mercury 1959)★★★★, *Songs Of Glory* (Columbia 1960)★★★, *Flatt And Scruggs And The Foggy Mountain Boys* (Harmony 1960)★★★, *Foggy Mountain Banjo* (Columbia 1961)★★★★, *Songs Of The Famous Carter Family* (Columbia 1961)★★★, *Folk Songs Of Our Land* (Columbia 1962)★★★★, *Flatt And Scruggs At Carnegie Hall* (Columbia 1962)★★★, *The Original Sound Of Flatt And Scruggs* (Mercury 1963)★★★, *Hard Travelin'/The Ballad Of Jed Clampett* (Columbia 1963)★★★★, *Recorded Live At Vanderbilt University* (Columbia 1964)★★★, *The Fabulous Sound Of Flatt And Scruggs* (Columbia 1964)★★★, *The Versatile Flatt And Scruggs* (Columbia 1965)★★★, *Pickin' Strummin' And Singin'* (Columbia 1965)★★★, one side is Jim And Jesse *Stars Of The Grand Ol' Opry* (Starday 1966)★★, *Town & Country* (Columbia 1966)★★★, *When The Saints Go Marching In* (Columbia 1966)★★★, with Doc Watson *Strictly Instrumental* (Columbia 1967)★★, *Hear The Whistle Blow* (Columbia 1967)★★, *The Original Theme From Bonnie & Clyde* (Mercury 1968)★★, with Bill Monroe *Bill Monroe With Lester Flatt & Earl Scruggs:The Original Bluegrass Band* (Decca 1978)★★★.

● COMPILATIONS: *Flatt And Scruggs Greatest Hits* (Columbia 1966)★★★, *The Original Foggy Mountain Breakdown* (Mercury 1968)★★★★, *World Of Flatt And Scruggs* (Columbia 1973)★★★, *The Golden Era 1950-1955* (Rounder 1977)★★★★, *Foggy Mountain Banjo* (1978)★★★★, *Blue Ridge Cabin Home* (Rebel 1979)★★★★, *Columbia Historic Edition* (Columbia 1982)★★★, *20 All Time Great Recordings* (Columbia 1983)★★★, *Country And Western Classics* 3-LP box set (Time-Life 1982)★★★, *Mercury Sessions, Volume 1* (Mercury 1987)★★★★, *Mercury Sessions, Volume 2* (Mercury 1987)★★★, *You Can Feel It In Your Soul* (County 1988)★★★, *Don't Get Above Your Raisin'* (Rounder 1992)★★★, *The Complete Mercury Sessions* (Mercury 1992)★★★★, *1949 -1959* 4-CD box set (Bear Family 1992)★★★★, *1959 - 1963* 5-CD box set (Bear Family 1992)★★★★, *1964 - 69, Plus* 6-CD box set (Bear Family 1996)★★★★, *'Tis Sweet To Be Remembered: The Essential* (Legacy/Columbia 1997)★★★★.

FLATT, LESTER

b. 28 June 1914, Overton County, Tennessee, USA, d. 11 May 1979, Nashville, Tennessee, USA. Versed in the old-time country music style prevalent in his rural environment, Flatt began playing guitar during the 30s. At the end of the decade he abandoned his job in a textile mill to pursue a career as a professional musician. Having made his debut on station WDBJ, Flatt became a popular entertainer throughout the south and by 1944 was a feature of the *Grand Ole Opry*. He then joined Bill Monroe's Bluegrass Boys where he later met banjoist Earl Scruggs. The two musicians left Monroe in 1948 and, as Flatt And Scruggs, redefined the modern bluegrass sound. For over 20 years the duo led various versions of their group, the Foggy Mountain Boys, which remained at the heart of America's traditional music circuit. They parted company in 1969 following which Flatt created another group, the Nashville Grass. He continued to tour and record, but his once-prolific work rate lessened considerably following open-heart surgery in 1975.

● ALBUMS: with Mac Wiseman *Lester 'N' Mac* (RCA Victor 1971)★★★, *Foggy Mountain Breakdown* (1973)★★★, with Wiseman *On The South Bound* (RCA Victor 1973)★★★, with Wiseman *Over Hills To Poor House* (RCA Victor 1973)★★★, *Before You Go* (1974)★★★, *Flatt Gospel* (1975)★★★, with John Hartford, Benny Martin *Tennessee Jubilee* (Flying Fish 1975)★★★, *Just Flatt Gospel* (1975)★★★, *Heaven's Bluegrass Band* (CMH 1976)★★★, *Lester Flatt* (1977)★★★, *Live At The Bluegrass Festival* (RCA 1986)★★★, *The Golden Era* (Rounder 1988)★★★★, *Lester Flatt's Greatest Performance* (CMH 1989)★★★.

FLAVIN, MICK

b. 3 August 1950, Gaigue, Ballinamuck, Co. Longford, Eire. After leaving school, he was apprenticed as a carpenter, but his love of the recordings of Hank Williams, George Jones and Charley Pride, plus his ambition to be a professional country singer, saw him form a band and begin to entertain in local venues. However, he spent over 12 years as a part-time entertainer and also successfully defeated a drink problem before he finally achieved his goal. In 1986, he recorded a self-financed cassette album sold only at gigs. It was well received and the following year, his recording debut, *I'm Going To Make It After All*, proved prophetically

correct and won him an award. Since then, he has worked hard to establish himself on the Irish and UK country scene and has made highly acclaimed appearances at several major shows. He made his English debut in 1988 at the Peterborough Festival and the following year proved very popular at the International Festival Of Country Music at Wembley. He joined the Ritz record label in 1990 and the following year, recorded a very popular duet album with Philomena Begley. However, it is his solo recordings that have helped make him one of the Ritz label's most popular singers and established him as a major UK artist.

● ALBUMS: *I'm Going To Make It After All* (Harmac 1987)★★★, *Introducing Mick Flavin* (Prism 1988)★★★★, *You're Only Young Once* (Harmac 1988)★★★, *In Concert* (Ritz 1990)★★★, *Travellin' Light* (Ritz 1990)★★★, with Philomena Begley *In Harmony* (Ritz 1991)★★★, *Sweet Memory* (Ritz 1992)★★★, *The Lights Of Home* (Ritz 1993)★★★, *Echoes Of My Mind* (Ritz 1994)★★★, *Country All The Way* (Ritz 1997)★★★.

● VIDEOS: *In Concert* (Ritz 1990), *Going Home Again* (1995).

FLECK, BELA

b. *c*.1953, New York City, New York, USA. Fleck has been credited with expanding the parameters of the banjo by combining traditional bluegrass with jazz and classical music, similar to what David Grisman did with the mandolin. Inspired by the song 'Duelling Banjos' in the film *Deliverance*, Fleck took up the banjo at the age of 14. He moved to Kentucky in his early 20s to start the bluegrass group Spectrum. In 1981 he relocated to Nashville, joining the influential New Grass Revival, with whom he stayed for eight years. In 1989 he formed the Flecktones with Howard Levy (keyboards, harmonica), Victor Wooten (bass) and Roy Wooten (drumitar - a guitar wired to electric drums). The group's debut album for Warner Brothers Records sold over 50,000 copies and reached the Top 20 on the *Billboard* jazz charts. Fleck is clearly an outstanding musician but there seems to be difficulty in establishing him beyond a jazz audience, which would seem not to be his most comfortable category - his music is more eclectic and would appeal to both rock and folk/roots audiences.

● ALBUMS: *Crossing The Tracks* (Rounder 1979)★★★, *Natural Bridge* (Rounder 1982)★★★, *Double Time* (Rounder 1984)★★★, with the New Grass Revival *Deviation* (Rounder 1985)★★, *In Roads* (Rounder 1986)★★★, *Drive* (Rounder 1988)★★, *Bela Fleck And The Flecktones* (Warners 1990)★★★, *Flight Of the Cosmic Hippo* (Warners 1991)★★★★, with Tony Trischka *Solo Banjo Works* (Rounder 1993)★★★★, *UFO TOFU* (Warners 1993)★★★, *Tales From The Acoustic Planet* (Warners 1995)★★★★, with Jie Bing Chen, V.M. Bhatt *Tabula Rasa* (Water Lily Acoustics 1996)★★★.

● COMPILATIONS: *Daybreak* (Rounder 1987), ★★★★, *Places* (Rounder 1987)★★★, *Live Art* (Warners 1996)★★★.

FLETCHER, TEX

b. Jerry Bisceglia, 8 March 1910, Harrison, New York, USA, d. 1986. A fine singer/yodeller and left-handed guitarist, although little is known of his early life. He probably made his debut as an entertainer with *Buffalo Bill's Wild West Show*. He worked briefly as a cowboy and sang on radio in Yankton, South Dakota, which probably led to later claims being made that he originated from that state. He spent most of his time in New York and between November 1936 and June 1937, he recorded 13 sides there for Decca, including two duets with Joe Rogers. He made 10 further recordings, this time with his Lonely Cowboys, between October 1937 and February 1938. The material varied from standard cowboy ballads ('The Zebra Dun') and family songs ('A Song For Mother') to the popular 'I Get The Blues When It Rains' and the strangely titled 'Meet Me Tonight In The Cowshed'. His Hollywood success consisted of a few musical shorts and his claim to being a singing cowboy was confined to a single starring role, in 1939, in *Six Gun Rhythm*. Grand National Pictures closed just as it was released and he was left to promote his film himself. He was drafted for army service during World War II, which prevented him from moving to another studio to continue his singing cowboy career. After his discharge, he returned to New York and for many years, he was popular as The Lonely Cowboy, on WOR radio. During the 50s and 60s, he also appeared fairly regularly on television. He published two songbooks and made countless personal appearances. Copies of his recordings, originally released on both Decca and Montgomery Ward, are rare, but 'The Yodelling Cowboy's Last Song' appears on MCA's *Cowboy Image* compilation.

FLORES, ROSIE

b. 10 September 1950, San Antonio, Texas, USA. Flores's background accounts for the strong Mexican influence in her brand of country music. When she was 12 years old, her family moved to San Diego, California, and she subsequently became part of an all-girl psychedelic band, Penelope's Children. She was then backed by a punk band, Rosie And The Screamers. Next came another all-girl cowpunk band, the Screamin' Sirens. In 1985, she was part of a compilation album of new country artists, *A Town South Of Bakersfield*, on which she sang 'Heartbreak Train' with Albert Lee. Her first album for Reprise, *Rosie Flores*, was produced with Pete Anderson and Dwight Yoakam, but her biggest single on the US country charts, 'Crying Over You', only reached number 51. Dropped by Reprise, she re-emerged five years later on Hightone with *After The Farm*. Flores remains one of those Texas artists more popular as a cult performer in Europe than in her home country. In 1994 she toured the UK as lead guitarist for Butch Hancock, but during the visit she badly broke her right arm, which ultimately delayed the recording of *Rockabilly Filly*. The album included duets with two of her rockabilly idols, Wanda Jackson and Janis Martin. She collaborated with cult rockabilly singer Ray Campi on her 1997 album, which featured tracks recorded over the previous seven years.
● ALBUMS: with The Screamin' Sirens *Fiesta* (Enigma 1984)★★★, *Rosie Flores* (Reprise 1987)★★★★, *After The Farm* (Hightone 1992)★★★, *Once More With Feeling* (Hightone 1993)★★★, *Rockabilly Filly* (Hightone 1995)★★★, *A Honky Tonk Reprise* 1987 Reprise album plus extra tracks (Rounder 1996)★★★★, with Ray Campi *A Little Bit Of Heartache* (Watermelon 1997)★★★.

FLYING BURRITO BROTHERS

The Flying Burrito Brothers initially referred to an informal group of Los Angeles musicians, notably Jesse Davis and Barry Tashain. The name was appropriated in 1968 by former Byrds Gram Parsons (b. 5 November 1946, Waycross, Georgia, USA, d. 19 September 1973; guitar, vocals) and Chris Hillman (b. 4 December 1942, Los Angeles, California, USA; guitar, vocals) for a new venture that would integrate rock and country styles. 'Sneaky' Pete Kleinow (pedal steel), Chris Ethridge (bass) plus various drummers completed the line-up featured on *The Gilded Palace Of Sin*, where the founding duo's vision of a pan-American music flourished freely. The material ranged from the jauntily acerbic 'Christine's Tune' to the maudlin 'Hippy Boy', but its highlights included Parsons' emotional reading of two southern soul standards, 'Dark End Of The Street' and 'Do Right Woman', and his own poignant 'Hot Burrito #1' and the impassioned 'Hot Burrito #2'. The album's sense of cultural estrangement captured a late 60s restlessness and reflected the rural traditions of antecedents the Everly Brothers. This artistic triumph was never repeated. *Burrito Deluxe*, on which Bernie Leadon replaced Ethridge and Michael Clarke (b. Michael Dick, 3 June 1944, Texas, USA), formerly of the Byrds, became the permanent drummer, showed a group unsure of direction as Parsons' role became increasingly questionable. He left for a solo career in April 1970 and with the arrival of songwriter Rick Roberts, the Burritos again asserted their high quality. The underrated *The Flying Burrito Brothers* was a cohesive, purposeful set, marked by the inclusion of Roberts' 'Colorado', Gene Clark's 'Tried So Hard' and Merle Haggard's 'White Line Fever', plus several other excellent Roberts originals. Unfortunately, the group was again bedevilled by defections. In 1971 Leadon joined the Eagles while Kleinow opted for a career in session work, but Hillman, Clarke and Roberts were then buoyed by the arrival of Al Perkins (pedal steel), Kenny Wertz (guitar), Roger Bush (bass) and Byron Berline (fiddle). *The Last Of The Red Hot Burritos* captured the excitement and power of the group live. The septet was sundered in 1971, with Wertz, Bush and Berline forming Country Gazette, Hillman and Perkins joining Manassas, while Roberts embarked on a solo career before founding Firefall with Clarke. However, much to the consternation of Hillman, 'Sneaky' Pete Kleinow later commandeered the Burritos' name and in 1975 completed *Flying Again* with Chris Ethridge, Gene Parsons (guitar, vocals) and Gib Guilbeau (fiddle). The last-named joined Kleinow in a full-scale reactivation during the 80s. The arrival of country veteran John Beland provided the group with a proven songwriter worthy of the earlier pioneering line-up. The 1997 line-up comprised Beland, Guilbeau, Kleinow, Larry Patton (bass) and Gary Kubal (drums).
● ALBUMS: *The Gilded Palace Of Sin* (A&M 1969)★★★★★, *Burrito DeLuxe* (A&M 1970)★★★, *The Flying Burrito Brothers* (A&M 1971)★★★, *The Last Of The Red Hot Burritos* (A&M 1972)★★★★, *Live In Amsterdam* (Bumble 1973)★★★, *Flying Again* (Columbia 1975)★★, *Airborne* (Columbia 1976)★★, *Flying High* (J.B. 1978)★★, *Live From Tokyo* (Regency 1978) reissued as *Close Encounters To The West Coast* (Relix 1991)★★, *Burrito Country* (Brian 1979)★★, *Cabin Fever* (Relix 1985)★★, *Live From Europe* (Relix 1986)★★, *Flying Burrito Bros Live* Holland only (Marlstone 1986)★★, *Back To The Sweethearts Of The Rodeo* (Disky 1987)★★★, *Southern Tracks* (Dixie Frog 1990)★★★, *Encore - Live In Europe* (Sundown 1991)★★, *Eye Of A Hurricane* (1993)★★★, *California Jukebox* (Ether 1997)★★.
Solo: Sneaky Pete Kleinow *Sneaky Pete* (Rhino 1979)★★★,

Legend And The Legacy (Shiloh 1994)★★★, *California Jukebox* (Ether/American Harvest 1997)★★★.
● COMPILATIONS: *Honky Tonk Heaven* (A&M 1972)★★, *Close Up The Honky Tonks* (A&M 1974)★★★★, *Bluegrass Special* (Ariola 1975)★★, *Hot Burrito - 2* (A&M 1975)★★, with Gram Parsons *Sleepless Nights* (A&M 1976)★★★, with Parsons *Dim Lights, Thick Smoke And Loud, Loud Music* (Edsel 1987)★★★, *Farther Along: Best Of* (A&M 1988)★★★★, *Hollywood Nights 1979-1981* (Sundown 1990)★★★, *Out Of The Blue* (Polygram Chronicles 1996)★★★.

FOGELBERG, DAN

b. 13 August 1951, Peoria, Illinois, USA. Having learned piano from the age of 14, Fogelberg moved to guitar and songwriting. Leaving the University of Illinois in 1971, he relocated to California and started playing on the folk circuit, at one point touring with Van Morrison. A move to Nashville brought him to the attention of producer Norbert Putnam. Fogelberg released *Home Free* for Columbia shortly afterwards. This was a highly relaxed album, notable for the backing musicians involved, including Roger McGuinn, Jackson Browne, Joe Walsh and Buffy Sainte-Marie. Despite the calibre of the other players, the album was not a success, and Fogelberg, having been dropped by Columbia, returned to session work. Producer Irv Azoff, who was managing Joe Walsh, signed Fogelberg and secured a contract with Epic. Putnam was involved in subsequent recordings by Fogelberg. In 1974, Fogelberg moved to Colorado, and a year later released *Souvenirs*. This was a more positive album, and Walsh's production was evident. From here on, Fogelberg played the majority of the instruments on record, enabling him to keep tight control of the recordings, but inevitably it took longer to finish the projects. Playing support to the Eagles in 1975 helped to establish Fogelberg. However, in 1977, due to appear with the Eagles at Wembley, he failed to appear onstage, and it was later claimed that he had remained at home to complete recording work on *Netherlands*. Whatever the reason, the album achieved some recognition, but Fogelberg has enjoyed better chart success in the USA than in the UK. In 1980, 'Longer' reached number 2 in the US singles charts, while in the UK it did not even reach the Top 50. Two other singles, 'Same Auld Lang Syne' and 'Leader Of The Band', both from *The Innocent Age*, achieved Top 10 places in the USA. The excellent *High Country Snows* saw a return to his bluegrass influences and was in marked contrast to the harder-edged *Exiles* that followed. From plaintive ballads to rock material, Fogelberg is a versatile writer and musician who continues to produce credible records and command a loyal cult following.
● ALBUMS: *Home Free* (Columbia 1973)★★, *Souvenirs* (Full Moon 1974)★★★, *Captured Angel* (Full Moon 1975)★★, *Netherlands* (Full Moon 1977)★★, with Tim Weisberg *Twin Sons Of Different Mothers* (Full Moon 1978)★★★★, *Phoenix* (Full Moon 1979)★★★★, *The Innocent Age* (Full Moon 1981)★★★★, *Windows And Walls* (Full Moon 1984)★★, *High Country Snows* (Full Moon 1985)★★★, *Exiles* (Full Moon 1987)★★, *The Wild Places* (Full Moon 1990)★★, *Dan Fogelberg Live - Greetings From The West* (Full Moon 1991)★★, *River Of Souls* (Sony 1993)★★.
● COMPILATIONS: *Greatest Hits* (Full Moon 1983)★★★,

Starbox (1993)★★★, *Portrait: The Music Of Dan Fogelberg From 1972-1997* 4-CD box set (Epic 1997)★★★★.

FOLEY, BETTY

b. 3 February 1933, Chicago, Illinois, USA, d. 1990. The daughter of country star Red Foley, her mother died in childbirth and she was raised by her stepmother in Berea, Kentucky. She learned guitar as a child and at 17, she began to appear regularly on the *Renfro Valley Barn Dance*, a show that her father had helped to create with John Lair around 1937. Her singing gained her a recording contract with Decca Records, and in 1954, she had a number 8 hit with 'As Far As I'm Concerned', followed the next year by a Top 3 with 'Satisfied Mind', both being duets with her father. She left the *Barn Dance* in 1954 and in 1956 and 1957, she was a regular on the *Midwestern Hayride* on WLW Cincinnati and also played on the *Grand Ole Opry*. In 1958, she starred on WNOX Knoxville's *Tennessee Barndance*, before moving to the *Louisiana Hayride* on KWKH Shreveport. After leaving Decca, she recorded for Bandera, gaining a number 7 hit (her last) with 'Old Moon' in 1959. She eventually became a resident performer, with her father, on the ABC's networked *Jubilee USA* television show on KWTO Springfield, Missouri. After retiring as a performer, she had a business interest in Kentucky Fried Chicken.

FOLEY, RED

b. Clyde Julian Foley, 17 June 1910, in a log cabin between Blue Lick and Berea, Kentucky, USA, d. 19 September 1968, Fort Wayne, Indiana, USA. The son of a fiddle player, he learned guitar as a child and was encouraged to sing by his parents. After high school, he attended Georgetown College, Kentucky, where he was discovered by a scout for the noted WLS National Barn Dance in Chicago. In 1930, he joined John Lair's Cumberland Ridge Runners and returned to Kentucky with Lair in 1937, to help him establish the now famous Renfro Valley Barn Dance. He returned to Chicago in 1941, co-starred with Red Skelton in the network country radio show *Avalon Time* and signed with Decca. The first number he recorded was 'Old Shep', a song he had written in 1933, about a dog he had owned as a child (in reality, the dog, sadly poisoned by a neighbour, had been a German shepherd named Hoover). The song, later recorded by many artists including Hank Snow and Elvis Presley, has become a country classic. His first chart success came in 1944, when the patriotic wartime song 'Smoke On The Water' was a US pop chart number 7 and a 13-week occupant of the number 1 position in the country charts. On 17 January 1945, Foley had the distinction of making the first modern country records recorded in Nashville. In April 1946, Foley became a regular member of the *Grand Ole Opry*, replacing Roy Acuff as the star of NBC's prestigious *Prince Albert Show*. When he left Chicago for Nashville, he took with him a young guitar player called Chet Atkins, one of the many artists he helped. During the next eight years Foley established himself as one of the most respected and versatile performers in country music. He acted as master of ceremonies, the straight man for *Opry* comedians Rod Brasfield and Minnie Pearl, and proved himself a vocalist who could handle all types of material. In 1954, he moved to KWTO Springfield, as the host of the *Ozark Jubilee*, which, in 1956, became one of the first successful network television shows. Between 1944 and

1959, Foley charted 41 solo country entries of which 38 were Top 10 hits. There were six more country number 1s, including his 1950 million-selling 'Chattanoogie Shoe Shine Boy', which also topped the pop charts. Several others achieved crossover pop chart success. During this time he also had many major hit duets with various artists including Evelyn Knight, his daughter Betty Foley, Ernest Tubb, ('Goodnight Irene') and six with Kitty Wells, including their country number 1, 'One By One', which remained on the charts for 41 weeks. His performances of gospel numbers were so popular that recordings of 'Steal Away' (1950) (recorded by Hank Williams as 'The Funeral'), 'Just A Closer Walk With Thee' (1950) and 'Peace In The Valley' (1951) all became million-sellers. He also recorded with the Andrews Sisters and in the late 50s, even cut some rock 'n' roll recordings such as 'Crazy Little Guitar Man'. Although he continued to tour and appear on network television shows, he also moved into acting in the early 60s and co-starred with Fess Parker in the ABC-TV series *Mr. Smith Goes To Washington*. His daughter Shirley married one-time pop and later gospel singer Pat Boone, and some ten years after Foley's death, his granddaughter Debby Boone had both country and pop success. Foley never lost his love for country music and, unlike Eddy Arnold, never sought success as a pop artist, even though many of his recordings did attain pop chart status. His voice was mellow and had none of the raw or nasal style associated with many of his contemporaries; some have even likened it to Bing Crosby. His importance to the country music scene is often overlooked and little has been written about him, but he was rightfully elected to the Country Music Hall of Fame in 1967. He was headlining a touring *Opry* show when, after playing the matinée and evening shows, Foley suffered a heart attack and died in his sleep at Fort Wayne, Indiana, on 19 September 1968. This prompted Hank Jnr., seemingly the last person to speak to him, to write and record (as Luke The Drifter Jnr) the tribute narration 'I Was With Red Foley (The Night He Passed Away)', which charted in November 1968. In the song, Hank Jnr. relates that after reminiscing about the problems faced by country singers such as himself and Hank Snr., Red's final words were: 'I'm awful tired now, Hank, I've got to go to bed'.

● ALBUMS: *Red Foley Souvenir Album* (Decca 1951)★★★★, *Lift Up Your Voice* (Decca 1954)★★★, with Ernest Tubb *Red & Ernie* (Decca 1956)★★★, *My Keepsake Album* (Decca 1958)★★★, *Beyond The Sunset* (Decca 1958)★★★★, *He Walks With Thee* (Decca 1958)★★, *Red Foley's Dickies Souvenir Album* (Decca 1958)★★★, *Let's All Sing To Him* (Decca 1959)★★, *Let's All Sing With Red Foley* (Decca 1959)★★★, *Company's Comin'* (Decca 1961)★★★, *Red Foley's Golden Favorites* (Decca 1961)★★★★, *Songs Of Devotion* (Decca 1961)★★★, with Kitty Wells *Kitty Wells & Red Foley's Greatest Hits* (Decca 1961)★★★★, *Dear Hearts And Gentle People* (Decca 1962)★★★, *The Red Foley Show* (Decca 1963)★★★, *The Red Foley Story* (Decca 1964)★★★★, *Songs Everybody Knows* (Decca 1965)★★★, *I'm Bound For The Kingdom* (Vocalion 1965)★★★, *Red Foley* (Vocalion 1966)★★★, *Songs For The Soul* (Decca 1967)★★★, with Kitty Wells *Together Again* (Decca 1967)★★★, *I Believe* (1969)★★★, *The Old Master* (1969)★★★, *Red Foley Memories* (1971)★★★★.

● COMPILATIONS: *Gospel Favorites* (1976)★★★, *Beyond The Sunset* (MCA 1981)★★★★, *Tennessee Saturday Night* (Charly 1984)★★★, *The Red Foley Story* (MCA 1986)★★★★, *Red Foley: Country Music Hall Of Fame Series* (MCA 1991)★★★★.

FORAN, DICK

b. John Nicholas Foran, 18 June 1910, Flemington, New Jersey, USA, d. 13 August 1979. Foran, the son of a US senator, studied geology at Princeton University. He worked briefly as a Pennsylvania Railroad investigator, before a desire to sing in films led him to Hollywood. In 1934, he made his debut in *Gentlemen Are Born* and in 1935, he appeared with Shirley Temple in the musical *Stand Up And Cheer*. He first appeared as a singing cowboy (complete with his palomino, Smoke) for Warner Brothers in *Moonlight On The Prairie*, late in 1935, thus becoming the second of the genre (Gene Autry beat him when *Tumbling Tumbleweeds* was released two months earlier). Between 1935 and 1937, Foran, Warner's only singing cowboy, starred in 12 B-westerns, including *Cowboy From Brooklyn* (1937), before moving to Universal in 1938, where he appeared in a variety of roles and two western serials, *Winners Of The West* (1940) and *Riders In Death Valley* (1941). The same year, he appeared with the Sons of the Pioneers in the radio series *Ten-Two-Four Ranch*. His successes as a singing cowboy were few when compared to Autry, but his acting ability saw him in various roles in well over 100 films, the last being in 1967. During the 50s, he also appeared in many television productions. Although he had had operatic training, his singing was readily accepted by his western audiences.

FORD, GERRY

b. 25 May 1943, Athlone, Co. Westmeath, Eire. When he was aged 16, Ford emigrated to England as an apprentice baker, and, on qualification, married and relocated to Edinburgh, where he joined the police force for 11 years. Since the late 60s he has been a country music performer, turning professional in 1976. He has recorded all his albums since 1981 in Nashville and has performed numerous times on the *Grand Ole Opry* as a guest of Opry star Jean Shepard. He has recorded six duets with Shepard, while Boxcar Willie added train whistles to Ford's tribute 'They Call Him Boxcar Willie'. Boxcar also wrote 'Jesus, I Need To Talk To You' for Ford's *All Over Again*. His easy-listening albums, which combine the new with the familiar, have helped to establish him as Scotland's 'Mr. Country'. In 1991, economy forced him to drop his band in favour of Nashville-made backing tapes, and they have been well received. *Thank God For The Radio* won an award as the UK country album of the year, and Ford has good cause to 'thank God for the radio', as he has presented country programmes on BBC Radio Scotland for 13 years.

● ALBUMS: *These Songs Are Just For You* (1977)★★★, *Someone To Give My Love To* (1978)★★★, *With Love* (1980)★★★, *On The Road* (Big R 1981)★★, *Let's Hear It For The Working Man* (Big R 1982)★★★, *Memory Machine* (Trimtop 1985)★★★, *Thank God For The Radio* (Trimtop 1986)★★★★, *All Over Again* (Trimtop 1988)★★★, *Stranger Things Have Happened* (Trimtop 1989)★★★, *Family Bible* (Trimtop 1990)★★, *Better Man* (Trimtop 1991)★★★, *Can I Count On You?* (1993)★★★.

● COMPILATIONS: *16 Country Favourites Volume One* (Trimtop 1990)★★★.

FORD, JOY

b. 10 March 1946, Brilliant, Alabama, USA. The eldest of eight children of musical parents, Ford picked cotton as a child. The family relocated to Chicago in 1959 and two years later to Poplar Bluff, Missouri. In 1963, she joined the *Century 21 Show* (a large touring carnival that played state fairs all over the USA) as an acrobatic dancer. Here she worked with Loretta Lynn who encouraged her to sing. She eventually moved to New York where, for a time, she pursued a successful acting career and sang at venues. She joined Country International Records and gained her first chart success in 1978 with 'Love Isn't Love Until You Give It Away'. In 1979, she toured with the Nashville Magic Band and during the 80s, she had four minor hits, the last coming in 1988 with 'Yesterday's Rain'. Outside of her music and acting she owns the Melody J Ranch in Dickson County, Tennessee, where she raises Appaloosa horses.

● ALBUMS: *Keep On Truckin'... Keep On Lovin'* (Country International 1983)★★★, *From The Heart Of Joy* (Country International 1983)★★★.

FORD, TENNESSEE ERNIE

b. Ernest Jennings Ford, 13 February 1919, Bristol, Tennessee, USA, d. 17 October 1991, Reston, Virginia, USA. It is difficult to categorize a performer with so many varied achievements, but Ford can be summarized as a master interpreter of melodic songs and hymns. The fact that he has been able to combine singing with his strong faith gives America's best-loved gospel singer great satisfaction. When only four years old, he was singing 'The Old Rugged Cross' at family gatherings, and from an early age, he wanted to be an entertainer. He pestered the local radio station until they made him a staff announcer in 1937 and he also took singing lessons. He subsequently worked for radio stations WATL in Atlanta and WROL in Knoxville, where he announced the attack on Pearl Harbor. He joined the US Army Air Corps in 1942 and married a secretary, Betty Heminger, whom he met at the bombardier's school. After the war, they moved to California and he worked as an announcer and a disc jockey of hillbilly music for KXFM in San Bernardino. He rang cowbells and added bass harmonies to the records he was playing and so developed a country yokel character, Tennessee Ernie. He continued with this on KXLA Pasadena and he became a regular on their *Hometown Jamboree*, which was hosted by bandleader Cliffie Stone. He was also known as the Tennessee Pea-Picker, using the catchphrase 'Bless your pea-pickin' hearts' and appearing on stage in bib overalls and with a blacked-out tooth. Lee Gillette, an A&R man for Capitol Records, heard Ford singing along with a record on air and asked Stone about him. His first record, in 1949, was 'Milk 'Em In The Morning Blues'. Ford began his chart success with 'Tennessee Border', 'Country Junction' and 'Smokey Mountain Boogie', a song he wrote with Stone. 'Mule Train', despite opposition from Frankie Laine, Gene Autry and Vaughn Monroe, was a national hit and a US country number 1. An attempt to write with Hank Williams did not lead to any completed songs, but Ford wrote 'Anticipation Blues' about his wife's pregnancy and it reached the US charts in 1949. Capitol teamed him with many of their female artists including Ella Mae Morse, Molly Bee and the Dinning Sisters, and his most successful duets were 'Ain't Nobody's Business But My Own' and 'I'll Never Be Free', a double-sided single with Kay Starr. The duet just missed gold record status, but he secured one, also in 1950, with his own song, 'Shotgun Boogie', which capitalized on the boogie craze and can be taken as a forerunner of rock 'n' roll. Its UK popularity enabled him to top a variety bill at the London Palladium in 1953. Ford recalls, 'When somebody told me that "Give Me Your Word" was number 1 in your charts, I said, "When did I record that?' because it wasn't big in America and I had forgotten about it!". Ford also had success with 'The Cry Of The Wild Goose' and the theme for the Marilyn Monroe film *The River Of No Return*, while the superb musicians on his records included Joe 'Fingers' Carr, who was given equal billing on 'Tailor Made Woman' in 1951, Speedy West and Jimmy Bryant. Ford hosted a US daytime television show for five days a week and, in 1955, Capitol informed him that he would be in breach of contract if he did not record again soon. He chose a song he had been performing on the show, Merle Travis's 'Sixteen Tons'. Ford says, 'The producer, Lee Gillette, asked me what tempo I would like it in. I snapped my fingers and he said, "Leave that in." That snapping on the record is me.' 'Sixteen Tons' topped both the US and the UK charts, and Ford was also one of many who recorded 'The Ballad Of Davy Crockett', the theme of a Walt Disney western starring Fess Parker, which made number 3 in the UK. His half-hour US television show, *The Ford Show* (guess the sponsor), ran from 1956-61. He closed every television show with a hymn, which led to him recording over 400 gospel songs. One album, *Hymns*, made number 2 in the US album charts and was listed for over five years. He has shared his billing with the Jordanaires on several albums including *Great Gospel Songs*, which won a Grammy in 1964. Ford says, 'Long before I turned pro, it was a part of my life. There are many different types of gospel music, ranging from black music to the plain old Protestant hymns. I've shown that you don't have to sing hymns with a black robe on.' Ford had further US hits with 'That's All', 'In The Middle Of An Island' and 'Hicktown' but, for many years, he concentrated on gospel. In 1961 he decided to spend more time with his family and moved to a ranch in the hills of San Francisco. He recorded albums of well-known songs, both pop and country, and he rates *Country Hits - Feelin' Blue* and *Ernie Sings And Glen Picks*, an album that showcases his deep, mellow voice alongside Glen Campbell's guitar, among his best work. Many collectors seek original copies of his albums of Civil War songs. Ford, who was elected to the Country Music Hall of Fame in 1990, remarked, 'People say to me, "Why don't you record another 'Sixteen Tons'?" And I say, "There is no other 'Sixteen Tons'".

● ALBUMS: *This Lusty Land* (Capitol 1956)★★★, *Hymns* (Capitol 1956)★★★, *Spirituals* (Capitol 1957)★★★, *C-H-R-I-S-T-M-A-S* (Capitol 1957)★★, *Tennessee Ernie Ford Favourites* (Capitol 1957)★★★, *Ol' Rockin' 'Ern* (Capitol 1957)★★★, *The Folk Album* (Capitol 1958)★★★, *Nearer The Cross* (Capitol 1958)★★★, *The Star Carol* (Capitol 1958)★★★, with the Jordanaires *Gather 'Round* (Capitol 1959)★★★★, with the Jordanaires *A Friend We Have* (Capitol 1960)★★★, *Sing A Hymn With Me* (Capitol 1960)★★★, *Sixteen Tons* (Capitol 1960)★★★★, *Sing A Spiritual With Me* (Capitol 1960)★★, *Come To The Fair* (Capitol 1960)★★★, *Sings Civil War Songs Of The North* (Capitol 1961)★★★★, *Sings Civil War Songs Of The South* (Capitol 1961)★★★★, *Ernie Ford Looks At Love* (Capitol 1961)★★, *Hymns At Home* (Capitol 1961)★★★, *Here*

Comes The Tennessee Ernie Ford Mississippi Showboat (Capitol 1962)★★, I Love To Tell The Story (Capitol 1962)★★★, Book Of Favourite Hymns (Capitol 1962)★★, Long, Long Ago (Capitol 1963)★★★, with the San Quentin Prison Choir We Gather Together (Capitol 1963)★★★, with the Roger Wagner Chorale The Story Of Christmas (Capitol 1963)★★, with the Jordanaires Great Gospel Songs (Capitol 1964)★★, Country Hits - Feeling Blue (Capitol 1964)★★★★, Let Me Walk With Thee (Capitol 1965)★★, Sing We Now Of Christmas (Capitol 1965)★★★, My Favourite Things (Capitol 1966)★★★, Wonderful Peace (Capitol 1966)★★, God Lives (Capitol 1966)★★, Aloha From Tennessee Ernie Ford (Capitol 1967)★★★, Faith Of Our Fathers (Capitol 1967)★★, with Marilyn Horne Our Garden Of Hymns (Capitol 1967)★★, with Brenda Lee The Show For Christmas Seals (Decca 1968)★★★, The World Of Pop And Country Hits (Capitol 1968)★★★, O Come All Ye Faithful (Capitol 1968)★★★, Songs I Like To Sing (Capitol 1969)★★★, New Wave (Capitol 1969)★★★, Holy Holy Holy (Capitol 1969)★★★, America The Beautiful (Capitol 1970)★★★, Sweet Hour Of Prayer (Capitol 1970)★★★, Tennessee Ernie Ford Christmas Special (Capitol 1970)★★★, Everything Is Beautiful (Capitol 1970)★★★, Abide With Me (Capitol 1971)★★★, Mr. Words And Music (Capitol 1972)★★★, It's Tennessee Ernie Ford (Capitol 1972)★★★, Country Morning (Capitol 1973)★★★, Ernie Ford Sings About Jesus (Capitol 1973)★★, Precious Memories (Capitol 1975)★★★, with Glen Campbell Ernie Sings And Glen Picks (Capitol 1975)★★★, Tennessee Ernie Ford Sings His Great Love (Capitol 1976)★★★, For The 83rd Time (Capitol 1976)★★★, He Touched Me (Capitol 1977)★★, with the Jordanaires Swing Wide Your Golden Gate (Capitol 1978)★★★★, Tell The Old, Old Story (Capitol 1981)★★★, There's A Song In My Heart (Word 1982)★★★, Sunday's Still A Special Day (Capitol 1984)★★★, Keep Looking Up (Word 1985)★★★.
● COMPILATIONS: Tennessee Ernie Ford Deluxe Set (Capitol 1968)★★★, The Very Best Of Tennessee Ernie Ford (MFP 1983)★★★, 16 Tons Of Boogie/The Best Of Tennessee Ernie Ford (Rhino 1989)★★★★, All Time Greatest Hymns (Curb 1990)★★★★, Capitol Collectors Series (Capitol 1991)★★★, Country Gospel Classics, Volumes 1 & 2 (Capitol 1991)★★★, Sings Songs Of The Civil War (Capitol 1991)★★★, Red, White & Blue (Capitol 1991)★★★, Sixteen Tons (Capitol 1995)★★★★, The Tennessee Ernie Ford Collection (1949-1965) (Razor & Tie 1997)★★★★.

FORESTER SISTERS

Kathy (b. 1955), June (b. 1956), Kim (b. 1960) and Christy Forester (b. 1962) are from Lookout Mountain, Georgia, USA. Kathy and June sang in church as children, obtained their college degrees and started playing professionally: by 1982, both Kim and Christy had joined them. They formed their own band and started to explore songs and harmonies (Kathy's husband on bass is also the group's road manager). In 1983 they recorded some demo tapes that led to a contract with WEA Records. Their first single, '(That's What You Do) When You're In Love', made the US country Top 10. Their glossy, professional sound (and looks) appealed to country fans and they had three number 1 country hits from their first album - 'I Fell In Love Again Last Night', 'Just In Case' and 'Mama's Never Seen Those Eyes'. In 1986 they teamed up with the Bellamy Brothers for another US number 1

country single, 'Too Much Is Not Enough', and they worked together on The Brothers And Sisters Tour. In 1987 they had a further chart-topper with the title track from You Again. More Than I Am in 1996 was firmly aimed at the Christian market.
● ALBUMS: The Forester Sisters (Warners 1985)★★★★, Perfume, Ribbons And Pearls (Warners 1987)★★★, You Again (Warners 1987)★★★★, A Christmas Card (Warners 1987)★★, Sincerely (Warners 1988)★★★, Family Faith (Warners 1988)★★, All I Need (Warners 1989)★★★, Come Hold Me (Warners 1990)★★★, Talkin' About Men (Warners 1991)★★★, I Got A Date (Warners 1992)★★★, More Than I Am (Warner Resound 1996)★★.
● COMPILATIONS: Greatest Hits (Warners 1989)★★★.

FORRESTER, HOWDY

b. Howard Wilson Forrester, 31 March 1922, Vernon, Hickman County, Kentucky, d. 1 August 1987, Nashville, Tennessee, USA. In 1933, the youngest of four Forrester boys, he was struck down by rheumatic fever and during eight months' convalescing, he learned to play a fiddle that his grandfather had acquired during service in the Civil War. Both his father (who died in an accident on an unmanned rail crossing in 1927) and an uncle were competent fiddlers and he learned much from his Uncle Bob. In the early 30s, he and brothers Clyde (guitar) and Joe (guitar, bass) began to play for local square dances. In 1936, after the family had relocated to Nashville, he played with a group on a local station. In 1938, he and Joe were playing on the Grand Ole Opry, as members of Harold Goodman's Tennessee Valley Boys. It was Goodman, a founder of the Opry singing trio the Vagabonds, who nicknamed him Howdy. Greatly influenced by Opry star Fiddlin' Arthur Smith, he left the Opry and played with various groups in Oklahoma and Texas where, in 1940, he met and married Billie Russell, a multi-instrumentalist and singer, who worked under the name of Sally Ann. They returned to Nashville, where between 1940 and 1943, he worked with Bill Monroe, until called for service with the US Navy in World War II (his wife continued to work with Monroe during the time he was away). When discharged in 1964, he moved to Texas, where he played with various bands and on WRLD Dallas. He recorded some Mercury Records sides and worked with fiddler Georgia Slim (b. Robert Rutland, 1916, d. 1969), whom he knew from his late 30s days on the Opry, on the Texas Roundup. In 1949, he returned to Nashville, where he worked on the Opry with Cowboy Copas, until he became a member of Roy Acuff's Smoky Mountain Boys, in 1951. This marked the start of a long association with Acuff that lasted until his death. He continued to play the Opry but stopped touring with Acuff in 1963 and from 1964-67, he worked as a booking agent and, later, on other administrative duties for Acuff-Rose Music. In 1967, he announced that he would not play professionally again but within three months, he was once again with Acuff on the Opry. In the middle of 1983, continuing chest pains gave rise for concern because of the rheumatic fever he had suffered as a boy and he retired from all but his Opry appearances with Acuff. In late 1986, he had major surgery for the removal of his stomach when he was found to have cancer. To everyone's amazement, he was soon playing again, and continued to play the Opry with Acuff until mid-June 1987, finally passing away at his home on 1 August that year. He

is justifiably rated one of country music's finest fiddlers and is especially remembered for his exceptional ability to perfect twin fiddle technics, which he first played with Georgia Slim but later developed further on recordings with Kenny Baker and Chubby Wise. Apart from his countless recordings with Acuff, he made solo recordings for several labels including Hickory, Stoneway, Capitol and MGM Records.
● ALBUMS: *Fancy Fiddlin' Country Style* i (Cub 1960)★★★, *Fancy Fiddlin' Country Style* ii (MGM 1962)★★★, *Fiddlin' Country Style* (United Artists 1963)★★★★, with Georgia Slim *Texas Roundup* radio transcriptions (Kanawha 1969)★★, *Howdy's Fiddle & Howdy Too* (Stoneway 1973)★★★, *Big Howdy* (Stoneway 1974)★★★★, with Chubby Wise *Sincerely Yours* (Stoneway 1974)★★★, with Wise *Fiddle Favorites* (Stoneway 1975)★★★, *Leather Britches* (Stoneway 1975)★★★, *Stylish Fiddling* (Stoneway 1976)★★, with Kenny Baker *Red Apple Rag* (County 1983)★★.

FOSTER AND LLOYD

During the early 80s, Radney Foster (b. 20 July 1959, Del Rio, Texas, USA) was playing in a local club when a producer suggested he move to Nashville. The new MTM music group employed him as a staff writer and there he met Bill Lloyd (b. 6 December 1955, Fort Hood, Texas, USA). Lloyd had worked in New York and Kentucky before coming to Nashville where they wrote for Sweethearts Of The Rodeo (Foster also co-wrote with Holly Dunn her US country hit single 'Love Someone Like Me'). By chance a recording contract was offered to them in preference to the songwriting agreement they were hoping to secure. A decision had to be taken quickly as they both had busy solo careers - they decided to take the risk and their debut was a huge success, spawning two US country chart Top 10 hits, 'Crazy Over You' and 'Sure Thing', followed by two further hits, 'What Do You Want From Me This Time' and 'Fair Shake', before the duo broke up. Their album, *Version Of The Truth*, includes an instrumental, 'Whoa', that features Duane Eddy. Foster continued a solo recording career and Lloyd continues as a songwriter.
● ALBUMS: *Foster And Lloyd* (RCA 1987)★★★, *Faster And Llouder* (RCA 1989)★★★, *Version Of The Truth* (RCA 1990)★★★.
● COMPILATIONS: *Essential Foster And Lloyd* (RCA 1996)★★★★.

FOSTER, RADNEY

b. 20 July 1959, Del Rio, Texas, USA. His father, who was a lawyer (as had been his grandfather and father before him), played guitar and sang and Radney, the second of four Foster children, followed his father's example with regard to music. In 1979, dreams of being a country singer saw him drop out of university and move to Nashville in the hope of fulfilling his ambition. However, he was, at that time, unsuccessful in his quest to be either a singer or a songwriter. Although very disappointed, he refused to give up hope, but after a year, he decided that he would first return home and complete his course at the University of the South, Texas. In the evenings, he sang in local clubs and continued to write songs. After he finally graduated, he returned to Nashville where, this time, he found work as a staff writer for MTM Publishing Company. Here he worked with songwriter Bill Lloyd (b. 6 December 1955, Fort Hood, Texas, USA) and after

acquiring a recording contract with RCA, they began performing as Foster And Lloyd. In 1992, after three albums and nine country chart hits and much discussion about the direction of their individual careers, they parted amicably. Foster later cited as a reason for the break-up the fact that he felt that many of the songs he was writing were not suited to the duo; for that and other reasons, which probably included a downturn in the duo's success, Foster became a solo artist in 1992. He joined the Arista label and his debut album was named after his birthplace and year of birth. He achieved immediate Top 10 success with 'Just Call Me Lonesome' and in 1993, three more songs, 'Nobody Wins' (a number 2), 'Easier Said Than Done' and 'Hammer And Nails', charted. The bespectacled and usually well-dressed Foster is a serious man, who once said: 'Being a songwriter is about being observant of your own life and the world you see around you'. Foster's songwriting and performing talents should make him remain popular with country music audiences for some time to come, although *Labor Of Love* did not achieve the same level of commercial success as his debut.
● ALBUMS: *Del Rio, TX 1959* (Arista 1992)★★★, *Labor Of Love* (Arista 1995)★★★.
● VIDEOS: *The Running Kind* (Arista 1994).

4 RUNNER

The 90s US vocal country group 4 Runner take their name from a type of Toyota four-wheel-drive estate car that also inspired the title of their song 'A Heart With 4 Wheel Drive'. The group consists of Craig Morris (lead vocal), Billy Crittenden (baritone), Lee Hilliard (tenor) and Jim Chapman (bass). Morris has toured with Marie Osmond and Dobie Gray and has written songs for Ray Charles, Reba McEntire and the Oak Ridge Boys. Crittenden sang in Tanya Tucker's band for five years and co-wrote Diamond Rio's 'Love A Little Stronger'. Hillard worked with Loretta Lynn for nine years. Their experience shows in their witty debut single, 'Cain's Blood', with its excellent four-part harmonies, which made the US country charts.
● ALBUMS: *4 Runner* (Polydor 1995)★★★.

FOWLER, WALLY

b. Wallace Fowler, 15 February 1917, near Adairsville, Georgia, USA, d. 3 June 1994, Hollow Lake, near Nashville, Tennessee, USA. His father was the cotton king of Bartow County, until the Depression left him broken both in health and financially. Fowler once worked in a florist's to support the family and began singing in the Harmony Quartet. In 1936, he became lead singer with the John Daniel Quartet, whose repertoire varied from gospel to variety songs and moved to Lubbock, Texas. He began to write songs and first sang his popular 'I'm Sending You Red Roses' (a number 2 hit for Jimmy Wakely in 1944) in Dallas. In 1940, the quartet relocated to Nashville, where they played on WSM and the *Grand Ole Opry*. In 1944, Fowler formed his own group, the Georgia Clodhoppers, which included Chet Atkins on lead guitar, to work on WNOX Knoxville. They became regulars on the *Mid-day Merry Go Round* and before long Fowler also formed his Harmony Quartet. Among many appearances, the quartet began to sing in weekly concerts for children at nearby Oak Ridge, Tennessee, which led to Fowler renaming the group the Oak Ridge Quartet. He moved to Nashville, and from 1946-50 became a regular part of the *Prince Albert*

Show on the *Grand Ole Opry*. After Red Foley continually introduced them as 'Wally Fowler And His Oak Ridge Boys', the name became permanent and the quartet became one of the country's most popular gospel groups. Fowler left them in 1952 but in 1970, after many personnel changes, the group turned to country music and have since registered many chart hits and won many awards. Apart from his activities with the quartet, Fowler became involved in promotional work and songwriting (Eddy Arnold enjoyed Top 5 country hits with 'That's How Much I Love You' and 'I Couldn't Believe It Was True'). In 1948, he organized his first *All-Night Singing* in Nashville, an event that proved so popular, it led to many more in other towns. During his career, Fowler often helped others, including the young Patsy Cline. He recorded for several labels, but in later years, he went into semi-retirement and tended to avoid publicity, although he continued to promote some gospel and variety shows in North Carolina. He also surprisingly gained a minor country chart hit, 'Lo And Behold', in 1984, singing with his Tennessee Valley Boys. He was elected to the *Gospel Music Hall Of Fame* in 1988. Fowler drowned on a fishing trip with his son-in-law in 1994 when he was found face down in a lake. A doctor believed he may have fallen in after suffering a heart attack.

● ALBUMS: *Call Of The Cross* (Decca 1960)★★★, with the Oak Ridge Quartet *Gospel Song Festival* (King 1960)★★, *Wally Fowler's All Nite Singing Gospel Concert* (Starday 1960)★★, *More Wally Fowler All Nite Singing Gospel Concert* (Starday 1964)★★, *Victory Through Jesus* (Pickwick/Hilltop 1965)★★★, *Gospel Sing* (Vocalion 1967)★★★, *Pure Country Gospel* (1976)★★★, *A Tribute To Elvis Presley* (Dove 1977)★★, *You Will Reap* (Pickwick 1978)★★★, *A Tribute To Mother* (Nashwood 1984)★★★.

FOX, CURLY, AND TEXAS RUBY

b. Arnim LeRoy Fox, 9 November 1910, Graysville, Tennessee, USA, d. 10 November 1995. At the age of 13 Fox, the son of a fiddler, was already touring with a medicine show before joining the Roane County Ramblers, with whom he made his first recordings in 1929. In the early 30s, he played with the Carolina Tarheels and in 1932 with his own band, the Tennessee Firecrackers, he was a popular performer on WSB Atlanta. In 1935, he cut some Decca recordings with the Shelton Brothers, including his noted instrumental, 'Listen To the Mocking Bird' (complete with special fiddle-made bird effects) and his vocal 'Curley's New Talking Blues'. In 1937, Fox teamed up with Texas Ruby (b. Ruby Owens, 4 June 1908, Wise County, Texas, USA, d. 29 March 1963, Nashville, Tennessee, USA). She was the sister of Tex Owens (the writer of 'Cattle Call') and had played on many radio stations, including the *Iowa Barn Dance Frolics* and appeared on the *Grand Ole Opry* in 1934 with Zeke Clements. Fox and Owens (often working with the Shelton Brothers) toured the south, where they appeared on numerous stations and where Fox won a great many fiddle contests. They were married in 1939 and became firm favourites on the *Opry*, where along with Rod Brasfield, they were stars of the Purina segment. During the 40s, they recorded for Columbia and King and between 1948 and 1955, they were regulars on a KPRC Houston television show but then returned to the *Opry* and also made further recordings for Starday. Their close partnership was ended in 1963,

when Texas Ruby was tragically killed by a fire that destroyed their trailer home. Fox was shattered and effectually retired from the business and though from the mid-70s, was, on occasions, persuaded to make special appearances at some bluegrass festivals, he has never got over his loss. He is rated by experts to to have been perhaps the greatest showman of all the early day country fiddlers. Texas Ruby initially billed herself as Radio's Original Yodeling Cowgirl but she was an outstanding vocalist. Equally at home with country ballads or blues songs, she was an undoubted influence on other female singers including Patsy Cline and Loretta Lynn.

● ALBUMS: *Curly Fox & Texas Ruby* (1963)★★★, *Travellin' Blues* (1963)★★★★, *Favorite Songs Of Texas Ruby* (1963)★★★, *Curly Fox, Champion Fiddler Volumes 1 & 2* (1973)★★★★.

FOXWORTHY, JEFF

b. USA. Jeff Foxworthy is the first comedian to be played on country radio and to make the US country charts. He walked out of a successful job at IBM to become a stand-up comedian. He developed the catchphrase: 'You might be a redneck if . . !', an example being: 'You might be a redneck if you lost a tooth opening a beer can.' The southern states have taken Foxworthy to heart and appreciate that his humour is affectionate. He collaborated with Little Texas for 'Party All Night' and he makes a guest appearance in Alan Jackson's video for 'I'm In Love With You Honey And I Don't Even Know Your Name'. His US television series is also very popular and the merchandising is big business. His albums have achieved extraordinary success, selling over 10 million copies in the USA.

● ALBUMS: *You Might Be A Redneck If...* (Warners 1994)★★★, *Games Rednecks Play* (Warners 1995)★★★, *The Redneck Test Volume 11* (Laughing Hyena 1994)★★, *The Redneck Test Volume 43* (Laughing Hyena 1995)★★, *The Original* (Laughing Hyena 1995)★★★, *Sold Out* (Laughing Hyena 1995)★★★, *Live* (Laughing Hyena 1996)★★, *Crank It Up - The Music Album* (Warner Bros 1996)★★★.

● VIDEOS: *You Might Be A Redneck If . . .* (1995).

● FURTHER READING: all of the following are by Jeff Foxworthy *Hick Is Chic - A Guide To Etiquette For The (Grossly) Unsophisticated. Red Ain't Dead. Check Your Neck. You're Not A Kid Anymore. Games Rednecks Play. You Might Be A Redneck If...*

FRANCIS, CLEVE

b. 22 April 1945, Jennings, Louisiana, USA. The eldest of six children, Francis had childhood ambitions to play the guitar and sing country music. He gained his first experience towards his ambition by singing and playing gospel music in the local church choir. After completing his college education, he attended medical school, where he qualified as a cardiologist. After relocating to Washington DC, he worked at his qualified profession during the day and gradually built a reputation as a singer by performing in local clubs in the evenings. He eventually attracted attention when his album *Lovelight* was released in the USA by Playback, whose distribution arrangement with the Cottage label also saw it released in the UK. A video of the title track attracted attention on CMT and TNN and led to him joining Liberty, where he then had the distinction of being, at the time, the only

black country singer signed to a major label. What was more distinctive, however, was his being signed to Liberty at the relatively advanced age of 48, and his decision to put on hold his medical career. His first album release for Liberty saw him gain three minor country chart entries, 'You Do My Heart Good', 'How Can I Hold You' and a re-recording of 'Lovelight'. 'Walkin', the title track of his follow-up album, also gained minor chart success in 1993, but a big hit has so far evaded him. However, his refined vocals and especially the more MOR material and musical backings that he has been given by his producers, seem unlikely to endear him to traditionally minded country fans, and it may be that his biggest success could come as a nightclub or cabaret singer.
● ALBUMS: *Lovelight* (Playback 1991, released in UK on Cottage 1992)★★★, *Tourist In Paradise* (Liberty 1992)★★★★, *Walkin'* (Liberty 1993)★★★, *You've Got Me Now* (Liberty 1994)★★★.

FRANK, J.L.

b. Joseph Lee Frank, 15 April 1900, Rossal, Limestone County, Alabama, USA, d. 4 May 1952. Orphaned at seven, he grew up in Tennessee and as a youth worked as a coalminer and a hotel bellboy. In 1923, he relocated to Chicago and after his marriage in 1925, he and his wife, Marie, became involved in artist management. Between 1928 and 1935, he was involved with WLS *Roundup*, and in 1929, he became manager of Gene Autry and Smiley Burnette. Between 1935 and 1939, he worked from Louisville, Kentucky, but, believing that Nashville was to become an important venue for country music, he opened an office there. His ability to promote country shows and organize tours for artists soon made him a popular and important figure in Music City. He was prominent in helping many artists, especially Pee Wee King (his son-in-law), Roy Acuff, Eddy Arnold, Hank Williams, Hank Snow, Minnie Pearl and Ernest Tubb, and managed numerous others. His association with a major theatre chain enabled country artists to be booked into venues that previously had been unavailable to the genre. Frank's ability to promote the artists also helped to promote the image of the *Grand Ole Opry* and he was instrumental in helping many to actual membership of the *Opry*, particularly Roy Acuff. He also wrote a few country songs, including 'Sundown And Sorrow' and 'Chapel On The Hill'. However, he was no vocalist, he did not play any instrument, nor could he read music. On 4 May 1952, he died of a major throat infection, while on a trip to Dallas to promote a show. In 1967, J.L. 'Joe' Frank was inducted into the Country Music Hall Of Fame. His plaque reads: 'Pioneer promoter of Country & Western Shows. His method of combining broadcasting and personal appearances moved country entertainers from rural schoolhouses into city auditoriums and coliseums. The unselfish, compassionate man was one of the industry's most loved members'.

FRAZIER, DALLAS

b. 27 October 1939, Spiro, Oklahoma, USA. Frazier wrote realistically about his family's move to Bakersfield in his song 'California Cottonfields', which was recorded by Merle Haggard. In his teens, he won a talent contest sponsored by Ferlin Husky and became part of his roadshow, with Husky subsequently recording 'Timber, I'm Falling!'. However, Frazier's first success as a songwriter was with a novelty

about a cartoon caveman, 'Alley-Oop'. This 1960 record by a studio band, the Hollywood Argyles, which included Frazier himself, was a US number 1 and the song was also covered by Dante And The Evergreens, the Beach Boys, Brian Poole And The Tremeloes, the Bonzo Dog Doo-Dah Band and the Dynasores. Frazier wrote several songs in the same vein, notably 'Mohair Sam', a hit for Charlie Rich, and 'Elvira', a minor US pop hit for Frazier himself in 1966. Frazier's writing displays versatility and his songs include 'There Goes My Everything' (Jack Greene, Engelbert Humperdinck, Elvis Presley), 'Son Of Hickory Holler's Tramp' (O.C. Smith), 'Beneath Still Waters' (Emmylou Harris), 'If My Heart Had Windows' (George Jones) and 'Fourteen Carat Mind' (Gene Watson). He wrote four US country number 1 hits for Charley Pride with A.L. 'Doodle' Owens ('All I Have To Offer You (Is Me)', '(I'm So) Afraid Of Losing You Again', 'I Can't Believe That You've Stopped Loving Me', 'Then Who Am I'). Although he has a fine voice, Frazier has only had moderate success as a performer, notably with 'Everybody Ought To Sing A Song', 'Sunshine Of My World' and 'The Birthmark Henry Thompson Talked About'. In addition to his own albums, both George Jones and Connie Smith have recorded albums of his songs. Smith's *If It Ain't Love* includes three duets with him. Although he has been involved with the ministry since 1976, many of his older songs have become successful. In 1981 the Oak Ridge Boys won a gold disc for their version of 'Elvira'.
● ALBUMS: *Elvira* (Capitol 1966)★★★★, *Tell It Like It Is* (Capitol 1967)★★★, *Singin' My Songs* (1970)★★★, *My Baby Packed Up My Mind And Left Me* (1971)★★★.

FRICKE, JANIE

b. Jane Frickie, 19 December 1947, on the family farm near South Whitney, Indiana, USA. Fricke, who adopted the spelling in 1986 to avoid mispronunciations, has sung in public since the age of 10. Her father was a guitarist and her mother a piano teacher and organist. Frickie sang jingles to pay her university fees and then moved to Los Angeles to find work as a session singer. As this was not productive, she moved to Nashville and joined the Lea Jane Singers, often recording three sessions a day, five days a week. Fricke has added background vocals to thousands of records, mostly country, including ones by Crystal Gayle ('I'll Get Over You'), Ronnie Milsap ('(I'm A) Stand By My Woman Man'), Elvis Presley ('My Way'), Tanya Tucker ('Here's Some Love') and Conway Twitty ('I'd Love To Lay You Down'). Frickie's uncredited contribution on Johnny Duncan's 'Jo And The Cowboy' led to several other records with Duncan. The disc jockeys and public alike were curious about the mystery voice on his country hits 'Stranger', 'Thinkin' Of A Rendezvous' and 'It Couldn't Have Been Any Better', and she was finally given equal billing on 'Come A Little Bit Closer'. This led to considerable interest in her first solo recordings and she had US country hits with 'What're You Doing Tonight?' and a revival of 'Please Help Me I'm Falling'. At first, she was reluctant to tour because she found herself in continuing demand as a session singer. She joined Vern Gosdin for 'Till The End' and 'Mother Country Music' and Charlie Rich for a US country number 1, 'On My Knees'. In 1982, Fricke had her first solo US country number 1 with 'Don't Worry 'Bout Me, Baby', co-written by 60s hitmaker Bruce Channel and featuring Ricky Skaggs' harmony vocals.

Johnny Rodriguez's road manager, Randy Jackson, proposed to Fricke on a radio phone-in show and has since married her and become her manager. Fricke, who toured with Alabama, had a US country number 1 with a similarly styled, high-energy performance, 'He's A Heartache (Looking For A Place To Happen)' (1983). It was taken from *It Ain't Easy*, which she made with her own Heart City Band and which was produced by Bob Montgomery. 'It Ain't Easy Bein' Easy' (1982) and 'Tell Me A Lie' (1983) were other US country number 1s from the same album. She joined Merle Haggard for another number 1, 'A Place To Fall Apart' (1985), which was based on a letter he had written about his ex-wife, Leona Williams, and Fricke's other duet partners include George Jones ('All I Want To Do In Life'), Ray Charles ('Who Cares?'), Tommy Cash ('The Cowboy And The Lady') and Larry Gatlin ('From Time To Time'). Her *Black And White* album was more blues-based, while *Labour Of Love* was produced by Chris Waters and included an ingenious song he had written with his sister, Holly Dunn, 'Love Is One Of Those Words', as well as Steve Earle's 'My Old Friend The Blues'. Fricke's fashions, based on her stage-wear, are popular in many US clothes stores. She has recorded albums for Intersound and Branson Entertainment in the 90s.

● ALBUMS: *Singer Of Songs* (Columbia 1978)★★★, *Love Notes* (Columbia 1979)★★★, with Johnny Duncan *Nice 'N' Easy* (Columbia 1979)★★, *From The Heart* (Columbia 1980)★★★, *I'll Need Someone To Hold Me When I Cry* (Columbia 1981)★★★, *Sleeping With Your Memory* (Columbia 1981)★★★, *It Ain't Easy* (Columbia 1982)★★★, *Love Lies* (Columbia 1983)★★★, *The First Word In Memory Is Me* (Columbia 1984)★★★, *Somebody Else's Fire* (Columbia 1985)★★, *Black And White* (Columbia 1986)★★★★, *After Midnight* (Columbia 1987)★★★, *Saddle The Wind* (Columbia 1988)★★★, *Labor Of Love* (Columbia 1989)★★★, *Janie Fricke* (Intersound 1990)★★★, *Crossroads* (Branson 1992)★★★, *Now & Then* (Branson 1993)★★★.

● COMPILATIONS: *Greatest Hits* (Columbia 1982)★★★, *The Very Best Of Janie Fricke* (Columbia 1986)★★★★, *17 Greatest Hits* (Columbia 1986)★★★, *Country Store: Janie Fricke* (Country Store 1988)★★★.

FRIEDMAN, KINKY

b. Richard Friedman, 31 October 1944, Rio Duckworth, Palestine, Texas, USA. Friedman, a Jew in Texas, remarks, 'Cowboys and Jews have a common bond. They are the only two groups to wear their hats indoors and attach a certain importance to it.' Friedman, whose father was a university lecturer, first recorded as part of the surfing band King Arthur And The Carrots, in 1966. One of the Carrots, Jeff Shelby, became Little Jewford Shelby in Friedman's band, the Texas Jewboys, the name satirizing Bob Wills' Texas Playboys. Chuck Glaser of the Glaser Brothers took him to Nashville for his first album, *Sold American*. The title song combined the qualities of Ralph McTell's 'Streets Of London' with Phil Ochs' 'Chords Of Fame', and has been recorded by Glen Campbell and Tompall Glaser, the latter version being co-produced by Friedman. His Jewish upbringing and culture was reinforced in songs such as 'We Refuse The Right To Refuse Service To You' and 'Ride 'Em Jewboy'. Friedman's single 'Carryin' The Torch', an offbeat look at the Statue of Liberty, was produced by Waylon Jennings. *Kinky Friedman* was a patchy mixture of blasphemy and ballads, and

included a good-natured romp produced by Willie Nelson, 'They Ain't Makin' Jews Like Jesus Anymore'. A hoarse recording of 'Sold American', recorded as part of Bob Dylan's Rolling Thunder Revue, was included on *Lasso From El Paso*. Buck Owens, who published 'Okie From Muskogee', refused to allow the album to be called Asshole From El Paso. 'Ol' Ben Lucas', about nose-picking, features Eric Clapton's guitar-picking, while 'Men's Room, L.A.' is about a shortage of toilet paper and features Ringo Starr as Christ wanting to use the toilet. Friedman's own career never shone as brightly as the 3-D portrait of Christ he had at his home, and in 1977, he dropped his touring band and went solo. He also improved his diction so that his insults could be understood. He sang the title song of the film *Skating On Thin Ice*, and he was murdered in his acting role in *Easter Sunday*, a film starring Dorothy Malone and Ruth Buzzi. Friedman has become a perceptive writer, writing on country music for *Rolling Stone*, and his novel, *Greenwich Killing Time*, is about a country singer-turned-detective. Friedman briefly returned to performing to promote this anthology, although his live sets merely reprised his old material. In recent years he has become a successful writer of crime novels, and he tries to write a new novel each year. Friedman says his autobiography will be printed backwards, like old Jewish texts. He also intends to write a mystery in which one of Willie Nelson's ex-wives is out to kill him - and has the full co-operation of the participants for this! On his promotional tours for his books, he goes 'singing the song that made me infamous and reading from the books that made me respectable'.

● ALBUMS: *Sold American* (Vanguard 1973)★★★, *Kinky Friedman* (ABC 1974)★★, *Lasso From El Paso* (Epic 1976)★★★, *Under The Double Ego* (Sunrise 1983)★★, *Old Testaments And New Revelations* (Fruit Of The Tune 1992)★★★, *From One Great American To Another* (Fruit Of The Tune 1995)★★★.

● FURTHER READING: *Greenwich Killing Time*, Kinky Friedman. *A Case Of Lone Star*, Kinky Friedman. *When The Cat's Away*, Kinky Friedman. *Frequent Flyer*, Kinky Friedman. *Musical Chairs*, Kinky Friedman. *The Kinky Friedman Crime Club*. Kinky Friedman. *Elvis, Jesus And Coca Cola*, Kinky Friedman. *More Kinky Friedman*, Kinky Friedman. *Armadillos And Old Lace*, Kinky Friedman. *God Bless John Wayne*, Kinky Friedman. *Roadkill*, Kinky Friedman.

FRIZZELL, DAVID

b. 26 September 1941, El Dorado, Texas, USA. In the mid-50s, David hitch-hiked to California to join and tour with his older brother Lefty Frizzell. He recorded some unsuccessful country rockabilly tracks for Columbia Records in 1958 and served in the US Army during the early 60s. After his discharge, he made further recordings for various labels and gained a Top 40 US country chart hit in 1970, after returning to Columbia, with 'I Just Can't Help Believing'. He worked for a time in the 70s for Buck Owens on his networked *Ranch Show* television programme, managed a nightclub and had minor hits on Cartwheel, Capitol and RSO. He first worked at the club with Shelly West (the daughter of singer Dottie West), who was at the time married to his younger brother Allen Frizzell (b. 1951). Allen was for a time Dottie West's lead guitarist and frontman. He had three minor country hits in the 80s, in his own right but became more involved with the business side of the industry than with performing. In 1978, the two brothers and Shelly West toured extensively. David and Shelly had a US country number 1 in 1981 with 'You're The Reason God Made Oklahoma', which featured in the Clint Eastwood film *Any Which Way You Can*. They had made a demo recording of the song some considerable time before, but it had been turned down by record companies until chosen by Eastwood for the film. Further country Top 10 hits followed including 'A Texas State Of Mind' and 'I Just Came Here To Dance'. He also had a popular solo recording, 'Lefty', a tribute to his brother, that also featured Merle Haggard. 1982 proved to be an important year for him with a US country number 1 with 'I'm Gonna Hire A Wino To Decorate Our Home', followed by a number 5 hit with 'Lost My Baby Blues'. Another duet recording with Shelly West called 'Please Surrender' was used by Eastwood in his film *Honkytonk Man*. Further solo hits include 'Where Are You Spending Your Nights These Days', 'A Million Light Beers Ago' and a further Top 20 duet with 'It's A Be Together Night'. A talented and capable singer, although by no means the equal of his legendary brother, even if at times there is a slight vocal resemblance.

● ALBUMS: *The Family's Fine But This One's All Mine* (Warners 1982)★★★, *On My Own Again* (Viva 1983)★★★, *Solo* (1984)★★★, *David Sings Lefty Frizzell* (1987)★★★, *My Life Is Just A Bridge* (1993)★★★; with Shelly West *Carrying On The Family Names* (Warners 1981)★★★, *Our Best To You* (Viva 1982)★★★, *In Session* (Viva 1983)★★★, *Golden Duets* (Viva 1984)★★★★.

FRIZZELL, LEFTY

b. William Orville Frizzell, 31 March 1928, Corsicana, Navarro County, Texas, USA, d. 19 July 1975. The eldest of eight children of an itinerant oilfield worker, he was raised mainly in El Dorado, Arkansas, but also lived in sundry places in Texas and Oklahoma. Greatly influenced by his parents' old 78s of Jimmie Rodgers, he sang as a young boy and when aged 12, he had a regular spot on KELD El Dorado. Two years later he was performing at local dances at Greenville and further exposure on other radio stations followed as the family moved around. At the age of 16, he was playing the honky tonks and clubs in places such as Waco and Dallas and grew into a tough character himself, performing the music of Jimmie Rodgers, plus some of his own songs. Some accounts suggest that it was at this time that he became known as Lefty after fighting in a Golden Gloves boxing match, but this appears to have been later publicity hype by Columbia Records. Both his father and his wife have steadfastly denied the story, maintaining that Lefty actually gained the nickname when he beat the school bully during his schooldays. It is further claimed that it was a schoolfriend and guitarist called Gene Whitworth who first called him Lefty (he was actually always known as Sonny to his family). In 1945, he was married, and his wife Alice became the inspiration for several of his songs over the 30 years the marriage lasted. More and more frequently, his drinking landed him in trouble with the authorities, and he was inspired to write his famous song, 'I Love You A Thousand Ways', while spending a night in a Texas country jail. He made his first recordings for Columbia in 1950, and had immediate success when 'If You've Got The Money, I've Got The Time' and 'I Love You A Thousand Ways' both

became US country number 1 hits. He became close friends with Hank Williams, who suggested Frizzell should join the *Grand Ole Opry*. Frizzell replied, 'Look, I got the number-one song, the number-two song, the number-seven song, the number-eight song on the charts and you tell me I need to join the *Opry*'; Williams thought for a while, and commented, 'Darned if you ain't got a hell of an argument'. The following year he had seven Top 10 entries, which included three more number 1 hits, 'I Want To Be With You Always' (which also gained Top 30 status in the US pop charts), 'Always Late (With Your Kisses)' and 'Give Me More More More (Of Your Kisses)'. Further Top 10s followed and as Merle Haggard later sang in his song 'The Way It Was in '51', 'Hank and Lefty crowded every jukebox'. In 1952, Frizzell did join the *Opry* but left after a few months, stating that he did not like it. In 1953, Frizzell moved from Beaumont, Texas, to Los Angeles, where he became a regular on *Town Hall Party*. He had by now become accepted as a national entertainer and he recorded regularly, although the hits became less frequent. His hard-drinking lifestyle was partly to blame, and certainly he and Williams suffered similar troubles. Charles Wolfe quotes Frizzell as once saying: 'All Hank thought about was writing. He did record a number he wrote because I was having trouble with my better half, called "I'm Sorry for You, My Friend"'. Some time later, the friendship between the two men was damaged when Frizzell refused to allow Williams to record 'What Am I Gonna Do With All This Love I Have For You', Frizzell intending to record it himself, although, for some reason, he never did so. Lefty Frizzell became upset about material not being released by Columbia and in 1954, he broke up his band and stopped writing songs; tired of the way he had been exploited, his behaviour became more unpredictable. He was joined in California by his brother David Frizzell, and for a time they toured together. Eventually he charted again with his version of Marty Robbins' 'Cigarettes And Coffee Blues' and in 1959, he enjoyed a number 6 US country hit with 'The Long Black Veil'. The *Town Hall Party* had closed in 1960 and late in 1961, Frizzell decided to move to Nashville. He played bookings wherever he could and made further recordings, achieving minor hits that included 'Don't Let Her See Me Cry'. His career received a welcome boost in 1964 when 'Saginaw, Michigan' became a country number 1 and also entered the US pop charts. This song must rate as one of country music's finest ballads and Frizzell's version has rightly become a standard and worthy of a place in any collection. Twelve more chart entries followed between 1964 and 1972, but only 'She's Gone Gone Gone' reached the Top 20. In the late 60s, he became despondent that Columbia were not releasing his material; the label issued some albums but released few singles that were potential chart hits. In 1968, he even recorded with June Stearns as Agnes And Orville but, concerned at the lack of promotion of his own material, his drinking worsened. In 1972, after 22 years with the label, he left Columbia and joined ABC. The change seemed to work wonders - he set about recording material for albums, resumed playing concerts all over the USA and appeared on network television. He charted with such songs as 'I Can't Get Over You To Change My Life', 'I Never Go Around Mirrors' and 'Railroad Lady', and his album releases proved very popular. His superb song 'That's The Way Love Goes' (his own recording was only issued as a b-side) became a US country number 1 for Johnny Rodriguez in 1974 and Merle Haggard in 1984. Frizzell developed high blood pressure, but refused to take medication to treat the condition since he thought the medicine would interfere with his alcohol consumption. Even in the depths of his drinking, he remained humorous, which led writer Bob Oermann to describe him as 'a lovable, punch-drunk, boozy, puddin'-headed, bear-like kind of a guy who never really got along with Nashville or the *Opry*'. He spent much time between concerts fishing at his home just outside Nashville, and maintained daily contact with his wife despite their recent separation. He was 47 (although he looked older), and aside from the blood pressure, seemed to be in reasonable health. It therefore came as a surprise to most when, on the morning of 19 July 1975, he suffered a massive stroke, and though rushed to Nashville's Memorial Hospital, he died later that evening of the resulting haemorrhage. Ironically, at the time of his death, he had a chart hit with the song 'Falling'.

Lefty Frizzell was a great songwriter and one of the best stylists that the world of country music has ever seen. His singing was distinctive, with a unique style of pronunciation and a laid-back delivery and gentle vibrato that may have appeared lazy, but was in fact part of a carefully designed pattern that he alone mastered. The bending of words as emphasized in 'Alway-yayys Lay-yate' (Always Late) and similar songs led to him being described as a genius for phrasing. John Pugh once described his singing as 'a compelling, ethereal, transcendent vocal quality that has produced some of the most hauntingly beautiful sounds ever to emanate from a pair of human vocal chords'. His influence is evident on later performers such as Merle Haggard, John Anderson, Stoney Edwards, Randy Travis and George Strait, who, although not perhaps intentionally trying to imitate their mentor, are readily identifiable as students of Frizzell. Since his death many artists have recorded tribute songs, while some have even recorded complete albums, including Willie Nelson (*To Lefty From Willie*) and brother David Frizzell (*David Sings Lefty*). Lefty Frizzell was elected to the Nashville Songwriters' Association International Hall Of Fame in 1972 and inducted into the Country Music Hall Of Fame in 1982.

● ALBUMS: *The Songs Of Jimmie Rodgers* 10-inch album (Columbia 1951)★★★★, *Listen To Lefty* 10-inch album (Columbia 1952)★★★★, shared with Carl Smith and Marty Robbins *Carl, Lefty & Marty* (Columbia 1956)★★★★, *The One And Only Lefty Frizzell* (Columbia 1959)★★★★, *Lefty Frizzell Sings The Songs Of Jimmie Rodgers* (Harmony 1960)★★★★, *Saginaw, Michigan* (Columbia 1964)★★★, *The Sad Side Of Love* (Columbia 1965)★★★, *Lefty Frizzell's Country Favorites* (Harmony 1966)★★★, *Lefty Frizzell Puttin' On* (Columbia 1967)★★★, *Mom And Dad's Waltz (& Other Great Country Hits)* (Harmony 1967)★★★, *Signed Sealed And Delivered* (1968)★★★, *The Legendary Lefty Frizzell* (1973)★★★, *The Classic Style Of Lefty Frizzell* (1975)★★★, *Remembering* (1975)★★★, *Lefty Frizzell In 1951* (1982)★★★, *His Last 2 Sessions* (1982)★★★, *Country Classics* (1983)★★★, *Lefty Goes To Nashville* (1983)★★★, *The Legend Lives On* (1983)★★★.

● COMPILATIONS: *Lefty Frizzell's Greatest Hits* (Columbia 1966)★★★★, *The ABC Collection-Lefty Frizzell* (ABC 1977)★★★★, *Treasures Untold: The Early Recordings Of Lefty* (Rounder 1980)★★★, *Lefty Frizzell* (Columbia Historic Edition 1982)★★★, *American Originals* (Columbia 1990)★★★, *The Best Of Lefty Frizzell* (Rhino 1991)★★★★, *His Life - His Music* 14-LP box set (Bear Family 1984)★★★★ reissued as *Life's Like Poetry* 12-CD set (Bear Family 1992)★★★★, *That's The Way Love Goes: The Final Recordings Of Lefty Frizzell* (Varese Sarabande 1997)★★★, *Look What Thoughts Will Do: The Essential, 1950-1963* (Columbia 1997)★★★★.

● FURTHER READING: *Lefty Frizzell His Life - His Music*, Charles Wolfe. *The Honky Tonk Life Of Country Music's Greatest Singer*, Daniel Cooper.

FROGGATT, RAYMOND

b. Raymond William Froggatt, 13 November 1941, Birmingham, England. Froggatt had a traumatic childhood, with his father dying when he was young, and his missing schooling because of tuberculosis. Froggatt joined the Birmingham scene in the mid-60s and his group, the Monopoly, was signed to Polydor. Their first single, 'House Of Lords', was written by the Bee Gees and, at Polydor's request, he used the stage name of Steve Newman - a cross between Steve McQueen and Paul Newman - but he soon reverted back to his own name. As part of the band the Raymond Froggatt, he recorded 'Red Balloon', explaining, 'I spent some time in Paris and there's a game in which children hold balloons on strings and weave in and out of them. If you get to the end of the balloons, you marry the farmer's daughter.' Dave Clark heard Froggatt's version, covered it with the Dave Clark Five, and reached number 7 in the UK chart. Although Froggatt's 'Big Ship' was rejected for Lulu in the *Eurovision Song Contest*, it became a Top 10 hit for Cliff Richard, who recorded several more of his songs. Other compositions include 'Rachel's Comin' Home' (Joan Baez), 'Only The Memories' (Gladys Knight And The Pips) and 'Everybody's Losin'' (Leon Russell). 'Louise', a track on *Bleach*, includes a concertina solo from an 82-year-old busker. In the mid-70s, Froggatt, with guidance from promoter Mervyn Conn, switched to country and made a popular easy listening album, *Southern Fried Frog*, in Nashville with top producer Larry Butler. This helped establish him as the UK's top country artist and for a time, at every live performance, fans would hold up toy frogs and sway with their 'Froggie' scarves. His rough-hewn features, shades, white dinner jacket and torn jeans made him a distinctive figure, and he was even accepted in Warsaw ('I was not allowed to do 'Teach Me Pa' as the authorities thought it was subversive'). 'Don't Let Me Cry Again' was a airplay hit on BBC Radio 2 in 1983 and, more recently, he recorded 'Maybe The Angels' in aid of leukaemia research. Hartley Cain has long provided lead guitar for Froggatt, who says of his own playing, 'I'm worse now than I was after a few lessons. It helps with my writing because I'm not restricted to certain chord sequences. Some of my songs sound clever but really it's a total lack of knowledge.' He was also one of the few musicians to be granted the Freedom of the City of Birmingham. He remains a popular if enigmatic performer, who makes little effort to conform to audience expectations.

● ALBUMS: *The Voice And Writing Of Raymond Froggatt* (1968)★★, *Bleach* (1972)★★, *Handle With Care* (Bell 70s)★★, *Let The Memphis Moon Shine On Me* (Jet 70s)★★, *Rogues And Thieves* (1974)★★, *Southern Fried Frog* (Jet

1978)★★★★, *Stay With Me* (Merco 1981)★★★, *Sooner Or Later* (1982)★★★, *Why* (Happy Face 1984)★★★, *Raymond Froggatt* (1986)★★★, *Live At Birmingham Odeon* (1987)★★, *Is It Rollin' Bob* (1988)★★★, *Tour '89* (1989)★★, *Here's To Everyone* (1992)★★★, *Songs From A Minstrel* (1992)★★★.

FROMHOLZ, STEVEN
b. 8 June 1945, Temple, Texas, USA. Fromholz's father worked for the Ford Motor Company and the family travelled around the country. At the age of 18, he met Michael Martin Murphey at North Texas State University and they formed the Dallas County Jug Band and then the Michael Murphey Trio. Fromholz became half of Frummox with Don McCrimmon, and their poor-selling 1969 album is prized by collectors. The duo split in 1971 and Fromholz and his wife ran a restaurant in Gold Hill, Colorado. Stephen Stills invited him to join Manassas on the road, but Fromholz left after six months because 'I'd had too much cocaine and was sick.' He dedicated a single he recorded for Michael Nesmith's Countryside label, 'Sweet Janey', to his wife, but the album he made for Nesmith, *How Long Is The Road To Kentucky?*, was never released. Willie Nelson had a US country hit with Fromholz's song 'I'd Have To Be Crazy', and featured him on his live album, *The Sound In Your Mind*. Fromholz's Capitol album, *A Rumour In My Own Time*, featuring Nelson, Doug Dillard and John Sebastian, is a fine example of outlaw country. He was not suited to the easy listening arrangements on *Frolicking In The Myth*, although the album contained good material. He did, however, sound fine next to Peter Fonda on the soundtrack of the film *Outlaw Blues*. He recorded an album for Willie Nelson's Lone Star label, *Jus' Playin' Along*, and his tribute to Hondo Crouch, the eccentric owner of Luckenbach, Texas, 'Hondo's Song', featured Nelson and was, surprisingly, released as a single in the UK.
● ALBUMS: as Frummox *From Here To There* (1969)★★, *A Rumour In My Own Time* (Capitol 1976)★★★, *Frolicking In The Myth* (Capitol 1977)★★★, *Jus' Playin' Along* (Lone Star 1978)★★★, *Fromholz - Live* (1979)★★, *Frummox 2* (1982)★★★.

FUNDIS, GARTH
The country music producer Garth Fundis was raised in Kansas, USA, but went to Nashville in 1971, where he was employed by the studio owner Jack Clement. He sang harmony on 'Amanda' by Don Williams, for whom he also worked as recording engineer until Williams elevated him to co-producer for records such as 'Tulsa Time' and 'Lay Down Beside Me'. Since then, he has made a succession of big-selling records with Williams, often finding him the songs to record. He has also produced Keith Whitley and gave him the song 'Don't Close Your Eyes', and thereby relaunched his career. Fundis also produced 'When You Say Nothing At All' and was mixing Whitley's next album when he heard of his death. He discovered Trisha Yearwood singing backing vocals for Pat Alger, and produced her first hit, 'She's In Love With The Boy'. He has also had some success producing Ty England.

GAFFNEY, CHRIS
b. Vienna, Austria. Although not born in the USA, the 90s country singer and accordian player Chris Gaffney was raised in Arizona and southern California and spent 10 years working in Los Angeles shipyards. He has been performing since the 60s and his music has evolved into a honky tonk mixture of Cajun, Tex-Mex, rock 'n' roll and western swing. His songs are full of stories, characters and unusual scenarios, such as the fear of a gangland reprisal in 'The Gardens' and the drunk soldier remembering his lost friend in Vietnam. Gaffney sings with a rough, world-weary voice and plays guitar and accordion. His band is called the Cold Hard Facts and he is assisted on record by musicians such as Dave Alvin and Jim Lauderdale. On 1995's *Loser's Paradise* he duetted with Lucinda Williams on a cover version of the Intruders' 'Cowboys To Girls'.
● ALBUMS: *Road To Indio* (Cactus Club 1986)★★★, *Chris Gaffney And The Cold Hard Facts* (ROM 1990)★★★, *Mi Vida Loca* (Hightone 1992)★★★, *Loser's Paradise* (Hightone 1995)★★★★.

GAITHER, BILL
b. USA. One of the heavyweights behind the re-emergence of US gospel as a viable commercial force in contemporary music, Gaither's list of credits include spells as a presenter, disc jockey and record/video compiler. In the latter respect he was responsible for the 'Gaither Gospel Series' of audio and video archive releases of the 90s, featuring nearly-forgotten southern gospel greats such as the Blackwoods and the Speer Family.

GARLAND, HANK
b. Walter Louis Garland, 11 November 1930, Cowpens, South Carolina, USA. A professional electric guitarist at the age of 15 who played on the *Grand Ole Opry* with Paul Howard for several weeks, before Howard found out he was violating the state's child labour laws and reluctantly sent the talented youngster home. Garland returned to Nashville on his sixteenth birthday, where he quickly became one of the most popular and respected session guitarists and played on recordings by countless artists. In 1949, he made his first solo recordings for Decca, even including a few vocals, which clearly failed to match his instrumental talent. His recording of 'Sugarfoot Rag' not only inspired his nickname, it also firmly established him in Nashville. During the 50s, he recorded for Decca and Dot, being remembered for versions of 'E-String Rag' and 'Guitar Shuffle' and also worked with Chet Atkins. In the late 50s, Garland's playing was a prominent part of the coming of the Nashville Sound and his work extended to rockabilly and recording with Elvis Presley. In 1959, it was Garland who played the lead on Jim Reeves' recording of 'He'll Have To Go' and later on Patsy

Cline's 'I Fall To Pieces'. He also became respected in other genres of music, particularly jazz, which he had always loved. He appeared at the 1960 Newport Jazz Festival and made jazz recordings with Gary Burton, Joe Benjamin and Joe Morello. On 8 September 1961, a serious car crash near Springfield, Tennessee, left him in a coma for some weeks and although he slowly recovered, the crash permanently affected his co-ordination. Considerable practice saw him managing to play a few bars but he could never remember what he was playing and his professional career ended. He left Nashville in 1963 and lived for a time in Milwaukee, but it is believed that after his wife's death in a car crash, he moved to South Carolina. It seems that in 1962, he was so respected by his fellow musicians that they often added his name to Musician Union forms indicating he should be paid for playing on sessions. Garland greatly influenced other guitarists including Willie Nelson and Albert Lee.

● ALBUMS: *Jazz Winds From A New Direction* (Columbia 1961)★★★, *The Velvet Guitar Of Hank Garland* (Columbia 60s)★★, *The Unforgettable Guitar* (RCA 60s)★★★, with Nashville All-Stars *After The Riot At Newport* (Bear Family 1989)★★★★.
● COMPILATIONS: *Hank Garland & His Sugarfooters* covers 1949-57 recordings (Bear Family 1992)★★★★.

GATELEY, JIMMY

b. James David Gateley, 1 May 1931, Springfield, Missouri, USA, d. 17 March 1985. Gateley learned to play fiddle and first appeared with a local band on KGBX Springfield in 1951. After a spell with the Red River Rustlers in Jamestown, North Dakota, he became a member of Dusty Owen's Rodeo Boys on *The Wheeling Jamboree* on WWVA Wheeling, West Virginia. He returned to Springfield in 1954, where, until 1963, he worked on radio and television with Red Foley on *The Ozark Jubilee* and *Jubilee USA*. In 1963, he started a long association with Bill Anderson, for whom he played fiddle, sang, acted as frontman and was also featured on many of Anderson's recordings. He became a regular on the *Grand Ole Opry* with Anderson and also in a double act with Harold Morrison. He made his first solo recordings for Cullman in 1959 but later recorded for several labels, including Starday, Decca, Columbia, Chart, Sapphire, B.T. and Constoga. He failed to achieve a chart hit with his own recordings but his talents as a songwriter led to some of his songs becoming hits when recorded by others. These include 'Alla My Love' (a number 5 in 1962 for Webb Pierce) and 'The Minute You're Gone' (a number 9 in 1963 for Sonny James). He co-wrote 'Bright Lights And Country Music' with Bill Anderson, whose recording of the song reached number 11 in 1965. He appeared in the films *The Road To Nashville* and *Las Vegas Hillbillies*. He became a deacon of his local Madison, Tennessee church and in the 70s, he became more inclined towards gospel music. In the early 80s, he released an album of gospel songs, and a further one, *My Kind Of Country*, was distributed by his local church after his death.
● ALBUMS: *Jimmy Gateley* (Constoga 1979)★★★, *The Dreamer* (Sapphire 1979)★★, *Lookin' Up* (B.T. 1982)★★★.

GATLIN, LARRY, AND THE GATLIN BROTHERS BAND

Larry (b. Larry Wayne Gatlin, 2 May 1948, Seminole, but raised in nearby Odessa, Texas, USA) and his brothers, Steve and Rudy (b. 4 April 1951 and 20 August 1952, respectively, Olney, Texas, USA), were encouraged in their fledgling talent by their father, an oil driller, and with their younger sister LaDonna, they sang at church functions, appeared on television and made an album. They worked together for several years until Larry enrolled at the University of Houston. In 1971, he was a temporary replacement in the Imperials gospel group, and then Dottie West recorded his songs 'Once You Were Mine' and 'You're The Other Half Of Me', and he moved to Nashville. Johnny Cash performed 'The Last Supper' and 'Help Me' in his documentary film *The Gospel Road*, and also sang with Kris Kristofferson on his *Jesus Was A Capricorn*. At Kristofferson's insistence, he was signed to Monument Records, and two singles were released simultaneously - the solo 'My Mind's Gone To Memphis' and the Gatlins' 'Come On In', which featured Steve, Rudy and LaDonna. In October 1973 Gatlin had his first US country hit with 'Sweet Becky Walker', which was followed by a personal collection of beautifully sung love songs, *The Pilgrim*, with liner notes by Johnny Cash. Further successes followed with 'Bigger They Are, The Harder They Fall' (later recorded by Elvis Presley, who also sang 'Help Me') and 'Delta Dirt'. Larry produced Johnny Duncan's 'Jo And The Cowboy' and 'Third Rate Romance', and Steve, Rudy and LaDonna joined him as part of Tammy Wynette's roadshow (Wynette, incidentally, recorded one of the quirkiest of Gatlin's compositions, 'Brown Paper Bag'). Wynette's autobiography recounts how her affair with Rudy created friction between him and Larry. After leaving the show, LaDonna married Tim Johnson and they worked as travelling evangelists. The Gatlin brothers, with Larry singing lead, Steve bass and Rudy tenor, had a US country Top 10 hit with 'Broken Lady', which won a Grammy as the Best Country Song of 1976. Larry recalls, 'the Eagles were very hot at the time with a lot of harmony and some real pretty acoustic guitars, so I decided to write something that had our voices up front without a lot of other things going on. That was "Broken Lady" and it set the style for the Gatlin Brothers from then on.' The Gatlin brothers had success with 'Statues Without Hearts', 'I Don't Wanna Cry' (the title line followed a chance remark to an American disc jockey), 'Love Is Just A Game' (Larry later said: 'I wrote that for Neil Diamond but then realized that he didn't need another hit record, and I did!'), and 'I Just Wish You Were Someone I Love' (his first US country number 1). Their first single for US Columbia, 'All The Gold In California', was another country number 1, but many US radio stations banned 'The Midnight Choir' as sacrilegious. Their success tailed off when Larry's songs stopped being so distinctive, and, with much reluctance, he agreed to perform songs by outside writers. *Houston To Denver* was one of their best albums but, ironically, the number 1 country single, 'Houston (Means I'm One Day Closer To You)', was Larry's own song. For some years, Larry had been an embarrassment to those who knew him, even causing songwriter Roger Bowling to include a snide reference to the Gatlins in 'Coward Of The County'. For example, Larry refused to sign autographs after shows - a cardinal sin for a country performer - saying, 'It's unfair to step off a stage after I've been singing my butt off and be met with 200 people sticking pencils in my face.' From 1979 to 1984 Larry Gatlin had spent an estimated $500,000 on cocaine, but, to the relief of his friends, he eventually underwent treatment. Once cured, he joined Nancy Reagan's 'Just Say No' anti-drug campaign. The *Smile* album included 'Indian Summer', co-written with Barry Gibb and featuring a tender-voiced Roy Orbison. Larry said, 'I think I have proven I can write great songs because those who are acknowledged as having written great songs say so.' The group disbanded in 1991, but still performed regularly at their own theatre in Branson, Missouri. In 1993 Larry took the lead in the Broadway Musical *The Will Rogers Follies*. The group signed to the Branson Entertainment label the same year, releasing the tribute album *Moments To Remember*.

N.B.: The Gatlin Boys who recorded the 1980 album *A Long Time Coming*, are a British country music band.

● ALBUMS: by the Gatlin Quartet *The Old Country Church* (Sword & Shield 1961)★★; by Larry Gatlin *The Pilgrim* (Monument 1973)★★★★, *Rain-Rainbow* (Monument 1974)★★★; by Larry Gatlin With Family And Friends *Larry Gatlin With Family And Friends* (Monument 1976)★★★; by Larry Gatlin With Brothers And Friends *High Time* (Monument 1976)★★★, *Broken Lady* (Monument 1976)★★★, *Love Is Just A Game* (Monument 1977)★★★, *Oh! Brother* (Monument 1978)★★★; by Gatlin Brothers Band *Straight Ahead* (Columbia 1979)★★★, *Help Yourself* (Columbia 1980)★★★, *Not Guilty* (Columbia 1981)★★★, *Sure Feels Like Love* (Columbia 1982)★★★, *A Gatlin Family Christmas* (Columbia 1983)★★, *Houston To Denver* (Columbia 1984)★★★, *Smile* (Columbia 1986)★★★, *Partners* (Columbia 1987)★★★, *Pure 'N' Simple* (Columbia 1989)★★★, *Cookin' Up A Storm* (Columbia 1990)★★★, *Adios* (Liberty 1991)★★★, *Moments To Remember* (Branson 1993)★★★, *Cool Water* (Branson 1994)★★.

● COMPILATIONS: *Greatest Hits* (Columbia 1978)★★★, *Greatest Hits, Volume 2* (Columbia 1983)★★★, *17 Greatest Hits* (Columbia 1985)★★★, *Biggest Hits* (Columbia 1988)★★★, *Best Of The Gatlins: All The Gold In California* (Columbia/Legacy 1996)★★★★.

GATTIS, KEITH

b. 1971, Austin, Texas, USA. This country singer-songwriter began to develop his ambitions in the music industry when in his mid-teens he purchased a second-hand guitar and an instruction book. Almost immediately, he formed a local country band and played impromptu concerts in the vicinity. In testament to his agricultural roots, he then founded a group with fellow members of the Future Farmers Of America. This group won a major national talent contest and performed in front of over 25,000 as headline act at the FFA Nationals in Kansas City. Gattis then pursued a degree in Performing Arts Technology, while developing his songwriting. This course allowed him access to the school studio, where he spent much of his time. Eventually he moved to Nashville to take a job at a steel guitar shop. By night he played 'hole in the wall dives and honky tonks', and this brought him to the attention of local legends Ernest Tubbs and Johnny Paycheck. A demo tape was eventually passed to producer Norro Wilson via Jim Dowell, then manager of Sammy Kershaw. Wilson secured a contract with RCA Records, for whom he recorded his *The Real Deal* debut in 1996. A traditional, somewhat conservative country record, its commercial fortunes improved when the attendant debut single, 'Little Drops Of My Heart', became a minor hit.

● ALBUMS: *The Real Deal* (RCA 1996)★★★.

GATTON, DANNY

b. 4 September 1945, Washington DC, USA, d. 20 October 1994, USA. Guitarist and songwriter Danny Gatton first picked up a guitar at the age of nine. Inspired by guitarist Charlie Christian and Bob Wills' Texas Playboys, Gatton soon developed a unique individual style. Much of this was due to his customization of a standard Les Paul guitar into what he termed the 'Les Paulveriser'. He enhanced this sound by making home recordings using two reel-to-reel tapes that produced an echo effect when one machine was played slightly out of synchronization with the other. Through his thirties and forties he played regularly in Washington to an audience who appreciated his unique take on jazz, bluegrass and rockabilly, issuing a series of exclusively mail-order albums that gradually expanded his audience. Eventually, one of these, *Unfinished Business*, provoked enough critical feedback to prompt Elektra Records into offering him a contract. However, despite further strong reviews, neither *88 Elmira Street* nor *Cruisin' Deuces* succeeded commercially. Gatton collaborated with jazz musician Joey DeFrancesco on his *Relentless* project but, depressed by the loss of his contract with Elektra, he committed suicide in October 1994.

● ALBUMS: *American Music* (1975)★★★, *Redneck Jazz* (NRG 1978)★★★, *Unfinished Business* (NRG 1988)★★★★, *88 Elmira Street* (Elektra 1991)★★★, *New York Stories* (Blue Note 1992), *Cruisin' Deuces* (Elektra 1993)★★★, with Joey DeFrancesco *Relentless* (Big Mo 1994)★★★.

GAY, CONNIE B.

b. Connie Barriot Gay, 22 August 1914, Lizard Lick, North Carolina, USA, d. 3 December 1989. After local education, Gay attended the State University and graduated in 1935. He first worked as a salesman in Washington DC, but in the early 40s, his interest in radio led to his joining the Department of Agriculture and becoming involved with its *National Farm And Home Hour*. In 1946, he became the presenter of *Town And Country*, a one-hour country music show on WARL Arlington, Virginia, working only for a percentage of the advertising monies, but he was shrewd enough to register 'Town And Country' as a trademark. Listener reaction soon saw the show increased to three hours and renamed *Gay Time*. In 1947, after promoting two major sell-out country shows starring Eddy Arnold, Gay moved more towards promotional work. His friendship with Jim Denny, a fellow promoter but also the manager of the *Grand Ole Opry*, led to Gay promoting *Opry* acts and quickly establishing himself as a major promoter. His shows gained network coverage on radio and television and he was never short of promotional gimmicks. He arranged train tours to Nashville, river cruises on the Potomac, country concerts starring the major acts at many prestigious 'intown' venues and even Special Service Road Shows, which toured to US bases overseas. In the late 50s, an alcohol problem ended his marriage and saw him disappear for a time when he entered Alcoholics Anonymous. In 1961, he remarried and with his wife's financial help, he relaunched his promotional activities. He promoted major radio and television shows, including *Town And Country Jamboree*, *Town And Country Time* and *Country Style*. His investments, at one time, made him the owner of nine radio stations. He was involved in the discovery of Patsy Cline and promoting Roy Clark and Jimmy Dean to major stardom. In 1960, after failing to become the Governor of the Virgin Islands, he relocated to McLean, Virginia. He was inducted into the Country Music Hall Of Fame in 1980. His plaque notes that he was an advisor to five Presidents and states: 'His pioneer use of the term country music and registered trademark "Town and Country" were instrumental in bringing country music "uptown". He has served as founding President of the Country Music Association and President of the Country Music Foundation'. Gay died of cancer, at his home in McLean, in 1989.

GAYLE, CRYSTAL

b. Brenda Gail Webb, 9 January 1951, Paintsville, Kentucky, USA. Gayle was the last of eight children born to Ted and Clara Webb. Her sister, Loretta Lynn, had her own story told in the film *Coal Miner's Daughter*. By the time Gayle was born, her father had a lung disease, and he died when she was eight. When Gayle was four, the family moved to Wabash, Indiana, where her mother worked in a nursing home. Clara Webb, who was musical, encouraged Gayle to sing at family gatherings and church socials. Unlike Lynn, her influences came from the Beatles and Peter, Paul And Mary. In the late 60s, after graduation, she signed with her sister's recording label, USA Decca. As the label already had Brenda Lee, a change of name was needed and, when they drove past a sign for Krystal hamburgers, Lynn said, 'That's your name. Crystals are bright and shiny, like you.' At first, she was managed by Lynn's husband, Mooney, and she was part of her stage show. She established herself with regular appearances on Jim Ed Brown's television show *The Country Place*. Lynn wrote some of her first records ('Sparklin' Look Of Love', 'Mama, It's Different This Time') and therein lay the problem - Crystal Gayle sounded like Loretta Lynn. Gayle first entered the US country charts in 1970 with 'I've Cried (The Blue Right Out Of My Eyes)', which was followed by 'Everybody Oughta Cry' and 'I Hope You're Having Better Luck Than Me'. There was nothing original about the records and Gayle, wanting a say in what she recorded, left the label. She joined United Artists and was teamed with producer Allen Reynolds, who was having success with Don Williams. Her first records had the easy-going charm of Williams' records, but her 1974 US country hit, 'Wrong Road Again', hinted at the dynamics in her voice. Reynolds, who wrote the song, did not have enough time to devote to composing but nurtured several songwriters (including Richard Leigh and Bob McDill) who supplied Gayle with excellent songs. Gayle also had a country hit with 'Beyond You', written by herself and her lawyer/manager/husband Vassilios 'Bill' Gatzimos. Gayle entered the US country Top 10 with the title song from *Somebody Loves You*, and followed it with her first number 1 country single, 'I'll Get Over You', written by Leigh. Reynolds, when time allowed, was a fine songwriter and his 'Ready For The Times To Get Better' was featured on *Crystal*. In 1976, Gayle was voted Female Vocalist of the Year by the Academy of Country Music, but Reynolds knew there was a bigger market than merely country fans for her records. He seized the opportunity when Leigh wrote the jazz-tinged ballad 'Don't It Make My Brown Eyes Blue', although United Artists had reservations. 'They thought it was a mistake', said Reynolds. 'It was gimmickless, straight ahead, soulful and classy, but that's all it takes.' The public found 'Don't It Make My Brown Eyes Blue'

irresistible and it went to number 2 in the US pop charts and reached number 5 in the UK. 'Don't It Make My Brown Eyes Blue' won Grammy awards for the Best Female Country Vocal Performance and for the Best Country Song. The album on which it appeared, *We Must Believe In Magic*, became the first album by a female country artist to sell over a million copies. Gayle, who was Female Vocalist of the Year for both the Academy of Country Music and the Country Music Association, said, 'There is no rivalry between me and Loretta and if there is, it is on a friendly basis. I know that Loretta voted for me at the CMA awards in Nashville.' In 1979, she became the first US country artist to perform in China. Although petite in stature, she had a mesmerizing stage act. With her back to the audience, they watched her luxurious hair sway back and forth. Gayle grows her hair to three inches off the floor: 'If it's on the ground, I find I step on it on stage. When you've hair like this, you cannot plan anything other than washing your hair and doing your concert.' Her fifth album, again produced by Reynolds, *When I Dream*, included the credit, 'Suggestions: Crystal'. It was a lavish production with 50 musicians being credited, including such established Nashville names as Hargus 'Pig' Robbins, Lloyd Green, Bob Moore and Kenny Malone. The title track, a torch ballad, brought out the best in Gayle's voice. The British writer Roger Cook, who had settled in Nashville, gave her a soulful ballad touching on the paranoia some lovers feel, 'Talking In Your Sleep'. Released as a single, it reached number 11 in the UK and number 18 in the USA. Another popular album track/single was 'Why Have You Left The One You Left Me For?'. In 1979 Gayle released her final album for United Artists, ironically called *We Should Be Together*. It included two more country hits with the ballads 'Your Kisses Will' and 'Your Old Cold Shoulder'. That year she joined US Columbia and quickly had a US pop hit with 'Half The Way'. She had three country number 1s among her 10 hits for the label. She recorded an excellent version of Neil Sedaka's 'The Other Side Of Me' and surprised many fans by reviving an early country record, Jimmie Rodgers' 'Miss The Mississippi And You'. In 1982 she moved to Elektra and worked on the soundtrack of the Francis Ford Coppola film *One From The Heart* with Tom Waits. Gayle has had many more country chart entries, including number 1s with a revival of Johnnie Ray's 'Cry' and duets with Eddie Rabbitt ('You And I') and Gary Morris ('Making Up For Lost Time'). In recent years, Gayle joined Capitol Records and her 1990 album, *Ain't Gonna Worry*, reunited her with Reynolds. Buzz Stone produced *Three Good Reasons*, which was a heartening return to her country roots. She is now signed to the Branson label.

● ALBUMS: *Crystal Gayle* (United Artists 1975)★★★, *Somebody Loves You* (United Artists 1975)★★★, *Crystal* (United Artists 1976)★★★, *We Must Believe In Magic* (United Artists 1977)★★★, *When I Dream* (United Artists 1978)★★★★, *I've Cried The Blue Right Out Of My Eyes* (MCA 1978)★★★, *We Should Be Together* (United Artists 1979)★★★, *Miss The Mississippi* (Columbia 1979)★★★★, *A Woman's Heart* (Columbia 1980)★★★★, *These Days* (Columbia 1980)★★★, *Hollywood/Tennessee* (Columbia 1981)★★★, *True Love* (Elektra 1982)★★★, with Tom Waits *One From The Heart* film soundtrack (Columbia 1982)★★★★, *Cage The Songbird* (Warners 1983)★★★, *Nobody Wants To Be Alone* (1985)★★★, *Crystal Gayle*

(1986)★★★, *Straight To The Heart* (1986)★★★, *A Crystal Christmas* (Warners 1986)★★, with Gary Morris *What If We Fall In Love* (Warners 1987)★★, *I Love Country* (Columbia 1987)★★, *Nobody's Angel* (Warners 1988)★★★, *Ain't Gonna Worry* (Capitol 1990)★★★, *Three Good Reasons* (Liberty 1992)★★★★.

● COMPILATIONS: *Classic Crystal* (United Artists 1979)★★★, *Favorites* (United Artists 1980)★★★, *Crystal Gayle's Greatest Hits* (Columbia 1983)★★★★, *Best Of Crystal Gayle* (Warners 1987)★★★, *All Time Greatest Hits* (Curb 1990)★★★, *50 Original Tracks* (1993)★★★★, *Best Always* (1993)★★★★.

● VIDEOS: *In Concert* (1993).

GEEZINSLAW BROTHERS

Based in Austin, USA, this novelty country music duo comprises Sam Aldred (b. 5 May 1934) and DeWayne 'Son' Smith. Very much in the vein of Homer And Jethro, they recorded 'Chubby (Please Take Your Love To Town)', the alternative 'Ruby, Don't Take Your Love To Town'. They recorded some duets with Willie Nelson. In the 90s and working as just the Geezinslaws, they had moderate success with 'Help, I'm White And I Can't Get Down', which was co-written with fiddle player Clinton Gregory.

● ALBUMS: *The Kooky World Of The Geezinslaw Brothers* (Columbia 1963)★★★, *Can You Believe* (Capitol 1966)★★★, *My Dirty, Lowdown, Rotten, Cotton-Pickin' Little Darlin'* (Capitol 1967)★★★, *Chubby (Please Take Your Love To Town)* (Capitol 1968)★★★, *The Geezinslaws Are Alive And Well* (Capitol 1969)★★★, *If You Think I'm Crazy* (Lone Star 1979)★★, *The Geezinslaws* (Step One 1989)★★★, *World Tour* (Step One 1990)★★★, *Feelin' Good, Gittin' Up, Gittin' Down* (Step One 1992)★★, *I Wish I Had A Job To Shove* (Step One 1994)★★★.

GENE AND DEBBE

Gene Thomas (b. 28 December 1938, Palestine, Texas, USA) was already a hit-maker in his own right before teaming up with Debbe Neville in 1967. Thomas had logged two chart hits: 1961's 'Sometime' and 1964's 'Baby's Gone', both country ballads. He met Neville when he was a staff songwriter for Acuff-Rose music in Nashville. Their first single, on TRX Records, 'Go With Me', was a minor hit but 'Playboy' the following year made it to the US Top 20. After one last collaboration, 'Lovin' Season', the duo split up, Thomas returned to his writing job and Neville disappeared from the pop music scene.

GENTRY, BOBBIE

b. Roberta Lee Streeter, 27 July 1944, Chicasaw County, Mississippi, USA. Gentry, of Portuguese descent, was raised on a poverty-stricken farm in Greenwood, Mississippi, and was interested in music from an early age. She wrote her first song at the age of seven ('My Dog Sergeant Is A Good Dog') and learned piano - black keys only! - guitar, banjo and vibes. By her teens, she was performing regularly and took her stage name from the film *Ruby Gentry*. After studying both philosophy and music, she was signed to Capitol Records and recorded 'Mississippi Delta' for an a-side. To her own guitar accompaniment, Gentry recorded for the b-side one of her own songs, 'Ode To Billie Joe', in 30 minutes. Violins and cellos were added, the song was reduced from its original seven minutes, and, as a result of disc jockeys' reactions, it became the a-side. Despite competition from Lee Hazlewood, Gentry's version topped the US charts for four weeks and reached number 13 in the UK. Capitol's truncated version added to the song's mystery: what did Billie Joe and his girlfriend throw off the Tallahatchie Bridge and why did Billie Joe commit suicide? The song's main thrust, however, was the callousness of the girl's family regarding the event, and it can be twinned with Jeannie C. Riley's subsequent story of 'Harper Valley PTA'. Gentry became a regular headliner in Las Vegas and she married Bill Harrah, the manager of the Desert Inn Hotel (Gentry's second marriage, in 1978, was to singer-songwriter Jim Stafford). Gentry made an easy listening album with Glen Campbell, which included successful revivals of the Everly Brothers hits 'Let It Be Me' (US Top 40) and 'All I Have To Do Is Dream' (US Top 30/UK number 3). Gentry, with good looks similar to Priscilla Presley, was given her own UK television series, *The Bobbie Gentry Show*, which helped her to top the charts in 1969 with the Burt Bacharach and Hal David song from *Promises, Promises*, 'I'll Never Fall In Love Again'. The 1976 film *Ode To Billy Joe* (sic), starred Robby Benson and Glynnis O'Connor, and had Billy Joe throw his girlfriend's ragdoll over the bridge and commit suicide because of a homosexual affair. Gentry herself retired from performing to devote time to her business interests.

● ALBUMS: *Ode To Billie Joe* (Capitol 1967)★★★, *Delta Sweetie* (Columbia 1968)★★★, with Glen Campbell *Bobbie Gentry And Glen Campbell* (Capitol 1968)★★★, *Local Gentry* (1968)★★, *Touch 'Em With Love* (Capitol 1969)★★★, *I'll Never Fall In Love Again* (Capitol 1970)★★★, *Fancy* (Capitol 1970)★★, *Patchwork* (1971)★★, *Sittin' Pretty/Tobacco Road* (1971)★★.

● COMPILATIONS: *Bobby Gentry's Greatest* (Capitol 1969)★★★, *Greatest Hits* (Curb 1990)★★★, *The Best Of* (Music For Pleasure 1994)★★★.

GERRARD, ALICE

b. 8 July 1934, Seattle, Washington, USA. Gerrard grew up in California and while still at college in the late 50s, she became greatly attracted to old-time and bluegrass music. She learned to play guitar and banjo and began writing her own material early in her career. At college, she had met (and married) Jeremy Foster (a friend and former classmate of Mike Seeger) and together they organized the Green County Stump Jumpers. In the early 60s, she met Hazel Dickens, and the two formed a partnership that saw them write songs about various aspects of life, as well as performing together at numerous folk festivals all over the south. In 1972, for some time, they joined with Mike Seeger (whom she had married in 1970), Tracy Schwartz and Lamar Greer to perform as the Strange Creek Singers. After their partnership ended amicably, she continued her career and worked various venues, sometimes with her husband. In the late 70s, along with Jeanie McLerie and Irene Herrmann, she formed the Harmony Sisters. They later recorded two albums for Flying Fish Records. She has also worked with and in some cases recorded with other artists including Peter Rowan and the Red Clay Ramblers. Like her friend Hazel Dickens, she continued to appear at festivals and around the bluegrass/folk music circuit. In the 80s, she relocated to Durham, North Carolina, where she founded and edited a music magazine called *The Old Time Herald* and also worked with a group called the Herald Angels. In 1994, using mainly her own material, she made further recordings for the Copper Creek label. In their work both together and apart, Hazel Dickens and Alice Gerrard have done much to influence countless traditional music fans as well as pioneering the role of women in bluegrass, which encouraged later artists such as Emmylou Harris.

● ALBUMS: with Hazel Dickens *Who's That Knocking & Other Bluegrass Music* (Folkways 1965)★★★, with Dickens *Won't You Come And Sing For Me* (Folkways 1973)★★★, *Alice Gerrard & Mike Seeger* (Greenhays 70s)★★★, *Pieces Of My Heart* (Copper Creek 1994)★★★.

As the Strange Creek Singers *The Strange Creek Singers* (Arhoolie 1972)★★★. With The Harmony Sisters *Harmony Pie* (Flying Fish 1982)★★★, *Second Helping* (Flying Fish 1984)★★★.

● COMPILATIONS: with Dickens *Hazel & Alice* (Rounder 1973)★★★, with Dickens *Hazel Dickens & Alice Gerrard* (Rounder 1976)★★★.

GIBBS, TERRI

b. 15 June 1954, Augusta, Georgia, USA. Gibbs was born blind and has been playing the piano since she was three. She listened to a wide repertoire of music and, even though she is regarded as a country singer, there are many other influences, notably Ray Charles. Gibbs sang gospel in her early teens and formed her own band, Sound Dimension. Meeting Chet Atkins, she was encouraged to become a professional performer. In 1975, she started a long residency at the Augusta Steak And Ale Restaurant, playing 50 songs a night. Her appearance had impressed an MCA executive, while her demo tapes had been noticed by producer/songwriter Ed Penney. Her debut single for MCA, the country soul of 'Somebody's Knockin', reached number 13 on the US pop charts. Subsequently, the only had country hits, which included 'Rich Man', 'Mis'ry River', 'Somedays It Rains All Day Long' and 'Anybody Else's Heart But Mine', but, despite her talent, she did not emerge as a major country star. In 1984, she recorded a duet, 'Slow Burning Fire', with George Jones and she said, 'His style and his phrasing had a big influence on my own singing.' She turned to gospel music in 1986, signing with the Word label, and enjoyed three Top Five singles on the Christian charts in 1988. She has since retired from the music business.

● ALBUMS: *Somebody's Knockin'* (MCA 1981)★★★, *I'm A Lady* (MCA 1981)★★★, *Some Days It Rains All Night* (MCA 1982)★★★, *Over Easy* (MCA 1983)★★★, *Hiding From Love* (MCA 1984)★★★, *Old Friends* (MCA 1985)★★★, *Turn Around* (Word 1987)★★★, *Great Day* (Morning Gate 1990)★★★.

● COMPILATIONS: *Best Of ...* (Varese Sarabande 1996)★★★★.

GIBSON, DON

b. 3 April 1928, Shelby, North Carolina, USA. If loneliness meant world acclaim, then Gibson, with his catalogue of songs about despair and heartbreak, would be a superstar. Gibson learnt the guitar from an early age and started performing while still at school. He worked some years around the clubs in Knoxville and he built up a reputation via local radio. His first records were made as part of the Sons Of The

Soil for Mercury in 1949. His first recorded composition was 'Why Am I So Lonely?'. Gibson recorded for RCA, Columbia and MGM (where he recorded the rockabilly 'I Ain't A-Studyin' You, Baby' in 1957), but with little chart success. However, Faron Young took his forlorn ballad 'Sweet Dreams' to number 2 in the US country charts in 1956. It has since been associated with Patsy Cline and also recorded by Emmylou Harris, Don Everly, Roy Buchanan, Reba McIntyre and Elvis Costello. 'I Can't Stop Loving You' was a US country hit for Kitty Wells and then, in 1962, a transatlantic number 1 for Ray Charles. In 1991, the song was revived by Van Morrison with the Chieftains. 'I Can't Stop Loving You' was also one side of the hit single (US number 7 pop, number 1 country) that marked his return to RCA in 1958. The other side, 'Oh Lonesome Me', which Gibson had originally intended for George Jones, is also a much-recorded country classic. Gibson actually sings 'Ole lonesome me' but a clerk misheard his vocal. Chet Atkins' skilful productions appealed to both pop and country fans and this single was followed by 'Blue Blue Day' (number 20 pop/number 1 country), 'Give Myself A Party', 'Don't Tell Me Your Troubles', 'Just One Time' and his own version of 'Sweet Dreams'. In 1961 Gibson made his UK chart debut with 'Sea Of Heartbreak', which was followed by the similar-sounding 'Lonesome Number One'. The sadness of his songs matched Roy Orbison's, who recorded an album *Roy Orbison Sings Don Gibson* in 1967 and had a hit single with 'Too Soon To Know'. His own bleak *King Of Country Soul*, which includes some country standards, is highly regarded. Gibson lost his impetus through his alcohol and drug dependency, but he recorded successful duets with both Dottie West and Sue Thompson. He had a US country number 1 with 'Woman (Sensuous Woman)' in 1972. Further hits with 'One Day At A Time' and 'Bring Back Your Love To Me' marked the end of Gibson's chart success, but he continued performing throughout the 80s and 90s.

● ALBUMS: *Oh Lonesome Me* (RCA Victor 1958)★★★★, *Songs By Don Gibson* (Lion 1958)★★, *No One Stands Alone* (RCA Victor 1959)★★★, *That Gibson Boy* (RCA Victor 1959)★★★, *Look Who's Blue* i (RCA Victor 1960)★★★, *Sweet Dreams* (RCA Victor 1960)★★★★, *Girls, Guitars And Gibson* (RCA Victor 1961)★★★★, *Some Favourites Of Mine* (RCA Victor 1962)★★★, *I Wrote A Song* (RCA Victor 1963)★★★, *God Walks These Hills* (RCA Victor 1964)★★, *Too Much Hurt* (RCA Victor 1965)★★★, *Don Gibson* (RCA Victor 1965)★★★, *The Fabulous Don Gibson* (RCA Victor 1965)★★★, *A Million Blue Tears* (RCA Victor 1965)★★★, *Hurtin' Inside* (RCA Victor 1966)★★★, *Don Gibson With Spanish Guitars* (RCA Victor 1966)★★, *Great Country Songs* (RCA Victor 1966)★★★, *All My Love* (RCA Victor 1967)★★★, *The King Of Country Soul* (RCA Victor 1968)★★★, *More Country Soul* (RCA Victor 1968)★★★, *I Love You So Much It Hurts* (RCA Victor 1968)★★★, *My God Is Real* (RCA Victor 1969)★★, with Dottie West *Dottie And Don* (RCA Victor 1969)★★★, *Don Gibson Sings All-Time Country Gold* (RCA Victor 1969)★★★, *Hits - The Don Gibson Way* (RCA Victor 1970)★★★, *A Perfect Mountain* (Hickory 1970)★★★, *Hank Williams As Sung By Don Gibson* (Hickory 1971)★★★, *Country Green* (Hickory 1972)★★★, *Woman (Sensuous Woman)* (Hickory 1972)★★★, *Sample Kisses* (Hickory 1972)★★★, *Am I That Easy To Forget?* (Hickory 1973)★★★, with Sue Thompson *The Two Of Us Together* (Hickory 1973)★★★, *Touch The Morning/That's*

What I'll Do (Hickory 1973)★★★, with Thompson *Warm Love* (Hickory 1973)★★★, *Just Call Me Lonesome* (Hickory 1973)★★★, *Snap Your Fingers* (Hickory 1974)★★★, *Bring Back Your Love To Me* (Hickory 1974)★★★, *Just One Time* (Hickory 1974)★★★, *I'm The Loneliest Man/There She Goes I Wish Her Well* (Hickory 1975)★★★, with Thompson *Oh How Love Changes* (Hickory 1975)★★★, *Don't Stop Loving Me* (Hickory 1975)★★★, *I'm All Wrapped Up In You* (Hickory 1976)★★★, *If You Ever Get To Houston (Look Me Down)* (Hickory 1977)★★★, *Starting All Over Again* (Hickory 1978)★★★, *Look Who's Blue ii* (Hickory 1978)★★★.
● COMPILATIONS: *20 Of The Best* (RCA 1982)★★★, *Rockin' Rollin' Gibson, Volume l* (Bear Family 1984)★★★★, *Rockin' Rollin' Gibson, Volume 2* (Bear Family 1984)★★★★, *Collector's Series* (RCA 1985)★★, *Don Gibson And Los Indios Tabajaras* (Bear Family 1986)★★, *Don Gibson - The Early Days* (Bear Family 1986)★★, *Collection: Don Gibson* (Castle 1987)★★★, *A Legend In His Time* (Bear Family 1988)★★★, *All Time Greatest Hits* (RCA 1990)★★★★, *The Singer: The Songwriter, 1949-60* (Bear Family 1991)★★★, *Currents* (1992)★★★, *The Singer: The Songwriter 1961-66* 4-CD box set (Bear Family 1993)★★★★.
● FURTHER READING: *Don Gibson - A Legend In His Own Time*, Richard Weize and Charles Wolfe.

GIBSON, LORNE

b. 1940, Edinburgh, Scotland. At the age of 17, Gibson, who was working in a cafe, developed an interest in country music when a customer played him a Hank Williams EP. He said, 'The songs were simple and easy to play and sing. It was several years before I realized how good they were.' In the early 60s, rock 'n' roll impresario Larry Parnes wanted to promote Gibson, who took his stage name from the make of guitar, as 'sweet rock'. Instead, Gibson signed with Tommy Sanderson, who went on to manage the Hollies and Lulu. The BBC Light Programme was looking for a British country performer, so he formed the Lorne Gibson Trio, the most regular members being Steve Vaughan (guitar) and Vic Arnold (bass). His *Side By Side* series featured various musical guests, including the Beatles, who had just released their first records; Gibson later guested on their series *Pop Go The Beatles!* Although Gibson did not have chart hits, cover versions of Jimmy Dean's 'Little Black Book' and Freddie Hart's 'Some Do, Some Don't' for Decca sold 60,000 apiece. Gibson never made an album for Decca, saying, 'They wouldn't let me. If I'd made an album it could only have been on my own terms. They didn't want me doing country and had me listed as a calypso singer.' Gibson sang the theme of the Peter Sellers comedy film *Heavens Above!*, and played the ghost in the pop film *The Ghost Goes Gear*. Gibson was only filmed from one side as an accident had necessitated several stitches on the other side of his face. Over a period of months, 'Red Roses For A Blue Lady' sold a respectable 175,000, but did not reach the charts. He says, 'I never expected to have a hit. I discovered early on that country music fans don't buy British records. They didn't then and, to a great extent, they still don't.' Gibson, who still performs occasionally, has maintained his repertoire - 'Devil Woman', 'Eighteen Yellow Roses', the tongue-twisting 'The Auctioneer' and an offbeat Jack Clement song, 'You've Got The Cleanest Mind In The Whole Wide World ('Cause You Change It Every Minute)'. Gibson's singles deserve to be col-

lected onto a compilation, while an album he recorded in 1978, *For The Life Of A Song*, was never released. He is, however, featured on the 1974 album based on the BBC Radio 2 series *Up Country*.

GIBSON/MILLER BAND

Dave Gibson (b. Arkansas, USA) was a folk musician in Chicago in the 70s, although he grew up influenced by the music of Hank Williams, Eddy Arnold and Elvis Presley. He moved to Nashville as a singer-songwriter in 1982. Several of his songs have been recorded by well-known artists, such as 'Jukebox In My Mind' (Alabama) and 'Ships That Don't Come In' (Joe Diffie). The Gibson/Miller Band were formed when producer Doug Johnson introduced Gibson to Blue Miller (b. Detroit, Michigan, USA), who had worked with Bob Seger and Isaac Hayes, and who at the time had no interest in country music. Johnson filled out their sound with bassist Bryan Grassmeyer (b. Nebraska, USA, ex-Vince Gill; Suzy Bogguss), steel guitarist Mike Daly (b. Cleveland, Ohio, USA) and ex-Sweethearts Of The Rodeo drummer Steve Grossman (b. West Islip, New York, USA). *Where There's Smoke* was well received and the singles 'Big Heart' and 'High Rollin'' were US country chart hits. *Red, White And Blue Collar* includes a cover version of Waylon Jennings' and Willie Nelson's 'Mamas, Don't Let Your Babies Grow Up To Be Cowboys'.
● ALBUMS: *Where There's Smoke* (Epic 1993)★★★, *Red, White And Blue Collar* (Epic 1994)★★★.

GILL, VINCE

b. Vincent Grant Gill, 5 April 1957, Norman, Oklahoma, USA. Gill's father, a lawyer who played in a part-time country band, encouraged his son to have a career in country music. While still at school, Gill joined the bluegrass group Mountain Smoke. He moved to Louisville in 1975 and joined Bluegrass Alliance with Sam Bush and Dan Crary. In 1979, he was able to demonstrate his vocal, guitar, banjo and fiddle talents in Pure Prairie League and he is present on their albums *Can't Hold Back*, *Firin' Up* and *Something In The Night*. Gill then became part of Rodney Crowell's backing group, the Cherry Bombs. He began his solo recording career with a six-track mini-album for RCA Records, *Turn Me Loose*. His duet with Rosanne Cash, 'If It Weren't For Him', was withdrawn due to contractual difficulties. He was among the musicians on Patty Loveless's albums, and she repaid the compliment by duetting with him on 'When I Call Your Name', which was named Single Of The Year by the Country Music Association. Gill married Janis Oliver from Sweethearts Of The Rodeo and he wrote 'Never Knew Lonely' while he was homesick in Europe. He added vocal harmonies to Dire Straits' bestselling album *On Every Street*, and Mark Knopfler in turn appears on his album *Pocket Full Of Gold*. In 1991, he had Top 10 US country chart hits with 'Pocket Full Of Gold', 'Liza Jane' and 'Look At Us' and was voted the Male Vocalist Of The Year at the 1991 Country Music Association's Annual Awards Show. In 1992, he went one better when he not only picked up the Male Vocalist Of The Year award but also the award for Song Of The Year with 'Look At Us', a song he co-wrote with Max D. Barnes. In 1992 additions to his chart successes included 'I Still Believe In You' (number 1) and 'Take Your Memory With You' (number 2). Gill later revealed he had turned down the offer to join Dire Straits for their 1992 world tour, preferring to concentrate on his own career. Among performers and public alike, Gill is now established as one of the most successful figures in country music. The excellent *When Love Finds You* included a tribute to Conway Twitty, 'Go Rest High On That Mountain', with harmonies from Patty Loveless and Ricky Skaggs. Gill has mainly concentrated on romantic ballads, although he proved he could turn his hand to soul music when he duetted with Gladys Knight on 'Ain't Nothing Like The Real Thing' (although, at the time, Knight was not even sure who he was). His duet with Dolly Parton on her incredibly successful 'I Will Always Love You' was a US country hit in 1995, after they performed it at the CMA awards. Gill also proved he has a long future in the limelight by being an excellent host at the awards ceremony. *High Lonesome Sound* explored several styles of American music, with varying degrees of success.

● ALBUMS: *Turn Me Loose* mini-album (RCA 1983)★★, *The Things That Matter* (RCA 1984)★★★, *Vince Gill* (RCA 1985)★★★, *The Way Back Home* (RCA 1987)★★★, *When I Call Your Name* (MCA 1989)★★★, *Pocket Full Of Gold* (MCA 1991)★★★, *I Never Knew Lonely* (MCA 1992)★★★, *I Still Believe In You* (MCA 1992)★★★★, *Let There Be Peace On Earth* (MCA 1993)★★, *When Love Finds You* (MCA 1994)★★★★, *High Lonesome Sound* (MCA 1996)★★★.

● COMPILATIONS: *Souvenirs* (MCA 1995)★★★★, *The Essential Vince Gill* (RCA 1996)★★★★, *Super Hits* (RCA 1996)★★★.

● VIDEOS: *I Still Believe In You* (1993).

GILLEY, MICKEY

b. 9 March 1936, Ferriday, Louisiana, USA. Gilley is a cousin to Jerry Lee Lewis and the evangelist Jimmy Swaggart. He grew up with his cousins and his mother, a waitress, who saved her money to buy him a piano when he was 12 years old. Gilley left Louisiana when he was 17 and started working in bars in Houston. His first record was 'Tell Me Why' for the aptly named Minor label in 1957. He had regional success in 1959 with 'Is It Wrong?', with Kenny Rogers on bass. In 1964 he started a record label, Astro, in Houston and again did well locally with 'Lonely Wine'; the resulting album is now valued at £200 a copy. In 1968 he signed with Louisiana's Paula label and had short-lived success with 'Now I Can Live Again'. He was heard at the Des Nesadel club in Houston by local businessman Sherwood Cryer. Cryer was impressed with Gilley's performance and invited him to his club, Shelley's, in Pasadena, Texas, with a view to establishing a partnership. In 1971, the club reopened as Gilley's, and through regular exposure on television, became very popular. Gilley himself was a resident performer and, to please a jukebox operator, he recorded Harlan Howard's 'She Called Me Baby' for his Astro label. The Houston disc jockeys preferred the b-side, a revival of George Morgan's country hit 'Room Full Of Roses'. In 1974, *Playboy* magazine, which had its own label, reissued it nationally and 'Room Full Of Roses' was a number 1 US country hit and also made the pop charts. Continuing his country 'flower power', he followed it with another chart-topping revival, 'I Overlooked An Orchid'. Gilley also made the US country Top 10 with 'Overnight Sensation', a duet with Playmate-turned-country singer Barbi Benton. His success on the US country charts was soon outstripping his cousin's as he had number 1 records with revivals ('City

Lights', 'Window Up Above', 'Bring It On Home To Me') and with new songs ('Don't The Girls All Get Prettier At Closing Time', 'She's Pulling Me Back Again'). However, most of his records, for the good or the worse, were strongly influenced by Jerry Lee Lewis and were made quickly and cheaply. After Gilley signed with Epic, the producer Jim Ed Norman was determined to take him out of Lewis's shadow and have him spend more time on his records. His revival of 'True Love Ways' was a US number 1 country hit in 1980 and was followed by 'Stand By Me', which he sang in *Urban Cowboy*, a film starring John Travolta - and a mechanical bull - and set in Gilley's. Gilley's was so successful that it had been extended to take 3,500 customers and Cryer, having the patent on the mechanical bull, made a fortune by selling them to other clubs. 'Stand By Me' made number 22 on the US pop charts, and Johnny Lee, the bandleader at Gilley's, also did well with 'Lookin' For Love'. Gilley continued his run of country number 1s with revivals of 'You Don't Know Me' and 'Talk To Me, Talk To Me' and also a duet with Charly McClain called 'Paradise Tonight'. In 1987 he split acrimoniously with Cryer, which resulted in the closure of Gilley's club. After a legal action, Gilley was awarded $17 million, which included considerable back-royalties on T-shirt sales alone. No longer confined to the club, Gilley has toured extensively, but has not tried to build a UK following. He also opened a theatre in Branson, Missouri in the 90s. Surprisingly, Gilley has only ever had three singles released in the UK ('Room Full Of Roses', 'Stand By Me' and 'You Don't Know Me'). Gilley mentions Jerry Lee Lewis in his stage show, also performing 'Great Balls Of Fire', and is keen to record an album with his cousin. He says, 'I've always given Jerry Lee credit for being the best talent in the family. He created that piano style and it rubbed off on me.'

● ALBUMS: *Lonely Wine* (Astro 1964)★★, *Down The Line With Mickey Gilley* (Paula 1967)★★★, *Room Full Of Roses* (Playboy 1974)★★★, *City Lights* (Playboy 1974)★★, *Mickey's Movin' On* (Playboy 1975)★★★, *Overnight Sensation* (Playboy 1975)★★★, *Gilley's Smokin'* (Playboy 1976)★★★, *First Class* (Playboy 1977)★★★, *Mickey Gilley Live At Gilley's* (Epic 1978)★★★, *Mickey Gilley* (Paula 1978)★★★, *Flying High* (Epic 1978)★★★, *The Songs We Made Love To* (Epic 1979)★★★, *That's All That Matters To Me* (Epic 1980)★★★, *Down The Line* (Charly 1980)★★★, *You Really Don't Know Me* (Epic 1981)★★★, *Christmas At Gilley's* (Epic 1981)★, *Put Your Dreams Away* (Epic 1982)★★★, *Fool For Your Love* (Epic 1983)★★★, *You've Really Got A Hold On Me* (Epic 1983)★★★, with Charly McClain *It Takes Believers* (Epic 1984)★★★, *Too Good To Stop Now* (Epic 1984)★★★, *From Pasadena With Love* (Sundown 1985)★★★, *I Feel Good* (1986)★★★, *Back To Basics* (1987)★★★, *Rockin' Rollin' Piano* (1987)★★★, *Chasing Rainbows* (1988)★★★.

● COMPILATIONS: *Mickey Gilley At His Best* (Paula 1974)★★★, *Gilley's Greatest Hits, Vol. 1* (Playboy 1976)★★★★, *Greatest Hits, Vol. 2* (Playboy 1977)★★★, *Biggest Hits* (Epic 1982)★★★, *20 Golden Songs* (Astan 1984)★★★, *Ten Years Of Hits* (Epic 1984)★★★.

GILMORE, JIMMIE DALE

b. 6 May 1945, Amarillo, Texas, USA. Gilmore is one of the many singer-songwriters to emerge from Lubbock; he says, 'People used to ask us why there is so much music in Lubbock and we'd say that maybe it was the UFOs that came through in the early 50s. There was a famous sighting that was known as the Lubbock Lights.' Apart from such extra-terrestrial help, Gilmore acknowledges the three common influences for American singer-songwriters: Hank Williams, Elvis Presley and Bob Dylan. His father played in an old-time country band, and Gilmore learned fiddle, trombone and guitar. He began to perform around coffee-houses in Lubbock and one of his earliest compositions was 'Treat Me Like A Saturday Night'. Joe Ely gave him a Townes Van Zandt record, which changed his life: 'It was a revelation to me because I heard both worlds, folk and country, in the same place.' Gilmore, Ely and Butch Hancock worked in different combinations until all three came together in the Flatlanders, which was formed in 1971. The acoustic band also featured Steve Wesson's musical saw, and fanciful commentators have likened its sound to the Lubbock wind. The Flatlanders took their name from the landscape and they played bars around Austin and Lubbock. Gilmore's nasal whine was as flat as that landscape, but it was suited to his laid-back, evocative songwriting. Under the name of Jimmie Dale, they released a single of Gilmore's 'Dallas', with its oft-quoted first line, 'Did you ever see Dallas from a DC-9 at night?'. Another key song was Gilmore's 'Tonight I Think I'm Gonna Go Downtown', but the album they made in 1972 was not released until 1980. The Flatlanders was over within a year but it is fondly remembered by Ely and Hancock, who have developed solo careers. Gilmore, meanwhile, spent much of his time studying philosophy. His two albums for Hightone, *Fair And Square* and *Jimmie Dale Gilmore*, have strong country roots and include some superb Butch Hancock songs ('Red Chevrolet', 'Just A Wave, Not The Water'). Hancock and Gilmour recorded together and Gilmore became part of Elektra's American Explorer series, excelling himself on his *After Awhile* album. Gilmore may never match Ely and Hancock, but he is a significant influence on their work. *Braver, Newer World* moved him away from his country-based music into what Gilmore described as 'west Texas psychedelic blues rockabilly'.

● ALBUMS: as the Flatlanders *One More Road (1972 Recording)* (Charly 1980)★★★, *Fair And Square* (Hightone 1988)★★★, *Jimmie Dale Gilmore* (Hightone 1989)★★★★, with Butch Hancock *Two Roads - Live In Australia* (Virgin Australia 1990)★★★, as the Flatlanders *More A Legend Than A Band* (Rounder 1990)★★★, *After Awhile* (Elektra 1991)★★★★, *Spinning Around The Sun* (Elektra 1993)★★★, *Braver, Newer World* (Elektra 1996)★★★. The albums *Fair And Square* and *Jimmie Dale Gilmore* were issued together on a single CD in 1989.

GIMBLE, JOHNNY

b. 30 May 1926, near Tyler, Texas, USA. The fifth of six brothers, Gimble grew up in a musical environment, and each of his brothers played a stringed instrument. By the age of 12, having already learned both fiddle and mandolin, he was playing with four of his brothers at local dances and made his first radio appearances while still at school. He left home when he was 17 and found work playing fiddle and banjo with the Shelton Brothers and also with Jimmie Davis on KWKH Shreveport. In 1949, he joined Bob Wills' Texas Playboys (for the first time) and moved with Wills from Oklahoma to Dallas, when he opened the Bob Wills Ranch House. Around 1951, he left full-time work with Wills but

later played with him on other occasions. Gimble continued to play local venues and did session work with several artists including Marty Robbins and Lefty Frizzell, but in 1955, seeking some work with security, he became a barber and moved to Waco. During the 60s, he returned to a full-time musical career. He realized that he could find a lot of work as a session musician and relocated with his family to Nashville. Here his talents were much in demand and he worked with many top artists including Merle Haggard, who used him, as an ex-Texas Playboy, on his tribute album to Bob Wills. Apart from his countless session recordings with others, he recorded in his own right and worked with the popular First Nashville Jesus Band. He moved to Austin in the late 70s but still continued with some session work in Nashville. He has toured with many artists including Willie Nelson, has been featured on the popular *Hee-Haw* and *Austin City Limits* television series and has made several appearances at the Wembley Festival in London. He is equally at home with western-swing, country, blues or jazz music and during his career he has won many awards in recognition of his outstanding fiddle-playing.

● ALBUMS: *Fiddlin' Around* (Capitol 1974)★★★, *Honky Tonk Hits* (1976)★★★, *Texas Dance Party* (Lone Star 1975)★★★★, with the Texas Swing Pioneers *Still Swingin'* (CMH 1976)★★★, *Honky Tonk Hurtin' Songs* (1981)★★, *More Texas Dance Hall Favorites* (1981)★★★, *I Saw The Light* (1981)★★★, with Joe Barnhill's Nashville Sound Company *Swingin' The Standards* (1981)★★★, *My Kinda Music* (1984)★★★, *Still Fiddlin' Around* (MCA 1988)★★★.

● COMPILATIONS: *Texas Fiddle Connection* (CMH 1981)★★★.

GIRLS NEXT DOOR

In 1982, the Nashville record producer Tommy West, formerly of Cashman And West, asked session singer Doris King (b. 13 February 1957, Nashville, Tennessee, USA) to find three other girls for a harmony group that could blend country with soul and big band music. King recruited Cindy Nixon (b. 3 August 1958, Nashville, Tennessee, USA), Tammy Stephens (b. 13 April 1961, Arlington, Texas, USA) and Diane Williams (b. 9 August 1959, Hahn, AFB, Germany), and they originally called themselves Belle. Changing their name to The Girls Next Door, they had moderate success on the US country charts, including a Top 10 entry with a revival of 'Slow Boat To China'.

● ALBUMS: *Girls Next Door* (1986)★★, *What A Girl Next Door Can Do* (1987)★★, *How 'Bout Us* (1990)★★.

GIRLS OF THE GOLDEN WEST

Mildred Fern Good (b. 11 April 1913) and Dorothy Laverne Good (b. 11 December 1915, d. 12 November 1967, Hamilton, Ohio, USA, both at Mount Carmel, Illinois, USA). During the 30s, when duets were extremely popular, the Good Sisters were the most famous of the female duet singers. The Good family were of German extraction (originally being named Goad), and their father had at times been a schoolteacher, a farmer and storekeeper before moving to East St. Louis, where he worked in a factory. Their mother played guitar, taught the young Dorothy the essentials and the girls made their radio debut as Mildred and Dorothy Goad on KMOX St. Louis around 1930. They soon became Millie and Dolly Good, but a smart agent dressed them in cowboy outfits with fringed skirts, announced that they came from Muleshoe, Texas, and billed them somewhat imaginatively as the Girls Of The Golden West. They were to maintain the erroneous Texas connection for the whole of their career. Using only Dolly's simple guitar accompaniment and drawing heavily on western-type songs, they developed a pleasant style, with Dolly singing lead vocals and Millie providing the harmony. They had both learned to yodel as children and their ability to do so in harmony made them almost unique in their field. Around 1931, they moved to WLS Chicago, where they joined the *National Barn Dance* and in July 1933, they made their first recordings for RCA-Victor. They made further recordings in 1934 and 1935 and in 1937 moved to WLW Cincinnati, appearing first on the *Renfro Valley Barn Dance* and then in 1939, they became stars of the *Boone County Jamboree* and *Midwestern Hayride*. They made their final Victor recordings in Chicago in 1938, which brought their recorded output to 64 tracks. During the 30s and 40s, they were a very popular act and toured extensively throughout the Midwest and parts of the south. They remained in Cincinnati until 1949 when, except for the occasional appearance in the 50s, they nominally retired. In 1963, they recorded for Bluebonnet and Dolly did some solo work. One of their popular songs was 'Silver Moon On The Golden Gate', which they found amusing since neither had ever seen the noted bridge or even been to San Francisco.

● COMPILATIONS: *Girls Of The Golden West Volumes 1 - 6* (1965)★★★★, *The Girls Of The Golden West (Selected Recordings)* (1980)★★★★, *Songs Of The West* (1981)★★★★.

GLASER, TOMPALL
(see Tompall And The Glaser Brothers)

GOLBEY, BRIAN
b. Brian James Golbey, 5 February 1939, Pyecombe, Sussex, England. Golbey inherited a love of early American country music from his father, who had also taught him to play harmonica and melodeon, by the time he was given a guitar for his eleventh birthday. He was soon playing along with Jimmie Rodgers recordings and in 1953, he earned his first money singing 'Little Joe The Wrangler' at a Coronation celebration party. He next learned to play a fiddle that his grandfather had brought back from France in World War I and began to entertain during National Service in the army. He played clubs during the folk revival of the early 60s and around 1965, he helped to start what was probably one of the first country music clubs in the UK. In 1966, he turned professional and made his recording debut playing fiddle on Paul Jones's first solo album. In 1967, he teamed up with banjoist Pete Stanley. They toured, made radio and television appearances and during 1969/70 played residencies in Florence and Rome. In 1970, Golbey became a solo act on the emerging British country scene and made his own first recordings. He also made his first visit to America, appearing in Nashville as the British representative on the International Show and on the *Midnight Jamboree*. He also appeared on the noted *Wheeling Jamboree* and the *Renfro Valley Barn Dance*. He toured the UK with Patsy Montana and Mac Wiseman, and in 1972, won the *Billboard/Record Mirror* award as Top UK Solo Performer and the Male Vocalist of the Year award from the British Country Music Association. A further trip to America followed. In 1975, he

and Allan Taylor formed the folk-orientated band Cajun Moon, but various problems and differences of opinion arose and after recording a single album, the band broke up. In 1977, Golbey again began to work partly with Stanley and until the mid-80s, when for personal reasons he decided to reduce travelling commitments, they toured on a regular basis to Switzerland, Germany, Norway, Belgium, Holland and France (Golbey and Stanley maintain their friendship and still appear on occasions together). Golbey married Sandra Youngman in 1969; the marriage produced two sons, James (b. 1971) and David (b. 1973), but ended in divorce. He married Sandi Stubbs in 1980 and they have a son Daniel (b. 1985). Over the years, Golbey has done voice-overs for radio and television commercials and also appeared in a film, *The American Way* (although he stresses it is through no fault of his own that the film sank without trace). He has played in locations ranging from the Shetland Islands to Lands End and Berne to Belfast and in venues that vary from small school halls to the Albert Hall and from pubs to the Palladium. Working as a session musician, he has played on countless recordings but fondly remembers contributing 'Widdicombe Fair' and 'My Darling Clementine' for a mid-80s nursery rhyme album by Tim Hart (of Steeleye Span) & Friends. Apart from his albums, other Golbey recordings appear on various compilation albums. In 1993, the BCMA (GB) honoured him with an award for his long and continuing service to country music. A pioneer of British country music and a knowledgeable expert on early country music artists, he regularly contributes to the UK magazine *Country Music People*.

● ALBUMS: *The Old And The New* (Lucky 1970)★★★, *Virginia Waters* (Phoenix 1972)★★★, *Silver Haired Daddy Of Mine* (Avenue 1973)★★★★, *Moments* (Emerald Gem 1974)★★★, *Cajun Moon* (Chrysalis 1976)★★★, *The London Tapes* (Waterfall 1977)★★, with Pete Stanley *When The Dealing Is Done* (Waterfront 1979)★★★, with Nick Strutt *Last Train South* (Waterfront 1983)★★★.

GOLDSBORO, BOBBY
b. 18 January 1941, Marianna, Florida, USA. Goldsboro first came to prominence as a guitarist in Roy Orbison's touring band in 1960. His major chart breakthrough as a solo singer occurred in 1964 with the self-penned US Top 10 hit 'See The Funny Little Clown'. During the mid-60s, he also enjoyed minor US hits with 'Whenever He Holds You', 'Little Things' (a UK hit for Dave Berry), 'Voodoo Woman', 'It's Too Late' and 'Blue Autumn'. His international status was assured in 1968 with the elegiacal 'Honey', a Bobby Russell composition, perfectly suited to Goldsboro's urbane, but anguished, vocal style. The song dominated the US number 1 position for five weeks and was arguably the most unlucky single never to reach number 1 in the UK, twice reaching the number 2 slot, in 1968 and 1975. Goldsboro enjoyed further hits in the early 70s, with 'Watching Scotty Grow' and the risqué 'Summer (The First Time)'. In an attempt to extend his appeal, Goldsboro subsequently turned to country music, and met with considerable success in the 80s.

● ALBUMS: with Del Reeves *Our Way Of Life* (United Artists 1967)★★★, *Honey* (United Artists 1968)★★★, *Word Pictures* (United Artists 1968)★★★, *Today* (United Artists 1969)★★★, *Muddy Mississippi Line* (United Artists 1970)★★★, *We Gotta Start Lovin'* (United Artists 1971)★★★,

Come Back Home (United Artists 1971)★★, *10th Anniversary Album* (United Artists 1974)★★, *A Butterfly For Bucky* (United Artists 1976)★★, *Goldsboro* (1977)★★, *Roundup Saloon* (1982)★★.
● COMPILATIONS: *Solid Goldsboro* (United Artists 1967)★★★, *Summer (The First Time)* (United Artists 1973)★★★, *Best Of Bobby Goldsboro* (MFP 1983)★★★★, *The Very Best Of Bobby Goldsboro* (C5 1988)★★★★, *All-Time Greatest Hits* (Curb 1990)★★★.

GOODACRE, TONY

b. 3 February 1938, Leeds, England. With up to 300 shows a year, Tony Goodacre has been among the hardest-working British country musicians. In his adolescence, Goodacre acted, sang and played piano but, realizing the advantages of being able to entertain on demand, he switched to guitar. He formed the Tigers Skiffle Group while in the Royal Air Force and conversations with American servicemen inspired his passion for country music. He borrowed dozens of rare American country records and set about learning the songs. In September 1956, Goodacre secured his first professional engagement singing country music. He had a day job in Leeds during the late 50s and 60s but he worked clubs and pubs in the evenings. In 1969 he began working regularly with steel guitarist Arthur Layfield, and they became the nucleus for a new group, Goodacre Country. Economics are such that Goodacre now usually works solo but he still occasionally teams up with Layfield as well as several seasoned musicians, many of whom have played on his albums. Ever since 1975, when he included eight original songs on *Grandma's Feather Bed*, Goodacre has championed the cause of British country songwriters. *Written In Britain* was totally that, and among the songwriters he has featured are Terry McKenna, Geoff Ashford, Sammy King and Stewart Ross. George Hamilton IV, president of his fan club, encouraged Goodacre to play in Nashville, which culminated in appearances at the *Grand Ole Opry* in 1977. The following year he returned to Nashville to record *Mr Country Music*, and his tours have encompassed the USA, Australasia and Europe. In 1980, along with his wife Sylvia, Goodacre formed the Sylvantone label, which has released albums by other British acts, some of whom received his management guidance. His albums - and videos - are sold at personal appearances and include 'Old Shep', 'The Country Hall Of Fame' and 'The Old Rugged Cross', as well as several of the original songs he has recorded over the years.
● ALBUMS: *Roaming 'Round In Nashville* (Outlet 1974)★★★, *Grandma's Feather Bed* (Outlet 1975)★★★, *Thanks To The Hanks* (Outlet 1976)★★★, *Written In Britain* (Outlet 1977)★★★★, *Mr. Country Music* (Outlet 1978)★★, *You've Made My Life Complete* (Outlet 1979)★★★, *Recorded Live In Ilkley* (Sylvantone 1980)★★, *25th Anniversary* (Sylvantone 1981)★★★, *Red Roses* (Sylvantone 1984)★★★, *Country Favourites* (Sylvantone 1988)★★, *Something Special* (Sylvantone 1989)★★★.
● COMPILATIONS: *The Tony Goodacre Collection* (Sylvantone 1986)★★★.

GOODMAN, STEVE

b. 25 July 1948, Chicago, Illinois, USA, d. 20 September 1984. An engaging singer-songwriter from Chicago, Goodman was a favourite with critics, although his albums rarely achieved the commercial success that reviews suggested they deserved. His first appearance on record came in 1970 on *Gathering At The Earl Of Old Town*, an album featuring artists who regularly performed at a Chicago folk club, the Earl Of Old Town, which was run by an enthusiast named Earl Plonk. Released initially on Dunwich Records and later by Mountain Railroad, the album included three tracks by Goodman, 'Right Ball', 'Chicago Bust Rag' (written by Diane Hildebrand) and his classic train song, 'City Of New Orleans'. By 1972, Goodman's talent had been spotted by Kris Kristofferson, who recommended him to Paul Anka. Anka, who was an admirer of Kris Kristofferson, convinced Buddah (the label to which Anka was signed at the time) to sign Goodman, while Goodman in turn recommended his friend and fellow singer-songwriter John Prine to both Anka and Kristofferson, resulting in Atlantic signing Prine. Unfortunately for Goodman, Prine's career took off and Goodman remained a cult figure. He made two excellent albums for Buddah; *Steve Goodman* (which was produced by Kristofferson) included his two best-known songs in commercial terms, 'You Never Even Call Me By My Name', which was David Allan Coe's breakthrough country hit in 1975, and 'City Of New Orleans', a 1972 US Top 20 hit for Arlo Guthrie that was also covered by dozens of artists. Recorded in Nashville, the album featured many Area Code 615 musicians including Charlie McCoy and Kenny Buttrey. It was followed by *Somebody Else's Troubles* (produced by Arif Mardin) which featured musicians including David Bromberg, Bob Dylan (under the alias Robert Milkwood Thomas) and members of the Rascals. Although his album had failed thus far to chart, Goodman quickly secured a new contract with Asylum, a label that specialized in notable singer-songwriters. While his next two self-produced albums, *Jessie's Jig And Other Favourites* (1975) and *Words We Can Dance To* (1976), were minor US hits, 1977's *Say It In Private* (produced by Joel Dorn and including a cover version of 'Two Lovers', the Mary Wells classic written by Smokey Robinson), 1979's *High And Outside* and 1980's *Hot Spot* failed to chart, and his days on major labels ended at this point. By this time, Goodman, who had been suffering from leukemia since the early 70s, was often unwell, but by 1983, he had formed his own record label, Red Pajamas, with the help of his (and Prine's) manager, Al Bunetta. The first album to be released on the label was a live collection covering 10 years of performances by Goodman. *Artistic Hair's* sleeve pictured him as almost bald, due to the chemotherapy he was receiving in a bid to cure his illness. Soon afterwards came *Affordable Art*, which also included some live tracks and at least one out-take from an Asylum album, and with John Prine guesting. Goodman's final album, *Santa Ana Winds*, on which Emmylou Harris and Kris Kristofferson guested, included two songs he co-wrote with Jim Ibbotson and Jeff Hanna of the Nitty Gritty Dirt Band, 'Face On The Cutting Room Floor' and 'Queen Of The Road', but in September 1984, he died from kidney and liver failure following a bone marrow transplant operation. In 1985, Red Pajamas Records released a double album *Tribute To Steve Goodman*, on which many paid their musical respects to their late friend, including Prine, Bonnie Raitt, Arlo Guthrie, John Hartford, Bromberg, Richie Havens and the Nitty Gritty Dirt Band. It is highly likely that the largely excellent catalogue of this notable performer will be re-evaluated in the future - while he cannot be aware of the posthumous praise he has received, few would regard it as less than well deserved.

● ALBUMS: *Gathering At The Earl Of Old Town* (Dunwich 1970)★★★, *Steve Goodman* (Buddah 1972)★★★★, *Somebody Else's Trouble* (Buddah 1973)★★★, *Jessie's Jig And Other Favourites* (Asylum 1975)★★★★, *Words We Can Dance To* (Asylum 1976)★★★★, *Say It In Private* (Asylum 1977)★★★, *High And Outside* (Asylum 1979)★★★, *Hot Spot* (Asylum 1980)★★★, *Artistic Hair* (Red Pajamas 1983)★★★, *Affordable Art* (Red Pajamas 1983)★★, *Santa Ana Winds* (Red Pajamas 1984)★★.

● COMPILATIONS: *No Big Surprise - The Steve Goodman Anthology* (Red Pajamas 1995)★★★.

GORDY, EMORY, JNR.

Emory Gordy Jnr. was first noted as the bass player for Elvis Presley's 70s band. At the same time he was playing with Gram Parsons and after Parsons' death, he became a member of Emmylou Harris's Hot Band. He was a session musician on many country rock albums, notably by Eric Andersen, the Bellamy Brothers, Jonathan Edwards, the Flying Burrito Brothers, Chris Hillman, Albert Lee, Lyle Lovett, Mickey Newbury and Ricky Skaggs. He also played on several Billy Joel albums. When he turned to record production, he had four US country number 1s with Earl Thomas Conley - 'What She Is (Is A Woman In Love)', 'We Believe In Happy Endings' (a duet with Emmylou Harris), 'What'd I Say' and 'Love Out Loud'. He also produced the Bellamy Brothers including 'Old Hippie' and 'Kids Of The Baby Boom'. In the mid-90s he tried to re-establish Alabama as a major chart act. Gordy is married to Patty Loveless and, naturally, produces her records.

GORKA, JOHN

b. New Jersey, USA. Singer-songwriter Gorka, who possesses a rich and emotive baritone, honed his craft in America's north-eastern folk scene of the early 80s before recording a succession of acclaimed albums. Influenced by Tom Paxton, Richard Thompson and Tom Waits, amongst others, his musical career began in 1986 when he was attending Moravian College in Bethlehem, with the intention of studying history and philosophy. A small coffee-house folk scene had sprung up at a nearby venue called Godfrey Daniels, and Gorka graduated from open-mic spots to leading a group, the Razzy Dazzy Spasm Band. However, he then packed his guitar and took his songs out to the wider world, playing throughout north-east America, then travelling to Texas where he won the Kerrville Folk Festival's New Folk Award in 1984. His debut album, *I Know*, was released on Red House Records in 1987, and featured the best of his early songwriting, including 'Blues Palace', 'Downtown Tonight' and 'Down In The Milltown'. Afterwards, he would enjoy a more stable relationship with High Street/Windham Hill Records. The ensuing albums explored a multi-faceted talent, with earnest vocals bedecking Gorka's dry wit and sharp observations and character sketches. By the advent of *Temporary Road* in 1993 the artist found increased exposure, touring with Mary-Chapin Carpenter and Nanci Griffith. Meanwhile, a single drawn from the album, 'When She Kisses Me', was voted the CMT Best Independent Video Of The Year. For *Out Of The Valley* Gorka relocated from

Bethlehem to Nashville, teaming up with producer/guitarist John Jennings. Together they recruited an all-star cast to accompany the singer, including Mary-Chapin Carpenter, Kathy Mattea, Leo Kottke and Dave Mattacks (Fairport Convention). Gorka also drew on the rich musical environment that surrounded him in the studio, using a guitar once owned by Buddy Holly, the piano with which Carole King had recorded *Tapestry* and a mixing board that had been used for sessions with Elvis Presley and Roy Orbison. This time the songs were less personally defined, using a third person mechanism to allow the artist to explore his characters, giving them individual motivation and colour.

● ALBUMS: *I Know* (Red House 1987)★★★★, *Land Of The Bottom Line* (Windham Hill 1990)★★★, *Jack's Crows* (High Street 1992)★★★, *Temporary Road* (High Street 1993)★★★, *Out Of The Valley* (High Street 1994)★★★★, *Between Five And Seven* (High Street 1996)★★★.

● VIDEOS: *Good Noise* (1994).

GOSDIN, VERN

b. 5 August 1934, Woodland, Alabama, USA. Vern's first steps in carrying out his wish to be a country singer-songwriter came in the early 50s, when as a result of singing with his two brothers in the local church, they became regulars as the Gosdin Family on WVOK Birmingham. In 1953, he moved to Atlanta where he sold ice cream and in 1956 to Chicago where he ran a country music nightclub. During this time he worked hard to develop his singing and writing, and also became a talented instrumentalist on guitar, banjo and mandolin. In 1960, he moved to California, where he joined his brother Rex (b. 1938, d. 23 May 1983), first in a bluegrass group called the Golden State Boys and then as members of Chris Hillman's bluegrass band the Hillmen. When Hillman moved on to rock as a founder-member of the Byrds, Vern also worked as a session musician while continuing to perform bluegrass with Rex. He recorded for several labels with no real success, and in 1966, even recorded an album with Gene Clark, who had recently left the Byrds. In 1967, the brothers finally achieved a US country chart hit with 'Hangin' On', but lacking any follow-up success, Vern soon returned to Atlanta and opened a glass and mirror shop, singing only in his spare time. His song 'Someone To Turn To' was recorded by the Byrds at the instigation of guitarist Clarence White. In 1976, Gosdin returned to recording, charting a version of 'Hangin' On' and enjoying Top 10 hits with 'Yesterday's Gone (both of which featured backing vocals by Emmylou Harris) and 'Till The End'. He left his sons to run the business and with Rex returned to touring and concerts. Between 1978 and 1988, he registered 27 more US country chart hits, including number 1s with 'I Can Tell By The Way You Dance (You're Gonna Love Me Tonight)' and 'Set 'Em Up Joe'. In 1979 and 1980, his brother Rex had three minor chart entries, the biggest being a duet with Tommy Jennings on 'Just Give Me What You Think Is Fair'. Rex died on 23 May 1983 at the age of 45, some two weeks before his recording of 'That Old Time Feelin'' entered the charts. Vern continues to record and perform although he was hospitalized in 1995 with a stroke, and was dropped by Columbia Records. He is a rare performer in that his solid country voice and heartbreaking songs are somewhat alien to much of Nashville's modern music scene. Like George Jones, he appears to improve with age. Even Tammy

Wynette once said, 'If anybody sounded like Jones other than Jones without really trying to, it is Vern Gosdin.'
● ALBUMS: with The Hillmen: *The Hillmen* (Together 1970)★★★, *Till The End* (Elektra 1977)★★★★, *Never My Love* (Elektra 1978)★★★, *You've Got Somebody* (Elektra 1979)★★★, *Passion* (Ovation 1981)★★★, *If You're Gonna Do Me Wrong, Do It Right* (1983)★★★, *Today My World Slipped Away* (1983)★★★, *Dream Lady* (1984)★★★, *There Is A Season* (Compleat 1984)★★★, *If Jesus Comes Tomorrow* (Compleat 1984)★★★, *Time Stood Still* (1985)★★★, *Chiseled In Stone* (Columbia 1988)★★★★, *Alone* (Columbia 1989)★★★, *Rough Around The Edges: A.M.I. Sessions* (RCA 1989)★★, *10 Years Of Hits - Newly Recorded* (Columbia 1990)★★★, *Out Of My Heart* (Columbia 1991)★★★, *Nickels And Dimes And Love* (Columbia 1993)★★★, *24 Karat Heartache* (American Harvest 1997)★★★. As The Gosdin Brothers: *Echoes (With The Gosdin Brothers)* (Columbia 1967)★★★★ reissued as *Gene Clark With The Gosdin Brothers* (Edsel 1997), *Sounds Of Goodbye* (Capitol 1968)★★★.
● COMPILATIONS: *The Best Of Vern Gosdin* (Columbia 1989)★★★★, *Super Hits* (Columbia 1994)★★★, *Warning: Contains Country Music (The Great Ballads Of Vern Gosdin)* (American Harvest 1997)★★★★.

GRAHAM, TAMMY
b. Tammy Wynette Graham, *c.*1968, Little Rock, Arkansas, USA. Named by her parents after Tammy Wynette, this country singer began to make some progress towards a similar level of name recognition in the mid-90s. However, it had been a long apprenticeship. Graham spent much of her youth as a child singer, before spending several years as one of the most successful acts at Caesar's Palace in Las Vegas. She had begun singing at the age of three, going on to teach herself piano by listening to Dr. John records. By the time she was 10 she was opening shows for Jerry Lee Lewis, moving to Nashville a year later. Although her demos failed to secure a contract, she continued to sing semi-professionally, working with gospel singer Wally Fowler and serving as support act to Faron Young and Danny Davis. When she became a teenager she elected to go on the road with a group for the first time: 'Me and my momma and daddy in the front seat and my three musicians in the back seat of a Lincoln Continental, pulling a U-Haul trailer. We went all over, from Florida to Mexico.' She began performing in Las Vegas casinos at the age of 17. Thus began her record-breaking seven-year, three shows a night, six nights a week residence at Caesar's Palace. She returned to Nashville only after one of these performances had been observed by Joe Diffie's manager, Danny Morrison. He introduced her to Tim DuBois, who signed her to Career Records after travelling to Las Vegas to see her play. Paired with producer Barry Beckett she made her long-playing debut in 1996. This self-titled collection utilized some of 'Music Row's' best writers, including Mark D. Snaders, Bob DiPiero and Bob McDill.
● ALBUMS: *Tammy Graham* (Career 1996)★★★.

GRAMMER, BILLY
b. William Wayne Grammer, 28 August 1925, Benton, Illinois, USA. Grammer was a coalminer's son and one of 13 children. His father played the fiddle, and by the time he was in his teens, Grammer was playing guitar, mandolin and banjo at local dances. After a spell in the forces, he started

in C&W radio on WRAL in Arlington, Virginia, in 1947, but established his reputation as a session guitarist in Washington. He played lead guitar for several country performers - Hawkshaw Hawkins, Grandpa Jones, T. Texas Tyler - and he worked with Jimmy Dean on his television series from 1955-59. Grammer first recorded as a solo performer in 1949, but in 1959, had a vocal success with the million-selling 'Gotta Travel On', a 19th century British melody that had previously been revived by the Weavers. Grammer's pop success was short-lived as the excellent double-sided 'Bonaparte's Retreat'/'The Kissing Tree' barely made the US Top 50. He had a country hit with 'I Wanna Go Home' in 1963, which Bobby Bare reworked as 'Detroit City'. He joined the *Grand Ole Opry* and became a session guitarist. His first model of the Grammer Flat-Top Guitar, which he now manufactures, is in the Country Music Hall of Fame.
● ALBUMS: *Travellin' On* (Monument 1961)★★★, *Gospel Guitar* (Decca 1962)★★, *Billy Grammer Sings Gotta Travel On* (Decca 1964)★★★, *Country Gospel Favourites* (Decca 1964)★★, *Country Guitar* (Decca 1965)★★★, *Sunday Guitar* (Epic 1967)★★, *Country Favourites* (Vocalion 1968)★★★, *Billy Grammer Plays* (1975)★★★ *Christmas Guitars* (1977)★★.

GRAND OLE OPRY
(see Hay, George D.)
● FURTHER READING: *The Grand Ole Opry History Of Country Music*, Paul Kingsbury.

GRAVES, JOSH
b. Burkett K. Graves, *c.*1925, Tellico Springs, Tennessee, USA. One of the greatest of all dobro players and probably the first to have played the instrument in bluegrass music. Historian Bill C. Malone summarized Graves' abilities as follows: 'Graves perfected a rolling syncopated style that enabled him to play galloping breakdowns as well as slow love songs or ballads'. He was attracted to the dobro as a child on hearing Cliff Carlisle play on Jimmie Rodgers' recordings, and he later met Carlisle, who gave him help and encouragement. He was also influenced in his early career by the dobro playing of Pete Kirby (Bashful Brother Oswald). He learned not only dobro but also guitar and bass, and in 1942, he made his professional debut with the Pierce Brothers. After then playing with Esco Hankins in Knoxville, he played with Molly O'Day and Mac Wiseman, before joining Wilma Lee And Stoney Cooper on the WWVA *Wheeling Jamboree*. In 1957, he moved with them to the *Grand Ole Opry*, where he first met Flatt And Scruggs. He soon became a permanent member of their Foggy Mountain Boys, initially playing bass, but soon changing to dobro. He was impressed by Scruggs' brilliant three-fingered style of banjo playing which, with Scruggs' help, he soon adapted to the dobro. When Flatt And Scruggs split in 1969, he became a member of Flatt's Nashville Grass until 1971, when he joined the Earl Scruggs Revue until 1974. During the 60s and early 70s, he played on albums by both Flatt and Scruggs and as a session musician, he played albums by other artists including Steve Young and Kris Kristofferson. In 1974, he left Scruggs to work as a session musician and to make solo appearances. He recorded his debut, *Alone At Last*, for Epic and also appeared on releases by Charlie McCoy, Boots Randolph and James Talley. In 1975, he recorded a duet

album with Jake Tullock as Uncle Jake And Uncle Josh (he had created Uncle Josh as an alter-ego comic character that he portrayed on stage, and he was friendly with Tullock from his days with Flatt And Scruggs). During the late 70s, he recorded with Bobby Smith and as one of Joe Maphis's Super Picker Pals, while also recording solo albums for CMH. In the 80s, Graves, Mike Auldridge and Jerry Douglas produced *Dobro Summit*, an educational video, and he also played as a member of the Masters, with Eddie Adcock, Kenny Baker and Jesse McReynolds. In 1988, he recorded an album with his son Billy Troy (guitar). In the 90s, Graves was still in demand for session work and was regularly making appearances on various radio and television shows.

● ALBUMS: *Alone At Last* (Epic 1974), *Uncle Josh & His Dobro* (Cottontown 70s)★★★, with Jake Tullock *Just Joshing* (Cottontown Jubilee 1975)★★, with Bobby Smith *Sweet Sunny South* (CMH 1976)★★★, *Bobby Smith & Josh Graves* (Vetco 1976)★★★, *Same Old Blues* (CMH 1978)★★★, with Smith *Smokin' Bluegrass* (CMH 1978)★★★, with Vassar Clements *Sing Away The Pain* (CMH 1979)★★★, *Josh Graves & Friends* 1962/3 recordings (Cowboy Carl 1979)★★, *Playing It Simple* (Vetco 1980)★★★, *King Of The Dobro* (CMH 1980)★★★, with Red Taylor *Living Legends* (Old Homestead 1984)★★★, with Billy Troy *Dad The Dobro Man* (CMH 1988)★★★, *The Real Josh* (Amber 1988)★★★, with Kenny Baker *The Puritan Sessions* (Rebel 1989)★★★.

GRAY, CLAUDE

b. 26 January 1932, Henderson, Texas, USA. During his schooldays, he showed more interest in music than sports and, learning to play the guitar, he began to perform locally. By the late 50s, he was playing venues over a wide area, for a time he worked as a disc jockey on WDAL Meridian, Mississippi, and made his first recordings for Decca Records. However, it was in 1960, on the 'D' label (a subsidiary of Mercury), that he gained his first US country chart hit, when his recording of Willie Nelson's 'Family Bible' peaked at number 10. This success led to him being moved to the major label and in 1961, he enjoyed major Top 5 hits with 'I'll Just Have Another Cup Of Coffee (Then I'll Go)' and Roger Miller's song 'My Ears Should Burn (When Fools Are Talked About)'. In 1966, after further Mercury successes, he recorded for Columbia and charted with 'Mean Old Woman', before returning to Decca. He formed the Graymen, which became a very popular touring band all over the USA, being especially popular on the nightclub circuit around Las Vegas. In the late 60s he had eight chart entries, including Top 20 hits with 'I Never Had The One I Wanted' and the truck-driving song 'How Fast Them Trucks Can Go'. He left Decca in 1971 but achieved a few small hits on the Million and Granny labels. In 1982 he had a minor hit with a duet recording with Norma Jean of 'Let's Go All The Way' (a 1964 solo hit for Norma Jean). Known as 'The Tall Texan' (for obvious reasons), Gray is much better as a live performer, it is said, than as a recording artist. This perhaps accounts for his inability to maintain chart hits. He is still active, his last chart entry having been a minor hit with Neil Diamond's 'Sweet Caroline' in 1986.

● ALBUMS: *Songs Of Broken Love Affairs* (Mercury 1962)★★★, with the Melody Singers *Country Goes To Town* (Mercury 1962)★★★, *Claude Gray Sings* (Decca 1967)★★★, *Treasure Of Love* (Hilltop 1967)★★, *The Easy Way Of Claude*

Gray (Decca 1968)★★, *Presenting Claude Gray* (Million 1972)★★★, *Great Country Roads* (Sunrise 1997)★★★.

GRAY, MARK

b. 24 October 1952, Vicksburg, Mississippi, USA. Singer-songwriter Gray first played piano at the age of 12 and headed his own gospel group at 19. He joined the Oak Ridge Boys as a writer with their publishing company, also becoming the keyboard player with their road band. Later he became a member of pop-country band Exile and was lead vocalist on two of their albums, *Don't Leave Me This Way* (1980) and *Heart And Soul* (1981). In the early 80s, three of his songs were US country number 1s, 'Take Me Down' and 'The Closer You Get', both for Alabama and 'It Ain't Easy Bein' Easy' for Janie Frickie. He signed with Columbia in 1983 and between 1983 and 1988, he registered 11 US country chart successes, including solo Top 10 hits with 'If The Magic Is Gone' and 'Please Be Love', but his highest chart entry came with his 1985 duet recording with Tammy Wynette of 'Sometimes When We Touch'. He had two minor duet hits in 1988 with Bobbi Lace, but has not achieved a solo hit since 1986.

● ALBUMS: *Magic* (Columbia 1984)★★★, *This Ol' Piano* (Columbia 1984)★★★, *That Feeling Inside* (Columbia 1986)★★★.

GRAY, OTTO, AND HIS OKLAHOMA COWBOYS

Around 1923, a group of musicians in Stillwater, Oklahoma, began playing as the Billy McGinty Cowboy Band. William McGinty, an old-time cowboy who had ridden with Roosevelt's Rough Riders, formed the band to preserve the music of the Old West and hired Otto Gray as the band's manager. Gray was born around 1890 at Ponca, on the Ponca Indian Reservation, in Indian Territory, Oklahoma, USA. Little is known of his early years but at the time McGinty hired him, he was a successful rancher. An adept promoter, he soon found the band work, only to discover that the original members would not tour. A talented fiddle player, Gray formed his own Oklahoma Cowboys, which included his wife (Mommie) as the featured vocalist and his son Owen, by recruiting genuine cowboy musicians working on Oklahoma ranches. They first broadcast in 1924 on KFRU Bristow, but later played on KVOO Tulsa and KFJF Oklahoma City and went on to play countless radio stations all over the USA. With shrewd organization, Gray assembled a show that featured, in addition to the music, himself and Mommie doing trick roping and whip cracking, a trained dog and speciality musical items. He publicized the show by advertising in national magazines such as *Billboard*, sending publicity men ahead to forthcoming venues and by using booking agencies in Chicago and New York to co-ordinate the band's appearances on various entertainment circuits. At one time their show was carried by over a 100 radio stations. Very likely the first touring cowboy stage show to perform genuine cowboy songs, they were also probably the first ever group to use custom-made cars to transport them on tour. Gray's personal vehicle, a $20,000 Cadillac, was even equipped for radio transmissions. By the time Gray finally disbanded the group (and disappeared into obscurity) in 1936, he had inspired other country groups to dress as cowboys, he had popularized 'western' music and he may even have been a candidate for the title of the first singing cowboy. It is probable that Gray's Cowboys were an inspiration to Bob Wills, who moved to Tulsa to organize his Texas Playboys. Gray was the first western star to have his photograph on the cover of *Billboard* magazine. Two of his Cowboys, Zeke Clements and 'Whitey' Ford (The Duke Of Paducah), went on to successful solo careers.

GRAYSON, G.B.

b. Gillam Bannon Grayson, 11 November 1887, Grayson, Ashe County, Tennessee, USA, raised in Laurel Bloomery, Johnson County, d. 16 August 1930. Although blinded as a child, Grayson learned the fiddle and began singing. When the family moved to Tennessee, he took to busking. Eventually, he teamed up with Clarence 'Tom' Ashley and Doc Walsh and forged a reputation in Virginia, Tennessee and North Carolina. He met Henry Whitter, who made the original recording of 'The Wreck Of The Southern Old '97', and recorded with him in 1927. In 1929 they made the first ever recording of 'Tom Dooley' (shortly after the civil war, Grayson's uncle had been involved in the capture of suspected murderer Tom Dula). Grayson died in a car crash near Damascus, Virginia, in August 1930, leaving a wife and six children. Today he is accepted as an important pioneer of country music and fiddle-playing, and is generally considered a superior vocalist to Whitter, having even sung lead on several records under Whitter's name.
● COMPILATIONS: *Grayson And Whitter, 1927-1930* (Old Homestead 1976)★★★, *Going Down The Highway* (1976)★★★.

GRAYSON, JACK

b. Jack Lebsock, Sterling, Colorado, USA. Singing from an early age, Lebsock appeared on shows with top artists, including Johnny Cash. However, he found little success and turning to songwriting, becoming a staff writer for ABC/Dot during the 70s. He co-wrote 'Bless Your Heart' (with Freddie Hart) and wrote 'Super Kind Of Woman', both of which became number 1 country hits for Hart in 1972 and 1973, respectively. He also wrote 'The First Time', a number 2 for Hart in 1975. He made his own chart debut as a recording artist on Capitol in 1973 when, as Jack Lebsock, he had a minor hit with 'For Lovers Only'. After a further minor hit the following year, he changed his name (in tribute to his mother); in 1979 and 1980, he recorded for Churchill and Hitbound, achieving four minor chart hits as Blackjack Jack Grayson. He next recorded for Koala (this time as Jack Grayson and Blackjack), gaining a Top 20 hit with his version of 'When A Man Loves A Woman' (a number 1 pop hit in 1966 for Percy Sledge). In the early 80s, he recorded for Joe-Wes and his last chart entry, 'Lean On Me' (another former pop number 1, recorded by Bill Withers in 1972), was on AMI in 1984.
● ALBUMS: *Jack Grayson Sings* (Joe-Wes 1982)★★★.

GREAT PLAINS

A US country rock group led by vocalist Jack Sundrud, Great Plains originally made their debut in 1991 with 'A Picture Of You'. Two further singles for Columbia Records, 'Faster Gun' and 'Iola', followed a year later, but immediately afterwards changes at their record company enforced a sabbatical from recording and touring. As a result, guitarist Russ Pahl left to

find session work and drummer Michael Young decided to spend more time on his business affairs, restoring vintage cars. The group's fourth founding member, bassist Danny Dadmun-Bixby, toured with Mary-Chapin Carpenter while Sundrud spent much of the period writing new songs, one of which, 'Cain's Blood', was recorded by 4Runner. Eventually Great Plains were reconvened when Sundrud and Dadmun-Bixby met multi-instrumentalist Lex Browning. The trio then signed with Magnatone Records, the label headed by long-time friend Brent Maher. Maher also produced the album *Homeland*, which featured the excellent single 'Dancing With The Wind'.
● ALBUMS: *Great Plains* (Columbia 1991)★★★, *Homeland* (Magnatone 1996)★★★.

GREEN, LLOYD

b. Lloyd L. Green, 4 October 1937, Mississippi, USA. Green's family moved to Mobile, Alabama, when he was four years old and he was raised there. He learned Hawaiian string guitar from the age of seven and graduated to steel guitar. He was playing professionally by the time he was 10, and recalls, 'I played in clubs a couple of nights a week with a rhythm guitarist called Emmanuel Abates, who was also a yo-yo champion. He wasn't a very good guitarist and eventually he went back to his yo-yos.' Green studied psychology at the University of Southern Mississippi, but he left at the age of 19 to seek fame in Nashville. In December 1956 he joined Faron Young's road band and stayed for 18 months. During that time, he played steel guitar on his first session, George Jones's 'Too Much Water Runs Under The Bridge'. He returned to Mobile and later came back to Nashville as a shoe salesman. When he told one customer that he could not afford $75 to renew his union card, she renewed it for him - she was the widow of the publisher Fred Rose. The first successful session on which Green played was Warner Mack's 'The Bridge Washed Out' in 1965. For the next 15 years, 'the steelworker' averaged 400 sessions a year, which included 'It's Four In The Morning' (Faron Young), 'Easy Lovin'' (Freddie Hart) and the Byrds' seminal country rock album, *Sweetheart Of The Rodeo*. He says, 'Bob Dylan had hinted and flirted with the steel guitar before the Byrds, but he'd only let Pete Drake colour the songs very lightly. "You Ain't Goin' Nowhere" took a whole day to record, which was a whole new revolution for me. I was used to sessions that were highly organized and where everyone was clock-watching.' He also played on Paul McCartney's 'Sally G' but turned down a US tour because he did not want to lose work in Nashville. He made several solo records, mostly easy-listening country music, although his technique is skilfully demonstrated on 'I Can See Clearly Now'. He popularized the blocking technique, used by Jimmy Day in the 50s, whereby the palm of the picking hand is used to mute the strings in order to lose the ringing effect. Green, who was not a solo attraction in the USA, made successful appearances at the Wembley Country Music Festival and his 1979 three-week UK tour with Billie Jo Spears was the longest he had been away from Nashville since 1964. He also worked in the UK with his fellow session musicians Charlie McCoy and Hargus 'Pig' Robbins. He says, 'It's laughable when I read of Nashville sessionmen getting together after hours and having a jam session. We play enough music in the studio. We'd rather get drunk and have a good time.'

● ALBUMS: *Big Steel Guitar* (Time 1964)★★★, *Day For Decision* (Little Darlin 1966)★★★, *The Hit Sounds* (1966)★★★, *Mr. Nashville Sound* (Chart 1968)★★★, *Cool Steel Man* (1968)★★★, *Green Country* (Little Darlin 1969)★★★, *Moody River* (1969)★★★, with Pete Drake *The Music City Sound* (1970)★★★, *Lloyd Green And His Steel Guitar* (Prize 1971)★★★, *Shades Of Steel* (Monument 1973)★★★, *Steel Rides* (Monument 1976)★★★, *Feelings* (1976)★★★, *Ten Shades Of Green* (Mid-Land 1976)★★★, *Lloyd's Of Nashville* (Mid-Land 1980)★★★, *Reflections* (1991)★★★.

GREENBRIAR BOYS

Formed in New York, USA, in 1958, the Greenbriar Boys were one of the leading exponents of urban bluegrass. The original line-up comprised John Herald (guitar, lead vocals), Bob Yellin (banjo, tenor vocals) and Eric Weissberg (banjo, mandolin, dobro, fiddle), but in 1959 the latter was replaced by Ralph Rinzler (mandolin, baritone vocals). The following year the group won the top award at the annual Union Grove Fiddlers' Convention, while Yellin secured the first of several hits as a solo artist. The Greenbriar Boys completed several excellent albums for the Vanguard label and became a highly popular attraction on the club, concert and festival circuits. Individually the members appeared as session musicians for, among others, Ramblin' Jack Elliott, Joan Baez and Patrick Sky. The trio was later augmented by vocalist Dian Edmondson; this reshaped unit recorded a lone release for Elektra Records. The group then underwent a radical change. Edmondson dropped out of the line-up, while Rinzler left for an administrative post with the Newport Folk Festival committee. Herald and Yellin added Frank Wakefield (mandolin) and Jim Buchanan (fiddle), but the Greenbriars' impetus was waning and the group was officially disbanded in 1966.

● ALBUMS: *The Greenbriar Boys* (Vanguard 1962)★★★★, *Ragged But Right!* (Vanguard 1964)★★★, *Dian And The Greenbriar Boys* (Elektra 1964)★★★, *Better Late Than Never* (Vanguard 1966)★★★.

● COMPILATIONS: *The Best Of John Herald And The Greenbriar Boys* (1972)★★★★.

GREENE, JACK

b. Jack Henry Greene, 7 January 1930, Maryville, Tennessee, USA. Greene took guitar lessons when he was eight years old, then added drumming to his abilities. Moving to Atlanta in the late 40s, he became part of the Cherokee Trio with Lem Bryant and Speedy Price. He then became a member of the Rhythm Ranch Boys and was a popular radio entertainer on *Georgia Jublilee* on WTJH. Greene's career was interrupted for military service in Korea, but he returned to Atlanta and joined the Peachtree Cowboys, also working as a salesperson and construction worker. In 1962 he joined Ernest Tubb And The Texas Troubadours as a drummer and occasional vocalist. He was featured on *Ernest Tubb Presents The Texas Troubadours*, and his performance on 'The Last Letter' led to solo recordings. Starting in 1965 with 'Ever Since My Baby Went Away', Greene had a succession of country hits, including number 1 hits with 'There Goes My Everything', 'All The Time', 'You Are My Treasure', 'Until My Dreams Come True' and 'Statue Of A Fool'. He did not leave Tubb's band until 1967, and only

then because Tubb tired of hearing calls for the drummer to sing. In 1969 he had a further hit with Hank Cochran's song 'I Wish I Didn't Have To Miss You', on which he was partnered by Cochran's wife, Jeannie Seely. She became part of his roadshow and they continued to record together. Capitalizing on the popularity of outlaw country, they changed the name of their band from the Jolly Greene Giants to the Renegades, but they stayed with middle-of-the-road country music. Although his last chart entry was with 'If It's Love (Then Bet It All)' in 1984, Greene, who joined the Grand Ole Opry in 1967, is still a regular performer.

● ALBUMS: *Jack Greene* (Decca 1965)★★★, *There Goes My Everything* (Decca 1966)★★★, *All The Time* (Decca 1967)★★★, *What Locks The Door* (Decca 1967)★★★, *You Are My Treasure* (Decca 1968)★★★, *I Am Not Alone* (Decca 1968)★★★, *Until My Dreams Come True* (Decca 1968)★★★, *Statue Of A Fool* (Decca 1969)★★★, *Back In The Arms Of Love* (Decca 1969)★★★, *There's A Whole Lot About A Woman A Man Don't Know* (Decca 1970)★★★, *Yours For The Taking* (1981)★★. By Jack Greene and Jeannie Seely: *I Wish I Didn't Have To Miss You* (Decca 1969)★★★, *Jack Greene And Jeannie Seely* (Decca 1970)★★★, *Two For The Show* (Decca 1971)★★, *Live At The Grand Ole Opry* (1978)★★★.

● COMPILATIONS: *Greatest Hits* (Gusto 1986)★★★★, *The Jolly Green Giant* (Edsel 1997)★★★★.

GREENE, RICHARD

b. 1945, Beverly Hills, California, USA. This virtuoso fiddle player began his career in 1962 in a duo called the Orange Coast Ramblers with Ken Frankel on mandolin. They broke up in 1963 when Frankel joined Jerry Garcia and Robert Hunter in the Hart Valley Drifters. Greene joined the Dry City Scat Band with David Lindley, Chris Darrow (both of whom were later in Kaleidoscope), Steve Cahill and Pete Maldem. Greene was with them until 1965 and he plays on their privately pressed EP and on the Elektra Records compilation *Sting Band Project*. After this, Greene was briefly a member of the Greenbriar Boys and between March 1966 and March 1967 served in Bill Monroe's Bluegrass Boys; he is featured on the Decca album *Blue Grass Time*. Greene joined Red Allen And The Kentuckians before switching to the Jim Kweskin Jug Band in time for *Garden Of Joy*. In 1968 he joined the Blues Project and played a pivotal role in revitalizing their career. Having moved from the east coast to west, the group took a new name, Sea Train, and with the addition of Peter Rowan (ex-Bill Monroe; Earth Opera), they played a well-regarded fusion of rock and traditional styles. In 1971 Greene and Rowan formed an offshoot project, Muleskinner, with David Grisman, Clarence White and Bill Keith, and together they recorded an album that was issued following White's premature death. After the break-up of Sea Train in 1973, Greene formed Richard Greene And Zone with Randy Resnick (guitar, ex-Pure Food And Drug Act), Larry Taylor (bass, ex-Pure Food And Drug Act), Ken Collier (drums) and Richard Martin (vocals). They recorded a disappointing album, after which Greene was involved with several traditional acts, notably Old And In The Way, the Great American String Band and Country Gazette. He also made three solo albums and in 1980 rejoined Peter Rowan for an album released only in Japan.

● ALBUMS: as Richard Greene And Zone *Richard Greene And Zone* (Warners 1973)★★★, *Duets* (Rounder 1978)★★★,

Rambling (Rounder 1980)★★★, with Peter Rowan *Peter Rowan, Richard Greene And The Red-Hot Pickers* (Nippon Columbia 1980)★★★★, *Blue Rondo* (Sierra 1982)★★★, with the Greene String Quartet *The String Machine* (Virgin 1991)★★★, *The Greene Fiddler* (Sierra 1995)★★★.
● VIDEOS: *Muleskinner - Live Video* (1991).

GREENWOOD, LEE
b. 27 October 1942, Los Angeles, California, USA. Because of his parents' divorce, Greenwood was brought up by his grandparents in Sacramento, California, but he inherited their musical talent (his mother played piano and his father woodwind). In his teens, he played in various bands in Sacramento and Los Angeles and was even part of a dixieland jazz band at Disneyland. He played saxophone for country star Del Reeves and then formed his own band, Apollo, which found work in Las Vegas in 1962. He turned down an opportunity to join the Rascals and for many years he was arranging and playing music for bands in casinos. The environment narrowed his vocal range and he developed a husky-voiced approach to ballads similar to Kenny Rogers. In 1979 his career took a major step forward when he was heard by Larry McFadden of Mel Tillis's band, who became his manager. His first MCA single, 'It Turns Me Inside Out', was a US country hit in 1981. This was followed by several other hits including two number 1s, 'Somebody's Gonna Love You' and 'Going, Going, Gone'. His songs were also recorded by several other performers including Kenny Rogers who found success with 'A Love Song'. In 1984 he recorded an album with Barbara Mandrell and they made the US country charts with 'You've Got A Good Love Coming To Me' and he also recorded his own patriotic song, 'God Bless The USA', which won the Country Music Association's Song Of The Year. His other number 1 country singles are 'Dixie Road', 'I Don't Mind The Thorns (If You're The Rose)', 'Don't Underestimate My Love For You', 'Hearts Aren't Made To Break (They're Made To Love)', and the sensual 'Mornin' Ride'. He has won numerous country awards but is best known in the UK for the original recording of 'The Wind Beneath My Wings', which entered the UK charts in 1984. He switched labels to Capitol Records, but this was not enough to stop the decline of his career during the 90s.
● ALBUMS: *Inside And Out* (MCA 1982)★★★, *Somebody's Gonna Love You* (MCA 1983)★★, *The Wind Beneath My Wings* (MCA 1984)★★★, with Barbara Mandrell *Meant For Each Other* (MCA 1984)★★★, *You've Got A Good Love Coming* (MCA 1984)★★★, *Christmas To Christmas* (MCA 1985)★★, *Streamline* (MCA 1985)★★★, *Love Will Find It's Way To You* (MCA 1986)★★★★, *If There's Any Justice* (MCA 1987)★★★, *This Is My Country* (MCA 1988)★★★, *If Only For One Night* (MCA 1989)★★★, *Holdin' A Good Hand* (Capitol 1991)★★★, *American Patriot* (Liberty 1992)★★★.
● COMPILATIONS: *Greatest Hits* (MCA 1985)★★★★, *Greatest Hits, Vol. 2* (MCA 1989)★★★.

GREER, JIM
b. James Marvin Greer, 3 September 1942, West Liberty, Logan County, Ohio, USA. Greer was attracted to country music by his sisters, Bonnie and Valeda, who, as the Greer Sisters, sang on several stations in the 50s, including the *Renfro Valley Barn Dance*, on WLW Cincinnati. After learning banjo, guitar and mandolin, he played with them, until

Bonnie tired of the travelling and they disbanded. Greer then formed his Mac-O-Chee Valley Folks, which featured himself on banjo, sister Valeda (guitar), Bob McPherson (guitar, mandolin), Dalton Burroughs (bass), Valeda's husband John Wentz (dobro) and later added Aaron Hicks or Herb Collins (fiddle). They played bluegrass and traditional music, plus a few numbers written by McPherson, as a semi-professional group appearing at various local shows or bluegrass festivals. Between 1965 and 1969, they also played weekly on *Jamboree USA* at WWVA Wheeling, West Virginia. They made their first recordings in the early 60s for Rite and Starday, but later recorded albums for Uncle Jim O'Neal's popular Rural Rhythm label, before returning to Rite's Golden Shield subsidiary for a gospel album. In the mid-70s, the band found themselves faced with a common problem for semi-professional bands. Faced with more work than they could handle on a part-time basis, they had to choose between going fully professional or disbanding. Since all members had full-time occupations that they were hesitant to give up, they reluctantly decided on the latter. Greer concentrated on running his West Liberty clothing store and apart from occasional local appearances has remained inactive. Collins has since died but the remainder of the band stayed in their beloved Mac-O-Chee Valley area.
● ALBUMS: *Bluegrass In Ohio* (Rite 1963)★★★★, *Log Cabin Songs* (Rural Rhythm 1965)★★★, *Memories In Song* (Rural Rhythm 1966)★★★, *Stars Of The WWVA Jamboree* (Rural Rhythm 1966)★★★, *Country Favorites* (Rural Rhythm 1967)★★★, *Gospel Singing Time* (Golden Shield 1970)★★.

GREGG, RICKY LYNN
The 90s country singer Ricky Lynn Gregg is of Native American descent. He formed two rock groups, the Ricky Lynn Project and Head East, and with them opened for Huey Lewis And The News and Heart. He then switched direction to honky tonk country and formed the band Cherokee Thunder with whom he played clubs in Dallas. He reached the US country charts with a revival of Mel Street's 'If I Had A Cheatin' Heart'.
● ALBUMS: *Ricky Lynn Gregg* (Liberty 1993)★★★, *Get A Little Closer* (Liberty 1994)★★★.

GRIBBIN, TOM
b. 2 January 1949, Florida, USA. Gribbin trained as a lawyer but formed a band, the Saltwater Cowboys, for weekend work. They mixed country with rock and Caribbean influences. To add to their diversity, they recorded the Clash's song 'Guns Of Brixton', but following the Brixton riots in south London, England, the record was considered too sensitive for UK airplay. Gribbin and his band were surprisingly well received at the Wembley Country Music Festival, which is usually a graveyard for more radical acts. His first album, *Son Of Lightning*, was issued with two distinct covers, one for the shops and one for Wembley. For a short period, Gribbin looked as though he might be the first new-wave country star to become established in the UK, but it did not happen.
● ALBUMS: *Son Of Lightning* (Country Roads 1981)★★★, *Useppa Island Rendezvous* (Range 1984)★★★.

GRIFF, RAY
b. John Ray Griff, 22 April 1940, Vancouver, Canada. The family relocated to Winfield, Alberta, where Griff played

drums for the Winfield Amateurs at the age of six. After learning piano and guitar, he was leading his own band on the club circuit by the time he was 18. His songwriting talent was first noted when Johnny Horton recorded 'Mr Moonlight', and in 1964, after recording his song 'Where Do I Go', Jim Reeves suggested Griff move to Nashville, where he worked as a writer and publisher and later formed his own publishing company. He eventually made some recordings and first reached the US country charts with 'Your Lily White Hands' in 1967. Recording for several different labels throughout the 70s, he had several minor hits, including his personal account, 'The Last Of The Winfield Amateurs', and Top 20 success with 'The Morning After Baby Let Me Down', 'You Ring My Bell' and 'If I Let Her Come In'. He also had his own television series on CBC. Among his popular songs recorded by other artists are 'Canadian Pacific' (George Hamilton IV), 'It Rains Just The Same In Missouri' (Mac Wiseman), 'Better Move It On Home' (Porter Wagoner and Dolly Parton), 'Step Aside' (Faron Young), 'Baby' (Wilma Burgess) and 'Who's Gonna Play This Old Piano' (Jerry Lee Lewis). Griff, in common with Mel Tillis, initially suffered from a stutter, but like Tillis, he has overcome his problem to find success in country music.

● ALBUMS: *A Ray Of Sunshine* (Dot 1968)★★★, *Ray Griff Sings* (1972)★★★, *Songs For Everyone* (1973)★★★, *Expressions* (1974)★★, *Ray Griff* (1976)★★★, *Last Of The Winfield Amateurs* (1976)★★★, *Raymond's Place* (1977)★★★, *Canada* (1979)★★★, *Maple Leaf* (1980)★★★, *Adam's Child* (1981)★★.

GRIFFIN, REX

b. 12 August 1912, Gasden, Alabama, USA, d. 11 October 1959. Griffin remains one of the relative unknowns of country music, except as the writer of a country classic. One popular theory, probably based on his accent, was that he was a Texan. He played guitar (he could also play piano) in string bands and worked on radio stations all over the south, before arriving in Dallas in the early 30s. He starred on KRLD's *Texas Roundup Show* and soon established a reputation across the station's broadcasting area. Between March 1935 and September 1939, Griffin recorded 36 sides for Decca. They included a mixture of yodels such as 'The Yodeling Cowboy's Last Song' and 'Love Call Yodel', which reflected his love of Jimmie Rodgers' work, and sentimental ballads such as 'Just For Old Time's Sake' and 'An Old Faded Photograph'. After the first four recordings, on which he was accompanied by banjoist Johnny Motlow, the majority of the recordings featured only Griffin and his guitar; on the last five, he was backed by the guitar and bass of Ted (Brooks) and Smitty (Smith). Undoubtedly his greatest claim to fame is as the writer of 'The Last Letter', which he recorded on 13 May 1937. The song, which he wrote in the Tutweiler Hotel, New Orleans, is now far better known than any facts about its writer. It has since been recorded by countless artists, including Gene Autry, Connie Smith, Ernest Tubb, Marty Robbins, Waylon Jennings, Willie Nelson (who had a country hit with it in 1976) and, perhaps more surprisingly, by old-time artists such as the Blue Sky Boys and the Carter Family. Griffin's version proved so popular that he recorded 'Answer To The Last Letter' on 25 September 1939. Further Griffin songs that became hits for other artists include 'My Hillbilly Baby' (Ernest Tubb) and 'Just Call Me Lonesome', a hit for

both Eddy Arnold and Jim Reeves. It would seem that Griffin worked with Hank Williams in the mid-40s and some have suggested that Williams' 1948 recording of 'Lovesick Blues', which launched him to stardom, bears more than a passing resemblance in delivery and yodel style to the version that Griffin recorded in September 1939. Griffin's version, in turn, bore comparison to the 1923 recording by blues singer Emmett Miller. By the late 40s, Griffin had disappeared from the music scene. The date and location of his death is unknown but he merits remembrance as an early pioneer of the genre of 'honky tonk' songs.

● COMPILATIONS: *Last Letter* 3-CD box set (Bear Family 1996)★★★.

GRIFFITH, NANCI

b. 6 July 1953, Seguin, Texas, USA. Singer-songwriter Griffith brilliantly straddles the boundary between folk and country music, with occasional nods to the mainstream rock audience. Her mother was an amateur actress and her father a member of a barbershop quartet. They passed on their interest in performance to Nanci, and although she majored in education at the University of Texas, she eventually chose a career in music in 1977, by which time she had been performing in public for 10 years. In 1978 her first album, *There's A Light Beyond These Woods*, was released by a local company, BF Deal Records. Recorded live in a studio in Austin, it featured mainly her own compositions, along with 'Dollar Matinee', written by her erstwhile husband Eric Taylor. The most notable song on the album was the title track, and as a souvenir of her folk act of the time, the album was adequate. In 1982, *Poet In My Window* was released by another local label, Featherbed Records; like its predecessor, this album was re-released in 1986 by the nationally distributed Philo/Rounder label. It displayed a pleasing maturity in composition, the only song not written by Griffith herself being 'Tonight I Think I'm Gonna Go Downtown', penned by Jimmie Gilmore and John Reed (once again, Eric Taylor was involved as associate producer/bass player), while the barbershop quartet in which her father, Marlin Griffith, sang provided harmony vocals on 'Wheels'.

By 1984 she had met Jim Rooney, who produced her third album, *Once In A Very Blue Moon*, released in 1985 by Philo/Rounder. This album featured such notable backing musicians as lead guitarist Phillip Donnelly, banjo wizard Bela Fleck, Lloyd Green and Mark O'Connor. It was recorded at Jack Clement's Nashville studio. As well as more of her own songs, the album included her version of Lyle Lovett's 'If I Was The Woman You Wanted', Richard Dobson's 'Ballad Of Robin Wintersmith' and the superb title track written by Pat Alger - Griffith named the backing band she formed in 1986 the Blue Moon Orchestra. Following on the heels of this artistic triumph came 1986's *Last Of The True Believers*. Released by Philo/Rounder, the album had a similar feel to its predecessor, and one that set it apart from run-of-the-mill albums by singer-songwriters. It included two songs that would later achieve US country chart celebrity as covered by Kathy Mattea, Griffith's own 'Love At The Five And Dime' and Pat Alger's 'Goin' Gone', as well as several other songs that would become Griffith classics, including the title track, 'The Wing And The Wheel' (which inspired Griffith's music publishing company), 'More Than A Whisper' and 'Lookin' For The Time (Working Girl)', plus the fine Tom Russell song

'St. Olav's Gate'. The album became Griffith's first to be released in the UK when it was licensed by Demon Records. Signed by MCA Records, her debut album for the label, *Lone Star State Of Mind*, was released in 1987, and was produced by MCA's golden-fingered Tony Brown, the influential A&R representative in Nashville who had signed Steve Earle and Lyle Lovett as well as Griffith herself (she also co-produced the album). The stunning title track again involved Alger as writer, while other notable tracks included the remake of 'There's A Light Beyond These Woods' from the first album, Robert Earl Keen Jnr.'s 'Sing One For Sister' and Griffith's own 'Ford Econoline' (about the independence of 60s folk singer Rosalie Sorrels). However, attracting most attention was Julie Gold's 'From A Distance', a song that became a standard by the 90s as covered by Bette Midler, Cliff Richard and many others, but which received its first major exposure with Griffith's own version. *Little Love Affairs*, released in 1988, was supposedly a concept album, but major songs included 'Outbound Plane', which she co-wrote with Tom Russell, veteran hit writer Harlan Howard's '(My Best Pal's In Nashville) Never Mind' and John Stewart's 'Sweet Dreams Will Come', as well as a couple of collaborations with James Hooker (ex-Amazing Rhythm Aces), and keyboard player of the Blue Moon Orchestra. Later that year Griffith recorded and released a live album, *One Fair Summer Evening*, recorded at Houston's Anderson Fair Retail Restaurant. Although it only included a handful of songs that she had not previously recorded, it was at least as good as *Little Love Affairs*, and was accompanied by a live video. However, it seemed that Griffith's appeal was falling between the rock and country audiences, the latter apparently finding her voice insufficiently radio-friendly, while Kathy Mattea, who recorded many of the same songs some time after Griffith, became a major star.

In 1989 came *Storms*, produced by the legendary Glyn Johns, who had worked with the Beatles, the Rolling Stones, the Eagles, Steve Miller, the Who, Joan Armatrading and many others. Johns deliberately geared the album's sound towards American radio, and it became Griffith's biggest seller. The album featured Hooker, Irish drummer Bran Breen (ex-Moving Hearts), Bernie Leadon (ex-Eagles), guitarist Albert Lee and Phil Everly of the Everly Brothers providing harmony vocals on 'You Made This Love A Teardrop'. Although it was a sales breakthrough for Griffiths, it failed to attract country audiences, although it reached the album chart in the UK, where she had regularly toured since 1987. However, her major European market was Ireland, where she was accorded near-superstar status. *Late Night Grande Hotel* was produced by the British team of Rod Argent and Peter Van Hook, and again included a duet with Phil Everly on 'It's Just Another Morning Here', while English singer Tanita Tikaram provided a guest vocal on 'It's Too Late'. In 1991, singing 'The Wexford Carol', she was one of a number of artists who contributed tracks to the Chieftains' *The Bells Of Dublin*. *Other Voices Other Rooms* was a wholehearted success artistically and commercially. Griffith interpreted some outstanding songs by artists such as Bob Dylan ('Boots Of Spanish Leather'), John Prine ('Speed Of The Sound Of Loneliness') and Ralph McTell ('From Clare To Here'). *Flyer*, another exquisite record, maintained her popularity with some excellent new material that indicated a strengthening and hardening of her vocals, with greater power and a hint of treble. She continues to fail to put a foot wrong.

● ALBUMS: *There's A Light Beyond These Woods* (BF Deal 1978)★★, *Poet In My Window* (Featherbed 1982)★★, *Once In A Very Blue Moon* (Philo 1985)★★★, *Last Of The True Believers* (Philo 1986)★★★★, *Lone Star State Of Mind* (MCA 1987)★★★★, *Little Love Affairs* (MCA 1988)★★★★, *One Fair Summer Evening* (MCA 1988)★★★★, *Storms* (MCA 1989)★★★★, *Late Night Grande Hotel* (MCA 1991)★★★★, *Other Voices Other Rooms* (Elektra 1993)★★★★, *Flyer* (Elektra 1994)★★★★, *Blue Roses From The Moon* (East West 1997)★★★★.

● COMPILATIONS: *The Best Of* (MCA 1993)★★★★.

GRISMAN, DAVID

b. 1945, Hackensack, New Jersey, USA. An accomplished mandolinist, Grisman forged his reputation on the mid-60s US bluegrass circuit as a member of several New York-based attractions, including the Washington Square Ramblers, the Galaxy Mountain Boys and the Even Dozen Jug Band. In 1966 Grisman joined Red Allen and the Kentuckians, but the following year teamed with fellow enthusiast and songwriter Peter Rowan in the Boston rock act Earth Opera. This fascinating unit completed two albums, after which Grisman moved to San Francisco where he renewed an acquaintance with Grateful Dead guitarist Jerry Garcia. The mandolinist contributed to the group's stellar *American Beauty* before participating in several informal aggregations, notably Muleskinner, Old And In The Way and the Great American String Band. Grisman then recorded as a solo act, and as leader of the David Grisman Quartet, which initially included Tony Rice (guitar), Darol Anger (fiddle) and Todd Phillips and/or Bill Amatneck (bass). The group pursued a hybrid of jazz and bluegrass, dubbed 'Dawg Music', and remained a highly inventive attraction despite numerous line-up changes. Grisman's reputation within America's traditional music fraternity grew throughout the 70s and 80s. He built a recording studio at his Mill Valley home and in 1990 founded the Acoustic Disc label. An early release, *Dawg 90*, received a Grammy nomination in the country instrumental category, and was followed in 1991 by a further collaboration with long-time associate Jerry Garcia.

● ALBUMS: *The David Grisman Album* (Rounder 1976)★★★★, *The David Grisman Quintet* (Rhino 1977)★★★, *Hot Dawg* (A&M 1979)★★★, *David Grisman And John Sholle* (1979)★★★, *Quintet: 80* (Warners 1980)★★★, with Stéphane Grappelli *Live* (1980)★★★★, *Mondo Mando* (Warners 1981)★★★, *Here Today* (Rounder 1982)★★★, *Dawg Jazz - Dawg Grass* (Warners 1983)★★★, *Acoustic Christmas* (1983)★★, with Andy Statman *Mandolin Abstractions* (Rounder 1983)★★★, *Acousticity* (Zebra 1985)★★★, *Home Is Where The Heart Is* (Rounder 1988)★★★, *Dawg 90* (Acoustic Disc 1990)★★★, with Jerry Garcia *Garcia Grisman* (Acoustic Disc 1991)★★★, *Bluegrass Reunion* (Acoustic Disc 1992)★★★★, with Jerry Garcia *Not For Kids Only* (1993)★★★, *Dawgood* (Acoustic Disc 1993)★★★, *Tone Poems* (Acoustic Disc 1994)★★★, *Dawganova* (Acoustic Disc 1995)★★★, *Tone Poems 2* (Acoustic Disc 1995)★★★, *DGQ-20* (Acoustic Disc 1996)★★★.

● COMPILATIONS: *Early Dawg* (Sugar Hill 1980)★★★.

● VIDEOS: *Muleskinner - Live Video* (1991).

GUITAR, BONNIE

b. Bonnie Buckingham, 25 March 1923, Seattle, Washington, USA. She learned several instruments as a child, was a talented guitarist and began to write songs before she completed her education. In the early 50s she recorded for Fabor and in the mid-50s worked as a session guitarist in Los Angeles. She made her debut in the US country charts in 1957 on Dot Records with her own song 'Dark Moon'. In 1958 she formed her own Dolton label in Seattle and began to record various local acts, including a pop trio called the Fleetwoods, who in 1959 had two million-selling records on her label with 'Come Softly To Me' and 'Mr Blue'. Her instrumental work, production and recording abilities with the Fleetwoods attracted the attention of Dot; wishing to concentrate on her own career, she sold Dolton and worked for Dot and ABC-Paramount, both on A&R and production and as a recording artist. In the 60s she had Top 10 country hits with 'I'm Living In Two Worlds', '(You've Got Yourself) A Woman In Love' (her biggest hit) and 'I Believe In Love'. In 1969 she also had a minor hit with 'A Truer Love You'll Never Find', a duet recording with Buddy Killen issued as Bonnie And Buddy. She also worked with songwriter Don Robertson and recorded 'Born To Be With You' with him as the Echoes. She was a popular touring artist in the 60s and early 70s, often working with Eddy Arnold. During the 70s, she recorded for Columbia and MCA and her last chart entry was a minor hit entitled 'Honey On The Moon' in 1980, by which time she had moved to the 4 Star label. In 1986 after a long absence, she doubtless pleased her fans by releasing two albums, called *Yesterday* and *Today*. She continues to record and change record labels with alarming regularity.

● ALBUMS: *Moonlight & Shadows* (Dot 1957)★★★, *Whispering Hope* (Dot 1959)★★★, *Dark Moon* (Dot 1962)★★★★, *Bonnie Guitar Sings* (Dolton 1965)★★★, *Merry Christmas From Bonnie Guitar* (Dot 1966)★★, *Miss Bonnie Guitar* (Dot 1966)★★★, *Two Worlds* (Dot 1966)★★★, *Favorite Lady Of Song* (Dot 1967)★★, *Green Green Grass Of Home* (Dot 1967)★★, *Bonnie Guitar-Award Winner* (Dot 1967)★★, *I Believe In Love* (Dot 1968)★★★, *Leaves Are The Tears Of Autumn* (1968)★★★, *Stop The Sun/A Woman In Love* (1968)★★, *Affair* (1969)★★★, *Night Train To Memphis* (1969)★★★, *Allegheny* (1970)★★, *Yesterday* (Tumbleweed 1986)★★★, *Today* (Tumbleweed 1986)★★★, *You're Still The Same* (Playback 1989)★★★.

● COMPILATIONS: *Dark Moon* (Bear Family 1991)★★★★.

GULLY JUMPERS

(see Warmack, Paul, And The Gully Jumpers)

GUTHRIE, WOODY

b. Woodrow Wilson Guthrie, 14 July 1912, Okemah, Oklahoma, USA, d. 3 October 1967, New York City, New York, USA. A major figure of America's folk heritage, Guthrie was raised in a musical environment and achieved proficiency on harmonica as a child. By the age of 16 he had begun his itinerant lifestyle, performing in a Texas-based magic show where he learned to play guitar. In 1935 Guthrie moved to California where he became a regular attraction on Los Angeles' KFVD radio station. Having befriended singer Cisco Houston and actor Will Geer, Guthrie established his left wing-oriented credentials with joint appearances at union meetings and migrant labour camps. Already a prolific songwriter, his reactions to the poverty he witnessed inspired several of his finest compositions, notably 'Pastures Of Plenty', 'Dust Bowl Refugees', 'Vigilante Man' and 'This Land Is Your Land', regarded by many as America's 'alternative' national anthem. Guthrie was also an enthusiastic proponent of Roosevelt's 'New Deal', as demonstrated by 'Grand Coolie Dam' and 'Roll On Columbia', while his children's songs, including 'Car Car', were both simple and charming. At the end of the 30s Guthrie travelled to New York where he undertook a series of recordings for the folk song archive at the Library Of Congress. The 12 discs he completed were later released commercially by Elektra Records.

Guthrie continued to traverse the country and in 1940 met Pete Seeger at a folk-song rally in California. Together they formed the Almanac Singers with Lee Hayes and Millard Lampell, which in turn inspired the Almanac House, a co-operative apartment in New York's Greenwich Village which became the focus of the east coast folk movement. In 1942 Guthrie joined the short-lived Headline Singers with Lead Belly, Sonny Terry and Brownie McGhee, before beginning his autobiography, *Bound For Glory*, which was published the following year. He and Houston then enlisted in the merchant marines, where they remained until the end of World War II, after which Guthrie began a series of exemplary recordings for the newly founded Folkways label. The artist eventually completed over 200 masters which provided the fledgling company with a secure foundation. Further sessions were undertaken for other outlets, while Guthrie retained his commitment to the union movement through columns for the *Daily Worker* and *People's World*. Guthrie's prolific output - he conscientiously composed every day - continued unabated until the end of the 40s when he succumbed to Huntington's Chorea, a hereditary, degenerative disease of the nerves. He was hospitalized in 1952, and was gradually immobilized by this wasting illness until he could barely talk or recognize friends and visitors. By the time of his death on 3 October 1967, Woody Guthrie was enshrined in America's folklore, not just because of his own achievements, but through his considerable influence on a new generation of artists. Bob Dylan, Ramblin' Jack Elliott, Roger McGuinn and Woody's son Arlo Guthrie were among his most obvious disciples, but the great number of performers, including Judy Collins, Tom Paxton, Richie Havens and Country Joe McDonald, gathered at two subsequent tribute concerts, confirmed their debt to this pivotal figure.

● ALBUMS: *Dust Bowl Ballads* 1940 recording (Folkways 1950)★★★★, *More Songs By Guthrie* (Meldisc 1955)★★★, *Songs To Grow On* (Folkways 1958)★★★, *Struggle* (Folkways 1958)★★★, *Bound For Glory* (Folkways 1958)★★★★, *Sacco & Vanzetti* (1960)★★★★, *Dust Bowl Ballads* 1940 recordings (Rounder 1964)★★★★, *Library Of Congress Recordings* 1940 recordinga (Folkways 1964)★★★★, *Bed On The Floor* (Verve/Folkways 1965)★★★, *Woodie Guthrie* (Xtra 1965)★★★, *Bonneville Dam And Other Columbia River Songs* (Verve/Folkways 1965)★★★, *Poor Boy* (Xtra 1966)★★★, *This Land Is Your Land* (Smithsonian/Folkways 1967)★★★★.

● COMPILATIONS: *The Greatest Songs Of Woody Guthrie* (Vanguard 1972)★★★★, *Woodie Guthrie* (Ember 1968)★★★, *A Legendary Performer* (RCA 1977)★★★, *Poor Boy* (Transatlantic 1981)★★★, *Columbia River Collection* (Rounder 1988)★★★, *Folkways: The Original Vision*

(1989)★★★★, *Long Ways To Travel The Unreleased Folkways Masters 1944-1949* (Smithsonian/Folkways 1994)★★★★, *Woody Guthrie Sings Folk Songs* (Smithsonian/ Folkways 1995)★★★, *Ballads Of Sacco & Vanzetti* (Smithsonian/Folkways 1996)★★★.
● VIDEOS: *Vision Shared: A Tribute To Woody Guthrie* (CMV Enterprises 1989).
● FURTHER READING: *Woody Guthrie Folk Songs*, Woody Guthrie. *American Folksong*, Woody Guthrie. *Born To Win*, Woody Guthrie and Robert Shelton (ed.). *A Mighty Hard Road: The Woody Guthrie Story*, Henrietta Yurchenco. *Bound For Glory*, Woody Guthrie. *Seeds Of Man: An Experience Lived And Dreamed*, Woody Guthrie. *Woody Guthrie: A Life*, Joe Klein. *Pastures Of Plenty-A Self Portrait*, Woody Guthrie. *Woody Guthrie: Roll On Columbia*, Bill Murlin (ed.).

HAGERS

John Hager (guitar, harmonica, drums, vocals) and Jim Hager (guitar, drums, vocals) were identical twins (b. 30 August 1946, Chicago, Illinois, USA, John being the elder by 20 minutes). They were adopted by Rev. John Hager and his wife and grew up with a love for music which, in their teens, saw them perform on local radio and television. They served in Germany and Vietnam during their US Army service and regularly entertained their fellow servicemen. After discharge, they spent two years working in a trio in the Chicago area, before relocating to California. They played at Disneyland and had a club residency, until Buck Owens made them part of his touring show for the next two years. In 1969, they became members of the cast of the popular *Hee Haw* television show and their vocals, comedy routines and impersonations saw them remain show favourites for 18 years, until 1987. They were signed by Capitol Records in 1969, and gained their first chart hit with the oddly titled 'Gotta Get To Oklahoma (Cause California's Getting To Me)'. In 1970, they registered three more Top 75 hits, including a version of Merle Haggard's now much recorded 'Silver Wings'. In 1971, their final entry, 'I'm Miles Away', just reached the Top 50 and proved prophetically correct as far as further hits were concerned. During the 70s, they recorded without chart success for Barnaby and Elektra Records and toured with their country show. They have also made successful acting appearances, including roles in the film *Twin Detectives* for ABC-TV in 1976, and in 1987, they co-pre-

sented *Country Kitchen* on TNN. Their uniqueness as identical twins has led to many television appearances, as well as work on commercials. In the 90s, they became noted for hosting their major annual fishing competition at Lakewood, Wisconsin, which they organize to benefit charities.
● ALBUMS: *The Hagers* (Capitol 1970)★★★, *Two Hagers Are Better Than One* (Capitol 1970)★★★, *Motherhood, Apple Pie And The Flag* (Capitol 1971)★★, *Countryside* (Barnaby 1972)★★, *The Hagers* (Elektra 1974)★★★.

HAGGARD, MERLE

b. 6 April 1937, Bakersfield, California, USA. 'Like a razor's edge, Merle Haggard sings' is how John Stewart described his voice in 'Eighteen Wheels', and that razor has been honed by his rough and rowdy ways. In the 30s Haggard's parents migrated from the Dustbowl to 'the land of milk and honey', California. Life, however, was almost as bleak there and Haggard himself was born in a converted boxcar. His father, who worked on the Santa Fe railway, died of a stroke when Haggard was nine. Many of Haggard's songs are about those early years: 'Mama's Hungry Eyes', 'California Cottonfields', 'They're Tearin' The Labour Camps Down' and 'The Way It Was In '51'. Haggard became a tearaway who, despite the efforts of his Christian mother ('Mama Tried'), spent many years in reform schools. When only 17, he married a waitress and they had four children during their ten years together. His wife showed disdain for his singing and Haggard says, 'Any listing of famous battlefields should include my marriage to Leona Hobbs'. Haggard provided for the children through manual labour and armed robbery. He was sent to San Quentin in 1957, charged with burglary; a Johnny Cash concert in January 1958 led to him joining the prison band. Songs from his prison experiences include 'Sing Me Back Home' and 'Branded Man'. Back in Bakersfield in 1960, Haggard started performing and found work accompanying Wynn Stewart. Only 200 copies were pressed of his first single, 'Singing My Heart Out', but he made the national charts with his second, Stewart's composition 'Sing A Sad Song', for the small Tally label. Capitol took over his contract and reissued '(All My Friends Are Going To Be) Strangers' in 1965. The record's success prompted him to call his band the Strangers, its mainstays being Roy Nichols on lead guitar and Norm Hamlet on steel. When 'I'm A Lonesome Fugitive' became a country number 1 in 1966, it was clear that a country star with a prison record was a very commercial proposition. Haggard recorded an album of love songs with his second wife, Bonnie Owens, but, despite its success, they never repeated it. In 1969 a chance remark on the tour bus led to him writing 'Okie From Muskogee', a conservative reply to draft-card burning and flower power. President Nixon declared Haggard his favourite country singer, while Ronald Reagan, then Governor of California, gave him a full pardon. Johnny Cash refused to perform the song at the White House and Phil Ochs, a spearhead of youth culture, sang it to annoy his own fans. Some suggest that the irony in Haggard's song has been overlooked, but he has since confirmed his dislike of hippies - though several rock bands, notably the Beach Boys, performed the song as a piece of counter-culture irony. Haggard sang more specifically about anti-Vietnam demonstrators in 'The Fightin' Side Of Me', but his song about an interracial love affair, 'Irma Jackson', was not released at first because Capitol thought it would harm his image. Around this time, Haggard wrote and recorded several glorious singles that rank with the best of country music and illustrate his personal credo: 'I Take A Lot Of Pride In What I Am', 'Silver Wings', 'Today I Started Loving You Again' and 'If We Make It Through December'. He also sang songs by other writers, notably Tommy Collins, and recorded tributes to Jimmie Rodgers (a double album, *Same Train, A Different Time*), Bob Wills (an album showing that Haggard is a fine fiddle player) and Lefty Frizzell (the song 'Goodbye Lefty'). Another of Haggard's consuming passions was model trains and he recorded an album titled *My Love Affair With Trains*. Like most successful country artists, he has also recorded Christmas and religious albums, *The Land Of Many Churches* being partly recorded at San Quentin jail (Haggard has not officially recorded a full prison album because he does not want to copy Johnny Cash). Between 1973 and 1976, Haggard achieved nine consecutive number 1 records on the US country charts and his tally of number 1 records has been surpassed only by Conway Twitty. In 1977, shortly after moving to MCA, he recorded a touching tribute album to Elvis Presley with the Jordanaires. In 1978 he divorced Bonnie Owens and married a backing singer, Leona Williams. She wrote several songs for him and also recorded a duet album, but in 1984, they too were divorced (Haggard divorced his fourth wife in 1991). Haggard had often written about alcohol ('Swinging Doors', 'The Bottle Let Me Down'), but his MCA albums reveal an increasing concern about his own drinking habits. Less introspective following a move to Epic in 1981, he had a major country hit with a revival of 'Poncho And Lefty' with Willie Nelson. He still writes prolifically ('I Wish Things Were Simple Again', 'Let's Chase Each Other Around The Room'), but he also revives songs of yesteryear, including 'There! I've Said It Again' and 'Sea Of Heartbreak'. Coming full circle, *Amber Waves Of Grain* showed his concern for the plight of the American farmer. Haggard appears pained and sad on most of his album covers, but this does not detract from the quality of his work. He has refused to compromise - for example, 'My Own Kind Of Hat'. By 1990 he had the incredible tally of 95 country hits on the *Billboard* chart, including a remarkable 38 chart toppers. Early in 1993, Haggard was declared bankrupt, though this setback seemed to do nothing to dampen his enthusiasm for touring. Although many of the 'new hats acts' owe much to Haggard, notably Randy Travis and Clint Black, Haggard himself became old hat for a couple of years. The reassessment of his work started with two tribute albums by contemporary performers, *Mama's Hungry Eyes* and *Tulare Dust*, and some fine recent work by the man himself. He also wrote 'Untanglin' My Mind' with Black. He was inducted into the Country Music Hall Of Fame and released *1996* shortly afterwards.

● ALBUMS: *Strangers* (Capitol 1965)★★★, with Bonnie Owens *Just Between The Two Of Us* (Capitol 1966)★★★, *Swinging Doors/The Bottle Let Me Down* (Capitol 1966)★★★, *I'm A Lonesome Fugitive* (Capitol 1967)★★★, *Branded Man* (Capitol 1967)★★★, *Sing Me Back Home* (Capitol 1968)★★★, *The Legend Of Bonnie And Clyde* (Capitol 1968)★★★, *Mama Tried* (Capitol 1968)★★★★, *Pride In What I Am* (Capitol 1969)★★★, *Instrumental Sounds Of Merle Haggard's Strangers* (Capitol 1969)★★★, *Same Train, Different Time* (Capitol 1969)★★★, *A Portrait Of Merle Haggard* (1969)★★★, *Okie From Muskogee* (Capitol 1970)★★★★, *Introducing My Friends, The Strangers* (Capitol 1970)★★★, *The Fightin' Side Of Me* (Capitol 1970)★★★, *A Tribute To The Best Damn Fiddle Player In The World (Or, My Salute To Bob Wills)* (Capitol 1970)★★★★, *Getting To Know Merle Haggard's Strangers* (Capitol 1970)★★★, *Hag* (Capitol 1971)★★★, *Honky Tonkin'* (Capitol 1971)★★★, *Someday We'll Look Back* (Capitol 1971)★★★, with Bonnie Owens, Carter Family *The Land Of Many Churches* (Capitol 1971)★★★, *Let Me Tell You About A Song* (Capitol 1972)★★★, *It's Not Love, But It's Not Bad* (Capitol 1972)★★★, *Totally Instrumental (With One Exception)* (Capitol 1973)★★★, *I Love Dixie Blues ... So I Recorded 'Live' In New Orleans* (Capitol 1973)★★★, *Merle Haggard's Christmas Present* (Capitol 1973)★★, *If We Make It Through December* (Capitol 1974)★★, *Merle Haggard Presents His 30th Album* (Capitol 1974)★★, *Keep Movin' On* (Capitol 1975)★★★, *It's All In The Movies* (Capitol 1976)★★, *My Love Affair With Trains* (Capitol 1976)★★★, *The Roots Of My Raising* (Capitol 1976)★★★, *Ramblin' Fever* (1977)★★★, *A Working Man Can't Get Nowhere Today* (1977)★★★, *My Farewell To Elvis - From Graceland To The Promised Land* (MCA 1977)★★★, *I'm Always On A Mountain When I Fall* (MCA 1978)★★★, *Serving 190 Proof* (MCA 1979)★★★, *The Way I Am* (MCA 1980)★★★, *Back To The Barrooms* (MCA 1980)★★★, *Rainbow Stew - Live At Anaheim Stadium* (MCA 1981)★★★, with Johnny Paycheck *Mr Hag Told My Story* (Epic 1981)★★★, *Songs For The Mama That Tried* (1981)★★★, *Big City* (Epic 1981)★★★, *Goin' Where The Lonely Go* (Epic 1982)★★★, with George Jones *A Taste Of Yesterday's Wine* (Epic 1982)★★★, *Going Home For Christmas* (Epic 1982)★★★, with Willie Nelson *Poncho And Lefty* (Epic 1983)★★★, with Leona Williams *Heart To Heart* (Mercury 1983)★★★, *That's The Way Love Goes* (Epic 1983)★★★, *The Epic Collection - Live* (Epic 1983)★★★, *It's All In The Game* (Epic 1984)★★★, *Kern River* (Epic 1985)★★★, *Amber Waves Of Grain* (Epic 1985)★★★, *Out Among The Stars* (Epic 1986)★★★, *A Friend In California* (Epic 1986)★★★, with Nelson *Seashores Of Old Mexico* (Epic 1987)★★★, *Chill Factor* (Epic 1988)★★★, *5:01 Blues* (Epic 1989)★★★, *Blue Jungle* (Curb 1990)★★★, *1994* (Curb 1994)★★★, *1996* (Curb 1996)★★★.

● COMPILATIONS: *Best Of Merle Haggard* (Capitol 1968)★★★, *Truly The Best Of Merle Haggard* (Capitol 1971)★★★★, *Songs I'll Always Sing* (Capitol 1976)★★★★, *Country Boy* (Pair 1978)★★★, *His Epic Hits: First Eleven To Be Continued* (Epic 1984)★★★, *Greatest Hits Of The 80s* (Epic 1990)★★★, *The Best Of Country Blues* (Curb 1990)★★★, *Capitol Collectors Series* (Capitol 1990)★★★, *More Of The Best* (Rhino 1990)★★★★, *18 Rare Classics* (Curb 1991)★★★, *Best Of The Early Years* (Curb 1991)★★★, *Super Hits* (Epic 1993)★★★, *Lonesome Fugitive: The Merle Haggard Anthology (1963-1977)* (Razor & Tie 1995)★★★★, *Untamed Hawk* 5-CD box set (Bear Family 1995)★★★★, *Vintage* (Capitol 1996)★★★, *Down Every Road* (Capitol 1996)★★★★, *Poet Of The Common Man* (Curb 1997)★★★★.

● VIDEOS: *The Best Of Merle Haggard* (1989), *Country Legends Live* (Prism 1990), *Same Train - A Different Time* (Bear Family 1993), *In Concert* (1993), *Poet Of The Common Man Plus Live In Concert* (Massive Video 1997).

● FURTHER READING: *Sing Me Back Home*, Merle Haggard with Peggy Russell.

HAGUE, MEL

b. 20 January 1943, Whiston, Rotherham, South Yorkshire, England. Though born in England, Hague grew up in Canada, where he first discovered his love of country music. He had moved there at age eight to obtain treatment for the cerebral palsy condition from which he suffered (doctors had originally diagnosed him as unlikely ever to walk). On arrival back in Rotherham, England, in 1961, he formed his first group, the Paladins, before putting together the Westernaires trio three years later. This outfit continued to tour widely, winning the West Country Music Association Most Entertaining Band Award in 1973 - which led to a recording contract with Jim Fowley, head of Look Records. A debut album, *The Winner*, was released, showcasing Hague's songwriting skills on tracks such as 'Don't Call Me A Cowboy', 'Lisa' and 'As Close To Me As You'. The band continued until 1976 when Hague went solo. Among many awards he has collected on his travels are the Daily Mirror's Golden Guitar Award (in a nationwide ballot sponsored by Aria Guitars) and nominations for the Top British Country Music Songwriter by the Country Music Association (coming second two years running). He has also worked extensively promoting country music on local radio, and raised money for the 1981 Year Of The Disabled by riding a bicycle from Doncaster to Wembley, arriving in time for the festival there (he had never ridden a bike before). In 1987 Hague elected to return to a band format, adding Nick Strutt (guitars, mandolin), Andy Seward (bass) and John Firminger (drums).

● ALBUMS: with the Westernaires *The Winner* (Look 1975)★★★★, *Old Gravel Boots* (Look 1977)★★★, *Live* (Look 1978)★★, *Merry Go Round* (Look 1979)★★★ *Live At The Queen Bess* (OGB 1981)★★, *I've Turned The Corner* (OGB 1984)★★★. As Mel Hague Band *What Is Done, Is Done* (OGB 1989)★★★, *Don't Want You Knockin' On My Door* (New Country 1992)★★★.

● VIDEOS: *Live In Blackpool* (1992).

HALE, MONTE

b. 8 June 1921, San Angelo, Texas, USA. He learned to ride, rope, play guitar and sing as a boy and entertained at local venues in the early 40s. In 1944, he played guitar and sang with Jimmy Wakely, which led to a contract with Republic. Between 1944 and 1946, he appeared in eight films with various cowboy stars before he went on to star with his horse, Pardner, in 19 B-westerns for that studio. The first of these, *Home On The Range* (1946), was the first of the genre that Republic made in colour. Hale was noted for his fancy 'Nudie'-made cowboy shirts and his fine singing voice was supported in many of his films by Foy Willing and the Riders Of The Purple Sage. Strangely, by the time he played his last cowboy lead in 1950, he no longer sang in the films. He appeared in some non-westerns including *Giant* (1955) and taught the star, James Dean, the rope trick that he had to perform in the film. During the 50s and 60s, he played in various television programmes, including *Tales Of Wells Fargo*. He recorded for Beltone and MGM in the late 40s, without major success. He apparently never showed any great ambition to be a star, usually professing that he was happier back home on the range. He finally retired to California, where his wife became the director of his great friend Gene Autry's *Western Heritage Museum*, and he continued to appear at rodeos and film festivals.

HALE, THERON, AND HIS DAUGHTERS

b. *c*.1883, Pikeville, Tennessee, USA, d. 1954, Nashville, Tennessee, USA. The fiddle-playing Hale and his two daughters, Mamie Ruth (mandolin, fiddle) and Elizabeth (piano), were one of the early acts on the *Grand Ole Opry*. Hale bought a dairy farm near Nashville around the time of World War I, but for some time he made his living as a sewing machine salesman (he later ran a piano shop in Nashville). The trio played on the *Opry* from 1926 until the early 30s, being especially remembered for their twin fiddle renderings of such numbers as 'Listen To The Mocking Bird' (Theron cleverly produced bird whistles with his fingerwork on the strings), 'Red Wing' and 'Over The Waves'. These twin fiddle harmonies, boosted by Elizabeth's piano accompaniment, gave them a sound that was significantly different to the other early *Opry* bands. In October 1928, when the Victor Company decided to record some of the early *Opry* acts, the Hales became one of the first bands to record in Nashville. They recorded six sides, including 'Mocking Bird', but they were not satisfied with the recordings. They played solely on WSM programmes and never toured. In the early 30s, Mamie Ruth, an excellent musician, left Nashville to get married and later became a violin teacher at Vanderbilt University. Theron (who was also a competent banjoist) and Elizabeth continued for a short time with other musicians taking Mamie Ruth's place, but the act soon folded and Theron quit playing on WSM. He later played some personal appearances with Sam McGee and banjoist Fred Colby.

HALEY SISTERS

Jo-Ann (b. 1973) and Becky (b. 1972) Haley were raised in Harden, West Yorkshire, England. In 1989 they formed the Applejack Trio with Kevin Raymond. The sisters decided to work as a duo in 1990 and they are managed by UK performer Tony Best. In a short time, they were winning UK country music awards and they have toured with Daniel O'Donnell and Raymond Froggatt. They are natural entertainers and their repertoire includes traditional country ('When I Stop Dreaming'), pop hits ('So Sad', 'Breakin' In A Brand New Broken Heart') and new country ('Victim Of The Game' and Sweethearts Of The Rodeo's aptly titled 'Sisters - Best Of Friends'). In 1996 they won the best UK group/duo award in the Great British Country Music Awards.

● ALBUMS: *Cowboys' Sweethearts* cassette only (TBL 1990)★★, with Dave Sheriff *Blue Moon Of Kentucky* (TBL 1991)★★★, *My Side Of The Story* includes most of *Cowboys' Sweethearts* (TBL 1991)★★★★, *Sisters - Best Of Friends* (TBL 1993)★★★, *A Little Bit Of Luck* (Leisure 1995)★★★★

HALL, GARY

b. Preston, Lancashire, England. Hall worked in various bands in Preston as a teenager. For six years from 1986, he worked with the Stormkeepers, playing around 500 gigs and recording his first three albums with them. He produced *Porch Songs* for his fiancée, Cathryn Craig. In 1995 he went to Nashville for *Twelve Strings And Tall Stories*, in which Hall, Craig and the British guitarist Mark Wilkinson tried to capture the feel of his live show. Traces of his musical heroes - Van Morrison, Gram Parsons and Tim Buckley - can be heard in songs such as 'Walk Slowly Through This Life' and 'The Queen Of Broken Dreams'.

● ALBUMS: *Wintertime Already* (Chooglin' 1987)★★★,

Garage Heart (Run River 1989)★★★, *Wide Open To The World* (Run River 1991)★★★, *What Goes Around* (Round Tower 1993)★★★, *Twelve Strings And Tall Stories* (Round Tower 1996)★★.

HALL, HILLMAN

b. 1938, Olive Hill, Kentucky, USA, d. 1989. Hillman was the younger brother of Tom T. Hall and, like his brother, a songwriter of some considerable ability. Some consider that although of similar style, he was a better vocalist than Tom T., even though he failed to register any chart hits. In 1975 he recorded an album of his own songs for Warner Brothers that was produced by Marijohn Wilkin. It included a very witty look at the B-movie western hero in 'Celluloid Cowboy', who was 'meek as a lamb and afraid of his horse', and was so short that the leading lady stood in a hole for the love scenes. His 'You Can't Fool A Country Music Fan' was his personal tribute to country music. He shared his brother's affinity for strange titles, as witnessed by 'Fair To Middlin', Lower Middle Class Plain Hard Working Man', and his 'One Pitcher Is Worth A Thousand Words' was undoubtedly semi-autobiographical. Wilma Burgess charted his 'Parting (Is Such Sweet Sorrow)' in 1969. Hall's album includes his own recording of 'Pass Me By', his biggest success as a songwriter, which, following hit recordings in 1973 by Johnny Rodriguez and in 1980 by Janie Frickie, has become a country standard.
● ALBUMS: *One Pitcher Is Worth A Thousand Words* (Warners 1975)★★★.

HALL, RICK

b. 31 January 1932, Franklin County, Mississippi, USA. Hall played in Carmol Taylor And The Country Pals before forming the Hallmarks. In 1958 he joined the Fairlanes, which included another successful producer-to-be, Billy Sherrill, with whom he started Spar Music and the Florence Alabama Music Enterprises (FAME), together with Tom Stafford. In 1961, differences forced a split; shortly afterwards, Arthur Alexander took a song, 'You Better Move On', to Stafford, who in turn sent Alexander along to Rick Hall. The result was a hit record in 1962, once Hall had managed to lease the master to Dot Records, who then promptly whisked Alexander away from Hall. However, although he had 'lost' Alexander, with the money he made from the singer's initial hit record, Hall was able to lease a studio at Avalon Boulevard, Muscle Shoals. However, it was his success in producing hits at Fame for other nationally distributed independent labels such as Atlantic and Chess that really established Hall's and Muscle Shoals' considerable reputation. A major part in that achievement was played by the several wonderful rhythm sections that Hall recruited to play at his studios, and who would feature on major hits by artists including Clarence Carter, Wilson Pickett, Arthur Conley, Etta James and, later, Candi Staton. Perhaps the best-known line-up of Fame musicians stemmed from the 1966/7 period and comprised Spooner Oldham (keyboards), Jimmy Johnson (guitar), Junior Lowe/David Hood (bass) and Roger Hawkins (drums), with Oldham soon to be replaced by Florida émigré Barry Beckett. It was Oldham, Johnson and Hawkins who played on Aretha Franklin's first and only session at Fame in January 1967, which produced 'I Never Loved A Man (The Way I Love You)'; Jerry Wexler

then 'borrowed' the same musicians for the New York sessions that produced her subsequent Atlantic successes. Many of the early Fame-originated songs came from writers such as Dan Penn, Spooner Oldham, and Donnie Fritts, with Penn in particular also playing an important role as a quasi-producer/A&R representative. After Penn's departure his role at Fame was taken on first by Jimmy Johnson (who also often engineered sessions) and later by multi-talented blind soulman Clarence Carter; however, it was Rick Hall who always remained 'the boss'. In the 70s Hall produced smash hits for acts including the Osmonds, Paul Anka and Bobbie Gentry. In the 80s he returned to country music and is now one of the most successful producers in that field.
● FURTHER READING: *Sweet Soul Music*, Peter Guralnick. *Say It One More Time For The Brokenhearted*, Barney Hoskyns. *Music Fell On Alabama*, Christopher S. Fuqua.

HALL, ROY

b. 6 January 1907, Haywood County, North Carolina, USA, d. 16 May 1943. Roy Hall and his brother Jay Hugh (b. 13 November 1910, Haywood County, North Carolina, USA, d. April 1974), both played guitar and in their teens, they began to entertain while working in the local textile mills. In 1937, they appeared as the Hall Brothers on WSPA Spartanburg, South Carolina, and made their first recordings for Bluebird Records. Further recordings were made in 1938, before the brothers split and Roy formed his string band, the Blue Ridge Entertainers. The band first played WSPA, before moving on to Asheville, Greensboro, Winston-Salem and finally to WDBJ Roanoke, Virginia, where it appeared twice daily. In late 1939, his Saturday evening *Blue Ridge Jamboree* regularly attracted major stars including Tex Ritter and Roy Rogers. Hall was an astute businessman and his show proved so popular that before long, he had to form two bands to meet all the bookings; the second band was led by his brother Jay Hugh, who had rejoined him in 1940 (early in 1940, Jay Hugh appeared and recorded with Clyde Moody and Steve Ledford as The Happy-Go-Lucky Boys). The bands played a mixture of old-time and modern music and were undoubtedly an influence on later bluegrass bands. Hall was one of the first bandleaders to feature the prominent use of the steel guitar. He recorded a 1938 version of 'Wabash Cannonball', which has been compared to Roy Acuff's, and he also recorded 'The Orange Blossom Special' approximately seven months before the Rouse Brothers, although because of a legal argument over publishing rights, it was never released. Among the songs Hall first featured in the early 40s were 'I Wonder Where You Are Tonight' and 'Don't Let Your Sweet Love Die'. By 1945, the sales of the latter exceeded 100,000. Hall did not live to enjoy the record's success, dying in a car crash on 16 May 1943. Jay Hugh Hall remained active in music until 1950 and lived in Roanoke until his death in 1974. (This artist should not be confused with Roy Hall [alias Sunny David], the writer of 'Whole Lotta Shakin' Goin' On', who recorded rockabilly in the 50s.)
● ALBUMS: *Roy Hall & The Blue Ridge Entertainers* (1977)★★★.

HALL, TOM T.

b. 25 May 1936, Olive Hill, Kentucky, USA. Hall was one of eight children and his father was a bricklayer and part-time minister. Hall described the family home as 'a frame house of pale-grey boards and a porch from which to view the dusty road and the promise of elsewhere beyond the hills - the birthplace of a dreamer'. Hall, who started to learn to play a schoolfriend's guitar at the age of 10, was influenced by a local musician who died of tuberculosis when only 22 years old, hence his classic song, 'The Year That Clayton Delaney Died'. Hall's mother died of cancer when he was 13 and, two years later, his father was injured in a shooting accident, which necessitated Hall leaving school to look after the family. A neighbour, Hurley Curtis (who was later the subject of Hall's 'A Song For Uncle Curt'), had a small, travelling cinema and Hall began to accompany him, playing bluegrass with other musicians. Curtis helped to find them a place on a programme on WMOR, Morehead, Kentucky, and Hall broadcast regularly as part of the Kentucky Travellers. When the band broke up, he continued at the station as a DJ, then joined the army in 1957. Several songs ('Salute To A Switchblade', 'I Flew Over Our House Last Night') relate to his army days. On leaving the army in 1961, he returned to WMOR and worked as both a DJ and a musician. He went to Roanoke, Virginia, to study journalism; another song, 'Ode To A Half A Pound Of Ground Round', indicates how little money he had at that time. At one stage, he stayed with an army friend ('Thank you, Connersville, Indiana') and tried to find acceptance in Nashville for his country songs. In 1963, his song 'DJ For A Day' was recorded by Jimmy C. Newman. In 1964 he moved to Nashville and married Iris 'Dixie' Dean, who had emigrated from Weston-super-Mare, England, and was the editor of *Music City News*. Hall wrote several songs about Vietnam - 'Goodbye Sweetheart, Hello Vietnam' (recorded by Johnny Wright) advocates support for the war, while 'Mama, Tell 'Em What We're Fightin' For' (Dave Dudley) assumes another stance. Margie Singleton asked Hall to write her a song like 'Ode To Billie Joe', and he produced 'Harper Valley PTA'; however, it was not passed on to Singleton, who was away at the time. The song instead went to Jeannie C. Riley, who took it to number 1 in the US pop charts. The lyric related to an incident in Hall's childhood; said Hall, 'I wrote about a lady who had criticized a teacher for spanking her child to get at her.' In 1968 Hall signed to Mercury Records, added a middle initial and became Tom T. Hall. His offbeat US country hits included 'Ballad Of 40 Dollars', which had been prompted by working in a graveyard, and the strummed 'Homecoming'. He then topped the US country charts with 'A Week In The County Jail'. Hall's best songs describe people and situations ('Pinto The Wonder Horse Is Dead', 'I Miss A Lot Of Trains'), while his philosophizing is often crass ('The World, The Way I Want It', '100 Children'). The light-hearted 'I Can't Dance' has also been recorded by Gram Parsons with Emmylou Harris, and 'Margie's At The Lincoln Park Inn', a return to the small-town hypocrisy of 'Harper Valley PTA', was a US country hit for Bobby Bare. Bare says, 'That song was written about the Capital Park Inn in Nashville, but he changed the name to protect the guilty. It's a great cheating song, one of the best'. Hall went on an expedition looking for songs and the result was his most consistent work, *In Search Of A Song*. Songs such as 'Ramona's Revenge' and 'Tulsa Telephone Book' described many scenes and moods, and he was backed by superlative Nashville musicians. His next album, *We All Got Together And ...* was not as strong but it did include 'Pamela Brown', in which he thanks a girl for not marrying

him, and 'She Gave Her Heart To Jethro', to which he adds 'and her body to the whole damn world'. *The Storyteller* included his finest song, a perceptive encounter with an ageing black cleaner, 'Old Dogs, Children And Watermelon Wine'. Hall's touring band, the Storytellers, included Johnny Rodriguez, who later became a solo star. Hall recorded with Patti Page and he championed the songwriter Billy Joe Shaver, recording his songs and writing the sleeve notes for his first album. Amongst his numerous awards and honours, Hall won a Grammy for his notes on *Tom T. Hall's Greatest Hits*. Ironically, Hall had his only substantial hit in the US pop charts (number 12 in 1974) with one of his weaker songs, 'I Love', a sentimental list of what he liked. He reworked Manfred Mann's 'Fox On The Run' for his bluegrass album *The Magnificent Music Machine*, and he also made a highly acclaimed, good-natured album with Earl Scruggs. His mellow *Songs In A Seashell* was inspired by a fishing trip and included both original songs and standards. Although his singing range is limited, Hall can be a fine interpreter of others' material, in particular 'P.S. I Love You' and Shel Silverstein's 'Me And Jimmie Rodgers'. In the 80s Hall concentrated on novel-writing and children's songs. He retired from recording in 1986 but, following 1995's box set compilation, a long overdue collection of new, adult songs appeared in 1996. The following year's *Home Grown* was Hall's strongest collection of songs since his 70s heyday.

● ALBUMS: *'The Ballad Of 40 Dollars' And Other Great Songs* (Mercury 1969)★★★, *Homecoming* (Mercury 1969)★★★, *I Witness Life* (Mercury 1970)★★★, *100 Children* (Mercury 1970)★★, *In Search Of A Song* (Mercury 1971)★★★★, *We All Got Together And...* (Mercury 1972)★★, *Tom T. Hall . . . The Storyteller* (Mercury 1972)★★, *The Rhymer And Other Five And Dimers* (Mercury 1973)★★★, *For The People In The Last Hard Town* (Mercury 1973)★★★, *Country Is* (Mercury 1974)★★★, *Songs Of Fox Hollow* (Mercury 1974)★★, *Faster Horses* (Mercury 1976)★★★, *The Magnificent Music Machine* (Mercury 1976)★★★, *About Love* (Mercury 1977)★★, *New Train - Same Rider* (RCA 1978)★★★, *Places I've Done Time* (RCA 1978)★★★, *Saturday Morning Songs* (RCA 1979)★★, *Ol' T's In Town* (RCA 1979)★★★, *Soldier Of Fortune* (RCA 1980)★★★, with Earl Scruggs *The Storyteller And The Banjoman* (1982)★★★★, *In Concert* (Mercury 1983)★★★, *World Class Country* (Mercury 1983)★★★, *Everything From Jesus To Jack Daniels* (1983)★★, *Natural Dreams* (Mercury 1984)★★, *Songs In A Seashell* (Mercury 1985)★★, *Country Songs For Kids* (Mercury 1988)★, *Songs From Sopchoppy* (Mercury 1996)★★, *Home Grown* (Mercury 1997)★★★.

● COMPILATIONS: *Greatest Hits, Vol. 1* (Mercury 1972)★★★★, *Greatest Hits, Vol. 2* (Mercury 1975)★★★, *Greatest Hits, Vol. 3* (Mercury 1978)★★★, *Essential Tom T. Hall* (Mercury 1988)★★★★, *Great Country Hits* (Special 1994)★★★, *Storyteller, Poet, Philosopher* 2-CD box set (Mercury 1995)★★★★.

● FURTHER READING: *The Songwriter's Handbook*, Tom T. Hall. *The Storyteller's Nashville*, Tom T. Hall. *The Laughing Man Of Woodmont Cove*, Tom T. Hall. *Spring Hill* (a novel), Tom T. Hall.

HALL, WENDELL

b. 23 August 1896, St. George, Kansas, USA, d. 2 April 1969, Alabama, USA. Hall was educated in Chicago and served in the armed forces during World War I. He learned to play several instruments and once worked as a staff musician on KYW Chicago. He was a friend of Carson Robison, whom he had first met in Kansas City and worked with for Victor in Chicago and New York. Around 1922, he began to use a ukulele, at the time a fairly obscure instrument, but Hall made it more internationally known. Billed as The Red Headed Music Maker, Hall became a very popular entertainer during the 20s and established an international reputation when, in 1923, he achieved one of the first hillbilly hit recordings. He wrote lyrics to an old country dance tune and to his own ukulele backing, he recorded 'It Ain't Gonna Rain No Mo''. Released on 16 November on Victor 19171, it proved to be Victor's top hit of the year. Hall's recording sold in excess of two million records and even more sheet music copies. Further major sales came with Vernon Dalhart, who recorded it twice, under his own name for Emerson and under his Bob White alias for Regal. Although Hall was not a country singer, he was popular in the south and Midwest, and the amazing sales achieved by this record undoubtedly prompted record companies to look for early-day country or hillbilly artists. He also performed as a singing xylophonist in vaudeville and with orchestras, and appeared in films and later on television. He toured extensively, including to Europe, singing and playing his own compositions, which included pieces especially written for the ukulele. In the 30s, he turned more to directing and promotional work, sometimes toured in the USA organizing talent shows and made guest appearances on the *National Barn Dance*. He remained fairly active in the music industry until his death in 1969.

HALLEY, DAVID

b. 1950, Oklahoma City, Oklahoma, USA. David Halley is one of the new generation of Texas singer-songwriters and Jimmie Dale Gilmore and Joe Ely have recorded his songs ('Rain Just Falls' on Gilmore's *Fair & Square* album and 'Hard Livin'' on Ely's *Musta Notta*). Growing up in Texas, Halley met artists such as Gilmore, Ely and Butch Hancock, and was soon performing in bands in Denver and Austin. His breakthrough came in 1987 when Keith Whitley enjoyed a Top 10 hit with Halley's song 'Hard Livin''. After that he teamed up with Gilmore as his bandleader. Other commissions followed, including spells with Nanci Griffith, Ray Wylie Hubbard and Darden Smith (playing guitar on his 'Two Dollar Novels'). He also played with Syd Straw, who played on Halley's *Stray Dog Talk*. Mainly rooted in the country tradition, this was a strong album of simple, direct compositions. Less linear and more abstract was the belated follow-up, *Broken Spell*, with influences drawn from rock and jazz.
● ALBUMS: *Stray Dog Talk* (Demon 1990)★★★, *Broken Spell* (dos 1994)★★★.

HAMBLEN, STUART

b. Carl Stuart Hamblen, 20 October 1908, Kellyville, Texas, USA, d. 8 March 1989. The son of a travelling Methodist preacher, Hamblen's childhood was spent travelling around Texas as his father's work decreed. His love of open spaces and yearning for the life of a cowboy is apparent in some of his early songs. He learned to rope and ride, and as a youngster combined working the rodeos with his college studies to be a teacher. He passed his exams but a desire to sing and

write songs led to him moving to California. He worked first with The Beverly Hill Billies, a singing group led by Zeke Manners, but soon hosted his own shows on radio and appeared at various west coast venues with his own band. He first recorded for Decca in 1934, when he cut his popular songs 'Texas Plains' and 'Ridin' Old Paint'. During the 30s and 40s, he proved a natural for Hollywood and appeared in many B-movie westerns, usually as the villain. At times, owing to an inability to hold his drink, he played out many of his screen roles in real life, and was often jailed after shooting out streetlights or brawling. He later said, 'I guess I was the original juvenile delinquent'. Fortunately for him, because of his radio popularity, his sponsors usually bailed him out. He continued to write songs, including 'My Mary' and 'Born To Be Happy', but it was not until 1949 that he registered his first US country chart entry with 'I Won't Go Huntin' With You Jake But I'll Go Chasin' Women'. Soon afterwards, 'Remember Me, I'm The One Who Loves You' was a Top 10 country hit for himself and for Ernest Tubb. His recording of 'Black Diamond', a semi-narration, was also popular; later Hank Snow's version became a much sought-after recording. In 1949, he attended a prayer meeting in Los Angeles given by a then lesser-known preacher named Billy Graham. He publicly announced that he was devoting his life to Christ and gave up his film and radio work, but maintained his songwriting and recording. Hamblen's new-found religious fervour led to him writing 'It Is No Secret (What God Can Do)'. The generally accepted version of events tells that Hamblen wrote the song following a conversation with his old drinking companion, film star John Wayne, who found Hamblen's zeal hard to believe, but then replied casually, 'Well it's no secret what God can do'. He first charted it himself as a Top 10 US country hit in 1951 but soon other artists had successful versions, including Red Foley with the Andrews Sisters, Jo Stafford and Bill Kenny and the Song Spinners. A few years later Elvis Presley recorded it with the Jordanaires and it became one of his best-known gospel recordings. In 1952 Hamblen decided to run for President of the USA on the pro-prohibition party ticket, but, as history records, he lost by approximately 27 million votes. He concentrated on writing songs of a religious nature such as 'His Hands' and 'Open Up Your Heart', and in 1954, achieved both US country and pop chart success himself with 'This Ole House' (he wrote the song after finding the dead body of an old prospector in a tumbledown hut miles from anywhere). Recorded by Rosemary Clooney it became a million-seller, even reaching number 1 in the British pop charts. Years later, an up-tempo 1981 version by pop singer Shakin' Stevens also topped the British charts. From the late 50s, for many years, he hosted religious television shows and continued to record, though he professed to be retired. In 1971, he began his popular KLAC Sunday morning network radio programme *The Cowboy Church Of The Air*, which ran for more than a decade. He died following an operation on a brain tumour on 8 March 1989.
● ALBUMS: *It Is No Secret* 10-inch album (RCA Victor 1954)★★★★, *It Is No Secret* (RCA Victor 1956)★★★★, *Grand Old Hymns* (RCA Victor 1957)★★★, *Hymns* (Harmony 1957)★★★, *Beyond The Sun* (Camden 1959)★★★, *Remember Me* (Coral 1960)★★, *The Spell Of The Yukon* (Columbia 1961)★★, *Of God I Sing* (Columbia 1962)★★, *In The Garden And Other Inspirational Songs* (Camden 1966)★★★, *This Old*

House Has Got To Go (There's A Freeway Coming Through) (Kapp 1966)★★★, *I Believe* (Harmony 1967)★★★, *A Man And His Music* (1974)★★★, *The Cowboy Church* (1974)★★★.

HAMILTON, GEORGE, IV

b. 19 July 1937, Winston-Salem, North Carolina, USA. George Hamilton IV is one of the few American country stars to have become a household name in Britain, although he is sometimes confused with the actor George Hamilton. 'George Hamilton I was a farmer in the Blue Ridge', he says, 'George Hamilton II was a railroad man who loved country music and collected Jimmie Rodgers' records. My father, George Hamilton III, was the general manager of a headache powder company. I'm a city boy from a middle-class family but my parents gave me an honest love of country music. We'd listen to the *Grand Ole Opry* on a Saturday night.' In 1956, while at the University of North Carolina, Hamilton persuaded a local label, Colonial, to record him. He recorded one of the first teen ballads, 'A Rose And A Baby Ruth', written by his friend John D. Loudermilk. Its regional success prompted ABC-Paramount to issue it countrywide - Hamilton found himself at number 6 in the nation's pop chart and the single became a million-seller. The b-side, 'If You Don't Know, I Ain't Gonna Tell You', heralded the subsequent direction of his music and became a US country hit in its own right in 1962. It is also one of the few songs that Hamilton has written himself. 'There are too many great writers around to bother with mediocre music,' he says now. The title, 'A Rose And A Baby Ruth', was too obscure for UK record-buyers - a Baby Ruth was a chocolate bar - but Hamilton did make the UK Top 30 with his second American Top 10 entry, 'Why Don't They Understand?'. The song, co-written by Joe 'Mr. Piano' Henderson, was one of the first hits about the 50s generation gap. Hamilton's other US hits were 'Only One Love', 'Now And For Always' and the curio 'The Teen Commandments Of Love' with Paul Anka and Johnny Nash. He made the UK Top 30 with 'I Know Where I'm Going'. Hamilton toured on rock'n'roll package shows with Buddy Holly, Eddie Cochran and Gene Vincent, and appeared on Broadway with Louis Armstrong. His leanings towards country music were satisfied when ABC-Paramount let him record a tribute album to Hank Williams. In 1958 Hamilton married his childhood sweetheart, Adelaide ('Tinky') Peyton, and moved to Nashville where they raised a family. Hamilton started recording for RCA in 1961 and returned to the US Top 20 with John D. Loudermilk's adaptation of a western song, 'Abilene', in 1963. His other country hits include 'Break My Mind', 'Fort Worth, Dallas Or Houston' and 'She's A Little Bit Country'. Hamilton pioneered the songs of Gordon Lightfoot ('Steel Rail Blues', 'Early Mornin' Rain'), which, in turn, led to a love affair with Canadian music. He recorded Joni Mitchell's 'Urge For Going' (the first artist to release one of her songs), Leonard Cohen's 'Suzanne' and Ian Tyson's 'Summer Wages', along with several albums of which *Canadian Pacific* is the best known. He comments, 'Country music is swamped with songs about the seamy side of life - love in a honky tonk, meet me at the dark end of the street, and does your husband know? There's so much more to life than adultery and I felt that the Canadians had a different approach to songwriting. They have a long-standing love of their land and Ray Griff's "Canadian Pacific" sums up that feeling.'

Hamilton appeared at the first Wembley country music festival and he has been a regular visitor to the UK ever since. Hamilton acknowledges that he has changed the UK public's perception of country music: 'When I first came here, people had the idea that country music was all hicks and hillbillies, cowboys and indians. I wanted to show it was an art form, a quality music. I wore a three-piece suit which was a bit formal for the music I was playing but I wouldn't have been comfortable in jeans and a stetson.' Hamilton has championed British country music by recording home-grown songs and also by recording with the Hillsiders. In 1979, Hamilton became the first country singer to play a summer season at a seaside resort (Blackpool). Although Hamilton moved to North Carolina in 1972, he sees little of his home. He tours so often that Bob Powell, a former editor of the UK magazine *Country Music People*, named him the International Ambassador of Country Music. In 1974 Hamilton became the first country artist to give concerts in the Soviet Union and he lectured at Moscow University. He has appeared at festivals in Czechoslovakia and recorded there. His pioneering work was recognized by *Billboard* magazine who gave him their Trendsetter award in 1975. Hamilton's best recordings were made in the late 70s when he made three albums with producer Allen Reynolds, *Fine Lace And Homespun Cloth*, *Feel Like A Million* and *Forever Young*. He nearly reached the UK charts with a revival of 'I Wonder Who's Kissing Her Now' from the first album. Increasingly in recent years, Hamilton has given Christian concerts. He has been part of Billy Graham's crusades and he regularly tours British churches. Hank Wangford parodies Hamilton's sincere eyebrows, and he takes it all in good spirit as he admits, 'I have no paranoia about what the critics say about me. I accept that some folks think I'm bland, easy listening and it's pretty obvious that I'm not a great vocalist. However, I can communicate with an audience and I do try to interpret songs which say something.' Hamilton sometimes works with his son, George Hamilton V (b. 11 November 1960, Nashville, Tennessee, USA), who had a US country hit with 'She Says' and also tours the UK country clubs in his own right. Like his father, he will sign autographs until the last person has left.

● ALBUMS: *George Hamilton IV On Campus* (ABC 1958)★★★, *Sing Me A Sad Song - A Tribute To Hank Williams* (ABC 1958)★★★, *To You And Yours (From Me And Mine)* (RCA Victor 1961)★★★, *Abilene* (RCA Victor 1963)★★★, *George Hamilton IV's Big 15* (ABC 1963)★★★, *Fort Worth, Dallas Or Houston* (RCA Victor 1964)★★★, *Mister Sincerity* (RCA Victor 1965)★★★, *By George* (ABC 1966)★★★, *Steel Rail Blues* (RCA Victor 1966)★★★, *Coast-Country* (RCA Victor 1966)★★★, *Folk Country Classics* (RCA Victor 1967)★★★, *Folksy* (RCA Victor 1967)★★★, *In The Fourth Dimension* (RCA Victor 1968)★★★, *The Gentle Sound Of George Hamilton IV* (RCA Victor 1968)★★★, *George Hamilton IV* (RCA Victor 1968)★★★, *Canadian Pacific* (RCA Victor 1969)★★★★, *Back Where It's At* (RCA Victor 1970)★★★, part with Skeeter Davis *Down Home In The Country* (RCA Victor 1970)★★★, *North Country* (RCA Victor 1971)★★★, with the Hillsiders *Heritage* (1971)★★★, *West Texas Highway* (RCA Victor 1971)★★★, *Country Music Is In My Soul* (RCA Victor 1972)★★★, *Down East Country* (RCA Victor 1972)★★★, *Travelin' Light* (RCA Victor 1972)★★★, *The International Ambassador Of Country Music* (RCA Victor 1973)★★★, with Arthur Smith *Singing On*

The Mountain (1973)★★, *Back To Down East Country* (1974)★★★, *Bluegrass Gospel* (Lamb And Lion 1974)★★★, *Trendsetter* (1975)★★★, *Back Home At The Opry* (RCA Victor 1976)★★★, *Fine Lace And Homespun Cloth* (1977)★★★, *Feel Like A Million* (Elektra 1978)★★★, *Forever Young* (MCA 1979)★★★, *Cuttin' Across The Country* (RCA 1981)★★★, *One Day At A Time* (Word 1982)★★★, *George Hamilton IV With Jiri Brabec And Country Beat* (1982)★★★, *Songs For A Winter's Night* (Ronco 1982)★★, *Music Man's Dream* (Range 1984)★★★, *Hymns Country Style* (Word 1985)★★★, *George Hamilton IV* (MCA 1986)★★★, *Give Thanks* (Word 1988)★★, *A Country Christmas* (Word 1989)★★, with the Moody Brothers *American Country Gothic* (Conifer 1990)★★★, with George Hege Hamilton V *Country Classics* (1992)★★★, *Thanksgiving In The Country* (Word 1994)★★★, *Canadian Country Gold And Unmined Treasures* (Broadland International 1995)★★★★, *Treasured Keepsakes* (Alliance 1996)★★★.
● COMPILATIONS: *The Best Of* (RCA Victor 1970)★★★★, *Greatest Hits* (RCA Victor 1974)★★★★, *The ABC Collection* (ABC 1977)★★★★, *The Very Best Of* (Country Store 1986)★★★, *To You And Yours, From Me And Mine* 6-CD box set (Bear Family 1996)★★★★, *Country Boy ... Best Of* (Camden 1997)★★★★.

HANCOCK, BUTCH
b. George Hancock, 12 July 1945, Lubbock, Texas, USA. Folk-rock singer-songwriter, and part-time painter, whose early leanings towards music were temporarily frustrated by architectural school. Hancock left to work on his father's farm, his interest in singing rekindled by long days of driving tractors on the dusty Texas plains of the 60s. Drawing heavily on the acoustic traditions of rock 'n' roll, and Bob Dylan in particular, he formed his first band, the Flatlanders, in 1970. Together with Joe Ely and Jimmy Gilmore, they recorded for the Plantation label run by Shelby Singleton. However, the results were not heard prior to Ely's rise to fame in the 70s. Continuing as a solo artist, Hancock relocated, first to Clarendon and finally to Austin, to release albums on his own Rainlight label. The late 70s and early 80s witnessed a stream of gentle, intelligent albums, including two recorded at the same show (the solo *1981: A Space Odyssey* and *Firewater (Seeks Its Own Level)*, which featured backing from local musicians). After a quiet spell, during which time he pursued his interests in photography and video production, in the mid-80s he returned with a more commercial set of songs that nevertheless maintained the standard of his good-humoured evaluations of Texas life. His most-recorded song is 'If I Was A Bluebird' (Joe Ely, Emmylou Harris, etc.); others include the whimsical 'West Texas Waltz', 'She Never Spoke Spanish To Me' and 'Standin' At The Big Hotel'.
● ALBUMS: *West Texas Waltzes & Dust-Blown Tractor Tunes* (Rainlight 1978)★★★, *The Wind's Dominion* (Rainlight 1979)★★, *Diamond Hill* (Rainlight 1980)★★★, *1981: A Space Odyssey* (Rainlight 1981)★★, *Firewater (Seeks Its Own Level)* (Rainlight 1981)★★★, with Marce Lacoutre *Yella Rose* (Rainlight 1985)★★★, *Split And Slide II (Apocalypse Now, Pay Later)* (Rainlight 1986)★★, with Jimmie Dale Gilmore *Two Roads - Live In Australia* (Virgin Australia 1990)★★★, *Cause Of The Cactus* (Rainlight 1991)★★★, *Own The Way Over Here* (Sugar Hill 1993)★★★, *Eats Away The Night* (Sugar Hill 1995)★★★, *You Coulda Walked Around The World* (Rainlight 1997)★★★.
● COMPILATIONS: *Own And Own* (Sugar Hill 1989)★★★.

HANK THE DRIFTER
b. Daniel Ray Andrade, 2 September 1929, Taunton, Massachusetts, USA. After learning to play guitar as a youth, he sang with a local group. Their successes in local talent competitions led to Andrade being given a 15-minute show on WPEP Taunton, as the Drifting Cowboy. He proved popular and soon gained sponsorship by *The New Bedford Times* for a weekly show on WNBH. He eventually relocated to Texas where, as Hank The Drifter (the name came from his adulation of Hank Williams and his music), he appeared on the *Cowtown Jamboree* in Fort Worth, *Corns A Poppin'* in Houston and *Big D Jamboree* in Dallas. His idolization of Williams was evident in his songs and led to him writing tributes such as 'Hank Williams Is Singing Again' and 'Hank Williams' Ghost'. He continued to perform at festivals, fairs, rodeos and numerous other venues into the 80s, his appearances ranging from Texas to the New England states and many others in between. He recorded for the New England label in Houston but some recordings have also been issued by the Canadian, Spartan and Quality companies. In 1980, Cattle of Germany released an album of his New England recordings, which contained 12 self-penned songs, including the two tributes listed earlier.
● COMPILATIONS: *Hank Williams Is Singing Again* (Cattle 1980)★★★.

HANLON, JERRY
b. 28 December 1933, near Kickapoo, Peoria County, Illinois, USA. He first played piano and sang as a child, before teaching himself the guitar, being inspired by Jimmie Rodgers. He served in the US Air Force, where he pursued his interest in country music. During his service career, he won several awards from the American Red Cross for his work entertaining in hospitals. He began writing songs and in 1958, one, a tribute to Rodgers, led to him meeting the latter's widow, Carrie. Impressed by Hanlon, she encouraged him and introduced him to Ernest Tubb, who offered him appearances on his radio shows and took him on some tours. In 1961, he guested on Tubb's *Midnight Jamboree*, singing 'Boy With A Future' (after Tubb's death, Hanlon showed his appreciation of his help by recording the tribute 'E.T. We're Missing You'). His easy singing style and the occasional yodel saw him go on to play the *Grand Ole Opry* and form his own band, the Midwest Playboys, with whom he toured extensively in the 60s. He had various single releases between 1964 and 1978, although none charted. Between 1987 and 1994, he completed 10 very successful European tours that saw him play various venues in Ireland, Scotland and Scandinavia. His Irish ancestry has helped him become especially popular in Ireland, where his song 'The Calling (Home)' has been recorded by Irish country singers, including Sean Cuddy. In January 1993, he underwent open-heart surgery but surprised everybody with his speedy return to his personal appearance commitments. He devotes a great deal of time entertaining for the Drug and Alcohol Rehabilitation Organisation in America and for the handicapped, both in America and Ireland.
● ALBUMS: *Memories* (Universal-Athena 1980)★★★,

Everybody Wants To Be A Cowboy (Universal-Athena 1985)★★★★, *My Kind Of Country* cassette only (Universal-Athena 1991)★★★, *My Country, My Heritage* (Universal-Athena 1992)★★★, *If The Good Lord Is Willing* (Universal-Athena 1992)★★, *Walking Talking Dolly* (Universal-Athena 1993)★★★, *Livin' On Dreams* (Universal-Athena 1996)★★★.

HANLY, MICK

b. Limerick, Eire. Singer-songwriter Hanly was inspired by mid-50s rock 'n' roll before he became more interested in folk in the 60s. After performing Woody Guthrie songs in his spare time, in the late 60s and early 70s he turned to the Irish traditional music of his youth. Together with Michael O'Domhnaill, he formed Monroe, and supported Planxty on their 1973 tour, subsequently releasing *Folk Weave*, before O'Domhnaill left for the Bothy Band in 1975. Hanly went to France for two years, and, on his return to Ireland, recorded two acclaimed solo albums with Donal Lunny, Andy Irvine and Declan Sinnott. He then toured Ireland and Europe with Irvine, who had recently left Planxty. In 1981, Hanly joined Moving Hearts as a vocalist, and contributed his own songs to *Live Hearts*. After the demise, in 1985, of one of Ireland's most successful and innovative traditional bands, he went solo again, and moved towards country music. His songs were covered by Christy Moore, Mary Black and the country singer Hal Ketchum, who took Hanly's 'Past The Point Of Rescue' into the Top 10 of the US country chart in 1993.

● ALBUMS: as Monroe *Folk Weave* (1974)★★, *A Kiss In The Morning Early* (1977)★★★, *As I Went Over Blackwater* (1979)★★★, with Moving Hearts *Live Hearts* (1983)★★, *Warts And All* (1993)★★★, *Happy Like This* (1994)★★★.

HARDEN, ARLENE

b. 1 March 1945, England, near Pine Bluff, Arkansas, USA. Harden sang with her brother Bobby and sister Robbie as the Harden Trio on *Barnyard Frolics*, when all three were teenagers in Little Rock. Later they were featured on the *Ozark Mountain Jubilee*, the *Louisiana Hayride* and in 1966, the *Grand Ole Opry*. The trio recorded for Columbia and early in 1966, they had a US country and pop hit with Bobby Harden's song 'Tippy Toeing'. Another of his songs, 'Sneaking 'Cross The Border', also became a Top 20 country hit. Their last chart entry, 'Everybody Wants To Be Somebody Else', seemed to be somewhat prophetic because in 1968, they disbanded. Arlene had begun to pursue a solo career in 1967 and had minor hits that year with 'Fair Weather Love' and 'You're Easy To Love'. Between 1967 and 1978, she accrued 17 more country chart entries, the most successful being 'Lovin' Man' (a female version of the Roy Orbison number 1, 'Oh Pretty Woman'). She also charted with a version of Orbison's 'Crying', and after moving to Capitol in 1974, she recorded a country version of the Helen Reddy pop hit 'Leave Me Alone (Ruby Red Dress)', although for some reason she appears as 'Arleen' on this release. Bobby Harden duetted with his sister in 1968 on 'Who Loves Who' and had a minor solo country chart entry in 1975 with 'One Step'. Arlene moved to Elektra in 1977, where her last chart entry was a 1978 minor hit with 'You're Not Free And I'm Not Easy'.

● ALBUMS: *What Can I Say* (Columbia 1968)★★★, *Sings Roy Orbison* (Columbia 1970)★★, *I Could Almost Say Goodbye* (Capitol 1975)★★★. By Bobby Harden *Nashville*

Sensation (Starday 1969)★★★. As the Harden Trio *Tippy Toeing* (Columbia 1966)★★★, *Sing Me Back Home* (Columbia 1968)★★★, *Great Country Hits* (Harmony 1970)★★★.

HARGROVE, LINDA

b. 3 February 1950, Jacksonville, Florida, but was raised in Tallahassee. Hargrove learnt piano and guitar from an early age and played french horn in the school band. She was imitating Carole King's songwriting from the age of 14. She played with a local rock band and then, in 1970, she decided to try her luck in Nashville. Sandy Posey recorded her material and steel guitarist Pete Drake offered her session work and subsequently produced her records. She befriended Michael Nesmith and they wrote 'Winonah', which Nesmith recorded, and the country standard 'I've Never Loved Anyone More', which has been recorded by Lynn Anderson, Eddy Arnold, Billie Jo Spears and Marty Robbins. An album for Michael Nesmith's Countryside label was never released, and her first (released) album for Elektra, *Music Is Your Mistress*, included a duet with Melba Montgomery, 'Don't Let It Bother You'. Her songs include 'Let It Shine' (Olivia Newton-John), 'Just Get Up And Close The Door' (Johnny Rodriguez), 'New York City Song' (Jan Howard, Tanya Tucker) and 'Something I Can Forget' (Moe Bandy), but she saved the wonderfully titled 'Time Wounds All Heels' for herself. She had a US country hit in 1975 with 'Love Was (Once Around The Dance Floor)'. *Impressions* was an album with a Spanish flavour. She became a born-again Christian, married Charlie Bartholomew and now performs gospel concerts as Linda Bartholomew, regarding Linda Hargrove as a different person and denouncing her past life of writing secular songs and indulging in drink and drugs. She recently recovered from leukemia and has started singing again.

● ALBUMS: *Music Is Your Mistress* (Elektra 1973)★★★, *Blue Jean Country Queen* (Elektra 1974)★★★, *Love, You're The Teacher* (Capitol 1975)★★★★, *Just Like You* (Capitol 1976)★★★★, *Impressions* (Capitol 1977)★★★, *A New Song* (1981)★★★, *Greater Works* (1987)★★★.

HARRELL, BILL

b. 14 September 1934, Marion, Virginia, USA. Harrell learned to read music and for a time, as a child, he had piano lessons, before becoming interested in bluegrass music during his studies at the University of Maryland. He learned guitar and mandolin, playing the latter in a band that he formed with other students. After leaving university, he worked with several bluegrass bands in the Washington DC area, including the Rocky Mountain Boys. In 1957, he was called for military service, during which he was involved in a serious car accident that left him hospitalized for 12 months. In 1960, by then specializing in the guitar, he formed his band, the Virginians. They recorded an album for United Artists Records and another, *Ballads & Bluegrass*, under the name of Buck Ryan And Smitty Irvin for Monument (the latter two were actually the fiddle and banjo players in the Virginians). They played regularly on television on WSVA Harrisonburg, guested on various other stations and appeared at numerous venues throughout several states. In 1966, Harrell disbanded the Virginians to work with Don Reno And The Tennessee Cut-Ups. He played and toured with the group until he and Reno parted amicably in 1977 (between 1970 and 1971, they were joined by Reno's old partner Red Smiley). They recorded for several labels, including King, Starday and Monument. Harrell then formed a new version of the Virginians, which, with variations in personnel, he continued to front into the 90s. They recorded albums for Adelphi, Leather and Rebel. Harrell's contribution to the genre over almost 40 years has been of major importance in the development and lasting popularity of bluegrass music.

● ALBUMS: With the Virginians *The Wonderful World Of Bluegrass* (United Artists 1963)★★★, *Ballads & Bluegrass* (Adelphi 1978)★★★★, *Bluegrass Gospel Pure and Simple* (Leather 1980)★★, *I Can Hear Virginia Calling Me* (Rebel 1980)★★★, *Blue Ridge Mountain Boy* (Leather 1981)★★★, *L&N Don't Stop Here Anymore* (Leather 1981)★★★, *Walking In The Early Morning Dew* (Rebel 1983)★★★, *Do You Remember* (Rebel 1985)★★★, *Blue Virginia Blue* (Rebel 1986)★★★, *A Song For Everyone* (Rebel 1987)★★★, *After Sunrise* (Rebel 1990). As Don Reno And Bill Harrell And Tennessee Cut-Ups *Bluegrass Favorites* (Jalyn 1967)★★★, *Reno & Harrell* (Rural Rhythm 1967)★★★, *Yellow Pages* (Derbytown 1967)★★★, *All The Way To Reno* (King 1968)★★★, *A Variety Of Sacred Songs* (King 1968)★★, *The Most Requested Songs* (Jalyn 1968)★★★, *I'm Using My Bible For A Road Map* (King 1970)★★, with Red Smiley *Together Again* (Rome 1971)★★★, with Smiley *Letter Edged In Black* reissued by Rebel as *Songs Of Yesterday* 1988 (Wango 1971)★★★, *Bluegrass On My Mind* (Starday 1973)★★★, *Rivers & Roads* (King Bluegrass 1974)★★★, *Tally Ho* (King Bluegrass 1974)★★★, *Spice Of Life* (King Bluegrass 1975)★★★, *Bi-Centennial Bluegrass* (Monument 1975)★★★, *Dear Old Dixie* (CMH 1976)★★★, *The Don Reno Story* (CMH 1976)★★★, *Home In The Mountains* (CMH 1977)★★★, with Smiley *Live At The Lone Star Festival* (Atteiram 1977)★★.

HARRELL, KELLY

b. Crockett Kelly Harrell, 13 September 1889, Draper Valley, Wythe County, Virginia, USA, d. 9 July 1942. Harrell grew up in Fries and like another of the early country pioneers, Henry Whitter, he worked in a local textile mill. In January 1925, no doubt believing, like many others, that he could better Whitter's vocals, he went to New York and recorded four sides for Victor Records, including 'New River Train' and 'Roving Gambler'. In August 1925, he and Whitter both recorded for OKeh Records in Asheville, North Carolina, with Whitter actually playing guitar or harmonica on Harrell's recordings. He returned to New York in June 1926 and recorded 13 more sides for Victor, including re-recordings of the first four. After moving to Henry County to work at a mill offering better wages, Harrell began to sing with the Virginia String Band, which included noted fiddler Posey Rorer. Between 1927 and 1929, he recorded a further 19 sides for Victor, including two duets with Henry Norton. The Depression saw the end of his Victor recording career, but the Virginia String Band continued to play local venues, while the members continued working in the mills. Harrell, a fine vocalist, who sang in a style far removed from the harsh nasal tones of contemporaries such as Whitter, also composed several songs, the best-known being 'Away Out On The Mountain', which was very successfully recorded by Jimmie Rodgers. Harrell always longed to make further recordings himself and regularly contacted other companies. Before he could meet with any success, however, he suffered a heart attack at work on 9 July 1942 and was found to be dead on arrival at the hospital.

● COMPILATIONS: *Kelly Harrell And The Virginia String Band* (County 1977)★★★, *The Complete Kelly Harrell* (Bear Family 1985)★★★.

HARRIS, EMMYLOU

b. 12 April 1947, Birmingham, Alabama, USA. Starting as a folk singer, Harris tried her luck in the late 60s in New York's Greenwich Village folk clubs, making an album for the independent Jubilee label in 1970, *Gliding Bird*, which was largely unrepresentative of her subsequent often stunning work. It included cover versions of songs by Bob Dylan, Fred Neil and Hank Williams, as well as somewhat mundane originals and a title track written by her first husband, Tom Slocum. Harris then moved to Washington DC, where latter-day Flying Burrito Brother Rick Roberts heard her singing in a club, and recommended her to Gram Parsons, who was looking for a female partner. Parsons hired Harris after discovering that their voices dovetailed perfectly, and she appeared on his two studio albums, *GP* (1973) and *Grievous Angel* (1974). The latter was released after Parsons died, as was a live album recorded for a US radio station that was released some years later.

Eddie Tickner, who had been involved with managing the Byrds, and who was also managing Parsons at the time of his drug-related demise, encouraged Harris to make a solo album using the same musicians who had worked with Parsons. The cream of Los Angeles session musicians, they were collectively known as the Hot Band, and among the 'pickers' who worked in the band during its 15-year lifespan backing Harris were guitarist James Burton (originally lead guitarist on 'Suzy Q' by Dale Hawkins, and simultaneously during his time with Harris, lead player with Elvis Presley's Las Vegas band), pianist Glen D. Hardin (a member of the Crickets post-Buddy Holly, and also working simultaneously with both Harris and Presley), steel guitarist Hank DeVito, bass player Emory Gordy Jnr. (now a highly successful Nashville-based producer), John Ware (ex-Michael Nesmith's First National Band, and a member of Linda Ronstadt's early 70s backing group), and the virtually unknown Rodney Crowell. Backed by musicians of this calibre (subsequent Hot Band members included legendary British lead guitarist Albert Lee and Ricky Skaggs, later a country star in his own right), Harris released a series of artistically excellent and often commercially successful albums, starting with 1975's *Pieces Of The Sky*, and also including *Elite Hotel* (1976), *Luxury Liner* (1977) and *Quarter Moon In A Ten Cent Town* (whose title was a line in the song 'Easy From Now On', co-written by Carlene Carter and Susanna Clark, wife of singer-songwriter Guy Clark). *Blue Kentucky Girl* was closer to pure country music than the country rock that had become her trademark and speciality, and 1980's *Roses In The Snow* was her fourth album to reach the Top 40 of the US pop chart. *Light Of The Stable*, a 1980 Christmas album also featuring Linda Ronstadt, Dolly Parton, Willie Nelson and Neil Young, was surprisingly far less successful. Two more albums in 1981 (*Evangeline* and *Cimmaron* - the latter featuring a cover of the Poco classic, 'Rose Of Cimmaron') were better sellers, but a 1982 live album, *Last Date*, was largely ignored. The following year's *White Shoes* was Harris's final album produced by Canadian Brian Ahern, her second husband, who had established a reputation for his successful work with Anne Murray, prior to producing all Harris's classic albums up to this point. Harris and Ahern subsequently separated both personally and professionally, marking the end of an era that had also seen her appearing on Bob Dylan's *Desire* in 1976 and *The Last Waltz*, the farewell concert/triple album/feature film by the Band from 1978. Around this time, Harris was invited by producer Glyn Johns and British singer-songwriter Paul Kennerley to participate in a concept album written by the latter, *The Legend Of Jesse James* (Kennerley's follow-up to the similarly conceptual *White Mansions*). Harris and Kennerley later married, and together wrote and produced *The Ballad Of Sally Rose* (a concept album that by her own belated admission reflected her relationship with Gram Parsons) and the similarly excellent *13*, but neither recaptured Harris's previous chart heights. In 1987 there were two albums involving Harris: *Trio*, a multi-million selling triumph that won a Grammy award, was a collaboration between Harris, Linda Ronstadt and Dolly Parton, but Harris's own *Angel Band*, a low-key acoustic collection, became the first of her albums not to be released in the UK, where it was felt to be too uncommercial. This fall from commercial grace occurred simultaneously (although perhaps coincidentally) with the virtual retirement of manager Eddie Tickner, who had guided and protected Harris through 15 years of mainly classic albums. *Bluebird* was a definite return to form with production by Richard Bennett and featuring a title track written by Butch Hancock, but a commercial renaissance did not occur. *Duets*, a compilation album featuring Harris singing with artists including Gram Parsons, Roy Orbison, George Jones, the Desert Rose Band, Don Williams, Neil Young and John Denver, was artistically delightful, but appeared to be an attempt on the part of the marketing department of WEA (to whom she had been signed since *Pieces Of The Sky*) to reawaken interest in a star who they feared might be past her commercial peak. The same year's *Brand New Dance* was not a success compared with much of her past catalogue, and in that year, the much-changed Hot Band was dropped in favour of the Nash Ramblers, a bluegrass-based acoustic quintet composed of Sam Bush (mandolin, fiddle, duet vocals, ex-New Grass Revival), Al Perkins (dobro, banjo, ex-Manassas; Flying Burrito Brothers; Souther Hillman Furay), *Grand Ole Opry* double bass player Roy Huskey Jnr., drummer Larry Atamanuik and 22-year-old new boy John Randall Stewart (acoustic guitar, harmony vocal - the Rodney Crowell replacement). In 1991, Harris and the Nash Ramblers were permitted to record a live album at the former home of the *Grand Ole Opry*, the Ryman Auditorium in Nashville. The record was poorly received in some quarters, however, and at the end of 1992, it was reported that she had been dropped by Warner Brothers Records, ending a 20-year association. Harris remained in the incongruous position of being a legendary figure in country music, always in demand as a guest performer in the studio, but unable to match the record sales of those younger artists who regarded her as a heroine. Her 1995 album represented the severing of the cord; she boldly stepped away from country-sounding arrangements and recorded the stunning Daniel Lanois-produced *Wrecking Ball*. The title track is a Neil Young composition and other songs featured were written by Lanois, Steve Earle and Anna McGarrigle. Harris described this album as her 'weird'

record: its wandering and mantric feel creeps into the psyche and the album represents one of the most rewarding releases of her underrated and lengthy career. She picked up a Grammy for the work in 1996 as the Best Contemporary Folk Album.

● ALBUMS: *Gliding Bird* (Jubilee 1970)★★, *Pieces Of The Sky* (Reprise 1975)★★★★, *Elite Hotel* (Reprise 1976)★★★, *Luxury Liner* (Reprise 1977)★★★★, *Quarter Moon In A 10 Cent Town* (Reprise 1978)★★★, *Blue Kentucky Girl* (Reprise 1979)★★★, *Roses In The Snow* (Reprise 1980)★★★★, *Light Of The Stable* (Reprise 1980)★★★, *Evangeline* (Reprise 1981)★★★, *Cimmaron* (Reprise 1981)★★★, *Last Date* (Reprise 1982)★★★, *White Shoes* (Warners 1983)★★★, *The Ballad Of Sally Rose* (Reprise 1985)★★★, *13* (Reprise 1986)★★★, with Dolly Parton, Linda Ronstadt *Trio* (Warners 1987)★★★, *Angel Band* (Reprise 1987)★★★, *Bluebird* (Reprise 1988)★★★, *Duets* (Warners 1990)★★★★, *Brand New Dance* (Reprise 1990)★★★, *At The Ryman* (Reprise 1992)★★★, with Carl Jackson *Nashville Country Duets* (1993)★★★, *Cowgirl's Prayer* (Asylum 1993)★★★, *Songs Of The West* (Warners 1994)★★★, *Wrecking Ball* (Grapevine 1995)★★★★.

● COMPILATIONS: *Profile (The Best Of Emmylou Harris)* (Reprise 1978)★★★★, *Profile II (The Best Of Emmylou Harris)* (Reprise 1984)★★★, *Her Best Songs* (K-Tel 1980)★★★, *Portraits* 3-CD box set (Reprise Archives 1996)★★★★.

● VIDEOS: *Thanks To You* (1990), *At The Ryman* (1992).

HARRIS, GIL

Little is known of this New Zealand-born friend of Tex Morton, who was sufficiently inspired by Morton's success to go to Australia to record four sides for Regal-Zonophone on 12 May 1939. A talented yodeller (in the style of Goebel Reeves), he was billed as the Whispering Yodeller, and the recordings, which included fine versions of 'True Blue Gil' and 'The Hobo's Meditation', suggested that he had a great future as a country singer. However, soon after making the recordings, he was offered a post with job security outside the music industry. Obviously realizing the unreliability of the financial side of life as a singer, he accepted the post and consequently disappeared from the music scene.

HARRIS, TED

b. Theodore Clifford Harris, 2 August 1937, Lakeland, Florida, USA. Harris first worked for a local newspaper but from an early age knew he wanted to be a songwriter. In 1958, with some early examples of his work, he relocated to Nashville. He became friendly with Ted Daffan and Joe Talbot, and had spells writing for both RCA/Victor and Columbia Records but mainly worked in various stores to earn a living. In 1960, somewhat disenchanted, he tried his luck, unsuccessfully, in Memphis but eventually returned to Nashville. In 1965, he formed Harbot Music with Joe Talbot, and immediately achieved success when Carl Belew's recording of 'Crystal Chandelier' became a number 12 country hit. Further Top 20 hits soon followed with 'Rainbows And Roses' (Roy Drusky) and 'Paper Mansions' (Dottie West). When Talbot and Harris amicably parted two years later, Harris formed Contention Music and further hits followed. Many top artists, including Waylon Jennings and Charley Pride, recorded his songs. Pride's subsequent recording of 'Crystal Chandelier' ensured that the song is now always associated with him, particularly in the UK, but, in spite of being recorded by around 50 artists over the years, Belew's remains the only version to chart. In 1960, Anita Bryant had a Top 5 US pop hit with Harris's song 'Paper Roses', while in the UK, the Kaye Sisters' version reached number 7 in the pop charts. In 1973, Marie Osmond's recording of the song became a crossover hit in the USA and also reached number 2 in the UK pop charts. In 1972, the University of Tennessee appointed Harris to lecture on a course for songwriters. He became a director of the Country Music Association and has won numerous awards for his songwriting, including being elected to the Nashville Songwriters' Hall Of Fame in 1990. Among his other hit songs are 'Dark Side Of Fame', 'The Happiness Of Having You', 'Here I Go Again' and 'The Hand That Rocks The Cradle'. Throughout his career, to date, Harris has never worked with other writers.

HART, FREDDIE

b. Fred Segrest, 21 December 1926, Lochapoka, Alabama, USA. Hart was one of 10 boys and five girls born to a family of sharecroppers. He left school at the age of 12 and started working for his parents. When he was only 15, he lied about his age - and his parents signed the papers - so that he could join the marines. He saw action at both Guam and Iwo Jima. Four years later he was back as a civilian and taught karate to the Los Angeles police. He acquired a black belt, but in 1951, he went into country music when he joined Lefty Frizzell's band. In 1953 he was given a recording contract with Capitol Records, but it was not until 1959 that he had his first hit - 'The Wall' with Columbia. He recorded further country hits with Monument and Kapp, including 'Hank Williams' Guitar', and, in 1969, he rejoined Capitol as a successful country performer. In 1971 Hart went to number 17 in the US pop charts with 'Easy Loving', which won the Country Music Association's Song of the Year award two years running. He explained its success as follows: 'I try to put down in my songs what every man wants to say, and what every woman wants to hear. A song like "Easy Loving" has brought a lot of people together. Many people have told me that they have fallen in love and gotten married because of that song.' This method of songwriting has led Hart into some obscure corners, none more so than 'The Child' in which he plays a baby in his mother's womb! His country hits include 'My Hang Up Is You', 'Bless Your Heart', 'The Pleasure's Been All Mine' and 'Why Lovers Turn To Strangers'. His compositions include 'Skid Row Joe' for Porter Wagoner and 'I Ain't Goin' Hungry Anymore' for Charlie Rich. His UK debut at the Wembley country music festival in 1978 was too overblown for some - at one stage, it looked as though he would thank every individual member of the audience. In the early 80s, he had success with 'Roses Are Red' and 'You Were There' on the small Sunbird label, but by then he was no longer fully committed to country music. With shrewd investing, Hart became wealthy, and in the 80s, he concentrated on his acres of plum trees, his trucking company and his 200 breeding bulls. He now runs a school for handicapped children in Burbank, California. In 1988, he returned with a collection of songs that he had written 'with the Lord in my heart'.

● ALBUMS: *The Spirited Freddie Hart* (Columbia 1962)★★★, *Hart Of Country Music* (1965)★★★★, *Straight From The Hart* (Kapp 1966)★★★★, *A Hurtin' Man* (1967)★★★, *Neon And The Rain* (1967)★★★, *Born A Fool* (1968)★★★, *Togetherness* (1968)★★★, *California Grapevine* (1970)★★★, *New Sounds* (1970)★★★, *Easy Loving* (1971)★★★, *My Hang Up Is You* (1972)★★★, *Bless Your Heart* (1972)★★★, *Got The All-Overs For You* (1972)★★★, *Lonesome Love* (1972)★★★, *A Trip To Heaven* (1973)★★★, *Super Kind Of Woman* (1973)★★★, *If You Can't Feel It* (1973)★★★, *You Are My World* (1973)★★★, *Hang In There Girl* (1974)★★★, *Heart 'N' Soul* (1974)★★★, *The First Time* (1975)★★★, *Freddie Hart Presents The Hartbeats* (1975)★★, *That Look In Her Eyes* (1976)★★★, *People Put To Music* (1976)★★★, *The Pleasure's Been All Mine* (1977)★★★, *Only You* (1978)★★★, *My Lady* (1979)★★★, *Sure Thing* (1980)★★★, *Somebody Loves You* (1984)★★★, *I Will Never Die* (1988)★★.

● COMPILATIONS: *Freddie Hart's Greatest Hits* (Kapp 1969)★★★★, *World Of Freddie Hart* (Columbia 1972)★★★, *The Best Of Freddie Hart* (1975)★★★, *Best Of Freddie Hart* (MCA 1975)★★★★.

HARTFORD, JOHN

b. 30 December 1937, New York, USA. A child prodigy, Hartford was raised in St. Louis, and mastered the fiddle by the time he was 13. He then turned to banjo and dobro, and later played rock guitar in the clubs and honky tonks of St. Louis and Memphis. After leaving university, he worked at several jobs before moving to Nashville in 1965, where he quickly earned a reputation as a session player. In the following year he signed for RCA, and released 'Tall Tall Grass'. A year later, he recorded his best-known composition, 'Gentle On My Mind', which entered the US country charts, and was included on his *Earthwords And Music* album. In 1967, the song won several Grammy awards, and subsequently became a minor US hit for Glen Campbell. In 1969, Dean Martin's version went to number 2 in the UK, and sold over a million copies. Hartford's own solo career received a massive boost from this exposure, and he appeared regularly on television in the late 60s, guesting on the *Smothers Brothers Comedy Hour* and the *Glen Campbell Goodtime Hour*. He continued to work as a session musician, most notably on the groundbreaking Byrds set *Sweetheart Of The Rodeo*. After several years with RCA, he switched to Warner Brothers in 1971 and released *Aero-Plain*, a country-flavoured album containing the heartfelt 'They're Tearing Down The Grand Ole Opry'. In 1976, some of Hartford's most satisfying work was included on *Mark Twang*, for which he received a Grammy in the ethnic-traditional category. Despite his uneven output in later years, Hartford continues to be a respected artist on the US roots scene and records regularly, albeit to an ever decreasing audience. He formed his own label, Small Dog A-Barkin', and also performs with his son.

● ALBUMS: *Earthwords And Music* (RCA 1967)★★★, *The Love Album* (RCA 1968)★★, *John Hartford* (RCA 1969)★★, *Iron Mountain Depot* (RCA 1970)★★, *Aero-Plain* (Warners 1971)★★, *Morning Bugle* (Rounder 1972)★★★, *Down On The River* (Flying Fish 1972)★★★, with Lester Flatt, Benny Martin *Tennessee Jubilee* (Flying Fish 1975)★★★, *Nobody Knows What You Do* (Flying Fish 1976)★★, *Mark Twang* (Flying Fish 1976)★★★. As Dillard Hartford Dillard *Dillard-Hartford-Dillard* (Sonet 1975)★★★, *Permanent Wave* (Flying Fish 1980)★★★.

HARVEY, ROY

b. Roy Cecil Harvey, 24 March 1892, Monroe County, West Virginia, USA, d. 11 July 1958. Harvey loved music and learned to play guitar as a child, but a greater love for trains led to his working for the Virginian Railway. By 1923, he was working as an engineer, when a dispute caused a strike and his participation in it cost him his post. While working in a music shop in Beckley, he met Charlie Poole and their friendship led to Harvey becoming the guitarist with Poole's North Carolina Ramblers. From September 1926-30, he played on all Poole's Columbia recordings. He also recorded solo numbers and duets with Poole, Posey Rorer and noted yodeller Earl Shirkey (b. 1900, d. 1951), as well as guitar duets with Leonard Copeland. Harvey's repertoire was considerable and varied from ballads such as his self-penned 'The Virginian Strike Of '23' (written about the event that lost him his job) and old standards such as 'Mary Dear', to the comedy numbers 'Where The Roses Bloom For The Bootlegger' (with sales around 72,500, one of Columbia's top-selling records in 1928) and 'The Bootlegger's Dream Of Home'. He also played guitar when fiddler Jess Johnston (b. 1898, d. 1952) recorded the first version of 'Guitar Rag' ever recorded by white musicians, for Gennett (it was later popularized as 'Steel Guitar Rag' by Leon McAuliffe). In May 1931, Poole died and Harvey and Johnston, with Ernest Branch (banjo) and Bernice Coleman (fiddle), recorded as the West Virginia Ramblers, including an early version of 'Footprints In The Snow'. Harvey made his last recordings later that year for OKeh Records, the recordings being released as Branch And Coleman. In the late 30s, still saddened by Poole's death, Harvey grew more distant from music and joined the Beckley police. In 1942, he returned to his first love when, after relocating to Florida, he became an engineer for the Florida East Coast Railway. Early in 1958, he retired from the railroad and from music after giving his beloved Gibson to a friend in Daytona Beach. He died of cancer in 1958 and was buried at New Smyrna Beach. Rated as one of the 'smoothest of the old time guitarists', some of his solo and duet recordings may be found on various compilation albums by County, JEMF, Old Homestead and Vetco, and he is also featured on *The North Carolina Ramblers 1928-1930* (Biograph 1972).

HAWKINS, HAWKSHAW

b. Harold Franklin Hawkins, 22 December 1921, Huntingdon, West Virginia, USA, d. 5 March 1963, Camden, Tennessee, USA. Hawkins started on guitar but became proficient on many instruments. Success in a talent contest in 1937 led to paid work on radio stations in Huntingdon and Charleston. In 1942, he performed on radio in Manila when stationed in the Phillippines. After his discharge, he signed with King Records and did well with 'Sunny Side Of The Mountain', which became his signature tune. He was a regular member of the WWVA's *Wheeling Jamboree* from 1946 to 1954, which he left to join the *Grand Ole Opry*. In 1948 he became one of the first country artists to appear on network television. He had US country hits with 'Pan American', 'I Love You A Thousand Ways', 'I'm Just Waiting For You' and 'Slow Poke'. The tall, handsome country singer married fellow artist Jean Shepard, and they lived on a farm near Nashville where Hawkins bred horses. Their first son, Don Robin, was named after their friends Don Gibson and Marty

Robbins. In 1963 Hawkins released his best-known recording, Justin Tubb's song 'Lonesome 7-7203'. The song entered the US country charts three days before Hawkins died on 5 March 1963 in the plane crash that also claimed Patsy Cline and Cowboy Copas. 'Lonesome 7-7203' was his only number 1 record in the US country charts. Shepard was pregnant at the time and their son was named Harold Franklin Hawkins II in his memory.

● ALBUMS: *Hawkshaw Hawkins, Vol. 1* (King 1958)★★★, *Hawkshaw Hawkins Sings Grand Ole Opry Favourites* (King 1958)★★★, *Hawkshaw Hawkins* (King 1959)★★★, *The All New Hawkshaw Hawkins* (King 1963)★★★, *The Great Hawkshaw Hawkins* (1963)★★★ *Taken From Our Vaults, Volume 1* (King 1963)★★★, *Taken From Our Vaults, Volume 2* (King 1963)★★★, *Taken From Our Vaults, Volume 3* (King 1964)★★★, *Hawkshaw Hawkins Sings* (Camden 1964)★★★, *The Country Gentleman* (Camden 1966)★★★, *Lonesome 7-7203* (King 1969)★★.

● COMPILATIONS: *16 Greatest Hits Of Hawkshaw Hawkins* (Starday 1987)★★★, *Hawk, 1953-61* 3-CD box set containing previously unissued material (Bear Family 1991)★★★★

HAWKINS, RONNIE

b. 10 January 1935, Huntsville, Arkansas, USA. Hawkins, who is rock 'n' roll's funniest storyteller says: 'I've been around so long, I remember when the Dead Sea was only sick'. Hawkins' father played at square dances and his cousin, Dale Hawkins, staked his own claim to rock 'n' roll history with 'Susie Q'. Hawkins, who did some stunt diving for Esther Williams' swimming revue, earned both a science and physical education degree at the University of Arkansas, but his heart was in the 'chitlin' starvation circuit' in Memphis. Because the pay was poor, musicians went from one club to another using the 'Arkansas credit card' - a siphon, a rubber hose and a five gallon can. Hawkins befriended Elvis Presley: 'In 1954 Elvis couldn't even spell Memphis; by 1957 he owned it'. After Hawkins' army service, he followed Conway Twitty's recommendation by working Canadian clubs. While there, he made his first recordings as the Ron Hawkins Quartet, the tracks being included on *Rrrracket Time*. In 1959 Hawkins reached number 45 on the US charts with 'Forty Days', an amended version of Chuck Berry's 'Thirty Days'. He explains, 'Chuck Berry had simply put new lyrics to 'When The Saints Go Marching In'. My record company told me to add ten days. They knew Chess wouldn't sue as they wouldn't want to admit it was "The Saints"'. Hawkins' version of Young Jessie's 'Mary Lou' then made number 26 in the US charts. With his handstands and leapfrogging, he became known as Mr. Dynamo and pioneered a dance called the Camel Walk. In 1960 Hawkins became the first rock 'n' roller to involve himself in politics with a plea for a murderer on Death Row, 'The Ballad Of Caryl Chessman', but to no avail. The same year Hawkins with his drummer, Levon Helm, travelled to the UK for the ITV show *Boy Meets Girls*. He was so impressed by guitarist Joe Brown that he offered him a job, but, on returning home, the Hawks gradually took shape - Levon Helm, Robbie Robertson, Garth Hudson, Richard Manuel and Rick Danko. Their wild 1963 single of two Bo Diddley songs, 'Bo Diddley' and 'Who Do You Love', was psychedelia before its time. 'Bo Diddley' was a Canadian hit, and by marrying a former Miss Toronto, Hawkins made the country his home. He supported local talent and refused, for example, to perform in clubs that did not give equal time to Canadian artists. Meanwhile, the Hawks recorded for Atlantic Records as Levon and the Hawks and were then recruited by Bob Dylan, becoming the Band. The various incarnations of the Hawks have included many fine musicians, notably the pianist Stan Szelest. Hawkins had Canadian Top 10 hits with 'Home From The Forest' and 'Bluebirds Over The Mountain', while his experience in buying a Rolls-Royce was recounted in Gordon Lightfoot's 'Talkin' Silver Cloud Blues'. In 1970 Hawkins befriended John Lennon and Yoko Ono, and the promotional single on which Lennon praises Hawkins' 'Down In The Alley' is a collector's item. Kris Kristofferson wrote humorous liner notes for Hawkins' album *Rock And Roll Resurrection*, and it was through Kristofferson that Hawkins had a role in the disastrous film *Heaven's Gate*. Hawkins is better known for his extrovert performance in the Band's film *The Last Waltz*. The burly singer has also appeared in Bob Dylan's Rolling Thunder Revue and he has some amusing lines as 'Bob Dylan' in the film *Renaldo And Clara*; Hawkins' segment with 'happy hooker' Xaviera Hollander includes the line: 'Abraham Lincoln said all men are created equal, but then he never saw Bo Diddley in the shower'. In 1985 Hawkins joined Joni Mitchell, Anne Murray, Neil Young and several others for the Canadian Band Aid record, 'Tears Are Not Enough', by Northern Lights. Hawkins has a regular Canadian television series, *Honky Tonk*, and owns a 200 acre farm and has several businesses. It gives the lie to his colourful quote: '90 per cent of what I made went on women, whiskey, drugs and cars. I guess I just wasted the other 10 per cent'.

● ALBUMS: *Ronnie Hawkins* (Roulette 1959)★★, *Mr. Dynamo* (Roulette 1960)★★, *The Folk Ballads Of Ronnie Hawkins* (Roulette 1960)★★, *Ronnie Hawkins Sings The Songs Of Hank Williams* (Roulette 1961)★★, *Ronnie Hawkins* (1969)★★, *Ronnie Hawkins* (Cotillion 1970)★★, *Arkansas Rock Pile* (Roulette 1970)★★, *The Hawk* i (1971)★★, *Rock And Roll Resurrection* (Monument 1972)★★, *The Giant Of Rock And Roll* (1974)★★, *The Hawk* ii (United Artists 1979)★★, *Rrrracket Time* (Charly 1979)★★, *A Legend In His Spare Time* (1981)★★, *The Hawk And Rock* (1982)★★, *Making It Again* (1984)★★, *Hello Again ... Mary Lou* (1991)★★.

● COMPILATIONS: *The Best Of Ronnie Hawkins & His Band* (Roulette 1970)★★★, *The Best Of Ronnie Hawkins And The Hawks* (Rhino 1990)★★★.

● VIDEOS: *The Hawk In Concert* (MMG VIdeo 1988), *This Country's Rockin' - Reunion Concert* (1993).

● FURTHER READING: *The Hawk: The Story Of Ronnie Hawkins & The Hawks*, Ian Wallis.

HAY, GEORGE D.

b. George Dewey Hay, 9 November 1895, Attica, Indiana, USA, d. 8 May 1968. On completion of his education, Hay began his working career with a company involved in property and sales. He later changed to journalism and by 1919, was working for the Memphis *Commercial Appeal*. Part of his duties was to cover court cases and as a result of what he saw and heard there, he began to write a column that he called 'Howdy Judge'. The column presented, in a humorous and inoffensive manner, the conversations between a white judge and the unfortunate blacks who came before him on various charges. The stories, all written in dialect, quickly became extremely popular with the readers of the paper and won for their writer the nickname of 'Judge' (in 1926, Hay published some of the stories in a book). In 1923, the owners of the paper decided that they should try the new field of radio and founded WMC in Memphis. Hay was selected to be the newspaper's radio announcer and editor. Initially reluctant but quick to see the opportunities it offered, he began to develop a radio style. He realized from the start that immediate identification was essential and he took to using a chanting form of vocal delivery preceded by a blast from a toy wooden steamboat whistle, which he called 'Hushpuckiny'. He also gained national recognition by being the first announcer to inform the world of the death of President Harding. In 1924, his successful radio work at WMC saw him move to the Sears company to become the chief announcer on their new and more powerful WLS station in Chicago. He changed his steamboat whistle for a train whistle and soon became involved with the station's *WLS Barn Dance* (later known as the *National Barn Dance*). He began to refer to himself as the 'Solemn Old Judge' and established such a reputation that his services were much in demand. By the end of the year he had been awarded a gold cup by *Readers Digest* as the most popular announcer in the USA. Hay's reputation led to him being invited to Nashville to attend the dedication ceremony on 5 October 1925 of the new WSM station owned by National Life and Accident Insurance Co. Ltd. (The WSM letters stood for We Shield Millions.) While there he was offered the post of director of the station and a few weeks later, he took up his new position. He assessed the programme schedules against the potential audience figures, and quickly decided that too much emphasis was being placed on Nashville itself and that the station could not last if it only catered for the limited audience found within the city. He knew from his experience in Chicago of the importance of appealing to a rural audience. His views were not completely shared by the governing body but he was given the opportunity to prove his point. Fully aware of the success of the *WLS Barn Dance*, he decided that the station should feature a musical content of more interest to the outlying areas, particularly those to the south. On 28 November 1925, Hay's *WSM Barn Dance* started with a programme of fiddle music played by the 77-year-old Uncle Jimmie Thompson, who was accompanied by his niece Eva Thompson Jones on piano. Hay, naturally, provided announcements, and it was noticed that he had once again reverted to using his steamboat whistle, which he now called Old Hickory as a mark of respect to Nashville's hero, Andrew Jackson.

After this initial performance, the show became a regular Saturday evening programme on WSM. It extended to three hours' duration and Hay featured many noted local artists on it. Though immensely popular in the outlying areas, the show did have its adversaries within the city. Attempts were made to have 'the hillbilly programme' stopped, with claims that it was detrimental to the good name of Nashville. Hay successfully defended his creation and in 1927, fully aware of the fact that the station carried the NBC Grand Opera broadcasts from New York, he parodied the name by changing it from the Barn Dance to the *Grand Ole Opry*. Hay was eventually replaced as station manager of WSM by Harry Stone in 1930 but continued with his duties on the

Opry. His blasts on the steamboat whistle and shouts of 'Let her go, boys' became nationally known as the show opener. He also always closed with a special little verse and a final whistle blast. His instruction to musicians was always 'Keep it down to earth, boys' and he totally objected to any instrument being used that was not of the accepted acoustic variety. In the 30s and 40s, he continued to organize the *Opry*, he auditioned new talent and was responsible for the final *Opry* popularity of a great many artists, including Uncle Dave Macon (the *Opry*'s first real star), Roy Acuff and Eddy Arnold. Hay retired from active participation in the *Opry* in 1951 and moved to his daughter's home in Virginia. In 1953, his book, *A Story Of The Grand Ole Opry*, was published in Nashville. He was elected to the Country Music Hall Of Fame in 1966 for his services to the music and returned to Nashville for the occasion. It marks the esteem in which he was held by WSM to note that from his retirement in 1951 up to his death on 8 May 1968, at Virginia Beach, Virginia, he was to all intents and purposes still available for work and was paid by WSM.
● FURTHER READING: *A Story Of The Grand Ole Opry*, George D. Hay.

HAYES, WADE

b. 1971, Bethel Acres, Oklahoma, USA. Hayes was virtually born with a guitar in his hand, arriving into a family that lived and breathed country music. His father, Don Hayes, was a professional musician and bought Wade his first proper guitar at the age of 11. The family suffered a traumatic period during the mid-80s when his father secured a record contract and moved the family to Nashville. The record company went bankrupt owing Hayes Sr. a considerable amount of money - consequently, the family home was repossessed and they moved back to Oklahoma. Hayes Jr. started his professional career playing in his father's band as guitar and second vocalist. In 1992 Hayes met with the successful record producer Don Cook, and in a flurry of signings Hayes found himself with Columbia Records and a songwriting contract with Tree Publishing. He made his recording debut in 1995 with *Old Enough To Know Better*, an album that was featured widely on US country radio, and justifiably became a sizeable hit. The title song was also a substantial country hit, while the track 'Family Reunion' was about a son burying his mother beside his long-lost father. Other impressive tracks include 'Don't Make Me Come To Tulsa' and a great Cook, Brooks And Dunn song, 'Steady As She Goes'. Hayes' tunnel vision for country music and success has to be admired; it is evident that he is determined to make his career in country music a long one. Hayes continued to show startling maturity with his second effort, an accomplishment way beyond his years.
● ALBUMS: *Old Enough To Know Better* (Columbia 1995)★★★★, *On A Good Night* (Columbia 1996)★★★.

HAZLEWOOD, LEE

b. Barton Lee Hazlewood, 9 July 1929, Mannford, Oklahoma, USA. Hazlewood, the son of an oil worker, served in Korea, and on his return, became a DJ in Phoenix. He set himself up as an independent record producer and wrote 'The Fool', 'Run Boy Run' and 'Son Of A Gun' for Sanford Clark. On Clark's recordings, Hazlewood experimented with ways of recording Al Casey's guitar, often using echo. In 1957, after 'The Fool' had become a US pop hit for the Dot label, Hazlewood formed his own Jamie label, with publisher Lester Sill and television host Dick Clark. Hazlewood created the 'twangy guitar' by slowing down Duane Eddy's notes and deepening his sound. Hazlewood and Eddy co-wrote many instrumental hits including 'Rebel Rouser', 'Cannon Ball', 'Shazam!' and, with a minimal lyric, 'Dance With The Guitar Man'. Eddy was the first major performer to include musicians' names on album sleeves and, similarly, Hazlewood was acknowledged as the producer. Eddy also backed Hazlewood on a single, 'The Girl On Death Row'/'Words Mean Nothing'. Much of Eddy's success stemmed from his regular appearances on Dick Clark's *American Bandstand*, and Clark's payola allegations subsequently harmed Eddy's career. Hazlewood formed his LHI label and he produced the *Safe At Home* album by the International Submarine Band (including Gram Parsons). At Reprise in 1965, he wrote and produced US hits by Dean Martin ('Houston') and Dino, Desi And Billy, who included Martin's son ('I'm A Fool'). When Hazlewood was assigned to Nancy Sinatra, the daughter of the label's owner, who had made several unsuccessful singles, he promised to secure her hits. Nicknaming her 'Nasty Jones', he gave her 'These Boots Are Made For Walkin'', which had been written for a man, and said, 'You gotta get a new sound and get rid of this babyness. You're not a virgin anymore so let's do one for the truck drivers. Bite the words'. Sinatra's boots stomped over the international charts, and she followed it with other Hazlewood songs including 'How Does That Grab You, Darlin'', 'Sugartown' and 'Lightning's Girl'. Their duets include the playful 'Jackson' and the mysterious 'Some Velvet Morning' and 'Lady Bird'. The partnership folded because Sinatra tired of singing Hazlewood's songs, although she has made few records since. Hazlewood tried for the US country charts with a cover version of 'Ode To Billie Joe', and he also produced Waylon Jennings' *Singer Of Sad Songs*. His own albums include *Trouble Is A Lonesome Town*, a sombre collection about the characters in a western town, and *Requiem For An Almost Lady*, a sincere tribute to a girl-friend who had died. His *Poet, Fool Or Bum* was dismissed in one word by the *New Musical Express* - 'Bum'. One track, 'The Performer', emphasized his disillusionment, and he moved to Sweden, making records for the Scandinavian market. He reappeared in 1995, touring America with Nancy Sinatra.
● ALBUMS: *Trouble Is A Lonesome Town* (Mercury 1964)★★★, *The N.S.V.I.P.'s* soundtrack (1965)★★, *Lee Hazlewood Sings Friday's Child* (Reprise 1966)★★★, *The Very Special World Of Lee Hazlewood* (MGM 1966)★★★, *Hazlewoodism - Its Cause And Cure* (MGM 1966)★★, *Love And Other Crimes* (Reprise 1968)★★★, with Nancy Sinatra *Nancy And Lee* (Reprise 1968)★★★★, *Cowboy In Sweden* (1970)★★★, with Ann-Margret *The Cowboy And The Lady* (LHI 1971)★★★, *Forty* (LHI 1971)★★★, *Requiem For An Almost Lady* (1971)★★, with Sinatra *Nancy And Lee Again* (RCA 1972)★★★, *13* (1972)★★★, *I'll Be Your Baby Tonight* (1973)★★, *Poet, Fool Or Bum* (Capitol 1973)★★, *The Stockholm Kid* (1974)★★, *A House Safe For Tigers* film soundtrack (1975)★, *20th Century Lee* (1976)★★, *Movin' On* (1977)★★, *Back On The Street Again* (1977)★★.
● COMPILATIONS: with Sinatra *Fairytales And Fantasies* (Rhino 1989)★★★, *The Many Sides Of Lee* (Request 1991)★★★★.

HEAD, ROY

b. 1 September 1941, Three Rivers, Texas, USA. This respected performer first formed his group, the Traits, in 1958, after moving to San Marcos. The line-up included Jerry Gibson (drums) who later played with Sly And The Family Stone. Head recorded for several local labels, often under the supervision of famed Texas producer Huey P. Meaux, but it was not until 1965 that he had a national hit when 'Treat Her Right' reached number 2 on both the US pop and R&B charts. This irresistible song, with its pumping horns and punchy rhythm, established the singer alongside the Righteous Brothers as that year's prime blue-eyed soul exponent. Head's later releases appeared on a variety of outlets, including Dunhill and Elektra Records, and embraced traces of rockabilly ('Apple Of My Eye') and psychedelia ('You're (Almost) Tuff'). However, by the 70s he had honed his style and was working as a country singer, and in 1975 he earned a notable US C&W Top 20 hit with 'The Most Wanted Woman In Town'. He continued to have country hits well into the 80s.

● ALBUMS: *Roy Head And The Traits* (TNT 1965)★★★, *Treat Me Right* (Scepter 1965)★★★, *A Head Of His Time* (Dot 1968)★★★, *Same People* (Dunhill 1970)★★, *Dismal Prisoner* (1972)★★, *Head First* (Dot 1976)★★, *Tonight's The Night* (ABC 1977)★★, *Boogie Down* (1977)★★, *Rock 'N' Roll My Soul* (1977)★★, *In Our Room* (1979)★★, *The Many Sides Of Roy Head* (1980)★★.

● COMPILATIONS: *His All-Time Favourites* (1974)★★★, *Treat Her Right* (Bear Family 1988)★★★, *Slip Away: His Best Recordings* (Collectables 1993)★★, *Treat Her Right: Best Of Roy Head* (Varèse Vintage 1995)★★★★.

HEAP, JIMMY, AND THE MELODY MASTERS

b. James Arthur Heap, 3 March 1922, Taylor, Texas, USA, d. 4 December 1977. Heap graduated from high school in 1941 and joined the US Air Force. Self-taught (either before or during his military service), he became a competent lead guitarist and on his discharge in 1945, he began to assemble his Melody Masters. They began broadcasting on KTAE Taylor in 1948 and remained there until 1958. By 1949, the band members were Houston 'Perk' Williams (b. November 1926, near Chriesman, Texas; fiddle), Cecil 'Butterball' Harris (b. 1929, Sharp, Texas; steel guitar), Bill Glendinning (b. 5 May 1924, Taylor, Texas; electric bass fiddle), Horace Barnett (b. 18 October 1914, near Beaukiss, Texas; guitar) and Arlie Carter (b. 9 September 1911, Lexington, Texas; piano, guitar) (fiddler Louis Renson was also an original member). They played local state dances and clubs and also opened shows for Bob Wills, Ernest Tubb and Hank Williams. In 1949, they recorded for Imperial Records, including the Heap-Carter song 'Haunted Hungry Heart', which became a hit for Slim Whitman, then an Imperial artist, and the definitive version of 'The Wild Side Of Life' (also co-written by Carter). Their version sold well in Texas but since Imperial had no major distribution at that time, it failed to become a national hit. Heap recommended his friend Hank Thompson to record it for Capitol Records, requesting in return that if it became a hit, Thompson should secure Heap a Capitol contract. Thompson's version sold a million and the song has since been recorded by countless artists. Thompson kept his promise and between

November 1951 and December 1955, Heap recorded 37 sides for Capitol. Heap played lead guitar and, never keen on singing, he left most of the vocals to Perk Williams; although Williams had run his own band prior to joining Heap, he had never sung before, but soon proved to be an excellent vocalist. Several of the recordings sold well but the most popular was 'Release Me', which in 1954, became a Top 5 US country hit and Heap's only chart entry (in 1967, it became a smash pop hit for Engelbert Humperdinck, reaching number 4 in the USA, while topping the UK pop charts). In 1954, George Harrison (b. 13 March 1926, Fort Worth, Texas, USA; drums) joined the band. In 1956, Williams' wife died in a car crash near Milano (very close to the spot where Johnny Horton also died in 1960) and he never recovered from his loss. He was also growing disenchanted with the rockabilly music they played and only tolerated pop songs when played in a country style. He decided to leave the band to play as a solo performer. In 1955, Heap left Capitol and formed his own Fame label, on which he released a series of party records. The Melody Masters, with the addition of a trumpet player and a comedian, continued to play the Texas dancehall circuits and in Las Vegas. Heap later boasted they could play anything from the 'Flight Of The Bumble Bee' to the 'Orange Blossom Special'. Heap was a shrewd businessman and he kept the band running until July 1977 when, tired of the travelling and long hours, he dissolved the group. On 4 December 1977, while fishing on Lake Buchanan, his boat capsized and he was drowned. Heap and his Melody Masters were an important act in the development of country music but they have rarely been afforded the credit their input deserves. In 1992, Bear Family Records issued a CD containing all his Capitol recordings, five being previously unissued.

● COMPILATIONS: *The Early Hillbilly Years* (CowgirlBoy 1990)★★★, *Release Me: Jimmie Heap And The Melody Masters* (Bear Family 1992)★★★★.

HEARTS AND FLOWERS

Formed in 1964 at the Troubador Club in Los Angeles, California, when Rick Cunha (guitar, vocals) and Dave Dawson (autoharp, vocals), then working as a duo, met Larry Murray (guitar, vocals, ex-Scotsville Squirrel Barkers). Together they formed an acoustic country/folk act that quickly became an integral part of the west coast circuit. *Now Is The Time For Hearts And Flowers* revealed a group of breathtaking confidence, whose three-part harmonies and gift for melody brought new perspectives to a range of material drawn from Donovan, Carole King, Tim Hardin and Kaleidoscope. Terry Paul and Dan Woody were then added to the line-up, but Hearts And Flowers were a trio again for *Of Horses, Kids And Forgotten Women*. Although Rick Cunha had been replaced by another former Barker, Bernie Leadon, the blend of styles remained the same with Murray emerging as the group's chief songwriter. Commercial success did not ensue, and the band broke up soon after the album's release. Leadon and associate bassist David Jackon reappeared in Dillard And Clark and while Dawson dropped out of music altogether, both Murray and Cunha recorded as solo artists.

● ALBUMS: *Now Is The Time For Hearts And Flowers* (Capitol 1967)★★★, *Of Horses, Kids And Forgotten Women* (Capitol 1968)★★, *Now Is The Time For Hearts And Flowers/Of Horses, Kids And Forgotten Women* (Edsel 1995)★★★.

HEARTWOOD, KIYA

When the R&B label Malaco Records set up a country music subsidiary in 1993, the first signing was the country singer Kiya Heartwood. The album was recorded in Muscle Shoals Studio in Alabama but the results were uninspiring.
● ALBUMS: *True Frontiers* (Waldoxy 1993)★★★.

HEE HAW

This popular US television programme was the brainchild of John Aylesworth and Frank Peppiatt, two Canadians, who owned a production company. It first appeared on the CBS-TV network in the middle of 1968 and became a syndicated programme in 1971. Compered by Buck Owens and Roy Clark, it included a mixture of country music, a few serious songs and what is usually termed in the USA 'cornball' or 'rube' humour, probably drawing inspiration for its presentation from the *Rowan & Martin Laugh In*. The show, produced at WLAC-TV, was the first of its kind actually to be produced in Nashville and then syndicated. It was directed by Bill Davis and had George Richey (Tammy Wynette's husband) and sometimes Charlie McCoy supervising the musical content, which was usually provided by Buck Owens' Buckeroos or by guesting Nashville session musicians. Regular artists to supply the comedy over the years have included Minnie Pearl, Archie Campbell, Junior Samples, Grandpa Jones, Stringbean, Roni Stoneman and Kenny Price. There had been over 600 shows recorded when, in 1994, the show's then owners, Gaylord Syndicom, decided to cease production. Instead, they programmed a series taken from recordings of the show that was called *Hee Haw Silver*. During 1994, a programme called *Hee Haw Live* was also running in the Acuff Theatre in Opryland USA.

HELM, LEVON

b. Mark Levon Helm, 26 May 1942, Marvell, Arkansas, USA. Drummer Helm was part of the Ron Hawkins Quartet and when he graduated, he and Hawkins moved to Canada, developing into Ronnie Hawkins And The Hawks. When the group left Hawkins, they began playing the bars and clubs in their own right and recorded for Atlantic Records as Levon And The Hawks. In 1965 Bob Dylan invited them to accompany him on concert dates. They also made their own records as the Band. Their first albums, *Music From Big Pink* and *The Band*, feature American music at its best and encompass many styles, little of which could have been predicted before they met Dylan. When the Band disbanded, Helm, who had developed into an fine, intense vocalist, made solo albums and took acting roles. He was brilliantly cast as Loretta Lynn's father in the film *Coal Miner's Daughter* and, after recording 'Blue Moon Of Kentucky' for the soundtrack album, he used the same musicians for a country album, *American Son*. Helm played good ol' boys in several other films and was also featured as Jesse James on the concept album *The Legend Of Jesse James*, and he was a drummer alongside Ringo Starr when the latter formed his All-Starr Band in 1990. The Band re-formed in 1991 and relationships may have been strained when Helm published his no-holds-barred autobiography *This Wheel's On Fire*, in 1993.
● ALBUMS: *Levon Helm And The RCO All-Stars* (ABC 1977)★★★, *Levon Helm* (ABC 1978)★★, *American Son* (MCA 1980)★★★, *Levon Helm* (Capitol 1982)★★.
● FURTHER READING: *This Wheel's On Fire*, Levon Helm

with Stephen Davis. *Across The Great Divide: The Band And America*, Barney Hoskyns.

HELMS, BOBBY

b. Robert Lee Helms, 15 August 1933, Bloomington, Indiana, USA, d. 19 June 1997, Martinsville, Indiana, USA. Helms was something of a child prodigy, who was playing guitar and singing a mixture of pop and country on local radio at the age of 12, and from 1946-54, he regularly appeared on WWTV Bloomington. He made his debut on the *Grand Ole Opry* in 1950, having impressed WSM officials so much that they had him flown to Nashville to appear. He signed with Decca and in 1957, his recording of Lawton Williams' 'Fraulein', his first US country chart entry, was a number 1 (even reaching number 36 in the US pop charts). The song stayed in the country charts for 52 weeks, which, according to Joel Whitburn's *Record Research*, is the second longest chart tenure of all time. The same year also saw him with two further hits, 'My Special Angel' and the original version of 'Jingle Bell Rock', both of which became million sellers and made the Top 10 in the US pop charts. The former, another US country number 1, managed a Top 30 appearance in the UK charts, but lost out to the Top 10 cover version by Malcolm Vaughan (Max Bygraves made the UK Top 10 with his version of 'Jingle Bell Rock' in 1959). Helms had further country/pop success the following year with 'Jacqueline', from the film *The Case Against Brooklyn* (the record also charted in the UK) and a US country number 10 with 'Just A Little Lonesome'. In the late 60s, he left Decca and recorded for Little Darlin' but achieved no further major chart hits. Throughout the 70s and 80s, he continued to tour, often with his wife Dori and he released an album in 1989. He is still remembered because of seasonal appearances of 'Jingle Bell Rock' but his last chart hit, 'Mary Goes Round', was on the Certron label in 1970. Interestingly, it was a cover version of Helms' recording of 'Schoolboy Crush' that became the b-side of Cliff Richard's first recording.
● ALBUMS: *Bobby Helms Sings To My Special Angel* (Decca 1957)★★★, *Country Christmas* (1958)★★, *Bobby Helms* (Vocalion 1965)★★★, *I'm The Man* (Kapp 1966)★★★, *Sorry My Name Isn't Fred* (Kapp 1966)★★★, *Bobby Helms Sings Fraulein* (Harmony 1967)★★★, *All New Just For You* (Little Darlin' 1968)★★★, *Jingle Bell Rock* (1974)★★, *Pop A-Billy* (MCA 1983)★★★, *Bobby Helms Country* (Playback 1989)★★★.
● COMPILATIONS: *The Best Of Bobby Helms* (Columbia 1963)★★, *Greatest Hits* (1975)★★★, *Fraulein: The Classic Years* (Bear Family 1994)★★★★.
● FURTHER READING: *My Special Angel*, Dave Davis.

HENDERSON, MIKE

b. 7 July 1951, Independence, Missouri, USA. Beginning with a harmonica at the age of five and then graduating to guitar, 90s country singer Mike Henderson became immersed in music at an early age. At first he played the rock music of the day, but at the University of Missouri, he fell in with bluegrass musicians, mostly playing mandolin. He then joined a blues band, the Bel-Airs, which helped to develop his distinctive guitar style, which he describes as 'half Bill Monroe, half Muddy Waters'. Henderson and his wife moved to Nashville in 1985 and became part of the Roosters and then the Snakes, who played at the Bluebird Cafe and made an album for Curb Records in 1989. Because of his dexterity on so many instruments, Henderson was offered session work, playing on albums by Emmylou Harris (*Bluebird*), John Hiatt (*Stolen Moments*) and Joy Lynn White (*Between Midnight And Hindsight*). He has also played guitar for Kevin Welch. Several acts have recorded his songs and 'Powerful Stuff' by the Fabulous Thunderbirds was included in the film *Cocktail*. His albums are in the honky-tonk blues tradition.

● ALBUMS: *Country Music Made Me Do It* (RCA 1994)★★★, *The Edge Of Night* (Dead Reckoning 1995)★★★, with the Bluebloods *First Blood* (Dead Reckoning 1996)★★★.

HENDRICKS, SCOTT

Hendricks met Tim DuBois and Greg Jennings at Oklahoma State University in 1975. Then, three years later, while working at Opryland, he met Paul Gregg. Gregg and Jennings formed Restless Heart and DuBois and Hendricks were the record producers. Between them, they produced a series of highly successful country singles and albums. Since then, Hendricks has produced Brooks And Dunn, Alan Jackson, John Michael Montgomery, Lee Roy Parnell, Larry Stewart and Steve Wariner. He has a personal as well as a professional relationship with Faith Hill and he produced her 1996 US country number 1, 'It Matters To Me'.

HERNDON, TY

b. Butler, Alabama, USA. 90s country singer Ty Herndon grew up with a background of family singing, both at home and in church. He went to Nashville to seek his fortune, but through bad management agreements, he made no progress and his mother lost her house. 'Hat Full Of Rain' summarizes his problems: 'I've been ridin' through the storm, feelin' weary and worn.' He kept plugging away at his music and in 1993, he became the Texas Entertainer of the Year. Nashville has now welcomed him back and his debut album included guest vocals from Joe Diffie and Patty Loveless. The title track, a dramatic ballad, was a US country hit, while he dipped into the Jim Croce songbook for 'You Don't Mess Around With Jim'. The 1996 follow-up was a disappointment, suffering from a shortage of standout material.

● ALBUMS: *What Mattered Most* (Epic 1995)★★★★, *Living In A Moment* (Epic 1996)★★.

HICKS, DAN

b. 9 December 1941, Little Rock, Arkansas, USA. A former folk musician, Hicks joined the Charlatans in 1965, replacing original drummer Sam Linde. This trailblazing group is credited with pioneering the 60s San Francisco sound, although they sadly failed to reap due commercial rewards. Frustrated with his limited role, Hicks emerged from behind the drumkit to play guitar, sing and compose before establishing a new group, Dan Hicks And His Hot Licks, with David LaFlamme (violin - later of It's A Beautiful Day) and Bill Douglas (bass). However, within months the leader had reshaped the venture around Sid Page (violin), Jaime Leopold (bass) John Webber (b. 1947; guitar) and singers Tina Gancher (b. 1945) and Sherri Snow. *Original Recordings* established Hicks' 'folk-swing' style, which drew on country, 30s vocal jazz and the singer's quirky, deadpan humour to create a nostalgic, yet thriving, music. It included the mesmerizing 'I Scare Myself', later revived successfully by Thomas Dolby. Webber then dropped out of the group,

while Gancher and Snow were replaced by Maryanne Price and Naomi Ruth Eisenberg. *Where's The Money*, recorded live at the Los Angeles Troubadour, confirmed the promise of its predecessor, while *Striking It Rich*, which introduced newcomer John Girton (guitar), was arguably Hicks' strongest collection. *Last Train To Hicksville* completed this idiosyncratic unit's catalogue before Hicks decided to pursue a solo career. *It Happened One Bite* nonetheless drew support from Page, Girton and Price, but this disappointing set lacked the verve and interplay of earlier releases. During the 80s Hicks formed the Acoustic Warriors with James 'Fingers' Shupe (fiddle, mandolin) and Alex Baum (bass) with whom he continued his unique vision.

● ALBUMS: with the Hot Licks *The Original Recordings* (Epic 1969)★★★, *Where's The Money?* (Blue Thumb/MCA 1971)★★★, *Striking It Rich!* (Blue Thumb/MCA 1972)★★★, *Last Train To Hicksville...The Home Of Happy Feet* (Blue Thumb/MCA 1973)★★, *It Happened One Bite* (Warners 1978)★★★, with the Acoustic Warriors *Shootin' Straight* (Private Music 1994)★★★.

● COMPILATIONS: *Rich And Happy In Hicksville - Very Best Of Dan Hicks And His Hot Licks* (See For Miles 1986)★★★.

HIGHWAY 101

Like the Monkees, Highway 101 is a manufactured US group. Chuck Morris, the manager of the Nitty Gritty Dirt Band and Lyle Lovett, wanted to form a group that would play 'traditional country with a rock 'n' roll backbeat'. He recruited session man Scott 'Cactus' Moser to help him. He worked with bassist Curtis Stone, the son of Cliffie Stone, in the film *Back To School*, and then added session guitarist Jack Daniels. Morris then heard some demos by Paulette Carlson. She had had songs recorded by Gail Davies and Tammy Wynette and had a cameo role as a nightclub singer in the film *Twins*. Their first single, 'Some Find Love', was not successful, but in 1987, they had their first US country hits with 'The Bed You Made For Me' (number 4), which Carlson wrote, and 'Whiskey, If You Were A Woman' (number 2). They topped the US country charts with 'Somewhere Tonight' with its songwriting credit of 'old' and 'new' country, Harlan Howard and Rodney Crowell. In 1988 they had further chart-toppers with 'Cry, Cry, Cry' (which was a new song and not a revival of the Johnny Cash hit), 'If You Love Me, Just Say Yes' (being based on the slogan of Nancy Reagan's anti-drugs campaign, 'Just say no') and 'Who's Lonely Now' in 1989. Paulette Carlson took a turn off the Highway in 1990, and Nikki Nelson was recruited for *Bing Bang Boom*. The title track was an infectious and successful single, but the album failed to sell in the same quantities as before. Daniels quit in 1992 and the group made, *The New Frontier*, before disbanding. In 1995 Carlson initiated a reunion, missing only 'Cactus' from the line-up, and the band released a new album.

● ALBUMS: *Highway 101* (Warners 1987)★★★, *101 2* (Warners 1988)★★★, *Paint The Town* (Warners 1989)★★★, *Bing Bang Boom* (Warners 1991)★★★, *The New Frontier* (Liberty 1993)★★★, *Reunited* (Willow Tree 1996)★★★.

● COMPILATIONS: *Greatest Hits* (Warners 1990)★★★★.

HILL, FAITH

b. Audrey Faith Perry, 21 September, 1967, Jackson, Mississippi, USA. Raised in the small town of Star, Mississippi, USA, the 90s country singer Faith Hill was

singing at family gatherings from the age of three. She was influenced by Reba McEntire and formed her first band when she was 17 years old, performing at local rodeos. She moved to Nashville in 1989 and her first job was selling T-shirts at the Country Music Fan Fair. Attempts to make a name for herself in Nashville were fruitless, and Hill eventually accepted a secretarial job with a music publisher. Legend has it that the publisher/singer Gary Morris urged her to leave the job and take up singing as a career. She befriended songwriter Gary Burr, who produced her demo tape, and suitably impressed Warner Brothers Records. Hill has subsequently recorded several of Burr's songs, including 'I Would Be Stronger Than That', 'Just Around The Eyes' and 'Just About Now'. Her first album was produced by Scott Hendricks, who had previously had some success with Brooks And Dunn and Restless Heart. Her sparkling debut US country single, the rocking 'Wild One', topped the country charts and she followed it with a version of Janis Joplin's 'Piece Of My Heart', another cheerful country-rocker. *Take Me As I Am* was successful, but surgery on her vocal cords delayed the making of *It Matters To Me*. This included a song about wife-beating, 'A Man's Home Is His Castle', a duet with Shelby Lynne, 'Keep Walkin' On', and a song written for her by Alan Jackson, 'I Can't Do That Anymore'. Her regular band features Trey Grey (drums), Steve Hornbeak (keyboards), Tom Rutledge (guitar, fiddle), Anthony Joyner (bass), Lou Toomey (lead guitar), Karen Staley (guitar, vocals) and is masterminded by dobro and steel guitarist Gary Carter. Much of Hill's popularity has been fuelled by having one of the best touring bands in the business. 'It Matters To Me' was a further US country chart topper in 1996. In 1997 she recorded with her husband Tim McGraw, resulting in the number 1 hit and CMA Award-winning 'It's Your Love'.
● ALBUMS: *Take Me As I Am* (Warners 1993)★★★, *It Matters To Me* (Warners 1995)★★★★.
● VIDEOS: *Piece Of My Heart* (Deaton Flanigen 1994).

HILLMAN, CHRIS

b. 4 December 1942, Los Angeles, California, USA. Originally a mandolin player of some distinction, Hillman appeared in the Scottsville Squirrel Barkers, the Blue Diamond Boys and the Hillmen before Jim Dickson offered him the vacant role of bassist in the fledgling Byrds in late 1964. The last to join that illustrious group, he did not emerge as a real force until 1967's *Younger Than Yesterday*, which contained several of his compositions. His jazz-influenced, wandering basslines won him great respect among rock *cognoscenti*, but it soon became clear that he hankered after his country roots. After introducing Gram Parsons to the Byrds, he participated in the much-acclaimed *Sweetheart Of The Rodeo* and went on to form the highly respected Flying Burrito Brothers. A line-up with Stephen Stills in Manassas and an unproductive period in the ersatz supergroup Souther Hillman Furay Band was followed by two mid-70s solo albums of average quality. A reunion with Roger McGuinn and Gene Clark in the late 70s proved interesting but short-lived. During the 80s, Hillman recorded two low-budget traditional bluegrass albums, *Morning Sky* and *Desert Rose*, before forming the excellent and highly successful Desert Rose Band. They enjoyed considerable but diminishing success and the unit folded in 1993. Hillman and Herb Pederson worked as a duo in the

mid-90s and released a traditionally flavoured album, *Bakersfield Bound*, in 1996.
● ALBUMS: with The Hillmen *The Hillmen* (Together 1970)★★★, *Slippin' Away* (Asylum 1976)★★★, *Clear Sailin'* (Asylum 1977)★★, *Morning Sky* (Sugar Hill 1982)★★★, *Desert Rose* (Sugar Hill 1984)★★★, with Herb Pederson *Bakersfield Bound* (Sugar Hill 1996)★★★★, with Pedersen, Tony Rice, Larry Rice *Out Of The Woodwork* (Rounder 1996)★★★★.

HILLSIDERS

The Hillsiders played country when country was not cool - as the UK's leading country band, they have now introduced thousands of people to the music. The group's origins go back to 1959 when lead singer/rhythm guitarist Kenny Johnson (b. 11 December 1939, Liverpool, England) formed the Country Three. Johnson, joined by guitarist Joe Butler (b. 12 January 1939, Liverpool, England), changed the group to Sonny Webb and the Country Four, taking his stage name from the American country stars Sonny James and Webb Pierce. In 1961, following an argument, Johnson regrouped as Sonny Webb And The Cascades. Butler played bass and they were joined by lead guitarist Frank Wan, who had been with Clinton Ford, and Brian 'Noddy' Redman, of the Fourmost and Kingsize Taylor And The Dominoes. Playing the beat venues frequented by Merseybeat groups, they brought their tough environment to country music and so pioneered country rock before the Byrds. Their publicity proclaimed, 'For that country flavour and the best in pops', and their repertoire can be gauged from their recordings at the Rialto Ballroom in Liverpool for Oriole's *This Is Merseybeat* albums. The songs included George Jones' 'Who Shot Sam?', Bob Luman's 'You've Got Everything', Hank Locklin's 'Border Of The Blues' and Buck Owens' 'Excuse Me'. At Ozzie Wade's country music club in Liverpool in May 1964, Sonny Webb and the Cascades became the Hillsiders. Brian Hilton from Group One joined as lead guitarist when Frank Wan switched to steel. Wan, who tired of life on the road, was subsequently replaced by Ronnie Bennett in 1966. The Hillsiders had a residency at the Black Cat club in Liverpool but they spent time touring, working in Germany with Red Sovine and often backing visiting American artists. Bobby Bare and George Hamilton IV both made albums with the group. The Hillsiders made numerous records in their own right, starting with an appearance on Decca's album *Liverpool Goes Country*. They won numerous country awards and became well known through the radio programmes *Country Meets Folk* and *Up Country*. The packaging for their album *By Request* features genuine requests and shows their most popular stage numbers - 'Proud Mary', 'Crying In The Rain' and 'Me And Bobby McGee'. However, they were also writing more and more of their own material, leading to their self-penned album *Our Country*, which included the excellent 'Across The Mountain' and 'Blue Kentucky Morning', a song they had written for Patsy Powell. The promising Butler-Johnson partnership ceased when Johnson left the Hillsiders in January 1975 to be replaced by Kevin McGarry from another Liverpool band, the Westerners. As the Hillsiders sold more of their Polydor albums at shows than in the shops, they were encouraged to set up their own label, Stile. Ronnie Bennett left the Hillsiders to develop his own steel guitar company and he was replaced by Dave Rowlands. Both the Hillsiders and Kenny Johnson, with his new group Northwind, have moved towards a more powerful-sounding country music and both have developed strong, original material. The *15 - 25* album, their fifteenth in 25 years, included guest apperances by Kenny Johnson and Ronnie Bennett and featured a new version of their first single, Diggy Liggy Lo'. Butler left the Hillsiders in 1993, largely because of his commitments as a broadcaster on local radio. He was replaced by Mick Kinney from another Merseyside band, Phil Brady And The Ranchers. Butler now plays in a well-established part-time band, Hartford West. The Hillsiders were notable for being the first UK band to pick up on the potential of the Mavericks; says McGarry, 'We were performing their songs long before anyone had heard of them and then they got known through CMT. People have said to us "That American act is doing your songs"'.

● ALBUMS: *The Hillsiders Play The Country Hits* (60s)★★★, *The Hillsiders* (60s)★★★, with Bobby Bare *The English Countryside* (1967)★★, *The Leaving Of Liverpool* (1969)★★★, with George Hamilton IV *Heritage* (1971)★★★, *By Request* (1972)★★, *Our Country* (1973)★★★, *To Please You* (1975)★★★, *Goodbye Scottie Road* (1976)★★★, *On The Road* (70s)★★, *A Day In The Country* (LP 1979)★★★, *15 - 25* (1990)★★★.
Solo: Kenny Johnson *Let Me Love You Once* (1980)★★★, *The Best Of Kenny Johnson* (1982)★★★.

HOBBS, BECKY

b. Rebecca A. Hobbs, 24 January 1950, Bartlesville, Oklahoma, USA. Hobbs' father loved big band music and her mother country, two strong influences on her later work. She was given a piano when she was nine years old, and began playing the piano parts on rock 'n' roll records, notably those of Jerry Lee Lewis. At the age of 15, she formed an all-girl group, the Four Faces Of Eve, and from 1971, she worked with a bar band, Swamp Fox, in Baton Rouge. The band went to Los Angeles in 1973, but they soon broke up. Hobbs recorded what is now a highly obscure album for MCA (Helen Reddy recorded one of the songs, 'I'll Be Your Audience'), and then recorded for Tattoo, finally achieving some entries on the US country charts with 'Honky Tonk Saturday Night' and 'I Can't Say Goodbye To You'. Her duet with Moe Bandy, 'Let's Get Over Them Together', was a US country hit and then came a top-selling single, 'Hottest Ex In Texas'. Her compositions include 'I Want To Know Who You Are Before We Make Love' (Alabama, Conway Twitty), 'Still On A Roll' (Moe Bandy and Joe Stampley, Kelvin Henderson), 'I'll Dance A Two Step' (Shelley West) and 'Feedin' The Fire' (Zella Lehr). Her effervescent style is well to the fore on her honky tonk album *All Keyed Up*, which was co-produced by Richard Bennett, Steve Earle's guitarist. She has also recorded what is arguably the best of all tributes to George Jones, 'Jones On The Jukebox'. There was a six-year gap between *All Keyed Up* and *The Boots I Came To Town With*, during which the impetus had left her career. The latter album, still a good one, included her version of 'Angels Among Us', an original song that Alabama had first recorded. During a hiatus between albums, she recorded briefly with Curb Records, which included an interesting version of the 1963 Ernest Ashworth hit (also a hit for Johnny Tillotson later that year), 'Talk Back Trembling Lips'.

● ALBUMS: *Becky Hobbs* (MCA 1974)★★★, *From The Heartland* (Tattoo 1975)★★★, *Everyday* (Tattoo 1977)★★★, *Becky Hobbs* (Liberty 1984)★★★, *All Keyed Up* (RCA 1988)★★★, *The Boots I Came To Town With* (Intersound 1994)★★★.

HOFNER, ADOLPH

b. 8 June 1916, Moulton, Lavaca County, Texas, USA. His father was part-German and his mother Czechoslovakian, and Hofner grew up initially speaking Czech and with a love of polka music. He and his brother Emil (b. 1918) both learned to play stringed instruments and by the early 30s, with Emil playing steel and Adolph standard guitar and aspiring to be a vocalist, the two played in a trio around the clubs of San Antonio, where the family had relocated in 1928. Adolph joined Jimmy Revard's Oklahoma Playboys in 1935 and made his first recordings with them. By 1939, Adolph was a popular vocalist with his own band, the San Antonians, although during the war his name caused some problems until he became Dolph Hofner. He recorded a mixture of country, Texan and Czech music and later claimed to be the first artist to record 'Cotton Eyed Joe'. When, in the late 40s, polka music again became popular in Texas, Hofner was quick to add it to his band's repertoire, and even recorded several polkas, including 'Julida Polka'. He was sponsored by Pearl Beer and with his band renamed the Pearl Wranglers, playing a mixture of country, Tex-Mex, western swing and German-style polka music, he commenced a regular programme that was carried by several radio stations, and also toured extensively. In 1994, still active, Adolph Hofner was honoured at a special show in his favourite San Antonio dancehall to commemorate his fifty-fifth anniversary in country music.

● ALBUMS: *Dance-O-Rama* 10-inch album (Decca 1955)★★, *South Texas Swing (His Early Recordings 1935-1955)* (Arhoolie 1964)★★★★.

HOGAN, JOHN

b. 31 August, Kilbeggan, County Westmeath, Eire. After completing his education, Hogan worked as a supervisor in a peat briquette factory in Croghan, County Offaly. Inspired by Jim Reeves and Hank Williams, he dreamed of a singing career. Early in 1988, using the money scheduled as the next instalment on his mortgage to finance the project in a local studio, he recorded a demo tape of an old song that his mother had sung as a child, called 'Brown Eyes'. Air play on local radio provoked considerable interest and led to him quitting his job to concentrate on a singing career. He formed a band and with the help of appearances on some major television shows and a great deal of hard work, he gradually built his reputation and gained successes in the Irish charts. He also began to write songs such as 'My Feelings For You' and 'Turn Back The Years' and made his first recordings for K-Tel Records. His appearances extended to the UK, where he became very popular around the country club circuit. In 1990, he joined the Ritz label and early in 1993, he achieved an ambition when the label decided that he should record an album in Nashville. He has also released an in-concert video, *My Kind Of Country*, which helped increase his popularity, not only in his native Ireland, where he lives in County Offaly (near to the factory where he used to work), but also in the UK. He continues to write some of his own material, such as the semi-autobiographical 'My Guitar' and 'Stepping Stone', while Foster And Allen recorded his song 'My Christmas'.

● ALBUMS: *My Feelings For You* (K-Tel 1988)★★, *Turn Back The Years* (K-Tel 1989)★★★, *Humble Man* (Ritz 1991)★★★, *The Nashville Album* (Ritz 1993)★★★★, *Loving You* (Ritz 1996)★★★.

● VIDEOS: *My Kind Of Country* (1994).

HOLLOWAY, KEN

b. 1965, Lafayette, Louisiana, USA. Holloway was a promising country singer working in bars and hoping for a contract with a major label, but his career was changed when his wife, Connie, became a born-again Christian. He says, 'I woke up one night and Connie was praying for me. She thought I was asleep but I could hear her saying, "God, he's my best friend. I love him so much, I don't want to go to heaven without him. You do what you have to do to get him saved"' (this event is recorded in his song 'I Don't Wanna Go Alone'). Holloway attended church meetings and a few months later, after witnessing a fight at a honky tonk, he put down the microphone and walked out of the club, resolving never to sing in one again. He studied theology and became an ordained minister. At the same time, a new strand of religious music was developing that sounded like state-of-the-art country. Paul Overstreet and Russ Taff led the way, but at the forefront of the new Christian Country videos on CMT was Ken Holloway. As energetic as Alan Jackson and Ken Diffie, his songs are full of moral dilemmas, Christian sentiments and the joys of family life. The analogies are forced - heaven is seen as an endless honky-tonk party in 'Hoedown', and in another he states that 'the old rugged cross became our family tree' - best is 'Unplug the jukebox/I won't need it anymore/No more lonely nights walking the floor/I've found a new love that's worth waiting for.' Most of Holloway's concerts take place in churches and he has never returned to honky tonks.

● ALBUMS: *Ken Holloway* (Ransom 1994)★★, *He Who Made The Rain* (Ransom 1995)★★★, *The Ordinary* (Ransom 1997)★★★.

HOLLY, DOYLE

b. Hoyle F. Hendricks, 30 June 1936, Perkins, Oklahoma, USA. Holly worked in oilfields in Kansas, Oklahoma and California and made some of his first musical appearances as a member of Johnny Burnette's band. Between 1963 and 1970, a fine guitarist, he was a regular member of Buck Owens' Buckeroos, playing bass guitar and singing harmony as well as solo vocals. He also appeared on many of Owens' recordings. Holly sings a fine solo version of 'Streets Of Laredo' on Owens' 1965 *I've Got A Tiger By The Tail*. In 1970, he decided to form his own band, the Vanishing Breed. He signed to Barnaby Records and made his chart debut in 1972 with 'My Heart Cries For You'. The following year, he registered the first charted version of 'Queen Of The Silver Dollar' and his only Top 20 success, 'Lila', which reached number 17 in 1973. His last chart entries came in 1974, when he had three minor hits, including 'Just Another Cowboy Song'. Holly later played with other bands but nothing has been heard of him in recent years.

● ALBUMS: *Doyle Holly* (Barnaby 1973)★★★, *Just Another Cowboy Song* (Barnaby 1973)★★★.

HOLM, JUNE

b. 14 June 1925, Brisbane, Queensland, Australia (but grew up on a farm by the Clarence River in New South Wales), d. 31 December 1966. One of the first female Australian country artists, and in spite of her relatively short career, she is held in very high esteem by followers of the music for her excellent guitar playing and exceptionally clear vocals and yodelling. Her mother played steel guitar and ukulele but it is claimed that June taught herself to play guitar while riding her pony to school, and only took up singing and yodelling in protest of the fact that all the popular country music singers were men. She made her first public appearance in 1935 and for a time sang with Beverley Thorn, mainly featuring Hawaiian-type music; however, Holm leaned more towards hillbilly music, and the duo split in 1939. She recorded some radio transcription discs that year and appeared on ABC. In the early 40s, she established herself and during the war years, working with a Red Cross entertainment unit, she was very popular with Australian servicemen. On 28 January 1942, she made her only six recordings, which included 'Happy Yodelling Cowgirl' and 'Daddy Was A Yodelling Cowboy'. In view of the popularity of her records and the fact that she remained active on stage and radio for several years after making them, it is strange that she made no further recordings. After the war, she toured all the Australian states with a Stage Spectacular show. In 1948, she married a man called Hayes (Leo or Tom), a government official, whose work took him to various overseas postings, and they spent some years in Nigeria and Suva. She appeared on Brisbane radio in 1958 but retired from entertaining two years later. Tragedy struck when her mother and father died and then, early in 1966, her husband died suddenly, leaving her three months pregnant with twins. She became very depressed and underwent medical treatment. She died on 31 December 1966, as a result of an overdose of barbiturates - whether accidental or deliberate is still open to conjecture. She was buried in an unmarked grave on 3 January 1967, the day before the twins celebrated their first birthday, leaving them and her other three children orphans. In 1980, an EP was released to raise funds to provide a memorial for her grave and in December 1981, her six recordings, plus a souvenir booklet and six songs by Zeta Burns (who had fronted the memorial campaign), were released. June Holm was known as Australia's Yodelling Cowgirl and the three Regal-Zonophone 78s of her recordings are now collectable records.

● COMPILATIONS: *Songs To Be Remembered* (Queensland Country Style 1981)★★★.

HOLMES BROTHERS

Sherman Holmes (b. 29 September 1939, Plainfield, New Jersey, USA), Wendell Holmes (b. 19 December 1943, Plainfield, New Jersey, USA), Popsy Dixon (b. 26 July 1942, Virginia Beach, Virginia, USA) and Gib Wharton (b. 15 September 1955, Mineral Wells, Texas, USA). The Holmes Brothers took almost three decades to become an overnight sensation. Both Sherman and Wendell sang in the church choir in Christchurch (now Salud), Virginia, where they grew up. Sherman studied clarinet and piano before taking up the bass he plays onstage, while Wendell learned trumpet, organ and guitar. In 1959, Sherman took a break from studying music theory and composition at Virginia

State University to visit New York and never returned south. When Wendell graduated from high school in 1963, his brother brought him to New York. After working with Jimmy Jones and Charlie And Inez Foxx, they formed their own band, the Sevilles, which lasted from 1963 to 1966, after which they worked in a variety of Top 40 bands. The Holmes Brothers band finally came together in 1980, when they were joined by drummer Popsy Dixon, who subsequently proved to be the possessor of a strong tenor voice. Steel guitarist Geb Wharton played in Texas country groups until he decided to move to New York in 1988. The band's albums reveal the breadth of their repertoire, which they have claimed contains some 250 songs. Their long experience of playing all forms of popular music has enabled them to fuse elements of gospel, C&W, R&B and soul and present them in an easily assimilable form.

● ALBUMS: *In The Spirit* (Rounder 1989)★★★, *Where It's At* (Rounder 1991)★★★★, *Soul Street* (Rounder 1993)★★★, *Lotto Land: Original Soundtrack Recording* (Stony Plain 1996)★★, *Promised Land* (Rounder 1997)★★★.

HOMER AND JETHRO

Homer (b. Henry D. Haynes, 27 July 1920, d. 7 August 1971, Chicago, Illinois, USA) and Jethro (b. Kenneth C. Burns, 10 March 1920, d. 4 February 1989, Evanston, Illinois, USA) were both from Knoxville, Tennessee, USA. They went to the same school and learned to play stringed instruments as young children. In 1932, they began to work together as musicians on WNOX Knoxville, where they performed in a quartet known as the String Dusters. With Homer on guitar and Jethro on mandolin, they mainly played instrumental pop music and any vocals were usually performed as a trio. Somewhat bored with the regular format, they developed a comedy act that they used backstage. They began to present comedy versions of popular songs by maintaining the melody but changing the lyrics, and before long, they were encouraged to perform them live on the radio. They were given the names of Homer and Jethro by the programme director, Lowell Blanchard. The act quickly proved a popular part of the String Dusters' routine. In 1936, they left the group to work solely as Homer and Jethro but stayed at WNOX until 1939. They then became regulars on the *Renfro Valley Barn Dance* in Kentucky, but in 1941, they were both called up for military service. In 1945, they were back together as regulars on the *Midwestern Hayride* on WLW Cincinnati, and between 1946 and 1948, they recorded their humorous songs for the local King label. In 1949, after a move to RCA Records, they had Top 10 US country chart success with a recording with June Carter of 'Baby It's Cold Outside'. In the late 1940s, they toured with their own tent show but eventually joined Red Foley on KWTO Springfield. In 1949, they toured the USA as part of orchestra leader Spike Jones' show and in 1951, while in Chicago with Jones, they were invited to become regulars on the *National Barn Dance* on WLS, where they remained until 1958. During the 50s and 60s, they toured extensively, their humour proving very popular in many varied venues, including Las Vegas. Their biggest country chart hit came in 1953, when 'How Much Is That Hound Dog In The Window' reached number 2. In 1959, they had a US pop Top 20 hit with 'The Battle Of Kookamonga', their parody of Johnny Horton's hit 'Battle Of New Orleans'. Proving that no song was safe from the

couple's attentions in 1964, they had their last chart entry with their version of the Beatles' 'I Want To Hold Your Hand'. They also made commercials for Kellogg's Cornflakes during the 60s, which made them household names in the USA, but might have prompted a drop in sales had they been shown in Britain. The zany comedy tended to overshadow the fact that the duo were fine musicians. They made instrumental albums and in 1970, they recorded with Chet Atkins (Jethro's brother-in-law) as the Nashville String Band (it was not until the album had reached the charts that RCA revealed the identities of the musicians). Atkins rated Homer as one of the best rhythm guitarists he ever knew. Jethro was also noted as an excellent mandolin player and one who, even in his early days, did much to make the instrument acceptable in jazz music. The partnership came to an end after 39 years on 7 August 1971, when Homer suffered a heart attack and died. Jethro was deeply affected by Homer's death but eventually returned to work as a musician. In the late 70s, he toured and recorded with Steve Goodman. Jethro died of cancer at his home in February 1989. Homer and Jethro's parodies included such titles as 'The Ballad Of Davy Crew-Cut' and 'Hart Brake Motel', and few could match album titles such as *Songs My Mother Never Sang, Ooh! That's Corny* (named after their catchphrase) or, bearing in mind they had been steadily turning out albums for 16 years, to suddenly decide to call one simply *Homer & Jethro's Next Album*. They never enjoyed success in the UK but were an institution in the USA.

● ALBUMS: *Homer & Jethro Fracture Frank Loesser* 10-inch album (RCA Victor 1953)★★★, *The Worst Of Homer & Jethro* (RCA Victor 1957)★★★★, *Barefoot Ballads* (RCA Victor 1957)★★★, *Life Can Be Miserable* (RCA Victor 1958)★★★★, *Musical Madness* (Audio Lab 1958)★★★, *They Sure Are Corny* (King 1959)★★★★, *At The Country Club* (RCA Victor 1960)★★★, *Songs My Mother Never Sang* (RCA Victor 1961)★★★, *Homer & Jethro At The Convention* (RCA Victor 1962)★★★, *Homer & Jethro Strike Back* (Camden 1962)★★★, *Playing It Straight* (RCA Victor 1962)★★★, *Cornier Than Corn* (King 1963)★★★★, *Zany Songs Of The 30s* (RCA Victor 1963)★★★, *Homer & Jethro Go West* (RCA Victor 1963)★★★, *Ooh, That's Corny!* (RCA Victor 1963)★★★, *The Humorous Side Of Country Music* (Camden 1963)★★★, *Cornfucius Say* (RCA Victor 1964)★★★, *Fractured Folk Songs* (RCA Victor 1964)★★★, *Homer & Jethro Sing Tenderly And Other Love Ballads* (RCA Victor 1965)★★★, *The Old Crusty Minstrels* (RCA Victor 1965)★★★, *Songs To Tickle Your Funny Bone* (Camden 1966)★★★, *Wanted For Murder* (RCA Victor 1966)★★★, *Any News From Nashville* (RCA Victor 1966)★★★, *It Ain't Necessarily Square* (RCA Victor 1967)★★★, *Nashville Cats* (RCA Victor 1967)★★★, *24 Great Songs In The Homer & Jethro Style* (King 1967)★★★, *Something Stupid* (RCA Victor 1967)★★★, *Songs For The 'Out' Crowd* (RCA Victor 1967)★★★, *The Playboy Song* (Camden 1968)★★★, *There's Nothing Like An Old Hippie* (RCA Victor 1968)★★, *Homer & Jethro Live At Vanderbilt University* (RCA Victor 1968)★★★, *Cool Crazy Christmas* (RCA Victor 1968)★★, *Homer & Jethro's Next Album* (RCA Victor 1969)★★★, *The Far Out World Of Homer & Jethro* (RCA Victor 1972)★★★. With The Nashville String Band *Down Home* (RCA Victor 1970)★★★, *Identified* (RCA Victor 1970)★★★, *Strung Up* (RCA Victor 1971)★★★.
By Jethro Burns: with Joe Venuti, Curly Chalker, Eldon

Shamblin *S'Wonderful (4 Giants Of Swing)* (Flying Fish 1977)★★★, *Jethro Burns* (Flying Fish 1977)★★★, *Jethro Burns Live* (Flying Fish 1978)★★★, with Tiny Moore *Back To Back* (Flying Fish 1980)★★★, *Tea For One* (Flying Fish 1982)★★★, with Red Rector *Old Friends* (Flying Fish 1983)★★★.
● COMPILATIONS: *The Best Of Homer & Jethro* (RCA Victor 1966)★★★, *Country Comedy* (Camden 1971)★★★, *Assault On The Rock 'N' Roll Era* (Bear Family 1989)★★★, *The Best Of* (RCA 1992)★★★, *America's Favorite Song Butchers: The Weird World Of Homer & Jethro* (Razor & Tie 1997)★★★★.

HOOSIER HOT SHOTS

The group consisted of Hezzie Trietsch (drums, song whistle, alto horn, washboard), brother Kenny Triesch (guitar, bass, banjo, horn), Frank Kettering (bass, guitar, banjo, flute, piano, piccolo) and Gabe Ward (clarinet). After starting out as a dance band, they found comedy routines were more enjoyable to perform and consequently, by 1935, when they became regulars on the WLS *National Barn Dance* in Chicago, they had become a novelty act. Their rousing stage entrance, preceded by the cry 'Are you ready, Hezzie', inspired a national catchphrase, and for years they worked the NBC *Alka Seltzer Show* segment with Uncle Ezra. Songs that they made popular include 'Meet Me In The Icehouse Lizzie', 'Red Hot Fannie' and 'The Man With Whiskers'. They toured extensively and recorded for ARC, Vocalion and Mercury Records, but their comedy and zany behaviour firmly established their live appeal. They toured with the WLS tours and historian Bill C. Malone states in *Country Music USA* that they 'frequently grossed between $3,000 and $5,000 dollars for one-day stands'. They visited Hollywood and even made appearances in several films. Naturally, over the years, there were personnel changes and other artists who appeared as members included Nathan Harrison, Keith Milheim and Gil Taylor.
● ALBUMS: *The Hoosier Hot Shots* (Tops 1959)★★★★, *The Hoosier Hot Shots Hoop It Up (Wha Hoo)* (Golden Tone 1960)★★★★, *The Original Hoosier Hot Shots* (Dot 1964)★★★★, *It's The Hoosier Hot Shots (National Barn Dance)* (Sunbeam 1975)★★★, *Nashville's Original Hoosier Hot Shots - Country Kiddin'* (Spin-O-Rama 70s)★★★.
● COMPILATIONS: Rural Rhythm (Columbia/ Legacy 1992)★★★★.

HOPKINS, DOC

b. 26 January 1900, Harlan County, Kentucky, USA, d. 3 January 1988, Chicago, Illinois, USA. Hopkins, who grew up in the Renfro Valley, is remembered as an old-time singer and guitarist, but he originally learned banjo from blind Kentucky player Dick Burnett. He saw army service during World War I and on his discharge, he spent 10 years working on medicine shows that saw him tour all over the USA, frequently playing Hawaiian music. In 1930, he moved to WLS Chicago, where he became a prominent member of the Cumberland Ridge Runners. He also worked with Bradley Kincaid and Karl And Harty and established himself as a regular on the *National Barn Dance*. Although he was more interested in working on the radio than in records, he did record for Broadway and ARC, and in March 1941, he cut six sides for Decca, including 'My Little Georgia Rose' and 'Wreck Of The Old Thirty-One'. He also made around 200 radio transcriptions for the MM Cole Company. He basically retired from performing in the 50s and became well known as a teacher of the banjo.

HORSBURGH, WAYNE

b. 11 June 1955, Lima, near Benalla, Victoria, Australia. Horsburgh grew up on the family's dairy farm and was given his first guitar at the age of eight. His interest in country music began when he used to listen to his father's Hank Snow and Wilf Carter records. When he was aged 11, he sang with a local dance band and made the finals of a national television programme in Melbourne. After completing his high school studies in 1971, he spent four years working for the State Savings Bank, first in Benalla and later in Melbourne. However, in August 1973, after seeing Slim Whitman during an Australian tour, he decided upon a career in country music. Impressed by Whitman's clever use of falsetto, he practised and soon became a proficient yodeller, a talent that endeared him to his American audiences when, some years later, he made regular visits to the USA. He finally achieved his breakthrough in 1978, when he was offered the opportunity to tour with the travelling show of Australian legend Buddy Williams. He benefited greatly from this experience and soon built up a popular stage act of his own. Now a household name in Australia thanks to major television shows such as Reg Lindsay's *Country Homestead* and the *Midday Show* and countless country radio shows, he has already won many awards. He divides his time between Australia and the USA, where he has toured and appeared with such stars as Roy Rogers, Riders In The Sky and the Sons Of The Pioneers. His recordings have resulted in Australian hits such as 'Lover's Carousel', 'Shepherd's Farewell', 'September's Sweet Child' (released in the UK on *Yodelling Crazy* by EMI in 1992) and 'Give 'Em Another Encore'. In 1991, he recorded an album of songs of the singing cowboys, which, as a lover of the style of Rogers and Gene Autry, represented the fulfilment of a lifelong ambition. He made a brief visit to the UK in 1992, where his yodelling and country ballads endeared him to British country music audiences. In 1994, he recorded his first Nashville-based album. His all-round friendly and courteous manner, in addition to the fact that he always finds time to meet his fans, places Horsburgh as one of the most popular of the modern Australian artists.
● ALBUMS: with Desree Ilona Crawford *I Run Alone* (Country-City 1984)★★★, with Deniese Morrison *Sequins And Satins, Buckles And Britches* (Country-City 1984)★★★, *Yodelling For You* (Country-City 1985)★★★, *Now & Then & Again* (Country-City 1986)★★, *Where In The World* (Country-City 1989)★★★, *I've Always Wanted To Be A Singing Cowboy* (Rich River 1992)★★★, *In Every Stone There's A Diamond* (Country-City 1992)★★★, *From Nashville To You* (Rotation 1994)★★★.

HORTON, JOHNNY

b. 3 April 1925, Los Angeles, California, USA, d. 5 November 1960, Texas, USA. Horton was raised in Tyler, Texas, where his sharecropping family settled in search of work. He learned the guitar from his mother and, due to his athletic prowess, won scholarships at Baylor University and later the University of Seattle. For a time he worked in the fishing industry but began his singing career on KXLA Pasadena in

1950, quickly acquiring the nickname of 'The Singing Fisherman'. He recorded for Cormac in 1951 and then became the first artist on Fabor Robinson's Abbott label. In 1952 he moved to Mercury Records but was soon in conflict with the company about the choice of songs. He married Hank Williams' widow, Billie Jean, in September 1953, who encouraged him to better himself. With Tillman Franks as his manager, Horton moved to Columbia Records, and their co-written 'Honky Tonk Man' marked his debut in the US country charts. Horton recorded 'Honky Tonk Man' the day after Elvis Presley recorded 'Heartbreak Hotel' and Presley's bass player, Bill Black, was on the session. The song was successfully revived by Dwight Yoakam in 1986, while George Jones revived another song recorded that day, 'I'm A One Woman Man', in 1989. Other fine examples of Horton's rockabilly talents are 'All Grown Up' and the hard-hitting 'Honky Tonk Hardwood Floor'. In 1959, Horton switched direction and concentrated on story songs, often with an historical basis, and had his first US country number 1 with a Tillman Franks song, 'When It's Springtime In Alaska'. This was followed by his version of Jimmie Driftwood's 'The Battle Of New Orleans', which became a number 1 pop and country hit in the USA. Lonnie Donegan's 'Battle Of New Orleans' made number 2 in the UK, but Horton's number 16 was respectable, especially in view of the fact that his version was banned by the BBC for referring to 'the bloody British'. Horton's next record was another historical song, 'Johnny Reb', backed with the up-tempo novelty, 'Sal's Got A Sugar Lip'. Told simply to cover Horton's latest record, Donegan mistakenly covered 'Sal's Got A Sugar Lip' - and still managed to have a hit! Horton's 'Sink The Bismarck', inspired by the film, made number 3 in the US charts, while he sang the title song of the John Wayne film *North To Alaska* and took it to number 4 in the USA and number 23 in the UK. It also topped the US country charts for five weeks.

On 5 November 1960, Horton died on the way to hospital after a head-on collision with a pick-up truck near Milano, Texas. Tillman Franks received head and chest injuries that required hospital treatment and guitarist Tommy Tomlinson suffered a very serious leg injury which, because of his diabetes, failed to heal and a few months later the leg was amputated. He later played guitar for a time with Claude King but never really recovered from the crash (the driver of the other vehicle, James Davis, aged 19, also died). Billie Jean (who later stated that before he left for the last time, Horton kissed her on exactly the same place on the same cheek that Hank Williams had kissed her when he set off for his final trip) became a country star's widow for the second time in 10 years. Horton, who has been described as the last major star of the *Louisiana Hayride*, is buried in Hillcrest Cemetery, Bossier City, Louisiana. Much of his up-tempo material did not appeal to the traditionalists but somebody once wrote that 'he was ten years older than most of the rockabillies but with his cowboy hat hiding a receding hairline, he more or less looked the part'. However, his 'saga' songs have certainly guaranteed that he is not forgotten.

● ALBUMS: *Honky Tonk Man* (Columbia 1957)★★★, *Done Rovin'* (Briar Internatonal 1958)★★, *Free And Easy Songs* (Sesac 1959)★★, *The Fantastic Johnny Horton* (Mercury 1959)★★★, *The Spectacular Johnny Horton* (Columbia 1960)★★★, *Johnny Horton Makes History* (Columbia 1960)★★★, *Honky Tonk Man* (Columbia 1962)★★★, *Johnny Horton* (Dot 1962)★★★, *I Can't Forget You* (Columbia 1965)★★★, *The Voice Of Johnny Horton* (Hilltop 1965)★★★, *Johnny Horton On The Louisiana Hayride* (Columbia 1966)★★★, *All For The Love Of A Girl* (Hilltop 1968)★★, *The Unforgettable Johnny Horton* (Harmony 1968)★★★, *Johnny Horton On The Road* (Columbia 1969)★★, *The Battle Of New Orleans* (Harmony 1971)★★★.

● COMPILATIONS: *Johnny Horton's Greatest Hits* (Columbia 1961)★★★, *America Remembers Johnny Horton* (Columbia Special Products 1980)★★★, *Rockin' Rollin' Johnny Horton* (Bear Family 1981)★★★★, *American Originals* (Columbia 1989)★★★, *The Early Years* 7-LP box set (Bear Family 1991)★★★, *Johnny Horton 1956-1960* 4-CD box set (Bear Family 1991)★★★★, *Honky Tonk Man: The Essential Johnny Horton 1956-1960* (Columbia/Legacy 1996)★★★★, *Somebody's Rockin'* (Bear Family 1996)★★★.

● FURTHER READING: *Johnny Horton: Your Singing Fisherman*, Michael LeVine.

HOUSE, JAMES

b. 21 March 1955, Sacramento, California, USA. His father and his uncles sang a cappella country music, but House was more interested in rock music as he grew up. He started performing as a solo acoustic act but then formed his own group, the House Band, which was signed to Warner and then moved to Atlantic. He started to write country music and, with the advent of more rock-based musicians in the genre such as Steve Earle, he was signed to MCA. House made the US country charts with 'Don't Quit Me Now', 'Hard Times For A Honest Man', 'You Just Get Better All The Time' and 'That'll Be The Last Thing'. He acted as vocal coach for Dustin Hoffman on the film *Ishtar*, and played a solo acoustic set when he came to the UK with Randy Travis.

● ALBUMS: *James House* (MCA 1989)★★★★, *Hard Times For A Honest Man* (MCA 1990)★★★, *Days Gone By* (Epic 1994)★★.

● VIDEOS: *A Real Good Way To Wind Up Lonesome* (Planet 1994).

HOUSTON, DAVID

b. 9 December 1938, Bossier City, Louisiana, USA, d. 30 November 1993, Bossier City, Louisiana, USA. Houston's forefathers included Sam Houston, who fought for Texas's independence from Mexico, and the Civil War general Robert E. Lee. His parents were friends of 20s singer Gene Austin, who was his godfather and encouraged him. Houston made his debut on *Louisiana Hayride* when aged only 12. He continued with his studies and, encouraged by his manager, Tillman Franks, made a one-off single for Sun Records in Memphis, 'Sherry's Lips'/'Miss Brown'. In 1963 he was signed to Epic Records, who wanted to break into the country market. His first release, 'Mountain Of Love', made number 2 in the US country charts, and was followed by further hits including 'Livin' In A House Of Love' and 'Sweet, Sweet Judy'. In 1966, a song partly written by his producer Billy Sherrill, 'Almost Persuaded', topped the US country charts and also made the Top 30. It established him as one of country music's top balladeers, and he had further country chart-toppers with 'With One Exception', 'My Elusive Dreams' (a duet with Tammy Wynette), 'You Mean The World To Me', 'Have A Little Faith', 'Already In Heaven' and 'Baby Baby (I Know You're A Lady)'. He also appeared in the 1967 country film *Cotton-Pickin' Chicken Pluckers*. He never repeated his success with Tammy Wynette and she says in her autobiography, *Stand By Your Man*, 'If he was the last singer on earth, I'd never record with him again'. However, Houston has recorded several successful duets with other singers, including 'I Love You, I Love You' and 'After Closing Time', with Barbara Mandrell. His last Top 10 country success was with 'Can't You Feel It?' in 1974, and when he left Epic, he recorded with seven other labels. During his career, Houston had seven number 1 country records and 61 chart entries, the last, 'A Penny For Your Thoughts Tonight Virginia', a minor hit on the Country International label in 1989. In 1991, he appeared in the UK at Wembley's International Festival of Country Music. Houston, who joined the *Grand Ole Opry* in 1972, made his last appearance on the show on 6 November 1993. He suffered a ruptured brain aneurism on 25 November and remained in a coma until his death five days later. He is remembered by his country music associates for his knowledge of the music and its artists.

● ALBUMS: *David Houston (New Voice From Nashville)* (Epic 1964)★★★, *David Houston Sings Twelve Great Country Hits* (Epic 1965)★★★, *Almost Persuaded* (Epic 1966)★★★, *Golden Hymns* (Epic 1967)★★, *My Elusive Dreams with Tammy Wynette* (Epic 1967)★★★★, *You Mean The World To Me* (Epic 1967)★★★, *Already, It's Heaven* (Epic 1968)★★★, *Kiss Away* (Epic 1968)★★★, *David* (Epic 1969)★★★, *Baby Baby* (Epic 1970)★★★, *The Wonders Of The Wine* (Epic 1970)★★★, *A Woman Always Knows* (Epic 1971)★★★, *Gentle On My Mind* (Harmony 1972)★★★, *The Day Love Walked In* (Epic 1972)★★★, with Barbara Mandrell *A Perfect Match* (Epic 1972)★★★, *Good Things* (Epic 1973)★★★, *Old Time Religion* (Harmony 1973)★★★, *What A Night* (Epic 1976)★★★, *A Man Needs Love* (Epic 1975)★★★, *David Houston* (Starday 1977)★★, *From The Heart Of Houston* (Derrick 1979)★★, *Next Sunday I'm Gonna Be Saved* (Excelsior 1980)★★, *From Houston To You* (Excelsior 1981)★★, *David Houston Sings Texas Honky Tonk* (Delta 1982)★★, *Mountain Of Love* (51 West 1982)★★, with Mandrell *Back To Back* (51 West 1983)★★★, *Houston Country* (51 West 1984)★★.

● COMPILATIONS: *Greatest Hits* (Epic 1969)★★★★, *Greatest Hits, Vol. 2* (Epic 1972)★★★, *The Best Of David Houston* (Gusto 1978)★★★, *The Best Of David Houston* (First Base 1985)★★★, *American Originals* (Epic 1989)★★★★, *Almost Persuaded - 20 Greatest Hits* (Country Stars Collection 1994)★★★.

● FILMS: *Carnival Rock* (1957), *Cotton-Pickin' Chicken Pluckers* (1967).

HOWARD, CHUCK

b. Flat Fork, Kentucky, USA, d. 15 August 1983. In 1963, Howard produced the ridiculous pop hit 'Surfin' Bird', for the Trashmen. He wrote the mean-spirited 'Happy Birthday Darlin'' for Conway Twitty and in 1980 made the US country chart himself with 'I've Come Back (To Say I Love You One More Time)'.

HOWARD, HARLAN

b. Harlan Perry Howard, 8 September 1929, Lexington, Harlan County, Kentucky, USA. Howard was raised in Detroit and began songwriting when he was 12. After graduation, he spent four years as a paratrooper and was able to spend weekends in Nashville. His talent was recognized by Johnny Bond and Tex Ritter, who published his early songs. Wynn Stewart recorded 'You Took Her Off My Hands' and Howard had his first US country hit in 1958 with 'Pick Me Up On Your Way Down' for Charlie Walker, which was followed by 'Mommy For A Day' by Kitty Wells. Many songs were recorded by Buck Owens including 'Above And Beyond', 'Excuse Me (I Think I've Got A Heartache)', 'Under The Influence Of Love', 'I've Got A Tiger By The Tail' (based on a campaign for Esso petrol) and 'Foolin' Around', most of them being co-written with Owens. In 1959 Guy Mitchell recorded Ray Price's country hit 'Heartaches By The Number' for the pop market and went to number 1 in the US and number 5 in the UK. He married country singer Jan Howard in 1960 and they moved to Nashville, where she recorded many of his demos. One of Patsy Cline's best-known recordings, 'I Fall To Pieces', was written by Howard and Hank Cochran, and he also wrote her US country Top 10 single 'When I Get Through With You (You'll Love Me Too)'. Howard wrote two of Jim Reeves' best recordings, 'I Won't Forget You' and 'The Blizzard', as well as 'The Image Of Me', a Reeves demo discovered in the 80s. Other country successes include 'Don't Call Me From A Honky Tonk' (Johnny And Jonie Mosby), 'Still In Town' (Johnny Cash), 'Three Steps To The Phone' (George Hamilton IV), 'You Comb Her Hair' (with Hank Cochran for George Jones), 'Your Heart Turned Left (And Mine Was On The Right)' (George Jones) and 'Yours Love' (Willie Nelson). Other crossover hits were 'Too Many Rivers' (Kitty Wells and then Brenda Lee), 'Busted' (Johnny Cash and then Ray Charles) and 'The Chokin' Kind' (Waylon Jennings and then Joe Simon). He wrote numerous songs for folk singer Burl Ives when he started recording for the country market, including 'Call Me Mr. In-Between' and 'I'm The Boss'. Bob Dylan praised his song 'Ole Podner', Howard's tribute to a sick fishing buddy, producer Happy Wilson, while Richard Thompson has called 'Streets Of Baltimore', written by Howard and Tompall Glaser, 'a wonderfully succinct story told in three verses with every line a killer.' Howard's sentimental 'No Charge', has been recorded by Melba Montgomery and Tammy Wynette and was a UK number 1 for J.J. Barrie. Howard has made several albums, and although he had a US country hit with 'Sunday Morning Christian' in 1971, the albums are little more than collections of demos for other artists. In 1975, a long-forgotten Howard song, 'She Called Me Baby', was revived very successfully by Charlie Rich. In 1977 the UK division of RCA Records released a 16-track compilation album, *The Songs Of Harlan Howard*. He spends his time pitching his songs at Tree Music in Nashville and he often works with younger writers. In 1984 he wrote a US country number 1 for Conway Twitty, 'I Don't Know A Thing About Love (The Moon Song)', and subsequent number 1s have included 'Why Not Me?' (with Sonny Throckmorton and Brent Maher for the Judds), 'Somebody Should Leave' (with Chick Rains for Reba McEntire) and 'Somewhere Tonight' (with Rodney Crowell for Highway 101). Other 80s compositions include 'You're A Hard Dog To Keep Under The Porch' (with Susanna Clark for Gail Davies), 'I Don't Remember You' (with Bobby Braddock for John Conlee) and 'Never Mind' for Nanci Griffith. Howard cites 'Another Bridge To Burn' (Ray Price, Little Jimmy Dickens) as his best song.

● ALBUMS: *Harlan Howard Sings Harlan Howard* (Capitol

1961)★★★★, *All Time Favourite Country Songwriter* (Monument 1965)★★★, *Mr. Songwriter* (RCA Victor 1967)★★★, *Down To Earth* (RCA Victor 1968)★★, *To The Silent Majority, With Love* (Nugget 1971)★★, *Singer And Songwriter* (1981)★★.

HOWARD, JAN

b. Lula Grace Johnson, 13 March 1930, Kansas City, Missouri, USA. Howard, with a mixture of Cherokee and Irish blood, was raised in poverty, married at 15 and had three sons in quick succession. Her husband beat her and squandered what little money they had, and she divorced him in 1953. A few weeks later, she 'married' a serviceman, who was supposedly divorced, and when that relationship collapsed, she moved to Los Angeles in the hope of finding work as a singer. She met and married aspiring songwriter Harlan Howard within 30 days. She sang on his demonstration records and her version of 'Mommy For A Day' (for Kitty Wells) led to her own recording contract. Her first record was a duet with Wynn Stewart, 'Yankee Go Home', which was followed by her first US country hit, 'The One You Slip Around With', in 1960. The Howards moved to Nashville and she skilfully combined the roles of housewife and country star. Harlan Howard wrote several of her country hits including 'Evil On Your Mind', 'What Makes A Man Wander', 'Wrong Company' and 'I Don't Mind'. In 1968 she recorded her own personal song, 'My Son', for Jimmy in Vietnam. Before the record could be released, her son died in action. The marriage subsequently broke up and a second son committed suicide. Howard worked herself out of the crisis, touring with Bill Anderson and finding success with several duets: 'I Know You're Married', 'For Loving You' (a number 1 US country hit), 'If It's All The Same To You', 'Someday We'll Be Together' and 'Dissatisfied'. She also has long spells on the road with Johnny Cash and Tammy Wynette, and with the *Grand Ole Opry*. She published her best-selling autobiography in 1987.

● ALBUMS: with Wynn Stewart *Sweethearts Of Country Music* (Challenge 1961)★★★, *Jan Howard* (Dot 1962)★★★, with the Jordanaires *Sweet And Sentimental* (Capitol 1962)★★★★, *Bad Seed* (1966)★★★, *Jan Howard Sings 'Evil On Your Mind'* (1966)★★★, *This Is Jan Howard Country* (1967)★★★, *Lonely Country* (1967)★★★, with Bill Anderson *For Loving You* (Decca 1967)★★★, with Stewart *Wynn Stewart And Jan Howard Sing Their Hits* (Starday 1968)★★★★, *Count Your Blessings, Woman* (1968)★★★, *The Real Me* (1968)★★★, *Jan Howard* (1969)★★, *For God And Country* (1970)★★, *Rock Me Back To Little Rock* (1970)★★, with Anderson *If It's All The Same To You* (1971)★★★, *Love Is Like A Spinning Wheel* (1972)★★★, with Anderson *Bill And Jan (Or Jan And Bill)* (MCA 1972)★★★, with Anderson *Singing His Praise* (MCA 1972)★★, *Sincerely* (1976)★★, *Tainted Love* (1984)★★★, *The Life Of A Country Girl Singer* (1987)★★.

● FURTHER READING: *Sunshine And Shadow*, Jan Howard.

HOWARD, RANDY

b. 1960, Georgia, USA. The fiddle player Randy Howard was encouraged by his father to play an instrument - first, the drums, then the electric guitar and then the fiddle. Howard developed an affinity with the fiddle and joined his father and cousin in a bluegrass band. In 1979, aged 18, Randy

Howard became the youngest person to win the World Championship Fiddling Contest in Union Grove, North Carolina, and he has won numerous fiddling - and mandolin - contests since. Howard's first sessions were with the southern rock bands Charlie Daniels, Marshall Tucker and the Allman Brothers Band. Howard had a minor US country hit with 'All American Redneck' in 1983 and had to wait until 1988 for another one, which was a revival of 'Ring Of Fire'. In 1990, encouraged by his friend Mark O'Connor, he moved to Nashville and has played on sessions with Blackhawk, Vince Gill, Kennedy Rose, Shelby Lynne and his namesake, Randy Howard. He often tours with Kathy Chiavola's band. Howard says, 'I'd like to be remembered as a musician who was creative, who has never played mechanically and who always gave each song his best shot.'

● ALBUMS: *Survival Of The Fiddlist* (Survival Of The Fiddlist 1993)★★★.

HOWARD, RANDY (RANDALL LAMAR)

b. Randall Lamar Howard, 9 May 1950, Macon, Georgia, USA. After working in local clubs he made his name on the Bobby Lord television series, after which he had his own show. He wrote 'God Don't Live In Nashville, Tennessee' and 'She's A Lover' and had a minor US country hit with his 'All-American Redneck' in 1983. He had to wait until 1988 for another one, which was a revival of 'Ring Of Fire'. *Macon Music* is a mixture of southern rock and country with titles typical of the era - 'The Last Rebel Yell' and 'Heaven, Hell Or Macon'. The album includes some quickfire fiddling from the fiddle player also called Randy Howard and also from Georgia.

● ALBUMS: *Randy Howard* (Atlantic 1988)★★, *Macon Music* (Sweet Lake 1994)★★.

HUBBARD, RAY WYLIE

b. 13 November 1946, Soper, Oklahoma, USA. Much of Hubbard's fame rests on his songwriting. Jerry Jeff Walker recorded his composition 'Up Against The Wall, Redneck Mother', turning it into a left-field country standard. He formed the Cowboy Twinkies who released a self-titled debut for Warner Brother Records in 1975, but the album's failure led to the band's break-up. Hubbard went on to record his solo debut, before performing with Walker's old back-up band as the Ray Wylie Hubbard Band. His solo work has attracted increasing critical and commercial success. His collection, *Lost Train Of Thought*, was self-released in 1992 and sold at shows throughout his home state of Texas. Despite its low-key origins, it introduced many to his intelligent, uncompromising songwriting. The contents included a moving duet with Willie Nelson ('These Eyes'), plus several further excellent Hubbard standards such as 'When She Sang Amazing Grace'. *Loco Gringo's Lament* followed two years later, earning rave reviews from several quarters including *Rolling Stone* magazine, who described it as 'the most welcome comeback by a Texas honky-tonker since Billy Joe Shaver's'. *Dangerous Spirits* was another left-field classic that featured Hubbard backed by several guest artists, including Tony Joe White and Lucinda Williams.

● ALBUMS: *Off The Wall* (Lone Star 1978)★★★, *Lost Train Of Thought* (Misery Loves Company 1992)★★★, *Loco Gringo's Lament* (Deja 1994)★★★★, *Dangerous Spirits* (Continental Song City 1997)★★★★.

HUGHEY, JOHN

b. c.1935, Elaine, Arkansas, USA. The steel guitarist John Hughey was given a Gene Autry flat-top guitar when he was nine, but in his teens switched to steel guitar. He initially joined the Phillips County Ramblers and later joined Slim Rhodes And Mother's Best Mountaineers when their steel player was drafted to Vietnam and stayed with them for 15 years. In 1968 he met up with his childhood friend Conway Twitty and became a member of Twitty's backing band, the Lonely Blue Boys. His steel guitar playing was featured on Twitty's first US country number 1, 'Next In Line'. The Lonely Blue Boys evolved into the Twitty Birds and for a time, also included John's brother, Gene. His steel guitar with its 'crying' sound was featured on most of Conway's chart-topping singles, but by 1980 Hughey was becoming frustrated. Twitty had sold the franchise for his souvenirs to another company and so his backing musicians no longer received their percentage cut on the sales. Twitty was also moving away from the steel guitar and after several unhappy years, Hughey finally left in 1988. He worked for Loretta Lynn for a year and since then, has worked for Vince Gill. His session work has included two albums with Elvis Presley (*From Elvis In Memphis* and *Back In Memphis*) as well as albums with Joe Diffie, Alan Jackson, Reba McEntire, Dean Martin and Dolly Parton.

HUMMON, MARCUS

b. Washington DC, USA. The country singer Marcus Hummon was the son of a US diplomat and grew up travelling the world, living in Africa, Italy and the Philippines. Hummon developed a love of country music but his influences also include James Taylor and John Denver. While at college, he played many clubs in the Washington area with his three sisters and built up a strong reputation. In 1986, he moved to Nashville and had his first success as a songwriter with 'Pilgrims On The Way (Mathew's Song)' for Michael Martin Murphey. He wrote 'Only Love', a Grammy-nominated hit for Wynonna, 'Cheap Seats' (Alabama), 'Over My Shoulder' (Patty Loveless), 'Every Little Word' (Hal Ketchum) and 'Honky Tonk Mona Lisa' (Doug Stone). He has also written 'The Pathway To The Moon' for the British group MN8. His band is called Red Wing, but he came to the UK with just his steel player, Darrell Scott, for dates supporting Alison Krauss in 1995.
● ALBUMS: *All In Good Time* (Columbia 1995)★★★.

HUNLEY, CON

b. Conrad Logan Hunley, 9 April 1945, Luttrell, Knox County, Tennessee, USA. The Hunley family were known as a local gospel singing group and from an early age Con appeared with them. He grew up an admirer of Chet Atkins and for a time sought to emulate his idol; however, he quickly realized that the guitar was not to be his instrument and instead turned his attention to the piano. Influenced by Ray Charles and singing somewhat like Charlie Rich, he began to play in groups during his high school years and during his time in the US Air Force, played in various bands. After his discharge he returned to Knoxville, first working in a mill but soon found work in local country clubs. In 1976, he formed his own band and recorded five singles for the minor Prairie Dust label. Some were his own compositions and three of the recordings became minor hits in the US

country charts, helping to build his reputation. He decided to move to Nashville in 1977 and as a result of appearances at George Jones' *Possum Holler*, he managed to secure a contract with Warner Brothers. His first release on that label was Jimmy C. Newman's song 'Cry, Cry Darling' which went to number 34 in the charts. He followed this with 11 successive Top 20 hits, including 'Week End Friend', 'You've Still Got A Place In My Heart', 'I've Been Waiting For You All Of My Life' (a pop hit for Paul Anka two years later) and in 1982, 'Oh Girl', which had been a number 1 pop hit for the Chi-Lites 10 years earlier. During the 80s the hits became less frequent. He recorded a version of 'Satisfied Mind' that featured a guest vocal from Porter Wagoner (who had a hit with the song in 1955) and in 1986, he charted with 'Blue Suede Shoes'. Perhaps prophetically, his last successful record was in 1986 with a song called 'Quittin' Time' - whether it was remains to be seen.
● ALBUMS: *Con Hunley* (Warners 1979)★★, *I Don't Want To Lose You* (Warners 1980)★★★, *Don't It Break Your Heart* (Warners 1980)★★★, *Ask Any Woman* (Warners 1981)★★, *Oh Girl* (Warners 1982)★★.

HUNTER, IVORY JOE

b. 10 October 1911, Kirbyville, Texas, USA, d. 8 November 1974. Although Hunter was a well-known figure in Texas through his radio shows, it was not until the 40s, when he moved to the west coast, that his career flourished. He established his own record companies, Ivory and Pacific, the latter of which provided the outlet for Hunter's first R&B chart-topper, 'Pretty Mama Blues'. Joe continued his success with several singles recorded with sidemen from the Duke Ellington Orchestra before one of his most enduring compositions, 'I Almost Lost My Mind', became a second R&B number 1 in 1950. A re-recorded version also proved popular when the singer moved to Atlantic label later in the decade, but Pat Boone's opportunistic cover was a greater commercial success. However, a further fine Hunter original, 'Since I Met You Baby', then swept to the top of the R&B chart in 1956 and to number 12 in the national pop chart. Unhappy at being labelled an R&B act, this talented and prolific artist was equally adept with pop, ballad or spiritual styles and in later years became a popular C&W attraction, so much so, that a benefit concert was held for him at Nashville's *Grand Ole Opry* shortly before his death from lung cancer in 1974.
● ALBUMS: *I Get That Lonesome Feeling* (1957)★★★, *Ivory Joe Hunter* (Sound 1957)★★, *Ivory Joe Hunter* (Atlantic 1958)★★★★, *Ivory Joe Hunter Sings The Old And The New* (1958)★★★, *Ivory Joe Hunter* (Sage 1959)★★, *The Fabulous Ivory Joe Hunter* (1961)★★★, *This Is Ivory Joe Hunter* (1964)★★★, *The Return Of Ivory Joe Hunter* (1971)★★★, *I've Always Been Country* (1974)★★★.
● COMPILATIONS: *Sixteen Of His Greatest Hits* (1958)★★★, *Ivory Joe Hunter's Greatest Hits* (1963)★★★, *7th Street Boogie* (1980)★★★, *The Artistry Of Ivory Joe Hunter* (1982)★★★, *This Is Ivory Joe* (1984)★★, *I Had A Girl* (1987)★★, *Jumping At The Dewdrop* (1987)★★★, *Since I Met You Baby* (1988)★★, *Sings 16 Greatest Hits* (1992)★★★.

HUNTER, TOMMY

b. Thomas James Hunter, 20 March 1937, London, Ontario, Canada. Hunter developed a keen interest in country music as a child, after seeing Roy Acuff during a Canadian tour, and by his early teens, he had mastered the guitar and was playing and singing locally. He played on CBC radio in 1952 and the following year, he left home to tour in Canada and the USA. In 1956, he became a regular on the Canadian television programme *Country Hoedown* (remaining on the show until 1965) and also presented the daily *Tommy Hunter Show* on radio. In 1962, it also became a very popular syndicated television programme which ran until 1989. He made his first recordings for RCA/Victor Records in 1956 and the first of many appearances on the *Grand Ole Opry* in 1965. He later recorded for Capitol and Columbia Records, and, in 1990, he formed his own Edith label. Curiously, he has never placed much emphasis on the recording aspect of his long association with country music. His recorded output includes many albums but unfortunately few appeared to be readily available outside his native Canada, and although a superstar there, he is far less known in other countries. He remained active into the 90s, regularly performing with his band. He has received several awards over the years, including Canada's highest civilian award, the Order Of Canada, in 1986.

● ALBUMS: *Tommy Hunter Readings* (Edith 90s)★★★, *Songs Of Inspiration* (Edith 90s)★★★, *Tommy Hunter Sings For You* (Edith 90s)★★★.

● FURTHER READING: *My Story*, Tommy Hunter.

HUSKY, FERLIN

b. 3 December 1925, on a farm near Flat River, Missouri, USA. Husky learned to play guitar as a child and during World War II served in the US Merchant Navy. His mother wanted him to be a preacher and his father a farmer, but after discharge, he found radio work as an announcer and disc jockey but gradually turned to performing while at KXLW St. Louis. In the late 40s he moved to California, where he appeared on the Los Angeles *Hometown Jamboree* and played clubs in the Bakersfield area. Believing that Ferlin Husky, his real name, was unsuitable, he first called himself Tex Preston, then changed again to Terry Preston. He also developed an alter ego country philosopher character, Simon Crum, whom he introduced into his act. (A few years later, Sheb Wooley also adopted a similar practice with his character Ben Colder, who sought to entertain with his supposed humorous parodies on popular and country songs.) In the early 50s, he recorded for Capitol and worked with Tennessee Ernie Ford. In 1953, as Ferlin Huskey, he recorded 'A Dear John Letter' with Jean Shepard, which became a smash US country number 1, as well as reaching number 4 on the US pop charts. An answer version called 'Forgive Me John', also had success in both charts. Following success with his self-penned 'Hank's Song' (a tribute to Hank Williams), Huskey finally dropped the name of Terry Preston. In 1957, now minus the 'e' again, Husky joined the *Grand Ole Opry* and achieved another smash hit number 1 with his million-selling recording of 'Gone', which, ironically, he had first recorded unsuccessfully as Preston five years earlier. In 1960, he charted a further country number 1 with the gospel/country 'Wings Of A Dove', which also became a Top 20 pop hit. He recorded 'The Drunken Driver', a tear-jerking narrative about a father who runs over his son, which has been rated a classic by some and one of the worst recordings ever made by others. He became a popular entertainer on many network television shows, including hosting

the *Arthur Godfrey Show* and appearing as a dramatic actor on *Kraft TV Theatre*. While not always singing traditional country material, he maintained his country popularity through the character of Simon Crum. In this guise, he demonstrated a great talent for impersonating other country stars, presenting rustic comedy, and even managed a number 2 country hit with 'Country Music's Here To Stay'. He recorded an album of pop songs called *Boulevard Of Broken Dreams* in 1957 and also recorded several rock 'n' roll singles such as 'Wang Dang Do'. Husky has appeared in several films including *Mr. Rock & Roll* and *Country Music Holiday*. From the 60s to the mid-70s, he toured extensively with his band, the Hush Puppies, and had regular country chart entries including 'Once', 'Just For You', 'True True Lovin'' and 'Freckles And Polliwog Days'. He moved to ABC Records in 1973 and achieved a country chart entry (his last) in 1975 with 'An Old Memory Got In My Eye'. Husky has been married six times and has nine children, one of whom is called Terry Preston. His career was slowed in 1977 by a heart operation but he recovered and continued to perform, and later recorded once more.

● ALBUMS: with Jean Shepard *Ferlin Husky And Jean Shepard* (Capitol 1955)★★★, *Ferlin Husky's Songs Of The Home And Heart* (Capitol 1956)★★★, *Boulevard Of Broken Dreams* (Capitol 1957)★★, *Born To Lose* (Capitol 1959)★★★, *Ferlin Husky - Country Tunes From The Heart* (King 1959)★★★, *Sittin' On A Rainbow* (Capitol 1959)★★★, *Gone* (Capitol 1960)★★★, *Easy Livin'* (King 1960)★★★, *Ferlin's Favorites* (Capitol 1960)★★★, *Some Of My Favorites* (Capitol 1960)★★★, *Walkin' & Hummin'* (Capitol 1961)★★★, *Memories Of Home* (Capitol 1963)★★★, *The Heart & Soul Of Ferlin Husky* (Capitol 1963)★★★, *The Unpredictable Simon Crum* (Capitol 1963)★★, *By Request* (Capitol 1964)★★★, *True True Lovin'* (Capitol 1965)★★★, *I Could Sing All Night* (Capitol 1966)★★★, *Songs Of Music City, USA* (Capitol 1966)★★★, *Christmas All Year Long* (Capitol 1967)★★, *What Am I Gonna Do Now* (Capitol 1967)★★★, *Where No One Stands Alone* (Capitol 1968)★★★, *Just For You* (Capitol 1968)★★★, *White Fences And Evergreen Trees* (Capitol 1969)★★★, *That's Why I Love You So Much* (Capitol 1969)★★★, *Your Love Is Heavenly Sunshine* (Capitol 1970)★★★, *Your Sweet Love Lifted Me* (Capitol 1970)★★★, *One More Time* (Capitol 1971)★★★, *Just Plain Lonely* (Capitol 1972)★★★, *Sweet Honky Tonk* (1973)★★★, *True True Lovin'* (1973)★★★, *Champagne Ladies & Blue Ribbon Babies* (ABC 1974)★★★, *Freckles & Polliwog Days* (ABC 1974)★★★, *Mountain Of Everlasting Love* (ABC 1974)★★, *The Foster & Rice Songbook* (ABC 1975)★★, *Ferlin Husky* (1982)★★★, *Live* (1983)★★.

● COMPILATIONS: *Hits Of Ferlin Husky* (Capitol 1963)★★★★, *The Best Of Ferlin Husky* (Capitol 1969)★★★, *Collector's Series* (Capitol 1989)★★★★, *Greatest Hits* (Curb 1990)★★★★, *Vintage* (Capitol 1996)★★★★.

INMAN, AUTRY

b. Robert Autry Inman, 6 January 1929, Florence, Alabama, USA, d. 6 September 1988. An early prodigy, Inman played guitar at the age of five and at 12, he formed his band, the Alabama Blue Boys. He played on various local radio stations and in the mid-40s, he began to appear on the WWVA *Wheeling Jamboree*. He appeared on the *Grand Ole Opry* in 1947, where he became friendly with Cowboy Copas. In 1949/50, he played bass for Copas's Oklahoma Cowboys, before spending the next two years playing with George Morgan. In 1953, recording for Decca Records, he enjoyed a number 4 country hit with 'That's All Right', but failed to achieve a follow-up hit with the label. He made further recordings for RCA/Victor Records (1958-60), United Artists Records (1960) and Mercury Records (1962), without finding chart success (in 1961, he formed his own Lakeside label and released a live album). In 1963, his Sims recording of 'The Volunteer' made the Top 25. He recorded two risqué live albums for Jubilee the following year and eventually returned to the charts in 1968, with 'The Ballad Of Two Brothers', a patriotic narrative delivered over strains of the 'Battle Hymn Of The Republic'. It reached number 14 in the country charts and also crossed over to become a Top 50 pop hit. He appeared in two films, *A Face In The Crowd* (1957) and *Music City USA* (1966), and released further albums, but achieved no further chart success.
● ALBUMS: *Autry Inman At The Frontier Club* (Lakeside 1961)★★★★, reissued on Sims 1964, *Autry Inman i* (Mountain Dew 1963)★★★, *Riscotheque-Saturday Night* (Jubilee 1964)★★, *Riscotheque Adult Comedy Volume 2 - New Year's Eve With Autry Inman* (Jubilee 1964)★★, *Ballad Of Two Brothers* (Epic 1968)★★, *Autry Inman ii* (Jubilee 1969)★★, *Autry Inman - Great Country & Western Singer* (Guest Star 70s)★★★ *Country Gospel* (Guest Star 70s)★★.
● COMPILATIONS: *12 Country Hits From Autry Inman* (Alshire 1969)★★★, *Country Love Songs* (CowgirlBoy 90s)★★★.

INTERNATIONAL SUBMARINE BAND

This country rock group was formed in New England, USA, in 1965 by Gram Parsons (vocals, keyboards, guitar), Ian Dunlop (bass, vocals), John Nuese (guitar, ex-Trolls) and Tom Snow (piano), who was later replaced by a drummer, Mickey Gauvin. It was Gauvin and Dunlop who suggested the group's new name - a reference to the 'International Silverstream Submarine Band' from the 'Our Gang' film series of the 1930s. They moved to New York where they backed former child actor Brandon De Wilde on a series of demos for RCA Records and also made two singles. The first, an instrumental version of the title song to the film *The Russians Are Coming, The Russians Are Coming*, was backed by a version of Buck Owens' 'Truck Driving Man' and was issued on Ascot Records in 1966. Later that year the quartet switched to Columbia for 'Sum Up Broke'/'One Day Week', the a-side of which was an impressive synthesis of folk rock and pop. When these singles were unsuccessful, the group followed De Wilde to Los Angeles where they supported several acts, including Love and Iron Butterfly, but their blend of R&B, C&W and rock 'n' roll was at odds with prevailing psychedelic trends. Footage of the ISB appeared in the film *The Trip*. Lee Hazlewood showed interest in the C&W element of their music but internal disputes broke apart the founding line-up. In 1967 Dunlop and Gauvin left to form the original Flying Burrito Brothers while Parsons and Nuese were joined in the International Submarine Band by Bob Buchanan (bass) and Jon Corneal (drums). *Safe At Home* was released on Hazlewood's LHI label. It featured material by Johnny Cash and Merle Haggard, alongside four Parsons originals, notably 'Luxury Liner' and 'Blue Eyes'. Both of these songs were completed prior to Buchanan's arrival and feature Chris Ethridge on bass. The album, however, was not a success and the band dissolved. Parsons briefly joined the Byrds, then formed a revamped Flying Burrito Brothers, initially including both Corneal and Ethridge. Gauvin formed Vegelava with two ex-members of the Blues Magoos before retiring from music. Dunlop returned to his native Cornwall where he formed the Muscletones, while Nuese fronted a version of the International Submarine Band during the early 70s. At the same time Parsons was enjoying an influential solo career.
● ALBUMS: *Safe At Home* (LHI 1967)★★★.

INTVELD, JAMES

b. Compton, California, USA. John Intveld and his brother Ricky grew up watching their father play with a local band. He was given a guitar when he was eight and he sang in the church choir. In 1981, after playing with various bands, he (vocals, guitar) and Ricky (drums) formed the Rockin' Shadows with Pat Woodward (double bass). In 1983 they opened for Ricky Nelson who was so impressed that he invited both Ricky and Pat Woodward to join his Stone Canyon Band. Two years later Nelson and his entire band were killed in a aeroplane crash. Intveld worked as a solo artist in Pasadena and enrolled at an acting school. He wrote a US country hit for Rosie Flores, 'Cryin' Over You', and found work as a session player, notably for rockabilly performer Ray Campi. He provided Johnny Depp's singing voice in the film *Cry Baby*, and later appeared in the film *Indian Runner*. He is part of the Blasters and also a member of an occasional band with Harry Dean Stanton and Billy Swan, the Repo Men.
● ALBUMS: *James Intveld* (Bear Family 1996)★★★.

IONA AND ANDY

Iona and Andy started performing together in 1980, the year they were married. They harmonize together and Iona plays guitar and Andy bass. One of their most-requested songs is 'An Old Cottage Home In The Country'. In 1994 they released what is possibly the first bilingual country music album, with half the tracks sung in Welsh. The success of this album has led to increased bookings and they also plan an unplugged show as a trio with Jim Donaldson.
● ALBUMS: including *Across The Mountain* (Barge

1987)★★★, *Spirit Of The Night* (Sain 1994)★★★, *Milltiroedd - 100 Miles* (Sain 1996)★★★.

IRBY, JERRY

b. Gerald Irby, 20 October 1917, New Braunfels, Texas, USA, d. 1983. Irby was raised by his wealthy grandmother, a fact that contradicted his claim to have struggled 'with just a cheap guitar and a few songs'. In 1933, he moved to Houston playing honky tonks, and in 1936 formed a duo with Ted Daffan. In 1938, they split when Daffan joined the Bar X Cowboys and Irby briefly fronted his Serenaders in Beaumont. In 1940, thanks to grandmother's finances, he opened Jerry's Country Palace, but in June 1941, it closed and he became the vocalist with the Bar X Cowboys (Daffan had by this time left to form his Texans). In 1945, although still with the Cowboys, Irby made solo recordings for Gulf, achieving local state success with his song 'Driving Nails In My Coffin'. He also made recordings with the Cowboys but when further solo recordings for Globe caused disagreements, he left the Cowboys to form his Texas Ranchers. He later recorded for Mercury, Imperial and 4 Star, before joining MGM Records in 1948. He achieved success with 'Roses Have Thorns' and his songs were recorded by Bob Wills and Bill Boyd. In 1948, he opened his *Texas Corral Nite Club* (with grandmother's backing) and played there until the early 50s, when, plagued by a drink problem and almost broke, he sold the club to go into farming. He was equally unsuccessful in this area and by 1955, he was back in Houston. In December 1955, his old friend Daffan recorded him singing 'Tangled Mind', for his Daffan label. It proved a hit and he formed a band and made further recordings, including 'A Man Is A Slave'. Sadly, he failed to make a return to the good times and left music for a time during the 60s, helping his wife to run a beauty salon. After they divorced, he returned to singing around 1971, even opening a club. He remarried and, in 1973, became an evangelist. He recorded albums of gospel music and even gave some of his old songs new religious lyrics. He was quoted as saying, 'I'm still in the country music business; it just has a different message'. In 1977, he had a popular television programme in Houston. His recordings for the Daffan label were included on Bear Family Records' 2-CD *The Daffan Records*, released in 1995, but few others are available.

● ALBUMS: *Hot Line To Heaven* (Bagatelle 1975)★★, *Are You Ready* (World Witness 1976)★★.

ISAACS, BUD

b. 26 March 1928, Bedford, Indiana, USA. Isaacs was playing steel guitar professionally at the age of 16 and after playing on some local stations, he relocated to Nashville. He began to play on the *Grand Ole Opry* in 1951 with Eddie Hill, later joining Little Jimmy Dickens. In 1953, he was responsible for the addition of foot and knee pedals to a steel guitar. By careful footwork, he was able to vary the tension on individual strings and could consequently change the pitch of a single string so as to alter individual chords. His idea caused a sensation as it had previously been considered impossible to change anything less than an whole chord at one time. The first recording to feature his new invention was when Isaacs played it on Webb Pierce's hit recording of 'Slowly' in 1954. (Jimmy Day had played steel on earlier versions by Pierce). His idea revolutionized the sound of steel guitars on

country recordings and most of the leading exponents of the instrument soon followed his lead. He was much in demand for session work but he also made solo recordings that year for RCA Records, including his lilting 'The Waltz You Saved For Me'. In 1955, he became a member of the *Ozark Jubilee*, appearing on radio and television programmes with the star, Red Foley. It has been recorded that Isaacs played on the 11 top country hits of the year in 1955. In 1958, Isaacs, with Chet Atkins, Homer Haynes, Jethro Burns (Homer And Jethro) and Dale Potter, recording as the Country All-Stars, cut *String Dustin'*, a very up-tempo release. Isaacs married Geri Mapes, a yodeller, singer and bass player and they worked together with an act they called the Golden West Singers. He continued to play on countless recordings and was inducted into the Steel Guitar Hall Of Fame; they eventually retired to Arizona. Isaacs will always be remembered for his dazzling steel guitar playing, especially his catchy 'Bud's Bounce'. His 1955 RCA/Victor Records EP, *Crying Steel Guitar*, is now a highly prized collectable.

JACKSON, ALAN

b. 17 October 1958, Newman, Georgia, USA. Jackson, the son of a motor mechanic, had a love of gospel music through church and his family. His roots can be heard in 'Home' (written for Mother's Day), 'Chattahoochee' and his tribute to Hank Williams, 'Midnight In Montgomery'. He has also revived several songs from his youth including Eddie Cochran's 'Summertime Blues' and a joint composition from Roger Miller and George Jones, 'Tall Tall Trees'. He tried several jobs, but in 1986, he moved with his wife, Denise, to Nashville to try to succeed as a country performer. Through a chance meeting with Glen Campbell, he gained an audition with his publishing company, and he became the first artist to be signed to Arista Records' Nashville division. He wrote most of his debut album, *Here In The Real World*, which remained on the US country album chart for over a year. He had immediate success with 'Blue Blooded Woman' and then four more singles from the album topped the US country charts - 'Here In The Real World', 'Wanted', 'Chasin' That Neon Rainbow' and 'I'd Love You All Over Again'. The UK magazine *Country Music People* said of him, 'He's uncontroversial, stands for the flag, Mom and apple pie, looks like he washes every day and sings for middle America.' The lanky, quiet-spoken Georgian is one of the Hat brigade and he joined the *Grand Ole Opry* in 1991. *Don't Rock The Jukebox* confirmed that his initial success was no fluke and the album spawned five number 1 singles - 'Don't Rock The Jukebox', 'Someday', 'Midnight In Montgomery', 'Dallas' and 'Love's Got A Hold On You'. He also wrote songs with Randy Travis, including the latter's number 1 hit 'Forever Together', and his own 'She's Got The Rhythm And I Got The Blues', another number 1 from 1992. The album on which it featured, *A Lot About Livin'*, is Jackson's most successful to date, selling six million copies to the end of August 1995. Even his *Honky Tonk Christmas* has notched up a respectable 700,000. This album includes Alison Krauss, the Chipmunks and a duet with the deceased Keith Whitley. Other number 1s from *A Lot About Livin'* are 'Tonight I Climbed The Wall', 'Chattahoochee' and 'Who Says You Can't Have It All'. His next album, *Who I Am*, included four more country number 1s, 'Summertime Blues', 'Livin' On Love', 'Gone Country' and 'I Don't Even Know Your Name', giving him 16 chart-topping records to that time. 'Gone Country' wittily parodies people who turned to country music when it became fashionable: 'I heard down there, it's changed, you see/They're not as backward as they used to be.' He has contributed to tribute albums to the Eagles and Merle Haggard and displayed his traditional side by recording a duet of 'A Good Year For The Roses' with its originator, George Jones. Jackson wrote 'Job Description' to explain to his daughters, Mattie Denise and Alexandra Jane, why he was rarely home, and he has won a succession of industry awards, establishing himself as a top ranking country star, not too far behind Garth Brooks. He stands for simple truths in straightforward, well-crafted songs and he says, 'I don't dance, I don't swing from ropes, I just stand there.'

● ALBUMS: *Here In The Real World* (Arista 1990)★★★, *Don't Rock The Jukebox* (Arista 1991)★★★★, *A Lot About Livin' (And A Little 'Bout Lovin)* (Arista 1992)★★★★, *Honky Tonk Christmas* (Arista 1993)★★, *Who I Am* (Arista 1994)★★★, *Everything I Love* (Arista 1996)★★★★.

● COMPILATIONS: *The Greatest Hits Collection* (Arista 1995)★★★★.

● VIDEOS: *Here In The Reel World* (1990), *Livin', Lovin', And Rockin' That Jukebox* (1994), *Who Says You Can't Have It All* (DNA 1994), *The Greatest Video Hits Collection* (6 West Home Video 1995).

JACKSON, CARL

b. 18 September 1953, Louisville, Mississippi, USA. Carl Jackson started at the age of 13 by accompanying his father and his uncle on the banjo in a bluegrass band. One of his compositions, 'Banjo Man', describes how he learnt Earl Scruggs' licks by listening to his records. Jackson toured with Jim And Jesse and during that time made his first solo album, *Bluegrass Festival*. In 1972, he joined Glen Campbell's band, and Campbell produced his Capitol album, *Banjo Player*. The interplay between Campbell and Jackson, particularly on 'Duellin' Banjos', has been much admired, but staying with Campbell prevented him from developing his own musical personality. He has now branched out on his own and his fine musicianship can be heard on his album with John Starling, *Spring Training*, which won a Grammy for Best Bluegrass Album.

● ALBUMS: *Bluegrass Festival* (Prize 1971)★★★ *Banjo Player* (Capitol 1973)★★★, *Old Friends* (Capitol 1978)★★, *Banjo Man* (Sugar Hill 1981)★★★★, *Song Of The South*

(Sugar Hill 1982)★★★, *Banjo Hits* (Sugar Hill 1983)★★★, with John Starling and the Nash Ramblers *Spring Training* (Sugar Hill 1991)★★★, with Emmylou Harris *Nashville Country Duets* (1993)★★★.

JACKSON, LARRY

b. 15 June 1947, Gadsden, Alabama, USA. His father died in a car accident four months before he was born. He began playing guitar as a child and made his first performance at the age of 10 singing at a local theatre. He relocated to Columbus, Georgia, in 1957 where he lived with his two sisters until the mid-50s, when he moved to Atlanta. He began songwriting in 1962 and in later years, he formed his own publishing company, Mountain Water Publishing. He made his first recordings in 1986 in Nashville for the Columbus-based Trish label, owned by his sister Pat. In June 1986, the death of his mother saw him lose all interest in the music industry for almost two years and the recordings were never issued. He returned to the recording studios in 1988 and his recording of 'Country Music Never Let Me Down', recorded for JDS in Atlanta, had independent chart success. He subsequently moved to Nashville, where he hopes that his talent for writing on a wide range of subjects and his personal appearances will see him fulfil his ambition of country stardom. He formed his own Loree label and, in addition to his own recordings, works on producing other artists. His first album, which contained two of the unissued Trish tracks, namely 'Damn Those Memories' and 'Sarah', has received air play in America and Japan and also Eastern Europe. In 1994, he co-wrote Tim McGraw's hit 'Don't Take The Girl'.

● ALBUMS: *The Blue Highway* (Loree 1991)★★★.

JACKSON, SHOT

b. Harold B. Jackson, 4 September 1920, Wilmington, North Carolina, USA, d. 24 January 1991. He grew up on a farm in Georgia, with a childhood nickname of 'Buckshot', which was curtailed in adulthood to 'Shot'. Impressed by the dobro playing of Pete Kirby (Bashful Brother Oswald), he learned to play and was proficient enough to start his career in 1941. He relocated to Nashville in 1944, where he played on the *Grand Ole Opry* with Cousin Wilbur (Westbrooks). After service in the US Navy, he became steel guitarist for the Bailes Brothers, with whom he recorded and played regularly on the *Louisiana Hayride*, until 1951. Between 1951 and 1957, he played dobro for Johnnie And Jack and electric steel guitar for Kitty Wells, appearing on numerous recordings. Jackson then played steel guitar for Roy Acuff for almost five years. In the early 60s, he, Buddy Emmons and Jimmy Day were responsible for the manufacture of Sho-Bud pedal steel guitars. It was a small project that started in their garage but quickly became a major business enterprise. He still played with Acuff but also managed Melba Montgomery and played on her recordings, including her noted duets with George Jones. He was critically injured and pinned in the wreckage following a car crash, while travelling with Acuff, on 10 July 1965. When he was eventually fit enough to work again, he toured for a time with his wife, Donna Darlene, a featured singer on *The Wheeling Jamboree*. He also produced a seven-string guitar which he named Sho-Bro. He continued to make appearances at various venues, including on *Hee Haw* and at special events, including reunion shows with his old friends, the Bailes Brothers. In the mid-70s, he cut down on his performing and worked at making and repairing instruments. He sold his Sho-Bud interest in 1980 and his repair business in 1983, when he decided to retire completely. Some eight weeks later, he suffered a stroke. He survived but the lasting effect left him without speech and unable to play. In June 1990, a further stroke left him completely incapacitated, before his death on 24 January 1991. His old friend Walter Bailes conducted the funeral. Jackson made various solo recordings during his career and gained induction to the Steel Guitar Hall Of Fame in 1986.

● ALBUMS: *Singing Strings Of Steel Guitar And Dobro* (Starday 1962)★★, *Bluegrass Dobro* (Cumberland 1965)★★★, *The Hurtin' Side Of Country* (Arc 60s)★★★, *Steelin' With A Dobro* (Arc 60s)★★★, *Nashville Northwest* (Wasp 60s)★★★, with Merle Travis, Charlie Collins *Shot Jackson & Friends* (Vetco 1977)★★★.

JACKSON, STONEWALL

b. 6 November 1932, Tabor City, North Carolina, USA. Jackson's family tree does in fact extend to the famous Confederate general of the American Civil War - hence his name. After the death of his father when Stonewall was aged two, his mother relocated to Moultrie, Georgia, where, at the age of eight, he worked on his uncle's farm. When he was 10 he swapped his bicycle for a guitar and learned to play by watching others. He joined the army in 1948, lying about his age, but the error was soon discovered. The next year he joined the navy legally and began his singing career by entertaining his shipmates. After discharge in 1954, he spent two years working on a farm but in 1956, with no professional singing experience, he decided to try his luck in Nashville. He impressed Wesley Rose enough for him to record some demo discs of his songs; after auditioning for George D. Hay, Jackson became one of the few performers without a recording contract to become a member of the *Grand Ole Opry*. In fact, he recalled, 'I found out later it's the only time anybody's ever come and just was hired off the street'. He signed for Columbia Records in 1957 and first worked on Ernest Tubb's roadshow. He made his US country chart debut in 1958 when his recording of George Jones's prison saga, 'Life To Go', reached number 2. In 1959, Jackson's recording of John D. Loudermilk's 'Waterloo' became a million-selling country number 1, also reaching number 4 in the US pop charts. Between 1959 and 1963 further successes followed, including 'Why, I'm Walking', 'A Wound Time Can't Erase', 'Leona' and 'Old Showboat', before he achieved another country number 1 with 'B.J. The D.J.' Throughout the mid-60s and early-70s he charted regularly, including his own songs 'Don't Be Angry' (a song he had initially recorded as a demo for Wesley Rose eight years earlier), 'I Washed My Face In Muddy Water' and 'Stamp Out Loneliness'. ('Don't Be Angry' was revived in 1987 by Daniel O'Donnell on his album *Don't Forget To Remember*). Jackson's style gradually went out of fashion but he did make the country Top 10 in 1971 with a country version of 'Me And You And A Dog Named Boo'. During the Vietnam War he recorded a patriotic single, 'The Minute Men Are Turning In Their Graves', and even renamed his band the Minute Men to emphasize the point. *The Great Old Songs* contains many folk ballads, including arguably his best track, 'The Black Sheep'. He also has the distinction of being the first artist to record a live in-concert album at the *Opry*. He still resides in Nashville and maintains his *Opry* appearances.

● ALBUMS: *The Dynamic Stonewall Jackson* (Columbia 1959)★★★, *Sadness In A Song* (Columbia 1963)★★, *I Love A Song* (Columbia 1963)★★★, *Trouble And Me* (Columbia 1964)★★★, *The Exciting Stonewall Jackson* (Columbia 1966)★★★, *All's Fair In Love 'N' War* (Columbia 1966)★★★, *Help Stamp Out Loneliness* (1967)★★★, *Stonewall Jackson Country* (1967)★★★, *The Great Old Songs* (1968)★★★★, *Thoughts Of A Lonely Man* (1968)★★★, *Nothing Takes The Place Of Loving You* (1968)★★★, *I Pawned My Past Today* (1969)★★★, *The Old Country Church* (1969)★★, *A Tribute To Hank Williams* (1969)★★★, *The Real Thing* (1970)★★★, *The Lonesome In Me* (1970)★★★, *Stonewall Jackson Recorded Live At The Grand Ole Opry* (1971)★★★, *Waterloo* (1971)★★★★, *Me And You And A Dog Named Boo* (1971)★★★, *World Of Stonewall Jackson* (1972)★★★, *Nashville* (1974)★★★, *Stonewall (Platinum Country)* (1979)★★★, *My Favorite Sin* (1980)★★★, *Stonewall Jackson* (1982)★★★, *Solid Stonewall* (1982)★★, *Alive* (1984)★★, *Up Against The Wall* (Allegience 1984)★★.

● COMPILATIONS: *Stonewall Jackson's Greatest Hits* (Columbia 1965)★★★, *American Originals* (Columbia 1989)★★★.

● FURTHER READING: *From The Bottom Up: The Stonewall Jackson Story*, Billy Henson (ed.).

JACKSON, TOMMY

b. Thomas Lee Jackson Jnr., 31 March 1926, Birmingham, Alabama, USA, d. 9 December 1979. His parents relocated to Nashville when Jackson was a baby and he grew up listening to the *Grand Ole Opry*. Greatly influenced by 'Fiddlin'' Arthur Smith, at the age of seven Jackson was playing in bars and on street corners. When he was 12, he toured with Johnny And Jack, before leading the Tennessee Mountaineers on Nashville radio. In the early 40s, he played regularly on the *Opry* with Curley Williams and Paul Howard, before serving as a rear gunner in Flying Fortress bombers during World War II, for which he received five decorations. In April 1946, he returned to Nashville and began to work with various *Opry* stars but played regularly in Red Foley's Cumberland Valley Boys (the band, consisting of Jackson alongside Zeke Turner on electric guitar, Jerry Byrd on steel guitar, Louis Innis on rhythm guitar, were also perhaps Nashville's first real session musicians). His dislike of touring saw him increasingly seeking work as a session musician and it was in this capacity that, in 1947, he made his first recordings playing fiddle behind Hank Williams (Jackson provided the brilliant fiddlework on 'I Saw The Light', 'Lovesick Blues' and several other Williams hits). In 1948, after moving with Foley to Cincinnati, he also worked with Cowboy Copas, Hawkshaw Hawkins and Grandpa Jones, as well as playing on sessions for King. He made his first solo recordings for Mercury Records in the early 50s, but in 1953, he joined Dot Records, where he recorded a whole series of albums and singles for square dancing. They not only popularized the dancing but also led to many new players becoming attracted to the fiddle. In 1954, having more session work than he could cope with, he ceased working with Foley or any specific artist. He continued to play into the 70s, by which time he had worked with or played on recordings by almost every major star, including

Faron Young, Ray Price, George Jones, Bill Monroe, Jim And Jesse and Hank Snow. Jackson died in December 1979 after a long period of poor health. Noted historian Charles. K. Wolfe accurately described Jackson as 'the first great Nashville session fiddler who virtually invented the standard country fiddle back-up style and in the early 50s, his string of albums both reflected and stimulated the square dance craze'.

● ALBUMS: *Popular Square Dance Music Without Calls* (Dot 1957)★★★, *Square Dance Tonight* (Dot 1958)★★★, *Square Dance Fiddle Favorites* (Mercury 1958)★★★, *Do-Si-Do* (Dot 1959)★★★, *Square Dances Without Calls* (Decca 1959)★★★, *Square Dance Festival Volumes 1 & 2* (Dot 1960)★★★, *Swing Your Partner* (Dot 1962)★★★, *Square Dance Festival Volume 3* (Dot 1963)★★★, *Let's Dance To Country Pops* (Somerset 1964)★★★, *Bluegrass Square Dance Jamboree* (Hamilton 1964)★★, *Square Dances* (Dot 1964)★★★, with Lloyd Ellis *Guitar & Fiddle Country Style* (Mercury 1965)★★★, with Pete Wade *Twin Fiddles Play Country's Greatest Waltzes* (Cumberland 1965)★★.

● COMPILATIONS: *Square Dance Music* 14 volumes EPs (Dot 1957)★★★, *Greatest Bluegrass Hits* (Dot 1962).

JACKSON, WANDA

b. Wanda Jean Jackson, 20 October 1937, Maud, Oklahoma, USA. Jackson started her career as one of the rawest of female rockabilly singers before going on to successful work in both country and gospel music. Her family moved to California when she was four, settling in the city of Bakersfield, but moved back to Oklahoma when she was 12. There Jackson won a talent contest that led to her own radio programme. Country singer Hank Thompson liked her style and hired her to tour with his band. In 1954 Jackson signed to Decca Records, recording 15 country tracks, one of which, 'You Can't Have My Love', a duet with Billy Gray, made the country Top 10. The following year Jackson joined Red Foley's touring company and met Elvis Presley. He advised her to change her style to the new rock 'n' roll. When she signed with Capitol Records in 1956, she recorded a number of singles, one side of each a rocker, the other a honky-tonk country number. Only one of these rockabilly records, 'I Gotta Know', made the country charts, but her other recordings for Capitol, such as 'Honey Bop', 'Fujiyama Mama' and 'Hot Dog That Made Him Mad', are prized by collectors decades later. Only one, 'Let's Have A Party', earlier recorded by Elvis, made the US pop charts when Capitol belatedly released it in 1960. Backed by the Blue Caps, this song is delivered in raucous style and it remains an extraordinary vocal delivery. That same year, Jackson chose to stay with country and recorded her own composition, 'Right Or Wrong', which has since become a hit for both Ronnie Dove and George Strait. 'Right Or Wrong' and 'In The Middle Of a Heartache' became the last of Jackson's Top 10 country songs in 1961/2, although she placed 30 singles in that chart in total. She recorded nearly two dozen albums for Capitol in the 60s. By the early 70s Jackson began recording Christian music for Capitol and later the Word and Myrrh labels, returning to rock 'n' roll for one album, *Rock 'N' Roll Away Your Blues*, in 1984. In 1995 she duetted on Rosie Flores' *Rockabilly Filly*, and supported the singer on her US tour.

● ALBUMS: *Wanda Jackson* (Capitol 1958)★★★★, *Rockin' With Wanda* (Capitol 1960)★★★★, *There's A Party Goin' On* (Capitol 1961)★★★, *Right Or Wrong* (Capitol 1961)★★★, *Lovin' Country Style* (Decca 1962)★★★, *Wonderful Wanda* (Capitol 1962)★★★, *Love Me Forever* (Capitol 1963)★★★, *Two Sides Of Wanda Jackson* (Capitol 1964)★★★★, *Blues In My Heart* (Capitol 1964)★★★, *Wanda Jackson Sings Country Songs* (Capitol 1966)★★★, *Salutes The Country Music Hall Of Fame* (Capitol 1966)★★★, *Reckless Love Affair* (Capitol 1967)★★★, *You'll Always Have My Love* (Capitol 1967)★★★, *Cream Of The Crop* (Capitol 1968)★★★, *The Happy Side Of...* (Capitol 1969)★★★, *In Person At Mr. Lucky's In Phoenix, Arizona* (Capitol 1969)★★★, *The Many Moods Of...* (Capitol 1969)★★★, *Country!* (Capitol 1970)★★★, *Woman Lives For Love* (Capitol 1970)★★★, *I've Gotta Sing* (Capitol 1971)★★★, *I Wouldn't Want You Any Other Way* (Capitol 1972)★★★, *Praise The Lord* (Capitol 1972)★★★, *When It's Time To Fall In Love Again* (Myrrh 1973)★★★, *Country Keepsakes* (Myrrh 1973)★★★, *Now I Have Everything* (Myrrh 1974)★★★, *Closer To Jesus* (Word 1982)★★★, *Rock 'N' Roll Away Your Blues* (1984)★★★.

● COMPILATIONS: *The Best Of Wanda Jackson* (Capitol 1967)★★★★, *Her Greatest Country Hits* (EMI 1983)★★★★, *Early Wanda Jackson* (Bear Family 1984)★★★, *Rockin' In The Country: The Best Of ...* (Rhino 1990)★★★★, *Right Or Wrong 1954-62* (1993)★★★★, *16 Rock 'N' Roll Hits* (1993)★★★★, *Capitol Country Music Classics* (Capitol 1993)★★★★, *Vintage Collection Series* (Capitol 1996)★★★★.

JAE, JANA

b. Jana Margaret Meyer, 30 August 1942, Great Falls, Montana, USA. Her parents both studied classical violin and she began playing at the age of three. However, her maternal grandfather, a country fiddler, influenced her musical direction. After her parents divorced, Jae grew up with her mother in Colorado and Idaho, gaining musical experience playing in school orchestras and talent contests. She qualified in classical music at a Denver college and gained a scholarship to study for a year at the Vienna Academy in Austria. Between 1967 and 1970, she was married, raised two children, was divorced and resumed a musical career, winning national fiddle championships in 1973 and 1974. In 1974, while playing in a bluegrass band, she was heard by Buck Owens. When, in 1975, Don Rich died in a motor cycle accident, she replaced him in Owens' Buckeroos and regularly played with them on tour and on *Hee Haw*. In 1977, after recording a solo album of Owens' songs without permission, she was sacked, but later, she and Owens married: it proved a stormy relationship. First, Owens divorced her; they then remarried, but soon afterwards she divorced Owens. She continued to play with him until 1979, when she became a solo artist and recorded for Lark Records. Apart from her country fiddling, with her trademark blue fiddle, she has a love of jazz music, which has even seen her play at the Montreux Jazz Festival in Switzerland. In the 80s, with her band Hotwire, she continued to perform and also worked on commercials and promotional work for a major chain store company. She gained the nickname of Fiddling Femme Fatale and stands as the first female musician to become a member of Owens' band.

● ALBUMS: *I Love Fiddling* (American Heritage 70s)★★★, *The Devil You Say* (Lark 80s)★★★, *Live* (Lark 80s)★★, *Symphony Pops* (Lark 80s)★, *By Request* (Lark 80s)★★, *Don't Rock The Bow* (Lark 80s)★★★.

JAMES, SONNY

b. James Loden, 1 May 1929, Hackleburg, Alabama, USA. The Country Music Hall Of Fame includes a guitar that Sonny James' father made for him when he was three years old. James has been performing since that time and has played fiddle and guitar with the Lodens' family revue. Sonny won several junior fiddle championships, although he was to play guitar on his records. He was signed by Capitol Records in 1953 and marketed as Sonny James by producer Ken Nelson. James had his first US country hits with 'That's Me Without You', 'She Done Give Her Heart To Me' and 'For Rent', and made the UK Top 30 with a record that is now a children's favourite, 'The Cat Came Back'. He had a number 1 record on the US pop charts with 'Young Love' in 1957, which was also a number 1 record for film star Tab Hunter. Hunter repeated his success in the UK charts, but James only reached number 11. (The original version of 'Young Love' by composer Rick Cartey is long-forgotten.) 'First Date, First Kiss, First Love' made number 25 in the US pop charts and James had 19 other records in the Hot 100. Because he was tall, quiet, respectable and good-looking, he became known as the Southern Gentleman. He left Capitol and recorded for NRC and RCA but returned to Capitol and enjoyed numerous country hits between 1963 and 1971, including 16 consecutive number 1s. His hits included 'You're The Only World I Know', 'Behind The Tear', 'Take Good Care Of Her', 'The Minute You're Gone', which was covered by Cliff Richard, and 'A World Of Our Own' and 'I'll Never Find Another You', two of the Seekers' pop hits that he covered for the country market. He appeared in several low-budget country films - *Second Fiddle To An Old Guitar*, *Nashville Rebel*, *Las Vegas Hillbillies* (with Jayne Mansfield) and *Hillbilly In A Haunted House* (with Basil Rathbone and Lon Chaney). James has also revived pop songs for the country market including 'Only The Lonely', 'It's Just A Matter Of Time' and 'Running Bear', all three being number 1 records. His 1972 number 1, 'That's Why I Love You Like I Do', was a remade and retitled version of the b-side of 'Young Love', 'You're The Reason (I'm In Love)'. He switched to Columbia in 1972 and continued his success with 'When The Snow Is On The Roses', 'Is It Wrong (For Loving You)?' (both reaching number 1), 'Little Band Of Gold' and 'Come On In'. He produced Marie Osmond's transatlantic Top 10 revival of 'Paper Roses' and made an album inside Tennessee State Prison. The 57-year-old singer recorded a new version of 'Young Love' for Dot Records, but the album, particularly the track 'You've Got Your Troubles', exposed some shaky vocals. In total, Sonny James has had 72 records in the US country charts including 23 number 1s, which makes him one of the most successful country artists in history.
● ALBUMS: *Sonny* (Capitol 1957)★★★, *The Southern Gentleman* (Capitol 1957)★★★, *Honey* (Capitol 1958)★★★★, *The Sonny Side* (Capitol 1959)★★★, *This Is Sonny James* (Capitol 1959)★★★★, *Young Love* (Dot 1962)★★★, *The Minute You're Gone* (Capitol 1964)★★★, *You're The Only World I Know* (Capitol 1965)★★★, *I'll Keep Holding On (Just To Your Love)* (Capitol 1965)★★★, *Behind The Tear* (Capitol 1965)★★★, *True Love's A Blessing* (Capitol 1966)★★★, *Till The Last Leaf Shall Fall* (Capitol 1966)★★★, *My Christmas Dream* (Capitol 1966)★★, *Young Love And Other Songs Of The Heart* (Capitol 1967)★★★, *I'll Never Find Another You* (Capitol 1967)★★★, *Born To Be With You*

(Capitol 1968)★★★, *A World Of Our Own* (Capitol 1968)★★★, *Heaven Says Hello* (Capitol 1968)★★, *Need You* (Capitol 1968)★★★, *Close Up* (Capitol 1969)★★★, *The Astrodome Presents - In Person - Sonny James* (Capitol 1969)★★, *Only The Lonely* (Capitol 1969)★★★, *Traces* (Capitol 1970)★★★, *It's Just A Matter Of Time* (Capitol 1970)★★★, *My Love/Don't Keep Me Hanging On* (Capitol 1970)★★★, *Number One (The Biggest Hits In Country Music History)* (Capitol 1970)★★★, *Empty Arms* (Capitol 1971)★★★, *Here Comes Honey Again* (Capitol 1971)★★★, *The Sensational Sonny James* (Capitol 1971)★★★, *That's Why I Love You Like I Do* (1972)★★, *When The Snow Is On The Roses* (Columbia 1972)★★★, *The Greatest Country Hits Of 1972* (Columbia 1973)★★, *The Gentleman From The South* (Columbia 1973)★★★, *If She Just Helps Me Get Over You* (Columbia 1973)★★★, *Sonny James* (Columbia 1973)★★★, *Young Love* (Columbia 1973)★★★, *Is It Wrong?* (Columbia 1974)★★★, *Country Male Artist Of The Decade* (Columbia 1975)★★★, *A Little Bit South Of Saskatoon* (Columbia 1975)★★★, *The Guitars Of Sonny James* (Columbia 1975)★★★, *200 Years Of Country Music* (Columbia 1976)★★, *When Something Is Wrong With My Baby* (Columbia 1976)★★★, *A Mi Esposa Con Amor* (Columbia 1977)★★, *Sonny James In Prison - In Person* (Columbia 1977)★★, *You're Free To Go* (Columbia 1977)★★★, *This Is The Love* (Columbia 1978)★★★, *Favorites* (Columbia 1979)★★★, *Sonny's Side Of The Street* (Monument 1979)★★★, *I'm Lookin' Over The Rainbow* (Dimension 1982)★★★, *Sonny James* (Dot 1986)★★★.
● COMPILATIONS: *The Best Of Sonny James* (Capitol 1965)★★★, *American Originals* (Columbia 1989)★★★, *Capitol Collector's Series* (Capitol 1990)★★★, *Greatest Hits* (Columbia 1992)★★★.

JARAMILLO, JERRY

b. 7 March 1954, Belen, New Mexico, USA. Jaramillo became interested in music as a child and his father gave him his first guitar when he was 12. He began performing locally and eventually formed his Brown River Road Band, with which he played a residency at an Albuquerque nightclub. He has acted as opener for several artists including Loretta Lynn and Faron Young. In 1988, he gained some indie chart successes with 'Face To The Wall', 'Jeanie Loved The Roses' and his self-penned 'Honky Tonk Cinderella'. His recordings generally feature a mixture of down-to-earth honky tonk, bar-room ballads and Tex-Mex, while his bilingual talent, like that of Johnny Rodriguez, sometimes gives rise to Spanish as well as English vocals.
● ALBUMS: *Jerry Jaramillo* (LRJ 1988)★★★, *Favorites* (LRJ 1989)★★.

JARRELL, TOMMY

b. 1901, near Round Peak, Surry County, North Carolina, USA, d. 28 January 1985, Mount Airy, USA. Jarrell was an old-time fiddler, banjoist and singer, but never became a professional musician, nor was heard outside his home locale, until he was nearly 70 years old. The Jarrells were of Scots-Irish descent and he learned his fiddle playing and much of his vast repertoire of songs from his father, Ben Jarrell, a noted old-time fiddler who played and recorded with Da-Costa Woltzs Southern Broadcasters in the late 20s. Tommy was also influenced by Fred Cockerham, another fiddler. The family moved to Mount Airy in 1921 and from 1925 to his retirement in 1966, Jarrell worked for the State Highways Department. After his wife died in 1967, he began to play the fiddle again. He became recognized as an authority on old-time music and was much in demand for appearances at various folk festivals and colleges. Jarrell recorded several albums, both as a solo artist and also with Cockerham and Oscar Jenkins, and his versatility was showcased on his 1974 album *Come And Go With Me*, which featured all banjo tracks. Jarrell was invited to perform at President Reagan's inaugural ceremony but was not well enough to attend. Many of his best performances are available on record and a film, *Sprout Wings And Fly*, was made about him. Some of his last recordings were made in June 1984, when, along with Alice Gerrard, Andy Cahan and Verlen Clifton, he proved that, even at the age of 83, he was still a most competent fiddle performer. Jarrell died following an heart attack at his home in 1985.

● ALBUMS: *June Apple* (1972)★★★, *Joke On The Puppy* (1972)★★★, with Oscar Jenkins, Fred Cockerham *Down At The Cider Mill* (c.1973)★★★, *Jenkins, Jarrell & Cockerham, Vol. 2 (Back Home In Blue Ridge)* (c.1973)★★★, *Stay All Night* (1973)★★★, *Come And Go With Me* (1974)★★★★, *Sail Away Ladies* (1976)★★★, *Pickin' On Tommy's Porch* (1983)★★★, *Rainbow Sign* (1986)★★.

JAYE, JERRY

b. Gerald Jaye Hatley, 19 October 1937, Manila, Arkansas, USA. A singer/guitarist whose material sometimes leaned more towards rock than traditional country, Jaye made his first recordings for his own label in 1966, before gaining an album release on Hi Records the following year. In 1975, recording for Columbia, Jaye had a minor hit with his version of Tommy Edwards' 1958 pop number 1, 'It's All In The Game'. The following year, he returned to the Hi label and registered two minor hits, 'Honky Tonk Women Love Red Neck Men', being the highest placing at number 32. Since then he has been conspicuous by his absence from the country charts.

● ALBUMS: *My Girl Josephine* (Hi 1967)★★, *Honky Tonk Women Love Red Neck Men* (Hi 1976)★★★, *My Girl Josephine* UK release (Demon 1992)★★.

JEFFRIES, HERB

b. 24 September 1916, Detroit, Michigan, USA. Early in his career Jeffries sang with the Erskine Tate band, for many years one of the most popular bands residing in Chicago. In 1931 he joined Earl Hines and was then briefly with Blanche Calloway. A tall, striking-looking man, in the late 30s Jeffries appeared in a number of films made by black producer-director Oscar Micheaux. In *The Bronze Buckaroo* and similar tales, Jeffries appeared as a black equivalent to the then popular white singing cowboys such as Gene Autry. In the early 40s Jeffries sang with Duke Ellington and his recording of 'Flamingo' was hugely successful. In the 50s Jeffries sang in clubs, often on the west coast, recording with artists including Lucky Thompson and Bobby Hackett. A re-recording of 'Flamingo', this time with Les Brown, was also successful. In the 70s and 80s Jeffries continued performing as a singer and actor, operated his own record label, United National, and appeared, exuding charm, bonhomie and good humour, as singer and master of ceremonies at several of the Ellington reunion conventions in the USA and UK. At one

such reunion in Los Angeles in the summer of 1991, Jeffries received excellent notices for his performance in a revival of Ellington's *Jump For Joy*, half a century after his first appearance in the show.

● ALBUMS: *Calypso Joe* (1957)★★★, *Flamingo* (c.1957)★★, *Say It Isn't So* (1957)★★★, *If I Were A King* (c.1960)★★★, *I Remember Bing* (c.1960)★★.

● COMPILATIONS: with Earl Hines *Swingin' Down* (1932-33)★★★, with Duke Ellington *The Blanton-Webster Band* (1940-42)★★★★★, *The Bronze Buckaroo Rides Again* (Warner Western 1995)★★★.

JENNINGS, TOMMY

b. 8 August 1938, USA. Both his parents and his brother, Waylon Jennings, were musical but Tommy only started performing when he left the US Army. He played bass with his brother's group, the Waylors, for five years. He managed Waylon for a time and they adapted 'Delia's Gone' together. Waylon also recorded Tommy's 'Life Goes On'. Jennings has recorded spasmodically, sounding reasonably like his brother, but US country chart placings tell the story - 'Make It Easy On Yourself' (number 96, 1975), 'Don't You Think It's Time' (number 71, 1978) and with Rex Gosdin, 'Just Give Me What You Think Is Fair' (number 51, 1980).

● ALBUMS: *Equal Opportunity Lovin' Man* (1982)★★★.

JENNINGS, WAYLON

b. Wayland Arnold Jennings, 15 June 1937, Littlefield, Texas, USA. Jennings' mother wanted to christen him Tommy but his father, William Alvin, insisted that the family tradition of 'W.A.' should be maintained. His father played guitar in Texas dancehalls and Jennings' childhood hero was Ernest Tubb, with whom he later recorded. When only 12 years old, he started as a radio disc jockey and then, in Lubbock, befriended an aspiring Buddy Holly. In 1958, Holly produced his debut single 'Jole Blon' and they co-wrote 'You're The One', a Holly demo that surfaced after his death. Jennings played bass on Holly's last tour, relinquishing his seat for that fatal plane journey to the Big Bopper. Jennings named his son, Buddy, after Holly and he recalled their friendship in his 1976 song 'Old Friend'. Much later (1996) he contributed a poignant version of 'Learning The Game' with Mark Knopfler to the Buddy Holly tribute album *not-fadeaway*. After Holly's death, Jennings returned to radio work in Lubbock, before moving to Phoenix and forming his own group, the Waylors. They began a two-year residency at a new Phoenix club, J.D's, in 1964. The album of their stage repertoire has worn well, but less satisfying was *Don't Think Twice*, Jennings' album for A&M. 'Herb Alpert heard me as Al Martino,' says Waylon, 'and I was wanting to sound like Hank Williams'. Bobby Bare heard the A&M album and recommended Jennings to record producer Chet Atkins. Jennings started recording for RCA in 1965 and made the US country charts with his first release, 'That's The Chance I'll Have To Take'. He co-wrote his 1966 country hit, 'Anita, You're Dreaming', and developed a folk-country style with 'For Loving Me'. He and Johnny Cash shared two wild years in Nashville, so it was apt that he should star in *Nashville Rebel*, a dire, quickly made film. Jennings continued to have country hits - 'Love Of The Common People', 'Only Daddy That'll Walk The Line' and, with the Kimberlys, 'MacArthur Park'. However, he was uncomfortable with session men, feeling that the arrangements were overblown. He did his best, even with the string-saturated 'The Days Of Sand And Shovels', which was along the lines of Bobby Goldsboro's 'Honey'. When Jennings was ill with hepatitis, he considered leaving the business, but his drummer Richie Albright, who has been with him since 1964, talked him into staying on. Jennings recorded some excellent Shel Silverstein songs for the soundtrack of *Ned Kelly*, which starred Mick Jagger, and the new Jennings fell into place with his 1971 album, *Singer Of Sad Songs*, which was sympathetically produced by Lee Hazlewood. Like the album sleeve, the music was darker and tougher, and the beat was more pronounced. Such singles as 'The Taker', 'Ladies Love Outlaws' and 'Lonesome, On'ry And Mean' showed a defiant, tough image. The cover of *Honky Tonk Heroes* showed the new Jennings and the company he was keeping. His handsome looks were overshadowed by dark clothes, a beard and long hair, which became more straggly and unkempt with each successive album. The new pared-down, bass-driven, no-frills-allowed sound continued on *The Ramblin' Man* and on his best album, *Dreaming My Dreams*. The title track is marvellously romantic, and the album also included 'Are You Sure Hank Done It This Way?', 'Bob Willis Is Still The King', a tribute to his roots, and 'Let's All Help The Cowboys (Sing The Blues)', an incisive look at outlaw country with great phased guitar. *Wanted! The Outlaws* and its hit single, 'Good Hearted Woman', transformed both Willie Nelson and Waylon Jennings' careers, making them huge media personalities in the USA (the 1996 Anniversary reissue added nine tracks, plus the brand new Steve Earle song 'Nowhere Road', sung by Nelson and Jennings). The first of the four 'Waylon And Willie' albums is the best, including the witty 'Mammas, Don't Let Your Babies Grow Up To Be Cowboys' and 'I Can Get Off On You'. In his autobiography, Nelson subsequently revealed a constant drug habit, while in his own autobiography, *A Man Called Hoss*, Jennings admitted to 21 years' addiction in an ode bidding farewell to drugs. Jennings was tired of his mean and macho image even before it caught on with the public. He topped the US country charts for six weeks and also made the US Top 30 with a world-weary song for a small township, 'Luckenbach, Texas', which is filled with disillusionment. Further sadness followed on 'I've Always Been Crazy' and 'Don't You Think This Outlaw Bit's Done Got Out Of Hand?'. He aged quickly, acquiring a lined and lived-in face which, ironically, enhanced his image. His voice became gruffer but it was ideally suited to the stinging 'I Ain't Living Long Like This' and 'It's Only Rock & Roll'. His theme for *The Dukes Of Hazzard* made the US Top 30, but the outlaw deserved to be convicted for issuing such banal material as 'The Teddy Bear Song' and an embarrassing piece with Hank Williams Jnr., 'The Conversation'. The latter was included on *Waylon And Company*, which also featured duets with Emmylou Harris and actor James Garner. Jennings has often recorded with his wife, Jessi Colter, and he and Johnny Cash had a hit with 'There Ain't No Good Chain Gang' and made an underrated album, *Heroes*. His albums with Nelson, Cash and Kris Kristofferson as the Highwaymen were also highly successful. Jennings and Cash had major heart surgery at the same time and recuperated in adjoining beds. A change to MCA and to producer Jimmy Bowen in 1985 had improved the consistency of his work, including brilliant reworkings of Los Lobos' 'Will The

Wolf Survive?' and Gerry Rafferty's 'Baker Street'. His musical autobiography, *A Man Called Hoss* (Waylon refers to everyone as 'hoss'), included the wry humour of 'If Ole Hank Could Only See Us Now'. Despite his poor health, Jennings still looks for challenges and *Waymore's Blues (Part II)* was produced by Don Was. On the *Red Hot And Country* video, his thought-provoking 'I Do Believe' showed him at his best, questioning religious beliefs. Willie and Waylon will be remembered as outlaws and certainly they did shake the Nashville establishment by assuming artistic control and heralding a new era of grittier and more honest songs. Whether they justify the tag 'outlaws' is a moot point - Jerry Lee Lewis is more rebellious than all the so-called Nashville outlaws put together. Bear Family Records have repackaged Jennings' recordings in a 15-album series, *The Waylon Jennings Files*, which includes many previously unissued titles. In 1996 he signed to Justice Records and released the impressive *Right For The Time*.

● ALBUMS: *Waylon Jennings At J.D's* (Bat 1964)★★, *Don't Think Twice* (A&M 1965)★★, *Waylon Jennings - Folk/Country* (RCA 1966)★★, *Leaving Town* (RCA 1966)★★, *Nashville Rebel* (RCA 1966)★★★, *Waylon Sings Ol' Harlan* (RCA 1967)★★, *The One And Only Waylon Jennings* (Camden 1967)★★★, *Love Of The Common People* (RCA 1967)★★, *Hangin' On* (RCA 1968)★★, *Only The Greatest* (RCA 1968)★★★, *Jewels* (RCA 1968)★★★, *Waylon Jennings* (Vocalion 1969)★★★, with the Kimberlys *Country Folk* (RCA 1969)★★★, *Just To Satisfy You* (RCA 1969)★★★, *Ned Kelly* film soundtrack (United Artists 1970)★★, *Waylon* (RCA 1970)★★★, *Singer Of Sad Songs* (RCA 1970)★★★, *The Taker/Tulsa* (RCA 1971)★★★, *Cedartown, Georgia* (1971)★★, *Good Hearted Woman* (RCA 1972)★★★, *Ladies Love Outlaws* (RCA 1972)★★★, *Lonesome, On'ry And Mean* (RCA 1973)★★★, *Honky Tonk Heroes* (RCA 1973)★★★★, *Nashville Rebel* film soundtrack (RCA 1973)★★★, *This Time* (RCA 1974)★★★, *The Ramblin' Man* (RCA 1974)★★, *Dreaming My Dreams* (RCA 1975)★★★★, *Mackintosh And T.J.* (RCA 1976)★★★, with Willie Nelson, Jessi Colter, Tompall Glaser *Wanted! The Outlaws* (RCA 1976)★★★★, *Are You Ready For The Country?* (RCA 1976)★★★, *Waylon 'Live'* (RCA 1976)★★, *Ol' Waylon* (RCA 1977)★★★, with Nelson *Waylon And Willie* (RCA 1978)★★★★, with Colter, John Dillon, Steve Cash *White Mansions* (1978)★★★, *I've Always Been Crazy* (RCA 1978)★★★, *The Early Years* (RCA 1979)★★, *What Goes Around Comes Around* (RCA 1979)★★★, *Waylon Music* (RCA 1980)★★★, *Music Man* (RCA 1980)★★, with Colter *Leather And Lace* (RCA 1981)★★, with Nelson *WWII* (RCA 1982)★★★★, with Colter *The Pursuit Of D.B. Cooper* film soundtrack (1982)★★, *Black On Black* (RCA 1982)★★, *It's Only Rock & Roll* (RCA 1983)★★★, *Waylon And Company* (RCA 1983)★★, with Nelson *Take It To The Limit* (Columbia 1983)★★★, *Never Could Toe The Mark* (RCA 1984)★★, *Turn The Page* (RCA 1985)★★, *Will The Wolf Survive?* (MCA 1985)★★★★, with Nelson, Johnny Cash, Kris Kristofferson, *Highwayman* (Columbia 1985)★★★★, with Cash *Heroes* (Columbia 1986)★★★, *Hangin' Tough* (MCA 1987)★★★, *A Man Called Hoss* (MCA 1987)★★, *Full Circle* (MCA 1988)★★★, with Cash, Kristofferson, Nelson *Highwayman 2* (Columbia 1990)★★★, *The Eagle* (Epic 1990)★★★, with Nelson *Clean Shirt* (Epic 1991)★★, *Too Dumb For New York City - Too Ugly For L.A.* (Epic 1992)★★★, *Cowboys, Sisters, Rascals & Dirt* (Epic 1993)★★★, *Waymore's Blues (Part II)*

(Epic 1994)★★, with Nelson, Cash, Kristofferson *The Road Goes On Forever* (Liberty 1995)★★, *Ol' Waylon Sings Ol' Hank* (WJ 1995)★★★, *Right For The Time* (Justice 1996)★★★, with Nelson, Colter, Glaser *Wanted! The Outlaws (1976-1996, 20th Anniversary)* (RCA 1996)★★★★.
● COMPILATIONS: *Greatest Hits* (RCA 1979)★★★★, *Greatest Hits, Volume 2* (RCA 1985)★★★, *Waylon: Best Of Waylon Jennings* (RCA 1985)★★★, *New Classic Waylon* (MCA 1989)★★★, *Silver Collection* (RCA 1992)★★★, *Only Daddy That'll Walk The Line: The RCA Years* (RCA 1993)★★★, *The Essential Waylon Jennings* (RCA 1996)★★★★.
● VIDEOS: *Renegade Outlaw Legend* (Prism 1991), *The Lost Outlaw Performance* (1991), *America* (1992).
● FURTHER READING: *Waylon Jennings*, Albert Cunniff. *Waylon - A Biography*, R. Serge Denisoff. *Waylon And Willie*, Bob Allen. *The Waylon Jennings Discography*, John L. Smith (ed.). *Waylon: An Autobiography*, Waylon Jennings with Lenny Kaye.

JIM AND JESSE

The McReynolds Brothers, Jim (b. 13 February 1927) and Jesse (b. 9 July 1929, both on a farm at Coeburn, in the Clinch Mountain region of Virginia, USA), came from a musical family; their grandfather was a noted fiddle player, who had recorded for RCA Victor. The brothers learned to play several stringed instruments as children and as teenagers played at local dances. They made their radio debut in 1947 on WNVA Norton, by which time Jim usually played guitar and Jesse mandolin. Playing bluegrass/country material, they made their first recordings around 1951 for the small Kentucky label, but in 1952, after moving to WVLK Lexington, they joined Capitol. Owing to the Korean War, Jesse spent two years in the Armed Forces, one in Korea, where he worked as an entertainer with Charlie Louvin. In 1954, he rejoined his brother at WNOX Knoxville, where they first worked on the *Tennessee Barn Dance*. Later they moved on to various radio and/or television stations in Alabama, Georgia and North Florida, and with their band, the Virginia Boys, they quickly established a reputation. The brothers' singing, with Jesse taking lead vocals and Jim adding high-pitched tenor harmonies, was obviously influenced by other brother duos such as the Blue Sky Boys and the Louvins. Jesse's 'crosspicking' mandolin work was a prominent feature in their usual bluegrass instrumental line-up. Their touring show included comedy routines and they performed a variety of material ranging from new songs to old standards and from bluegrass instrumentals to bluegrass versions of country hits. In 1959, some of their broadcasts were sponsored by Martha White Mills, making them that company's number two advertising unit after Flatt And Scruggs. They first appeared on the *Grand Ole Opry* in 1961 and became regulars in 1964. Their style of music made them popular at many venues, including a successful appearance at the 1963 Newport Folk Festival. In 1960, they joined Columbia, having recorded for Starday during the late 50s and in 1962, the label released their work on their Epic label. Although the recordings were steady sellers, they had limited US country chart success with only minor hits, including 'Cotton Mill Man' (1964). Their only Top 20 hit was 'Diesel On My Tail' (1967). In 1971, after moving to Capitol, they recorded an album of modern bluegrass using electrified instruments, but soon resorted back

to their preferred acoustic sounds, and by 1972, they were producing their own albums. They have presented their own network television shows and have easily maintained their popularity as top bluegrass performers. They have appeared at all major venues and toured extensively, both in the USA and overseas, including appearances at London's Wembley Festival. They charted in 1982 with 'North Wind' (a trio recording with Charlie Louvin) and again in 1986 with 'Oh Louisiana'.
● ALBUMS: *Sacred Songs* (1961)★★, *Bluegrass Classics* (Epic 1963)★★★, *Bluegrass Special* (Epic 1963)★★★★, *The Old Country Church* (Epic 1964)★★, *Y'All Come: Bluegrass Humour* (Epic 1964)★★★, *Berry (Chuck) Pickin' In The Country* (Epic 1965)★★★, one side is Flatt And Scruggs *Stars Of The Grand Ole Opry* (Starday 1966)★★★, *Sacred Songs We Love* (Epic 1966)★★, *Sing Unto Him A New Song* (Epic 1966)★★★, *Diesel On My Tail* (Epic 1967)★★★, *All-Time Great Country Instrumentals* (Epic 1968)★★★, *Jim And Jesse Salutin' The Louvin Brothers* (Epic 1969)★★★, *Wildwood Flower* (Harmony 1970)★★★, *We Like Trains* (Epic 1970)★★★, *Freight Train* (Capitol 1971)★★★★, *The Jim & Jesse Show* (Capitol 1972)★★★, *Superior Sounds Of Bluegrass* (Capitol 1974)★★★, *Jesus Is The Key To The Kingdom* (1975)★★, *Paradise* (1975)★★★, *Live In Japan* (1975)★★, *Songs About Our Country* (1976)★★★, *Jim & Jesse* (1976)★★★, *Palace Of Songs* (1977)★★★, *Radio Shows* (1978)★★★, *Early Recordings* (1978)★★★, *Songs Of Inspiration* (1978)★★★, *Jim & Jesse Today* (1980)★★, *Back In Tokyo Again* (1981)★★, *Jim & Jesse & Charlie Louvin* (1982)★★★, *Homeland Harmony* (1983)★★★, *Air Mail Special* (1985)★★★, *Somewhere My Love* (1986)★★★, *In The Tradition* (Rounder 1987)★★★, *Some Old, Some New, Some Borrowed, Some Blue* (1987)★★★, *Music Among Friends* (Rounder 1991)★★★.
By Jesse McReynolds: *Mandolin Workshop* (1972)★★★, *Me And My Fiddles* (1973)★★★, with Marion Sumner *Old Friends* (1979)★★★, *Guitar Pickin' Showcase* (1980)★★★, with Sumner *Fiddle Fantastic* (1986)★★★, *A Mandolin Christmas* (1988)★★, *The Mandolobro* (1991)★★★.
● COMPILATIONS: *Twenty Great Songs* (Capitol 1969)★★★★, *Jim And Jesse Story: 24 Greatest* (CMH 1980)★★★★, *Jim & Jesse: 1952-1955* (Bear Family 1992)★★★★, *Bluegrass And More* (Bear Family 1994)★★★★.

JIMINEZ, FLACO

b. Leonardo Jiminez, 11 March 1939, San Antonio, Texas, USA. Jiminez's grandfather, Patricio, learned the accordion from German neighbours and played in towns in southern Texas at the turn of the century. Jiminez's father, Santiago, was a noted accordionist and played lively dance music around San Antonio. His best-known composition is the polka 'Viva Seguin', named after a small town near San Antonio. Santiago, who started recording in 1936 and made some records for RCA, played the two-button accordion and made no attempt to integrate his music with other American forms. Jiminez, nicknamed El Flaco 'the skinny one', played bajo sexto with his father and made his recording debut in 1955 on 'Los Tecolotes'. He recorded with a group, Los Caminantes, and often had regional successes by considering contemporary lifestyle such as 'El Pantalon Blue Jean' and 'El Bingo'. His albums for Arhoolie attracted a following outside Texas, and his appearance alongside Bob Dylan on

Doug Sahm And Band in 1973, brought him to the attention of rock fans. Ry Cooder began touring and recording with him, and Jiminez can be heard on Cooder's *Chicken Skin Music*, *Show Time*, *The Border* and *Get Rhythm*. Their key collaborations are the free-flowing 'He'll Have To Go' and the sombre 'Dark End Of The Street'. *Tex-Mex Breakdown* showed that Jiminez was thinking in terms of a wider audience. He has also worked with Peter Rowan and a key track is 'Free Mexican Airforce'. Jiminez tours in his own right and is popular at arts centres and folk venues throughout the UK. His father died in 1984 and his younger brother, Santiago Jnr., is also a professional accordionist with several albums to his name.

● ALBUMS: *El Principe Del Acordeon* (1977)★★★, *Flaco Jiminez Y Su Conjunto* (Arhoolie 1978)★★★★, with Santiago Jiminez *El Sonido De San Antonio* (Arhoolie 1980)★★★, *Mis Polkas Favorites* (UK Viva Seguin) (1983)★★★, *Tex-Mex Breakdown* (1983)★★★, *On The Move* (1984)★★★, with Los Paisanos, Los Hnos Barron, Los Formales *Augie Meyers Presents San Antonio Saturday Night* (1986)★★★, *Ay Te Dejo En San Antonio* (Arhoolie 1986)★★★, with Ry Cooder, Fred Ojeda, Peter Rowan *The Accordion Strikes Back* (1987)★★★★, *Flaco's Amigos* (Arhoolie 1988)★★★★, *Partners* (Warners 1992)★★★, *Un Mojada Sin Licencia And Other Hits From The 1960s* (Arhoolie 1993)★★★.

● COMPILATIONS: *Arriba El Norte* (Rounder 1988)★★★, *San Antonio Soul* (Rounder 1991)★★★, *Flaco's First!* 1956-58 recordings (Arhoolie 1996)★★★.

JOHNNIE AND JACK

This popular singing duo comprised Johnnie Wright and Jack Anglin. They first worked together as the Dixie Early Birds on WSIX Nashville in 1939. The following year, after forming a band, they became Johnnie And Jack And The Tennessee Hillbillies (soon changing it to the Tennessee Mountain Boys) and between 1940 and Anglin's death in March 1963, they built themselves a considerable reputation. During the early 40s, they were resident on several radio stations, including WBIG Greensboro (1940) and WCHS Charleston (1941), before moving to WNOX Knoxville in 1942. When Anglin was drafted for military service, Wright's friend, Smilin' Eddie Hill, agreed to deputize. At WNOX, they played on the *Mid-Day Merry-Go-Round*, working for a time with a young fiddle player (but later guitarist) named Chet Atkins. At this time, Wright's wife, Muriel Deason, became Kitty Wells, and during these years, she only occasionally appeared with the band, as she was raising her first two children, Ruby and Bobby Wright. However, following Anglin's return when the war ended, the line-up often toured as Johnnie And Jack Featuring Kitty Wells, with appearances on numerous radio stations, including Raleigh, Decatur and Birmingham. In 1947, Johnnie And Jack returned to Nashville to spend a year on the *Grand Ole Opry* and made their first recordings on the Apollo label. They tended to play gospel songs and old-time ballads, such as 'The Paper Boy' and 'Lord Watch O'er My Daddy'. In 1948, they became regulars on the newly formed *Louisiana Hayride* on KWKH Shreveport, where they remained until December 1951. Late in 1948, with the assistance of their friend Chet Atkins, they joined RCA Victor and in January 1949, backed Kitty Wells on her first recordings; further recordings with her followed before she left the label. (The

next year she started her highly successful Decca career.) In 1951, their repertoire began to include more modern country songs and they registered Top 5 US country chart hits of their own with 'Poison Love' and 'Crying Heart Blues'. They returned as *Opry* regulars in January 1952 and promptly registered a Top 10 hit with 'Three Ways Of Knowing'. During the 50s, working usually with Kitty Wells, they played their weekly *Opry* commitments and toured extensively, often working the same tours as Roy Acuff. In 1954, they had a country number 1 with 'I Get So Lonely' and a number 3 with 'Goodnight Sweetheart Goodnight'. Other Top 10 hits included 'Kiss Crazy Baby' and 'Stop The World (And Let Me Off)'. They are also still remembered for two songs that surprisingly did not chart for them, 'Ashes Of Love' and the rumba-rhythmed 'Down South In New Orleans'. The Tennessee Mountain Boys featured talented musicians including steel guitarist 'Shot' Jackson, fiddler Paul Warren and mandolinist Clyde Baum. Their last chart hit came in 1962, a Top 20 with 'Slow Poison'. At a time when they were one of country music's most popular and respected acts, Anglin died in a car crash on 7 March 1963, on his way to a memorial service for Patsy Cline.

● ALBUMS: *Johnnie & Jack And The Tennessee Mountain Boys* (RCA Victor 1958)★★★, *Hits By Johnnie & Jack* (RCA Victor 1959)★★, *Smiles & Tears* (Decca 1962)★★★, *Poison Love & Other Country Favorites* (Camden 1963)★★, *Sincerely* (Camden 1964)★★★, *Here's Johnnie & Jack* (Vocalion 1968)★★, with Kitty Wells *At KWKH* (Bear Family 1994)★★★.

● COMPILATIONS: *All The Best Of Johnnie & Jack* (RCA Victor 1970)★★★, *And The Tennessee Mountain Boys* (Bear Family)★★★.

JOHNSON MOUNTAIN BOYS

A popular bluegrass group which, when founded in 1978, consisted of Dudley Connell (b. Dudley Dale Connell, 18 February 1956, Scherr, West Virginia, USA; guitar, banjo, lead vocals), Richard Underwood (b. 14 July 1956, Seabrook, Maryland, USA; banjo, bass, vocals), David McLaughlin (b. David Wallace McLaughlin, 13 February 1958, Washington DC, USA; mandolin, lead vocals), Eddie Stubbs (b. 25 November 1961, Gaithersburg, Maryland, USA; fiddle, vocals) and Larry Robbins (b. 25 April 1945, Montgomery County, Maryland, USA; bass fiddle). When McLaughlin left later that year, his place was taken by Ed D'Zmura (mandolin). They made their first recordings in 1978, which resulted in an album and EP release on Copper Creek and soon gained a following with their appearances in the Washington DC area. In 1981, McLaughlin returned and they established themselves further afield with the help of some fine album releases on Rounder Records and some notable concert performances. The personnel remained constant until 1986, when Robbins left and Marshall Willborn replaced him on bass fiddle, while a little later Underwood was replaced by Tom Adams. They toured extensively in the USA and Canada and also made very popular appearances in the UK. Among special venues were the White House and the *Grand Ole Opry*. In February 1988, with some members tired of the travelling and also a little disappointed that they had not been favoured by network television, the band formally announced their retirement from performing as a full-time unit. A farewell concert was recorded and later

released by Rounder. In 1989, they made a welcome appearance at two festivals and in the following two years, they were persuaded to make many more. Earl Yager became the bass player, while past member Underwood played the 1989/90 venues and Adams returned in 1991. In 1993, they released a CD and in 1994, they were still making some appearances.
● ALBUMS: *The Johnson Mountain Boys* (Rounder 1981)★★★, *Walls Of Time* (Rounder 1982)★★★, *Working Close* (Rounder 1983)★★★, *The Johnson Mountain Boys* (Copper Creek 1984)★★★★, *Live At The Birchmere* (Rounder 1984)★★, *We'll Still Sing On* (Rounder 1985)★★★, *Let The Whole World Talk* (Rounder 1987)★★, *Requests* (Rounder 1988)★★, *At The Old Schoolhouse* (Rounder 1989)★★★ *Blue Diamond* (Rounder 1993)★★★.
● COMPILATIONS: *Favorites* (Rounder 1987)★★★.

JOHNSON, KENNY

b. 11 December 1939, Liverpool, England. In the early 60s, Johnson was the lead singer/rhythm guitarist of the country Merseybeat band Sonny Webb And The Cascades. They developed into the Hillsiders, which for many years was the UK's top country band, recording with Bobby Bare and George Hamilton IV. Johnson left in 1975 and soon formed his own band, Kenny Johnson And Northwind, which, for many years, has been regarded as one of the best bands on Merseyside. Johnson's passionate vocals are enhanced by Bobby Arnold's driving electric guitar. They play contemporary country music, often written by Johnson, but occasionally perform oldies gigs as Sonny Webb And The Cascades. Johnson's song 'Today' is a favourite on request shows and at Merseyside weddings. Johnson takes his time over his recordings but *Summer Nights* featured 16 of his own compositions with no fillers. John Fogerty and John Anderson influences are apparent on the album, but there is also much of Johnson's own originality including a touching song about growing up on Merseyside, 'Old Hutte Lane'. Johnson writes for West Virginia and he produced Julie Finney's *Something Called Love*. His weekly programme on BBC Radio Merseyside has the highest listening figures for any regional country show.
● ALBUMS: *Let Me Love You Once* (O.B.M. 1980)★★★, *The Best Of Kenny Johnson* (O.B.M. 1982)★★★, *Summer Nights* (Stox 1991)★★★.

JOHNSON, LARRY C.

b. 21 February 1952, Charlotte, North Carolina, USA. Johnson grew up in Mountain City, Tennessee, but moved to Chicago in his teens. His mother taught him guitar and, inspired by Hank Williams, George Jones and Marty Robbins, Johnson gained his first professional experience, under an assumed name (he was under-age), singing in the honky tonks of Illinois. He has a fondness for country music with a gospel flavour and early in his career, he privately recorded two volumes called *Songs Of Reality*, the majority of the numbers being self-penned. Operating from Fort Payne, Alabama, he continues to perform and achieved some success with the title track of his first Nashville-recorded album. A recent album of western swing and traditional country songs all composed by Col. Buster Doss also attracted air play on European and Scandinavian country stations. His avowed intention is to preserve traditional country music for future generations and he has plans to develop a country music park on his farm in Mentone, Alabama.
● ALBUMS: *Drinkin' Whisky* (Ye Old Heritage 1992)★★★, *Rainbow Of Roses* (Stardust 1994)★★★.

JOHNSON, MICHAEL

b. 8 August 1944, Alamosa, Colorado, USA. With a taste catholic enough to embrace both Charlie Byrd and Chuck Berry, Johnson was taught rudimentary guitar by an older brother before spending a year in Barcelona studying flamenco with Graciano Tarrago. After returning to the USA, the 22-year-old toured with the Chad Mitchell Trio (with John Denver). In 1971, his first solo album was overseen by Peter Yarrow (of Peter, Paul And Mary) and Phil Ramone, but he had to wait until 1978 when 'Bluer Than Blue' reached number 12 in the US charts. It was followed by lesser entries with 'Almost Like Being In Love' and 'This Night Won't Last Forever'. Transferring from EMI-America to RCA, Johnson next addressed himself to the C&W field, beginning well with 'I Love You By Heart', a commercially successful duet with Sylvia. He was to top the country chart twice with singles from the movie *Wings* - 'Give Me Wings' (co-written by Rhonda Fleming) and Hugh Prestwick's 'The Moon Is Over My Shoulder' (featuring a galvanizing acoustic guitar solo by Don Potter). Further hits with 'Crying Shame', Randy Vanwarmer's 'I Will Whisper Your Name' and - another Prestwick opus - 'That's That', established Johnson as a star of the genre by the 90s. However, illness and poor sales of his 1991 album threatened his new-found status.
● ALBUMS: *Michael Johnson* i (1971)★★, *Wings* (RCA 1987)★★★★, *Life's A Bitch* (RCA 1989)★★★, *Michael Johnson* ii (1991)★★, *Departure* (Vanguard 1995)★★.
● COMPILATIONS: *The Best Of Michael Johnson* (RCA 1990)★★★.

JONES, COLEY

Jones led the Dallas String Band, the sole recorded exemplars of black Texan string band music, although their line-up on record of two mandolins, guitar and bass omits the violin (and sometimes clarinet and trumpet) that was usually included on live dates. Jones was an indifferent guitarist, but a brilliant mandolinist, at his best on the sparkling 'Dallas Rag'. The band also played pop songs and blues (although, like all their repertoire, the blues were played more as entertainment than for personal expression). As a soloist, Jones performed comic songs such as 'Drunkard's Special' and 'Travelling Man', and humorous monologues. In duet with the female singer Bobbie Cadillac, he pandered to more up-to-date tastes, recording four variants of 'Tight Like That', but it is his, and his band's, songster material that is of more enduring value.
● ALBUMS: *Coley Jones & The Dallas String Band* (1983)★★★.

JONES, DAVID LYNN

b. 15 January 1950, Bexar, Arkansas, USA. David Lynn Jones' forefathers lived on the same acres for generations. His father was the village postmaster and his mother a preacher. His neighbours have also formed the nucleus of his band. His most successful record, 'Bonnie Jean', is about his sister ('She's got a heart of gold and nerves of steel/Little sister rolls them eighteen wheels'). His first album, produced by

Waylon Jennings' producer Richie Albright, showed the influences of Bruce Springsteen alongside country music. Waylon sang with Jones on his US country hit, 'High Ridin' Heroes'. Jones left Mercury Records, and moved to Liberty, after he claimed there had been too much interference with the recording of his second album. His best-known song is 'Living In The Promiseland', a US country hit for Willie Nelson.

● ALBUMS: *Hard Times On Easy Street* (Mercury 1987)★★★, *Wood, Wind And Stone* (Mercury 1989)★★★, *Mixed Emotions* (Liberty 1992)★★, *Play By Ear* (Liberty 1994)★★★.

JONES, GEORGE

b. George Glenn Jones, 12 September 1931, Saratoga, Texas, USA. Jones is the greatest of honky tonk singers but he has also been a victim of its lifestyle. He learned guitar in his youth, and in 1947, was hired by the husband-and-wife duo Eddie And Pearl. This developed into his own radio programme and a fellow disc jockey, noting his close-set eyes and upturned nose, nicknamed him 'The Possum'. He married at 18 but the couple separated within a year. Jones joined the marines in 1950 and, after being demobbed in November 1953, was signed by Pappy Daily to the new Starday label. He had his first country hit in 1955 with 'Why Baby Why', a pop hit for Pat Boone. He recorded some rockabilly tracks including 'Rock It', which Daily released under the name of Thumper Jones. Jones has so strongly disassociated himself from these recordings that he is apt to destroy any copies that he sees. Daily also leased cover versions of well-known songs by Jones and other performers, including Sleepy La Beef, to others for budget recordings. Jones's work, for example, was issued under the pseudonyms of Johnny Williams, Hank Davis and Glen Patterson, but collectors should bear in mind that these names were also used for other performers. In 1959 he had his first country number 1 with 'White Lightning', written by his friend the Big Bopper. The single made number 73 on the US Top 100 and, despite numerous country hits, it remains his biggest pop hit, perhaps because his voice is too country for pop listeners. (Jones has never reached the UK charts, although he and the Big Bopper supplied the backing vocals for Johnny Preston's 'Running Bear'.) Jones's second US country number 1 was with the sensitive 'Tender Years', which held the top spot for seven weeks. He demonstrated his writing skills on 'The Window Up Above', which was subsequently a hit for Mickey Gilley, and 'Seasons Of My Heart', recorded by both Johnny Cash and Jerry Lee Lewis. His flat-top hairstyle and gaudy clothes may look dated to us now, but he recorded incredibly poignant country music with 'She Thinks I Still Care' and 'You Comb Her Hair', as well as the up-tempo fun of 'Who Shot Sam?'. The American public kept up with the Joneses for 'The Race Is On', but Jack Jones was the winner in the charts. George Jones recorded prolifically for the Musicor label, although most of his numerous albums are less than 30 minutes long. He recorded successful duets with other performers; Gene Pitney ('I've Got Five Dollars And It's Saturday Night') and Melba Montgomery ('We Must Have Been Out Of Our Minds'). In 1970 he recorded the original version of 'A Good Year For The Roses', later a hit for Elvis Costello, and 'Tell Me My Lying Eyes Are Wrong', a concert favourite for Dr. Hook. His stormy marriage to Tammy Wynette (1969-75) included duet albums of lovey-dovey songs and bitter recriminations. A solo success, 'The Grand Tour', is a room-by-room account of what went wrong. His appalling behaviour (beating Wynette, shooting at friends, missing concerts) is largely attributable to his drinking. An album of superstar duets was hampered when he missed the sessions and had to add his voice later. His partners included Elvis Costello ('Stranger In The House'), James Taylor ('Bartender's Blues') and Willie Nelson ('I Gotta Get Drunk'). His album with Johnny Paycheck is a collection of rock 'n' roll classics. By the late 70s, his drinking and cocaine addiction had made him so unreliable that he was known as 'No Show Jones', although a song he recorded about it suggested he was proud of the name. When he did appear, he sometimes used Donald Duck's voice instead of his own. In 1979 he received medical treatment, and, with support from the music industry, staged a significant comeback with *I Am What I Am*, which included his greatest single, 'He Stopped Loving Her Today', and a further duet album with Wynette. Further trouble ensued when he beat up another fiancée, but a divorcee, Nancy Sepulveda, tolerated his mistreatment and married him in 1983. Jones's behaviour has improved in recent years, although, as he would have it, 'If you're going to sing a country song, you've got to have lived it yourself.' In short, George Jones's major asset is his remarkable voice which can make a drama out of the most mundane lyrics (James O'Gwynn recorded a tribute 'If I Could Sing A Country Song (Exactly Like George Jones)'). Jones has had more records (almost 150) in the US country charts than any other performer, although his comparatively low tally of 13 number 1s is surprising. Undoubtedly, he would have had another with a duet with Dolly Parton, 'Rockin' Years', but following an announcement that he was to move to MCA, his voice was replaced by Ricky Van Shelton's. His first MCA album, *And Along Came Jones*, included a tribute to his deceased mother. In 1995 he renewed his artistic partnership with ex-wife Wynette for *One*. It was as good as anything they had made together, and included an affectionate nod to new country artists: 'I've even heard a few/that sound like me and you'. Jones may no longer sell records in the quantities he used to, but his albums now show more consistency. He is still regarded by many as the world's leading honky-tonk singer. In April 1996 he released his autobiography, *I Lived To Tell It All*, which was soon followed by a new album of the same title.

Being a George Jones completist is an exhausting task because he has had 450 albums released in the USA and UK alone. The listing concentrates only on albums of new recordings, collections of singles on albums for the first time, and compilations where previously unissued tracks have been added. In addition, in the early 70s, RCA Records in America reissued 15 compilations from his Musicor albums, usually with additional tracks, but they are not included below. Jones has recorded such key tracks as 'Ragged But Right' several times. Surprisingly, however, only two live albums have been issued, both in the 80s.

● ALBUMS: *Grand Ole Opry's Newest Star* (Starday 1956)★★★, *Grand Ole Opry's New Star* (Mercury 1957)★★★, *Country Church Time* (Mercury 1958)★★★, *George Jones Sings White Lightning* (Mercury 1959)★★★, *George Jones Salutes Hank Williams* (Mercury 1960)★★★, *The Crown Prince Of Country Music* (Starday 1960)★★★, *Sings His*

Greatest Hits (Starday 1962)★★★, The Fabulous Country Music Sound Of George Jones (Starday 1962)★★★, George Jones Sings Country And Western Hits (Mercury 1962)★★★, From The Heart (Mercury 1962)★★★, with Margie Singleton Duets Country Style (Mercury 1962)★★★, The New Favourites Of George Jones (United Artists 1962)★★★, The Hits Of His Country Cousins (United Artists 1962)★★★, Homecoming In Heaven (United Artists 1962)★★★, My Favourites Of Hank Williams (United Artists 1962)★★★, George Jones Sings Bob Wills (United Artists 1962)★★★, I Wish Tonight Would Never End (United Artists 1963)★★★, with Melba Montgomery What's In Our Heart (United Artists 1963)★★★, More New Favourites Of George Jones (United Artists 1963)★★★, The Novelty Side Of George Jones (Mercury 1963)★★★, The Ballad Side Of George Jones (Mercury 1963)★★★, Blue And Lonesome (Mercury 1963)★★★, C&W No. l Male Singer (Mercury 1964)★★★, Heartaches And Tears (Mercury 1964)★★★, with Montgomery Bluegrass Hootenanny (United Artists 1964)★★★, George Jones Sings Like The Dickens (United Artists 1964)★★★, Jones Boys' Country And Western Songbook (instrumentals) (Musicor 1964)★★★, with Gene Pitney For The First Time (Musicor 1965)★★★, Mr. Country And Western Music (Musicor 1965)★★★, New Country Hits (Musicor 1965)★★★, Old Brush Arbors (Musicor 1965), I Get Lonely In A Hurry (United Artists 1965)★★★, Trouble In Mind (United Artists 1965)★★★, The Race Is On (United Artists 1965)★★★, King Of Broken Hearts (United Artists 1965)★★★, The Great George Jones (United Artists 1965)★★★, Singing The Blues (Mercury 1965)★★★, George Jones (Starday 1965)★★★, Long Live King George (Starday 1966)★★★, with Pitney It's Country Time Again! (Musicor 1966)★★★, Love Bug (Musicor 1966)★★★, I'm A People (Musicor 1966)★★★, We Found Heaven At 4033 (Musicor 1966)★★★, with Montgomery Blue Moon Of Kentucky (United Artists 1966)★★★, with Montgomery Close Together (Musicor 1966)★★★, Walk Through This World With Me (Musicor 1967)★★★, Cup Of Loneliness (Musicor 1967)★★★, with Montgomery Let's Get Together/Party Pickin' (Musicor 1967)★★★, Hits By George (Musicor 1967)★★★, The George Jones Story (Starday 1967)★★★, The Young George Jones (United Artists 1967)★★★, Songbook And Picture Album (Starday 1968)★★★, with Dolly Parton George Jones & Dolly Parton (Starday 1968)★★, The Songs Of Dallas Frazier (Musicor 1968)★★★, If My Heart Had Windows (Musicor 1968)★★★, The George Jones Story (Musicor 1969)★★★, with Montgomery Great Country Duets Of All Time (Musicor 1969)★★★, My Country (Musicor 1969)★★★, I'll Share My World With You (Musicor 1969)★★★, Where Grass Won't Grow (Musicor 1969)★★★, My Boys - The Jones Boys (Musicor 1969)★★★, Will You Visit Me On Sunday? (Musicor 1970)★★, George Jones With Love (Musicor 1971)★★★, The Great Songs Of Leon Payne (Musicor 1971)★★★, with Tammy Wynette We Go Together (Epic 1971)★★★, George Jones (We Can Make It) (Epic 1972)★★★, with Wynette Me And The First Lady (Epic 1972)★★★, A Picture Of Me (Epic 1972)★★★, with Wynette We Love To Sing About Jesus (Epic 1972)★★, with Wynette Let's Build A World Together (Epic 1973)★★★, Nothing Ever Hurt Me (Epic 1973)★★★, with Wynette We're Gonna Hold On (Epic 1973)★★★, In A Gospel Way (Epic 1974)★★★, The Grand Tour (Epic 1974)★★★, George, Tammy And Tina (Epic 1975)★★★, Memories Of Us (Epic 1975)★★★, The Battle (Epic 1976)★★, Alone Again (Epic 1976)★★★, with Wynette Golden Ring (Epic 1976)★★★, The Battle (Epic 1976)★★, Alone Again (Epic 1976)★★★, with Wynette Golden Ring (Epic 1976)★★★, Bartender's Blues (Epic 1978)★★, My Very Special Guests (Epic 1979)★★★, with Johnny Paycheck Double Trouble (Epic 1980)★★★, I Am What I Am (Epic 1980)★★★★, with Wynette Together Again (Epic 1980)★★★, Still The Same Ole Me (Epic 1981)★★★, with Merle Haggard A Taste Of Yesterday's Wine (Epic 1982)★★★, Shine On (Epic 1983)★★★, You've Still Got A Place In My Heart (Epic 1984)★★★, By Request (1984)★★★, Ladies Choice (Epic 1984), Who's Gonna Fill Their Shoes? (Epic 1985)★★★, Wine Coloured Roses (Epic 1986)★★★, Salutes Bob Wills & Hank Williams (Liberty 1986)★★★, Live At Dancetown USA (Ace 1987)★★★, Too Wild Too Long (Epic 1988)★★★, One Woman Man (Epic 1989)★★★, Hallelujah Weekend (1990)★★★, You Oughta Be Here With Me (Epic 1990)★★★, Friends In High Places (Epic 1991)★★★, And Along Came Jones (MCA 1991)★★★, Walls Can Fall (MCA 1992)★★★, High Tech Redneck (MCA 1993)★★★, The Bradley Barn Sessions (MCA 1994)★★★, with Wynette One (MCA 1995)★★★, I Lived To Tell It All (MCA 1996)★★★.

● COMPILATIONS: Greatest Hits (Mercury 1961)★★★, The Best Of George Jones (United Artists 1963)★★★, Greatest Hits, Volume 2 (Mercury 1965)★★★, Greatest Hits (Musicor 1967)★★★, Golden Hits, Volume1 (United Artists 1967)★★★, Golden Hits, Volume 2 (United Artists 1967)★★★, Golden Hits, Volume 3 (United Artists 1968)★★★, The Golden Country Hits Of George Jones (Starday 1969)★★★, The Best Of George Jones (Musicor 1970)★★★, The Best Of Sacred Music (Musicor 1971)★★★, with Wynette Greatest Hits (Epic 1977)★★★, The Best Of George Jones (Epic 1978)★★★, with Wynette Encore: George Jones & Tammy Wynette (Epic 1981)★★★★, Anniversary: Ten Years Of Hits (Epic 1982)★★★★, White Lightnin' (Ace 1984)★★★, The Lone Star Legend (Ace 1985)★★★, Burn The Honky Tonk Down (Rounder 1986)★★★, with Wynette Super Hits (Epic 1987)★★★, Don't Stop The Music (Ace 1987)★★★, Greatest Country Hits (Curb 1990)★★★, The Best Of George Jones, Vol. 1: Hardcore Honky Tonk (Mercury 1991)★★★★, The Best Of 1955-1967 (Rhino 1991)★★★★, Cup Of Loneliness: The Mercury Years (Mercury 1994)★★★★, The Spirit Of Country: The Essential George Jones (Epic/Legacy 1994)★★★★, All-Time Greatest Hits (Liberty 1994)★★★, White Lightning (Drive Archive 1994)★★, with Gene Pitney George Jones & Gene Pitney (Bear Family 1995)★★★, with Melba Montgomery Vintage Collection Series (Capitol 1996)★★★.

● VIDEOS: with Tammy Wynette Country Stars Live (Platinum Music 1990), Same Ole Me (Prism 1990), Golden Hits (Beckmann Communications 1994), Live In Tennessee (Music Farm Ltd 1994).

● FURTHER READING: Ragged But Right - The Life And Times Of George Jones, Dolly Carlisle. George Jones - The Saga Of An American Singer, Bob Allen. I Lived To Tell It All, George Jones.

JONES, GRANDPA

b. Louis Marshall Jones, 20 October 1913, Niagara, Henderson County, Kentucky, USA. The youngest of the 10 children of a tobacco farmer, Jones learned guitar and first appeared on radio in 1929, soon after securing his own programme on WJW Akron, where he became known as 'The Young Singer of Old Songs'. He worked on the *Lum and Abner* radio show but in 1935 joined Bradley Kincaid's touring company. Kincaid maintained that he sounded like a grumpy old man on their early morning WBZ Boston show and nicknamed him 'Grandpa'. Jones adopting the name and became a permanent 'Grandpa' at the tender age of 22. He left Kincaid in 1937, readily finding work on many stations including WWVA Wheeling, WCHS Charleston and WMMN Fairmont, before, in 1942, joining the *Boone County Jamboree* on WLW Cincinnati, where he first worked with Merle Travis, the Delmore Brothers and Ramona Riggins (his future wife). He first recorded for the newly formed King label in 1943, recording two sides with Merle Travis that were released as the Shepherd Brothers. Further recordings were made in 1944 before he joined the army, finally serving in the military police in Germany, where he broadcast daily on AFN radio with his band the Munich Mountaineers. After his discharge in 1946 he returned to Cincinnati, but later that year moved to Nashville and became a *Grand Ole Opry* regular. Between 1947 and 1951 he recorded extensively for King and after changing his style of music from ballads to up-tempo songs and comedy numbers, produced his well-known recordings of 'Eight More Miles To Louisville', 'Mountain Dew' and 'Old Rattler', using the banjo for the first time on record on the latter. He also made some fine recordings with Merle Travis and the Delmores as the gospel group the Brown's Ferry Four. He recorded for RCA from 1952-55 and later for several other labels. He entered the US country charts in 1959 with 'The All-American Boy', a pop hit for Bill Parsons, and reached number 5 in 1963 with his recording of the old Jimmie Rodgers song, 'T for Texas'. The popularity of his recordings and his *Opry* performances led to him joining the cast of the CBS network television show *Hee-Haw* in 1969, where his comedy routines with Minnie Pearl became very popular. Grandpa Jones was elected to the Country Music Hall Of Fame in 1978 and still performs regularly at the *Opry*. He published his autobiography in 1984. On 3 January 1998, following an *Opry* performance, he suffered a stroke.

● ALBUMS: *Grandpa Jones Sings His Greatest Hits* (King 1958)★★★, *Grandpa Jones-Strictly Country Tunes* (King 1959)★★★, *Do You Remember (When Grandpa Jones Sang These Songs)* (King 1962)★★★, *Grandpa Jones Makes The Rafters Ring* (Monument 1962)★★★, *An Evening With Grandpa Jones* (Decca 1963)★★★, *Grandpa Jones Yodeling Hits* (Monument 1963)★★★, *Rolling' Along With Grandpa Jones* (King 1963)★★★, *Grandpa Jones Sings Real Folk Songs* (Monument 1964)★★, *Other Side Of Grandpa Jones (At Home/On Stage)* (King 1964)★★, *Grandpa Jones Remembers The Brown's Ferry Four* (Monument 1966)★★★, *Everybody's Grandpa* (Monument 1968)★★★, *Living Legend Of Country Music* (King 1969)★★★, *Grandpa Jones Sings Hits From Hee-Haw* (Monument 1969)★★★, *Grandpa Jones Live* (Monument 1970)★★★, *What's For Supper?* (1974)★★★, with Ramona And the Brown's Ferry Four *The Grandpa Jones Story* (CMH 1976)★★★, with Ramona Jones *Old Time Country Music Collection* (1978)★★★, with Ramona and their four children *Grandpa Jones' Family Album* (CMH 1979)★★★, *Family Gathering* (1981)★★★, with Roy Clark, Buck Owens, Kenny Price *The Hee-Haw Gospel Quartet* (Songbird 1981)★★★, with Merle Travis *Merle And Grandpa's Farm And Home Hour* (1985)★★★. As a member of the Brown's Ferry Four: *Sacred Songs* (King 1957)★★★, *Sacred Songs Volume 2* (King 1958)★★★, *16 Sacred Gospel Songs* (King 1963)★★★, *Wonderful Sacred Songs* (King 1964)★★★.

● COMPILATIONS: *Good Ole Mountain Dew* (Sony 1995)★★★, *Everybody's Grandpa* 5-CD box set (Bear Family 1996)★★★★.

● FURTHER READING: *Everybody's Grandpa (Fifty Years Behind The Mike)*, Louis M. 'Grandpa' Jones.

JORY, SARAH

b. 20 November 1969. Jory's musical talents were quickly recognized and as she loved her parents' country records, she began playing steel guitar since the age of five. She appeared in a club the following year and this was followed by her television debut when she was eight. Her father became her manager and she joined Colorado Country. Her first album, however, *Sarah's Steel Line*, was made with the Warrington band Poacher. She worked with Colorado Country for four years, followed by an assortment of gigs while she completed her schooling. She regularly went to the USA and appeared on steel guitar conventions. She made her first vocal tape, *No Time At All*, in 1986 and spent some time developing a new act around the pub circuit in Bristol. She formed a new, fully professional band, and in 1991 she opened for Eric Clapton in Dublin and undertook a nation-wide tour with Glen Campbell. She plays banjo, mandolin, guitar and keyboards as well as steel guitar, but, now signed to Ritz, her main chance of stardom is as a vocalist. One 1994 single was an unremarkable revival of Jackie DeShannon's 'When You Walk In The Room', which had also been recently revived by Pam Tillis. She was featured in a major UK television documentary about female country singers on the *South Bank Show*. *Love With Attitude* was recorded in Nashville with the songs and musicians of Music City USA.

● ALBUMS: *Sarah's Steel Line* (1980)★★, *Cross Country* (Sara 1986)★★★, *No Time At All* (1986)★★★, *Sarah's Dream* (Hitsound 1991)★★★, *New Horizons* (Ritz 1992)★★★★, *The Early Years - 20 Steel Guitar Favourites* (Ritz 1993)★★★, *The Early Years - 20 Classic Songs* (Ritz 1993)★★★, *Web Of Love* (Ritz 1994)★★★★, *Love With Attitude* (Ritz 1995)★★★.

● VIDEOS: *An Evening With* (1992).

JUDD, CLEDUS 'T', (NO RELATION)

b. Barry Poole, Crow Springs, Georgia, USA. A rather unlikely star of the 90s country scene, Cledus 'T' Judd (No Relation) has won many admirers for his cheeky renditions of current hits, and his merciless lampooning of the Nashville hierarchy. After high school, he briefly flirted with a career as a professional basketball player before dropping out of his scholarship to attend the Roffler Hair Design College. Based at the Don Shaw Hairdressers in Atlanta, he began competing in international hairstyling events. At this time he began to write his first 'country-rap' songs, which he would improvise over country records in talent contests. He subsequently moved to Nashville where he continued to work as a hairdresser, but he also sent in his songs to radio for the first time. The first two songs to receive extensive air play were 'Indian In-Laws' (based on Tim McGraw's 'Indian Outlaw') and 'Gone Funky' (based on Alan Jackson's 'Gone Country'). As a result, Judd was signed by the Walter Yetnikoff-backed independent label Razor & Tie. Within a

few months of his impersonations/parodies airing on radio, being the subject of Judd's humorous attack had become one of the acid tests of an artist's popularity and name recognition. One of his victims, Shania Twain, was so charmed by Judd she agreed to appear in the video for his 1996 single, '(She's Got A Butt) Bigger Than The Beatles', a parody of Joe Diffie's hit, 'Bigger Than The Beatles'. Judd also secured a four-night support slot to Tammy Wynette in Las Vegas, as many proclaimed him as the 'Weird Al Yankovic of country'.
● ALBUMS: *Cledus T. Judd (No Relation)* (Razor & Tie 1995)★★★, *I Stoled This Record* (Razor & Tie 1996)★★★.

JUDD, NAOMI
(see the Judds).

JUDDS
Freshly divorced, Naomi Judd (b. Diana Ellen Judd, 11 January 1946, Ashland, Kentucky, USA) moved with her daughters Wynonna (b. Christina Ciminella, 30 May 1964, Ashland, Kentucky, USA) and Ashley (b. 1968) from California back to Morrill, Kentucky, where she worked as a nurse in a local infirmary. Outside working and school hours, she and the children would sing anything from bluegrass to showbiz standards for their own amusement. However, when Wynonna nurtured aspirations to be a professional entertainer, her mother lent her encouragement, to the extent of moving the family to Nashville in 1979. Naomi's contralto subtly underlined Wynonna's tuneful drawl. While tending a hospitalized relation of RCA Records producer Brent Maher, Naomi elicited an audition in the company's boardroom. With a hick surname and a past that read like a Judith Krantz novel, the Judds - so the executives considered - would have more than an even chance in the country market. An exploratory mini-album, which contained the show-stopping 'John Deere Tractor', proved the executives correct when, peaking at number 17, 'Had A Dream' was the harbinger of 1984's 'Mama He's Crazy', the first of many country chart-toppers for the duo. The Judds would also be accorded a historical footnote as the earliest commercial manifestation of the form's 'new tradition' - a tag that implied the maintenance of respect for C&W's elder statesmen. This was shown by the Judds' adding their voices to *Homecoming*, a 1985 collaboration by Jerry Lee Lewis, Roy Orbison, Johnny Cash and Carl Perkins (who later co-wrote Naomi and Wynonna's 1989 smash, 'Let Me Tell You About Love'). The Judds' repertoire also featured revivals of Ella Fitzgerald's 'Cow Cow Boogie', Elvis Presley's 'Don't Be Cruel' and Lee Dorsey's 'Working In A Coal Mine'. Self-composed songs included Naomi's 1989 composition 'Change Of Heart', dedicated to her future second husband (and former Presley backing vocalist), Larry Strickland. Maher too contributed by co-penning hits such as 1984's Grammy-winning 'Why Not Me', 'Turn It Loose', 'Girls Night Out' and the title track of the Judds' second million-selling album, *Rockin' With The Rhythm Of The Rain*. The team relied mainly on songsmiths such as Jamie O'Hara ('Grandpa Tell Me About The Good Old Days'), Kenny O'Dell ('Mama He's Crazy'), Mickey Jupp, Graham Lyle and Troy Seals ('Maybe Your Baby's Got The Blues') and Paul Kennerley ('Have Mercy', 'Cry Myself To Sleep'). Most Judds records had an acoustic bias - particularly on the sultry ballads selected for *Give A Little Love*. They also have an occasional penchant for star

guests that have included the Jordanaires ('Don't Be Cruel'), Emmylou Harris 'The Sweetest Gift' (*Heartland*), Mark Knopfler on his 'Water Of Love' (*River Of Time*) and Bonnie Raitt playing slide guitar on *Love Can Build A Bridge*. In 1988, the pair became the first female country act to found their own booking agency (Pro-Tours) but a chronic liver disorder forced Naomi to retire from the concert stage two years later. Naomi and Wynonna toured America in a series of extravagant farewell concerts, before Wynonna was free - conveniently, cynics said - to begin her long-rumoured solo career. This she did in style, with a remarkable album that touched on gospel, soul and R&B, and confirmed her as one of the most distinctive and powerful female vocalists of her generation.
● ALBUMS: *The Judds: Wynonna & Naomi* mini-album (Curb/RCA 1984)★★, *Why Not Me?* (Curb/RCA 1984)★★★, *Rockin' With The Rhythm Of The Rain* (Curb/RCA 1985)★★★, *Give A Little Love* (Curb/RCA 1986)★★★, *Heartland* (Curb/RCA 1987)★★, *Christmas Time With The Judds* (Curb/RCA 1987)★★, *River Of Time* (Curb/RCA 1989)★★★, *Love Can Build A Bridge* (Curb/RCA 1990)★★★.
● COMPILATIONS: *Greatest Hits* (Curb/RCA 1988)★★★★, *Collector's Series* (Curb/RCA 1993)★★★, *Greatest Hits, Volume 2* (Curb/RCA 1991)★★★, *The Judds Collection 1983 - 1990* 3-CD box set (RCA 1991)★★★, *Number One Hits* (Curb 1995)★★★, *The Essential Judds* (RCA 1995)★★★★, *The Judds Collection* (Curb/The Hit 1996)★★★.
● VIDEOS: *Their Final Concert* (1992), *The Farewell Tour* (1994).
● FURTHER READING: *The Judds: Unauthorized Biography*, Bob Millard. *Love Can Build A Bridge*, Naomi Judd.

KANE, KIERAN
b. 7 October 1949, Queens, New York, USA. The 90s country singer and record company owner Kieran Kane initially enjoyed a certain amount of success as half of the O'Kanes alongside Jamie O'Hara. The duo split in 1989 to resume their solo careers, mostly as songwriters. The acoustic *Find My Way Home* did not sell sufficiently well for Atlantic Records to want to try again with the artist. This worked to Kane's advantage as, with Mike Henderson, he established his own label, Dead Reckoning, which has already developed into one of the most creative labels in Nashville and whose signings include Kevin Welch, Tammy Rogers and Harry Stinson, all of whom work outside of the mainstream. Regarding Kane's own work, the acoustic *Dead Rekoning* cost

only $10,000 to make. 'This Dirty Little Town' features harmony vocals from Emmylou Harris and Lucinda Williams. Emmylou Harris has in fact recorded one of his songs, 'If I Could Be There', and Kathy Mattea has recorded 'Forgive And Forget'. Kane has much faith in Dead Reckoning, although he is cynical about the industry in general: 'Record companies rarely have anything to do with music.'

● ALBUMS: *Find My Way Home* (Atlantic 1993)★★★, *Dead Rekoning* (Dead Reckoning 1995)★★★.

KAPLANSKY, LUCY

b. Chicago, Illinois, USA. Kaplansky sang backing vocals on albums by Nanci Griffith, John Gorka and Shawn Colvin, but, being a qualified psychologist, she delayed her debut album to work with the homeless in New York. She was part of a duo with Shawn Colvin and Colvin produced *The Tide*. She is a fine singer-songwriter with folk and country roots and has a good line in cover versions, including Police's 'Secret Journey' and Richard Thompson's 'When I Get To The Border' and 'Don't Renege On Our Love' (from the accomplished follow-up, Flesh And Bone). She sang with Dar Williams on 'The Christians And The Pagans'.

● ALBUMS: *The Tide* (Red House 1994)★★★★, *Flesh And Bone* (Red House 1996)★★★★.

KARL AND HARTY

Karl Davis and Hartford Connecticut Taylor (both b. 1905, Mount Vernon, Kentucky, USA). They grew up listening to the musicians who regularly played in their town and learned many songs from their parents and from Brag Thompson, the pianist for the silent films that were shown at the local cinema. By the age of 12, Karl had learned to play the mandolin from Doc Hopkins (a noted local singer) and Harty had taught himself to play the guitar. By 1929, they were regularly appearing with Hopkins as the Kentucky Krazy Kats on WHAS Louisville. The following year, Bradley Kincaid was instrumental in their moving to WLS Chicago, where they featured on several programmes including the *National Barn Dance* and appeared with such artists as Red Foley in the Cumberland Ridge Runners. In 1933, Karl wrote 'I'm Here To Get My Baby Out Of Jail', which they recorded the following year. It proved so successful that almost every other duet group recorded it and the song went on to become a country standard. The two benefited from the new microphone and broadcasting equipment, which meant that the old mountain shouting style of singing was no longer necessary. During the 30s, their quieter style of close harmony vocal work became the form copied by other acts including the Blue Sky Boys, the Delmore Brothers and, years later, the Everly Brothers. They played on WLS until 1937 and then moved to *Suppertime Frolics* on Chicago WJJD, becoming popular over an even larger area. By the mid-40s, the changing times and the record companies' constant search for jukebox records found the pair forced to record more modern songs aimed at the honky-tonk market. They consequently recorded songs such as 'Seven Beers With The Wrong Woman' and 'Don't Mix Whiskey With Women', while continuing to sing their more usual style of number, such as 'Wreck On The Highway' and 'The Prisoner's Dream', on their radio programmes. They later commented: 'We were like Dr. Jekyll and Mr. Hyde and we didn't much like that either'. In the 50s, they retired from

performing when live radio and country music in Chicago declined. Karl remained active as a songwriter and had songs recorded by artists including Emmylou Harris and Linda Ronstadt. There is little doubt that Karl's best-known song is 'Kentucky'. He wrote it as a tribute to his home state and when it was recorded in January 1941, it became very popular with US servicemen in World War II. However, it was not their own version but that of the Blue Sky Boys, in 1947, that turned the song into a country classic (Karl received the honour of being named a Kentucky Colonel in 1970 by the grateful state). Harty died in 1963 and Karl in 1979.

● COMPILATIONS: *Early Recordings* (1981)★★★.

KASH, MURRAY

The Canadian Murray Kash spent many years promoting country music in the UK, working as a radio presenter and compere. He has had series on the BBC and Radio Luxembourg. He worked for promoter Mervyn Conn for some years and was the Festival Director for the International Festivals of Country Music at Wembley from 1969-79. He is married to the cabaret entertainer Libby Morris, and he wrote one of the first country books to be published in the UK, *Murray Kash's Book Of Country* (Star Books, 1981). He has recorded narrations for RCA ('Sleeping Beauty', 1968) and Columbia ('What Is A Boy?', 1974).

KAZEE, BUELL

b. 29 August 1900, Burton Fork, Magoffin County, Kentucky, USA, d. 31 August 1976. Kazee, a banjo-playing minister, has been described as 'the greatest white male folk singer in the United States'. Charles Wolfe considered him the 'epitome of the Kentucky mountain songster . . . a high, tight, 'lonesome' voice, accompanied only by a banjo 'geared' to unusual tunings'. Kazee started learning songs from his parents and first played banjo at the age of five. During his time at Georgetown College, where he studied for a ministerial career, he developed a keen interest in old English ballads. He also took lessons from a professional tenor and on graduating in 1925, he gave concerts of folk music. Accompanied by a pianist, and dressed in tie and tails, he played banjo and guitar, sang songs and lectured on music at important venues. In 1927, he went to Brunswick's New York studio where, in his trained tenor style, he first sang a mixture of popular ballads and religious numbers. The company were not interested, until they convinced him that he should play his banjo and sing in his natural manner. Between 1927 and 1929, he subsequently recorded over 50 songs of which 46 were issued. These included what has been described as the finest recorded version of 'Lady Gay'. His bestsellers proved to be 'Little Mohee' and 'Roving Cowboy' and some recordings were even released in the UK and Australia. Brunswick wanted him to tour but Kazee had just married and had no wish for a professional career. He became a Baptist minister but sang at revival-style meetings and remained at a church in Morehead for 22 years. He wrote music including a cantata, an operetta ('The Wagoner Lad'), three religious books and a book on banjo playing, as well as an unpublished autobiography. In the 1960s, revived interest among the young devotees to folk music saw Kazee make appearances at the Newport Folk Festival and also give further lectures in spite of failing health. He died in 1976 but his music was continued by his son Philip who, in addition to singing and playing some of his father's material, is also a minister.

● ALBUMS: *Buell Kazee Sings & Plays* (Smithsonian/Folkways 1959)★★★, *Buell Kazee* (June Appal 1976)★★★.

KEEN, ROBERT EARL

b. 11 January 1956, Houston, Texas, USA. In the mid-70s, Keen befriended Lyle Lovett at Texas A&M University, an establishment that combined academic and military activities. They often sang and played guitar together and they wrote 'This Old Porch', which appeared on Lovett's first album. Keen also formed a bluegrass band, the Front Porch Boys. In 1981, he moved to Austin and worked as the Incredible Robert Keen and Some Other Guys Band. He financed an album on loans of $4,500, *No Kinda Dancer*, which has twice been reissued. *The Austin Chronicle* nominated him Songwriter of the Year, an honour that invariably went to Butch Hancock. On Steve Earle's advice that there were too many distractions in Austin - namely, pretty women and drugs - Keen moved to Nashville, although he returned to Texas in 1987. He was a backing singer on Nanci Griffith's 'St. Olav's Gate' and she recorded his songs 'Sing One For Sister' and 'I Would Change My Life'. He appeared on the recording of the 1986 Kerrville Folk Festival and then recorded a live album for Sugar Hill. In 1989, he made a spirited album about Texas life, *West Textures*. His rough-hewn voice suited the bittersweet songs, which included a country music parody worthy of David Allan Coe, 'It's The Little Things (That Piss Me Off)'. The stand-out track, ironically, was a song he did not write - Kevin Farrell's western tale of 'Sonora's Death Row'. Although Keen is a frequent performer, he prefers to write at home: 'I'm not a very good writer on the road because I only come up with lonely hotel songs.' *Gringo Honeymoon* was another excellent album, full of narratives and the telling observation that 'there are just two ways to go - dyin' fast or livin' slow'. *Number 2 Live Dinner* was a raucous live album recorded in Texas. His major label debut was a typically uncompromising collection comprised largely of Keen originals, and featuring Margo Timmins of Cowboy Junkies on the duet 'Then Came Lo Mein'.

● ALBUMS: *No Kinda Dancer* (Philo 1984)★★★★, *The Live Album* (Sugar Hill 1988)★★, *West Textures* (Sugar Hill 1989)★★★, *A Bigger Piece Of Sky* (Sugar Hill 1993)★★★, *Gringo Honeymoon* (Special Delivery 1994)★★★★, *Number 2 Live Dinner* (Sugar Hill 1996)★★★, *Picnic* (Arista 1997)★★★★.

KEITH, BILL

b. October 1939, Boston, Massachusetts, USA. Keith is known for his innovative banjo style, and is credited with helping the development of the progressive bluegrass mode of playing, partly attributed to his chromatic technique. Having started out learning the piano, Keith moved on to tenor banjo. In 1957, after seeing Pete Seeger of the Weavers, Keith bought a five-string banjo and gradually worked his way round the folk clubs and bars of New England with his partner Jim Rooney. In September 1962, Keith won the Philadelphia Folk Festival banjo contest. His first professional job was playing with Red Allen and mandolin player Frank Wakefield from Tennessee, eventually joining Bill

Monroe's Blue Grass Boys and also the Country Gentlemen. In 1964, Keith recorded with Wakefield and Allen for the Folkways label, and the same year, joined the Jim Kweskin Jug Band, which featured Geoff and Maria Muldaur and Richard Greene. When the group split up in 1968, Keith joined Ian And Sylvia Tyson's Great Speckled Bird, a country rock outfit, in which he also played steel guitar. After approximately a year, he went on tour with Jonathan Edwards, and later Judy Collins. From his work with the Blue Velvet Band, he then formed Muleskinner with David Grisman, Clarence White, Richard Greene and Peter Rowan. Keith spent much of the following period in session work and touring with Rooney, both in Europe and the UK. For *Something Auld, Something Newgrass, Something Borrowed, Something Bluegrass* he is backed by Vassar Clements (fiddle), Tony Rice (guitar) and David Grisman (mandolin). The album includes a cover version of a Mick Jagger/Keith Richard composition, 'No Expectations', as well as Duke Ellington's 'Caravan'. During the 80s, he toured a number of British clubs along with long-time colleague Jim Rooney as Keith And Rooney, before forming the New Blue Velvet Band with Rooney, Eric Weissberg and Kenny Koseck.

● ALBUMS: *Sweet Moments With The Blue Velvet Band* (1969)★★★, *Something Auld, Something Newgrass, Something Borrowed, Something Bluegrass* (Rounder 1976)★★★★, *Bill Keith And Jim Collier* (Hexagone 1979)★★, *Banjoistics* (Rounder 1984)★★★, with Rooney *Collection* (Waterfront 1984)★★★.

● VIDEOS: *Muleskinner - Live Video* (1991).

KEITH, TOBY

b. 8 July 1961, Elk Town, Clinton, Oklahoma, USA. The 90s country singer Toby Keith grew up on an Oklahoma farm listening to his father's favourite, Bob Wills, and finding his own hero in Merle Haggard. He tested broncs and bulls for a rodeo during his summers in high school. Oil was found in Elk Town and Keith worked as a roughneck and then an operational manager. This experience inspired 'Boomtown', of which he says, 'The wells ran dry. The rich people got rich by saving their money. The fools who spent it were broke.' Keith himself had formed the Easy Money Band, originally playing Alabama's hits but then widening the repertoire as they accumulated new and better equipment. He was signed by Harold Shedd, who produced his first album, *Toby Keith*. It included a tribute to the film stars of yesteryear, 'Should've Been A Cowboy', a number 1 country record that also became the anthem of the Dallas Cowboys football team. The album included further hits with 'Wish I Didn't Know Now', 'Ain't Worth Missing' and 'A Little Less Talk (And A Lot More Action)'. *Billboard* named him the Top New Country Artist of 1993. His number 1 country song 'Who's That Man' started as a joke: 'You know the old one that goes, "What do you get if you play country music backwards? Answer: your wife back, your dog back, your house back and your car back." I was kicking that idea round as a fun song when I hit upon the line, "Who's that man running my life?" It dawned on me that it would work better as a serious song.' In 1995 he released a sentimental seasonal album, *Christmas To Christmas*, which featured songs from the cream of Nashville's songwriters. In 1996 he appeared in the film *Burning Bridges*, with Tanya Tucker and Vanessa Williams. The same year he had a major country hit with 'Does That

Blue Moon Ever Shine On You' and a huge hit album with *Blue Moon*. He followed up with 1997's superior *Dream Walkin'*, featuring the hit single 'We Were In Love'.
● ALBUMS: *Toby Keith* (Polygram 1993)★★★, *Boomtown* (Polygram 1995)★★★, *Christmas To Christmas* (Polygram 1995)★★★, *Blue Moon* (A&M 1996)★★★★, *Dream Walkin'* (Mercury 1997)★★★★.
● VIDEOS: *Who's That Man* (1994).

KELLY, SANDY
b. 27 February 1954, Ballintogher, Co. Sligo, Eire, but raised in Wales. Kelly became a professional in her teens, singing with the Fairways Showband in Ireland and then with her younger sister Barbara and two cousins as the Duskeys. They represented Ireland in the 1982 Eurovision Song Contest. After developing a successful solo career in Ireland as a middle-of-the-road country singer, Kelly decided to promote the songs of her favourite performer, Patsy Cline. In her 1992 K-Tel video *The Voice Of Sandy Kelly - The Songs Of Patsy Clyne* (sic), she sang 13 songs by her musical hero, backed by the Jordanaires. Kelly was teamed with George Hamilton IV in the stage show *Patsy Cline - A Musical Tribute*, which toured the UK and Ireland for a year, including a three-month West End run. Sandy's husband, Michael, plays bass and acts as musical director while her sister, Barbara Ellis (b. 8 October 1961, Mohill, Co. Leitrim, Eire) records for K-Tel (Ireland), releasing an album, *Breakin' Ground*, in 1994. Kelly's 1994 album *Kelly's Heroes* includes duets with Willie Nelson, Johnny Cash and both George Hamilton IV and V.
● ALBUMS: *Paradise Tonight* (CBS Ireland 1986)★★★, *I Need To Be In Love* (K-Tel Ireland 1989)★★★★, *An Evening With Sandy Kelly* (K-Tel Ireland 1990)★★, *The Voice Of Sandy Kelly - The Songs Of Patsy Cline* subsequently repackaged as *A Musical Tribute To Patsy Cline* (K-Tel Ireland 1991)★★★, *Everytime You Need A Friend* (K-Tel Ireland 1992)★★★, *Kelly's Heroes* (K-Tel Ireland 1994)★★★.
● VIDEOS: *An Evening With Sandy Kelly* (Prism 1990).

KEMP, WAYNE
b. 1 June 1941, Greenwood, Arkansas, USA. Kemp's father was a motor mechanic and as a teenager Kemp drove racing cars. His interest changed to music and, forming his own band, he toured the south-west. In 1963, he gained fame as a songwriter when George Jones had a big hit with 'Love Bug'. After his own recording of 'The Image Of Me' had made little impression, Conway Twitty's version became a number 5 country hit. Twitty had further major success with Kemp's songs 'Next In Line', 'Darling You Know I Wouldn't Lie' and 'That's When She Started To Stop Loving You'. Kemp's own first hit came in 1969 with his Decca recording of 'Won't You Come Home'. Between then and 1982, also recording on MCA, United Artists and Mercury, he charted 20 more hits, the only Top 20 entrant being 'Honky Tonk Wine' (1973). In 1983, he had a minor hit on Door Knob with his song 'Don't Send Me No Angels' (the song was later successfully recorded by both Ricky Van Shelton and George Jones). Kemp remains active as a writer but his last chart hit was a duet with Bobby G. Rice, 'Red Neck And Over Thirty', in 1986.
● ALBUMS: *Wayne Kemp* (1972)★★★, *Kentucky Sunshine* (1974)★★.

KENDALLS
Royce Kendall (b. 25 September 1934, St. Louis, Missouri, USA) and Jeannie Kendall (b. 30 November 1954, St. Louis, Missouri, USA). Royce learned guitar from the age of five and formed a duo, the Austin Brothers, with his brother Floyce. After serving in the US Army, Royce and his wife Melba started a hairdressing business in St. Louis. Their only child, Jeannie, began harmonizing with her father on old-time country songs, and they were soon entertaining family and friends. Their first record, for a small local label, was 'Round Round Round', and their talents were recognized in Nashville by Pete Drake, although they simply recorded country versions of pop hits such as 'Leavin' On A Jet Plane', 'Proud Mary' and 'You've Lost That Lovin' Feelin''. Jeannie Kendall was among the backing singers on Ringo Starr's Nashville album *Beaucoups Of Blues*. The family moved to Hendersonville, just outside Nashville, and the Kendalls had success with Dot Records, notably 'Two Divided By Love' and 'Everything I Own'. In the mid-70s, Ovation Records started a country division and the Kendalls, who had a contemporary sound with traditional overtones, were to test the market. When a single of 'Live And Let Live' was released, Ovation found that country disc jockeys preferred the b-side, 'Heaven's Just A Sin Away'. It topped the US country charts and became the Country Single of the Year. The father and daughter followed the record with other 'cheating' songs, notably 'It Don't Feel Like Sinnin'' To Me' and 'Pittsburg Stealers'. They had a further US country number 1 with the double-sided 'Sweet Desire'/'Old Fashioned Love', plus further Top 10 hits with 'I'm Already Blue' and Dolly Parton's 'Put It Off Until Tomorrow'. In 1981, they moved to Mercury and continued their success with 'Teach Me How To Cheat' and 'If You're Waiting On Me (You're Backing Up)'. They had their third chart-topper in 1984 with 'Thank God For The Radio'. Jeannie, who takes most of the lead vocals, married band member Mack Watkins. The Kendalls' chart success has deserted them, but they continue to tour.
● ALBUMS: *Meet The Kendalls* (Stop 1970)★★★, *Two Divided By Love* (Dot 1972)★★★, *Leavin' On A Jet Plane* (1974)★★★, *Let The Music Play* aka *Heaven's Just A Sin Away* (1977)★★★, *Old Fashioned Love* (1978)★★★, *1978 Grammy Awards Winners: Best Country Duo* (Gusto 1978)★★, *Just Like Real People* (1979)★★★, *Heart Of The Matter* (1979)★★★, *Lettin' You On A Feelin'* (Mercury 1981)★★, *Stickin' Together* (Mercury 1982)★★★, *Moving Train* (Mercury 1983)★★, *Two Heart Harmony* (Mercury 1985)★★★, *Fire At First Sight* (MCA 1986)★★★, *Break The Routine* (Step One 1987)★★★, *Make A Dance* (Branson 1995)★★★.
● COMPILATIONS: *16 Greatest Hits* (Deluxe 1988)★★★.

KENNEDY ROSE
Mary Ann Kennedy and Pam Rose, who together form 90s country duo Kennedy Rose, are session singers who decided to work together. Pam Rose had a few minor entries on the US country charts in the late 70s, the most notable being 'It's Not Supposed To Be That Way', which featured Willie Nelson's vocals. Mary Ann Kennedy wrote 'Ring On Her Finger, Time On Her Hands' (Lee Greenwood) and 'I'll Still Be Loving You' (Restless Heart). Together they provided backing vocals for Emmylou Harris and Sting, who signed them to his company, Pangaea. Their songs have been covered by Reba McEntire, Art Garfunkel and Restless Heart,

and they wrote Martina McBride's 1995 country hit 'Safe In The Arms Of Love'. They feature a driving, acoustic-based country rock sound, playing many of the instruments themselves and, unusually for Nashville, including instrumentals. Their first album, *Hai Ku*, featured 'Love Like This'. *Walk The Line* features guest appearances by Emmylou Harris and Sting and owes as much to rock as to country.
● ALBUMS: *Hai Ku* (IRS 1989)★★, *Walk The Line* (IRS 1994)★★★★.

KENNEDY, JERRY

b. Jerry Glenn Kennedy, 10 August 1940, Caddo Parish, Shreveport, Louisiana, USA. Kennedy has been a featured session guitarist for many top Nashville country stars and in the early 60s, he played lead guitar on some of Elvis Presley's recordings. He also worked with guitarist Charlie Tomlinson and recorded several guitar albums with him under the name of Tom And Jerry. After he became a record producer with Mercury/Phonogram, he produced the recordings of many artists including Roy Orbison, Bobby Bare, Charlie Rich, Patti Page, Roger Miller, the Statler Brothers, Reba McEntire and Becky Hobbs. He was responsible for Jerry Lee Lewis's commercial renaissance in the late 60s, when he steered him back towards the country market. He has also worked in several administration posts within the music industry, including that of Vice-President of A&R of the Country Division of Mercury.
● ALBUMS: *Jerry Kennedy's Dancing Guitars (Rock Elvis' Hits)* (1962)★★ *Jerry Kennedy's Guitars & Strings Play The Golden Standards* (Smash 1963)★★, *From Nashville To Soulville* (Smash 1965)★★, *Jerry Kennedy Plays With All Due Respect To Kris Kristofferson* (Mercury 1971)★★★, *Jerry Kennedy & Friends* (1974)★★★; as Tom And Jerry *Guitar's Greatest Hits Volume 1* (Mercury 1961)★★, *Guitar's Greatest Hits Volume 2* (Mercury 1962)★★, *Guitars Play The Sound Of Ray Charles* (Mercury 1962)★★, *Surfin' Hootenanny* (Mercury 1963)★★.

KENNEDY, RAY

b. 13 May 1954, Buffalo, New York, USA. Kennedy's father worked as a credit manager for Sears, and his demanding career kept the family on the move. Kennedy dropped out of college in the mid-70s and lived in a cabin in the woods of Oregon. After a year developing his style, he began performing in the Pacific Northwest. In 1980 he took his songs to Nashville and 'The Purple Heart' and 'The Same Old Girl' were recorded by David Allan Coe and John Anderson, respectively. Kennedy built his own 24-track studio, and in 1990 he wrote, produced, engineered, sang and played all the instruments except steel guitar on his debut *What A Way To Go*. He made the US country charts with the title track, 'Scars' and 'I Like The Way It Feels', and his highly danceable music is described as 'hi-tech hillbilly'. The second album was equally strong but featured other musicians and only one song was self-penned.
● ALBUMS: *What A Way To Go* (Atlantic 1990)★★★, *Guitar Man* (Atlantic 1993)★★★.

KENNERLEY, PAUL

b. 1948, Hoylake, Wirral, England. Kennerley moved to London and worked in advertising, ran a small pub-rock booking agency and managed the Winkies. He was drawn to country music after hearing Waylon Jennings sing 'Let's All

Help The Cowboys Sing The Blues' on the radio. His knowledge of American history was apparent on *White Mansions*, a concept album about the Civil War, produced by Glyn Johns and featuring Waylon and his wife, Jessi Colter. This was followed by *The Legend Of Jesse James*, which included Levon Helm and Johnny Cash as Jesse and Frank James, respectively, as well as Emmylou Harris and Albert Lee. The album was coincidentally released at the same time as *The Long Riders*, a film about the James brothers. One song, 'The Death Of Me', was later recorded by Emmylou Harris with the lyric altered to 'Born To Run'. In 1981 the Paul Kennerley Band had success at the Wembley Festival. He moved to America, wrote a concept album with Harris, *The Ballad Of Sally Rose*, and subsequently married her. Kennerley wrote several songs for her and played on her albums. He also wrote for the Judds including 'Have Mercy', 'Cry Myself To Sleep', both country number 1s, and 'Give A Little Love'. On her first solo album, Wynonna sang 'Live With Jesus' simply by recording her voice over Paul Kennerley's demo. He has also written 'Everybody Knows' (Prairie Oyster) and 'World Without You' (Kelly Willis). Kennerley's marriage to Harris ended, but both he and Albert Lee have been the most successful Brits in country music, and both have found success through Emmylou Harris.
● ALBUMS: *White Mansions* (A&M 1978)★★★★, *The Legend Of Jesse James* (A&M 1981)★★★.

KENTUCKY COLONELS

Fêted as one of the finest ever bluegrass groups, the Kentucky Colonels evolved out of a family-based ensemble, the Three Little Country Boys. The White brothers (born Le Blanc), Roland (mandolin, vocals), Clarence White (b. 6 June 1944, Lewiston, Maine, USA, d. 14 July 1973; guitar, vocals) and Eric (bass, vocals), began performing during the mid-50s, but Billy Ray Latham (banjo) and Leroy Mack (dobro) later joined the founding trio. The unit was then renamed the Country Boys. Roger Bush replaced Eric White in 1961, after which the quintet became known as the Kentucky Colonels. Their progress was undermined following Roland White's induction into the army, although the group completed its debut album, *New Sounds Of Bluegrass America*, in his absence. The Colonels enjoyed their most prolific spell on his return. Fiddler Bobby Slone replaced Leroy Mack and the revitalized quintet recorded the classic *Appalachian Swing*. However, Clarence White grew increasingly unhappy with the music's confines and harboured ambitions towards a more electric style. The group attempted an awkward compromise, offering sets both traditional and contemporary, but this forlorn balance failed to satisfy either party. A new fiddler, Scotty Stoneman, joined, but by April 1966, the Colonels had all but collapsed. Roland and Eric White did attempt to revive the group the following year, adding Dennis Morris (guitar) and Bob Warford (banjo), but although this proved short-term, numerous other reunions have taken place. Latham and Bush, meanwhile, joined Dillard And Clark, while Clarence White was drafted into the Byrds.
● ALBUMS: *New Sounds Of Bluegrass America* (Briar 1963)★★★, *Appalachian Swing* (World Pacific 1964)★★★, *Kentucky Colonels* (United Artists 1974)★★★, *The White Brothers Live In Sweden* (Rounder 1979)★★★.
● COMPILATIONS: *Livin' In The Past* (Briar 1975)★★★,

The Kentucky Colonels With Scotty Stoneman (1975)★★★, *Kentucky Colonels 1966* (Shiloh 1978)★★★, *Kentucky Colonels 1965-1966* (Rounder 1979)★★★, *Clarence White And The Kentucky Colonels* (Rounder 1980)★★★, *On Stage* (Rounder 1984)★★★.

KENTUCKY HEADHUNTERS

The Kentucky Headhunters come, naturally enough, from Kentucky. Ricky Lee Phelps (lead vocal) and his brother, Doug, played in various groups around Kentucky before meeting Greg Martin (lead guitar) in 1984. He introduced them to his cousins, the brothers Richard Young (rhythm guitar) and Fred Young (bass). Previously, the Young brothers and Martin had been in a group together, Itchy Brother, which was almost signed to Led Zeppelin's own label Swan Song. Since then, Fred Young had played Patsy Cline's drummer in the film, *Sweet Dreams*. This time, taking their name from Muddy Waters' band, the Headchoppers, the five musicians financed their own album, *Pink*, in 1988, and the tracks were subsequently released by Mercury, with additional material, on *Pickin' On Nashville*. Their first US country hit was with a revival of Bill Monroe's 'Walk Softly On This Heart Of Mine'. This was followed by their anthemic tribute to a 74-year-old marbles champion, Dumas Walker, and then by a revival of Don Gibson's 'Oh Lonesome Me'. Their boisterous stage act included some magic from Ricky Lee Phelps. The Kentucky Headhunters, like Lynyrd Skynyrd before them, are a controversial band who bring heavy metal influences to country music, and vice versa: on *Electric Barnyard*, they thrash through 'The Ballad Of Davy Crockett'. The decision of the two Phelps brothers to quit the Headhunters in 1992 delayed the release of their third album, *Rave On*. Replaced by Anthony Kenney and Mark Orr the band concentrated on the heavier side of their sound. Doug Phelps rejoined in 1996 before the release of *Stompin' Grounds*.
● ALBUMS: *Pickin' On Nashville* (Mercury 1989)★★★, *Electric Barnyard* (Mercury 1991)★★★, *Rave On!* (Mercury 1993)★★, with Johnnie Johnson *That'll Work* (Elektra 1993)★★★, *Stompin' Grounds* (BNA 1997)★★★.
● COMPILATIONS: *Best Of The Kentucky Headhunters: Still Pickin'* (Mercury 1994)★★★★.

KERNAGHAN, LEE

b. 1965, Australia. The 90s country singer Lee Kernaghan is the son of country music performer Ray Kernaghan, best known for his album *Me And Louis On The Road*. Lee joined his father on the road from an early age and won a recording contract with RCA Records. He appeared with his father at the International Fan Fair show in Nashville in 1986, and spent time writing with Nashville songwriters. Returning to Australia, he was invited to record again by songwriter/producer Garth Porter. They wrote songs that celebrated their Australian roots and *The Outback Club* became a top-selling country album in Australia. The follow-up, *Three Chain Road*, is regarded as a high point of New Country, perhaps the Australian equivalent of Garth Brooks and selling 100,000 copies. It included a song about a man's love for his 4WD truck, 'She's My Ute', and a duet with Slim Dusty about a much-loved horse, 'Leave Him In The Longyard'. There is also a plea for Australia to become a republic, 'Southern Son'. His 1995 album included the sentimental '1959' and a ver-

sion of Porter Wagoner's 'This Cowboy's Hat', rewritten to reflect Australian life. Lee's sisters, Tania and Fiona, are also country performers, respectively releasing the albums *December Moon* and *Cypress Grove* in 1995.
● ALBUMS: *The Outback Club* (ABC 1992)★★★, *Three Chain Road* (ABC 1994)★★★★, *1959* (ABC 1995)★★★, *1959* reissue with bonus CD featuring new solo material and duets (ABC 1997)★★★.

KERR, ANITA

b. Anita Jean Grob, 31 October 1927, Memphis, Tennessee, USA. Kerr took piano lessons from the age of four and she was soon appearing on her mother's radio show in Memphis. By the age of 14, she was the staff pianist and was making vocal arrangements of church music for the station. In 1949, she formed the Anita Kerr Quartet (later Singers) with Gil Wright (tenor), Dorothy Ann 'Dottie' Dillard (alto) and Louis D. Nunley (baritone). They established themselves as session singers, particularly in Nashville. By the early 60s, they were featured on, it is estimated or alleged, a quarter of all the country records being made there, including records by Chet Atkins, Floyd Cramer, Jim Reeves and Hank Snow as well as pop records by Brook Benton, Perry Como, Connie Francis, Brenda Lee and Roy Orbison. Kerr also produced Skeeter Davis's 'The End Of The World'. In 1960, the quartet made the US Top 10 with 'Forever' under the name of the Little Dippers. In 1962, this time as the Anita And Th' So-And-So's, they had a minor US hit with 'Joey Baby'. From the mid-60s, the Anita Kerr Singers made several easy-listening albums and also accompanied Rod McKuen on his best-selling poetry albums as the San Sebastian Strings And Singers.
● ALBUMS: *Voices In Hi-Fi* (1958)★★★, *Georgia On My Mind* (1965)★★★, *We Dig Mancini* (1966)★★, *Slightly Baroque* (1967)★★★, *The Anita Kerr Singers Reflect On The Hits Of Burt Bacharach And Hal David* (Dot 1969)★★, *Velvet Voices And Bold Brass* (Dot 1969)★★★, *The Look Of Love* (1970)★★★, *The Simon And Garfunkel Songbook* (Bainbridge 1971)★★, *Grow To Know Me* (1972)★★★, *Anita Kerr's Christmas Story* (1972)★★, *Daytime, Nighttime* (1973)★★★, *Precious Memories* (1974)★★★, *Grow To Know Me* (1974)★★★, *Halleluah Brass* (1975)★★, *Gentle As Morning* (1975)★★★, *Halleluah Guitarists* (1976)★★★, *Walk A Little Slower* (1976)★★★, *Anita Kerr & The French Connection* (RCA 1977)★★.

KERSH, DAVID

b. 1970, Texas, USA. Kersh is another anonymous, good-looking country newcomer, but his debut album has been well received. The album is mostly up-tempo but the key track is the slow dance tune 'Goodnight Sweetheart', which made the US country Top 10 in 1996.
● ALBUMS: *Goodnight Sweetheart* (Curb 1996)★★★.

KERSHAW, DOUG

b. 24 January 1936, Tiel Ridge, Louisiana, USA. This renowned fiddle player and vocalist is a major figure in Cajun, or acadian circles, the traditional music of Louisiana's French-speaking minority. He was introduced to music by 'Daddy Jack' and 'Mama Rita', who subsequently appeared on many of the artist's compositions, and joined a family-based band, the Continental Playboys, on leaving high school. When Kershaw's songwriting talent resulted in a publishing and recording contract, he formed a duo with one of his brothers, and as Rusty And Doug quickly became popular throughout the southern USA. By 1956, they were a regular attraction on *The World's Original Jamboree*, a weekly showcase for local talent, and the following year enjoyed a residency on the famed *Grand Ole Opry*. Three of Kershaw's original compositions, 'Louisiana Man', 'Joli Blon' and 'Diddy Liggy Lo', not only became Cajun standards, but have been the subject of numerous cover versions by both pop and country acts. The brothers embarked on separate careers in 1964, but despite the approbation of their peers, Kershaw did not secure a larger audience until 1968, when he guested on *The Johnny Cash Show*. This appearance coincided with the release of *The Cajun Way*, the artist's debut for Warner Brothers Records, which affirmed his new-found popularity. Cameos on albums by Bob Dylan and John Stewart endeared Kershaw to the rock fraternity, while a series of stellar 70s recordings confirmed his talent as a flamboyant musician and gifted composer. He signed with Scotti Bros. in 1981, and achieved his highest chart position (number 29) with 'Hello Woman' the same year. After an enforced absence through substance abuse, he returned to the charts in 1988 with 'Cajun Baby', on which he duetted with Hank Williams Jr.

● ALBUMS: *The Cajun Way* (Warners 1969)★★★, *Spanish Moss* (Warners 1970)★★★, *Swamp Grass* (Warners 1971)★★★, *Doug Kershaw* (Warners 1972)★★★★, *Devil's Elbow* (Warners 1972)★★★, *Douglas James Kershaw* (Warners 1973)★★★, *Mama Kershaw's Boy* (Warners 1974)★★★, *Alive & Pickin'* (Warners 1975)★★★★, *Ragin' Cajun* (Warners 1976)★★★, *Flip, Flop & Fly* (Warners 1977)★★★, *Louisiana Man* (Warners 1978)★★★, *Hot Diggity Doug* (BMG 1989)★★★.

● COMPILATIONS: *The Best Of Doug Kershaw* (Warners 1989)★★★★. As Rusty And Doug *Louisiana Man And Other Favorites* (Warners 1971)★★★★, *Cajun Country Rockers* (Bear Family 1979)★★★★, *Cajun Country Rockers 2* (Bear Family 1981)★★★★, *Instant Hero* (Scotti Bros 1981)★★★, *Cajun Country Rockers 3* (Bear Family 1984)★★★, *More Cajun Country Rock* (Bear Family 1984)★★★, *Jay Miller Sessions Volume 22* (Flyright 1986)★★★, *Rusty, Doug, Wiley And Friends* (Flyright 1989)★★★, *The Best Of Doug And Rusty Kershaw* (Curb 1991)★★★.

KERSHAW, SAMMY

b 24 February 1958, Kaplan, Louisiana, USA. He is related to Doug Kershaw and hence there is a strong Cajun feel to his work. Among his other influences are Cal Smith and Mel Street. Sammy Kershaw started playing country clubs when he was 12 years old, working with local musician J.B. Perry. During his eight years with Perry, they opened for George Jones and Ray Charles (years later he would duet with Jones on 'Never Bit A Bullet Like This'). He joined a local band, Blackwater, but after a few years, decided to leave the industry and help design shops for the Wal-Mart Corporation. Some of his early tracks were released in the USA in 1993 on a MTE album, *Sammy Kershaw*, that was designed to look like his current product. He was encouraged back into music by a contract with Mercury Records in 1990. Kershaw had his first country hit with 'Cadillac Style' and ended up as spokesman for their 1992 sales campaign.

He courted controversy when he recorded 'National Working Women's Holiday' but he is well able to deal with hecklers, having once been a stand-up comic. He topped the US country charts with 'She Don't Know She's Beautiful' in 1993. He has been married three times and says, 'I'm a ballad-singing fool and I've lived all those songs at one time or another.' Following a greatest hits compilation, Kershaw released the disappointing *Politics, Religion And Her*, but bounced back with *Labor Of Love*.

● ALBUMS: *Don't Go Near The Water* (Mercury 1991)★★★, *Haunted Heart* (Mercury 1993)★★★, *Sammy Kershaw* (MTE 1993)★★, *Feelin' Good Train* (Mercury 1994)★★★, *Christmas Time's A Comin'* (Mercury 1994)★★, *Politics, Religion And Her* (Mercury 1996)★★, *Labor Of Love* (Mercury 1997)★★★.

● COMPILATIONS: *The Hits Chapter 1* (Mercury 1995)★★★.

● VIDEOS: *The Hit Video Collection* (1994).

KESSINGER BROTHERS

Clark Kessinger (b. 27 July 1896, South Hills, Kanawha County, West Virginia, USA, d. 4 June 1975) spent most of his life in the county either at St. Albans or South Charleston. He learned to play the banjo as a very young child and was playing the fiddle at the age of five. He made his professional debut when seven years old (earning more than his father's foundry wage), playing in the local saloons and later, as a teenager, also for country dances and on radio WOBU Charleston. He served in the US Army during World War I and on discharge started to play regularly with his nephew Luches (b. 1906, Kanawha County, West Virginia, USA, d. 1944; guitar). The record company believed that they would market better if classed as brothers and so they became known primarily as the Kessinger Brothers, but also recorded as the Wright Brothers, the Arnold Brothers and the Birmingham Entertainers. They made their first recordings for Brunswick-Vocalion in 1928 and by 1930, they were instrumental stars with some 29 single records released on Brunswick's *Songs From Dixie* series. Clark Kessinger recorded additional fiddle tunes for Vocalion releases with the material varying from old-time traditional fiddle tunes such as 'Sally Goodin' and 'Turkey In The Straw' to local tunes such as 'Kanawha March' and 'Going Up Bushy Fork'. He has been described by noted authority Ivan M. Tribe as 'an outstanding breakdown fiddler, but he was probably unexcelled in his ability to play slower and more difficult waltzes and marches with almost equal dexterity'. During the 30s, Clark met and discussed playing styles with world-famous classical violinist Fritz Kreisler, when he appeared in Charleston. The Kessingers played together around the Charleston area until 1944, when Luches died. After his nephew's death, Clark continued to play at local dances and worked as a painter during the day. In 1964, he won a state fiddling contest in Virginia, which led to new successes and publicity. He played various folk festivals including Newport, the Smithsonian Folklife Society, appeared at the *Grand Ole Opry* and on network television and recorded four albums. In July 1971, he suffered a stroke soon after he had recorded an album for Rounder. He died four years later in June 1975, on his way to hospital following a further stroke.

● ALBUMS: *The Legend Of Clark Kessinger (Sweet Bunch Of Daisies)* (1965)★★★, *Old Time Music With Fiddle And Guitar* (Rounder 1971)★★★, *The Kessinger Brothers (1928-1930 Recordings)* (1975)★★★, *The Legend Of Clark Kessinger*

(1975)★★★, *Memorial Album* (1976)★★★, *Live At Union Grove* (Smithsonian/Folkways 1977)★★★, *Old-Time Country Music* (70s)★★★, *Old-Time Country Music Volume 2* (70s)★★★.

KETCHUM, HAL

b. Hal Michael Ketchum, 9 April 1953, Greenwich, New York, USA. Ketchum credits his early influences as Buck Owens, Merle Haggard and Marty Robbins, but he was equally inspired by John Steinbeck's novels. His early musical career included playing drums for an R&B band and guitar in a blues band. He then began to establish himself as a singer and songwriter at the Kerrville Folk Festival. In 1987, he recorded his self-produced, first album as Hal Michael Ketchum, which was initially only released in cassette form. In 1989, it was reissued on CD by the German Sawdust label. In 1991, Ketchum joined Curb Records and, with his grey hair, he could hardly be marketed as a New Country act. *Past The Point Of Rescue*, however, produced US country chart singles: 'Small Town Saturday Night' was a US country number 1 and he followed it with 'Past The Point Of Rescue' and 'Somebody's Love'. His producer, Allen Reynolds, had written the Vogues' 1965 US hit 'Five O'Clock World', and Ketchum worked up a new version of the song. *Sure Love* was a confident second album, including tributes to his working-class roots in 'Mama Knows The Highway' and 'Daddy's Oldsmobile'. He made a cameo appearance in the movie *Maverick* singing 'Amazing Grace', and became a member of the *Grand Ole Opry* in 1994. Ketchum tours with his band, the Alibis, and is touted by many to develop into a major country star. He says, 'I have a two hundred song catalogue which is, by Nashville standards, not a lot.' Ketchum also paints and writes children's stories, should his two-hundred song catalogue prove insufficient. His most recent release, *Hal Yes*, was produced by Stephen Bruton (ex-Kris Kristofferson guitarist) and proved to be one of his finest albums.

● ALBUMS: *Threadbare Alibi* (Watermelon 1989)★★★, *Past The Point Of Rescue* (Curb 1991)★★★, *Sure Love* (Curb 1992)★★★, *Every Little Word* (Curb/Hit 1994)★★★, *Hal Yes* (Curb/Hit 1997)★★★★.
● COMPILATIONS: *Hal Ketchum The Hits* (Curb 1996)★★★★.
● FILMS: *Maverick*.

KILGORE, MERLE

b. Merle Wyatt Kilgore, 9 August 1934, Chickasha, Oklahoma, USA. Kilgore was raised in Louisiana when the family moved to Shreveport. He learned to play guitar as a boy and started working on the radio station KENT as a disc jockey at the age of 16. By the time he was 18, he was the leading guitarist on the *Louisiana Hayride* and had also appeared on the *Grand Ole Opry* in Nashville and the *Big D Jamboree* in Dallas. Between 1952 and 1954 he was also a regular on KFAZ-TV in Monroe, Louisiana. His songwriting ability soon became apparent. In 1954, his song 'More And More' became a hit for both Webb Pierce and Guy Lombardo and in 1959, 'Johnny Reb' was a country and pop hit for Johnny Horton. Throughout the 50s, Kilgore was very active as a disc jockey, club performer and regular member of the *Hayride*, and had his own first US country chart hits on the Starday label in 1960 with 'Dear Mama' and 'Love Has Made

You Beautiful' and although it never charted, his song '42 in Chicago' is something of a country standard. In 1962, he teamed with Claude King to write 'Wolverton Mountain'. King's subsequent recording sold a million copies and became a US country and pop hit. It later transpired that the trigger-happy old mountain man in the song, Clifton Clowers, was Kilgore's uncle. (Kilgore had originally offered the song to Johnny Horton, who believed it to be the worst song Kilgore had written, and when he offered it to George Jones, the latter told Kilgore that he hated mountain songs.) The following year, Kilgore teamed up with June Carter to write 'Ring Of Fire', which repeated the million-selling success when recorded by Carter's future husband, Johnny Cash. Kilgore recorded for several labels but his releases never proved great sellers. Through the 60s and 70s, he worked steadily, including film appearances in *Country Music On Broadway*, *Nevada Smith* (for which he wrote and recorded the title song) and *Five Card Stud*. He starred in shows in Las Vegas, played Carnegie Hall, New York, but gradually became more involved with music publishing, production and management. He was the opening act for Hank Williams Jnr. for 21 years and later became his manager and the vice-president of Hank Williams Jnr. Enterprises. Kilgore portrayed himself in the television movie *Living Proof: The Hank Williams Jnr. Story* in 1983.

● ALBUMS: *There's Gold In Them Thar Hills* (Starday 1963)★★★★, *Ring Of Fire* (1965)★★★, *Merle Kilgore, The Tall Texan* (Mercury/Wing 1966)★★, *Big Merle Kilgore* (Starday 1973)★★.
● COMPILATIONS: *Teenager's Holiday* (1991)★★★.

KILLEN, BUDDY

b. 13 November, Florence, Alabama, USA. Little appears to be known of Killen's early life or where he gained his first musical experience. However, after arriving in Nashville, he became a regular session musician playing stand-up bass, and also regularly appeared as a sideman on the *Grand Ole Opry*. In the early 50s, Jack Stapp, the President of Tree Publishing, employed Killen to work with the company. Killen proved to be a very talented independent record producer and was instrumental in helping many artists on the way to stardom, including Bill Anderson, Dottie West, Mel Tillis and Roger Miller. He also signed up a young singer-songwriter named Dolly Parton, when she first arrived in Nashville. Killen proved so successful in his work and promotion of the company that, in 1975, when Stapp moved on to become the chairman of the company's many enterprises, he promoted Killen to the position of co-owner and president. When Stapp died in 1980, Killen became sole owner and as such, one of the music industry's most powerful businessmen. Everyone has their failures, and Killen certainly had one in 1957 when, after listening to an unknown folk/country singer called Jimmie Driftwood sing two verses of a song called 'Battle Of New Orleans', he told him: 'Son, if that's the kind of stuff you've got, you'd better go home. We couldn't sell one record of that.' Two years later, after Driftwood's own recording had charted and Johnny Horton's had become a country and pop number 1, Driftwood met Killen again; on seeing Driftwood approach, Killen bent over and said, 'Kick me'. Over the years, Killen has held many executive posts in Nashville and the music industry, including President of the National Academy Of Recording

Arts And Sciences (NARAS). Although never noted as a recording artist, in 1969 he actually made the *Billboard* country charts singing a duet with Bonnie Guitar called 'A Truer Love You'll Never Find Than Mine'.

● FURTHER READING: *By The Seat Of My Pants: My Life In Country Music*, Buddy Killen with Tom Carter.

KINCAID, BRADLEY

b. 13 July 1895, near Lancaster, Garrard County, Kentucky, USA, d. 23 September 1989. Kincaid grew up strumming folk tunes, mountain ballads and vaudeville songs on an old 'hound dog' guitar, so-called because his father had swapped a hunting dog for it. He gained a college education in Chicago and lectured on folk music to learned societies. Kincaid described himself as a folk-singer rather than a hill-billy (a term he hated), and he became known as the Kentucky Mountain Boy. In 1926, he gained a regular spot on WLS Chicago and became the star of its *National Barn Dance*. Kincaid began recording in 1927 and his pseudonyms included Dan Hughey, John Carpenter and Harley Stratton. His best-known records are 'Barbara Allen', 'The Fatal Derby Day', 'The Legend Of The Robin's Red Breast' and 'The Letter Edged In Black'. Like A.P. Carter of the Carter Family, he collected songs, and the individual sales of his 12 folios, *My Favourite Mountain Ballads And Old Time Songs*, were as many as 100,000. Sears manufactured a replica of his 'hound dog' guitar. Kincaid toured extensively, and in 1936, he discovered Lewis Marshall Jones, whom he renamed Grandpa Jones. Between 1944 and 1947, Kincaid was a regular on the *Grand Ole Opry* and he then bought his own radio station, WWSO Springfield. He retired in 1953, although he still performed at folk festivals. In 1963, he recorded 162 songs in four days, but only six albums from that session were ever released. He died in September 1989 in Springfield, Ohio, USA.

● ALBUMS: *American Ballads* 10-inch album (Varsity 1955)★★★★, *Bradley Kincaid Sings American Ballads And Folk Songs* (Varsity 1957)★★★★, *Bradley Kincaid - Mountain Ballads And Old Time Songs* 6 volumes (mid-60s)★★★★, *Family Gospel Album* (1971)★★, *Bradley Kincaid - The Kentucky Mountain Boy* (1973)★★, *Mountain Ballads And Old Time Songs* (1976)★★★, *Favourite Old Time Songs* (1984)★★★, *Old Time Songs And Hymns* (1984)★★★, *Mountain Ballads And Old Time Songs, Volume 7* (1989)★★★.

● FURTHER READING: *Radio's Kentucky Mountain Boy - Bradley Kincaid*, Loyal Jones.

KING, CLAUDE

b. 5 February 1923, on a farm near Keithville, Shreveport, Louisiana, USA. His date of birth has, since 1961, frequently been cited incorrectly owing to promotional material released by his then manager, Tillman Franks, who at the time thought it tactful to lose a decade from his new client's age. King showed an early interest in music and was a proficient guitarist by the age of 12. He won a sports scholarship to the University of Idaho, intending to pursue an athletic career, but changed his mind and returned to Shreveport to work on the *Louisiana Hayride*. During the 50s, he played various local venues and took to writing songs. He first recorded for Gotham in 1952, but it was in 1961, after he signed for Columbia, that he achieved his first US country and pop chart hits with 'Big River, Big Man' and 'The

Comancheros'. In 1962, he teamed with Merle Kilgore to write 'Wolverton Mountain'. After the song was rejected by Johnny Horton and George Jones, King decided to record it himself and promptly found that he had a million-selling country and pop hit on his hands. During the 60s, King had an impressive list of 23 country chart hits. They included Top 10 successes with 'The Burning Of Atlanta', 'Tiger Woman' and his version of Johnny Horton's song 'All For The Love Of A Girl'. (In 1969, King recorded a tribute album to his great friend Horton.) In the early 70s, he found things more difficult, and his only Top 20 hit came with 'Mary's Vineyard'. The total of King's country chart hits stands at 30, the last being 'Cotton Dan' in 1977. During his career he made appearances in several films including *Swamp Girl*, and in 1982, he also acted in the television mini-series *The Blue And The Grey*.

● ALBUMS: *Meet Claude King* (Columbia 1962)★★★, *Tiger Woman* (Columbia 1965)★★★, *I Remember Johnny Horton* (Columbia 1969)★★, *Friend, Lover, Woman, Wife* (Columbia 1970)★★★, *Chip 'N' Dales Place* (Columbia 1971)★★★.

● COMPILATIONS: *The Best Of Claude King* (Harmony 1968)★★★, *Greatest Hits* (True 1977)★★★, *Claude King's Best* (Gusto 1980)★★★, *American Originals* (Columbia 1990)★★★, *Claude King More Than Climbing That Mountain, Wolverton Mountain That Is* 5-CD box set (Bear Family 1994)★★★★.

KING, PEE WEE

b. Julius Frank Anthony Kuczynski, 18 February 1914, Milwaukee, Wisconsin, USA. His parents, whose families had been Polish immigrants, relocated to Abrams when he was a child and he grew up in the Polish community there. His father, who played fiddle and concertina, ran a polka band and the boy was encouraged to play instruments from an early age. He first played concertina and then fiddle, but at the age of 14, he changed to accordion. He made appearances with his father's band but while still at high school and calling himself Frankie King, he formed a five-piece band that played on radio at Racine, Wisconsin. After graduating in 1932, he fronted a band he called the King's Jesters and played various radio stations and venues in Wisconsin, Michigan and Illinois. In 1934, he was given the chance to tour with Gene Autry as the accordionist with his group. In 1935, he moved to WHAS Louisville, where Autry headed a band called the Log Cabin Boys. Here he found three members of the band called Frank and, being a mere 5 feet 6 inches tall, he was given the nickname of Pee Wee, a name he later took legally. When Autry left for Hollywood in 1936, King took over the band and renamed it the Golden West Cowboys. In 1937, he moved to Nashville and became a member of the *Grand Ole Opry*, where he remained until 1947. His band included, at different times, such noted country music performers as Ernest Tubb, Eddy Arnold, Cowboy Copas, Redd Stewart and Clell Summey. In 1941, he and his band, with other Opry acts including Minnie Pearl, toured extensively with *The Grand Ole Opry Camel Caravan*. In 1938, he made his film debut with Autry in *Goldmine In The Sky* and later appeared in other B-movie westerns, not only with Autry, but other cowboy stars including Johnny Mack Brown and Charles Starrett. In 1947-57, he had his own radio and television series on WAVE, Louisville. He recorded for RCA-Victor and in 1948, he achieved his first US country and pop chart hit with 'Tennessee Waltz'. Inspired by Bill Monroe's 'Kentucky Waltz', King and Redd Stewart merely added lyrics to Monroe's theme song, the 'No Name Waltz'. King quickly followed with his other 'state' song hits, 'Tennessee Tears' and 'Tennessee Polka', as well as his co-written 'Bonaparte's Retreat'. In 1951, he had a US country and pop number 1 with his song 'Slowpoke', which topped the country charts for 15 weeks and went on to sell a million (it was also a Top 10 hit for Hawkshaw Hawkins). When released in Britain, it was for some reason called 'Slow Coach'. Other King songs to become Top 10 country hits for him were 'Silver And Gold', 'Busybody', 'Changing Partners' (a UK hit for both Kay Starr and Bing Crosby) and 'Bimbo' (later recorded successfully by Jim Reeves). In all cases, the vocals were performed by Redd Stewart. In the late 50s and early 60s, King had four television shows in different venues but in 1962, work pressure forced him to abandon them. Between 1952 and 1956, he won every available award for western bands. Noted country authority Colin Escott once wrote that Bill Haley and rock 'n' roll owed a great debt to Pee Wee King, as far as instrumentation was concerned. By 1959, King found that this very genre badly affected his music and he broke up his band. For the next four years, he worked with Redd Stewart in Minnie Pearl's Roadshow. In 1963, she gave up touring but King continued to run the show until, in 1968, he once again disbanded the group. He later relied on local musicians to back him on his appearances. In 1969, he retired from performing to concentrate on the business side of the music industry and through the 70s spent much time on promotional work. He was one of the first members elected to the Nashville Songwriters' International Hall Of Fame when it was founded in 1970 and his many varied services to the country music industry also earned him the honour of election to the Country Music Hall Of Fame in 1974. He later became a director of the Country Music Foundation in Nashville. In 1986, he appeared on the *Opry*'s 60th Anniversary Show. He has suffered two strokes in the 90s.

● ALBUMS: *Pee Wee King* 10-inch album (RCA Victor 1954)★★★, *Pee Wee King* 10-inch album (RCA Victor 1955)★★★, *Waltzes* 10-inch album (RCA Victor 1955)★★★, *Swing West* 10-inch album (RCA Victor 1955)★★★★, *Swing West* (RCA Victor 1956)★★★, with the New Golden West Cowboys *Back Again (With The Songs That Made Them Famous)* (Starday 1964)★★, *Country Barn Dance* (Camden 1965)★★★, *The Legendary (Live Transcriptions)* (Longhorn 1967)★★, *Golden Olde Tyme Dances* (Briar 1975)★★★, *Ballroom King* (Detour 1982)★★★, *Hog Wild Too!* (Zu Zazz 1990).

● COMPILATIONS: *Biggest Hits* (Capitol 1966)★★★, *Best Of Pee Wee King And Redd Stewart* (Starday 1975)★★★, *Rompin', Stompin', Singin', Swingin'* (Bear Family 1983)★★★, *Pee Wee King And His Golden West Cowboys* 6-CD box set (Bear Family 1995)★★★★.

● FURTHER READING: *Hell-Bent For Music: The Life Of Pee Wee King*, Wade Hall.

KIRBY, PETE

b. Beecher Kirby, c.1915, near Gatlinburg, Sevier County, Tennessee, USA. The Kirbys were a musical family with all 10 siblings playing some instrument, though not professionally. Kirby learned guitar and banjo but worked in mills and

on a farm before finding work as a guitarist in an Illinois club. After hearing a dobro, he also mastered that instrument. In 1939, he became a member of Roy Acuff's Smoky Mountain Boys, starting an association that lasted to Acuff's death in 1992. Kirby's dobro became a distinctive feature of the Acuff sound and he has become known as one of the instrument's finest exponents. He was also a fine harmony vocalist. He figured in the comedy routines that were part of Acuff's show and, wearing his bib and brace overalls and playing a banjo for his solo spots, he became known as Bashful Brother Oswald and a great favourite of the *Grand Ole Opry* audiences. He played on many of Acuff's recordings but recorded in his own right for Starday in 1962 and for Rounder in the 70s, including two fine albums with fellow Acuff band member Charlie Collins. He was also one of the stars chosen to play on the Nitty Gritty Dirt Band's famous *Will The Circle Be Unbroken* project in 1972.

● ALBUMS: *Bashful Brother Oswald* (Starday 1962)★★, *Brother Oswald* (Rounder 1972)★★★, *Banjo & Dobro* (Rounder 1974)★★★, with Charlie Collins *That's Country* (Rounder 1975)★★★, with Collins *Os & Charlie* (Rounder 1976)★★★, *Don't Say Aloha* (1978)★★★.

KIRK, EDDIE

b. Edward Merle Kirk, 21 March 1919, on a ranch near Greeley, Colorado. The ranch hands taught him cowboy songs and he was singing and tap-dancing with a small band at the age of nine. In 1934, he relocated to California where, for a time, he worked with the Beverly Hill Billies. He was National Yodelling Champion in 1935 and 1936 and between 1933 and 1937, he earned a reputation as an amateur boxer. He worked in films and made personal appearances until 1943, when he joined the navy. He returned to California in 1945, appearing in films, and directed the Hollywood Barn Dance choir. In the late 40s, he appeared on Gene Autry's radio show and also on the *Town Hall Party* in Compton. He made his recording debut for Capitol in 1947 and in 1948/9, he registered Top 10 country hits with 'The Gods Were Angry With Me' (which included a recitation by Tex Ritter) and 'Candy Kisses'. He later developed a fondness for flying.

KIRKPATRICK, ANNE

b. 4 July 1952, Sydney, Australia. Slim Dusty, that is David Kirkpatrick, is Australia's best-loved country performer and his wife, Joy McKean, is the 'Queen of Aussie Cowgirls'. Their daughter, Anne Kirkpatrick, allegedly gave her first performance at the age of two when she strayed onto the stage in her nightdress while her father was singing and subsequently stole the show. She also presented her father with a gold disc for 'A Pub With No Beer'. By the time she was 12, she was working regularly with the Slim Dusty Show and doing her studying by correspondence courses. She sang and played bass on many of his recordings and her first solo album was released while she was at university. After graduating, she formed the Anne Kirkpatrick Band and built up a reputation in Sydney. The first phase of her career is neatly summarized in the aptly titled *Annie's Songs*, and she can also be heard to good advantage on the live double album *Slim Dusty - The Entertainer*. After taking time off to raise a family, she remodelled herself as a contemporary country music performer. She often records US country hits ('Sight For Sore Eyes', 'A Bottle Of Wine And Patsy Cline') but is also a fine songwriter in her own right and has won several awards in Australia.

● ALBUMS: *Shoot The Moon* (EMI 1979)★★, *Merry Go Round Of Love* (Nulla 1986)★★★★, *Come Back Again* (1988)★★★, with Slim Dusty *Two Singers, One Song* (EMI 1990)★★★, *Out Of The Blue* (ABC 1992)★★★, *The Game Of Love* (ABC 1994)★★★, *Live - 21st Anniversary Concert* (ABC 1995)★★. All the record labels are Australian.

KIRWAN, DOMINIC

b. Omagh, County Tyrone, Northern Ireland. Kirwan's mother was a talented pianist who played in local theatres, but his first connections with the stage came when, at the age of five, he joined a school to learn Irish dancing. He toured as a dancer appearing at festivals in the UK and at the age of 12, as the Ulster minor champion, he appeared at a major Norwegian festival. He began singing semi-professionally in the late 70s and worked with several different groups while supporting himself through his daytime occupation as a car salesman. He formed his own band in 1988 and after winning two major talent competitions, he recorded his debut album. These recordings proved popular enough to attract the attention of Ritz Records and he subsequently signed to that label. His career received a boost in 1990, when he toured the UK with Charley Pride. This led to further appearances as a guest on a UK tour by Tammy Wynette. His music ranges from modern easy listening to country standards, as well as Irish ballads such as 'My Wild Irish Rose'. In 1993, a duet, 'I'll Walk Beside You', with fellow Ritz artist Tracey Elsdon, proved very popular. In his stage act, Kirwan incorporates a routine that shows that he can still compete with the best when it comes to Irish dancing.

● ALBUMS: *The Green Fields Of Ireland* (Music Box 1988)★★, *Try A Little Kindness* (Ritz 1989)★★★ *Love Without End* (Ritz 1990)★★★★ *Evergreen* (Ritz 1991)★★★★, *Today* (Ritz 1993), *Irish Favourites* (Ritz 1994)★★★★, *On The Way To A Dream* (Ritz 1995)★★★.

● VIDEOS: *Live In Concert* (Ritz 1990), *Christmas Party* (1994).

KNOX, BUDDY

b. Buddy Wayne Knox, 14 April 1933, Happy, Texas, USA. Knox was one of the first 'pop-abilly' hitmakers in the 50s. With bassist Jimmy Bowen, he formed the country band the Rhythm Orchids in 1956, adding Don Lanier (guitar) and Dave Alldred (drums). The following year Knox sang lead vocals on 'Party Doll', recorded at Norman Petty's Oklahoma studio. First issued locally on the Triple-D label, it became the first release on Roulette, formed by New York nightclub owner Maurice Levy. 'Party Doll' went to number 1 in the USA. At the same session Bowen recorded another hit, 'I'm Stickin' With You'. With his light voice skimming over the insistent rhythms, Knox was the first in a line of Texan rockers that included Buddy Holly and Roy Orbison. Both 'Rock Your Little Baby To Sleep' and the gimmicky 'Hula Love' were Top 20 hits later in 1957, when he also appeared in the film *Disc Jockey Jamboree*. Although he toured frequently with Alan Freed's package shows, 'Somebody Touched Me' (1958) was his only later hit and in 1960, Knox and Bowen moved to Los Angeles. There, Knox turned to 'teenbeat' material such as 'Lovey Dovey', 'Ling Ting Tong' and 'She's Gone' (a minor UK hit in 1962) with producer

Snuff Garrett. During the mid-60s he returned to country music, recording in Nashville for Reprise and had a hit with 'Gypsy Man', composed by ex-Crickets' Sonny Curtis. This led to film appearances in *Travellin' Light* (with Waylon Jennings) and *Sweet Country Music* (with Boots Randolph and Johnny Paycheck). Knox was now based in Canada, where he set up his own Sunnyhill label. He also visited Europe with rockabilly revival shows during the 70s and early 80s. Jimmy Bowen became one of Nashville's most powerful A&R men, working for Dot, MCA and latterly Capitol.

● ALBUMS: *Buddy Knox* (Roulette 1958)★★★, with Jim Bowen *Buddy Knox And Jimmy Bowen* (Roulette 1959)★★★, *Buddy Knox In Nashville* (1967)★★★, *Gypsy Man* (United Artists 1969)★★★, *Four Rock Legends* (1978)★★, *Sweet Country Music* (Rockstar 1981)★★, *Texas Rockabilly Man* (Rockstar 1987)★★, *Travellin' Light* (Rundell 1988)★★.

● COMPILATIONS: *Buddy Knox's Golden Hits* (Liberty 1962)★★★, *Rock Reflections* (Sunset 1971)★★★, *Party Doll* (Pye 1978)★★★, *Greatest Hits* (Rockhouse 1985)★★★, *Liberty Takes* (Charly 1986)★★★, *Party Doll And Other Hits* (Capitol 1988)★★★, *The Best Of Buddy Knox* (Rhino 1990)★★★★, with Jim Bowen *The Complete Roulette Recordings* (Sequel 1996)★★★★.

● FILMS: *Jamboree* aka *Disc Jockey Jamboree* (1957).

KOLLER, FRED

b. Chicago, Illinois, USA. Fred Koller has been a professional songwriter since he was 23. He hitchhiked to Nashville and his first songs were recorded by the Sons Of The Pioneers, Tex Williams and Rosemary Clooney. He befriended Shel Silverstein and they wrote many songs together, notably 'Jennifer Johnson And Me' (Mac Davis), ' This Guitar Is For Sale' (Bobby Bare) and 'Rock Star's Lament' (Bobby Bare). He co-wrote the country standard 'Lonestar State Of Mind' (Nanci Griffith) with Pat Alger and Gene Levine. Another song first recorded by Nanci Griffith, 'Goin' Gone', written by Koller, Alger and Bill Dale, was a US country number 1 for Kathy Mattea. Mattea has also recorded 'Life As We Knew It' and 'She Came From Fort Worth'. The Jeff Healey Band had a pop hit with another of Koller's songs, 'Angel Eyes', and other songs include 'Boom Town' (Lacy J. Dalton), 'The TV Tells Me So' (Smothers Brothers), 'Lord, I Want My Rib Back' (Gene Watson) and 'Circumstantial Evidence' (Jerry Lee Lewis). Koller makes his own eccentric records in a corncrake voice, as though Dave Van Ronk were recording novelty songs. The best-known of his novelty songs are 'Let's Talk Dirty In Hawaiian', which he wrote with John Prine, and 'Juanita', which was recorded by David Allan Coe and Burl Ives. Koller has done much to encourage other songwriters by writing magazine columns and the book *How To Pitch And Promote Your Songs*.

● ALBUMS: *Songs From The Night Before* (Alcazar 1988)★★★, *Night Of The Living Fred* (Alcazar 1989)★★★ *Where The Fast Lane Ends* (Alcazar 1990)★★★.

● FURTHER READING: *How To Pitch And Promote Your Songs*, Fred Koller.

KRAUSS, ALISON

b. 23 July 1971, Decatur, Illinois, USA. Krauss is unique in the 90s crop of female country singers in that she leans strongly towards more traditional forms of country music, especially bluegrass. She began learning classical music on violin at the age of five and won her first fiddle contest at the age of eight when she took the honours in the Western Longbow competition. In 1983 at the age of 12, she met singer-songwriter John Pennell, who introduced her to old bluegrass cassettes. By the end of the same year she had been awarded the Most Promising Fiddle Player (Mid West) accolade by the Society For The Preservation of Bluegrass Music. Pennell encouraged her to join his group Silver Rail when she was 14 years old. After two years with them she spent a year playing in Indiana group Classified Grass, with whom she recorded the demo tape that successfully attracted the attention of Rounder Records' head, Ken Irwin. Krauss then returned to Pennell's group, who had changed their name to Union Station, replacing their fiddler Andrea Zonn. In 1987 she recorded *Too Late To Cry* with them; it included the fiddle classic 'Dusty Miller', alongside six originals by Pennell. The album also included noted acoustic musicians such as Sam Bush and Jerry Douglas. Union Station again joined her for the Grammy-nominated follow-up album, which included a duet of 'Wild Bill Jones' with her lead guitarist, Jeff White. Inspired by Ricky Skaggs, who had brought bluegrass back into contemporary country music's mainstream, she worked hard to achieve similar acclaim. Though *I've Got That Old Feeling* was subsequently awarded a Grammy as best bluegrass recording of 1990, she insisted on maintaining her links with Union Station and remained with the independent Rounder label despite offers from several major labels. Her popularity was furthered in 1993 as opening act on a major Garth Brooks tour. Her video for 'Steel Rails' topped the CMT video chart and she made a successful debut in London in 1994. She has recorded albums of gospel songs with the Cox Family from Louisiana and her harmony vocals and fiddle playing can be heard to good advantage on Dolly Parton's *Eagle When She Flies* and *Heartsongs* and Michelle Shocked's *Arkansas Traveller*. She contributed 'When You Say Nothing At All' with Union Station to the tribute album to Keith Whitley and also performed 'Teach Your Children' with Crosby, Stills And Nash on *Red Hot + Country*. She subsequently became the youngest member of the *Grand Old Opry*. On inducting her, Bill Monroe opined, 'Alison Krauss is a fine singer and she really knows how to play bluegrass music like it should be played.' In 1995 she received five nominations at the annual Country Music Association awards, though one had to be withdrawn when the organizers realized that the platinum-selling compilation *Now That I've Found You* did not meet the criteria for Album Of The Year, which requires 60% new material. She did, however, win all other sections for which she was nominated, including Female Vocalist, Horizon Award, Single Of The Year (for 'When You Say Nothing At All') and Vocal Event (her collaboration with Shenandoah). *So Long So Wrong*, her first new album with Union Station in five years, proved to be an outstanding collection of songs that justified all the accolades.

● ALBUMS: with Union Station *Too Late To Cry* (Rounder 1987)★★★, with Union Station *Two Highways* (Rounder 1989)★★★, with Union Station *I've Got That Old Feeling* (Rounder 1990)★★★, with Union Station *Every Time You Say Goodbye* (Rounder 1992)★★★★, with the Cox Family *Everybody's Reaching Out For Someone* (Rounder 1993)★★★, with the Cox Family *I Know Who Holds Tomorrow* (Rounder 1994)★★★, with the Cox Family *Beyond The City* (Rounder 1995)★★★, with Union Station *So Long So Wrong* (Rounder 1997)★★★★.

● COMPILATIONS: *Now That I've Found You: A Collection* (Rounder 1995)★★★★.

KRISTOFFERSON, KRIS

b. 22 June 1936, Brownsville, Texas, USA. Kristofferson, a key figure in the 'New Nashville' of the 70s, began his singing career in Europe. While studying at Oxford University in 1958 he briefly performed for impresario Larry Parnes as Kris Carson, while for five years he sang and played at US Army bases in Germany. As Captain Kristofferson, he left the army in 1965 to concentrate on songwriting. After piloting helicopters part-time he worked as a cleaner at the CBS studios in Nashville, until Jerry Lee Lewis became the first to record one of his songs, 'Once More With Feeling'. Johnny Cash soon became a champion of Kristofferson's work and it was he who persuaded Roger Miller to record 'Me And Bobby McGee' (co-written with Fred Foster) in 1969. With its atmospheric opening ('Busted flat in Baton Rouge, waiting for a train/feeling nearly faded as my jeans'), the bluesy song was a country hit and became a rock standard in the melodramatic style of Janis Joplin and the Grateful Dead. Another classic among Kristofferson's early songs was 'Sunday Morning Coming Down', which Cash recorded. In 1970, Kristofferson appeared at the Isle of Wight pop festival while Sammi Smith was charting with the second of his major compositions, the passionate 'Help Me Make It Through The Night', which later crossed over to the pop and R&B audiences in Gladys Knight's version. Knight was also among the numerous artists who covered the tender 'For The Good Times', a huge country hit for Ray Price, while 'One Day At A Time' was a UK number 1 for Lena Martell in 1979. Kristofferson's own hits began with 'Loving Her Was Easier (Than Anything I'll Ever Do Again)' and 'Why Me', a ballad that was frequently performed in concert by Elvis Presley. In 1973, Kristofferson married singer Rita Coolidge and recorded three albums with her before their divorce six years later. Kristofferson had made his film debut in *Cisco Pike* (1971) and also appeared with Bob Dylan in *Pat Garrett And Billy The Kid*, but he achieved movie stardom when he acted opposite Barbra Streisand in a 1976 remake of the 1937 picture *A Star Is Born*. For the next few years he concentrated on his film career (until the 1979 disaster *Heaven's Gate*, the same year he split from Coolidge), but returned to country music with *The Winning Hand*, which featured duets with Brenda Lee, Dolly Parton and Willie Nelson. A further collaboration, *Highwaymen* (with Nelson, Cash and Waylon Jennings), headed the country chart in 1985. The four musicians subsequently toured as the Highwaymen and issued two further collaborative albums. A campaigner for radical causes, Kristofferson starred in the post-nuclear television drama *Amerika* (1987) and came up with hard-hitting political commentaries on *Third World Warrior*. Kristofferson compered and performed at the Bob Dylan Tribute Concert in 1992, during which he gave Sinead O'Conner a sympathetic shoulder to cry on after she was booed off stage. His recording career took an upturn with the release of *A Moment Of Forever* in 1995.

● ALBUMS: *Kristofferson* (Monument 1970)★★, *The Silver-*

Tongued Devil And I (Monument 1971)★★★, *Me And Bobby McGee* (Monument 1971)★★★, *Border Lord* (Monument 1972)★★★, *Jesus Was A Capricorn* (Monument 1972)★★★, with Rita Coolidge *Full Moon* (A&M 1973)★★★, *Spooky Lady's Sideshow* (Monument 1974)★★, with Coolidge *Breakaway* (A&M 1974)★, *Who's To Bless ... And Who's To Blame* (Monument 1975)★★, *Surreal Thing* (Monument 1976)★★, five tracks on *A Star Is Born* film soundtrack (Monument 1976)★★★, *Easter Island* (Monument 1977)★★, with Coolidge *Natural Act* (A&M 1979)★★, *Shake Hands With The Devil* (Monument 1979)★★★, *To The Bone* (Monument 1981)★★, with Dolly Parton, Brenda Lee, Willie Nelson *The Winning Hand* (Monument 1983)★★★, with Willie Nelson *Music From Songwriter* film soundtrack (Columbia 1984)★★★, with Nelson, Johnny Cash, Waylon Jennings *Highwayman* (Columbia 1985)★★★★, *Repossessed* (Mercury 1986)★★, *Third World Warrior* (Mercury 1990)★★, with Nelson, Cash, Jennings *Highwayman 2* (Columbia 1990)★★★, *Live At The Philharmonic* (Monument 1992)★★★, with Nelson, Cash, Jennings *The Road Goes On Forever* (Liberty 1995)★★, *A Moment Of Forever* (Justice 1995)★★.
● COMPILATIONS: *The Songs Of Kristofferson* (Monument 1977)★★★, *Country Store* (Starblend 1988)★★★, *The Legendary Years* (Connoisseur Collection 1990)★★★, *Singer/Songwriter* (Monument 1991)★★★, *The Best Of Kristofferson* (Sony 1995)★★★★.
● FURTHER READING: *Kris Kristofferson*, Beth Kalet.
● FILMS: *The Last Movie* (1970), *Cisco Pike* (1972), *Blume In Love* (1973), *Pat Garrett And Billy The Kid* (1973), *Bring Me The Head Of Alfredo Garcia* (1974), *Alice Doesn't Live Here Any More* (1975), *The Sailor Who Fell From Grace With The Sea* (1976), *A Star Is Born* (1976), *Vigilante Force* (1976), *Semi-Tough* (1978), *Convoy* (1978), *Heaven's Gate* (1980), *Rollover* (1981), *Flashpoint* (1984), *Songwriter* (1984), *Trouble In Mind* (1985), *Blood And Orchids* television movie (1986).

KRUGER, JEFFREY

b. England. Kruger has enjoyed a long and distinguished career in the music and entertainment industry. Under his management, the Kruger Organisation (TKO) grew from its ownership of the Flamingo Club, one of the most prominent early 50s London jazz clubs, to an international entertainment corporation with interests in film, video, music publishing, recording and concerts, spanning musical genres from classical to country, blues, pop and jazz. In that time Kruger has amassed an impressive list of musical firsts. He established Ember Records, the UK's first independent label, produced Tony Crombie And The Rockets, the first British rock 'n' roll group to make the UK charts, and co-produced *Rock You Sinners*, the first English rock 'n' roll film. His involvement in the music industry began in the 50s. During this time he was employed selling *Batman* and *Superman* serials for Columbia Pictures, while playing piano by night for various pick-up bands. Finally he formed his own band, Sonny Kruger And The Music Makers. His business career began when he sensed that London's thriving jazz scene required a more 'upmarket' venue. Hence, he established the Flamingo club, where artists such as Billie Holiday and Sarah Vaughan made their British debuts. Kruger then formed his own talent and management agencies in the late 50s. The new decade saw him introduce Glen Campbell to

the UK market for the first time, and he also organized his first tour in the territory. The Flamingo club, meanwhile, continued to prove its popularity with all manner of musicians, offering period entertainment that included such stellar acts as Jimi Hendrix, Black Sabbath, Yes, the Moody Blues and Genesis. As well as opening the door to European tours by Marvin Gaye, Kruger also invited Gladys Knight And The Pips to perform before they had made their name in the USA. This paved the way for tours by Barry White, the Jacksons, Temptations, Supremes, Isaac Hayes and black country star Charlie Pride. His involvement with country music increased throughout the 70s and 80s. This period saw him working with Johnny Cash, Nanci Griffiths, Kris Kristofferson and Tammy Wynette, as well as the promotion of festivals including the Country Music Festival in Peterborough. TKO went public in the USA in 1986, the expansion including the purchase of music publishing companies (Full Armor Music and Whole Armor Music, two Nashville Christian concerns), adding film and video properties to its film library and launching a marketing campaign to raise the company profile and awareness of its product. TKO has also continued to promote tours, including dance and theatre productions (Bolshoi and Kirov ballets, Rudolph Nureyev, Placido Domingo, Harlem Globe Trotters) plus a backbone of musical works (Chuck Berry, Julio Iglesias). Among many other awards, Kruger has subsequently been made an Honorary Citizen of the State of Tennessee by the Governor for services to country music, and received a similar honour from the governor of Kansas. He is a member of the Academy Of Motion Pictures and Arts and Sciences, and the Performing Rights Society.

L

LA BEEF, SLEEPY

b. Thomas Paulsley La Beff, 11 July 1935, Smackover, Arkansas, USA. This singing guitarist cut a popular if portly figure during a reawakening of enthusiasm for rockabilly in the late 70s. The youngest of 10 children in a watermelon farming family, his drooping eyelids earned him a nickname that became a lifelong *nom de theatre*. His musical career began in gospel groups, performing at weekends while he worked as a surveyor in Houston, Texas and then Nashville, Tennessee. In 1956, he was engaged by Starday Records to release budget-priced copies of current hits before a transfer to Columbia three years later. Though he was allowed to develop his own *basso profundo* hybrid of blues and C&W, the company dropped the hitless La Beef, whose discs were then issued on several smaller labels - notably Sun Records, for whom he would be the sole remaining signing when it was bought out in 1969. The previous year, he had made his US country chart debut with 'Every Day'. Further hits preceded a number of interesting projects during the 70s and 80s, such as a proliferation of record releases during the rockabilly craze, a co-related part in Peter Guralnick's *Lost Highway* movie, a 1980 album on which he was backed by the cream of Nashville session players (including D.J. Fontana), a live album (*Nothin' But The Truth*) from Harper's Ferry (a club local to his home in Alston, Massachusetts), and a remarkable 1987 appearance in Hank Wangford's British television series, *The A-Z Of Country Music*. His two most recent albums are astonishingly energetic for a man over 60 years old.

● ALBUMS: *Black Land Farmer* (Plantation 1971)★★★, *The Bulls Night Out* (Sun 1974)★★★, *Western Gold* (Sun 1976)★★★, *Rockabilly '77* (Sun 1977)★★★, *Downhome Rockabilly* (Sun 1979)★★★, *Electricity* (1979)★★★, *It Ain't What You Eat It's The Way That You Chew It* (Rounder 1980)★★★, *Ain't Got No Home* (Rounder 1983)★★★, *Nothin' But The Truth* (Rounder 1985)★★★, *Strange Things Happening* (Rounder 1994)★★★, *I'll Never Lay My Guitar Down* (Rounder 1996)★★★.

● COMPILATIONS: *Early Rare And Rockin' Sides* (Baron 1979)★★★, *Larger Than Life* 6-CD box set (Bear Family 1997)★★★.

LA COSTA

b. LaCosta Tucker, 6 April 1951, Seminole, Texas, USA. The elder sister of Tanya Tucker. During the 60s, she worked briefly with her sister in a group called the Country Westerners in Phoenix, but became disenchanted with a musical career and left to work in a hospital in Toltrec, Arizona. After sister Tanya's chart hit with 'Delta Dawn' in 1972, she returned to music and between 1974 and 1978, recording as La Costa for Capitol, she registered 12 country chart hits. These included Top 20 successes with 'Get On My Love Train', 'He Took Me For A Ride', 'This House Runs On Sunshine' and 'Western Man'. Since then, in spite of a change of label to Elektra, only two further hits (both minor) have followed; the last, 'Love Take It Easy On Me', released under her full name of LaCosta Tucker, was in 1982.

● ALBUMS: *Get On My Love Train* (Capitol 1974)★★★, *With All My Love* (Capitol 1975)★★, *Lovin' Somebody* (Capitol 1976)★★★, *Changing All The Time* (Elektra 1980)★★.

LACE, BOBBI

Model, actress and singer from Florida, USA. She had a minor role in the 1984 film *Scarface*, and then, as Bobbi Lace, she had several minor US country hits including 'It's Gonna Be Love' with Mark Gray and a revival of Dusty Springfield's 'Son Of A Preacher Man'. She has now dropped the name and performs as Lori Smith.

LAIR, JOHN

b. 1 July 1894, on a farm near Livingston, Kentucky, USA, d. 13 November 1985, Lexington, Kentucky, USA. Lair developed a childhood interest to become a respected authority on and a collector of old-time music. After military service in World War I, he ran the family farm until, concerned by the threatened over-development of Renfro Valley, he moved to Battle Creek, Michigan. Here, he worked as a teacher and an insurance agent, before becoming a programme director at WLS Chicago in 1927. He immediately began to organize the station's *National Barn Dance* programme and formed a band of musicians and singers that he called the Cumberland Ridge Runners. He occasionally played harmonica and jug, but, being no great musician himself, he usually confined himself to narrations, writing material and announcing duties. In 1937, Lair left WLS for WLW Cincinnati, where he helped create the *Boone County Jamboree* and soon afterwards the *Renfro Valley Barn Dance*, which, through his business acumen and some help from others, including Red Foley and Slim Miller, Lair moved to his own home in Renfro Valley, Kentucky, in 1939. The programme, which took place in a barn, was soon carried by WHAS Louisville, whose transmissions in turn were carried by other stations, even, eventually, by the NBC Network. The programme helped to launch the careers of many artists including the Coon Creek Girls and on its 25th anniversary in 1962, the State Governor proudly declared Lair's show 'a Kentucky institution'. The Barn Dance was only one of the many folk music activities that Lair organized and his beloved Valley eventually became a noted tourist attraction with its festivals, museum and shops.

LALOR, TRUDI

b. 23 March 1972, Portlaoise, County Laoise, Eire. She grew up with an interest in music and in her teens sang with local musical societies. Successful appearances at local concerts led to her joining Hazel records where her first release, a four-track EP, *Money Talks*, gained her considerable air play. Lalor's break came in September 1993, when the very popular Louise Morrissey was incapacitated by a serious car crash. During Morrissey's absence, the talented Lalor fronted her band, fulfilled all her Irish and UK commitments and quickly established herself as one of the best young singers on the British and Irish country scene. She has since

fronted her own Country Band and has created a considerable impression at concerts all over Ireland and the UK. At one concert, she even greatly impressed Garth Brooks, who unexpectedly arrived at the show during his visit to Ireland. Her debut album, produced by Ray Lynam, clearly demonstrates her ability to handle new country material such as Jamie O'Hara's 'For Reasons I've Forgotten' and Eurovision composer Teresa O'Donnell's 'If This World Could Love', as well as old-time favourites, all interspersed with the expected country and Irish, especially her stunning rendition of 'Lovely Laoise'.
● ALBUMS: *Next Time 'Round* (Hazel 1995)★★★.

LAMBCHOP

Led by singer and guitarist Kurt Wagner, Lambchop are a large, Nashville, Tennessee-based ensemble whose instrumentation is highly unique within the popular music tradition. Wagner's world-weary vocals (which in an earlier age would have delineated him as a 'crooner') are backed by an eight-piece orchestra featuring clarinet, lap steel guitar, saxophone, trombone, organ, cello and 'open-end wrenches'. While the group appear immaculately dressed in suits for their live appearances, Wagner's urbane, often seedy narratives offer a highly contrary proposition, describing such delights as suicide and romantic allure on their highly praised alternative country debut, *I Hope You're Sitting Down*. For the follow-up collection, 1996's *How I Quit Smoking*, Lambchop employed the services of arranger John Mock, previously best known for his work with Kathy Mattea, to embellish the lush orchestral backdrop. This was aided by the presence of a string quartet. The results were excellent, allowing Wagner to indulge himself in the sort of grandiose country melodramas not heard since the heyday of Jim Reeves.
● ALBUMS: *I Hope You're Sitting Down* (Merge 1994)★★★, *How I Quit Smoking* (Merge 1996)★★★, *Hank* (City Slang 1996)★★★.

LANDSBOROUGH, CHARLIE

b. Charles Alexander Landsborough, 26 October 1941, Wrexham, Clywd, Wales. Landsborough's family come from Birkenhead and he has spent his life on Merseyside. After several jobs, he trained as a teacher, but music has been the mainstay of his life. He was part of a local beat group, the Top Spots, but developed his own style by writing gentle, melodic, romantic ballads, albeit influenced by the American singer-songwriter Mickey Newbury. Because of his teaching commitments and transport problems with 'unreliable cars', he is little known outside Merseyside. His main strength is as a songwriter. Foster And Allen entered the UK charts with the astute reflections of 'I Will Love You All My Life', and Roly Daniels put 'Part Of Me' into the Irish charts. The repertoire of many Irish country artists includes 'The Green Hills Are Rolling Still', while 'Heaven Knows', which suggests that people should be colour-coded according to their deeds, has been recorded by George Hamilton IV. Landsborough does not stray from his niche of astute social or romantic observations, and, sooner or later, a big-name artist will convert one of his songs into a standard. The most likely contenders are 'No Time At All' and 'I Will Love You All My Life'.
● ALBUMS: *Heaven Knows* (1989)★★★ *Songs From The Heart* (1992)★★★, *What Colour Is The Wind?* (Ritz 1994)★★★, *With You In Mind* (Ritz 1996)★★★, *Further Down The Road* (Ritz 1997)★★★.
● VIDEOS: *An Evening With Charlie Landsborough* (1995).

LANE, CRISTY

b. Eleanor Johnston, 8 January 1940, Peoria, Illinois, USA. Lane was the eighth of 12 children brought up in a economically depressed area. In 1959, she married country music fan Lee Stoller, who encouraged her to sing country, and, after many local performances, she made her first single, 'Janie Took My Place', in Nashville in 1968. She and her husband sold their Peoria nightclub, Cristy's Inc., and moved to Nashville in 1972. Stoller formed LS Records, chiefly to release his wife's product. Her first entry on the US country charts was with 'Tryin' To Forget About You' in 1977. She then had Top 10 country hits with 'Let Me Down Easy', 'I'm Gonna Love You Anyway', 'Penny Arcade' and 'I Just Can't Stay Married To You'. Further country hits followed but Stoller was jailed for financial irregularities. She moved to United Artists and had a US country number 1 in 1980 with a gospel song written by Marijohn Wilkin and Kris Kristofferson, 'One Day At A Time'. Her husband, released from jail and inspired by Slim Whitman's album sales through television advertising, took over her career and started marketing her in a similar way. Cristy Lane has continued performing into the 90s, basing herself in Branson, Missouri.
● ALBUMS: *Cristy Lane...Is The Name* (LS Records 1977)★★, *Love Lies* (LS Records 1978)★★★, *Simple Little Words* (United Artists 1979)★★★, *I Have A Dream* (United Artists 1980)★★, *Ask Me To Dance* (United Artists 1980)★★★, *Fragile - Handle With Care* (United Artists 1981)★★★, *Amazing Grace* (United Artists 1982)★★★, *Here's To Us* (United Artists 1983)★★★, *Christmas Is The Man From Galilee* (United Artists 1983)★★, *Amazing Grace, Vol. 2* (Arrival 1986)★★, *All In His Hands* (Heartwarming 1989).
● COMPILATIONS: *Footprints In The Sand* (United Artists 1983)★★★, *My Best To You* (Arrival 1992)★★★.
● FURTHER READING: *Cristy Lane: One Day At A Time*, Lee Stoller with Pete Chaney.

LANE, RED

b. Hollis R. DeLaughter, 9 February 1939, near Bogalusa, Louisiana, USA. A singer-songwriter who learned guitar as a child, Lane moved to Nashville in the early 60s, where he worked with Justin Tubb and as a session musician. In 1967, he became frontman for Dottie West's band and co-wrote with West her 1968 hit 'Country Girl'. In the early 70s, he recorded for RCA and charted four minor hits, the biggest being 'The World Needs A Melody' and the last, 'It Was Love While It Lasted', in 1972. Since then he has remained active as a session musician and toured as a guitarist with Merle Haggard. Some of his songs have been recorded by top artists but he has failed to achieve further chart successes of his own.
● ALBUMS: *The World Needs A Melody* (RCA 1971)★★.

LANG, K.D.

b. Kathryn Dawn Lang, 2 November 1961, Consort, Alberta, Canada. She prefers the lower case appearance of her name because 'it's generic and unlike Cherry Bomb, it's a name, not a sexuality'. This farmer's daughter had become a skilled pianist and guitarist by adolescence and, on leaving school, scratched a living in the performing arts, classical and *avant garde* music, before choosing to sing country - a genre that she had once despised as the corniest in pop. However, forsaking much of its rhinestoned tackiness for a leaner, more abandoned approach on *A Truly Western Experience*, she moved from a Canadian label to Sire Records. She was known for her slightly skewered sensibility and a tough backing combo consisting in 1983 of Gordon Matthews (guitar), Ben Mink (violin, mandolin), Mike Creber (piano), John Dymond (bass) and Michel Pouliot (drums). She named them the Reclines - a genuflexion towards Patsy Cline. Overseen by Dave Edmunds, *Angel With A Lariat* was favoured by influential rock journals such as *Rolling Stone* (who voted lang Female Vocalist of the Year), but many country radio stations refused to play it, prejudiced as they were by lang's spiky haircut, vegetarian stance and ambiguous sexuality (she would only go public on the latter subject in a June 1992 interview with *Advocate* magazine). Nevertheless, she charted via 'Cryin'', a duet with Roy Orbison for 1987's *Hiding Out* comedy movie soundtrack. The following year, she gained a breakthrough with the lush *Shadowland*, which was rendered agreeable to country consumers through a Nashville production by Owen Bradley and the presence of the Jordanaires, Brenda Lee, Loretta Lynn, Kitty Wells and other credible guest stars. Tracks such as the tear-jerking 'I Wish I Didn't Love You So' and Chris Isaak's 'Western Stars' exemplified what lang described as 'torch and twang' - an expression incorporated into the title of her next collection. Mostly self-composed with Mink, it set the seal on the grudging acceptance of her by bigots and, more to the point, confirmed her as a behemoth of country's New Tradition. In 1992, she became newsworthy and featured in dozens of magazines in Europe and the USA; having 'discovered' Garth Brooks, they finally picked up on the considerable talent of k.d. lang when the acclaimed *Ingenue* was released. This excellent release was, however, far removed from country, C&W or new country; it was a sensual and deep collection firmly putting her in sight of major honours. The same year showed lang as possessing a promising acting ability in her debut film role in *Salmonberries*. *Drag* featured cover versions including a highly original interpretation of Steve Miller's 'The Joker'.

● ALBUMS: *A Truly Western Experience* (Bumstead 1984)★★, *Angel With A Lariat* (Sire 1987)★★★, *Shadowland* (Sire 1988)★★★, *Absolute Torch And Twang* (Sire 1989)★★★, *Ingenue* (Sire/Warners 1992)★★★★, *Even Cowgirls Get The Blues* film soundtrack (Sire/Warners 1993)★★, *All You Can Eat* (Sire/Warners 1995)★★★, *Drag* (Warners 1997)★★★.

● VIDEOS: *Harvest Of Seven Years* (Warner Music Video 1992).

● FURTHER READING: *Carrying The Torch*, William Robertson. *k.d. lang*, David Bennahum. *All You Get Is Me*, Victoria Starr.

● FILMS: *Salmonberries* (1992).

LANOR RECORDS

Lanor Records is the brainchild of famed Cajun producer Lee Lavergne, a native of rural town Church Point, near Crowley in Louisiana, USA. He formed the label in 1960 as an adjunct to his day job as a cleric in a wholesale grocery.

Influenced by Hank Williams and other country artists as a child, Lavergne began to record local artists after being demobbed from the army. The first release on which he worked was with Shirley Bergeron, a local artist popular in Lafetyette. 'J'ai Fait Mon Edée' sold out of its pressing of 2,000 copies and established the Lanor Records label in the area. Although inexperienced with the production process, he knew enough to supervise his musicians on direction and sound, gradually accumulating knowledge as the label grew. Booking studios such as J.D. Miller's in Crowley or Cosimo's in New Orleans, he engaged a number of prominent Cajun artists. Eventually, with studio rates escalating, he built his own studio with a cheap mixing board and reel-to-reel recorder. By 1972 he was also running his own music store, which would help finance his activities with the label. His first big hit came with Elton Anderson, after that artist was dropped by Mercury Records. 'Life Problem' became a major local seller and was picked up for national distribution by Capitol Records. Later, Billy Matte and Charles Mann ('Red Red Wine') furthered the label's reputation with sustained singles success. However, despite some 150 singles by the turn of the 90s, it is only relatively recently that Lanor has issued cassette albums and compact discs. Despite its sporadic recording activity and limited discography, Lanor has become a Mecca for fans of Cajun and zydeco music passing through Louisiana.

LARKIN, PATTY

b. Wisconsin, USA. Expert guitarist and singer-songwriter Patty Larkin has described her style as 'folk music meets the beat generation meets rock 'n' roll.' In the meantime critics have described her acoustic, electric and slide guitar technique and presentation as 'comparable to the best of Bonnie Raitt'. Larkin studied classical piano for four years before she took up slide guitar as her primary instrument during her seventh grade. Her first songs were written a year later. She enrolled at Berklee College Of Music in the 70s after first attending the University Of Oregon and studying jazz guitar privately. Her time at Berklee saw her researching composition skills and music theory and history, also playing mandolin and guitar in a Celtic band that busked on the streets of Cambridge, Massachusetts. It was during this time that she developed her distinctive playing style, a highly percussive and melodic framework derived from her education in Irish folk tunes by John Martyn and jazz by various local musicians. In the early 80s Larkin formed a rock band as rhythm and lead guitarist, before electing to embark on her own solo career, influenced by Ry Cooder and Richard Thompson. Regularly playing about 150 shows a year, Larkin made her album debut in 1985 with *Step Into The Light*. Though well received, the subsequent *I'm Fine* collection was the more enduring, with fine compositions including the feisty 'If I Was Made Of Metal'. After a lively recording of her potent stage show (*In The Square*), she moved over to High Street Records. *Tango* added more studio polish, and included guest appearances by fellow High Street/Windham Hill associates Darol Anger and John Gorka. By this time she was well into her record run of nine Boston Music Awards (she lives in Cape Cod, Massachusetts), and she had also gained the Distinguished Alumnae Award from Berklee College. *Angels Running* was another highly acclaimed release, placing Larkin in the Top

10 of the AAA (Adult Album Alternative) charts. *Strangers World* united her with multi-instrumentalist producer John Leventhal (a veteran of work with Shawn Colvin, Marc Cohn and Rosanne Cash), and was described by the artist as a 'song cycle'. Certainly it evaded the dichotomy of old, where Larkin would often craft either instrumentals or comedic pieces. The effect was startling and confirmed a talent that seems capable of sustaining itself for many years to come.

● ALBUMS: *Step Into The Light* (Philo 1985)★★, *I'm Fine* (Philo 1988)★★★, *In The Square* (Philo 1990)★★★, *Tango* (High Street 1990)★★, *Angels Running* (High Street 1993)★★★, *Strangers World* (High Street 1994)★★★, *Perishable Fruit* (High Street 1997)★★.

LARSON, NICOLETTE

b. 1952, Helena, Montana, USA, d. 16 December 1997, Los Angeles, California, USA. Larson moved to California where she became a member of touring road-bands with Hoyt Axton and Commander Cody. By the 70s she had become established as a session singer and appeared on albums by Emmylou Harris (*Luxury Liner*), Linda Rondstadt (*Mad Love*) and Neil Young (*American Stars And Bars, Comes A Time*). She began her solo career in 1978 with *Nicolette*, which featured support from James Burton and Klaus Voorman as well as members of Little Feat and the Doobie Brothers. Despite the all-star cast, the singer's voice retained its individuality and she was rewarded when the track 'Lotta Love' reached the US Top 10. After three strong albums she moved to Nashville and recorded *Say When*; the album showed her to be equally adept at country music, which was well suited to her high, clear intonation. Larson nonetheless retained contact with her associates from the past, singing backing vocals on Young's *Harvest Moon* and *Unplugged* albums. *Sleep, Baby, Sleep* was a collection of lullabies and a difficult album to market. The duets with Graham Nash, David Crosby and Ronstadt made it an album for adults, yet it was presumably intended to send children to sleep. Larson died in December 1997 of complications arising from cerebral edema.

● ALBUMS: *Nicolette* (Warners 1978)★★★, *In The Nick Of Time* (Warners 1979)★★, *Radioland* (Warners 1981)★★★, *All Dressed Up With No Place To Go* (Warners 1982)★★★, *Say When* (MCA 1985)★★★, *Sleep, Baby, Sleep* (Sony 1994)★★★.

LAUDERDALE, JIM

b. 11 April 1957, Statesville, North Carolina, USA. His father was a minister and his mother a music teacher and choir director. Lauderdale played drums in the school band and after graduation decided to become a solo performer in New York. He impressed record producer Pete Anderson while in the Los Angeles production of *Pump Boys And Dinettes* and was recorded for the compilation *A Town South Of Bakersfield, Volume 2*. He then sang backing vocals for various artists including Carlene Carter and Dwight Yoakam, and had his songs recorded by Vince Gill and George Strait. *Planet Of Love* is an impressive album that was co-produced by Rodney Crowell and John Leventhal and included Marc Cohn and Shawn Colvin among the musicians. Lauderdale himself wrote all the songs and performs them in a variety of styles ranging from western swing to Jerry Lee Lewis. He has also written several songs for Kelly Willis and he appears on the chorus of Carlene Carter's 'Little Love Letters'.

Persimmons was another accomplished album sprinkled with classy country rock and ballads with a formidable list of helpers - Emmylou Harris, Dan Dugmore (guitar), Al Perkins (guitar), Pat Buchanan (guitar) and Larry Knechel (piano).

● ALBUMS: *Planet Of Love* (Reprise 1991)★★★★, *Pretty Close To The Truth* (Atlantic 1993)★★★, *Every Second Counts* (Atlantic 1995)★★★, *Persimmons* (Upstart 1996)★★★★.

LAWRENCE, TRACY

b. 27 January 1968, Atlanta, Texas, USA. The son of a banker, Lawrence was raised in Foreman, Arkansas, and sang in the church choir. He started working in honky tonks when he was 17 years old and moved to Nashville in 1990. He recorded his first album and the future looked bright until he and his girlfriend were accosted by four thugs in a hotel parking lot. He suffered gunshot wounds and his album was put on hold for five months while he recovered. *Sticks And Stones* sold 500,000 copies and he had country hits with 'Today's Lonely Fool', 'Runnin' Behind' and 'Somebody Paints The Wall'. In 1993, he had a hat trick of number 1s, 'Alibis', 'Can't Break It To My Heart' and 'My Second Home'. He recorded 'Hillbilly With A Heartache' as a duet with John Anderson and his video for 'My Second Home' is a who's who of New Country music. In 1996 he reached number 1 again with 'Time Marches On'. His road band is called Little Elvis, even though the most likely crown he could steal would be Garth Brooks' and not Presley's.

● ALBUMS: *Sticks And Stones* (Atlantic 1991)★★★, *Alibis* (Atlantic 1993)★★★, *I See It Now* (Atlantic 1994)★★★★, *Tracy Lawrence Live* (Atlantic 1995)★★, *Time Marches On* (Atlantic 1996)★★★, *The Coast Is Clear* (Atlantic 1997)★★★.

● VIDEOS: *I See It Now* (A*Vision 1994), *In The Round* (Warner Vision 1996).

LAWSON, DOYLE

b. Doyle Wayne Lawson, 20 April 1944, Fordtown, near Kingsport, Tennessee, USA. His father sang in a gospel quartet and he was attracted to both gospel and bluegrass music as a child. By the time he reached his teens, he could play mandolin, banjo and guitar but captivated by Bill Monroe's playing, he specialized in the former. He began his professional career in 1963, playing banjo with Jimmy Martin's Sunny Mountain Boys. In 1966, he began an association with J.D. Crowe, first playing guitar but soon becoming the mandolinist with Crowe's Kentucky Mountain Boys and, in the late 60s, he played on two albums with Crowe and also recorded with Red Allen for Rebel. He joined the Country Gentlemen in 1971, and remained a member until 1979. During this time, he toured to Japan and Europe, recorded 10 albums with the group and also recorded a solo mandolin instrumental album. In 1979, he left the Gentlemen and formed his own group, Quicksilver. The group initially comprised Lawson, Terry Baucom (banjo), Jimmy Haley (guitar) and Lou Reid (bass), but over the years, there have been several changes of personnel. In 1979, they recorded *Doyle Lawson & Quicksilver* on Sugar Hill Records and followed it, throughout the 80s, with a series of albums, some gospel, some bluegrass, but eventually the albums were a mixture of both genres. Guest musicians on recordings have included Sam Bush, Mike Auldridge and Jerry Douglas. The group

were noted for their harmonies and a cappella singing and on *Heaven's Joy Awaits*, they included no musical accompaniment. During the 80s, Lawson also recorded a series of five albums for Rounder with J.D. Crowe, Tony Rice and Bobby Hicks as the Bluegrass Album Band. In 1990, Lawson moved his recording work to Brentwood Music and in the mid-90s, was still a very active and respected figure in bluegrass and gospel music.
● ALBUMS: *Tennessee Dream* (County 1977)★★★, *Doyle Lawson & Quicksilver* (Sugar Hill 1980)★★★, *Rock My Soul* (Sugar Hill 1981)★★★, *Quicksilver Rides Again* (Sugar Hill 1982)★★, *Heavenly Treasures* (Sugar Hill 1983)★★★, *Once And For Always* (Sugar Hill 1985)★★★, *Beyond The Shadows* (Sugar Hill 1986)★★★, *The News Is Out* (Sugar Hill 1987)★★★, *Heaven's Joy Awaits* (Sugar Hill 1987)★★★, *Hymn Time In The Country* (Sugar Hill 1988)★★, *I'll Wander Back Someday* (Sugar Hill 1988)★★★, *I Heard The Angels Singing* (Sugar Hill 1989)★★★, *My Heart Is Yours* (Sugar Hill 1990)★★★, *Treasures Money Can't Buy* (Brentwood Music 1992)★★, *Pressing On Regardless* (Brentwood Music 1992)★★, *Never Walk Away* (Sugar Hill 1995)★★★, *There's A Light Guiding Me* (Sugar Hill 1996)★★★.

LAWSON, TIM

b. 1953, London, Ontario, Canada. Lawson played guitar as a child, but he went into business when he left school. In the early 90s, he began to write songs and his debut album, *The Quiet Canadian*, is full of thoughtful, reflective work. The title track is a tribute to Canada's wartime intelligence expert, Sir William Stephenson, the man called Intrepid. 'Wartime Letters' was inspired by correspondence between his parents, and the multimedia version gives considerable background information.
● ALBUMS: *The Quiet Canadian* (Timberholme 1995)★★★.

LAWTON, JIMMY

Lawton was born in the USA but he is mainly known as a country artist in Europe. He settled in the Netherlands and built himself a reputation in various European venues, but although he made tours in the UK, he was unable to match his level of support in mainland Europe. He has recorded with European musicians, including an excellent version of Merle Haggard's song 'Somewhere Between' with Dutch country girl Ine Masseurs.
● ALBUMS: *Arizona Sunday* UK release (Westwood 1978)★★★, *Jimmy Lawton* European release (Arcade 1986)★★★.

LAY, RODNEY

b. Coffeyville, Kansas, USA. Lay worked as a DJ and singer on KGGF Coffeyville, and in the mid-60s, toured with Wanda Jackson. In 1973, he gained a small acting role in *Pat Garrett And Billy The Kid* which starred Kris Kristofferson. Lay became musical director and leader of Roy Clark's band. When not working with Clark, he fronted his own band, the Wild West. Recording with them, he enjoyed six minor hits during the 80s, including 'Happy Country Birthday Darling', and his version of the 1973 Mel Street hit 'Walk Softly On The Bridges', but his fondness for rock and rockabilly material did little to attract the traditionalists.
● ALBUMS: *Desert Rock* (Sun 1979)★★★, *Rockabilly Nuggets* (Sun 1980)★★★, *Silent Partners* (Sun 1981)★★★.

LE ROUX

Formed in the mid-70s in Louisiana, USA, Le Roux was originally called Louisiana's Le Roux and consisted of Jeff Pollard (guitar, vocals), Tony Haselden (guitar), Rod Roddy (keyboard), Bobby Campo (horn), Leon Medica (bass) and David Peters (drums). They were originally session musicians backing blues, folk and Cajun artists, and took the name Le Roux from the Cajun word for the gravy used in gumbo, a traditional Louisiana dish. Discovered by William McEuen, manager of the Nitty Gritty Dirt Band, they signed to Capitol Records, and released their debut, *Louisiana's Le Roux*, in 1978. Their first three albums only glanced the charts and they signed to RCA Records in 1982 (having shortened their name to Le Roux). The single 'Nobody Said It Was Easy (Lookin' For The Lights)' became their only major hit, reaching US number 18 that year. *Last Safe Place* became their biggest album, making number 64. They had two further chart singles after the hit, but by 1983 there were personnel changes and the group disappeared from the music scene.
● ALBUMS: *Louisiana's Le Roux* (Capitol 1978)★★, *Keep The Fire Burnin'* (Capitol 1979)★★★, *Up* (Capitol 1980)★★, *Last Safe Place* (RCA 1982)★★★★, *So Fired Up* (1983)★★.

LEAKE COUNTY REVELLERS

One of the best and most respected of the old-time string bands. They were formed in 1926, when the members began to play together for relaxation in the evenings or for local dances at Sebastopol, Scott County, Mississippi, USA. The band comprised Will Gilmer (b. William Bryant Gilmer, 27 February 1897, Leake County, USA, d. 28 December 1960; fiddle), R.O. Mosley (b. R. Oscar Mosley, 1885, Sebastopol, Scott County, Mississippi, USA, d. early 30s; mandolin), Jim Wolverton (b. 1895, Leake County, USA, d. 50s; banjo) and Dallas Jones (b.17 December 1889, Sebastopol, Scott County, Mississippi, USA; guitar). Their local popularity grew and led to them making their first four recordings for Columbia Records in 1927. Their recording of 'Wednesday Night Waltz', for which they are best remembered, proved so successful that it became one of the bestselling records of old-time music. In the late 20s, further Columbia sessions led to over 20 releases and their popularity saw them tour and gain their own programmes on WJDX Jackson. Their repertoire, much at variance with most of the early string bands, consisted mainly of waltzes or slow numbers and experts in the music have attributed much of their success to Gilmer's gentle fiddle playing. After Mosley's death, in the early 30s, the Revellers disbanded (arguably, they should have been the Scott and not Leake County Revellers - geographically Sebastopol was in the former county; they were actually named by Columbia). Gilmer and Jones both continued to play for some years, although with different bands.
● COMPILATIONS: *The Leake County Revellers 1927-1930* (County 1975)★★★.

LEDFORD, STEVE

b. Steven Walter Ledford, 2 June 1906, Bakersville, Mitchell County, North Carolina, USA, d. 19 September 1980. One of 12 children, with help from his father, he started playing fiddle aged seven and won a competition two years later. His first professional work came as a member, with two siblings, of the Carolina Ramblers String Band. In 1931, the band travelled to New York, where they played on radio and in February 1932, they recorded 20 sides for ARC, eight of which gained release on various labels including Perfect. Soon afterwards, they disbanded and Ledford returned to North Carolina, where he married and became a farmer. He returned to music in the late 30s, working with J.E. Mainer, Wade Mainer and Zeke Morris on various radio stations and tours, during which time he also made several recordings with Mainer's Mountaineers, including a version of 'Little Maggie', that has since led to the song always being associated with him. Ledford also recorded with Jay Hugh Hall and Clyde Moody as the Happy-Go-Lucky Boys and in the early 40s, he worked for some time at WDBJ Roanoke, Virginia, with Jay Hugh and Roy Hall. The bands played a mixture of old-time and modern music and undoubtedly were an influence on later bluegrass bands. In 1942, Ledford retired to work his farm but several years later, he, with his brother Wayne and James Gardner, re-formed a version of the Carolina Ramblers, which played a long residency in Maggie Valley. In 1971, as the Ledford String Band, they recorded for Rounder Records. Ledford continued to play at some venues until shortly before his death in September 1980.

● ALBUMS: *Ledford String Band* (Rounder 1971)★★★.

LeDoux, Chris

b. 2 October 1948, Biloxi, Mississippi, USA. LeDoux's father was an airforce pilot who was posted to various parts of the USA. His grandfather, who had served in the US cavalry and fought against Pancho Villa, encouraged LeDoux to ride horses on his Wyoming farm. LeDoux attended high school at Cheyenne, Wyoming, and, while still at school, he twice won the state's bareback title. In 1967, after graduating, he won a rodeo scholarship and received a national title in his third year. In 1976, he became the Professional Rodeo Cowboys Association's world champion in bareback riding. LeDoux has been playing guitar and harmonica and writing songs since his teens, and he used his musical ability as a means of paying his way from one rodeo to another. Since 1971, he has been recording songs about 'real cowboys', although his voice would not win world championships and he has never had a substantial US country hit. His albums combine his own compositions about rodeo life with old and new cowboy songs. He describes his music as 'a combination of western soul, sagebrush blues, cowboy folk and rodeo rock 'n' roll'. For all his tough image, his music has a soft centre ('God Must Be A Cowboy At Heart') and the narration 'This Cowboy's Hat'), but one of his love songs is titled 'If You Loved Me, You'd Do It'. Charlie Daniels, Johnny Gimble and Janie Frickie are among the musicians on his records and Garth Brooks pays tribute to him in 'Much Too Young (To Feel This Damn Old)'. LeDoux lives with his family on a ranch in Wyoming and farms sheep. He is a popular entertainer with his band, Western Underground, particularly on the rodeo circuit. All his albums are released on his own label, American Cowboy Songs, but only *Rodeo's Singing Bronc Rider* has been released in the UK. Garth Brooks' testimony, together with the success of a single, 'Ridin' For A Fall', brought him to the attention of Liberty Records, who signed LeDoux for new recordings and have reissued his earlier work. He moved to Capitol Records in 1995.

● ALBUMS: *Songs Of Rodeo Life* (American Cowboy Songs

1971)★★★, *Chris LeDoux Sings His Rodeo Songs* (American Cowboy Songs 1972)★★★, *Rodeo Songs - Old And New* (American Cowboy Songs 1973)★★★, *Songs Of Rodeo And Country* (American Cowboy Songs 1974)★★★, *Songs Of Rodeo And Living Free* (American Cowboy Songs 1974)★★★, *Life As A Rodeo Man* (American Cowboy Songs 1975)★★★, *Songbook Of The American West* (American Cowboy Songs 1976)★★★, *Sing Me A Song, Mr. Rodeo Man* (American Cowboy Songs 1977)★★, *Songs Of Rodeo Life* a re-recording of the 1971 album (American Cowboy Songs 1977)★★★, *Western-Country (Cowboys Ain't Easy To Love)* (American Cowboy Songs 1978)★★★, *Paint Me Back Home In Wyoming* (American Cowboy Songs 1979)★★★, *Rodeo's Singing Bronc Rider* (American Cowboy Songs 1979)★★, *Western Tunesmith* (American Cowboy Songs 1980)★★★, *Sounds Of The Western Country* (American Cowboy Songs 1980)★★★, *Old Cowboy Heroes* (American Cowboy Songs 1980)★★★, *He Rides The Wild Horses* (American Cowboy Songs 1981)★★★, *Used To Want To Be A Cowboy* (American Cowboy Songs 1982)★★★, *Thirty Dollar Cowboy* (American Cowboy Songs 1983)★★★, *Old Cowboy Classics* (American Cowboy Songs 1983)★★★, *Wild And Wooly* (American Cowboy Songs 1986)★★★, *Melodies And Memories* (American Cowboy Songs 1984)★★★, *Powder River* (American Cowboy Songs 1990)★★★, *Western Underground* (Liberty 1991)★★★, *What Ya Gonna Do With A Cowboy* (Liberty 1992)★★★, *Under This Old Hat* (Liberty 1993)★★★, *Haywire* (Liberty 1994)★★★, *Stampede* (Capitol 1996)★★★★, *Live* (Capitol 1997)★★.

● COMPILATIONS: *Best Of Chris Le Doux* (Liberty 1994)★★★, *Rodeo Rock And Roll Collection* (Liberty 1995)★★★.

● FURTHER READING: *Gold Buckle, The Rodeo Life Of Chris LeDoux*, David G. Brown.

Lee, Albert

b. 21 December 1943, Leominster, Herefordshire, England. Lee is a country rock guitarist of breathtaking ability. If a poll of polls were taken from leading guitarists in the field, Lee would be the likely winner. During the early 60s he was the guitarist in the R&B-influenced Chris Farlowe And The Thunderbirds. He departed in 1967, as by then offers of session work were pouring in. During that time he joined Country Fever, playing straight honky-tonk country music, before recording as Poet And The One Man Band with Chas Hodges (later of Chas And Dave). The unit evolved into Heads Hands And Feet, a highly respected band, playing country rock. It was during this stage in his career that Lee became a 'guitar hero'; he was able to play his Fender Telecaster at breakneck speed and emulate and outshine his American counterparts. Lee played with the Crickets in 1973-74 and spent an increasing amount of time in America, eventually moving out there. After appearing on a reunion album with Chris Farlowe in 1975, he joined Emmylou Harris's Hot Band, replacing one of his heroes, the legendary James Burton. During the late 70s and early 80s Lee performed in touring bands with Eric Clapton, Jackson Browne, Jerry Lee Lewis and Dave Edmunds. His solo on 'Sweet Little Lisa' on Edmund's *Repeat When Necessary* is a superb example of the man's skill. Lee played a major part in the historic reunion of the Everly Brothers at London's Royal Albert Hall in 1983, and he continues to be a member of their regular touring band. He has made several solo albums which are impressive showcases for one of Britain's finest guitarists.

● ALBUMS: *Hiding* (A&M 1979)★★★★, *Albert Lee* (Polydor 1982)★★★, *Speechless* (MCA 1987)★★★, *Gagged But Not Bound* (MCA 1988)★★, *Black Claw And Country Fever* (Line 1991)★★, with Hogan's Heroes *Live At Montreux* 1992 recording (Round Tower 1994)★★, *Undiscovered - The Early Years* (Diamond 1998)★★★.

● COMPILATIONS: *Country Guitar Man* (Magnum 1986)★★★.

LEE, BRENDA

b. Brenda Mae Tarpley, 11 December 1944, Lithonia, Georgia, USA. Even in early adolescence, Lee had an adult husk of a voice that could slip from anguished intimacy through sleepy insinuation to raucous lust, even during 'Let's Jump The Broomstick', 'Speak To Me Pretty' and other jaunty classics that kept her in the hit parade from the mid-50s to 1965. Through local radio and, by 1956, wider exposure on Red Foley's Ozark Jubilee broadcasts, 'Little Brenda Lee' was ensured enough airplay for her first single, a revival of Hank Williams' 'Jambalaya', to crack the US country chart before her *Billboard* Hot 100 debut with 1957's 'One Step At A Time'. The novelty of her extreme youth facilitated bigger triumphs for 'Little Miss Dynamite' with the million-selling 'Rockin' Around The Christmas Tree' and later bouncy rockers, before the next decade brought a greater proportion of heartbreak ballads, such as 'I'm Sorry' and 'Too Many Rivers' - plus an acting role in the children's fantasy movie *The Two Little Bears*. 1963 was another successful year - especially in the UK with the title song of *All Alone Am I*, 'Losing You' (a French translation), 'I Wonder' and 'As Usual' each entering the Top 20. While 1964 finished well with 'Is It True' and 'Christmas Will Be Just Another Lonely Day', only minor hits followed. Although she may have weathered prevailing fads, family commitments caused Lee to cut back on touring and record only intermittently after 1966's appositely titled *Bye Bye Blues*. Lee resurfaced in 1971 with a huge country hit in Kris Kristofferson's 'Nobody Wins'; this and later recordings established her as a star of what was then one of the squarest seams of pop. When country gained a younger audience in the mid-80s, respect for its older practitioners found her guesting with Loretta Lynn and Kitty Wells on k.d. lang's *Shadowland*. - produced in 1988 by Owen Bradley (who had also supervised many early Lee records). In Europe, Brenda Lee remained mostly a memory - albeit a pleasing one as shown by Coast To Coast's hit revival of 'Let's Jump The Broomstick', a high UK placing for 1980's *Little Miss Dynamite* greatest hits collection and Mel Smith And Kim Wilde's 'Rockin' Around The Christmas Tree'. Lee is fortunate in having a large rock 'n' roll catalogue destined for immortality, in addition to her now high standing in the country music world. In 1993, billed as 'the biggest-selling female star in pop history', Brenda Lee toured the UK and played the London Palladium, headlining a nostalgia package that included Chris Montez, Len Barry and Johnny Tillotson. From her opening 'I'm So Excited', through to the closing 'Rockin' All Over The World', she fulfilled all expectations, and won standing ovations from packed houses. In keeping with many of their packages, the Bear Family box set is a superb retrospective.

● ALBUMS: *Grandma, What Great Songs You Sang* (Decca 1959)★★, *Brenda Lee* (Decca 1960)★★★★, *This Is ... Brenda* (Decca 1960)★★★★, *Miss Dynamite* (Brunswick 1961)★★★★, *Emotions* (Decca 1961)★★★, *All The Way* (Decca 1961)★★★, *Sincerely Brenda Lee* (Decca 1962)★★★★, *Brenda, That's All* (Decca 1962)★★★★, *All Alone Am I* (Decca 1963)★★★, *Let Me Sing* (Decca 1963)★★★, *Sings Songs Everybody Knows* (Decca 1964)★★★, *By Request* (Decca 1964)★★★, *Merry Christmas From Brenda Lee* (Decca 1964)★★★, *Top Teen Hits* (Decca 1965)★★★, *The Versatile Brenda Lee* (Decca 1965)★★★, *Too Many Rivers* (Decca 1965)★★★, *Bye Bye Blues* (Decca 1965)★★★, *Coming On Strong* (Decca 1966)★★★, *Call Me Brenda* (Decca 1967)★★★, *Reflections In Blue* (Decca 1967)★★★, *Good Life* (Decca 1967)★★★, with Tennessee Ernie Ford *The Show For Christmas Seals* (Decca 1968)★★★, with Pete Fountain *For The First Time* (Decca 1968)★★★, *Johnny One Time* (Decca 1969)★★★, *Memphis Portrait* (Decca 1970)★★★, *Let It Be Me* (Vocalion 1970)★★★, *A Whole Lotta* (MCA 1972)★★★, *Brenda* (MCA 1973)★★★, *New Sunrise* (MCA 1974)★★★, *Brenda Lee Now* (MCA 1975)★★★, *The LA Sessions* (MCA 1977)★★★, *Even Better* (MCA 1980)★★★, *Take Me Back* (MCA 1981)★★★, *Only When I Laugh* (MCA 1982)★★★, with Dolly Parton, Kris Kristofferson, Willie Nelson *The Winning Hand* (Monument 1983)★★★, *Feels So Right* (MCA 1985)★★★, *Brenda Lee* (Warners 1991)★★★, *A Brenda Lee Christmas* (Warners 1991)★★★, *Greatest Hits Live* (MCA 1992)★★★, *Coming On Strong* (Muskateer 1995)★★★.

● COMPILATIONS: *10 Golden Years* (Decca 1966)★★★, *The Brenda Lee Story - Her Greatest Hits* (MCA 1973)★★★★, *Little Miss Dynamite* (MCA 1976)★★★★, *Greatest Country Hits* (MCA 1982)★★★, *25th Anniversary* (MCA 1984)★★★★, *The Early Years* (MCA 1984)★★★, *The Golden Decade* (Charly 1985)★★★★, *The Best Of Brenda Lee* (MCA 1986)★★★★, *Love Songs* (MCA 1986)★★★, *Brenda's Best* (Ce De 1989)★★★★, *Very Best Of Brenda Lee Volume 1* (MCA 1990)★★★★, *Very Best Of Brenda Lee Volume 2* (MCA 1990)★★★, *The Brenda Lee Anthology Volume One, 1956-1961* (MCA 1991)★★★★, *The Brenda Lee Anthology Volume Two, 1962-1980* (MCA 1991)★★★, *Little Miss Dynamite* 4-CD box set (Bear Family 1996)★★★★, *The EP Collection* (See For Miles 1996)★★★★.

LEE, DICKEY

b. Richard Lipscombe, 21 September 1941, Memphis, Tennessee, USA. Lee was a country singer and composer whose most recorded composition was 'She Thinks I Still Care', made famous by George Jones. At high school in Memphis, he sang rock 'n' roll and recorded the Elvis Presley-influenced 'Dreamy Nights' and 'Good Lovin'' with the Collegiates for the local Sun label. When producer Jack Clement left Sun to set up his own studio in Beaumont, Texas, Lee went with him. There he concentrated on pop material, releasing an unsuccessful revival of the 1953 hit tune 'Oh Mein Papa', before recording his biggest success, the million-selling 'Patches' (1961). Produced by Clement, this lachrymose death-ballad was composed by Barry Mann and Larry Kolber. The follow-up, 'I Saw Linda Yesterday', was also a hit but Lee's later teen-ballads made little impact until another song about a deceased girlfriend, 'Laurie (Strange Things Happening)', reached the US Top 20 in 1965. By now, however, Lee was based in Nashville and had established himself as a successful country songwriter following Jones's 1962 hit version of 'She Thinks I Still Care'. Among the numerous artists who later recorded the song were Elvis Presley, Michael Nesmith and Anne Murray. During the late 60s and 70s Lee himself recorded for RCA and had a country number 1 with 'Never Ending Song Of Love' in 1971. In Britain, the song was a Top 10 hit for the New Seekers. Nearly 30 more singles by Lee were US country hits over the next decade. They included 'Rocky' (1975), 'Ashes Of Love' (1976), '9,999,999 Tears' (1976), 'It's Not Easy' (1978) and 'Lost In Love' (1980). Among those who successfully recorded Lee's compositions were Don Williams, Glen Campbell and Brenda Lee. He moved to Mercury Records in 1979.

● ALBUMS: *The Tale Of Patches* (Smash 1962)★★★, *Dickey Lee Sings Laurie And The Girl From Peyton Place* (TCF Hall 1965)★★, *Never Ending Song of Love* (RCA 1971)★★, *Crying Over You* (RCA 1972)★★★★, *Sparklin' Brown Eyes* (RCA 1973)★★★, *Rocky* (1975)★★★, *Ashes Of Love* (RCA 1976) *Angels, Roses And Rain* (RCA 1976)★★★, *Baby Bye Bye* (RCA 1977)★★★, *Dickey Lee* (Mercury 1980)★★★, *Everybody Loves A Winner* (Mercury 1981)★★★.

LEE, JOHNNY

b. John Lee Ham, 3 July 1946, Texas City, Texas, USA. Lee was raised on a dairy farm in Alta Loma, Texas, but his main interest was rock 'n' roll and he led a high school band, Johnny Lee And the Roadrunners. He worked through the 60s by playing popular hits in Texas clubs and bars. In 1968, he began a 10-year working relationship with Mickey Gilley, both on the road and at his club Gilley's in Pasadena. He had moderate US country successes in the mid-70s with 'Sometimes', 'Red Sails In The Sunset' and 'Country Party', and appeared in the 1979 television movie *The Girls In The Office*. Lee was featured in the film *Urban Cowboy*, which was shot at Gilley's, and in 1980, he had a US number 1 country single and US Top 5 pop hit with a song from the film, 'Lookin' For Love', which had previously been turned down by 20 different performers. Further number 1 country hits came with 'One In A Million' and 'Bet Your Heart On Me'. Another US country hit, 'Cherokee Fiddle', featured Michael Martin Murphey and Charlie Daniels. Lee married actress Charlene Tilton (who played Lucy in the television series *Dallas*) on St. Valentine's Day 1982 in a much-publicized wedding at Tony Orlando's house, with Gilley as best man. Lee contributed a track, 'Lucy's Eyes', to an album by the stars of *Dallas*. However, their stormy marriage only lasted three years and Lee remarried in 1987. He had a further number 1 country single with a theme from a short-lived television soap opera, *The Yellow Rose*, with actress-singer Lane Brody, who was in the country music film *Tender Mercies*. His final solo number 1 country single was with 'You Could've Heard A Heart Break' in 1984. Lee was in the right place at the right time, but unfortunately for him, a stringent management contract meant that he enjoyed very few financial rewards. Setting up a rival club to Gilley's, called Johnny Lee's, was not a wise career move. He reappeared in 1991 with a country version of Chris De Burgh's 'Lady in Red'.

● ALBUMS: *For Lovers Only* (JMS 1977)★★★, *Lookin' For Love* (Asylum 1980)★★★, *Bet Your Heart On Me* (Full Moon 1981)★★, *Party Time* (Full Moon 1981)★★, *Sounds Like Love* (Full Moon 1982)★★★, *Country Party* (Full Moon 1983)★★★, *Hey Bartender* (Full Moon 1983)★★★, *Till The*

Bars Burn Down (Full Moon 1983)★★★, *Workin' For A Livin'* (1984)★★★, with Willie Nelson *Johnny Lee And Willie Nelson* (Astan 1984)★★★, *Keep Me Hangin' On* (1985)★★★, *New Directions* (Curb 1989)★★.

● COMPILATIONS: *Greatest Hits* (Full Moon 1983)★★★.
● FURTHER READING: *Looking For Love*, Johnny Lee with Randy Wiles.

LEE, ROBIN

b. Robin Lee Irwin, 7 November 1953, Nashville, Tennessee, USA. In spite of early glowing praise for her vocal abilities from some critics, Lee has so far failed to establish herself as a top country singer. Between 1983 and 1988, she charted 13 minor *Billboard* country chart hits, one, 'Paint The Town Blue', being a duet with Lobo. Most were on the Evergreen label, but in 1990, her Atlantic recording of 'Black Velvet' (a song about Elvis Presley that was a 1990 number 1 hit for Alannah Myles), peaked at number 10. However, she failed to maintain that standard and by the mid-90s she had only managed three more minor chart entries, the last, 'Nothin' But You', a modest number 51 in 1991.

● ALBUMS: *Evergreen* (Atlantic 1986)★★★, *Black Velvet* (Atlantic 1990)★★★, *Heart On A Chain* (Atlantic 1991)★★, *This Old Flame* (Atlantic 1994)★★.

LEGARDE TWINS

This popular duo, also on occasions referred to as Australia, comprises identical twins Tom (the eldest by 30 minutes) and Ted Legarde (b. 15 March 1931, Mackay, Queensland, Australia), the youngest members of a family of nine. They were raised on the family farm, both becoming expert horsemen. At the age of 15, clutching an old guitar and influenced by cowboy films and the recordings of Wilf Carter, they left home. They worked on Queensland's largest cattle ranch, took part in cattle drives and rode in rodeos, and they began singing at a Victoria rodeo, when they failed to win any prize money but needed to eat. They joined Buddy Williams' touring rodeo and circus and, at the age of 17, became Australia's youngest professional rodeo riders. They soon found singing to be less painful than rodeo work and concentrated on it. In 1950, they made their first recordings for Rodeo, but between 1952 and 1957, they had several single releases on Regal Zonophone. In 1954, they toured Australia with their boyhood idol Hopalong Cassidy (William Boyd), but in 1957, they decided to seek success in America. They first played shows in Canada but later hosted their own television series in Los Angeles. Between 1958 and 1963, they relocated to Nashville, where they recorded singles for Dot and Liberty Records and made appearances on the *Grand Ole Opry*, debuting with their own song, 'Cooee Call'. They returned to Australia, where they briefly ran a country show from a Paddington, Sydney theatre, recorded albums for Columbia Records and compered two local country shows. In 1965, they returned to the USA where, under 'Colonel' Tom Parker's management, they worked in Las Vegas and even appeared in television's *Star Trek*. They recorded for numerous labels and in 1978, as the Le Gardes, they achieved a minor hit with 'True Love' (a cover of the 1956 Bing Crosby/Grace Kelly pop hit) on Raindrop. A further minor hit came in 1978, with 'I Can Almost Touch The Feeling' on 4 Star. In 1980, as the Legarde Twins, they achieved a minor hit, 'Daddy's Making Records In Nashville', for Invitation 101. In 1987, they were awarded Hall Of Fame status at Australia's prestigious Tamworth Country Festival and during the 80s, they launched their own Boomerang label and made several appearances in the UK, including at the Wembley Festival. Their last US country chart entry reached number 92, 'Crocodile Man From Walk-About-Creek', in 1988. During the 90s, they have operated their own theatre near Nashville's Music Row.

● ALBUMS: *Ballads Of The Bushland* (Columbia 1964)★★★, *Twincerely Yours* (Columbia 1964)★★★, *Songs Of Slim & Buddy* (Columbia 1964)★★, *Australia Down Under Country Volume 1* (Boomerang 1983)★★★, *Australia - Down Under Country Volume 2* (Boomerang 1984)★★.

LEIGH, RICHARD

b. Virginia, USA. In 1974, immediately following his graduation, the songwriter Richard Leigh went to Nashville. Within a year he had written Crystal Gayle's first country number 1, 'I'll Get Over You', and shortly after that he also wrote her third, 'Don't It Make My Brown Eyes Blue'. He had initially believed that 'Don't It Make My Brown Eyes Blue' would suit Shirley Bassey, but Gayle took the song, for which Leigh won a Grammy, and made it a worldwide hit (it reached number 5 in the UK). Leigh also co-wrote the following country number 1 singles: 'That's The Thing About Love' by Don Williams (co-written with Gary Nicholson), 'Put Your Dreams Away' by Mickey Gilley (co-written with Wayland Holyfield) and 'Life's Highway' by Steve Wariner (co-written with Roger Murrah). Other songs he has written include 'The Greatest Man I Never Knew' (Reba McEntire), 'I Wouldn't Have It Any Other Way' (Aaron Tippin), 'It's All I Can Do' (Anne Murray) and 'It Ain't Gonna Worry My Mind' (Ray Charles and Mickey Gilley). He has said of his songwriting talent: 'I work from my own experiences because that makes it possible to put details in and make it believable. Without details, people are tipped off that it's just fiction.'

● ALBUMS: *Richard Leigh* (United Artists 1980)★★.

LEWIS, BOBBY

b. 9 May 1946, Hodgenville, Hardin County, Kentucky, USA. Lewis, who comes from the birthplace of Abraham Lincoln, began to play the guitar at the age of nine and made his television debut at 13. He joined *The Old Kentucky Barn Dance* on WHAS Louisville, where he also appeared on the CBS-networked *Saturday Night Country Style*, before joining the WHAS-TV weekly *Hayloft Hoedown*. Being only 5 feet 4 inches tall, he found his Gibson J-200 guitar heavy and cumbersome and took to playing a lute (he had bought the instrument under the inital impression that it was a strange-shaped, but much lighter, guitar when he saw it in a music shop window). After stringing it with steel guitar strings, he began to use it in his act. He is, in all probability, the first and only person in country music to use a lute as his main instrument. Influenced and helped by Ernest Tubb, he moved to Nashville in 1964 and recorded for United Artists. In 1966, he gained his first US country chart entry with 'How Long Has It Been?', which peaked at number 6. Further Top 20 country hits included 'Love Me And Make It All Better', 'From Heaven To Heartache' and in 1970, his version of 'Hello Mary Lou' (a pop hit for Rick Nelson in 1961). He guested on the *Grand Ole Opry*, played venues all across the

USA and made tours to both Europe and the Far East. After 1973, he recorded for various labels and achieved some minor chart entries, the best being 'Too Many Memories', a number 21 country hit in 1973. His last chart entry came in 1985, with a song called 'Love Is An Overload', after which he seems to have disappeared from the music scene.

● ALBUMS: *Tossin' And Turnin'* (Beltone 1961)★★★, *Little Man With A Big Heart* (United Artists 1966)★★, *How Long Has It Been* (United Artists 1967)★★, *A World Of Love* (United Artists 1967)★★★, *An Ordinary Miracle* (United Artists 1968)★★★, *From Heaven To Heartache* (United Artists 1969)★★★, *Things For You And I* (United Artists 1969)★★★, *Too Many Memories* (1973)★★★, *Portrait In Love* (1977)★★★, *Soul Full Of Music* (1977)★★.

● COMPILATIONS: *The Best Of Bobby Lewis* (United Artists 1970)★★★.

LEWIS, JERRY LEE

b. 29 September 1935, Ferriday, Louisiana, USA. The 'Killer' is the personification of 50s rock 'n' roll at its best. He is rowdy, raw, rebellious and uncompromising. The outrageous piano-pounder has a voice that exudes excitement and an aura of arrogance that becomes understandable after witnessing the seething hysteria and mass excitement at his concerts. As a southern boy, Lewis was brought up listening to many musical styles in a home where religion was as important as breathing. In 1950, he attended a fundamentalist bible school in Waxahachie, Texas, but was expelled. The clash between the secular and the religious would govern Lewis's life and art for the remainder of his career. He first recorded on the *Louisiana Hayride* in 1954 and decided that Elvis Presley's label, Sun Records, was where he wanted to be. His distinctive version of country star Ray Price's 'Crazy Arms' was his Sun debut, but it was his second single, a revival of Roy Hall's 'Whole Lotta Shakin' Goin' On' in 1957 that shot him to international fame. The record, which was initially banned as obscene, narrowly missed the top of the US chart, went on to hit number 1 on the R&B and country charts and introduced the fair-haired, one-man piano wrecker to a world ready for a good shaking up. He stole the show from many other stars in the film *Jamboree* in which he sang the classic 'Great Balls Of Fire', which became his biggest hit and topped the UK chart and made number 2 in the USA. He kept up the barrage of rowdy and unadulterated rock with the US/UK Top 10 single 'Breathless', which, like its predecessor, had been written by Otis Blackwell.

Problems started for the flamboyant 'god of the glissando' when he arrived in Britain for a tour in 1958, accompanied by his third wife, Myra, who was also his 13-year-old second cousin. The UK media stirred up a hornet's nest and the tour had to be cancelled after only three concerts, even though the majority of the audience loved him. The furore followed Lewis home and support for him in his homeland also waned; he never returned to the Top 20 pop chart in the USA. His last big hit of the 50s was the title song from his film *High School Confidential*, which made the UK Top 20 in 1959 and number 21 in the USA. Despite a continued high standard of output, his records either only made the lower chart rungs or missed altogether. When his version of Ray Charles' 'What'd I Say' hit the UK Top 10 in 1960 (US number 30) it looked like a record revival was on the way, but it was not to be. The fickle general public may have disowned the hard-living, hellraiser, but his hardcore fans remained loyal and his tours were sell-outs during the 60s. He joined Smash Records in 1963 and although the material he recorded with the company was generally unimaginative, there were some excellent live recordings, most notably *The Greatest Live Show On Earth* (1964).

In 1966, Lewis made an unexpected entry into rock music theatre when he was signed to play Iago in Jack Good's *Catch My Soul*, inspired by *Othello*. After a decade playing rock 'n' roll, Lewis decided to concentrate on country material in 1968. He had often featured country songs in his repertoire, so his new policy did not represent an about-face. This changeover was an instant success - country fans welcomed back their prodigal son with open arms. Over the next 13 years Lewis was one of country's top-selling artists and was a main attraction wherever he put on his 'Greatest Show On Earth'. He first appeared at the *Grand Ole Opry* in 1973, playing an unprecedented 50-minute set. He topped the country chart with records such as 'There Must Be More To Love Than This' in 1970, 'Would You Take Another Chance On Me?' in 1971 and a revival of 'Chantilly Lace' a year later. The latter also returned him briefly to the transatlantic Top 40. However, he also kept the rock 'n' roll flag flying by playing revival shows around the world and by always including his old 50s hits in his stage shows. In fact, old fans have always been well catered for - numerous compilations of top-class out-takes and never previously issued tracks from the 50s have regularly been released over the last 20 years. On the personal front, his life has never been short of tragedies, often compounded by his alcohol and drug problems. His family has been equally prone to tragedy. In November 1973, his 19-year-old son, Jerry Lee Jnr., was killed in a road accident following a period of drug abuse and treatment for mental illness. Lewis's own behaviour during the mid-70s was increasingly erratic. He accidentally shot his bass player in the chest - the musician survived and sued him. Late in 1976, Lewis was arrested for waving a gun outside Elvis Presley's Gracelands home. Two years later, Lewis signed to Elektra Records for the appropriately titled *Rockin' My Life Away*. Unfortunately, his association with the company ended with much-publicized lawsuits. In 1981, Lewis was hospitalized and allegedly close to death from a haemorrhaged ulcer. He survived that ordeal and was soon back on the road. In 1982, his fourth wife drowned in a swimming pool. The following year, his fifth wife was found dead at his home following a methodone overdose. The deaths brought fresh scandal to Lewis's troubled life. Meanwhile, the IRS were challenging his earnings from the late 70s in another elongated dispute. A sixth marriage followed, along with more bleeding ulcers and a period in the Betty Ford Clinic for the treatment of a pain-killer addiction. Remarkably, Lewis's body and spirit have remained intact, despite these harrowing experiences. During his career he has released dozens of albums, the most successful being *The Session* in 1973, his sole US Top 40 album, on which many pop names of the period backed him, including Peter Frampton and Rory Gallagher. Lewis was one of the first people inducted into the 'Rock 'n' Roll Hall Of Fame' in 1986. In 1989, a biopic of his early career, *Great Balls Of Fire*, starring Dennis Quaid, brought him briefly back into the public eye. In 1990, a much-awaited UK tour

had to be cancelled when Lewis and his sixth wife failed to show. He moved to Dublin, Eire, to avoid the US taxman, but eventually returned to Memphis. In 1995, he jammed with Bruce Springsteen at the opening of the Rock 'n' Roll Hall Of Fame building in Cleveland. His cousin Mickey Gilley is an accomplished country artist, while another cousin, Jimmy Lee Swaggart, has emerged as one of America's premier television evangelists. Any understanding of the career of Jerry Lee Lewis is inextricably linked with the parallel rise and fall of Swaggart. They were both excellent piano players, but whereas Lewis devoted his energies to the 'devil's music', Swaggart damned rock 'n' roll from the pulpit and played gospel music. Lewis has often described his career as a flight from God, with Swaggart cast in the role of his conscience and indefatigable redeemer. The relationship, however, was more complex than that, and the spirits of these two American institutions were latterly revealed as more complementary than antithetical. When Swaggart was discovered with a prostitute in a motel, the evangelist created a scandal that surpassed even his cousin's series of dramas. Tragedy, scandal and, above all, rock 'n' roll have seldom played such an intrinsic role in one musician's life.

● ALBUMS: *Jerry Lee Lewis* (Sun 1957)★★★★, *Jerry Lee Lewis And His Pumping Piano* (London 1958)★★★, *Jerry Lee's Greatest* (Sun 1961)★★★★, *Rockin' With Jerry Lee Lewis* (Design 1963)★★★, *The Greatest Live Show On Earth* (Smash 1964)★★★, with the Nashville Teens *Live At The Star Club, Hamburg* (Philips 1965)★★, *The Return Of Rock* (Smash 1965)★★★, *Country Songs For City Folks* (Smash 1965)★★★, *Whole Lotta Shakin' Goin' On* (London 1965)★★★★, *Memphis Beat* (Smash 1966)★★★, *By Request - More Greatest Live Show On Earth* (Smash 1966)★★★, *Breathless* (London 1967)★★★, *Soul My Way* (Smash 1967)★★★, *Got You On My Mind* (Fontana 1968)★★★, *Another Time, Another Place* (Mercury 1969)★★★, *She Still Comes Around* (Mercury 1969)★★★, *I'm On Fire* (Mercury 1969)★★★, *Jerry Lee Lewis' Rockin' Rhythm And Blues* (Sun 1969)★★★, with Linda Gail Lewis *Together* (Mercury 1970)★★★, *She Even Woke Me Up To Say Goodbye* (Mercury 1970)★★★, *A Taste Of Country* (Sun 1970)★★★, *There Must Be More To Love Than This* (Mercury 1970)★★★, *Johnny Cash And Jerry Lee Lewis Sing Hank Williams* (Sun 1971)★★★, *Touching Home* (Mercury 1971)★★★, *In Loving Memories* (Mercury 1971)★★★, *Would You Take Another Chance On Me* (Mercury 1972)★★★, *The Killer Rocks On* (Mercury 1972)★★★, *Old Tyme Country Music* (Sun 1972)★★★, with Johnny Cash *Sunday Down South* (Sun 1972)★★, *The Session* (Mercury 1973)★★★, *Live At The International, Las Vegas* (Mercury 1973)★★★, *Great Balls of Fire* (Hallmark 1973)★★★, *Southern Roots* (Mercury 1974)★★★, *Rockin' Up A Storm* (Sun 1974)★★★, *Rockin' And Free* (Sun 1974)★★★, *I'm A Rocker* (Mercury 1975)★★★, *Odd Man In* (Mercury 1975)★★★, *Jerry Lee Lewis* (Elektra 1979)★★★, *Killer Country* (Elektra 1980)★★★, *When Two Worlds Collide* (Elektra 1980)★★★, with Johnny Cash, Carl Perkins *The Survivors* (Columbia 1982)★★★, *My Fingers Do The Talking* (MCA 1983)★★★, *I Am What I Am* (MCA 1984)★★★, with Webb Pierce, Mel Tillis, Faron Young *Four Legends* (1985)★★★, with Johnny Cash, Carl Perkins, Roy Orbison *The Class Of '55* (1986)★★★, *Keep Your Hands Off It* (Zu Zazz 1987)★★★, *Don't Drop It* (Zu Zazz 1988)★★★, *Live In Italy* (Magnum Force 1989)★★, *Great Balls Of Fire!* film

soundtrack (Polydor 1989)★★★, *Rocket* (Instant 1990)★★★, *Live At The Vapors Club* (Ace 1991)★★★, *Young Blood* (Sire/Elektra 1995)★★★, *Jerry Lee Lewis At Hank Cochran's* recorded 1987 (Trend 1996)★★★.
● COMPILATIONS: *Golden Hits* (Smash 1964)★★★★, *Country Music Hall Of Fame Hits Vol. 1* (Smash 1969)★★★★, *Country Music Hall Of Fame Hits Vol. 2* (Smash 1969)★★★★, *Original Golden Hits Vol. 1* (Sun 1969)★★★★, *Original Golden Hits Vol. 2* (Sun 1969)★★★, *The Best Of Jerry Lee Lewis* (Smash 1970)★★★★, *Original Golden Hits Vol. 3* (Sun 1971)★★★, *Monsters* (Sun 1971)★★★, *Rockin' With Jerry Lee Lewis* (Mercury 1972)★★★★, *Fan Club Choice* (Mercury 1974)★★★, *Whole Lotta Shakin' Goin' On* (Hallmark 1974)★★★★, *Good Rockin' Tonight* (Hallmark 1975)★★★, *Jerry Lee Lewis And His Pumping Piano* (Charly 1975)★★★, *Rare Jerry Lee Lewis Vol. 1* (Charly 1975)★★★, *Rare Jerry Lee Lewis Vol. 2* (Charly 1975)★★★, *The Jerry Lee Lewis Collection* (Hallmark 1976)★★★★, *Golden Hits* (Mercury 1976)★★★★, *The Original Jerry Lee Lewis* (Charly 1976)★★★★, *Nuggets* (Charly 1977)★★★★, *Nuggets Vol. 2* (Charly 1977)★★★, *The Essential Jerry Lee Lewis* (Charly 1978)★★★★, *Shakin' Jerry Lee* (Arcade 1978)★★★, *Back To Back* (Mercury 1978)★★★, *Duets* (Sun 1979)★★★, *Jerry Lee Lewis* (Hammer 1979)★★★, *Good Golly Miss Molly* (Bravo 1980)★★★, *Trio Plus* (Sun 1980)★★★, *Jerry Lee's Greatest* (Charly 1981)★★★★, *Killer Country* i (Elektra 1981)★★★★, *Jerry Lee Lewis* (Mercury 1981)★★★, *The Sun Years* 12-LP box set (Sun 1984)★★★★, *18 Original Sun Greatest Hits* (Rhino 1984)★★★★, *Milestones* (Rhino 1985)★★★★, *The Collection* (Deja Vu 1986)★★★★, *The Pumpin' Piano Cat* (Sun 1986)★★★, *Great Balls Of Fire* (Sun 1986)★★★★, *The Wild One* (Sun 1986)★★★, *At The Country Store* (Starblend 1987)★★★, *The Very Best Of Jerry Lee Lewis* (Philips 1987)★★★★, *The Country Sound Of Jerry Lee Lewis* (Pickwick 1988)★★, *The Classic Jerry Lee Lewis* 8-CD box set (Bear Family 1989)★★★★, *The Classic Jerry Lee Lewis* (Ocean 1989)★★★, *Killer's Birthday Cake* (Sun 1989)★★★, *Killer's Rhythm And Blues* (Sun 1989)★★★★, *Killer: The Mercury Years, Volume One, 1963-1968* (Mercury 1989)★★★, *Killer: The Mercury Years, Volume Two, 1969-1972* (Mercury 1989)★★★, *Killer: The Mercury Years, Volume Three, 1973-1977* (Mercury 1989)★★★, *Great Balls Of Fire* (Pickwick 1989)★★, *The EP Collection* (See For Miles 1990)★★★★, *The Jerry Lee Lewis Collection* (Castle 1990)★★★, *The Best Of Jerry Lee Lewis* (Curb 1991)★★★, *Pretty Much Country* (Ace 1992)★★★, *All Killer, No Filler: The Anthology* (Rhino 1993)★★★★, *The Complete Palamino Club Recordings* (1993)★★★, *The EP Collection Vol. 2 ... Plus* (See For Miles 1994)★★★★, *The Locust Years . . . And The Return To The Promised Land* 8-CD box set (Bear Family 1995)★★★★, *Sun Classics* (Charly 1995)★★★★, *Killer Country* ii (Mercury 1995)★★★.
● VIDEOS: *Carl Perkins & Jerry Lee Lewis Live* (BBC Video 1987), *Jerry Lee Lewis* (Fox Video 1989), *I Am What I Am* (Charly Video 1990), *The Killer* (Telstar Video 1991), *Killer Performance* (Virgin Vision 1991), *The Jerry Lee Lewis Show* (MMG Video 1991).
● FURTHER READING: *Jerry Lee Lewis: The Ball Of Fire*, Allan Clark. *Jerry Lee Lewis*, Robert Palmer. *Whole Lotta Shakin' Goin' On: Jerry Lee Lewis*, Robert Cain. *Hellfire: The Jerry Lee Lewis Story*, Nick Tosches. *Great Balls Of Fire: The True Story Of Jerry Lee Lewis*, Myra Lewis. *Rockin' My Life Away: Listening To Jerry Lee Lewis*, Jimmy Guteman. *Killer!*, Jerry Lee Lewis And Charles White.
● FILMS: *Jamboree* aka *Disc Jockey Jamboree* (1957), *Beach Ball* (1964), *Be My Guest* (1965), *American Hot Wax* (1976).

LEWIS, LITTLE ROY

b. 24 February 1942, Lincolnton, Georgia, USA. The youngest member of the popular gospel and bluegrass singing group, the Lewis Family. He played banjo at the age of six and gained his nickname by playing full-time with the family group at the age of nine, when an elder brother, Esley, who usually played the instrument for the group, was called for military service. When Esley returned, he found himself upstaged by his young sibling and happily moved to playing bass until he left the group. In 1954, when the Lewis Family started a long residency on WJBF-TV Augusta, Roy played with them. He subsequently played on all the family's recordings but during the 60s, he also made solo recordings for Starday, the first, in 1962, being an EP release. Over the years, he has also played guitar, bass and autoharp as well as adding vocals to his input to the family show. Lewis has also become very popular for the comedy that he brings to the proceedings, which takes the form of constant chatter, good-natured badinage aimed at the other members and the amusing sound effects he adds to some of the songs. During the 70s and 80s, he may no longer have been little but he remained very much the focal point of the Lewis Family, both live and on record.
● ALBUMS: *Golden Gospel Banjo* (Starday 1962)★★★, *Gospel Banjo* (Canaan 1972)★★★, *The Entertainer* (Canaan 1977)★★★, *Super Pickin'* (Canaan 1981)★★, *In The Heart Of Dixie* (Canaan 1984)★★.
● COMPILATIONS: *The Best Of Little Roy Lewis* (Canaan 1985)★★★.

LEWIS, TEXAS JIM

b. James Lewis Jnr., 15 October 1909, Meigs, Georgia, USA, d. 23 January 1990. His mother died when he was five and his father remarried and raised two more children. In 1919, the family relocated to Fort Myers, Florida, where Lewis stayed until 1928, when he relocated to Texas. Here, he began singing and also acquired his nickname. By 1930, the family were in Detroit and he returned home and played local bars with 14-year-old Jack Rivers (in reality his half-brother Rivers Lewis). In 1932, he returned to Texas where, until 1934, he played with the Swift Jewel Cowboys in Houston. Returning to Detroit, he joined Jack West's Circle Star Cowboys and also worked on WJR. He then formed his own Lone Star Cowboys, which included Jack Rivers and Smokey Rogers, and moved to New York, where they remained for five years. With a repertoire of western swing and popular numbers, they played a residency at the Village Barn, various theatres and clubs and made regular radio appearances. They recorded for Vocalion Records and between August 1940 and February 1944 cut almost 40 sides for Decca Records. They ranged from the gentle 'Molly Darling', to the comedy of 'When There's Tears In The Eye Of A Potato (Then I'll Be Crying For You)'. They also recorded numerous transcription discs and toured as far as California. Lewis became noted for the strange musical instrument that he called Hootenanny. It consisted of washboards, motor horns, cowbells, sirens and guns that actually

fired. When Lewis was drafted in 1942, Spade Cooley became leader of the band. When he returned to the music in 1944, he formed a new band, opened a club and toured until 1950, when he relocated to Seattle. Here he presented a radio show and then established his *Rainier Ranch* and his very popular *Sheriff Tex's Safety Junction* children's show on KING-TV, which lasted for seven years. He also appeared on Canadian television with the programme. Most of his recordings at this time were children's records. After his children's show ended, he continued to play around the Seattle clubs and over the years, he has been afforded many tributes for his dedicated work in promoting western swing music. He appeared in several films including *Badmen From Red Butte* (1940), *Pardon My Gun* (1942), *Law Of The Canyon* and *The Stranger From Ponca City* (both 1947). He also successfully recorded 'Squaws Along The Yukon', several years before the Hank Thompson version and had a number 3 US country hit, 'Too Late To Worry Too Blue To Cry', on Decca Records, in 1944. Although few of his recordings are available on US labels, in the 80s Cattle Records of Germany issued several albums of his early work and also one, *Just Plain Old Ordinary Me* (1985), by Jack Rivers.
● COMPILATIONS: *Texas Jim Lewis & His Lone Star Cowboys Volume 1 & 2* (Cattle 1981)★★★, *Squaws Along The Yukon* (Cattle 1985)★★★, *Rootin' Tootin, Hootenanny* (Cattle 1985)★★★ *The King Of North Western Swing* (Cattle 1985)★★★.

LIGHT CRUST DOUGHBOYS

A western swing group that originally featured Bob Wills (fiddle), Herman Arnspiger (guitar) and Milton Brown (vocals), who were then performing as the Aladdin Laddies (sponsored by the Aladdin Mantle Lamp Company) on WBAP Fort Worth, Texas. When Burrus Mill and Elevator Company, the makers of Light Crust flour, sponsored a show on KFJZ in 1931, their general manager Wilbert Lee O'Daniel decided to use them for his show. During their first broadcast for the new sponsors, after originally being named the Fort Worth Doughboys, the station announcer referred to them as the Light Crust Doughboys. The public wrote in for more, although the group did not get paid. O'Daniel actually sacked them two weeks later, claiming to dislike 'their hillbilly music'. The station continued to use them without a sponsor and O'Daniel relented, later appearing on the programme himself. Arnspiger had left (being replaced by Sleepy Johnson) and Brown's brother Durwood had joined, when the group made their first recordings for Victor on 9 February 1932. In 1932, Milton Brown left to follow a very successful career with his own swing band, the Musical Brownies, until his death in a car crash in 1936. In 1933, Wills, after an acrimonious association with O'Daniel, left to form his famed Texas Playboys. The Doughboys, although undergoing many changes of personnel, remained with Burrus Mills until 1942 and made many popular recordings. After a short spell as the Coffee Grinders (due to sponsorship by Duncan Coffee) and without Burrus Mill's sponsorship, they once again became the Light Crust Doughboys. Throughout the 50s and 60s, they worked on radio and television, played live shows and recorded for several labels.
● ALBUMS: *The Light Crust Doughboys* (Audio Lab 1959)★★★.
● COMPILATIONS: *String Band Swing Volumes 1 & 2*

(Longhorn 1981)★★★, *We're The Light Crust Doughboys From Burrus Mills*, *The Light Crust Doughboys Original Hit Songs*, *The Light Crust Doughboys 1936-1939* (Texas Rose 1982)★★★, *Live 1936* (Jambalaya 1990)★★★.

LILLY BROTHERS

Mitchell B. Lilly (b. 15 December 1921) and Charles Everett Lilly (b. 1 July 1923) were both born at Clear Creek, near Beckley, West Virginia, USA. Always known as Bea and Everett, the two brothers began performing in the mid-30s, being especially influenced by Bill Monroe and the Blue Sky Boys. In the late 30s, using mandolin and guitar to back their high harmony vocals, they began their professional career. In 1939, they played the *Old Farm Hour*, at the radio station WCHS Charleston, as the Lonesome Holler Boys. They sometimes played three radio shows a day as well as evening dances, and in late 1939 and 1940, they were a very popular act on WJLS Beckley. When America became involved in World War II, Everett joined the armed forces. In 1945, they played with Molly O'Day at Beckley and also at KRLD Dallas and WNOX Knoxville. They next formed the Smiling Mountain Boys, which included Paul Taylor, Burk Barbour (fiddle) and Lonnie Glosson (harmonica), but surprisingly, they refused the opportunity to record for the King label. Between 1948 and 1950, they were a featured duet with Red Belcher And His Kentucky Ridge Runners and played WWVA Wheeling with him. The brothers split up in 1950 when Everett joined Lester Flatt and Earl Scruggs, playing mandolin and taking tenor vocals. In 1951, he appeared on the classic Flatt and Scruggs Columbia recordings of such numbers as 'Somehow Tonight', 'Tis Sweet To Be Remembered' and 'Over The Hills To The Poorhouse' (he was the only sideman of their band to receive a billing on a record label). Late in 1952, the brothers reunited and relocated to Boston, where with Don Stover (banjo) and Tex Logan (fiddle), and initially calling themselves the Confederate Mountaineers, they played local radio, television and clubs for several years until for a short time in 1958. Everett again joined Flatt And Scruggs. In 1959, the Lillys and Stover began to play at Boston's *Hillbilly Ranch*, where they stayed for approximately 16 years. In 1960, they were recorded live at this venue by Robert Tainaka and a tape of their act gained album release in Japan, with the result that the Lilly Brothers became the most popular act of its kind in that country. Everett Lilly retired, heartbroken, back to West Virginia following the death in a car crash of his son, Giles, in 1970. Bea stayed in Boston and Stover went on to form his own band. In 1973, the brothers and Stover were persuaded to re-form and not only recorded an album for the County label but actually made two tours of Japan. Their success was described as 'nothing less than phenomenal' and the live recording of one concert resulted in the release of three albums. Everett later worked for a Japanese company and arranged further tours for American bluegrass groups to tour Japan. They continued to play their mountain, folk and old-time music on occasions at folk festivals and colleges. In 1979, they featured as the subjects of an educational film, *True Facts In A Country Song*. There were many brother harmony acts in West Virginia but only the Lillys, along with the Bailes Brothers, really gained a reputation of any significance outside their own state.
● ALBUMS: with Don Stover *Live At Hillbilly Ranch*

(1960)★★, with Stover *Folk Songs Of The Southern Mountains* (Folkways 1961)★★★ *Bluegrass Breakdown* (Folkways 1963)★★★★ *Country Songs Of The Lilly Brothers* (Folkways 1964)★★★ with Stover *Early Recordings* (Rebel 1971)★★★, *What Will I Leave Behind* (County 1973)★★★, *Holiday In Japan (Volumes 1-3)* (1973)★★.

LINDE, DENNIS

b. 13 March 1943, Abilene, Texas, USA. Dennis Linde (pronounced Lin-dy) played in a group called the Starlighters in the 60s and by the 70s he occasionally played bass guitar on Elvis Presley's recordings. His song 'Burning Love' was originally recorded by Arthur Alexander, but became a worldwide hit for Presley, who also recorded Linde's ballad 'For The Heart'. Linde has played in Kris Kristofferson's band and produced his album *Jesus Was A Capricorn*. Kristofferson said about him, 'Dennis Linde may be a genius, he certainly is weird, possibly the most creative and prolific songwriter in the business.' He wrote several songs for Roy Orbison's *Regeneration* and his compositions include 'Long Long Texas Road' (Roy Drusky), 'The Love She Found In Me' (Gary Morris), 'Vanessa' (Shakin' Stevens), 'Walkin' A Broken Heart' (Don Williams) and 'Cast Iron Heart' (Blackhawk). He wrote US country number 1 hits for Eddy Raven, 'I'm Gonna Get You' and 'In A Letter To You'; when Raven heard 'In A Letter To You', he told the publishers that it sounded like Don Williams' 'Then It's Love' - it transpired that Linde had written that song too. From time to time he makes his own records, including the 1973 single 'Hello, I Am Your Heart'.
● ALBUMS: *Linde Manor* (Intrepid 1968)★★★, *Dennis Linde* (Elektra 1973)★★★, *Trapped In The Suburbs* (Elektra 1974)★★★, *Surface Noise* (Monument 1976)★★★, *Under The Eye* (Monument 1977)★★★.

LINDSAY, REG

b. 7 July 1930, Parkes, New South Wales, Australia. The family's ancestors had arrived from the UK to seek gold but found only hard work, which led ultimately to the boy growing up in an inland farming area known as the Golden West. He learned to play fiddle and mandolin from his father and is reputed to have played 'The Wheel Of The Wagon Is Broken' on the harmonica at the age of four. He developed a great interest in country music from the recordings of such singers as Wilf Carter and Tex Morton. The family relocated to Adelaide but whenever possible, Lindsay spent his free time out of town, working on farms and learning the life of a cowboy. During this time, he mastered the banjo and guitar and worked hard on his singing and yodelling. After leaving school, he worked in the shearing sheds and as a fencing contractor before being hurt in a rodeo accident. In 1951, while confined to bed recuperating, he heard of a major talent show being held in Sydney that was organized by top country singer Tim McNamara. He made the long trip to Sydney and, singing 'Streamlined Yodel Song', won the contest, pushing Shorty Ranger into second place. The prize was a recording contract with Rodeo Records, but the win also led to demands for personal appearances and considerable radio work. Throughout the 50s and 60s, he had popular radio shows on major Australian stations including 2CH, 2SM and 2KY. In the mid-60s, he also added television work to his busy schedule, which included touring with his own show. In 1954, he married Heather McKean (Slim

Dusty's sister-in-law) and worked some tours with his brother-in-law (the marriage produced three daughters but the couple later divorced). The same year, Lindsay was booked to accompany his idol, Wilf Carter, on his Australasian tour and when (after a week) Carter was forced through throat problems to quit, Lindsay continued the tour with his own show. He proved so popular that the 'tour' went on for over five years. In 1968, he made his first visit to the USA, where he appeared on the *Grand Ole Opry*. A later appearance saw him become the first Australian country artist to play the networked Saturday Night *Opry* segment. He has since made many trips to the USA and has made several recordings in Nashville and even worked on record production there. Over the years, he has released a steady stream of records, on EMI (after Rodeo) until the late 60s, then the Festival label, another spell with EMI, and subsequently the Seven label, which led to his recordings being released in America on Con Brio. He is probably the first Australian artist to use an electric lead guitar and he even used a didgeridoo on records (on 'Walkabout Rock 'n' Roll'). His many recordings have included rockabilly, bluegrass, boogie and on occasions, he has used orchestral backings. Though rated by many to be one of the best exponents around, he dropped the yodel during the late 50s, citing overkill of the technique, but in more recent times, he has used it again to great effect. In a career now lasting over four decades, he has become one of Australia's most popular and versatile entertainers. He has won many awards, including being made an honorary citizen of Tennessee for his promotion of country music worldwide. He also starred on the first ever country music show at the Sydney Opera House. In 1984, he became the ninth artist to be elected to the Country Music Roll Of Renown (Australia's equivalent to Nashville's Country Music Hall Of Fame). Surprisingly, although he is a major star in his own hemisphere and well known in the USA, he is still relatively unknown in the UK and Europe, except to the devout band of followers of Australian country music.
● ALBUMS: *Country Music Comes To Town* (EMI 1961)★★★★, *Reg Lindsay Favourites* (EMI 1962)★★★, *Country And Western Singalong* (EMI 1963)★★★, *Songs For Country Folk* (EMI 1964)★★★, *Another Country And Western Singalong* (EMI 1964)★★★, *Reg Lindsay Encores* (EMI 1964)★★★, *Reg Lindsay's National Country & Western Hour* (Festival 1965)★★★, *Country & Western Million Sellers* (Festival 1966)★★★, *Glory Land Way* (Festival 1967)★★★, with Heather McKean *Country Duets From Reg And Heather* (Festival 1968)★★★, *TV Requests* (Festival 60s)★★★, *Roadside Mail Box* (Festival 60s)★★★, *Reg Lindsay On Tour* (Festival 60s)★★, *Australia's Country Music Man* (Festival 60s)★★★★, *Hot Shot Country* (Festival 60s)★★★, *She Taught Me To Yodel* (Festival 1970)★★★, *Armstrong* (Festival 1970)★★★, *Out On The Lone Prairie* (Columbia 70s)★★★★, *Country & Western Greats* (WRC 1972)★★★, *Country Music Jamboree* (Summit 1973)★★★, *Australia's King Of The Road* (Summit 1973)★★★, *21st Anniversary Album* (Festival 1973)★★★, *Country Favourites* (Summit 1974)★★★, *Country Classics* (Summit 1974)★★★, *Reg Lindsay* (Festival 1974)★★★, *Country And Western Greats* (Calendar 1974)★★★, *Reg Lindsay In Nashville* (Festival 1975)★★★, *The Travellin' Man* (Festival 1976)★★★, *Silence On The Line* (EMI 1977)★★★, *Play Me A Simple Song* (EMI 1978)★★★,

The World Of Rodeo (EMI 1978)★★★, *Some Of The Best* (EMI 1978)★★★, *Standing Tall* (Brook 1979)★★★, *Ten Ten Two And A Quarter* (Brook 1980)★★★, *If You Could See Me Now* (Telmak 1981)★★★, *Will The Real Reg Lindsay* (Powderworks 1982)★★, *I've Always Wanted To Do That* (RCA 1985)★★★, *Lifetime Of Country Music* (Hammard 1987)★★★.
● COMPILATIONS: *20 Golden Country Greats* (Festival 1965)★★★★, *Classics* (EMI 1981)★★★★

LINDSEY, JUDY

b. Austin, Texas, USA. The country singer Judy Lindsey attended North Texas State University and then took a job at the Bauder Fashion College where she taught modelling and psychology. She had her own modelling career and took part in a long-running campaign for Dodge cars. She wanted to be a singer and when she met Johnny Carroll in 1977, she encouraged Carroll to start performing again; they formed the Judy And Johnny Band, which had a residency at the Hilton Hotel in Fort Worth. By 1983, Lindsey had added Wanda Jackson's rock 'n' roll hits to her repertoire, which proved popular with audiences. She released 'Fujiyama Mama' as a single and as time went on, she recorded more and more on her own. She had a minor hit in 1989 with 'Wrong Train'.

LINDSEY, LaWANDA

b. 12 January 1953, Tampa, Florida, USA. Lindsey's family moved to Savannah, Georgia, soon after her birth; her father was the manager of a local country music radio station and played on air with his group the Dixie Showboys. From the age of five, Lindsey was featured with the band. Conway Twitty was impressed by her talent and, through his help, she signed with Chart Records in 1967. Her first singles included 'Beggars Can't Be Choosers', 'Wave Bye Bye To The Man' and two duets with Kenny Vernon, 'Eye To Eye' and 'Pickin' Wild Mountain Berries', which was her biggest-selling record. In 1970, she had a solo hit on the US country charts with 'Partly Bill'. Although she continued to record and had several minor successes, she did not manage to establish herself as an adult country artist.
● ALBUMS: *Swingin' And Singin' My Songs* (Chart 1969)★★★, *We'll Sing In The Sunshine* (Chart 1970)★★★, with Kenny Vernon *Pickin' Wild Mountain Berries* (Chart 1970)★★★, *This Is LaWanda Lindsey* (Capitol 1974)★★.
● COMPILATIONS: *Greatest Hits* (Chart 1971)★★★.

LITTLE TEXAS

Following their 1992 debut album, *First Time For Everything*, Little Texas emerged as one of America's biggest 'new country' phenomena. The band comprised Tim Rushlow (vocals), Del Gray (drums), Porter Howell (guitar, bass), Duane Propes (bass, backing vocals), Jeff Huskins and Brady Seals (keyboards, guitar, backing vocals), and they were rewarded soon after their debut with the American Country Music award for Top Vocal Group. With sales of the album achieving gold status, Little Texas toured the USA with artists including Travis Tritt and Trisha Yearwood. *First Time For Everything* produced a run of successful singles, as did its follow-up, *Big Time*, whose sales figures would reach platinum status. They promptly recorded a third set, *Kick A Little* (their first to be released outside the USA), which contained more strong material including 'Your Days Are

Numbered', 'A Night I'll Never Remember' and 'Southern Grace'. The band's self-titled fourth album was released in 1996, but poor sales and diverging interests led to their split the following year.
● ALBUMS: *First Time For Everything* (Warners 1992)★★★, *Big Time* (Warners 1993)★★★, *Kick A Little* (Warners 1994)★★★, *Little Texas* (Warners 1996)★★.
● COMPILATIONS: *Greatest Hits* (Warners 1995)★★★.
● VIDEOS: *Kick A Little* (Warner Reprise 1994), *Greatest Hits* (Warner Reprise 1995)

LIVINGSTONE, JOHN GRAEME

b. 21 February 1951, Nelson, Lancashire, England. Livingstone is a singer-songwriter mostly working around his home in the Lake District. 'Wings Of Fire' was a powerful single, influenced by his love of John Stewart. 'Ship Of The Sky' is about the courage of the Archbishop of Canterbury's envoy, Terry Waite. A new album, *Innocent Bystander*, featuring Wes McGhee and Cathryn Craig, is set for release in 1997. He has also completed a series of songs about soldiers fighting Napoleon's forces in Spain, 'Just A Little War'. Livingstone owns Stillwater Records and Fair Oaks Entertainer. He has brought singer-songwriter Dave Mallett and Don-Oja Dunaway to the UK as well as promoting concerts by Bill Zorn, now with the Limeliters.
● ALBUMS: *House Full Of Strangers* (Stillwater 1988)★★★.

LOCKLIN, HANK

b. Lawrence Hankins Locklin, 15 February 1918, McLellan, Florida, USA. A farm boy, Locklin worked in the cottonfields as a child and on the roads during the Depression of the 30s. He learned to play the guitar at the age of 10 and was soon performing on local radio and at dances. His professional career started in 1938 and after an interruption for military service, he worked various local radio stations, including WALA Mobile and KLEE Houston. In 1949, he joined the *Louisiana Hayride* on KWKH Shreveport and achieved his first country chart entry with his Four Star recording of his self-penned 'The Same Sweet One'. In 1953, 'Let Me Be The One' became his first country number 1. After moving to RCA Records in the mid-50s, he had Top 10 US country hits with 'Geisha Girl', his own 'Send Me The Pillow You Dream On', both also making the US pop charts, and 'It's A Little More Like Heaven'. His biggest chart success came in 1960, when his million-selling recording of 'Please Help Me I'm Falling' topped the US country charts for 14 successive weeks and also reached number 8 in the pop charts. It also became one of the first modern country songs to make the British pop charts, peaking at number 9 in a 19-week chart stay. (An answer version by Skeeter Davis called '(I Can't Help You) I'm Falling Too' also became a US country and pop hit the same year.) Locklin became a member of the *Grand Ole Opry* in 1960 and during the next decade, his fine tenor voice and ability to handle country material saw him become one of the most popular country artists. He registered over 20 US chart entries including 'We're Gonna Go Fishing' and a number 8 hit with what is now a country standard, 'The Country Hall Of Fame', in 1967. He hosted his own television series in Houston and Dallas in the 1970s and during his career has toured extensively in the USA, Canada and in Europe. He is particularly popular in Ireland, where he has toured many times, and in 1964, he recorded an album of Irish songs. Although a popular artist in Nashville, he always resisted settling there. In the early 60s, he returned to his native Florida and built his home, the Singing L, on the same cottonfield where he had once worked as a boy. After becoming interested in local affairs, his popularity saw him elected mayor of his home-town of McLellan. Although Locklin's last chart success was a minor hit in 1971, he remained a firm favourite with the fans and still regularly appeared on the *Opry*. He is now retired from the music business.

● ALBUMS: *Foreign Love* (RCA Victor 1958)★★★, *Please Help Me I'm Falling* (RCA Victor 1960)★★★, *Encores* (King 1961)★★, *Hank Locklin* (Wrangler 1962)★★, *10 Songs* (Design 1962)★★, *A Tribute To Roy Acuff, The King Of Country Music* (RCA Victor 1962)★★★, *This Song Is Just For You* (Camden 1963)★★★, *The Ways Of Life* (RCA Victor 1963)★★★, *Happy Journey* (RCA Victor 1964)★★★, *Irish Songs, Country Style* (RCA Victor 1964)★★★, *Hank Locklin Sings Hank Williams* (RCA Victor 1964)★★★, *Born To Ramble* (Hilltop 1965)★★★, *My Kind Of Country Music* (Camden 1965)★★★, *Down Texas Way* (Metro 1965)★★★, *Hank Locklin Sings Eddy Arnold* (RCA Victor 1965)★★★, *Once Over Lightly* (RCA Victor 1965)★★★, with the Jordanaires *The Girls Get Prettier* (RCA Victor 1966)★★★, *The Gloryland Way* (RCA Victor 1966)★★★, *Bummin' Around* (Camden 1967)★★, *Send Me The Pillow You Dream On* (RCA Victor 1967)★★★, *Sings Hank Locklin* (1967)★★★, *Nashville Women* (RCA Victor 1967)★★★, *Queen Of Hearts* (Hilltop 1968)★★★, *My Love Song For You* (RCA Victor 1968)★★★, *Softly - Hank Locklin* (RCA Victor 1969)★★★, *That's How Much I Love You* (Camden 1969)★★★, *Wabash Cannonball* (Camden 1969)★★★, *Best Of Today's Country Hits* (RCA Victor 1969)★★★, *Lookin' Back* (RCA Victor 1969)★★★, *Bless Her Heart - I Love Her* (RCA Victor 1970)★★, *Candy Kisses* (Camden 1970)★★★, *Hank Locklin & Danny Davis & The Nashville Brass* (RCA Victor 1970)★★, *The Mayor Of McLellan, Florida* (RCA Victor 1972)★★★, *There Never Was A Time* (1977)★★★, with various artists *Carol Channing & Her Country Friends* (1977)★★, *All Kinds Of Everything* (Topspin 1979)★★★, *Please Help Me I'm Falling* (Topline 1986)★★★.

● COMPILATIONS: *The Best Of Hank Locklin* (King 1961)★★, *The Best Of Hank Locklin* (RCA Victor 1966)★★★, *Country Hall Of Fame* (RCA Victor 1968)★★★★, *The First Fifteen Years* (RCA Victor 1971)★★★, *Famous Country Music Makers* (RCA 1975)★★, *The Golden Hits* (1977)★★★, *The Best Of Hank Locklin* (RCA 1979)★★★, *20 Of The Best* (RCA 1982)★★★, *Please Help Me I'm Falling* 4-CD box set (Bear Family 1995)★★★★, *Send Me The Pillow That You Dream On* 3-CD box set (Bear Family 1997)★★★★.

LOGAN, JOSH

b. Richmond, Kentucky, USA. One of the New Country's hat brigade with a difference - his hat is of the Humphrey Bogart variety. Logan's favourite country performer was Mel Street and his own vocals were very close to the latter's. He had the misfortune of having his single, 'I Made You A Woman For Somebody Else', covered by Conway Twitty, and thereby lost any possible success. He eventually made the US charts with 'Everytime I Get To Dreamin''. His debut album included Street's 'Easy Lovin'' Kind' and the good-natured 'Somebody Paints The Wall': 'Everytime I make my mark, somebody paints the wall.' There was an excellent cover by George

Jones under the title, 'Somebody Always Paints The Wall', but Logan disappeared for several years before bouncing back with 1996's *Something Strange*.

● ALBUMS: *Somebody Paints The Wall* (Curb 1989)★★★, *Something Strange* (Bob Grady 1996)★★★.

LOGSDON, JIMMY

b. James Lloyd Logsdon, 1 April 1922, Panther, Kentucky, USA. The son of a Methodist minister, he began singing in his father's church choir at the age of 12 and first played clarinet at school before changing to guitar. Between 1944 and 1946, he served in the Air Force and on release opened a record shop in LeGrange, Kentucky. By 1948, he was performing locally and received a break in 1950, when he won his own 15-minute country radio show, first on WLOU but later on WINN Louisville. In October 1952, Decca Records heard him singing on his own show and signed him to the label. He was also helped by his friendship with Hank Williams, by whom he was greatly influenced (at times his style was very similar) and with whom he toured in 1952. In January 1953, his double-side tribute release, 'The Death Of Hank Williams' and 'Hank Williams Sings The Blues No More', gained him considerable acclaim, although it failed to make the national country charts. Soon afterwards, together with his band, the Golden Harvest Boys, he began his live *Country & Western Music Show* on WHAS-TV, as well as maintaining a country radio show on WKLO. During the late 50s, after three further Decca singles, he also recorded singles for Dot and Starday and two more rockabilly-type numbers as Jimmy Lloyd for Roulette. In the early 60s, he appeared on various major NBC and CBS radio shows, the *Louisiana Hayride* and the *Grand Ole Opry*. In July 1962, Logsdon was chosen to replace Wayne Raney as the presenter on WCKY Cincinnati's major night-time country music show and that same year, he recorded an album for the King label. In the late 60s, he presented major shows on WTVF Mobile and WCLU Louisville. He remained fairly active as a performer and as a radio presenter on various stations until around 1976, when he took up a post with the Kentucky Labour Department. During his career, he wrote many songs, some of which were recorded by other artists including Johnny Horton, Carl Perkins and even Woody Herman, who recorded Logsdon's 'No True Love'.

● ALBUMS: *Howdy Neighbors* (King 1963)★★★, *Doin' It Hank's Way* (Castle 1980)★★★.

● COMPILATIONS *I Got A Rocket In My Pocket* (Bear Family 1993)★★★★.

LONE PINE, HAL, AND BETTY CODY

Harold John Breau (b. 5 June 1916, Pea Cove, Maine, USA, d. 26 March 1977; guitar, vocals) and Rita M. Coté (b. 17 August 1921, Sherbrooke, Quebec, Canada; guitar, vocals). In the mid-30s, Breau sang on radio in his native state and became the leader of the Lone Pine Mountaineers. He first met Coté in 1938, after her family had relocated to Aubourn, Maine, where, greatly influenced by Patsy Montana, she started her singing career as the vocalist with Curly And The Country Boys on WCOU Lewiston. They were married in June 1940 and changing her name from the French to the English spelling, they worked together for over 10 years with the Lone Pine Mountaineers, on radio and shows in the New England area and over the border to Canada's Maritime

Provinces. In the early 50s, they recorded both solo and duet numbers for RCA Records, achieving particular success with their duets 'It's Goodbye And So Long To You' and 'Trail Of The Lonesome Pine'. In 1953, Cody's 'Tom Tom Yodel' was a Canadian hit, while 'I Found Out More Than You Ever Knew' reached number 10 in the US country chart (the song was the 'answer' version of the Davis Sisters' hit 'I Forgot More Than You'll Ever Know'). In June 1953, the couple became regulars on the *Wheeling Jamboree*, where they remained for several years. After relocating to Manitoba in the late 50s, they divorced. Breau, usually only known then as Hal Lone Pine, later recorded for Arc Records, including duets with Jean Ward. He returned to Maine, where he remarried and continued to play in the area where he had started his career years earlier, until his death in 1977. Cody retired for a time to look after her family, but in the early 70s, she toured with Dick Curless and between 1972 and 1982, played a residency. She eventually returned to Lisbon Falls, Maine, where she made occasional appearances with her son, Dennis. The Breaus' eldest son, Leonard, became the jazz guitarist Lenny Breau, who was murdered in 1984. Lone Pine is remembered as the writer of two popular Canadian country songs, 'When It's Apple Blossom Time In Annapolis Valley' and 'Prince Edward Island Is Heaven To Me', both of which have been recorded by many artists, including Wilf Carter and George Hamilton IV. In the 80s, Cattle Records of Germany released albums of their recordings.

● ALBUMS: *Lone Pine & His Mountaineers* (RCA 60s)★★★, *Hal Lone Pine* (Arc 60s)★★★, *More Show Stoppers* (Arc 60s)★★, *Songs Everyone Remembers* (Arc 60s)★★, *Coast Of Maine* (Arc 60s)★★★, *Betty Cody Sings Again* (1979)★★★, *Hal Lone Pine & His Mountaineers* i (Cattle 1979)★★★, *Betty Cody's Country Souvenir Album* (Cattle 1985)★★★, *Duets & Memories* (Elmwood Station 1992)★★★, *Hal Lone Pine & His Mountaineers* ii (Castle 1995)★★★.

LONESOME PINE FIDDLERS

This noted early bluegrass band, whose input did much to help popularize the music, was initially formed at WHIS Bluefield, West Virginia, in 1938, by Ezra Cline (b. 13 January 1907, Baisden, West Virginia, USA, d. 11 July 1984; bass fiddle, vocals) and his cousins/brothers-in-law, Curly Ray Cline and Ned Cline and Gordon Jennings (singer, guitarist). World War II hindered the band's career and Ned Cline, serving in the US Army, died in the Normandy landings. When the band re-formed at WHIS, Charlie Cline joined his relatives. In 1949, Charlie and Curly Ray both left, although the latter rejoined in 1951. The early 50s saw various personnel changes, and among contributing musicians were Ray Morgan, Bob Osborne, Larry Richardson, Jimmy and Paul Williams and Ray and Melvin Goins. In 1952, the band relocated, first to WOAY Oak Hill, then WJR Detroit, but in 1953, they moved to WLSI Pikeville, where they played daily radio shows for several years. In the late 50s, other musicians who played with the band included James Carson, Billy Edwards and Udell McPeak. In 1957, the band was comprised of Ezra, Curly Ray, Charlie and his wife Lee, and for two years, they varied their output, even electrifying some instruments. They played a regular television show on WSAZ Huntington, and in 1961, also WCYB Bristol, Virginia. Ezra, Curly Ray and the Goins brothers eventually returned to their normal bluegrass style and even recorded with Hylo

Brown. In 1964, the Fiddlers ceased full-time playing but a unit consisting of Ezra (bass), Curly Ray (fiddle), Lowell Verney (banjo) and Landon Messer (guitar) played bluegrass shows, until Curly Ray left to join the Stanley Brothers, after which the Fiddlers basically ceased to exist. Over the years, they recorded for several labels including Cozy, RCA/Victor and Starday. Ezra continued to run his Pikeville restaurant for a time but eventually retired to Gilbert, West Virginia, where he made some appearances at purely local events, before he died on 11 July 1984. There is little doubt that the Lonesome Pine Fiddlers made a major contribution to bluegrass music. It has even been suggested that the only reason that they are not ranked with Bill Monroe and other bluegrass legends is because, for some reason, Ezra refused the opportunity for the band to star in the *Martha White Flour* segment on the *Grand Ole Opry*, on WSM Nashville. The programme was then offered to Flatt And Scruggs. In 1988, Curly Ray, Charlie and Ray and Melvin Goins recorded a reunion album on which Curly Ray's son, Timmy, took Ezra's place. In 1992 Bear Family Records issued a CD containing all of the Cozy and RCA masters.

● ALBUMS: *The Lonesome Pine Fiddlers* (Starday 1961)★★★, *14 Mountain Songs With 5-String Banjo* (Starday 1962)★★★, *Bluegrass* (Starday 1962)★★★, *More Bluegrass* (Starday 1963)★★★, *Hylo Brown Meets The Lonesome Pine Fiddlers* (Starday 1963)★★★, *Kentucky Bluegrass* (Nashville 1966)★★★, *Bluegrass Music '52 & '53* (London 1969)★★★, *Lonesome Pine Fiddlers Reunion* (Riverside 1988)★★★. As Charlie Cline And The Lonesome Pine Fiddlers: with Lee Cline *Shalom (Peace)* (Atteiram 1977)★★★, *Bluegrass Gospel* (Shiloh 1977)★★★, *Lonesome Pines* (Old Homestead 1978)★★★, *Strictly Cline* (Atteiram 1978)★★★, *Why Ray Ralph* (Old Homestead 1979)★★★, *Brushy Creek Bluegrass* (Old Homestead 1981)★★★, *Sunset Is Coming* (Old Homestead 1983)★★★.

● COMPILATIONS: *The Best Of The Lonesome Pine Fiddlers* (London 1971)★★★, *Lonesome Pine Fiddlers* (Collectors Classic 1974)★★★, *Early & Great Bluegrass Volume 1* (Old Homestead 1979)★★★★, *Early & Great Bluegrass Volume 2* (Old Homestead 1983)★★★★, *Windy Mountain* (Bear Family 1992)★★★★.

LONESOME STRANGERS

Lonesome Strangers is a Los Angeles-based country band formed during the cowpunk explosion of the 80s. Their lead vocalist, Jeff Rhymes, writes most of their material, while other members include Randy Weeks, Lorne Rall and Mike McLean. Opening regularly for Dwight Yoakam, they built up a strong reputation that led to them being signed by Hightone Records in 1988. Their debut album was released to great acclaim, and they had minor US country hits with 'Goodbye Lonesome, Hello Baby Doll' and 'Just Can't Cry No More'. McLean and Rall left the band, before the follow-up finally appeared in 1997. The new line-up included Greg Perry (drums) and Jeff Roberts (bass).

● ALBUMS: *The Lonesome Strangers* (Hightone 1989)★★★★, *Land Of Opportunity* (Little Dog 1997)★★★.

LONESTAR

This US country rock band signed to RCA Records in the 90s after establishing their reputation through a touring schedule that regularly encompassed over 200 performances a year. Comprising Richie McDonald (lead vocals, guitar), John Rich (lead vocals, bass), Michael Britt (guitar), Keech Rainwater (drums) and Sean Sams (keyboards), the group formed in Nashville, Tennessee, though all the members are natives of Texas. They made their debut in January 1995 when BNA Records released the *Lonestar Live* EP, recorded at Nashville's renowned Wildhorse Saloon. The group's harmonies and deep-rooted affection for the country tradition soon won supporters, and the successful singles 'Tequila Talkin'' and 'No News', made them a hot property in contemporary country circles. When the latter release made number 1 on the *Billboard* Hot Country Singles & Tracks chart, it built interest for the release of the group's self-titled debut album. This was promoted by a rigorous touring schedule, which had initially given Lonestar much of their fanbase. As a result the group were invited to perform at the annual ACM telecast, where five years previously, McDonald had heard a Miller Lite beer jingle he had sung air during the commercial break. 'Come Cryin' To Me' was another number 1 single taken from *Crazy Nights*. Rich left the band shortly afterwards.

● ALBUMS: *Lonestar* (BNA 1995)★★★, *Crazy Nights* (BNA 1997)★★★.

LONG, HUBERT

b. 3 December 1923, Poteet, Texas, USA, d. 7 September 1982, Nashville, Tennessee, USA. Long grew up in Freer, Texas, and after completing high school in 1942, he joined the US Navy. In 1945, he returned to Texas, working in a record store until 1946, when he worked briefly with both Decca and RCA Records. After meeting 'Colonel' Tom Parker, he became involved in promotional work, initially with Eddy Arnold, whom Parker was then managing, and relocated to Nashville. Around 1950, he became the manager of the *Louisiana Hayride* in Shreveport, where he first became involved with the booking and management of artists. In 1952, he formed the Hubert Long Agency, and in 1955, he created Nashville's first country music management company, the Stable Of The Stars, which represented many of the music's major artists. In 1959, he formed his first music publishing business, Moss Rose, and was responsible for the construction of Nashville's SESAC building. By 1960, his business interests were numerous, involving advertising, publishing and publications, not only in the USA but in many overseas locations, including England, Australia, Japan, South Africa and several European countries. He was also involved in real estate and owned many prestigious properties, including some on Nashville's Music Row. He was the first person to be elected both Chairman and President of the Country Music Association and was involved in the formation of both the CMA and the CMA Foundation. Long had to undergo surgery for a brain tumour in March 1982, but the operation failed to effect a long-term cure, and on 7 September, he died in Nashville's Baptist Hospital. Long's services to country music saw him win many awards, not least his induction to the Country Music Hall Of Fame in 1979.

LONZO AND OSCAR

A vocal and instrumental comedy duo that for many years consisted of John Sullivan (b. 7 July 1917, Edmonton, Kentucky, USA, d. 5 June 1967, Nashville, Tennessee, USA;

bass fiddle, guitar) and his brother Rollin Sullivan (b. 19 January 1919, Edmonton, Kentucky, USA; mandolin, guitar). The brothers toured the south as a duo in the late 30s and appeared on WTJS Jackson, Tennessee, where they worked with Eddy Arnold. In 1942, Rollin played on the *Grand Ole Opry* as a member of Paul Howard's band, but the following year, he joined that of Eddy Arnold. A fellow band member was Ken Marvin (b. Lloyd George, 27 June 1924, Haleyville, Alabama, USA; bass fiddle, guitar) and the two men immediately resumed a comedy act that they had started at WTJS. Initially known as Cicero (Marvin) And Oscar (Rollin), they were soon renamed Lonzo And Oscar by Arnold. Dressed in ill-fitting costumes and singing novelty songs in country harmony, interspersed by inane banter (John Sullivan wrote material for them), they were a well-established act when war service intervened. After their discharge, they resumed as part of Arnold's touring show and played with him at WAVE Louisville but in 1946, Marvin retired. John Sullivan assumed the role of Lonzo and they remained as part of Arnold's group until they became regular *Opry* members in their own right in 1947. In January 1948, an RCA-Victor recording of 'I'm My Own Grandpa' charted to give them a major Top 5 hit on both juke-box and country charts (the song, attributed to Dwight Latham and Moe Jaffe, was based on a humorous Mark Twain anecdote). The original single was made by Ken Marvin and Rollin but the brothers later made their own version. Their partnership lasted two decades until John's death following a heart attack in 1967. During this period they maintained their *Opry* status, proved a very popular touring act and appeared frequently on network television. They recorded for several other labels including Starday, Decca and their own Nugget label but only achieved one further chart hit, 'Country Music Time'. Their songs varied from the sublime 'Ole Buttermilk Sky' to the ridiculous 'You Blacked My Blue Eyes Once Too Often' and 'There's A Hole In The Bottom Of The Sea'. Late in 1967, the act was re-formed when David Hooten (b. St. Claire, Missouri, USA) took over the role of Lonzo. They resumed the touring and the *Opry* shows and, recording for Columbia, they found some success with 'Did You Have To Bring That Up While I Was Eating?'. The comedy continued but surprisingly, on a 1974 GRC album, the hillbilly harmony is completely missing. Some of the material may almost be classed as gospel and their fine harmony work saw them chart with the title track 'Traces Of Life'. Further recordings appeared in the early 80s on the Brylen label. The original 'I'm My Own Grandpa' appears on RCA's mid-60s compilation *Stars Of The Grand Ole Opry*.

● ALBUMS: *America's Greatest Country Comedians* (Starday 1960)★★★, *Lonzo & Oscar* i (Starday 1961)★★★, *Country Comedy Time* (Decca 1963)★★★, *Country Music Time* (Starday 1963)★★★, *Lonzo & Oscar* ii (Hilltop 1965)★★, *Mountain Dew* (Columbia 1968)★★★, *Hole In The Bottom Of The Sea* (Nugget 1969)★★★, *Traces Of Life* (GRC 1974)★★★, *Old & New Songs* (Brylen 1982)★★.

LORD, BOBBY

b. 6 January 1934, Sanford, Florida, USA. Lord's singing career began in his teens, singing jazz on Paul Whiteman's New York television show. With the intention of pursuing a medical career, he returned to Florida to study at the University of Tampa, but a casual appearance on television

prompted a change of mind, and in 1953, he was hosting *Bobby Lord's Homefolks Show* on television. He moved to Springfield, Mississippi, in the late 50s, as a member of Red Foley's *Jubilee USA*. He gained a number 10 US country hit in 1956, with his Columbia recording, 'Without Your Love'. In 1960, he became a member of the *Grand Ole Opry* in Nashville and began to appear on other major televised country shows. In the early 60s, he recorded for Hickory, achieving a number 21 in 1964 with his self-penned 'Life Can Have Meaning'. In 1965, he was given his own syndicated televised *Bobby Lord Show*, which ran for some years. Between 1968 and 1971, he scored seven further chart hits when recording for Decca Records. The biggest was 'You And Me Against The World', a number 15 in 1970, and the last was the prophetically titled 'Goodbye Jukebox', a number 75 and his only 1971 hit. In 1969, he wrote *Hit The Glory Road*, a book that looked at religion and country music. He eventually returned to Florida and supervised his business enterprises, including property. He continued to make limited appearances at local venues and sometimes, when in Nashville, even played on the *Opry*.
● ALBUMS: *The Bobby Lord Show* (Hickory 1965)★★, *Bobby Lord* (Decca 1970)★★.
● COMPILATIONS: *Bobby Lord's Best* (Harmony 1964)★★★.
● FURTHER READING: *Hit The Glory Road!*, Bobby Lord.

LORE AND THE LEGENDS

Lore Cayote Orion (b. Ramona, California, USA) developed an esoteric form of country music by combining Spanish influences with his love of rock music. He wrote 'That's What Made Me Love You', a US country hit for Bill Anderson and Mary Lou Turner. He worked as part of Bandera in the early 80s and then built up a UK following as Lore And The Legends. One UK single was released as a picture disc. Lore currently manages a dude ranch.
● ALBUMS: *One Step Ahead Of The Law* (Colt 1987)★★★, *Lore Cayote Orion* (PT 1988)★★.

LOST AND FOUND

A bluegrass group founded, in 1973, by Allen Mills (b. Allen Herman Mills, 4 November 1937, Danville, Virginia, USA; bass, guitar, vocals, MC), Gene Parker (b. 28 April 1942; banjo, guitar, vocals), Dempsey Young (b. 1 July 1954, Richmond, Virginia, USA; mandolin, guitar, banjo, bass, vocals) and Roger Handy (guitar, vocals). They soon established a reputation on the bluegrass festival circuit with their repertoire of old standards and new numbers, some penned by Mills. They recorded three albums for Outlet before moving to Rebel in 1980, where they recorded a steady series of albums until they moved to Copper Creek in 1994. There have been changes in personnel over the years which, after Handy left, led to appearances on guitar and vocals by several other musicians, in order of membership, Bubba Chandler, Steve Wilson and Ronnie Bowman. Founder-member Parker remained with the group until 1987, when Jody King became the banjoist for a time. In 1991, Barry Berrier (b. 10 October 1960, Mount Airy, North Carolina, USA; guitar, vocals) and Lynwood Lunsford (b. 31 January 1962, Roxboro, North Carolina, USA; banjo, vocals) joined founder-members Mills and Young, and continued to uphold the expected high standard of this popular bluegrass band. In 1995, Mills, Young and Parker were together again with

Wilson or Steve Thomas on fiddle for another Rebel album. Mills' song 'Sweet Rosie By The River', which they recorded on *The Deal*, has become a very popular number in bluegrass music.
● ALBUMS: *First Time Around* (Outlet 1975)★★★, *The Second Time Around* (Outlet 1976)★★★, *The Third Time Around* (Outlet 1978)★★★, *The Lost & Found* (Rebel 1980)★★★, *Endless Highway* (Rebel 1982)★★★, *The Sun's Gonna Shine* (Rebel 1985)★★★, *The Deal* (Rebel 1987)★★★, *Hymn Time* (Rebel 1988)★★★, *New Day* (Rebel 1989)★★★, *Bluegrass Classics* (Rebel 1991)★★★★, *January Rain* (Rebel 1992)★★★, *Just Pickin'* (Copper Creek 1994)★★★, *Across The Blue Ridge Mountains* (Rebel 1995)★★★.
● COMPILATIONS: *The Best Of Lost & Found* Outlet material (Rebel 1984)★★★★.

LOST GONZO BAND

In the early 70s many country and rock musicians settled in Austin, Texas, and a key venue was the Armadillo World Headquarters. Here Jerry Jeff Walker recruited the musicians to back him on an album to made in Luckenbach, Texas. The album, recorded in August 1973, was called *Viva Terlingua* and the musicians were named the Lost Gonzo Band. The mainstays were Gary P. Nunn (keyboards, vocals) and Bob Livingston (bass, vocals), along with Michael McGeary, Herb Steiner, Craig Hillis and Kelly Dunn. The band toured with Walker for five years and cut solo albums. The line-up changed but an important addition was John Inmon (lead guitar). They did session work individually and also worked with Ray Wylie Hubbard. In 1990 Jerry Jeff Walker re-formed the band (Inmon, Livingston and drummer Freddie Krc) for the Gonzo Compadres. The Lost Gonzo Band has now recorded two more albums, the current personnel being Inmon, Livingston, Riley Osborne (keyboards), Tomas Ramirez (saxophone), Paul Pearcy (drums) and producer Lloyd Maines (steel guitar). They describe themselves quite accurately as 'a rock 'n' roll jazz country reggae R&B Texas roadhouse band.'
● ALBUMS: *The Lost Gonzo Band* (MCA 1975)★★★, *Thrills* (MCA 1976)★★★★, *Signs Of Life* (Capitol 1979)★★, *Rendezvous* (Amazing 1992)★★★★, *Hands Of Time* (Vireo 1995)★★★.

LOUDERMILK, JOHN D.

b. 31 March 1934, Durham, North Carolina, USA. Loudermilk's first musical experience was banging a drum for the Salvation Army; he played various instruments as a child and appeared regularly on the radio from the age of 11. In 1956, George Hamilton IV recorded his song 'A Rose And A Baby Ruth', which went from the local to the national charts, reaching number 6. A few months later, Eddie Cochran made his debut in the US Top 20 with 'Sittin' In The Balcony', another Loudermilk song that he had recorded himself under the pseudonym Johnny D. When Loudermilk moved to Nashville, a stream of hits followed, the UK chart successes being 'Waterloo' (Stonewall Jackson, 1959), 'Angela Jones' (Michael Cox, 1960), 'Tobacco Road' (Nashville Teens, 1964), 'Google Eye' (which was a catfish, Nashville Teens, 1964), 'This Little Bird' (Marianne Faithfull, 1965, and subsequently parodied by the Barron Knights), 'Then You Can Tell Me Goodbye' (Casinos, 1967, and a US country number 1 for Eddy Arnold), 'It's My Time' (the

Everly Brothers, 1968), 'Indian Reservation (The Lament Of The Cherokee Reservation Indian)' (Don Fardon, 1970 and a US number 1 for the Raiders, 1971) and 'Sunglasses' (a revival of a Skeeter Davis record by Tracey Ullman, 1984). His controversial 'death' song, 'Ebony Eyes', was the b-side of the Everly Brothers' 1961 number 1, 'Walk Right Back'. Other successful b-sides include 'Weep No More My Baby' (Brenda Lee's 'Sweet Nuthins'), 'Stayin' In' (Bobby Vee's 'More Than I Can Say'), 'Heaven Fell Last Night' (the Browns' 'The Three Bells') and 'In A Matter Of Moments' (Louise Cordet's 'I'm Just A Baby'). Near misses include 'All Of This For Sally' (Mark Dinning), 'The Guitar Player (Him And Her)' for Jimmy Justice and 'To Hell With Love' for Adam Faith. He arranged an old song, 'Abilene', for George Hamilton IV, which made the US charts in 1963 and became a country standard. His other country music successes include 'Talk Back Trembling Lips' (Ernest Ashworth and Johnny Tillotson), 'Bad News' (Johnny Cash and Boxcar Willie), 'Break My Mind' (George Hamilton IV, Gram Parsons and the Hillsiders), 'You're Ruinin' My Life' (Hank Williams Jnr.) and 'Half-Breed' (Marvin Rainwater). He wrote clever novelty songs for Bob Luman ('The Great Snowman' and 'The File') and for Sue Thompson ('Sad Movies (Make Me Cry)', 'Norman', 'James (Hold The Ladder Steady)' and 'Paper Tiger', all US Top 30 hits). Loudermilk had his own hit with 'The Language Of Love', which made number 13 in the UK in 1962. He made several albums of his own material and they have been collected on two Bear Family compilations, *Blue Train* and *It's My Time*, which contain two previously unreleased tracks in 'The Little Wind Up Doll' and 'Giving You All My Love'. He has often worked in the UK and performs his songs in a similar manner to Burl Ives. He produced Pete Sayers' best album, *Bogalusa Gumbo*, in 1979, but an album that he recorded at the same sessions has not been released. He now spends his time studying ethnomusicology.

● ALBUMS: *The Language Of Love* (RCA Victor 1961)★★★, *Twelve Sides Of Loudermilk* (RCA Victor 1962)★★★, *John D. Loudermilk Sings A Bizarre Collection Of Unusual Songs* (RCA Victor 1965)★★★, *Suburban Attitudes In Country Verse* (RCA Victor 1967)★★, *Country Love Songs* (RCA Victor 1968)★★, *The Open Mind Of John D. Loudermilk* (RCA Victor 1969)★★, *Elloree* (1975)★★, *Just Passing Through* (1977)★★.

● COMPILATIONS: *The Best Of John D. Loudermilk* (RCA 1970)★★★, *Encores* (RCA 1975)★★★, *Blue Train* (Bear Family 1989)★★★, *It's My Time* (Bear Family 1989)★★★, *Sittin' In The Balcony* (Bear Family 1995)★★★.

LOUISIANA HAYRIDE, THE

This popular radio show was first broadcast on station KWKH Shreveport on 3 April 1948, the brainchild of the manager Henry Clay, the programme director Horace Logan and the commercial manager Dean Upson (a former member of the *Grand Ole Opry* singing trio, the Vagabonds). The programme, a three-hour Saturday night show broadcast live from Shreveport's Municipal Auditorium, quickly attracted the public's attention. It was soon rated by many to be second only to Nashville's *Opry* as the important venue for would-be country stars to reach. The *Opry* had already been established for over 20 years but the *Hayride* did not have the budget to compete with the mighty WSM, and consequently, it became the practice that artists first established

themselves on the *Hayride* and then moved up to the *Opry*. In its way, therefore, if only as a final grooming place for stardom, the show became a very important part of country music and soon acquired the nickname of 'the cradle of the stars'. The first *Hayride* show actually featured some established acts, including the Bailes Brothers and Johnny And Jack (plus Johnny's then unknown wife, Kitty Wells), but within four months, under the careful management of its director and compere Horace Logan, the show had its own new star in Hank Williams (Hank would later return to play the *Hayride* in November 1952, after he was dropped by the *Opry*). From that point, the country music side of KWKH's programming saw a steady progression of future stars, including Red Sovine, Webb Pierce, George Jones, Faron Young, Johnny Horton, Jimmy C. Newman, Floyd Cramer, Hank Locklin, Slim Whitman and Elvis Presley (Whitman recorded two of his biggest hits, 'Indian Love Call' and 'Love Song Of The Waterfall', for Imperial Records in the studio of KWKH). Jim Reeves launched his career with KWKH, first as an announcer and DJ before being given the chance to sing one night on the *Hayride* in 1952, when Hank Williams failed to arrive. Johnny Cash also started on the road to stardom as a member of the *Hayride* in 1955. In its heyday, the *Hayride* show was broadcast over CBS national network and also carried internationally on the Armed Forces Network. Recordings of performances on the show by some artists, including one by Presley, have been issued on CD. When the show finally ended, after undergoing various formats, in the early 90s, it marked the end of a piece of country music history.

LOUVIN BROTHERS

Brothers Lonnie Ira Loudermilk (b. 21 April 1924, d. 20 June 1965) and Charlie Elzer Loudermilk (b. 7 July 1927) were both born in Rainesville, Alabama, USA. They were raised on a 40-acre farm in Henegar, Alabama, but only half of it could be cultivated. Despite their poverty, their parents sang gospel songs and encouraged their sons' musical talents. Ira took up the mandolin and Charlie the guitar, and they created perfect harmonies for country and gospel music, inspired, in particular, by the Blue Sky Boys. In 1943, after winning a talent contest in Chattanooga, they began broadcasting regularly, leading to three shows a day for WMPS in Memphis. They recorded for Decca, MGM and Capitol, but they found it hard to make ends meet and worked night shifts in the Post Office. Some radio broadcasts to promote a songbook, *Songs That Tell A Story*, have been released and show the Louvin Brothers at their best, with no additional instruments. Their career was also interrupted by Charlie's military service in Korea (their 'Weapon Of Prayer' was an emotional plea for peace). They performed as the Louvin Brothers because the family name was considered too long for stage work, although their cousin, John D. Loudermilk, was to have no such qualms. Capitol Records re-signed the brothers as gospel artists but a tobacco company sponsoring a portion of the *Grand Ole Opry* told them to sing secular songs as 'you can't sell tobacco with gospel music'. They crossed over to the country market with their own composition 'When I Stop Dreaming', which is now a standard. Their secular US country hits included 'I Don't Believe You've Met My Baby' (their only number 1), 'Hoping That You're Hoping', 'You're Running Wild' and 'My Baby's Gone', but

Charlie says, 'I don't think we ever did a show without some gospel music. Our mother would have thrashed us if we hadn't done that!'

By the late 50s, their sound was old-fashioned and their songs too melodramatic for the rock 'n' roll era. The Everly Brothers, who acknowledged their debt to the Louvins, may also have contributed unwittingly to their downfall. Charlie says, 'Ken Nelson told Ira, in 1958, that the mandolin was hindering the sales of our music, so my brother lost total interest in the mandolin and never picked another note on it on a record. He had put 25 years of his life into mastering that instrument, and it messed his head to hear a good friend whose opinion he respected say, "You're the problem, you've got to throw that thing away".' Ira's drink problem worsened, their own relationship deteriorated and their last success together was, ironically, 'Must You Throw Dirt In My Face?'. Charlie broke up the partnership on 18 August 1963: 'He had said a lot of times he was going to quit, but it was the first time I had ever said it.' Charlie went on to have solo hits with 'I Don't Love You Anymore' and 'See The Big Man Cry, Mama'. Ira started his solo career with 'Yodel Sweet Molly' but he was shot and badly injured by his wife, Faye, whom he then divorced. He then married Florence, who sang on his shows as Anne Young, but soon afterwards they both perished in a car crash in Jefferson City, Missouri, USA, on 20 June 1965. Ira and Bill Monroe had pledged that whoever lived the longest would sing at the other's funeral, and Monroe sang 'Where No One Stands Alone'. Gram Parsons introduced their songs to a new audience, recording 'The Christian Life' with the Byrds, and 'Cash On The Barrelhead' and 'The Angels Rejoiced In Heaven Last Night' with Emmylou Harris. After Parsons' death, Harris continued recording their songs: 'If I Could Only Win Your Love', 'When I Stop Dreaming', 'You're Learning' and, with Don Everly, 'Everytime You Leave'. Charlie Louvin had a country hit with 'You're My Wife, She's My Woman' and made two successful albums with Melba Montgomery. A single, 'Love Don't Care' with Emmylou Harris, made the US country charts.

● ALBUMS: by the Louvin Brothers *Tragic Songs Of Life* (Capitol 1956)★★★★, *Nearer My God To Thee* (Capitol 1957)★★★, *The Louvin Brothers* (MGM 1957)★★★★, *Ira And Charlie* (Capitol 1958)★★★, *The Family Who Prays* (Capitol 1958)★★★★, *Country Love Ballads* (Capitol 1959)★★★, *Satan Is Real* (Capitol 1960)★★★, *Those Louvin Brothers Sing The Songs Of The Delmores* (Capitol 1960)★★★, *My Baby's Gone* (Capitol 1960)★★★, *Encore* (Capitol 1961)★★★, *Country Christmas With The Louvin Brothers* (Capitol 1961)★★★, *Weapon Of Prayer* (Capitol 1962)★★★, *Keep Your Eyes On Jesus* (Capitol 1963)★★★, *The Louvin Brothers Sing And Play Their Current Hits* (Capitol 1964)★★★, *Thank God For My Christian Home* (Capitol 1965)★★★, *Two Different Worlds* (Capitol 1966)★★★, *The Louvin Brothers Sing The Great Roy Acuff Songs* (Capitol 1967)★★★, *Country Heart And Soul* (Tower 1968)★★★, *Live At The New River Ranch* recorded 1956 (Copper Creek 1989)★★★, *Running Wild* (1992)★★★.
Solo: Charlie Louvin *Less And Less/I Don't Love You Anymore* (Capitol 1965)★★★, *The Many Moods Of Charlie Louvin* (Capitol 1966)★★★★, *Lonesome Is Me* (Capitol 1966)★★★, *I'll Remember Always* a tribute to Ira Louvin (Capitol 1967)★★★, *I Forgot To Cry* (Capitol 1967)★★★,

Will You Visit Me On Sundays? (Capitol 1968)★★★, *Hey Daddy* (Capitol 1968)★★★, *The Kind Of Man I Am* (Capitol 1968)★★★, *Here's A Toast To Mama* (Capitol 1969)★★★, *Ten Times Charlie* (Capitol 1970)★★★, with Melba Montgomery *Something To Brag About* (Capitol 1971)★★★, with Montgomery *Baby, You've Got What It Takes* (Capitol 1971)★★★, *It Almost Felt Like Love* (1974)★★, *Country Souvenirs* (1981)★★★, *Charlie Louvin* (1982)★★★, *Jim And Jesse And Charlie Louvin* (1982)★★★, *Charlie Louvin* (1989)★★★, *Then, Now And Forever* (1990)★★, *50 Years Of Making Music* (Cottage 1991)★★★, with Charles Whitstein *Hoping That You're Hoping* (Copper Creek 1992)★★★. Ira Louvin *The Unforgettable Ira Louvin* (Capitol 1965)★★★.
● COMPILATIONS: *The Great Gospel Singing Of The Louvin Brothers* (1973)★★★, *Songs That Tell A Story* (Rounder 1981)★★★, *Radio Favourites 1951-1957* (CMF 1987)★★★, *Close Harmony* 8-CD box set (Bear Family 1992)★★★★, *Capitol Country Music Classics* (1993)★★★, *When I Stop Dreaming: The Best Of The Louvin Brothers* (Razor & Tie 1995)★★★★.

LOVELESS, PATTY

b. Patricia Ramey, 4 January 1957, Pikeville, Kentucky, USA. The youngest of eight children, she began to write songs and sing in local venues with her brother Roger, after the family relocated to Louisville. When she was 14 years old they visited Nashville, where her singing and songwriting so impressed the Wilburn Brothers (although they felt she was not mature enough to record), that they offered her the opportunity to work on their shows. She combined singing and schooling, but in 1973, after marrying Terry Lovelace, who played drums with the Wilburns, she relocated to North Carolina, and for a time, finding the current country music did not suit her more traditional preferences, she left the music scene. During this time her marriage ended and a second marriage to a rock musician also floundered in the mid-80s, seemingly because he told her to give up country. Eventually, she resumed her singing career (even singing some rock 'n' roll in local clubs) and, using the name Loveless to avoid being confused with porn actress Linda Lovelace, she moved to Nashville in 1985. She became a staff writer at Acuff-Rose and her brother Roger (acting as her manager) persuaded his friend Emory Gordy Jnr., a producer and musician at MCA, to record her. She made her chart debut in 1985 with 'Lonely Days, Lonely Nights' and her career was firmly established by her debut album, *Patty Loveless*, in 1987. In 1988, she had her first Top 10 successes with 'If My Heart Had Windows', which George Jones had first charted 21 years earlier, and her version of Steve Earle's 'A Little Bit Of Love'. Loveless established herself with UK audiences by her fine performances at the 1987 and 1988 Wembley Festivals. She became a member of the *Grand Ole Opry* in 1988 and in 1989, she married Emory Gordy Jnr. She continued to record chart-making songs, enjoying number 1s with 'Timber, I'm Falling In Love' and 'Chains'. In 1992, she recorded a successful duet, 'Send A Message To My Heart', with Dwight Yoakam. Also late in 1992, she underwent surgery for a leaking blood vessel on her vocal cords, and in spite of some initial concern, she soon recovered. Believing that it was time to make some changes, she reluctantly dispensed with her brother's management and moved to the Epic label. She is quoted as saying, 'The goal was to find a real good style and just have a lot of fun with it'. She quickly gained a number 1 country hit, 'Blame It On Your Heart', which also nudged the pop charts. There seems little doubt that her vocal stylings will see her achieve continued success. Indeed, her 1995 hit, 'Here I Am', reinforced her approach; adhering to her belief in hard country music, she says, 'You're gonna hear that old bluegrass style, those blues licks when I sing. It's who I am - and I can't leave that behind. What we sang growing up was more old mountain style music, white man's blues, and that'll always be in there'. Although she never mentioned the fact when she was struggling to make her name, she is actually a cousin of Loretta Lynn, Crystal Gayle, Peggy Sue and Jay Lee Webb. Cousin Loretta finally broke the news one day on live television. A further number 1 came in March 1996 with 'You Can Feel Bad'. Loveless was voted Best Female Vocalist at the 1997 CMA awards.

● ALBUMS: *Patty Loveless* (MCA 1987)★★, *If My Heart Had Windows* (MCA 1988)★★, *Honky Tonk Angel* (MCA 1988)★★, *On Down The Line* (MCA 1990)★★★, *Up Against My Heart* (MCA 1991)★★★★, *Only What I Feel* (Epic 1993)★★★★, *When Fallen Angels Fly* (Epic 1994)★★★, *The Trouble With The Truth* (Epic 1996)★★★, *Long Stretch Of Lonesome* (Epic 1997)★★★.

● COMPILATIONS: *Greatest Hits* (MCA 1993)★★★★.

● VIDEOS: *You Don't Even Know My Name* (Sony 1995).

LOVETT, LYLE

b. 1 November 1957, Houston, Texas, USA. Singer-songwriter Lovett grew up 25 miles north of Houston in the rural Klein community (an area largely populated by farmers of German extraction), which was named after his grandfather, Adam Klein. During his teenage years, as Houston's borders expanded, Lovett was exposed to more urban influences, and attended Texas A&M University where he studied journalism and then German. During this period (late 70s), he began writing songs; his early heroes included Guy Clark (who later wrote a dedication on the sleeve of Lovett's first album), Jerry Jeff Walker and Townes Van Zandt. Having visited Europe (to improve his German) in the late 70s, he met a local country musician named Buffalo Wayne (who apparently took his name from his favourite western heroes), and remained in touch after returning to Texas - when Wayne was organizing an event in Luxembourg in 1983, he booked Lovett, and also on the bill was an American band from Phoenix whose members included Matt Rollings (keyboards) and Ray Herndon (guitar), who were later involved with Lovett's albums. Lovett worked the same Texas music circuit as Nanci Griffith, singing on two of her early albums, *Once In A Very Blue Moon* (1984, which included one of his songs, 'If I Were The Woman You Wanted') and *Last Of The True Believers* (1985), on the cover of which he is pictured. When Guy Clark heard a demo tape by Lovett in 1984, he passed it on to Tony Brown of MCA Records, and by 1986, Lovett had signed to MCA/Curb. His self-titled debut album was idiosyncratic, to say the least, including both the song covered by Griffith and 'Closing Time', which was covered by Lacy J. Dalton, as well as a fine song he co-wrote with fellow singer-songwriter Robert Earl Keen Jnr., 'This Old Porch'. However, his acceptance was slow in US country music circles, and Lovett first received substantial critical acclaim when the album was eventually

released in Europe. The follow-up, *Pontiac*, was released in 1987 after Lovett had successfully toured Europe backed only by cellist John Hagen. The album made it clear that Lovett was rather more than a folk or country artist, with such songs as the surreal 'If I Had A Boat' and 'She's Hot To Go', while guests on the album included Emmylou Harris. By this time, Lovett was talking about both recording and touring with what he called His Large Band, with several saxophone players and a female backing singer, Francine Reed, as well as a regular rhythm section, and his third album, released in 1989, was indeed titled *Lyle And His Large Band*. Including an insidiously straight cover version of the Tammy Wynette standard 'Stand By Your Man', and a version of the R&B oldie 'The Glory Of Love', this again delighted critics by its very humour and eclecticism, but further confused record buyers, especially in the USA, who were unsure whether this was a country or jazz record or something quite different.

At this point Lovett moved away from Nashville, where he was regarded as too weird, and as a result, his fourth album, produced by Los Angeles heavyweight George Massenburg, was not released until early 1992. Its title, *Joshua Judges Ruth* (three consecutive books in the Old Testament, but meaning something very different if read as a phrase), was symptomatic of Lovett's intelligence, but perhaps equally so of his idiosyncratic approach. As usual, critics loved it, although it included hardly any traces of country music, and seemed to portray him as a Tom Waits-like figure - ultra-sophisticated, but somewhat off the wall. In 1992, Lovett was chosen as the opening act for many of the dates on the first world tour during the 90s by Dire Straits. This exposed him to a huge international audience, but seems to have done little to extend his cult following. In the same year, Lovett met the Hollywood actress Julia Roberts on the set of *The Player*, a high-grossing film, in which Lovett played the role of a detective. They married in June 1993; the following year their marriage was floundering, and by 1995 it appeared to be over. Presumably Lovett will now resume his career as one of the sharpest and wittiest songwriters to come out of America in recent times. He performed 'You've Got A Friend In Me' with Randy Newman for the soundtrack of the hugely successful movie *Toy Story*. *The Road To Ensenada* mixed Lovett's razor wit with pathos. Long-standing observers of Lovett's lyrics will read much into this album and pontificate for hours about their relevance to his relationship with Roberts.

● ALBUMS: *Lyle Lovett* (MCA/Curb 1986)★★★★, *Pontiac* (MCA/Curb 1987)★★★★, *Lyle Lovett And His Large Band* (MCA/Curb 1989)★★★, *Joshua Judges Ruth* (MCA/Curb 1992)★★★, *I Love Everybody* (MCA/Curb 1994)★★★, *The Road To Ensenada* (MCA/Curb 1996)★★★.

LULU BELLE AND SCOTTY

Lulu Belle (b. Myrtle Eleanor Cooper, 24 December 1913, Boone, North Carolina, USA) and Scott Wiseman (b. 8 November 1909, Spruce Pine, near Ingalls, North Carolina, USA, d. 31 January 1981). Lulu Belle learned to play the guitar and sing mountain songs as a child, but after the family relocated to Evanston, Illinois, in 1929, she first worked as a clerk. In 1932, she successfully auditioned at WLS television company Chicago and was given a spot on the *National Barn Dance* programme, where she initially worked with Red Foley. Wiseman grew up on the family farm and developed his first musical skills by learning to play a home-made banjo. He became interested in a musical career after seeing Bradley Kincaid perform and by working in his school holidays, he bought himself a guitar. In 1927, he made his radio debut, singing and playing in a manner that showed a distinct Kincaid influence, on WRVA Richmond. Initially doubtful that he could make his living by music, he decided to study for a teaching career. From 1929-32, he attended the Teachers College at Fairmont, West Virginia and obtained a degree. During these years, he wrote songs and, appearing as Skyland Scotty, was regularly featured on WMMN Fairmont. In 1933, he joined the *National Barn Dance*, where he began to work with Lulu Belle. He made his first recordings (solo) in December 1933, when, playing his guitar for one of the few times on record, he cut four songs for RCA-Victor. One of the songs was 'Home Coming Time In Happy Valley', which soon became a popular song for the duo. They were married on 13 December 1934, by which time they had become a very popular act. On stage, Scotty wore plain, casual attire and played banjo, while Lulu Belle dressed in old gingham styled dresses, pantalettes and usually wore pigtails. Their simple harmony singing, interspersed with comedy and novelty songs, endeared them to the network audience and gained them the nickname of the Sweethearts of Country Music. In 1936, Lulu Belle was voted the most popular woman on American radio and between 1938 and 1944, their national popularity saw them appear in seven films including *Shine On Harvest Moon*. They remained stars of the WLS *National Barn Dance* from 1933-58 but also had a spell on the *Boone County Jamboree* (later the *Midwestern Hayride*) on WLW Cincinnati, as well as playing on the *Grand Ole Opry* and the *Ozark Jubilee*. They were also regulars on WNNBQ-TV Chicago from 1949-57. Over the years, they recorded for various labels including Conqueror, Vocalion, and Bluebird. They popularized many songs including 'Mountain Dew' (written by Scotty with Bascombe Lunsford), 'Remember Me', 'My Heart Cries For You', 'Tying The Leaves' and 'Does Your Spearmint Lose Its Flavour On The Bed Post Overnight?' (a UK pop hit for Lonnie Donegan with 'Chewing Gum' substituted for 'Spearmint' in 1959). Perhaps their best-known song is one that originated at a time when Scotty was hospitalized with appendix trouble. During a visit, Lulu Belle said 'Have I told you lately that I love you' and it inspired him to write a song. Gene Autry recorded it in November 1945 and in 1946, it was a Top 5 US country hit for Autry, Tex Ritter, Red Foley and Foy Willing. It went on to become a country standard and has been recorded over the years by many artists, including Bing Crosby with the Andrews Sisters, Jim Reeves, Van Morrison and Elvis Presley. In 1958, after Scotty had obtained an MA Teaching degree at Northwestern University at Evanston, they semi-retired from the entertainment business. They moved back to Spruce Pine, where Scotty taught people with speech problems at the college. They also bought a cattle farm but still made a few concert appearances and recorded for the Starday label in the 60s. At one time, they presented their *Breakfast In The Blue Ridge* radio show supposedly live from their home, but in reality, it was taped in Chicago. They appeared at the 1975 *Fan Fair* in Nashville and on the *Opry*, but generally during the 70s, Scotty continued to teach and they restricted themselves to local appearances. In 1971, his many songs saw him elected to the Nashville Songwriters' International Hall of Fame. Lulu Belle became interested in politics and in 1974, she was elected to the North Carolina House of Representatives. Scotty died following a heart attack when driving home from Gainsville, Florida. Lulu Belle remarried in 1983 (Ernest Stamey, an old family friend) and in 1986, she recorded a solo album for the Old Homestead label.

● ALBUMS: *Lulu Belle & Scotty* (Super 1963)★★★, *The Sweethearts Of Country Music* (Starday 1963)★★★★, *Down Memory Lane* (Starday 1964)★★★, *Lulu Belle & Scotty (Sweethearts Still)* (Starday 1965)★★★, *Just A Closer Walk With Thee* (Birch 1974)★★, *Have I Told You Lately That I Love You* (Old Homestead 1974)★★.
Solo: Lulu Belle *Snickers & Tender Memories* (Old Homestead 1986)★★.

● COMPILATIONS: *Early And Great Volume 1* (1985)★★★, *Country & Western Memories, Volume 3: Lulu Belle & Scotty* (1986)★★★, *Tender Memories Recalled Volumes 1 & 2* (1989)★★★, *Tender Memories Recalled Volume 3* (1991)★★.

LUMAN, BOB

b. Robert Glynn Luman, 15 April 1937, Blackjack, near Nacogdoches, Texas, USA, d. 27 December 1978, Nashville, Tennessee, USA. Luman's father, Joe, a school caretaker, bus driver and gifted musician, taught his son country music, but Luman's first love was baseball, which he played on a semi-professional basis until 1959. He was influenced by seeing Elvis Presley in concert, later saying, 'That was the last time I tried to sing like Webb Pierce or Lefty Frizzell'. His band then won a talent contest sponsored by the Texas Future Farmers of America and judged by Johnny Horton. In 1955, Luman recorded the original version of 'Red Cadillac And A Black Moustache' and also a scorching 'Red Hot' for Imperial Records. He joined *Louisiana Hayride* as replacement for Johnny Cash and came into contact with guitarist James Burton and bass player James Kirkland, whom he recruited for his band. Unfortunately for Luman, Ricky Nelson was so impressed by Luman's musicians that he made them a better offer. After a brief, unsuccessful period with Capitol Records, Luman moved to Warner Brothers, who released 'Class Of '59' and 'Dreamy Doll', both featuring Roy Buchanan. He had a transatlantic hit with Boudleaux Bryant's satire on 'death discs' such as 'El Paso' and 'One Of Us (Will Weep Tonight)' in 'Let's Think About Living'. 'If we keep losing our singers like this,' he concluded, 'I'll be the only one you can buy.' He failed to repeat his success, despite such clever novelties as 'The Great Snowman' and 'Private Eye'. After spending part of the early 60s in the army due to the draft laws, he became a member of the *Grand Ole Opry* in 1964 and made many country records for the Hickory label, including John D. Loudermilk's witty 'The File'. He became a big-selling US country artist via his Epic recordings, 'When You Say Love', 'Lonely Women Make Good Lovers' and 'Neither One Of Us Wants To Be The First To Say Goodbye', subsequently a pop hit for Gladys Knight And The Pips. In 1976, he underwent major surgery and then, prompted and produced by Johnny Cash, he recorded *Alive And Well*. Despite the title, he collapsed and died shortly after an appearance at the *Grand Ole Opry*. In recent years, Luman's work has been reassessed with retrospectives and, like Johnny Burnette, it is his early, rockabilly work that most interests collectors. To quote one of his country hits, 'Good Things Stem From Rock 'n' Roll.'

● ALBUMS: *Let's Think About Living* (Warners 1960)★★★★, *Livin' Lovin' Sounds* (Hickory 1965)★★★, *Ain't Got Time To Be Unhappy* (Epic 1968)★★★, *Come On Home And Sing The Blues To Daddy* (Epic 1969)★★★, *Getting Back To Norman* (Epic 1970)★★★, *Is It Any Wonder That I Love You?* (Epic 1971)★★★, *A Chain Don't Talk To Me* (Epic 1971)★★★, *When You Say Love* (Epic 1972)★★★, *Lonely Women Make Good Lovers* (Epic 1972)★★, *Neither One Of Us* (Epic 1973)★★, *Red Cadillac And A Black Moustache* (Epic 1974)★★★, *Still Loving You* (Epic 1974)★★, *A Satisfied Mind* (Epic 1976)★★, *Alive And Well* (1977)★★, *Bob Luman* (Polydor 1978)★★, *The Pay Phone* (Polydor 1978)★★, *Try Me* (Rockstar 1988)★★.

● COMPILATIONS: *The Rocker* (Bear Family 1984)★★★, *More Of That Rocker* (Bear Family 1984)★★★, *Still Rockin'* (Bear Family 1984)★★★, *Carnival Rock* (Bear Family 1988)★★★, *Wild-Eyed Woman* (Bear Family 1988)★★★, *American Originals* (Columbia 1989)★★★★, *Let's Think About Living* (Castle 1994)★★★.

● FILMS: *Carnival Rock* (1957).

LUNDY, TED

b. Teddy Joe Lundy, 26 January 1937, Galax, Virginia, USA, d. 23 June 1980. It was hardly surprising that Lundy had a great interest in music. His great-uncle, Emmett Lundy, was a famous old-time fiddler and both his parents played instruments. He first played guitar aged eight, but after hearing Earl Scruggs' new style of banjo playing, as opposed to the more common old-time clawhammer style, he adopted the banjo as his main instrument. After playing on local radio in 1951, he joined Jimmy Williams' Shady Valley Boys, with whom he played at WHIS Bluefield, West Virginia and WCYB Bristol, Tennessee. After relocating to Delaware, he played on a part-time basis with several artists, including Rome Johnson. He recorded for Starday with Alex Campbell in the early 60s, before forming his own Southern Mountain Boys, which included his cousin Jerry Lundy (fiddle), Fred Hannah (mandolin) and Bob Paisley (guitar). They recorded a few sides for New River in 1962 but did not release an album until 10 years later. After one album for the German-owned GHP label, they moved to Rounder Records. The band continued to play the circuits and appeared at festivals through to 1980, although there were several changes of personnel, including Paisley, who formed his own group in 1979. The Southern Mountain Boys disbanded after Lundy committed suicide in 1980.

● ALBUMS: *Ted Lundy & The Southern Mountain Ramblers* (GHP 1972)★★★, *The Old Swinging Bridge* (Rounder 1973)★★★. As Ted Lundy And Bob Paisley And The Southern Mountain Boys *Slipping Away* (Rounder 1976)★★★, *Lovesick & Sorrow* (Rounder 1978)★★★.

LUNN, ROBERT

b. Robert Rainey Lunn, 28 November 1912, Franklin, Tennessee, USA, d. 1966. Little is known of Lunn's early life, probably because of the fact that he apparently expected writers to pay for interviews. He may well have worked in vaudeville before he arrived on the *Grand Ole Opry* in 1930, with an act that included comedy and ventriloquism, but mainly the gimmick that led to him acquiring the pseudonym of 'the Talking Blues Man'. A left-handed guitarist, he used a heavy guitar vamp as a backing, while he talked his way through recitations that sometimes contained countless verses (the practice had previously been used in the 20s by a vaudeville artist called Chris Bouchillon, whom Lunn may have seen). It is unlikely that comedy numbers such as 'Tooth Picking Time In False Teeth Valley' would ensure stardom today, but by the mid-30s, with his band the Talking Blue Boys, he was a very popular *Opry* act and remained so for many years (he also worked on occasions with Roy Acuff and his talking blues style was used later by folk-singer Woody Guthrie). A noted practical joker, Lunn would sometimes stand at the stage door and audition any would-be *Opry* members, who wrongly assumed him to be the stage manager, in the street. Apart from a break during military service in World War II, he remained on the *Opry* until 1958 and toured with Acuff to Australia and Hawaii in 1959. He very rarely sang and his recording career consisted of a single Starday album. Lunn died following a heart attack in 1966.

● ALBUMS: *The Original Talking Blues Man* (Starday 1962)★★★.

LUTHER, FRANK

b. Frank Luther Crow, 5 August 1900, near Hutchinson, Kansas, USA, d. 16 November 1980. A competent musician, Luther was one of the early pioneers who popularized western songs with city dwellers, via his personal appearances and radio performances. Sometimes working with his brother Phil, he toured and by the mid-20s, had established a considerable reputation. He had noted the success of Carson Robison and Vernon Dalhart with their country ballads and cowboy songs and performed similar material. In 1928, Robison and Dalhart split and Luther and Robison began to work together. They recorded under various names including the Highhatters, the Homespun Trio and Men About Town. They even used some of Dalhart's own pseudonyms, and Luther was very adept at imitating the latter's nasal tones. However, they are perhaps best remembered for their fine recordings as Bud and Joe Billings. Their recordings proved good sellers and were released in various countries; the 1929 Regal Zonophone recording, 'Will The Angels Play Their Harps For Me', was very popular in the UK. Another combination in 1931 saw 'In The Cumberland Mountains' listed as Bud And Joe Billings and Carson Robison (brother Phil Crow being the extra vocalist). They occasionally performed as the Carson Robison Trio with Luther's wife, Zora Layman, as the third member. (Layman, a Kansas-born singer and fiddler, also recorded in her own right, being especially remembered for her recording of 'Seven Years With The Wrong Man'. She and Luther divorced in 1940, but continued to worked together for several years. A pioneer of early country music, she later worked as a singing teacher and died in October 1981.) In 1934, Luther made recordings with singing cowboy Ray Whitley. The use of pseudonyms, and the fact that in those days, artists recorded for different labels, saw Luther appear on a vast number of recordings. It has been suggested that, in one year, he made over 500 recordings and it has been estimated that he probably appeared on 3,000 in all. In the mid-30s, he became interested in recording cowboy and other songs especially for children. He finally worked on the production of children's material for Decca. He co-wrote 'Barnacle Bill

The Sailor' with Robison and some of their recordings may be found on *Just A Melody* (Old Homestead).

LYNCH, CLAIRE

b. Hazel Green, Alabama, USA. In her childhood Lynch discovered the magic of old bluegrass recordings, and by 1973 had joined the Hickory Wind group. Subsequently evolving into the Front Porch String Band, between 1975 and 1981 they released three albums before agreeing to part company. Afterwards, Lynch moved to Nashville with the intention of working as a songwriter. Her accomplished backing vocals and writing skills soon found her regular employment with artists such as Patty Loveless, Kathy Mattea and Tanya Tucker. All three artists recorded her songs, while her backing vocals were also employed by Linda Ronstadt, Emmylou Harris, Charlie Sizemore and Dolly Parton. She re-formed the Front Porch String Band with her former colleagues in 1991, with whom she recorded the well-received *Lines And Traces*. Her solo debut came in 1993 with *Friends For A Lifetime*, a record that accrued further excellent reviews. Three years then passed before *Moonlighter*, her debut for Rounder Records, which further enhanced her profile with its sweet singing belying more bittersweet lyrics. *Silver And Gold* was an even more accomplished follow-up from this masterly singer.
● ALBUMS: *Friends For A Lifetime* (1993)★★★, *Moonlighter* (Rounder 1996)★★★, *Silver And Gold* (Rounder 1997)★★★★.

LYNN, JUDY

b. Judy Voiten, 12 April 1936, Boise, Idaho, USA. The daughter of bandleader Joe Voiten (who once worked with Bing Crosby), she grew up to be a teenage rodeo rider. She also became a yodelling champion and in 1955, she represented her state in the Miss America contest. Later the same year, when the touring *Grand Ole Opry* show played Boise, she deputized for the indisposed Jean Shepard, which resulted in her joining the show. In 1957, she co-hosted with Ernest Tubb the first national television showing of the *Opry*. This led to appearances on many major television shows and after leaving the touring *Opry* show, in 1960 she formed her own band and started her own television series. 'Footsteps Of A Fool' became her first and only US country Top 10 hit, when it charted in 1962. Noted for her beauty and elegance, her colourful western-style Nudie costumes and with a repertoire that ran from big ballads to yodels, she became very popular. She was one of the first country singers to appear in Las Vegas and was a featured artist around the Nevada casino circuit for over twenty years, being a frequent performer at such major venues as the Golden Nugget Club and Caesar's Palace. She recorded for several labels including ABC, United Artists, Musicor and Columbia Records and her last country chart hit was 'Padre' in 1975. She retired from the music industry in 1980 to become a church minister. (She is not related to country star Loretta Lynn.)
● ALBUMS: with the Sunshine Boys *Sings At The Golden Nugget* (United Artists 1962)★★★, *Here Is Our Gal Judy Lynn* (United Artists 1963)★★★, *Number One Most Promising New Country And Western Girl Singer* (United Artists 1964)★★★, *The Judy Lynn Show* (United Artists 1964)★★★, *The Judy Lynn Show Act 2* (United Artists 1965)★★★, *The Judy Lynn*

Show Plays Again (Musicor 1966)★★, with the Jordanaires *Honey Stuff* (Musicor 1966)★★★, *Judy Lynn In Las Vegas* (Unart 1967)★★★, *Golden Nuggets* (Musicor 1967)★★★, *Judy Lynn Sings At Caesar's Palace* (Columbia 1969)★★, *Parts Of Love* (1971)★★★, *Naturally* (1973)★★.
● COMPILATIONS: *The Best Of Judy Lynn* (United Artists 1966)★★★.

LYNN, LORETTA

b. Loretta Webb, 14 April 1935, Butcher Hollow, Kentucky, USA. Lynn is a coalminer's daughter, being the second of the eight children of Ted and Clara Webb. She is one-quarter Cherokee and her name came from her mother's fondness for film star Loretta Young. She was raised in a small shack during the Depression and was attracted to country music as an 11-year-old, when the family acquired a radio and she heard the singing of Molly O'Day. Her autobiography tells of her makeshift wardrobe and how, at the age of 13, she married a serviceman, Oliver Vanetta Lynn, known to his friends as Doolittle or Mooney (short for Moonshine). He took her to Custer, Washington, and she had four children and several miscarriages by the time she was 18. They had six children in all and Lynn was a grandmother at the age of 29. 'Mooney', recognizing her talent, encouraged her to sing in local clubs and her band, the Trailblazers, included her brother, Jay Lee Webb, on guitar. Her talent was recognized by Don Grashey of Zero Records, who took her to Los Angeles in February 1960 where she recorded four of her own songs. Zero had no money for promotion so she and Mooney promoted 'I'm A Honky Tonk Girl' themselves, the song taking its style from Kitty Wells' 'It Wasn't God Who Made Honky Tonk Angels'. Mooney said that 'they drove 80,000 miles to sell 50,000 copies', but it reached number 14 in the US country charts and enabled her to appear regularly on the *Grand Ole Opry*. Many female singers were jealous of her success, but Patsy Cline sprang to her defence and they became close friends (Lynn released a tribute album to her in 1977). When they moved to Nashville, she became a regular on a weekly television show with the Wilburn Brothers, who also managed her. Kitty Wells and Patsy Cline were two of her major influences and she was pleased to be assigned to their producer, Owen Bradley, by USA Decca Records. 'Success', her second country hit, peaked at number 6 in 1962, and she had further hits with 'Before I'm Over You' and 'Blue Kentucky Girl'. She then developed a hard-hitting persona as the wife who stood no nonsense from her rivals ('You Ain't Woman Enough', 'Fist City') or her husband (her first country number 1, 'Don't Come Home A-Drinkin' (With Lovin' On Your Mind)' from 1966, 'Your Squaw Is On The Warpath'). Her best-known record, the autobiographical 'Coal Miner's Daughter', was a US country number 1 in 1970. Shel Silverstein, ironically a *Playboy* cartoonist, wrote 'One's On The Way' in which she was harassed by her children and an insensitive husband. She answered Tammy Wynette's 'Stand By Your Man' in 1975 with the double standards of 'The Pill', which was banned by several US radio stations. By way of contrast, she subsequently had a country hit with a song called 'Pregnant Again'.

Although her first duets were with Ernest Tubb, she formed a regular team with Conway Twitty and the combination of the two distinctive voices worked well, especially in 'After The Fire Is Gone', 'As Soon As I Hang Up The Phone', 'The

Letter' and the amusingly-titled 'You're The Reason Our Kids Are Ugly'. When she fell out with the Wilburn Brothers, she formed United Talent Inc. with Twitty. As the brothers still owned her publishing, she was reluctant to record her own material, although subsequently she was elected to the Nashville Songwriters International Hall of Fame. In 1972, Lynn was the first woman to become the Country Music Association's Entertainer of the Year and she also shared the Vocal Duo of the Year award with Twitty. In 1973, she made the cover of *Newsweek* and was the first woman in country music to become a millionaire. However, she met with little UK success and some of her UK releases sold less than 200 copies. Her bestselling autobiography, *Coal Miner's Daughter*, showed how the human spirit could combat poverty and sickness, but also illustrated that the problems of endless touring could be as traumatic. Lynn's musicians call her 'Mom' and share their problems with her. Sissy Spacek won an Oscar for her portrayal of Lynn, which included reproducing her singing, in the 1980 film *Coal Miner's Daughter*; the film also featured Tommy Lee Jones as her husband and Levon Helm of the Band as her father. Her country music success includes 16 number 1 singles, 60 other hits, 15 number 1 albums and numerous awards, but she has never sought pop success. Her last Top Ten single was 'I Lie' in 1982. She owns a huge ranch 70 miles outside of Nashville, which has the whole town of Hurricane Mills in its grounds. Another part of the property, the Loretta Lynn Dude Ranch, is a tourist attraction with camping facilities. Despite her prolific output in the 60s and 70s, she has not recorded much recently, although she teamed up with Tammy Wynette and Dolly Parton for 1993's *Honky Tonk Angels* album. To quote Roy Acuff, 'A song delivered from Loretta is from the deepest part of her heart.' She received the Legend Award at 1996's 3rd Annual Country Music Awards.

● ALBUMS: *Loretta Lynn Sings* (Decca 1963)★★★, *Before I'm Over You* (Decca 1964)★★★, *Songs From My Heart* (Decca 1965)★★★★, *Blue Kentucky Girl* (Decca 1965)★★★★, *Hymns* (Decca 1965)★★, with Ernest Tubb *Mr. And Mrs. Used To Be* (Decca 1965)★★★★, *I Like 'Em Country* (Decca 1966)★★★, *You Ain't Woman Enough* (Decca 1966)★★★★, *A Country Christmas* (Decca 1966)★★, with Tubb *Ernest Tubb & Loretta Lynn Singin' Again* (Decca 1967)★★★★, *Don't Come Home A-Drinkin'* (Decca 1967)★★★, *Singin' With Feelin'* (Decca 1967)★★★, *Who Says God Is Dead* (Decca 1968)★★★, *Fist City* (Decca 1968)★★★, *Your Squaw Is On The Warpath* (Decca 1969)★★★, *A Woman Of The World/To Make A Man* (Decca 1969)★★★, with Tubb *If We Put Our Heads Together* (Decca 1969)★★★★, *Here's Loretta Singing 'Wings Upon Your Horns'* (Decca 1970)★★★, *Loretta Writes 'Em And Sings 'Em* (Decca 1970)★★★, *Coal Miner's Daughter* (Decca 1971)★★★★, *I Want To Be Free* (Decca 1971)★★★★, *You're Lookin' At Country* (Decca 1971)★★★, with Conway Twitty *We Only Make Believe* (Decca 1971)★★★★, with Twitty *Lead Me On* (Decca 1971)★★★, *One's On The Way* (Decca 1972)★★★, *God Bless America Again* (Decca 1972)★★★, *Alone With You* (Decca 1972)★★★, *Here I Am Again* (Decca 1972)★★★, *Entertainer Of The Year* (MCA 1973)★★★★, with Twitty *Louisiana Woman, Mississippi Man* (MCA 1973)★★★, *Love Is The Foundation* (MCA 1973)★★★, *They Don't Make 'Em Like My Daddy* (MCA 1974)★★★, with Twitty *Country*

Partners (MCA 1974)★★★, with Twitty *Feelins'* (MCA 1975)★★★, *Back To The Country* (MCA 1975)★★★, *Home* (MCA 1975)★★★, *When The Tingle Becomes A Chill* (MCA 1976)★★★, *Somebody Somewhere* (MCA 1976)★★★, *On The Road With Loretta And The Coal Miners* (MCA 1976)★★, with Twitty *United Talent* (MCA 1976)★★★, *I Remember Patsy* (MCA 1977)★★★, with Twitty *Dynamic Duo* (MCA 1977)★★★, *Out Of My Head And Back In My Bed* (MCA 1978)★★★, with Twitty *Honky Tonk Heroes* (MCA 1978)★★★, *Greatest Hits Live* (K-Tel 1978)★★★, with Twitty *Diamond Duet* (MCA 1979)★★★, *We've Come A Long Way Baby* (MCA 1979)★★★, *Loretta* (MCA 1980)★★★, *Lookin' Good* (MCA 1980)★★★, with Twitty *Two's A Party* (MCA 1981)★★★, *Making Love From Memory* (MCA 1982)★★★, *I Lie* (MCA 1982)★★★, *Lyin', Cheatin', Woman Chasin', Honky Tonkin', Whiskey Drinkin' You* (MCA 1983)★★★, *Just A Woman* (MCA 1985)★★★, with Twitty *Making Believe* (MCA 1988)★★★, *Who Was That Stranger* (MCA 1989)★★★, with Tammy Wynette, Dolly Parton *Honky Tonk Angels* (Columbia 1993)★★★.

● COMPILATIONS: *Loretta Lynn's Greatest Hits* (Decca 1968)★★★, *Here's Loretta Lynn* (Vocalion 1968)★★★, with Ernest Tubb *The Ernest Tubb/Loretta Lynn Story* (MCA 1973)★★★★, *Greatest Hits Volume 2* (MCA 1974)★★★, with Twitty *The Very Best Of Conway And Loretta* (MCA 1979)★★★★, *Great Country Hits* (MCA 1985)★★★, *Golden Greats* (MCA 1986)★★★, *20 Greatest Hits* (MCA 1987)★★★, *The Very Best Of Loretta Lynn* (Platinum 1988)★★★, *The Country Music Hall Of Fame: Lorette Lynn* (MCA 1991)★★★★, *Coal Miner's Daughter: The Best Of ...* (Music Collection 1993)★★★, *Honky Tonk Girl: Collection* 3-CD box set (MCA 1994)★★★★, *The Very Best Of Loretta Lynn* (Half Moon 1997)★★★.

● VIDEOS: *Loretta Lynn Live* (MSD 1988), *Coal Miners Daughter* (Prism Video 1991), *Loretta Lynn* (Telstar Video 1992).

● FURTHER READING: *Coal Miner's Daughter*, Loretta Lynn with George Vecsey. *The Story Of Loretta Lynn*, Robert K. Krishef. *Loretta Lynn's World Of Music: Including An Annotated Discog*, Laurence J. Zwisohn.

LYNNE, SHELBY

b. Shelby Lynn Moore, 22 October 1968, Quantico, Virginia, USA. The exceptionally talented Lynne was raised in Jackson, Alabama, and her life reads like a soap opera: there were long arguments with her father who had her jailed on a trumped-up charge, and later, she saw her father shoot her mother dead and then commit suicide. When she appeared on the *Nashville Now* talent show at the age of 18, it was evident that she was a very good singer with a rather unusual, deep voice. Billy Sherrill offered to produce her records and her first album included the standards 'I Love You So Much It Hurts Me' and 'I'm Confessin''. Her first single, 'If I Could Bottle This Up', was with another of Sherrill's artists, George Jones. She is a very determined country performer who does not kowtow to the media by turning on smiles for the photographers. Her reputation made it difficult to obtain a record contract after parting with Epic. *Temptation* was a radical album, employing a full horn section, and sounded closer to Harry Connick Jnr. than country music. Her video for 'Feelin' Kind Of Lonely Tonight' indicated her wish to tour with an orchestra. *Restless* marked something of a return to traditional country, although there were still jazz and R&B overtones. Despite her talent, she has yet to win over US radio stations.

● ALBUMS: *Sunrise* (Epic 1989)★★★, *Tough All Over* (Epic 1990)★★★★, *Soft Talk* (Epic 1991)★★★, *Temptation* (Morgan-Creek 1993)★★★, *Restless* (Magnatone 1995)★★★.
● VIDEOS: *Tell Me I'm Crazy* (1993).

MAC AND BOB

Mac (b. Lester MacFarland, 2 February 1902, Gray, Kentucky, USA, d. 25 July 1984, Oliver Springs, Tennessee, USA; mandolin, harmonica, fiddle, tenor vocals) and Bob (b. Robert Alexander Gardner, 16 December 1987, Oliver Springs, Tennessee, USA, d. 30 September 1978, Knoxville, Tennessee, USA; guitar, lead vocals) were one of the very first close harmony duet acts to sing in country music. Both blind, they first met, in 1915, while studying at Louisville's Kentucky School For The Blind and began to sing together. In 1922, they began playing the vaudeville circuit and local venues, but by 1925, as MacFarland And Gardner, they were an established act on WNOX Knoxville. Their very effective style saw Gardner singing lead and playing guitar, while MacFarland picked the instrumental lead on his mandolin and added tenor harmony. During the 30s, his mandolin playing did much to popularize the instrument in country music. In 1926, in New York, they recorded 24 sides for Vocalion Records, with their version of 'When The Roses Bloom Again' proving so successful that they made further recordings that year. Vocalion arranged tours for them, in 1927, and held further recording sessions. When, in April 1931, they relocated to Chicago, to become regulars on WLS *National Barn Dance*, they also became Mac And Bob. Leaving Vocalion, they made recordings for ARC in 1933, which the company marketed, not only on different labels such as Perfect and Oriole, but also under pseudonyms such as Bob Lester And Bud Green, the Harper Brothers, Parsons And Kent, the Perry Brothers and several others. It has been estimated that they made over 250 recordings for various labels during their career. In the late 30s, they moved briefly to Pittsburgh, but returned to WLS in 1939. They remained popular performers there until 1950, when they withdrew from full-time performing. They popularized such country songs as 'Tis Sweet To Be Remembered', 'Twenty One Years' and 'The Knoxville Girl' (all since recorded by numerous acts, especially including the Blue Sky Boys, the Louvin Brothers and Mac Wiseman). However, their wide repertoire

ran to gospel material, as well as popular songs such as 'I'm Forever Blowing Bubbles'. In later years, they made a few more recordings and Mac actually sang on *Precious Memories* with Patsy Montana. Gardner, a religious man, became an evangelist and MacFarland worked for some years in a Chicago hospital. In the early 70s, they both moved back to the Knoxville area, where Gardner died in 1978. MacFarland died at his home in Oliver Springs in 1984. In addition to the albums listed, some recordings have appeared on compilations of old-time music.

● ALBUMS: *Precious Memories* (Birch 1977)★★★, *Mac & Bob Early Recordings Vol. 1* (Old Homestead 1983)★★★.

MACK, LONNIE

b. 1941, Harrison, Indiana, USA. Lonnie Mack began playing guitar while still a child, drawing early influence from a local blues musician, Ralph Trotts, as well as established figures Merle Travis and Les Paul. He later led a C&W act, Lonnie And The Twilighters, and by 1961 was working regularly with the Troy Seals Band. The following year, Mack recorded his exhilarating instrumental version of Chuck Berry's 'Memphis'. By playing his Gibson 'Flying V' guitar through a Leslie cabinet, the revolving device that gives the Hammond organ its distinctive sound, Mack created a striking, exciting style. 'Memphis' eventually reached the US Top 5, while an equally urgent original, 'Wham', subsequently broached the Top 30. *The Wham Of That Memphis Man* confirmed the artist's vibrant skill, which drew on blues, gospel and country traditions. Several tracks, notably 'I'll Keep You Happy', 'Where There's A Will' and 'Why', also showed Mack's prowess as a soulful vocalist, and later recordings included a rousing rendition of Wilson Pickett's 'I Found A Love'. The guitarist also contributed to several sessions by Freddy King and appeared on James Brown's 'Kansas City' (1967). Mack was signed to Elektra in 1968 following a lengthy appraisal by Al Kooper in *Rolling Stone* magazine. *Glad I'm In The Band* and *Whatever's Right* updated the style of early recordings and included several notable remakes, although the highlight of the latter set was the extended 'Mt. Healthy Blues'. Mack also added bass to the Doors' *Morrison Hotel* (1970) and undertook a national tour prior to recording *The Hills Of Indiana*. This low-key, primarily country album was the prelude to a six-year period of seclusion that ended in 1977 with *Home At Last*. Mack then guested on Michael Nesmith's *From A Radio Engine To The Photon Wing*, before completing *Lonnie Mack And Pismo*, but this regeneration was followed by another sabbatical. He re-emerged in 1985 under the aegis of Texan guitarist Stevie Ray Vaughan, who co-produced the exciting *Strike Like Lightning*. Released on the Alligator label, a specialist in modern blues, the album rekindled this talented artist's career, a rebirth that was maintained on the fiery *Second Sight*.

● ALBUMS: *The Wham Of That Memphis Man* (Fraternity 1963)★★★★, *Glad I'm In The Band* (Elektra 1969)★★★, *Whatever's Right* (Elektra 1969)★★★, *The Hills Of Indiana* (Elektra 1971)★★★, *Home At Last* (1977)★★, *Lonnie Mack And Pismo* (1977)★★, *Strike Like Lightning* (Alligator 1985)★★★, *Second Sight* (1987)★★★.

● COMPILATIONS: *For Collectors Only* (Elektra 1970)★★★, *The Memphis Sound Of Lonnie Mack* (1974)★★★.

MACK, WARNER

b. Warner McPherson, 2 April 1938, Nashville, Tennessee, USA. Warner Mack is one of the few country musicians to be born in Nashville, although at the age of seven he moved to Jackson, Tennessee, and when he was nine, to Vicksburg, Mississippi. Mack, whose father was a minister, tells his story in the song 'Tennessee Born, Mississippi Raised'. He played at various school functions and started performing on the radio show *Louisiana Hayride*. In 1957, he wrote and recorded 'Is It Wrong (For Loving You)?', which was later a number 1 country hit for Sonny James. In 1964 Mack had success with a Jim Glaser song, 'Sitting In An All Night Cafe', but while it was climbing the country charts, he suffered serious injuries in a car accident. Mack, whose stage name came about through a mistake on a record label, had a US country number 1 with his own composition, 'The Bridge Washed Out', and had further success with 'Talking To The Walls' and 'How Long Will It Take?'. He was the first country artist to record a national commercial for Coca-Cola. His last US country chart entry was 'These Crazy Thoughts' in 1977. Mack has completed successful tours of UK country clubs, always closing with an emotional version of 'He Touched Me'.
● ALBUMS: *Warner Mack's Golden Country Hits, Vol. 1* (Kapp 1961)★★★★, *Warner Mack's Golden Country Hits, Vol. 2* (Kapp 1962)★★★, *Great Country And Western Hits* (1964)★★★, *The Bridge Washed Out* (1965)★★★, *The Country Touch* (1966)★★★, *Everybody's Country Favourites* (Decca 1966)★★★, *Drifting Apart* (Decca 1967)★★★, *The Many Moods Of Warner Mack* (Decca 1968)★★, *The Country Beat Of Warner Mack* (Decca 1969)★★★, with his sister Dean *Songs We Sang In Church And Home* (Decca 1969)★★★, *I'll Still Be Missing You* (Decca 1969)★★★, *Love Hungry* (Decca 1970)★★, *You Make Me Feel Like A Man* (Decca 1971)★★★, *Great Country* (Decca 1973)★★★, *The Prince Of Country Blues* (1983)★★★, *At Your Service* (1984)★★, *Warner Mack - The England Tour* (1984)★★.
● COMPILATIONS: *The Best Of The Best Of Warner Mack* (1978)★★★★.

MACON, UNCLE DAVE

b. David Harrison Macon, 7 October 1870, Smart Station, Warren County, Tennessee, USA, d. 22 March 1952, Readyville, Tennessee, USA. Macon's family moved to Nashville when his father, a Confederate captain in the Civil War, bought the city's Broadway Hotel. Macon learned to play the banjo and acquired songs from the vaudeville artists who stayed at the hotel. He married in 1889 and started the Macon Midway Mule And Wagon Transportation Company, which was later described in the song 'From Here To Heaven'. His mule-drawn wagons carried goods between Murfreesboro and Woodbury. Macon performed at venues along the way. However, the business collapsed following the advent of a motorized competitor in 1920. Although he had worked as a jovial entertainer for many years, he never thought of turning professional until a pompous farmer asked him to play at a wedding. Macon demanded $15, certain that he would be turned down; it was accepted and became his first professional booking. At the age of 52, when Uncle Dave Macon launched his professional career, his songs and humour proved so popular that he was soon known all over the south. He became the first star of the Grand Ole Opry when it was launched in 1925 with material covering folk tunes, vaudeville, blues, country and gospel music. In 1927, Macon formed the Fruit Jar Drinkers with Sam And Kirk McGee and Mazy Todd - their tracks among the finest produced by old-time string bands. In 1931 he was the main attraction of the *Opry*'s first touring show, working with his son, Dorris, and the Delmore Brothers. Between 1924 and 1938, he recorded over 170 songs, which makes him among the most recorded of the early-day country stars. Despite the age of the recordings, his whooping and hollering brings them to life, and notable successes included 'Arkansas Traveller' and 'Soldier's Joy'. 'Hill Billie Blues' is possibly the first recorded song ever to use hillbilly in its title. His 1927 recording of 'Sail Away Ladies' was converted into the 50s skiffle hit, 'Don't You Rock Me, Daddy-O'. Macon appeared with Roy Acuff in the 1939 film *Grand Ole Opry*, which showed that, even at an advanced age, he was a fine showman. Macon stopped touring in 1950 and he made his last appearance at the *Opry* on 1 March 1952. After his death at Murfreesboro in 1952, a monument was erected near Woodbury by his fellow *Opry* associates and he was elected to the Country Music Hall Of Fame in 1966.
● COMPILATIONS: *Uncle Dave Macon - First Featured Star Of The Grand Ole Opry* (Decca 1966)★★★, *Uncle Dave Macon - Early Recordings, 1925-1935* (1971)★★★, *Go Long Mule* (1972)★★★, *The Gayest Old Dude In Town* (1974)★★★, *Dixie Dewdrop* (1975)★★★, *Uncle Dave Macon At Home - His Last Recordings* (Bear Family 1976)★★★, *Keep My Skillet Good And Greasy* (1979)★★★, *Laugh Your Blues Away* (Rounder 1979)★★★, *Country Music Hall Of Fame* (MCA 1992)★★★★, *Travelin' Down The Road* (Country/BMG 1995)★★★★.
● FURTHER READING: *Uncle Dave Macon: A Bio Discography*, Ralph Rinzler & Norman Cohen.

MADDOX, ROSE

b. Roselea Arbana Maddox, 15 December 1926, near Boaz, Alabama, USA. In the Depression days of 1933, Charlie and Lula Maddox took their five young children (Cal, Henry, Fred, Don and Rose), whose ages ranged from 7 to 16, illegally boarded freight trains and headed for California, eventually settling near Bakersfield. They followed the various harvests, working as 'fruit tramps', and were soon joined by eldest son Cliff. All were musical, and to help their income, they began to play for local dances, with the 12-year-old Rose providing the vocals, even in noisy honky tonks. They first appeared on radio on KTRB Modesto in 1937, but by 1941, when they disbanded owing to Cal, Fred, and Don being drafted, they had become a popular act, due initially to appearances on the powerful KFBK Sacramento station. In 1946, they re-formed as the Maddox Brothers And Rose and became popular over a wide area. Their bright and garish stage costumes earned them the title 'the most colourful hillbilly band in America'. Cliff died in 1948, and his place was taken by Henry. By the early 50s, with an act that included comedy as well as songs, they were regulars on the *Louisiana Hayride*, played concerts and also appeared on the *Grand Ole Opry*. In 1947, they recorded for Four Star before moving to Columbia in 1951. Their successes included Rose's stirring recordings of 'The Philadelphia Lawyer' and 'The Tramp On The Street'. Rose also recorded with her sister-in-law, Loretta, as Rosie And Rita. By the mid-50s, Rose was beginning to look to a solo career. In 1957, she signed for Capitol and about that time the Maddox Brothers nominally disbanded. Rose soon established herself as a solo singer and, during the 60s, had several chart hits including 'Gambler's Love', 'Conscience I'm Guilty' and her biggest hit 'Sing A Little Song Of Heartache'. She also had four very successful duet recordings with Buck Owens, namely 'Mental Cruelty', 'Loose Talk', 'We're The Talk Of The Town' and 'Sweethearts In Heaven'. In the late 60s, she suffered the first of several heart attacks that have affected her career, but by 1969 she had recovered and made the first of her visits to Britain. She continued to work when health permitted throughout the 70s, but had no chart success. After leaving Capitol in 1967, she recorded for several labels including Starday, Decca and King. In the 80s, she recorded two albums for Arhoolie Records and her famous Varrick album *Queen Of The West*, on which she was helped by Merle Haggard and the Strangers and Emmylou Harris. Her son, Donnie, died in 1982 and she sang gospel songs with the Vern Williams band at his funeral. She frequently appeared with Williams, a popular west coast bluegrass musician who also provided the backing on some of her 80s recordings. In 1987, Maddox suffered a further major heart attack which left her in a critical condition for some time. Her situation was aggravated by the fact that she had no health insurance but benefit concerts were held to raise the funds. Rose Maddox possessed a powerful, emotive voice and was gifted with the ability to sing music of all types. Her recordings range from early hillbilly songs and gospel tunes through to rockabilly numbers that have endeared her to followers of that genre. Later she worked with long-time friend and rockabilly artist Glen Glenn, recording the album *Rockabilly Reunion* with him at the Camden Workers Club, London, in March 1987. Many experts rate the album *Rose Maddox Sings Bluegrass* as her finest recorded work. On it she is backed by such outstanding bluegrass musicians as Don Reno, Red Smiley and Bill Monroe. In 1995 she was nominated for a Grammy for the last mentioned album.

● ALBUMS: *Precious Memories* (Columbia 1958)★★★, *Glorybound Train* (Capitol 1960)★★★, *The One Rose* (Capitol 1960)★★★, *A Big Bouquet Of Roses* (Capitol 1961)★★★, with Bill Monroe *Sings Bluegrass* (Capitol 1962)★★★★, *Alone With You* (Capitol 1963)★★★, *Rosie* (1970)★★★, *Reckless Love & Bold Adventure* (1977)★★★, *This Is Rose Maddox* (Arhoolie 1980)★★★, *A Beautiful Bouquet* (Arhoolie 1983)★★★, with Merle Haggard & The Strangers, Emmylou Harris *Queen Of The West* (Varrick 1983)★★★, with Glen Glenn *Live In London - Rockabilly Reunion* (1988)★★★, *Rose Of The West Coast Country* (1991)★★★, with Fred Maddox *50 Years Of Country Music* (1993)★★★, *$35 And A Dream* (Arhoolie 1995)★★★, *The Moon Is Rising* (Country Town Music 1996)★★★.

● COMPILATIONS: Rose Maddox *The One Rose - The Capitol Years* 4 CD box set(Bear Family 1994)★★★★. As The Maddox Brothers & Rose: *A Collection Of Standard Sacred Country Songs* (King 1959)★★★, *I'll Write Your Name In The Sand* (King 1961)★★★, *The Maddox Brothers & Rose* (Wrangler 1962)★★★, *The Maddox Brothers & Rose 1946-1951 Vols. 1 & 2* (Arhoolie 1964)★★★★, *The Maddox Brothers & Rose Go Honky Tonkin'* (Hilltop 1965)★★★, *Family Folks* (Bear Family 1982)★★★★, *Rockin' Rollin'* (Bear Family 1982)★★★★, *The Maddox Brothers & Rose On The Air Vol. 1* (Arhoolie 1983)★★★, *The Maddox Brothers & Rose*

On The Air Vol. 2 (Arhoolie 1983)★★★, *The Maddox Brothers & Rose: Their Original Hits* (Arhoolie 1986)★★★★, *America's Most Colorful Hillbilly Band* (Arhoolie 1993)★★★.

● FURTHER READING: *The Life And Career Of Rose Maddox*, Jonny Whiteside.

MAINER, J.E.

b. Joseph Emmett Mainer, 20 July 1898, in a one room log house in Buncombe County, North Carolina, USA, d. 12 June 1971. Mainer played banjo at the age of nine but later became an accomplished fiddle player. He worked in textile mills from the age of 12 but began playing locally with other musicians in the 20s. He eventually formed Mainer's Mountaineers which consisted of his banjo-playing brother Wade Mainer and guitarists Daddy John Love and Claude 'Zeke' Morris. In 1932, Mainer played regularly on radio in Gastonia but in 1934, sponsored by Crazy Water Crystals, and performing as the Crazy Mountaineers, they became regulars on WBT Charlotte. They later moved to WPTF Raleigh but also played in New Orleans and on the Mexican border stations. Over the years there were various changes of personnel including Steve Ledford, Snuffy Jenkins and Morris's brothers Wiley and George. They first recorded as J.E. Mainer's Mountaineers for Bluebird in 1935 and are still remembered for their recordings of 'Johnsons's Old Grey Mule', 'Take Me In The Lifeboat' and 'Maple On The Hill'. By the end of the 40s, Mainer's RCA recordings exceeded 200 but he later recorded for King and during the 60s, made recordings for the folk music archives of the Library of Congress and a whole series of albums for Rural Rhythm. Mainer's Mountaineers were one of the most important of all the early-day string bands and greatly influenced later bands and musicians. Mainer remained active and regularly appeared at bluegrass and folk festivals until his death from a heart attack.

● ALBUMS: *Good Ole Mountain Music* (King 1960)★★★, *J.E. Mainer Variety Album* (King 1961)★★★, *Legendary Family From The Blue Ridge Mountains* (Arhoolie 1963)★★★, *70th Happy Birthday* (1968)★★★, *J.E. Mainer* (1968)★★★.

● COMPILATIONS: *J.E. Mainer's Crazy Mountaineers. Volumes 1 & 2* (1963)★★★, *The Legendary J.E. Mainer Volumes 1-20* (1966-71)★★★, *At Home With Family And Friends Volumes 1 & 2* (1981)★★★.

MAINER, WADE

b. 21 April 1907, near Weaverville, North Carolina, USA. The younger brother of J.E. Mainer and a fine singer and talented banjoist who developed a clever two-fingered style that made his playing readily identifiable. In 1937, after initially playing with his brother's Mountaineers, he formed his own Sons of The Mountaineers, which at times included Wade Morris, Jay Hugh Hall, Steve Ledford and Clyde Moody. He recorded for Bluebird until 1941, being especially remembered for his 1939 recording of 'Sparkling Blue Eyes'. He later made some recordings for King before moving in the 50s to work for Chevrolet in Flint, Michigan. After retirement from that in the 70s, he returned to recording with the Old Homestead label.

● ALBUMS: *Soulful Sacred Songs* (King 1961)★★★★, *Early Radio* (1971)★★★, *Wade Mainer & The Mainer Mountaineers* (1971)★★★, *Sacred Songs Of Mother And Home* (Old Homestead 1971)★★★, *Rock Of My Soul* (1972)★★★,

Mountain Sacred Songs (1972)★★★, *From The Maple On The Hill* (1973)★★★, *Old Time Songs* (1982)★★★, *In The Land Of Melody* (June Appal 1987)★★★.
● COMPILATIONS: *Wade Mainer & The Sons Of The Mountaineers* (Old Homestead 1979)★★★, *Early And Great Volumes 1 & 2* (1983)★★★.

MALLETT, DAVE

b. 1950, Maine, New England, USA. One of country singer Dave Mallett's most poignant songs is 'My Old Man', in remembrance of his father. By the age of 10, Mallett was performing as a country duo with his brother Neil. Following several years as a performer in clubs and coffee-houses, Mallett befriended Paul Stookey of Peter, Paul And Mary and they co-produced his debut, which included 'Garden Song', also recorded by Stookey himself, John Denver, Pete Seeger and Arlo Guthrie. His first albums were issued under the name of David Mallett but he has worked as Dave Mallett since *Vital Signs*. He has written several songs with Hal Ketchum, notably 'Old Soldiers' and 'Daddy's Oldsmobile'. Ketchum was featured along with Nanci Griffith, Michael Johnson and Kathy Mattea on *this town*. His compositions include 'Red Red Rose' (Emmylou Harris). He says, 'In your twenties you find your tools; in your thirties, you learn how to use your tools; in your forties, you have your tools and you know how to use them. So I feel glad to be in my forties.' A contented man, he has written about the virtues of middle-age and also contributed to albums of children's songs.
● ALBUMS: *David Mallett* (Neworld 1977)★★★, *Pennsylvania Sunrise* (Neworld 1979)★★★, *Hard Light* (Neworld 1981)★★★, *Open Doors And Windows* (Flying Fish 1983)★★★, *Vital Signs* (Flying Fish 1986)★★★, *For A Lifetime* (Flying Fish 1988)★★★, *this town* (Vanguard 1993)★★★, *...in the falling dark* (Vanguard 1995)★★★.
● COMPILATIONS: *Inches And Miles: 1977-1980* (Flying Fish 1990)★★★★.

MALONE, GENEVA

b. Texas, USA. One of the rising stars of her thriving local country music scene, Malone has been called 'the most listened to country singer in Texas today.' A regular on the honky-tonk circuit, where audiences have responded well to her natural, self-consciously conservative style, she claims to have played 'almost every country venue in the Lone Star State'. This earnest, hard-working singer brought her backing group, the five-piece Southern Rain, to the UK in 1996, headlining a 'Texas Country Music Show', also featuring Shannon McCaw and Dennis Raley.

MANDRELL, BARBARA

b. 25 December 1948, Houston, Texas, USA, but raised in Oceanside, near Los Angeles, California. Mandrell comes from a musical family: her father, Irby, sang and played guitar and her mother, Mary, played piano and taught music. At the age of 12, Mandrell demonstrated the steel guitar at a national convention and then worked in Las Vegas with Joe Maphis and Tex Ritter. By her teens, she also played saxophone, guitar, banjo and bass. Her parents formed the Mandrells with herself and two boys, one of whom, drummer Ken Dudney, became her husband in 1967. Their extensive touring schedule included forces bases in Vietnam. Mandrell first recorded in 1966 for the small Mosrite label, and her sobbing 'Queen For A Day', with Glen Campbell on guitar, was reissued with a revised accompaniment in 1984. Mandrell signed with Columbia in 1969, and, for a time, she concentrated on country versions of soul hits - 'I've Been Lovin' You Too Long', 'Treat Him Right', 'Show Me' and 'Do Right Woman - Do Right Man'. Despite her glossy Las Vegas look, she joined the *Grand Ole Opry* in 1972, switched to ABC-Dot in 1975 and had her first Top 5 country single with 'Standing Room Only'. In 1977 she had her first US country number 1 with 'Sleepin' Single In A Double Bed', which was written by Kye Fleming and Dennis Morgan, who also wrote further number 1 hits, including 'Years' and 'I Was Country When Country Wasn't Cool', which was released during *Urban Cowboy*'s popularity and featured George Jones. Her version of the soul hit '(If Loving You Is Wrong) I Don't Want To Be Right' was another country number 1 and also a US pop hit, leading her to name her band the Do-Rites. Mandrell also covered Poacher's 'Darlin'' for the US country market. Her television series, *Barbara Mandrell And The Mandrell Sisters*, ran from 1980-82 and was also screened in the UK. There was good-humoured interplay between Mandrell and her sisters, Irlene (b. Ellen Irlene Mandrell, 29 January 1956, California, USA) and Louise Mandrell, and the diminutive Barbara had the same vivacious appeal as Dolly Parton. She had further US country number 1 singles, 'Til You're Gone' and 'One Of A Kind Pair Of Fools', and also fared well with 'To Me', a duet with Lee Greenwood. In 1984 she and her two children were badly injured when her car was hit head-on. She was unable to work for a year, although she had another child, and she lost much credibility when she sued, on her insurer's advice, the late driver's family for $10 million. Her records for Capitol did not see much chart success as her style of music fell out of favour, but she maintained that the accident had strengthened her faith. During the 90s she has published her autobiography and kept up a busy touring schedule.
● ALBUMS: *Treat Him Right* (Columbia 1971)★★★, with David Houston *A Perfect Match* (Columbia 1972)★★, *The Midnight Oil* (Columbia 1973)★★★, *This Time I Almost Made It* (Columbia 1974)★★★, *This Is Barbara Mandrell* (ABC 1976)★★★, *Midnight Angel* (ABC 1976)★★★, *Lovers, Friends And Strangers* (ABC 1977)★★★, *Love's Ups And Downs* (ABC 1978)★★★, *Moods* (ABC 1978)★★, *Just For The Record* (1979)★★★, *Love Is Fair* (1980)★★★, *Looking Back* (Columbia 1981)★★★, *Live* (MCA 1981)★★, *In Black And White* (MCA 1982)★★★, *He Set My Life To Music* (1982)★★, *Spun Gold* (1983)★★★, with Houston *Back To Back* (1983)★★★, *Clean Cut* (MCA 1984)★★★, with Lee Greenwood *Meant For Each Other* (1984)★★★, *Christmas At Our House* (1984)★★, *Get To The Heart* (MCA 1985)★★★, *Moments* (1986)★★, *Sure Feels Good* (Capitol 1987)★★, *I'll Be Your Jukebox Tonight* (Capitol 1988)★★, *Morning Sun* (1990)★★, *No Nonsense* (1991)★★, *Key's In The Mailbox* (1991)★★.
● COMPILATIONS: *The Best Of Barbara Mandrell* (MCA 1979)★★★★, *Greatest Hits* (MCA 1985)★★★, *Greatest Country Hits* (Curb 1987)★★★, *Best Of Barbara Mandrell* (Liberty 1992)★★★.
● FURTHER READING: *Get To The Heart: My Story*, Barbara Mandrell with George Vecsey. *The Barbara Mandrell Story*, Charles Paul Conn.

MANDRELL, LOUISE

b. Thelma Louise Mandrell, 13 July 1954, Corpus Christi, Texas, USA. Mandrell began playing guitar, banjo and fiddle as a child and joined her sister, Barbara Mandrell, in the latter's band on bass in 1969. She had a short-lived marriage with Ronny Shaw, who opened for Barbara Mandrell, and her second marriage also failed. She was a featured singer with Merle Haggard's roadshow in the mid-70s. She signed to Epic and had US country hits with 'Put It On Me', 'Everlasting Love' and 'Reunited' (which was a duet with her third husband, R.C. Bannon). She had further success with RCA and was the butt of her sister's jokes on the television series *Barbara Mandrell And The Mandrell Sisters*. In 1983, she had solo country hits with 'Save Me' and 'Too Hot To Sleep', which led to her own television series. Her 1988 single with Eric Carmen, 'As Long As We Got Each Other', made the US country charts despite only promotional copies being issued.

● ALBUMS: with R.C. Bannon *Inseparable* (Epic 1979)★★★, with Bannon *Love Won't Let Us Go* (Epic 1980)★★★, *Louise Mandrell* (Epic 1981)★★★, with Bannon *Me And My R.C.* (RCA 1982)★★★, with Bannon *(You're My) Superwoman, (You're My) Incredible Man* (RCA 1982)★★, *Close Up* (RCA 1983)★★★, *Too Hot To Sleep* (RCA 1983)★★, *I'm Not Through Loving You Yet* (RCA 1984)★★, *Maybe My Baby* (RCA 1985)★★.

MANIFOLD, KEITH

b. Keith Cyril Manifold, 2 April 1947, Biggin By Hartington, near Buxton, Derbyshire, England. Manifold learned to play guitar and after completing his education, he sought a singing career. He was influenced by such artists as Jimmie Rodgers and Hank Williams. He was also greatly inspired by the recordings and particularly the yodels of Wilf Carter and quickly became one of the few British artists to become completely proficient in the art of yodelling. He made his professional debut at a local club in Derbyshire in June 1965. In 1974, he became the first UK country artist to benefit from appearances on television's *Opportunity Knocks*, eventually finishing second to the series' overall winner Lena Zavaroni. He made his first recordings for the Westwood label in 1974. In 1975, he performed the winning song, 'Who's Gonna Bring Me Laughter', in the 1975 *Opportunity Knocks* Songwriters Competition, which led him to record for a major label, and he was also voted the *Billboard* Best British Solo Artist at London's Wembley Festival. In 1977, he recorded for DJM and in September 1978, he was sponsored and taken to the USA to record an album in Nashville, using Nashville musicians. In 1986, he varied his style to record a gospel album, on which he was backed by the Pilling Brass Ensemble. Manifold has maintained his popularity over the years, still tours extensively in the British Isles and has also regularly played in several European venues. Occasionally he is joined onstage by his two daughters. He also owns an entertainments agency and is involved with promotional work and a recording studio.

● ALBUMS: *Casting My Lasso* (Westwood 1974)★★★, *Let's Sit Down* (Westwood 1974)★★★, *Yodelling Just For You* (Westwood 1975)★★★, *Danny Boy* (Westwood 1976)★★★, *Inheritance* (DJM 1977)★★★, *In Nashville* (1978)★★★, *Remembering* (Westwood 1979)★★★, *Old Folks Home* (1983)★★★, *Time* (Future Earth 1985)★★★, *Keith Manifold*

& White Line Fever (1986)★★, *Old Rugged Cross* (1986)★★★, *She's Mine* (1989)★★★, *I Dreamed About Mama Last Night* (1989)★★★, *Love Hurts* (1991)★★.

MANN, CARL

b. 24 August 1942, Huntingdon, Tennessee, USA. Mann was a rockabilly artist who recorded his only two chart singles for Phillips International, owned by Sam Phillips, proprietor of the legendary Sun Records. Mann was a singer and pianist whose group, the Kool Kats, was based in Jackson, Tennessee, when they recorded their first tracks for the small Jaxon label, owned by Jim Stewart (who later founded Stax Records). Those songs were published by Knox Music, a company owned by Phillips. Phillips signed Mann and had him record the standard 'Mona Lisa', which had been a hit for Nat 'King' Cole in the early 50s. It reached number 25 in the US in 1959 and became Mann's biggest hit. He recorded a total of seven singles and an album for Phillips International before leaving in 1962, but only one other single, 'Pretend', another Cole song, charted, also in 1959. He toured with fellow rockabilly artist Carl Perkins from 1962-64 and left music between 1967 and 1974, after which he returned on the ABC/Dot Records label, with a remake of the Platters' 'Twilight Time'.

● ALBUMS: *Like Mann* (Phillips 1960)★★★.

● COMPILATIONS: *Gonna Rock 'N' Roll Tonight* (Charly 1978)★★★, *The Rocking Mann* (Charly 1987)★★★. Archival albums: *The Sun Story, Vol. 6* (1977), *14 Unissued Sides* (1985).

MANNERS, ZEKE

b. Leo Mannes, San Francisco, California, USA. An accordion- and piano-playing vocalist, songwriter and co-founder, with Glen Rice, of the Beverly Hill Billies, who made their debut on KMPC Los Angeles in April 1930. Manners had originally gone to Hollywood in the hope of making a career in films and initially had no interest in country music. With the Hill Billies, he became known as Leo 'Zeke Craddock' Manners, which eventually led to the permanent change of surname. It was Manners who discovered Elton Britt and brought him to the Hill Billies. When the original group split in late 1932, Rice moved to San Francisco forming a new Beverly Hill Billies, while Manners remained on KMPC with a new group, Zeke And His City Fellers, which included Elton Britt. They also recorded transcriptions as the Langworth Hill Billies. Eventually, around 1933, Manners and Britt moved to New York where, under various aliases, they performed and recorded for ARC. They eventually went their separate ways, with Britt going on to solo stardom. Zeke Manners later recorded for several labels, including RCA, but they were reunited in 1959, when Britt recorded an album with Manners' band.

● ALBUMS: with Elton Britt *The Wandering Cowboy* (ABC-Paramount 1959)★★★, *Those Fabulous Beverly Hill Billies* gold vinyl (Rar Arts 1961)★★★.

MAPHIS, JOE, AND ROSE LEE

b. Otis W. ('Joe') Maphis, 12 May 1921, near Suffolk, Virginia, USA, d. 27 June 1986, Nashville, Tennessee, USA. His father taught him to play the fiddle as a child and he was performing at local dances by the age of 10. By the time he was 16, Maphis was a featured musician on WBRA Richmond, where he also played guitar, mandolin and bass. During the

40s, he starred on several top country shows, including *Boone County Jamboree* (later the *Midwestern Hayride*) (WLW Cincinnati), *National Barn Dance* (WLS Chicago) and *Old Dominion Barn Dance* (WRVA Richmond), where he first met his future wife Rose Lee (b. 29 December 1922, Baltimore, Maryland, USA). She was singing and playing the guitar before she reached her teens and at the age of 15, as Rose Of The Mountains, she had her own show on radio in Hagerstown, Maryland. In 1948, she met Joe and they were soon married. They moved to Los Angeles in 1951, where they became regulars on Cliffie Stone's *Hometown Jamboree* and later stars of the televised *Town Hall Party* from KFI Compton. Joe also worked with Merle Travis on occasion and they recorded two duet albums together. In the 50s, apart from their own recordings they worked as session musicians. Joe, with his super-fast picking on his unusual double-necked guitar, was much in demand by both country and pop artists and he recorded with rockabilly singers such as Wanda Jackson and Ricky Nelson, with whom he also toured. Maphis appeared with many of the major country stars, including Jimmy Dean and Jerry Lee Lewis on network television shows. From the 50s, for almost 30 years, he and Rose Lee toured with their own show, joined later by their three children, Jody, Dale and Lorrie. During this time they not only played in every American state but also in Europe and the Far East. They made their home in Nashville in the 60s, where Joe's multi-instrumental skills were much in demand for session work. He played the background music on several films and television series, including *Thunder Road*, *Have Gun Will Travel*, *The Virginian* and *The FBI Story*. Their abilities won them the nickname of 'Mr & Mrs Country Music'. Over the years, they recorded in their own right for several labels, including Capitol, Starday and CMH. In 1960, Joe gave 11-year-old Barbara Mandrell her first big break in country music when he included her on his show at the Showboat Hotel and Casino, Las Vegas (contrary to many reference books, although Mandrell referred to him as Uncle Joe, he was not her real uncle). Joe Maphis, who was Bert Weedon's favourite picker, became known as the King Of The Strings and ranks alongside the likes of great guitarists such as Merle Travis and Chet Atkins.
● ALBUMS: by Joe Maphis *Fire On The Strings* (Columbia 1957)★★★, *Hi-Fi Holiday For Banjo* (Harmony 1959)★★★, with Merle Travis *Two Guitar Greats* (Capitol 1964)★★★, *Hootenanny Star* (Kapp 1964)★★★, *Golden Gospel Guitar* (Starday 1965)★★★, *The Amazing Joe Maphis* (Starday 1966)★★★, *Country Guitar Goes To The Jimmy Dean Show* (Starday 1966)★★★, *New Sound Of Joe Maphis* (Mosrite 1967)★★★, *Gospel Guitar* (1970)★★★, *Gospel Guitar Vol. 2* (1971)★★★, with Jody Maphis *Guitaration Gap* (Chart 1971)★★★, with Jackie Phelps *Nashville Guitars* (Nashville 1973)★★★, *Grass 'N' Jazz* (1977)★★★, with Merle Travis *Country Guitar Giants* (CMH 1979)★★★, *Flat Picking Spectacular* (1982)★★★; by Joe and Rose Lee Maphis: *Rose Lee Maphis* (Columbia 1961)★★★★, *Rose Lee & Joe Maphis with the Blue Ridge Mountain Boys* (Capitol 1962)★★★, *Mr & Mrs Country Music* (Capitol 1964)★★★, with Dale Maphis *Dim Lights, Thick Smoke* (CMH 1978)★★★, *Boogie Woogie Flat Top Guitar Pickin' Man* (CMH 1979)★★★, *Honky Tonk Cowboy* (CMH 1980)★★★.
● COMPILATIONS: *Flying Fingers* (Bear Family 1997)★★★★.

MARGO

b. Margaret O'Donnell, 6 February 1951, Kincasslagh, County Donegal, Eire. Influenced by Patsy Cline and while still at school, she began her own musical career in 1964 as a member of a local showband, the Keynotes. Her first success came with her recordings of 'Bonny Irish Boy' and 'Road By The River' in 1968, which led to appearances on major television shows. In the early 70s, she formed her own band, Country Folk, topped the Irish charts with an old Irish ballad, 'I'll Forgive And I'll Try To Forget', and registered a very successful appearance at the 1972 Wembley Festival. Margo was the victim of a road accident in the mid-70s, which saw her hospitalized for months and inactive for over a year. In 1976, she fronted the Country Blue Boys, toured extensively and enjoyed a major duet hit, 'Hello Mr Peters', with Larry Cunningham. Since that time, she has continued to entertain audiences, not only in the UK but also in the USA and Australia. Her major achievements include appearances at Carnegie Hall, New York and London's Royal Albert Hall, plus a very successful series on RTE Television. In 1983, her younger brother, Daniel O'Donnell, joined her band and gained some experience before launching his own solo career. In 1988, after joining the Ritz label, Margo recorded 'Two's Company' with Daniel. In 1989, she was honoured, in Kincasslagh, at an event that included a surprise appearance from her brother, in recognition of her 25 years in showbusiness. In 1991, she formed a new band, Sweet Dreams, which featured John Glenn as her co-vocalist, but she later reverted to using her original band name of Country Folk. In 1994, Ritz released *New Beginnings*, which included her hit single 'The Eyes Of My Child', as well as a new version of her old hit 'I'll Forgive And Try To Forget', but in 1995, she joined the Hazel label. Once asked for a comment on her successful longevity in the business, she is quoted as saying, 'Keep your head very level and stay away from the drink at all costs.' A very accomplished entertainer, she has never strayed far from her early influences, in either her concert appearances or her recorded output of almost 30 albums, which has led many people to affectionately call Margo 'The Queen of Country and Irish'.
● ALBUMS: *Margo And The Country Folk* (Ruby 1971)★★★, *From Margo With Love* (ARA 1972)★★★, *Country Lovin'* (ARA 1973, issued in UK, One Up 1973)★★★, *At Home In Ireland* (ARA 1974)★★★, *Margo - The Girl From Donegal* (IRL 1975)★★★, with Larry Cunningham *Yes Mr Peters* (Release 1977)★★★, *A Toast To Claddagh* (ARA 1978)★★★, *Galway Bay* (ARA 1978)★★★, *Irish Requests* (ARA 1979)★★★, *Country Style* (ARA 1979)★★★, *Country Girl* (Homespun 1980)★★★, *Margo's Favourites* (Harp 1980)★★★, *Trip To Ireland* (Homespun 1982)★★★, *Three Leaf Shamrock* (Homespun early-80s)★★★, *Just Margo* (Homespun early-80s)★★★, *I'll Settle For Old Ireland* (Homespun early-80s)★★★, *Destination Donegal* (ARA 1982)★★★, *18 Irish Songs* (ARA 1982)★★★, *Toast From An Irish Colleen* (Stoic 1984)★★★, *Girl From Donegal* (IMHC 1987)★★★, *Margo Now* (Unicorn 1987, reissued with different sleeve Ritz 1988)★★★, *I Long To See Old Ireland Free Once More* (Outlet 1988)★★★, *Ireland Must Be Heaven* (EMI-Ireland 1988)★★★, *A Trip Through Ireland* (I&B 1989)★★★, *Ireland On My Mind* (Ritz 1992)★★★, *New Beginnings* (Ritz 1994)★★★.
● COMPILATIONS: *Greatest Hits: Margo* (Ara 1978)★★★★, *All Time Hits* (ARA 1979)★★★.

MARTELL, LINDA

b. Leesville, South Carolina, USA. Initially a R&B singer who included some country material in her repertoire. In 1969, while working the clubs and military bases in her home state, she attracted the attention of Shelby Singleton, who signed her to his Plantation label. In 1969 and 1970, she registered three *Billboard* country hits, namely 'Color Him Father', her version of the Freddy Fender hit 'Before The Next Teardrops Falls' and 'Bad Case Of the Blues'. Further chart success eluded her but she is credited with being the first black female country singer to appear on the *Grand Ole Opry* after her appearance there in August 1969.

● ALBUMS: *Color Me Country* (Plantation 1970)★★★.

MARTIN, ASA

b. 28 June 1900, Winchester, Clark County, Kentucky, USA, d. 15 August 1979. Martin learned to play guitar as a child (later adding musical saw) and gained his first professional work in vaudeville and minstrel shows. He recorded for Gennett with Doc Roberts and for some years from the late 20s, he worked as a duo with young James Roberts (Doc's son). Between 1928 and 1934, they recorded a mixture of old-time songs, new numbers and parodies, on some sessions being accompanied by Roy Hobbs (mandolin). Roberts tired of the music, in 1937, and joined the navy but later, he rejoined Martin, who had a band at WLAP Lexington on Martin's popular *Morning Roundup*. Amongst his musicians were Stringbean and the Amburgey Sisters; one of them, Irene, married Roberts and they performed as James And Martha (Carson). Martin, who also worked on WHAS Louisville and WLW and WCKY Cincinnati, made further recordings, mainly comedy numbers, for Vocalion Records in 1938. Throughout the 30s, Martin appeared on countless recordings for Paramount, Gennett and ARC. He once even recorded a sketch ('The Beer Party') with some friends to celebrate the end of prohibition. In 1940, he relocated to WCMI Ashland but during World War II, he withdrew from full-time performing and moved to Ohio, where he worked in a steel plant. He retired in the mid-60s and settled near Irvine, Kentucky, where he formed and played locally with his Cumberland Rangers. In 1971, Martin and Doc and James Roberts (the original Fiddlin' Doc Roberts Trio) were reunited to play a reunion concert at Berea College. In 1974, Martin and the Cumberland Rangers recorded an album for Rounder Records, but sadly, little of his immense recorded output is available, except for occasional tracks on some old-time compilations. He continued to make concert appearances with his group, sometimes beyond his own state and even, on one occasion, to Japan. Martin, a fine vocalist and a much respected rhythm guitarist, has helped many young musicians. In later years, his brilliant memory made him a source of knowledge on the early days of the music. On 15 August 1979, Martin, after spending the morning and afternoon fishing, returned to his garden to collect cucumbers for tea; his daughter-in-law subsequently found him dead, the victim of a heart attack.

● ALBUMS: *Doctor Ginger Blue* (Rounder 1974)★★★.

MARTIN, BENNY

b. 8 May 1928, Sparta, Tennessee, USA. Martin grew up in a musical family (his father and two sisters played as the Martin Family) and he was taught to play the guitar, man-dolin and fiddle as a child - receiving tuition on the latter from Lester Flatt's father. After making his radio debut on WHUB Cookeville around 1939, he became a member of Big Jeff And The Radio Playboys on the *Mid-Day Merry-Go-Round* at WNOX Knoxville, and in 1942, moved with them to WLAC Nashville. They relocated to Chattanooga, playing WDOD and WAPO, and toured with Bisby's Comedians tent show, where they worked with Rod Brasfield. In 1946, they returned to WLAC and Martin left the band and joined WSM. He worked briefly as a member of the Musical Millers on the *Martha White Show* before his musical talents as a fiddle player and vocalist found him in demand. During the late 40s and 50s, he played with many famous acts, including Bill Monroe, Roy Acuff, Lester Flatt and Earl Scruggs (he also played on their Columbia recordings made between November 1952 and August 1953) and Johnny And Jack. He toured extensively, particularly during his time with Roy Acuff with whom he visited Germany in 1949. He made some solo vocal recordings for Mercury Records in the early 50s, and from 1953-60, he was a member of the *Grand Ole Opry*. He had minor US country hits in the 60s, with 'Rosebuds And You' and a duet with bluegrass musician Don Reno on the patriotic offering 'Soldier's Prayer in Viet Nam'. Martin, always a popular entertainer, continued to play with various acts throughout the 70s and 80s and has recorded albums with several other top instrumentalists, as well as appearing as a guest on other artists' albums. The *Tennessee Jubilee*, made with John Hartford and Lester Flatt, includes his tribute to the early days of bluegrass, 'Lester, Bill And Me'. During the 50s, he worked on perfecting an unusual eight-string fiddle, which he often used on the *Opry*; he was inspired to develop the instrument after playfully using his fiddle bow on Bill Monroe's mandolin.

● ALBUMS: *Country Music's Sensational Entertainer* (Starday 1961)★★★, *Old Time Fiddlin' & Singin'* (Mercury 1964)★★★, with Bobby Sykes *Benny Martin with Bobby Sykes* (Hilltop 1965)★★★, with Don Reno *Bluegrass Gospel Favorites* (1967)★★★, with John Hartford, Lester Flatt *Tennessee Jubilee* (Flying Fish 1975)★★★, *Turkey In The Grass* (1977)★★★, *Southern Bluegrass Fiddle* (1980)★★★, with Buddy Spicer *Great American Fiddle Collection* (1980)★★★, with Reno *Gospel Songs From Cabin Creek* (1990)★★★.

● COMPILATIONS: *The Fiddle Collection* (CMH 1977)★★★, *Big Daddy Of The Fiddle And Bow* (CMH 1979)★★★★.

MARTIN, GRADY

b. Thomas Grady Martin, 17 January 1929, Chapel Hill, Marshall County, Tennessee, USA. As a boy, Martin was obsessed with both the fiddle and guitar, and he attended all the shows he could in order to watch and learn. When aged only 15, he was taken to Nashville to play with the Bailes Brothers on the *Grand Ole Opry*. He and his friend, Jabbo Arrington, travelled to Chicago to play on 1946 recordings by fiddler Curly Fox and his wife, Texas Ruby. He became a resident musician on the *Grand Ole Opry*, but in 1949, he and Arrington joined a band formed by Little Jimmy Dickens. Their twin guitars can be heard on Dickens' country hits, 'A-Sleepin' At The Foot Of The Bed' and 'Hillbilly Fever'. Martin formed a group of session musicians, the Slewfoot Five, who recorded in their own right and were credited on hit records by Bing Crosby ('Till The End Of The World') and Burl Ives ('The Wild Side Of Life'). Martin played on sessions for Red

Foley, Bobby Helms, Webb Pierce and Marty Robbins ('El Paso'). He also played on Buddy Holly's Nashville sessions, including 'Love Me' and 'Modern Don Juan', and the distinctive introduction to Johnny Horton's 'Battle Of New Orleans'. A failure in electrical equipment led to him 'inventing' feedback on Marty Robbins' US hit, 'Don't Worry'. Martin and Chet Atkins are the only musicians to have accompanied both Hank Williams and Elvis Presley. Martin played on Presley's recording sessions from 1962-65, and he became a mainstay of the so-called Nashville sound. He also worked with Joan Baez, J.J. Cale, Kris Kristofferson ('Why Me Lord'), Roy Orbison ('Oh Pretty Woman') and Leon Russell. Martin has also toured with Jerry Reed and latterly with Willie Nelson, and can be seen in his film *Honeysuckle Rose*. Nelson says, 'Grady Martin has been my hero forever. There's nobody to have in the studio than Grady Martin, because not only does he play great guitar, he knows what everybody else is supposed to be doing too.'

● ALBUMS: *Dance-O-Rama* 10-inch album (Decca 1955)★★★, *Powerhouse Dance Party* (Decca 1956)★★★, *Jukebox Jamboree* (Decca 1956)★★★, *The Roaring Twenties* (Decca 1957)★★, *Hot Time Tonight* (Decca 1959)★★★, *Big City Lights* (1960)★★★, *Swinging Down The River* (1962)★★★, *Songs Everybody Knows* (1964)★★★, *Instrumentally Yours* (1965)★★, *A Touch Of Country* (1967)★★★, *Cowboy Classics* (1967)★★.

MARTIN, JIMMY

b. James Henry Martin, 10 August 1927, on a farm near Sneedville, Tennessee, USA. He learned to play the guitar as a boy and first appeared on radio in Morristown in 1948. He joined Bill Monroe in 1949 and remained with him (except for a short break) until 1954. Many rate Martin to be the finest lead singer and guitarist ever to work with Monroe. He played on some of Monroe's best recordings and sang notable duets with him, including '20-20 Vision', before eventually forming his own Sunny Mountain Boys. Martin went on to become a legend of bluegrass music, he played the WJR Detroit *Barn Dance, Louisiana Hayride* and all major venues. Over the years his band has contained some great bluegrass musicians, including J.D. Crowe, Doyle Lawson and Alan Munde. He recorded for Decca and had some chart successes including 'Rock Hearts' (1958) and 'Widow Maker' (1964). He also achieved acclaim for his work on the Nitty Gritty Dirt Band's legendary 1972 album *Will The Circle Be Unbroken*. Many experts believe that Martin has never been afforded full credit for his contributions over the years. It may be that his frankness and the perfection that he expects from his musicians have at times worked against him.

● ALBUMS: *Good 'N' Country* (Decca 1960)★★★, *Country Music Time* (Decca 1962)★★★, *This World Is Not My Home* (Decca 1963)★★★, *Widow Maker* (Decca 1964)★★★, *Sunny Side Of The Mountain* (Decca 1965)★★★, *Mr. Good 'N' Country Music* (Decca 1966)★★★, *Big And Country Instrumentals* (Decca 1967)★★, *Tennessee* (Decca 1968)★★★, *Free Born Man* (Decca 1969)★★★, *All Day Singing* (Decca 1970)★★★, *I'd Like To Be Sixteen Again* (Decca 1972)★★★, *Moonshine Hollow* (Decca 1973)★★★, *Jimmy Martin & The Sunny Mountain Boys* (Decca 1973)★★★, *Fly Me To Frisco* (Decca 1974)★★★, *Me 'N' Old*

Pete (Gusto 1978)★★★, *To Mother At Christmas* (Gusto 1980)★★, with Ralph Stanley *First Time Together* (Gusto 1980)★★, *Will The Circle Be Unbroken* (Gusto 1980)★★★, *One Woman Man* (Gusto 1983)★★★, *With The Osborne Brothers* (Gusto 1983)★★★, *Big Jam Session* (Gusto 1984)★★★, *Stormy Waters* (King Of Bluegrass 1985)★★★, *Hit Parade Of Love* (King Of Bluegrass 1987)★★.

● COMPILATIONS: *You Don't Know My Mind (1956-1966)* (Rounder 1990)★★★★, *Jimmy Martin And The Sunny Mountain Boys* 6-CD box set (Bear Family 1994)★★★★.

MARTIN, JUDY

b. Eva Alaine Overstake, 16 July 1918, Decatur, Illinois, USA, d. November 1951. She learned to play guitar as a child and first sang at Salvation Army gatherings with her elder sisters, Evelyn (b. 1913) and Lucille (b. 1915, d. 1978). In 1931, singing as the Three Maids, they became regulars on WLS Chicago, where they worked with Red Foley. In 1933, after she married Foley, the act broke up (Evelyn and Lucille went on to work as solo acts, with Lucille later achieving lasting country music fame as singer-songwriter Jenny Lou Carson). Eva became a regular on the WLS *National Barn Dance* programme until 1947. During this time, she and Foley raised three children; the elder, Shirley Lee, later married singer Pat Boone and is the mother of pop singer Debbie Boone. Eva also brought up Betty Foley, whose mother, Foley's first wife Axie Pauline (Cox), had died in childbirth. In the late 40s, Eva followed a solo career, performing as Judy Martin, but in November 1951, she ended her life with an overdose of sleeping tablets. Her reasons were unclear but reports indicated that it was mainly because of Foley's friendship with Sally Sweet, who later became his third wife. She made some recordings with Foley and may be heard on *Red Foley* (Vocalion 1966).

MARTIN, MAC, AND THE DIXIE TRAVELERS

b. William D. Colleran, 26 April 1925, Pittsburg, Pennsylvania, USA. Colleran began his career as a teenager singing with Ed Brozi in a touring medicine show, and was influenced by acts such as the Monroe Brothers and the Blue Sky Boys. After World War II, he became interested in bluegrass music. In 1949, he and his band played regularly on WHJB Greensburg, Pennsylvania, and since there were three members of the band called Bill, he decided he would become Mac Martin. In the early 50s, he was noted for his banjo playing and fine vocal work, and in 1953, was playing with a band on WHOD Homestead, Pennsylvania, which was likened to that of Lester Flatt and Earl Scruggs. In 1957, he and his band took a residency at Walsh's Lounge in Pittsburg where they played weekly for the next 15 years. In 1963, the Travelers recorded two albums for Gateway records, although only one was released. A few years later, they recorded four albums for Rural Rhythm. Noted mandolin specialist Bob Artis (b. 26 July 1946, Santa Monica, California, USA) joined the band and when Mac Martin left for a time in 1972, Artis took over. In 1974, when the band recorded for County, Martin had returned. In addition to his playing, Artis wrote many articles for publications such as *Bluegrass Unlimited* and *Muleskinner News*, and his book *Bluegrass* was published in 1975.

● ALBUMS: *Folk And Bluegrass Favorites* (Rural Rhythm

1966)★★★, *Traveling Blues* (Rural Rhythm 1968)★★★, *Goin' Down The Country* (Rural Rhythm 1968)★★★, *Just Like Old Times* (1970)★★★, *Back Trackin'* (1971)★★★, *Dixie Bound* (County 1974)★★★, *Travelin' On* (1978)★★★, *Basic Bluegrass* (1987)★★★, *Traveler's Portrait* (1989)★★★.

● FURTHER READING: *Bluegrass*, Bob Artis.

MARVIN, JOHNNY AND FRANKIE

Johnny (b. John Senator Marvin, 11 July 1897, Butler, Oklahoma, USA, d. 20 December 1945, Hollywood, California, USA) and brother Frankie (b. Frank James Marvin, 27 January 1904, Butler, Oklahoma, USA). Around 1913, Johnny (who played guitar and banjo and had previously left home at the age of 12 to join a travelling show called the Royal Hawaiians, where he learned the steel guitar and ukulele. After naval service in World War I, he moved into vaudeville and as Honey Duke And His Uke, he worked his way to New York where, for five years, he had a daily radio show on network NBC. He made records and even appeared on Broadway in the musical *Honeymoon Lane*. In 1928, he was joined by Frankie (also a good steel guitarist) and using several differing names, he was soon recording for several labels. The Marvins befriended and arranged auditions for the young Gene Autry, when he first visited New York seeking a recording contract. Autry never forgot their help and from that time he began to provide work for them. In the late 20s, Frankie also worked with the Duke of Paducah (Benjamin Francis 'Whitey' Ford, b. 12 May 1901, DeSoto, Missouri, USA, d. 20 June 1986, Nashville, Tennessee, USA) in a comedy duo known as Ralph And Elmer (Ford also later worked as MC on Autry's radio show before becoming a long-time regular on the *Grand Ole Opry*). The Marvins moved to Hollywood with Autry in 1934, and for about 20 years, Frankie's distinctive steel guitar was an important part of the Autry sound on recordings and radio shows. He also worked on Autry's films, both in acting roles and as a stuntman - a job that he reckoned paid better than acting. Although Johnny recorded for Decca in the mid-30s, the Depression had basically ended his solo career. He worked with Autry as a writer and producer on the *Melody Ranch Show* and wrote around 80 songs for Autry's films, including 'Dust'. During World War II, Johnny made several tours to the South Pacific to entertain army personnel and in 1943, in the Papuan jungles, he contacted dengue fever, which ultimately led to his death from a heart attack in 1945. In the mid-50s, when the *Melody Ranch Show* was taken off air, Frankie become something of a recluse. However, when the television version of *Melody Ranch* appeared on Autry's own KTLA station, Frankie worked on it both on and off camera. In the early 70s, he retired to Frazier Park, California, and underwent open heart surgery. He was not a prolific songwriter like his brother but he co-wrote the well-known song 'Cowboy's Heaven' with Autry in 1934. He was an avid angler all his life and when once asked why he never tried to resume his own recording career, he replied, 'Heck, I ain't got time. I'd rather go fishing'.

MASON DIXON

Jerry Dengler (b. 29 May 1955, Colorado Springs, Colorado, USA), Frank Gilligan (b. 2 November 1955, Queens, New York, USA) and Rick Henderson (b. 29 May 1953, Beaumont, Texas, USA). Mason Dixon is the brainchild of three gradu-

ates of Lamar University in Beaumont, Texas. They recorded their mixture of folk and country for several small labels in the 80s and then signed with Capitol Records in 1988, releasing two albums. Their most successful singles were '3935 West End Avenue', 'When Karen Comes Around' and 'Exception To The Rule'. Henderson was replaced by Terry Casburn in 1989.

● ALBUMS: *The Spirit Of Texas* (Texas 1985)★★★, *Exception To The Rule* (Capitol 1988)★★★, *Reach For It* (Capitol 1990)★★★.

MASSEY, LOUISE, AND THE WESTERNERS

b. Victoria Louise Massey, 10 August 1902, Hart County, Texas, USA, d. 22 June 1983. The family relocated first to Midland and then to the K Bar Ranch, near Roswell, Lincoln County, New Mexico, to an area still influenced by the legacy of Billy the Kid. The Masseys became a very popular vocal and instrumental family band of the 30s and 40s and one of the first to adopt elaborate cowboy outfits as their stage attire. The band originally comprised Henry 'Dad' Massey and three of his eight children, namely Louise (d. 22 June 1903, San Angelo, Texas) and brothers Curt (b. 3 May 1910) and Allen. 'Dad' taught his children to play various instruments, although Curt usually played fiddle, but in later years, he also played trumpet and piano. When Louise was 15, she married Milton Mabie who then became the fifth member of the group. The Massey Five's career began in the 20s, when they played and sang at local shows and church socials. This led to a two-year tour of the USA and Canada, as well as a radio show on KMBC Kansas City. In 1930, 'Dad' retired to his ranch and a Californian, Larry Wellington, replaced him. In 1933, they became regulars on the *National Barn Dance* on WLS Chicago, before moving to New York in 1935, where they featured on the NBC-networked *Show Boat*, and the following year, they gained their own networked *Log Cabin Dude Ranch* on NBC-WJZ. They had, by this time, first become the Westerners but when Louise, with her flamboyant Spanish-style costumes, became more and more the focal point of the act, she received lead billing. They made popular personal appearances over a wide area and even returned to WLS to star on *Plantation Party* and other shows. In 1938, they made a film appearance in Tex Ritter's Monogram B-western *Where The Buffalo Roam*. They recorded for several labels including Vocalion, OKeh and Conqueror and are best remembered for their fine version of 'My Adobe Hacienda'. Louise wrote the song, based on a house that she and Milt were building in 1941. She needed the music properly transcribed for publication before it could be used on NBC and this was done by a family friend, Lee Penny. He had no professional connection with the band or with the writing of the song but Louise credited him as co-writer for his work. After the group disbanded, Curt became the musical director and theme songwriter for the television shows *Beverly Hillbillies* and *Petticoat Junction* (which he actually sang).

MASTERS FAMILY

Formed in 1946, the Family are noted for their country and gospel performances. They comprised Johnnie Masters (b. John Mace Purdom, 27 May 1913, Jacksonville, Florida, USA, d. 21 January 1980; songwriter, guitar, mandolin, vocals), Lucille Masters (b. Lucille Ferdon, 13 September

1917, Homerville, Georgia, USA; songwriter, vocals) and their son Owen (b. John Owen Masters, 3 February 1935, Jacksonville, Florida, USA; songwriter, guitar, vocals). Purdom, who adopted the name Masters after his mother's remarriage, learned guitar as a boy and was performing on local radio in 1933. He met and married Lucille Ferdon in 1934, and in the early 40s, they sang as the Dixie Sweethearts on Jacksonville radio stations and made their first recordings for Rich-R-Tone in 1946. When young Owen and, on occasions, daughter Deanna, began to sing with them, they became the Masters Family. They recorded for Mercury Records in the late 40s and relocated to Knoxville, where they were regulars on WROL. Between 1950 and 1956, they recorded numerous sides for Columbia Records, most being gospel orientated, including their noted 'Gloryland March' (James Roberts, of James And Martha Carson, sang lead on some of the later recordings). After 1952, they became the first gospel group to adopt a normal country backing, rather than the limited piano or guitar accompaniment usual on gospel recordings at that time. Owen Masters was badly injured in a car crash in 1955 and his long absence affected the group's activities. They returned to Jacksonville and mainly played at church venues but recorded again, in the early 60s, for Starday and Decca Records. The Masters divorced but later remarried. In the late 70s, Johnnie planned for some comeback appearances but when he died, in January 1980, following a heart attack, the idea was forgotten. His widow, Evelyn and Deanna moved to Florida, while Owen settled in Mount Juliet, Tennessee. All members were prolific songwriters and many of their numbers have become country or gospel standards including 'Medals For Mothers', 'Cry From The Cross', 'Honeymoon On A Rocket Ship', 'That Little Country Church House', and many others.
● ALBUMS: *Sacred Songs* (Harmony 1959)★★★, *Everlasting Joy* (Harmony 1962)★★★, *Gospel Sing* (Decca 1962)★★★, *Spiritual Wings* (Harmony 1963)★★★, *The Gloryland March* (Starday 1963)★★★.

MATHIS, COUNTRY JOHNNY

b. 28 September 1933, Maud, Texas, USA. Not to be confused with his more successful namesake, this Johnny Mathis is a country singer-songwriter. He appeared on the *Big D Jamboree*, Dallas, but moved to Shreveport and made his debut on the *Louisiana Hayride* in 1953. In 1954, he and Jimmy Lee Fautheree recorded as Jimmy And Johnny and gained a number 3 US country chart hit with his song 'If You Don't Somebody Else Will'. During his days at Shreveport, Mathis worked with Johnny Horton and co-wrote some songs with him including 'I'll Do It Everytime'. Horton also recorded some of Mathis's songs. Although Mathis appeared on the *Grand Ole Opry*, he had no solo chart hits after 'Please Talk To My Heart' in 1963. The following year that song became a Top 10 hit for Ray Price and, 16 years later, charted again for Freddy Fender. His songs have been recorded by many stars, including George Jones, Faron Young, Charley Pride and Engelbert Humperdinck. Mathis recorded both country and gospel material for Little Darlin' and Hilltop Gospel during the 60s and 70s, but despite being around the country music scene for three decades, he basically remains an unknown.
● ALBUMS: *Country Johnny Mathis* (Hilltop 1965)★★★, *He*

Keeps Me Singing (Little Darlin' 1967)★★★, *Come Home To My Heart* (Little Darlin' 1970)★★, *Country Heartfelt* (President 1981)★★.
● COMPILATIONS: *Great Country Hits* (1964)★★★, *The Best Of My Country* (1973)★★★. As Jimmy & Johnny *If You Don't, Somebody Else Will* (Bear Family 1997)★★★.

MATTEA, KATHY

b. 21 June 1959, Cross Lane, West Virginia, USA. During her teens, Mattea began playing with her guitar at church functions and, when she attended university, she joined a bluegrass group, Pennsboro. She decided to go with the bandleader to Nashville and, among several jobs, she worked as a tour guide at the Country Music Hall Of Fame. Despite the competition, her vocal talents were appreciated and she was soon recording demos, jingles and commercials. In 1982, she became part of Bobby Goldsboro's roadshow. She signed with Mercury and worked with Don Williams' producer, Allen Reynolds. Her first single, 'Street Talk', made the US country charts, and then, after some minor successes, her version of Nanci Griffith's 'Love At The Five And Dime' reached number 3. She topped the US country charts with 'Goin' Gone', written by the delightfully eccentric Fred Koller, and had further chart-toppers with '18 Wheels And A Dozen Roses', 'Life As We Knew It', 'Come From The Heart' and 'Burnin' Old Memories'. Mattea is married to Jon Vezner, who won awards for writing the best country song of the year with Mattea's 'Where've You Been', written about his grandparents' love. Her 1991 album, *Time Passes By*, includes her version of 'From A Distance' which she recorded in Scotland with her friend, folk-singer Dougie MacLean. Her song, 'Leaving West Virginia', is used by the West Virginia Department of Tourism. Mattea overcame persistent throat problems to record *Lonesome Standard Time* in 1992. Since then she has become part of the new wave of contemporary country females currently leading the way. The compilation *Ready For The Storm* testifies to the quality and consistency of her work. *Love Travels* leaned more towards pop, with half the album recorded in New York.
● ALBUMS: *Kathy Mattea* (Mercury 1984)★★★, *From My Heart* (Mercury 1985)★★★, *Walk The Way The Wind Blows* (Mercury 1986)★★★★, *Untasted Honey* (Mercury 1987)★★★, *Willow In The Wind* (Mercury 1989)★★★, *Time Passes By* (Mercury 1991)★★★★, *Lonesome Standard Time* (Mercury 1992)★★★, *Untold Stories* (1993)★★★, *Good News* (Mercury 1993)★★★, *Walking Away A Winner* (Mercury 1994)★★★, *Love Travels* (Mercury 1997)★★★.
● COMPILATIONS: *A Collection Of Hits* (Mercury 1990)★★★★, *Ready For The Storm Favourite Cuts* (Mercury 1995)★★★★.
● VIDEOS: *The Videos* (1994).

MAVERICKS

This country-rock band was formed in Miami, Florida, a region better known for its dance and rock music than any fondness for country. Lead singer and songwriter Raul Malo (vocals, guitar) was born in Miami of Cuban descent. His parents' record collection was full of American roots music and rockabilly, and led to his discovery of Johnny Cash, Elvis Presley and Bill Haley. He also grew particularly fond of the dramatic intensity of the ballads sung by Roy Orbison and Patsy Cline. However, nobody at his school shared his taste, until he came across Robert Reynolds (bass). Reynolds was also a fan of older bands, and had previously been unable to find anyone to share his fascination with old country records. His best friend was Paul Deakin (drums), who had played with local progressive rock bands for several years. They played the Florida rock circuit, having realized that the few country venues wanted covers bands only. They used the opportunity to set about building a set of strong original songs, steering away from too close an approximation of their heroes because, as Reynolds conceded, 'it's one thing to touch the nerve of older styles, it's another to let yourself be engulfed by them'. The band independently released a 13-song album in 1990. This eventually reached the ears of the Nashville record companies, and MCA Records flew them to the country music capital for a showcase. Legend has it that the company decided to make their offer before the end of the band's sound-check. Their debut for MCA, *From Hell To Paradise*, was a minor success, but it was with *What A Crying Shame* that they made their breakthrough when it sold over half a million copies. It was produced by Don Cook (who had also worked with Mark Collie and Brooks & Dunn) and it included cover versions such as Bruce Springsteen's 'All That Heaven Will Allow' and Jesse Winchester's 'O What A Thrill'. The group then added a second guitarist, Nick Kane. The Mavericks are not to be confused with the UK band of the same name formed in the 90s by the former Sex Pistols bass player, Glenn Matlock. 1995 proved to be their crowning year with a CMA award and their finest album to date, *Music For All Occasions*.

● ALBUMS: *The Mavericks* (Y&T 1990)★★★, *From Hell To Paradise* (MCA 1992)★★★, *What A Crying Shame* (MCA 1994)★★★★, *Music For All Occasions* (MCA 1995)★★★★.

MAYNARD, KEN

b. 21 July 1895, Vevay, Indiana, USA, d. 23 March 1973, California, USA. Maynard, who could play guitar, banjo and fiddle, worked in rodeos until he broke into films as a stuntman. He became the first motion picture singing cowboy, when he sang in *The Wagon Master* in 1929. In this part-talkie (it was 40% silent), he sang 'The Lone Star Trail' and 'The Cowboy's Lament'. He recorded eight cowboy songs for Columbia in 1930. A cowboy song was used for a film title for the first time in Maynard's 1930 film *The Strawberry Roan*. His career as a singing cowboy ended with the film debut of Gene Autry in Maynard's 1934 film, *In Old Sante Fe*. His singing, which has been described as rustic, was not comparable to that of Autry, Roy Rogers or later singing cowboys, but he continued for some years as a noted cowboy actor. (His brother Kermit Maynard [1898-1971] was also a cowboy actor.)

McANALLY, MAC

b. Lyman McAnally Jnr., 1 July 1959, Belmont, Mississippi, USA. McAnally's early life is described in his US country hit song, 'Back Where I Came From'. Inspired by his mother's gospel piano playing, he started working in clubs from a young age, and eventually had a US pop hit in 1977 with 'It's A Crazy World'. His first album for Geffen Records featured the quaintly titled 'E = MC Squared'. *Simple Life* included harmonies from Tammy Wynette and Ricky Skaggs, but McAnally is better known for his songwriting, which, unusually for Nashville, he generally does on his own. He has

written 'It's My Job', 'Back Where I Come From' (both Jimmy Buffett), 'Two Dozen Roses' and 'She's All I Got Going' (both Shenandoah), and the classic story-song, 'Crime Of Passion' for Ricky Van Shelton. He wrote 'Company Time' for Linda Davis and the amusing video showed an MCP receiving a public humiliation for his behaviour. He also co-produced Ricky Skaggs' album *My Father's Son*.

● ALBUMS: *It's A Crazy World* (Ariola 1977)★★★, *Finish Lines* (Geffen 1980)★★★, *Nothin' But The Truth* (Geffen 1989)★★★, *Simple Life* (Warners 1990)★★★★, *Live And Learn* (MCA 1992)★★★, *Knots* (MCA 1994)★★★.

McAULIFFE, LEON

b. William Leon McAuliffe, 1 March 1917, Houston, Texas, USA, d. 20 August 1988, Tulsa, Oklahoma, USA. McAuliffe learned both guitar and steel guitar while at school, and when aged 16 joined the Light Crust Doughboys. In March 1935, he joined Bob Wills' Texas Playboys as steel guitarist, remaining with him until December 1942, when military service intervened. Wills' entreaties of 'Take It Away Leon' became an expected shout, both on live and recorded performances. He formed his own band, the Western Swing Band, in 1946, but after becoming the owner of the Cimarron Ballroom, Tulsa, in the early 50s, changed the band's name to the Cimarron Boys. He recorded for Majestic, Columbia, Dot and Starday, finding success with such numbers as 'Steel Guitar Rag' and 'Panhandle Rag', and played regularly on KVOO and KRMG, Tulsa. In the late 50s and for most of the 60s, McAuliffe and his band toured extensively in the USA, appeared on many television shows and even visited Europe. He formed Cimarron Records in 1961, and the next year had US country chart success with his version of 'Faded Love', before moving to Capitol in 1964. He retired in the late 60s, but in 1973, he played on the famous last recordings made by Wills and soon afterwards was persuaded to front a line-up of ex-Texas Playboys. This band played successfully during the 70s and early 80s, and recorded for Capitol and Delta. He died in August 1988, and is remembered as one of the great steel guitarists.

● ALBUMS: *Take Off* (Dot 1958)★★★, *The Swinging Western Strings Of Leon McAuliffe* (Cimarron 1960)★★★, *Cozy Inn* (ABC-Paramount1961)★★★, *Mister Western Swing* (Starday 1962)★★★, *The Swinging West With Leon McAuliffe & His Cimarron Boys* (Starday 1964)★★★, *The Dancin'est Band Around* (Capitol 1964)★★★, *Everybody Dance, Everybody Swing* (Capitol 1964)★★★, *Take It Away, Leon* (1973)★★★, *For The Last Time* (1975)★★★, *Steel Guitar Rag* (1982)★★★, *Leon McAuliffe & His Western Swing Band* (Columbia 1984)★★★.

● COMPILATIONS: *Golden Country Hits* (Dot 1966)★★★.

McBRIDE AND THE RIDE

Terry McBride (b. 16 September 1958, Austin, Texas, USA; lead vocals, bass), Ray Herndon (b. 14 July 1960, Scottsdale, Arkansas, USA; guitar, vocals) and Billy Thomas (b. 24 October 1953, Fort Myers, Florida, USA; drums, vocals). MCA producer Tony Brown noticed that Alabama were losing their appeal and so he formed a new country group to take over the market. He experimented with McBride, Herndon and Thomas, liked what he heard and gave them a contract; within two months, they were making their first album. The title track of *Sacred Ground* is a neat twist on adultery, written by Kix Brooks of Brooks And Dunn and Vernon Rust. Herndon and Thomas left in 1993 and were replaced by Kenny Vaughn (guitar), Randy Frazier (bass) and Keith Edwards (drums); the band were then renamed Terry McBride And The Ride. They are featured performing 'No More Cryin'' in the rodeo film 8 Seconds. Terry McBride's father, incidentally, was Dale McBride, an original member of the Downbeats, who had several minor country successes in the 70s.

● ALBUMS: *Burnin' Up The Road* (MCA 1990)★★★, *Sacred Ground* (MCA 1992)★★★★, *Hurry Sundown* (MCA 1993)★★★, *Terry McBride And The Ride* (MCA 1994)★★★.

McBRIDE, LAURA LEE

b. Laura Frances Owens, 16 May 1920, Bridport, Oklahoma, USA. McBride first sang with her sister as Joy And Jane on her father Tex Owens' radio programme on KMBC Kansas City, Missouri, in the mid-30s. When, in 1943, she was hired by Bob Wills, she became not only the first female vocalist with Wills but, in fact, the first featured woman singer of western swing music. She devoted her life to the genre and became affectionately known as the Queen of Western Swing. She recorded with Wills on Armed Forces Radio Transcriptions in 1943/4 and some MGM recordings in 1950. In the late 40s, she married guitarist/bandleader Dickie McBride who, as a member of Cliff Bruner's Texas Wanderers, provided the vocal for the first recording of the country standard 'It Makes No Difference Now' in September 1938 (between 1938 and 1941, Dickie McBride fronted his own band the Village Boys and recorded for Decca). In the late 70s, Laura Lee McBride made some appearances with surviving members of Bob Wills' Texas Playboys at various functions.

McBRIDE, MARTINA

b. Martina Mariea Schiff, 29 July 1966, Sharon, Kansas, USA. One of the leaders in contemporary country music, McBride has also won converts within more puritanical country factions for the respect she affords the roots of the music. She and her husband sold T-shirts at Garth Brooks concerts, and she graduated to becoming his opening act. *The Time Has Come*, her debut album, impressed many with its cultured treatment of traditional material such as 'Cheap Whiskey' and 'That's Me'. Her breakthrough came as the result of two singles in 1993, 'My Baby Loves Me The Way That I Am' and the much removed 'Independence Day', which gave her considerable momentum on country radio. The latter single's accompanying video also won the Country Music Association's Video Of The Year category in 1993. This time the subject matter was far from traditional, depicting an abused wife who takes justice into her own hands. Sales of her second album, *The Way That I Am*, climbed to the half million mark as a result of this exposure. She won the CMA Video Of The Year award in 1994 for 'Independence Day'. In 1995 RCA Records launched a major campaign to back her third album, *Wild Angels*, with numerous television appearances (including the CMT Showcase Artist Of The Month) and special retail promotion via the K-mart chain. Preceded by the single 'Safe In The Arms Of Her Love', *Wild Angels* was produced by McBride alongside Paul Worley and Ed Seay. Its composition relied heavily on the melancholy and sadness of her earlier releases, with her compassionate,

third-person songs reflecting sympathetically on relationships with a series of characters. 'Safe In The Eyes Of Love' was a country hit although for many, her revival of Delbert McClinton's 'Two More Bottles Of Wine' was a stronger track. Other songs, such as 'Born To Give My Love To You' which addressed the birth of her daughter Delaney, were more optimistic (her baby daughter gurgles on the number 1 hit 'Wild Angels'). In addition to the release of the album and extensive touring commitments she joined Reba McEntire, Trisha Yearwood and Linda Davis in a new version of the Michael McDonald/Patti LaBelle hit, 'On My Own'. The opening track on 1997's *Evolution*, 'I'm Little But I'm Loud', featured the recorded talents of a seven year old McBride, but overall the album strays too close to slick MOR to match *Wild Angels*.

● ALBUMS: *The Time Has Come* (RCA 1992)★★★, *The Way That I Am* (RCA 1993)★★★★, *Wild Angels* (RCA 1995)★★★★, *Evolution* (RCA 1997)★★★.
● VIDEOS: *Independence Day* (1994).

McCALL, C.W.

b. William Fries, 15 November 1928, Audubon, Iowa, USA. Fries loved country music as a child, but had a successful career in advertising in Omaha, culminating in a 1973 campaign for the Metz bread company that involved a truck-driver called C.W. McCall: 'It was just a name that came out of thin air,' says Fries. He had done the voice-over himself and developed the character on record. McCall had a US country hit with 'The Old Home Filler-Up And Keep On A-Truckin' Cafe', and then reached the pop chart with a tale of brake failure on 'Wolf Creek Pass'. President Nixon had imposed a 55 miles per hour speed limit during an oil shortage, and CB radio, which had previously been confined to farmers and radio hams, became in demand so that motorists could warn each other of radar traps. McCall told the story of 'Convoy' in CB jargon and the accompanying press release enabled DJs to explain the song to their listeners. 'Convoy' soared to number 1 on both the US pop and country charts, also making number 2 in the UK. A parody, 'Convoy G.B.', by Laurie Lingo And The Dipsticks (in actuality, BBC Radio 1 disc jockeys Dave Lee Travis and Paul Burnett) made number 4. McCall's record was the inspiration for a film of the same name, directed by Sam Peckinpah and starring Kris Kristofferson. The soundtrack featured 'Convoy' and previously released material by other artists. McCall went to number 2 on the US country charts with the narration 'Roses For Mama', and enjoyed a minor US pop hit with 'There Won't Be No Country Music (There Won't Be No Rock'n'Roll)', but he soon returned to advertising. In 1982, he moved to Ouray, Colorado, and was elected mayor in 1986.

● ALBUMS: *Black Bear Road* (MGM 1975)★★★, *Wolf Creek Pass* (MGM 1975)★★, *Wilderness* (MGM 1976)★★, *Rubber Duck* (MGM 1976)★★, *Roses For Mama* (MGM 1977)★★★, *C.W. McCall And Co.* (MGM 1978)★★.
● COMPILATIONS: *C.W. McCall's Greatest Hits* (Polygram 1990)★★★.

McCALL, DARRELL

b. 30 April 1940, New Jasper, Oklahoma, USA. Honky-tonk vocalist McCall was briefly successful both in the early 60s, as first a pop and then a country singer, and then again in

the mid-70s when outlaw country was at the height of its popularity. Raised in Oklahoma, McCall moved down to Nashville in 1958 in an attempt to record as a duo with his childhood friend Johnny Paycheck. When this plan failed he found work as a studio harmony vocalist and band member for artists including George Jones, Ray Price and Faron Young. In 1959 McCall met Nashville producer Buddy Killen who persuaded him to join the Little Dippers, alongside Delores Dinning, Emily Gilmore and Hurshel Wigintin. They placed a Top 10 pop single in 1960 ('Forever'), but by 1961 McCall had signed a solo contract with Capitol Records, releasing two unsuccessful singles for the pop market ('My Kind Of Lovin'' and 'Call The Zoo') before the label dropped him. Moving to Phillips Records in 1962, McCall switched back to recording country material, and immediately placed on the charts with the number 17 single 'A Stranger Was Here' in January 1963. Unable to repeat this success, McCall temporarily abandoned music for a film career, appearing in *Nashville Rebel* (1965), *Road To Nashville* and *What Am I Bid* (both 1966), and also worked briefly as a cowboy. He returned to music in 1968, signing up to the independent label Wayside Records for whom he released several singles and an album. When his contract expired in 1971, McCall signed to Tree International as a professional songwriter (Hank Williams Jnr had recently taken his 'Eleven Roses' to number 1) before resuming his recording career in 1974 with Atlantic Records. By 1975 he had left Atlantic for Columbia Records where he enjoyed a brief period of chart success, achieving two Top 40 singles with 'Lily Dale' (a duet with Willie Nelson) and the solo 'Dreams Of A Dreamer'. His popularity soon faded and by 1980 he was back on an independent label, Hillside Records, before switching briefly to RCA Records for the minor hit 'Long Line Of Empties'. McCall's final chart placing was with 1986's 'Memphis In May' on Indigo Records. The same year, he released two albums, but has not recorded since. German label Bear Family Records have released a comprehensive box set of McCall's recordings.
● ALBUMS: *Meet Darrell McCall* (Wayside/Mercury 1970)★★★, with the Tennessee Volunteers *Reunion* (BGM 1986)★★★, with Johnny Bush *Hot Texas Country* (1986)★★★.
● COMPILATIONS: *The Real McCall* 5-CD box set (Bear Family 1996)★★★★.

McCANN, EAMON

b. 6 November 1955, Creggan, Omagh, Co. Tyrone, Northern Ireland. McCann's interest in music came from his father, who played in a ceilidh band. After learning to play guitar as a boy, he gained his first experience of country music playing local venues with his two brothers. He recorded a demo cassette, *Eamon McCann Sings Country*, in 1990 on No Sweat, which led to him being signed to the Harmac label the following year. In 1992, he formed his own band, Pure Country, which soon became a popular touring band on the Irish country scene. He joined Ritz Records in 1994 and has collected several awards for his modern approach to country music. He sings in a style that strongly suggests the influence of Randy Travis and Merle Haggard. *Everything That I Am* included seven of his own songs. It has also led Irish devotees of line dancing to create a new dance routine, The Eamon McCann Shuffle, which they perform to his

recording of 'Its All Over Now'. McCann now regularly tours in the UK and his growing popularity and the airplay his records are receiving should ensure future success.
● ALBUMS: *Gold In The Mountains* (Harmac 1991)★★★, *Everything That I Am* (Ritz 1994)★★★, *Touch Wood* (Ritz 1997)★★★★.

McCARTERS

Jennifer and twins Lisa and Teresa McCarter were born in the late 60s, in Dolly Parton's home-town of Sevierville, Sevier County, Tennessee, USA. Their father, a factory foreman, played banjo in local bands, and their mother was a gospel singer. When Jennifer was 11 years old and her siblings were nine, they were performing clog dancing routines they had learned from watching the groups on the *Grand Ole Opry*. Three years later, realizing that they would not make a living in that occupation, Jennifer learned to play the guitar and sing, and soon the twins were adding harmony vocals. Around 1984, they made their debut on a Knoxville television station and gained further experience working with *Opry* stars Stu Philips and Archie Campbell, as well as busking on the streets of their home-town. In 1986, after some persistent and persuasive telephoning by Jennifer, the girls managed to get an audition with Kyle Lehning, Randy Travis's record producer, which led to them signing for Warner Brothers. They made their US country chart debut in January 1988, with Top 10 hits named 'Timeless And True Love' and 'The Gift', the title track of their first album. Soon after, they became part of the Randy Travis show and toured extensively in the USA and Europe. They have also appeared on many top US network television shows. Their close-harmony singing is similar to the 'Trio' recordings of Dolly Parton, Linda Ronstadt and Emmylou Harris. Jennifer also showed a talent for songwriting and with Carl Jackson co-wrote their beautifully descriptive ballad 'Letter From Home'. By the time their second album appeared in 1990, they had become known as Jennifer McCarter And The McCarters. Shortly after its release they were dropped by their record company, but they have continued to maintain their following by constantly touring USA and Europe. A new album of acoustic country songs was planned for the latter part of 1996. Says Jennifer McCarter, 'We've learnt from everything that went wrong in our career, and it's been better for us. When it happens again, and it will, we will be ready.'
● ALBUMS: *The Gift* (Warner Bros 1988)★★★★, *Better Be Home Soon* (Warner Bros 1990)★★★.

McCLAIN, CHARLY

b. Charlotte Denise McClain, 26 March 1956, Jackson, Tennessee, USA. McClain began her musical career when only nine years old with her brother in a band called Charlotte And The Volunteers. For six years they worked locally and also had television appearances. She then started modelling swimsuits, changed her name to Charly and was signed to Epic in 1976. She had US country hits with 'Lay Down', 'Make The World Go Away', 'Surround Me With Love' and a duet with Johnny Rodriguez, 'I Hate The Way I Love It'. McClain had her first US country number 1 with the soap opera saga of 'Who's Cheatin' Who'. This was followed by 'Sleepin' With The Radio On' and two duets with Mickey Gilley, 'Paradise Tonight' (a number 1) and 'Candy Man'. In

1983, she married Wayne Massey, a star of the television soap *One Life To Live*, and they had success with the duets 'With Just One Look In Your Eyes' and 'You Are My Music, You Are My Song'. Massey encouraged her to record 'Radio Heart', also a US country number 1, and he became her record producer when she switched from Epic to Mercury Records. McClain has appeared in the television series *Hart To Hart* and *Fantasy Island*, and has been featured in numerous commercials.

● ALBUMS: *Here's Charly McClain* (Epic 1977)★★★, *Let Me Be Your Baby* (Epic 1978)★★★, *Alone Too Long* (Epic 1979)★★★, *Women Get Lonely* (Epic 1980)★★★, *Who's Cheatin' Who* (Epic 1981)★★★, *Encore* (Epic 1981)★★★, *Surround Me With Love* (Epic 1981)★★★, *Too Good To Hurry* (Epic 1982)★★★, *Paradise* (Epic 1983)★★★, *The Woman In Me* (Epic 1983)★★★, with Mickey Gilley *It Takes Believers* (Epic 1984)★★★, *Charly* (Epic 1984)★★★, *Radio Heart* (Mercury 1985)★★★, *Still I Stay* (Mercury 1987)★★★, *Charly McClain* (Mercury 1988)★★★.

● COMPILATIONS: *Greatest Hits* (Epic 1982)★★★★, *Biggest Hits* (Epic 1985)★★★★.

McCLINTOCK, HARRY

b. 8 October 1882, Knoxville, Tennessee, USA, d. 24 April 1957, San Francisco, California, USA. He learned guitar and sang as a child but left home in 1896 to travel. He worked briefly with a travelling show, before he hoboed his way to New Orleans. During his career, he was referred to as Haywire Mac, Radio Mac and sometimes just plain Mac. By 1897, he was busking on the streets where, for the first time, he sang his self-penned 'Big Rock Candy Mountain' (the song later became internationally popular and has been recorded by many artists). In 1898, he worked as a mule driver in the Philippines, delivering supplies to American troops involved in the war with Spain. In 1899, he assisted journalists reporting on the Boxer Rebellion in China, before visiting Australia. He moved to Africa and worked for the railroad delivering supplies to the British during the Boer War. In 1902, after visiting London to watch the coronation of Edward VII, he worked in Argentina, Barbados and St. Croix before returning to the USA to work on the west coast and in Alaska. He became involved with the Industrial Workers of the World and wrote several songs and poems for their publications, including his famous 'Hallelujah, I'm A Bum'. In 1925, while working as a brakeman, he gained a daily programme on KFRC San Francisco where both he and the aforementioned song soon proved very popular. In 13 sessions, between 1928 and 1932, he recorded 41 sides for Victor, including 'Hallelujah, I'm A Bum', 'The Bum Song' and 'The Bum Song #2'. The material also included hobo songs ('My Last Dollar'), cowboy ballads ('The Texas Rangers') and novelty numbers ('Ain't We Crazy'). Some were recorded with what was described as his Haywire Orchestra. In 1938, he re-recorded his three 'Bum' songs and 'Big Rock Candy Mountain' for Decca. He relocated to Hollywood in 1938 and made some film appearances, including several with Gene Autry. He also did regular radio work and wrote articles, plays and stories for several publications, sometimes under pseudonyms. His popular column 'The Railroad Boomer', for *Railroad Magazine*, ran for 10 years and in 1953, he returned to San Francisco to appear on the radio and television show *The Breakfast Hour*, until he

officially retired in 1955. He continued, however, to make appearances by request whenever he felt inclined.

● COMPILATIONS: *Hallelujah, I'm A Bum* covers 1928-29 (Rounder 1975)★★★.

McCLINTON, O.B.

b. Obie Burnett McClinton, 25 April 1940, Senatobia, Mississippi, USA, d. 23 September 1987. The son of a Baptist preacher, McClinton was dissuaded from listening to R&B, but took solace in country music. Having worked for a time as a disc jockey at radio station WDIA in Memphis, he forged a career as a songwriter, penning country-soul ballads for Otis Redding ('Keep Your Arms Around Me'), before finding the ideal foil in James Carr. Two of McClinton's compositions, 'You've Got My Mind Messed Up' (1966) and 'A Man Needs A Woman' (1968), stand among this singer's finest work. McClinton then became a staff writer at the Stax label and, in January 1971, began recording as a C&W artist on the company's Enterprise subsidiary. His albums there offered varied material, including versions of Wilson Pickett's 'Don't Let The Green Grass Fool You' (1972) - his most successful country chart single - and Merle Haggard's 'Okie From Muskogee'. McClinton briefly moved to Mercury in 1976, where he had a hit with 'Black Speck', before moving to Epic, where he scored half a dozen minor C&W hits. One of the few successful black country singers, McClinton died of abdominal cancer in September 1987.

● ALBUMS: *O.B. Clinton Country* (Enterprise 1972)★★★, *Obie From Senatobie* (Enterprise 1973)★★★, *O.B. McClinton Live At Randy's Rodeo* (Enterprise 1973)★★, *Chocolate Cowboy* (Epic 1981)★★★.

McCOY, CHARLIE

b. 28 March 1941, Oak Hill, West Virginia, USA. When McCoy was eight years old, he ordered a harmonica for 50 cents and a box-top, but he was more interested in the guitar. He played in rock 'n' roll bands in Miami, where Mel Tillis heard him and suggested that he visit Nashville to work as a singer. Although his singing career did not take off, he played drums for US hitmakers Johnny Ferguson and Stonewall Jackson. In 1961, McCoy recorded as a singer for US Cadence Records and entered the charts with 'Cherry Berry Wine'. He then formed a rock 'n' roll band, Charlie McCoy And The Escorts, which played in Nashville clubs for several years. McCoy played harmonica on Ann-Margret's 'I Just Don't Understand' and Roy Orbison's 'Candy Man', and the success of the two records led to offers of session work. McCoy became the top harmonica player in Nashville, playing up to 400 sessions a year. He worked with Bob Dylan, playing harmonica on 'Obviously Five Believers', trumpet on 'Rainy Day Women, Nos. 12 And 35', and bass on several other tracks. The success of Dylan and other rock musicians in Nashville prompted McCoy and other sessionmen to form Area Code 615. McCoy had a US chart hit in 1972 with a revival of 'Today I Started Loving You Again', but, considering his love of blues harmonica player Little Walter, his records are comparatively unadventurous and middle-of-the-road. Nevertheless, he often reached the US country charts with instrumental interpretations of over-worn country songs. McCoy joined Barefoot Jerry and was featured on the group's 1974 US country hit, 'Boogie Woogie'. He now limits his session appearances, largely because he is musical director of the television series *Hee-Haw*. McCoy frequently visits the UK and has played the Wembley Country Festival with other Nashville musicians. He appeared with other Nashville session men on Ween's oddball *12 Golden Country Greats* in 1996.

● ALBUMS: *The Real McCoy* (Monument 1969)★★★, *Charlie McCoy* (Monument 1972)★★★, *Goodtime Charlie* (Monument 1973)★★★, *Fastest Harp In The South* (Monument 1973)★★★, *The Nashville Hit Man* (Monument 1974)★★★, *Christmas Album* (Monument 1974)★★, *Harpin' The Blues* (Monument 1975)★★★, *Charlie My Boy* (Monument 1975)★★, *Play It Again, Charlie* (Monument 1976)★★★, *Country Cookin'* (Monument 1977)★★★, *Appalachian Fever* (Monument 1979)★★★, *One For The Road* (1986)★★, *Charlie McCoy's 13th* (Step One 1988)★★★, *Beam Me Up, Charlie* (Step One 1989)★★★, *Out On A Limb* (Step One 1991)★★★.

● COMPILATIONS: *Greatest Hits* (Monument 1990)★★★★.

McCOY, NEAL

b. Hubert Neal McGauhey Jnr. (surname pronounced McGoy), 30 July 1963, Jacksonville, Texas, USA. McCoy grew up with a love of country as well as pop, soul and big band music. He started performing as Neal McGoy and his break came when Janie Fricke was a judge in a talent contest that he won. She mentioned McCoy to Charley Pride, who signed him to a booking and management contract and asked him to be his opening act. His debut single was 'That's How Much I Love You' on 16th Avenue Records, but in 1991, he moved to Atlantic Records and adjusted his name to Neal McCoy. After several minor hits, including 'If I Built You A Fire', 'Where Forever Begins', 'Now I Pray For Rain' and 'No Doubt About It', he found success with his excellent third album and had his first US country number 1s with the title track, 'No Doubt About It', and 'Wink'. 'You Gotta Love That' was a Top 10 hit, and stayed on the US country singles chart for over a year. Further singles and albums have proved equally successful.

● ALBUMS: *At This Moment* (Atlantic 1991)★★★, *Where Forever Begins* (Atlantic 1992)★★★, *No Doubt About It* (Atlantic 1994)★★★★, *You Gotta Love That* (Atlantic 1995)★★★, *Neal McCoy* (Atlantic 1996)★★★, *Be Good At It* (Atlantic 1997)★★★.

● COMPILATIONS: *Greatest Hits* (Atlantic 1997)★★★.

● VIDEOS: *You Gotta Love That!* (Warner Music Video 1994).

McCREADY, MINDY

The 21-year-old McCready (b. Malinda Gayle McCready, Fort Myers, Florida, USA) is one of the brightest new voices in country music, updating the traditional values of the genre for a new generation of listeners. Born and raised in southern Florida, she moved to Nashville when she was 18. Meeting up with producer David Malloy, she spent almost a year performing and preparing her demo tape, before signing with RLG Records. Released in April 1996, her debut *Ten Thousand Angels* was an assertive and confident collection that revealed McCready as an icon of female independence and self-reliance. The album gained strong reviews and by 1997 had gone platinum. The follow-up, *Don't Stay The Night*, was released in November 1997 to further acclaim. Though McCready does not write any of her own material, she covers songs that deal frankly with relationships and sexual dilemmas, and on tracks such as 'What If I Do' and 'This Is Me', she sounds like a country version of Alanis Morissette. Her rising status was confirmed by recent support slots for George Strait, Alan Jackson and Tim McGraw.

● ALBUMS: *Ten Thousand Angels* (BNA 1996)★★★, *If I Don't Stay The Night* (BNA 1997)★★★★.

McDANIEL, MEL

b. 6 September 1942, Checotah, Oklahoma, USA. McDaniel began working in bands around Tulsa - first on trumpet, then on guitar - and J.J. Cale wrote and produced his first single, 'Lazy Me'. He moved to Nashville in 1969, and after two years of knocking on doors, his brother found him steady work at a club in Anchorage, Alaska. In the mid-70s, he began recording demos for a Nashville publisher and his singing talents were then recognized. In 1976 he entered the US country charts with 'Have A Dream On Me' and he had a considerable success with 'Gentle To Your Senses'. A record about a synthetic lover, 'Plastic Girl', was banned by radio stations. He recorded many songs by Bob McDill including 'Louisiana Saturday Night', 'Right In The Palm Of Your Hand', 'I Call It Love' and his US country number 1, 'Baby's Got Her Blue Jeans On'. He wrote Conway Twitty's tribute to the *Grand Ole Opry*, 'The Grandest Lady Of Them All', while his hippie anthem 'Roll Your Own' has been recorded by Hoyt Axton, Arlo Guthrie and Commander Cody.

● ALBUMS: *Gentle To Your Senses* (Capitol 1977)★★★, *Mello* (Capitol 1978)★★★, *The Farm* (Capitol 1978)★★★, *Countrified* (Capitol 1981)★★★, *Take Me To The Country* (Capitol 1982)★★★, *Naturally Country* (Capitol 1983)★★★, *Mel McDaniel & Oklahoma Wind* (Capitol 1984)★★★, *Let It Roll* (Capitol 1985)★★★, *Stand Up* (Capitol 1985)★★★, *Just Can't Sit Down Music* (Capitol 1986)★★★, *Now You're Talkin'* (1988)★★★, *Rockabilly Boy* (1989)★★★, *Country Pride* (1991)★★★.

● COMPILATIONS: *Greatest Hits* (Capitol 1987)★★★★.

McDOWELL, RONNIE

b. 26 March 1950, Fountain Head, Tennessee, USA. McDowell initially built his career on his ability to imitate the voice of Elvis Presley, a talent he was often called upon to utilize in films and television programmes. He also recorded his own music, however, and by the 80s, was a major star in his own right in the country field. McDowell began trying out his Presley imitation while in the US Navy in 1968. Upon his discharge, he worked as a sign painter in Nashville while trying to sell his songs. Among the country artists who recorded his compositions were Roy Drusky and Billy Walker. He recorded for minor record labels such as Chart and Scorpion during the mid-70s, with no success, and released a cover version of Roy Orbison's 'Only The Lonely' in 1976, which also did not chart. McDowell's first single to chart was 'The King Is Gone', his tribute to his departed hero, which he wrote (with Lee Morgan) and recorded on Scorpion two months after Presley's death. It reached number - 13 on both the country and pop charts. His real breakthrough came later that year with 'I Love You, I Love You, I Love You', which reached number 5 on the country chart (it was also his last single to cross over to pop, although it placed near the bottom of that chart). McDowell continued to place singles on the country charts through 1980, having switched to Epic Records in 1979. That same year he supplied the voice of Presley for the soundtrack of the film *Elvis*. At the start of 1981, he began a long string of country Top 10 singles with 'Wandering Eyes', which was followed by the number 1 'Older Women' and 10 other Top 10 country hits. By the middle of the 80s, he was able to release music with little remaining of the Elvis sound, and could finally claim to have succeeded on the merits of his own voice. Later, he returned to his early vocation as the voice of Elvis in the short-lived 1989 television series titled *Elvis*. McDowell switched labels to MCA Records' Curb division in 1986. One of his biggest hits of the late 80s was a remake of the old Conway Twitty hit 'It's Only Make Believe', with the originator supplying a guest vocal.

● ALBUMS: *The King Is Gone* (Scorpion 1977)★★★, *Live At The Fox* (Scorpion 1978)★★, with the Jordanaires *A Tribute To The King* (Scorpion 1979)★★★, *Elvis* film soundtrack (Dick Clark 1979)★★, *Rockin' You Easy, Lovin' You Slow* (Epic 1979)★★★, *Love So Many Ways* (Epic 1980)★★★, *Going, Going...Gone* (Epic 1980)★★★, *Good Time Lovin' Man* (Epic 1981)★★★, *Love To Burn* (Epic 1982)★★★, *Personally* (Epic 1983)★★★, *Country Boy's Heart* (Epic 1983)★★★, *Willing* (Epic 1984)★★★, *In A New York Minute* (Epic 1985)★★★, *All Tied Up In Love* (Epic 1986)★★★, *Your Precious Love* (Curb 1991)★★★, *Unchained Melody* (Curb 1991)★★, *Country Dances* (Curb 1993)★★★.

● COMPILATIONS: *Greatest Hits* (Epic 1982)★★★, *Older Women And Other Greatest Hits* (Epic 1987)★★★★, *Best Of Ronnie McDowell* (Curb 1990)★★★.

● FILMS: *Elvis - The Movie* (1979).

McEnery, David

b. 15 December 1914, San Antonio, Texas, USA, close to the Alamo. Being a Texan, McEnery naturally became interested in things appertaining to the western life and as a boy at school, took to playing the guitar and singing cowboy songs. His fondness for 'Red River Valley' led to his nickname, Red River Dave, when he started his professional career. He played on local radio in the early 30s, but during the decade he also played many stations in various places, including New York State, where the northern audiences were taken with the singing cowboy and his strange saga songs. He developed a penchant for writing songs of historic events such as 'The Battle Of The Alamo' and 'Pony Express', and his first real break came in 1937 with his saga song 'Amelia Earhart's Last Flight'. Following this, he moved to Chicago for a time and in 1939, was invited to New York to sing his song of the lost aviator and others on the first commercial television broadcast at the World's Fair. In the early 40s, he returned to San Antonio, Texas, and began regular appearances on Border Radio station XERF where, billing himself as 'your favourite Texas Farmboy', he sang his songs and sold his sets of six songbooks, which he classed as 'a complete library of cowboy, hillbilly and sacred songs'. He also appeared on local US stations and during the 40s and 50s, recorded for several labels. He wrote many songs including 'I'm A Convict With Old Glory In My Heart' (about the man who wanted to fight but was in jail) and as the war ended, he tugged at his listeners' heartstrings with such maudlin numbers as 'The Blind Boy's Dog' (later recorded with success by Hank Snow). He has never been short on gimmicks; in 1936, he claimed to be the first (and probably the last) singing

cowboy to broadcast from an airship when, from the Goodyear blimp, high above Miami, he sang 'Way Out There' over the airwaves of CBS. In 1946, he was handcuffed to a piano for 12 hours and wrote songs from titles that people selected from magazines. By the end, he claimed a total of 52 completed songs. In the 40s, he appeared in several films, including *Swing In The Saddle, Hidden Valley* and *Echo Ranch* but had made some appearances in earlier films in the 30s. Although he was a singer of cowboy songs for many years and is an expert on them, he is probably now best remembered for his saga songs. After the success of the Amelia Earhart song, he continued over the years to turn out such numbers of news interest including 'Ballad Of Emmett Till', 'The Flight Of Gary Powers', 'The Flight Of Apollo Eleven' and 'The Ballad Of Patty Hearst'. He has appeared on countless radio and television programmes and built the reputation of being something of a character, as well as becoming an ordained Pentecostal minister. Many of the major stars have recorded his songs and among his many tribute songs, he once recorded a dedication to his friend, Bob Wills, called 'Somewhere I Hear Angels Singing The San Antone Rose'. He moved to Nashville in the mid-70s, where he became noted for his flamboyant western dress with gold boots, his long white hair and goatee beard, all of which made him look somewhat like a modern Buffalo Bill Cody. He later returned to his native Texas, where he dispensed with the white locks and beard and reverted to more conventional attire, but still maintained his regular public appearances at folk festivals and similar events in many parts of the USA.

● ALBUMS: *Red River Dave* 10-inch album (Varsity 1951)★★★, with the Texas Tophands *Songs Of The Rodeo* (Place 1961)★★★, *Red River Dave Sings* (Continental 1962)★★★.

● COMPILATIONS: *Red River Dave Volumes 1* and *2* (Bluebonnet 1975)★★★, *Days Of The Yodeling Cowboys* (80s)★★★, *More Days Of Yodeling Cowboys Volume 2* (80s)★★★, *Yodelin' Cowboy Memories* (80s)★★★.

McEntire, Pake

b. Dale Stanley McEntire, 1952, Chockie, Oklahoma, USA. Brother of Reba McEntire, Pake sang at rodeos with her and their other sister Susie as the Singing McEntires in the early 70s. He has competed professionally in roping events for many years. McEntire had his first US country success with 'Every Night' in 1986; 'Savin' My Love For You' went to number 3. Reba sang harmony on his 1987 chart entry, 'Heart Vs. Heart'.

● ALBUMS: *Too Old To Grow Up Now* (1986)★★★, *My Whole World* (1988)★★★.

McEntire, Reba

b. Reba Nell McEntire, 28 March 1955, Chockie, Oklahoma, USA. One of four children, McEntire recorded 'The Ballad Of John McEntire', which was about her grandfather. The family owned a 7,000-acre ranch and participated in rodeos; this background later inspired McEntire's song 'Daddy'. She sang with her sister Susie and brother Pake McEntire as the Singing McEntires, and in 1972, they recorded for the small Boss label. In 1974, she was asked to sing 'The Star-Spangled Banner' at the National Rodeo Finals in Oklahoma City. Honky-tonk singer Red Steagall heard her, which led to a recording contract with Mercury. Her first single, 'I Don't

Want To Be A One Night Stand', made the US country charts in 1976, the year in which she married rodeo rider Charlie Battles. It was followed by several minor successes, including a revival of 'Sweet Dreams' and two duets with Jacky Ward ('Three Sheets To The Wind' and 'That Makes Two Of Us'). She made the US country Top 10 with '(You Lift Me) Up To Heaven', the Top 5 with 'Today All Over Again', and in 1982, number 1 with 'Can't Even Get The Blues'. She often recorded country waltzes and had another chart-topper in 1983 with 'You're The First Time I've Thought About Leaving'. She then left Mercury for MCA, although the label was to release an album of out-takes, *Reba Nell McEntire*, in 1986. She continued her country hits with 'Just A Little Love', 'He Broke Your Memory Last Night', 'Have I Got A New Deal For You', and the number 1 hits 'How Blue' and 'Somebody Should Leave'. Her best-known single and title track of a bestselling album was 'Whoever's In New England'. McEntire's own battles with Battles ended in their divorce in 1987, and she married her bandleader, Narvel Blackstock, in 1989. Several of her successes, although not written for her ('I Know How He Feels' and 'New Fool At An Old Game'), have overtones from her own life. She has won numerous country music awards, but her 1988 album *Reba*, although very successful, irritated traditionalists who questioned her revival of a pop hit, 'Sunday Kind Of Love', and her version of Otis Redding's 'Respect'. McEntire was adamant: 'I can sing any kind of song, but whatever I sing, it'll come out country.' She appeared, killing graboids with an elephant gun, in the well-reviewed horror film *Tremors*. On 16 March 1991, tragedy struck when Chris Austin, Kirk Cappello, Joey Cigainero, Paula Kaye Evans, Terry Jackson, Michael Thomas, Tony Saputo - seven of the nine members of McEntire's band - died in a plane crash shortly after taking off from San Diego. The following year, McEntire herself was involved in a forced landing at Nashville airport, evoking memories of the earlier tragedy. She dedicated her next album, *For My Broken Heart*, to her friends and collegues. It proved to be one of her most successful projects, and the title track was a major hit single. She tried to come to terms with the previous tragedy in 'If I Had Only Known', but the whole song selection evoked memories of it. Despite its melancholia, the album became one of her biggest hits. Having committed her feelings to record, McEntire then had a massive success via the dramatic video for the 'cheating' song, 'Does He Love You', which she sang with Linda Davis. When McEntire performed at the 1993 CMA awards, her low-cut dress was the most controversial aspect of the evening's entertainment. It might have been more telling to ask if she was singing soul or country. In 1995 she looked to her roots for an album of her favourite songs, *Starting Over*, including 'Talking In Your Sleep' and 'By The Time I Get To Phoenix'. For 'On My Own', she was joined by Linda Davis, Martina McBride and Trisha Yearwood. The follow-up, *What If It's You*, featured the excellent singles 'The Fear Of Being Alone' and 'I'd Rather Ride Around With You'. She is trying to establish herself as a film actress and has played alongside Kenny Rogers in *The Gambler Returns: The Luck Of The Draw*, Burt Reynolds in *The Man From Left Field* and Bruce Willis in *North*. As one of the best interpreters of any kind of popular song McEntire is on her way to selling more records than any other female country artist.
● ALBUMS: *Reba McEntire* (Mercury 1977)★★, *Out Of A*

Dream (Mercury 1979)★★★, *Feel The Fire* (Mercury 1980)★★★, *Heart To Heart* (Mercury 1981)★★★, *Unlimited* (Mercury 1982)★★★, *Behind The Scene* (Mercury 1983)★★★, *Just A Little Love* (MCA 1984)★★★, *Have I Got A Deal For You* (MCA 1985)★★★, *My Kind Of Country* (MCA 1986)★★★, *Whoever's In New England* (MCA 1986)★★★, *Reba Nell McEntire* (MCA 1986)★★★, *What Am I Gonna Do About You* (MCA 1986)★★★, *The Last One To Know* (MCA 1987)★★★, *So So So Long* (MCA 1988)★★★, *Merry Christmas To You* (MCA 1988)★★★, *Reba* (MCA 1988)★★★, *Sweet Sixteen* (MCA 1989)★★★, *Live* (MCA 1989)★★★, *Rumour Has It* (MCA 1990)★★★, *For My Broken Heart* (MCA 1991)★★★, *It's Your Call* (MCA 1992)★★★★, *Read My Mind* (MCA 1994)★★★★, *Starting Over* (MCA 1995)★★★★, *What If It's You* (MCA 1996)★★★.
● COMPILATIONS: *The Best Of Reba McEntire* (Mercury 1985)★★★★, *The Very Best Of Reba McEntire* (Country Store 1987)★★★, *Greatest Hits* (MCA 1987)★★★★, *Greatest Hits Vol. 2* (MCA 1993)★★★★.
● VIDEOS: *Reba In Concert* (1992), *For My Broken Heart* (1993), *Greatest Hits* (MCA 1994), *Why Haven't I Heard From You* (Picture Vision 1994), *Reba Live* (MCA 1995), *And Still* (MCA 1995), *Reba Celebrating 20 Years* (MCA 1996).
● FURTHER READING: *Reba: Country Music's Queen*, Don Cusic. *Reba - My Story*, Reba McEntire with Tom Carter.

McEuen, John

b. 19 December 1945, Garden Grove, California, USA. McEuen was exposed to many forms of music through his brother William McEuen, who was a disc jockey and concert promoter. John formed his own folk group, the Illegitimate Jug Band, so called because they did not have a jug player. The group evolved into the Nitty Gritty Dirt Band and brother Bill became their manager. McEuen usually played banjo but he also played accordion, guitar, mandolin, dulcimer, steel guitar and fiddle. His guest appearances include Hoyt Axton's *Rusty Old Halo*, David Allan Coe's *Just Divorced*, Marshall Tucker Band's *Long Hard Ride*, and Bill Wyman's *Monkey Grip*. Since leaving the Dirt Band in 1986, McEuen has made records in the progressive bluegrass field, that is, bluegrass music that combines other sources such as Irish traditional music and jazz. He made his only solo appearance on the US country charts to date with a revival of Buddy Holly's 'Blue Days, Black Nights'. He arranged the music for one of Steve Martin's television specials and says, 'I could go down in history as the man who taught Steve Martin how to play the banjo.' In 1989 he returned to the Dirt Band for the double album *Will The Circle Be Unbroken, Volume 2*, and was understandably annoyed when only asked to play on one song. In 1990 he produced and directed the in-concert video and album for the Dillards, *A Night In The Ozarks*. He recorded the music for the television mini-series *The Wild West* in 1993, which was followed by a cable special, *The Music Of The Wild West*. He also scored the film *The Good Old Boys*, starring Tommy Lee Jones. *String Wizards II* features a guest appearance from José Feliciano. *Acoustic Traveller* includes a rare vocal on 'I Am A Pilgrim' and is a collection of songs from around the world. McEuen says, 'Most songs tell you what they're doing all the way through, but five people can listen to an instrumental and have five different opinions as to how it made them feel.'
● ALBUMS: *String Wizards* (Vanguard 1991)★★★, *String*

Wizards II (Vanguard 1994)★★★, *Acoustic Traveller* (Vanguard 1996)★★★.

MᴄEᴠᴏʏ, Jᴏʜɴɴʏ

b. Banagher, Co. Offaly, Eire. After serving an apprenticeship around the Irish folk clubs, McEvoy established himself on the country music scene in the mid-60s. Since then he has become one of the most important and respected Irish country singer-songwriters. He made his first recordings in 1965 and topped the Irish charts the following year with 'Mursheen Durkin'. In the mid-70s, he furthered his reputation with his popular country show on British television and had his own series *My Ireland* on RTE. He has toured extensively in the UK, USA and Canada. McEvoy has written and recorded many fine songs based on true-life incidents. They range from 'The Ballad Of John Williams' (the story of a couple who sailed on the Titanic), 'Lincoln's Army' (a song of an Irish emigrant to the USA), 'Michael' (the story of Irish patriot Michael Collins), 'I'll Write Whenever I Can' (written after he saw homeless living on London's streets), to the beautifully descriptive 'Rich Man's Garden', about childhood memories, and 'Leaves In The Wind', a moving story of 'old Rosie Atkinson' who had been widowed by the war. McEvoy has become something of a living legend in Ireland and many artists including Foster And Allen have recorded his songs.

● ALBUMS: *Johnny McEvoy* (Hawk 1973)★★★, *Sings Country* (Hawk 1974)★★★, *Sounds Like McEvoy* (Hawk 1974)★★★, *All Our Wars Were Merry, All Our Songs Were Sad* (Hawk 1974)★★★, *Sings Hank Williams* (Hawk 1975)★★★, *Where My Eileen Is Waiting* (Hawk 1975)★★★, *Long Before Your Time* (Hawk 1976)★★★, *Christmas Dreams* (Hawk 1976)★★★, *Leaves In The Wind* (Hawk 1977)★★★, *I'll Spend A Time With You* (Hawk 1978)★★★, with Gloria *Golden Duets* (Pickwick/Harp 1980)★★★, *Johnny McEvoy Goes Country* (Pickwick/Harp 1980)★★★, *My Favourite Irish Songs* (Pickwick/Harp 1981)★★★, *Since Maggie Went Away* (MCA 1985)★★★, *Songs Of Ireland* (MCA 1986)★★★, *Sings For You* (Play 1988)★★★, *The Original* (Play 1991)★★★.

● COMPILATIONS: *Golden Hour Of Johnny McEvoy* covers 70s (Polydor 1988)★★★, *20 Greatest Hits* (Dolphin 1988)★★★, *20 More Hits* (Dolphin 1988)★★★,

MᴄGᴇᴇ, Sᴀᴍ Aɴᴅ Kɪʀᴋ

Samuel Fleming McGee (b. 1 May 1894, d. 21 August 1975) and David Kirkland McGee (b. 4 November 1899, d. 24 October 1983) were both born and raised on the family farm near Franklin, Williamson County, Tennessee, USA. Their father was a noted fiddle player, and the brothers learned to play the banjo as children but changed their style in their teens. Sam worked as a blacksmith, but around 1910, he became interested in the guitar and learned to play from black street musicians. During his career he became so proficient that he has been a major influence on many musicians and was most likely the first white musician to use the guitar as a solo instrument, instead of a mere accompaniment for vocals or fiddle music. Kirk concentrated on the banjo, although he later played guitar, mandolin and fiddle, and also developed into a fine vocalist. In 1925, Sam first met and played with Uncle Dave Macon, and the following year, made his first appearance with Macon on the *Grand Ole Opry*. Soon afterwards, they were joined by Kirk and both

played with Macon, as well as performing as a duo. In 1927, together with fiddler Mazy Todd, they went to New York with Macon and recorded as Uncle Dave Macon And His Fruit Jar Drinkers. They recorded with Macon until the mid-30s, as well as recording as a duo, including their noted 1934 recording of 'Brown's Ferry Blues'. They were among the first members of the *Opry* ever to record, which later led to Sam stating, 'They recorded us because we were outstanding in the field and that's where they found us - outstanding in the field'. In 1930, they also teamed up with Fiddlin' Arthur Smith and both toured and played the *Opry* with him as the Dixieliners. They worked with Smith until 1938, when he left for Hollywood. Strangely, though recognized as one of the *Opry*'s most influential bands, they never actually recorded with Smith until years later in the 60s, when they were reunited by Mike Seeger. During the 40s, they toured with Bill Monroe, appeared occasionally with Macon and still played the *Opry*. It seems likely that Sam was the first member to play an electric guitar on the *Opry*, consisting of an amplified Spanish guitar and an early electric lap steel. However, this soon incurred the wrath of George D. Hay, who quickly told Sam to 'Keep it down to earth'. In the 50s and 60s, the folk revival found them touring and still on the *Opry*. In later years, Kirk went into the property business and Sam continued to work the farm until he died in a tractor accident in 1975, at the age of 82. After Sam's death, Kirk played the *Opry* as a member of the *Opry*'s own Fruit Jar Drinkers String Band, frequently playing fiddle rather than banjo. He died after a heart attack at his home in Franklin in 1983, having appeared on the *Opry* only a few days previously. It is interesting to note that, in 1924, Sam had learned to play the guitar-banjo, and his recordings using it, made with Macon in 1926 and 1927, are probably the only known examples of this difficult instrument being played by a white musician. The brothers' contribution to the history of country music, with their gospel, blues, instrumentals and old folk ballads, is considerable, and although they made many recordings during their long careers, few are now available.

● ALBUMS: with Arthur Smith *Fiddlin'* (1961)★★★, one side each act *Opry Old Timers Sam & Kirk McGee And The Crook Brothers* (Starday 1962)★★★, with Arthur Smith *Rare Old Fiddle Tunes (Fiddlin' Arthur Smith & His Dixieliners)* (Folkways 1962)★★★, with Smith *Old Timers Of The Grand Ole Opry* (1964)★★★, with Smith *Milk 'Em In The Evening Blues* (1965)★★★, *Opry Old Time Songs And Guitar Tunes, Volume One* (1985)★★★.

Solo: Sam McGee: *The Grandad Of The Country Guitar Pickers* (Arhoolie1963)★★★. Kirk McGee: *Mister Kirk* (1980)★★★. They also appear on several album releases of Uncle Dave Macon and sundry individual tracks appear on various artists albums of old-time music.

MᴄGʜᴇᴇ, Wᴇs

b. 26 October, 1948, Lutterworth, Leicestershire, England. One of the very few British performers whose Texas-inspired country music is regarded as creditable in the USA, McGhee has suffered more than most from the British refusal to accept homegrown country music as genuine. He has worked with noted Texan artists including Ponty Bone and Freddie Krc (for both of whom he produced albums in the 80s), Butch Hancock, Jimmie Dale Gilmore and Kimmie

Rhodes. As a promising teenage guitarist, McGhee was involved with the celebrated Reg Calvert (who worked as patron for a number of emergent musicians in the 60s from a large country house, where several groups, none of which became famous, lived communally). During the late 60s, McGhee worked in Hamburg as one of many musicians following the Merseybeat trail - his first wife was German. During the early 70s, he fronted an early pub/rock combo known as McGhee, but management problems, among other things, conspired to sabotage the recording contract he had been promised. By the mid-70s, McGhee had become friendly with Arthur Anderson, a musician he had met on the gig circuit, and they joined forces to record an album of McGhee's original material, with Anderson engineering and producing. The result, *Long Nights And Banjo Music*, was released on their own label, Terrapin Records, in 1978, with McGhee as lead vocalist and lead guitarist, plus assistance from, among others, Bob Loveday (violin, later with the Penguin Cafe Orchestra and the post-Boomtown Rats Bob Geldof band) and Rick Lloyd (later a member of the chart-topping Flying Pickets). The achievement of completing the album was of far greater significance than much of the self-conscious country rock it contained, and McGhee and Anderson scraped together enough finance - by renting out their home-made studio and by McGhee writing and recording radio commercials - to release a second album in 1980, *Airmail*, which gave notice that he was a considerable songwriting talent. Before *Landing Lights* was released in 1983, Anderson had left the partnership, although he worked on part of the album, some of which was recorded in Texas with local musicians including Krc (ex-Jerry Jeff Walker), Bone and Lloyd Maines (ex-Joe Ely), Gilmore and Rhodes. Probably McGhee's best original studio album to date in terms of original songs, it was released on his own TRP label, as was 1985's *Thanks For The Chicken*, a live double album made in Texas with a mixed British/Texan band, including Krc, Bone, Rhodes and Texan fiddler Alvin Crow, plus McGhee's long-time backing vocalist Ian Bartholomew (primarily an actor), Patti Vetta, and Irish multi-instrumentalist Dermot O'Conner. As well as numerous fine McGhee originals, the album included cover versions of Richard Thompson's 'Tear Stained Letter', Joe 'King' Carrasco's 'Mexcal Road' and the sublime 'Contrabandistas', written by Rhodes' husband, record producer Joe Gracey, and his partner, Bobby Earl Smith. The album even included a song sung in Mexican - McGhee had developed a cult following in Mexico owing to his semi-successful attempts to cater for the Hispanic audience. American music publisher Bug Music signed him during the second half of the 80s as his fifth album, *Zacatecas*, was released in 1986. A much more measured collection, it was his first studio album made without cost-cutting, and included a remarkable epic titled 'Monterey', plus a cover version of the 60s hit by Troy Shondell, 'This Time'. As usual, there was little commercial interest in Britain, although McGhee began working frequently in Texas, both on his own account and as lead guitarist with Kimmie Rhodes, who had duetted with him on a track from *Thanks For The Chicken*, and on several of whose albums he had played. Finally, in 1991, a UK label, Minidoka, was interested enough in McGhee to release a compilation of remixed tracks from his previous studio albums titled *Neon And Dust*, although this again did not achieve the success its quality so richly deserved. His acoustic album *Border Guitars* in 1995 featured Rhodes, Krc and Bone. His great ability to write in the same West Texas style as Joe Ely and Butch Hancock suggests that he was born in the wrong country.

● ALBUMS: *Long Nights And Banjo Music* (Terrapin 1978)★★★★, *Airmail* (TRP 1980)★★★, *Landing Lights* (TRP 1983)★★★, *Thanks For The Chicken* (TRP 1985)★★★, *Zacatecas* (TRP 1986)★★★, *Border Guitars* (Road Goes On Forever 1995)★★★.

● COMPILATIONS: *Neon And Dust* (Minidoka 1991)★★★, *Heartache Avenue: Classic Recordings 1978-1992* (Road Goes On Forever 1997)★★★★, *Backbeat* (Road Goes On Forever 1997)★★★.

McGRAW, TIM

b. 1 May 1967, Delhi, Louisiana, USA. He was raised in Start, Louisiana, and is the son of Frank Edwin 'Tug' McGraw, a noted left-handed relief pitcher for the New York Mets and Philadelphia Phillies, who retired in 1984 after a 19-year major league baseball career. Tim began his musical career singing in local clubs and also worked as a demo singer. He was signed to Curb Records in 1990 but did not achieve his first chart entry until 1992 with 'Welcome To The Club'. In 1993, he had two further minor hits with 'Memory Lane' and 'Two Steppin' Mind', all three of these songs taken from his debut album. He appeared on the Honky Tonk Attitude tour with Joe Diffie. McGraw's career took off with the release, early in 1994, of the single 'Indian Outlaw'. The song, written by John D. Loudermilk, caused considerable controversy in the USA, where some claimed that it degraded the accepted image of the American Indian. Controversy always helps sales, and the recording, with its war-dance, rhythmic drum beat, quickly gave McGraw his first country number 1 record. The song naturally appeared on his second album, from which he also gained further chart success with the recording of 'Down On The Farm' and the title track. The album, *Not A Moment Too Soon*, entered the *Billboard* country chart at number 1. The album sales topped four million and it remained in the Top 5 for over a year. The following album, *All I Want*, also amassed huge sales and McGraw topped the country singles chart with 'I Like It, I Love It' and just missed with 'Can't Be Really Gone'. Many see him as the successor to Garth Brooks, and although his records are not quite as distinctive, he does seem determined to remain a country artist (whatever that means today) with titles such as 'Don't Mention Memphis', 'Give It To Me Strait', 'It Doesn't Get Any Countrier Than This' and his 1996 US country number 1 'She Never Lets It Go To her Heart'. His run of success continued with *Everywhere* in 1997, and a CMA Award for Vocal Event Of The Year on 'It's Your Love' (with his wife Faith Hill).

● ALBUMS: *Tim McGraw* (Curb 1993)★★★, *Not A Moment Too Soon* (Curb 1994)★★★★, *All I Want* (Curb/Hit 1995)★★★★, *Everywhere* (Curb 1997)★★★★.

● VIDEOS: *Indian Outlaw* (Curb 1994), *Refried Dreams* (Curb 1995), *An Hour With Tim* (Curb 1995).

McKINLAY, BOB

b. 13 May 1942, Ashton-in-Makerfield, near Wigan, Lancashire, England. Like many others, McKinlay learned guitar from Bert Weedon's *Play In A Day*. He was a member

of the north-west beat group The Long And The Short, which made the UK Top 30 in 1964 with 'The Letter', featuring session musician Jimmy Page on lead guitar. They appeared in the film *Gonks Go Beat*, and then McKinlay was offered a place in the Mojos. He soon, however, returned to Wigan and a job in a printing works. He became a mature student and gained a degree in sociology and a teaching diploma. He visited Nashville in 1977, and on his return, formed a country group. He decided to become a full-time professional and toured the UK country clubs with American singer-songwriter Steve Young. McKinley is enormously popular around country clubs and manages to support a band. His songs include his personal credo, 'English Born - Dixie Fried', and this Wigan peer has made several cassettes to sell at his shows. He has emulated Bert Weedon by issuing his own guitar tutor.
● ALBUMS: *English Born - Dixie Fried* (1979)★★★, *Country Good And Rollin'* (1982)★★★, *My Songbird* (1984)★★★, *Country Tapestry* (1985)★★★, *Roots And Offshoots* (1987)★★★, *Once More* (1989)★★★, *Singer-Songwriter* (1990)★★★.

McLAIN, TOMMY
b. 15 March 1940, Jonesville, Louisiana, USA. McLain was a practitioner of a musical style briefly popular in that state during the 50s and 60s called 'swamp pop'. He is best known for his 1966 hit 'Sweet Dreams', written by country singer Don Gibson and previously a hit for Patsy Cline. It peaked at number 15 in the US charts. McLain first came to notice as bassist for Clint West And The Boogie Kings, a popular Louisiana 'blue-eyed soul' band. He recorded 'Sweet Dreams' on his own, and news of its modest sales was brought to the attention of producer Floyd Soileau, who re-recorded the song for his Jin label. The subsequent national success forced the distribution of the disc onto the newly formed MSL Records, and it eventually sold a million copies. McLain released six further singles on Soileau's Jin Records label and Soileau later released two albums of his material but none charted. He was still performing in Louisiana in the early 90s.
● ALBUMS: *Tommy McLain* (Jin 1973)★★★.
● COMPILATIONS: *The Best of Tommy McLain* (Jin 1977)★★★.

McMILLAN, TERRY
b. USA. Before launching his solo career in the gospel/Christian rock tradition, Terry McMillan was a well-known and respected Nashville session musician. Having worked alongside Eric Clapton, Garth Brooks, Amy Grant, Chet Atkins and Ray Charles, the decision to pursue a solo career was initially prompted by Giant Records Nashville president, James Stroud. Despite McMillan's proclamations that he did not sing country music, Stroud insisted that he would be pleased to release whatever McMillan offered ('He didn't care if I cut a polka'). The resultant album, *Somebody's Comin'*, featured guest musicians Ron Hemby (guitar), Michael Rodes and Tommy Sims (bass), Steve Nathan (keyboards) and Lonnie Wilson (drums). Among the backing vocalists were Chris Rodriguez, Nicol Smith and Michael McDonald. McMillan went to Nashville for the first time in 1973, initially to play drums and blues harmonica in a covers band. He then became the drummer in Eddy Raven's

band, before touring as Chet Atkins' harmonica player. From there, his reputation spread, and McMillan was one of the musicians at Live Aid, backing Neil Young. He was also one of the select band of musicians to be invited to perform at President Clinton's Inaugural Ball. *Somebody's Comin'* featured a number of standards, such as 'Amazing Grace', alongside songs co-written by McMillan. The decision to make it a Christian project was a surprise to some, but not the artist himself: 'I've been through a whole lot in my life. My house burned down. Both my parents were dead of alcohol at a young age. I was headed down that road, and I got spared. My whole priorities changed. I'm meaning it from the heart: I'd rather see souls changed than be a star.'
● ALBUMS: *Somebody's Comin'* (Giant 1997)★★★.

McNAMARA, TIM
b. Timothy Edmund McNamara, 10 October 1922, Lucknow, near Orange, New South Wales, Australia, d. 16 April 1983, Sydney, Australia. A pioneer of Australian country music, not only by his own performances but by the help he gave fellow performers. The youngest of 11 children, he worked as a boundary rider on a sheep station when he was 12. The following year, when the family relocated to Sydney, he refused to accompany them. Instead, having quit school, he spent the next four or five years working on dairy farms. He learned to play guitar, sing and yodel the hillbilly songs that he heard on the radio by such singers as Tex Morton. In 1940, he married Daphne Ford, a top horse rider and she encouraged him to pursue a singing career. He saw service with the Air Force during World War II, some of it overseas but sang whenever the opportunity arose. Returning to civilian life in 1945, writing much of his own material, he resumed the life of an entertainer, sometimes working as a duo with his brother Tommy Mack. By 1948, he was a well-established artist and appeared in the film *Into The Straight*. He sang two of his own songs, 'Riding Along' and 'We're Going To The Rodeo Today', both of which he later recorded, with four other songs, at his first recording session in August that year. In 1949, he joined 2SM Sydney as the presenter of their country show. Here he played records, sang a few songs and interviewed any available guests. Both Slim Dusty and Gordon Parsons gained initial career boosts through their appearances on the programme. In August 1950, McNamara persuaded 2SM and Rodeo Records to sponsor a national talent show, with a recording contract as the prize to be won at the grand final in Sydney's Town Hall. The first show attracted massive interest, eventually being won by Reg Lindsay with Shorty Ranger in second place. The process was repeated in other years and many artists achieved a breakthrough following appearances on McNamara's show. In 1950, McNamara had joined Rodeo Records and during the 50s, he recorded around 52 sides for the label, with many being self-penned numbers. In 1952, he became more active in production and with his wife, promoted shows in many areas that featured most of the top Australian artists. He recorded six sides for Festival in 1956 but made no further recordings until the 70s, when he recorded albums for EMI and Picture before returning to EMI. He maintained regular appearances around the Australian country circuit and even played the *Grand Ole Opry* in 1959 during an American visit. In 1981, his dedicated commitment to the Australian country music scene

saw him become only the sixth person elected to the Country Music Roll Of Renown (Australia's equivalent to Nashville's Country Music Hall Of Fame). McNamara remained active promoting shows and helping fellow artists, until he finally lost his battle against cancer and with his wife, son Tim and old friend Smoky Dawson at his bedside, died in a Sydney hospital on 16 April 1983.

● ALBUMS: *Relaxin'* (EMI 1971)★★★, *Campfire Of Dreams* (Picture 1974)★★★.

MCNEIL, RITA

b. Big Pond, Cape Breton Island, Nova Scotia, Canada. McNeil appeared on the music scene in Britain almost overnight, and has had a degree of success in the field of country and folk music. In 1985, she went to Tokyo to perform at the Canada Expo pavilion, and in 1987, *Flying On Your Own* was released. The title track was also recorded by fellow Canadian Anne Murray. That same year, McNeil sang at the Edinburgh Folk Festival, and won a Canadian Juno award as Most Promising Female Vocalist. She first appeared in London, England, in September 1990, and Polydor released three of her albums, *Flying On Your Own, Reason To Believe* and *Rita*. In the same year, McNeil's *Reason To Believe* toppled Madonna from the top of the Australian album charts. Mixing country, folk and elements of Gaelic drawn from the fact that her family originally came from Scotland, McNeil has had less success in Britain than on her home ground, but still charted with 'Working Man', which reached the UK Top 20. Her albums have achieved platinum sales in Canada and she was the subject of a 1991 documentary, *Home I'll Be*.

● ALBUMS: *Flying On Your Own* (Polydor 1987)★★★, *Reason To Believe* (Polydor 1990)★★★, *Home I'll Be* (Polydor 1991)★★★.

MELLONS, KEN

b. Kenneth Edward Mellons, 10 July 1965, Nashville, Tennessee, USA. Mellons is one of the few country artists to have been raised in Nashville and he has wanted to play country music since he was three years old. He grew up attending shows, festivals and the *Grand Ole Opry* and he worked at Opryland USA impersonating country performers. This led to an appearance on the *Opry* itself. Mellons is a honky tonk singer and songwriter and had a US country Top 10 hit with 'Jukebox Junkie'. On his first CD, he thanks his 'Honky Tonk Teachers', Lefty Frizzell, George Jones, Merle Haggard, Hank Williams and Keith Whitley 'for the lessons I've learned'. John Anderson and George Jones offer vocal support on a classic honky tonk song, 'He'll Never Be A Lawyer ('Cause He Can't Pass The Bar)'. He spent several months on the road opening for Billy Ray Cyrus and he has done much fund-raising for a Memphis children's hospital.

● ALBUMS: *Ken Mellons* (Epic 1994)★★★, *Where Forever Begins* (Epic 1995)★★★.

MEYERS, AUGIE

b. 1941, San Antonio, Texas, USA. Meyers is best known as the organist in the Sir Douglas Quintet on their 60s hits, including 'She's About A Mover' and 'Mendocino'. He has recorded on his own, and more importantly, perhaps, has influenced the keyboard players in groups such as Elvis

Costello's Attractions and Joe 'King' Carrasco's Crowns. Meyers, who also plays accordion, first appeared on record in 1958, with a group called Danny Ezba And The Goldens. In 1964, producer Huey P. Meaux was assembling a Texan rock group to combat the British Invasion and teamed Meyers with San Antonio singer/songwriter/guitarist Doug Sahm. The Sir Douglas Quintet disbanded in 1967, when Sahm moved to San Francisco and Meyers formed Lord August and the Visions Of Lite. He then joined Sahm in San Francisco and the Quintet was reborn, only to break up again in 1971. Meyers began releasing a string of solo albums that year. In 1990, he teamed up with Sahm and fellow Texans Flaco Jimenez and Freddy Fender for an album called *Texas Tornados*.

● ALBUMS: *Augie's Western Head Music Co.* (1971)★★★, *You Ain't Rollin' Your Roll Rite* (1973)★★, *Live At The Longneck* (1975)★★, *Finally In Lights* (1977)★★★, *Still Growing* (1982)★★, *August In New York* (1984)★★, *Augie's Back* (1986)★★, *My Main Squeeze* (1987)★★, with Doug Sahm, Flaco Jimenez, Freddy Fender *Texas Tornados* (1990)★★★

MIKI AND GRIFF

Miki (b. Barbara MacDonald Salisbury, 20 June 1920, Ayrshire, Scotland, d. 20 April 1989) was raised on Rothesay on the Isle of Bute. When she joined the George Mitchell Choir, she met Griff (b. Emyr Morus Griffith, 9 May 1923, Holywell, Wales, d. 24 September 1995). They learned vocal discipline and stagecraft there. They married in 1950, and after leaving Mitchell, developed a comedy act with props and novelty numbers such as 'Spooks' and 'Ol' McDonald's Farm'. Griff's moustache became a recognizable trademark. In 1958, they fell in love with the Everly Brothers' album of traditional country ballads, *Songs Our Daddy Taught Us*, as well as country albums by the Louvin Brothers, and they would sing these songs for their own amusement in dressing-rooms. Lonnie Donegan heard them and invited them to perform on his television series. He arranged a contract with Pye Records and produced their first records. In 1959, 'Hold Back Tomorrow' made the UK Top 30, and they made very successful EPs, *Rockin' Alone (In An Old Rockin' Chair)* and *This Is Miki - This Is Griff*, which topped the EP charts. They appeared on several of Donegan's own records, including 'Virgin Mary' and 'Michael Row The Boat'. Miki recorded a tender version of 'I Never Will Marry' with only Donegan's whistling and acoustic guitar for accompaniment, and they were to work with him until 1964. In 1962, Miki And Griff's only UK Top 20 hit came when they covered Burl Ives' 'A Little Bitty Tear', and the following year they made the Top 30 with a cover version of Steve Lawrence and Eydie Gorme's US hit, 'I Want To Stay Here'. Lesser-known records such as 'This Time I Would Know', 'Oh, So Many Years' and Harlan Howard's humorous 'Automation' were just as good. Although they often covered songs by other performers, their records were always instantly recognizable. Record producer Tony Hatch used to say, 'Miki can create a better harmony than I can ever write for her.' Visiting the USA, they received a standing ovation on Roy Acuff's portion of the *Grand Ole Opry* in 1964. Miki And Griff are easily the most-recorded UK country act, with most of their recordings being for Pye. They did, however, record two albums for Major-Minor and included the weepie 'Two Little Orphans'. In later years, they performed as a duo to the accompaniment of Miki's piano. Griff's humour was always evident, and his emotion-charged version of 'These Hands' was always a showstopper. Miki developed into a fine songwriter - in particular, 'God Was Here (But I Think He Left Early)'. They always had time for their fans, but Miki, who disguised her illness on stage for some months, died of cancer in April 1989. Understandably, Griff did not return to performing. The duo are fondly remembered by many listeners for introducing them to country music, and they were a fine, middle-of-the-road act in their own right.

● ALBUMS: *Miki And Griff* (Pye 1961)★★★, *The Country Style Of Miki And Griff* (Pye 1962)★★★, *I Want To Stay Here* (Pye 1963)★★★, *Those Rocking Chair People* (Pye 1969)★★★, *Two Little Orphans* (Pye 1970)★★★, *Tennessee Waltz* (Pye 1970)★★★, *Lonesome* (Pye 1970)★★★, *The Country Side Of Miki And Griff* (Pye 1972)★★★, *Let The Rest Of The World Go By* (Pye 1973)★★★, *Country Is* (Pye 1974)★★★, *Two's Company* (Pye 1975)★★★, *This Is Miki - This Is Griff* (Pye 1976)★★★, *Etchings* (Pye 1977)★★★, *Country* (Pye 1978)★★★, *At Home With Miki And Griff* (Scotdisc 1987)★★★, *Little Bitty Tear* (1993)★★★.

● COMPILATIONS: *The Best Of Miki And Griff* (Castle 1983)★★★, *The Very Best Of ...* (Sound Waves 1994)★★★★.

MILES, GARRY

b. James E. Cason, 27 November 1939, Nashville, Tennessee, USA. Miles had a busy career as solo singer, group member and songwriter in the 60s. His best-known song as Garry Miles was 'Look For A Star', a Top 20 hit in 1960 on Liberty Records. Before that, he had played guitar with Brenda Lee and performed as part of a trio called the Statues, who achieved a Top 100 cover version of the ballad 'Blue Velvet'. 'Look For A Star' had been featured in the UK film *Circus Of Horrors* in 1960. Released under the Miles pseudonym, it reached number 16. (N.B. Garry Mills, who had a hit with the same song, was a different artist.) A few other singles were issued under the Miles name, and as the Statues, but none were hits. Cason then recorded under his other nickname, Buzz Cason, for several labels but did not have any hits under that name. He did, however, co-write the hit 'Sandy' for Ronny And The Daytonas, and sang background for artists including Elvis Presley, Kenny Rogers and Jimmy Buffett.

MILLER, BILL

b. Stockbridge-Munsee Reservation, Wisconsin, USA. Miller is a Native American from the Mohican tribe, and much of his songwriting concerns itself with the plight of his people since the frontier days of the nineteenth century. American society's general intolerance and vilification of 'red Indians' is something, sadly, that Miller continues to encounter to the present day. He recalls a particularly galling meeting with record company executives in Nashville where he was promised a recording contract if he 'dropped that Indian shit'. He has never had any intention of betraying his heritage, and a cursory glance at his songbook, including titles such as 'Geronimo's Cadillac', 'Trail Of Freedom' and 'Reservation Road', demonstrate his continuing advocacy of his cultural background. In 1992 he was finally awarded a major recording contract via Jim Ed Norman at Warner Brothers Records, ironically due to the success of the Hollywood film *Dances With Wolves* (from the same industry

so responsible for the demonizing of native Americans in their 'cowboy and indians' films). Miller was born on a reservation in Wisconsin and brought up with nine siblings. He quickly descended into alcoholism, just like his father and grandfather before him. However, he was determined that it was time to break the cycle of dependency and abuse. His first musical experience came when playing guitar in his uncle's Wisconsin polka band, but he embarked on a fine arts degree before dedicating himself to music. His first two albums were both recorded for his own Windspirit label, preceding three more for Rosebud Records, which he co-owns with Kathy Mattea's manager. His first properly distributed album, *The Red Road*, was finally released in 1993 and confirmed him as a natural peer of fellow Native American activist John Trudell. He subsequently contributed the flute passage in Vanessa Williams' 'Colors Of The Wind', which was included on the *Pocahontas* film soundtrack. However, as he conceded to *Billboard* magazine in 1995, 'I felt real limited at Warner Western. I said "I want to rock, so can I get out of this corral?"'. The subsequent *Raven In The Snow* collection, which saw him move to Reprise Records, included 'Pile Of Stones', a typically autobiographical song detailing how much he missed his children when on tour. The album's title was inspired by a return to his home reservation: 'With my music, my viewpoint, my belief system, I stand out like a raven in the snow.'

● ALBUMS: *The Red Road* (Warner Western 1993)★★★, *Raven In The Snow* (Reprise 1995)★★★.

MILLER, EMMETT

b. USA. A major but unrecognised influence on the development of country music and by inference rock 'n' roll, Emmett Miller was widely known as 'the Minstrel man'. Part of the reason for the lack of acknowledgement accorded his legacy can be ascribed to the dubious nature of minstrel-singing: in more enlightened times the sight of white actors 'blacked-up' as negroes, using accentuated singing voices, is hardly likely to be considered acceptable. Despite this, Miller deserves to be accredited as a fine singer whose innovations were adopted by much better-known figures including Jimmie Rodgers, Bob Wills, Hank Williams and Merle Haggard. Though the voice was decidedly country, Miller's minstrel act stemmed from the jazz tradition. So too did his band, the Georgia Crackers, featuring Tommy Dorsey, Jimmy Dorsey, Jack Teagarden and Gene Krupa. Sadly, much of his career took place before suitable equipment was available to record his songs. However, his was the first recorded version of 'Lovesick Blues' in 1925, though this tape has subsequently been 'lost'. However, it was recut in 1929, and archivists have noted that Hank Williams' later version of the song is almost note-for-note identical. Others inspired by Miller included Jimmie Rodgers (who, like Miller, yodelled) and Tommy Duncan. Bob Wills, meanwhile, cited Miller as his favourite singer. By the 30s Miller's career was effectively over, and it was not until 1996 that anybody thought it noteworthy enough to prepare a compilation. However, when they did they were rewarded with glowing reviews, many offering the observation that Miller has been the missing link in country music's early development.

● COMPILATIONS: *The Minstrel Man From Georgia* (Sony/Legacy 1996)★★★.

MILLER, FRANKIE

b. 17 December 1931, Victoria, Texas, USA. Miller was a moderately successful honky-tonk singer during the late 50s and early 60s, reaching the height of his fame with the Top 5 hit 'Black Land Farmer'. He originally formed the Drifting Texans at college, before signing to the Houston-based Guilt Edge in 1951 and recording several sides. After a spell of service in Korea, Miller signed to Columbia Records in 1954 and recorded a dozen sides. After several one-off singles for independent labels, he was signed to Starday Records by Don Pierce in 1959. 'Black Land Farmer' was an immediate hit, followed by 'Family Man' (number 7) in October. Miller was never as successful again, with only 'Baby Rocked Her Dolly' (1960) and 'A Little South Of Memphis' (1964) breaking the Top 40. He moved to United Artists Records in 1965, but by the late 60s had retired from music to work as a car salesman in Arlington, Texas.

● ALBUMS: *Country Music's New Star* (Starday 1961)★★★, *True Country Style Of Frankie Miller* (Starday 1962)★★★, *Fine Country Singing Of Frankie Miller* (Audio Lab 1963)★★★, *Blackland Farmer* (Starday 1965)★★★.
● COMPILATIONS: *Rockin' Rollin'* (Bear Family 1983)★★★, *Hey! Where You Going?* (Bear Family 1984)★★★, *The Very Best Of Frankie Miller* (Capitol 1993)★★★★, *Sugar Coated Baby* (Bear Family 1996)★★★.

MILLER, J.D. 'JAY'

b. 1923, El Campo, Texas, USA, d. 23 March 1996, Lafayette, Louisiana, USA. One of the best-known and most successful record producers from Louisiana, Miller started out as a musician, playing with country and Cajun bands around Lake Charles from the late 30s. After a spell in the services, he started to make records aimed at a small localized market for Cajun music in south-west Louisiana; these, by artists such as Lee Sonnier and Amidie Breaux, were among the first records in the idiom to appear after the war, and established his position as a pioneer in the field. He continued to record Cajun music and C&W on his Feature and Fais Do-Do labels, including the earliest records by Jimmie C. Newman and Doug Kershaw, and later on Kajun and Cajun Classics, which featured important figures such as Nathan Abshire and Aldus Roger. However, it was when he turned his attention in the mid-50s to black music that Miller began to develop his best-known and most enduring legacy. Between 1954, when he first recorded Lightnin' Slim, and the early 60s, he established an extraordinary list of blues and country artists, including Slim, Lonesome Sundown, Slim Harpo, Lazy Lester, Lefty Frizzell, Kitty Wells, Silas Hogan and many others, whose work he leased to the Nashville label Excello. He also continued to release records on labels of his own, Zynn and Rocko, including rockabilly and local pop by artists such as Johnny Jano and Warren Storm, and in the 70s, on Blues Unlimited. His list of artists was enormous, but just as important was the characteristic sound he achieved in his studio in Crowley, which became inextricably linked with the indigenous sounds of Louisiana. He died following complications from quadruple bypass surgery in 1996.

MILLER, JODY

b. 29 November 1941, Phoenix, Arizona, USA, but raised in Blanchard, Oklahoma. Miller's father loved country music and played fiddle, and all her four sisters were singers. She led a folk trio while still at school and, after graduation, moved to California to pursue a singing career, but a severe car accident forced her to return home. She established herself locally after appearing on Tom Paxton's television show, and gained a reputation as a folk-singer. Actor Dale Robertson introduced her to Capitol Records, and her first album, *Wednesday's Child*, was a blend of folk and pop music. Her first US chart success was with 'He Walks Like A Man' and then she went to number 12 with the answer to Roger Miller's 'King Of The Road', 'Queen Of The House'. As a result, she won a Grammy for the best female country performance. She recorded a dramatic teen anthem about being misunderstood, 'Home Of The Brave', which was more significant than its chart placings imply (US 25/UK 49). This, however, was a one-off as she then recorded more conventional country hits, having some success with 'Long Black Limousine'. In 1968, she left the business to raise a daughter, but returned to work with producer Billy Sherrill in Nashville in 1970. Her first success was with a Tony Hatch song, 'Look At Mine'. She then scored with country versions of pop hits, 'He's So Fine', 'Baby I'm Yours' and 'Be My Baby'. A duet with Johnny Paycheck, 'Let's All Go Down The River', also fared well. She made little attempt to change with the times and in the early 80s, she retired to breed quarter horses on a 1,000-acre ranch in Blanchard, Oklahoma. She returned with 1987's *My Country*, an album of patriotic songs that led to Miller being asked to perform at George Bush's inaugural ball in 1988. She then formed an unsuccessful duo with her daughter Robin.

● ALBUMS: *Wednesday's Child Is Full Of Woe* (Capitol 1963)★★★, *Home Of The Brave* (Capitol 1965)★★★, *Queen Of The House* (Capitol 1965)★★★, *Jody Miller Sings The Great Hits Of Buck Owens* (Capitol 1966)★★, *The Nashville Sound Of Jody Miller* (Epic 1969)★★, *Look At Mine* (Epic 1970)★★★, *There's A Party Goin' On* (Epic 1972)★★★, *He's So Fine* (Epic 1972)★★★, *Good News* (Epic 1973)★★★, *House Of The Rising Sun* (Epic 1974)★★, *Country Girl* (Epic 1975)★★★, *Will You Love Me Tomorrow?* (Epic 1976)★★★, *Here's Jody Miller* (Epic 1977)★★, *My Country* (1987)★★.
● COMPILATIONS: *The Best Of Jody Miller* (Capitol)★★★.

MILLER, NED

b. Henry Ned Miller, 12 April 1925, Raines, Utah, USA. When Miller was a small child, the family moved to Salt Lake City, Utah where, after completing his education, he worked as a pipe fitter. He became interested in songwriting and country music and learned to play the guitar, but had no real inclination to be a performer. In the mid-50s, he married and moved to California, where he hoped to sell some of his songs, and joined the Fabor label as a writer and/or performer. Early in 1957, a deal between Fabor and Dot Records, which gave the latter label first choice of all Fabor masters, saw two of his songs, 'Dark Moon' and 'A Fallen Star', both become US country and pop hits for Bonnie Guitar and Jimmy C. Newman, respectively. Miller himself played guitar on the former recording, which also was a number 4 US pop hit for Gale Storm. The song became a UK Top 20 pop hit for Tony Brent and was also recorded by the Kaye Sisters and Joe Loss And His Orchestra. In July 1957, Miller's most famous song appeared when, as a result of a game of patience, he wrote 'From A Jack To A King'. Both his own version and a pop one by Jim Lowe were released by

Dot, but created no major impression. From the start, Miller had little interest in a career as a singer and detested touring; he suffered constantly with stage fright and shyness, and was always a most reluctant performer. Stories are told of him on occasions actually sending a friend to perform as Ned Miller in his place. Although he made some further recordings, including 'Lights In The Street' and 'Turn Back', he achieved no chart success and concentrated on his writing. Between 1959 and 1961, he recorded briefly for Jackpot and Capitol. In 1962, he persuaded Fabor Robison to reissue his recording of 'From A Jack To A King' and this time, despite Miller's reluctance to tour and publicize the song, it became a number 2 country and number 6 pop hit. Released in the UK on the London label, it also soon reached number 2 in the UK pop charts. 'From A Jack To A King', an old-fashioned, traditional-sounding country song, was hardly a record that was ahead of its time, but it became an extraordinary success in Britain, where, in April 1963, it held the number 2 position for four weeks - in spite of the fact that there was no promotion from either the artist or label, and it went against the grain of songs that were hits at the time. It obviously says much for the quality of the song. Further Fabor recordings followed and Miller had Top 20 US country and pop hits with 'Invisible Tears' (1964) and 'Do What You Do Do Well' (1965). He returned to Capitol in 1966, and had five minor hits before being dropped by the label, again due to his unwillingness to tour. He moved to Republic where, in 1970, he achieved his last chart entry with 'The Lover's Song'. He then gave up recording and after moving to Prescott, Arizona, finally wrote his last song in the mid-70s. After eight years at Prescott, he settled in Las Vegas where he completely withdrew from all public appearances and gave up songwriting. In 1991, the German Bear Family label released a 31-track CD of his work, which included some previously unissued material.
● ALBUMS: *From A Jack To A King* i (Fabor 1963)★★★★, *Ned Miller (Sings The Songs Of Ned Miller)* (Capitol 1965)★★★, *Teardrop Lane* (Capitol 1967)★★★, *In The Name Of Love* (Capitol 1968)★★, *Ned Miller's Back* (Republic 1970)★★.
● COMPILATIONS: *The Best Of Ned Miller* (Capitol 1966)★★★, *From A Jack To A King* ii (Bear Family 1991)★★★★.

MILLER, ROGER

b. 2 January 1936, Fort Worth, Texas, USA, d. 25 October 1992, Los Angeles, California, USA. Miller was brought up in Erick, Oklahoma, and during the late 50s, moved to Nashville, where he worked as a songwriter. His 'Invitation To The Blues' was a minor success for Ray Price, as was '(In The Summertime) You Don't Want Love' for Andy Williams. Miller himself enjoyed a hit on the country charts with the portentously titled 'When Two Worlds Collide'. In 1962, he joined Faron Young's band as a drummer and also wrote 'Swiss Maid', a major hit for Del Shannon. By 1964, Miller was signed to Mercury's Smash label, and secured a US Top 10 hit with 'Dang Me'. The colloquial title was reinforced by some humorous, macabre lyrics ('They ought to take a rope and hang me'). The song brought Miller several Grammy awards, and the following year, he enjoyed an international Top 10 hit with 'King Of The Road'. This stoical celebration of the hobo life, with its jazz-influenced undertones, became

his best-known song. The relaxed 'Engine Engine No. 9' was another US Top 10 hit during 1965, and at the end of the year, Miller once more turned his attention to the UK market with 'England Swings'. This affectionate, slightly bemused tribute to swinging London at its zenith neatly summed up the tourist brochure view of the city ('bobbies on bicycles two by two . . . the rosy red cheeks of the little children'). Another international hit, the song was forever associated with Miller. The singer's chart fortunes declined the following year, and a questionable cover version of Elvis Presley's 'Heartbreak Hotel' barely reached the US Top 100. In 1968, Miller secured his last major hit with a poignant reading of Bobby Russell's 'Little Green Apples', which perfectly suited his understated vocal style. Thereafter, Miller moved increasingly towards the country market and continued performing regularly throughout America. In 1982, he appeared on the album *Old Friends* with Ray Price and Willie Nelson. Miller's vocals were featured in the Walt Disney cartoon *Robin Hood*, and in the mid-80s he wrote a Broadway musical, *Big River*, based on Mark Twain's *The Adventures Of Huckleberry Finn*. Roger Miller finally lost his battle with cancer when, with his wife Mary and son Roger Jnr. at his bedside, he died on 25 October 1992. A most popular man with his fellow artists, he was also a great humorist and his general outlook was once neatly summed up when he told the backing band on the *Grand Ole Opry*, 'I do this in the key of B natural, which is my philosophy in life.'
● ALBUMS: *Roger Miller* (Camden 1964)★★★, *Roger And Out* (Smash 1964)★★★, *Wild Child* aka *The Country Side Of Roger Miller* (Starday 1965)★★★, *The Return Of Roger Miller* (Smash 1965)★★★, *The 3rd Time* (Smash 1965)★★★, *Words And Music* (Smash 1966)★★★, *Walkin' In The Sunshine* (Smash 1967)★★★, *A Tender Look At Love* (Smash 1968)★★★, *Roger Miller* (Smash 1969)★★★, *Roger Miller* (Smash 1970)★★, *Waterhole Three* film soundtrack (Columbia 1973)★★, *Off The Wall* (Windsong 1978)★★★, *Making A Name For Myself* (20th Century 1980)★★, *Motive Series* (Mercury 1981)★★★, with Willie Nelson *Old Friends* (Columbia 1982)★★★, *The Big Industry* (Fundamental 1988)★★★.
● COMPILATIONS: *Golden Hits* (Smash 1965)★★★★, *Little Green Apples* (Pickwick 1976)★★★★, *Best Of Roger Miller* (Phillips 1978)★★★★, *Greatest Hits* (RCA 1985)★★★★, *Best Of Roger Miller, Vol. 1: Country Tunesmith* (Polygram 1991)★★★★, *The Best Of Roger Miller, Vol. 2: King Of The Road* (Mercury 1992)★★★★, *King Of The Road* 3-CD box set (Mercury Nashville 1995)★★★★, *Super Hits* (Epic 1996)★★.

MILSAP, RONNIE

b. Ronnie Lee Millsaps, 16 January 1943, Robbinsville, North Carolina, USA. Milsap's mother had already experienced a stillbirth and the prospect of raising a blind child made her mentally unstable. Milsap's father took him to live with his grandparents and divorced his mother. What little vision young Ronnie had was lost after receiving a vicious punch from a schoolmaster; both his eyes have now been removed. He studied piano, violin and guitar at the State School for the Blind in Raleigh, and although he had the ability to study law, he chose instead to be a professional musician. After some workouts with J.J. Cale and a 1963 single, 'Total Disaster', for the small Princess label, he toured *Playboy* clubs with his own band from 1965. Among his recordings for Scepter were early compositions by Ashford And Simpson, including the memorable 'Let's Go Get Stoned', relegated to a b-side. A few months later it was a million-selling single for another blind pianist, Ray Charles. Following a residency at TJ's club in Memphis, Milsap performed at the 1969 New Year's Eve party for Elvis Presley. Presley invited him to sing harmony on his sessions for 'Don't Cry Daddy' and 'Kentucky Rain', ironically the only time he has been part of a UK chart hit. After several recordings with smaller labels, Milsap made *Ronnie Milsap* for Warner Brothers Records, with top soul and country musicians. He worked throughout 1972 at Roger Miller's King Of The Road club in Nashville, and then signed with RCA Records. *Where The Heart Is* was a tuneful, country collection including the US country hits 'I Hate You' and 'The Girl Who Waits On Tables'. 'Pure Love' is an uplifting country great, while Don Gibson's 'I'd Be A Legend In My Time' was even more successful. In 1975, Milsap came to the UK as Glen Campbell's opening act, and the strength of his concert performances can be gauged from RCA's *In Concert* double album, hosted by Charley Pride, in which he duets with Dolly Parton on 'Rollin' In My Sweet Baby's Arms' and tackles a wild rock 'n' roll medley. His live album from the *Grand Old Opry* shows a great sense of humour - 'You don't think I'm gonna fall off this stage, do you? I got 20 more feet before the edge. That's what the band told me.' He had a crossover hit - number 16 on the US pop charts - with Hal David's 'It Was Almost Like A Song'. Milsap bought a studio from Roy Orbison, GroundStar, and continued to record prolifically. In 1979, RCA sent an unmarked, pre-release single to disc jockeys, inviting them to guess the performer. The funky seven-minute disco workout of 'Hi-Heel Sneakers' was by Milsap, but, more often than not, he was moving towards the Barry Manilow market. Milsap also helped with the country music score for Clint Eastwood's film *Bronco Billy*, and he recorded a flamboyant tribute album to Jim Reeves, *Out Where The Bright Lights Are Glowing*. A revival of Chuck Jackson's 'Any Day Now (My Wild Beautiful Bird)' reached number 14 on the US pop charts and also became *Billboard*'s Adult Contemporary Song Of The Year. His *Lost In The Fifties Tonight* album had doo-wop touches, but the album should have remained completely in that mould. Milsap also recorded a duet with Kenny Rogers, 'Make No Mistake, She's Mine'. He moved away from synthesizers and sounded more country than ever on 'Stranger Things Have Happened'. Enjoying his 35th US country number 1 with a Hank Cochran song, 'Don't You Ever Get Tired (Of Hurtin' Me)', Milsap remained a formidable force in US country music, only Conway Twitty and Merle Haggard having had more chart-toppers. It showed remarkable consistency by an artist with little traditional country to his name. His last number 1 was 'A Woman In Love' in 1989, after which his commercial fortunes finally began to decline. He left RCA in 1992 and signed to Liberty Records, but has been unable to break back into the charts.

● ALBUMS: *Ronnie Milsap* (Warners 1971)★★★, *Where The Heart Is* (RCA 1973)★★★, *Pure Love* (RCA 1974)★★★, *A Legend In My Time* (RCA 1975)★★★, *Night Things* (RCA 1975)★★★, *A Rose By Any Other Name* (RCA 1975)★★★, *20-20 Vision* (RCA 1976)★★★, *Mr. Mailman* (RCA 1976)★★★, *Ronnie Milsap Live* (RCA 1976)★★★, *Kentucky Woman* (RCA 1976)★★★, *It Was Almost Like A Song* (RCA 1977)★★★, *Only One Love In My Life* (RCA 1978)★★★, *Images* (RCA 1979)★★★, *Milsap Magic* (RCA 1980)★★★, *There's No Gettin' Over Me* (RCA 1980)★★★★, *Out Where The Bright Lights Are Glowing* (RCA 1981)★★★, *Inside* (RCA 1982)★★★, *Keyed Up* (RCA 1983)★★★★, *One More Try For Love* (RCA 1984)★★★, *Lost In The Fifties Tonight* (RCA 1986)★★★, *Christmas With Ronnie Milsap* (RCA 1986)★★, *Heart And Soul* (RCA 1987)★★, *Stranger Things Have Happened* (RCA 1989)★★★, *Back To The Grindstone* (RCA 1991)★★★, *True Believer* (Liberty 1993)★★★.
● COMPILATIONS: *Greatest Hits* (RCA 1980)★★★★, *Greatest Hits Vol. 2* (RCA 1985)★★★, *Greatest Hits Vol. 3* (RCA 1991)★★★, *The Essential Ronnie Milsap* (RCA 1995)★★★, *Sings His Best Hits For Capitol Records* (Capitol 1996)★★★.
● FURTHER READING: *Almost Like A Song*, Ronnie Milsap with Tom Carter.

MITCHELL, GUY

b. Albert Cernick, 22 February 1927, Detroit, Michigan, USA. An enormously popular singer in the USA and especially the UK, particularly during the 50s, with a straightforward style and affable personality. Although his birthplace is often given as Yugoslavia, his parents' homeland, Mitchell confirmed in a 1988 UK interview that he was born in Detroit, and was brought up there until the family moved to Colorado, and then to Los Angeles, California, when he was 11 years old. In Los Angeles, he successfully auditioned for Warner Brothers and, for the next few years, was groomed for a possible movie career as a child star, in addition to singing on the Hollywood radio station KFWB. The possibility of the world having another Mickey Rooney was averted when the family moved again, this time to San Francisco. Mitchell became an apprentice saddle-maker, and worked on ranches and in rodeos in the San Joaquin Valley, and also sang on cowboy singer Dude Martin's radio show. His affection for country music stayed with him for the remainder of his career. After a spell in the US Navy, Mitchell joined pianist Carmen Cavallero, and made his first records with the band, including 'I Go In When The Moon Comes Out' and 'Ah, But It Happens'. He then spent some time in New York, making demonstration records, and also won first place on the *Arthur Godfrey Talent Show*. In 1949, he recorded a few tracks for King Records, which were subsequently reissued on *Sincerely Yours* when Mitchell became successful.

In 1950, he was signed to Columbia Records by Mitch Miller, who is said to have been responsible for changing Cernick to Mitchell, Miller's full Christian name. Their first success came in 1950, with 'My Heart Cries For You' and 'The Roving Kind', which were followed by a string of hits throughout the decade, mostly jaunty novelty numbers, usually with Miller arrangements which used French horns to considerable effect. Several of the songs were written by Bob Merrill, including 'Sparrow In The Tree Top', 'Pittsburgh, Pennsylvania', 'My Truly, Truly Fair', 'Feet Up (Pat Him On The Po-Po)', 'Belle, Belle, My Liberty Belle' and 'She Wears Red Feathers', which contained the immortal Merrill couplet: 'An elephant brought her in, placed her by my side/While six baboons got out bassoons, and played "Here Comes The Bride"!' Other US Top 30 entries during this period included 'You're Just In Love', a duet with another Miller protégée, Rosemary Clooney, 'Christopher

Columbus', 'Unless' (a 30s Tolchard Evans number), 'Sweetheart Of Yesterday', 'There's Always Room At Our House', 'I Can't Help It', 'Day Of Jubilo', ''Cause I Love You, That's A-Why', 'Tell Us Where The Good Times Are' (the latter two duets with Mindy Carson), and 'Ninety-Nine Years (Dead Or Alive)'. 'Singing The Blues' (with Ray Conniff And His Orchestra) became his most successful record, staying at number 1 in the US charts for 10 weeks in 1956. In the UK, Tommy Steele had a hit with his cover version, but Mitchell also succeeded by reaching number 1. Further infectious hits followed: 'Knee Deep In The Blues', the irritatingly catchy 'Rock-A-Billy' ('rock-a-billy, rock-a-billy, rock-a-billy, rock-a-billy, ooh rock rock'), and his last US chart entry in 1959, 'Heartaches By The Number' (number 1). Of these, five sold over a million copies. Most of Mitchell's US hits were also successful in the UK, where he was highly popular, touring regularly, appearing at the London Palladium for the first time in 1952, and performing at the 1954 Royal Variety Performance. Additional chart entries in the UK included 'Pretty Little Black-Eyed Susie', 'Look At That Girl' (number 1), 'Cloud Lucky Seven', 'Cuff Of My Shirt', 'Dime And A Dollar' and 'Chicka Boom'. The latter was featured in Mitchell's first movie, a 3-D musical entitled *Those Redheads From Seattle* (1953), with Rhonda Fleming, Gene Barry and Teresa Brewer. Brewer and Mitchell proved a pleasant combination on the Johnny Mercer/Hoagy Carmichael song 'I Guess It Was You All The Time'. In 1954, Mitchell appeared with Gene Barry again, in the spoof western movie *Red Garters*, which also starred Rosemary Clooney, and contained another Mitchell 'special', 'A Dime And A Dollar'. In contrast to the somewhat perky style, so effective on his singles, some of Mitchell's albums revealed him to be an excellent ballad singer, particularly *A Guy In Love*, with Glenn Osser and his Orchestra, which contained standards such as 'The Moon Got In My Eyes', 'Allegheny Moon', 'East Of The Sun' and 'East Side Of Heaven'. *Sunshine Guitar*, with its guitar choir, was 'carefree and breezy, full of infectious gaiety', with a country 'feel' on several of the numbers. With the 60s beat boom imminent, Mitchell's contract with Columbia ended in 1962, and he released some singles on the Joy and Reprise labels. In 1967, he signed for the Nashville-based Starday label, but shortly after his *Travelling Shoes* and *Singing Up A Storm* were released, the company went out of business. During some periods of the 60s and 70s, Mitchell ceased performing. He issued only a few tracks on his own GMI label - partly because of poor health and serious alcohol problems. In 1979, he toured Australia, and started to play nightclubs in the USA. In the 80s he made several appearances in the UK, and released the old Elvis Presley favourite 'Always On My Mind', backed with 'Wind Beneath My Wings' from the Bette Midler hit movie *Beaches*. This was followed by *Garden In The Rain*, a set of British numbers that included 'My Kind Of Girl', 'Yesterday', 'I Hadn't Anyone Till You' and Noël Coward's theme tune, 'I'll See You Again'. In the 90s, the old hits were still being repackaged and sold to a younger audience following Mitchell's appearance in John Byrne's UK television drama, *Your Cheatin' Heart*, in 1990. During the filming in the UK he took the opportunity to play a number of country festival gigs. In 1991 during a tour of Australia he had a horse-riding accident that resulted in serious internal injuries. He spent some time in intensive care but made a

complete recovery. He has a loyal following in the UK (where arguably he was more popular); these devotees of 50s nostalgia subscribe to a regular magazine *Mitchell Music* - it is remarkable that their enthusiasm remains as strong 40 years after his heyday. Mitchell typified 50s pop more than any other performer, and his catalogue of hits remains formidable. His work is destined to endure.

● ALBUMS: *Songs Of The Open Spaces* 10-inch album (Columbia 1952)★★★ UK title *Guy Mitchell Sings* (Columbia 1954)★★★, *Red Garters* film soundtrack (Columbia 1954)★★★, *The Voice Of Your Choice* (Philips 1955)★★★, *A Guy In Love* (Columbia/Philips 1959)★★★, as Al Grant *Sincerely Yours* (1959)★★★, *Sunshine Guitar* (Columbia 1960)★★★, *Traveling Shoes* (Starday 1967)★★★, *Singin' Up A Storm* (Starday 1968)★★★, *Heartaches By The Number* (Nashville 1970)★★★, *The Roving Kind* (1981)★★★, *A Garden In The Rain* (President 1985)★★★.

● COMPILATIONS: *Guy Mitchell's Greatest Hits* (Columbia 1958)★★★★, *Showcase Of Hits* (Philips 1958)★★★★, *The Best Of Guy Mitchell* (Columbia 1966)★★★, *American Legend - 16 Greatest Hits* (1977)★★★★, *20 Golden Greats* (1979)★★★★, *Hit Singles 1950-1960* (Columbia 1981)★★★★, *20 Golden Pieces of Guy Mitchell* (Bulldog 1984)★★★★, *Guy's Greatest Hits* (Columbia 1984)★★★★, *Singing The Blues* (Castle 1986)★★★★, *Portrait Of A Song Stylist* (Masterpiece 1989)★★★, *Sweep Your Blues Away* (1989)★★★, *Heartaches By The Number* (Bear Family 1990)★★★★, *Your Cheatin' Heart* soundtrack (1990)★★★, *20 All Time Hits* (MFP 1991)★★★★, *16 Most Requested Songs* (Columbia/Legacy 1992)★★★★, *The Essential Collection* (1993)★★★★.

● FURTHER READING: *Mitchell Music*, privately published UK fanzine.

MIZE, BILLY

b. 29 April 1929, Kansas City, Kansas, USA. Raised in the San Joaquin Valley of California, Mize first learned to play guitar as a child, but converted to steel guitar when he received one for his 18th birthday. Originally, he was influenced by the music of Bob Wills and when he moved to Bakersfield, he formed his own band and played residences at local venues. He also worked as a disc jockey on KPMC. In 1953, he appeared on *The Cousin Herb Trading Post Show* on KERO-TV Bakersfield, and became affectionately known as Billy The Kid. He was a regular with the show for 13 years, including hosting it at one stage. Mize still played his other appearances, and in 1955, began to appear on the *Hank Penny Show* on Los Angeles television. In 1957, his popularity grew to the extent that, for several years, he managed to appear on seven Los Angeles television stations weekly, including *Town Hall Party*, and still maintained his Bakersfield commitments. He naturally developed into a television personality and, in 1966 and 1967, he became host/singer of Gene Autry's *Melody Ranch* network show on KTLA. He also commenced his own syndicated *Billy Mize Show* from Bakersfield. He first recorded for Decca in the 50s, and later for Challenge and Liberty, before making the US country charts in 1966 with his Columbia recording of 'You Can't Stop Me'. Between 1966 and 1977, he totalled 11 US chart entries, including his own composition, 'Make It Rain'. Some of his songs were hits for other artists, such as 'Who Will Buy The Wine' (Charlie Walker), 'My Baby Walks All Over Me' (Johnny Sea) and 'Don't Let The Blues Make

You Bad' (Dean Martin). He maintained rigorous schedules throughout the 60s and 70s, and appeared in the television series *RFD Hollywood*. He later became a television producer with his own production company. He has also worked as a musician on numerous recording sessions, including playing steel and rhythm guitar on many of Merle Haggard's recordings. His brother Buddy (b. 5 August 1936, Wichita, Kansas, USA) is a noted country songwriter, record producer and radio personality. He also relocated to Bakersfield, and his songs have been recorded by Buck Owens, Johnny Cash, Marty Robbins, Hank Snow and many others. In the early 80s, Buddy and Billy worked together on various television projects. Billy currently heads Billy Mize Productions, making television spectaculars with Merle Haggard.

● ALBUMS: *This Time And Place* (Imperial 1969)★★★, *You're Alright With Me* (United Artists 1970)★★★, *Love'N'Stuff* (1976)★★.

MIZELL, HANK

b. Bill Mizell, Asheville, North Carolina, USA. Mizell was a minor rockabilly artist best known for the 1957 recording 'Jungle Rock'. He served in the US Navy in 1947, and upon his discharge began both singing and preaching. In the early 50s he and his five-piece country band went to Montgomery, Alabama, to record. A disc jockey there nicknamed him Hank after the recently deceased Hank Williams, and the name stuck. In 1957, working with guitarist Jim Bobo, drummer Bill Collins and pianist Eddie Boyd in Chicago, Mizell recorded 'Jungle Rock' for the local EKO label. King Records picked up distribution, but the record did not sell, and Mizell gave up performing professionally. He became a preacher and moved between Chicago, Mississippi and Nashville for the next few years. Although several country singles were recorded in the 60s and 70s, Mizell remained virtually unknown until 1976, when rockabilly collectors in Europe discovered the King single. 'Jungle Rock' transcended cult credibility to reach the UK Top 10, and prompted Charly Records to release other rediscovered Mizell recordings. Mizell made a few other rockabilly and country recordings in the 80s, but remained unknown outside of hardcore rockabilly circles.

● COMPILATIONS: *Jungle Rock* (Charly 1976)★★★, *Higher* (1977)★★, *We're Gonna Bop Tonight* (1982)★★★.

MOFFATT, HUGH

b. 10 November 1948, Fort Worth, Texas, USA. Unlike most country performers, Moffatt played trumpet in his high school band and had a fondness for big band jazz. He gained a degree in English from Rice University in Houston and learned to play the guitar. Moffatt played acoustic sets in Austin and Washington and then, in 1973, moved to Nashville. He says, 'I was interested in Nashville purely because of Kris Kristofferson. He proved that you can take the folk and the literary tradition, and you can be in Nashville, too.' In 1974, Ronnie Milsap recorded Moffatt's 'Just In Case'. Moffatt recorded two singles for Mercury - a cover version of 'The Gambler' and his own 'Love And Only Love' - but the contract then terminated. In the early 80s he formed the band Ratz, which included Moffatt's wife, Pebe Sebert, and released a five-track EP, *Putting On The Ratz*. In 1987, his superb album *Loving You* was released, and

included a song written with Sebert, 'Old Flames (Can't Hold A Candle To You)'. He admits, 'That title and the ideas were Pebe's. We wrote it three months after we were married. We spent three months writing it, as we wanted it to be right. Everybody knew it would be a hit.' The song has been successfully recorded by Joe Sun, Dolly Parton and Foster And Allen. The only other song they wrote together was 'Wild Turkey', which was recorded by Lacy J. Dalton. Other Moffatt songs include 'Love Games' (Jerry Lee Lewis), 'Praise The Lord And Pass Me The Money' (Bobby Bare), 'Why Should I Cry Over You?' (George Hamilton IV) and 'Words At Twenty Paces' (Alabama). His sister, Katy Moffatt, is also a recording artist, at home with both acoustic and hard-rocking material. Hugh and Katy released a duet of 'Rose Of My Heart', which has also been recorded by Johnny Rodriguez and Nicolette Larson. *The Wognum Sessions* is so-called because Moffatt and two other musicians recorded an album in a small church in Holland. Moffatt now seems content to play club dates, without aiming for more major commercial success.

● ALBUMS: *Loving You* (Philo 1987)★★★, *Troubadour* (Philo 1989)★★★★, *Live And Alone* (Philo 1991), with Katy Moffatt *Dance Me Outside* (Philo 1992)★★★, *The Wognum Sessions* (Strictly Country 1995)★★★, *The Life Of A Minor Poet* (Watermelon 1996)★★★.

MOFFATT, KATY

b. 19 November 1950, Fort Worth, Texas, USA. Moffatt is a Texan singer-songwriter whose country-based folk has won a limited, yet loyal, following. Originally from Fort Worth, her early influences included Leonard Cohen and Tracy Nelson. She spent the early 70s playing folk clubs and small rock venues, mainly in Colorado, before signing to CBS, and releasing two commercially slanted records in the mid to late 70s. Disillusioned with the music business, Moffatt kept a low profile during the early 80s, but during the mid-80s she received a nomination from the Academy Of Country Music as Best New Female Vocalist. Her appearance on the semi-legendary compilation *A Town South Of Bakersfield* (1985) was a key career move, and her performance at the Kerrville Folk Festival a year later was another important step; she met the respected songwriter Tom Russell, and they began a fruitful collaboration. In 1989, Moffatt gained favourable reviews for *Walkin' On The Moon*, her first album for 11 years. Throughout her career she has supported many musicicans including Warren Zevon, Roy Orbison, the Everly Brothers, and Don Williams, and has recorded regularly for a variety of independent labels. She has recorded an album with her brother Hugh Moffatt. Strange but true: one of the factors that helped former 60s star P.J. Proby recover from his alcoholic oblivion was hearing Katy perform one of his lesser-known songs, 'In A Moment'. He bought a CD Walkman and played it continuously while drying out.

● ALBUMS: *Katy* (Columbia 1976)★★★, *Kissing In The California Sun* (Columbia 1978)★★★, *Walkin' On the Moon* (Philo 1989)★★★★, *Child Bride* (Philo 1990)★★★, *The Greatest Show On Earth*, with Hugh Moffatt *Dance Me Outside* (Philo 1992)★★★, *Indoor Fireworks* (Red Moon 1992)★★★, *The Greatest Show On Earth* this album was retitled *Evangeline Hotel* after the Ringling Brothers, Barnum and Bailey claimed infringement of copyright (Round Tower 1993)★★★★, *Hearts Gone Wild* (Watermelon

1994)★★★, *Midnight Radio* (Rounder 1996)★★★, with Kate Brislin *Sleepless Nights* (Rounder 1996)★★★.

MONROE, BILL

b. William Smith Monroe, 13 September 1911, on a farm near Rosine, Ohio County, Kentucky, USA, d. 9 September 1996. The Monroes were a musical family; his father, known affectionately as Buck, was a noted step-dancer, his mother played fiddle, accordion and harmonica, and was respected locally as a singer of old-time songs. Among the siblings, elder brothers Harry and Birch both played fiddle, and brother Charlie and sister Bertha played guitar. They were all influenced by their uncle, Pendleton Vanderver, who was a fiddler of considerable talent, and noted for his playing at local events. (Monroe later immortalized him in one of his best-known numbers, 'Uncle Pen', with tribute lines such as 'Late in the evening about sundown; high on the hill above the town, Uncle Pen played the fiddle, oh, how it would ring. You can hear it talk, you can hear it sing'). At the age of nine, Monroe began to concentrate on the mandolin; his first choice had been the guitar or fiddle, but his brothers pointed out that no family member played mandolin, and as the baby, he was given little choice, although he still kept up his guitar playing. His mother died when he was 10, followed soon after by his father. He moved in to live with Uncle Pen and they were soon playing guitar together at local dances. Bill also played with a black blues musician, Arnold Schultz, who was to become a major influence on the future Monroe music. After the death of his father, most of the family moved away in their search for work. Birch and Charlie headed north, working for a time in the car industry in Detroit, before moving to Whiting and East Chicago, Indiana, where they were employed in the oil refineries. When he was 18, Bill joined them, and for four years worked at the Sinclair refinery. At one time, during the Depression, Bill was the only one with work, and the three began to play for local dances to raise money.

In 1932, the three Monroe brothers and their girlfriends became part of a team of dancers and toured with a show organized by WLS Chicago, the radio station responsible for the *National Barn Dance* programme. They also played on local radio stations, including WAE Hammond and WJKS Gary, Indiana. In 1934, Bill, finding the touring conflicted with his work, decided to become a full-time musician. Soon afterwards, they received an offer to tour for Texas Crystals (the makers of a patent purgative medicine), which sponsored radio programmes in several states. Birch, back in employment at Sinclair and also looking after a sister, decided against a musical career. Bill married in 1935, and between then and 1936, he and Charlie (appearing as the Monroe Brothers) had stays at various stations, including Shenandoah, Columbia, Greenville and Charlotte. In 1936, they moved to the rival and much larger Crazy Water Crystals and, until 1938, they worked on the noted *Crazy Barn Dance* at WBT Charlotte for that company. They became a very popular act and sang mainly traditional material, often with a blues influence. Charlie always provided the lead vocal, and Bill added tenor harmonies.

In February 1936, they made their first recordings on the Bluebird label of RCA Victor, which proved popular. Further sessions followed, and in total they cut some 60 tracks for the label. Early in 1938, the brothers decided that they

should follow their own careers. Charlie kept the RCA recording contract and formed his own band, the Kentucky Pardners. Since he had always handled all lead vocals, he found things easier and soon established himself in his own right. Prior to the split, Bill had never recorded an instrumental or a vocal solo, but he had ideas that he wished to put into practice. He moved to KARK Little Rock, where he formed his first band, the Kentuckians. This failed to satisfy him, and he soon moved to Atlanta, where he worked on the noted *Crossroad Follies*; at this point, he formed the first of the bands he would call the BlueGrass Boys. In 1939, he made his first appearance on the *Grand Ole Opry*, singing his version of 'New Muleskinner Blues', after which George D. Hay (the Solemn Old Judge) told him, 'Bill, if you ever leave the Opry, it'll be because you fire yourself' (over 50 years later, he was still there).

During the early 40s, Monroe's band was similar to other string bands such as Mainer's Mountaineers, but by the middle of the decade, the leading influence of Monroe's driving mandolin and his high (some would say shrill) tenor singing became the dominant factor, and set the Blue Grass Boys of Bill Monroe apart from the other bands. This period gave birth to a new genre of music, and led to Monroe becoming affectionately known as the Father of Bluegrass Music. He began to tour with the *Opry* roadshows, and his weekly network WSM radio work soon made him a national name. In 1940 and 1941, he recorded a variety of material for RCA Victor, including gospel songs, old-time numbers and instrumentals such as the 'Orange Blossom Special' (the second known recording of the number). Wartime restrictions prevented him from recording between 1941 and early 1945, but later that year, he recorded for Columbia. In 1946, he gained his first country chart hits when his own song, 'Kentucky Waltz', reached number 3, and his now-immortal recording of 'Footprints In The Snow' reached number 5 in the US country charts. By 1945, several fiddle players had made their impact on the band's overall sound, including Chubby Wise, Art Wooten, Tommy Magness, Howdy Forrester and in 1945, guitarist/vocalist Lester Flatt and banjo player Earl Scruggs joined. Stringbean had provided the comedy and the banjo playing since 1942, although it was generally reckoned later that his playing contributed little to the overall sound that Monroe sought. Scruggs' style of playing was very different, and it quickly became responsible for not only establishing his own name as one of the greatest exponents of the instrument, but also for making bluegrass music an internationally identifiable sound. It was while Flatt and Scruggs were with the band that Monroe first recorded his now-immortal song 'Blue Moon Of Kentucky'. By 1948, other bands such as the Stanley Brothers were beginning to reflect the influence of Monroe, and bluegrass music was firmly established. During the 40s, Monroe toured with his tent show, which included his famous baseball team (the reason for Stringbean's first connections with Monroe), which played against local teams as an attraction before the musical show began. In 1951, he bought some land at Bean Blossom, Brown County, Indiana, and established a country park, which became the home for bluegrass music shows. He was involved in a very serious car accident in January 1953, and was unable to perform for several months. In 1954, Elvis Presley recorded Monroe's 'Blue Moon Of Kentucky' in a 4/4 rock tempo and sang it at his solitary appearance on the *Opry*. A dejected Presley found the performance made no impact with the *Opry* audience, but the song became a hit. It also led to Monroe re-recording it in a style that, like the original, started as a waltz, but after a verse and chorus featuring three fiddles, it changed to 4/4 tempo; Monroe repeated the vocal in the new style (Paul McCartney's 1991 *Unplugged* album features a version in both styles). Monroe toured extensively throughout the 50s, and had chart success in 1958 with his own instrumental number, 'Scotland'. He used the twin fiddles of Kenny Baker and Bobby Hicks to produce the sound of bagpipes behind his own mandolin - no doubt his tribute to his family's Scottish ancestry. By the end of the decade, the impact of rock 'n' roll was affecting his record sales and music generally. By this time, Flatt and Scruggs were firmly established with their own band and finding success on television and at folk festivals. Monroe was a strong-willed person and it was not always easy for those who worked with him, or for him, to achieve the perfect arrangement. He had stubborn ideas, and in 1959, he refused to play a major concert in Carnegie Hall, because he believed that Alan Lomax, the organizer, was a communist. He was also suspicious of the press and rarely, if ever, gave interviews. In 1962, however, he became friendly with Ralph Rinzler, a writer and member of the Greenbriar Boys, who became his manager.

In 1963, Monroe played his first folk festival at the University of Chicago. He soon created a great interest among students generally and, with Rinzler's planning, he was soon busily connected with festivals devoted solely to bluegrass music. In 1965, he was involved with the major Roanoke festival in Virginia, and in 1967, he started his own at Bean Blossom. During the 60s, many young musicians benefitted from their time as a member of Monroe's band, including Bill Keith, Peter Rowan, Byron Berline, Roland White and Del McCoury. In 1969, he was made an honorary Kentucky Colonel, and in 1970, was elected to the *Country Music Hall Of Fame* in Nashville. The plaque stated: 'The Father of Bluegrass Music. Bill Monroe developed and perfected this music form and taught it to a great many names in the industry'. Monroe has written many songs, including 'Memories Of Mother And Dad', 'When The Golden Leaves Begin To Fall', 'My Little Georgia Rose' and 'Blue Moon Of Kentucky' (the latter a much-recorded country standard) and countless others. Many have been written using pseudonyms such as Albert Price, James B. Smith and James W. Smith. In 1971, his talent as a songwriter saw him elected to the Nashville Songwriters' Association International Hall Of Fame. He kept up a hectic touring schedule throughout the 70s, but in 1981, he was diagnosed with cancer. He survived after treatment and, during the 80s, maintained a schedule that would have daunted much younger men. In 1984, he recorded the album *Bill Monroe And Friends*, which contains some of his songs sung as duets with other artists, including the Oak Ridge Boys ('Blue Moon Of Kentucky'), Emmylou Harris ('Kentucky Waltz'), Barbara Mandrell ('My Rose Of Old Kentucky'), Ricky Skaggs ('My Sweet Darling') and Willie Nelson ('The Sunset Trail'). Johnny Cash, who also appears on the album, presumably did not know any Monroe songs because they sang Cash's own 'I Still Miss Someone'.

Over the years since Monroe first formed his bluegrass band, some of the biggest names in country music have played as members before progressing to their own careers. These include Clyde Moody, Flatt And Scruggs, Jim Eanes, Carter Stanley, Mac Wiseman, Jimmy Martin, Sonny Osborne, Vassar Clements, Kenny Baker and his own son James Monroe. Amazingly, bearing in mind his popularity, Monroe's last chart entry was 'Gotta Travel On', a Top 20 country hit in March 1959. However, his records are still collected and the German Bear Family label has released boxed sets on compact disc of his Decca recordings. (Between 1950, when he first recorded for Decca and 1969, he made almost 250 recordings for the label.) He continued to play the *Opry*, and in 1989, he celebrated his 50th year as a member, the occasion being marked by MCA (by then the owners of Decca) recording a live concert from the *Opry* stage, which became his first ever release on CD format. He underwent surgery for a double coronary bypass on 9 August 1991, but by October, he was back performing and once again hosting his normal *Opry* show. The acknowledged 'father of bluegrass music' died a few days before his 85th birthday in 1996.

● ALBUMS: *Knee Deep In Bluegrass* (Decca 1958)★★★, *I Saw The Light* (Decca 1959)★★★, *Mr. Bluegrass* (Decca 1960)★★★, *The Great Bill Monroe & The BlueGrass Boys* (Harmony 1961)★★★, *Bluegrass Ramble* (Decca 1962)★★★, with Rose Maddox *Rose Maddox Sings Bluegrass* (Decca 1962)★★★, *The Father Of Bluegrass Music* (Decca 1962)★★★, *My All-Time Country Favorites* (Decca 1962)★★★, *Bluegrass Special* (Decca 1963)★★★★, *Bill Monroe Sings Country Songs* (Decca 1964)★★★, *I'll Meet You In Church Sunday Morning* (Decca 1964)★★★, *Original Bluegrass Sound* (Harmony 1965)★★★, *Bluegrass Instrumentals* (Decca 1965)★★★, *The High Lonesome Sound Of Bill Monroe* (Decca 1966)★★★, *Bluegrass Time* (Decca 1967)★★★, *I Saw The Light* (Decca 1969)★★★, *A Voice From On High* (Decca 1969)★★★, *Bluegrass Style* (Vocalion 1970)★★★, *Kentucky Bluegrass* (Decca 1970)★★★, *Bill Monroe's Country Hall Of Fame* (Decca 1971)★★★★, *Uncle Pen* (Decca 1972)★★★, *Bean Blossom* (Decca 1973)★★★, with James Monroe *Father And Son* (Decca 1973)★★★, *The Road Of Life* (Decca 1974)★★★, with Birch Monroe *Brother Birch Monroe Plays Old-Time Fiddle Favorites* (Decca 1975)★★★, with Doc Watson *Bill & Doc Sing Country Songs* (FBN 1975)★★★, with Kenny Baker *Kenny Baker Plays Bill Monroe* (Decca 1976)★★★, *Weary Traveller* (Decca 1976)★★★, *Sings Bluegrass, Body And Soul* (Decca 1977)★★★, *Bluegrass Memories* (Decca 1977)★★★, with James Monroe *Together Again* (Decca 1978)★★★, *Bill Monroe With Lester Flatt & Earl Scruggs:The Original Bluegrass Band* (Rounder 1979)★★★★, *Bluegrass Classic (Radio Shows 1946-1948)* (MCA 1980)★★★, *Bean Blossom 1979* (MCA 1980)★★★, *Orange Blossom Special (Recorded Live At Melody Ranch)* (MCA 1981)★★, *Master Of Bluegrass* (MCA 1981)★★★, *Live Radio* (1982)★★★, *Bill Monroe & Friends* (MCA 1984)★★★, *Bluegrass '87* (MCA 1987)★★★, *Southern Flavor* (MCA 1988)★★★, *Live At The Opry: Celebrating 50 Years On The Grand Ole Opry* (MCA 1989)★★★, *Muleskinner Blues 1940-1941 recordings* (RCA 1991)★★★. As The Monroe Brothers *Early Bluegrass Music* (Camden 1963)★★★, *The Monroe Brothers, Bill & Charlie* (Decca 1969)★★★, *Feast Here Tonight* (Bluebird 1975)★★★.

● COMPILATIONS: *Bill Monroe & His Blue GrassBoys (16 Hits)* (Columbia 1970)★★★, *The Classic Bluegrass Recordings*

Volume 1 (County 1980)★★★, *The Classic Bluegrass Recordings Volume 2* (County 1980)★★★, *MCA Singles Collection Volumes 1, 2 & 3* (MCA 1983)★★★, *Columbia Historic Edition* (Columbia 1987)★★★, *Bill Monroe Bluegrass 1950-1958* 4-CD box set (Bear Family 1989)★★★★, *Country Music Hall Of Fame* (MCA 1991)★★★, *Bill Monroe Bluegrass 1959-1969* 4-CD box set (Bear Family 1991)★★★★, *The Essential Bill Monroe 1945-1949* (Columbia/Legacy 1992)★★★★, with the Blue Grass Boys *Live Recordings 1956-1969: Off The Record Volume 1* (Smithsonian/Folkways 1993)★★★, with Doc Watson *Live Duet Recordings 1963-80* (Smithsonian/Folkways 1993)★★★, *The Music Of Bill Monroe* 4-CD box set (MCA 1994)★★★★, *Bluegrass (1970-1979)* 4-CD box set (Bear Family 1995)★★★★, *16 Gems* (Columbia/Legacy 1996)★★★★.
● FURTHER READING: *Bossmen: Bill Monroe And Muddy Waters*, J. Rooney. *Bill Monroe And His Blue Grass Boys*, Neil V. Rosenberg.

MONROE, BIRCH

b. 1901, on a farm near Rosine, Ohio County, Kentucky, USA, d. 15 May 1982. Birch was the fiddle-playing elder brother of Bill Monroe who, after the death of his parents, moved to Detroit with brother Charlie Monroe. Here, they worked for a time in the motor industry, before moving to work in the oil refineries at Whiting and East Chicago, Indiana. In 1929, they were joined by brother Bill, and during the Depression, the three began to play at local venues; eventually Bill and Charlie worked professionally together as the Monroe Brothers. From the mid-to late 40s, he worked with brother Bill's band, playing bass and taking bass vocals, as well as acting as their manager and booking agent. He remained connected with his brother's business enterprises, and from 1951 to the end of the 70s, he managed the country park at Bean Blossom, Indiana, which featured the weekly *Brown County Jamboree*. His recording career was limited to those recordings made with his brother's band, except in the mid-70s, when, accompanied by the BlueGrass Boys and under the production of Bill, he recorded an album of fiddle music. Birch Monroe died in 1982, and is buried in the Monroe family plot on Jerusalem Ridge, Rosine, Kentucky.
● ALBUMS: with Bill Monroe *Brother Birch Monroe Plays Old-Time Fiddle Favorites* (Decca 1975)★★★.

MONROE, CHARLIE

b. 4 July 1903, on a farm near Rosine, Ohio County, Kentucky, USA, d. 27 September 1975. Charlie was the elder brother of Bill Monroe who, after the death of his parents, moved to Detroit with fiddle-playing brother Birch Monroe. Here they worked for a time in the motor industry, before moving to work in the oil refineries at Whiting and East Chicago, Indiana. In 1929, they were joined by brother Bill and during the Depression, the three began to play at local venues; eventually Bill and Charlie worked professionally together as the Monroe Brothers. In 1938, they decided to pursue their own careers. At the time of the split, they had a contract with RCA-Victor, for whom they had recorded 60 songs; Charlie, who had always taken the lead vocals (though Bill had written many of their songs), kept this contract. Throughout the 40s, he toured and recorded for RCA-Victor, and at times his band, the Kentucky Pardners, which

became one of North Carolina's most popular hillbilly bands, included notable musicians such as guitarist Lester Flatt and mandolin players Red Rector, Ira Louvin and Curly Sechler. He differed from his brother in that his band played a mixture of country and bluegrass, and Charlie, a highly respected guitarist, frequently used an electric guitar. He made many fine recordings, and although he never achieved a chart hit, Monroe is remembered for his versions of numbers such as 'Down In The Willow Garden' (an old folk song) and his own compositions 'Rubber Neck Blues', 'It's Only A Phonograph Record' and 'Who's Calling You Sweetheart Tonight?'. He joined Decca around 1950, and although they made some concert appearances together, further recordings with brother Bill never materialized. In the early 50s, tired of the touring, he broke up his band and semi-retired to his Kentucky farm. In 1957, he supposedly retired to manage a coalmine and yard near Rosine, but made some special appearances, and during the early 60s, recorded two albums on the Rem label. His wife became ill with cancer, and to meet the medical expenses, Monroe left Kentucky and worked in Indiana for a lift company until his wife died. He remarried in 1969 when he moved to Tennessee, and in 1972, he was persuaded to appear with Jimmy Martin at a Gettysburg bluegrass festival, which led him to make some further appearances at similar events. He relocated to Reidsville, North Carolina, and in late 1974, he, too, was diagnosed as suffering from cancer. He made his last public performance in his old home area of Rosine, Kentucky, around early August, and died at his home in Reidsville in September 1975, but is buried in the Monroe family plot on Jerusalem Ridge, Rosine, Kentucky. Although his work was not as important as that of brother Bill, he nevertheless made a significant contribution to the formation of what is now known as bluegrass music.
● ALBUMS: *Bluegrass Sound* (1963)★★★, *Lord Build Me A Cabin* (Starday 1965)★★★, *Charlie Monroe Sings Again* (Starday 1966)★★★, *Who's Calling You Sweetheart Tonight?* (Camden 1969)★★★, *Noon-Day Jamboree (Radio Shows 1944)* (1970)★★★, *Songs Of Charlie Monroe & the Kentucky Pardners (Vintage Radio Recordings)* (1970)★★★, *Live At Lake Norman Music Hall* (1975)★★★, *Tally Ho* (1975)★★★, one side of second album by Phipps Family *Memories Of Charlie Monroe* (1975)★★★, *Charlie Monroe's Boys:The Early Years* (1982)★★★, *Vintage Radio 1944* (1990)★★★. As The Monroe Brothers *Early Bluegrass Music* (Camden 1963)★★★, *The Monroe Brothers, Bill & Charlie* (Decca 1969)★★★, *Feast Here Tonight* (Bluebird 1975)★★★.

MONROE, JAMES

b. James William Monroe, 1941. Son of Bill Monroe. James began his musical career in 1964, playing upright bass with his father's BlueGrass Boys. In 1969, he became the band's guitarist and also began to take lead vocals. He left the Bluegrass Boys in 1972, and formed his own bluegrass band, the Midnight Ramblers, but later recorded two albums with his father. In the mid-70s, he recorded several albums for Atteiram, including a tribute to his uncle, Charlie Monroe, on which his father also appeared. Soon afterwards he drastically reduced his performing to help with the running of his father's business affairs.
● ALBUMS: with Bill Monroe *Father And Son* (Decca 1973)★★★, *Sings Songs of 'Memory Lane' Of His Uncle*

Charlie Monroe (Atteiram 1976)★★★, *Together Again* (Decca 1978)★★★. With the Midnight Ramblers *Something New! Something Different! Something Good!* (Atteiram 1974)★★★, *Midnight Blues* (Atteiram 1976)★★★, *Satisfied Mind* (1984)★★★.

MONROE, MELISSA

b. Melissa Katherine Monroe, 1936, d. December 1990. Daughter of Bill Monroe. A singer and instrumentalist, Monroe toured with her father's roadshow during the 40s and 50s. She made some solo recordings for Columbia in the early 50s, but did not achieve any chart success.

MONTANA ROSE

Montana Rose is a goodtime country band from Gallatin Gateway, Montana, USA. It is fronted by Claudia Appling Williams and her bandleader/bassist husband, Kenny. The band also features Rick Winkling (guitar) and Mike Gillan (drums) with accordion playing from Fats Kaplan on *Star Of Bannack*. Their cynical look at modern country music in 'Hillbilly With A Record Deal' did well and they may become hillbillies with a major record deal themselves.
● ALBUMS: *Highway 191* (Cowboy Heaven 1995)★★★, *Star Of Bannack* (Cowboy Heaven 1996)★★★.

MONTANA SLIM

(see Carter, Wilf)

MONTANA, PATSY

b. Rubye Blevins, 30 October 1912, Hot Springs, Arkansas, USA, d. 3 May 1996, San Jacinto, California, USA. Montana was the eleventh child and first daughter of a farmer, and in her childhood she learned organ, guitar, violin and yodelling. In 1928 she worked on radio in California as Rubye Blevins, the Yodelling Cowgirl from San Antone. In 1931 she joined Stuart Hamblen's show, appearing on radio and at rodeos as part of the Montana Cowgirls. Hamblen renamed her Patsy as it was 'a good Irish name'. In 1933 she joined the Kentucky Ramblers, who, because of their western image, became the Prairie Ramblers. In 1935 Montana recorded her self-penned 'I Want To Be A Cowboy's Sweetheart', the first million-seller by a female country singer. She recorded many other western songs including 'Old Nevada Moon' and 'Back On The Montana Plains' (several of her songs had Montana in the title). She appeared in several films including *Colorado Sunset* with Gene Autry. During the war, she recorded with the Sons Of The Pioneers and the Lightcrust Doughboys; her 'Goodnight Soldier' was very popular. She continued with her cowgirl image after the war but retired in 1952 and moved to California. She returned to touring in the 60s, often with her daughter Judy Rose, and recorded for Starday with Waylon Jennings on lead guitar. She won popularity outside the USA, particularly in the UK, with her appearances in country clubs. Montana, who presented a picture of independence through her cowgirl image, has inspired many yodelling singers including Rosalie Allen, Texas Ruby and Bonnie Lou. In 1993 she received the Living Legends Of Western Music award. She died in May 1996, and was inducted into the Country Music Hall Of Fame the same year.
● ALBUMS: *New Sounds Of Patsy Montana At The Matador Room* (Sims 1964)★★★, *Precious Memories* (Burch

1977)★★★, *Mum And Me* (Look 1977)★★★, *I Want To Be A Cowboy's Sweetheart* (1977)★★★, *Patsy Montana Sings Her Original Hits* (Cattle 1980)★★.
● COMPILATIONS: *Early Country Favourites* (Old Homestead 1983)★★★, *Patsy Montana And The Prairie Ramblers* (1984)★★★, *The Cowboy's Sweetheart* (Flying Fish 1988)★★★.

MONTGOMERY, BOB

b. 1936, Lambasas, Texas, USA. While attending Lubbock's Hutchinson High School, this rhythm guitarist was partnered by Buddy Holly as a 'Singer of Western and Bop' when entertaining at parents' evenings, parties and, indeed, 'anywhere we could get to a microphone'. Sometimes augmented by the younger Larry Welborn on double bass, they were heard regularly on local radio with Montgomery as main vocalist in a repertoire that embraced his (and Holly's) own compositions. Among these were 'Flower Of My Heart' and other items taped as demos in the mid-50s. With superimposed backing, these would be released after Holly's death gave them historical importance, as it was Buddy who was singled out by Decca Records in 1956 as the most commercial talent. However, not begrudging him his luck, Montgomery continued to write songs with his friend, among them 'Wishing', 'Love's Made A Fool Of You' and other Holly hits. After serving as engineer in Norman Petty's Clovis studio, Montgomery moved to Nashville in 1959 where, as a songwriter, he provided Wilma Burgess with 'Misty Blue' (revived in 1976 by Dorothy Moore), 'Two Of A Kind' (written with Earl Sinks) for Sue Thompson and Roy Orbison, and 1965's 'Wind Me Up' for Cliff Richard. Among other recipients of Montgomery pieces were Bob Luman and Mel Tillis. In 1966 he became a United Artists staff producer. His most enduring labours in this sphere were for Bobby Goldsboro (including 'Honey' and 'Summer The First Time') but other ventures into what was to be named 'country-pop' included records by Bill Dees, Johnny Darrell, Buddy Knox, Del Reeves and Earl Richards. In the early 70s Montgomery founded House Of Gold, one of Nashville's most respected music publishing concerns.
● ALBUMS: with Buddy Holly: *Holly In The Hills* (1965, reissued as *Wishing* in 1968)★★★, with Holly *Western And Bop* (1977)★★★.

MONTGOMERY, JOHN MICHAEL

b. 20 January 1965, Danville, Kentucky, USA. Montgomery arrived on the country music scene in 1993 with a debut album, *Life's A Dance*, that became the only million-seller on the country charts by a new artist that year. Its title track was also a number 1 single. *Kickin' It Up* was number 1 on both the US Country and Adult Contemporary charts, and produced two more successful singles, 'I Swear' and 'Rope The Moon'. However, Montgomery remained unchanged by his success, and refused to leave Lexington to go to Nashville. Instead he continued to enjoy traditional rock 'n' roll pursuits such as fishing and golfing. His musical talent had been initially encouraged by his father, who performed in a local country band and taught his son his first chords. Montgomery joined the family band as guitarist, before taking the lead singing role when his parents divorced. Afterwards, he made a frugal living on the local honky tonk scene as a solo artist playing what he referred to as 'working man's country'. Eventually, Atlantic Records signed him, although it was Montgomery himself rather than the record company who rejected his own material for inclusion on his debut ('Mine just weren't good enough'). There were problems during the recording, typified in an anecdote regarding a late-night call to the head of Atlantic that resulted in a change of producer. Atlantic's faith in their artist was subsequently rewarded by Montgomery's swift rise, even though some questioned his political correctness with songs such as 'Sold'. *Kickin' It Up* and *John Michael Montgomery* were massive hits, both number 1 albums. In the mid-90s he stands as one of the hottest artists in country music, appealing to lovers of both Garth Brooks and Lynyrd Skynyrd. *What I Do The Best,* though a slightly disappointing album, showed no signs of his commercial appeal waning.

● ALBUMS: *Life's A Dance* (Atlantic 1992)★★★, *Kickin' It Up* (Atlantic 1994)★★★★, *John Michael Montgomery* (Atlantic 1995)★★★★, *What I Do The Best* (Atlantic 1996)★★★.
● COMPILATIONS: *Greatest Hits* (Atlantic 1997)★★★★.
● VIDEOS: *I Swear* (1993), *Kickin' It Up* (1994).

MONTGOMERY, MELBA

b. 14 October 1938, Iron City, Tennessee, USA. Born into a musical family, Montgomery's father ran a church choir and both her brothers, Carl and Earl, became country songwriters, often supplying her with material. In 1958 she and her brothers were finalists in a nationwide talent contest sponsored by Pet Milk - another finalist was Johnny Tillotson. Her success led to an appearance on the *Grand Ole Opry,* where she impressed Roy Acuff. He added her to his roadshow and she spent four years touring the USA and its military bases abroad. In 1962 she recorded two singles, 'Happy You, Lonely Me' and 'Just Another Fool Along The Way', for Lonzo and Oscar's Nugget label. She recorded prolifically for United Artists and Musicor, and made the US country charts with 'Hall Of Shame' and 'The Greatest One Of All', although Melba is better known for her duets with George Jones ('We Must Have Been Out Of Her Minds', which she wrote) and Gene Pitney ('Baby, Ain't That Fine'). Substantial success eluded her at Capitol, although she recorded duets with Charlie Louvin, notably 'Something To Brag About'. She gave Elektra a number 1 country single with 'No Charge', written by Harlan Howard, although it was covered for the UK market by J.J. Barrie. She has spent the past decade raising her family.
● ALBUMS: with George Jones *What's In Our Heart* (United Artists 1963)★★★, *Melba Montgomery - America's Number One Country And Western Girl Singer* (United Artists 1964)★★★, *Down Home* (United Artists 1964)★★★, with Jones *Bluegrass Hootenanny* (United Artists 1964)★★★, *I Can't Get Used To Being Lonely* (United Artists 1965)★★★, shared with Dottie West *Queens Of Country Music* (Starday 1965)★★★, with Jones *Blue Moon Of Kentucky* (United Artists 1966)★★★, *Country Girl* (Musicor 1966)★★★, *Hallelujah Road* (Musicor 1966)★★★, with Gene Pitney *Being Together* (Musicor 1966)★★★, with Jones *Close Together* (Musicor 1966)★★★, *The Mood I'm In* (Unart 1967)★★★, *Melba Toast* (Musicor 1967)★★★, with the Jordanaires *Don't Keep Me Lonely Too Long* (Musicor 1967)★★★, *I'm Just Living* (Musicor 1967)★★★, with Jones *Let's Get Together/Party Pickin'* (Musicor 1967)★★★, with Jones *Great Country Duets Of All Time* (Musicor 1969)★★★,

The Big Country World Of Melba Montgomery (1969)★★★, with Charlie Louvin *Somethin' To Brag About* (Capitol 1971)★★★, with Louvin *Baby, You've Got What It Takes* (Capitol 1971)★★★, *Melba Montgomery - No Charge* (Elektra 1973)★★★, *Aching Breaking Heart* (1975)★★★, *Don't Let The Good Times Fool You* (1975)★★★, *The Greatest Gift Of All* (1975)★★★, *Melba* (1976)★★★, *Melba Montgomery* (1978)★★★.
● COMPILATIONS: with Jones *Vintage Collection Series* (Capitol 1996)★★★.

MOODY, CLYDE

b. 19 September 1915, Cherokee, North Carolina, USA, d. 7 April 1989, Nashville, Tennessee, USA. Raised in Marion, North Carolina, Moody had learned the guitar by the age of eight and soon after became a professional musician. He left home when he was 14. He first worked with Jay Hugh Hall, initially as Bill And Joe on WSPA Spartanburg, South Carolina, in 1929, but later with Steve Ledford, they became the Happy-Go-Lucky Boys. (He also played some semi-professional baseball with Asheville, South Carolina.) Between 1937 and 1940, while continuing to appear as a duo, they also played with Wade Mainer's Sons Of The Mountaineers and recorded for Bluebird, both as a duo and with the group. They performed on many Carolina radio stations until they left Wade Mainer and joined his brother, J.E. Mainer, in Alabama. In 1941 Moody had a disagreement with both Hall and Mainer, and left to join Bill Monroe back in North Carolina. During his time with Monroe, Moody appeared on various recordings including the classic version of his own song 'Six White Horses', which was coupled with 'Mule Skinner Blues' as Monroe's Blue Grass Boys' first Bluebird single release. Moody soon left, and hiring Lester Flatt as his partner, he worked WHBB Burlington as the Happy-Go-Lucky Boys; however, in 1942, he rejoined Monroe and stayed with him until 1945. When he finally left, his place was taken by Flatt. Moody worked with Roy Acuff for a short time but soon went solo and made his first solo recordings that year. He played the *Grand Ole Opry* during the late 40s but left to work on early television in Washington DC. His 1947 recording of 'Shenandoah Waltz' (co-written with Chubby Wise) is reputed to be the top-selling record for the King label, having had sales in excess of three million. The song is now a bluegrass standard, although most experts would say that Moody's original version is more that of a country ballad singer, such as Red Foley, than that of a bluegrass artist. He began to specialize in waltz numbers, having such success that he acquired the nickname of The Hillbilly Waltz King. In 1948, he had Top 20 US country chart hits with 'Carolina Waltz' and 'Red Roses Tied In Blue', and in 1950, his recording of 'I Love You Because' reached number 8. He left King in 1951 and recorded for Decca, but from 1957 to the early 60s, he was less active on the music scene. He returned to North Carolina, where he developed business interests in mobile homes and for a long time hosted his own daily television show, *Carolina In The Morning* in Raleigh. During the 60s, he recorded for Starday, Wango and Little Darlin'. He returned to Nashville in 1971 and once more became involved with the music scene. He guested on the *Opry,* played various bluegrass festivals, toured extensively with his friend Rambling Tommy Scott's Medicine Show and recorded for Old Homestead. During the mid-70s, his health began to suffer but he continued to perform whenever he was able, until he died on 7 April 1989.

● ALBUMS: *The Best Of Clyde Moody* (King 1964)★★★, *All Time Country & Western Waltzes* (1969)★★★, *Moody's Blues* (1972)★★★, *A Country Tribute To Fred Rose* (Old Homestead 1976)★★★, with Tommy Scott *We've Played Every Place More Than Once* (Starday 1978)★★★, with Scott *Early Country Favorites* (1980)★★★.

MOORE, BOB

b. 30 November 1932, Nashville, Tennessee, USA. A popular studio musician who progressed from bass player to musical director for Red Foley, Brenda Lee and Connie Francis, Moore then toured with Elvis Presley. His accompaniments for Roy Orbison earned him a solo contract with Monument Records (London in the UK) for his own combo, which released 'Hot Spot', 'My Three Sons' and 'Mexico'. The first and last were issued back to back in Britain, the second and third as Moore's contribution to the anthological *Demand Performance* album, with other tracks by Orbison, Billy Grammer, Jerry Byrd, Jack Eubanks and the Velvets. 'Mexico' reached number 7 in the US charts and earned Moore a Gold Disc in 1961, but this was the peak of his achievement. Two albums were issued on London in the late 60s but little else has been heard from him in recent years.

● ALBUMS: *Mexico And Other Great Hits!* (Monument 1961)★★★, *Viva!* (Hickory 1967)★★★, *Good Time Party* (London 1968)★★★.

MORGAN, GEORGE

b. 28 June 1924, Waverley, Tennessee, USA, d. 7 July 1975. Morgan was raised in Barberton, Ohio, and by the time he was nine, he was performing his own songs on guitar. He enlisted in the US Army during the war but was discharged three months later on medical grounds. He formed a band and found work on a radio station in Wooster, Ohio, and wrote 'Candy Kisses' after a broken romance. RCA showed an interest in Morgan, who performed 'Candy Kisses' on the *Grand Ole Opry* to great acclaim, but their tardiness led to US Columbia signing him instead. 'Candy Kisses' was a US country number 1 in 1949 despite competition from cover versions from Elton Britt, Red Foley and Eddie Kirk. However, there was friction between Morgan and Hank Williams, who regarded 'Candy Kisses' as 'stupid' and its singer 'a cross-eyed crooner'. Morgan, a crooner in the vein of Eddy Arnold, called his band the Candy Kids and he consolidated his reputation with 'Please Don't Let Me Love You', 'Room Full Of Roses', 'Almost', 'You're The Only Good Thing' and 'Mr. Ting-A-Ling (Steel Guitar Man)'. In 1953 Morgan became the first country performer to record with a symphony orchestra. In 1964 Morgan's duet of 'Slippin' Around' with Marion Worth was very successful, but by then Morgan was finding hits hard to come by. In 1967 he moved to Starday and then Nashville, Stop, US Decca and 4 Star, all with only minor successes. Morgan, a CB buff, suffered a heart attack while helping a friend install an aerial on his roof. Later that year, he celebrated his birthday at the *Opry* with the debut of his daughter, Lorrie. Within a few days he was undergoing open heart surgery but died on 7 July 1975. In 1979, a posthumous duet with Lorrie, 'I'm Completely Satisfied With You', made the US country charts.

● ALBUMS: *Morgan, By George* (Columbia 1957)★★★,

Golden Memories (Columbia 1961)★★★, *Tender Lovin' Care* (Columbia 1964)★★★, with Marion Worth *Slippin' Around* (Columbia 1964)★★★, *Red Roses For A Blue Lady* (Columbia 1965)★★★, *A Room Full Of Roses* (Starday 1967)★★★, *Candy Kisses* (Starday 1967)★★★, *Country Hits By Candlelight* (Starday 1967)★★★, *Steal Away* (Starday 1968)★★★, *Barbara* (Starday 1968)★★★, *Sounds Of Goodbye* (Starday 1969)★★★, *Misty Blue* (Nashville 1969)★★★, *George Morgan Sings Like A Bird* (Stop 1969)★★★, *The Real George* (Stop 1969)★★★, *Red Roses From The Blue Side Of Town* (Decca 1974)★★★, *A Candy Mountain Melody* (Deccaq 1974)★★★, *George Morgan - From This Moment On* (4-Star 1975)★★★.

● COMPILATIONS: *The Best Of* (Starday 1970)★★★, *Remembering The Greatest Hits* (Columbia 1975)★★★, *George Morgan - Country Souvenirs Of The 1950s* (1990), *Room Full Of Roses: The Best Of George Morgan* (Razor & Tie 1996)★★★★, *Candy Kisses* 8-CD box set (Bear Family 1996)★★★★.

MORGAN, JAYE P.

b. Mary Margaret Morgan, 1932, Mancos, Colorado, USA. Morgan performed with the Morgan Family Variety Troupe until her father's death in 1945. At 18, her voice had matured to the husky contralto that would land her a job as featured singer with Frank de Vol's orchestra and then that of Hank Penny, an RCA recording artist. Through Penny, the company signed Morgan who reached a wider audience during two years of weekly radio exposure on New York's *Robert Q. Lewis Show* and, less regularly, on the nationally transmitted *Stop The Music*. After 'That's All I Want From You' came close to topping the US chart in 1954, 'Danger! Heartbreak Ahead', 'The Longest Walk' and 'Pepper-Hot Baby' were smashes the following year - as were 'Chee Chee Oo Chee' and 'Two Lost Souls' (from Broadway musical *Damn Yankees*) - duets with Perry Como. However, a link-up on record with Eddy Arnold proved a flop, and that Christmas, 'If You Don't Want My Love' barely scraped into the Top 40. Subsequently, though still planting feet in both the C&W and pop camps, only 1959's 'Are You Lonesome Tonight' and a 1960 version of Johnny Cash's 'I Walk The Line' could be even remotely classed as 'hits'. Nevertheless, established as an all-American showbusiness 'personality', she would appear on television variety spectaculars and talk programmes as late as the mid-80s.

MORGAN, LORRIE

b. Loretta Lynn Morgan, 27 June 1959, Nashville, Tennessee, USA. The youngest daughter of country crooner and *Grand Ole Opry* star George Morgan, she followed in her father's footsteps. She naturally began singing with Dad and made her own *Opry* debut at the age of 13 at the old Ryman Auditorium, where her rendition of 'Paper Roses' gained her a standing ovation. After her father's death in 1975, she worked as a backing singing with George Jones's roadshow and for a time was married to Ron Gaddis, who played steel guitar in Jones's band. In 1979, she scored her first minor chart successes with 'Two People In Love' and 'Tell Me I'm Only Dreaming', as well as with a duet recording made earlier with her late father, 'I'm Completely Satisfied With You'. The same year, she had a daughter but her marriage ended and, tiring of life on the road, she basically retired. In 1984, the lure of the music enticed her back; she became a member of the *Opry* and relaunched her career. She met and married singer Keith Whitley in 1986 but the marriage ended when Whitley's heavy drinking finally took his life in May 1989 (she later recorded a tribute to Whitley, 'If You Came Back From Heaven', which appeared on her 1994 album *War Paint*). In 1988, she joined RCA and had a Top 20 hit with 'Trainwreck Of Emotion', but it was a number 9 weepy, 'Dear Me', entering the charts just a few weeks before Whitley's death, that finally established her as a major star. In 1990, she achieved her first number 1 with 'Five Minutes' and from that point, she has registered a regular stream of hit recordings. They include 'Til A Tear Becomes A Rose' (a duet made with Whitley), 'Except For Monday' and 'A Picture Of Me Without You' (a brave and very successful cover version of a 1972 George Jones hit) on RCA. A change of label to BNA in 1992, immediately produced a number 2 with 'Watch Me' and a further number 1 with 'What Part Of Me'. She is equally at home with up-tempo numbers or with ballads that call for the 'big voice' technique, such as her brilliant recording of 'Something In Red', which peaked at number 14. She attempted something different in 1993, when she recorded a Christmas album that had the New World Philharmonic Orchestra providing the music and featured duets with Tammy Wynette, Andy Williams and Johnny Mathis (the music was recorded in London and the vocals added in Nashville, Branson or L.A.). In 1993, she gained a Top 10 hit with 'Half Enough' and a minor placement for her version of 'Crying Time', which came from the movie *The Beverly Hillbillies*. In 1995, the release of *Greatest Hits* led to further chart successes. 'I Didn't Know My Own Strength' gave her another number 1 and soon afterwards, 'Back In Your Arms Again', a Fred Knobloch/Paul Davis song, with a catchy chorus, peaked at number 4. Her stunning version of 'Standing Tall', a Larry Butler/Ben Peters song that Billie Jo Spears had taken to number 15 in 1980, followed. A video of her singing the number, actually filmed on the stage of the old Ryman Auditorium home of the *Opry*, gained her recording major exposure on CMT and probably represents her best vocal performance since 'Something In Red'. There seems little doubt that Morgan will easily beat her father's record of 35 country chart entries, unless she is lost to country music in favour of the bright lights and highly paid circuits of venues such as Las Vegas.

● ALBUMS: *Leave The Light On* (RCA 1989)★★★, *Something In Red* (RCA 1991)★★★, *Watch Me* (BNA 1992)★★★★, *Merry Christmas From London* (BNA 1993)★★★, *War Paint* (BNA 1994)★★★, *Greater Need* (BNA 1996)★★★, *Shakin' Things Up* (BNA 1997)★★★.

● COMPILATIONS: *Greatest Hits* (BNA 1995)★★★★.

● VIDEOS: *War Paint - Video Hits* (1994), *I Didn't Know My Own Strength* (1995).

MORRIS BROTHERS

Wiley (d. 1990; mandolin, guitar, vocals) and Claude 'Zeke' Morris (guitar, vocals) are one of the many brother acts remembered for their fine harmony singing. At different times both worked with other bands including those of J.E. Mainer, Wade Mainer and Charley Monroe. They made their first recordings (accompanied by fiddler Homer Sherrill) for Bluebird in January 1938 and their next session (in September) yielded their noted version of 'Let Me Be Your Salty Dog'. They retired in the late 40s but did make some rare appearances later, including at the 1964 Newport Folk Festival and on a special television programme with Earl Scruggs. They were actually the first musicians ever to employ noted banjoists Earl Scruggs and Don Reno in their band. A third brother George Morris also played with them on occasions.

● ALBUMS: with Homer Sherrill *Wiley, Zeke & Homer* (Rounder 1972)★★★.

MORRIS, GARY

b. 7 December 1948, Fort Worth, Texas, USA. Morris sang in a church choir and learned guitar, playing along to the Beatles' records. When he and two friends auditioned for a club owner in Denver, they were told they were 'on in 15 minutes . . . providing they played country music'. They stayed at the club for five years and then Morris returned to Texas. He started campaigning for Jimmy Carter and in 1978, after Carter's election, Morris performed on a country show at the White House. As a result, he was signed to MCA, but when the singles did not sell, he moved to Colorado and formed a band, Breakaway. Producer Norro Wilson, who had been at the White House, signed him to Warners, but when Wilson moved to RCA, Morris found himself in limbo. Eventually, he had US country hits with 'Headed For A Heartache', 'Dreams Die Hard', 'Don't Look Back' and 'Velvet Chains'. In 1983, he became the first artist to put 'The Wind Beneath My Wings' on the US country charts and also had hits with 'The Love She Found In Me', 'Why Lady Why?' and a duet with Lynn Anderson, 'You're Welcome To Tonight'. He first appeared on the *Grand Ole Opry* in 1984, the same year he appeared on Broadway in *La Bohème* (alongside Linda Ronstadt). Morris had his first US country number 1 in 1985 with 'Baby Bye Bye' and he has had further US number 1 records with 'I'll Never Stop Loving You', 'Making Up For Lost Time' (a duet with Crystal Gayle), '100% Chance Of Rain' and 'Leave Me Lonely'. He returned to Broadway in 1987 for the main role in *Les Misérables* and was also featured on the 1988 symphonic recording. He moved from opera to soap opera by playing the blind country singer Wayne Masterson in *The Colbys*. Morris has the vocal and acting ability to take his career in any number of directions, although his commercial standing had dropped substantially by the early 90s.

● ALBUMS: *Gary Morris* (Warners 1982)★★★, *Why Lady Why* (Warners 1983)★★★, *Faded Blue* (Warners 1984)★★★, *Anything Goes...* (Warners 1985)★★★, *Second Hand Heart* (Warners 1986)★★★, *Plain Brown Wrapper* (Warners 1986)★★, with Crystal Gayle *What If We Fell In Love* (Warners 1987)★★, *Stones* (Liberty 1989)★★★, *Full Moon, Empty Heart* (Liberty 1991)★★.

● COMPILATIONS: *Hits* (Warners 1987)★★★★, *Greatest Hits, Vol. 2* (Warners 1990)★★★.

MORRISSEY, LOUISE

b. 23 March 1961, Bansha, Co. Tipperary, Eire. She grew up with a love of music and after completing her schooling, began to sing with her brothers, Billy and Norman, as the Morrisseys Folk And Ballad Group. She made her first recording, 'Farewell To Carlingford', in 1978. The group recorded several successful albums, including *Ireland's Morrisseys* and *On Stage (Live From Olympia)*. In 1988, encouraged by the popularity of Irish singers such as Ray

Lynam and Philomena Begley, she gave up folk music in favour of the ever-popular country and Irish (Norman became the bass guitarist in her band and Billy the band's manager). Her second country music recording, 'The Night Daniel O'Donnell Came To Town' (based on Johnny Cash's hit 'The Night Hank Williams Came To Town'), was a big hit for her in Ireland and quickly established her as a major Irish country singer. In 1990, in Zurich, competing against 14 countries, she won the European Country Music Gold Star Award singing 'Tipperary On My Mind', and since then she has continued to build her reputation with fine record releases. Her video *Memories Of Home* (1990) has sold in large numbers and she proved very popular on an appearance at the Wembley International Festival Of Country Music. Her touring has seen her play venues in the USA, Denmark and the Lebanon. On 26 September 1993, she survived a head-on car crash when travelling to a concert. She was scheduled to fly to Nashville the following day to record another album and make US concert appearances, but her injuries were so severe that it was six months before she was able to perform again. During her absence, the talented Trudi Lalor, a promising young vocalist, fronted Louise's band and fulfilled all her Irish and UK commitments. In 1995, completely recovered, Morrissey toured the UK with Charley Pride, receiving glowing tributes for her singing. She is equally at home with Irish ballads such as 'The Rose Of Allendale', country standards like 'Blue Eyes Crying In The Rain' or modern songs, including 'Achy Breaky Heart', one of the 14 tracks she recorded on an earlier visit to Nashville. She is the possessor of one of the finest female voices currently performing around the Irish and UK country music scene.
● ALBUMS: *Louise* (CMR 1988)★★★, *When I Was Yours* (CMR/Ritz 1990)★★★, *Here I Am In Love Again* (CMR/RTE 1991)★★★, *Silver Threads Among The Gold - Reflections* (CMR 1993)★★★, *You'll Remember Me* (Ritz 1994)★★★.
● VIDEOS: *Memories Of Home* (Ritz 1990).

MORTON, TEX

b. Robert William Lane, 8 August 1916, Nelson, New Zealand, d. 23 July 1983, Sydney, Australia. A Maori neighbour taught Morton his first guitar chords and he became so obsessed with music that, at the age of 15, he ran away from home and busked on the streets of Waihi. When asked one day by the town's policemen if his name was Bobby Lane, he noticed a nearby garage sign that gave the name of 'Morton' and quickly informed the officer that his name was Bob Morton and that he was a street singer and entertainer. He worked on various jobs, including one with a travelling troupe known as the Gaieties Of 1932. He made some aluminium disc recordings in Wellington (never commercially released), which proved very popular on local radio and may well be the first country music records made outside the USA. In 1932, he moved to Australia and worked with travelling shows, where, in addition to singing, he worked as a magician, a boxing booth fighter, with wild animals, as the stooge for others, and even rode as a Wall Of Death rider. In 1934, with a repertoire of Australian bush ballads as well as the early country songs that he had heard on record, he moved to Sydney. He undertook whatever jobs he could find, including going to sea as a stoker and electrician, and once worked as a labourer for the firm responsible for

installing the lighting on Sydney Harbour Bridge. After eventually winning a major talent show, he made his first recordings for Regal Zonophone in February 1936 when, among the four tracks recorded, two, 'Happy Yodeller' and 'Swiss Sweetheart', were his own compositions. The records sold well, further sessions soon followed and by 1937, Tex Morton the Yodelling Boundary Rider was a nationally known star. When he played his first concert in Brisbane, the crowd totalled 50,000. He continued to record throughout the late 30s, the material ranging from known country songs and his own numbers to recitations of the works of famous Australian poets Henry Lawson and Banjo Patterson. He published his Tex Morton songbook and a newspaper even ran a comic strip of his adventures. In 1939, a major star, he had established his own travelling circus/rodeo, where apart from singing, he entertained with trick shooting, fancy riding, a memory act and magic. World War II forced him to close his show and he invested heavily in a dude ranch, losing all his money when the project failed. After the war, he re-formed his rodeo, linked it with another major touring zoo and circus and toured all over Australia. In 1949, he decided to move to the USA and, having by then learned an act using hypnotism as well as his other talents, he moved to Los Angeles. After spending two years working as a singer and acting on radio and in some films, he began to appear as The Great Doctor Robert Morton - the World's Greatest Hypnotist. In 1951, he toured the USA and Canada with his one-man show on which he sang, did recitations, trick shooting, mind reading and hypnotism. He proved so popular that he set attendance records in many cities, including St. Louis, Boston and Vancouver and in Toronto his show outran *South Pacific*. Ever the showman, he used many gimmicks to attract the crowd, including stunts such as walking blindfold on the parapet of the tallest building in the town. In the early 60s, with many similar acts now performing, he gave up the hypnotism and, for a time, he worked on the stage and in films as Robert Morton. He briefly and unsuccessfully resurrected The Great Morton upon his return to Australia in 1965. He toured for a while with a small rodeo show but soon found that television had made such entertainment no longer viable. He continued to record and in 1973 released 'The Goodiwindi Grey' (a tribute to a famous racehorse), recorded at what turned out to be his last recording session. Throughout the 70s, he appeared on television and in Australian films. It is estimated that during his long career he recorded over 1,000 songs and had many national hits with numbers such as 'Beautiful Queensland', 'The Black Sheep' (his best-selling song) and 'Good Old Droving Days'. Morton died from pneumonia in 1983.
● ALBUMS: including *The Tex Morton Story* (1959)★★★, *Tex Morton Looks Back* (1961)★★★, *Songs Of The Outback* (1961)★★★, *The Versatile Tex Morton* (1962)★★★, *Sing, Smile And Sigh* (1964)★★★, *Encores* (60s)★★★, *Hallelujah I'm A Bum* (60s)★★★, *The Travelling Showman* (60s)★★★, *Tex Morton Today* (1970)★★★, *Tex Morton's Australia* (1973)★★★, early tracks some with sister Dorrie *Red River Valley* (1975)★★★.

MOSBY, JOHNNY AND JONIE

Mosby (b. 26 April c.30s, Ft. Smith, Arkansas, USA) moved to Los Angeles when a child and during the 50s built a reputation around the local country circuit, soon fronting his own

band. He first met Jonie (b. Janice Irene Shields, 10 August 1940, Van Nuys, Los Angeles, California, USA) when she successfully auditioned for the post of female vocalist with his band early in 1958, and that same year they married. They made their first recordings for a minor label in 1959 and had local chart success with 'Just Before Dawn'. They were later signed to Columbia Records and achieved their first US country chart entry in 1963 with a Harlan Howard song called 'Don't Call Me From A Honky Tonk'. They left Columbia and joined Capitol in 1964, and by 1973 had 16 further hits to their credit. These included 'Trouble In My Arms', 'Keep Those Cards And Letters Coming In' and 'Just Hold My Hand'. They also showed a penchant for recording, with minor success, country versions of songs that were pop hits, such as 'Hold Me, Thrill Me, Kiss Me' (Mel Carter), 'I'm Leaving It Up To You' (Dale And Grace) and 'My Happiness' (Connie Francis). Jonie and Johnny limited their touring in favour of raising their family, but appeared on various television shows and for several years had their own *Country Music Time* on Los Angeles television. They moved to Nashville in the 70s but achieved no chart hits after 1973.
● ALBUMS: *The New Sweethearts Of Country Music* (Starday 1965)★★★, *Mr & Mrs Country Music* (Columbia 1965)★★★, *Make A Left And Then A Right* (Capitol 1968)★★★, *Hold Me* (Capitol 1969)★★★, *I'll Never Be Free* (Capitol 1969)★★, *Just Hold My Hand* (Capitol 1969)★★★, *My Happiness* (Capitol 1970)★★★, *Oh, Love Of Mine* (Capitol 1970)★★.

MOWREY, DUDE

Dude Mowrey is a typical 90s country singer - young, good-looking and able to hold a tune, but ultimately fairly bland and anonymous. He is managed by Mel Tillis and, although his records have sold reasonably well, he has yet to make a big breakthrough.
● ALBUMS: *Honky Tonk* (Capitol 1991)★★, *Dude Mowrey* (Arista 1993)★★★.

MULESKINNER

Formed in San Francisco, California, USA, in 1971, Muleskinner was a superior bluegrass ensemble originally known as the Bluegrass Dropouts. Commitments to other groups meant they were largely a part-time project although they remained active for two years. Muleskinner featured the talents of Peter Rowan (guitar, lead vocals), Richard Greene (violin, bass vocals), both of Seatrain, David Grisman (mandolin, harmony vocals), Bill Keith (banjo) and Byrds guitarist Clarence White. White's death in 1973 brought the group to an end, prompting the release of *Muleskinner*, which was dedicated to his memory. White's unique playing style is one of the many highlights on offer, but the warmth of the ensemble's collective musicianship makes this a truly captivating set. Rowan, Grisman and Greene later formed Old And In The Way with auxiliary Muleskinner bassist John Kahn.
● ALBUMS: *Muleskinner* (Warners 1974)★★★.

MULLICAN, MOON

b. Aubrey Mullican, 29 March 1909, Corrigan, Polk County, Texas, USA, d. 1 January 1967, Beaumont, Texas, USA. Mullican was raised on a farm that was manned by black workers. One sharecropper, Joe Jones, taught Mullican how to play blues guitar. His father bought an old pump organ so

that the family could practise hymn-singing, but Aubrey preferred to pound out boogie-woogie and the blues. When Mullican was 14 years old, he went into a cafe in nearby Lufkin and sat at the piano; he came out two hours later with $40 in tips. When aged 16, and after an argument with his father, he moved to Houston and started playing the piano in brothels and honky tonks. He would work all night and sleep all day, hence his nickname 'Moon'. In the late 30s Mullican made his first recordings for US Decca as part of Cliff Bruner's Texas Wanderers, taking the lead vocal for 'Truck Driver Blues', arguably the first trucking song. He also recorded as part of Leon Selph's Blue Ridge Playboys. He helped musician Jimmie Davis became the State Governor of Louisiana and later joined his staff. In 1944 he invested his savings in 10 large juke-boxes but they were confiscated by the authorities because he refused to pay the appropriate tax. In 1946 he was signed by Sid Nathan to the new King label and 'New Pretty Blonde', a parody in pigeon French of 'Jole Blon', became a million-seller. He won another gold disc with 'I'll Sail My Ship Alone', and also found success with a tribute to mothers, 'Sweeter Than The Flowers', the double-sided 'Mona Lisa'/'Goodnight Irene' and 'Cherokee Boogie', which was one of a succession of boogie records. In 1949 he wrote 'Jambalaya' with Hank Williams, although he was not given a credit. This is probably unjust because the style of the song - and the subject matter of food! - were more in keeping with Mullican's other work than Williams'. In the mid-50s, Mullican delighted in the advent of rock 'n' roll as he said he had been doing that all along. Backed by the hit-making Boyd Bennett And His Rockets, he recorded 'Seven Nights To Rock'. However, he was too portly and bald for teenage record buyers. Jerry Lee Lewis acknowledges Mullican as a major influence - in particular, Mullican's playing of the melody with just two fingers on his right hand - and has recorded 'I'll Sail My Ship Alone'. He recorded for Coral and Starday but alcohol and too much jambalaya got the better of him. When asked why he chose the piano, Mullican replied, 'Because the beer kept sliding off my fiddle.' In 1962, the 19-stone Mullican collapsed on stage in Kansas City. He stopped drinking and returned to performing, making an album for Kapp, *The Moon Mullican Showcase*, produced by Jack Clement. He recorded the novelty number 'I Ain't No Beatle (But I Want To Hold Your Hand)' for Spar. On New Year's Eve 1966, he resolved to cut down on pork chops but died the following day. Governor Jimmie Davis sang at his funeral.
● ALBUMS: *Moon Over Mullican* (Coral 1958)★★★, *Moon Mullican Sings His All-Time Greatest Hits* (King 1958)★★★, *The Old Texan Sings And Plays 16 Of His Favorite Tunes* (King 1959)★★★, *The Many Moods Of Moon Mullican* (King 1960)★★★, *Instrumentals* (Audio Lab 1962)★★★, *Playin' And Singin'* (Starday 1963)★★★, *Mr. Piano Man* (Starday 1964)★★★, *Moon Mullican Sings 24 Of His Favorite Tunes* (King 1965)★★★, *Good Times Gonna Roll* (Hilltop 1966)★★★, *Moon Mullican's Unforgettable Great Hits* (Starday 1967)★★★, *The Moon Mullican Showcase* (Kapp 1968)★★, *I'll Sail My Ship Alone* (Nashville 1970)★★.
● COMPILATIONS: *Seven Nights To Rock: The King Years, 1946-1956* (Western 1983)★★★★, *Sweet Rockin' Music* (Charly 1984)★★★, *Moonshine Jamboree* (Ace 1993)★★★★.

MURPHEY, MICHAEL MARTIN

b. 13 March 1945, Dallas, Texas, USA. Having been influenced by gospel music at an early age, Murphey aspired to become a Baptist minister. From 1965-70, as a staff songwriter for Screen Gems, Murphey was writing theme tunes and soundtrack material for television. He grew disillusioned with the poor financial rewards, and left. For a short time he was a member of the Lewis And Clark Expedition, which he formed, before going solo. *Geronimo's Cadillac* was produced in Nashville by Bob Johnston, who was responsible for Murphey's signing with A&M Records. The title track was released as a single, and achieved a Top 40 place in the USA. As well as folk, country and blues, Murphey's early gospel leanings are evident in the overall sound of what is an excellent album. He signed to Epic in 1973 after releasing *Cosmic Cowboy Souvenir*, which continued the urban cowboy theme of his earlier work. His albums followed a more middle-of-the-road format after this, with occasional glimpses of his better work, as in *Peaks, Valleys, Honky-Tonks And Alleys*. However, he did reach number 3 in the US singles charts in 1975, achieving a gold disc with 'Wildfire'. Murphey has never had the degree of commercial success his writing would indicate that he is capable of. However, as a writer, Murphey has had songs covered by John Denver, Cher, Claire Hamill, Hoyt Axton, Bobby Gentry and the Monkees, for whom he wrote 'What Am I Doin' Hangin' 'Round'. He also wrote songs for Michael Nesmith including 'The Oklahoma Backroom Dance'. Murphey later played at Ronnie Scott's club in London, for a press presentation, and was supported on the occasion by J.D. Souther, Don Henley, Dave Jackson and Gary Nurm. *Geronimo's Cadillac* is probably his best-remembered work. *Michael Martin Murphey* included a number of songs Murphey had co-written with Michael D'Abo. Murphey was featured in the film *Urban Cowboy*, which included his song 'Cherokee Fiddle'. Much of the film was shot at Mickey Gilley's Bar. Murphey has continued recording easy-listening country and, in 1987, had a number 1 country single with a wedding song, 'A Long Line Of Love'. He had US country hits with 'A Face In The Crowd', a duet with Holly Dunn, and 'Talkin' To The Wrong Man', which featured his son, Ryan. He went off at a tangent in the 1990s and, like Ian Tyson, he has chosen to revive old cowboy songs as well as writing his own. He is a superb performer of this material, but whether this will prove to be a good career move remains to be seen, as many country performers want to forget the music's cowboy roots. He could be described as a latter-day Marty Robbins and *Cowboy Songs III* does include, with the aid of modern technology, a seamless duet with Robbins on 'Big Iron'. However, he is far more ambitious than Robbins, recording *Sagebrush Symphony* with the San Antonio Symphony Orchestra.

● ALBUMS: *Geronimo's Cadillac* (A&M 1972)★★★, *Cosmic Cowboy Souvenir* (A&M 1973)★★★, *Michael Murphey* (Epic 1973)★★★, *Blue Sky - Night Thunder* (Epic 1975)★★★★, *Swans Against The Sun* (Epic 1976)★★★★, *Flowing Free Forever* (Epic 1976)★★★, *Lone Wolf* (Epic 1977)★★★, *Peaks, Valleys, Honky-Tonks And Alleys* (Epic 1979)★★★, *Michael Martin Murphey* (Liberty 1982)★★★, *The Heart Never Lies* (Liberty 1983)★★★, *Tonight We Ride* (Warners 1986)★★★, *Americana* (Warners 1987)★★★, *River Of Time* (Warners 1988)★★★, *Land Of Enchantment* (Warners 1989)★★★, *Cowboy Songs* (Warners 1990)★★★, *Cowboy Christmas - Cowboy Songs II* (Warners 1991)★★★, *Cowboy Songs III* (Warners 1993)★★★, *Sagebrush Symphony* (Warners 1995)★★★, *The Horse Legends* (Warners 1997)★★★.

● COMPILATIONS: *The Best Of Michael Martin Murphey* (EMI 1982)★★★★.

MURPHY, DAVID LEE

b. Herrin, Illinois, USA. Although it took Murphy more than 10 years to secure a major label recording contract with MCA Records, he quickly regained ground with the success of his debut album, *Out With A Bang*, which topped *Billboard*'s Heatseekers chart in 1995. Murphy had first been spotted by MCA Nashville president Tony Brown while leading his country band, Blue Tick Hounds, in 1985. However, a full decade passed before Brown offered Murphy a contract, though the artist conceded that his former band was 'too edgy for country radio at the time or, at least, too edgy to get a deal'. In the intervening period Murphy worked as a professional songwriter, writing 'Red Roses Won't Work Now' for Reba McEntire's 1985 debut album and 'High Weeds And Rust' for Doug Stone. A version of that song was also included on *Out With A Bang*, alongside other original material such as the singles 'Fish Ain't Bitin'' and 'Just Once', which featured on the soundtrack to the *8 Seconds* film. 'Every Time I Get Around You' was the hit single that previewed *Gettin' Out The Good Stuff*, but album sales have failed to live up to the success of his debut.

● ALBUMS: *Out With A Bang* (MCA 1994)★★★★, *Gettin' Out The Good Stuff* (MCA 1996)★★★, *We Can't All Be Angels* (MCA 1997)★★★.

MURPHY, RALPH

b. 1944, Wallaceburg, Ontario, Canada. Murphey wanted to be a songwriter from an early age and, receiving little encouragement in Canada, tried both Los Angeles and Liverpool, even landing a recording contract as part of the Guardsmen in the UK in 1964. His first hit song was 'Call My Name' for James Royal. Moving back to Canada, Murphy formed Double M Records and produced April Wine and Roadhouse. His first US country hit was with 'Good Enough To Be Your Wife' (Jeannie C. Riley). Going into partnership with Roger Cook, they wrote 'Talking In Your Sleep' and 'Half The Way' (both Crystal Gayle), 'He Got You' (Ronnie Milsap) and '18 Wheels And A Dozen Roses' (Kathy Mattea). He re-established himself in Canada with 'Bad Day For Trains' for Patricia Conroy. In the 90s Little Texas had success with 'Inside'. Murphy is currently Director of Artists Relations for ASCAP in Nashville and believes that much of his work lies in helping songwriters learn their craft. His advice is 'Listen to the best because that is your real competition. Don't try and be as good as the guy playing down the street in the bar.' Another piece of advice might be to take Murphy's place when he cannot make a gig: when he could not appear at the Bluebird one night, Garth Brooks stepped in and was offered his Capitol recording contract!

MURRAY, ANNE

b. 20 June 1946, Springhill, Nova Scotia, Canada. Sometimes known as 'The Singing Sweetheart Of Canada', Murray graduated from the University of New Brunswick with a degree in physical education, and then spent a year as a teacher.

After singing simply for pleasure for a time, in 1964 she was persuaded to audition for *Sing Along Jubilee*, a regional television show, but was selected instead for the same network's *Let's Go*, hosted by Bill Langstroth (her future husband). Income from a residency on the programme and solo concerts was sufficient for Murray to begin entertaining professionally in a vaguely folk/country rock style, though she could also acquit herself admirably with both R&B and mainstream pop material. Like Linda Ronstadt - seen by some as her US opposite number - she was mainly an interpreter of songs written by others. Issued by Arc Records, *What About Me* (1968) created sufficient impact to interest Capitol Records, who signed her to a long-term contract. Two years later, her version of Gene MacLellan's remarkable 'Snowbird', taken from the album *This Was My Way*, soared into *Billboard*'s Top 10. Despite regular appearances on Glen Campbell's *Goodtime Hour* television series, subsequent releases - including the title track to *Talk It Over In The Morning* - sold only moderately until 1973 when she scored another smash hit with 'Danny's Song', composed by Kenny Loggins (with whom she duetted 11 years later on 'Nobody Loves Me Like You Do', a country chart-topper). She was rated *Billboard*'s second most successful female artist in 1976, but family commitments necessitated a brief period of domesticity before 'You Needed Me' won her a Grammy award for best female pop vocal performance in 1978. While revivals of Bobby Darin's 'Things' and the Monkees' 'Daydream Believer' were aimed directly at the pop market, it was with the country audience that she proved most popular. 'He Thinks I Still Care' (originally a b-side) became her first country number 1. However, along with 'Just Another Woman In Love', 'Could I Have This Dance' (from the film *Urban Cowboy*), the bold 'A Little Good News' (1983) and other country hits, she had also recorded a collection of children's ditties (*Hippo In My Tub*), commensurate with her executive involvement with Canada's Save The Children Fund. In 1989 Springhill's Anne Murray Center was opened in recognition of her tireless work for this charity. Three years later she played Las Vegas, with a show that amply demonstrated her excellent delivery and superior choice of songs. These strengths were consistently reflected in her recorded output during the 90s.

● ALBUMS: *What About Me* (Arc 1968)★★, *This Was My Way* (Capitol 1970)★★★, *Snowbird* (Capitol 1970)★★★★, *Anne Murray* (Capitol 1971)★★★★, *Talk It Over In The Morning* (Capitol 1971)★★★, *Anne Murray/Glen Campbell* (Capitol 1971)★★★, *Annie* (Capitol 1972)★★★, *Danny's Song* (Capitol 1973)★★★★, *Love Song* (Capitol 1974)★★★, *Country* (Capitol 1974)★★★★, *Highly Prized Possession* (Capitol 1974)★★★, *Together* (Capitol 1975)★★★, *Love Song* (Capitol 1975)★★★, *Keeping In Touch* (Capitol 1976)★★★, *Let's Keep It That Way* (Capitol 1977)★★★★, *Hippo In My Tub* (Capitol 1979)★★★, *New Kind Of Feeling* (Capitol 1979)★★★★, *I'll Always Love You* (Capitol 1980)★★★★, *Somebody's Waiting* (Capitol 1980)★★★, *Where Do You Go To When You Dream* (Capitol 1981)★★★, *Christmas Wishes* (Capitol 1981)★★★, *The Hottest Night Of The Year* (Capitol 1982)★★★, *A Little Good News* (Capitol 1983)★★★, *Heart Over Mind* (Capitol 1985)★★★, *Something To Talk About* (Capitol 1986)★★★, *Talk It Over In The Morning* (Capitol 1986)★★★, *Christmas Wishes* (Capitol 1986)★★★, *Songs Of The Heart* (Capitol 1987)★★★, *As I Am* (Capitol 1988)★★★, *Harmony* (Capitol 1989)★★★, *You Will* (Capitol 1990)★★★, *Yes I Do* (Capitol 1991)★★★, *Croonin'* (Capitol 1993)★★★, *Anne Murray* (Capitol 1996)★★★.

● COMPILATIONS: *A Country Collection* (1980)★★★, *Greatest Hits* (Capitol 1980)★★★★, *The Very Best Of Anne Murray* (Capitol 1981)★★★★, *Country Hits* (Capitol 1987)★★★, *Greatest Hits, Vol. 2* (Capitol 1989)★★★★, *15 Of The Best* (Capitol 1992)★★★, *The Best ... So Far* (EMI 1994)★★★★, *Now And Forever* 3-CD box set (EMI 1994)★★★★.

● FURTHER READING: *Snowbird: The Story Of Anne Murray*, Barry Grills.

MYLES, HEATHER

b. 31 July 1962, Riverside, California, USA. Myles was raised on a horse ranch in Texas and her brother was a rodeo rider. Heavily influenced by Merle Haggard, Patsy Cline, Tammy Wynette, Doris Day, Judy Garland and Buck Owens, she spent several years playing the honkytonk circuit. Dwight Yoakam's fiddler, Brantley Kearns, also plays for Myles. She made her recording debut on HighTone's Western Beat sampler, *Points West*, with her songs 'Lovin' The Bottle' and 'Rum And Rodeo', which was written about old-time rodeo rider Casey Tibbs. An excellent country writer, her debut album caused a stir, not so much because of the songs, but because she looked like Princess Diana on the cover. She tours with her band the Cadillac Cowboys. 'Call me a bitch, but you've got to be a bitch to make it in this business' is one of her theories, the other as relayed to *Country Music People* is: 'I'm in it for the long haul, sink or swim, come hell or high water, I'll make it in this business or I'll die trying'.

● ALBUMS: *Just Like Old Times* (HighTone 1992)★★★, *Rum And Rodeo* (HighTone 1994)★★★, *Untamed* (Demon 1995)★★★, *Sweet Little Dangerous: Heather Myles Live At The Bottom Line* (Demon 1996)★★.

NAPIER, BILL

b. William Napier, 17 December 1935, near Grundy, Wize County, Virginia, USA. A love of the Stanley Brothers' music saw him learn to play mandolin, and in 1954, after relocating to Detroit to find factory work, he played in the evenings with a local band, Curly Dan And Wilma Ann With The Danville Mountain Boys. He began to play lead guitar, and in 1957, he became a member of the Stanley Brothers' Clinch Mountain Boys. He recorded his own 'Daybreak In Dixie' with them and introduced acoustic lead guitar work to the Stanleys' recordings. In 1960, he left the Stanleys and he and Charlie Moore formed the Dixie Partners. They worked together with their band until 1967, during which time they recorded nine albums for King, the last being released after they split. During this time, Napier played lead guitar or banjo (which he used for the first time) and rarely played his mandolin. They appeared regularly on radio and television shows in South Carolina and Florida and made countless festival appearances in various states. After he and Moore parted, Napier, who maintained his home in the Detroit area, became semi-retired. He made appearances from time to time, and in the 70s, he again played with Curly Dan And Wilma Ann. He made some recordings with them, and in 1978, seven with Charlie Moore. In 1984, he recorded his only solo album with a group called the Mountain Music Clan for Old Homestead, before he began to work and record with Larry Taylor and his Waterloo Bluegrass Boys.

● ALBUMS: *Hillbilly Fever* (Old Homestead 1984)★★★, with Larry Taylor *We Salute The Stanley Brothers* (Old Homestead 1987)★★★, with Taylor *Country Boy's Life* (Old Homestead 1987)★★★. As Charlie Moore And Bill Napier *Folk 'N' Hill* (King 1963)★★★, *Country Hymnal* (King 1964)★★★, *City Folk Back On The Farm* (King 1964)★★★, *Country Music Goes To Vietnam* (King 1966)★★★, *Songs For All Lonesome Truck Drivers* (King 1966)★★, *Brand New Vocal Country & Western Songs* (King 1967)★★★, *Gospel & Sacred Songs* (King 1967)★★★, *Spectacular Instrumentals* (King 1967)★★, *Truckin' On* (Gusto 1979)★★★.

● COMPILATIONS: *Best Of Moore & Napier* (King 1963)★★★, *Best Of Charlie Moore & Bill Napier* (Starday 1975)★★★, *Charlie Moore & Bill Napier Collector's Classics* (Old Homestead 1978)★★★.

NASHVILLE BLUEGRASS BAND

NBB are without doubt one of the best of the modern bluegrass bands. They were founded in 1984 by Alan O'Bryant (b. 26 December 1955, Reidsville, North Carolina, USA; banjo, vocals), Pat Enright (b. *c.*1939, Huntington, Indiana, USA; guitar, vocals), Mike Compton (b. Meridian, Mississippi, USA; mandolin, vocals) and Mark Hembree (b. Appleton, Wisconsin, USA; acoustic bass, vocals). O'Bryant,

who began his bluegrass career as a teenager, and Enright, who had already had success fronting his own band on the west coast, met and began playing together in 1974, when they both relocated to Nashville. In 1976, they linked up with Compton and the three played local venues. Hembree played with Tony Trischka in Monroe Doctrine in 1977, before moving to Nashville in 1979 to spend almost five years with Bill Monroe. He subsequently became acquainted with Enright and the four recorded *My Native Home*, on which they were joined by fiddler Blaine Sprouse, for Rounder Records in 1985. Stuart Duncan (b. 14 April 1964, Quantico, Virginia, USA; fiddle,mandolin), who had worked with Larry Sparks before becoming a popular session musician, also joined the band. In 1986, the NBB had the distinction of becoming the first bluegrass band to perform in China. In 1987, they recorded two further albums for Rounder before moving to Sugar Hill Records. In July 1988, after a successful tour of several Middle Eastern countries, their bus was involved in a very serious road accident near Roanoke, Virginia. Hembree suffered such serious injuries that he left the group and was followed soon afterwards by Compton. Nick Haney (sadly a leukaemia victim) briefly played bass for the band until Gene Libbea (b. Southern California, USA; acoustic bass, ukulele, vocals) took over later that year. The band was also boosted by the arrival of ex-Kentucky Colonel and Country Gazette member Roland White (b. 23 April 1938, Lewiston, Maine, USA; mandolin, banjo, vocals), who also had great experience from his days playing with Flatt And Scruggs and Bill and James Monroe. In 1988, the NBB played with Peter Rowan on his noted *New Moon Rising*. In 1990, they made a very successful tour of several European countries, including England. Their *Waitin' For The Hard Times To Go* won them a well-deserved Grammy for Best Bluegrass Album in 1993. Duncan, who has won many awards for his fiddle prowess, released his solo *Stuart Duncan* on Sugar Hill in 1992. O'Bryant has written many fine songs, which have proved successful for the band and in some cases for other artists. His song 'Those Memories Of You' became a Top 5 hit for Dolly Parton, Emmylou Harris And Linda Ronstadt recording as Trio. Enright is also a competent writer. The members' high standard of musicianship make the NBB great favourites throughout the world of bluegrass music.

● ALBUMS: *My Native Home* (Rounder 1985)★★★★, *Idle Time* (Rounder 1987)★★★★, *To Be His Child* (Rounder 1987)★★★, *The Boys Are Back In Town* (Sugar Hill 1990)★★★, *Home Of The Blues* (Sugar Hill 1991)★★★, *Waitin' For The Hard Times To Go* (Sugar Hill 1993)★★★, *Still Unpleased* (Sugar Hill 1995)★★, *Unleashed* (Sugar Hill 1995)★★★.

● COMPILATIONS: *The Nashville Bluegrass Band* (Rounder 1987)★★★.

NASHVILLE WEST

A short-lived but pivotal California-based country group, Nashville West included former member of the Kentucky Colonels, Clarence White (b. 6 June 1944, Lewiston, Maine, USA, d. July 1973; guitar), and three ex-members of the Castaways - Wayne Moore (guitar, bass, vocals), Gene Parsons (b. 14 September 1944, Los Angeles, California, USA; drums, vocals) and Gib Guilbeau (fiddle, vocals). Popular in Bakersfield and El Monte's Nashville West club, the quartet's archive recordings reveal a mixture of contemporary hits ('By The Time I Get To Phoenix', 'Ode To Billy Joe') and country favourites ('Send Me Back Home', 'Sweet Mental Revenge'). The group split up in August 1968 when Parsons and White joined the Byrds. However, the duo paid homage to their former ensemble by including the instrumental 'Nashville West' on *Dr. Byrds And Mr. Hyde*.

● ALBUMS: *Nashville West* (Sierra 1978)★★★.

NATIONAL BARN DANCE, THE

Many radio stations broadcast 'barn dance' programmes, with WBAP Fort Worth probably the first in 1923. One of the longest-running and the one to gain the most nationwide acceptance was the *National Barn Dance* broadcast by WLS Chicago. WLS (World's Largest Store), owned by Sears-Roebuck Company, first broadcast in April 1924. The first barn dance programme was broadcast from the Sherman Hotel and featured the local Isham Jones dance band and a group of country musicians, who probably included fiddler Tommy Dandurand and banjo player Jesse Doolittle. The listeners enjoyed the programme and the development of the *National Barn Dance* began. It featured a mixture of popular numbers and folk/country songs and the show gradually began to produce its first stars. One of the best-loved was singer Grace Wilson (b. 10 April 1890, Owesso, Michigan, USA), who sang on the show from 1924 until she retired in 1960. After 1925, the show took on a more hillbilly format, with the arrival of performers such as Bradley Kincaid and Chubby Parker. In the early days, the show's development owed much to its announcer, George D. Hay (the Solemn Old Judge), a journalist from Memphis. With regular blasts of his steamboat whistle to emphasize his words, he popularized the show, before heading for WSM Nashville, where in November 1925, he launched a barn dance programme that soon became the *Grand Ole Opry*. Sears-Roebuck sold WLS to the *Prairie Farmer* newspaper in 1928, by which time the programme was well established and continued to produce stars such as Luther Ossenbrink, who, as Arkie The Woodchopper, arrived in 1929 and stayed until WLS ended the programme in 1960. During the 30s, the show's popularity increased, owing to performers such as Lulu Belle And Scotty, the Cumberland Ridge Runners, Karl And Harty, Red Foley and Gene Autry. In 1932, WLS moved the show to the Eighth Street Theatre, where it remained until the late 50s. In 1933, an hour-long Saturday evening section of the programme was sponsored by Alka-Seltzer and networked by NBC (it remained a networked NBC programme until 1946). This publicity led to tours being made by the show's performers and other radio stations broadcasting their own barn dance programmes. In 1944, Paramount Pictures released *The National Barn Dance* film, which described the programme as 'America's Favorite Radio Show'. It featured Lulu Belle And Scotty, Dinning Sisters, Hoosier Hotshots, Arkie and many others. The Kentucky Ramblers, who joined in 1933, remained a popular act until 1948. Bob Atcher achieved major success during his days on the show and in later years, Rex Allen, Johnny Bond and even Bill Haley were members. The show finally lost out to the much larger *Opry*. WLS dropped the programme in 1960 but it was broadcast by WGN Chicago until 1968, when the *National Barn Dance*, country music's first jamboree, finally played the last waltz.

NAYLOR, JERRY

b. Jerry Naylor Jackson, 6 March 1939, Stephenville, Texas, USA. Naylor sang country music from an early age; when aged only 14, he appeared on *Louisiana Hayride*. While in the US Army, he broke his back, an injury that has continued to plague him since then. He befriended Glen Campbell in Albuquerque, New Mexico, and in 1961 moved with him to Hollywood. He found work as a disc jockey and a single, 'You're Thirteen', was released in the UK. He and Campbell joined the Crickets in 1962 and he was featured on 'Don't Ever Change', 'My Little Girl' and 'Teardrops Fall Like Rain'. In 1964 he had a heart attack, brought about, he says, 'by the stress of being Buddy Holly's replacement'. He played the leading role in a concept album, a country opera entitled *The Legend Of Johnny Brown*, in 1966. He returned to the Crickets for their 1971 album *Rockin' 50s Rock And Roll*, but mostly he has followed a solo career, making numerous singles for US labels including Motown's country division. His best-known record is 'Is That All There Is To A Honky Tonk?' in 1975. He now works as a disc jockey in Angoura, California, and he is known to Buddy Holly fans for his outrageous claims to have been a Cricket throughout their hit-making years.

● ALBUMS: *Happy Birthday USA* (1976)★★, *Love Away Her Memory* (1977)★★, *Once Again* (1978)★★.

NELSON, RICKY

b. Eric Hilliard Nelson, 8 May 1940, Teaneck, New Jersey, USA, d. 31 December 1985, De Kalb, Texas, USA. Nelson came from a showbusiness family and his parents had sung in bands during the 30s and 40s. They had their own US radio show, *The Adventures Of Ozzie And Harriet*, soon transferred to television, in which Ricky and his brother David appeared. By 1957 Nelson embarked on a recording career, with the million-selling, double-sided 'I'm Walkin''/'A Teenager's Romance'. A third hit soon followed with 'You're My One And Only Love'. A switch from the label Verve to Imperial saw Nelson enjoy further success with the rockabilly 'Be-Bop Baby'. In 1958 Nelson formed a full-time group for live work and recordings, which included James Burton (guitar), James Kirkland (later replaced by Joe Osborn) (bass), Gene Garf (piano) and Richie Frost (drums). Early that year Nelson enjoyed his first transatlantic hit with 'Stood Up' and registered his first US chart-topper with 'Poor Little Fool'. His early broadcasting experience was put to useful effect when he starred in the Howard Hawks movie western *Rio Bravo* (1959), alongside John Wayne and Dean Martin. Nelson's singles continued to chart regularly and it says much for the quality of his work that the b-sides were often as well known as the a-sides. Songs such as 'Believe What You Say', 'Never Be Anyone Else But You', 'It's Late', 'Sweeter Than You', 'Just A Little Too Much' and 'I Wanna Be Loved' proved that Nelson was equally adept at singing ballads and up-tempo material. One of his greatest moments as a pop singer occurred in the spring of 1961 when he issued the million-selling 'Travelin' Man', backed with the exuberant Gene Pitney composition 'Hello Mary Lou'. Shortly after the single topped the US charts, Nelson celebrated his 21st birthday and announced that he was changing his performing name from Ricky to Rick. Several more pop hits followed, most notably 'Young World', 'Teenage Idol', 'It's Up To You', 'String Along' (his first for his new label, Decca), 'Fools

Rush In' and 'For You'. With the emergence of the beat boom, Nelson's clean-cut pop was less in demand and in 1966 he switched to country music. His early albums in this vein featured compositions from such artists as Willie Nelson, Glen Campbell, Tim Hardin, Harry Nilsson and Randy Newman. In 1969 Nelson formed a new outfit, the Stone Canyon Band, featuring former Poco member Randy Meisner (bass), Allen Kemp (guitar), Tom Brumley (steel guitar) and Pat Shanahan (drums). A version of Bob Dylan's 'She Belongs To Me' brought Nelson back into the US charts, and a series of strong, often underrated, albums followed. A performance at Madison Square Garden in late 1971 underlined Nelson's difficulties at the time. Although he had recently issued the accomplished *Rick Sings Nelson*, on which he wrote every track, the audience were clearly more interested in hearing his early 60s hits. Nelson responded by composing the sarcastic 'Garden Party', which reaffirmed his determination to go his own way. The single, ironically, went on to sell a million and was his last hit record. After parting with the Stone Canyon Band in 1974, Nelson's recorded output declined, but he continued to tour extensively. On 31 December 1985, a chartered plane carrying him to a concert date in Dallas caught fire and crashed near De Kalb, Texas. Nelson's work deserves a place in rock history, as he was one of the few 'good looking kids' from the early 60s who had a strong voice which, coupled with exemplary material, remains durable.

● ALBUMS: with various artists *Teen Time* (Verve 1957)★★, *Ricky* (Imperial 1957)★★, *Ricky Nelson* (Imperial 1958)★★, *Ricky Sings Again* (Imperial 1959)★★, *Songs By Ricky* (Imperial 1959)★★★, *More Songs By Ricky* (Imperial 1960)★★, *Rick Is 21* (Imperial 1961)★★, *Album Seven By Rick* (Imperial 1962)★★, *Best Sellers By Rick Nelson* (Imperial 1962)★★, *It's Up To You* (Imperial 1962)★★★, *A Long Vacation* (Imperial 1963)★★, *Million Sellers By Rick Nelson* (Imperial 1963)★★★★, *For Your Sweet Love* (Decca 1963)★★, *Rick Nelson Sings For You* (Decca 1963)★★★, *Rick Nelson Sings 'For You'* (Decca 1963)★★★, *The Very Thought Of You* (Decca 1964)★★, *Spotlight On Rick* (Decca 1964)★★★, *Best Always* (Decca 1965)★★, *Love And Kisses* (Decca 1965)★★, *Bright Lights And Country Music* (Decca 1966)★★, *On The Flip-Side* film soundtrack (Decca 1966)★, *Country Fever* (Decca 1967)★★, *Another Side Of Rick* (Decca 1968)★★, *Perspective* (Decca 1968)★★, *Ricky Nelson In Concert* (Decca 1970)★★★, *Rick Sings Nelson* (Decca 1970)★★★, *Rudy The Fifth* (Decca 1971)★★★, *Garden Party* (Decca 1972)★★★★, *Windfall* (1974)★★, *Intakes* (Epic 1977)★★, *Playing To Win* (Capitol 1981)★★★, *Memphis Sessions* (Epic 1986)★★★, *Live 1983-1985* (Rhino 1989)★★★.

● COMPILATIONS: *The Very Best Of Rick Nelson* (Decca 1970)★★★★, *Legendary Masters* (United Artists 1971)★★★★, *The Singles Album 1963-1976* (United Artists 1977)★★★★, *The Singles Album 1957-63* (United Artists 1977)★★★★, *Greatest Hits* (Rhino 1984)★★★, *Rockin' With Ricky* (Ace 1984)★★★★, *String Along With Rick* (Charly 1984)★★★, *All My Best* (MCA 1985)★★★★, *Best Of 1963-1975* (MCA 1990)★★★★, *Best Of Rick Nelson, Vol. 2* (Capitol 1991)★★★★, *1969-1976* (Edsel 1995)★★★.

● FURTHER READING: *Ricky Nelson: Idol For A Generation*, Joel Selvin. *The Ricky Nelson Story*, John Stafford and Iain Young. *Ricky Nelson: Teenage Idol, Travelin' Man*, Philip Bashe.

NELSON, WILLIE

b. Willie Hugh Nelson, 30 April 1933, Abbott, Texas, USA. Following their mother's desertion and the death of their father, Nelson and his sister Bobbie were raised by their grandparents. Bobbie was encouraged to play the piano and Willie the guitar. By the age of 7 he was writing cheating-heart-style songs. 'Maybe I got 'em from soap operas on the radio,' he said, 'but I've always seemed to see the sad side of things.' Bobbie married the fiddle player Bud Fletcher, and they both played in his band. When Fletcher booked western swing star Bob Wills, the 13-year-old Willie Nelson joined him for a duet. After graduation he enlisted in the US Air Force, but was invalided out with a bad back, which has continued to plague his career to the present day. In 1953 Nelson began a traumatic marriage in Waco, Texas. 'Martha was a full-blooded Cherokee Indian,' says Nelson, 'and every night was like Custer's last stand.' When they moved to Fort Worth, Texas, Nelson was criticized for playing beer-joints and inappropriately evangelizing - he fortunately gave up the latter. A Salvation Army drummer, Paul English, has been his drummer ever since, and is referred to in 'Me And Paul' and 'Devil In A Sleepin' Bag'. Nelson's first record, 'Lumberjack', was recorded in Vancouver, Washington, in 1956 and was written by Leon Payne. Payne, then a radio disc jockey, advertised the records for sale on the air. For $1, the listener received the record and an autographed 8 x 10 inch photo of Nelson; 3,000 copies were sold by this method. In Houston he sold 'Family Bible' to a guitar scholar for $50 and when it became a country hit for Claude Gray in 1960, Nelson's name was not on the label. He also sold 'Night Life' for $150 to the director of the same school; Ray Price made it a country hit and there have now been over 70 other recordings. Nelson moved to Nashville where his offbeat, nasal phrasing and dislike of rhinestone trimmings made him radically different from other country musicians. He recorded demos in 1961, which he later rescued from a fire. The demos were spread over three collections, *Face Of A Fighter*, *Diamonds In The Rough* and *Slow Down Old World*, but they are often repackaged in an attempt to pass off old material as new. These one-paced collections feature little to attract new fans, as the songs are either bleak, very bleak or unbearably bleak. From time to time, Nelson has re-recorded these songs for other albums.

In 1961 three of Nelson's country songs crossed over to the US pop charts: Patsy Cline's 'Crazy', Faron Young's 'Hello Walls' and Jimmy Elledge's 'Funny How Time Slips Away'. Ray Price employed Nelson to play bass with his band, the Cherokee Cowboys, not knowing that he had never previously played the instrument. Nelson bought a bass, practised all night and showed up the next day as a bass player. Touring put further pressures on his marriage and he was divorced in 1962. The following year Nelson had his first country hits as a performer, first in a duet with Shirley Collie, 'Willingly', and then on his own with 'Touch Me'. His 40 tracks recorded for Liberty Records were top-heavy on strings, but they included the poignant 'Half A Man' and the whimsical 'River Boy'. He also wrote a witty single for Joe Carson, 'I Gotta Get Drunk (And I Sure Do Dread It)'. When Liberty dropped their country performers, Nelson moved to Monument. He gave Roy Orbison 'Pretty Paper', which made the UK Top 10 in 1964 and became Nelson's most successful composition in the UK. Some Monument tracks were revamped for *The Winning Hand*, which gave the misleading impression that Nelson had joined forces with Kris Kristofferson, Brenda Lee and Dolly Parton for a double album. In 1965 Nelson married Shirley Collie and took up pig-farming in Ridgetop, Tennessee. During the same year Ray Price refused to record any more of Nelson's songs after an accident when Nelson shot his fighting rooster. However, they eventually joined forces for an album. Chet Atkins produced some fine albums for Nelson on RCA Records, including a tribute to his home state, *Texas In My Soul*. Nelson was only allowed to record with his own musicians on the live *Country Music Concert* album, which included an emotional 'Yesterday' and a jazzy 'I Never Cared For You'. He recorded around 200 tracks for the label, including well-known songs of the day such as 'Both Sides Now', 'Help Me Make It Through The Night' and, bizarrely, the UK comedy team Morecambe And Wise's theme song, 'Bring Me Sunshine'. *Yesterday's Wine* remains his finest RCA album, although it begins rather embarrassingly with Nelson talking to God. Nelson wrote seven of the songs in one night, under the influence of alcohol and drugs; 'What Can You Do To Me Now?' indicated his anguish and instability.

During 1970 his showbusiness lawyer, Neil Rushen, thought Nelson should record for Atlantic Records in New York. The singer used his own band, supplemented by Doug Sahm and Larry Gatlin. Atlantic did not feel that *The Troublemaker* was right for the label and it only surfaced after he had moved to Columbia. *Shotgun Willie* was closer to rock music and included Leon Russell's 'A Song For You' and the reflective 'Sad Songs And Waltzes'. *Phases And Stages* (1974), made in Muscle Shoals, Alabama, examined the break-up of a marriage from both sides - the woman's ('Washing The Dishes') and the man's ('It's Not Supposed To Be That Way'). Nelson also recorded a successful duet with Tracy Nelson (no relation) of 'After The Fire Is Gone'. He toured extensively and his bookings at a rock venue, the Armadillo World Headquarters in Austin, showed that he might attract a new audience. Furthermore, Waylon Jennings' hit with 'Ladies Love Outlaws' indicated a market for 'outlaw country' music. The term separated them from more conventional country artists, and, with his pigtail and straggly beard, Nelson no longer looked like a country performer. Ironically, they were emphasizing the very thing from which country music was trying to escape - the cowboy image. In 1975 Nelson signed with Columbia and wanted to record a lengthy, old ballad, 'Red Headed Stranger'. His wife suggested that he split the song into sections and fit other songs around it. This led to an album about an old-time preacher and his love for an unfaithful woman. The album consisted of Willie's voice and guitar and Bobbie's piano. Columbia thought it was too low-key, too religious and needed strings. They were eventually persuaded to release it as it was and *Red Headed Stranger* (1975) has since become a country classic. Nelson's gentle performance of the country standard 'Blue Eyes Crying In The Rain' was a number 1 country hit and also made number 21 on the US pop charts in 1975. With brilliant marketing, RCA then compiled *Wanted! The Outlaws* with Jennings, Nelson, Jessi Colter and Tompall Glaser. It became the first country album to go platinum and included a hit single, 'Good Hearted Woman', in which Jennings' thumping beat and Nelson's sensitivity were combined beautifully (the 1996 Anniversary

reissue added nine tracks, plus the brand new Steve Earle song 'Nowhere Road', sung by Nelson and Jennings). The first *Waylon And Willie* (1978) album included Ed Bruce's witty look at outlaw country, 'Mammas, Don't Let Your Babies Grow Up To Be Cowboys', and two beautifully restrained Nelson performances, 'If You Can Touch Her At All' and 'A Couple More Years'. Their two subsequent albums contained unsuitable or weak material and perfunctory arrangements, although the humorous *Clean Shirt* (1991) was a welcome return to form. Since then, they have added Johnny Cash and Kris Kristofferson for tours and albums as the Highwaymen. Nelson has also recorded two albums with Merle Haggard, including the highly successful 'Poncho And Lefty', as well as several albums with country stars of the 50s and 60s. His numerous guest appearances include 'Seven Spanish Angels' (Ray Charles), 'The Last Cowboy Song' (Ed Bruce), 'Are There Any More Real Cowboys?' (Neil Young), 'One Paper Kid' (Emmylou Harris), 'I Gotta Get Drunk' (George Jones), 'Waltz Across Texas' (Ernest Tubb), 'They All Went To Mexico' (Carlos Santana) and 'Something To Brag About' (Mary Kay Place). Utilizing modern technology, he sang with Hank Williams on 'I Told A Lie To My Heart'. He invited Julio Iglesias to join him at the Country Music Awards and their duet of Albert Hammond's 'To All The Girls I've Known Before' was an international success.

Nelson has recorded numerous country songs, including a tribute album to Lefty Frizzell, but more significant has been his love of standards. He had always recorded songs like 'Am I Blue?' and 'That Lucky Old Sun', but *Stardust* (1978), which was produced by Booker T. Jones of the MGs, took country fans by surprise. The weather-beaten, top-hatted character on the sleeve *was* Willie Nelson but the contents resembled a Bing Crosby album. Nelson sang ten standards, mostly slowly, to a small rhythm section and strings. The effect was devastating as he breathed new life into 'Georgia On My Mind' and 'Someone To Watch Over Me', and the album remained on the US country charts for nearly 10 years. Nelson recorded 103 songs in a week with Leon Russell but their performance of standards falls far short of *Stardust*. Nelson tried to recapture the magic of *Stardust* on the lethargic *Without A Song*, which contained the first Nelson/Iglesias duet, 'As Time Goes By'. In terms of both performance and arrangement, his Christmas album, *Pretty Paper* (1979), sounds like a mediocre act at a social club, but the jaunty *Somewhere Over The Rainbow* (the Harold Arlen/E.Y. 'Yip' Harburg classic) is much better. In 1982 Johnny Christopher showed Nelson a song he had written, 'Always On My Mind'. Nelson had originally wanted to record the song with Merle Haggard, but Haggard did not care for it; Nelson recorded an emotional and convincing version on his own, and it went to number 5 in the US charts. It was some time before Nelson learnt that Elvis Presley had previously recorded the song. The resulting album, which included 'Let It Be Me' and 'A Whiter Shade Of Pale', showed his mastery of the popular song. Other modern songs to which he has added his magic include 'City Of New Orleans', 'Wind Beneath My Wings' and 'Please Come To Boston'. He sang another Presley hit, 'Love Me Tender', on the soundtrack of *Porky's Revenge*. When Robert Redford met Nelson at a party, he invited him to join the cast of *The Electric Horseman*. Willie had an entertaining role as Redford's manager, and he made a major contribution to the soundtrack with 'My Heroes Have Always Been Cowboys'. Redford wanted to star in the film of *Red Headed Stranger* (1987) but it was eventually cast with Nelson in the title role. His other films include *Barbarosa* (in which he played an old gunfighter), a remake of *Stagecoach* with his outlaw friends, and the cliché-ridden *Songwriter* with Kris Kristofferson. He is more suited to cameo roles and has the makings of a latter-day Gabby Hayes.

Nelson's record label, Lone Star, which he started in 1978 with Steven Fromholz and the Geezinslaw Brothers, was not a commercial success, but he later developed his own recording studio and golf course at Pedernales, Texas; he produced *Timi Yuro - Today* there in 1982. He took over the Dripping Springs Festival and turned it into a festival of contemporary country music: Willie Nelson's Fourth of July Picnic. He has organized several Farm Aid benefits, and he and Kenny Rogers represented country music on the number 1 USA For Africa single, 'We Are The World'. With all this activity, it is hardly surprising that his songwriting has suffered and he rarely records new compositions. He wrote 'On The Road Again' for the country music film in which he starred, *Honeysuckle Rose*, and he also wrote a suite of songs about the old west and reincarnation, *Tougher Than Leather*, when he was in hospital with a collapsed lung. Among the many songs that have been written *about* Willie Nelson are 'Willy The Wandering Gypsy And Me' (Billy Joe Shaver), 'Willie, Won't You Sing A Song With Me' (George Burns), 'Crazy Old Soldier' (Lacy J. Dalton), 'Willon And Waylee' (Don Bowman), 'The Willie And Waylon Machine' (Marvin Rainwater), 'Willie' (Hank Cochran and Merle Haggard) and 'It's Our Turn To Sing With Ol' Willie' (Carlton Moody And The Moody Brothers). Nelson's touring band, Family, is a very tight unit featuring musicians who have been with him for many years. Audiences love his image as an old salt, looking rough and playing a battered guitar, and his headbands have become souvenirs in the same way as Elvis's scarves. His greatest testimony comes from President Jimmy Carter, who joined him onstage and said, 'I, my wife, my daughter, my sons and my mother all think he's the greatest'. Unfortunately, the USA's Inland Revenue Service took a different view, and in an effort to obtain $16 million in back-taxes, they had Nelson make an acoustic album, which was sold by mail order. His collaboration with artists such as Bob Dylan and Paul Simon on *Across The Borderline* brought him back into the commercial mainstream for the first time in several years. In 1991 Nelson married Annie D'Angelo and they now have a young family. Albums have flowed fast and furiously as Nelson brings himself back into the black financially, and *Just One Love* was the high point of his prolific 90s period. Nelson is a true outlaw and probably the greatest legend and performer in country music since Hank Williams.

● ALBUMS: *... And Then I Wrote* (Liberty 1962)★★★, *Here's Willie Nelson* (Liberty 1963)★★★, *Country Willie - His Own Songs* (RCA Victor 1965)★★★, *Country Favorites - Willie Nelson Style* (RCA Victor 1966)★★★, *Country Music Concert (Live At Panther Hall)* (RCA Victor 1966)★★★, *Make Way For Willie Nelson* (RCA Victor 1967)★★★, *The Party's Over* (RCA Victor 1967)★★★, *Texas In My Soul* (RCA Victor 1968)★★★, *Good Times* (RCA Victor 1968)★★★, *My Own Peculiar Way* (RCA Victor 1969)★★★, *Both Sides Now* (RCA Victor 1970)★★★, *Laying My Burdens Down* (RCA Victor 1970)★★★, *Willie Nelson And Family* (RCA Victor 1971)★★★, *Yesterday's Wine* (RCA Victor 1971)★★★, *The Words Don't Fit The Picture* (RCA Victor 1972)★★★, *The Willie Way* (RCA Victor 1972)★★★, *Shotgun Willie* (Atlantic 1973)★★★, *Phases And Stages* (Atlantic 1974)★★★, *What Can You Do To Me Now* (RCA 1975)★★, *Red Headed Stranger* (Columbia 1975)★★★★★, with Waylon Jennings, Jessi Colter, Tompall Glaser *Wanted! The Outlaws* (RCA 1976)★★★★, *The Sound In Your Mind* (Columbia 1976)★★★★, *Phases And Stages* 1964 recording (Atlantic 1976)★★, *Willie Nelson - Live* (RCA 1976)★★, *The Troublemaker* (Columbia 1976)★★★, *Before His Time* (RCA 1977)★★, *To Lefty From Willie* (Columbia 1977)★★★, *Stardust* (Columbia 1978)★★★★, *Face Of A Fighter* 1961 recording (Lone Star 1978)★★★, *Willie And Family Live* (Columbia 1978)★★★, with Jennings *Waylon And Willie* (RCA 1978)★★★★, with Leon Russell *One For The Road* (Columbia 1978)★★★★, *The Electric Horseman* (Columbia 1979)★★★★, *Willie Nelson Sings Kristofferson* (Columbia 1979)★★, *Pretty Paper* (Columbia 1979)★, *Sweet Memories* (RCA 1979)★★★, *Danny Davis And Willie Nelson With The Nashville Brass* (RCA 1980)★★★, with Ray Price *San Antonio Rose* (Columbia 1980)★★★, *Honeysuckle Rose* (Columbia 1980)★★★★, *Family Bible* (MCA Songbird 1980)★★★, *Somewhere Over The Rainbow* (Columbia 1981)★★★, *Minstrel Man* (RCA 1981)★★, with Roger Miller *Old Friends* (Columbia 1982)★★★, *Diamonds In The Rough* (1982)★★, with Johnny Bush *Together Again* (1982)★★★, *Always On My Mind* (Columbia 1982)★★★★, with Jennings *WWII* (RCA 1982)★★★★, with Webb Pierce *In The Jailhouse Now* (Columbia 1982)★★★, with Kris Kristofferson, Brenda Lee, Dolly Parton *The Winning Hand* (Monument 1982)★★★, with Merle Haggard *Poncho And Lefty* (Epic 1983)★★★, *Without A Song* (Columbia 1983)★★, *Tougher Than Leather* (Columbia 1983)★★★, *My Own Way* (RCA 1983)★★★, with Jennings *Take It To The Limit* (Columbia 1983)★★★, with Jackie King *Angel Eyes* (Columbia 1984)★★, *Slow Down Old World* (1984)★★★★, *City Of New Orleans* (Columbia 1984)★★, with Kristofferson *Music From Songwriter* film soundtrack (Columbia 1984)★★★, with Faron Young *Funny How Time Slips Away* (Columbia 1984)★★★, with Johnny Cash, Jennings, Kristofferson *Highwayman* (Columbia 1985)★★★★, with Hank Snow *Brand On My Heart* (Columbia 1985)★★★, *Me And Paul* (Columbia 1985)★★★, *Half Nelson* (Columbia 1985)★★, *The Promiseland* (Columbia 1986)★★, *Partners* (Columbia 1986)★★★, *Island In The Sea* (Columbia 1987)★★★, with Haggard *Seashores Of Old Mexico* (Epic 1987)★★★, with J.R. Chatwell *Jammin' With J.R. And Friends* (1988)★★★, *What A Wonderful World* (Columbia 1988)★★★, *A Horse Called Music* (Columbia 1989)★★★, with Cash, Jennings, Kristofferson *Highwayman 2* (Columbia 1990)★★★, *Born For Trouble* (Columbia 1990)★★★, with Jennings *Clean Shirt* (Epic 1991)★★, *Who'll Buy My Memories - The IRS Tapes* (Columbia 1991)★★★, with Willie Nelson *Together Again* (1982)★★★, *Across The Borderline* (Columbia 1993)★★★★, *Healing Hands Of Time* (Liberty 1994)★★★, *Moonlight Becomes You* (Justice 1994)★★, with Curtis Porter *Six Hours At Pedernales* (Step One 1994)★★, with Don Cherry *Augusta* (Coast To Coast 1995)★★, with Cash, Jennings, Kristofferson *The Road Goes On Forever* (Liberty 1995)★★, *Just One Love* (Transatlantic 1995)★★★, *Spirit* (Island 1996)★★★, with Waylon Jennings,

Jessi Colter, Tompall Glaser *Wanted! The Outlaws (1976-1996, 20th Anniversary)* (RCA 1996)★★★★, with Bobbie Nelson *How Great Thou Art* (Finer Arts 1996)★★.
● COMPILATIONS: *The Best Of Willie Nelson* (United Artists 1973)★★★, *Willie Nelson's Greatest Hits (And Some That Will Be)* (Columbia 1981)★★★, *20 Of The Best* (RCA 1982)★★★, *Country Willie* (Capitol 1987)★★★, *The Collection* (Castle 1988)★★★, *Across The Tracks - The Best Of Willie Nelson* (1988)★★★, *Nite Life: Greatest Hits And Rare Tracks, 1959-1971* (Rhino 1990)★★★★, *King Of The Outlaws* (1993)★★★, *Heartaches* (1993)★★★, *45 Original Tracks* (EMI 1993)★★★, *The Early Years* (Scotti Bros 1994)★★★, *The Early Years: The Complete Liberty Recordings Plus More* 2-CD set (Liberty 1994)★★★, *Super Hits* (Columbia 1994)★★★, *A Classic And Unreleased Collection* 3-CD box set (Rhino 1995)★★★, *Revolutions Of Time: The Journey 1975-1993* (Columbia/Legacy 1995)★★★★, *The Essential Willie Nelson* (RCA 1995)★★★.
● VIDEOS: *Honeysuckle Rose, First Time Together (with Ray Charles), My Life - Biography, Willie Nelson And Family In Concert* (CBS-Fox 1988), *The Best Of* (Vestron Video 1990), *The Original Outlaw/On The Road Again* (Hughes Leisure 1994), *Nashville Superstar* (Magnum Music 1997).
● FURTHER READING: *Willie Nelson Family Album*, Lana Nelson Fowler (ed.). *Willie Nelson - Country Outlaw*, Lola Socbey. *Willie*, Michael Bane. *I Didn't Come Here And I Ain't Leavin'*, Willie Nelson with Bud Shrake. *Heartworn Memories - A Daughter's Personal Biography Of Willie Nelson*, Susie Nelson. *Willie: An Autobiography*, Willie Nelson and Bud Shrake.

NEON PHILHARMONIC
Neon Philharmonic was essentially the work of two musicians, the Nashville, Tennessee-based singer-songwriter Don Gant (b. 1942, d. 6 March 1987) and the arranger, conductor and composer Tuppy Saussy. Gant's career included writing songs with Roy Orbison and singing solo and background for country artists such as Don Gibson and John D. Loudermilk. He produced records for many artists, including Bobby Bland, Jimmy Buffett and Lefty Frizzell. Gant also ran ABC-Dunhill Records and was president of the Nashville branch of the National Academy of Recording Arts and Sciences (NARAS). Gant teamed with Saussy in 1969 and recorded the latter's 'Morning Girl' for Warner Brothers Records with a chamber group comprised of members of the Nashville Symphony Orchestra. The record made the US Top 20 and one follow-up single also reached the charts. The 'group' released two albums and five further singles, but the novelty had diminished.
● ALBUMS: *Moth Confesses* (Warners 1969)★★, *Neon Philharmonic* (Warners 1969)★★.

NERVOUS NORVUS
b. Jimmy Drake, 1912, d. 1968. The California-based ex-truck driver's first record was the country ballad 'Gambling Fury', which he recorded as Singing Jimmy Drake on the Indiana label Claudra. He joined Dot Records in 1956 and had two of the biggest novelty hits of that year. His first hit, 'Transfusion', concerned the thoughts of a drink-driver who is in need of a blood transfusion after a car crash. Despite the sick subject matter, it was hilarious, though the British public were spared it when London Records refused its

release. The follow-up to this US Top 10 hit was 'Ape Call', a tale about cavemen recorded in hip language, with jungle calls courtesy of Red Blanchard. After his few months in the spotlight he returned to obscurity, despite later unsuccessful recordings on Big Ben and Embee.
● COMPILATIONS: *Transfusion* (1985)★★.

NESMITH, MICHAEL
b. Robert Michael Nesmith, 30 December 1942, Houston, Texas, USA. Although best-known as a member of the Monkees, Nesmith enjoyed a prolific career in music prior to this group's inception. During the mid-60s folk boom he performed with bassist John London as Mike and John, but later pursed work as a solo act. Two singles, credited to Michael Blessing, were completed under the aegis of New Christy Minstrels mastermind Randy Sparks, while Nesmith's compositions, 'Different Drum' and 'Mary Mary', were recorded, respectively, by the Stone Poneys and Paul Butterfield. Such experience gave the artist confidence to demand the right to determine the Monkees' musical policy and his sterling country-rock performances represented the highlight of the group's varied catalogue. In 1968 he recorded *The Witchita Train Whistle Sings*, an instrumental set, but his independent aspirations did not fully flourish until 1970 when he formed the First National Band. Former colleague London joined Orville 'Red' Rhodes (pedal steel) and John Ware (drums) in a group completing three exceptional albums that initially combined Nashville-styled country with the leader's acerbic pop, (*Magnetic South*), but later grew to encompass a grander, even eccentric interpretation of the genre (*Nevada Fighter*). The band disintegrated during the latter's recording and a Second National Band, on which Nesmith and Rhodes were accompanied by Johnny Meeks (bass; ex-Gene Vincent and Merle Haggard) and Jack Panelli (drums), completed the less impressive *Tantamount To Treason*. The group was disbanded entirely for the sarcastically titled *And The Hits Just Keep On Comin'*, a haunting, largely acoustic, set regarded by many as the artist's finest work. In 1972 he founded the Countryside label under the aegis of Elektra Records, but despite critically acclaimed sets by Iain Matthews, Garland Frady and the ever-present Rhodes, the project was axed in the wake of boardroom politics. The excellent *Pretty Much Your Standard Ranch Stash* ended the artist's tenure with RCA, following which he founded a second label, Pacific Arts. *The Prison*, an allegorical narrative that came replete with a book, was highly criticized upon release, although recent opinion has lauded its ambition. Nesmith reasserted his commercial status in 1977 when 'Rio', culled from *From A Radio Engine To The Photon Wing*, reached the UK Top 30. The attendant video signalled a growing interest in the visual arts which flourished following *Infinite Rider On The Big Dogma*, his biggest-selling US release. In 1982 *Elephant Parts* won the first ever Grammy for a video, while considerable acclaim was engendered by a subsequent series, *Michael Nesmith In Television Parts*, and the film *Repo Man*, which the artist financed. Having refused entreaties to join the Monkees' 20th Anniversary Tour, this articulate entrepreneur continues to pursue his various diverse interests including a highly successful video production company (Pacific Arts).
● ALBUMS: *Mike Nesmith Presents The Wichita Train Whistle Sings* (Dot 1968)★★, *Magnetic South* (RCA 1970)★★★, *Loose*

Salute (RCA 1971)★★★, *Nevada Fighter* (RCA 1971)★★★★, *Tantamount To Treason* (RCA 1972)★★, *And The Hits Just Keep On Comin'* (RCA 1972)★★★, *Pretty Much Your Standard Ranch Stash* (RCA 1973)★★★, *The Prison* (Pacific Arts 1975)★★, *From A Radio Engine To The Photon Wing* (Pacific Arts 1977)★★★, *Live At The Palais* (Pacific Arts 1978)★★, *Infinite Rider On The Big Dogma* (Pacific Arts 1979)★★★, *Tropical Campfires* (Pacific Arts 1992)★★★, *The Garden* (Rio Royal 1994)★★.

● COMPILATIONS: *The Best Of Mike Nesmith* (RCA 1977)★★★, *The Newer Stuff* (Awareness 1989)★★★, *The Older Stuff* (Rhino 1992)★★★★, *Complete* (Pacific Arts 1993)★★★.

● VIDEOS: *Elephant Parts* (Awareness 1992).

● FILMS: *Head* (1968).

NEVADA SLIM

b. Dallas Turner, 27 November 1927, Walla Walla, Washington, USA. Given away by his mother and then by a nurse, who was supposedly looking after him, he was finally adopted by the Turners, who raised him on their ranch in Elko, Nevada. He listened intently to the cowboy singers that he heard on Border Radio, being particularly influenced by Cowboy Slim Rinehart. In the mid-40s, after learning to play guitar, he hoboed to the Border stations, where Rinehart befriended him. They became great friends and it was Turner who put a tombstone on Rinehart's unmarked grave, after he was killed in a car crash in 1948 (*Cowboy Slim Rinehart's Folio Of Country Song Hits* was published by Dallas Turner in Reno, Nevada in 1983). Turner appeared on various programmes on XERF, XELO and XEG, sometimes singing under his own name but usually under an alias such as Nevada Slim or Yodellin' Slim Dallas. He proved popular with sponsors of the programmes, since he was a most competent 'pitchman' for their products. He also sold his own songbooks by mail order and remained a favourite on Border Radio for around 30 years, at times even being involved with the running of stations. He played few US stations, probably due to differences of opinion over marketing his wares, but in the 60s, he recorded transcription programmes that were broadcast by several important US stations including WWVA Wheeling and WCKY Cincinnati. In the mid-60s, he recorded several albums for Rural Rhythm, which he also sold by mail order. After seven years, he succeeded in curing a drink problem, brought on after his son died in a fire. He related how, lonely and sad in a motel room, he had held a gun to his head and was about to pull the trigger, when he heard a gospel song, 'God Put A Rainbow In The Clouds', playing on his bedside radio. He put down the gun, picked up the Gideon bible on the table and from that day, he found religion. He later became a minister and presented evangelistic programmes, as well as recording a gospel album. He became acknowledged as an noted historian of Western material and Border Radio. He has also sung authentic cowboy material in documentaries and appeared at the annual *Elko Cowboy Poetry Gathering*, instigated by Waddie Mitchell. A great deal of information about this most interesting and authoritative character may be found in the 1987 book *Border Radio* by Gene Fowler and Bill Crawford.

● ALBUMS: *Songs Of The Wild West Volumes 1,2,3* and *4* (Rural Rhythm 1964)★★★, *Nevada Slim Sings A Heart Song* (Rural Rhythm 1965)★★★, *Reverend Dallas Turner Sings*

Pentecostal Revival Songs (Rural Rhythm 1967)★★★, *Old Time Country Favorites* (Rural Rhythm 1968)★★★.

NEW GRASS REVIVAL

The New Grass Revival evolved around the fiddle talents of Sam Bush, who also plays guitar, mandolin and sings. Another long-standing member is bass player John Cowan, who, somewhat surprisingly, contributed soaring R&B-styled vocals to an acoustic band. The other founding members were Courtney Johnson (b. 20 December 1939, d. 7 June 1996) and Ebo Walker. The four-piece band had some success with the Leon Russell song 'Prince Of Peace'. They toured with Russell and cut a live album and video together at Perkins' Palace in Pasadena. In 1984 the band moved to Sugar Hill Records and their albums, while essentially bluegrass, also feature elements of jazz, reggae and soul. Amongst the later members of the Revival is the highly respected banjo player Bela Fleck. In 1991 Emmylou Harris formed an acoustic band, the Nash Ramblers, to accompany her, the leader of the group being Sam Bush. Bush's involvement with Harris seems to have curtailed any future activities, but the New Grass Revival's legacy is as the most significant acoustic country band in the USA.

● ALBUMS: *Arrival Of The New Grass Revival* (Starday 1972)★★★, *Fly Through The Country* (Flying Fish 1975)★★★★, *Commonwealth* (Flying Fish 1976)★★★, *When The Storm Is Over* (Flying Fish 1977)★★★, *Too Late To Turn Back Now* (Flying Fish 1978)★★★, *Barren Country* (Flying Fish 1979)★★★, *Leon Russell And The New Grass Revival* (1981)★★★, *Live* (Sugar Hill 1984)★★★, *On The Boulevard* (Sugar Hill 1984)★★★, *New Grass Revival* (EMI 1986)★★★, *Hold On To A Dream* (Capitol 1987)★★★, *Friday Night In America* (Capitol 1989)★★★.

● COMPILATIONS: *New Grass Anthology* (Capitol 1990)★★★, *Best Of New Grass Revival* (Liberty 1994)★★★★.

NEWBURY, MICKEY

b. Milton J. Newbury Jnr., 19 May 1940, Houston, Texas, USA. Newbury began by singing tenor in a harmony group, the Embers, who recorded for Mercury Records. He worked as an air traffic controller in the US Air Force and was stationed in England. He later wrote 'Swiss Cottage Place', which was recorded by Roger Miller. In 1963 he worked on shrimp boats in Galveston, Texas and started songwriting in earnest. In 1964 he was signed to Acuff-Rose Music in Nashville. Among his early compositions are 'Here Comes The Rain, Baby' (Eddy Arnold and Roy Orbison), 'Funny Familiar Forgotten Feelings' (Don Gibson and Tom Jones), 'How I Love Them Old Songs' (Carl Smith) and 'Sweet Memories' (Willie Nelson). In 1968 Kenny Rogers And The First Edition had a US pop hit with the psychedelic 'Just Dropped In (To See What Condition My Condition Was In)'. Newbury recorded low-key albums of his own but his voice was so mournful that even his happier songs sounded sad. After two albums for RCA, he moved to Mercury and wrote and recorded such sombre songs as 'She Even Woke Me Up To Say Goodbye' (later recorded by Jerry Lee Lewis), 'San Francisco Mabel Joy' (recorded by John Denver, Joan Baez, David Allan Coe and Kenny Rogers) and 'I Don't Think About Her (Him) No More', which has been recorded by Don Williams and Tammy Wynette, and also by Bobby Bare, under the title of 'Poison Red Berries'. Newbury, who by now lived on a houseboat, was intrigued by the way his wind chimes mingled with the rain, thus leading to the sound effects he used to link tracks. His gentle and evocative 'American Trilogy' - in actuality a medley of three Civil War songs ('Dixie', 'The Battle Hymn Of The Republic' and 'All My Trials') - was a hit in a full-blooded version by Elvis Presley in 1972. Says Newbury, 'It was more a detriment than a help because it was not indicative of what I could do.' Nevertheless, his *Rusty Tracks* also features reworkings of American folk songs. Amongst his successful compositions are 'Makes Me Wonder If I Ever Said Goodbye' (Johnny Rodriguez) and 'Blue Sky Shinin'' (Marie Osmond). He has scarcely made a mark as a performer in the US country charts (his highest position is number 53 for 'Sunshine'), but he was elected to the Nashville Songwriters' International Hall of Fame in 1980. Ironically, he has released few new songs since and his 'new age' album in 1988 featured re-recordings of old material. His 1996 album, *Lulled By The Moonlight*, was dedicated to first American pop songwriter Stephen Foster.

● ALBUMS: *Harlequin Melodies* (RCA Victor 1968)★★, *Mickey Newbury Sings His Own* (RCA 1968)★★★, *Looks Like Rain* (Mercury 1969)★★★, *'Frisco Mabel Joy* (Elektra 1971)★★★★, *Heaven Help The Child* (Elektra 1973)★★★, *Live At Montezuma* also issued as a double album with *Looks Like Rain* (Elektra 1973)★★★, *I Came To Hear The Music* (Elektra 1974)★★★, *Lovers* (Elektra 1975)★★★, *Rusty Tracks* (Hickory 1977)★★, *His Eye Is On The Sparrow* (Hickory 1978)★★★, *The Sailor* (Hickory 1979)★★★, *After All These Years* (Mercury 1981)★★★, *In A New Age* (Airborne 1988)★★★, *Nights When I Am Sane* (Winter Harvest 1994)★★★, *Lulled By The Moonlight* (Mountain Retreat 1996)★★★.

● COMPILATIONS: *Sweet Memories* (MCA 1986)★★★, *The Best Of Mickey Newbury* (Curb 1991)★★.

NEWMAN, JIMMY C.

b. Jimmy Yves Newman, 27 August 1927, Big Mamou, Louisiana, USA. Since he was of French origin, speaking both English and French, and grew up in the heart of the Cajun area of the state, it is no surprise that he went on to become one of the main artists to bring that genre of music into the field of country music. He left school prematurely when his father died to help support his eight siblings. Newman first became interested in country music through hearing his brother Walter play guitar and sing Jimmie Rodgers songs. In the mid-40s he played in a local Cajun band and made his first recording in French in 1946. Later, he formed his own band, played local radio and small venues around the state, and eventually presented his own programme on KPLC-TV in Lake Charles, where his mixture of Cajun and country music quickly proved popular. In 1949 he recorded the original version of the Webb Pierce hit 'Wondering'. The release failed to chart but, determined to find a hit song, he wrote and recorded 'Cry Cry Darling'. Listeners to his early recordings will note a prominent hiss on his pronunciation of the letter 'S', caused by a badly fitted gold tooth. Fred Rose tried to eliminate the problem by changing lyrics, such as in 'Cry Cry Darling', where 'sunshine' became 'moonlight' (a little later a partial denture replaced the offending tooth and permanently cured the problem). Also through the auspices of Fred Rose, Newman

joined Dot Records. In 1954 a new recording of 'Cry Cry Darling' reached number 4 on the US country charts and led to his joining the *Louisiana Hayride*. Between 1955 and 1957 he had five more Top 10 country hits, the biggest being his recording of Ned Miller's 'A Fallen Star', which became a number 2 country and number 23 pop hit. Newman acquired the 'C' in his name when the drummer on the recording of the song, T. Tommy Cutrer, labelled him Jimmy 'Cajun' Newman and the initial stuck. He did not like rocka-billy or novelty songs, but did record 'Bop-A-Hula' and the Jim Reeves song 'Step Aside Shallow Waters'. In 1958 he moved to MGM, where Top 10 country hits included 'You're Making A Fool Out Of Me' and 'A Lovely Work Of Art'. In 1961 he left MGM because he felt he was losing his Cajun roots. He joined Decca and in the next nine years charted 16 country hits including such popular recordings as 'DJ For A Day' and 'Artificial Rose', and Cajun numbers including 'Alligator Man', 'Bayou Talk' and 'Louisiana Saturday Night'. His last chart hit came in 1970 with a song called 'I'm Holding Your Memory'. He later recorded for several minor labels including Plantation. From the mid-50s through the 70s he toured extensively throughout the USA, played some overseas concerts and has also appeared on all major net-work radio and television shows. He became a member of the *Grand Ole Opry* in 1956 and still maintains his regular appearances, often hosting one of the show's segments. Newman's plaintive tenor vocals and traditional fiddle and steel guitar backing were ideally suited to the country music of the 50s and 60s and at times, except for his Cajun num-bers, his vocal work was comparable with that of Webb Pierce. He has always proved a great favourite with UK audi-ences on the occasions when he has appeared at the Wembley Festival, and he continues to tour with veteran Cajun musicians, including fiddle player Rufus Thibodeaux.

● ALBUMS: *This Is Jimmy Newman* (MGM 1959)★★★, *Songs By Jimmy Newman* (MGM 1962)★★★, *Folk Songs Of The Bayou Country* (Decca 1963)★★★, *Artificial Rose* (Decca 1966)★★★, *Country Crossroads* (Dot 1966)★★★, *A Fallen Star* (Dot 1966)★★★, *Jimmy Newman Sings Country Songs* (Decca 1966)★★★, *The World Of Country Music* (Decca 1967)★★★, *The Jimmy Newman Way* (Decca 1967)★★★, *Born To Love You* (Decca 1968)★★★, *The Jimmy Newman Style* (Decca 1969)★★★, *Country Time* (Decca 1970)★★, *Progressive C.C* (Charly 1977)★★★, with Hank Locklin, Rita Remington *Carol Channing & Her Country Friends* (1977)★★, *The Cajun Cowboy* (Plantation 1978)★★★, *The Happy Cajun* (Plantation 1979)★★★, *Cajun Country* (RCA 1982)★★★, *Wild 'N' Cajun* (RCA 1984)★★★, *Cajun & Country Too* (Swallow 1987)★★★, *Lache Pas La Patate* (La Louisiane 1987)★★★, *Louisiana Saturday Night* (Charly 1987)★★★, *The Alligator Man* (Rounder 1991)★★★.

● COMPILATIONS: *Greatest Hits Volume 1* (1981)★★★, *Jimmy Newman & Al Terry - Earliest Recordings 1949-1952* (1981)★★★, *Cajun Country Classics* (Charly 1986)★★★, *Bop A Hula* compiles Dot material (Bear Family 1990)★★★★.

NEWMAN, ROY

b. c.1900, Dallas, Texas, USA, d. 23 February 1981, Dallas, Texas, USA. Nothing is known now of Newman's childhood or of his teenage years but he grew up to become one of the pioneers of western swing music. By his mid-20s, he played piano, piano accordion and guitar and worked as a staff musician at WRR Dallas. In 1926, apart from his studio duties, he began to play piano as one half of the Mystery Duo, with John Thorvald (guitar). In 1931, he played guitar as part of a quartet known as the Wanderers, where he became associated with guitarist Jim Boyd. The group moved to WFAA in 1932, but Newman and Boyd with different musicians returned to WRR, as Roy Newman And His Boys, the following year. Also at WRR at that time was Bill Boyd, who played and recorded with musicians known as the Cowboy Ramblers. In reality, some of the musicians who played and recorded with Newman also played on Boyd's recordings, but each band managed an individual sound and both played on WRR's popular *Noon Hour Varieties*. Newman And His Boys (who sometimes numbered 10 musicians) recorded 72 sides between 1934 and 1939, and established a considerable reputation through their broadcasts and appearances in the Dallas and Fort Worth areas. Although never afforded the publicity gained by Bob Wills or Milton Brown, Newman, who probably played more jazz than his contemporaries, played his part in popularizing western swing music, before he disbanded in 1940. Important group members over the years, apart from Jim Boyd, were fiddlers Art Davis and Thurman Neal and Holly Horton (clarinet). Newman continued to work as a staff musician at WRR and/or WFAA until his retirement. He died at his home in 1981, the same year that an album of his early work was released. Recordings have also appeared on Rambler compilation albums.

● COMPILATIONS: *Roy Newman And His Boys 1934-1938* (Original Jazz Library 1981)★★★.

NEWTON, JUICE

b. Judy Kaye Cohen, 18 February 1952, Lakehurst, New Jersey, USA. This singing daughter from a military family spent most of her childhood in Virginia. While completing a formal education in California, she fronted Dixie Peach, a country rock combo that was renamed Silver Spur for their RCA albums in the mid-70s. Despite assistance from top Los Angeles session musicians, immediate solo success was dogged by Bonnie Tyler's version of 'It's A Heartache' eclipsing Newton's own, though she gained a US country hit by proxy when the Carpenters covered her self-composed 'Sweet Sweet Smile' in 1978. Two years later, she arrived in *Billboard*'s Top 5 with a revival of Chip Taylor's 'Angel Of The Morning' (her only UK hit) and then 'Queen Of Hearts' (also a hit for Dave Edmunds), while the *Juice* album containing both peaked at number 22. She enjoyed more hits in the pop charts with 'Love's Been A Little Hard On Me', *Quiet Lies* and a 1983 overhaul of the Zombies' 'Tell Her No', but it was the country market that came to provide the bulk of her success. After an encouraging response when she performed 'The Sweetest Thing I've Ever Known' at 1981's annual Country Radio Seminar, this old Silver Spur track was remixed for a single to become a country number 1 the following year. Other genre successes included a reworking of Brenda Lee's 'Break It To Me Gently', Dave Loggins' 'You Make Me Want To Make You Mine', 'Hurt' and a duet with Eddie Rabbitt, 'Born To Each Other'. She later married polo star Tom Goodspeed and concentrated on the nightclub circuit.

● ALBUMS: with Silver Spur *Juice Newton And Silver Spur* (RCA 1975)★★★, with Silver Spur *After The Dust Settles* (RCA 1977)★★★, with Silver Spur *Come To Me* (Capitol

1977)★★, *Well Kept Secret* (Capitol 1978)★★★, *Take A Heart* (Capitol 1979)★★★, *Juice* (Capitol 1981)★★★★, *Quiet Lies* (Capitol 1982)★★★, *Dirty Looks* (Capitol 1983)★★★, *Can't Wait All Night* (RCA 1984)★★★, *Old Flame* (RCA 1986)★★★, *Emotion* (RCA 1987)★★★, *Ain't Gonna Cry* (RCA 1989)★★.

● COMPILATIONS: *Collection* (EMI 1983)★★★, *Greatest Hits* (Capitol 1984)★★★★, *Greatest Country Hits* (Curb 1990)★★★.

NICHOLS, COWBOY SAM

b. 31 August 1918, Eula, Texas, USA. With the encouragement of his grandfather, he started singing cowboy songs and playing guitar as a child. In the early 30s, he played regularly on KNEL Brady but by 1937, he was performing, as Sam Nichols The Roaming Cowboy, on the powerful XEPN Border Radio station at Eagle Pass. Here, like contemporaries Slim Rinehart and Nevada Slim, he dressed the part, sold his songbooks and proved a popular artist. He remained at XEPN until he joined the US Navy during World War II. After his discharge, he relocated to California, where he worked the clubs, made a few brief film appearances and toured with Gene Autry and Spade Cooley. He recorded for Memo in 1946, before being signed by MGM Records, and he recorded for that label with session musicians, led by Porky Freeman, dubbed for the recordings the Melody Rangers. He wrote several songs that were also recorded by others, especially 'That Wild And Wicked Look In Your Eye', which in 1948 became a Top 10 hit for Ernest Tubb, and 'I'm Telling You', which proved popular for Nichols but suffered at the hands of an Audrey Williams recording. He left the music business in 1972 and settled on a small ranch near Sonora, Texas.

● COMPILATIONS: *Sam Nichols With The Melody Rangers* (Cattle 1987)★★★.

NIELSEN-CHAPMAN, BETH

b. Harlington, Texas, USA. Nielsen-Chapman sang harmony on Tanya Tucker's 1988 US number 1 country single 'Strong Enough To Bend', which she wrote with Don Schlitz. She also sang harmony and wrote Willie Nelson's 1989 US country number 1, 'Nothing I Can Do It About It Now'. Her debut album for Reprise Records failed to secure her career as a singer, however, although it included her version of 'Down On My Knees' (covered by Trisha Yearwood). The 1993 follow-up was an equally strong set, moving further away from country into adult-orientated pop music.

● ALBUMS: *Beth Nielsen-Chapman* (Reprise 1990)★★★, *You Hold The Key* (Reprise 1993)★★★.

NITTY GRITTY DIRT BAND

Formed in Long Beach, California, in 1965, this enduring attraction evolved from the region's traditional circuit. Founder-members Jeff Hanna (b. 11 July 1947; guitar, vocals) and Bruce Kunkel (guitar, vocals) had worked together as the New Coast Two, prior to joining the Illegitimate Jug Band. Glen Grosclose (drums), Dave Hanna (guitar, vocals), Ralph Barr (guitar) and Les Thompson (bass, vocals) completed the embryonic Dirt Band line-up, although Grosclose and Dave Hanna quickly made way for Jimmie Fadden (drums, guitar) and Jackson Browne (guitar, vocals). Although the last musician only remained for a matter of months - he was replaced by John McEuen - his songs remained in the group's repertoire throughout their early career. *Nitty Gritty Dirt Band* comprised jug-band, vaudeville and pop material, ranging from the quirky 'Candy Man' to the orchestrated folk/pop of 'Buy For Me The Rain', a minor US hit. *Ricochet* maintained this balance, following which Chris Darrow, formerly of Kaleidoscope (US), replaced Kunkel. The Dirt Band completed two further albums, and enjoyed a brief appearance in the film *Paint Your Wagon*, before disbanding in 1969. The group reconvened the following year around Jeff Hanna, John McEuen, Jimmie Fadden, Les Thompson and newcomer Jim Ibbotson. Having abandoned the jokey elements of their earlier incarnation, they pursued a career as purveyors of superior country rock. The acclaimed *Uncle Charlie And His Dog Teddy* included excellent versions of Mike Nesmith's 'Some Of Shelly's Blues', Kenny Loggins' 'House At Pooh Corner' and Jerry Jeff Walker's 'Mr. Bojangles', a US Top 10 hit in 1970. *Will The Circle Be Unbroken*, recorded in Nashville, was an expansive collaboration between the group and traditional music mentors Doc Watson, Roy Acuff, Merle Travis and Earl Scruggs. Its charming informality inspired several stellar performances and the set played an important role in breaking down mistrust between country's establishment and the emergent 'long hair' practitioners. Les Thompson left the line-up following the album's completion, but the remaining quartet, buoyed by an enhanced reputation, continued their eclectic ambitions on *Stars And Stripes Forever* and *Dreams*. In 1976 the group dropped its 'Nitty Gritty' prefix and, as the Dirt Band, undertook a pioneering USSR tour the following year. Both Hanna and Ibbotson enjoyed brief sabbaticals, during which time supplementary musicians were introduced. By 1982 the prodigals had rejoined Fadden, McEuen and newcomer Bob Carpenter (keyboards) for *Let's Go*. The Dirt Band were, by then, an American institution with an enduring international popularity. 'Long Hard Road (Sharecropper Dreams)' and 'Modern Day Romance' topped the country charts in 1984 and 1985, respectively, but the following year a now-weary McEuen retired from the line-up. Former Eagles guitarist Bernie Leadon augmented the group for *Working Band*, but left again on its completion. He was, however, featured on *Will The Circle Be Unbroken Volume Two*, on which the Dirt Band rekindled the style of their greatest artistic triumph with the aid of several starring names, including Emmylou Harris, Chet Atkins, Johnny Cash, Ricky Skaggs, Roger McGuinn and Chris Hillman. The set deservedly drew plaudits for a group about to enter the 90s with its enthusiasm still intact. *Acoustic*, released in 1994, was a credible and well-produced set.

● ALBUMS: *The Nitty Gritty Dirt Band* (Liberty 1967)★★★, *Ricochet* (Liberty 1967)★★★, *Rare Junk* (Liberty 1968)★★, *Alive* (Liberty 1969)★★, *Uncle Charlie And His Dog Teddy* (Liberty 1970)★★★, *All The Good Times* (United Artists 1972)★★★, *Will The Circle Be Unbroken* triple album (United Artists 1972)★★★★, *Stars And Stripes Forever* (United Artists 1974)★★, *Dreams* (United Artists 1975)★★★. As Dirt Band *Dirt Band* (United Artists 1978)★★, *An American Dream* (United Artists 1979)★★, *Make A Little Magic* (United Artists 1980)★★, *Jealousy* (United Artists 1981)★★. As Nitty Gritty Dirt Band *Let's Go* (United Artists 1983)★★, *Plain Dirt Fashion* (Warners. 1984)★★★, *Partners, Brothers And Friends* (Warners 1985)★★★, *Hold On* (Warners 1987)★★★, *Workin'*

Band (Warners. 1988)★★★, *Will The Circle Be Unbroken Volume II* (Warners. 1989)★★★★, *The Rest Of The Dream* (MCA 1991)★★★, *Not Fade Away* (Liberty 1992)★★, *Acoustic* (Liberty 1994)★★★.

● COMPILATIONS: *Pure Dirt* (Liberty UK 1968)★★, *Dead And Alive* (Liberty UK 1969)★★, *Dirt, Silver And Gold* (United Artists 1976)★★★, *Gold From Dirt* (United Artists UK 1980)★★★, *Early Dirt 1967-1970* (Decal UK 1986)★★, *Twenty Years Of Dirt* (Warners 1987)★★★, *Country Store: The Nitty Gritty Dirt Band* (Country Store 1987)★★, *The Best Of The Nitty Gritty Dirt Band Vol 2* (Atlantic 1988)★★, *More Great Dirt: The Best Of The Nitty Gritty Dirt Band, Volume 2* (Warners 1989)★★.

NOACK, EDDIE

b. De Armand A. Noack Jnr., 29 April 1930, Houston, Texas, USA, d. 5 February 1978. Noack who gained degrees in English and Journalism at the University of Houston, made his radio debut in 1947 and first recorded for Goldstar in 1949. In 1951, he cut several songs for Four Star including 'Too Hot To Handle'. Leased to the TNT label, it drew attention to his songwriting and was recorded by several artists. He joined Starday in 1953 (beginning a long association with 'Pappy' Daily), where his immediate success came as a writer when several of his songs were recorded by top artists including Hank Snow, who scored a major hit with 'These Hands' in 1956. Noack moved with Daily to his D label, where in 1958, after recording rockabilly tracks as Tommy Wood, he had a country hit with 'Have Blues Will Travel'. During the 60s, Noack quit recording to concentrate on songwriting and publishing and had many of his songs including 'Flowers For Mama', 'Barbara Joy', 'The Poor Chinee', 'A Day In The Life Of A Fool' and 'No Blues Is Good News' successfully recorded by George Jones. Noack did make some further recordings in the 70s, including arguably some of his best for his fine tribute album to Jimmie Rodgers. He moved to Nashville and in 1976, recorded an album that found release in Britain (where he had toured that year) on the Look label. He worked in publishing for Daily and in an executive role for the Nashville Songwriters Association until his death from cirrhosis in 1978. A fine performer somewhat in the style of Hank Williams, he is perhaps more appreciated today as a singer than he was in his own time.

● ALBUMS: *Remembering Jimmie Rodgers* (1972)★★★, *Eddie Noack i* (Look 1976)★★, *Eddie Noack ii* (Chiswick 1980)★★★, *Gentlemen Prefer Blondes* (1981)★★.

NOLAN, BOB

b. Robert Clarence Nobles, 1 April 1908, Point Hatfield, New Brunswick, Canada, d. 16 June 1980. Bob Nolan was an important member of the Sons Of the Pioneers. Although Canadian, his father joined the US Army in World War I and served in France. He suffered gas poisoning and on discharge, changed his name to Nolan and relocated to Arizona for health reasons. During his father's absence, the young Bob received some education while living with aunts in Boston, but at the age of 14, he moved to Tucson to join his father. While attending the University of Arizona, he began writing poetry, some of which became the basis for the songs that he later wrote. In 1927, a desire to travel led him to hobo his way west. The sound of the trains were the reason for his first song, 'Way Out There', and the later sequel, 'One More Ride'. In 1929, he moved to California, where he worked on beaches as a lifeguard and sang with a group, which inspired him to seek a musical career. In mid-1931, he answered an advertisement placed by Leonard Slye (later Roy Rogers) in an Los Angeles newspaper for a tenor singer/yodeller to join the Rocky Mountaineers. The pair and fiddler Bob Nichols worked for a time with the Mountaineers until Nolan, disheartened by their lack of success, left to become a caddy at Bel Air Country Club. Late in 1933, Slye and Tim Spencer persuaded Nolan to become the third member of the Pioneer Trio. The trio subsequently went on to become the Sons Of The Pioneers, with Nolan a most important part of the act, not only for his singing but also for his songwriting. Rated by many as the most poetic of all the western songwriters, Nolan was responsible for many of the group's biggest hits. These include 'At The Rainbow's End', 'The Touch Of God's Hand', 'Chant Of The Wanderer' and his two classics, 'Cool Water' and 'Tumbling Tumbleweeds'. He retired from active performing in 1949 but recorded with the group until 1957. He finally tired of the music scene and adopted a solitary existence. He was persuaded to record a solo album in 1979 which contained some of his old hits and Marty Robbins' 'Man Walks Among Us', which included an appearance from the writer. Nolan died, following a heart attack, on 16 June 1980. His last request was that his ashes should be spread on the Nevada desert.

● ALBUMS: *Sound Of A Pioneer* (Elektra 1979)★★★.

NORMA JEAN

b. Norma Jean Beasley, 31 January 1938, near Wellston, Oklahoma, USA. Norma Jean showed an early interest in singing and after the family relocated to Oklahoma City, when she was five years old, she was given guitar tuition by an aunt. At the age of 13 she had her own thrice-weekly show on KLPR and in 1958, after working with several other artists including Leon McAuliffe, she became a regular on Red Foley's *Ozark Jubilee* television show, where she first dropped her surname and where her melodic singing soon attracted nationwide attention. In 1960 she moved to Nashville and became the featured vocalist with Porter Wagoner on both his network television show and also on the *Grand Ole Opry*. She recorded for Columbia in the early 60s but only gained her first US country chart success, 'Let's Go All The Way', in 1964, by which time she had joined RCA. (The Columbia material is contained on her only Columbia album, *Country's Favorite*; released in 1966 on their Harmony subsidiary - it is now highly sought after by collectors.) Further hits followed, including country Top 10s with 'Go Cat Go' and 'I Wouldn't Buy A Used Car From Him' and a Top 5 recording of 'The Game Of Triangles' with Bobby Bare and Liz Anderson. Equally at home with up-tempo songs such as 'Truck Driving Woman', country monologues such as 'Old Doc Brown' or a country weepie on the lines of 'There Won't Be Any Patches In Heaven', she built up a considerable reputation. She married in 1967 and left Wagoner's show and though she continued to record regularly into the early 70s, she abandoned most of her public appearances to concentrate on her home - a 1000-acre farm near Oklahoma City (Wagoner filled the vacancy with a young girl called Dolly Parton). She recorded in the 80s and her last chart entry was a very minor hit in 1982, with a duet recording with Claude Gray of her first hit, 'Let's Go All The Way'.

● ALBUMS: with Porter Wagoner *The Porter Wagoner Show* (RCA Victor 1963)★★★, with Wagoner *Porter Wagoner In Person* (RCA Victor 1964)★★★, *Let's Go All The Way* (RCA Victor 1964)★★★, *Pretty Miss Norma Jean* (RCA Victor 1965)★★★, *Country's Favorite* (Harmony 1966)★★★, with Wagoner *Live - On The Road* (RCA Victor 1966)★★★, *Norma Jean Sings A Tribute To Kitty Wells* (RCA Victor 1966)★★★, *Please Don't Hurt Me* (RCA Victor 1966)★★★, *Norma Jean Sings Porter Wagoner* (RCA Victor 1967)★★★★, *Jackson Ain't A Very Big Town* (RCA Victor 1967)★★★, with Bobby Bare, Liz Anderson *The Game Of Triangles* (RCA Victor 1967)★★★, *The Body And Mind* (RCA Victor 1968)★★★, *Heaven Help The Working Girl* (Camden 1968)★★★, *Heaven's Just A Prayer Away* (RCA Victor 1968)★★★, *Love's A Woman's Job* (RCA Victor 1968)★★★, *Country Giants* (RCA Victor 1969)★★★, *It's Time For Norma Jean* (RCA Victor 1970)★★★, *Another Man Loved Me Last Night* (RCA Victor 1970)★★★, *Norma Jean* (Bearsville 1971)★★★, *Sings Hank Cochran Songs* (1971)★★★, *It Wasn't God Who Made Honky Tonk Angels* (1971)★★★, *I Guess That Comes From Being Poor* (1972)★★★, *Thank You For Loving Me* (1972)★★★, *The Only Way To Hold Your Man* (1973)★★★, *Norma Jean* (1978)★★★.

● COMPILATIONS: *The Best Of Norma Jean* (RCA Victor 1969)★★★★, *My Best To You* (Roma 1996)★★★★.

NOTTING HILLBILLIES

On 31 May 1986, Mark Knopfler played a low-key gig at the Grove pub in Holbeck, Leeds, with old friends Steve Phillips and Brendan Croker. They were billed as the Notting Hillbillies and each received the princely sum of £22 for their performance. Phillips first met Knopfler in 1968 when both interviewed a local blues and country guitarist (also called Steve Phillips) for the *Yorkshire Post*. As both journalists played guitar they formed the Duolian String Pickers duo and played together during the late 60s. They split when Knopfler went to university in 1970. When he finished studying three years later he went to London and eventually formed Dire Straits. Meanwhile, Phillips formed the Steve Phillips Juke Band to play rockabilly. In 1976 Bradford-born Croker met Phillips and when the Juke Band split they toured as Nev And Norriss. In 1980, Phillips temporarily retired from music to concentrate on art, and Croker eventually formed the 5 O'Clock Shadows. In 1986 Knopfler, flushed with success through Dire Straits, decided the time was right to do something a little different and all three musicians came together. Dire Straits manager Ed Bicknell was recruited as drummer (he had previously played in Mogul Thrash) and with backing musicians such as Guy Fletcher (guitar), Paul Franklin (pedal steel) and Marcus Cliff (bass, of the 5 O'Clock Shadows), they set out on a tour. They made just one album before returning to concentrate on their main bands.

● ALBUMS: *Missing ... Presumed Having A Good Time* (Vertigo 1990)★★.

● VIDEOS: *Notting Hillbillies: Missing* (Channel 5 1990).

NUDIE

b. Nudie Cohen, 1902, Kiev, Russia, d. May 1984. The surname has also been given as Cohn but he is usually referred to as just 'Nudie'. His father was a bootmaker in the Russian army and as a boy he began to learn the trade of a tailor. Around 1911, because of anti-Jewish purges in Russia, he and an elder brother emigrated to the USA, where they initially settled in Brooklyn. Around 1920, he began travelling around the USA, struggling to make a living. He had a brief and financially unrewarding career as a flyweight boxer, appeared as a Hollywood film extra and did tailoring work in the costume department of Warner Brothers. In New York, he even worked on costumes for striptease acts. In the early 40s, in Los Angeles, he became friendly with country singer Tex Williams, and persuaded Williams that he could make stage costumes for him and his band that would attract attention. Williams was delighted with the result, ordered further costumes and widely advertised their designer. The popularity of his suits quickly spread and soon other West Coast artists, especially singing cowboys such as Gene Autry, Roy Rogers and Rex Allen were wearing brightly coloured, rhinestone-studded Nudie creations. Nudie designed a 'free' suit, whose pattern included wagon wheels and cacti, for Porter Wagoner, then a struggling young hopeful. It was a very shrewd investment on Nudie's part. Wagoner, who continued to wear Nudie suits on the *Grand Ole Opry* for a great many years, became Nudie's best and longest-running advert. The attraction soon passed on to other country singers and during the 40s and 50s, most of Nashville's major stars were dressed by Nudie. His first cowboy designs were mainly elaborately decorated western wear, but for the country stars, he designed the clothes for the individual, as he had done with the wagon wheels for Wagoner. Hawkshaw Hawkins' jacket had a large hawk on the back, Ferlin Husky had husky dogs and Jimmy C. Newman had alligators (after his hit 'Alligator Man'). Hank Williams regularly wore Nudie-designed drape suits and was actually buried in one. Nudie also designed the stage costumes of Bill Anderson and his band, and Hank Snow, another long-time flamboyant dresser, regularly wore his rhinestone-studded creations. It was Nudie who created the $10,000 gold lamé tuxedo worn by Elvis Presley and later the flashy suits worn by the Flying Burrito Brothers, which had marijuana leaves embroidered on them, and stage costumes for the Rolling Stones. However, not all of his creations were so brightly coloured, since it was Nudie who was responsible for Johnny Cash's Man in Black image. Nudie obviously became a wealthy man and his own suits usually attracted considerable interest, as did his penchant for jewellery, which often saw him wearing $25,000 worth of gold (he was once described as 'a caricature of an American cowboy drawn by an enraged Russian cartoonist'). He was also noted for his famous white Pontiac convertible. The hood had giant Texas longhorn horn ornaments, while the interior contained patterned hand tool leather, with a silver saddle between the rear seats. There were 14 guns mounted in varying positions, which included Colt revolvers that worked as arm rests and door handles, gear lever and direction indicators and three rifles on the rear boot lid. The interior was decorated with hundreds of silver dollars, the front bumper had chrome quarter horses and the tape player could blast out a recording of a cattle stampede, whilst the horn played Dale Evans singing 'Happy Trails'. It seems that when they were going out together, Nudie's wife not surprisingly used to suggest that they took her car. Naturally, the car was at one point stolen, but the police appear to have had little trouble finding it again. Later there were several other Nudie-designed cars, which over the years have had several owners, including Webb Pierce and Hank Williams Jnr. Nudie died from natural causes in May 1984 but his wife continued to operate their store. Nudie, who was once quoted as saying, 'If Tom Mix got out of his grave and saw my clothes, he'd get back in again', was always proud of his achievements but never forgot the early days of struggle. A reminder was the photograph sent to him by famous American strip artist Lili St. Cyr, and autographed with: 'If I ever wear clothes, they'll be yours', which he proudly displayed in his store. For many years, clothes bearing a label that said 'Nudie's Rodeo Tailors, North Hollywood, California', were very much a status symbol to country artists. Nudie also played mandolin and apparently recorded an album featuring himself on that instrument, but recording data is seemingly not readily available. (In 1974, Manual Cuevas, who had started to work for Nudie in the late 50s, left to form his own Manual's Western Wear in North Hollywood, from which he carried on the traditions of dressing film stars and singers, including Dolly Parton, Marty Stuart and Dwight Yoakam, in the styles that he had learned during his years with Nudie.)

NULL, CECIL

b. 26 April 1927, East War, McDowell County, West Virginia, USA. He played guitar and wrote songs as a boy but actually began his entertaining career in the US Navy in World War II. After discharge, he played as a member of the Pioneer Pals on WOPI Bristol, Tennessee, gave guitar tuition and turned his attention to the autoharp. He moved to WCYB Bristol in 1948, as a member of Cousin Zeke's Band, with whom he recorded. He began to teach autoharp, so effectively that the manufacturers contracted him to work as a consultant and demonstrate the instrument at shows. He also published an instruction book, *Pickin' Style Auto-Harp*. Between 1950 and 1958, he was a member of the Tennessee Serenaders and from 1952, he made recordings. In 1958, he and Semie Moseley created an electrified autoharp that gained Null considerable television exposure as a folk-country crossover. In 1964, he began appearing as a duo with his wife Annette (b. 30 September 1939), who sang, yodelled, played autoharp and also guitar. They subsequently made recordings for Briar, Epic and a gospel instrumental album for Decca Records. They were very popular and worked on various major television shows including *Bobby Lord TV Show* (1965), *Ralph Emery* (1966-68) and from 1967, they appeared regularly on the *Grand Ole Opry*. They never achieved a chart hit, perhaps because, while the country fans liked their music, they were possibly unsure whether they were exactly country or folk. Null wrote numerous songs but his best-known is 'I Forgot More Than You'll Ever Know' (a US country number 1 and pop number 18 for the Davis Sisters in 1953 and since recorded by countless artists, including Jeanne Pruett who charted it again in 1972). In 1964, he penned 'Mother Maybelle', a tribute to his autoharp inspiration, Maybelle Carter.
● ALBUMS: *New Sounds In Folk Music* (Briar 1964)★★★, *Folk Instrumentals* (Jed 1967)★★★, *Instrumental Country Hymns* (Decca 1968)★★.

NUNN, GARY P.

b. Austin, Texas, USA. A singer-songwriter and guitarist who lived and worked around Austin. Nunn and some other musicians started working with the 70s progressive musician Jerry Jeff Walker, and they eventually coalesced in the progressive country group, the Lost Gonzo Band. The high spot of *Viva Terlingua!* in 1973 was when Walker generously allowed Nunn to take the lead vocals on his song about life on the road, 'London Homesick Blues'. It was also recorded by David Allan Coe and became the theme song for the long-running television series *Austin City Limits*. The Lost Gonzo Band worked on four more albums with Jerry Jeff Walker and also recorded under their own name. Nunn himself was married to singer-songwriter Karen Brooks, and their songs 'Couldn't Do Nothin' Right' (Karen) and 'Kara Lee' (Gary) comment on their relationship. Willie Nelson recorded his song 'The Last Thing I Needed The First Thing This Morning'. He works with the Sons Of The Bunkhouse Band and he was reunited with Walker as part of the Gonzo Compadres on *Viva Luckenbach!*, which included his lead vocal on 'What I Like About Texas'.

● ALBUMS: *Nobody But Me* (Turnrow 1980)★★★, *Home With The Armadillo* (Guacamole 1985)★★★, *Border States* (Dixie Frog 1988)★★★, *For Old Times Sake* (AO 1989)★★★, *Under My Hat* (Campfire 1997)★★★.

O'BRIEN, TIM

b. Wheeling, West Virginia, USA. While he was growing up, O'Brien became proficient on guitar, mandolin, fiddle and a guitar-shaped bouzouki and used to sing with his sister Mollie. In 1979 he and the banjo player Pete Wernick formed a bluegrass band, Hot Rize, with O'Brien on lead vocals, mandolin and fiddle. They also performed as their own opening act, as Red Knuckles And The Trailblazers, a western swing band. Hot Rize had run its course by 1984 and O'Brien, after making a solo album, teamed up with his sister again. Kathy Mattea had a US country hit with O'Brien's 'Walk The Way The Wind Blows' and O'Brien also sang on her version of 'The Battle Hymn Of Love'. In 1988 they made their first album together, which included John Prine's 'Unwed Fathers'. Because of a change in record company management, a solo album for RCA was never released and he returned to Sugar Hill Records for a traditional album, *Odd Man In.* He has said of his music: 'I go by own

my own rules and I've made a place for myself that I'm comfortable with. There are lots more of us out there that don't fit in.' In 1996 he released an album of Bob Dylan cover versions.

● ALBUMS: *Guess Who's In Town* (Biscuit City 1979)★★★, *Hard Year Blues* (Flying Fish 1984)★★★, *Odd Man In* (Sugar Hill 1993)★★★, *Oh Boy! Oh Boy!* (Sugar Hill 1994)★★★, *Red On Blonde* (Sugar Hill 1996)★★★; as Hot Rize *Hot Rize* (Flying Fish 1979)★★★, *Radio Boogie* (1981)★★, *In Concert* (Flying Fish 1984)★★★, *Traditional Ties* (Sugar Hill 1985)★★★, *Untold Stories* (Sugar Hill 1987)★★★, *Take It Home* (Sugar Hill 1990)★★★; as Red Knuckles And The Trailblazers *Red Knuckles And The Trailblazers* (Flying Fish 1982)★★★, *Shades Of The Past* (Sugar Hill 1988)★★; as Tim And Mollie O'Brien *Take Me Back* (Sugar Hill 1988)★★★, *Remember Me* (Sugar Hill 1992)★★★, *Away Out On The Mountain* (Sugar Hill 1994)★★★; with the O'Boys *Rock In My Shoes* (Sugar Hill 1995)★★★, *Red On Blonde* (Sugar Hill 1996)★★★.

O'CONNELL, MAURA

b. County Clare, Eire. Folk singer Maura O'Connell began her career working with Mike Hanrahan before becoming a full-time member of Stockton's Wing then De Dannan. However, after that band had enjoyed substantial success with *Star Spangled Molly*, O'Connell relocated to Nashville in 1985 to launch her solo career. She went there because of its reputation for songwriters, and the fact that all the major publishing houses were represented there - increasing the types and styles of songs available to her many times over. On arrival she quickly formed a musical partnership with dobro player Jerry Douglas, who has been a constant companion throughout her solo work. A succession of albums followed, before she joined Rykodisc Records in 1996 for the release of *Stories*. This included material drawn from established and disparate sources such as Shawn Colvin ('Shotgun Down The Avalanche'), Paul Brady (the title track), Hal Ketchum ('Ordinary Day') and Mary-Chapin Carpenter ('Wall Around Your Heart'). There was also a Beatles song, 'If I Fell', to further demonstrate O'Connell's diversity and her move away from a straightforward country or folk heritage. *Wandering Home* marked a return to her Irish folk roots, and saw O'Connell covering a diverse range of standards including 'West Coast Of Clare' and 'Down By The Sally Gardens'.

● ALBUMS: *Just In Time* (Philo 1988)★★★, *Helpless Heart* (Warners 1989)★★★, *A Real Life Story* (Warners 1991)★★★, *Blue Is The Colour Of Hope* (Warners 1992)★★★, *Stories* (Rykodisc 1996)★★★, *Wandering Home* (Rykodisc 1997)★★★★.

O'CONNOR, MARK

b. 4 August 1962, Seattle, Washington, USA. O'Connor is a naturally gifted instrumentalist, who first began to play the guitar at the age of six and won a University of Washington classical/flamenco guitar contest when he was aged 10. A year later, tiring of just playing the guitar, he turned to the fiddle and within weeks was playing it at square dances. Influenced by noted Texas fiddler Benny Thomasson, he played at festivals and contests. By the age of 14, he had already won two National Fiddle Championships, a Grand Masters Fiddle Championship, the National Guitar

Flatpicking Championship and had also produced two albums. After graduation in 1979, he toured extensively on the festival circuits, where he worked with several noted bluegrass musicians. After touring Japan with Dan Crary, he became the guitarist with David Grisman's quintet, where he also worked on a tour with the jazz violinist Stéphane Grappelli. In 1981, while O'Connor was recovering from a broken arm sustained in a skiing accident, Grisman reduced to a quartet and O'Connor became the fiddle player with the Dixie Dregs. He left in 1983 and began to work with many artists including John McKuen, Peter Rowan, Chris Hillman and the legendary Doc Watson. His multi-instrumental ability has seen him much in demand and he has played on countless recordings as a session musician. By the late 80s, his music mixed various genres including bluegrass, rock, jazz and classical. In 1990, he began to follow a more independent career and, writing much of his own material, he began to concentrate more on his own recordings. His collaboration with the cream of country sessionmen on *New Nashville Cats* won him much critical acclaim, and his revival of Carl Perkins' 'Restless', with vocals by Ricky Skaggs, Steve Wariner and Vince Gill, won several CMA Awards. O'Connor then began work on a record of duets with famous violinists from the classical as well as country fields. His flatpicking guitar work has been compared to Doc Watson and many now rate him Nashville's top fiddle player. He is also an accomplished banjoist and in 1983, he won the World Mandolin Championship.

● ALBUMS: *Mark O'Connor Four-Time National Junior Fiddle Champion* (1975)★★★, *Pickin' In The Wind* (1976)★★★, *Texas Jam Session* (1977)★★★, *In Concert* (1977)★★★, *Markology* (Rounder 1980)★★★, *On The Rampage* (Rounder 1980)★★★, with Fred Carpenter *Cuttin' Loose* (1980)★★★, with David Grisman Quintet *Quintet: '80* (Warners 1980)★★★, *Soppin' The Gravy* (Rounder 1981)★★★, *False Dawn* (Rounder 1982)★★★, with Doc and Merle Watson *Doc & Merle Watson Guitar Album* (Flying Fish 1983)★★★, *Meanings Of* (Warners 1986)★★★, *Stones From Which The Arch Was Made* (Warners 1988)★★★, *Elysian Forest* (Warners 1988)★★★, *On The Mark* (Warners 1989)★★★, *The New Nashville Cats* (Warners 1991)★★★★, *Heroes* (Warners 1993)★★★★, *The Fiddle Concerto* (Warners 1995)★★★.

● COMPILATIONS: *The Championship Years* (Country Music Foundation 1990)★★★★.

● VIDEOS: *The Devil Came Back To Georgia* (1993).

O'DANIEL, WILBERT LEE

b. 1890, Malta, Ohio, USA, d. 1969. The family relocated to Kansas, where he grew up and worked for several milling companies. In 1925, he moved to Fort Worth, Texas, to become the sales manager of the Burrus Mill And Elevator Company. A very competent salesman, he soon made the sales of the company's Light Crust Flour increase enormously, an achievement that saw him promoted to general manager of Burrus Mill. In 1930, he believed he could boost sales further by means of a radio programme, although he initially professed that he did not like hillbilly music. Early in 1931, the Light Crust Doughboys, which included both Milton Brown and Bob Wills, began broadcasting, first on KFJZ before moving to the more powerful WBAP. O'Daniel, determined to make the advertising exactly as he wanted it, began to carry out all announcing duties himself. He wrote promotional ditties and songs, arranged tours for the band and in 1932, the band recorded for RCA-Victor. Eventually differences of opinion with O'Daniel saw both Brown and Wills leave to pursue their own careers. In 1935, when O'Daniel was fired by Burrus Mill (probably for promoting himself more than his employers), he formed his own company and began to market Hillbilly Flour. He also had political aspirations and to assist in this and to advertise his product, he formed his band, the Hillbilly Boys, which included his sons Pat and Mike, singer/yodeller Leon Huff and Kitty Williamson (aka Texas Rose). The band proved very popular and made recordings, which included material that O'Daniel wrote. It also proved a useful and popular attraction during his successful 1938 campaign for the office of State governor. He was re-elected in 1940 and in 1941, on the death of the State senator, in a campaign that was far from pleasant, he was elected to the Senate (the person he beat for the office was Lyndon Baines Johnson, who later served as President from 1963 to 1969). At the end of his term, O'Daniel retired and an attempted comeback in 1956 failed miserably. During his career, he composed several songs that have remained popular in country music including 'Beautiful Texas' and 'Put Me In Your Pocket'.

O'DAY, MOLLY

b. LaVerne Lois Williamson, 9 July 1923, McVeigh, Pike County, Kentucky, USA, d. 5 December 1987. O'Day learned several instruments and first sang with her brother Cecil 'Skeets' Williamson on WCHS Charleston in 1939, initially using the name Mountain Fern but soon changing to Dixie Lee. In 1940, she joined the Forty Niners, a group led by singer/guitarist Leonard (Lynn) Davis (b. 15 December 1914, Paintsville, Kentucky, USA), whom she married in April 1941. In 1942, she changed her stage name to Molly O'Day and together with Davis, worked on a variety of radio stations, including WHAS Louisville and WNOX Knoxville. Between 1946 and 1951, with their band the Cumberland Mountain Folks, they recorded almost 40 sides for Columbia. These included such heart-rending numbers as 'The Drunken Driver' and 'Don't Sell Daddy Any More Whiskey'. She was the first artist to record Hank Williams' songs ('When God Comes To Gather His Jewels' and 'Six More Miles') after hearing Williams in 1942 singing 'Tramp On The Street', which also became one her most requested numbers. In the early 50s, she and her husband turned to religious work (Davis later becoming an evangelist), but her singing was slowed by tuberculosis, which led to the removal of part of a lung, although they later recorded some religious material for Rem and GRS. Throughout the 60s and 70s, they did limited radio work centred around their home in Huntington, West Virginia. O'Day's individual emotional style prompted some to dub her 'the female Hank Williams or Roy Acuff'; she died of cancer in 1987.

● ALBUMS: *Hymns For The Country Folks* (Audio Lab 1960)★★★, *Molly O'Day Sings Again* (1961)★★★, *The Unforgettable Molly O'Day* (Harmony1963)★★★, *The Living Legend Of Country Music* (Starday 1966)★★★★, *A Sacred Selection* (1975)★★★, *Skeets Williamson & Molly O'Day* (1975)★★★.

● COMPILATIONS: *Molly O'Day Radio Favorites* (1981)★★★, *The Soul Of Molly O'Day Volume 1* (Old Homestead 1983)★★★, *The Soul Of Molly O'Day Volume 2*

(Old Homestead 1984)★★★, *In Memory* (Old Homestead 1990)★★★, *Molly O'Day And The Cumberland Mountain Folks* (Bear Family 1992)★★★★.

O'DELL, KENNY

b. Kenneth Gist, Jnr., c.early 40s, Oklahoma, USA. O'Dell began writing songs in his early teens and after completing his education, he formed his own Mar-Kay record label in California. In the early 60s, he recorded his own 'Old Time Love' but it failed to chart. After working for a time with Duane Eddy, he formed a group, Guys And Dolls, with which he toured for some five years. In 1966, he wrote and recorded 'Beautiful People', which became a smash hit in Atlanta. Liberty Records told Bobby Vee he could record a better version and have a national hit; Vee later said he should never have listened to them, but in spite of split sales, both versions made the US Top 40. After further unsuccessful attempts at chart success, he moved to Nashville in 1969, where he managed Bobby Goldsboro's publishing company. He continued with his songwriting, sometimes with Larry Henley and in 1972, after producer Billy Sherrill had heard O'Dell's own recording, Sandy Posey charted with their song 'Why Don't We Go Somewhere And Love'. Sherrill became interested in O'Dell's songs and had Charlie Rich record 'I Take It On Home'. In 1973, Rich had a smash country and pop hit with 'Behind Closed Doors', which won O'Dell the CMA's *Song Of The Year* award (he actually played guitar on Rich's recording). In the latter half of the 70s, he tried to relaunch his singing career with Capricorn. He had a Top 10 country hit with 'Let's Shake Hands And Come Out Lovin'' in 1978 but 'Medicine Woman' in 1979 has so far proved to be his last country hit. He will always be remembered for, and was infinitely more successful with, his writing rather than his singing. Many artists have benefited by recording his songs, including Anthony Armstrong Jones ('I've Got Mine'), Tanya Tucker ('Lizzie And The Rainman'), both Billie Jo Spears (1977) and the Bellamy Brothers & Forrester Sisters (1986) ('Too Much Is Not Enough'), Dottie West ('When It's Just You And Me'), the Judds ('Mama He's Crazy') and many others.
● ALBUMS: *Beautiful People* (Vegas 1968)★★★, *Kenny O'Dell* (Capricorn 1973)★★★, *Let's Shake Hands And Come Out Lovin'* (Capricorn 1978)★★.

O'DONNELL, DANIEL

b. 12 December, 1961, Kincasslagh, Co. Donegal, Eire. O'Donnell is without doubt the biggest-selling act in history in the musical genre known as 'Country 'n' Irish'. He is a clean-cut and gimmick-free vocalist with leanings towards sentimental MOR material. He first emerged in Britain in 1985, although he was already popular in Ireland. His first attempts at singing came when he worked as a backing vocalist in the band that backed his sister, folk/country singer Margo O'Donnell (see Margo), during the early 80s, and his popularity among the female audiences increased at high speed. After a handful of early recordings (later released after he came to fame as 'The Boy From Donegal'), he signed to Michael Clerkin's Ritz Records, an Irish label based in London, and *Two Sides Of Daniel O'Donnell* was released in 1985. It was promoted by the first in a continuing series of nationwide UK tours that attracted capacity audiences (largely composed of fans of artists such as the late

Jim Reeves - O'Donnell usually features in his stage show a medley of songs connected with Reeves). In 1986 came a second O'Donnell release, *I Need You*, which in March 1987 was his first to reach the UK country album charts. That year's album *Don't Forget To Remember* (featuring a cover version of the hit by the Bee Gees as its title track) was O'Donnell's first to enter the UK country chart at number 1, a feat he has repeated with his five subsequent original albums, although the next one to be released in chronological terms, *The Boy From Donegal*, consisted mainly of material recorded in 1984 before he signed to Ritz, and was released in the UK by Prism Leisure. In 1988, Ritz licensed O'Donnell's next release, *From The Heart*, to Telstar Records, a television marketing company, and as well as entering the UK country chart at number 1, the album also reached the UK pop album chart in the autumn of that year, while a video, *Daniel O'Donnell Live In Concert*, was released. 1989 brought *Thoughts Of Home*, an album and video that were both heavily advertised on television by Telstar - the album made the Top 40 of the pop chart and the video became O'Donnell's first to reach the UK Music Video chart; once again, all his subsequent video releases have featured in the latter chart, which the original *Live In Concert* also entered in the wake of *Thoughts From Home*. By 1990, O'Donnell was back with an album, *Favourites*, and a companion video, *TV Show Favourites*, which was composed of material filmed for a hugely successful Irish television series. However, of far greater interest in 1990 was the news that he was making an album in Nashville with noted producer Allen Reynolds (who had enjoyed major success with Don Williams, Crystal Gayle, Kathy Mattea and latterly, Garth Brooks) - the first since O'Donnell's breakthrough that he had recorded with his original producer John Ryan. Released in late 1990, *The Last Waltz* was somewhat closer to genuine country music than its predecessors, and once again entered the UK country album charts at the top and charted strongly in the UK pop equivalent. During 1991, it was decided that nearly all of O'Donnell's album catalogue was MOR rather than country, and at a stroke, the UK country album chart - in which O'Donnell usually occupied the majority of the Top 10 places - hardly featured his albums at all. This produced an avalanche of complaints (including one from a nun) and public demonstrations urging that the decision be reversed and his albums be reinstated in the country list, which eventually occurred in late 1991. Another release, *The Very Best Of Daniel O'Donnell*, a compilation composed partly of previously released items along with some newly recorded material, continued O'Donnell's remarkable success story. In musical terms, what O'Donnell records is unadventurous, yet his immense popularity in the UK and Eire makes it clear that his output has been brilliantly targeted. As yet, he has not released an album in the USA, although imported albums have sold prodigiously in areas with populations of Irish extraction, and several concert appearances, including one at New York's Carnegie Hall in 1991, have been commercial triumphs. *Songs Of Inspiration* and *I Believe*, his most recent albums, were lacklustre gospel collections.
● ALBUMS: *Two Sides Of Daniel O'Donnell* (Ritz 1985)★★★, *I Need You* (Ritz 1986)★★★, *Don't Forget To Remember* (Ritz 1987)★★★, *The Boy From Donegal* 1984 recording (Ritz 1987)★★★, *From The Heart* (Telstar 1988)★★★, *Thoughts From Home* (Telstar 1989)★★★, *Favourites* (Ritz 1990)★★★,

The Last Waltz (Ritz 1990)★★★, *Follow Your Dream* (Ritz 1992)★★★, *Especially For You* (Ritz 1994)★★★, with Mary Duff *Timeless* (Ritz 1996)★★★, *Songs Of Inspiration* (Ritz 1996)★★, *I Believe* (Ritz 1997)★★★.
● COMPILATIONS: *The Very Best Of Daniel O'Donnell* (Ritz 1991)★★★★, *Irish Collection* (Ritz 1996)★★★.
● VIDEOS: *Live In Concert* (Ritz 1988), *Thoughts Of Home* (Telstar Video 1989), *TV Show Favourites* (Ritz 1990), *An Evening With Daniel O'Donnell* (Ritz 1990), *Follow Your Dream* (Ritz 1992), *And Friends Live* (Ritz 1993), *Just For You* (Ritz 1994), *Christmas With Daniel O'Donnell* (Ritz 1996).

O'GWYNN, JAMES

b. James Leroy O'Gwynn, 26 January 1928, Winchester, Mississippi, USA. He grew up on a farm in Hattiesburg, Mississippi, and was taught to play guitar by his mother. After completing his education, he spent four years in the US Marines, during which time, greatly influenced by the music of Hank Williams and Jimmie Rodgers, he decided to seek a singing career. In 1954, he became a cast member of Bif Collie's *Houston Jamboree*, which at the time also included George Jones. In 1956, he made his first recordings for Starday and also relocated to Shreveport to join the *Louisiana Hayride*. He gained his first chart entries in 1958, with two self-penned numbers on the D label, 'Talk To Me Lonesome Heart' (a number 16) and 'Blue Memories' (a number 28). In 1959, he moved to Mercury Records and, working under producer Shelby Singleton, he achieved further hits in 1959 with two co-written numbers, 'How Can I Think Of Tomorrow' and 'Easy Money'. He left the *Hayride*, moved to Nashville in 1961, and regularly played on the *Grand Ole Opry* until 1963. In 1961, he charted with 'House Of Blue Lovers' and in 1962, he gained his final chart entry 'My Name Is Mud', which peaked at number 7. During the 60s, he made further recordings for United Artists Records, Hickory and Stop and, in 1971, for Plantation, where he renewed his association with Singleton but achieved no major successes. O'Gwynn, known affectionately as the Smiling Irishman Of Country Music, finally retired to Dardanelle, Arkansas, where, apart from some casual appearances locally, he tended to withdraw from the music scene. In the 80s, his fan club was still active and Cattle Records of Germany issued three albums of recordings - some made for various labels and some live *Hayride* appearances.
● ALBUMS: *Heartaches And Memories* (Mercury/Wing 1964)★★★, *Country Dance Time* (Plantation 1978)★★★.
● COMPILATIONS: *The Best Of James O'Gwynn* (Mercury 1962)★★★★, *James O'Gwynn's Greatest Hits* (Plantation 1971)★★★★, *Star Of The Louisiana Hayride Volumes 1 & 2* German release, 50s recordings (Cattle 1982)★★★, *The Louisiana Hayride Presents James O'Gwynn* (Cattle 1985)★★★.

O'HARA, JAMIE

b. 8 August 1950, Toledo, Ohio, USA. The 90s country singer Jamie O'Hara had already enjoyed a certain amount of success with the O'Kanes with Kieran Kane when the duo split up in 1989. Prior to that he had been a halfback footballer, but had to retire following a knee injury. He went to Nashville and became a writer for Tree Publishing. O'Hara wrote 'Wandering Eyes' and 'Older Women' for Ronnie

McDowell and 'For Reasons I've Forgotten' for Trisha Yearwood. His own version is included on *Rise Above It*, which was produced by Garth Fundis. It also includes '50,000 Names', a song about the wall in Washington listing those who died in Vietnam. O'Hara wrote five songs on Shelby Lynne's *Temptation*.
● ALBUMS: *Rise Above It* (RCA 1994)★★★.

O'KANES

Jamie O'Hara (b. 8 August 1950, Toledo, Ohio, USA) planned to be a professional American footballer until knee injuries forced him to change his mind. He says, 'My father gave me a guitar as a gift. Two years later, I was in Nashville. That either shows a lot of confidence, a lot of arrogance or a lot of stupidity.' He wrote 'Grandpa (Tell Me 'Bout The Good Old Days)' for the Judds and befriended another songwriter, Kieran Kane. Kane (b. Queens, New York, USA) had worked with rock acts in Los Angeles in the early 70s and then moved to Nashville. He wrote 'Gonna Have A Party' for Alabama. O'Hara and Kane became friends, sharing their frustration at not having songs recorded, and they began collaborating on material. They recorded demos in Kane's attic studio, which Columbia Records considered good enough to release on their own account. The acoustic recordings (two guitars, bass, fiddle, mandolin, accordion, drums) made a stunning album debut in 1987. Their harmonies were reminiscent of a mellow version of the Louvin Brothers. They made the US country Top 10 with their first single, 'Oh Darlin' (Why Don't You Care For Me No More)', and then topped the chart with 'Can't Stop My Heart From Loving You'. Although their album was quiet and low-key, their rousing shows won them further acclaim. They were among the 'new traditionalists' in country music, but they stopped performing when Columbia failed to renew their recording contract. Their final chart entry was 'Rocky Road' from *Tired Of The Runnin'*. Following the recording of a third album, Kane and O'Hara split up and concentrated on solo careers.
● ALBUMS: *The O'Kanes* (Columbia 1987)★★★, *Tired Of The Runnin'* (Columbia 1988)★★★, *Imagine That* (Columbia 1990)★★.

OAK RIDGE BOYS

Originally called the Country Cut-Ups, the Oak Ridge Boys were formed in 1942 in Knoxville, Tennessee. They often performed at the atomic energy plant in Oak Ridge, where, in the midst of a war, their optimistic gospel songs were welcomed, and hence they were renamed the Oak Ridge Quartet. They recorded their first records in 1947 and there were many changes in personnel, although Wally Fowler (b. c.1916, d. 3 June 1994, Tennessee, USA) remained its leader. The group disbanded in 1956, only to emerge as the New Oak Ridge Quartet with a new leader, Smitty Gatlin. Handled by Fowler, they recorded their first records in 1947, moving their base to Nashville, but disbanded in 1956. A year later, they re-formed in a revised line-up organized by an original member, Smitty Gatlin. They became full-time professionals in 1961 and the album on which they changed from the Oak Ridge Quartet to the Oak Ridge Boys included strings and horns, an unusual move for a gospel group. William Lee Golden (b. 12 January 1939, near Brewton, Alabama, USA), who had admired the group since he saw them as an adolescent, became their baritone in 1964. When

Gatlin decided to become a full-time minister, Golden recommended Duane David Allen (b. 29 April 1943, Taylortown, USA), who became the group's lead vocalist in 1966. They established themselves as the best-loved white gospel group in the USA and won numerous awards and Grammys. Further changes came in 1972 with bass singer Richard Anthony Sterban (b. 24 April 1943, Camden, New Jersey, USA) and in 1973 with tenor Joseph Sloan Bonsall (b. 18 May 1948, Philadelphia, Pennsylvania, USA) becoming part of the group. Although most gospel fans enjoyed their high-energy, criss-crossing performances, they were criticized for adding a rock 'n' roll drummer to their band. They recorded a single, 'Praise The Lord And Pass The Soup', with Johnny Cash and the Carter Family in 1973. In 1975, they switched to country music, but their first secular single, 'Family Reunion', only reached number 83 in the US country charts. Their total income fell to $75,000 in 1975 and they made a loss in 1976. Columbia Records dropped them, ironically at the same time as they were accompanying their labelmate, Paul Simon, on 'Slip Slidin' Away', which featured sentiments diametrically opposite to gospel music. They opened for Johnny Cash in Las Vegas, played the USSR with Roy Clark, and had a major country hit with 'Y'All Come Back Saloon.' They topped the US country charts with 'I'll Be True To You' (a death disc), the classic 'Leavin' Louisiana In The Broad Daylight' and 'Trying To Love Two Women'. In 1981 they made number 5 on the US pop charts with 'Elvira' and followed it with 'Bobbie Sue' (number 12). Ronald Reagan, in a presidential address, said: 'If the Oak Ridge Boys win any more gold, they'll have more gold in their records than we have in Fort Knox.' Further country hits followed with 'American Made', 'Love Song', 'I Guess It Never Hurts To Hurt Sometime' (written by Randy Vanwarmer), 'Make My Life With You' and 'Come On In (You Did The Best You Could)'. In award ceremonies, they ousted the Statler Brothers as the top country vocal group, and their band has won awards in its own right. Golden, who stopped cutting his hair in 1979, became a mountain man, going bear hunting and sleeping in a teepee. When he was dismissed in 1986 for 'continuing musical and personal differences', he filed a $40 million suit, which was settled out of court. He released a solo album, *American Vagabond*, also in 1986, and has since formed a family group called the Goldens. His replacement was their rhythm guitarist, Steve Sanders (b. 17 September 1941, Richmond, Georgia, USA), formerly a child gospel performer and Faye Dunaway's son in the film *Hurry Sundown*. The Oak Ridge Boys continue with their philosophy to 'Keep it happy, keep it exciting', and do nothing that might tarnish their image. They turn down beer commercials and only sing positive songs. To quote Joe Bonsall, 'We're just an old gospel group with a rock 'n' roll band playing country music.' In 1996 Golden returned to the band when they signed to A&M Records.

● ALBUMS: *The Oak Ridge Boys Quartet* (Cadence 1959)★★★, *Wally Fowler's All Nite Singing Gospel Concert Featuring The Oak Ridge Quartet* (1960)★★, *The Oak Ridge Boys With The Sounds Of Nashville* (Warners 1962)★★★, *Folk Minded Spirituals For Spiritual Minded Folk* (Warners 1962)★★★, *The Oak Ridge Quartet In Concert* (Cumberland 1963)★★, *The Oak Ridge Boys Sing For You* (Skylite 1964)★★★, *The Oak Ridge Quartet Sing And Shout* (Skylite 1964)★★★, *I Wouldn't Take Nothing For My Journey Now*

(Skylite 1965)★★★, *At Their Best* (United Artists 1966)★★★★, *Solid Gospel Sound Of The Oak Ridge Quartet* (Skylite 1966)★★★, with the Harvesters *Together* (Canaan 1966)★★★, *The Oak Ridge Quartet Sings River Of Love* (Skylite 1967)★★★, *International* (Heartwarming 1971)★★★, *The Light* (Heartwarming 1972)★★★, *Hymns* (1973)★★★, *Street Gospel* (1973)★★★, *The Oak Ridge Boys* (Columbia 1974)★★★, *Super Gospel - Four Sides Of Gospel Excitement Heartwarming* (1974)★★, *Sky High* (Columbia 1975)★★★, *Old Fashioned, Down Home, Handclappin' Footstompin', Southern Style, Gospel Quartet Music* (Columbia 1976)★★★, *Y'All Come Back Saloon* (ABC 1977)★★★, *Live* (ABC 1977)★★, *Room Service* (ABC 1978)★★★, *The Oak Ridge Boys Have Arrived* (1979)★★★, *Together* (MCA 1980)★★★, *Fancy Free* (MCA 1981)★★★, *Bobbie Sue* (MCA 1982)★★★, *Christmas* (MCA 1982)★★, *American Made* (MCA 1983)★★★, *The Oak Ridge Boys Deliver* (MCA 1983)★★★, *Friendship* (MCA 1983)★★★, *Seasons* (MCA 1985)★★★, *Step On Out* (MCA 1985)★★★, *Where The Fast Lane Ends* (MCA 1986)★★, *Christmas Again* (MCA 1986)★★, *Monongahela* (MCA 1987)★★, *New Horizons* (MCA 1988)★★★, *American Dreams* (MCA 1989)★★★, *Unstoppable* (MCA 1991)★★★, *The Long Haul* (MCA 1992)★★★.

● COMPILATIONS: *The Sensational Oak Ridge Boys From Nashville, Tennessee* (Starday 1965)★★★, *Greatest Hits, Vol. 1* (MCA 1980)★★★★, *Greatest Hits, Vol. 2* (MCA 1984)★★★, *Greatest Hits, Vol. 3* (MCA 1989)★★★, *The Collection* (MCA 1992)★★★.

● FURTHER READING: *The Oak Ridge Boys - Our Story*, with Ellis Winder and Walter Carter.

ODELL, MAC

b. Odell McLeod, 31 May 1916, Roanoke, Alabama, USA. Odell, who sang, wrote songs and played harmonica, guitar and mandolin equally well, was a popular radio entertainer. He grew up listening to early country stars such as Jimmie Rodgers, the Skillet Lickers and especially the harmonica wizard Deford Bailey. He first worked with Slim Bassett and hoboed for a time around several states before they gained a regular show, as Mac And Slim in New Orleans, in 1935. After he married, he worked with his wife as Mac And Little Addie. They played WJJD Chicago's *Supper Time Frolics* for some time but their career was interrupted by World War II. Odell worked in a Michigan factory but continued to write songs as a staff writer for Roy Acuff (he wrote Acuff's popular 'Radio Station SAVED' and 'That Glory Bound Train'). After the war, he and his wife resumed their career on WLAC Nashville, remaining there until 1957. During this time he did daily shows with Addie and also appeared solo. He recorded for Mercury Records in 1949 but in 1952, he joined King. Many of his recordings were self-penned numbers, with the vast majority being of a gospel nature. These included 'Thirty Pieces Of Silver' (popularized by Wilma Lee Cooper) and 'From The Manger To The Cross', both of which have become much-recorded country standards. In 1957, he relocated to Benton Harbor, Michigan, where for some years, he neglected music to run Odell's Signs, until a 1974 heart attack forced him to give up sign writing. In the late 70s, he was persuaded to make further recordings for Folk Variety of Germany, who also released some of his earlier material. In 1985, he and Addie made a tour of Holland with the popular gospel singing Dutch duo, A.G. And Kate. In the late 80s, he

was entertaining locally with three old friends as the Silver Threads. Odell also wrote 'Purple Robe', 'The Stone Was Rolled Away' and the Flatt And Scruggs hit 'Cora Is Gone'.
● ALBUMS: *Hymns For The Country Folks* (Audio Lab 1961)★★★, *Be On Time* (Folk Variety 1977)★★★, *Wild Rose Of The Mountain* (Folk Variety 1978)★★★, *Seven Seven Nashville Session* (Folk Variety 1978)★★★, *Austin, Texas Git Together* (Folk Variety 1981)★★★, *Early Radio* (Old Homestead 1981)★★★.

OLD AND IN THE WAY

Formed in San Francisco, California, USA, Old And In The Way were active between 1973 and 1976. Founders Peter Rowan (lead vocals, guitar), David Grisman (mandolin, vocals), Richard Greene (violin, vocals) and John Kahn (bass) were previously members of superior bluegrass ensemble Muleskinner. The similarly styled Old And In The Way was buoyed by the inclusion of the Grateful Dead's Jerry Garcia (banjo, vocals). Vassar Clements replaced Greene prior to *Old And In The Way*, which showcased the group's informal dexterity. As well as traditional material, the set featured a version of the Rolling Stones' 'Wild Horses' and a Rowan original, 'Panama Red', also recorded by the New Riders Of The Purple Sage. Garcia was later replaced by Bill Keith, another ex-member of Muleskinner, but commitments to contemporary projects brought Old And In The Way to an end. Garcia, Grisman and Greene were later reunited in the Great American String Band.
● ALBUMS: *Old And In The Way* (Round 1975)★★★.

ORBISON, ROY

b. 23 April 1936, Vernon, Texas, USA, d. 6 December 1988, Madison, Tennessee, USA. Critical acclaim came too late for one of the leading singers of the 60s. He became the master of the epic ballad of doom-laden despair, possessing a voice of remarkable range and power, and often finding it more comfortable to stay in the high register. The former reluctant rockabilly singer, who worked with Norman Petty and Sam Phillips in the 50s, moved to Nashville and became a staff writer for Acuff-Rose Music. He used his royalties from the success of 'Claudette', recorded by the Everly Brothers, and written for his first wife, to buy himself out of his contract with Sun Records, and signed with the small Monument label. Although his main intention was to be a songwriter, Orbison found himself glancing the US chart with 'Up Town' in 1960. A few months later, his song 'Only The Lonely' was rejected by Elvis Presley and the Everly Brothers, and Orbison decided to record it himself. The result was a sensation: the song topped the UK charts and narrowly missed the top spot in the USA. The trite opening of 'dum dum dum dummy doo wah, yea yea yea yea yeah', leads into one of the most distinctive pop songs ever recorded. It climaxes with a glass-shattering falsetto, and is destined to remain a modern classic.

The shy and quiet-spoken Orbison donned a pair of dark-tinted glasses to cover up his chronic astigmatism, although early publicity photos had already sneaked out. Over the next five years he enjoyed unprecedented success in Britain and America, repeating his formula with further stylish but melancholy ballads, including 'Blue Angel', 'Running Scared', 'Crying', 'Dream Baby', 'Blue Bayou' and 'In Dreams'. Even during the takeover of America by the Beatles

(of whom he became a good friend), Orbison was one of the few American artists to retain his ground commercially. During the Beatles' peak chart year he had two UK number 1 singles, the powerful 'It's Over' and the hypnotic 'Oh Pretty Woman'. The latter has an incredibly simple instrumental introduction with acoustic guitar and snare drum, and it is recognized today by millions, particularly following its use in the blockbuster film *Pretty Woman*. Orbison had the advantage of crafting his own songs to suit his voice and temperament, yet although he continued to have hits throughout the 60s, none except 'It's Too Soon To Know' equalled his former heights; he regularly toured Britain, which he regarded as his second home. He experienced appalling tragedy when, in 1966, his wife Claudette was killed as she fell from the back of his motorcycle, and in 1968, a fire destroyed his home, also taking the lives of his two sons. In 1967 he starred as a singing cowboy in *The Fastest Guitar Alive*, but demonstrated that he was no actor. By the end of the decade Orbison's musical direction had faltered and he resorted to writing average MOR songs such as the unremarkable 'Penny Arcade'. The 70s were barren times for his career, although a 1976 compilation topped the UK charts. By the end of the decade he underwent open-heart surgery. He bounced back in 1980, winning a Grammy for his duet with Emmylou Harris on 'That Lovin' You Feelin' Again' from the film *Roadie*, and David Lynch used 'In Dreams' to haunting effect in his chilling film *Blue Velvet* in 1986. The following year Orbison was inducted into the Rock 'n' Roll Hall of Fame; at the ceremony he sang 'Oh Pretty Woman' with Bruce Springsteen. With Orbison once again in favour, Virgin Records signed him, and he recorded an album of his old songs using today's hi-tech production techniques. The result was predictably disappointing; it was the sound and production of the classics that had made them great. The video *A Black And White Night* showed Orbison being courted by numerous stars, including Springsteen, Tom Waits and Elvis Costello. This high profile led him to join George Harrison, Bob Dylan, Tom Petty and Jeff Lynne as the Traveling Wilburys. Their splendid debut album owed much to Orbison's major input. Less than a month after its critically acclaimed release, Orbison suffered a fatal heart attack in Nashville. The posthumously released *Mystery Girl* in 1989 was the most successful album of his entire career, and not merely as a result of morbid sympathy. The record contained a collection of songs that indicated a man feeling happy and relaxed; his voice had never sounded better. The uplifting 'You Got It' and the mellow 'She's A Mystery To Me' were impressive epitaphs to the legendary Big 'O'.
● ALBUMS: *Lonely And Blue* (Monument 1961)★★, *Exciting Sounds Of Roy Orbison (Roy Orbison At The Rockhouse)* (Sun 1961)★★, *Crying* (Monument 1962)★★★, *In Dreams* (Monument 1963)★★★, *Oh Pretty Woman* (1964)★★★★, *Early Orbison* (Monument 1964)★★, *There Is Only One Roy Orbison* (MGM 1965)★★, *Orbisongs* (Monument 1965)★★, *The Orbison Way* (MGM 1965)★★, *The Classic Roy Orbison* (MGM 1966)★★, *Roy Orbison Sings Don Gibson* (MGM 1966)★★★, *Cry Softly, Lonely One* (MGM 1967)★★, *The Fastest Guitar Alive* (MGM 1968)★, *Roy Orbison's Many Moods* (MGM 1969)★★, *The Big O* (MGM 1970)★★, *Hank Williams: The Roy Orbison Way* (MGM 1970)★★, *Roy Orbison Sings* (MGM 1972)★★, *Memphis* (MGM 1972)★★, *Milestones* (MGM 1973)★★, *I'm Still In Love With You* (Mercury 1975)★★,

Regeneration (Monument 1976)★★, *Laminar Flow* (Asylum 1979)★★, with Jerry Lee Lewis, Johnny Cash, Carl Perkins *The Class Of '55* (1986)★★★, *Mystery Girl* (Virgin 1989)★★★★, *Rare Orbison* (Monument 1989)★★★, *A Black And White Night Live* (Virgin 1989)★★, *King Of Hearts* (Virgin 1992)★★★★.

● COMPILATIONS: *Roy Orbison's Greatest Hits* (Monument 1962)★★★★, *More Of Roy Orbison's Greatest Hits* (Monument 1964)★★★, *The Very Best Of Roy Orbison* (Monument 1965)★★★★, *The Great Songs Of Roy Orbison* (Monument 1970)★★★★, *All-Time Greatest Hits Of Roy Orbison, Volumes 1 & 2* (Monument 1976)★★★, *Golden Days* (Monument 1981)★★★, *My Spell On You* (Hits Unlimited 1982)★★★, *Big O Country* (Decca 1983)★★, *Problem Child* (Zu Zazz 1984)★★, *In Dreams: The Greatest Hits* (Virgin 1987)★★★★, *The Legendary Roy Orbison* (Sony 1988)★★★, *For The Lonely: A Roy Orbison Anthology 1956-1965* (Rhino 1988)★★★★, *The Classic Roy Orbison (1965-1968)* (Rhino 1989)★★★, *Sun Years* (Rhino 1989)★★★★, *Our Love Song* (Monument 1989)★★★, *Singles Collection* (Polygram 1989)★★★, *The Sun Years 1956-58* (Bear Family 1989)★★★, *The Legendary Roy Orbison* (Columbia 1990)★★★★, *Best Loved Moments* (1993)★★★, *The Gold Collection* (Tristar 1996)★★★, *The Very Best Of Roy Orbison* (Virgin 1996)★★★★.

● FURTHER READING: *Dark Star*, Ellis Amburn. *Only The Lonely*, Alan Clayson.

● FILMS: *The Fastest Guitar Alive* (1966).

ORRALL, ROBERT ELLIS

In the early 80s the US country singer Robert Ellis Orrall worked with Carlene Carter and then moved to Nashville. He wrote country hits for Mason Dixon ('When Karen Comes Around') and Shenandoah ('Next To Me, Next To You'). His album, *Flying Colours*, has a similar pop/country mix to Dr. Hook's records.

● ALBUMS: *Flying Colours* (RCA 1993)★★★.

OSBORNE BROTHERS

Bobby Van (b. 7 December 1931; mandolin, vocals) and Sonny (b. 29 October 1937, both at Hyden, Kentucky, USA; banjo, vocals) formed this talented bluegrass duo. Bobby had played with the Lonesome Pine Fiddlers in 1949 and in 1951, they recorded as a duo with Jimmy Martin. During Bobby's military service in 1952, Sonny, though barely 15 years old, was playing and appearing on the *Grand Ole Opry* with Bill Monroe. They were reunited in 1953, appeared on WROL Knoxville and made further recordings with Martin. From 1956-59, they played the WWVA *Wheeling Jamboree* and, recording with Red Allen, they had a 1958 hit on MGM with 'Once More'. In 1963 they joined the *Opry* and after changing to the Decca label had several country chart successes, including 'Rocky Top'. Never afraid to modernize their bluegrass (Sonny actually once stated that he did not care too much for the genre), they added other musicians and used electrified instruments including a steel guitar, piano and drums, which caused some traditionalists to criticize their work. In spite of the instrumental innovations, their unique harmonies saw them readily accepted and they survived the competition of rock and pop music much better than some of the other bluegrass groups. They toured with major stars including Conway Twitty and Merle Haggard and also played non-country venues such as nightclubs and even a concert at the White House. In the mid-70s. they began recording for the new CMH label and later recorded several albums, including one with Mac Wiseman with whom they charted 'Shackles And Chains' in 1979. They have continued recording and performing throughout the 80s and 90s.

● ALBUMS: with Red Allen *Country Pickin' & Hillside Singin'* (MGM 1959)★★★, *Bluegrass Music* (MGM 1962)★★★, *Bluegrass Instrumentals* (MGM 1962)★★★, *Cuttin' Grass* (MGM 1963)★★★, *Voices In Bluegrass* (Decca 1965)★★★, *Up This Hill And Down* (1966)★★★, *Modern Sounds Of Bluegrass* (Decca 1967)★★★, *Yesterday, Today & The Osborne Brothers* (Decca 1968)★★★, *Favorite Hymns By The Osborne Brothers* (Decca 1969)★★★, *Up To Date & Down To Earth* (Decca 1969)★★★, *Ru-Beeee* (Decca 1970)★★, *The Osborne Brothers* (Decca 1971)★★★, *Country Roads* (Decca 1971)★★★, *Georgia Pinewoods* (Decca 1971)★★★, *Bobby & Sonny* (Decca 1972)★★★, *Bluegrass Express* (Decca 1973)★★★, *Midnight Flyer* (Decca 1973)★★★, *Fastest Grass Alive* (Decca 1974)★★★, *Pickin' Grass And Singin' Country* (Decca 1975)★★★, *Number One* (CMH 1976)★★★, *From Rocky Top To Muddy Bottom* (CMH 1977)★★★, *Bluegrass Collection* (CMH 1978)★★★, with Mac Wiseman *Essential Bluegrass Album* (CMH 1979)★★★★, with Buddy Spicher *Bluegrass Concerto* (CMH 1979)★★★, *I Can Hear Kentucky Calling Me* (CMH 1980)★★★, *Bluegrass Spectacular* (CMH 1982)★★★, *Bluegrass Gold* (CMH 1982)★★★, *Some Things I Want To Sing About* (Sugar Hill 1985)★★★, *Once More Volumes 1 & 2* (Sugar Hill 1986)★★★, *Favorite Memories* (Sugar Hill 1987)★★★, *Singing, Shouting Praises* (Sugar Hill 1988)★★★, *Hillbilly Fever* (CMH 1991)★★★.
Solo: Bobby Osborne *Bobby Osborne & His Mandolin* (CMH 1981)★★★. Sonny Osborne *Early Recordings Volumes 1, 2,.3* (1979)★★★, *Sonny Osborne & His Sunny Mountain Boys* (70s), *Songs Of Bluegrass, Five String In Hi-Fi*.

● COMPILATIONS: with Allen *The Osborne Brothers & Red Allen* (Rounder 1977)★★★, with Mac Wiseman *The Essential Bluegrass AIbum* (CMH 1979)★★★★, *Bluegrass 1956-1968* 4-CD box set (Bear Family 1995)★★★★, *Bluegrass 1968-1974* 4-CD box set (Bear Family 1995)★★★★,

OSBORNE, JIMMIE

b. James Osborne Jnr., 8 April 1923, Winchester, Kentucky, USA, d. 26 December 1957. After someone gave him a guitar, Osborne decided to be a singer and at 16 he was appearing regularly on WLAP Lexington. World War II disrupted his plans and, for a time, he entertained only in the evenings and weekends, while working days in a factory. After the war, he performed on several stations including WLAP, before arriving at KWKH Shreveport in 1947. His vocal work there with the Bailes Brothers and on the *Louisiana Hayride* led to him recording for King. In 1948, he scored a number 10 country hit with his first release, 'My Heart Echoes'. He returned to WLEX Lexington, working as a disc jockey and singer. He always called himself the Kentucky Folk Singer and he had a penchant, like Red River Dave, for writing songs about topical events. In 1949, his recording of one such number, 'The Death Of Little Kathy Fiscus', the story of the tragic death of a young girl in California, became a number 7 hit for him. (The song has since been successfully recorded by many others, including Howard Vokes and Kitty Wells). During the Korean War, Osborne produced an almost endless line of story songs, most of a patriotic nature such as

'God Please Protect America', which gave him another Top 10 hit in 1950. Others included 'Thank God For Victory In Korea' and 'The Voice Of Free America'. He made appearances on Nashville's *Grand Ole Opry* and on WLS Chicago's *National Barn Dance*. In 1952, he opened a record shop in Louisville, where he also became very popular for his show on WKLO. He made further King recordings until 1955 but he achieved no further hits. Osborne suffered bouts of depression and during one of these, for some unknown reason, he committed suicide on 26 December 1957. In 1988, a Dutch record label released an album that contained some of his King singles. (He should not be confused with the Osborne Brothers.)

● ALBUMS: *Jimmie Osborne Singing Songs He Wrote* (Audio Lab 1959)★★★, *The Legendary Jimmie Osborne* (King 1961)★★★, *Golden Harvest* (King 1963)★★★, *Jimmie Osborne's Gold Harvest (24 Songs)* (King 1965)★★★.

● COMPILATIONS: *The Very Best Of Jimmie Osborne* (King 1964)★★★, *The Voice Of Free America* Dutch release (Strictly Country 1988)★★★.

OSLIN, K.T.

b. Kay Toinette Oslin, 1943, Crossitt, Arkansas, USA. Oslin was raised in Mobile, Alabama, and then in Houston, Texas. She loved Hank Williams and the Carter Family, but hated early 60s country music because 'it was middle-aged men singing about drinking whiskey and cheating on their wives'. She attended drama school and worked in Houston as a folk trio with Guy Clark and radio producer David Jones. A live album she made with Texas singer Frank Davis was never released. She was in the chorus for the Broadway production of *Hello, Dolly!* starring Betty Grable, and for many years, she played bit parts, did session work and sang commercials to make a living. She sang harmony on the 1978 album *Guy Clark*, but her 1981 Elektra singles of 'Clean Your Own Tables' and 'Younger Men (Are Startin' To Catch My Eye)', released as Kay T. Oslin, did not sell. In 1982 Gail Davies recorded her song 'Round The Clock Lovin'', which prompted her to borrow $7,000 from an aunt to form a band for a Nashville showcase. The Judds recorded her song 'Old Pictures', while her own piano-based ballad, '80's Ladies', was a Top 10 country single and an anthem for older, single women (Oslin herself is unmarried). An album of songs written from the female perspective, also called *80's Ladies*, was a top-selling country album that crossed over to the pop market. Tom T. Hall described her as 'everybody's screwed-up sister'. Her number 1 country singles are 'Do Ya' (she stopped a faster take being released when she realized it worked much better at half-tempo), 'I'll Always Come Back' and the partly narrated 'Hold Me'. As a self-confessed 'aging sex bomb', it is unusual for a woman to have made her first mark on country music so late in life; it seems doubtful that she can maintain the momentum, particularly as she seems to have exhausted her original flow of songs, and because of the heart bypass operation she had to undergo in 1995. She released an imaginative covers album a year later, featuring songs picked from the past two centuries.

● ALBUMS: *80's Ladies* (RCA 1987)★★★, *This Woman* (RCA 1988)★★★, *Love In A Small Town* (RCA 1990)★★★★, *My Roots Are Showing...* (BNA 1996)★★★.

● COMPILATIONS: *Greatest Hits: Songs From An Aging Sex Bomb* (RCA 1993)★★★★.

OVERSTREET, PAUL

b. 17 March 1955, Newton, Mississippi, USA. Overstreet moved to Nashville in 1973 and was married for a short time to Dolly Parton's sister Frieda. It was not until 1982 that he made an impression as a songwriter. George Jones had a US country hit with 'Same Old Me' and Overstreet was able to 'buy a lot of booze and drugs and a new car'. The country hits continued with 'Diggin' Up Bones', 'On The Other Hand' and 'Forever And Ever, Amen', all for Randy Travis, and 'You're Still New To Me', a duet for Marie Osmond and Paul Davis. In 1985 and with the help of his new wife, Julie, Paul Overstreet decided to giving up drinking and drugs and devote his time to God and his family. This new lifestyle is reflected in many of his songs. He was part of the band SKO in 1986/7 and then had another US country number 1 with 'I Won't Take Less Than Your Love', which he performed with Tanya Tucker and Paul Davis. He wrote 'When You Say Nothing At All' (Keith Whitley), 'A Long Line Of Love' (Michael Martin Murphey) and 'Love Can Build A Bridge' (Judds) as well as having his own country hits with 'Seein' My Father In Me', 'Richest Man On Earth' and 'Daddy's Come Around', which was a number 1.

● ALBUMS: *Paul Overstreet* (RCA 1982)★★★, *Sowin' Love* (RCA 1989)★★★, *Heroes* (RCA 1991)★★★, *Love Is Strong* (RCA 1992)★★, *Time* (Scarlett Moon 1996)★★★.

● COMPILATIONS: *The Best Of Paul Overstreet* (RCA 1994)★★★★.

OVERSTREET, TOMMY

b. Thomas Cary Overstreet, 10 September 1937, Oklahoma City, Oklahoma, USA. Overstreet grew up in Houston, the home-town of his uncle, the 30s pop singer Gene Austin, and learned to play the guitar at the age of 14. Here he first appeared on KTHT radio and in a local production of *Hit The Road*, but after completing high school, he moved to Abilene. During 1956-57, he studied radio and television production at the University of Texas and also featured on Slim Willett's local television show, at one time appearing as Terry Dean from Abilene. Between 1957 and 1964 (military service excepted), he toured with Gene Austin, after which he worked for a time as a songwriter with Pat Boone's Cooga Music in Los Angeles. He recorded, without success, for Dunhill and eventually returned to Texas. In 1967, he moved to Nashville, where his University training saw him become manager of Dot Records' office. He also recorded for the label and after two minor hits, he had a Top 5 US country and minor pop hit with 'Gwen (Congratulations)'. This launched his career, and during the 70s, he registered 27 *Billboard* country chart hits. Although he never achieved a number 1, he did have Top 3 hits with 'Ann (Don't Go Runnin')', 'Heaven Is My Woman's Love' and '(Jeannie Marie) You Were A Lady'. Overstreet was never solely a country performer and with his band Nashville Express, he toured extensively both in the USA and Europe. He was at one time especially popular in Germany, where a recording of 'Heaven Is My Woman's Love', sung in German, was a hit. He appeared on most of the top US television programmes and made guest appearances on the *Grand Ole Opry* and *Hee-Haw*. He left Dot in 1979 and had six minor hits on Elektra, including 'What More Could A Man Need', but by the early 80s he was recording for minor labels. By this time, he had become a polished cabaret-style entertainer, far removed from any country roots; many may perhaps doubt that any ever really existed. He had a minor chart hit with 'Next To You' in 1986.

● ALBUMS: *Gwen (Congratulations)* (Dot 1971)★★★, *This Is Tommy Overstreet* (Dot 1972)★★★, *Heaven Is My Woman's Love* (Dot 1972)★★★, *My Friends Call Me T.O.* (Dot 1973)★★, *Woman Your Name Is My Song* (Dot 1974)★★, *I'm A Believer* (Dot 1975)★★★, *Live From The Silver Slipper* (Dot 1975★★★, *Turn On To Tommy Overstreet* (Dot 1976)★★★, *Vintage '77* (Dot 1977)★★, *Hangin' Around* (Dot 1977)★★★, *A Better Me (10th Anniversary Album)* (Dot 1978)★★★, *There'll Never Be Another First Time* (Dot 1978)★★★, *The Real Tommy Overstreet* (Dot 1979)★★★, *I'll Never Let You Down* (Elektra 1979)★★★, *I Can Hear Kentucky Calling* (Elektra 1980)★★, *Tommy Overstreet* (1982)★★, *Dream Maker* (1983)★★.

● COMPILATIONS: *Solid Gold Hits* (Bulldog 1988)★★★.

OWEN, JIM

b. 21 April 1941, Robards, Kentucky, USA. When he was eight years old, Owen saw Hank Williams sing and from that time he became completely fascinated by the star and his music. After completing his education, he worked variously as a journalist and as a golf coach until 1969 when, with Mel Tillis's help, he relocated to Nashville to work as a songwriter. Over the next few years, several artists had chart hits with his songs. These included 'Too Lonely Too Long' and 'One More Drink' (both Mel Tillis), 'Little Boy's Prayer' (Porter Wagoner), 'Sweet Baby On My Mind' (June Stearns), 'Southern Loving' and 'Broad Minded Man' (both Jim Ed Brown), 'The Telephone' (Jerry Reed) and arguably the best-known of all, 'Louisiana Woman, Mississippi Man' (Conway Twitty and Loretta Lynn). He never lost his obsession with Hank Williams and encouraged by his wife, who once dreamed that she saw Owen onstage at the *Grand Ole Opry* but that it was Williams' voice that she heard coming from him, he began to recreate his idol. He talked with people that had known or worked with Williams and practised his mannerisms and stage presentation. In 1976, he presented *Hank*, a one-hour PBS television special that won him an Emmy award for the best show of the year on public television. He then produced a 90-minute one-man live stage show, *An Evening With Hank Williams*, which had backing tracks provided by Hank's band, the Drifting Cowboys. He commenced touring extensively with the show and regularly drew audiences of thousands at countless venues. He also starred in the 1980 film *Hank Williams: The Man And His Music*, for which he received an Emmy nomination. In 1978, his Epic recording of 'Lovesick Blues', recorded with the Drifting Cowboys, was a minor chart hit and in the early 80s, he scored two more minor hits with 'Ten Anniversary Presents' and 'Hell Yes, I Cheated'. In 1985, he wrote and produced a 10-hour Hank Williams radio show which, on New Year's Day, was broadcast on various US stations as a tribute. Owen has also appeared as Hank Williams for the noted *Legends In Concert* at the Imperial Palace, Las Vegas, and made many appearances on the *Opry*, including a special one on 1 January 1993, the 40th anniversary of Williams' death, which gained him a standing ovation. He continued to tour with his show into the 90s, still writes songs and, at times, works as an auctioneer near his Henderson, Tennessee home. He is also noted for his collection of classic cars.

● ALBUMS: with the Drifting Cowboys *A Song For Us All - A Salute To Hank Williams* (Epic 1977)★★★, *Hank* (Sun 1982)★★.

● FILMS: *Hank Williams: The Man And His Music* (1980).

OWENS, BONNIE

b. Bonnie Campbell, 1 October 1932, Blanchard, Oklahoma, USA. Bonnie was a yodelling country singer, who married Buck Owens in 1947. Their son, Alvis Alan Owens (b. 22 May 1948), became the singer Buddy Alan. Buck and Bonnie Owens toured together and had a radio series in Arizona. They divorced in 1953 but both moved to Bakersfield in the early 60s, where she made her first records, 'Dear John Letter', 'Why Daddy Don't Live Here Anymore' and 'Don't Take Advantage Of Me'. After a relationship with Merle Haggard's manager, Fuzzy Owen, she married Haggard in 1965, becoming part of his stage show and recording a successful duet album with him. Their marriage was unusual in that Owens tolerated Haggard's affairs - 'I don't care what you do so long as you don't flaunt it in my face', she is reputed to have said. In 1970 they co-wrote 'Today I Started Loving You Again'. She stopped performing in 1975 to look after their family and business interests. They divorced in 1978 but she is now an integral part of his roadshow.

● ALBUMS: *Don't Take Advantage Of Me* (Capitol 1965)★★★, with Merle Haggard *Just Between The Two Of Us* (Capitol 1966)★★★, *Your Tender Loving Care* (Capitol 1967)★★★, *All Of Me Belongs To You* (Capitol 1967)★★★, *Somewhere Between* (Capitol 1968)★★★, *Hi-Fi To Cry By* (Capitol 1969)★★, *Lead Me On* (Capitol 1969)★★★, *Mother's Favourite Hymns* (Capitol 1971)★★.

OWENS, BUCK

b. Alvis Edgar Owens Jnr., 12 August 1929, Sherman, Texas, USA. Buck Owens became one of the leading country music stars of the 60s and 70s, along with Merle Haggard, the leading exponent of the 'west coast sound'. Owens gave himself the nickname Buck at the age of three, after a favourite horse. When he was 10, his family moved to Mesa, Arizona, where Owens picked cotton, and at 13 years of age he began playing the mandolin. He soon learned guitar, horns and drums. Owens performed music professionally by the age of 16, starring, along with partner Ray Britten, in his own radio programme. He also worked with the group Mac's Skillet Lickers, and at 17 married their singer, Bonnie Campbell, who later launched her own career as Bonnie Owens. The couple bore a son, who also had a country music career as Buddy Alan. In 1951 Owens and his family moved to Bakersfield, California, at the suggestion of an uncle who said work was plentiful for good musicians. Owens joined the Orange Blossom Playboys, with whom he both sang and played guitar for the first time, and then formed his own band, the Schoolhouse Playboys. Owens made ends meet by taking on work as a session guitarist in Los Angeles, appearing on recordings by Sonny James, Wanda Jackson, Tommy Sands and Gene Vincent. When the Playboys disbanded in the mid-50s Owens joined country artist Tommy Collins as singer and guitarist, recording a few tracks with him.

In 1955-56 Owens recorded his first singles under his own name, for Pep Records, using the name Corky Jones for rockabilly and his own name for country recordings. Owens signed to Capitol Records in March 1957. It was not until his fourth release, 'Second Fiddle', that he made any mark, reaching number 24 on *Billboard*'s country chart. His next, 'Under Your Spell Again', made number 4, paving the way for over 75 country hits, more than 40 of which made that chart's Top 10. Among the biggest and best were 'Act Naturally' (1963), later covered by the Beatles, 'Love's Gonna Live Here' (1963), 'My Heart Skips A Beat' (1964), 'Together Again' (1964), 'I've Got A Tiger By The Tail' (1965), 'Before You Go' (1965), 'Waitin' In Your Welfare Line' (1966), 'Think Of Me' (1966), 'Open Up Your Heart' (1966) and a cover version of Chuck Berry's 'Johnny B. Goode' (1969), all of which were number 1 country singles. Owens recorded a number of duets with singer Susan Raye, and also with his son Buddy Alan. He also released more than 100 albums during his career. In addition, his compositions were hits by other artists, notably Emmylou Harris ('Together Again') and Ray Charles ('Crying Time'). Owens' band, the Buckaroos (guitarist Don Rich, bassist Doyle Holly, steel guitarist Tom Brumley and drummer Willie Cantu), was also highly regarded. Their back-to-basics, honky-tonk instrumental style helped define the Bakersfield sound - Owens' recordings never relied on strings or commercialized, sweetened pop arrangements. The Buckaroos also released several albums on their own. In 1969, Owens joined as co-host the country music television variety programme *Hee Haw*, which combined comedy sketches and live performances by country stars. He stayed with the show until the mid-80s, long after his Capitol contract expired, and he had signed with Warner Brothers Records in 1976. Although Owens continued to place singles in the country charts with Warners, his reign as a top country artist had faltered in the mid-70s and he retired from recording and performing to run a number of business interests, including a radio station and recording studio in Bakersfield. In 1988, country newcomer Dwight Yoakam convinced Owens to join him in recording a remake of Owens' song 'Streets Of Bakersfield'. It reached number 1 in the country chart and brought new attention to Owens. He signed with Capitol again late in 1988 and recorded a new album, *Hot Dog*, featuring re-recordings of old Owens songs and cover versions of material by Chuck Berry, Eddie Cochran and others. Although Owens had not recaptured his earlier status by the early 90s, he had become active again, recording and touring, including one tour as a guest of Yoakam. In 1996 he was inducted into the Country Music Hall Of Fame.

● ALBUMS: *Buck Owens* (LaBrea 1961)★★★, *Buck Owens Sings Harlan Howard* (Capitol 1961)★★★, *Under Your Spell Again* (Capitol 1961)★★★, *The Fabulous Country Music Sound Of Buck Owens* (Starday 1962)★★★, *You're For Me* (Capitol 1962)★★★, *Buck Owens On The Bandstand* (Capitol 1963)★★★, *Buck Owens Sings Tommy Collins* (Capitol 1963)★★★, *Together Again/My Heart Skips A Beat* (Capitol 1964)★★★, *I Don't Care* (Capitol 1964)★★★, *I've Got A Tiger By The Tail* (Capitol 1965)★★★, *Before You Go/No One But You* (Capitol 1965)★★★, *The Instrumental Hits Of Buck Owens And The Buckaroos* (Capitol 1965)★★★, *Christmas With* (Capitol 1965)★★★, *Roll Out The Red Carpet* (Capitol 1966)★★★, *Dust On Mother's Bible* (Capitol 1966)★★★, *Carnegie Hall Concert* (Capitol 1966)★★★, *Open Up Your Heart* (Capitol 1967)★★★, *Buck Owens And His Buckaroos In Japan* (Capitol 1967)★★★, *Your Tender Loving Care* (Capitol 1967)★★★, *It Takes People Like You To Make People Like Me* (Capitol 1968)★★★, *A Night On The Town* (Capitol 1968)★★★, *Sweet Rosie Jones* (Capitol 1968)★★★, *Christmas Shopping* (Capitol 1968)★★★, *Buck Owens The Guitar Player* (Capitol 1968)★★★, *Buck Owens In London* (Capitol 1969)★★★, *Tall Dark Stranger* (Capitol 1969)★★★, *Big In Vegas* (Capitol 1970)★★★, with Susan Raye *We're Gonna Get Together* (Capitol 1970)★★★, with Raye *The Great White Horse* (Capitol 1970)★★★, *A Merry Hee Haw Christmas* (Capitol 1970)★★★, *I Wouldn't Live In New York City* (Capitol 1971)★★★, *Bridge Over Troubled Water* (Capitol 1971)★★★, with Raye *Merry Christmas From Buck Owens & Susan Raye* (Capitol 1971)★★, *The Songs Of Merle Haggard* (Capitol 1972)★★★, *Buck Owens Live At The Nugget* (Capitol 1972)★★★, *'Live' At The White House* (Capitol 1972)★★, *In The Palm Of Your Hand* (Capitol 1973)★★★, *Ain't It Amazing, Gracie* (Capitol 1973)★★★, with Raye *The Good Old Days Are Here Again* (Capitol 1973)★★, *Arms Full Of Empty* (Capitol 1974)★★★, *41st Street Lonely Hearts' Club/ Weekend Daddy* (Capitol 1975)★★, *Buck 'Em* (Warners 1976)★★, with Roy Clark, Grandpa Jones, Kenny Price *The Hee-Haw Gospel Quartet* (Songbird 1981)★★★, *Hot Dog!* (Capitol 1988)★★★, *Act Naturally* (Capitol 1989)★★★, *Blue Love* (1993)★★★.

● COMPILATIONS: *Country Hit Maker #1* (Starday 1964)★★★, *The Best Of Buck Owens* (Capitol 1964)★★★★, *The Best Of Buck Owens, Volume 2* (Capitol 1968)★★★★, *The Best Of Buck Owens, Volume 3* (Capitol 1969)★★★, *Close Up* (Capitol 1969)★★★, *Buck Owens* (Capitol 1970)★★★, *The Best Of Buck Owens, Volume 4* (Capitol 1971)★★★, with Susan Raye *The Best Of Buck Owens & Susan Raye* (Capitol 1972)★★★, *The Best Of Buck Owens, Volume 5* (Capitol 1974)★★★, *The Best Of Buck Owens, Volume 6* (Capitol 1976)★★★, *All-Time Greatest Hits, Vol. 1* (Curb 1990)★★★, *The Buck Owens Collection (1959-1990)* 3-CD box set (Rhino 1992)★★★★, *Very Best Of Buck Owens, Vol. 1* (Rhino 1994)★★★★, *Very Best Of Buck Owens, Vol. 2* (Rhino 1994)★★★★, *The Buck Owens Story Vol. 1 (1956-64)* (Personality 1994)★★★★, *The Buck Owens Story Vol. 2 (1964-68)* (Personality 1994)★★★★, *The Buck Owens Story Vol. 3 (1969-89)* (Personality 1994)★★★★, *Duets: Half A Buck* (K-Tel 1996)★★★.

OWENS, TEX

b. Doie Hensley Owens, 15 June 1892, Killeen, Texas, USA, d. 9 September 1962, New Baden, Texas, USA. The eldest of the 13 children of a sharecropper family that included sister Texas Ruby, who married fiddler Curly Fox, and who was a very popular country singer at the time of her tragic death in 1963. The family relocated to Oklahoma where, at 15 as 'Tex', he worked on ranches and briefly with touring shows as a singer and guitarist. For some years, he drifted around and worked on oilfields and railroad bridge building. He married Maude Neal in 1916. From 1920-22, he was a town marshal in Kansas and in the mid-20s, was working as a mechanic for a Chevrolet dealer. In 1932, after beginning to write songs seriously, he had his own show on KMBC Kansas City, Missouri, and also appeared on KMBC's *Brush Creek Follies*. In 1934, he made two recordings with a KMBC group, the Texas Rangers (who appeared on his show but were not his band) and four solo numbers including his now famous 'Cattle Call'. His show, which at times included his two daughters singing as Joy And Jane, proved so popular that it was networked by CBS and lasted on KMBC for over 11 years. It is possible that the show even appeared on early television broadcasts in 1932. Ten 1936 RCA-Victor recordings were unissued and seemingly are now lost. After KMBC, he starred on and co-hosted *Boone County Jamboree* in Cincinnati, before moving to KHJ Hollywood to do radio and film work. He broke his back when his horse fell on him during filming for the John Wayne film *Red River* (Owens spent over a year in hospital and later found that his scenes had been cut from the movie). He made his final four recordings in Hollywood in 1953-54, with backing that included his guitarist brother Charles. In 1960, he retired to his native State where he died at New Baden, on 9 September 1962. He wrote over 100 songs, and in 1971, he was posthumously elected to the Nashville Songwriters' Hall Of Fame. His song 'Cattle Call' has become a country standard, recorded by countless artists but none with more success than the million-selling RCA-Victor version made by Eddy Arnold in 1955. Owens' eldest daughter (as Laura Lee McBride) later became known for her vocal work with Bob Wills.

● COMPILATIONS: *Tex Owens - Cattle Call* (Bear Family 1994)★★★.

OXFORD, VERNON

b. 8 June 1941, Benton County, Arkansas, USA. Oxford comes from a musical, church-going family, and his father passed his fiddle-playing talent on to his son. He was given a guitar when he was 13 years old and has been singing country and country/gospel ever since. In 1964 he moved to Nashville with his wife, Loretta, and, after being turned down by several companies, RCA Records signed him, releasing a single and an album, both called 'Woman, Let Me Sing You A Song'. Oxford's recordings are a throwback to the rural honky-tonk sound of Hank Williams, with a voice to match, but he claims, 'I am being me. I sing a lot of Hank's songs but I never set out intentionally to imitate him. I guess we're both country boys and we both sing from the heart.' RCA dropped Oxford when his records did not sell, but a contingent of British fans lobbied RCA so hard that they reversed the decision. RCA released a UK double album in its *Famous Country Music Makers* series, although Oxford was anything but famous at the time. Oxford won more British fans with UK appearances, particularly at Wembley Country Music Festivals. He made the US country charts with 'The Shadows Of My Mind' and then, in 1976, with his controversial 'Redneck! (The Redneck National Anthem)', written by Mitchell Torok, and in the same vein, 'Redneck Roots' and 'A Good Old Fashioned Saturday Night Honky Tonk Barroom Brawl'. He also recorded a humorous duet with Jim Ed Brown called 'Mowing The Lawn'. He claims he just dreamed the words and music of his own songs, 'She's Always There' and 'Better Way Of Life'. Since 1977, Oxford has not had chart success in the USA, but that is not one of his objectives. He says, 'Going to church doesn't make you a Christian, and, in 1978, I was born again, even though I was a Baptist already'. However, Oxford, the subject of a BBC Television documentary, says, 'I do cheating songs but now I do them to represent what sin is: I use them to make a point about Jesus Christ. "Redneck!" shows what I used to be before I was saved. I sing gospel songs at the end of every show and tell them about the Truth. Sometimes I combine singing with preaching. When I called a girl out of the audience once, the power of God knocked her down and she slithered like a snake across the floor. I have found peace and happiness and I would like to help others to find it too.'

● ALBUMS: *Woman, Let Me Sing You A Song* (RCA Victor 1967)★★★, *By Public Demand* (RCA 1975)★★★, *America's Unknown Superstar* (RCA 1976)★★★, *I Just Want To Be A Country Singer* (RCA 1976)★★★, *Tribute To Hank Williams* (Meteor 1978)★★★, *Nobody's Child* (1978)★★★, *If I Had My Wife To Love Over* (Rounder 1979)★★★, *Keepin' It Country* (1979)★★, *I Love To Sing* (1980)★★★, *His And Hers* (1980)★★, *A Better Way Of Life* (Minit 1981)★★, *Pure Country* (1982)★★★, *The Tradition Continues* (1983)★★, *Power In The Blood* (BBC 1989)★★, *100% Country* (1990)★★★, *The Gospel Truth* (Rocade 1997)★★★.

● COMPILATIONS: *Famous Country Music Makers* (RCA 1974)★★★, *Twenty Of The Best* (RCA 1984)★★★, *Keeper Of The Flame* 5-CD box set (Bear Family 1995)★★★★.

OZARK JUBILEE, THE

The show was the brainchild of four Springfield, Missouri men, led by a promoter named Ely E. 'Si' Siman, who was initially connected with KWTO Springfield radio. In the early 50s, KWTO broadcast country radio programmes and Siman recognized the potential success of a networked televised country show. When KYTV Springfield began to televise local country shows, Siman and his three associates, Ralph Foster, Lester Cox and John Mahaffey, formed Crossroads Television Productions, Inc. and gave up their interest in the purely local radio shows. On 26 December 1953, the first of the new televised shows was broadcast and the following year, Siman succeeded in talking Red Foley, an established *Grand Ole Opry* star in Nashville, into becoming the MC and star of the Springfield show. In September 1954, the show was transmitted from the Jewell Theatre, Springfield, back to KYTV's studio and then relayed from there. Siman soon succeeded in selling the show to ABC-TV and on 22 January 1955, part of it was broadcast live on that network. There were some initial transmission difficulties and for 22 Saturdays, the show was transmitted from KOMU Columbia, Missouri. In April 1955, the *Jubilee* returned to Springfield, where it ran until its final show in January 1961 (Red Foley's departure because of income tax problems with the IRS has been cited as one reason for the show's demise). It was then replaced by the *Five Star Jubilee*, a colour show, which made KYTV the first station outside of Los Angeles, Chicago and New York, to have a regular colour programme. It broadcast 29 shows from the Landers Theatre, Springfield, before the series ended. Many future stars benefited from their appearances on the *Jubilee* programme including Porter Wagoner, Bobby Lord, Wanda Jackson, Jean Shepard, Carl Smith and Billy Walker. Amusingly Willie Nelson, then the frontman and bass guitarist in Ray Price's band (and washing dishes in a restaurant to help eke out a living), was once told by the show's producers that he was 'not yet ready for national television'. The *Ozark Jubilee*, sometimes referred to as *Jubilee USA*, did not survive for as long as some of its contemporaries, nor did it ever attain the popularity of the *Opry* or the *Louisiana Hayride*, but it did establish its place in the history of country music by the fact that it was the first to be aired on network television. Siman died of cancer in Springfield on 16 December 1994.

OZARK MOUNTAIN DAREDEVILS

One of country rock's more inventive exponents, the Ozark Mountain Daredevils featured the songwriting team of John Dillon (b. 6 February 1947, Stuttgart, Arkansas, USA; guitar, fiddle, vocals) and Steve Cash (b. 5 May 1946, Springfield, Missouri, USA; harmonica, vocals) with Randle Chowning (guitar, vocals), Buddy Brayfield (keyboards), Michael 'Supe' Granda (b. 24 December 1950, St. Louis, Missouri, USA; bass) and Larry Lee (b. 5 January 1947, Springfield, Missouri, USA; drums). The group were originally based in Springfield, Missouri. Their acclaimed debut album, recorded in London under the aegis of producer Glyn Johns, contained the US Top 30 single 'If You Want To Get To Heaven', while a second success, 'Jackie Blue', which reached number 3, came from the group's follow-up collection, *It'll Shine When It Shines*. Recorded at Chowning's ranch, this excellent set showcased the Ozarks' strong harmonies and intuitive musicianship, factors maintained on subsequent releases, *The Car Over The Lake Album* and *Men From Earth*. A 1978 release, *It's Alive*, fulfilled the group's obligation to A&M Records and two years later they made their debut on CBS. Paradoxically the Ozarks' subsequent work lacked the purpose of those early releases although the unit continues to enjoy a cult popularity. The group was reactivated in the late 80s by Dillon and Cash with Granda, Steve Canaday (b. 12 September 1944, Springfield, Missouri, USA; drums) and D. Clinton Thompson (guitar) and the resulting album, *Modern History*, released on the UK independent Conifer label, found the Ozarks with a new lease of life.
● ALBUMS: *The Ozark Mountain Daredevils* (A&M 1974)★★★, *It'll Shine When It Shines* (A&M 1974)★★★★, *The Car Over The Lake Album* (A&M 1975)★★★★, *Men From Earth* (A&M 1976)★★★, *Don't Look Down* (A&M 1977)★★, *It's Alive* (A&M 1978)★★, *Ozark Mountain Daredevils* (Columbia 1980)★★, *Modern History* (Request/Conifer 1990)★★★.
● COMPILATIONS: *The Best Of The Ozark Mountain Daredevils* (A&M 1983)★★★.

PAGE, PATTI

b. Clara Ann Fowler, 8 November 1927, Tulsa, Oklahoma, USA. A popular singer who is said to have sold more records during the 50s than any other female artist, Page's total sales (singles and albums) are claimed to be in excess of 60 million. One of eight girls in a family of 11, Clara Fowler started her career singing country songs on radio station KTUL in Tulsa, and played weekend gigs with Art Klauser and his Oklahomans. She successfully auditioned for KTUL's *Meet Patti Page* show, sponsored by the Page Milk Company, and took the name with her when she left. Jack Rael, who was road manager and played baritone saxophone for the Jimmy Joy band, heard her on the radio and engaged her to sing with them; he later became her manager for over 40 years. In 1948 Page appeared on the top rated *Breakfast Club* on Chicago radio, and sang with the Benny Goodman Septet. In the same year she had her first hit record, 'Confess', on which, in the cause of economy, she overdubbed her own voice to create the effect of a vocal group. In 1949, she used that revolutionary technique again on her first million-seller, 'With My Eyes Wide Open I'm Dreaming'. The song was re-released 10 years later with a more modern orchestral backing. Throughout the 50s, the hits continued to flow: 'I Don't Care If The Sun Don't Shine', 'All My Love' (US number 1), 'The Tennessee Waltz' (said to be the first real 'crossover' hit from country music to pop, and one of the biggest record hits of all time), 'Would I Love You (Love You, Love You)', 'Mockin' Bird Hill' (a cover version of the record made by Les Paul and Mary Ford, who took multi-tracking to the extreme in the 50s), 'Mister And Mississippi', 'Detour' (recorded for her first country music album), 'I Went To Your Wedding', 'Once In Awhile', 'You Belong To Me', 'Why Don't You Believe Me', '(How Much Is) That Doggie In The Window', written by novelty song specialist Bob Merrill, and recorded by Page for a children's album, 'Changing Partners', 'Cross Over The Bridge', 'Steam Heat', 'Let Me Go, Lover', 'Go On With The Wedding', 'Allegheny Moon', 'Old Cape Cod', 'Mama From The Train' (sung in a Pennsylvanian Dutch dialect), 'Left Right Out Of Your Heart', and many more. Her records continued to sell well into the 60s, and she had her last US Top 10 entry in 1965 with the title song from the Bette Davis-Olivia De Havilland movie *Hush, Hush, Sweet Charlotte*. Page also appeared extensively on US television during the 50s, on shows such as the *Scott Music Hall*, the *Big Record* variety show, and her own shows for NBC and CBS. She also made several films, including *Elmer Gantry* (1960), *Dondi* (1961, a comedy-drama, in which she co-starred with David Janssen) and *Boys Night Out* (1962). In the 70s, she recorded mainly country material, and in the 80s, after many successful years with Mercury and Columbia Records, signed for the Nashville-based company

Plantation Records, a move that reunited her with top record producer Shelby Singleton. In 1988, Page gained excellent reviews when she played the Ballroom in New York, her first appearance in that city for nearly 20 years.

● ALBUMS: *Songs* (Mercury 1950)★★★, *Folksong Favorites* 10-inch album (Mercury 1951)★★★, *Christmas* (Mercury 1951)★★, *Tennessee Waltz* 10-inch album (Mercury 1952)★★★★, *Patti Sings For Romance* (Mercury 1954)★★★, *Song Souvenirs* (Mercury 1954)★★★, *Just Patti* (Mercury 1954)★★★, *Patti's Songs* (Mercury 1954)★★★, *And I Thought About You* (Mercury 1954)★★★, *So Many Memories* (Mercury 1954)★★★, *Romance On The Range* (Mercury 1955)★★★, *Page I* (Mercury 1956)★★★, *Page II* (Mercury 1956)★★★, *Page III* (Mercury 1956)★★★, *You Go To My Head* (Mercury 1956)★★★, *In The Land Of Hi Fi* (EmArcy 1956)★★★, *Music For Two In Love* (Mercury 1956)★★★, *The Voices Of Patti Page* (Mercury 1956)★★★, *Page IV* (Mercury 1956)★★★, *Let's Get Away From It All* (Mercury 1956)★★★, *I've Heard That Song Before* (Mercury 1956)★★★, *My Song* (1956)★★★, *The East Side* (EmArcy 1956)★★★, *Manhattan Tower* (Mercury 1956)★★★, *The Waltz Queen* (Mercury 1957)★★★, *The West Side* (EmArcy 1958)★★★, *Patti Page On Camera* (Mercury 1959)★★★, *I'll Remember April* (Mercury 1959)★★★, *Indiscretion* (Mercury 1959)★★★, *Sings And Stars In 'Elmer Gantry'* (Mercury 1960)★★, *Three Little Words* (Mercury 1960)★★★, *Just A Closer Walk With Thee* (Mercury 1960)★★, *Country And Western Golden Hits* (Mercury 1961)★★, *Go On Home* (1962)★★★, *Golden Hit Of The Boys* (Mercury 1962)★★★, *Patti Page On Stage* (1963)★★★, *Say Wonderful Things* (Columbia 1963)★★, *Blue Dream Street* (1964)★★, *The Nearness Of You* (1964)★★★, *Hush, Hush, Sweet Charlotte* (Columbia 1965)★★★, *Gentle On My Mind* (Columbia 1968)★★, *Patti Page With Lou Stein's Music, 1949* (Hindsight 1988)★★★.

● COMPILATIONS: *Patti Page's Golden Hits* (Mercury 1961)★★★, *Patti Page's Golden Hits, Volume 2* (Mercury 1963)★★★, *The Best Of Patti Page* (Creole 1984)★★★, *The Mercury Years, Vol. 1* (Mercury 1991)★★★★, *The Mercury Years, Vol. 2* (Mercury 1991)★★★★.

PAGE, STU

b. 12 May 1954, Leeds, Yorkshire, England. Page, who has been playing the guitar since he was 10 years old, began his career with session work around Leeds. In 1973, after helping out an American bluegrass band, the Warren Wikeson Band, he was invited to join them in Boston for a year. When he returned to the UK, he took various day jobs, but played in several semi-pro bands. In 1984 he formed Stu Page And Remuda, and says, 'It's a word for a spare horse and that's what we were. We only got the gigs when someone had let the organizer down.' Besides being a talented guitarist, Page has a powerful voice that belies his small stature, and his band includes Terry Clayton (bass), Andy Whelan (guitar), Pat McPartling (drums) and Tim Howard (pedal steel). They have recorded several cassettes for sale at shows, together with the excellent album *The Stu Page Band*, which was produced by Joe Butler of the Hillsiders for Barge Records. Page's major influence is Merle Haggard and the band's singles include 'He Made The Whole World Sing', 'Are You Still In Love With Me?' and the double a-side, 'Florida Feelin''/'Honeysuckle Dreamin''.

● ALBUMS: *Radio Nights* (1984)★★★, *Front Page News* (1985)★★★, *The Stu Page Band* (Barge 1989)★★★★, *Fresh Pages* (1990)★★★, *Can't Sing The Blues* (Milltown 1995)★★★.

PAISLEY, BOB

b. James Robert Paisley, 14 March 1931, Ashe County, North Carolina, USA. His parents soon relocated to Pennsylvania, where he grew up and where, as a youth, he learned to play guitar and harmonica and developed a keen interest in country music, particularly the old-time acts such as the Blue Sky Boys. He gained his first experience playing in a country band during his military service but on his discharge first worked, for some time, in a chemist's shop. In 1964, with banjoist Ted Lundy and others, he formed the Southern Mountain Boys and played with the band until 1979, during which time they recorded several albums. (The Southern Mountain Boys disbanded after Lundy committed suicide on 23 June 1980). Severe hip problems caused Paisley to retire from music for a time but sometimes reliant on a walking stick, he eventually returned and with his son Dan and Landy's cousin Jerry, he re-formed as Southern Grass. They soon became popular playing the US bluegrass circuit and in the early 80s, they recorded for Rounder Records and embarked on a major European tour. They played in several countries, recorded a live album in Holland with Dutch duo A.G. And Kate and proved a great hit at their UK appearances. During the 80s, like his namesake, the manager of Liverpool Football Club, Paisley made several more European tours. In the 90s, he continued to play the US bluegrass festival circuit with a line-up that included his sons Dan and Mike.

● ALBUMS: with Ted Lundy *Ted Lundy & The Southern Mountain Ramblers* (GHP 1972)★★★, with Lundy *The Old Swinging Bridge* (Rounder 1973)★★★, as Ted Lundy And Bob Paisley And The Southern Mountain Boys *Slipping Away* (Rounder 1976)★★★, *Lovesick & Sorrow* (Rounder 1978)★★★, *Bob Paisley And Southern Grass* (Rounder 1981)★★★, *An Old Love Affair* (Brandywine 1982)★★★, with A.G And Kate *Pickin' In Holland* (Strictly Country 1984)★★★, *I Still Love You Yet* (Mountain Laurel 1985)★★★, *Home Of Light And Love* (Mountain Laurel 1988)★★★, *No Vacancy* (Brandywine 1992)★★.

PALOMINO ROAD

The 90s US country group Palomino Road consists of four musicians who have lived in Nashville for some years. The main songwriter, Ronnie Guilbeau (vocals), is the brother of Gib Guilbeau of the Burrito Brothers, and he worked with his father's band until moving to Nashville in the mid-80s. His best-known song is 'Call It Love' recorded by Poco. J.T. Corenflos (guitar) came to Nashville in 1982, and worked on the *Grand Ole Opry* and as a member of Joe Stampley's band. Randy Frazier (bass) played for Sammy Kershaw, while James Lewis (drums), originally from Kansas City, has been playing in Nashville since 1970. Palomino Road was formed in 1992 and unlike many bands, they are a self-contained unit with no outside musicians or session singers involved. They made the US country charts with a spirited revival of George Jones' 'Why Baby Why'.

● ALBUMS: *Palomino Road* (Liberty 1993)★★★.

PARKER, ANDY, AND THE PLAINSMEN

b. 1913, Mangum, Oklahoma, USA. Little is known of Parker's childhood but he began a 12-year spell on local radio in the Midwest in 1926. Then, in 1938, after relocating to San Francisco, he began to appear as the Singing Cowboy in *Death Valley Days* on NBC radio. He also sang on KGO on *Dude Martin's Roundup*, before moving to Los Angeles. Here in 1944, Parker, Charlie Morgan and Hank Caldwell became the Plainsmen, a vocal and swing instrumentalist trio. They made their film debut in *Cowboy Blues* with Ken Curtis and by 1946, they had record releases on the Coast label. They appeared regularly on the *Hollywood Barn Dance* on CBS radio and *Sunrise Salute* on KNX Los Angeles. When Caldwell departed, he was replaced by Paul 'Clem' Smith and the act then became Andy Parker And The Plainsmen. They recorded for Capitol, including more than 200 radio transcription discs and appeared in eight Eddie Dean B-westerns and many television shows. Other artists who became band members over the years include Deuce Spriggens (who later became a member of the Sons Of The Pioneers) and Noel Boggs. When Morgan decided to leave in 1956, Parker broke up the group. Parker wrote many songs, including the popular 'Trail Dust' and he and Morgan sang the theme song with Marilyn Monroe for the 1954 film *River Of No Return*.

PARKER, BILLY

b. Billy Joe Parker, 19 July 1937, Tuskegee, Oklahoma, USA. Parker is recognized by some mainly as a country disc jockey. However, his 22 *Billboard* chart entries represent a considerable achievement, more so than many artists who have attracted far more publicity as singers. Influenced by Hank Williams and George Jones, he learned guitar as a boy and was singing on a local Tulsa station at the age of 14, later spending some time on the *Ozark Jubilee*. He made his first recordings for Sims in 1963, when he was a regular radio disc jockey in Wichita, Kansas. His listeners voted him Mr DJ USA, which award also saw him guest on Nashville's WSM. He recorded for Decca Records in 1966 and between 1968 and 1971, he played as a member of Ernest Tubb's Texas Troubadours. In 1971, he began working on KVOO Tulsa and two years later, he was the station's Programme Controller. He gained his first chart hit in 1976 and, in the next three years, added 10 more, including, in 1979, his tribute to Tubb, 'Thanks E.T. Thanks A Lot'. None were major hits and many were gentle ballads, such as the overly sentimental 'Lord If I Make It To Heaven (Can I Bring My Own Angel Along)'. In the 80s, recording for Soundwaves, he recorded duet hits with some friends, including 'Who's Gonna Sing The Last Country Song' (with Darrell McCall) and 'Too Many Irons In The Fire' (with Cal Smith). He moved to Canyon Creek Records in 1988 and scored three more minor hits, including 'It's Time For Your Dreams To Come True' (number 87, 1989). Parker was voted Disc Jockey Of The Year in 1975, 1977, 1978 and 1984 and was inducted to the Country Music Disc Jockey Hall Of Fame in 1992. He managed to combine his singing, disc jockey work and Programme Controller's duties so efficiently that he was eventually appointed Executive Director at KVOO. In 1990, Bear Family Records issued a CD containing all his Soundwaves recordings, together with a booklet giving biographical information about the artist.
● ALBUMS: *Average Man* (Sunshine County 1976)★★★★,

Billy Parker (Sunshine County 1977)★★★, *Always Country* (Canyon Creek 1988)★★★, *I'll Speak Out For You Jesus* (Canyon Creek 1990)★★★.
● COMPILATIONS: with various other artists *Who's Gonna Sing The Last Country Song* (Soundwaves 1982)★★★, with various other artists *Something Old, Something New* (Soundwaves 1983)★★★, *Billy Parker And Friends* (Bear Family 1990)★★★.

PARKER, BYRON

b. Byron Harry Parker, 6 September 1911, Hastings, Iowa, USA, d. 6 October 1948. Parker's career started as one half of the Gospel Twins, a duo who appeared regularly in the early 30s on a local station in Shenandoah, Iowa. Between 1934 and 1937, he worked with the Monroe Brothers, originally just as their programme announcer but he also sang bass in their gospel quartet. In 1937, he left the Monroes, and nicknaming himself the Old Hired Hand, he formed his Hillbillies, which included J.E. Mainer and banjoist Snuffy Jenkins, at WIS Columbia. Soon afterwards fiddler Homer Sherrill joined but the group saw several changes of personnel. In 1940, he recorded 16 sides for Bluebird Records as Byron Parker's Mountaineers and four further sides for DeLuxe in 1946. Parker mainly acted as announcer or MC and rarely performed but he was so good at selling things on the programmes that he was never without a sponsor. Someone allegedly once commented that if he had wanted, Parker could have sold used matches. His shows proved immensely popular and his regular closing 'Goodbye, good luck, and may God Bless you everyone' was known by thousands. Parker continued to lead a group until 1947 when, because of increasing heart problems, his doctor told him to drastically cut down on his workload and travelling. He finally settled for working as a station announcer at WFIX Columbia, which he did until his premature death at the age of 37. After his death, Jenkins and Sherrill, as a mark of respect to their dead friend, renamed the group the Hired Hands and continued to play well into the 80s. Bill Anderson has always maintained that, as a boy, he was greatly influenced by Parker.
● COMPILATIONS: *Bluegrass Roots* (Old Homestead 1985)★★★.

PARNELL, LEE ROY

b. 21 December 1956, Abilene, Texas, USA. Bob Wills was a close family friend and Parnell sang on stage with him when he was only six years old, an incident he mentions in his 1993 song 'Country Down To My Soul'. Growing up in a household that loved western swing, Parnell found that his own tastes included blues and rock 'n' roll. He formed his own band when he was aged 19 and spent 10 years playing Texas honky tonks. In 1987 he moved with his family to Nashville and built up a reputation at the Bluebird Cafe. His first album was produced by R&B producer Barry Beckett and mixed soul with country. It did reasonably well but his career took off when he recorded *Love Without Mercy* with a small rhythm group. It included his US country hits 'What Kind Of Fool Do You Think I Am' and 'The Rock' ('I am your rock, but I'm rolling away') as well as a duet with Delbert McClinton, 'Road Scholar', a pun in reference to Kris Kristofferson being a Rhodes scholar. Parnell's superb guitar-playing is highlighted on 'Workin' Man Blues' which he cut with Steve Wariner and Diamond Rio; he wanted to call their group, Merle Jam, but was persuaded to settle for the less witty Jed Zepplin. Parnell plays electric slide guitar on Mary Chapin Carpenters's 'Shut Up And Kiss Me' and she joined him for the title track of *We All Get Lucky Sometimes*. Parnell is the only new country artist to be praised by Kinky Friedman; possibly he cut his teeth in the Kinkster's band. *Every Night's A Saturday Night* was a consistent album that looked set to maintain Parnell's recent popularity.

● ALBUMS: *Lee Roy Parnell* (Arista 1990)★★, *Love Without Mercy* (Arista 1992)★★★, *On The Road* (Arista 1993)★★★, *We All Get Lucky Sometimes* (Career 1995)★★★★, *Every Night's A Saturday Night* (Career 1997)★★★.

PARSONS, BILL

b. 8 September 1934, Crossville, Tennessee, USA. Parsons was a friend of country singer Bobby Bare. Prior to entering the US Army, Bare agreed to help Parsons, who was just leaving the service, make a record. Due to a mix-up at Fraternity Records, for which Bare recorded, the 1959 single titled 'The All American Boy', co-written by Parsons and Bare (using the name Orville Lunsford), was credited to Parsons, although it was Bare singing on the record. It rose to number 2 in the US pop charts as the real Bill Parsons stood on the sidelines watching. As Bare had not yet gained any attention within country music, the deception was continued for one other single, which did not chart. Bare then reverted to his true name and, beginning in 1962, launched a very successful country career. As for the real Bill Parsons, he retired from the music business after recording two unsuccessful singles for Starday Records in 1960.

PARSONS, GENE

b. Eugene Victor Parsons, 4 September 1944, Los Angeles, California, USA. Parsons began his musical career playing in the Castaways and subsequently formed a duo with Gib Guilbeau. This was followed by the formation of country group Nashville West, in which Parsons played alongside the celebrated guitarist Clarence White. When the latter was inducted into the Byrds in 1968, Parsons was soon enrolled as their drummer. He remained with them until 1972, appearing on the albums *Dr Byrds & Mr Hyde*, *The Ballad Of Easy Rider*, *(Untitled)*, *Byrdmaniax* and *Farther Along*. Parsons' drumming skills were notable on the extended arrangement of 'Eight Miles High' that the Byrds included in their live sets and on an entire side of *(Untitled)*. Parsons was also a guitarist, banjoist and talented songwriter. Arguably his finest moment as a composer occurred on the excellent 'Gunga Din' from *The Ballad Of Easy Rider*. His other compositions included 'Yesterday's Train' and, in conjunction with Clarence White, the instrumentals 'Green Apple Quick Step' and 'Bristol Steam Convention Blues'. Parsons and White were also responsible for inventing the 'String Bender', an instrument that duplicated the sound of a steel guitar. Following his dismissal from the Byrds, Parsons signed to Warner Brothers and released the impressive *Kindling*. Parsons subsequently joined a latter-day version of the Flying Burrito Brothers for two minor albums, *Flying Again* and *Airborne*. His second solo album, *Melodies*, included a moving tribute to his former partner, the late Clarence White. He also appeared in various offshoot-Byrds reunion concerts, notably with Michael Clarke, before continuing his

recording career with *Birds Of A Feather*, recorded with his wife Meridian Green.

● ALBUMS: *Kindling* (Warners 1973)★★★★, *Melodies* (Sierra 1979)★★, as Parsons Green *Birds Of A Feather* (Sierra 1987)★★★.

● COMPILATIONS: *The Kindling Collection* (Sierra 1995)★★★.

● FURTHER READING: *Timeless Flight: The Definitive Biography Of The Byrds*, Johnny Rogan.

PARSONS, GORDON

b. 24 December 1926, Paddington suburb, Sydney, New South Wales, Australia, d. 17 August 1990. At the age of three the family relocated into the bush to Cooks Creek, where he grew up listening to the radio to break the monotony of the lonely area. He owned his first guitar at the age of 11 and, initially influenced by recordings he heard of Jimmie Rodgers, he was soon known around the area, especially at local dances, for his singing, yodelling and guitar playing. School held little attraction and he left home at 14, when he was offered a job cutting sleepers for the railroad. His father's words to the employer's invitation are reputed to have been: 'You might as well take the mongrel - he's no use here' (he in fact became a skilled axeman, later winning several awards for his abilities). Gaining further influence from recordings of Wilf Carter and fellow Australians Tex Morton and Buddy Williams, he established a reputation as an entertainer. An appearance on a talent show led to him recording six sides for Regal-Zonophone in May 1946. These included 'Where The Bellinger River Flows' and 'The Passing of Cobber Jack'. He toured with Goldwyn Bros Circus, where he met and married Zelda Ashton of the Ashton Circus family (they eventually parted but their daughter, Gail, was born in 1949). He began to tour with various artists, including Slim Dusty and Tex Morton, but he was unable to maintain regular work for long periods. He loved the quiet life, and later saying, 'I never could handle anything long and drawn out', he disappeared from the music scene into the bush to write more songs - sometimes he worked on farms and on others he just 'went fishing'. During the 50s, he made further recordings but he was never a prolific recording artist, in fact, his total recorded output seemingly only amounted to 21 singles and seven albums. Undoubtedly, the best-known song associated with him is 'The Pub With No Beer', which in 1957, became an international hit for his great friend Slim Dusty. There has been some contention over the years regarding the actual authorship of the song. Parsons had once been given some lines of verse and from them, he had written the song. It was later found that a poem by Dan Sheahan called 'A Pub Without Beer', which contained many similarities in the wording, had been printed in a 1944 newspaper. Dusty, who later became Sheahan's friend and recorded several of his songs, has always maintained that Parsons had believed the lines that he had been given were from some anonymous work. Noted Australian writer Eric Watson summed up the controversy by saying that, in his opinion, Sheahan's was the better poem, while Parsons' was the better song. In any event, those who knew of Parsons' fondness for beer later jokingly said that he not only wrote the song, he actually caused it. The song is in fact credited with being Australia's only gold 78 although, surprisingly, it is not actually listed as a million-seller in Murrells' *The Book*

Of Golden Discs. During the 60s, he made further recordings, including his own version of 'The Pub' but his reluctance to maintain routine appearances disappointed his fans. He gradually withdrew from performing except for the occasional show and at one time worked as a warden of a wildlife sanctuary. He married for the third time in 1978 and relocated to Sydney, although he kept a caravan at a fishing place near Gosford, which offered him immediate escape from the humdrum of city life. In the 80s, he released three albums on the Selection label. Over the years, he has won several major awards for his contributions to Australian country music, including having his effigy in the wax museum at Tamworth. In 1982, he received the ultimate honour when he became only the seventh artist to be elected to the Country Music Roll Of Renown (Australia's equivalent to Nashville's Country Music Hall Of Fame). His songs have ranged from the comedy of 'The Pub', to the descriptive ballad 'Ellenborough Falls' and the sadness of 'The Passing Of Cobber Jack'. Known affectionately as the Old GP or just plain Ned, he earned a reputation as a pioneer of Australian country music. Many would say that as a fine singer-songwriter and yodeller, he could have become as well known as any of his contemporaries, had he so wished. When asked why he did not make records he usually replied, 'I dunno, Mate. I'd just as soon poke around the bush and split a few posts' or 'I'd rather be fishing than anything else'.

● ALBUMS: *Rhythm Of The Range* (EMI 70s)★★★, *Gordon Parsons* (Hadley 1976)★★★, *The Old G.P.* (Selection 1980)★★★, *Just Passin' Through* (Selection 80s)★★★, *Throw In A Line* (Selection 80s)★★★.

PARSONS, GRAM

b. Cecil Ingram Connor, 5 November 1946, Winter Haven, Florida, USA, d. 19 September 1973, Joshua Tree, California, USA. Parsons' brief but influential career began in high school as a member of the Pacers. This rock 'n' roll act later gave way to the Legends which, at various points, featured country singer Jim Stafford as well as Kent Lavoie, later known as Lobo. By 1963 Parsons had joined the Shilos, a popular campus attraction modelled on clean-cut folk attraction the Journeymen. The quartet - Parsons, George Wrigley, Paul Surratt and Joe Kelly - later moved to New York's Greenwich Village, but Parsons left the line-up in 1965 upon enrolling at Harvard College. His studies ended almost immediately and, inspired by the concurrent folk rock boom, founded the International Submarine Band with John Nuese (guitar), Ian Dunlop (bass) and Mickey Gauvin (drums). Two excellent singles followed, but having relocated to Los Angeles, Parsons' vision of a contemporary country music found little favour amid the prevalent psychedelic trend. The group was nonetheless signed by producer Lee Hazelwood, but with Dunlop and Gauvin now absent from the line-up, Bob Buchanan (guitar) and Jon Corneal (drums) joined Parsons and Nuese for *Safe At Home*. This excellent set is now rightly viewed as a landmark in the development of country rock, blending standards with several excellent Parsons originals, notably 'Luxury Liner'. However, by the time of its release (April 1968), the quartet had not only folded, but Gram had accepted an offer to join the Byrds.

His induction resulted in *Sweetheart Of The Rodeo*, on which the newcomer determined the group's musical direction. This synthesis of country and traditional styles followed the mould of *Safe At Home*, but was buoyed by the act's excellent harmony work. Although Parsons' role as vocalist was later diminished by Hazelwood's court injunction - the producer claimed it breached their early contract - his influence was undeniable, as exemplified on the stellar 'Hickory Wind'. However, within months Parsons had left the Byrds in protest over a South African tour and instead spent several months within the Rolling Stones' circle. The following year he formed the Flying Burrito Brothers with another ex-Byrd, Chris Hillman, 'Sneaky' Pete Kleinow (pedal steel guitar) and bassist Chris Ethridge (bass). *The Gilded Palace Of Sin* drew inspiration from southern soul and urban country music and included one of Parsons' most poignant compositions, 'Hot Burrito #1'. *Burrito Deluxe* failed to scale the same heights as internal problems undermined the unit's potential. Parsons' growing drug dependency exacerbated this estrangement and he was fired from the group in April 1970. Initial solo recordings with producer Terry Melcher were inconclusive, but in 1972 Parsons was introduced to singer Emmylou Harris and together they completed *G.P.* with the assistance of Elvis Presley's regular back-up band. An attendant tour leading the Fallen Angels - Jock Bartley (guitar), Neil Flanz (pedal steel), Kyle Tullis (bass) and N.D. Smart II (drums) - followed, but Parsons' appetite for self-destruction remained intact. Parsons lived the life of a true 'honky tonk hero' with all the excesses of Hank Williams, even down to his immaculate, embroidered, Nudie tailored suits. Sessions for a second album blended established favourites with original songs, many of which had been written years beforehand. Despite its piecemeal content, the resultant set, *Grievous Angel*, was a triumph, in which plaintive duets ('Love Hurts', 'Hearts On Fire') underscored the quality of the Parsons/Harris partnership, while 'Brass Buttons' and 'In My Hour Of Darkness' revealed a gift for touching lyricism. Parsons' death in 1973 as a result of 'drug toxicity' emphasized its air of poignancy, and the mysterious theft of his body after the funeral, whereupon his road manager, Philip Kaufman, cremated the body in the desert, carrying out Gram's wishes, added to the singer's legend. Although his records were not a commercial success during his lifetime, Parsons' influence on a generation of performers, from the Eagles to Elvis Costello, is a fitting testament to his talent. Emmylou Harris adopted his mantle with a series of superior country rock releases, while an excellent concept album, *Ballad Of Sally Rose* (1985), undoubtedly drew on her brief relationship with this star-struck singer. Parsons' catalogue is painfully small compared with his enormous importance in contemporary country rock, and his work is destined to stand alongside that of his hero Hank Williams.

● ALBUMS: *G.P.* (Reprise 1972)★★★★, *Grievous Angel* (Reprise 1973)★★★★, *Sleepless Nights* (A&M 1976)★★★, *Gram Parsons And The Fallen Angels - Live 1973* (Sierra 1981)★★, *Cosmic American Music* 1972 demos (Sundown 1995)★★★.

● COMPILATIONS: *Gram Parsons* (Warners 1982)★★★, *The Early Years 1963-1965* (Sierra 1984)★★★, *Warm Evenings, Pale Mornings, Bottled Blues* (Raven 1992)★★★.

● FURTHER READING: *Gram Parsons: A Music Biography*, Sid Griffin (ed.). *Hickory Wind: The Life And Times Of Gram Parsons*, Ben Fong-Torres.

PARTON, DOLLY

b. 19 January 1946, Locust Ridge, Tennessee, USA. Dolly
Rebecca Parton's poor farming parents paid the doctor in
cornmeal for attending the birth of the fourth of their 12 offspring. After her appearances as a singing guitarist on local
radio as a child, including the *Grand Ole Opry* in Nashville,
Parton left school in 1964. Her recorded output had included
a raucous rockabilly song called 'Puppy Love' for a small
label as early as 1958, but a signing to Monument in 1966 -
the time of her marriage to the reclusive Carl Dean - yielded
a C&W hit with 'Dumb Blonde', as well as enlistment in the
prestigious *Porter Wagoner Show* as its stetsoned leader's
voluptuous female foil in duets and comedy sketches. While
this post adulterated her more serious artistic worth, she
notched up further country smashes, among them 'Joshua',
the autobiographical 'Coat Of Many Colours' and, with
Wagoner, 'Last Thing On My Mind' (the Tom Paxton folk
standard), 'Better Move It On Home' and 1974's 'Please
Don't Stop Loving Me'. On the crest of another solo hit with
'Jolene' on RCA that same year, she resigned from the show
to strike out on her own - though she continued to record
periodically with Wagoner. Encompassing a generous portion of her own compositions, her post-1974 repertoire was
less overtly country, even later embracing a lucrative stab at
disco in 1979's 'Baby I'm Burning' and non-originals ranging
from 'House Of The Rising Sun' to Jackie Wilson's 'Higher
And Higher'. 'Jolene' became a 'sleeper' UK Top 10 entry in
1976 and she continued her run in the US country chart with
singles such as 'Bargain Store' (banned from some radio stations for 'suggestive' lyrics), 'All I Can Do' and 'Light Of A
Clear Blue Morning' (1977). That same year, 'Here You
Come Again' crossed into the US pop Hot 100, and her siblings basked in reflected glory - particularly Randy, who
played bass in her backing band before landing an RCA contract himself, and Stella Parton, who had already harried the
country list with 1975's 'Ode To Olivia' and 'I Want To Hold
You With My Dreams Tonight'. Their famous sister next ventured into film acting, starring with Lily Tomlin and Jane
Fonda in 1981's *9 To 5* (for which she provided the title
theme), and with Burt Reynolds in the musical *Best Little
Whorehouse In Texas*. Less impressive were *Rhinestone* and
1990's *Steel Magnolias*. She also hosted a 1987 television
variety series which lost a ratings war. Nevertheless, her success as a recording artist, songwriter and big-breasted 'personality' remained unstoppable. As well as ploughing back
royalties for 70s cover versions of Parton numbers by
Emmylou Harris, Linda Ronstadt and Maria Muldaur into
her Dollywood entertainment complex, she teamed up with
Kenny Rogers in 1983 to reach the number 1 position in the
USA and Top 10 in the UK with a Bee Gees composition,
'Islands In The Stream'. With Rogers too, she managed
another US country number 1 two years later with 'Real
Love'. Although other 80s singles such as 'I Will Always Love
You' and 'Tennessee Homesick Blues' were not major chart
hits, they became as well-known as many that did. *Trio* with
Ronstadt and Harris won a Grammy for best country album
in 1987. Her CBS debut, *Rainbow*, represented her deepest
plunge into mainstream pop - though 1989's *White Limozeen*
(produced by Ricky Skaggs) retained the loyalty of her multi-
national grassroots following. Her celebration of international womanhood, 'Eagle When She Flies', confirmed her
return to the country market in 1991. In 1992, Whitney

Houston had the biggest-selling single of the year in the UK
with Parton's composition 'I Will Always Love You', which
she sang in the film *The Bodyguard*. Her excellent 1995
album reprised the latter song as a duet with Vince Gill.
Treasures paid tribute to singer-songwriters of the 60s and
70s, including songs by Cat Stevens and Neil Young alongside the expected country material.

● ALBUMS: *Hello, I'm Dolly* (Monument 1967)★★, with
Porter Wagoner *Just Between You And Me* (RCA Victor
1968)★★★, with George Jones *Dolly Parton And George Jones*
(Starday 1968)★★, *Just Because I'm A Woman* (RCA
1968)★★★, with Wagoner *Just The Two Of Us* (RCA Victor
1968)★★★, with Wagoner *Always, Always* (RCA Victor
1969)★★★, *My Blue Ridge Mountain Boy* (RCA 1969)★★★,
with Wagoner *Porter Wayne And Dolly Rebecca* (RCA Victor
1970)★★★, *A Real Live Dolly* (RCA 1970)★★★, with Wagoner
Once More (RCA Victor 1970)★★★, with Wagoner *Two Of A
Kind* (RCA Victor 1971)★★★, *Coat Of Many Colours* (RCA
1971)★★★★, with Wagoner *The Right Combination* (RCA
Victor 1972)★★★, with Wagoner *Together Always* (RCA
Victor 1972)★★★, with Wagoner *Love And Music* (RCA
Victor 1973)★★★, with Wagoner *We Found It* (RCA Victor
1973)★★★, *My Tennessee Mountain Home* (RCA 1973)★★★★,
with Wagoner *Porter 'N' Dolly* (RCA 1974)★★★, *Love Is Like A
Butterfly* (RCA 1974)★★★★, *Jolene* (RCA 1974)★★★★, with
Wagoner *Say Forever You'll Be Mine* (RCA 1975)★★★, *The
Bargain Store* (RCA 1975)★★★★, *Dolly* (RCA 1976)★★★, *All I
Can Do* (RCA 1976)★★★, *New Harvest ... First Gathering*
(RCA 1977)★★★★, *Here You Come Again* (RCA 1977)★★,
Heartbreaker (RCA 1978)★★, *Dolly Parton And Friends At
Goldband* (1979)★★, *Great Balls Of Fire* (RCA 1979)★★, with
Wagoner *Porter Wagoner & Dolly Parton* (RCA 1980)★★★★,
Dolly Dolly Dolly (RCA 1980)★★, *9 To 5 And Odd Jobs* (RCA
1980)★★★, *Heartbreak Express* (RCA 1982)★★, *The Best Little
Whorehouse In Texas* film soundtrack (MCA 1982)★★, with
Kris Kristofferson, Brenda Lee, Willie Nelson *The Winning
Hand* (Monument 1983)★★★, *Burlap And Satin* (RCA
1983)★★, *The Great Pretender* (RCA 1984)★★, *Rhinestone*
film soundtrack (RCA 1984)★★, with Kenny Rogers *Once
Upon A Christmas* (RCA 1984)★★★, *Real Love* (RCA
1985)★★★, with Linda Ronstadt, Emmylou Harris *Trio*
(Warners 1987)★★★, *Rainbow* (Columbia 1987)★★, *White
Limozeen* (Columbia 1989)★★★, *Eagle When She Flies*
(Columbia 1991)★★★, *Straight Talk* film soundtrack
(Hollywood 1992,)★★, *Slow Dancing With The Moon*
(Columbia 1993)★★★, with Wagoner *Sweet Harmony*
(1993)★★, with Tammy Wynette, Loretta Lynn *Honky Tonk
Angels* (Columbia 1993)★★★★, *Heartsongs - Live From Home*
(Columbia 1994)★★★, *Something Special* (Columbia
1995)★★★, *Treasures* (Rising Tide 1996)★★★.

● COMPILATIONS: with Wagoner *The Best Of Porter
Wagoner And Dolly Parton* (RCA Victor 1971)★★★★, *The Best
Of Dolly Parton* (RCA 1973)★★★★, *The Best Of Dolly Parton
Volume 2* (RCA 1975)★★★★, with Wagoner *Hits Of Dolly
Parton And Porter Wagoner* (RCA 1977)★★★★, *The Dolly
Parton Collection* (Pickwick 1979)★★★, *The Very Best Of Dolly
Parton* (RCA 1981)★★★★, *The Dolly Parton Collection*
(Monument 1982)★★★, *Greatest Hits* (RCA 1982)★★,
Collector's Series (RCA 1985)★★★, *The World Of Dolly Parton,
Vol. 1* (Monument 1988)★★★, *The World Of Dolly Parton, Vol.
2* (Monument 1988)★★★, *Greatest Hits Volume 2* (RCA
1989)★★, *Anthology* (Connoisseur 1991)★★★, *The RCA

Years 1967-1986 2-CD set (RCA 1993)★★★★, *The Essential Dolly Parton - Volume One* (RCA 1995)★★★, *The Greatest Hits* (Telstar 1995)★★★, with Wagoner *The Essential Porter And Dolly* (RCA 1996)★★★★, *I Will Always Love You And Other Greatest Hits* (Columbia 1996)★★★, *The Essential Dolly Parton - Volume Two* (RCA 1997)★★★.

● VIDEOS: *Dolly Parton In London* (RCA/Columbia 1988), with Kenny Rogers *Real Love* (RCA/Columbia 1988).

● FURTHER READING: *Dolly Parton: Country Goin' To Town*, Susan Saunders. *Dolly Parton*, Otis James. *The Official Dolly Parton Scrapbook*, Connie Berman. *Dolly*, Alanna Nash. *Dolly Parton (By Scott Keely)*, Scott Keely. *Dolly Parton*, Robert K. Krishef. *Dolly, Here I Come Again*, Leonore Fleischer. *My Story*, Dolly Parton.

PARTON, STELLA

b. 4 May 1949, Locust Ridge, near Sevier County, Tennessee, USA. Parton, the sixth of 12 children, made her radio debut with her sister, Dolly Parton, in 1955. She sang in local clubs and arrived in Nashville in 1972. She recorded, without success, for the small Royal American and Music City labels and toured with a gospel group. She returned to country music in 1975 with a defence of Olivia Newton-John's awards from the Country Music Association called 'Ode To Olivia'. She spent 18 weeks in the US country charts with 'I Want To Hold You In My Dreams Tonight' for the Country Soul label before switching to Elektra. She then made the US country Top 20 with 'Danger Of A Stranger', 'Standard Lie Number 1' and 'Four Little Letters'. Parton is a slim blonde but the cover of her 1978 album, *Stella Parton*, was airbrushed to give her similar assets to her famous sister! On that album, 10 members of the Parton family join her on 'Down To Earth', while she is also featured on the soundtrack of her sister's film *Rhinestone*. She has also played in a stage version of the film *The Best Little Whorehouse In Texas*, taking the role Dolly originally played in the film. She returned to music after a long absence with 1996's *A Woman's Touch*.

● ALBUMS: *I Want To Hold You In My Arms Tonight* (Country Soul 1975)★★★, *Country Sweet* (Elektra 1977)★★★, *Stella Parton* (Elektra 1978)★★★, *Love Ya* (Elektra 1979)★★, *So Far...So Good* (Elektra 1982)★★★, *A Woman's Touch* (SPPI 1996)★★.

PATTERSON, RAY AND INA

A highly popular husband-and-wife harmony duo originally formed in 1947. It comprised Ray Patterson (b. 17 April 1926, near Clayton, New Mexico, USA; mandolin, guitar, most other stringed instruments, vocals) and Ina (b. Ina Lee Phelps, 13 March 1929, Dexter, Texas, USA; guitar, vocals). Patterson's family had hopes of him becoming a classical violinist but he had differing ideas, and by the time he was 17, he played guitar and mandolin. He was badly wounded in Europe during World War II and while convalescing in a hospital in Colorado, he met Ina. They were married in 1945 and made their home in Roswell, Texas, where the Patterson family had relocated in 1934. They began to sing together, and in 1947, they became regulars on Roswell's *Saturday Night Jamboree*. Until 1960, they continued to be popular performers on numerous stations that ranged from Ohio to Texas and Alabama and Carolina to Colorado, where they finished at KPIK Colorado Springs, appearing there on radio and television. They recorded for several minor labels, cut

transcription programmes for Border Radio and published a very popular songbook. Between 1962 and 1985, they lived in Woodland Park, Colorado, where Ray worked as a photographer but they still sang their old-time songs at special events. They made further recordings in 1966 and 1973, which led to their appearance at some major festivals. Ina developed hearing difficulties in 1881 and they more or less retired from music to live at Colorado Springs. Noted authority Ivan M. Tribe commented: 'The duo possessed some of the finest harmony in the history of the genre although they arrived on the scene a little too late to have the impact of the Blue Sky Boys'. In reality, they succeeded, singing in a style that had seen its best days a quarter of a century earlier and yet they were good enough to prove popular for many years. Sadly for them, they never had the opportunity to record for a major label during their best days.

● ALBUMS: *Old Time Ballads & Hymns* (County 1967)★★★, *Old Time Songs* (County 1969)★★★, *Songs Of Home And Childhood* (County 1973)★★★.

PAUL, LES

b. 9 June 1915, Wankesha, Wisconsin, USA. Paul began playing guitar and other instruments while still a child. In the early 30s he broadcast on the radio and in 1936 was leading his own trio. In the late 30s and early 40s he worked in New York, where he was featured on Fred Waring's radio show. He made records accompanying singers such as Bing Crosby and the Andrews Sisters. Although his work was in the popular vein, with a strong country leaning, Paul was highly adapatable and frequently sat in with jazz musicians. One of his favourites was Nat 'King' Cole, whom he knew in Los Angeles, and the two men appeared together at a Jazz At The Philharmonic concert in 1944, on which Paul played some especially fine blues. Dissatisfied with the sound of the guitars he played, Paul developed his own design for a solid-bodied instrument, which he had made at his own expense. Indeed, the company, Gibson, were so cool towards the concept that they insisted their name should not appear on the instruments they made for him. In later years, when it seemed that half the guitarists in the world were playing Les Paul-style Gibson guitars, the company's attitude was understandably a little different. Paul's dissatisfaction with existing techniques extended beyond the instrument and into the recording studios. Eager to experiment with a multi-tracking concept, he built a primitive studio in his own home. He produced a succession of superb recordings on which he played multi-track guitar, among them 'Lover', 'Nola', 'Brazil' and 'Whispering'. During the 50s Paul continued his experimentation with other, similar recordings, while his wife, Mary Ford (b. 7 July 1928, d. 30 September 1977), sang multiple vocal lines. Other major record successes were 'The World Is Waiting For The Sunrise', 'How High The Moon', which reached number 1, and 'Vaya Con Dios', another US number 1 hit. By the early 60s Paul had tired of the recording business and retired. He and Ford were divorced in 1963 and he spent his time inventing and helping to promote Gibson guitars. In the late 70s he returned to the studios for two successful albums of duets with Chet Atkins, but by the end of the decade he had retired again. A television documentary in 1980, *The Wizard Of Wankesha*, charted his life and revived interest in his career.

In 1984 he made a comeback to performing and continued to make sporadic appearances throughout the rest of the decade. He was even performing at the guitar festival in Seville, Spain in 1992. A remarkably gifted and far-sighted guitarist, Paul's contribution to popular music must inevitably centre upon his pioneering work on multi-tracking and his creation of the solid-bodied guitar. It would be sad, however, if his efforts in these directions wholly concealed his considerable abilities as a performer.

● ALBUMS: with Mary Ford *Hawaiian Paradise* (Decca 1949)★★, *Galloping Guitars* (Decca 1952)★★★, with Ford *New Sound, Volume 1 & 2* (Capitol 1950)★★★, *Bye, Bye Blues* (Capitol 1952)★★★★, with Ford *The Hitmakers* (Capitol 1955)★★★, with Ford *Les And Mary* (Capitol 1955)★★★★, with Ford *Time To Dream* (Capitol 1957)★★★, *More Of Les* (Decca 1958)★★★, with Ford *Lover's Luau* (Columbia 1959)★★★, with Ford *Warm And Wonderful* (Columbia 1962)★★★, with Ford *Bouquet Of Roses* (Columbia 1962)★★★, with Ford *Swingin' South* (Columbia 1963)★★★, *Les Paul Now* (Decca 1968)★★★, with Chet Atkins *Chester And Lester* (RCA Victor 1976)★★★, with Atkins *Guitar Monsters* (RCA Victor 1978)★★★.

● COMPILATIONS: with Ford *The Hits Of Les And Mary* (Capitol 1960)★★★★, with Ford *The Fabulous Les Paul And Mary Ford* (Columbia 1965)★★★, *The Very Best Of Les Paul And Mary Ford* (1974)★★★★, with Ford *The Capitol Years* (Capitol 1989)★★★★, *The Legend And The Legacy* 4-CD box set (Capitol 1991)★★★★.

● VIDEOS: *He Changed The Music* (Excalibur 1990), *Living Legend Of The Electric Guitar* (BMG 1995).

● FURTHER READING: *Les Paul: An American Original*, Mary Alice Shaughnessy. *Gibson Les Paul Book: A Complete History Of Les Paul Guitars*, Tony Bacon and Paul Day.

PAYCHECK, JOHNNY

b. Donald Eugene Lytle, 31 May 1938, Greenfield, Ohio, USA. His date of birth is often disputed, and varies between 1938 and 1941. The title of Paycheck's 1977 country hit, 'I'm The Only Hell (Mama Ever Raised)', is apt as he has been in trouble throughout his life; the wild eyes on his album sleeves give the picture. Although only 5 feet 5 inches, he is tougher than most and served two years for assaulting an officer while in the US Navy. He moved to Nashville and played bass and sometimes steel guitar for Porter Wagoner, Faron Young, Ray Price and chiefly, George Jones. He made several records with Jones, singing tenor on *I'm A People* and the hit singles 'Love Bug' and 'The Race Is On'. At first, he recorded rockabilly as Donny Young in 1959 ('Shaking The Blues', written by Jones) and then sang country on Mercury Records ('On Second Thoughts'). Most people think the name Johnny Paycheck was a parody of Johnny Cash, but it came from a heavyweight boxer who was KO'd by Joe Louis in two rounds in 1940 and was close to Paycheck's own Polish family name. By now, he had developed Jones's mannerisms and he had country hits with 'A-11' and 'Heartbreak, Tennessee'. He wrote Tammy Wynette's first hit, 'Apartment No. 9', and Ray Price's 'Touch My Heart'. He formed his own Little Darlin' Records in 1966 and had country hits with 'The Lovin' Machine', Bobby Bare's composition 'Motel Time Again' and 'Don't Monkey With Another Monkey's Monkey'. His supposedly live album from Carnegie Hall was actually recorded in a studio on April Fool's Day 1966. Paycheck

became an alcoholic, the label went bankrupt and he was arrested for burglary. He moved to Los Angeles, living hand to mouth, spending what little money he had on drink and drugs. Record producer Billy Sherrill rehabilitated him and he had a massive country hit with 'Don't Take Her, She's All I Got' in 1971. This was followed by 'Someone To Give My Love To', 'Mr. Lovemaker' and 'Song And Dance Man'. Paycheck also had success on the US country charts with a gospel-flavoured duet with Jody Miller, 'Let's All Go Down To The River'. Further troubles led to bankruptcy and a paternity suit in 1976. In 1977, at the height of outlaw country, he had his biggest country hit with David Allan Coe's anthem to working people, 'Take This Job And Shove It', and its b-side, 'Colorado Cool-Aid', was successful in its own right. He is well known in country circles in the UK for his narration 'The Outlaw's Prayer', from *Armed And Crazy*. His lifestyle is reflected in 'Me And The I.R.S.', 'D.O.A. (Drunk On Arrival)', and '11 Months And 29 Days', which was his sentence for passing a dud cheque at a Holiday Inn - a case of Johnny Badcheck. A law suit with his manager followed and his friends, George Jones and Merle Haggard, made albums with him. In 1981, after he went back to a woman's house after a concert, he was arrested for allegedly raping her 12-year-old daughter. The charges were reduced - he was fined and given probation - but he was dropped by Epic Records, although he maintained, 'I dropped them. I couldn't stand the back-stabbing stench there anymore'. Then, in 1985, he got into a bar-room argument with a stranger - and shot him. While awaiting trial, he recorded with the 'de-frocked' evangelist John Wesley Fletcher. Paycheck claimed he had the gun because he had emphysema and so could not fight physically! He was found guilty and entered prison in 1989, recording a live album with a visiting Merle Haggard while incarcerated. In 1991 his sentence was commuted, subject to community services. PayCheck (note the new spelling) also recorded a duet with George Jones, 'The Last Outlaw's Alive And Doing Well'. Whether his latest work will meet with commercial success remains uncertain, but various performers gave him their support at a tribute concert. If he is short of cash, he should be able to sell his extraordinary story to the movies. It may be the only way in which he can resolve his debts to the IRS.

● ALBUMS: *Johnny Paycheck At Carnegie Hall* (Little Darlin' 1966)★★★, *The Lovin' Machine* (Little Darlin' 1966)★★★, *Gospeltime In My Fashion* (Little Darlin' 1966)★★★, *Jukebox Charlie* (Little Darlin' 1967)★★★, *Country Soul* (Little Darlin' 1968)★★★, *Wherever You Are* (Little Darlin' 1969)★★★, *Johnny Paycheck Again* (Centron 1970)★★★, *She's All I Got* (1971)★★★, *Heartbreak, Tennessee* (Epic 1972)★★★, *Mr. Lovemaker* (Epic 1972)★★★, *Song And Dance Man* (Epic 1972)★★★, *Somebody Love Me* (Epic 1973)★★★, *Slide Off Your Satin Sheets* (Epic 1977)★★★, *Take This Job And Shove It* (Epic 1978)★★★★, *Armed And Crazy* (Epic 1978)★★★, *11 Months And 29 Days* (Epic 1979)★★★★, with George Jones *Double Trouble* (Epic 1980)★★★, *Everybody's Got A Family - Meet Mine* (Epic 1980)★★★, *New York Town* (Epic 1980)★★★, with Merle Haggard *Mr. Hag Told My Story* (Epic 1981)★★★, *Lovers And Losers* (Epic 1982)★★, *Back On The Job* (Astan 1984)★★★, *I Don't Need To Know That Right Now* (Allegience 1984)★★★, *Apartment No. 9* (President 1985)★★★, *Modern Times* (1987)★★★, *Honky Tonk And Slow Music* (Sundown 1988)★★★, *Outlaw At The Cross* (1989)★★,

Live In Branson, MO, USA (Playback 1993)★★, *The Difference In Me* (Playback 1993)★★★.
● COMPILATIONS: *Biggest Hits* (Epic 1983)★★★, *16 Greatest Hits* (1988)★★★, *The Real Mr. Heartache: The Little Darlin' Years* (Country Music Foundation 1996)★★★★.

PAYNE, JIMMY

b. 12 April 1936, Leachville, Arkansas, USA. The Payne family moved to Gideon, Missouri, in 1944 and Jimmy enjoyed country music and singing in church. He had a gospel programme on the radio on Saturdays and was picking cotton during the week. In 1957, he moved to St. Louis to work as a professional country singer. He met Chuck Glaser while in the US Army and played guitar with the Glaser Brothers band. Chuck Glaser took over his management when he formed his band, the Payne Gang. He made several singles including 'Ladder To The Sky', 'What Does It Take (To Keep A Woman Like You Satisfied)' and 'My Most Requested Song'. He first appeared on the *Grand Ole Opry* in 1966. He cut several singles including his own composition, 'Woman, Woman', which had national success in 1967 when it was recorded by Gary Puckett And The Union Gap. He continued to have only minor success as a solo artist - 'L.A. Angels', 'Rambling Man' and 'Turning My Love On' - but he wrote Charley Pride's US number 1 country single, 'My Eyes Can Only See As Far As You'. He wrote the popular title track of his gospel album, *Walk With Me The Rest Of The Way*, with Jim Glaser. In 1986 he recorded a duet, 'Ugly Women And Pickup Trucks', with Tompall Glaser.
● ALBUMS: *Woman, Woman, What Does It Take* (1968)★★★, *Live At Broadmoor* (1976)★★, *Walk With Me The Rest Of The Way* (1978)★★★, *The Best That Love Can Give* (1980)★★, *The Album Version* (1986)★★.

PAYNE, LEON

b. Leon Roger Payne, 15 June 1917, Alba, Texas, USA, d. 11 September 1969. Payne became blind as a young child following the application of the wrong medication for an eye complaint. Between 1924 and 1935, he attended the Texas School for the Blind in Austin, where he studied music and learnt to play guitar, banjo, organ, piano, trombone and drums. After graduating, he worked briefly as a one-man band. In 1935, he appeared as a vocalist on KWET Palestine and during the 30s, he worked with several bands including, in 1938, that of Bob Wills. In spite of his blindness, he travelled extensively (often hitchhiking to venues) and appeared on many Texas stations as well as the *Louisiana Hayride*. In 1948, he played with Jack Rhodes' Rhythm Boys, but in 1949, he formed his own band, the Lone Star Buddies, and played the *Grand Ole Opry*. Although a fine vocalist, he is best remembered for his songwriting and from the late 40s, his songs were regularly hits for other artists. These included 'Cry Baby Heart' (George Morgan), 'Lost Highway' and 'They'll Never Take Her Love From Me' (Hank Williams), 'For Now And Always' and 'There Wasn't An Organ At Our Wedding' (Hank Snow), 'You Can't Pick A Rose In December' (Ernest Ashworth) and 'Blue Side Of Lonesome' (Jim Reeves and George Jones). There is little doubt that the song for which he will always be remembered is 'I Love You Because'. Written in 1949 for his wife Myrtie, it has been recorded by countless artists including Ernest Tubb, Carl Smith, Johnny Cash and Elvis Presley. In the UK,

it is always associated with Jim Reeves, whose recording was a number 5 UK pop hit in 1964. The fact is often overlooked that, in 1949, Payne's own recording was a US country number 1, the only version actually to top the charts. In 1956, he recorded a cover version of Presley's 'My Baby Left Me', under the pseudonym of Rock Rogers. He refused to use his own name for rock 'n' roll, in the fear that it might upset country music fans. During his career, Payne recorded for various labels including MGM, Bluebird, Bullet, Capitol, Decca and Starday. One album made for the latter label featured songs appertaining to events in the Old West. In 1965, he suffered a heart attack and retired to San Antonio, where he died following a further heart attack on 11 September 1969. He was one of the first members elected to the Nashville Songwriters' International Hall Of Fame when it was founded in 1970. Two radically different performers have paid tribute to his work - Elvis Costello with a recording of Payne's most bizarre song, the mass-murder saga 'Psycho', and George Jones with an album devoted to Payne's compositions.
● ALBUMS: *Americana* (Starday 1963)★★★, *Leon Payne: A Living Legend Of Country Music* (Starday 1963)★★★★, *Gone But Not Forgotten* (1988)★★★.

PEARL, MINNIE

b. Sarah Ophelia Colley, 25 October 1912, Centerville, Tennessee, USA, d. 4 March 1996, Nashville, Tennessee, USA. The daughter of a prominent businessman, she, unlike many country artists, grew up in relative luxury though under the strict supervision of her mother, who played the local church organ. She developed an interest in the stage as a small child and later, when permitted, watched vaudeville shows at a Nashville theatre, being very impressed by the act of comedienne Elviry Weaver. After graduating from high school, she attended Nashville's Ward-Belmont College, a fashionable finishing school for young ladies, where, in 1932, she acquired a degree in speech and drama. She worked as a teacher in her home-town for two years, before finding work with a company that toured the south, producing amateur plays in rural areas. In 1936, after meeting what was later described as 'an amusing old mountain woman' when touring in Alabama, she began to develop her alter ego. Colley worked hard over the next few years, gradually building her act and it was not until November 1940 that she first auditioned for the *Grand Ole Opry*. Although the *Opry* management had some misgivings that she would be accepted as a country character, because of her known upper-class education, she was permitted to appear on the late evening show. Roy Acuff was impressed and a few weeks later signed her to his roadshow. The audience on the night were amused and Minnie Pearl was on the *Opry* to stay, and destined to become one of its most popular stars. Minnie Pearl, dressed in her cheap frilly cotton dress and wearing a wide-brimmed hat with the price label still attached, became an *Opry* legend. After an opening catch-phrase of 'How-dee, I'm just so proud to be here', she chattered incessantly about the community of Grinder's Switch (an actual small railway switching point near Centerville), told appallingly corny jokes, recited comic monologues, sang (badly), included a little dance and related how one day she would catch her boyfriend, Hezzie.
Since 1940, Minnie Pearl worked with most major country

stars and once featured in popular routines with *Opry* comedian Rod Brasfield. In 1947, she appeared on the first country show to play Carnegie Hall, New York (she returned with a second show in 1961) and also married Henry Cannon, a commercial pilot, who became her manager. She later joked, 'I married my transportation'. She toured extensively with *Opry* and other shows in America and Canada and appeared in Europe, including a 1949-50 tour with her friends Hank Williams, Red Foley and Rod Brasfield. Over the years she appeared on all major network radio and television shows. She recorded for several labels but not being a recognized vocalist, failed to find chart success to match that of her stage act. Her only country chart entry came in 1966 with a Top 10 hit in 'Giddyup Go - Answer', the woman's reply to Red Sovine's country number 1. During her long career she received many awards, the most important being her election to the Country Music Hall of Fame in 1975. Her plaque reads: 'Humor is the least recorded but certainly one of the most important aspects of live country music.' In the early 80s, three attacks of breast cancer led to double mastectomy surgery in 1985. She was fitted with a pacemaker in 1990, but on each occasion, she soon returned to her *Opry* commitments. She made her final appearance there on 14 June 1991, when, during her usual cross-patter routine with Roy Acuff, she completely forget her lines. Acuff managed to cover the mistake, but Pearl ran off stage calling to her husband, 'Henry, we've got to go home . . . right now'. Three days later, a stroke that left her partially paralysed on the left side, brought to an end her 51-year association with the show. In 1992, by her own wishes, she entered a retirement home and from that time, she usually refused to see any visitors. Her condition slowly worsened and she died on 4 March 1996, following a further stroke. In addition to her many country music awards, in 1992 she was also presented with the National Medal of Arts by President Bush, and in 1994, she was inducted into the National Comedy Hall Of Fame.

● ALBUMS: *Howdee (Cousin Gal From Grinder's Switch At The Party)* (Starday 1963)★★★, *Laugh-A-Long* (Pickwick/Hilltop 1964)★★★, *America's Beloved Minnie Pearl* (Starday 1965)★★★, *The Country Music Story* narrated by Minnie Pearl but songs by others (Starday 1966)★★★, *Howdy!* (Sunset 1967)★★★, *Looking For A Feller* (Nashville 1970)★★★, *Grand Old Opry Stars (Grandpa Jones & Minnie Pearl)* (RCA Camden 1975)★★★.

PEER, RALPH

b. Ralph Sylvester Peer, 22 May 1892, Kansas City, Missouri, USA, d. 19 January 1960, Hollywood, California, USA. A leading talent scout, recording engineer and record producer in the field of country music in the 20s and 30s, Peer went on to form the famous Southern Music Publishing Company. After working for his father, who sold sewing machines, phonographs and records, he spent several years with Columbia Records in Kansas City, until around 1920, when he was hired as recording director of General Phonograph's OKeh label. In the same year he supervised what is said to be the first blues recording, Mamie Smith's 'Crazy Blues', and followed that, in June 1923, with another 'first', when he set up mobile recording equipment in Atlanta, Georgia, to make what was reputedly the first genuine country record, Fiddlin' John Carson's 'Little Old Log Cabin In The

Lane'/'That Old Hen Cackled And The Rooster's Goin' To Crow'. Early in 1925 Peer recorded some sides with Ernest V. 'Pop' Stoneman, the pivotal figure of the Stoneman Family. Out of these sessions came 'The Sinking Of The Titanic', one of the biggest-selling records of the 20s. In 1926 Peer moved to Victor Records, and began to tour the southern states in search of new talent. He struck gold in August of the following year, when he recorded Jimmie Rodgers and the Carter Family on the same session. Rodgers, who later became known as the 'Father Of Country Music', cut 'The Soldier's Sweetheart' and 'Sleep, Baby, Sleep', while the Carters' first sides included 'Single Girl, Married Girl'. Another historic session took place in 1931 when Peers recorded Rodgers and the Carters performing together. In 1928, together with Victor, Peer formed the Southern Music Company, to publish and promote the expanding catalogue of country music.

Within two years, he had extended his interests to jazz, having added the legendary names and songs of Fats Waller, Jelly Roll Morton, Louis Armstrong and Count Basie to Southern's roster. Shortly afterwards Peer broadened his canvas even further by moving into popular music, with songs as diverse as Hoagy Carmichael and Stuart Gorrell's 'Georgia On My Mind' and the French waltz 'Fascination', written by F.D. Marchetti, Maurice de Feraudy and Dick Manning. Ten years after 'Rockin' Chair', Southern published 'Lazy River', another Carmichael standard, which was successfully revived in 1961 by Bobby Darin. In 1932 Peer acquired sole ownership of Southern from Victor and, in the same year, opened a London office headed by Harry Steinberg. Steinberg was able to place Southern copyrights with top bandleaders such as Henry Hall, enabling them to be heard on the popular radio programmes of the day. The 30s were boom years for sheet music, and it was not uncommon to sell over a million copies of a particular tune. In 1934 Southern had a smash hit in the UK with Fred Hillebrand's 'Home James And Don't Spare The Horses', which was popularized by Elsie Carlisle and Sam Browne with the Ambrose Orchestra. Back in the USA, Benny Goodman opened and closed his programmes with 'Let's Dance' and 'Goodbye', both Southern copyrights. In the early 30s Peer had visited Mexico and picked up several songs such as 'Granada' and 'Maria Elena', but in 1938, Southern's situation completely changed, and the publishing company moved dramatically into the big league. After further journeys to Central America, Peer flooded the world market with that region's music, and transformed it into enormous hits. Songs such as 'Frenesi', 'Brazil', 'Tico Tico', 'Perfidia' (a hit in 1941 for Glenn Miller and revived 20 years later by the Ventures), 'Baia', 'Ba-Ba-Lu', 'Amor', 'Besame Mucho' and 'El Cumbanchero' endured as some of Southern's most lucrative copyrights. 'Time Was' ('Duerme'), successful for bandleader Jimmy Dorsey in 1941, was still heard regularly in the UK in the 90s, in a version by Nelson Riddle's Orchestra, as the signature tune of veteran broadcaster Hubert Gregg's long-running radio show, *Thanks For The Memory*. Southern had another big hit with the title song from the 1939 movie *Intermezzo*, which starred Ingrid Bergman and Leslie Howard. It was especially popular in the UK, where the film's title was *Escape To Happiness*. In 1940 there came another watershed when the dispute between the ASCAP and US radio stations, led to the inauguration of the rival Broadcast Music Incorporated (BMI). BMI supported music by blues, country and hillbilly artists, and Peer, through his Peer-International company, soon contributed a major part of BMI's catalogue.

During World War II, and just afterwards, Peer published many fondly remembered songs such as 'Deep In The Heart Of Texas' and 'You Are My Sunshine' (both hits for Bing Crosby), 'Humpty Dumpty Heart' (Glenn Miller), 'You're Nobody 'Till Somebody Loves You' (Russ Morgan), 'The Three Caballeros' (Andrews Sisters), 'Say A Prayer For The Boys Over There' (Deanna Durbin), 'I Should Care' and 'The Coffee Song' (both Frank Sinatra), 'That's What I Like About The South' (Phil Harris), 'You've Changed' (Connie Russell), 'I Get the Neck Of The Chicken' (Freddie Martin) and 'Can't Get Out Of This Mood' (Johnny Long). Hot on the trail of the liberating forces, Peer was back in Europe in 1945, and published Jean Villard and Bert Reisfeld's composition 'Les Trois Cloches' ('The Three Bells'), which was recorded by Edith Piaf, and subsequently became a hit for the Browns in 1952, when it was also known as 'The Jimmy Brown Song'. Around that time, Peer was still publishing such music as 'Mockingbird Hill', a million-seller for Patti Page and Les Paul And Mary Ford, 'Sway' (Dean Martin and Bobby Rydell), 'Busy Line' (Rose Murphy) and the novelty 'I Know An Old Lady' (Burl Ives). Then came the rock 'n' roll revolution, during which Southern published hits by Buddy Holly, Little Richard, the Big Bopper and the Platters. In 1956 Peer-Southern's Mexican office signed Perez Prado, who is credited with having created the Latin-American jazz style of the mambo. He added evergreens such as 'Patricia' and 'Mambo Jambo' to the catalogue. By then Peer had relinquished control of the Peer-Southern empire, which was represented by over 20 offices throughout the world, and handed over the running to his son, Ralph Peer II. Peer Snr was devoting more time to copyright law, and to his absorbing interest in horticulture, especially camellias, on which he was a leading authority. In the 60s Southern had successful copyrights with songs such as 'Running Bear' (Johnny Preston), 'What In the World's Come Over You' (Jack Scott), 'Little Boy Sad' (Johnny Burnette), 'Clementine' (Bobby Darin), 'Love Me With All Your Heart' (Karl Denver), 'Catch The Wind' (Donovan), 'Detroit City' (Bobby Bare) and 'Winchester Cathedral' (New Vaudeville Band). The original country connection was retained with material such as Mel Tillis's 'Ruby, Don't Take Your Love To Town', which was a big hit for Kenny Rogers. Sadly, Peer did not live to hear those songs.

PENNY, HANK

b. Herbert Clayton Penny, 18 August 1918, Birmingham, Alabama, USA, d. 17 April 1992, California, USA. His father, who became a hypnotist, learned to play the guitar and wrote poetry after being disabled in a mine accident, gave him his first guitar tuition and his interest in entertaining. At the age of 15, he joined the act of Hal Burns on WAPI, playing banjo and learning comedy routines. In 1936, he moved to New Orleans where he worked with Lew Childre on WWL. He disliked the *Grand Ole Opry*'s hillbilly music and became somewhat obsessed by what he termed Texas fiddle music, being the Western-Swing music of Bob Wills and Milton Brown. He returned to Birmingham, formed his band the Radio Cowboys and began to present his swing

music, first on WAPI and WKBC Birmingham and then at WDOD Chattanooga. Penny made his first recordings for ARC (with Art Satherley) in 1938, recording such up-tempo swing-jazz-country tunes as 'Hesitation Blues'. In 1939, he moved to WSB Atlanta and joined the *Crossroads Follies*. Here, Boudleaux Bryant and steel guitarist Noel Boggs joined the band. In July 1939, he recorded 'Won't You Ride In My Little Red Wagon', which became his signature tune. The group disbanded in 1940 and for a time Penny worked solo on WSB but recorded with a 'pickup' band in 1941. In 1942, he moved to WLW Cincinnati, appeared regularly on the *Boone County Jamboree* and *Mid-Western Hayride* and worked with Merle Travis and Grandpa Jones. He toured with various shows and also fronted a group called the Plantation Boys, with whom he recorded for King Records in 1944.

He moved to Hollywood in 1945, re-formed his band and played the ballroom circuits of California. Later that year, he took over the band of Deuce Spriggins, played a residency at the famed *Riverside Rancho* and had his own show on KXLA and KGIL. He made further recordings for King and also appeared in four Charles Starrett B-movie westerns. He registered his first US country chart hits in 1946 with 'Steel Guitar Stomp' and 'Get Yourself A Redhead' (both reaching number 4). In 1947, apart from his band work, he played on ABC's network *Roundup Time* as a comedian. He had a further number 4 country hit in 1950 with 'Bloodshot Eyes', which also was a hit for R&B artist Wynonie Harris. Penny also joined his friend Spade Cooley's network television show as a comedian, but still maintained a rigorous schedule of playing dancehalls with his band, now known as the Penny Serenaders. He recorded for RCA-Victor in 1950, using an enlarged band that recorded as Hank Penny And His California Cowhands. In 1951, he left Spade Cooley and became the comedian with the Dude Martin stage and television show and he was also one of the founders of the Palomino Club in North Hollywood. He married country singer Sue Thompson in 1953, for a time hosted his own show on KHJ-TV and also moved from RCA to Decca. In the late 50s, the effects of rock music saw him move to Las Vegas and begin to include pop music in his repertoire. He divorced in 1963 but married his vocalist Shari Bayne in 1966. (During the 70s, his ex-wife, Sue Thompson, had chart successes with solo hits as well as duet hits with Don Gibson for Hickory Records.) Penny quit Las Vegas in 1968 and after a spell back in California, he moved to Nashville in 1970. Disliking the city and its music, he worked as a DJ on KFRM Wichita, and with his wife, he played the local club circuit. In 1976, he returned to California, where he remained active, played in a few films and organized reunion concerts of some of the television and western-swing music celebrities of the 50s, including Cliffie Stone. He died of a heart attack in 1992. He ranks as one of the most important exponents of western-swing music, although he rarely receives the publicity given to the likes of Wills, Brown and Cooley. There are several country musicians who benefited from their experience as a member of Hank Penny's band, including Herb Remington, Curly Chalker and Roy Clark.

● COMPILATIONS: *Tobacco State Swing* (Rambler 1981)★★★, *Rompin', Stompin', Singin', Swingin'* (Bear Family 1983)★★★★, *Country And Western Memories* (1986)★★★.

PERFECT STRANGER

Formed in Carthage, Texas, USA, Perfect Stranger circumvented the major labels' monopoly of country music by releasing a debut single, 'You Have The Right To Remain Silent', on the independent Pacific Records. They then saw it become a major success despite distribution problems. Signed afterwards to Curb Records, a debut album of the same title was released in June 1995 and achieved a Top 10 placing on the *Billboard* Top Country Albums chart (this collection was mainly an update of the group's limited pressing debut album for Pacific, *It's Up To You*). Comprising Richard Raines, Steve Murray, Shayne Morrison and Andy Ginn, the group were judged by the country music press to represent a new breed of 'raw' country acts. As Morrison told *Billboard* magazine in 1995, 'We don't want the slick production sound of today's country music.'
● ALBUMS: *It's Up To You* (Pacific 1995)★★★, *You Have The Right To Remain Silent* (Curb 1995)★★★.

PERKINS, AL

Al Perkins was with Don Henley, later of the Eagles, in the late 60s band Shiloh. He replaced 'Sneaky' Pete Kleinow in the Flying Burrito Brothers in 1971, a time when they were frustrated at their lack of progress. However, their final album, *The Last Of The Red Hot Burritos*, is regarded by many as their best work. Within six months, he and fellow Burrito Chris Hillman had joined Manassas with Stephen Stills. Perkins has played on numerous record dates and credits include Gene Clark, Bob Dylan, the Eagles, Roger McGuinn, Randy Newman, Dolly Parton, the Rolling Stones, Al Stewart and James Taylor.

PERKINS, CARL

b. Carl Lee Perkins, 9 April 1932, Ridgely, Tennessee, USA (his birth certificate misspelled the last name as Perkings), d. 19 January 1998, Nashville, Tennessee, USA. Carl Perkins was one of the most renowned rockabilly artists recording for Sun Records in the 50s and the author of the classic song 'Blue Suede Shoes'. As a guitarist, he influenced many of the next generation of rock 'n' rollers, most prominently George Harrison and Dave Edmunds. His parents, Fonie 'Buck' and Louise Brantley Perkins, were sharecroppers during the Depression and the family was thus very poor. As a child Perkins listened to the *Grand Ole Opry* on the radio, exposing him to C&W (or hillbilly) music, and he listened to the blues being sung by a black sharecropper named John Westbrook across the field from where he worked. After World War II the Perkins family relocated to Bemis, Tennessee, where he and his brothers picked cotton; by that time his father was unable to work due to a lung infection. Having taught himself rudimentary guitar from listening to such players as Butterball Page and Arthur Smith, Perkins bought an electric guitar and learned to play it more competently. In 1953 Carl, his brothers Jay (rhythm guitar) and Clayton (upright bass), and drummer W.S. 'Fluke' Holland formed a band that worked up a repertoire of hillbilly songs performing at local honky tonks, primarily in the Jackson, Tennessee area, where Carl settled with his wife Valda Crider in 1954. Borrowing some of his technique from the black musicians he had studied set Perkins apart from the many other country guitarists in that region at that time; his style of playing lead guitar fills around his own vocals was similar to

that used in the blues. Encouraged by his wife, and by hearing a record by Elvis Presley on the radio, Perkins decided in 1954 to pursue a musical career. That October the Perkins brothers travelled to Memphis to audition for Sam Phillips at Sun Records. Phillips was not overly impressed, but agreed that the group had potential. In February 1955 he issued two songs from that first Perkins session, 'Movie Magg' and 'Turn Around', on his new Flip label. Pure country in nature, these did not make a dent in the market. Perkins' next single was issued in August, this time on Sun itself. One track, 'Let The Jukebox Keep On Playing', was again country, but the other song, 'Gone! Gone! Gone!' was pure rockabilly. Again, it was not a hit. That November, after Phillips sold Presley's Sun contract to RCA Records, Phillips decided to push the next Perkins single, an original called 'Blue Suede Shoes'. The song had its origins when Johnny Cash, another Sun artist, suggested to Perkins that he write a song based on the phrase 'Don't step on my blue suede shoes'. It was recorded at Sun on 19 December 1955, along with three other songs, among them the b-side 'Honey Don't', later to be covered by the Beatles. 'Blue Suede Shoes' entered the US *Billboard* chart on 3 March 1956 (the same day Presley's first single entered the chart), by which time several cover versions had been recorded, by a range of artists from Presley to Lawrence Welk. Perkins' version quickly became a huge hit and was also the first country record to appear on both the R&B chart and the pop chart, in addition to the country chart. Just as Perkins was beginning to enjoy the fruits of his labour, the car in which he and his band were driving to New York was involved in a severe accident near Dover, Delaware, when their manager, Stuart Pinkham, fell asleep at the wheel. Perkins and his brother Clayton suffered broken bones; brother Jay suffered a fractured neck; and the driver of the truck they hit, Thomas Phillips, was killed. 'Blue Suede Shoes' ultimately reached number 2 on the pop chart, a number 1 country hit and an R&B number 2. Owing to the accident, Perkins was unable to promote the record, the momentum was lost, and none of his four future chart singles would climb nearly as high. In the UK, 'Blue Suede Shoes' became Perkins' only chart single, and was upstaged commercially by the Presley cover version. Perkins continued to record for Sun until mid-1958, but the label's newcomers, Johnny Cash and Jerry Lee Lewis, occupied most of Sam Phillips' attention. Perkins' follow-up to 'Blue Suede Shoes', 'Boppin' The Blues', only reached number 70, and 'Your True Love' number 67. While still at Sun, Perkins did record numerous tracks that would later be revered by rockabilly fans, among them 'Everybody's Trying To Be My Baby' and 'Matchbox', both of which were also covered by the Beatles. On 4 December 1956, Perkins was joined by Lewis and a visiting Presley at Sun in an impromptu jam session which was recorded and released two decades later under the title 'The Million Dollar Quartet'. (Johnny Cash, despite having his photograph taken with Presley, Lewis and Carl, did not take part in the 'million dollar session' - he went shopping instead.) One of Perkins' last acts while at Sun was to appear in the film *Jamboree*, singing a song called 'Glad All Over'. In January 1958, Perkins signed with Columbia Records, where Cash would soon follow. Although some of the songs he recorded for that label were very good, only two, 'Pink Pedal Pushers' and 'Pointed Toe Shoes', both obvious attempts to recapture the success of his first footwear-oriented hit, had a minor impression on the charts. Later that year Jay Perkins died of a brain tumour, causing Carl to turn alcoholic, an affliction from which he would not recover until the late 60s. In 1963 Perkins signed with Decca Records, for which there would be no successful releases. He also toured outside of the USA in 1963-64; while in Britain, he met the Beatles, and watched as they recorded his songs. Perkins, who, ironically, was becoming something of a legend in Europe (as were many early rockers), returned to England for a second tour in October 1964. By 1966 he had left Decca for the small Dollie Records, a country label. In 1967 he joined Johnny Cash's band as guitarist and was allotted a guest singing spot during each of Cash's concerts and television shows. In 1969, Cash recorded Perkins' song 'Daddy Sang Bass', a minor hit in the USA. By 1970, Perkins was back on Columbia, this time recording an album together with new rock revival group NRBQ. In 1974 he signed with Mercury Records. Late that year his brother Clayton committed suicide and their father died. Perkins left Cash in 1976 and went on the road with a band consisting of Perkins' two sons, with whom he was still performing in the 90s. A tribute single to the late Presley, 'The EP Express', came in 1977 and a new album, now for the Jet label, was released in 1978. By the 80s Perkins' reputation as one of rock's pioneers had grown. He recorded an album with Cash and Lewis, *The Survivors* (another similar project, with Cash, Lewis and Roy Orbison, *The Class Of '55*, followed in 1986). Perkins spent much of the 80s touring and working with younger musicians who were influenced by him, among them Paul McCartney and the Stray Cats. In 1985 he starred in a television special to mark the 30th anniversary of 'Blue Suede Shoes'. It co-starred Harrison, Ringo Starr, Dave Edmunds, two members of the Stray Cats, Rosanne Cash and Eric Clapton. In 1987 Perkins was elected to the Rock And Roll Hall of Fame. He signed to the Universal label in 1989 and released *Born To Rock*. His early work has been anthologized many times in several countries. He was unwell for much of the 90s and suffered from a heart condition that took its toll in January 1998.

● ALBUMS: *The Dance Album Of Carl Perkins* (Sun 1957)★★★★, *Whole Lotta Shakin'* (Columbia 1958)★★★, *Country Boy Dreams* (Dollie 1968)★★★, *Blue Suede Shoes* (Sun 1969)★★★, *On Top* (Columbia 1969)★★★, with the NRBQ *Boppin' The Blues* (Columbia 1970)★★★, *My Kind Of Country* (Mercury 1973)★★★, *Carl Perkins Show* (1976)★★★, *From Jackson, Tennessee* (1977)★★★, *Ol' Blue Suede's Back* (Jet 1978)★★★, with Jerry Lee Lewis, Johnny Cash *The Survivors* (Columbia 1982)★★★, *The Heart And Soul Of Carl Perkins* (Allegience 1984)★★★, with Jerry Lee Lewis, Johnny Cash, Roy Orbison *The Class Of '55* (1986)★★★, *Born To Rock* (Universal/MCA 1989)★★★, *Friends, Family & Legends* (1992)★★★, with Scotty Moore *706 Reunion-A Sentimental Journey* (1993)★★★, *Hound Dog* (Muskateer 1995)★★★, with various artists *Go Cat Go!* (BMG 1996)★★★.

● COMPILATIONS: *Carl Perkins Greatest Hits* (Columbia 1969)★★★, *The Sun Years* 3-LP box set (Sun 1982)★★★★, *Up Through The Years, 1954-1957* (Bear Family 1986)★★★★, *Original Sun Greatest Hits* (Rhino 1986)★★★, *Honky Tonk Gal: Rare And Unissued Sun Masters* (Rounder 1989)★★, *Jive After Five: Best Of Carl Perkins (1958-1978)* (Rhino 1990)★★★, *The Classic Carl Perkins* 5-CD box set (Bear Family 1990)★★★★, *Restless: The Columbia Recordings* (Columbia 1992)★★★, *Country Boy's Dream: The Dollie Masters* (Bear Family 1994)★★★.

● VIDEOS: *Rockabilly Session* (Virgin Vision 1986), *Carl Perkins & Jerry Lee Lewis Live* (BBC Video 1987), *This Country's Rockin'* (1993).

● FILMS: *Jamboree a.k.a. Disc Jockey Jamboree* (1957).

● FURTHER READING: *Discipline In Blue Suede Shoes*, Carl Perkins. *Go, Cat, Go: Life And Times Of Carl Perkins The King Of Rockabilly*, Carl Perkins with David McGee.

PERRYMAN, LLOYD

b. Lloyd Wilson Perryman, 29 January 1917, Ruth, Arkansas, USA, d. 31 May 1977. An important member of the Sons Of The Pioneers. The family relocated to California in 1928, where Perryman learned to play guitar and showed his first interest in music during his high school years. He first appeared on radio on KERN Bakersfield but in 1932, he left home and moved to the Los Angeles area. During the next few years, he sang with various groups, including the 4-S Ranch Boys, the Beverly Hillbillies, Jack And His Texas Outlaws and Jimmy LeFevre And His Saddle Pals. In September 1936, Bob Nolan invited him to take over from Tim Spencer who was leaving the Sons Of The Pioneers. Spencer returned in 1938, by which time Perryman had become an important part of the Pioneers. Between April 1943 and January 1946, he was drafted for military service and his place in the group was taken by Ken Carson. In 1949, when Spencer and Nolan left, Perryman became the leader of the group. He acted as compere at their concerts and was also responsible for all vocal arrangements, although he actually wrote very few songs himself. Perryman, a natural baritone, originally sang tenor, but it was a well-known fact that he could sing any part in the trio harmonies of the group, for any of the hundreds of songs in their repertoire. He died after a short illness in May 1977.

PHILLIPS, BILL

b. William Clarence Phillips, 28 January 1936, Canton, North Carolina, USA. Phillips grew up in an area steeped in country music and learned guitar and began singing before leaving high school to work as an upholsterer. In 1955, he joined the *Old Southern Jamboree* on WMIL Miami and sang at local clubs, before moving to Nashville in 1957. He joined Cedarwood Publishing as a songwriter and soon gained attention when he penned Webb Pierce's 1958 Top 10 country hit 'Falling Back To You'. This success saw Phillips signed to Columbia and in 1959 and 1960, he registered his first two Top 30 hits with 'Sawmill' and 'Georgia Town Blues', both with Mel Tillis, and he appeared on the *Grand Ole Opry*. He joined Decca in 1963 and by 1971, had registered 12 more hits, the biggest being 'Put It Off Until Tomorrow' (1966) which, with Dolly Parton (the song's co-writer) on harmony vocal, reached number 6. Other Top 10s included 'The Company You Keep' (1966), 'The Words I'm Gonna Have To Eat' and 'Little Boy Sad' (1969), the latter having previously been a 1961 pop hit for Johnny Burnette. During the 70s, he registered five more minor hits, when recording on the United Artists or Soundwaves label. From the early 70s, he began to work as part of the Kitty Wells-Johnny Wright Show, although continuing to make a few recordings as a solo artist. In 1995, he suffered a stroke and Wells, Wright and other country music friends played a charity show to raise money for him.

● ALBUMS: *Bill Phillips Best* (Harmony 1964)★★★, *Put It Off Until Tomorrow* (Decca 1966)★★★, *Bill Phillips Style* (Decca 1967)★★★, *Country Action* (Decca 1968)★★★, *Little Boy Sad* (Decca 1970)★★★.

PHILLIPS, SAM

b. 1923, Florence, Alabama, USA. Although harbouring ambitions as a criminal lawyer, Phillips was obliged to drop out of high school to support his family. In 1942 he took up a post as disc jockey at station WLAY in Muscle Shoals, before moving to WREC in Memphis as an announcer four years later. In 1950 he opened Sam's Memphis Recording Studio at 706 Union Avenue and although initial work largely consisted of chronicling weddings and social gatherings, Phillips' main ambition was to record local blues acts and license the resultant masters. Howlin' Wolf, Bobby Bland, Ike Turner, B.B. King and Roscoe Gordon were among the many acts Phillips produced for independent outlets Chess, Duke and RPM. Their success inspired the founding of Sun Records in February 1952, a venture that flourished the following year when Rufus Thomas scored a notable R&B hit with 'Bear Cat'. Success was maintained by 'Little' Junior Parker and Billy 'The Kid' Emerson, while Phillips looked to expand the label's horizons by recording country acts. His wish to find a white singer comfortable with R&B was answered in 1954 with the arrival of Elvis Presley. The singer's five singles recorded with Phillips rank among pop's greatest achievements, and although criticized for allowing his protégé to sign for RCA Records, the producer used the settlement fee to further the careers of Carl Perkins, Johnny Cash and, later, Jerry Lee Lewis. Phillips' simple recording technique - single track, rhythmic string bass and judicious echo - defined classic rockabilly and for a brief period the label was in the ascendant. The style, however, proved too inflexible and by the beginning of the 60s new Memphis-based studios, Stax and Hi Records, challenged Sun's pre-eminent position. Phillips also became increasingly distracted by other ventures, including mining concerns, radio stations and, more crucially, his share of the giant Holiday Inn hotel chain. In 1969 he sold the entire Sun empire to entrepreneur Shelby Singleton, thus effectively ending an era. Sam Phillips is nonetheless still revered as one of the leading catalysts in post-war American music and, if nothing else, for launching the career of Elvis Presley.

PHILLIPS, STEVE

b. Nicholas Stephen Phillips, 18 February 1948, London, England. The son of sculptor Harry Phillips, Steve first started playing guitar in 1961, at the time emulating rockabilly artists from the Sun label. Phillips was influenced by such artists as Robert Johnson and Scotty Moore, an influence that became apparent later in his country blues playing. Up until 1964, Phillips had played piano in a jug band, called Easy Mr. Steve's Bootleggers, but by 1965 he switched to blues. By the end of 1968, he was being booked regularly in the folk and blues clubs of his local area. During 1968, Phillips met Mark Knopfler, at the time a junior reporter in Leeds, and together they formed a duo, the Duolian String Pickers. This lasted until Knopfler moved to

London, later to form Dire Straits. From 1974-76 Phillips fronted the Steve Phillips Juke Band, which included his brother on bass. He met Brendan Croker in 1976, and they played occasionally as a duo. During this time, Phillips had been supporting his music working as a guitar repairer and a furniture and picture restorer. Following a brief period of unemployment, he took up landscape painting until 1986. Long-time friend Croker coaxed Phillips out of his 'retirement' by organizing bookings. BBC disc jockey Andy Kershaw, using the growing popularity of 'roots music', helped create a demand that enabled Phillips to turn professional in 1986. Phillips achieved a higher profile with his appearances as support to acts such as the Blues Band and Nanci Griffith. He was then approached by Knopfler, who offered to produce an album by Phillips. The project developed into the Notting Hillbillies, which included Guy Fletcher from Dire Straits, and Brendan Croker. Steve Phillips' recorded output is limited and is no reflection on his obvious talent. In 1991, he recorded two tracks, 'Stones In My Passway' and 'When You Got A Good Friend', for a Robert Johnson compilation. *The Best Of Steve Phillips* consists of recordings made during the previous 10 years, but is not a compilation in the strict sense of the word.

● ALBUMS: *The Best Of Steve Phillips* (Unamerican Activities 1987)★★★, *Steel Rail Blues* (Unamerican Activities 1990)★★★, with the Notting Hillbillies *Missing Presumed Having A Good Time* (Vertigo 1990)★★★, *Just Pickin'* (Revival 1997)★★★.

● VIDEOS: *Notting Hillbillies: Missing* (Channel 5 1990).

PIE PLANT PETE

b. Claud J. Moye, 9 July 1906, on a farm, near Shawneetown, Gallatin County, Illinois, USA, d. 7 February 1988. He learned to play guitar as a child and in his early teens, added harmonica. In 1927, with a considerable repertoire of the old-time songs his mother sang, he relocated to Chicago and made his professional debut on WLS on 5 May. Using a frame, he played harmonica and guitar together, calling the combination his 'two-cylinder cob-crusher'. He called himself Pie Plant Pete (for comedy reasons) and soon proved popular with WLS listeners. Between 1929 and 1934, after receiving a better offer, he became a regular on WTAM Cleveland. In 1929/30, he recorded 26 sides for Gennett and had releases on Superior as Jerry Wallace and on Champion as Asparagus Joe. Between 1934 and 1936, he made further recordings for Decca Records and ARC. In 1936, he began to work with Joe Troyan (Bashful Harmonica Joe), whom he had first met in Cleveland in 1935. They worked stations in Cleveland, Boston and Rochester, before their career was interrupted by World War II. Pete served briefly in the Quartermaster Corps but was discharged due to his age and he and Joe resumed their partnership at Cleveland until 1942, when Joe was drafted into the US Air Force. After the war, they relaunched their partnership working at Cleveland, Rochester and Detroit. In 1947, they recorded 20 sides for Process records of Buffalo, New York, which were released as 10 singles. They eventually parted and Pete worked on children's television before opening a company that produced radio jingles for advertising products in Ridgeway, Illinois. He died in 1988 and is buried in the Asbury Cemetery, Omaha, Illinois. It would appear that none of his early recordings have been reissued, but in 1989,

Cattle Records of Germany issued an album containing all the Process recordings.

● COMPILATIONS: *The Oldtime Country Music Collection Of Pie Plant Pete And Bashful Harmonica Joe* (Cattle 1989)★★★.

PIERCE, DON

b. 10 October 1919, Seattle, Washington, USA. Although destined to become a very respected record company director and producer, Pierce had no interest in music throughout his school years or his military service in World War II. During these years, golf held a great attraction and his interest in music came only after he became friendly with Hoagy Carmichael. In 1947, he risked his $12,000 savings by investing in the new 4 Star Record Company and (probably to help safeguard his money at a shaky time for the label) he also worked as a salesman. He became friendly with country singer T. Texas Tyler and began to take an active part in the production of some of the singer's very successful recordings. In October 1953, he profitably sold his 4 Star interest and apparently for $333 purchased a third share in the recently formed Starday label, of Jack Starnes Jnr. and Pappy Daily, and its connected Starrite Publishing. Two years later, Starnes left and Pierce became co-owner of the label. A shrewd businessman, with an eye for a hit record and many contacts from his 4 Star days, Pierce soon attracted attention to the label with George Jones's recording of 'Why Baby Why'. For five years Starday, while maintaining all copyrights, operated an agreement with Mercury Records, but in 1958, the agreement ended and Daily and Pierce parted amicably. Pierce, by then the actual owner of the label, moved to Nashville to relaunch Starday. He found immediate success with hit recordings by several artists, including Red Sovine and Cowboy Copas. During the 60s, after also turning his attention to bluegrass music, Flatt And Scruggs, Jim Eanes, Bill Clifton, Carl Story and the Stanley Brothers were some of the stars of that genre to successfully record for Starday. Realizing that the major labels were ignoring a public demand for recordings by old-time artists still active, he also recorded Sam And Kirk McGee, Lew Childre and the Blue Sky Boys. Pierce organized mail-order supplies and also caused some controversy by reissuing early recordings of some of the top stars of the day. There were complaints by some artists that such action was not in their best interests. In 1968, when his friend Syd Nathan of King Records died, he arranged an agreement to merge the two labels. In 1969, realizing that he was fighting a losing battle against the major labels, he sold Starday to LIN Broadcasting, a wise move for, within two years, the label went into liquidation and changed hands. Pierce, who later went into the real estate business, was a founder-member of the Country Music Association. His love of golf saw him become a founder of the Pro-Celebrity Tournament, which raises money for needy Nashville causes and he also initiated his Golden Eagle Master Achievement Award (the eagle was Starday's motif) which is presented at the annual Reunion Of Professional Entertainers.

PIERCE, WEBB

b. 8 August 1921, near West Monroe, Louisiana, USA, d. 24 February 1991, Nashville, Tennessee, USA. His father died when Pierce was only three months old, his mother remarried and he was raised on a farm seven miles from Monroe.

Although no one in the family performed music, his mother had a collection of country records which, together with Gene Autry films, were his first country music influences. He learned to play guitar and when he was 15 was given his own weekly radio show on KMLB Monroe. During World War II he served in the army, married Betty Jane Lewis in 1942 and after his discharge, they relocated from Monroe to Shreveport where, in 1945, he found employment in the men's department of the Sears Roebuck store. In 1947, he and his wife appeared on an early morning KTBS show as 'Webb Pierce with Betty Jane, the Singing Sweetheart'. He also sang at many local venues and developed the style that became so readily identifiable and was later described as 'a wailing whiskey-voiced tenor that rang out every drop of emotion'. He recorded for 4-Star in 1949 and soon afterwards moved to KWKH, where he became a member of the *Louisiana Hayride* on its inception that year. In 1950, he and Betty Jane were divorced and Pierce began building his solo career. He founded Pacemaker Records and a publishing company with Horace Logan, the director of the *Hayride*. His recording of 'Drifting Texas Sands', labelled as 'Tillman Franks and the Rainbow Valley Boys', due to Pierce still being under contract to 4-Star, created attention. His growing popularity attracted US Decca and in March 1951 he made his first recordings for that label. His third Decca release, 'Wondering', a song from the 30s by Joe Werner and the Riverside Ramblers, began a phenomenal success when, in March 1952, it spent four weeks at number 1 in the US country charts and gave Pierce his nickname of 'The Wondering Boy'. Two more number 1s, 'That Heart Belongs To Me' (a self-penned song) and 'Back Street Affair', followed - all three remaining charted in excess of 20 weeks. (The latter song also led to Kitty Wells' second chart hit with the 'answer' version, 'Paying For That Back Street Affair', early in 1953.) In November 1952 he married again, this time to Audrey Grisham, and finally gave up his job at Sears Roebuck. He left the *Hayride* and replaced Hank Williams on the *Grand Ole Opry*. During his days at Shreveport his band included such future stars as Goldie Hill, Floyd Cramer, Jimmy Day, the Wilburn Brothers and Faron Young. He remained a member of the *Opry* roster until 1955, leaving because of his heavy touring commitments, but he rejoined briefly in 1956 before a disagreement with the management caused him to leave once again. The problem concerned the fact that Pierce was having to turn down lucrative Saturday concerts elsewhere to return to Nashville to meet his *Opry* commitments, for which he received only the standard *Opry* fee. Pierce's chart successes during the 50s and 60s totalled 88 country hits. Further number 1 singles included 'It's Been So Long', 'Even Tho'', 'More And More', 'I Don't Care', 'Love Love Love' and a duet with Red Sovine of George Jones's song 'Why Baby Why'. Arguably his best-remembered number 1 hits are his version of the old Jimmie Rodgers song 'In The Jailhouse Now', which held the top spot for 21 weeks and his co-written 'Slowly', which remained there for 17, both songs charting for more than 35 weeks. The recording of 'Slowly' is unique because of Bud Isaacs' electric pedal steel guitar, which created a style that was copied by most other country bands. He also had nine US pop chart hits, the biggest being 'More And More', which reached number 22 in 1954. Pierce recorded rockabilly and rock 'n' roll numbers, having Top 10 country chart success with the first recorded version of 'Teenage Boogie' and with the Everly Brothers' 'Bye Bye Love', but his vocal version of 'Raunchy' failed to chart. In the mid-50s Pierce and the *Opry* manager, Jim Denny, formed Cedarwood Music, which handled other artists' songs as well as Pierce's own, and also bought three radio stations. When Denny died in 1963, Pierce retained the radio stations and left the publishing company to his late partner's family (he later acquired two more stations but eventually sold all five for a sum reputed to be almost $3 million). He toured extensively and appeared in the films *Buffalo Guns* (his co-stars being Marty Robbins and Carl Smith), *Music City USA*, *Second Fiddle To A Steel Guitar* and *Road To Nashville*, and during his career, dressed in rhinestone-studded suits; he became known as one of the most flamboyant, even by country standards, of the singers of his era. During the 60s he had two Pontiac cars fancily studded with silver dollars, large cattle horns mounted as a decoration on the radiator, ornamental pistols and rifles and even leather seats that resembled saddles. Later, his expensive Oak Hill, Nashville home, with its guitar-shaped swimming pool, attracted so many tourist buses to the usually quiet area that he had problems with his neighbours, particularly Ray Stevens. Pierce totally ignored suggestions that he was bringing country music into disrepute, maintaining that the fans had paid for his pool and were therefore entitled to see it. After heated court proceedings he was forced to erect a sign warning fans to stay away. His comment on Stevens, who had been the organizer of the objectors, was: 'That's what he gets for livin' across the street from a star'. Johnny Cash mentions the event in his song 'Let There Be Country', when he sings: 'Pierce invites the tourists in and Ray keeps them away'.

After 'Honky Tonk Song' in 1957, Pierce never gained another number 1 record but he did add eight further country hits during the 70s on Decca and Plantation. When the Columbia duet version of 'In The Jailhouse Now', which he recorded with Willie Nelson, charted in 1982 to register his 97th and last country hit, it gave him the distinction of having charted records in four decades. In the early 1980s he sold his Oak Hill home and retired to the Brentwood area of Nashville. He retired from touring but made special appearances when it pleased him and, reflecting on his career, he said, 'I've been blessed with so much. I guess it turned out the way I wanted it'. In 1985 he made a goodtime album with his friends Jerry Lee Lewis, Mel Tillis and Faron Young, but contractual problems led to it being withdrawn shortly after issue. Asked about recording again in 1986, he commented, 'Hell, I might get a hit and then everybody would be botherin' me again'. Late in the 80s his health began to fail; he survived open-heart surgery, but early in 1990 it was diagnosed that he was suffering with cancer. He underwent several operations but finally died in Nashville on 24 February 1991. He had been nominated for membership of the Country Music Hall of Fame in August 1990: most authorities expected that he would be elected but it was not to be. The honour may be bestowed before long but, sadly, it will come too late for him to know. Pierce was, without any doubt, one of country music's most successful and popular honky-tonk singers.

● ALBUMS: *That Wondering Boy* 10-inch album (Decca 1953)★★★★, *Webb Pierce* (Decca 1955)★★★, *That Wondering Boy* (Decca 1956)★★★★, *Just Imagination* (Decca 1957)★★★, *Webb!* (Decca 1959)★★★, *Bound For The Kingdom* (Decca 1959)★★★, *The One & Only Webb Pierce* (King 1959)★★★, *Walking The Streets* (Decca 1960)★★★, *Webb With A Beat* (Decca 1960)★★★★, *Fallen Angel* (Decca 1961)★★★, *Cross Country* (Decca 1962)★★★, *Hideaway Heart* (Decca 1962)★★★, *Bow Thy Head* (Decca 1963)★★★, *I've Got A New Heartache* (Decca 1963)★★★, *Sands Of Gold* (Decca 1964)★★★★, *Country Music Time* (Decca 1965)★★★, *Just Webb Pierce* (Hilltop 1965)★★★, *Memory Number One* (Decca 1965)★★★, *Sweet Memories* (Decca 1966)★★★, *Webb Pierce* (Vocalion 1966)★★★, *Webb's Choice* (Decca 1966)★★★, *Where'd Ya Stay Last Night?* (Decca 1967)★★★, *Fool, Fool, Fool* (Decca 1968)★★★, *Country Songs* (Vocalion 1969)★★★, *Saturday Night* (Decca 1969)★★★, *Webb Pierce Sings This Thing* (Decca 1969)★★★, *Love Ain't Never Gonna Be No Better* (Decca 1970)★★★, *Merry Go Round World* (Decca 1970)★★★, *Country Favorites* (Vocalion 1970)★★★, *Webb Pierce Road Show* (Decca 1971)★★, *I'm Gonna Be A Swinger* (Decca 1972)★★★, *Without You* (Decca 1973)★★★, *Carol Channing & Webb Pierce-Country & Western* (Plantation 1976)★★, *Faith, Hope And Love* (Plantation 1977)★★★, with Willie Nelson *In The Jailhouse Now* (Columbia 1982)★★★, with Jerry Lee Lewis, Mel Tillis, Faron Young *Four Legends* (1985)★★★.

● COMPILATIONS: *Golden Favorites* (Decca 1961)★★★, *The Webb Pierce Story* (Decca 1964)★★★, *Webb Pierce's Greatest Hits* (Decca 1968)★★★★, *Golden Hits Volume 1* (Plantation 1976)★★★, *Golden Hits Volume 2* (Plantation 1976)★★★, *The Living Legend Of Webb Pierce* (1977)★★★, *Webb 'The Wondering Boy' Pierce 1951-1958* 4-CD box set (Bear Family 1990)★★★★, *The One And Only...* (1993)★★★, *Webb Pierce: King Of The Honky Tonk: From The Original Master Tapes* (Country Music Foundation 1994)★★★★.

PILLOW, RAY

b. 4 July 1937, Lynchburg, Virginia, USA. A singer, guitarist and songwriter, who had no initial thoughts of a singing career, Pillow dropped out of high school in the eleventh grade and enlisted in the US Navy, where he completed his high school diploma. In 1958, he was discharged and entered college, and one day for a dare, he deputized for the singer in the college rock band. He found that he enjoyed singing and also learned to play the guitar, but still had no immediate ideas of a singing career. In 1961, he travelled to Nashville and competed in the National Pet Milk Talent Contest. He did not win but the WSM radio judges placed him in second place. He returned to Lynchburg and after completing his college degree, he found work with a trucking company. However, he decided that now he wanted to be an entertainer and returned to Nashville. He played small clubs, honky tonks and local radio stations and gradually built enough of a reputation that in 1964, he was given a recording contract by Capitol. His first charted in 1965 with 'Take Your Hands Off My Heart' and followed it with a Top 20 hit in 1966 with 'Thank You Ma'am'. Capitol also paired him with Jean Shepard and the duo had major successes with 'I'll Take The Dog', 'Mr Do It Yourself' and 'Heart We Did All We Could'. Pillow joined the *Grand Ole Opry* in 1966 and for a time toured with the *Martha White Show*. Although he never achieved any further major hits, he continued to record for various labels including ABC, Mega and MCA having minor hits with such songs as 'Gone

With The Wine', 'Wonderful Day', 'Countryfied' and 'Living In The Sunshine Of Your Love'. His last chart entry, 'One Too Many Memories', came in 1981 on First Generation. A fine singer with a pleasant style of delivery, Pillow continues to appear on the *Opry* and make personal appearances. In the late 80s he worked in A&R at Capitol.

● ALBUMS: *Presenting Ray Pillow* (Capitol 1965)★★★★, with Jean Shepard *I'll Take The Dog* (Capitol 1966)★★, *Even When It's Bad It's Good* (Capitol 1967)★★★, *Wonderful Day* (1968)★★★, *Ray Pillow Sings* (ABC 1969)★★, *People Music* (1970)★★★, *Slippin' Around With Ray Pillow* (Mega 1972)★★★, *Countryfied* (1974)★★★, *Ray Pillow* (1982)★★, *One Too Many Memories* (Allegience 1984)★★★.

PINK, CELINDA

b. 1957, Celinda Cosby, Tuscaloosa, Alabama, USA. The 90s country singer Celinda Pink once recorded 'I've Earned The Right To Sing The Blues' and the song could not be more appropriate. Her father was in the Alabama state prison and her mother abandoned her children when Celinda was only five. She absconded from foster homes and children's homes and was sent to a reform school. A quick learner, she graduated at 16 and then went to Nashville to trace her mother. She married a local musician, Hal Brock, but their relationship was short-lived and she became a heroin addict. After a number of relationships, she teamed up with one of Ernest Tubb's Texas Troubadours, Pete Mitchell. He encouraged her to sing the blues as well as country. However, he left her on the day she was to record *Victimised*. 'I felt he did that on purpose to upset me', reflects Pink. 'When I went in there, I sung those songs with pain and feeling.' The album's dedication reads, 'Special thanks to Pete for breaking my heart.' Her albums feature the throatiest blues in Nashville and yet have enough country to appeal to that market as well. Indeed, she records for one of the most traditional labels in Nashville, Step One. Her son Jonathan now plays guitar in her band.

● ALBUMS: *Victimised* (Step One 1993)★★★, *Unchained* (Step One 1995)★★★.

PITTMAN, BARBARA

b. Memphis, Tennessee, USA. Pittman was one of the few women who recorded for the legendary Sun Records. She heard blues music on Beale Street in Memphis as a child and began performing in Memphis clubs such as the Eagle's Nest, where a young Elvis Presley, whom Pittman dated, also honed his act during the mid-50s. In 1955 she went on the road as a singer with cowboy movie star Lash LaRue's travelling show. In 1956 she signed with Sun; although she released a number of singles on the label, none were hits. During the 60s Pittman moved to California where she sang on soundtracks for such 'motorcycle movies' as *Wild Angels*, *Wild On Wheels* and *Hells Angels*, under the name Barbara And The Visitors. She also recorded for Del-Fi Records but nothing was ever released. Pittman never recorded an album under her own name.

PLAVA TRAVA ZABORAVA

The seven-piece Croatian bluegrass band Plava Trava Zaborava (Croatian for 'Bluegrass festival') were formed in 1982. Although they play mainly bluegrass, they also play other styles of country music and their repertoire includes Rodney Crowell's 'Voila An American Dream' and Billy Joe Shaver's 'Georgia On A Fast Train'. Jimmy Matestic (vocals) sings without a discernible accent and also writes their original material. The instrumental 'Yugo Goes To Nashville' allows the individual members to shine.

● ALBUMS: *Live, Country* (Crazy)★★★, *Hat Trick* (Crazy)★★★, *Dance All Night-Live* (Crazy 1993)★★★, *5* (Crazy 1993)★★★.

POOLE, CHARLIE

b. 22 March 1892, Alamance County, North Carolina, USA, d. 21 May 1931. A talented five-string banjo player who, because of a childhood hand injury, played in a thumb and three-fingered picking style that was later further developed by Earl Scruggs. In 1917, Poole teamed up with fiddle player Posey Rorer (b. 22 September 1891, Franklin County, Virginia, USA, d. March 1935) and the two played throughout West Virginia and North Carolina. In 1922, they added a guitarist, initially Clarence Foust, but when they made their first Columbia recordings on 27 July 1925, the regular guitarist was Norman Woodlieff. Perhaps in reference to their itinerant lifestyle, they adopted the name of North Carolina Ramblers in 1923 and as such, they became one of the most influential of the early string bands. They are still remembered for their recording of 'Don't Let Your Deal Go Down'. In 1926, Roy Harvey (b. 24 March 1892, Monroe County, West Virginia, USA) replaced Woodlieff and in 1928, following a disagreement, Poole replaced Rorer with Lonnie Austin. Working with other musicians, including his son Charlie Jnr. (b. James Clay Poole, 1913), Poole continued to play but made his last recordings on 9 September 1930. (Woodlieff and Rorer made further recordings with other musicians and Harvey also recorded with his own North Carolina Ramblers band.) Poole was in real life very much a rambler, a trait that saw an early end to his 1911 marriage. He was also a heavy drinker and met a premature death from a heart attack in 1931, while celebrating an offer to play music for a Hollywood Western. Posey Rorer died in 1935 and was buried near Poole.

● COMPILATIONS: *Charlie Poole & The North Carolina Ramblers 1925-1930, Volumes 1 - 4* (Historical 1965-71)★★★, *Charlie Poole & The Highlanders, Charlie Poole 1926-1930* (Historical 1990)★★★★, *Old Time Songs* (County 1993)★★★.

● FURTHER READING: *Charlie Poole And The North Carolina Ramblers*, Clifford Rorer.

POSEY, SANDY

b. Martha Sharp, 18 June 1947, Jasper, Alabama, USA. As a teenager Posey moved to west Memphis where she embarked on a career as a studio session singer. Her contributions to innumerable records impressed producer Chips Moman, who encouraged the artist as both a songwriter and performer. Posey's debut single, 'Born A Woman', reached number 12 in the US charts in 1966, while its pithy lyric - 'If you're born a woman, you're born to be hurt' - brought a new maturity to the often maudlin approach common to female country singers. 'Single Girl', its equally accomplished follow-up, scaled the UK and US Top 20s, before 'What A Woman In Love Won't Do', 'I Take It Back' and 'Are You Never Coming Home' (all 1967) continued her run of success. Posey was one of several singers backing Elvis Presley when he undertook sessions at Moman's American studios. She was featured on 'Mama Liked The Roses', and also appeared with the singer during his first Las Vegas engagement in 1969. However, while retaining a popularity within the country market, Posey's distinctive approach as a solo act latterly proved too specialized for pop. She released albums for Columbia Records, Monument and Warner Brothers Records, charting for the last time with 1979's 'Love Is Sometimes Easy'. After releasing an independent album in 1983, Posey concentrated on session work.

● ALBUMS: *Born A Woman* (MGM 1966)★★★★, *I Take It Back* (MGM 1967)★★★, *Single Girl* (MGM 1967)★★★, *Looking At You* (MGM 1968)★★★, *Sandy Posey* (MGM 1970)★★★, *Why Don't We Go Somewhere And Love* (Columbia 1972)★★★, *Tennessee Rose* (Audiograph 1983)★★.

● COMPILATIONS: *The Best Of Sandy Posey* (MGM 19670.)★★★, *Best Of Sandy Posey* (Collectables 1996)★★★★, *All American Country* (Spectrum 1997)★★★.

POTTER, DALE

b. Allen Dale Potter, 28 April 1930, Puxico, Missouri, USA, d. 13 March 1996, USA. A regular at the *Grand Ole Opry*, fiddle player Dale Potter contributed to records by many of the stellar country artists of the post-war period, including Hank Williams, Little Jimmy Dickens, Bill Monroe and Cowboy Copas. Taught fiddle and guitar by his father from an early age, Potter gravitated to country music after listening to Bob Wills' KVOO Tulsa radio performances. This event proved axiomatic in the development of his style - unaware that Wills' Texas Playboys featured more than one fiddle player, he adapted his technique to enable him to play both harmony and melody. Potter soon landed a regular radio spot himself, before being summoned to Nashville to join Milton Estes' Musical Millers. He was only 18 when he made his stage debut at the *Grand Ole Opry*, playing a version of Tex Owens' 'Cattle Call'. Zeb Turner then engaged him in recording work to boost his income. His first session was with Hank Williams in 1949, resulting in songs including 'Wedding Bells' and 'Lost Highway'. He subsequently became an in-demand session player, working on Red Foley's Top 10 hit, 'Sugarfoot Rag', and a series of hits by Webb Pierce, Ray Price, Johnny Paycheck and Faron Young. Potter also appeared on the very first Everly Brothers recording session in 1955. Later he joined the Country All-Stars, which featured Chet Atkins, who described him as 'the best all-round fiddler in the business.' He worked with Judy Lynn in 1960, then the Sons Of The West in Dallas, before ill health curtailed his career.

PRAIRIE RAMBLERS

The group was originally formed as the Kentucky Ramblers by Charles 'Chick' Hurt (b. 1901, d. 1967; mandolin) and 'Happy' Jack Taylor (b. *c.*1900, d. 1962; tenor banjo). Both men were born in the Summershade area, near Glasgow, Kentucky, USA. Hurt moved to Kewanne, Illinois, as a young man and there organized his first band, but a few years later was reunited with Taylor, his childhood friend. They joined forces with Shelby David 'Tex' Atchison (b. 1912; fiddle, lead vocals) and Floyd 'Salty' Holmes (guitar, harmonica, jug player), both born near Rosine, Ohio County, Kentucky, USA (Atchison was actually born on the farm adjoining that of

Bill Monroe's father). In 1932, they made their radio debut on WOC Davenport, Iowa, and later the same year, they moved to WLS Chicago, first working on the *Merry-Go-Round* and then the *National Barn Dance*. In June 1933, they joined forces with Patsy Montana, who recorded with them when they made their first recordings for RCA-Victor's Bluebird label in December that year. By this time, with the growing interest in cowboy songs and music, the band had become the Prairie Ramblers. In 1934, they spent six months at WOR New York and returned to WLS specializing more in pop-styled cowboy songs and swing music. They emphasized the cowboy image, appearing at venues on horseback and western dress, and even using the Gene Autry song 'Ridin' Down The Canyon' as their signature tune. They joined ARC records and by the end of 1936, they had recorded over 100 sides for that label. Their repertoire covered a wide variety of songs including gospel numbers such as 'How Beautiful Heaven Must Be', but in 1935, they were persuaded to record some numbers that were somewhat risqué. Hurt was not happy with this and to change their overall sound, they added the clarinet and vocals of Bill Thawl and recorded them under the name of the Sweet Violet Boys, although it was an open secret as to who the band really were. Some of the songs were written by Bob Miller (he also played piano on many of the Ramblers' recordings), who sought anonymity by copyrighting them under the rather poorly camouflaged pseudonym of Trebor Rellim. Among the songs were numbers such as 'There's A Man Who Comes To Our House Every Single Day (Poppa Comes Home And The Man Goes Away)', 'Jim's Windy Mule' and 'I Love My Fruit' - a song that has been suggested as being the first gay hillbilly song. (It seems that they made the young Patsy Montana leave the studio when this material was being recorded.) Atchison and Holmes left in 1938 and were replaced by fiddler Alan Crockett and guitarist/vocalist Kenneth Houchens. In the early 1940s, they added the accordion of Augie Kline and electric guitarist George Barnes. Patsy Montana left around 1941 to pursue her solo career. The Ramblers appeared in various films, some with Gene Autry, and also later recorded with Rex Allen. They made their final recordings for Mercury Records in December 1947, by which time their material was no longer of any specific type. At the time when they left WLS and disbanded in 1948, one of their songs was 'You Ain't Got No Hillbilly Anymore' - a fact with which many people agreed. Hurt and Taylor continued to work around the Chicago area as a duo for a time until they eventually retired.

● COMPILATIONS: *Tex's Dance* (1982)★★★, *Patsy Montana And The Prairie Ramblers* (1984)★★★, *Sing It Fast And Hot* (1989)★★★.

PRESLEY, ELVIS

One of Elvis's first nicknames was 'The Hillbilly Cat' and there was a strong country music component in much of his work. Although initially recording in a blues town, Memphis, he cut several country songs for Sun; his first single was an up-tempo revival of Bill Monroe's 'Blue Moon Of Kentucky'. He appeared on the *Grand Ole Opry* (none too successfully) and *Louisiana Hayride* (50 appearances), and toured alongside country musicians, with many of whom his manager, Tom Parker, had previously worked. His first stage performances were on country shows alongside the likes of

Slim Whitman, Hank Snow and Faron Young. The relationship between established country performers and the new pretender was acted out, with some amusement, in the fictional film *Loving You*. Over at RCA, Presley worked with numerous country musicians including Floyd Cramer and Chet Atkins, and his singles regularly made the pop, country and R&B charts. He topped the US country charts for five weeks in 1955 with 'I Forgot To Remember To Forget'. 'Heartbreak Hotel', written by Mae Boren Axton, topped the US country charts for 17 weeks. His records include '(Now And Then There's) A Fool Such As I' (originally recorded by Hank Snow), 'Old Shep' (Red Foley) and 'Is It So Strange?' (Faron Young). His drab material of the 60s changed when he discovered Jerry Reed and cut 'Guitar Man' and 'U.S. Male'. From then on, his arrangements were overblown, but country songs formed an increasingly large part of his repertoire, both live and on record, including renditions of 'There Goes My Everything', 'He'll Have To Go', 'She Thinks I Still Care' and 'I Really Don't Want To Know'. The maudlin nature of much country music particularly appealed to him once his marriage was over. In all, Presley recorded around 60 country songs, including *Elvis Country* in 1970. Many consider his finest record to be the amalgam of three Civil War songs put together by country writer Mickey Newbury as 'An American Trilogy'. Since his death, he has been a regular topic for country songwriters, and many contemporary country performers paid tribute to him in Memphis in 1994 at the concert released as *It's Now Or Never*.

● ALBUMS: *Elvis Presley* (RCA Victor 1956)★★★★, *Elvis* (RCA Victor 1956)★★★★★, *Rock 'N' Roll* (1956)★★★★, *Rock 'N' Roll No. 2* (1957)★★★★, *Loving You* film soundtrack (RCA Victor 1957)★★★★, *Elvis' Christmas Album* (RCA Victor 1957)★★★, *King Creole* (RCA Victor 1958)★★★★, *Elvis' Golden Records* (RCA Victor 1958)★★★★★, *For LP Fans Only* (RCA Victor 1959)★★★★, *A Date With Elvis* (RCA Victor 1959)★★★★, *Elvis' Golden Records, Volume 2* (RCA Victor 1960)★★★★★, *Elvis Is Back!* (RCA Victor 1960)★★★★, *G.I. Blues* (RCA Victor 1960)★★★, *His Hand In Mine* (RCA Victor 1961)★★★, *Something For Everybody* (RCA Victor 1961)★★★, *Blue Hawaii* (RCA Victor 1961)★★★, *Pot Luck* (RCA Victor 1962)★★★, *Girls! Girls! Girls!* (RCA Victor 1963)★★★, *It Happened At The World's Fair* (RCA Victor 1963)★★, *Fun In Acapulco* (RCA Victor 1963)★★, *Elvis' Golden Records, Volume 3* (1964)★★★★, *Kissin' Cousins* (RCA Victor 1964)★★, *Roustabout* (RCA Victor 1964)★★, *Girl Happy* (RCA Victor 1965)★★, *Flaming Star And Summer Kisses* (1965)★★, *Elvis For Everyone* (RCA Victor 1965)★★★, *Harem Holiday* (RCA Victor 1965)★★, *Frankie And Johnny* (RCA Victor 1966)★★, *Paradise, Hawaiian Style* (RCA Victor 1966)★★, *California Holiday* (RCA Victor 1966)★★, *How Great Thou Art* (RCA Victor 1967)★★★, *Double Trouble* (RCA Victor 1967)★★, *Clambake* (RCA Victor 1968)★★, *Elvis' Golden Records, Volume 4* (RCA Victor 1968)★★★★, *Speedway* (RCA Victor 1968)★★, *Elvis - TV Special* (RCA 1968)★★★, *From Elvis In Memphis* (RCA 1970)★★★★, *On Stage February 1970* (RCA 1970)★★★★, *I'm 10,000 Years Old - Elvis Country* (RCA 1970)★★★, *That's The Way It Is* (RCA Victor 1971)★★★, *Love Letters From Elvis* (RCA 1971)★★★, *Elvis Sings The Wonderful World Of Christmas* (RCA 1971)★★★, *Elvis Now* (RCA 1972)★★★, *He Touched Me* (RCA 1972)★★★, *Elvis As Recorded At Madison Square Garden* (RCA 1972)★★★, *Aloha From Hawaii Via Satellite* (RCA 1973)★★★, *Elvis* (RCA 1973)★★★, *Raised On Rock* (RCA 1973)★★★, *A Legendary Performer, Volume 1* (RCA 1974)★★★★, *Good Times* (RCA 1974)★★★, *Elvis Recorded On Stage In Memphis* (RCA 1974)★★★★, *Hits Of The 70s* (1974)★★★, *Promised Land* (RCA 1975)★★★, *Having Fun With Elvis On Stage* (1975)★★, *Today* (RCA 1975)★★★, *The Elvis Presley Sun Collection* (RCA 1975)★★★★★, *From Elvis Presley Boulevard, Memphis, Tennessee* (RCA 1976)★★★, *Moody Blue* (RCA 1977)★★★, *Welcome To My World* (RCA 1977)★★★, *A Legendary Performer* (RCA 1977)★★★★, *He Walks Beside Me* (RCA 1978)★★★, *Elvis - A Canadian Tribute* (RCA 1978)★★★, *The '56 Sessions, Vol. 1* (1978)★★★★, *Elvis's 40 Greatest* (RCA 1978)★★★★★, *Elvis - A Legendary Performer, Volume 3* (RCA 1979)★★★★, *Our Memories Of Elvis* (RCA 1979)★★★, *Our Memories Of Elvis Vol 2* (RCA 1979)★★★, *The '56 Sessions, Vol. 2* (1979)★★★★, *Elvis Presley Sings Leiber And Stoller* (RCA 1979)★★★★, *Elvis Aaron Presley* (RCA 1979)★★★, *Elvis Sings The Wonderful World Of Christmas* (RCA 1979)★★★, *The First Year* (1979)★★★, *The King...Elvis* (RCA 1980)★★★, *This Is Elvis* (RCA 1981)★★★, *Guitar Man* (RCA 1981)★★★, *Elvis Answers Back* (1981)★★★, *The Ultimate Performance* (RCA 1981)★★★, *Personally Elvis* (1982)★★★, *The Sound Of Your Cry* (1982)★★★, *Jailhouse Rock/Love In Las Vegas* (1983)★★★, *I Was The One* (RCA 1983)★★★, *The First Live Recordings* (Music Works 1984)★★★, *Rocker* (RCA 1984)★★★★, *A Golden Celebration* (1984)★★★, *A Valentine Gift For You* (RCA 1985)★★★, *Rare Elvis* (1985)★★★, *Essential Elvis* (1986)★★★★, *The Number One Hits* (RCA 1987)★★★★★, *The Top Ten Hits* (RCA 1987)★★★★, *The King Of Rock 'n' Roll: The Complete 50s Masters* (RCA 1992)★★★★★, *Elvis From Nashville To Memphis: The Essential '60s Masters* 5-CD box set (RCA 1993)★★★★★, *Elvis Gospel: 1957-1971* (RCA 1994)★★★, *If Every Day Was Like Christmas* (RCA 1994)★★★, *Walk A Mile In My Shoes: Elvis 56* (RCA 1996)★★★★★, *A Hundred Years From Now* (RCA 1996)★★★, *Presley - The All Time Greats* (RCA 1996)★★★★, *Great Country Songs* (RCA 1997)★★★, *Platinum - A Life In Music* 4-CD box set (RCA 1997)★★★★, *At The Louisiana Hayride 1954-1955* (Stomper Time 1997)★★.

● VIDEOS: *One Night With You* (1986), *Elvis Presley In Concert* (1986), *68 Comeback Special* (1986), *Memories* (1987), *This Is Elvis* (1988), *Graceland* (1988), *Great Performances Vol 2* (1990), *Great Vocal Performances Vol. 1* (1990), *Young Elvis* (1991), *Sun Days With Elvis* (1991), *Elvis On Tour* (1991), *Elvis; A Portrait By His Friends* (1991), *56 In the Beginning* (1991), *Private Elvis* (1993), *Elvis In Hollywood* (1993).

● FURTHER READING: *I Called Him Babe: Elvis Presley's Nurse Remembers*, Marian J. Cocke. *The Three Loves Of Elvis Presley: The True Story Of The Presley Legend*, Robert Holmes. *A Century Of Elvis*, Albert Hand. *The Elvis They Dig*, Albert Hand. *Operation Elvis*, Alan Levy. *The Elvis Presley Pocket Handbook*, Albert Hand. *All Elvis: An Unofficial Biography Of The 'King Of Discs'*, Philip Buckle. *The Elvis Presley Encyclopedia*, Roy Barlow. *Elvis: A Biography*, Jerry Hopkins. *Meet Elvis Presley*, Favius Friedman. *Elvis Presley*, Paula Taylor. *Elvis*, Jerry Hopkins. *The Elvis Presley Scrapbook 1935-1977*, James Robert Paris. *Elvis And The Colonel*, May Mann. *Recording Sessions 1954-1974*, Torben Holum, Ernst Jorgensen and Erik Rasmussen. *Elvis Presley: An Illustrated Biography*, W.A. Harbinson. *Elvis: The Films And Career Of Elvis Presley*, Steven and Boris Zmijewsky. *Presley Nation*, Spencer Leigh. *Elvis*, Peter Jones. *Presley: Entertainer Of The*

Century, Antony James. *Elvis And His Secret*, Maria Gripe. *On Stage, Elvis Presley*, Kathleen Bowman. *The Elvis Presley American Discography*, Ron Barry. *Elvis: What Happened* , Red West, Sonny West and Dave Hebler. *Elvis: Tribute To The King Of Rock*, Dick Tatham. *Elvis Presley*, Todd Slaughter. *Elvis: Recording Sessions*, Ernst Jorgensen, Erick Rasmussen and Johnny Mikkelsen. *The Life And Death Of Elvis Presley*, W.A. Harbinson. *Elvis: Lonely Star At The Top*, David Hanna. *Elvis In His Own Words*, Mick Farren and Pearce Marchbank. *Twenty Years Of Elvis: The Session File*, Colin Escott and Martin Hawkins. *Starring Elvis*, James W. Bowser. *My Life With Elvis*, Becky Yancey and Cliff Lindecker. *The Real Elvis: A Good Old Boy*, Vince Staten. *The Elvis Presley Trivia Quiz Book*, Helen Rosenbaum. *A Presley Speaks*, Vester Presley. *The Graceland Gates*, Harold Lloyd. *The Boy Who Dared To Rock: The Definitive Elvis*, Paul Lichter. *Eine Illustrierte Dokumentation*, Bernd King and Heinz Plehn. *Elvis Presley Speaks*, Hans Holzer. *Elvis: The Legend Lives! One Year Later*, Martin A. Grove. *Private Elvis*, Diego Cortez. *Bill Adler's Love Letters To Elvis*, Bill Adler. *Elvis: His Life And Times In Poetry And Lines*, Joan Buchanan West. *Elvis '56: In The Beginning*, Alfred Wertheimer. *Elvis Presley: An Illustrated Biography*, Rainer Wallraf and Heinz Plehn. *Even Elvis*, Mary Ann Thornton. *Elvis: Images & Fancies*, Jac L. Tharpe. *Elvis In Concert*, John Reggero. *Elvis Presley: A Study In Music*, Robert Matthew-Walker. *Elvis; Portrait Of A Friend*, Marty Lacker, Patsy Lacker and Leslie E. Smith. *Elvis Is That You?*, Holly Hatcher. *Elvis: Newly Discovered Drawings Of Elvis Presley*, Betty Harper. *Trying To Get To You: The Story Of Elvis Presley*, Valerie Harms. *Love Of Elvis*, Bruce Hamilton and Michael L. Liben. *To Elvis With Love*, Lena Canada. *The Truth About Elvis*, Jess Stearn. *Elvis: We Love You Tender*, Dee Presley; Rick Billy and David Stanley. *Presleyana*, Jerry Osborne and Bruce Hamilton. *Elvis: The Final Years*, Jerry Hopkins. *When Elvis Died*, Nancy and Joseph Gregory. *All About Elvis*, Fred L. Worth and Steve D. Tamerius. *Elvis Presley: A Reference Guide And Discography*, John A. Whisler. *The Illustrated Discography*, Martin Hawkins and Colin Escott. *Elvis: Legend Of Love*, Marie Greenfield. *Elvis Presley: King Of Rock 'N' Roll*, Richard Wooton. *The Complete Elvis*, Martin Torgoff. *Elvis Special 1982*, Todd Slaughter. *Elvis*, Dave Marsh. *Up And Down With Elvis Presley*, Marge Crumbaker with Gabe Tucker. *Elvis For The Record*, Maureen Covey. *Elvis: The Complete Illustrated Record*, Roy Carr and Mick Farren. *Elvis Collectables*, Rosalind Cranor. *Jailhouse Rock: The Bootleg Records Of Elvis Presley 1970*, Lee Cotten and Howard A. DeWitt. *Elvis The Soldier*, Rex and Elisabeth Mansfield. *All Shook Up: Elvis Day-By-Day, 1954-1977*, Lee Cotten. *Elvis*, John Townson, Gordon Minto and George Richardson. *Priscilla, Elvis & Me*, Michael Edwards. *Elvis On The Road To Stardom: 1955-1956*, Jim Black. *Return To Sender*, Howard F. Banney. *Elvis: His Life From A To Z*, Fred L. Worth and Steve D. Tamerius. *Elvis And The Colonel*, Dirk Vallenga with Mick Farren. *Elvis: My Brother*, Bill Stanley with George Erikson. *Long Lonely Highway: 1950's Elvis Scrapbook*, Ger J. Rijff. *Elvis In Hollywood*, Gerry McLafferty. *Reconsider Baby: Definitive Elvis Sessionography*, Jorgensen, E., *Elvis '69, The Return*, Joseph Tunzi. *The Death Of Elvis: What Really Happened*, Charles C. Thompson and James P., Cole. *Elvis For Beginners*, Jill Pearlman. *Elvis, The Cool King*, Bob Moreland and Jan Van Gestel. *The Elvis Presley Scrapbooks 1955-1965*, Peter Haining (ed.). *The Boy Who Would Be King. An Intimate Portrait Of Elvis Presley By His Cousin*, Earl Greenwood and Kathleen Tracy. *Elvis: The Last 24 Hours*, Albert Goldman. *The Elvis Files*, Gail Brewer-Giorgio. *Elvis, My Dad*, David Adler and Ernest Andrews. *The Elvis Reader: Texts And Sources On The King Of Rock 'n' Roll*, Kevin Quain (ed.). *Elvis Bootleg Buyer's Guide, Pts 1& 2*, Tommy Robinson. *Elvis: The Music Lives On- The Recording Sessions 1954-1976*, Richard Peters. *The King Forever*, no author listed. *Dead Elvis: A Chronicle Of A Cultural Obession*, Greil Marcus. *Elvis People: Cult Of The KIng*, Ted Harrison. *In Search Of The King*, Craig Gelfand, Lynn Blocker-Krantz and Rogerio Noguera. *Aren Med Elvis*, Roger Ersson and Lennart Svedberg. *Elvis And Gladys*, Elaine Dundy. *King And I: Little Gallery of Elvis Impersonators* , Kent Barker and Karin Pritikin. *Elvis Sessions: The Recorded Music Of Elvis Aron Presley 1953-1977*, Joseph Tunzi. *Elvis: The Sun Years*, Howard A. DeWitt. *Elvis In Germany: The Missing Years*, Andreas Schroer. *Graceland: The Living Legend Of Elvis Presley*, Chet Flippo. *Elvis: The Secret Files*, John Parker. *The Life And Cuisine Of Elvis Presley*, David Adler. *Last Train To Memphis: The Rise Of Elvis Presley*, Peter Guralnick. *In His Own Words*, Mick Farren. *Elvis: Murdered By The Mob*, John Parker. *The Complete Guide To The Music Of ...*, John Robertson. *Elvis's Man Friday*, Gene Smith. *The Hitchhiker's Guide To Elvis*, Mick Farren. *Elvis, The Lost Photographs 1948-1969*, Tunzi and O'Neal Joseph. *Elvis Aaron Presley: Revelations From The Memphis Mafia*, Alanna Nash. *The Elvis Encyclopaedia*, David E. Stanley. *E: Reflections On The Birth Of The Elvis Faith*, John, E. Strausbaugh. *Elvis Meets The Beatles: The Untold Story Of Their Entangled Lives*, Chris Hutchins and Peter Thompson. *Elvis, Highway 51 South, Memphis, Tennessee*, Joseph A. Tunzi. *Elvis In The Army*, William J. Taylor Jnr. *Everything Elvis*, Pauline Bartel. *Elvis In Wonderland*, Bob Jope. *Elvis: Memories And Memorabilia*, Richard Bushkin.
● FILMS: *Love Me Tender* (1956), *Loving You* (1957), *Jailhouse Rock* (1957), *King Creole* (1958), *G.I. Blues* (1960), *Flaming Star* (1960), *Wild In The Country* (1961), *Blue Hawaii* (1961), *Kid Galahad* (1962), *Girls Girls Girls* (1962), *Follow That Dream* (1962), *It Happened At The World's Fair* (1963), *Fun In Acapulco* (1963), *Roustabout* (1964), *Viva Las Vegas* (1964), *Kissin' Cousins* (1964), *Tickle Me* (1965), *Harum Scarum* aka *Harem Holiday* (1965), *Girl Happy* (1965), *Spinout* (1966), *Paradise Hawaiin Style* (1966), *Frankie And Johnny* (1966), *Easy Come Easy Go* (1967), *Clambake* (1967), *Live A Little Love A Little* (1968), *Speedway* (1968), *Stay Away Joe* (1968), *Double Trouble* (1968), *The Trouble With Girls* (1969), *Charro!* (1969), *Change Of Habit* (1969), *This Is Elvis* compilation (1981).

PRICE, KENNY

b. 27 May 1931, Florence, Kentucky, USA, d. 4 August 1987, Florence, Kentucky, USA. Price was raised on a farm in Boone County, Kentucky, and he was given a guitar when he was five years old. He played guitar as a teenager on a radio station in Cincinnati and then entertained the troops when he was in the forces. His break came in 1957 when he was invited to appear on Arthur Godfrey's television show in what was the first colour transmission in the USA - perhaps they were attracted to his highly coloured Nudie suits! He moved to Nashville in the early 60s and, after signing with the new Boone label in 1965, he had several US country hits - 'Walkin'

On New Grass', 'Happy Tracks', 'Pretty Girl, Pretty Clothes, Pretty Sad', 'Grass Won't Grow On A Busy Street' and 'My Goal For Today'. He was a comedian and because he weighed 20 stone, he was known as 'The Round Mound Of Sound'. He became a regular member of the *Hee Haw* television show. He moved to RCA and had US Top 10 country singles with 'Northeast Arkansas Mississippi County Bootlegger', 'Biloxi' and 'The Sheriff Of Boone County'. In 1973 Craig Baguley, the editor of *Country Music People*, wrote a tribute to him, 'Kenny Price', which was recorded by the Johnny Young Four. His final chart entries included 'Afraid You'd Come Back', 'Well Rounded Travellin' Man' and, ironically, 'She's Leavin' (And I'm Almost Gone)'. Kenny Price died from a heart attack in 1987.

● ALBUMS: *One Hit Follows Another* (Boone 1967)★★★, *Southern Bound* (Boone 1967)★★★, *Walkin' On New Grass* (RCA 1969)★★★, *Happy Tracks* (RCA 1969)★★★, *Heavyweight* (RCA 1970)★★★, *Northeast Arkansas Mississippi County Bootlegger* (RCA 1970)★★★, *The Sheriff Of Boone County* (RCA 1971)★★★, *The Red Foley Songbook* (RCA 1971)★★★, *Charlotte Fever* (RCA 1971)★★★, *Super Sideman* (RCA 1972)★★★, *You Almost Slipped My Mind* (RCA 1972)★★★, *Sea Of Heartbreak And Other Don Gibson Tunes* (RCA 1973)★★★, *30 California Women* (RCA 1973)★★★, *Turn On Your Lovelight And Let It Shine* (RCA 1974)★★★, *Best Of Both* (1980)★★★, with Roy Clark, Grandpa Jones, Buck Owens *Hee-Haw Gospel Quartet* (Songbird 1981)★★★, *A Pocket Full Of Tunes* (1982)★★★.

PRICE, RAY

b. Ray Noble Price, 12 January 1926, on a farm near Perryville, Cherokee County, Texas, USA. Price grew up on a farm and by the time he left high school, was already singing and playing guitar locally. In 1942, while studying veterinary medicine at Abilene's North Texas Agricultural College, he was drafted into the Marines. He returned to his studies in 1946, but also began performing at local clubs, and as the Cherokee Cowboy, he appeared on KRBC. He still had thoughts of a career as a rancher but in 1949, the opportunity to join the *Big D Jamboree* in Dallas finally convinced him that his future lay in country music. He first recorded for a minor label, Bullet, and had some success in Texas with 'Jealous Lies', but in 1952 he joined Columbia Records and had immediate US country Top 10 hits with 'Talk To Your Heart' and 'Don't Let The Stars Get In Your Eyes'. Price moved to Nashville, where he became a member of the *Grand Ole Opry*. He was also befriended by Hank Williams, with whom he lived for a time and on occasions worked with the Drifting Cowboys on shows that Hank missed. When he later formed his own band, the Cherokee Cowboys, quite apart from appearances by members of the old Hank Williams band, it was occasionally to include Willie Nelson, Johnny Paycheck, Johnny Bush, Buddy Emmons and Roger Miller. Price's vocals and the excellence of the Cherokee Cowboys represented some of the finest honky-tonk country music of all time. The immense popularity Price gained may be judged by his chart successes. In the 20 years between 1954 and 1974 he amassed a total of 64 US country chart hits, only 11 of which failed to make the Top 20 and 13 also crossed over to the pop charts. He registered 7 country number 1 hits including 'Crazy Arms' (his first million-seller), 'My Shoes Keep Walking Back To You', 'City Lights'

(his second million-seller, which also launched Bill Anderson's songwriting career) and 'For The Good Times', a third million-seller which first introduced the songwriting talent of a young Nashville janitor called Kris Kristofferson. He also recorded what is probably the most popular country version of 'Release Me', a song that 13 years later became a UK pop chart number 1 for Engelbert Humperdinck. In 1967, Price moved from honky-tonk music to a more pop-orientated approach. His backings began to feature strong orchestral accompaniment, far removed from the traditional fiddle and steel guitar influence of his mentor, Hank Williams. Price maintained that most of his songs were ballads and that the strings provided the soul. In concert, he often used up to ten violins in his backing but for his records there were often many more; when he recorded his version of 'Danny Boy', the backing was by an orchestra that consisted of forty-seven musicians. He also dispensed with his western-style dress and took to appearing in smart evening suits; the Cherokee Cowboy was dead. He toured extensively and appeared on all major network radio and television shows. By 1973, Price had grown rather tired of the touring and semi-retired to his ranch near Dallas to breed horses. Five years later, he found that he missed the musical life and once more was to be found back on the circuit. From the mid-70s through to the late 80s, he recorded for Myrrh, ABC, Monument, Dimension, Warner Brothers, Viva and Step One, and although there were few Top 20 hits after 1974, he continued regularly to register country chart entries. In 1980, in an effort to boost his somewhat flagging chart successes, he asked Willie Nelson to record an album with him. Nelson obliged his old boss and their duet of 'Faded Love', from the album *San Antonio Rose*, charted at number 3. A feud had existed for many years between Price and Nelson dating back to when they were neighbours. Nelson had shot and eaten one of Price's fighting roosters for killing some of his hens and Price swore he would never record another Nelson song (the reason why Price kept fighting roosters is open to conjecture). He eventually overcame his anger, but Nelson had no real reason to agree to the request to record the album since Price had not recorded any of his songs for a long time. Price also appeared in the Clint Eastwood film *Honkytonk Man*. From the mid-80s, some of his recordings were of dubious country content, such as his versions of the Frank Sinatra pop hit 'All The Way' and the 1931 Gene Austin hit 'Please Don't Talk About Me When I'm Gone', but on others he tended to revert more to the simple country backings of his early days. When 'I'd Do It All Over Again' charted in December 1988, it took his tally of country hits to 108 and in the statistics produced by Joel Whitburn for his *Record Research*, based on country music chart success from 1944-88, Price stands at number 6 in the Top 200 country artists of all time. He currently performs at his own theatre in Branson, Missouri In 1996 he was inducted into the Country Music Hall Of Fame.

● ALBUMS: *Ray Price Sings Heart Songs* (Columbia 1957)★★★, *Talk To Your Heart* (Columbia 1958)★★★★, with orchestra and chorus *Faith* (Columbia 1960)★★★, *Sings San Antonio Rose (A Tribute To The Great Bob Wills)* (Columbia 1962)★★★★, *Night Life* (Columbia 1963)★★★, *Love Life* (Columbia 1964)★★★, *Burning Memories* (Columbia 1965)★★★, *Western Strings* (Columbia 1965)★★★, *The Other Woman* (Columbia 1965)★★★,

Another Bridge To Burn (Columbia 1966)★★★, *Touch My Heart* (Columbia 1967)★★★, *Born To Lose* (Harmony 1967)★★★, *Danny Boy* (Columbia 1967)★★★, *She Wears My Ring* (Columbia 1968)★★★, *Take Me As I Am* (Columbia 1968)★★★, *I Fall To Pieces* (Harmony 1969)★★★, *Ray Price's Christmas Album* (Columbia 1969)★★, *Sweetheart Of The Year* (Columbia 1969)★★★, *For The Good Times* (Columbia 1970)★★★, *The World Of Ray Price* (Columbia 1970)★★★, *You Wouldn't Know Love* (Columbia 1970)★★★, *Make The World Go Away* (Harmony 1970)★★★, *I Won't Mention It Again* (Columbia 1971)★★★, *Release Me* (Columbia 1971)★★★, *The Lonesomest Lonesome* (Columbia 1972)★★★, *She's Got To Be A Saint* (Columbia 1973)★★★, *Like Old Times Again* (Columbia 1974)★★★, *This Time Lord* (Myrrh 1974)★★★, *You're The Best Thing That Ever Happened To Me* (Myrrh 1974)★★★, *If You Ever Change Your Mind* (ABC 1975)★★★, *Say I Do* (ABC 1975)★★, *Hank 'N' Me* (ABC 1976)★★★, *Rainbows And Tears* (ABC 1976)★★★, *Help Me* (Columbia 1977)★★★, *How Great Thou Art* (1977)★★★, *Reunited - Ray Price And The Cherokee Cowboys* (ABC 1977)★★★, *Precious Memories* (ABC 1977)★★★, *There's Always Me* (Monument 1979)★★★, with Willie Nelson *San Antonio Rose* (Columbia 1980)★★★, *Ray Price* (Dimension 1981)★★★, *Town And Country* (Dimension 1981)★★★, *Tribute To Willie & Kris* (Dimension 1981)★★★, *Diamonds In The Stars* (Dimension 1981)★★★, *Loving You* (Dimension 1982)★★★, *Somewhere In Texas* (Dimension 1982)★★★, *Master Of The Art* (Viva 1983)★★★, *Portrait Of A Singer* (1985)★★★, *Welcome To The Country* (1985)★★★, *A Revival Of Old Time Singing* (Step One 1987)★★★, *The Heart Of Country Music* (Step One 1987)★★★, *A Christmas Gift For You* (Step One 1987)★★, *Just Enough Love* (Step One 1988)★★, *Sometimes A Rose* (1992)★★★, with Faron Young *Memories That Last* (1992)★★★.

● COMPILATIONS: *Ray Price's Greatest Hits* (Columbia 1961)★★★, *Ray Price - Collector's Choice* (Harmony 1966)★★★, *Ray Price's Greatest Hits, Volume 2* (Columbia 1967)★★★, *Welcome To My World* (1971)★★★, *Ray Price's All-Time Greatest Hits* (1972)★★★, *The Best Of Ray Price* (Columbia 1976)★★★, *Happens To Be The Best* (Pair 1983)★★★, *Greatest Hits, Volume 1, 2 & 3* (1986)★★★, *By Request - Greatest Hits, Volume 4* (1988)★★★, *American Originals* (Columbia 1989)★★★, *The Essential Ray Price (1951-1962)* (Columbia 1991)★★★★, *Ray Price And The Cherokee Cowboys: The Honky Tonk Years (1950-1966)* 10-CD box set (Bear Family 1995)★★★★.

PRIDE, CHARLEY

b. 18 March 1938, Sledge, Mississippi, USA. Charley Pride was born on a cotton farm, which, as a result of his success, he was later able to purchase. Pride says, 'My dad named me Charl Frank Pride, but I was born in the country and the midwife wrote it down as Charley'. Harold Dorman, who wrote and recorded 'Mountain of Love', also hails from Sledge and wrote 'Mississippi Cotton Pickin' Delta Town' about the area, for Pride. As an adolescent, Pride followed what he heard on the radio with a cheap guitar, breaking with stereotypes by preferring country music to the blues. He played baseball professionally but he reverted to music when the Los Angeles Angels told him that he did not have a 'major league arm'. In 1965 producer Jack Clement brought Pride to Chet Atkins at RCA Records. They consid-

ered not disclosing that he was black until the records were established, but Atkins decided that it was unfair to all concerned. 'The Snakes Crawl at Night' sold on its own merit and was followed by 'Just Between You And Me' which won a Grammy for the best country record by a male performer. On 7 January 1967 Ernest Tubb introduced him at the *Grand Ole Opry*, 42 years after the first black performer to appear there, DeFord Bailey in 1925. Prejudice ran high but the quality of Pride's music, particularly the atmospheric live album from Panther Hall, meant that he was accepted by the redneck community. At one momentous concert, Willie Nelson kissed him on stage. Pride has had 29 number 1 records on the US country charts, including six consecutive chart-toppers between 1969 and 1971 - an extraordinary feat. His most significant recordings include 'Is Anybody Goin' to San Antone?', which he learnt and recorded in 15 minutes, and 'Crystal Chandelier', which he took from a Carl Belew record and is still the most requested song in UK country clubs. Strangely enough, 'Crystal Chandelier' was not a US hit, where his biggest single is 'Kiss An Angel Good Mornin''. Unfortunately, Pride fell into the same trap as Elvis Presley by recording songs that he published, so he did not always record the best material around. Nevertheless, over the years, Charley Pride has encouraged such new talents as Kris Kristofferson, Ronnie Milsap, Dave And Sugar (who were his back-up singers) and Gary Stewart (who was his opening act). In 1975 Pride hosted a live double album from the *Opry*, *In Person*, which also featured Atkins, Milsap, Dolly Parton, Jerry Reed and Stewart. By the mid-80s, Pride was disappointed at the way RCA was promoting 'New Country' in preference to established performers so he left the label. He then recorded what is arguably his most interesting project, a tribute album to Brook Benton. Sadly, it was not released as he signed with 16th Avenue Records, who preferred new material. Records such as 'I'm Gonna Love Her On The Radio' and 'Amy's Eyes' continued his brand of easy-listening country, but could not recapture his sales of the late 60s. Pride has had a long and contented family life and his son, Dion, plays in his band ('We took the name from Dion And The Belmonts. We just liked it'). Seeing him perform in concert underlines what a magnificent voice he has. Sadly, he does not choose to test it in other, more demanding musical forms, although he argues that 'the most powerful songs are the simple ones.' In 1994 he received the Academy Of Country Music's Pioneer Award.

● ALBUMS: *Country Charley Pride* (RCA 1966)★★★, *The Pride Of Country Music* (RCA 1967)★★★★, *The Country Way* (RCA 1967)★★★, *Make Mine Country* (RCA 1968)★★★, *Songs Of Pride ... Charley, That Is* (RCA 1968)★★★, *Charley Pride - In Person* (RCA 1968)★★★, *The Sensational Charley Pride* (RCA 1969)★★★★, *Just Plain Charley* (RCA 1970)★★★, *Charley Pride's Tenth Album* (RCA 1970)★★★, *Christmas In My Home Town* (RCA 1970)★★, *From Me To You (To All My Wonderful Fans)* (RCA 1971)★★★, *Did You Think To Pray?* (RCA 1971)★★, *I'm Just Me* (RCA 1971)★★★, *Charley Pride Sings Heart Songs* (RCA 1971)★★★, *A Sunshiny Day With Charley Pride* (RCA 1972)★★★, *Songs Of Love By Charley Pride* (RCA 1973)★★★, *Sweet Country* (RCA 1973)★★★, *Amazing Love* (RCA 1973)★★★, *Country Feelin'* (RCA 1974)★★★, *Pride Of America* (RCA 1974)★★, *Charley* (RCA 1975)★★★, *The Happiness Of Having You* (RCA 1975)★★★, *Sunday Morning With Charley Pride* (RCA 1976)★★★, *She's*

Just An Old Love Turned Memory (RCA 1977)★★★, Someone Loves You Honey (RCA 1978)★★★, Burgers And Fries (RCA 1978)★★★, You're My Jamaica (RCA 1979)★★, There's A Little Bit Of Hank In Me (RCA 1980)★★★, Roll On Mississippi (RCA 1981)★★★, Charley Sings Everybody's Choice (RCA 1982)★★★, Live (RCA 1982)★★, Night Games (RCA 1983)★★★, The Power Of Love (RCA 1984)★★★, After All This Time (16th Avenue 1987)★★★, I'm Gonna Love Her On The Radio (16th Avenue 1988)★★★, Moody Woman (16th Avenue 1989)★★★, Amy's Eyes (16th Avenue 1990)★★★, Classics With Pride (16th Avenue 1991)★★★★, My 6 Latest & 6 Greatest (Honest 1993)★★★, Just For The Love Of It (Ritz 1996)★★★.
● COMPILATIONS: The Best Of Charley Pride (RCA 1969)★★★★, The Best Of Charley Pride, Volume 2 (RCA 1972)★★★★, The Incomparable Charley Pride (RCA 1973)★★★, The Best Of Charley Pride, Volume 3 (RCA 1977)★★★, Greatest Hits (RCA 1981)★★★★, The Very Best Of ... (Ritz 1995)★★★★, Super Hits (RCA 1996)★★★, The Essential Charley Pride (RCA 1997)★★★★.
● VIDEOS: Charley Pride-Live (MSD 1988), Charley Pride (Telstar 1992), An Evening In Concert (Honest Entertainment 1996), My Latest And Greatest (Massive Video 1997).
● FURTHER READING: Charley Pride, Pamela Barclay. Pride; The Charley Pride Story, Charley Pride with Jim Henderson.

PRINE, JOHN

b. 10 October 1946, Maywood, Illinois, USA. Prine's grandfather had played with Merle Travis, and Prine himself started playing guitar at the age of 14. He then spent time in College, worked as a postman for five years, and spent two years in the army. He began his musical career around 1970, singing in clubs in the Chicago area. Prine signed to Atlantic Records in 1971, releasing the powerful John Prine. The album contained the excellent Vietnam veteran song 'Sam Stone', featuring the wonderfully evocative line: 'There's a hole in daddy's arm where all the money goes, and Jesus Christ died for nothing I suppose'. Over the years Prine achieved cult status, his songs being increasingly covered by other artists, 'Angel From Montgomery', 'Speed Of The Sound Of Loneliness', and 'Paradise' being three in particular. He was inevitably given the unenviable tag of 'the new Dylan' at one stage. His last album for Atlantic, Common Sense (produced by Steve Cropper), was his first album to make the US Top 100. While the quality and content of all his work was quite excellent, his other albums had only scratched the US Top 200. His first release for Asylum, Bruised Orange, was well received, but the follow-up, Pink Cadillac, was not so well accommodated by the public or the critics. However, The Missing Years changed everything with massive sales at home, and a Grammy award for best Contemporary Folk Album, making Prine almost a household name. His outstanding songs had been covered by the likes of Bonnie Raitt and John Denver over the years, and he co-wrote the hit 'I Just Want To Dance With You' with Daniel O'Donnell. His career has taken on a new lease of life in the 90s; Prine presented Town And Country for Channel 4 Television in the UK in 1992, a series of music programmes featuring singers such as Nanci Griffith and Rodney Crowell. In keeping with his career upswing, Lost Dogs & Mixed Blessings was another strong work. Prine's songs are

becoming even quirkier and only the author could know the meaning of many of them. In January 1998 he was reported to be seriously ill.
● ALBUMS: John Prine (Atlantic 1972)★★★★, Diamonds In The Rough (Atlantic 1972)★★★, Sweet Revenge (Atlantic 1973)★★★★, Common Sense (Atlantic 1975)★★★, Bruised Orange (Asylum 1978)★★★, Pink Cadillac (Asylum 1979)★★★, Storm Windows (Asylum 1980)★★★, Aimless Love (Oh Boy 1985)★★★, German Afternoons (Demon 1987)★★★, John Prine Live (Oh Boy 1988)★★★, The Missing Years (Oh Boy 1992)★★★★, Live (1993)★★★, Lost Dogs & Mixed Blessings (Rykodisk 1995)★★★, Live On Tour (Oh Boy 1997)★★★.
● COMPILATIONS: Prime Prine (Atlantic 1977)★★, Anthology: Great Days (Rhino 1993)★★★★.

PROPHET, RONNIE

b. 26 December 1937, Calumet, Quebec, Canada. Prophet, whose second cousin is Canadian country singer Orvel Prophet, was raised on a farm but spent his adolescence playing clubs in Montreal. In the late 60s Ronnie, deciding that this Prophet needed more than honour in his own country, established himself at the Carousel Club in Nashville. With his comedy and impressions, he stood apart from other country performers. Chet Atkins called him 'the greatest one-man show I've seen' and Prophet himself comments, 'I believe that if an audience goes to a live show, then they should get a live show. I'm irritated by artists who are walking jukeboxes.' In truth, Prophet has not had enough country hits to be a walking juke-box, and he has only had five minor successes on the US country charts, including 'Sanctuary' (number 26) and 'Shine On' (number 36). His serious records resemble Conway Twitty at his most mannered. In 1978, Prophet was a major success in the UK at the Wembley Country Music Festival, which led to further appearances, UK tours and his own television programmes. Although he is an excellent MC, Prophet has not sustained his popularity, possibly because 'Harry The Horny Toad' and 'The Phantom Of The Opry' wear thin.
● ALBUMS: Ronnie Prophet Country (RCA 1976)★★★, Ronnie Prophet (RCA 1977)★★★, Just For You (RCA 1978)★★★, Faces And Phrases (RCA 1980)★★★, Audiograph Alive (RCA 1982)★★, I'm Gonna Love Him Out Of You (RCA 1983)★★★, Ronnie Prophet And Glory-Anne (RCA 1985)★★, Ronnie Prophet (RCA 1987)★★★.

PRUETT, JEANNE

b. Norma Jean Bowman, 30 January 1937, Pell City, Oklahoma, USA. Pruett, one of 10 children, used to listen to the Grand Ole Opry with her parents and she harmonized with her brothers and sisters. She married Jack Pruett, and in 1956, they settled in Nashville where he became Marty Robbins' long-standing lead guitarist. She wrote several songs for Robbins, and 'Count Me Out' was a US country hit in 1966. After some unsuccessful records for RCA, she made the US country charts with 'Hold On To My Unchanging Love' for Decca in 1971. It was followed by a country number 1 in 1973, 'Satin Sheets', which was also a US pop hit. Another Top 10 country single, 'I'm Your Woman', was on the charts at the same time as a Robbins single she had written, 'Love Me' (after Robbins' death, a duet version of the same song was also a country hit). Although she did not repeat the success of 'Satin Sheets', she generated interest in 1979 with 'Please Sing Satin Sheets For Me'. Although she regularly appears at the *Grand Ole Opry*, Pruett has never been fully committed to her career as she values her home life and is a prize-winning cook and gardener.

● ALBUMS: *Love Me* (Decca 1972)★★★, *Satin Sheets* (MCA 1973)★★★★, *Welcome To The Sunshine* (MCA 1974)★★★, *Honey On His Hands* (MCA 1975)★★★, *Encore* (IBC 1979)★★★, *Country* (1982)★★, *Star Studded Nights* (Audiograph 1982)★★★, *Audiograph Alive* (Audiograph 1983)★★, *Stand By Your Man* (Allegiance 1984)★★, *Jeanne Pruett* (MCA 1985)★★★.

PUCKETT, RILEY

b. George Riley Puckett, 7 May 1894, near Alpharetta, Georgia, USA, d. 13 July 1946, East Point, Georgia, USA. Due to the accidental use of overly strong medication to treat a minor eye infection, he was blinded as a baby. In 1912, after graduating from the Georgia Academy for the Blind in Macon, where he first learned to play the banjo and piano, he sought the life of a musician and moved to Atlanta. He appeared at the Georgia Old Time Fiddler's Convention in 1916, drawing good reviews as 'the blind banjoist'. He also took to playing the guitar and singing and worked local dances and busked on the streets. In 1922, he made his radio debut on WSB as a special guest with the Hometown Band - a local band led by fiddler Clayton McMichen. The programmes of the powerful WSB could be heard across most of the United States and Puckett's performance attracted attention. He was a fine singer and listeners were also greatly impressed by his excellent yodelling. In 1923, he, McMichen and Gid Tanner began to play together as the Skillet Lickers. Puckett made his first recordings in New York in March 1924, when he and Tanner became the first hillbilly artists to appear on the Columbia label. He recorded such solo numbers as 'Little Old Log Cabin In The Lane' and 'Rock All My Babies To Sleep'. By yodelling on the latter, he probably became the first hillbilly singer to yodel on record - preceding the blue yodels of Jimmie Rodgers by three years (it has never been established just where he first learned this art). He was badly injured in a car crash in 1925 and subsequently married his nurse (they had one daughter, Blanche, but later parted). His recordings proved so popular that, by the end of the year, only the recordings of Vernon Dalhart received more orders among Columbia artists. The Skillet Lickers, who underwent various changes in line-up during their existence, made their first recordings in 1926 and proved very successful. Their 1927 recording of 'A Corn Licker Still In Georgia' very quickly sold a quarter of a million copies. During the years that Puckett played with the Skillet Lickers, he still made solo concert and recording appearances. When, because of the Depression, the Skillet Lickers disbanded in 1931, he was still much in demand as a solo artist. They re-formed briefly in 1934, when he and Tanner recorded together for the last time (Tanner tired of the music business and returned to chicken farming). During the 30s and early 40s, Puckett travelled extensively making personal appearances, and for some time he also had his own very popular tent show, which toured the Midwest, Texas, Oklahoma and the southern states. He was featured on various radio stations and at times ran his own bands. In 1945, he was a regular member of the *Tennessee*

Barn Dance on WNOX Knoxville, where he appeared with the Delmore Brothers, Chet Atkins and Sam And Kirk McGee. After leaving Columbia in 1934, he made recordings for RCA-Victor and Decca. His final recordings were made for RCA in 1941, in a session that included the pop-oriented 'Where The Shy Little Violets Grow' and Carson Jay Robison's 'Railroad Boomer'. The undoubted secret of Puckett's success, quite apart from his instrumental abilities, was his large repertoire. He could sing (and play) equally well any songs ranging from old-time folk ballads such as 'Old Black Joe' and 'John Henry' (his 1924 version is in all probability the first time the song was recorded) through to vaudeville numbers such as 'Wait Till The Sun Shines Nellie' and 'Red Sails In The Sunset'. His fine banjo playing included standards such as 'Cripple Creek' and 'Oh Susanna' and his unique guitar style, with its very fast, thumb-played bass string runs, has been equalled by very few other guitarists, one exception being another blind musician, Doc Watson. Prior to his untimely death in 1946, he was appearing regularly on WACA Atlanta, with a band called the Stone Mountain Boys. A boil on his neck caused blood poisoning and though he was rushed to hospital, it was too late and he died on 13 July. One of the pallbearers at his funeral was his old associate Gid Tanner. It seems ironic that, as with his blindness, the correct treatment at the appropriate time could no doubt have effected a proper cure. Puckett is one of country music's most interesting and talented but, unfortunately, now overlooked characters.

● COMPILATIONS: with Gid Tanner And The Skillet Lickers *Gid Tanner And His Skillet Lickers* (1973)★★★, *The Skillet Lickers* (1973)★★★, *Gid Tanner And His Skillet Lickers, Volume 2* (1975)★★★, *Kickapoo Medicine Show* (1977)★★★, *A Day At The County Fair* (1981)★★★, *A Corn Licker Still In Georgia* (1985)★★★.

● SOLO COMPILATIONS: *Waitin' For The Evening Train* (1977)★★★, *Old Time Greats, Volume 1* (Old Homestead 1978)★★★, *Old Time Greats, Volume 2* (Old Homestead 1978)★★★, *Red Sails In The Sunset* (Bear Family 1988)★★★★.

● FURTHER READING: *Riley Puckett (1894-1946)*, Charles K.Wolfe, with *Discography* by John Larson, Tony Russell, Richard Weize.

PURE PRAIRIE LEAGUE

Formed in 1971, this US country rock group comprised Craig Lee Fuller (vocals, guitar), George Powell (vocals, guitar), John Call (pedal steel guitar), Jim Lanham (bass) and Jim Caughlin (drums). Their self-titled debut album was a strong effort, and included the excellent 'Tears', 'You're Between Me' (a tribute to McKendree Spring) and 'It's All On Me'. The work also featured some novel sleeve artwork, using Norman Rockwell's portrait of an ageing cowboy as a symbol of the Old West. On *Pure Prairie League*, the figure was seen wistfully clutching a record titled 'Dreams Of Long Ago'. For successive albums, the cowboy would be portrayed being ejected from a saloon, stranded in a desert and struggling with a pair of boots. The image effectively gave Pure Prairie League a brand name, but by the time of *Bustin' Out*, Fuller and Powell were left to run the group using session musicians. This album proved their masterwork, one of the best and most underrated records produced in country rock. Its originality lay in the use of string arrangements, for which they recruited the services of former David Bowie acolyte Mick Ronson. His work was particularly effective on the expansive 'Boulder Skies' and 'Call Me Tell Me'. A single from the album, 'Amie', was a US hit and prompted the return of John Call, but when Fuller left in 1975 to form American Flyer, the group lost its major writing talent and inspiration. Powell continued with bassist Mike Reilly, lead guitarist Larry Goshorn and pianist Michael Connor. Several minor albums followed and the group achieved a surprise US Top 10 hit in 1980 with 'Let Me Love You Tonight'. Fuller is now with Little Feat, while latter-day guitarist Vince Gill, who joined Pure Prairie League in 1979, has become a superstar in the country market in the 90s.

● ALBUMS: *Pure Prairie League* (RCA 1972)★★★, *Bustin' Out* (RCA 1975)★★★★, *Two Lane Highway* (RCA 1975)★★★★, *If The Shoe Fits* (RCA 1976)★★★, *Dance* (RCA 1976)★★★, *Live!! Takin' The Stage* (RCA 1977)★★, *Just Fly* (RCA 1978)★★, *Can't Hold Back* (RCA 1979)★★, *Firin' Up* (Casablanca 1980)★★, *Something In The Night* (Casablanca 1981)★★.

● COMPILATIONS: *Pure Prairie Collection* (RCA 1981)★★★, *Mementoes 1971-1987* (Rushmore 1987)★★★, *Best Of Pure Prairie League* (Mercury Nashville 1995)★★★★.

R. CAJUN AND THE ZYDECO BROTHERS

R. Cajun were formed in 1979 by Chris Hall, a former member of Shufflin' Sam and a keen enthusiast of Cajun music. The original line-up was Chris Hall (b. 2 July 1952, Sheffield, Yorkshire, England; accordion, vocals), Tony Dark (fiddle), Alf Billington (guitar, vocals), and Veronica Matthews (triangle). The following year, Trevor Hopkins (bass) joined the line-up, but was soon replaced by Beeds (b. 13 October 1947, Derby, Derbyshire, England; guitar, harmonica). The line-up, which started to make some impact on the folk circuit in 1982, consisted of Hall, Billington, John Squire (fiddle, guitar, mandolin), who joined that year, as did Beeds, and Jan Hall (b. 17 January 1953, Sheffield, Yorkshire, England; triangle, percussion). *Bayou Rhythms* included the Zydeco Brothers, Graham Jones (bass) and Neil 'Freddy' Hopwood (b. 23 April 1947, Lichfield, Staffordshire, England; drums). Hopwood had formerly been a member of Dr. Strangely Strange and the Sutherland Brothers bands. The album contained some infectious pieces such as 'Cajun Two-Step', and 'Bayou Pom Pom Special', as well as standards such as 'Jambalaya' and 'Deportees', and quickly established

them as a popular group at festivals. In 1984, Dave Blant (b. 27 November 1949, Burton Upon Trent, Staffordshire, England; bass, vocals) joined, replacing Graham Jones. Having previously left the group, Tony Dark re-joined them in 1986, in turn replacing John Squire. The same year, Clive Harvey (b. 27 November 1945, Watford, Hertfordshire, England; guitar, vocals) was added. It was this line-up that recorded *Pig Sticking In Arcadia*. Three years later, Dark again left the group, to be replaced by Derek Richardson (fiddle), then Dave 'Mitch' Proctor (b. 8 December 1952, Heanor, Derbyshire, England; fiddle) joined in 1990, replacing Richardson. Despite the various personnel changes, the overall sound of the group has remained remarkably constant. Their blend of Cajun and zydeco, apart from being unusual, has added to the band's original sound and style. They continue playing festivals, both at home and abroad, where they are equally popular. Chris Hall is the co-owner of Swamp, an organization that runs Bearcat Records and the UK's top Cajun venue, The Swamp Club, in Derby.

● ALBUMS: *Bayou Rhythms* (Moonraker 1984)★★★, *Pig Sticking In Arcadia* (Disc Ethnique 1987)★★★, *Out Of The Swamp* (1990)★★★, *No Known Cure* (1993)★★★, *That Cajun Thing* (Bearcat 1994)★★★.

RABBITT, EDDIE

b. Edward Thomas Rabbitt, 27 November 1944, Brooklyn, New York City, USA. Rabbitt, whose name is Gaelic, was raised in East Orange, New Jersey. His father, Thomas Rabbitt, a refrigeration engineer, played fiddle and accordion and is featured alongside his son on the 1978 track 'Song Of Ireland'. On a scouting holiday, Rabbitt was introduced to country music and he soon became immersed in the history of its performers. Rabbitt's first single was 'Six Nights And Seven Days' on 20th Century Fox in 1964, and he had further singles for Columbia Records, 'Bottles' and 'I Just Don't Care No More'. Rabbitt, who found he could make no headway singing country music in New York, decided to move to Nashville in 1968. Sitting in a bath in a cheap hotel, he had the idea for 'Working My Way Up From The Bottom', which was recorded by Roy Drusky. At first, he had difficulty in placing other songs, although George Morgan recorded 'The Sounds Of Goodbye' and Bobby Lewis 'Love Me And Make It All Better'. He secured a recording contract and at the same time gave Lamar Fike a tape of songs for Elvis Presley. Presley chose the one he was planning to do himself, 'Kentucky Rain', and took it to number 16 in the US country charts and number 21 in the UK. Presley also recorded 'Patch It Up' and 'Inherit The Wind'. In 1974 Ronnie Milsap topped the US country charts with 'Pure Love', which Rabbitt had written for his future wife, Janine, the references in the song being to commercials for Ivory soap ('99 44/100th per cent') and 'Cap'n Crunch'. Rabbitt also recorded 'Sweet Janine' on his first album. He had his first US country success as a performer with 'You Get To Me' in 1974, and, two years later, topped the US country charts with 'Drinkin' My Baby (Off My Mind)', a goodtime drinking song he had written with Even Stevens. He also wrote with his producer, David Molloy. Rabbitt followed his success with the traditional-sounding 'Rocky Mountain Music' and two more drinking songs, 'Two Dollars In The Jukebox (Five In A Bottle)' and 'Pour Me Another Tequila', at which point

Rabbitt was criticized by the Women's Christian Temperance Union for damaging their cause. Further number 1s came with 'I Just Want To Love You', which he had written during the session, 'Suspicions' and the theme for the Clint Eastwood film *Every Which Way But Loose*, which also made number 41 in the UK. Rabbitt harmonized with himself on the 1980 country number 1 'Gone Too Far'. Inspired by the rhythm of Bob Dylan's 'Subterranean Homesick Blues', he wrote 'Drivin' My Life Away', a US Top 5 pop hit as well as a number 1 country hit, for the 1980 film *Roadie*. A fragment of a song he had written 12 years earlier gave him the concept for 'I Love A Rainy Night', which topped both the US pop and country charts. He had further number 1 country hits with 'Step By Step' (US pop 5) and the Eagles-styled 'Someone Could Lose A Heart Tonight' (US pop 15). He also had chart-topping country duets with Crystal Gayle ('You And I') and Juice Newton ('Both To Each Other (Friends And Lovers)'), the latter being the theme for the television soap opera *Days Of Our Lives*. Rabbitt's son Timmy was born with a rare disease in 1983 and Rabbitt cut back on his commitments until Timmy's death in 1985. Another son, Tommy, was born in good health in 1986. Rabbitt topped the US country charts by reviving a pure rock 'n' roll song from his youth in New York, Dion's 'The Wanderer'. During his son's illness, he had found considerable difficult but wrote his 1988 US country number 1 'I Wanna Dance With You'. His ambition is to write 'a classic, one of those songs that will support me for the rest of my life'. Despite serious illness he returned in 1997 with the aptly titled *Beatin' The Odds*.

● ALBUMS: *Eddie Rabbitt* (Elektra 1975)★★, *Rocky Mountain Music* (Elektra 1976)★★, *Rabbitt* (Elektra 1977)★★, *Variations* (Elektra 1978)★★, *Loveline* (Elektra 1979)★★, *Horizon* (Elektra 1980)★★, *Step By Step* (Elektra 1981)★★, *Radio Romance* (Elektra 1982)★★, *The Best Year Of My Life* (Warners 1984)★★, *Rabbitt Trax* (RCA 1986)★★, *I Wanna Dance With You* (RCA 1988)★★, *Jersey Boy* (Capitol Nashville 1990)★★, *Ten Rounds* (Capitol Nashville 1991)★★, *Beatin' The Odds* (Intersound 1997)★★★.

● COMPILATIONS: *The Best Of Eddie Rabbitt* (Elektra 1979)★★★, *Greatest Hits, Volume 2* (Warners 1983)★★★, *Greatest Country Hits* (Curb 1991)★★★, *All Time Greatest Hits* (Warners 1991)★★★.

RAINWATER, MARVIN

b. Marvin Karlton Percy, 2 July 1925, Wichita, Kansas, USA. A big-voiced, rockabilly singer-songwriter, who is a quarter Cherokee Indian (using his mother's maiden name on stage), Percy became a regular on Red Foley's *Ozark Mountain Jubilee* in the early 50s. After being spotted on Arthur Godfrey's Talent Scouts television show in the mid-50s, he was signed to Coral. The first of his two singles for them, 'I Gotta Go Get My Baby', became a hit for the label when their top act Teresa Brewer covered his record. Rainwater then joined MGM and his second release, the self-composed 'Gonna Find Me A Bluebird' in 1957, gave him his only US Top 40 hit. Later that year a duet with Connie Francis (before her string of hits), 'Majesty Of Love', graced the US Top 100. In 1958, another of his songs, 'Whole Lotta Woman', which only reached number 60 in his homeland, topped the UK chart, and his UK-recorded follow-up, 'I Dig You Baby', also entered the British Top 20. He later recorded without success for Warwick, Warner Brothers, United

Artists, Wesco, his own label Brave, as well as UK labels Philips, Sonet and Westwood. In subsequent years, the man who performed in full American Indian regalia has continued to play the rockabilly and country circuits on both sides of the Atlantic.

● ALBUMS: *Songs By Marvin Rainwater* (MGM 1957)★★★, *Marvin Rainwater Sings With A Beat* (MGM 1958)★★★★, *Gonna Find Me A Bluebird* (MGM 1962)★★★, *Marvin Rainwater* (Crown 1974)★★★, *Marvin Rainwater & Mike Cowdery* (Hoky 1981)★★.

● COMPILATIONS: *Rockin' Rollin' Rainwater* (Bear Family 1982)★★★, *Classic Recordings* (Bear Family 1992)★★★★, *Whole Lotta Woman* (Bear Family 1994)★★★★.

RANDALL, JON

b. Duncanville, Dallas, Texas, USA. Randall grew up in the Dallas suburb of Duncanville, where his influences included Elvis Presley and ZZ Top as well as old and new bluegrass artists. During his high school days, he toured surrounding states in a battered Cadillac as part of bluegrass combo Southern Heritage. After completing his studies, he moved to Nashville in an attempt to make an impact in the country music industry. By day holding down jobs that included courier and process server for a law firm, he also found time to continue playing the guitar and sing. He passed his first audition for Holly Dunn's band, playing the *Grand Ole Opry* on its 20th anniversary celebrations, before touring Alaska and Japan. This was followed by occasional gigs with Vince Gill and Steve Wariner, before Carl Jackson introduced him as a new member of Emmylou Harris's Nash Ramblers. Randall began his solo career as an RCA Records artist in 1994 with *What You Don't Know*. This featured compositions by respected artists and writers including Russell Smith, Carl Jackson, Jim Lauderdale, Vince Melamend, Kevin Welch and Jeff Black, as well as Randall's own material. Guest appearances from Harris, the Nash Ramblers, Trisha Yearwood and Vince Gill confirmed his standing in the country community. As the singer/guitarist commented: 'What you hear on the album is what I am. And what I am is a little bit mainstream, a little bit left field, a little bit bluegrass and a little bit rock 'n' roll.' Randall had already toured and/or recorded with Sam Bush, Carl Jackson and Steve Wariner in addition to Emmylou Harris, with whom he had participated in the 1992 Grammy award-winning live album *At The Ryman*. He insisted that he wanted his solo career to carry on both the intensity and musical integrity of his work with the Nash Ramblers. To promote it he set out as support act to Mary-Chapin Carpenter's 1994 UK tour.

● ALBUMS: *What You Don't Know* (RCA 1994)★★★.

RANDOLPH, 'BOOTS'

b. Homer Louis Randholph III, 3 June 1925, Paducah, Kentucky, USA. Known as 'Mr. Saxophone', Randolph was of that self-contained caste that improvised the orthodox 'Nashville sound' from a notation peculiar to city studios, and thus had first refusal on countless daily record dates in 'Music City USA' until well into the 60s. Although the 'Western Swing' element of C&W had always admitted woodwinds, his employment was vital in widening the genre's range of instrumentation, as the country capital beckoned purveyors of more generalized pop. Indeed, as a solo star, Randolph entered the US pop charts himself with 1963's

'Yakety Sax' *tour de force*. As well as refashioning on disc the diverse likes of 'Tequila', 'Hi Heel Sneakers', 'Willie And The Hand Jive' and 'Bridge Over Troubled Waters', he also ventured into the soul field with a version of the Phil Upchurch Combo's 'You Can't Sit Down'. Although 'Yakety Sax' resurfaced as the traditional closing theme to UK television's *Benny Hill Show*, Randolph will be remembered chiefly as an accompanist heading horn sections for artists of such immeasurable fame as Elvis Presley - notably on 1960's *Elvis Is Back* - and Roy Orbison for whom he became a 'good luck charm. I'd pay him even if he didn't play'.

● ALBUMS: *Yakety Sax* (RCA Victor 1960)★★★, *Boots Randolph's Yakety Sax* (Monument/London 1963)★★★, *The Yakin' Sax Man* (Camden 1964)★★★, *Sweet Talk* (Camden 1965)★★, *Boots Randolph Plays More Yakety Sax* (Monument/London 1965)★★, *Boots With Strings* (Monument 1967)★★, *Hip Boots* (Monument 1967)★★, *Boots Randolph With The Knightsbridge Strings And Voices* (1968)★★, *Sunday Sax* (Monument 1968)★★★, *Fantastic Boots Randolph* (Monument 1968)★★, *The Sound Of Boots* (Monument 1968)★★, *... With Love; The Seductive Sax Of Boots Randolph* (Monument 1969)★★, *Saxsational* (Monument 1969)★★, *Yakety Revisited* (Monument 1970)★★, *Hit Boots 1970* (Monument 1970)★★, *Boots With Brass* (Monument 1971)★★, *Homer Louis Randolph III* (Monument 1971)★★, *The World Of Boots Randolph* (Monument 1971)★★, *Boots Randolph Plays The Great Hits Of Today* (Monument 1972)★★, *Sentimental Journey* (Monument 1973)★★★, *Country Boots* (Monument 1974)★★★.

● COMPILATIONS: *Greatest Hits* (Monument 1976)★★★, *Yakety Sax* (Bear Family 1989)★★★.

RANEY, WAYNE

b. 17 August 1921, Wolf Bayou, near Batesville, Arkansas, USA, d. 23 January 1993. Raney became interested in music at an early age, due to the fact that a crippled foot prevented him playing games. He learned to play the harmonica and listened intently to the playing of Lonnie Glosson on Border radio station XEPN. In 1934, at the age of 13, he hitch-hiked to the station's studios in Eagle Pass and recorded some transcription records. He returned home, but when he was 17 he teamed up with Glosson and in 1938, the pair became favourites on KARK Little Rock and continued to play together on many occasions throughout the 40s. In 1941, Raney had his own show on WCKY in Cincinnati and sold a great many 'talking harmonicas' by mail order through the programme. In the late 40s, he became friendly with the Delmore Brothers and between 1946 and 1952, made many King recordings with them as the Delmore Brothers, the Brown's Ferry Four or under his own name (some recordings also included Glosson). One of his most popular was the 1946 recording of 'Harmonica Blues'. He enjoyed two Top 20 US country chart hits in 1948 with 'Lost John Boogie' and 'Jack And Jill Boogie'. In 1949, his recording of 'Why Don't You Haul Off And Love Me', which he co-wrote with Glosson, became a country number 1 and also made number 22 in the US pop charts. In the mid-50s, he left the King label and spent some time as a member of the *Grand Ole Opry* and toured with its shows. He recorded contributions to rock 'n' roll in 1957, such as his Decca version of 'Shake Baby Shake'. He left WCKY in 1961 and moved back to his native Arkansas, where he relocated to Concord, opened his own Rimrock recording studio and became involved with promotional work. He published his autobiography in 1990, three years before his death.

● ALBUMS: *Songs From The Hills* (King 1958)★★★, *Wayne Raney And The Raney Family* (Starday 1960)★★, *Don't Try To Be What You Ain't* (Starday 1964)★★★, *Gathering In The Sky* (Rimrock 1970)★★★, *We Need A Lot More Of Jesus* (Rimrock 1971)★★.

● COMPILATIONS: *Early Country Favorites* (1983)★★★, *Real Hot Boogie* (Charly 1986)★★★, *More Hot Boogie* (Charly 1987)★★★.

● FURTHER READING: *Life Has Not Been A Bed Of Roses*, Wayne Raney.

RANGER, SHORTY

b. Edwin Haberfield, 9 October 1925, Kempsey, New South Wales, Australia. He grew up on the adjoining farm at Nulla Nulla Creek to that occupied by the family of Slim Dusty. After first meeting at school, they became firm friends with a mutual love of music. Especially attracted to the songs and yodels that they heard on the recordings of such artists as Wilf Carter and Tex Morton, they aimed at a singing career. They learned to play guitar and, performing as a duo, at one time briefly as Buddy Bluebird and Buddy Blackbird, they entertained in their local area. During the 40s, they toured further afield, including Adelaide and Sydney, without lasting success. Although their careers separated in 1951, their friendship continued throughout the years. Shorty gained recognition and a recording contract with Rodeo Records that year, by virtue of his appearance on a national talent show organized by Tim McNamara, and Slim went on to international stardom. Shorty married in 1952 and the following year, when the first of four sons and two daughters arrived, he decided to concentrate on his family. From the mid-50s through to the early 70s, limiting his personal appearances, he made some recordings but mainly concentrated on his songwriting. In 1969, the legendary Australian singer Buddy Williams, who recorded almost 50 of Shorty's songs, released a tribute album called *Buddy And Shorty*. After 1973, with his family grown, he became more active both as a performer and recording artist. He released six albums on Hadley and later a series of 12 on his own Wildwood label. During the late 80s, he suffered a stroke and also a period of ill health as a result of poisoning from pest control chemicals. He survived and in 1989, he won the Songmaker of the Year award at the prestigious Tamworth Country Music Awards. In 1992, he celebrated 50 years of country by appearing on stage with old friend Slim Dusty. His health caused concern again in August 1994, which led to a brief hospital stay. In October, he was involved in a serious road accident, but by December, he was working on his first CD release. Since 1942, Shorty Ranger has written over 360 other songs, many of which have been recorded by other artists. 'Winter Winds', written in 1943, is undoubtedly the best known, owing to its use as his signature tune and to Slim Dusty's 1957 recording of it. The song, now rated as an Australian country classic, won Shorty a gold award in 1992. Over the years, he has received many other awards including a golden guitar. He has been honoured several times as a Pioneer of Country Music in Australia and in 1993, he was elected to the Country Music Roll Of Renown -

the Australian equivalent of Nashville's Country Music Hall of Fame.

● ALBUMS: *Heaven Country Style* (Hadley 1973)★★★, *The Man From Nulla Nulla* (Hadley 1976)★★★, *Sugarloaf Mountain Country* (Hadley 1978)★★★, *From Bullock Team To Diesels* (Hadley 1980)★★★, *A Tribute To Wilf Carter* (Hadley 1982)★★★, *38 Years Of Country Music* (Hadley 1983)★★, *Heaven Country Style* (Wildwood 1984)★★★, *The Land Where Time Stands Still* (Wildwood 1985)★★★, *Bush Balladeer* (Wildwood 1986)★★★★, *I'm In Love With The Country* (Wildwood 1987)★★★, *Shorty Ranger, The Singing Wanderer* (EMI 1987)★★★★, *Drifting Along With A Song* (Wildwood 1988)★★★, *Hillbilly Memories* (Wildwood 1989)★★★★, *The Vintage Collection* (Wildwood 1990)★★★, *True Country Style* (Wildwood 1990)★★★, *Wildwood Country Gospel* (Wildwood 1991)★★★, *Riding The Trail To My Home* (Wildwood 1992)★★★, *Take Me Back To The Country* (Wildwood 1993)★★★. (All Australian releases).

RANK AND FILE

Formed in Los Angeles in 1981, Rank And File comprised former members of the Dils, Chip Kinman (guitar, vocals) and Tony Kinman (bass, vocals), and ex-Nuns guitarist/vocalist Alejandro Escovedo. Drummer Slim Evans completed the line-up featured on *Sundown*, an exemplary blend of new wave and country. The album included 'Amanda Ruth', later recorded by the Everly Brothers. The Kinman brothers then took control of the group and, having moved to Austin, Texas, completed *Long Gone Dead* with session musicians, including Richard Greene (fiddle) and Stan Lynch, drummer with Tom Petty And The Heartbreakers. The new set emphasized the duo's love of pop melody, but the contents were still infused with C&W. A long hiatus ensued, but their third album proved a major disappointment, lacking the verve and charm of its predecessors. Rank And File was then disbanded with the Kinmans later founding Blackbird. Escovedo reappeared leading the acclaimed True Believers before embarking on a solo career.

● ALBUMS: *Sundown* (Slash 1982)★★★★, *Long Gone Dead* (Slash 1984)★★★, *Rank And File* (Slash 1987)★★.

RANKIN FAMILY

This Canadian folk quintet (all of whom are indeed members of the same family) consists of John Morris (b. 28 March 1959, Mabou, Nova Scotia, Canada), Raylene (b. 15 September 1960, Mabou, Nova Scotia, Canada), Jimmy (b. 28 May 1964, Mabou, Nova Scotia, Canada), Cookie (b. 4 May 1965, Mabou, Nova Scotia, Canada) and Heather (b. 24 October 1967, Mabou, Nova Scotia, Canada). The group was formed when they all gave up their respective careers to concentrate on music in the autumn of 1989. With instruments that include guitar, bass, piano, synthesizer, violin, mandolin and percussion, the Rankin Family produce a blend of traditional and contemporary music, dominated by the sweet vocals of the family sisters. The *Daily News* described their sound as 'the unpretentious good time charm of a maritime kitchen ceilidh with tight, lilting harmonies, dynamic musicianship and strong original songwriting'. Indeed, the 'wholesome' image of the band was supported by their appearance at the 1993 Cambridge Folk Festival at which they played two sets - one specially for children. The group's first album was released independently in 1989, and was followed by *Fare Thee Well Love* a year later (it was eventually re-pressed by EMI Records). *North Country* helped launch the band internationally, while their growing domestic profile was rewarded with four Canadian JUNO Awards: Single Of The Year; Canadian Entertainer Of The Year; Best Group; and Best Country Group.

● ALBUMS: *The Rankin Family* (Independent 1989)★★★, *Fare Thee Well Love* (Independent/EMI 1990)★★★, *North Country* (EMI 1993)★★★★, *Endless Seasons* (EMI 1995)★★★.

● CD ROM: *Rankin Family Collection* (EMI 1996).

RATTLESNAKE ANNIE

b. Rosanne Gallimore, 26 December 1941, Puryear, Tennessee, USA. Rattlesnake Annie, of Cherokee heritage, was born into a poor family of tobacco farmers. They had no electricity or modern conveniences, apart from a radio, on which Gallimore would hear country music from Nashville. Many of her songs ('Cotton Mama', 'Bulger Wilson', 'Good Ole Country Music') are about those years. As part of the Gallimore sisters, she appeared on the *Junior Grand Ole Opry* in 1954, but when she married Max McGowan, her ambitions were put on hold while she raised a family. David Allan Coe recorded her song 'Texas Lullaby', and she became Rattlesnake Annie through her habit of wearing a rattlesnake's tail on her right ear. Her first album, although self-financed, featured top Nashville musicians and established her as both a performer and songwriter. Perhaps because she shares a love of traditional country music with the likes of Boxcar Willie, she has been accepted in the UK, and even more so in Czechoslovakia, where her album with local country star Michal Tuny was a bestseller. She recorded 'Long Black Limousine' with Willie Nelson, a performer who favours the same casual approach to stage-wear. She signed to Sony Music Japan in 1991.

● ALBUMS: *Rattlesnakes And Rusty Water* (Rattlesnake 1980)★★★, with Michal Tuny *Rattlesnake Annie And The Last Cowboy* (Supraphone 1983)★★★, *Country Livin'* (Rattlesnake 1985)★★★★, *Rattlesnake Annie* (Columbia 1987)★★★, *Crossroads* (1990)★★★, *Indian Dreams* (Sony 1991)★★★, *Rattlesnake Annie Sings Hank Williams* (Sony 1991)★★★★, *Painted Bird* (Sony 1993)★★★.

RAUSCH, LEON

b. Edgar Leon Rausch, 2 October 1927, Springfield, Missouri, USA. Rausch grew up in Billings, learned to play several stringed instruments as a youngster and was playing guitar with his father in a local danceband by the time he was 11. During World War II, Rausch served three years in the US Navy and on his release, he began to play guitar with various local bands. In 1955, he worked in Tulsa but the following year, he joined the *Louisiana Hayride* and recorded for Central. In 1958, he joined Bob Wills' Texas Playboys, with whom he sang and played electric guitar until 1964. After a spell with Johnnie Lee Wills, he relocated to Fort Worth where, until 1968, he played the *Cowtown Jamboree* with the New Texas Playboys. They played the local area and for much of the time there, he also appeared regularly on local television. During these years, he recorded for Ric, Kapp and Longhorn, including his noted 'Someday I'll Sober Up'. He renewed his acquaintance with Wills to play bass on the

United Artists Records release *For The Last Time*, in December 1973. When, after Wills' death, the Original Texas Playboys re-formed, Rausch fronted the band and handled the vocals. They recorded three albums for Capitol Records in the late 70s and between 1976 and 1979, Rausch also had six solo minor US *Billboard* country hits on the Derrick label. These included 'Through The Bottom Of A Glass' and 'Palimony'. In 1983, Rausch, Johnny Gimble, Herb Remington and Eldon Shamblin and other old Playboys re-formed as Playboys II. In 1989, Rausch played bass guitar with Boxcar Willie at the Wembley Festival in London and in 1993, he played with Asleep At The Wheel on an album paying tribute to Bob Wills' music.

● ALBUMS: *From The Heart Of Texas* (Kapp 1966)★★★★, *For The Last Time* (United Artists 1974)★★★, *She's The Trip That I've Been On* (Derrick 1976)★★★, *Original Texas Playboys Live From Austin City Limits* (Delta 1976)★★, *Bob Wills Day, Live From Turkey, Texas* (Delta 1976)★★, *The Late Bob Wills Original Texas Playboys* (Capitol 1977)★★★, *Live And Kickin'* (Capitol 1978)★★, *Original Texas Playboys* (Capitol 1979)★★★★.

RAVEN, EDDY

b. Edward Garvin Futch, 19 August 1944, Lafayette, Louisiana, USA. Eddy, one of 11 children, was raised in bayou country. His father, a truck driver and blues guitarist, used to take him to honky tonks. He was given a guitar, and by the time he was 13 years old, he was playing in a rock 'n' roll band. When the family moved to Georgia in 1960, he worked for a radio station and recorded his own song, 'Once A Fool', as Eddy Raven for the small Cosmo label. They returned to Lafayette in 1963 and Raven worked in La Louisianne record store and also made singles for the owner's label. In 1969 he recorded *That Crazy Cajun Sound*, which impressed Jimmy C. Newman, who then secured Raven a songwriting contract in Nashville with Acuff-Rose. He also worked as lead singer for Jimmie Davis's band and toured with him during an election campaign for Governor of Louisiana. In 1971 Don Gibson had a Top 5 US country hit with Raven's 'Country Green', which was followed by Jeannie C. Riley's 'Good Morning, Country Rain'. He also wrote 'Back In The Country' (Roy Acuff), 'Sometimes I Talk In My Sleep' (Randy Cornor) and 'Touch The Morning' (Don Gibson). He had his first US country chart entry with 'The Last Of The Sunshine Cowboys' in 1974 for ABC Records and then recorded for Monument ('You're A Dancer') and Dimension ('Sweet Mother Texas', 'Dealin' With The Devil'). He had four country hits from his Elektra album, *Desperate Dreams*, including 'Who Do You Know In California?' and 'She's Playing Hard To Forget'. A second album for Elektra was never released and Raven spent two years resolving management problems. He wrote a Top 5 country record for the Oak Ridge Boys, 'Thank God For Kids'. He came back on RCA Records in 1984 with the escapist theme of 'I Got Mexico', a style he returned to in 1988 for 'Joe Knows How To Live'. He followed it with other hits, including 'I Could Use Another You', 'Shine Shine Shine' and 'You're Never Too Old For Young Love'. He went to number 1 with a bluesy song written by Dennis Linde and first recorded by Billy Swan, 'I'm Gonna Get You'. Linde also wrote his 1989 number 1, 'In A Letter To You', for the new Universal label. That year he also returned to the Cajun sounds of his youth

for 'Bayou Boys', in a mixture he described as 'electric cajun'. In 1991 he recorded for the ninth label of his career, Capitol Records. He struggled to secure record deals in the 90s, but released an impressive album with Jo-el Sonnier in 1997.

● ALBUMS: *That Cajun Country Sound* (La Louisianne 1969)★★★, *This Is Eddy Raven* (ABC/Dot 1976)★★★, *Eyes* (Dimension 1979)★★★, *Desperate Dreams* (Elektra 1981)★★★★, *I Could Use Another You* (RCA 1984)★★★, *Love And Other Hard Times* (RCA 1985)★★★, *Right Hand Man* (RCA 1987)★★★, *Temporary Sanity* (Capitol 1989)★★★, *Right For The Flight* (Capitol 1991)★★★, *Wide Eyed And Crazy* (Intersound 1994)★★★, with Jo-el Sonnier *Cookin' Cajun* (K-Tel 1997)★★★.

● COMPILATIONS: *The Best Of Eddy Raven* (RCA 1988)★★★★, *Greatest Country Hits* (Curb 1990)★★★★, *Greatest Hits* (Warners 1990)★★★, *Best Of Eddy Raven* (Liberty 1992)★★★.

RAY, DAVE

As a member of Koerner, Ray And Glover, with 'Spider' John Koerner and Tony Glover, Dave 'Snaker' Ray was in the vanguard of the folk revival of the 60s. An accomplished 6- and 12-string guitarist, the artist pursued a concurrent solo career with two compulsive country blues albums. The first included interpretations of material by, among others, Muddy Waters, Robert Johnson and Lead Belly, while the follow-up featured a greater emphasis on original material. The rise of electric styles obscured Ray's progress and it was 1969 before he re-emerged in Bamboo, a country-based duo he had formed with pianist Will Donight. Their eccentric album made little impression and Ray's subsequent profile was distinctly low-key. However, in 1990 Ray and Glover teamed up to record *Ashes In My Whiskey* for the Rough Trade label, winning critical acclaim.

● ALBUMS: *Fine Soft Land* (1967)★★★. As Koerner, Ray And Glover *Blues, Rags And Hollers* (1963)★★★, *More Blues, Rags And Hollers* (1964)★★★, *The Return Of Koerner, Ray And Glover* (1965)★★★, *Live At St. Olaf Festival* (60s/70s)★★, *Some American Folk Songs Like They Used To Be* (1974)★★, with Tony Glover *Ashes In My Whiskey* (Rough Trade 1990)★★★, with Glover *Picture Has Faded* (Tim/Kerr 1994)★★★.

RAY, WADE

b. Lyman Wade Ray, 6 April 1913, Evansville, Indiana, USA. Many country artists started their careers at an early age but Ray can certainly claim to be one of the youngest. He learned to play on an instrument his father had made from a cigar box and, billed as the World's Youngest Violin Player, he made his debut at the age of five. He also learned tenor banjo and from then onwards, he toured the vaudeville circuit until 1931 (it has been reported that he had been given 200 violins by the time he was 10). Between 1931 and 1943, he was the fiddler, vocalist and musical director for the National Champion Hillbillies on KMOX St. Louis. After a year in the army, he joined and recorded with Patsy Montana's Prairie Ramblers on the WLS *National Barn Dance* in Chicago. In 1949, he relocated to California and played the televised *Rex Allen Show*. Always in demand, he played residencies during the 50s and 60s, including various prestigious venues in Las Vegas, Reno, Lake Tahoe and during the 60s, the *Grand Ole Opry*. He was also a regular on ABC's televised *Roy Rogers Show*. In the mid-60s, he began playing as a session musician in Nashville and continued to do so through to 1979, when he relocated to Illinois, but ill health soon forced his retirement. During his career, he recorded for Capitol, RCA/Victor and ABC Records, but he never achieved a chart hit.

● ALBUMS: *A Ray Of Country Sun* (ABC-Paramount 1966)★★★, *Walk Softly* (RCA Camden 1966)★★★, with Homer And Jethro, Sonny Osborne and others *Down Yonder - The Country Fiddlers* (RCA Victor 1967)★★★★.

RAYE, COLLIN

b. Floyd Collin Wray, 22 August 1959, DeQueen, Arkansas, USA. Country rock and ballad performer Raye was raised in Texas, where his mother often opened shows for visiting star performers. For many years he and his brother Scott worked in Oregon and then in casinos in Las Vegas and Reno, but their contract to record for Warner Brothers as the Wray Brothers and as the Wray Brothers Band led nowhere, other than minor hits with 'Until We Meet Again', 'I Don't Want To Know Your Name', 'You Lay A Lotta Love On Me' and Tim Hardin's glorious song 'Reason To Believe'. When the brothers split, Collin was signed as a solo act to Epic by producer Bob Montgomery. A collection of romantic songs, *All I Can Be*, became an immediate bestselling country album in the USA and 'Love Me', 'In This Life' and 'That Was A River' all topped the US country charts. 'Love Me' has since become a popular song at funerals! The soft-voiced tenor was equally romantic on *In This Life*, and the title song became another US country number 1. By the time of his third album *Extremes*, Raye was expanding his balladeer image, and this forceful collection included 'That's My Story', which was written by Lee Roy Parnell, and 'Little Rock', about a recovering alcoholic. By 1995, Raye had achieved six country number 1s, and further hits in the Top 5. Although Raye is divorced he still lives with his ex-wife and children in Greenville, Texas. His album *I Think About You* includes the perplexing lyric of 'What If Jesus Came Back Like That', in which Christ returns to Earth as a vagrant and a single mother.

● ALBUMS: *All I Can Be* (Epic 1990)★★, *In This Life* (Epic 1992)★★★, *Extremes* (Epic 1994)★★★, *I Think About You* (Epic 1995)★★★★, *Christmas The Gift* (Epic 1996)★★.

● COMPILATIONS: *The Best Of Collin Raye - Direct Hits* (Epic 1997)★★★.

● VIDEOS: *My Kind Of Girl* (1994), *Little Rock* (Sherman Halsey 1994).

RAYE, SUSAN

b. 8 October 1944, Eugene, Oregon, USA. In 1961, with no personal thoughts of being a country singer, she found her mother had entered her in a talent show. She won and was soon singing and working as a disc jockey on local radio. By the mid-60s, she was a regular on the Portland television show *Hoedown*, where she was seen by Buck Owens' manager. Between 1968 and 1976, she worked with Owens, became a Capitol recording artist in her own right and was a regular performer on the top television show *Hee Haw*, which Owens co-hosted. Between 1970 and 1977, she registered 21 solo country hits, including 'I've Got A Happy Heart' and her version of Kay Starr's pop hit 'Wheel Of Fortune'. During this time she also recorded duets with

Owens, six of which charted, including a Top 10 with 'The Great White Horse'. She retired for a time but reappeared in the country charts in 1986 with 'I Just Can't Take The Leaving Anymore'.

● ALBUMS: *One Night Stand* (Capitol 1970)★★★, *Willy Jones* (Capitol 1971)★★★, *Pitty Pitty Patter* (Capitol 1971)★★★, *I've Got A Happy Heart* (1972)★★★, *Wheel Of Fortune/L.A International Airport* (Capitol 1972)★★★, *My Heart Has A Mind Of Its Own* (Capitol 1972)★★★, *Wheel Of Fortune* (Capitol 1972)★★★, *Love Sure Feels Good In My Heart* (Capitol 1973)★★★, *Cheating Game* (Capitol 1973)★★★, *Plastic Trains, Paper Planes* (Capitol 1973)★★★, *Hymns By Susan Raye* (Capitol 1973)★★, *Singing Susan Raye* (Capitol 1974)★★★,*Whatcha Gonna Do With A Dog ∙ Like That* (Capitol 1975)★★★, *Honey Toast And Sunshine* (Capitol 1976)★★★, *Susan Raye* (1977)★★, *There And Back* (1985)★★★, *Then And Now* (1986). With Buck Owens: *We're Gonna Get Together* (Capitol 1970)★★★, *The Great White Horse* (Capitol 1970)★★★, *Merry Christmas From Buck Owens & Susan Raye* (Capitol 1971)★★, *The Good Old Days Are Here Again* (Capitol 1973)★★.

● COMPILATIONS: With Buck Owens *The Best Of Buck Owens & Susan Raye* (Capitol 1972)★★★. *The Best Of Susan Raye* (Capitol 1974)★★★.

RECTOR, RED

b. William Eugene Rector, 15 December 1929, Marshall, North Carolina, USA, d. 31 May 1990. Rector became one of the best and most respected mandolin players in country and bluegrass music. He learned the instrument as a boy after listening to local radio, and as a teenager, he played with local groups. In 1946, he played with Johnnie And Jack, before moving to KNOX Knoxville to join Charlie Monroe's Kentucky Partners, with whom he made his first recordings. When Monroe relocated to Birmingham, Rector was unhappy and returned to Knoxville. He played and recorded with Carl Story And His Rambling Mountaineers, even moving with Story to Charlotte. He recorded with Don Reno and Red Smiley in 1953, and in 1955, he began to perform with Fred Smith as Red And Fred. Playing a mixture of serious songs and comedy, they proved a popular act on WNOX until *Mid-Day Merry-Go-Round* ended in 1958. He played for two years as a member of Hylo Brown's Timberliners, during which time he played on four 1958 sessions with Brown, even singing some lead vocals. After leaving Brown, he returned to Knoxville, where he became a regular (often with Fred Smith) on the daily *Cas Walker Show*. He remained with the programme, taping shows for use during his touring absences, until it ended in 1983. He worked on numerous Nashville recording sessions with other artists and played regularly on the bluegrass festival circuit, both as a solo act and with others, including Bill Clifton and Don Stover. He played venues in the UK in 1975 and toured Europe with Clifton in 1976, making many popular appearances in the UK. He recorded solo albums and duet ones with both Fred Smith and Norman Blake. His last album was recorded with another mandolinist, Jethro Burns (of Homer And Jethro), who, like Rector, was one of the instrument's greatest exponents. During the 80s, after the *Cas Walker Show* ended, he continued to play on recording sessions and made numerous personal appearances until he died suddenly, following a heart attack, on 31 May 1990.

Although usually noted as an instrumentalist, he was also a fine solo vocalist and an accomplished harmony singer, as proved on some of his recordings with Bill Clifton.

● ALBUMS: with Fred Smith *Songs From The Heart Of The Country* (County 1970)★★★, *Appaloosa* (Old Homestead 1975)★★★★, *Red Rector & Norman Blake* (County 1976)★★★, with Bill Clifton *Another Happy Day* (County 1976)★★★, with Clifton *In Europe* (WAM 1977)★★, *Are You From Dixie* (Bear Family 1977)★★★, *Red Rector & Friends* (Revonah 1978)★★★, *Back Home In Madison County* (Revonah 1981)★★★, with Jethro Burns *Old Friends* (Flying Fish 1983)★★★, with A.G. And Kate, Don Stover *Good Friends* (Strictly Country 1988)★★★.

RED RIVER DAVE
(see McEnery, David)

REED, BLIND ALFRED
b. 15 June 1880, Floyd, Virginia, USA, d. 17 January 1956. Born blind, but gifted with a fine singing voice, Reed, who was a very religious man, learned to play fiddle as a means of making a living. After marrying, he raised six children and spent most of his life around Princeton, West Virginia. He played on street corners and with other musicians for local dances. He also had a penchant for writing songs, often about special events, and had them printed on cards, which he sold for 10 cents. In August 1927, at the same sessions that started the careers of Jimmie Rodgers and the Carter Family, he recorded a song that he had just written about a train crash, 'The Wreck Of The Virginian', and three gospel numbers for Ralph Peer. He made further recordings in December in New York, this time accompanied by the West Virginia Night Owls (actually his guitarist son Arville and fiddler Fred Pendleton). He recorded his last session in November 1929, again with Arville playing guitar and adding vocals. He continued to play for a long time in the Princeton area, sometimes with another blind musician, Richard Harold (b. 1884, d. 1947), and for dances with the Night Owls. Eventually, new town bylaws regarding street entertainers saw him lose his main source of income. His songs feature some comedy numbers but frequently they were his means of commenting on some particular theme. He appeared chauvinistic when he sang about the rise of women's independence in 'We've Just Got To Have Them, That's All' and expressed his deep Christian beliefs in 'There'll Be No Distinction There', which informed 'we'll all be white in the heavenly light'. He also penned 'Explosion In The Fairmont Mines', which historians rated to be the only partially original song that he recorded, being basically a rewrite of 'Dream Of The Miner's Child'. Reed died in 1956 but Arville and Pendleton continued to play until the early 70s. Several of Reed's recordings have appeared on compilation albums but Rounder issued a complete album of them in 1972.

● COMPILATIONS: *How Can A Poor Man Stand Such Times And Live* (Rounder 1972)★★★★.

REED, JERRY
b. Jerry Hubbard, 20 March 1937, Atlanta, Georgia, USA. Reed has had three distinct careers: as a respected country guitarist, as a composer and singer of clever pop/country hits and as a genial, jokey television personality and film

actor. A cotton-mill worker, he was one of many youths brought up on country music who played rockabilly in the mid-50s. His own records for Capitol were unsuccessful but Reed's songs were taken up by Gene Vincent ('Crazy Legs') and Brenda Lee. After army service, Reed moved to Nashville, working as a session guitarist and achieving minor hits with 'Hully Gully Guitars' and the traditional 'Goodnight Irene'. He also wrote songs for Porter Wagoner ('Misery Loves Company') and Johnny Cash ('A Thing Called Love'). Reed's skill at the finger-picking guitar style was showcased on two duet albums with Chet Atkins in the 70s; Atkins also produced Reed's albums and singles. Reed's career gathered momentum after he signed a recording contract with RCA in 1965. Two years later he recorded the boastful 'Guitar Man' and 'U.S. Male', both of which were covered successfully by Elvis Presley in 1968. Reed had two big US pop hits in 1971 with the swamp rock-styled 'Amos Moses' and 'When You're Hot, You're Hot' (based on his television catchphrase), but his continuing popularity was with country audiences; the latter was a US country chart number 1 for five weeks. Another country number 1 followed with 'Lord Mr Ford' in 1973, a humorous attack on the cost of running a car in the 70s. During the late 70s he was less successful, but he returned to prominence with the recording of the Tim DuBois song 'She Got The Goldmine (I Got The Shaft)' for RCA in 1982. Produced by Rick Hall, it was a country number 1. Reed became well known to television viewers with appearances on Glen Campbell's show in the early 70s. This led to cameo roles in several Burt Reynolds movies including *W.W. And the Dixie Dance Kings* (1975), *Gator* (1976) and *Smokey And The Bandit* (1977).

● ALBUMS: *Tupelo Mississippi Flash* (RCA Victor 1967)★★★, *Alabama Wild Man* (RCA Victor 1968)★★★★, *Jerry Reed Explores Guitar Country* (RCA Victor 1969)★★★, *Cookin'* (RCA Victor 1970)★★★, *Georgia Sunshine* (RCA Victor 1970)★★★, with Chet Atkins *Me And Jerry* (RCA Victor 1970)★★, *When You're Hot You're Hot* (RCA Victor 1971)★★★★, *Ko Ko Joe* (RCA Victor 1971)★★★, *Smell The Flowers* (RCA Victor 1972)★★★, with Atkins *Me And Chet* (RCA Victor 1972)★★, *Jerry Reed* (RCA Victor 1972)★★★, *Hot A' Mighty!* (RCA Victor 1973)★★★, *Lord Mr Ford* (RCA Victor 1973)★★★, *The Uptown Poker Club* (RCA Victor 1974)★★★, *A Good Woman's Love* (RCA Victor 1974)★★★, *Red Hot Picker* (RCA Victor 1976)★★★, *Both Barrels* (RCA Victor 1976)★★★, *Jerry Reed Rides Again* (RCA Victor 1977)★★★, *East Bound And Down* (RCA Victor 1977)★★★, *Sweet Love Feelings* (RCA Victor 1978)★★★, *Half Singin' And Half Pickin'* (RCA Victor 1979)★★★, *Live At Exit Inn - Hot Stuff* (RCA Victor 1979)★★, *Jerry Reed Sings Jim Croce* (RCA Victor 1980)★★, *Texas Bound And Flyin'* (RCA Victor 1980)★★, *The Man With The Golden Thumb* (RCA Victor 1982)★★★, *The Bird* (RCA Victor 1982)★★, *Ready* (RCA Victor 1983)★★, *Lookin' At You* (1986)★★, with Chet Atkins *Sneakin' Around* (Columbia 1992)★★★, *Flyin' High* (Southern Tracks 1996)★★★.

● COMPILATIONS: *The Best Of Jerry Reed* (RCA Victor 1972)★★★★, *20 Of The Best* (RCA 1982)★★★★, *The Essential Jerry Reed* (RCA 1995)★★★★.

REED, OLA BELLE
b. 1915, in the mountains of western North Carolina, USA. Reed learned the clawhammer style of banjo playing as a

child and grew up singing the old-time songs of her local area. She played with the North Carolina Ridge Runners in the 30s and after World War II, with their band the New River Boys And Girls, she and her brother played at many North Carolina events. She featured on numerous radio stations and became an acknowledged authority on Appalachian tunes, as well as old-time gospel, bluegrass and folk music. Later she appeared with her husband Bud and son David, with whom she established the New River Ranch country park at Oxford, Pennsylvania. This venue attracted a great many lovers of her music from the New England area. In the late 70s, she recorded an album that ensured she would be rightly remembered, although she perhaps tempted fate somewhat prematurely by calling it *My Epitaph*.

● ALBUMS: *Ola Belle Reed* (Rounder 1975)★★★, *Ola Belle & Bud Reed, All In One Evening* (1976)★★★, *My Epitaph* (1977)★★, *Ola Belle Reed & Family* (Rounder 1978)★★.

REEVES, DEL

b. Franklin Delano Reeves, 14 July 1933, Sparta, North Carolina, USA. A singer, songwriter and multi-instrumentalist who had his own radio show at the age of 12, Reeves moved to California, where by the late 50s, he had his own television show. He first charted in 1961 with 'Be Quiet Mind' on Decca, but in 1965, he registered a US country number 1 with 'Girl On A Billboard' after moving to United Artists, with whom he stayed until 1980. A number 4 hit with 'The Belles Of Southern Bell' followed and he moved to Nashville. He became a regular on the *Grand Ole Opry* (having first guested on it in 1958) and remained on the roster through to the 80s. Between 1966 and 1986, he registered almost 50 country chart hits, including 'Looking At The World Through A Windshield', 'Good Time Charlies' and 'The Philadelphia Phillies'. He also achieved chart success with duet recordings with Bobby Goldsboro, Penny DeHaven and Billie Jo Spears. Reeves has appeared in several films including *Second Fiddle To An Old Guitar*, as well as hosting many television shows. He has toured extensively and, with his wife, written many popular country songs. A fine entertainer who also is noted for his comedy and impressions of other artists, his casual manner has led to him being called 'The Dean Martin Of Country Music'. He later moved into management and in 1992, he discovered Billy Ray Cyrus.

● ALBUMS: *Del Reeves Sings Girl On The Billboard* (United Artists 1965)★★★★, *Doodle-OO-Doo-Doo* (United Artists 1965)★★★, *Del Reeves Sings Jim Reeves* (United Artists 1966)★★, *Special Delivery* (United Artists 1966)★★★, *Getting Any Feed For Your Chickens?* (United Artists 1966)★★★, *Mr Country Music* (United Artists 1966)★★★, *Santa's Boy* (United Artists 1966)★★, *Struttin' My Stuff* (United Artists 1967)★★★, *Six Of One, Half A Dozen Of The Other* (United Artists 1967)★★★, *The Little Church In The Dell* (United Artists 1967)★★, with Bobby Goldsboro *Our Way Of Life* (United Artists 1967)★★★, *Running Wild* (United Artists 1968)★★★, *Looking At The World Through A Windshield* (United Artists 1968)★★★, *Down At Good Time Charlie's* (United Artists 1969)★★, *The Wonderful World Of Country Music* (Sunset 1969)★★★, *Big Daddy Del* (United Artists 1970)★★★, *Country Concert - Live* (United Artists 1970)★★★, *Out In The Country* (United Artists 1970)★★★, *The Del Reeves Album* (United Artists 1971)★★★★, *Friends & Neighbours* (United Artists 1971)★★★, *Before Goodbye* (United Artists 1972)★★★, *Trucker's Paradise* (United Artists 1973)★★★, *Live At The Palomino Club* (United Artists 1974)★★★, *With Strings And Things* (United Artists 1975)★★★, *Tenth Anniversary* (United Artists 1976)★★★, with Billie Jo Spears *By Request* (United Artists 1976)★★, *Del Reeves* (United Artists 1979)★★★, with Liz Lyndell *Let's Go To Heaven Tonight* (1980)★★, with Spears *Del And Billie Jo* (1982)★★.

COMPILATIONS: *The Best Of Del Reeves* (United Artists 1967)★★★, *The Best Of Del Reeves, Volume 2* (United Artists 1969)★★★, *The Very Best Of Del Reeves* (United Artists 1974)★★★★, *Baby I Love You* (Bear Family 1988)★★★.

REEVES, GOEBEL

b. Goebel Leon Reeves, 9 October 1899, Sherman, Texas, USA, d. 26 January 1959, Long Beach, California, USA. Reeves was one of the true characters of country music, one who managed to reverse the rags-to-riches story, and from his nomadic lifestyle, he acquired the nickname of the Texas Drifter. He received his early training from his mother, a talented musician, who taught both piano and singing. His father, once a salesman, was elected to the state legislature and when the family relocated to Austin, he secured Goebel a job as a page-boy in the government buildings. Reeves' long association with hobos started one cold night when, as he left work wearing an expensive new overcoat given to him for Christmas, he met a hobo. He subsequently arrived home, coatless, but engrossed by tales of hobo life. He began to spend more and more time talking to any hobo that he met in the neighbourhood. His parents provided a tutor to improve his education and, although intelligent, his interests turned to the lifestyle of the hobo and to music after hearing a vaudeville artist called Al Wilson. He was impressed by Wilson's singing and yodelling and it was probably Wilson who first taught him the yodel that he used so proficiently. He already played piano and trumpet but now turned to the guitar and began singing cowboy songs such as 'Little Joe the Wrangler'. In 1917, he joined the army (initially as a bugler) and saw action in Europe, where he was wounded and returned to the USA for discharge. Soon after, he left home and adopted the life of a hobo. He eked a living by singing on street corners and from that point many aspects of his life are unclear. He was known to fabricate facts - an early one being that he was born west of the Pecos and had been a hellraising cowboy. On occasions, Reeves has been branded a liar, yet sometimes his outlandish stories were found to be true. He certainly played WFAA Dallas in the early 20s and his claim to have befriended and worked with Jimmie Rodgers was not disproved by Nolan Porterfield in his definitive book on Rodgers. He apparently even claimed to have taught Rodgers how to yodel. However, Reeves was infinitely the more accomplished exponent of the art and since their yodels are dissimilar, this may have been just one of his inventions. Around 1921, he joined the merchant navy and spent several years in Europe, some in Italy but by the late 20s, he was back in Galvaston, Texas. Spurred by hearing a recording of Jimmie Rodgers, he sought the opportunity to record himself and made his first recordings for OKeh in San Antonio, on 25 June 1929. This proved to be the first of many recordings that he made into and during the 30s. He moved to New York and heeded advice not to commit himself to one label. His recordings subsequently appeared on numerous labels including Gennett, Challenge, Conqueror, Oriole, Banner and Perfect, and in the UK and Ireland on Panachord and Irish Rex. He avoided RCA-Victor, professing that he did not wish his recordings to clash with those of his friend Rodgers. Reeves also used the pseudonyms George Riley, Bert Knowles (Burton Knolds), Johnny Fay, the Broadway Wrangler and his own favourite, the Texas Drifter. He wrote most of the songs that he sang; many are autobiographical, drawn from his own life as a hobo, and in 1934, he even published a book containing the words to some of them. He drifted all over America and after playing network radio in New York (billed as the Singing Bum), he gained a contract with NBC, which saw him appear on the networked Rudy Vallee show. However, his rough country songs and his singing were totally unsuited to Vallee's more upper-class audiences and he soon quit. He played on Nashville's *Grand Ole Opry* and did programmes on numerous Canadian and American stations. His stories (true or invented) made him a most popular entertainer, although his refusal to settle in one place for more than a few months did not endear him to promoters. He appeared at the 1933 World's Fair in Chicago and played the WLS *National Barn Dance* in that city. He married in the mid-30s, but not surprisingly, because of his nomadic lifestyle, the marriage soon ended. Many of his later songs recounted stories of loneliness and lack of family life, again, no doubt, autobiographical. 'The Kidnapped Baby' recorded for Decca in January 1935, would seem to be his last professional recording; for some reason, it received a UK release but not a US one. The final Reeves recordings were the transcription discs that he made in 1938/9 for the Macgregor Company of California. Soon afterwards, tired of the same routines, he took a ship to Japan, where he quickly learned enough of the language to be actively employed with The Industrial Workers of the World. He returned to America before the start of World War II, but his entertaining career was basically over. He gave as his reason the fact that 'the songs were poor and current styles were artificial and insincere'. Becoming something of a recluse, he made his home in Bell Gardens, a small Los Angeles suburb, and worked in connection with the community's Japanese-American problems. He had lost all contact with family and friends; in fact, a sister lived within 30 miles of him for some years with neither knowing of the other's existence. In August 1957, Fred Hoeptner (writing in the booklet accompanying a 1994 Bear Family CD release of Reeves recordings), after initial work by John Edwards (the late Australian country authority), describes finally tracking down Reeves and gaining a taped interview with him. He found the Texas Drifter, still a showman and still inclined to bend the truth when it suited his purpose. In the 50s, Reeves had suffered heart problems and he eventually died of a heart attack in the Long Beach Veterans Hospital on 26 January 1959; he was buried in the Veterans' Cemetery five days later. Reeves made an important contribution to country music and his style influenced many other artists. Many of his songs, especially 'Hobo's Lullaby' (later also popularised by Woody Guthrie) and 'The Tramp's Mother', have been recorded by countless other artists while many people rate his amusing 'Station HOBO Calling' to be one of his best songs. Any genre of music

needs characters and, in Reeves, country music had one, which is why his work is still so popular; as Hoeptner emphasizes, 'he had the intellectual capacity to convert his experiences to recorded accounts, which were both artistically and commercially successful'.

● COMPILATIONS: *The Legendary Texas Drifter, Volume 1* (CMH 1972)★★★, *The Legendary Texas Drifter, Volume 2* (CMH 1973)★★★, *The Texas Drifter* (Glendale 1978)★★★, *Goebel Reeves - In Story And Song* (Glendale 1979)★★★, *Goebel Reeves - Hobo's Lullaby* (Bear Family 1994)★★★.

REEVES, JIM

b. James Travis Reeves, 20 August 1923, Galloway, Texas, USA, d. 31 July 1964 (Reeves' plaque in the Country Music Hall Of Fame mistakenly gives his date of birth as 1924). Reeves' father died when he was 10 months old and his mother was left to raise nine children on the family farm. Although only aged five, Reeves was entranced when a brother brought home a gramophone and a Jimmie Rodgers record, 'Blue Yodel No. 5'. When aged nine, he traded stolen pears for an old guitar he saw in a neighbour's yard. A cook for an oil company showed him the basic chords and when aged 12, he appeared on a radio show in Shreveport, Louisiana. By virtue of his athletic abilities, he won a scholarship to the University of Texas. However, he was shy, largely because of a stammer, which he managed to correct while at university (Reeves' records are known for perfect diction and delivery). His first singing work was with Moon Mullican's band in Beaumont, Texas, and he worked as an announcer and singing disc jockey at KGRI in Henderson for several years (Reeves eventually bought the station in 1959). He recorded two singles for a chain store's label in 1949. In November 1952 Reeves moved to KWKH in Shreveport, where his duties included hosting the *Louisiana Hayride.* He stood in as a performer when Hank Williams failed to arrive and was signed immediately to Abbott Records. In 1953, Reeves received gold discs for two high-voiced, country novelties, 'Mexican Joe' and 'Bimbo'. In 1955 he joined the *Grand Ole Opry* and started recording for RCA in Nashville, having his first hit with a song based on the 'railroad, steamboat' game, 'Yonder Comes A Sucker'. Chet Atkins considered 'Four Walls' a 'girl's song', but Reeves persisted and used the song to change his approach to singing. He pitched his voice lower and sang close to the microphone, thus creating a warm ballad style which was far removed from his hillbilly recordings. 'Four Walls' became an enormous US success in 1957, crossing over to the pop market and becoming a template for his future work. From then on, Atkins recorded Reeves as a mellow balladeer, giving him some pop standards and replacing fiddles and steel guitar with piano and strings (exceptions include an album of narrations, *Tall Tales And Short Tempers*).

Reeves had already swapped his western outfit for a suit and tie, and, in keeping with his hit 'Blue Boy', his group, the Wagonmasters, became the Blue Boys. He always included a religious section in his stage show and also sang 'Danny Boy' to acknowledge his Irish ancestry. 'He'll Have To Go' topped the US country charts for 14 weeks and made number 2 in the US pop charts. In this memorable song, Reeves conveyed an implausible lyric with conviction, and it has now become a country standard. A gooey novelty, 'But You Love Me Daddy', recorded at the same session with Steve, the nine-year-old son of bass player Bob Moore, was a UK Top 20 hit 10 years later. Having established a commercial format, 'Gentleman Jim' had success with 'You're The Only Good Thing', 'Adios Amigo', 'Welcome To My World' (UK number 6) and 'Guilty', which features French horns and oboes. His records often had exceptional longevity; 'I Love You Because' (number 5) and 'I Won't Forget You' (number 3) were on the UK charts for 39 and 25 weeks, respectively. He became enormously popular in South Africa, recording in Afrikaans, and making a light-hearted film there, *Kimberley Jim*, which became a local success. Reeves did not like flying but after being a passenger in a South African plane that developed engine trouble, he obtained his own daytime pilot's licence. On 31 July 1964 pilot Reeves and his pianist/manager, Dean Manuel, died when their single-engine plane ran into difficulties during a storm and crashed into dense woods outside Nashville. The bodies were not found until 2 August despite 500 people, including fellow country singers, being involved in the search. Reeves was buried in a specially landscaped area by the side of Highway 79 in Texas, and his collie, Cheyenne, was buried at his feet in 1967. Reeves continued to have hits with such ironic titles as 'This World Is Not My Home' and the self-penned 'Is It Really Over?'. Although Reeves had not recorded 'Distant Drums' officially - the song had gone to Roy Orbison - he had made a demo for songwriter Cindy Walker. Accompaniment was added and, in 1966, 'Distant Drums' became Reeves' first UK number 1. He had around 80 unreleased tracks and his widow followed a brilliant, if uncharitable, marketing policy whereby unheard material would be placed alongside previously issued tracks to make a new album. Sometimes existing tracks were remastered and duets were constructed with Deborah Allen and the late Patsy Cline. Reeves became a bestselling album artist to such an extent that *40 Golden Greats* topped the album charts in 1975. Both the Blue Boys and his nephew John Rex Reeves have toured with tribute concerts, and much of Reeves' catalogue is still available. Reeves' relaxed style has influenced Don Williams and Daniel O'Donnell, but the combination of pop balladry and country music is more demanding than it appears, and Reeves remains its father figure.

● ALBUMS: *Jim Reeves Sings* (Abbott 1956)★★, *Singing Down The Lane* (RCA Victor 1956)★★★, *Bimbo* (RCA Victor 1957)★★★, *Jim Reeves* (RCA Victor 1957)★★★, *Girls I Have Known* (RCA Victor 1958)★★★, *God Be With You* (RCA Victor 1958)★★★, *Songs To Warm The Heart* (RCA Victor 1959)★★★, *He'll Have To Go* (RCA Victor 1960)★★★★, *According To My Heart* (Camden 1960)★★★, *The Intimate Jim Reeves* (RCA Victor 1960)★★★★, *Talking To Your Heart* (RCA Victor 1961)★★★, *Tall Tales And Short Tempers* (RCA Victor 1961)★★★, *The Country Side Of Jim Reeves* (RCA Victor 1962)★★★, *A Touch Of Velvet* (RCA Victor 1962)★★★, *We Thank Thee* (RCA Victor 1962)★★★, *Good 'N' Country* (Camden 1963)★★★★, *Diamonds In The Sand* (Camden 1963)★★★, *Gentleman Jim* (RCA Victor 1963)★★★★, *The International Jim Reeves* (RCA Victor 1963)★★★, *Twelve Songs Of Christmas* (RCA Victor 1963)★★★, *Moonlight And Roses* (RCA Victor 1964)★★★★, *Have I Told You Lately That I Love You?* (RCA Victor 1964)★★★, *Kimberley Jim* (RCA Victor 1964)★★, *The Jim Reeves Way* (RCA Victor 1965)★★★, *Distant Drums* (RCA Victor 1966)★★★★, *Yours Sincerely, Jim Reeves* (RCA Victor 1966)★★★, *Blue Side Of Lonesome* (RCA Victor 1967)★★★, *My Cathedral* (RCA Victor 1967)★★★, *A Touch of Sadness* (RCA Victor 1968)★★★, *Jim Reeves On Stage* (RCA Victor 1968)★★★, *Jim Reeves - And Some Friends* (RCA Victor 1969)★★★, *Jim Reeves Writes You A Record* (RCA Victor 1971)★★★, *Something Special* (RCA Victor 1971)★★★, *Young And Country* (RCA Victor 1971)★★★, *My Friend* (RCA Victor 1972)★★★, *Missing You* (RCA Victor 1972)★★★, *Am I That Easy To Forget* (RCA Victor 1973)★★★, *Great Moments With Jim Reeves* (RCA Victor 1973)★★, *I'd Fight The World* (RCA Victor 1974)★★★, *Songs Of Love* (RCA Victor 1975)★★, *I Love You Because* (RCA Victor 1976)★★, *It's Nothin' To Me* (RCA Victor 1977)★★★, *Jim Reeves* (RCA Victor 1978)★★★, with Deborah Allen *Don't Let Me Cross Over* (RCA Victor 1979)★★, *There's Always Me* (RCA Victor 1980)★★, with Patsy Cline *Greatest Hits* (RCA Victor 1981)★★, *Dear Hearts & Gentle People* (1992)★★★, *Jim Reeves* (Summit 1995)★★★.

● COMPILATIONS: *The Best Of Jim Reeves* (RCA Victor 1964)★★★, *The Best Of Jim Reeves, Volume 2* (RCA Victor 1966)★★★, *The Best Of Jim Reeves, Volume 3* (RCA Victor 1969)★★★, *The Best Of Jim Reeves Sacred Songs* (RCA Victor 1975)★★★, *Abbott Recordings, Volume 1* (1982)★★, *Abbott Recordings, Volume 2* (1982)★★, *Live At The Grand Ole Opry* (CMF 1987)★★★, *Four Walls - The Legend Begins* (RCA 1991)★★★, *The Definitive Jim Reeves* (RCA 1992)★★★, *Welcome To My World: The Essential Jim Reeves Collection* (RCA 1993)★★★★, *Welcome To My World* 16-CD box set (Bear Family 1994)★★★★, *The Essential Jim Reeves* (RCA 1995)★★★★, *The Ultimate Collection* (RCA 1996)★★★★.

● FURTHER READING: *The Saga Of Jim Reeves: Country And Western Singer And Musician*, Pansy Cook.

REEVES, RONNA

b. Ronna Renee Reeves, 21 September 1958, Big Spring, Texas, USA. After starting singing and tap-dancing in local talent shows as a child prodigy, she fronted her own band at the age of 11. She went on to play Texas clubs and in the mid-70s, she was the opening act for George Strait and others, including Randy Travis. She joined Mercury Records in 1991 but her debut, *Only The Heart*, proved disappointing. In March 1992, her first country chart success, 'The More I Learn (The Less I Understand About Love)', reached number 49. Two further chart entries that year and two in 1993 just reached the Top 75, 'What If You're Wrong', a number 70, being the most successful. In 1993, after two more albums she left Mercury and seemingly still seeks the big hit needed to establish herself.

● ALBUMS: *Only The Heart* (Mercury 1991)★★, *The More I Learn* (Mercury 1992)★★★, *What Comes Naturally* (Mercury 1993)★★, *After The Dance* (River North 1995)★★.

REGINA REGINA

A well-manicured, airbrushed duo of female country singers, the participants in Regina Regina were christened 'the Thelma and Louise of country music' in 1996 by the head of their record label, James Stroud. Regina Leigh and Regina Nicks were brought to his attention after both had initially contemplated solo careers. Leigh had been singing backing vocals for Reba McEntire for three years, while Nicks had been McEntire's and her husband's personal assistant. However, the two Reginas did not decide to work together professionally until they met during a lunch break

in producer Willy Wilson's office and sang 'Amazing Grace' together. After that, they told *Billboard* magazine in 1996, 'we never looked back'. Wilson forwarded a cassette to Stroud, who was immediately impressed by the duo's ability to match each other's phrasing, pitch and harmonies - so much so that he initially thought they were sisters. They began work on their debut album in March 1996, using material written by Gary Burr/Tom Shapiro, Patty Smythe and Tia Sellers. Leigh explained that they had chosen 'strong women's songs. They're songs that women can identify with'. As one radio programmer wryly observed, 'Brooks And Dunn may have competition in the duo category now', although their album received mixed reviews upon release.
● ALBUMS: *Regina Regina* (Giant 1997)★★★.

REID, MIKE

b. 24 May 1947, Altoona, Pennsylvania, USA. Reid gained a degree in music from Penn State University but he was also an outstanding football player, becoming a professional for the Cincinnati Bengals. He won a national award as Defensive Rookie of the Year. Although he became a football star, he quit in 1975 to play keyboards for the Apple Butter Band in Cincinnati. He then became a solo performer with most bookings based on his previous fame including some performances as a guest pianist with symphony orchestras. In 1980, he moved to Nashville. He befriended Ronnie Milsap and wrote several US country hits for him, including 'Inside' (a number 1), 'Stranger In My House', 'Lost In The Fifties' and 'Old Folks', which was a duet. Since then, he has written numerous country successes including 'One Good Well' (Don Williams), 'Tell Him I'm Crazy' (Shelby Lynne), 'Love Without Mercy' (Lee Roy Parnell), 'Born To Be Blue' (Judds) and 'He Talks To Me' (Lorrie Morgan). He also wrote a contender for one of the best ever love songs, Willie Nelson's 'There You Are'. He wrote all the songs on his first album, *Turning For Home*, which was produced by Steve Buckingham, and topped the US country charts with 'Walk Of Faith'. In 1992 Collin Raye topped the charts with Reid's 'In This Life'.
● ALBUMS: *Turning For Home* (Columbia 1991)★★★, *Twilight Town* (Columbia 1992)★★★.

REMINGTONS

James Griffin (b. Memphis, Tennessee, USA), although over-shadowed by David Gates, was a singer-songwriter with Bread. After leaving the group, Griffin made an album with Terry Sylvester of the Hollies and was part of Black Tie with Billy Swan and Randy Meisner, who made a superb, good-time album, *When The Night Falls*, in 1990. Griffin then teamed up with Rick Yancey (b. 1948) and Richard Mainegra (b. 1948, New Orleans, Louisiana, USA), who had enjoyed a US pop hit with 'Rings' as part of Cymarron in 1971. Yancey had played guitar for Willie Nelson and Waylon Jennings, while Mainegra had written Elvis Presley's hit single 'Separate Ways'. As the Remingtons, they released a close-harmony single, 'A Long Time Ago', and an album that, in some respects, sounded similar to Bread.
● ALBUMS: *Blue Frontier* (BNA 1992)★★★.

RENO AND SMILEY

One of bluegrass music's most important bands, the Reno/Smiley partnership was formed in 1951 by Don Reno and Red Smiley, who had first met in 1949, at Roanoke, Virginia, and worked together in the Tennessee Buddies and the Blue Mountain Boys. In 1951, they formed their own band, the Tennessee Cut-ups. They first recorded for King in Cincinnati in 1952, and will always be remembered for their fine version of Reno's song 'I'm Using My Bible For A Road Map', recorded at that time. Although continuing to record several more sessions together, lack of full-time work for the band saw them semi-disbanded for a time in the early 50s. Reno And Smiley resumed their touring in the spring of 1955 and continued to play as a group until 1964. During these years, they became very popular on major country programmes, including the *Wheeling Jamboree* and the *Old Dominion Barn Dance*, and for many years, they did tele-vised programmes on WSVA Harrisonburg, Virginia, and a daily television show in Roanoke. They made numerous more recordings for King and a few for Dot Records. In 1961, they achieved a Top 20 US country hit with 'Don't Let Your Sweet Love Die' and also charted the novelty number 'Jimmy Caught The Dickens (Pushing Ernest In The Tubb)', under the pseudonym of Chick And His Hot Rod. At the end of 1964, diabetes and the worsening effects of wounds received during wartime service forced Smiley to give up the travelling. He continued to appear on a Roanoke television show, still recorded with the Cut-Ups and made some special appearances with Reno on the *Wheeling Jamboree*. In 1968, the Roanoke show ended when the station changed hands and Smiley partially retired. He rejoined Reno in 1970 but the long-standing Reno And Smiley partnership finally ended with Smiley's death in 1972.
● ALBUMS: *Sacred Songs* (King 1958)★★★, *Instrumentals* (King 1958)★★★, *Folk Ballads & Instrumentals* (King 1958)★★★★, *Good Ole Country Ballads* (King 1959)★★★, *Someone Will Love Me In Heaven* (King 1959)★★★, *A Variety Of Country Songs* (King 1959)★★★, *Hymns & Sacred Songs* (King 1960)★★, *New & Original Folk Songs Of The Civil War* (King 1961)★★★, *Wanted* (King 1961)★★★, *Country Songs* (King 1961)★★★★, *Banjo Special* (King 1962)★★★, *Another Day* (King 1962)★★★, *Country Folk Sing & Instrumentals* (King 1962)★★★, *Country Hits* (Angel 1962)★★★, *World's 15 Greatest Hymns* (King 1963)★★, *World's Best 5-String Banjo* (King 1963)★★★, *Bluegrass Hits* (Dot 1963)★★★, *Sweet Ballads Of The West* (Ember 1963)★★★, *True Meaning Of Christmas* (King 1963)★★, *Bluegrass Tribute To Cowboy Copas* (King 1964)★★★, *On The Road* (King 1964)★★, *Variety Show* (King 1966)★★★, *24 Country Songs* (King 1967)★★★, *Reno & Smiley* (London 1967)★★★, *Emotions* (Nashville 1969)★★★, *I Know You're Married But I Love You Still* (King 1969)★★★, *Together Again* (Rome 1971)★★★, *Last Time Together* (Starday 1973)★★★, *Songs For My Many* (Grassound 1976)★★★, *Live At The Lone Star Festival* (Atteiram 1977)★★.
● COMPILATIONS: *16 Gospel Greats* (Gusto 1978)★★★, *20 Bluegrass Originals* (Gusto 1978)★★★, *Instrumentals* (Gusto 1979)★★★, *Reno & Smiley Volumes 1 To 5* (Gusto 1983)★★★, *A Day In The Country* (Copper Creek 1989)★★★, *16 Greatest Hits* (Starday 1977)★★★★, *Early Years 1951-1959* 4-CD box set (King 1994)★★★★.

RENO, DON

b. Donald Wesley Reno, 21 February 1926, Spartanburg, South Carolina, USA, d. 16 October 1984. Reno, who began his career on local radio at 12 and was playing professionally with the Morris Brothers at 14, went on to become one of the world's greatest five-string banjo players. A fine tenor vocalist, he also played mandolin, guitar and harmonica. In 1941, he worked with Arthur 'Guitar Boogie' Smith, but between 1944 and 1946, his career was interrupted by military service. He returned from active service to South Carolina where, for the first six months, he fronted a local band. He and Earl Scruggs (whom he then replaced in Bill Monroe's band in 1948) popularized the three-finger roll technique of playing, initially introduced by Snuffy Jenkins in the late 30s. In 1949, Reno left Monroe to start his own band, the Tennessee Cut-Ups. Soon afterwards, guitarist Red Smiley joined him and, as Reno And Smiley, the two recorded and worked together at various major venues, including the *Wheeling Jamboree* and the *Old Dominion Barn Dance*. In the early 50s, Reno, wishing to expand the market for his playing, again worked with Arthur 'Guitar Boogie' Smith until May 1955. In 1955, with Smith playing a tenor banjo, they recorded the definitive version of 'Feuding Banjos'. The tune was later used (without their consent), under the title of 'Duelin' Banjos', for the soundtrack of the film *Deliverance*. Smith and Reno sued the film company and won. He was touring again with Smiley between 1955 and 1964, when ill health forced Smiley to give up travelling. In 1966, Reno began working with bluegrass singer and guitarist Bill Harrell. In 1970, Smiley returned to more full-time work with Reno until his death in 1972. After Smiley's death, Reno continued to work with Harrell until 1976 and made further recordings for CMH. He moved to Lynchburg, Virginia, to semi-retirement but still worked on occasion with his three sons, until his death 1984. Reno wrote many country songs, including 'I Know You're Married But I Love You Still' (chart hits for both Bill Anderson And Jan Howard and Red Sovine). A special memorial was erected on his grave in Lynchburg, Virginia, in 1996.

● ALBUMS: with Bill Harrell *Bluegrass Favorites* (Jalyn 1964)★★★, *Mr 5-String Plays Bluegrass* (Dot 1965)★★★, *A Song For Everyone* (Monument 1966)★★★, with Harrell *Most Requested Songs* (Jalyn 1966)★★★, with Benny Martin *Bluegrass Gospel Favorites* (Cabin Creek 1967)★★★, with Harrell *Yellow Pages* (Derby Town 1967)★★★, with Harrell *Reno & Harrell* (Rural Rhythm 1967)★★★, with Harrell *A Variety Of New Sacred Songs* (King 1968)★★★, with Harrell *All The Way To Reno* (King 1968)★★★, *Fastest Five String Alive* (King 1969)★★★, with Harrell *I'm Using My Bible For A Road Map* (King 1969)★★, with Eddie Adcock *Bluegrass Super Session* (London 1970)★★★, with Harrell *Bluegrass On My Mind* (Starday 1973)★★★, *Mr 5-String Banjo* (London 1973)★★★, with Harrell *Rivers & Roads* (King Bluegrass 1974)★★★, with Harrell *Tally Ho* (King Bluegrass 1974)★★★, with Harrell *Spice Of Life* (King Bluegrass 1975)★★★, *Don Reno Profile* (Wango 1975)★★, with Harrell *Bi-Centennial Bluegrass* (Monument 1976)★★★, with Harrell *Dear Old Dixie* (CMH 1976)★★★, with Harrell *Home In The Mountains* (CMH 1977)★★★ *Magnificent Bluegrass Band* (CMH 1978)★★★, *30th Anniversary Album* (CMH 1979)★★★, *Arthur Smith & Don Reno Feudin' Again* (1979)★★★, *Still Cutting Up* (Windy Ridge 1983)★★★, with Bobby Thompson *Banjo Bonanza* (Reader's Digest 1983)★★★, *The Final Chapter* (Step One 1986)★★★, *Family & Friends* (Kaleidoscope 1989)★★.

● COMPILATIONS: *The Best Of Don Reno* (Monument 1970)★★★★, with Bill Harrell *The Don Reno Story* (CMH 1976)★★★.

RENO, JACK

b. 30 November 1930, near Bloomfield, Iowa, USA. Reno, a singer and guitarist, first worked on radio at the age of 16 and, from 1955, was a regular member of the *Ozark Jubilee*. He continued working on radio, both in and out of the forces, and had his first record success in the US country charts with 'Repeat After Me' on the JAB label. His best-known single was 'I Want One' for Dot Records, but he also charted with country versions of pop hits, 'Hitchin' A Ride', 'Do You Want To Dance?', 'Beautiful Sunday' and 'Let The Four Winds Blow', with his last chart entry, 'Jukebox', in 1974. His awards include the Country Music Association's Disc Jockey Of The Year in 1978, but his career was curtailed by Hodgkin's disease. He recovered but, apart from duets with his daughter Sheila in 1986, he has become more involved in management and production.

● ALBUMS: *Meet Jack Reno* (Atco 1968)★★★, *I Want One* (Dot 1968)★★★, *I'm A Good Man In A Bad Frame Of Mind* (Dot 1969)★★, *Hitchin' A Ride* (Target 1972)★★, *Interstate 7* (Derbytown 1978)★★.

● COMPILATIONS: *The Best Of Jack Reno* (1990)★★★, *Hitchin' A Ride To The Country* (1990)★★★.

RESTLESS HEART

Comprising John Dittrich (b. 7 April 1951, Union, New Jersey, USA; drums, vocals), Paul Gregg (b. 3 December 1954; bass, vocals), Dave Innis (b. 9 April 1959, Bartlesville, Oklahoma, USA; keyboards, vocals), Greg Jennings (b. 2 October 1954, Oklahoma City, Oklahoma, USA; guitar, vocals), Larry Stewart (b 2 March 1959, Paducah, Kentucky, USA; lead vocals, guitar, keyboards), Restless Heart are a latter-day Eagles, continuing with the soft-rock sounds and harmonies of one of their favourite groups. They were formed by producers Tim DuBois and Scott Hendricks in 1983, originally as the Okie Project, but it took them two years to develop their sound and gain a record contract. Their first single, 'Let The Heartache Ride', attracted some attention and then, between 1986 and 1988, they topped the US country charts six times; 'That Rock Won't Roll', 'I'll Still Be Loving You' (also a pop hit and now much requested at weddings), 'Why Does It Have To Be (Wrong Or Right)', 'Wheels' (their best-known record, written by Dave Loggins, and in the same vein as the Eagles' 'Take It Easy'), 'Bluest Eyes In Texas' and the emotion-packed ballad 'A Tender Lie'. Stewart left for a solo career; his first solo album included guest appearances from Vince Gill and Suzy Bogguss. Restless Heart decided to continue as a quartet and won the ASCAP song of the year with 'When She Cries'. In the early 90s Innis left the band; *Matters Of The Heart* pictures the remaining members on the cover.

● ALBUMS: *Restless Heart* (RCA 1985)★★★, *Wheels* (RCA 1987)★★★, *Big Dreams In A Small Town* (RCA 1988)★★★, *Fast Movin' Train* (RCA 1990)★★★, *Big Iron Horses* (RCA 1992)★★★, *Matters Of The Heart* (BMG 1994)★★. Solo: Larry Stewart *Down The Road* (RCA 1993)★★★, *Why Can't You* (Columbia 1996)★★★.

● COMPILATIONS: *The Best Of Restless Heart* (RCA 1991)★★★★.

REYNOLDS, ALLEN

In the USA during the late 50s, Reynolds started his professional career as a record producer when he worked with his friend, country singer Dickey Lee, and they enjoyed a regional hit with 'Dream Boy'. He then worked at Sun Records in Memphis, becoming friends with producer Jack Clement, who recorded him singing 'Through The Eyes Of Love' for RCA in 1960. Reynolds was drafted and began a banking career, but he then wrote a pop hit, 'Five O'Clock World', for the Vogues. He was soon both a credible writer and producer of high-quality material. He worked with Crystal Gayle on 'Don't It Make My Brown Eyes Blue' and 'When I Dream'. Because of his production commitments, Reynolds has never been a prolific songwriter, but his small output includes 'Dreaming My Dreams' (Waylon Jennings, Don Williams), 'I Recall A Gypsy Woman' (Waylon Jennings, Don Williams), 'Somebody Loves You' (Crystal Gayle) and 'We Should Be Together' (Don Williams). Crystal Gayle is associated with 'Wrong Road Again', but Reynolds' own version made the US country charts, albeit a meagre number 95, in 1978. Some of his songs are written with Bob McDill, whose work is frequently performed by Reynolds' artists. In the late 80s, he established Kathy Mattea with his productions of 'Love At The Five And Dime' and 'Walk The Way The Wind Blows'. He had his biggest successes in the 90s with the multi-million-selling Garth Brooks and has also produced Daniel O'Donnell.

REYNOLDS, DONN

b. Winnipeg, Canada. Little seems known of Reynolds' early life or where he first learned his country music, but during World War II, he served in the Canadian Navy. In the late 40s, he spent two years touring Australia and New Zealand, where he worked on the radio and played the theatre circuit in New South Wales. He was initially attracted to yodelling by the recordings of Harry Torrani but soon developed his own style, which includes traces of both normal country and Bavarian yodels. On 16 September 1947, during his Australian tour, he recorded six sides for Regal-Zonophone, including his own composition 'The Stockman's Lullaby'. An urge to travel then prompted his return to the USA where, apart from his singing, he also appeared in films that starred Roy Rogers, Gene Autry and John Wayne. He later toured very successfully in South Africa. In the mid-50s, he played venues in the UK and Europe and in 1960, on a further UK visit, he married his wife, Cindy, a member of the Skylarks trio. They played venues together in the UK and he recorded tracks for Pye and HMV, before returning to Winnipeg in 1961, where he became popular on CTV's *Cross Country Barndance*. In the early 60s, he recorded two albums for the Canadian ARC label, one being a yodelling album. Reynolds is equally at home with gentle ballads and yodelling. It may be, however, that to some people, he is better known for his yodelling ability, since in 1956, this talent won him both the National and the World Yodelling Championships in the USA. In 1976, his name entered the *Guinness Book Of Records*, when he yodelled non-stop for seven hours and twenty-nine minutes.

● ALBUMS: *Springtime In The Rockies* (ARC 60s)★★★, *Blue Canadian Rockies* (ARC 60s)★★★★, *The Wild One* (Banff 60s)★★★, *Song Of The West* (Marathon 60s)★★★, *King Of The Yodellers* (Grand Slam 1979)★★★.

RICE, BOBBY G.

b. Robert Gene Rice, 11 July 1944, on a farm at Boscobel, Wisconsin, USA. The Rice Family were musical and all six siblings were taught instruments as children. After first playing for local parties, the family progressed to running the local Circle D Ballroom. Rice, who plays guitar and banjo, made his first appearances there with the family at the age of five. From the mid-50s, for almost seven years, the family also presented their own show on WRCO Richmond, Wisconsin, on which Bobby became the featured vocalist. In 1962, after graduation and after the family group disbanded, Bobby Rice pursued a musical career. He formed the Rock-A-Teens band, which played rock 'n' roll locally and on its own programme on WIST-TV. After two years, missing country music, he began to sing as a duo with his sister Lorraine. They proved popular in their area, hosted their own television show and sang backing harmonies on others. After Lorraine retired, he formed his own band, began songwriting and played what he termed modern country, which included country arrangements of pop songs. He moved to Nashville in the late 60s and recorded for Royal American. In the early 70s, his first five chart entries were all minor hits with songs that had been pop hits of the early 60s, including 'Sugar Shack' and 'Hey Baby'. Further hits followed, including Top 10s with 'You Lay So Easy On My Mind' (self-penned; a UK pop hit for Andy Williams in 1975), 'You Give Me You' and 'Freda Comes, Freda Goes'. Between 1976 and 1988, he charted 19 hits but only 'The Softest Touch In Town' made the Top 30, the last being 'Clean Livin' Folk' - a duet with Perry LaPointe in 1988. He recorded albums for several different labels but has seemingly failed to maintain the popularity he established in the 70s.

● ALBUMS: *Hit After Hit* (1972)★★, *You Lay So Easy On My Mind* (Metromedia 1973)★★★, *She Sure Laid The Lonelies On Me* (GRT 1974)★★★, *Write Me A Letter* (GRT 1975)★★★, *Bobby G. Rice* (1982)★★.

● COMPILATIONS: *Instant Rice - The Best Of Bobby G.* (GRT 1976)★★★, *Greatest Hits* (1980)★★★.

RICH, CHARLIE

b. 14 December 1932, Colt, Arkansas, USA, d. 25 July 1995. One of Rich's country hits was 'Life Has Its Little Ups And Downs', and the ups and downs of his own life were dramatic. Rich's parents were cotton farmers and he heard the blues from the pickers and gospel music from his parents, as his father sang in a choir and his mother played organ. Rich himself developed a passion for Stan Kenton's music, so much so that his friends nicknamed him 'Charlie Kenton'. He played piano and saxophone and studied music at the University of Arkansas. While in the US Air Force, he formed a small group in the vein of the Four Freshmen, the Velvetones, with his wife-to-be, Margaret Ann. After the forces, they bought a farm, but following bad weather, he opted for playing in Memphis clubs for $10 a night. At first, Sam Phillips felt that Rich was too jazz-orientated for his Sun label, but arranger Bill Justis gave him some Jerry Lee Lewis records and told him to return 'when he could get that bad'. Soon Rich was working on sessions at Sun including some for Lewis ('I'll Sail My Ship Alone'), Bill Justis and Carl Mann. He wrote 'The Ways Of A Woman In Love', 'Thanks A Lot' (both recorded by Johnny Cash), 'Break Up' (Ray Smith and Lewis), 'I'm Comin' Home' (Mann and then covered by

Elvis Presley) and the continuation of 'Don't Take Your Guns To Town', 'The Ballad Of Billy Joe' (Lewis and Rich himself). His first single, 'Whirlwind', was issued in the USA in August 1958 on the Sun subsidiary Phillips International. His first US hit came in 1960 when 'Lonely Weekends', a bright, echoey rock 'n' roll song that he had intended for Jerry Lee Lewis, made number 22 in the US charts. Time has shown it to be a fine rock 'n' roll standard but Rich's original recording was marred by heavy-handed chorus work from the Gene Lowery Singers.

Rich recorded 80 songs at Sun although only 10 singles and one album were released at the time. Many of the tracks have been issued since, some even being doctored to include an Elvis soundalike. Rich was not able to consolidate the success of 'Lonely Weekends' but some of his songs from that period, 'Who Will The Next Fool Be?', an R&B success for Bobby Bland and later Jerry Lee Lewis, 'Sittin' And Thinkin'' and 'Midnight Blues', have remained in his act. Rich's heavy drinking prompted his wife to leave with the children, but he convinced her that he would change. In 1962 Rich, like Presley before him, went from Sun to RCA Records, albeit to their subsidiary, Groove. From then on, Rich recorded in Nashville although Groove were grooming him as a performer of jazz-slanted standards ('I've Got You Under My Skin', 'Ol' Man River', 'Nice 'N' Easy'). He had no hits at the time but his reflective ballad 'There Won't Be Anymore' was a US Top 20 hit 10 years later; similarly, 'I Don't See Me In Your Eyes Anymore' and 'Tomorrow Night' were to become US country number 1s. Many regard Rich's period with producer Jerry Kennedy at Smash as his most creative, particularly as Margaret Ann was writing such excellent material as 'A Field Of Yellow Daisies'. He almost made the US Top 20 with Dallas Frazier's Coasters-styled novelty about a hippie, 'Mohair Sam', but he says, 'One hit like "Mohair Sam" wasn't much use. What I needed was a string of singles that would sell albums. I was also unlucky in that I put "I Washed My Hands In Muddy Water" on the b-side. Johnny Rivers heard it, copied my arrangement and sold a million records.' His next label, Hi, adopted another approach by pairing Rich with familiar country songs, but the album's sales were poor and he seemed destined to play small bars forever, although salvation was at hand. Billy Sherrill, who had worked as a recording engineer with Rich at Sun, signed him to Epic in 1967. He knew Rich's versatility but he was determined to make him a successful country singer. Choosing strong ballads, often about working-class marriage among the over-30s, and classy middle-of-the-road arrangements, he built up Rich's success in the US country charts, although it was a slow process. In 1968 his chart entries were with 'Set Me Free' (number 44) and 'Raggedly Ann' (number 45) and even Margaret Ann's cleverly written but thinly veiled comment on their own marriage, 'Life Has Its Little Ups And Downs', only reached number 41. His first substantial US country hit was with 'I Take It On Home' in 1972. In view of the material, Rich's lined face and grey hair became assets and he was dubbed 'The Silver Fox'. Although Rich's piano was often relegated to a supporting role, it complemented his voice on Kenny O'Dell's ballad 'Behind Closed Doors'. The 1973 song gave Rich a number 1 country and Top 20 pop hit and became the Country Song of the Year. Rich's recording was used to amusing effect to accompany Clyde the orang-utan's love affair in the Clint Eastwood film *Every Which Way But*

Loose. The follow-up, 'The Most Beautiful Girl', partly written by Sherrill, was a US number 1, and the b-side, 'Feel Like Goin' Home', was almost as strong (Rich had chosen the title after being the subject of the opening essay in Peter Guralnick's study of blues and rock 'n' roll, *Feel Like Going Home*). In the UK, 'The Most Beautiful Girl' made number 2 and was quickly followed by a Top 20 placing for 'Behind Closed Doors'. *Behind Closed Doors*, which contained both hits and songs written by himself, his wife and son Allan, was a smash and he topped the US country charts with 'There Won't Be Anymore' (number 18, pop), 'A Very Special Love Song' (number 11), 'I Don't See Me In Your Eyes Anymore', 'I Love My Friend' (number 24) and 'She Called Me Baby'. 'Everytime You Touch Me (I Get High)' also reached number 3 in the country and number 19 in the pop charts. Allan Rich, a member of his father's road band, recorded his father's 'Break Up', while Rich's evocative composition 'Peace On You' was also the title song of a Roger McGuinn album.

In 1974 Rich was voted the Entertainer of the Year by the Country Music Association of America. The next year, instead of announcing the winner (John Denver) on a live television show, he burnt the envelope. He says, 'I was ill and I should never have been there', but country fans were not so sympathetic and Rich lost much support. His records, too, were starting to sound stale as Sherrill had difficulty in finding good material and began to put too much emphasis on the strings. Nevertheless, there were gems, including 'Rollin' With The Flow', which returned Rich to the top of the US country charts, and a duet with Janie Fricke, 'On My Knees', also a country number 1. Rich made a gospel album, *Silver Linings*, with Billy Sherrill and says, 'We had a similar background of gospel music. His father was a Baptist preacher and he used to preach on horseback. That's him in the left-hand corner of the cover. I regard "Milky White Way" as one of my best recordings.' In 1978 Rich moved to United Artists where Larry Butler continued in the same vein. Occasionally the material was right - 'Puttin' In Overtime At Home', 'I Still Believe In Love' and the bluesy 'Nobody But You' - but, by and large, the records found Rich on automatic pilot. In 1980 he moved to Elektra Records where he recorded a fine version of Eric Clapton's 'Wonderful Tonight' and had a country hit with 'I'll Wake You Up When You Get Home'. There followed a long decade or more of silence from Rich, amid rumours that his occasionally self-destructive lifestyle had taken its toll. However, he returned triumphantly in 1992 with *Pictures And Paintings*, an album overseen by his long-time champion, journalist Peter Guralnick. Mixing jazzy originals with reinterpretations of songs from his past, the album proved to be Rich's most satisfying work since *The Fabulous Charlie Rich* 22 years earlier. He died in 1995 following a blood clot in his lung.

● ALBUMS: *Lonely Weekends With Charlie Rich* (Philips 1960)★★★, *Charlie Rich* (Groove 1964)★★★, *That's Rich* (RCA Victor 1965)★★★, *The Many New Sides Of Charlie Rich* (Smash 1965)★★★, *Big Boss Man* (RCA Victor 1966)★★★, *The Best Years* (Smash 1966)★★★, *Charlie Rich Sings Country And Western* (Hi 1967)★★★, *Set Me Free* (Epic 1968)★★★, *A Lonely Weekend* (Mercury 1969)★★★, *The Fabulous Charlie Rich* (Epic 1969)★★★★, *Boss Man* (Epic 1970)★★★, *Behind Closed Doors* (Epic 1973)★★★★, *Tomorrow Night* (RCA Victor 1973)★★★, *Fully Realized* (Mercury 1974)★★★, *There*

Won't Be Anymore (RCA 1974)★★, *Very Special Love Songs* (Epic 1974)★★★, *She Called Me Baby* (RCA 1974)★★★, *Sings The Songs Of Hank Williams And Others* (Hi 1974)★★, *The Silver Fox* (Epic 1974)★★★, *Everytime You Touch Me (I Get High)* (Epic 1975)★★★, *Silver Linings* (Epic 1976)★★★, *Take Me* (Epic 1977)★★, *Rollin' With The Flow* (Epic 1977)★★, *I Still Believe In Love* (United Artists 1978)★★, *The Fool Strikes Again* (United Artists 1979)★★, *Nobody But You* (1979)★★, *Once A Drifter* (Elektra 1980)★★★, *Pictures And Paintings* (Sire 1992)★★★★, *Charlie Rich Sings The Songs Of Hank Williams Plus The R&B Sessions* (Diablo 1994)★★★.

● COMPILATIONS: *The Best Of Charlie Rich* (Epic 1972)★★★, *Greatest Hits* (RCA Victor 1975)★★★, *Greatest Hits* (Epic 1976)★★★★, *Classic Rich* (Epic 1978)★★★, *Classic Rich, Volume 2* (Epic 1978)★★★, *American Originals* (Columbia 1989)★★★, *The Complete Smash Sessions* (Mercury 1992)★★★★, *The Most Beautiful Girl* (Pickwick 1995)★★★, *Lonely Weekends: Best Of The Sun Years* (AVI 1996)★★★★, *Sun Sessions* (Varèse Vintage 1996)★★★, *Feel Like Going Home: The Essential Charlie Rich* (Legacy/Columbia 1997)★★★★.

● FURTHER READING: *Charlie Rich*, Judy Eton.

RICHEY, KIM

b. 1 December 1956, Zanesville, Ohio, USA. By the mid-90s, country singer-songwriter Kim Richey had established an enviable reputation for the quality of her writing, so much so that she had earned credits working with Radney Foster ('Nobody Wins'), George Ducas ('Those Words We Said') and Trisha Yearwood ('Believe Me Baby (I Lied)'). Her own recording career had also begun in earnest, beginning with a superbly observed, self-titled song cycle for Mercury Records in 1995. Richey grew up singing in the Greenmont-Oak Park Community Church, thereafter forming a folk trio she named Blue Monday. They became the house act at the local Steak and Ale restaurant, before Richey took up studies at first Kentucky then Ohio University. The first song she wrote was for the short-lived Southern Star group, shortly before she graduated with a degree in environmental education. She was working with injured birds of prey when a friend persuaded her to move to Nashville in 1988. She sang on demo sessions for Radney Foster before securing a songwriting/publishing contract with Clearwater Music. The first time one of her songs was recorded, 'I Saw You Look At Her', it was by the Swedish country group Inger Nordstrom And Her Rhinestone Band. She soon established her reputation as a writer but remained keen to progress with her own material. The contract with Mercury has resulted in two albums of rare simplicity but ample emotive power. As Timothy White declared in *Billboard* magazine in 1997, 'Richey entices you with sad and unembellished music that reveals an original spirit - and then she ensnares you for keeps by making you consider all the noiseless sensations that no songs can ever contain.'

● ALBUMS: *Kim Richey* (Mercury Nashville 1995)★★★★, *Bitter Sweet* (Mercury Nashville 1997)★★★.

RICOCHET

US country vocal harmony group Ricochet comprise Heath Wright (lead singer, guitarist), Jeff Bryant (drums), Greg Cook (bass), Jeff's brother Junior Bryant (mandolin, fiddle), Teddy Carr (steel guitar) and Eddie Kilgallon (keyboards,

saxophone, guitar). Signed to Columbia Records in the mid-90s, all of the musicians except Jeff Bryant additionally provide back-up harmony singing to Wright's lead. The origins of Ricochet can be traced to Wright and the Bryant brothers' west Texas group Lariat, which broke up in the early 90s. Having recruited additional personnel and changed name, Ricochet then came to the attention of veteran producer Ron Chancey, best known for his work with the Oak Ridge Boys and Sawyer Brown. He saw them play a club in Columbia, Missouri, and tipped off his son Blake Chancey, who procured a development agreement for the group with Columbia. Their debut sessions were produced by Ed Seay, and, impressed with the four songs that resulted, Columbia converted their agreement into a full recording contract in February 1995. A self-titled debut album ensued the following year, highlighting the group's contemporary vocal sound, which echoed the earlier work of Diamond Rio and Blackhawk. The album's strongest ballad, 'What Do I Know?', also became a radio hit as the group set out on support tours with artists of the calibre of Merle Haggard and Doug Stone, before returning to the studio to record the follow-up *Blink Of An Eye*.

● ALBUMS: *Ricochet* (Columbia 1996)★★★, *Blink Of An Eye* (Columbia 1997)★★★.

RIDDLE, ALMEDA

b. 1898, White County, Arkansas, USA, d. 30 June 1986, Heber Springs, Arkansas, USA. A traditional and old-time singer from the Ozark Mountains. Music played an important part in her early family life and she grew up playing fiddle and organ and was taught to read music by her singing-teacher father. She acquired a large repertoire of Ozark and other folk ballads and later sang many old-time numbers unaccompanied. In 1959/60, she was recorded by Alan Lomax for the Library of Congress and also included on the set of his field recordings issued in 1961. During the 60s and 70s, she regularly appeared at folk and traditional music events all over the USA and at some major festivals, including Newport. During her career, she recorded for Vanguard, Rounder Records and other minor labels.

● ALBUMS: *Almeda Riddle: Songs And Ballads Of The Ozarks* (Vanguard 1964)★★★★, *Ballads And Hymns From The Ozarks* (Rounder 1973)★★★★, *More Ballads And Hymns From The Ozarks* (Rounder 1976)★★★, *Granny Riddle's Songs And Ballads* (Minstrel 1977)★★★.

● FURTHER READING: *A Singer And Her Songs*, Almeda Riddle.

RIDDLE, JIMMY

b. James Riddle, 3 September 1918, Dyersburg, Tennessee, USA, d. 10 December 1982, Nashville, Tennessee, USA. Riddle grew up in Memphis and as a boy learned to play the harmonica that his grandfather gave him for his fourth birthday. He later also played piano, piano accordion, guitar and bass. He played on street corners before joining Uncle Rube Turnipseed And The Pea Ridge Ramblers in the mid-30s. He then joined the Swift Jewel Cowboys, a western swing band, where he acted as a substitute player, and during his tenure with the band, he played whatever instrument was needed at the time; he played harmonica when he made his first recordings with them in 1939. He relocated to Houston, working first with the Crustene Roundup Gang and then with the Jolly Texans in Mississippi. During World War II, he briefly worked in a Houston shipyard, before in 1943, he became a member of Roy Acuff's Smoky Mountain Boys, where he played harmonica and piano. He saw military service from June 1944 to July 1946, after which he rejoined Acuff and worked with him for the remainder of his life, except for a short period around 1973. He toured worldwide with Acuff and also appeared with him in films. He made some solo recordings, and in later years, he did occasional work as a session musician. He was noted for making mouth music, a practice he learned from an old uncle, known as 'eephing'. He played tunes such as the 'William Tell' overture by slapping on his throat, made tap-dance noises on his teeth and did sundry vocal imitations, including an helicopter. These talents featured on a Decca Records single called 'Yakety Eeph'/'Wildwood Eeph'; Mike Seeger recorded him in the 70s and historian Charles K. Wolfe also recorded him for the PSB-TV *Southbound* series in 1979. (His son Steven has also been recorded performing in this unusual family tradition and seemingly there are duet recordings with his father in existence.) Early in 1982, failing heath forced him into retirement and he died in 1982.

● ALBUMS: *Country Harmonica* (Cumberland 1964)★★★, with the Smoky Mountain Boys *Country Music Cannonball* (Starday 1964)★★★, *Let's Go* (Briar 1967)★★, with Swift Jewel Cowboys *Chuck Wagon Swing* (String 1980)★★★.

RIDERS IN THE SKY

A Nashville-based trio consisting of Ranger Doug (b. Douglas B. Green, 20 March 1946, Great Lakes, Illinois, USA; guitar, baritone vocals), Woody Paul (b. Paul Woodrow Chrisman, 23 August 1949, Nashville, Tennessee, USA; fiddle, guitar, banjo, tenor vocals) and Too Slim (b. Fred LaBour, 3 June 1948, Grand Rapid, Michigan, USA; string bass, lead vocals), the group was initially founded in 1977, and before Woody Paul joined, both Bill Collins and Tommy Goldsmith had played as lead guitarists. The present trio formed their act to recreate (perhaps a little tongue-in-cheek) the music and entertaining facets of western groups such as the Sons Of The Pioneers and Riders Of The Purple Sage. Their fine harmonies and yodels are supported by sketches, humour and even rope-spinning and similar tricks. Their repertoire varies from old favourites such as 'Cool Water' and 'Tumbling Tumbleweeds', to a great deal of newer material of their own writing (often very humorous), but maintains their avowed intent to reproduce the music and songs of the Old West. In 1982, they became members of the *Grand Ole Opry* and the following year, they commenced their *Tumbleweed Theater* series, each episode of which featured a comedy skit, a few songs and a classic B-movie western, on the Nashville Network television channel. In 1988, National Public Radio began broadcasting *Riders Radio Theater* and in 1991-92, they had a Saturday morning children's show, *Riders In The Sky*, on CBS television. Outside of the act, Green is a respected Nashville historian and writer, who has edited several country music publications and is the author of *Country Roots (The Origins of Country Music)*. In 1995 they returned to their original home, Rounder Records, for the release of *Always Drink Downstream From The Herd*. Douglas Green released a solo album in 1997.

● ALBUMS: *Three On The Trail* (Rounder 1979)★★★, *Cowboy Jubilee* (Rounder 1980)★★★★, *Prairie Serenade* (Rounder 1981)★★★, *Weeds And Water* (Rounder 1982)★★★, *Live* (Rounder 1983)★★★, *Saddle Pals* (Rounder 1984)★★★, *New Trails* (Rounder 1986)★★★★, *The Cowboy Way* (MCA 1987)★★★, *Riders Radio Theater* (MCA 1988)★★★, *Riders Go Commercial* (MCA 1988)★★, *Horse Opera* (MCA 1990)★★, *Harmony Ranch* (Columbia 1991)★★★, *Saturday Morning With Riders In The Sky* (MCA 1992)★★★, *Merry Christmas From Harmony Ranch* (Columbia 1992)★★, *Cowboys In Love* (Columbia 1994)★★★, *Always Drink Downstream From The Herd* (Rounder 1995)★★★, *Public Cowboy Number 1: The Music Of Gene Autry* (Rounder 1996)★★★.
Solo: Douglas Green *Songs Of The Sage* (Rounder 1997)★★★.
● COMPILATIONS: *The Best Of The West* (Rounder 1987)★★★, *Best Of The West Rides Again* (Rounder 1987)★★★, *Cowboy Songs* (Easydisc 1997)★★★.
● FURTHER READING: *Riders In The Sky*, Ranger Doug, Woody Paul and Too Slim with Texas Bix Bender.

RILEY, JEANNIE C.

b. Jeannie Carolyn Stephenson, 19 October 1944, Anson, Texas, USA. Stephenson wanted to be a country singer, and after marrying her childhood sweetheart, Mickey Riley, she persuaded him to move to Nashville. He worked in a filling station, while she became a secretary on Music Row for music publisher Jerry Chesnut. She also recorded demo records for his writers and her voice appealed to record producer Shelby Singleton, who felt that Alice Joy's voice was too smooth on the demo for Tom T. Hall's song of small-town hypocrisy, 'Harper Valley PTA' (which owed much to Bobbie Gentry's 'Ode To Billie Joe'), and was more suited to a female singer than Hall himself. Riley recorded the song in one take and then rang her mother to tell her she had recorded a million-seller. It was an understatement, as 'Harper Valley PTA' topped the US charts and sold over six million. It was also a UK hit but only reached number 12. With her miniskirts and knee-length boots, Riley acted out the central character of 'Harper Valley PTA', and also recorded a concept album about others in Harper Valley. Her singles include 'The Girl Most Likely To', 'There Never Was A Time' and 'The Back Side Of Dallas', but she had no other substantial hits. She started drinking and her marriage ended in 1970. By 1976, she was a born-again Christian and she and Mickey had remarried. A successful film based on the song was produced in 1978 and led to a television series, both starring Barbara Eden. Riley will not work in clubs that serve alcohol and although she has made Christian albums, everyone remembers the day she 'socked it to the PTA', hence her record 'Return To Harper Valley' in 1987.

● ALBUMS: *Harper Valley PTA* (Plantation 1968)★★★★, *Sock Soul* (1968)★★★, *Yearbooks And Yesterdays* (Plantation 1968)★★★, *The Songs Of Jeannie C. Riley* (Plantation 1969)★★★, *Things Go Better With Love* (Plantation 1969)★★★, *Country Girl* (Plantation 1970)★★★, *The Generation Gap* (Plantation 1970)★★, *Jeannie* (Plantation 1972)★★, *Down To Earth* (MGM 1972)★★, *Give Myself A Party* (1972)★★, *When Love Has Gone Away* (MGM 1973)★★, *Just Jeannie* (MGM 1974)★★★, *Sunday After Church* (MGM 1975)★★, *Fancy Friends* (MGM 1977)★★, *Wings To Fly* (God's Country 1979)★★, *From Harper Valley To The Mountain Top* (God's Country 1981)★★★, *On The Road* (1982)★★, *Pure Country* (1982)★★, *Total Woman* (1987)★★.

● COMPILATIONS: *Jeannie C. Riley's Greatest Hits* (Plantation 1971)★★★, *The Best Of ...* (Varese Sarabande 1997)★★★.
● FURTHER READING: *From Harper Valley To The Mountain Top*, Jeannie C. Riley with Jamie Buckingham.

RIMES, LEANN

b. 28 August 1982, Jackson, Mississippi, USA. Rimes's father, Wilbur, was a part-time guitarist and, with his encouragement, LeAnn was singing and tap-dancing when aged only two and winning talent contests when five. The family moved to Texas and she sang 'The Star-Spangled Banner' at Dallas Cowboy games and the National Cutting Horse Championships in Fort Worth. Her parents recorded an album to sell at gigs when she was seven, and four years later she recorded *All That*, produced by her father, at Norman Petty's studio in Clovis, New Mexico. One track, an aching ballad, 'Blue', had been written by Bill Mack for Patsy Cline, who had died before it could be recorded. Roy Drusky and Kenny Roberts subsequently cut the song, but Bill Mack felt that it was ideal for Rimes. While listening to tapes on holiday, record executive Mike Curb heard Rimes's voice, rushed to a phone and offered her a contract with his nationally distributed label. On her debut album for Curb, she reworked 'Blue' and sang a duet with 78-year-old Eddy Arnold of his hit 'Cattle Call'. The new version of 'Blue' was an instant US hit, climbing high on the pop chart and topping the country chart. Her second country number 1 came with the up-tempo 'One Way Ticket (Because I Can)' with its Searchers-like guitars. *Blue* also topped the country albums chart - 22 weeks at the top and three million sales to February 1997. She was the youngest ever nominee at the 1996 Country Music Association Awards, although it was not until the 1997 event that she picked up the Horizon Award. American country fans shout 'LeAnn' in the way that recent UK music fans shout 'Liam', and providing she sticks to good, commercial material, she should emulate those other country child stars, Brenda Lee and Tanya Tucker. Like them, she sounds older than her age and she sings adult material - on 'My Baby' she tells us, 'My baby is a full-time lover, My baby is a full grown man.' At the 1997 Grammy Awards, Rimes won Best New Artist, Best Female Country and Best Country Song for 'Blue', and at the same year's *Billboard* Awards she won another six honours, including Artist Of The Year. Her excellent 1997 revival of 'Unchained Melody' is, however, another indication that her management is having difficulty finding appropriate material. Another is the remixed reissue of old material on *Unchained Melody/The Early Years*, although the album did debut at number 1 on the US album charts. With fashioned hair, Lolita sunglasses, AIDS ribbon and figure-hugging clothes, LeAnn Rimes looks much older than 15; there is even a credit for her manicurist on *Blue*. That aside, she does possess an extraordinary, rich voice for such a young singer.
● ALBUMS: *All That* (1993)★★, *Blue* (Curb 1996)★★★★, *Unchained Melody/The Early Years* (Curb 1997)★★, *You Light Up My Life/Inspirational Songs* (Curb 1997)★★★.

RINEHART, COWBOY SLIM

b. Nolan Rinehart, 12 March 1911, near Gustine, Texas, USA, d. 28 October 1948. Little is known of Rinehart, especially of his early life, but he grew up in a ranching area. A natural singer, he learned to play guitar and probably made his first broadcasts on local radio in Brady. In the 30s, his down-to-earth cowboy singing saw him become one of the most popular artists ever to appear on XEPN, a border radio station situated at Piedras Negras, just inside the Mexican border. In his early days at XEPN, he worked for a time with the then established Patsy Montana. She toured the east coast of America with Rinehart and was amazed to find how many people regularly listened to the powerful border radio broadcasts. His ability to sell his sponsor's products over the air led to him becoming known as the King Of Border Radio. He recorded many transcription discs, sometimes under differing names, which were broadcast as live programmes on various stations. A strong willed person, he was difficult to pin down, as singing cowboy Ken Maynard discovered, when he tried to arrange for Rinehart to audition for some appearances in his cowboy films. Maynard rated Rinehart the greatest cowboy singer that he had heard in his life. When eventually Rinehart went to Hollywood, he later maintained that the studio did not want him to perform with his guitar but as a crooner fronting an orchestra. They also wanted him to use Nolan, instead of the German-sounding Rinehart. It seems probable, since his prospected film career never happened, that Rinehart told the studio what to do with the job. He remained with border radio, where he sold vast numbers of his songbooks to his many fans, until his death. It has been written that, at the time, he was about to become involved more with the administrative side of border radio but this was never to happen. On 28 October 1948, he was killed in a car crash in Detroit, Michigan. He may have been making a few rare appearances away from border radio but it is also possible, since he had a recording contract from Decca in his pocket, that he was on his way to make his first commercial recordings.
● FURTHER READING: *Cowboy Slim Rinehart's Folio Of Country Song Hits*, Dallas Turner.

RITTER, TEX

b. Maurice Woodward Ritter, 12 January 1905, near Murvaul, Panola County, Texas, USA, d. 2 January 1974. The youngest of six children, he grew up on the farm that the Ritter family had worked for over 70 years. He attended High School in Beaumont and then entered the University of Texas in Austin. Here he began his studies for a law degree in Government and Political Science. He was active in the debating societies and sang with the University Glee Club. During this period, he developed a lasting interest in cowboy songs, being greatly influenced by the research of such authorities as John A. Lomax and J. Frank Dobie. He financed himself during his time at the university by working menial jobs but finally left in 1928, having completed only the first year of his Law School course. He sang cowboy and folk songs on KPCR Houston and struggled to make a living selling insurance. After meeting members of a touring operetta company in Austin, he joined them, finally arriving with the company in a Depression-gripped New York. He possibly sang on *Broadway in The New Moon* in September 1928, although some accounts place his arrival in the city a year later. After visiting Chicago, he decided to continue his studies for his Law degree and entered Northwestern University Law School in Evanston, Illinois, in September 1929. Without financial backing, he soon found himself unable to continue with the course and left to join a touring production of The New Moon in 1930. Late in 1930, he successfully auditioned for the part of Cord Elam in *Green Grow The Lilacs*. The producer said he wanted real cowboys who could sing, but farm boy Woodward reckoned he qualified (it was around this time that he acquired his nickname 'Tex'). After a test run in Boston, the company opened on Broadway on 26 January 1931, with Tex not only singing four songs as Elam but also understudying leading actor Franchot Tone. The play was very successful (it was later converted into the musical *Oklahoma*) and Tex stayed with it until it finally closed in Detroit. He sang on NBC radio and in 1932, he played the part of Sagebrush Charlie in a Broadway production of *The Roundup* and later appeared in *Mother Lode*. In the early 30s, he also worked on various radio programmes. He sang songs and told tales of the Old West in *Lone Star Rangers* and appeared in several radio dramas, including *Death Valley Days* and CBS's networked *Bobby Benson's Adventures* (later appearing in the music version *Songs Of The B-Bar-B*). In 1933, he starred in a daily children's cowboy radio show on WINS New York called *Cowboy Tom's Roundup*. His popularity also saw him appear on WHN radio with *Tex Ritter's Campfire* and *The WHN Barn Dance*. He made four recordings for ARC (American Record Corporation) in March 1933 but only 'Rye Whiskey' was released and he subsequently moved to Decca, where he made his first recordings, 'Sam Hall' and 'Get Along Little Dogie', on 21 January 1935. He went on to record a further 28 songs for the label, the last being in January 1939, in a session in Los Angeles, billed as Tex Ritter And His Texans, which produced four recordings including his version of the Vagabonds' hit 'When It's Lamp Lighting Time In The Valley'. Actually his 'Texans' were the Sons Of The Pioneers, a group more usually associated with Roy Rogers than Ritter. Many of the songs recorded were featured in his films, plus one or two popular numbers such as 'Nobody's Darling But Mine'. In 1936, Grand National Pictures decided that they, like other companies, should make some singing cowboy westerns. Unfortunately they had no singing cowboy under contract, but Edward Finney, a producer working with the company, promised he would find one. Ritter was drawn to his attention and Finney signed him to a personal contract, thus becoming his producer-agent. Ritter soon accepted a contract that promised to pay him, as the star, $2,400 per picture. The challenge of Hollywood was too good to refuse; Ritter found himself a horse, White Flash, and although more than competent with the singing aspect of his new career, he was coached by one-time outlaw Al Jennings on how to look equally convincing with a gun and his fists. The first of his 12 Grand National B-westerns, *Song Of The Gringo*, was shot in five days and was released in November 1936. *Headin' For The Rio Grande* followed shortly afterwards, and he co-starred with one Rita Cansino (later Rita Hayworth) in his fourth film, *Trouble In Texas* (1937). In 1938, after *Utah Trail*, Grand National's financial problems saw Finney move Ritter to Monogram, where by 1941, he had made 20 films, most of which received critical lashings. When his contract with Finney expired, Ritter decided to look after his own affairs and signed with Columbia Pictures. Financially, things improved, and in 1941, he co-starred with Bill Elliott in eight more films. When Elliott left for Republic, Ritter assumed that he would become the studio's only cowboy

star and was shocked when Columbia released him. He and White Flash moved to Universal, where he starred in seven films with Johnny Mack Brown and once again suffered by the double billing. In 1943, Brown moved on, leaving Ritter to star alone in his next three films, the last being *Oklahoma Raiders*. Financial problems then forced Universal to drop the series but many rate these as three of Ritter's best pictures. In 1944, he joined PRC (Producers Releasing Corporation), where he made a series of eight films that were later described as being little better than the low-budget Grand National series. On 15 October 1945, Tex Ritter's last singing cowboy film, *Flaming Bullets*, was released. Ritter married Dorothy Fay Southworth on 14 June 1941, a promising actress (known as Dorothy Fay) who had been his leading lady four times and also appeared in *The Philadelphia Story*. After their marriage, she gave up her career and subsequently raised their two sons, Thomas (Tom) and John (Jonathan Southworth Ritter). During his singing cowboy years, Ritter made countless personal appearances to promote his films and his stage shows with White Flash were very popular. A number of songbooks were issued, such as the *Tex Ritter Cowboy Song Folio* (1937) and *Tex Ritter: Mountain Ballads And Cowboy Songs* (1941). When he realized that his film career was over, he concentrated on his touring show, which he combined with his recording work. After his Decca contract ended, he did not resume his recording career until 1942, when he became the first C&W singer signed to the newly formed Capitol Records, with whom he stayed until his death. He achieved considerable success with 'Jingle Jangle Jingle', which topped the Hit Parade chart for several weeks in July and August 1942. In 1944, *Capitol 174* proved a smash hit for him with 'I'm Wastin' My Tears On You' (a country number 1/pop number 11) and 'There's A New Moon Over My Shoulder' (number 2 in the country chart and number 21 in the pop chart). Between 1945 and 1946, he registered seven successive Top 5 hits, including 'You Two Timed Me One Time Too Often', a country number 1 for 11 weeks. In 1948, 'Rye Whiskey' and his version of 'Deck Of Cards' both made the Top 10, while 'Pecos Bill' from the Walt Disney movie *Melody Time* also reached number 15. In 1950, 'Daddy's Last Letter (Private First Class John H McCormick)', based on an actual letter from a soldier killed in Korea, became a surprise hit for him. In the early 50s, the chart hits had dried up and it seemed that his career was nearing an end. He maintained his touring but was unable to gain television exposure other than guest appearances. The situation suddenly changed when he was asked to record the soundtrack song for the Fred Zinnemann film *High Noon* (which starred Gary Cooper and Grace Kelly). Ritter's US recording was made on 14 May 1952 without the drum beat so prominent in the film; it was dubbed on in August. In September or October, while touring the UK, he recorded a version in Decca's London studios (with an orchestra directed by Johnny Douglas) that contained the drumbeat and which is arguably Ritter's best recording of the song. This version was not released in the USA but was included on a Bear Family album in 1992. The resultant success of the film and the popularity of Ritter's recording relaunched his career. Surprisingly, he did not particularly like the song and had to be persuaded to sing it at the Academy Awards ceremony where it won an Oscar for Best Title Song. (Perhaps surprisingly, Ritter's recording of the song never actually made the country charts and in the UK it was Frankie Laine's version that became a Top 10 pop hit.) Following the success of 'High Noon', Ritter became the star of the Los Angeles television show *Town Hall Party*, which ran until 1961. He also guested on various western adventure programmes such as *Zane Grey Theatre* but one writer has been unkind enough to comment that 'none of the roles were memorable and his extra heft and advancing age, unfortunately, took away somewhat from the memory of his movie singing roles of previous years'. He also sang other movie and television themes, including 'The Marshal's Daughter', 'Trooper Hook', 'Gunsmoke' and 'The Searchers'. In 1963, Ritter was a founder-member of the Country Music Association and in 1964, he became only the fifth person and first singing cowboy to be elected to the Country Music Hall Of Fame. The plaque stated: 'One of America's most versatile stars of radio, television, records, motion pictures and Broadway stage. Untiring champion of the country and western music industry'. The following year when the *Grand Ole Opry* granted him life membership, he finally moved his home from California to Nashville. He played himself in *What Am I Bid?* (1967), in which he sang 'I Never Got To Kiss The Girl' - an amusing number based on fact, since he never did in any of his westerns. In 1970, Ritter was persuaded to run for election to the Senate but as a writer later reported, 'maybe the electorate did not want to lose him to Washington, they wanted him to stay at the Opry', and he was not elected. Ritter made his last film appearance in 1972, in *The Nashville Story*. In May 1973 he toured the UK and played three concerts in Scotland and 28 in England on successive days (he had first toured the UK and Europe in 1952). On 2 January 1974, at a time when he was working on arrangements for a further tour, he was told that one of his band members was in Nashville's jail over a matter of unpaid child support. He immediately went to the jail to arrange bail and while there, he suffered a heart attack from which he died within minutes. His final chart hit, 'The Americans', entered the charts a few days after his death. Although he starred in 58 B-westerns and appeared in over 20 other films, to a great many people Ritter was much more than merely a one-time singing cowboy. He was a respected statesman with a vast knowledge of the history of folk, country and cowboy music.

● ALBUMS: *Cowboy Favorites* 10-inch album (Capitol 1954)★★★★, *Songs From The Western Screen* (Capitol 1958)★★★★, *Psalms* (Capitol 1959)★★★, *The Texas Cowboy* (Capitol 1960)★★★, *Blood On The Saddle* (Capitol 1960)★★★, *The Lincoln Hymns* (Capitol 1961)★★, *Hillbilly Heaven* (Capitol 1961)★★★★, *Stan Kenton-Tex Ritter* (Capitol 1962)★★★, *Border Affair* (Capitol 1963)★★★, *The Friendly Voice Of Tex Ritter* (Capitol 1965)★★★, *Sings His Hits* (Hilltop 1966)★★★, *Just Beyond The Moon* (Capitol 1967)★★★, *Sweet Land Of Liberty* (Capitol 1967)★★★, *Tennessee Blues* (Hilltop 1967)★★★, *Tex Ritter's Wild West* (Capitol 1968)★★★, *Love You Big As Texas* (Hilltop 1968)★★★, *Bump Tiddil Dee Bum Bum* (Capitol 1968)★★★, *Chuck Wagon Days* (Hilltop 1969)★★★, *Tex* (Hilltop 1970)★★★, *Green Green Valley* (Capitol 1971)★★★, *Super Country Legendary Tex Ritter* (Capitol 1972)★★★, *Fall Away* (Capitol 1974)★★★, *Comin' After Ginny* (Capitol 1976)★★★.

● COMPILATIONS: *The Best Of Tex Ritter* (Capitol 1966)★★★, *An American Legend* triple album (Capitol 1973)★★★, *High Noon* 40s and 50s recordings (Bear Family 1983)★★★★, *Lady Killin' Cowboy* 1935-36 recordings (Bear Family 1986)★★★★, *Singing In The Saddle* 1937-39 recordings (Bear Family 1986)★★★★, *Greatest Hits* (Curb 1990)★★★, *Country Music Hall Of Fame* (MCA 1991)★★★, *High Noon* 1942-57 recordings (Bear Family 1992)★★★★.

● FURTHER READING: *The Tex Ritter Story*, Johnny Bond.

ROANE COUNTY REVELLERS

The Roane County Revellers of Tennessee are remembered because of recordings they made for Columbia Records in 1928 and 1929. The band was formed in the late 20s and was led by Jimmy McCarroll, an expert fiddler, who claimed Cherokee ancestry, had a farm near Oak Ridge and was something of an eccentric. The original members were Luke Brandon (guitar), John Kelly (mandolin) and Howard Wyatt (banjo). They never played as a fully professional unit, all had full-time employment which they were reluctant to give up. When offered the opportunity to record they declined travelling to New York and in consequence, they were actually recorded in Johnson City. The material included 'Johnson City Rag' and 'Free A Little Bird' and many of their tunes were recorded later by other early string bands. Nothing seems known of the various members, except that McCarroll later played with other units and Brandon's son, Luke Jnr., later established himself on several Knoxville stations including WNOX *Mid-Day Merry-Go-Round*.

ROBBINS, MARTY

b. Martin David Robinson, with twin sister Mamie, 26 September 1925, near Glendale, Arizona, USA, d. 8 December 1982, Nashville, Tennessee, USA. He later maintained that his father hated him and that his early childhood was unhappy. Reports indicate that John Robinson (originally a Polish immigrant named Mazinski) suffered from a drink problem that led to him abusing his family before eventually leaving his wife, Emma, to cope alone with their seven children plus the two from her previous marriage. At one time they lived in a tent in the desert, but in 1937 his parents divorced and Emma and the children moved to a shack in Glendale, where she took in laundry to support the family. In his early teens, Marty spent some time with an elder brother breaking wild horses on a ranch near Phoenix. Consequently his education suffered; he attended high school in Glendale but never graduated, and by the early 40s he was becoming involved in a life of petty crime. He left home to live the life of a hobo until he joined the US Navy in May 1943. It was during his three years in the service, where he saw action in the Pacific, that he learned to play the guitar and first started songwriting and singing. He also acquired a love of Hawaiian music that would surface several times during his career. After discharge in February 1946, he returned to Glendale, where he tried many jobs before starting to sing around the clubs and on local radio under the names of either Martin or Jack Robinson (his mother strongly disapproved of him singing in clubs and he used the name 'Jack' to try to prevent her finding out). By 1950, he had built a local reputation and was regularly appearing on KTYL Mesa and on both radio and in his own television show, *Western Caravan*, on KPHO Phoenix. He married Marizona Baldwin on 27 September 1948, a marriage that lasted until Marty's death. A son, Ronald Carson Robinson, was born in 1949 and 10 years later, their daughter Janet was born (Ronald eventually became a singer, performing both as Ronnie Robbins and as Marty Robbins Jnr.). Through the assistance of Little Jimmy Dickens, and by now known as Marty Robbins, he was signed by Columbia Records, for whom he first recorded in November 1951. In December 1952, 'I'll Go On Alone' became his first US country hit. It charted for 18 weeks, two of which were spent at number 1 (Marty wrote the song because initially his wife disliked his showbusiness life). He moved to Nashville in January 1953 and became a member of the *Grand Ole Opry*. Early in his career, he acquired the nickname of 'Mr Teardrop' and later wrote and recorded a song with that title. In 1955, his career, which by the end of 1954 appeared somewhat becalmed, received a welcome boost with the success of his recordings of rockabilly numbers, 'That's All Right' (originally written and recorded by Arthur 'Big Boy' Crudup in 1947 but more recently a hit for Elvis Presley) and 'Maybelline' both became Top 10 country hits. He had always realized that it would be advantageous to record in differing styles and accordingly his recordings varied from country to pop, from Hawaiian to gospel, and even some with his own guitar providing the sole accompaniment. In 1956, he achieved another country number 1 with his version of Melvin Endsley's 'Singing The Blues'. The song also made number 17 in the US pop charts, where Guy Mitchell's version was number 1. The following year, Marty turned Endsley's song 'Knee Deep In The Blues' into a number 3 country hit but again lost out in the pop charts to Mitchell, who had immediately covered Robbins' recording. Somewhat frustrated, Robbins made his next recordings in New York with Ray Conniff and his orchestra and during 1957-58, with what may be best termed teenage love songs, he registered three more country number 1s with his own song, 'A White Sports Coat (And A Pink Carnation)' (a million-seller), the Hal David-Burt Bacharach song, 'The Story Of My Life' and 'Stairway Of Love'. The first two were also major US pop hits for him (in the UK, the former was a hit for the King Brothers and Terry Dene, while Michael Holliday had Top 3 successes with the latter two).

During the late 50s, he formed a talent and booking agency and launched his own record label. Robbins had always had a love of the Old West. He always considered the cowboy state of Arizona to be his home (his maternal grandfather had once been a Texas Ranger), and in the late 50s he appeared in three B-movie westerns, *Raiders Of Old California*, *Badge Of Marshal Brennan* and *Buffalo Gun*. The first two were straight acting roles but the latter co-starred Webb Pierce and Carl Smith and included several songs. It was also at this time that he began to record the material that would see release on albums such as his now legendary *Gunfighter Ballads And Trail Songs* (he actually recorded the whole album in one day). In 1959, he wrote and charted the title track of the film *The Hanging Tree*, which starred Gary Cooper, before his classic 'El Paso' became a number 1 country and pop hit. It gave him a second million-seller and was also the first country music song to be awarded a Grammy. The success of this song established Robbins once and for all and songs such as 'Big Iron' and 'Running Gun' became firm favourites with audiences the world over. During the 60s, he registered 31 US country hits, 13 of which

also found success in the pop charts. The country number 1s included 'Don't Worry' (which has the distinction of being the first song to include the 'fuzz' sound on the recording: a fuse had blown in the control room channel carrying Grady Martin's lead guitar, with the result that it sounded fuzzy - Robbins liked the effect and left it in), 'Devil Woman' (a UK Top 5 pop hit for him), 'Ruby Ann', 'Ribbon Of Darkness', 'Tonight Carmen' and 'I Walk Alone'. In 1964, Robbins supported Barry Goldwater in his bid for President and also wrote 'Ain't I Right' and 'My Own Native Land', two protest songs against communism and anti-American war protesters. He felt the first would be a hit but Columbia, fearing racial repercussions, would not let him release them. However, his guitarist and backing vocalist Bobby Sykes' recordings of the songs were released on the Sims label. He used the pseudonym Johnny Freedom, but sounded so much like his boss that for years many people have believed the recordings were by Robbins himself (Robbins' own recordings were later released by Bear Family on the album *Pieces Of Your Heart*).

In 1969, Frankie Laine enjoyed a pop hit with Robbins' semi-autobiographical song 'You Gave Me A Mountain', while Johnny Bush released a country version. Surprisingly, Robbins' own recording was never released as a single. He also had a great interest in stock-car racing and during the 60s he began driving at the Nashville Speedway, an occupation that later saw him fortunate to survive several serious crashes. During the 60s, he also filmed a television series called *The Drifter*, appeared in eight films, including *Hell On Wheels*, *The Nashville Story*, *Ballad Of A Gunfighter*, *Road To Nashville* and *From Nashville With Music*, and wrote a Western novel, *The Small Man*. In August 1969, he suffered a heart attack on his tour bus near Cleveland and in January 1970 he underwent bypass surgery. He soon returned to his punishing schedules and in April he was starring in Las Vegas. The same year his moving ballad 'My Woman, My Woman, My Wife' became his second Grammy winner and the *Academy Of Country Music* voted him The Man of the Decade (originally, it had been intended that Frankie Laine should have the song but Robbins' wife told him to keep it for himself). He left Columbia for Decca Records in 1972 but returned in December 1975 and immediately registered two number 1 country hits with 'El Paso City' (a look back at his previous hit) and the old pop ballad 'Among My Souvenirs'. He had previously returned to El Paso with the nine-minute long 'Feleena (From El Paso)'. During the 70s, he had a further 30 country hits, made film appearances in *Country Music*, *Guns Of A Stranger*, *Country Hits* and *Atoka* as well as starring in his network television series *Marty Robbins Spotlight*.

His songwriting talents saw him elected to the Nashville Songwriters' International Hall Of Fame in 1975. His extensive touring schedules included crowd pleasing appearances at the 1975 and 1976 Wembley Festivals in London. He continued with these punishing schedules into the 80s but was again hospitalized following a second heart attack in January 1981. He returned to London for the April 1982 Festival, before making a tour in Canada. 'Some Memories Just Won't Die' became his biggest hit since 1978 and on 11 October 1982 he was inducted into the Country Music Hall Of Fame in Nashville. He toured on the west coast but in Cincinnati, on 1 December 1982, he played what turned out to be his last concert. The following day he suffered his third heart attack. He underwent major surgery but died of cardiac arrest on 8 December and was buried in Nashville three days later. A few days after his funeral, his recording of 'Honky Tonk Man', the title track of a Clint Eastwood film in which he had made a cameo appearance, entered the charts, eventually peaking at number 10. A quiet and withdrawn man offstage, Robbins possessed an onstage ability to communicate with and hold his audience, and his clever use of in-jokes, asides and sheer personality made him one of the finest entertainers to grace any genre of music. His tally of 94 *Billboard* country chart hits places him in eighth position in the list of most-charted country artists. He charted at least one song every year from 1952 (when he first recorded) to 1983 and during this period he also registered 31 pop hits.

● ALBUMS: *Rock 'N' Rollin' Robbins* 10-inch album (Columbia 1956)★★★, *The Song Of Robbins* (Columbia 1957)★★★, *Song Of The Islands* (Columbia 1957)★★★, *Marty Robbins* (Columbia 1958)★★★, *Gunfighter Ballads And Trail Songs* (Columbia 1959)★★★★, *More Gunfighter Ballads And Trail Songs* (Columbia 1960)★★★★, *The Alamo* film soundtrack (Columbia 1961)★★★, *Just A Little Sentimental* (Columbia 1961)★★★, *Devil Woman* (Columbia 1962)★★★★, *Marty After Midnight* (Columbia 1962)★★★, *Portrait Of Marty* (Columbia 1962)★★★, *Hawaii's Calling Me* (Columbia 1963)★★★, *Return Of The Gunfighter* (Columbia 1963)★★★, *R.F.D. Marty Robbins* (Columbia 1964)★★★, *Island Woman* (Columbia 1964)★★, *Turn The Lights Down Low* (Columbia 1965)★★★, *What God Has Done* (Columbia 1965)★★, *Saddle Tramp* (Columbia 1966)★★★, *The Drifter* (Columbia 1966)★★★, *Christmas With Marty Robbins* (Columbia 1967)★★, *My Kind Of Country* (Columbia 1967)★★★, *Tonight Carmen* (Columbia 1967)★★★, *By The Time I Get To Phoenix* (Columbia 1968)★★, *Bend In The River* (Columbia 1968)★★★, *I Walk Alone* (Columbia 1968)★★★, *Heart Of Marty Robbins* (Columbia 1969)★★★, *It's A Sin* (Columbia 1969)★★★, *Singing The Blues* (Columbia 1969)★★★, *My Woman, My Woman, My Wife* (Columbia 1970)★★★, *The Story Of My Life* (Columbia 1970)★★★, *From The Heart* (Columbia 1971)★★★, *Today* (Columbia 1971)★★★, *Marty Robbins Favorites* (Columbia 1972)★★★,with his Friends *Joy Of Christmas* (Columbia 1972)★★, *This Much A Man* (Decca 1972)★★★, *I've Got A Woman's Love* (Columbia 1972)★★★, *Bound For Old Mexico (Great Hits From South Of The Border)* (Columbia 1973)★★★, *Marty Robbins* (MCA 1973)★★★, *Good 'N' Country* (MCA 1974)★★★, *Have I Told You Lately That I Love You* (Columbia 1974)★★★, *No Sign Of Loneliness Here* (Columbia 1976)★★★, *El Paso City* (Columbia 1976)★★★, *Two Gun Daddy* (1976)★★★, *Adios Amigo* (Columbia 1977)★★★, *Don't Let Me Touch You* (Columbia 1977)★★★, *All Around Cowboy* (Columbia 1979)★★★, *The Performer* (Columbia 1979)★★★, *With Love* (1980)★★★, *Encore* (1981)★★★, *Everything I've Always Wanted* (1981)★★★, *The Legend* (1981)★★★, *Come Back To Me* (Columbia 1982)★★★, *Some Memories Just Won't Die* (Columbia 1982)★★★, *Sincerely* (Columbia 1983)★★★, *Forever Yours* (1983)★★★, *Twentieth Century Drifter* (1983)★★★★, *Just Me And My Guitar* (1983)★★★, *Hawaii's Calling Me* (1983)★★★, *Pieces Of Your Heart* (1985)★★★.

● COMPILATIONS: *Marty's Greatest Hits* (Columbia 1959)★★★, *More Greatest Hits* (Columbia 1961)★★★, *Marty Robbins' Greatest Hits, Volume 3* (Columbia 1971)★★★, *All Time Greatest Hits* (Columbia 1972)★★★, *Marty Robbins' Greatest Hits, Volume 4* (Columbia 1978)★★★, *Biggest Hits* (Columbia 1982)★★★, *Rockin' Rollin' Robbins Volumes 1-3* (Bear Family 1985)★★★★, *Marty Robbins Files Volumes 1-5* (1983-85)★★★★, *In The Wild West Parts 2, 4, 5* (1984-85)★★★★, *The Essential Marty Robbins: 1951-1982* (Columbia 1991)★★★★, *Marty Robbins Country 1951-58* 5-CD box set (Bear Family 1991)★★★, *Lost And Found* (Columbia 1994)★★★, *Country 1960-1966* 4-CD box set (Bear Family 1995)★★★★, *Under Western Skies* 4-CD box set (Bear Family 1995)★★★★, *The Story Of My Life: The Best Of Marty Robbins* (Columbia/Legacy 1996)★★★★.

● VIDEOS: *A Man & His Music* (90s), *The Drifter Vols. 1-4* (90s), *The Best Of The Marty Robbins Show Vol. 1 & 2* (1993), *The Best Of The Marty Robbins Show Vol. 3 & 4* (1993).

● FURTHER READING: *Marty Robbins: Fast Cars And Country Music*, Barbara J. Pruett.

ROBERTS, JAMES

b. 10 February 1918, Madison County, Kentucky, USA. The mandolin-playing son of legendary fiddler Doc Roberts, he first sang on recordings with his father and Asa Martin at the age of 10 and continued to work with Martin until, in 1937, tiring of the music, he joined the navy. He later returned to performing and while working at WLAP Louisville, on Asa Martin's *Morning Roundup*, he met Martha Lou Carson. They married, and singing as a duo, played various stations, including WHIS Bluefield, *The Renfro Valley Barn Dance* and in 1940, WSB Atlanta where, specializing in country gospel material and using the stage name of James And Martha Carson, the Barn Dance Sweethearts, they became a very popular act. In 1950, they moved to WNOX Knoxville's *Mid-Day Merry-Go-Round*. Between 1946 and 1950, they recorded 30 sides, initially with just their own guitar and mandolin accompaniment, but on the latter, backing vocals and hand-clapping were added. Their 1947 recordings of 'The Sweetest Gift' and Roberts' self-penned 'Man Of Galilee' are very highly rated. In 1951, they divorced and Roberts moved to WWVA Wheeling where he worked with Wilma Lee And Stoney Cooper and also led the station staff band, the Country Harmony Boys. Between 1952 and 1960, he returned to Knoxville. He recorded with the Lonesome Pine Fiddlers and the Masters Family and also, at times, played as a studio musician. He eventually retired to Lexington, but continued to make some personal appearances, usually of an evangelical nature.

● COMPILATIONS: with Martha Lou Carson *James & Martha Early Gospel Greats* 1940s recordings (ACM 1972)★★★.

ROBERTS, KENNY

b. 14 October 1927, Lenoir City, Tennessee, USA. After Roberts' mother died when he was a child, the family relocated to a farm near Athol, Massachusetts. He learned guitar, harmonica and fiddle and grew up listening to the music of the singing cowboys and the yodelling of Elton Britt. He won a talent competition when he was 13 years old and first played with the Red River Rangers on WHAI Greenfield in 1942. He moved to WKNE Keene, New Hampshire, the following year, where he became a member of the Down Homers. In 1946, the group moved to Fort Wayne, Indiana, where they regularly played the Barn Dance programme known as the *Hoosier Hop*. When the group relocated to Connecticut, Roberts decided it was time to launch his solo career. He had first recorded as a member of the group, but in early 1947 he recorded some solo tracks for Vita-Coustic. When these were not released, he moved to Coral. He worked regularly on stations in Fort Wayne and also KMOF St Louis, before moving to WLW Cincinnati in 1948. He acquired many nicknames during his career, not least of which was the Jumping Cowboy, a name he earned for his strange ability to jump several feet in the air while singing. He performed this feat regularly on his WLW children's television programme. He was an outstanding yodeller and naturally, many of his recordings demonstrate this talent with such fine examples as 'She Taught Me How To Yodel' and 'Yodel Polka'. Experts in the art rate that his speciality 'galloping yodel' made him the world's fastest yodeller. In 1949, he achieved his greatest hit when his recording of 'I Never See Maggie Alone' became a million-seller. It was a Top 10 hit in both US pop and country charts and also has the distinction of being possibly the first British composition to make the Top 10 in the US country charts (it dated from 1926 and featured lyrics by Harry Tilsley and music by Everett Lynton). In 1949-50, he had further US country chart hits with 'Wedding Bells', 'Jealous Heart' and 'Choc'late Ice Cream Cone'. During the 50s and mid-60s, he recorded for various labels, although few releases appeared, but in the late 60s, he recorded four complete albums for Starday. In the 70s, he recorded a tribute album to his idol Elton Britt and was asked to take Britt's place at a concert in 1972 in New Jersey on the night that Britt died. He semi-retired for a time in the late 50s but soon returned and has maintained an active participation ever since. He has fronted his own shows on radio and television on many stations and has appeared at all the major venues, including the *Wheeling Jamboree* and the *Grand Ole Opry*. With his wife Bettyanne (who writes some of his songs), he has toured in Australia, the Far East and throughout Europe. He is especially popular in the UK country clubs, where he is still rated by his best-known nickname of King Of The Yodelers.

● ALBUMS: *Indian Love Call (Kenny Roberts, America's King Of The Yodelers)* (Starday 1965)★★★, *Yodelin' Kenny Roberts Sings Country Songs* (Starday 1966)★★★, *The Incredible Kenny Roberts* (Starday 1967)★★★, *Country Music Singing Sensation* (Starday 1969)★★★, *Jealous Heart* (Starday 1970)★★★, *I Never See Maggie Alone* (Nashville 1971)★★, *Yodelin' With Kenny Roberts* (1971)★★★, *Tribute To Elton Britt* (1972)★★★, *Feelings Of Love* (1978)★★★, *Just Call Me Country* (1988)★★★, *You're My Kind Of People* (1991)★★.

● COMPILATIONS: *Jumpin' And Yodelin'* (Bear Family 1996)★★★.

ROBERTSON, ECK

b. Alexander Campbell Robertson, 20 November 1887, Delaney, Madison County, Arkansas, USA, d. 15 February 1975. He grew up in Texas and as a boy learned to play the fiddle, guitar and banjo, although it was as a fiddler that he established himself. The story exists that, as a boy who badly wanted a fiddle, he once made himself a substitute by skinning the family cat and stretching the skin over a gourd. In 1903, he toured with medicine shows but after his marriage in 1906, he confined his playing to more local venues, sometimes even providing musical backing for the silent western

films. His love of the Western image not only saw him become the first country musician to wear cowboy dress but, in 1918, he was known as the Cowboy Fiddler. In June 1922, he and fellow fiddler Henry Galliland, a 76-year-old Civil War veteran from Altus, Oklahoma, were engaged to play at a reunion of Old Confederate Soldiers in Richmond, Virginia. After the reunion, both men decided, without invitation, to head for New York to make records. They arrived at RCA-Victor's studios with Robertson still dressed as a cowboy and his colleague still wearing his Confederate uniform. Although shocked by their effrontery and dress, RCA-Victor did record them. They made duet recordings of the well-known fiddle tunes 'Arkansas Traveller' and 'Turkey In The Straw' on 30 June, and the following day, Robertson made solo recordings of 'Ragtime Annie' and 'Sallie Gooden' (a version now rated as a classic fiddle recording), plus two further recordings accompanied by the studio pianist (Galliland returned to his home in Altus, where he died a few years later). When RCA-Victor released a record containing 'Arkansas Traveller' and 'Sallie Gooden' on 1 September 1922, it seemingly became the first known hillbilly recording. When Robertson played these two tunes on WBAP Fort Worth on 23 March 1923, he effectively became the first country artist to promote his own records on the radio. He acquired legendary status throughout the southwest by his regular successes at fiddle contests, where his version of 'Ragtime Annie' was respected by all (his 1922 recording of this number appears on the RCA-Victor *Early Rural String Bands*). He often competed against Bob Wills and his father John and the rivalry between Robertson and the two Wills became known throughout the area. In later years, Bob Wills related, 'I could never beat Eck in a fiddle contest. Papa beat him lots of times but I never did'. After one monumental battle, where the elder Wills had augmented his playing with more than his usual volume of hollering, which seemingly pleased that day's judge, a bystander asked Robertson if Wills had outfiddled him. The reply was 'Hell, no. He didn't outfiddle me. That damned old man Wills outhollered me'. Robertson and wife Nettie (also a talented musician who played piano, guitar and mandolin) raised 10 children. Robertson made no further recordings until 1929 when, accompanied by Nettie, their son Eck Jnr. (banjo, guitar), a guitar-playing daughter and fiddler Dr. J.B. Cranfill (who played in the style of Galliland), they recorded 15 numbers, some of which featured vocals by Robertson. He continued to play for local events but also worked as a piano tuner. His fiddle playing provided great inspiration to many other musicians. In 1964, at the age of 76, he made a very successful appearance at the UCLA Folk Festival in Amarillo. Several of Robertson's recordings have appeared on County and RCA compilation albums. His noted 'Sallie Gooden' may be found on *The Smithsonian Collection Of Classic Country Music*, while Sonyatone reportedly released an album of his work.

ROBISON, CARSON JAY

b. 4 August 1890, Oswego, near Chetopa, Labette County, Kansas, USA, d. 24 March 1957, Pleasant Valley, New York, USA. Robison's father was a champion fiddle player and his mother a pianist and singer, and by the age of 14, Robison was competent enough to play the guitar professionally. He left home and worked with various dance bands and radio

stations, developing into a multi-instrumentalist. Victor Records were impressed when he made his first recording as a backing musician for Wendell Hall and employed him on a regular basis. They particularly liked his two-tone whistle, which was used to good effect on Felix Arnolt's piano novelty, 'Nola'. Between 1924 and 1928, Robison was associated with Vernon Dalhart, singing tenor harmony and playing guitar. They recorded 'The Wreck Of The Number 9', 'Little Green Valley', 'My Blue Ridge Mountain Home', 'Golden Slippers' and many topical songs. Robison recorded with Frank Luther (b. Francis Luther Crow, 4 August 1905, Kansas, USA) as Bud And Joe Billings and released 'Will The Angels Play Their Harps For Me?' and 'The Wanderer's Warning', both of which became popular in Britain in 1929, and 'Barnacle Bill'. In 1932 Carson Robison And The Buckeroos became the first country band to tour the UK, returning in 1936 and 1939. Proud of his success, Robison changed his band's name to the Pioneers and, following a commercial series on Radio Luxembourg, they became Carson Robison And The Oxydol Pioneers. During World War II, Robison maintained his popularity by writing topical songs that ridiculed Hitler, Mussolini and Hirohito, such as 'We're Gonna Have To Slap That Dirty Little Jap (And Uncle Sam's The Man That Can Do It)'. 'Turkey In the Straw' was rated the most popular song of 1942, and his songbooks included 'The Runaway Train', 'Carry Me Back To The Lone Prairie', 'Take Me Back To My Boots And Saddle' and 'Empty Saddles'. In 1947, Robison recorded his narration 'Life Gets Tee-Jus, Don't It', which was also successful for Peter Lind Hayes. Robison recorded square dance music for MGM in the 50s as well as bringing himself up to date with 'Rockin' And Rollin' With Granmaw'. He died in New York on 24 March 1957. Vernon Dalhart was elected to the Country Music Hall Of Fame in 1981 and although Robison played a crucial part in his success, he has yet to be elected himself.
● ALBUMS: *Square Dance* 10-inch album (Columbia 1955)★★★★, *Life Gets Tee-Jus, Don't It* (MGM 1958)★★★.
● COMPILATIONS: *The Immortal Carson Robison* (1978)★★★, *Just A Melody* (Old Homestead 1980)★★★, *Carson J. Robison, The Kansas Jayhawk* (Cattle 1987)★★★, *A Hillbilly Mixture* (Axis 1988)★★★, *Home Sweet Home On The Prairie* (ASV 1996)★★★★.

ROCKINGBIRDS

Six-piece London band playing country rock in the best traditions of Gram Parsons. The group was originally based in a Camden squat before eviction notices forced their departure. The initial line-up comprised Alan Tylor (vocals, guitar), Andy Hackett (guitar), Dave Golding (bass), Dave Morgan (drums; ex-Loft), Shaun Reid (percussion, backing vocals) and Patrick Harbuthnot (pedal steel guitar). Their second 45, 'Jonathan Jonathan', was a stirring tribute to Jonathan Richman, backed by a cover version of the Parsons/Chris Hillman tune 'Older Guys'. They also covered Tammy Wynette, with guest vocals, unlikely as it may seem, by Leslie of Silverfish. Another notable cover version was 'Deeply Dippy', as part of their record company's tribute to the genius of Right Said Fred. At the beginning of 1993 they were showcasing material for their second album and taking part in the Cambridge Folk Festival, by which time they had already played a significant part in a new-found, critical accommodation of country music. However, the move from

Heavenly Records proved unfortunate, and after line-up changes (losing Bill Prince to a solo career), they re-emerged in 1995 with a self-deprecating album (produced by Edwyn Collins) for Cooking Vinyl Records, whose title said everything about their commercial malaise.
● ALBUMS: *The Rockingbirds* (Heavenly 1992)★★★, *Whatever Happened To The Rockingbirds* (Cooking Vinyl 1995)★★.

RODGERS, JESSE

b. Jesse Otto Rodgers, 1911, Waynesboro, Mississippi, USA, d. 1973. Cousin of Jimmie Rodgers. A guitarist and singer, he may have worked with Jimmie in 1932 and so been influenced to pursue a career as an entertainer himself. He worked on the powerful Border radio stations XERA, XEPN and XELO and recorded Rodgers-type material until the late 30s, when his interest turned to things Western. He made his recording debut for RCA-Victor in San Antonio in March 1934, singing and yodelling in the manner of his cousin. When, in 1936, RCA released Jimmie's recording of 'My Good Gal's Gone Blues', Jesse's version of 'Leave Me Alone Sweet Mama' was on the b-side. This has raised the question of whether it was a case of mistaken identity or an attempt by the record company to test public reaction to Jesse as a possible successor to the then dead Singing Brakeman. In the late 40s, mainly based in Philadelphia, he recorded cowboy songs, appeared in the 1949 film *The Western Balladeer* and for some time, he had his own television show, *Ranger Jim*. In 1960, emphysema began to affect him and by 1963, he was forced to give up public performances. He wrote songs and cowboy stories until his death in 1973.
● COMPILATIONS: *His Country And Western Yodelling Days* (Cowgirl Boy 80s)★★★.

RODGERS, JIMMIE (THE SINGING BRAKEMAN)

b. James Charles Rodgers, 8 September 1897, Pine Springs, near Meridian, Mississippi, USA, d. 26 May 1933, New York, USA. Jimmie was the youngest of three sons of Aaron Woodberry Rodgers, who had moved from Alabama to Meridian to work as foreman of a railroad maintenance crew. In 1904, his mother Eliza (Bozeman) died (probably from tuberculosis), and following his father's remarriage, in 1906, he and elder brother Talmage went to live with their Aunt Dora, who ran the Bozeman family farm at Pine Springs. An ex-music teacher, his aunt probably sparked Rodgers' first real interest in music. Doubtless as the result of Jimmie's delinquent behaviour, in 1911 his father recalled him to Meridian, but his long absences at work led to Jimmie frequenting the local pool halls and barbershops, where he first began singing. At the age of 12, renderings of 'Steamboat Bill' and 'I Wonder Why Bill Bailey Don't Come Home' won him a local amateur talent contest. Flushed with this success, he decided to set up his own touring tent show, illicitly using his father's credit account to buy the tent. Shortly after his father brought him home, Jimmie ran away again with a travelling medicine show, but, soon disillusioned with the life, he was once more collected by his father. On this occasion, he was given the choice of returning to school or working with his father's gang on the railroad - he chose the latter. During the next decade, he worked on various railroad jobs, including call boy, flagman, baggage master and brakeman, in places that ranged from Mississippi to Texas and the Pacific Coast. He became noted as a flashy dresser (when funds allowed) and for his eye for the girls, although music was never far from his mind. On 1 May 1917, after a short courtship, he married Stella Kelly; by autumn, although she was pregnant, they had separated. Kelly said later, 'He was sweet as could be but he never had any money. He would strum away on some instrument and fool away his time and his money'. Divorced two years later, Rodgers continued his nomadic existence, and while working as a brakeman for the New Orleans & Northeastern Railroad, he met Carrie Williamson (b. 8 August 1902, Meridian, Mississippi, USA), the daughter of a Meridian minister. On 7 April 1920, with Carrie still at high school, they were married. Soon afterwards, Rodgers was laid off by the railroad, and was forced to do menial jobs to survive. He accepted any opportunity to entertain, resulting in absences from home and frequent changes in lodgings; the problems worsened on 30 January 1921 with the birth of the Rodgers' first daughter, Carrie Anita. When their second child, June Rebecca (b. 20 June 1923, d. 22 December 1923), died of diphtheria aged six months, Rodgers was away with a travelling show and was too poor to pay for the funeral. During his travels in the early 20s, possibly in New Orleans, he met and probably worked with Goebel Reeves, who later claimed to have taught Rodgers to yodel (Reeves, known as the Texas Drifter, was noted for his tall tales and this may have been one of them), although their differing styles make this claim very unlikely.

Rodgers' health had never been good, and late in 1924, a doctor diagnosed tuberculosis. Ignoring the fact that the disease usually proved fatal (as with his mother), he discharged himself from hospital. He formed a trio with his piano-playing sister-in-law Elsie McWilliams and fiddler Slim Rozell, and briefly played at local dances. He continued to work on the railroad, played blackface comedy with a touring show and later worked on the Florida East Coast Line. In 1926, believing the warm climate would alleviate his illness, he worked as a switchman for the Southern Pacific in Tucson, Arizona. He also sang and played banjo and guitar at local venues, until this interfered with his work. He was fired and the family moved back to Meridian to live with his in-laws. In 1927, he moved to Asheville, North Carolina, on his own, planning to work on the railroad, but his health was poor and he was unable to do the hard work required by the job. Instead, he drove a taxi, worked as a janitor and boosted his income by playing and singing at local functions and with a band on WWNC radio. He raised enough money for his family to join him, but was soon on the road again. This time he went to Johnson City, Tennessee, where he met Jack Pierce and brothers Claude and Jack Grant. Known as the Teneva Ramblers, the trio were a string band, struggling, like Rodgers, to make it as entertainers. He convinced the trio that he had a radio show in Asheville and they agreed to back him. The radio programme carried no pay but he used it to advertise himself, until the station dropped him. Leaving the family in Asheville, Rodgers and the trio took to the road. They played various venues as the Jimmie Rodgers Entertainers, before gaining a residency as a dance band at the affluent North Fork Mountain Resort. Rodgers then heard that Ralph Peer, a field representative for The Victor Talking Machine

Company, equipped with portable recording equipment, was in Bristol, Tennessee, seeking local acts to record. With Rodgers' persuasion, the band went to Bristol and were offered an audition, but they argued over the name of their act. The result was that the trio again became the Teneva Ramblers and Rodgers found himself minus his Entertainers. Nevertheless, he convinced Peer that he should record as a solo artist and consequently, on 4 August 1927, with only his own guitar accompaniment, Rodgers made his first recordings, 'The Soldier's Sweetheart' and 'Sleep Baby Sleep'. The two songs were released on 7 October 1927 (Vi 20864) and although the record did not become a major seller, it marked a first step towards musical success. When Rodgers knew the record had been released, he headed for New York, booked himself in at a hotel by telling them he was an RCA Victor recording artist, and contacted Peer. His impudence paid off and on 30 November 1927, he made four more recordings at RCA's Camden studios. It was the third recording, 'Blue Yodel' (often referred to as 'T for Texas'), that proved to be the boost Rodgers needed. It was coupled with Rodgers' version of Kelly Harrell's song 'Away Out On The Mountain' (Vi 21142). The wistful yodel, which eventually became a million-seller, became so popular that it led to him recording a series of 'Blue Yodel' numbers during his career and won him the nickname of 'America's Blue Yodeler'. Late in 1927, Rodgers, who had moved to Washington, appeared on a weekly show on WTFF billed as the Singing Brakeman (he always dressed as a brakeman on stage) and to help with family expenses, Carrie worked as a waitress. The northern climate, however, worsened his illness, and medication was expensive. In February 1928, Rodgers recorded eight more sides at Camden, including 'Blue Yodels #3 and #4', and a version of 'In The Jailhouse Now' that has become a country classic. Peer provided accompaniment from Julian Ninde (guitar) and Ellsworth T. Cozzens (steel guitar, mandolin, ukulele, banjo). Three further sessions were held that year, one at Camden and two in Atlanta, which produced 14 more sides. Peer constantly pressed him for new material, and Elsie McWilliams came to Rodgers' rescue. In a week, she and Rodgers wrote nine new songs. These included 'Daddy And Home', 'My Old Pal' and 'You And My Old Guitar', while Cozzens co-wrote 'Dear Old Sunny South By The Sea' and 'Treasures Untold', both very successful Rodgers recordings. By the end of the year, he was receiving a considerable sum in royalties and had played major tours in the south, allegedly receiving a weekly wage of $600 dollars for a 20-minute spot each night. He was hailed a hero on a visit to Meridian, but his health again gave cause for concern. By this time, he had forsaken his image and dress as the Singing Brakeman. He now sometimes dressed in a tuxedo and bowler hat and gloried in his billing as 'America's Blue Yodeler'. In February 1929, he recorded 11 sessions in New York (two), Dallas (four) and Atlanta (five). He also recorded the soundtrack for the short film *The Singing Brakeman*. He received backing on many of the recordings from Joe Kaipo (steel guitar), Billy Burkes (guitar) and Weldon Burkes (ukulele). Between the recording sessions, he played many venues, including a number on the major Radio-Keith-Orpheum Interstate Circuit tour (RKO), which visited cities in Texas, Oklahoma, Louisiana, Alabama and Georgia. Over 12 days during June and July 1930, Rodgers recorded a total of 16 tracks, including 'Pistol Packin' Papa' and 'Blue Yodel

'#8' (Muleskinner Blues) which featured only his guitar, while others had backing from Lani McIntire's Hawaiians ('Moonlight And Skies' and 'For The Sake Of Day's Gone By'). On the recording of 'Blue Yodel #9', he was backed by Lillian Armstrong (piano) and the trumpet of a young Louis Armstrong. Away from the studios, he suffered health and personal problems, including the reappearance of his first wife Stella. Accompanied by her daughter Kathryn (b. 16 February 1918), who bore a startling resemblance to Rodgers, Stella demanded money to support the child, evidently intending to capitalize on Rodgers' new-found financial success. On 3 February 1931, she launched a civil action; Rodgers did not dispute the parentage, but was perturbed by the huge sums being demanded. Rodgers decided to head west with his family, while his lawyer brother-in-law sorted out the problem (the final judgement in June 1932, ordered Rodgers to pay $50 per month until Kathryn was 18 years old - a total of $2,650). In January and February 1931, Rodgers worked with Will Rogers on a Red Cross tour to raise funds for families affected by the drought and Depression in Texas and Oklahoma. Rodgers also found that bookings were affected as a result of the Depression, and in consequence, he struggled to maintain his lifestyle. His health worsened, but he managed to keep up with his recording schedules. In January, he cut seven sides in San Antonio, among which was his now famous 'T.B. Blues'. (Four recordings, including an alternative cut of that song, were unissued by RCA Victor and remained so until released by Bear Family Records in 1992.) He moved his recording centre to Louisville, where, on 10 June, he made his only recordings with a female vocalist, one also being the only gospel number that he ever recorded. Sara Carter (a member of the Carter Family, who had also made their first recordings at the same Bristol sessions as Rodgers) duetted on 'Why There's A Tear In My Eye' and 'The Wonderful City', to the accompaniment of Mother Maybelle Carter's guitar. Two days later, Peer recorded two novelty items containing vocals and dialogue in 'Jimmie Rodgers Visits The Carter Family' and 'The Carter Family And Jimmy Rodgers In Texas'. Among the more serious songs were 'When The Cactus Is In Bloom', a self-penned number that evoked Rodgers' love for the Old West. He made 12 recordings in Dallas during a five-day period in February 1932, which included the prophetical 'My Time Ain't Long' and 'Blue Yodel #10'. A plan for Rodgers to tour the UK was never finalized, since his health prevented him from making the trip. In August, he travelled to Camden and with a backing that included Clayton McMichen and Slim Bryant, he managed 12 further recordings. Two of the numbers, 'Mother The Queen Of My Heart' and 'Peach Picking Time In Georgia', were written by Bryant and McMichen, respectively, and both have subsequently become country standards. He also recorded 'Whippin' That Old T.B.' - a brave but overly optimistic number. Two weeks later, Rodgers went to New York, insisting that Bryant accompanied him, and with other musicians, he made four recordings, including 'Prairie Lullaby' and his delightful version of 'Miss The Mississippi And You'. A promised network show on WEAF New York failed to materialize and his health had deteriorated so much that he was constantly taking painkillers and alcohol. He refused to surrender to his illness, and is quoted as telling McMichen: 'I want to die with my shoes on'. In late 1932 and the spring of 1933, Rodgers' desperate need for

money saw him alternate periods of enforced rest with appearances in tawdry venues in Texas, even appearing with vaudeville acts between films in nickelodeons. While living in San Antonio, he did for a time manage a weekly show on KMAC. In February 1933, he collapsed in Lufkin and was rushed to the Memorial Hospital, Houston. Realizing that money to support his family was still vitally needed, Rodgers contacted Peer and persuaded him to bring forward the proposed summer recording session to May. Realizing the financial and health problems involved, Peer agreed to pay Rodgers $250 dollars a side for 12 recordings. On 17 May, with only his own guitar, he recorded four songs in New York, including 'Blue Yodel #12' and another Western-orientated number in 'The Cowhand's Last Ride'. The following day he added 'Dreaming With Tears In My Eyes', 'Yodeling My Way Back Home' and 'Jimmie Rodgers' Last Blue Yodel'. He had to be carried out of the studio; after two days' rest, he made recordings of 'The Yodeling Ranger' and 'Old Pal Of My Heart'. Four days later, he returned to the studios. On the first three recordings, 'Old Love Letters', 'Mississippi Delta Blues' (its bluesy sadness has led many devotees to rate this one of his finest works) and 'Somewhere Below The Dixon Line', he had Tony Colicchio (guitar) and John Cali (steel guitar, guitar, banjo) providing instrumental backing. Rodgers had to rest on a cot during the recording, and with only his own guitar, he cut his final song, 'Years Ago'. After the sessions, Rodgers visited Coney Island pleasure beach; on his return to the hotel, he attempted to walk from the car but collapsed onto a fire hydrant after a short distance. He apparently told his brother-in-law, Alex Nelson, 'Let me take a blow'. Later that night, he developed a bad cough and began to haemorrhage badly. A doctor was called, but before he arrived at the hotel, Rodgers had slipped into a coma. He died in the early hours of 26 May, having literally drowned in his own blood. His body was taken by train to Meridian, where hundreds of mourners met it at Union Station in Meridian; on 29 May, his body lay in state. He was buried in Oak Grove Cemetery, next to the grave of June, his baby daughter. After Rodgers' death, his wife and daughter suffered severe financial problems. When it was discovered that Carrie had cancer and was in need of major surgery, friends started a fund to help with the costs. However, the treatment failed to halt the cancer and Carrie Williamson Rodgers died on 28 November 1961. Rodgers' daughter, Carrie Anita Rodgers Court, died from emphysema in San Antonio on 5 December 1993 and was taken to Meridian, where she was buried next to her father. She had requested that only Jimmie's recording of 'Sleep, Baby, Sleep' was to be played at her funeral (the second song he had recorded in Bristol in 1927, it was one he had often sung to her in her childhood). Following Rodgers' death, RCA Victor released very few of the unissued recordings, the last single being in 1938, to mark the fifth anniversary of his death. In the early 50s, no doubt through Peer's efforts, RCA released four 10-inch albums of his recordings. In 1956, they released the first 12-inch album. The interest it raised and the sales led to the release of seven more by 1964. In 1987, the Smithsonian Institution produced a boxed set of 36 recordings and later RCA released a boxed set in Japan. In the early 90s, Rounder issued a series of compact discs and cassettes, which included some alternative takes. In 1992, Bear Family released a definitive set of six compact discs of Rodgers' work. Among the countless tribute recordings that have been made over the years are those by Gene Autry (probably the first Rodgers soundalike in his early days), Bradley Kincaid and Ernest Tubb. In October 1936, even Mrs Carrie Rodgers made a recording, when, with Ernest Tubb accompanying her on Rodgers' guitar, she rendered the rather maudlin 'We Miss Him When The Evening Shadows Fall'. Arguably the best tribute is the long 'Jimmie Rodgers' Blues' by Elton Britt, which cleverly uses the titles of his songs within its lyrics. Later, several artists, including Hank Snow, Merle Haggard, Wilf Carter, Yodeling Slim Clark and Australia's Buddy Williams all recorded albums of Rodgers' songs. Naturally, there has also been much written about the artist. In 1935, his widow, with some persuasion and assistance, privately published her account of Rodgers' life. The book attracted little attention either then or in 1953, when it was reprinted to coincide with the first Jimmie Rodgers memorial celebration in Meridian (both Ernest Tubb and Hank Snow were greatly influenced in their early careers by Rodgers and the two singers worked together to establish the annual Meridian memorial event). It was reprinted again by the Country Music Foundation Press in 1975. Carrie Rodgers' book tended to avoid any controversial subject matter, but it does offer some insight into his family's lifestyle. Mike Paris and Chris Comber published a far more interesting volume in 1977, but the definitive book on the artist is undoubtedly the 1979 volume (revised 1992) written by Nolan Porterfield and published by the University Of Illinois Press as a volume in their series *Music In American Life*.

Jimmie Rodgers' influence on subsequent American (and other) artists is incalculable. Many of the top stars, including Gene Autry, Jimmie Davis, Hank Snow and Ernest Tubb started their careers virtually as Rodgers impersonators before developing their own styles. During his lifetime, Rodgers was not termed a 'country music singer', since the category did not truly exist at that time. He sang a mixture of folk ballads, blues and vaudeville and even semi-risqué numbers, such as 'Frankie And Johnny', which in his hands, became the accepted fare of not only the first generations of country music listeners and record buyers, but also those that have followed in the years since his death. Over the years, there has been a considerable amount of discussion concerning Rodgers' contribution to country music, a contribution that has seen him named as the 'Father Of Country Music' and elected as the first entrant to the Country Music Hall Of Fame in Nashville on its foundation in 1961. There is no doubt that, in his relatively short career, he established styles that many have followed. He was one of the first to successfully master the art of recording, his mournful yodel was magnetic to many people's ears and he was a very proficient entertainer, who loved to be in front of an audience.
● ALBUMS: *Travellin' Blues* 10-inch album (RCA Victor 1952)★★★★, *Memorial Album Volume 1* 10-inch album (RCA Victor 1952)★★★★, *Memorial Album Volume 2* 10-inch album (RCA Victor 1952)★★★, *Memorial Album Volume 3* 10-inch album (RCA Victor 1952)★★★, *Never No Mo' Blues* (RCA Victor 1956)★★★, *Train Whistle Blues* (RCA Victor 1958)★★★★, *My Rough And Rowdy Ways* (RCA Victor 1960)★★★, *Jimmie The Kid* (RCA Victor 1961)★★★, *Country Music Hall Of Fame* (RCA Victor 1962)★★★, *The Short But Brilliant Life Of Jimmie Rodgers* (RCA Victor 1963)★★★, *My Time Ain't Long* (RCA Victor 1964)★★★, *All*

About Trains one side Hank Snow (RCA Victor 1975)★★★★, *First Sessions 1927-28* (Rounder 1990)★★★, *The Early Years (1928-29)* (Rounder 1990)★★★★, *On The Way Up (1929)* (Rounder 1991)★★★, *Riding High (1929-30)* (Rounder 1991)★★★, *America's Blue Yodeller (1930-31)* (Rounder 1991)★★★★, *Down The Old Road (1931-32)* (Rounder 1991)★★★, *No Hard Times (1932)* (Rounder 1992)★★★, *Last Sessions (1933)* (Rounder 1992)★★★.
● COMPILATIONS: *The Best Of The Legendary Jimmie Rodgers* (RCA Victor 1965)★★★★, *Jimmie Rodgers, The Singing Brakeman* 6-CD box set (Bear Family 1992)★★★★, *American Legends #16* (LaserLight 1996)★★★, various artists tribute album *The Songs Of Jimmie Rodgers - A Tribute* (Columbia 1997)★★★.
● FURTHER READING: *My Husband Jimmie Rodgers*, Mrs Jimmie Rodgers. *Jimmie The Kid (The Life Of Jimmie Rodgers)*, Mike Paris and Chris Comber. *Jimmie Rodgers (The Life And Times Of America's Blue Yodeler)*, Nolan Porterfield.

RODMAN, JUDY
b. Judy Mae Robbins, 23 May 1951, Riverside, California, USA. Rodman, the daughter of an air-traffic controller, comes from a musical family that loved to entertain. She was raised in Miami and studied at Jacksonville University. In 1971 she moved to Memphis and shared rooms with Janie Frickie, with whom she recorded jingles and commercials. After marrying John Rodman and having a son, Peter, she moved to Nashville in 1980 and recorded many commercials. She sang background vocals on George Strait's US country number 1s, 'Let's Fall To Pieces Together' and 'You Look So Good In Love' as well as on T.G. Sheppard's 'Only One You' and Janie Frickie's album *It Ain't Easy*. While working for singer Ed Bruce, she impressed producer Tommy West and became the first signing to Mary Tyler Moore's new label, MTM, in 1984. Her first single, 'I've Been Had By Love Before', made the US country Top 40 and won Bob Dylan's patronage. In the booklet accompanying his *Biograph* set, Dylan says, 'At the moment I like Judy Rodman's "I've Been Had By Love Before" more than anything happening on the pop stations.' In 1986, she had a US country number 1 single with 'Until I Met You'. This was followed by 'She Thinks That She'll Marry', 'Girls Ride Horses Too' and, predictably, a revival of Bob Dylan's 'I'll Be Your Baby Tonight'. Unfortunately, her success could not prevent MTM from going into liquidation.
● ALBUMS: *Judy* (MTM 1986)★★★, *A Place Called Love* (MTM 1987)★★, *Goin' To Work* (1988)★★★.

RODRIGUEZ, JOHNNY
b. Juan Raul Davis Rodriguez, 10 December 1951, Sabinal, Texas, USA. Rodriguez grew up with a large family living in a shanty town 90 miles from the Mexican border. He was given a guitar when he was seven and, as a teenager, he sang with a beat group. His troubles with the law included goat rustling (he barbecued the goats). A Texas ranger, who heard him singing in his cell, found him a job at the Alamo village and he drove stagecoaches, rode horses and entertained tourists. Tom T. Hall recognized his talent and employed him as lead guitarist with his road band, the Storytellers. He was signed to Mercury Records, who particularly liked the way he could switch from English to Spanish. Rodriguez went to number 9 in the US country chart with his first

release, 'Pass Me By', in 1972 and he then had three consecutive number 1 records, 'You Always Come Back (To Hurting Me)', 'Riding My Thumb To Mexico' and 'That's The Way Love Goes'. He wrote many of his songs and occasionally wrote with Hall. In 1975 he had further number 1 country records with 'I Just Can't Get Her Out Of My Mind', 'Just Get Up And Close The Door' and 'Love Put A Song In My Heart'. In 1977, he had a Top 10 country hit with a revival of the Eagles' 'Desperado'. He moved to Epic Records in 1979 and found success with 'I Hate The Way I Love It', with newcomer Charly McClain. However, his drug addiction made him more erratic; he started to take less care over his records, and in 1983, he sacked his band. Rodriguez moved to Capitol Records in 1988 and had a country hit with a classy ballad, 'I Didn't (Every Chance I Had)'. He then had a further four minor hits with Capitol over a two-year period; 'I Wanta Make Up With You', 'You Might Want To Use Me Again', 'No Chance To Dance' and 'Back To Stay'. For some odd reason he recorded only one album for Capitol, and his 1994 album, *Run For The Border*, smacks of desperation - a few new songs and reworkings of his former glories.

● ALBUMS: *Introducing Johnny Rodriguez* (Mercury 1973)★★★, *All I Ever Meant To Do Was Sing* (Mercury 1973)★★★, *My Third Album* (Mercury 1974)★★★, *Songs About Ladies And Love* (Mercury 1974)★★, *Just Get Up And Close The Door* (Mercury 1975)★★★, *Love Put A Song In My Heart* (Mercury 1975)★★★, *Reflecting* (Mercury 1976)★★, *Practice Makes Perfect* (Mercury 1977)★★, *Just For You* (Mercury 1977)★★, *Love Me With All Your Heart* (Mercury 1978)★★, *Rodriguez Was Here* (1979)★★, *Rodriguez* (Epic 1979)★★, *Sketches* (1979)★★, *Gypsy* (Epic 1980)★★, *Through My Eyes* (Epic 1980)★★, *After The Rain* (Epic 1981)★★, *For Every Rose* (Epic 1983)★★, *Fooling With Fire* (Epic 1984)★★, *Full Circle* (Epic 1986)★★★, *Gracias* (Capitol 1988)★★★, *Run For The Border* (Intersound 1994)★★, *You Can Say That Again* (Hightone 1996)★★.

● COMPILATIONS: *The Greatest Hits Of Johnny Rodriguez* (Mercury 1976)★★★, *Biggest Hits* (Epic 1982)★★★, *Super Hits* (Epic 1995)★★★.

ROGERS, DAVID

b. 27 March 1936, Atlanta, Georgia, USA, d. 10 August 1993, Atlanta, Georgia, USA. From 1952 (military service excepted), his ambition to entertain saw him playing local venues, including almost six years at the Egyptian Ballroom until 1967, when he joined the *Wheeling Jamboree* on WWVA. Rogers made his US country chart debut on Columbia in 1968 with 'I'd Be Your Fool Again' and soon moved to Nashville. In 1972, his recording of 'Need You' reached number 9, a position equalled in 1974 by 'Loving You Has Changed My Life', after he became the first country artist on the Atlantic label. During the late 70s, he registered 13 minor hits on Republic but in the early 80s, he recorded for several minor labels. In total, Rogers had 37 country chart entries, the last, 'I'm A Country Song', being a minor hit on the Hal Kat label in 1984. In 1991, in spite of failing health, he appeared at several country clubs during a UK visit, being warmly welcomed by his British fans. He died after a long illness, in Atlanta, Georgia, on 10 August 1993, just a few days before he was scheduled to receive a Pioneer Award from the Georgia Country Music Hall Of Fame. Rogers is perhaps best remembered for his excellent 1973 album

recalling the *Grand Old Opry's* years at the Ryman Auditorium.

● ALBUMS: *The World Called You* (Columbia 1970)★★★, *She Don't Make Me Cry* (Columbia 1971)★★★, *Need You* (Columbia 1972)★★★, *Just Thank Me* (Atlantic 1973)★★★★, *Farewell To The Ryman* (Atlantic 1973)★★★, *Hey There Girl* (Atlantic 1974)★★★, *Country* (Hal Kat 1984)★★★.

ROGERS, KENNY

b. Kenneth David Rogers, 21 August 1938, Houston, Texas, USA. Rogers was the fourth of eight children, born in a poor area, where his father worked in a shipyard and his mother in a hospital. By sheer perseverance, he became the first member of his family to graduate. By 1955 Rogers was part of a doo-wop group, the Scholars, who recorded 'Poor Little Doggie', 'Spin The Wheel' and 'Kangewah', which was written by gossip columnist Louella Parsons. At the age of 19, he recorded 'That Crazy Feeling' as Kenneth Rogers for a small Houston label. Rogers' brother Lelan, who had worked for US Decca, promoted the record and its limited success prompted the brothers to form their own label, Ken-Lee, although Rogers' single 'Jole Blon' was unsuccessful. Rogers also recorded 'For You Alone' for the Carlton label as Kenny Rogers The First. When Lelan managed Mickey Gilley, Rogers played bass on his 1960 single 'Is It Wrong?', and he also played stand-up bass with the Bobby Doyle Three and appears on their 1962 album of standards, *In A Most Unusual Way*. After recording solo for Mercury, Rogers joined the New Christy Minstrels (he appears on their 1967 album of pop hits, *New Kicks!*) while forming a splinter group with other Minstrels - Mike Settle, Thelma Camacho and Terry Williams. They took their name, the First Edition, from the flyleaf of a book and developed a newsprint motif, dressing in black and white and appearing on black and white sets. They signed with Reprise and Rogers sang lead on their first major hit, Mickey Newbury's song about the alleged pleasures of LSD, 'Just Dropped In (To See What Condition My Condition Was In)'. *The First Edition* was in the mould of the Association and Fifth Dimension, but they had developed their own style by *The First Edition's 2nd*. The album did not produce a hit single and was not released in the UK, but the First Edition returned to the US charts with Mike Settle's ballad 'But You Know I Love You', which was also recorded by Buddy Knox and Nancy Sinatra. The First Edition had heard Roger Miller's low-key arrangement of 'Ruby, Don't Take Your Love To Town' and they enhanced it with an urgent drumbeat. Mel Tillis's song was based on an incident following the Korean war, but it also had implications for Vietnam. The record, credited to Kenny Rogers And The First Edition, reached number 6 in the US charts and number 2 in the UK. Its follow-up, 'Reuben James', about a coloured man who was blamed for everything, was only moderately successful, but they bounced back with Mac Davis's sexually explicit 'Something's Burning' (US number 11, UK number 8). The b-side, Rogers' own 'Momma's Waitin'', incorporates the major themes of country music - mother, prison, death, God and coming home - in a single song. The group had further US success with 'Tell It All Brother' and 'Heed The Call', performed the music for the Jason Robards film *Fools*, and hosted a popular television series. In 1972, all the stops were pulled out for the beautifully packaged double album *The Ballad Of Calico*, written by

Michael Murphey and dealing with life in a silver-mining town. After leaving Reprise, Rogers formed his own Jolly Rogers label which he has since described as 'a lesson in futility', and when the group broke up in 1974, he owed $65,000. In 1975 Rogers signed with United Artists and his producer, Larry Butler, envisaged how he could satisfy both pop and country markets. Impotence was an extraordinary subject for a hit record, but 'Lucille' (US number 5, UK number 1) established Rogers as a country star. He wrote and recorded 'Sweet Music Man', although the song is more appropriate for female singers and has been recorded by Billie Jo Spears, Anne Murray, Tammy Wynette, Dolly Parton and Millie Jackson. Rogers, who had a second solo hit with 'Daytime Friends', toured the UK with Crystal Gayle, and, although plans to record with her did not materialize, he formed a successful partnership with Dottie West. Don Schlitz's story-song, 'The Gambler', was ideal for Rogers and inspired the television movies *The Gambler, The Gambler II* and *The Gambler Returns* which featured Rogers. His love for poignant ballads about life on the road, such as 'She Believes In Me' (US number 5), is explained by his own life. Rogers had the first of four marriages in 1958 and blames constant touring for the failure of his relationships (although Rogers says the worst aspect of touring is being bombarded with grey-bearded lookalikes!). His fourth marriage was to Marianne Gorden, a presenter of the US television series *Hee-Haw* and an actress who appeared in *Rosemary's Baby*. His stage show promoted his happy family life and included home movies of their child, Christopher Cody. 'You Decorated My Life' was another US hit and then came 'Coward Of The County' (US number 3, UK number 1). This song, too, became a successful television movie, and the album *Kenny* sold five million copies. Rogers also made the documentary *Kenny Rogers And The American Cowboy*, and a concept album about a modern-day Texas cowboy, *Gideon*, led to a successful duet, 'Don't Fall In Love With A Dreamer' (US number 4), with one of its writers, Kim Carnes. Rogers also had success with 'Love The World Away' from the soundtrack of the film *Urban Cowboy*, and 'Love Will Turn You Around' from *Six Pack*, a light-hearted television movie in which he starred. Rogers' voice was ideal for Lionel Richie's slow-paced love songs and 'Lady' topped the US charts for six weeks. This was followed by 'I Don't Need You' (US number 3) from the album Richie produced for Rogers, *Share Your Love*. Rogers and Sheena Easton revived the Bob Seger song 'We've Got Tonight' (US number 6). Having sold 35 million albums for United Artists, Rogers moved to RCA and *Eyes That See In The Dark* was produced by Barry Gibb and featured the Bee Gees. It included 'Islands In The Stream' (US number 1, UK number 7) with Dolly Parton, which was helped by her playful approach on the video. Further US hits include 'What About Me?' with James Ingram and Kim Carnes and 'Make No Mistake, She's Mine' with Ronnie Milsap. Surprisingly, Rogers has not recorded with his close friend Glen Campbell, although he took the cover photograph for his album *Southern Nights*. Rogers was also featured on USA For Africa's highly successful 'We Are The World'. George Martin was an inspired choice of producer for *The Heart Of The Matter*, which led to two singles that topped the US country charts, 'Morning Desire' and 'Tomb Of The Unknown Love'. The title track from *They Don't Make Them Like They Used To* was the theme song for

the film *Tough Guys*, but overall, Rogers' services on RCA may have disappointed its management, who had spent $20 million to secure his success. Rogers returned to Reprise but the opening track of his first album, 'Planet Texas', sounded like a joke. His son, Kenny Rogers Jnr., sang background vocals on his father's records and launched his own career in 1989 with the single 'Take Another Step Closer'. Rogers now breeds Arabian horses and cattle on his 1,200-acre farm in Georgia and has homes in Malibu, Bel Air and Beverly Hills. He owns entertainment centres and recording studios and has 200 employees. This is impressive for someone who was described by *Rolling Stone* as an 'overweight lightweight'. He says, 'I've never taken my talent that seriously. At one time I had a three-and-a-half octave range and sang the high parts in a jazz group. Now I don't use it because I don't have to. If Muhammad Ali can beat anyone without training, why train?' Rogers now records for independent label Magnatone.

● ALBUMS: by the First Edition *The First Edition* (Reprise 1967)★★, *The First Edition's 2nd* (Reprise 1968)★★, *The First Edition '69* (Reprise 1969)★★. By Kenny Rogers And The First Edition *Ruby, Don't Take Your Love To Town* (Reprise 1969)★★★, *Something's Burning* (Reprise 1970)★★★★, *Fools* film soundtrack (1970)★★★, *Tell It All Brother* (Reprise 1971)★★★, *Transition* (Reprise 1971)★★★, *The Ballad Of Calico* (Reprise 1972)★★★, *Backroads* (Jolly Rogers 1972)★★★, *Monumental* (Jolly Rogers 1973)★★★, *Rollin'* (Jolly Rogers 1974)★★. By Kenny Rogers *Love Lifted Me* (United Artists 1976)★★★, *Kenny Rogers* (United Artists 1976)★★, *Daytime Friends* (United Artists 1977)★★★, with West *Every Time Two Fools Collide* (United Artists 1978)★★★, *Love Or Something Like It* (United Artists 1978)★★★, *The Gambler* (United Artists 1978)★★★★, with Dottie West *Classics* (United Artists 1979)★★, *Kenny* (United Artists 1979)★★★★, *Gideon* (United Artists 1980)★★★, *Share Your Love* (Liberty 1981)★★★, *Christmas* (Liberty 1981)★★, *Love Will Turn You Around* (Liberty 1982)★★★, *We've Got Tonight* (Liberty 1983)★★★★, *Eyes That See In The Dark* (RCA 1983)★★★★, with Dottie West, Kim Carnes, Sheena Easton *Duets* (Liberty 1984)★★★, *What About Me?* (RCA 1984)★★★, with Dolly Parton *Once Upon A Christmas* (RCA 1984)★★★, *Love Is What We Make It* (Liberty 1985)★★, *The Heart Of The Matter* (RCA 1985)★★, *Short Stories* (1986)★★, *They Don't Make Them Like They Used To* (RCA 1986)★★, *I Prefer The Moonlight* (RCA 1987)★★, *Something Inside So Strong* (Reprise 1989)★★, *Christmas In America* (Reprise 1989)★★, *Love Is Strange* (Reprise 1990)★★★, *You're My Kind Of People* (1991)★★★, *Some Prisons Don't Have Walls* (1991)★★, *Back Home Again* (Reprise 1991)★★★, *If Only My Heart Had A Voice* (1993)★★★, *The Gift* (Magnatone 1996)★★★, *Across My Heart* (Magnatone 1997)★★★.

● COMPILATIONS: Kenny Rogers And The First Edition *Greatest Hits* (Reprise 1971)★★★. Kenny Rogers *Ten Years Of Gold* (United Artists 1978)★★★, *Kenny Rogers' Greatest Hits* (Liberty 1980)★★★★, *Twenty Greatest Hits* (Liberty 1983)★★★, *25 Greatest Hits* (EMI 1987)★★★, *The Very Best Of Kenny Rogers* (Warners 1990)★★★, *All Time Greatest Hits* 3-CD box set (CEMA 1996)★★★.

● VIDEOS: with Dolly Parton *Real Love* (RCA/Columbia 1988).

● FURTHER READING: *Making It In Music*, Kenny Rogers and Len Epand. *Kenny Rogers - Gambler, Dreamer, Lover*, Martha Hume.

ROGERS, ROY

b. Leonard Franklin Slye, 5 November 1911, Cincinnati, Ohio, USA. Rogers worked on the west coast picking fruit and, after several singing jobs, he formed the Sons Of The Pioneers in 1933. They performed in many Western films, and, as a result of Republic's dispute with Gene Autry, Rogers received his first starring role, playing a singing congressman in the 1938 film *Under Western Skies*. When he and John Wayne jumped off a cliff in *Dark Command*, Hollywood's treatment of horses was severely questioned, which led to the formation of the Society for Prevention of Cruelty to Animals. In 1946 his wife died shortly after giving birth to their son, Roy Jnr. On 31 December 1947 he married an actress he met on the set of the film *The Cowboy And The Senorita*, Dale Evans. His films include *King Of The Cowboys*, *Son Of Paleface* with Bob Hope and Jane Russell, and *Hollywood Canteen*, in which he sang 'Don't Fence Me In'. Rogers' four-legged friend, Trigger ('the smartest horse in the movies'), had been ridden by Olivia de Havilland in *The Adventures Of Robin Hood* and cost Rogers $2,500. His films and television series (100 shows between 1951 and 1957) also featured a lovable, toothless and fearless old-timer, George 'Gabby' Hayes. They featured no sex and little violence (he would wing the baddies in black hats), and his wholesome image found favour when he toured UK theatres in the 50s. High prices are now paid for Roy Rogers memorabilia, whether it be cut-out dolls, thermos flasks or holster sets. Rogers' records include 'Blue Shadows On The Trail', 'These Are The Good Old Days', a tribute to the past, 'Hoppy, Gene And Me' and 'Ride, Concrete Cowboy, Ride' from the film *Smokey And The Bandit 2*. His palomino Trigger died in 1965 at the age of 33 and was stuffed and mounted, as referred to in Jimmy Webb's song 'P.F. Sloan'. Rogers became a successful businessman with a chain of restaurants, and he and Evans confined their appearances to religious ones. He made his first film in 16 years in 1975, *Mackintosh And T.J.*, while his son, Roy Rogers Jnr., made an album, *Dusty*, in 1983. Don McLean recorded Rogers' famous signature tune, 'Happy Trails', and Rogers revived it with Randy Travis in 1990. San Francisco rock band the Quicksilver Messenger Service used Rogers' *Happy Trails* as the title of their album in 1968 as well as recording the song as the closing track. He returned to the US country chart with his album *Tribute* in 1991, which included guest appearances from contemporary country performers. Clint Black helped to revitalize his career, the first time Rogers had accepted help from a man in a black hat. In 1992, a feature-length documentary entitled *Roy Rogers, King Of The Cowboys*, was shown at the Rotterdam Film Festival, and in the same year Rogers was reported to have signed a contract with Republic Pictures that involved an animated film based on Hollywood's most famous 'good guy'.

● ALBUMS: *Souvenir Album* 10-inch album (RCA Victor 1952)★★★, with Spade Cooley *Skip To My Lou And Other Square Dances* (1952)★★★, *Roy Rogers Roundup* (1952)★★★★, with Dale Evans *Hymns Of Faith* 10-inch album (RCA Victor 1954)★★, with Evans *Sweet Hour Of Prayer* (RCA Victor 1957)★★, with Evans *Jesus Loves Me* (RCA Victor 1959)★★, with Evans *The Bible Tells Me So* (Capitol 1962)★★, with The Sons Of The Pioneers *Pacos Bill* (Camden 1964)★★★★, *Lore Of The West* (Camden 1966)★★★, with Evans *Christmas Is Always* (Capitol

1967)★★, *The Country Side Of Roy Rogers* (Capitol 1970)★★★, *A Man From Duck Run* (Capitol 1971)★★★, *Take A Little Love And Pass It On* (Capitol 1972)★★★, with Evans *In The Sweet Bye And Bye* (Word 1973)★★★, *Happy Trails To You* (20th Century 1975)★★★★, with Evans *The Good Life* (Word 1977)★★★, with The Sons Of The Pioneers *King Of The Cowboys* (1983)★★★★, *Roy Rogers* (Columbia 1984)★★★, with Evans, Roy Rogers Jnr. *Many Happy Trails* (1984)★★★, *The Republic Years* (1985)★★★, *Tribute* (RCA 1991)★★★.

● COMPILATIONS: *Roll On Texas Moon* (Bear Family 1986)★★★, *The Best Of Roy Rogers* (Curb 1990)★★★, *Country Music Hall Of Fame* (MCA 1992)★★★, with Evans *Peace In The Valley* (Pair 1996)★★★.

● FURTHER READING: *Roy Rogers: King Of The Cowboys*, Georgia Morris and Mark Pollard.

ROGERS, SMOKEY

b. Eugene Rogers, McMinnville, Tennessee, USA. Rogers was raised in Detroit and was playing guitar and tenor banjo on radio at the age of 12, later working with Texas Jim Lewis And The Lone Star Cowboys in a residency at the *Village Barn*, in New York. In the early 40s, after a variety of club work in the Washington DC area, he relocated to Hollywood to join western swing king Spade Cooley. He actually wrote 'Shame On You', which Cooley adopted as his theme song. After he left Cooley, he and Tex Williams formed their own band, the Western Caravan, which played the west coast club and dancehall circuit. In 1947, Rogers and Deuce Spriggens both sang with Tex Williams on Williams' number 1 country and pop hit, 'Smoke Smoke Smoke (That Cigarette)', Capitol Records' first million-selling record. In 1950, Rogers bought the Bostonia Ballroom at El Cajon near San Diego, California, and soon afterwards, began a daily television show. In 1957, Ferlin Husky scored a major country and pop hit with Rogers' song 'Gone'. Later in his career, he became a much respected ballad singer, continuing to perform around southern California, and also became very popular for his radio work.

● COMPILATIONS: *Smokey Rogers (The Complete Entertainer)* (Shasta 1976)★★★.

RONSTADT, LINDA

b. Linda Maria Ronstadt, 15 July 1946, Tucson, Arizona, USA. The daughter of a professional musician, Ronstadt's first singing experience was gained with her sisters in the Three Ronstadts. She met guitarist Bob Kimmel at Arizona's State University and together the two aspirants moved to Los Angeles, where they were joined by songwriter Kenny Edwards. Taking the name the Stone Poneys, the trio became popular among the city's folk fraternity and had a US Top 20 hit with 'Different Drum'. Ronstadt embarked on a solo career in 1968. Her early solo albums, *Hand Sown, Home Grown* and *Silk Purse*, signalled a move towards country-flavoured material, albeit of a more conservative nature. The singer's third album marked a major turning point and featured a core of excellent musicians, including Don Henley, Glen Frey, Bernie Leadon and Randy Meisner, who subsequently formed the Eagles. The content emphasized a contemporary approach, with songs by Neil Young, Jackson Browne and Eric Anderson, and the set established Ronstadt as a force in Californian rock. The artist's subsequent two albums showed the dichotomy prevalent in her music. *Don't Cry Now* was largely undistinguished, chiefly because the material was weaker, while *Heart Like A Wheel*, paradoxically given to Ronstadt's former label to complete contractual obligations, was excellent. This platinum-selling set included 'You're No Good', a US number 1 pop hit, and a dramatic version of Hank Williams' 'I Can't Help It', which won Ronstadt a Grammy award for best female country vocal. This highly successful release set the pattern for the singer's work throughout the rest of the decade. Her albums were now carefully constructed to appease both the rock and country audiences, mixing traditional material, singer-songwriter angst and a handful of rock 'n' roll/soul classics, be they from Tamla/Motown ('Heatwave'), Roy Orbison ('Blue Bayou') or Buddy Holly ('That'll Be The Day'). Despite effusive praise from the establishment media and a consistent popularity, this predictable approach resulted in lethargy, and although *Mad Love* showed a desire to break the mould, Ronstadt was increasingly trapped in an artistic cocoon.

The singer's work during the 80s has proved more divergent. Her performance in Joseph Papp's production of *The Pirates Of Penzance* drew favourable reviews, although her subsequent role in the more demanding *La Boheme* was less impressive. Ronstadt also undertook a series of releases with veteran arranger/conductor Nelson Riddle, which resulted in three albums - *What's New, Lush Life* and *For Sentimental Reasons* - consisting of popular standards. In 1987 a duet with James Ingram produced 'Somewhere Out There', the theme to the film *An American Tail*; this gave her a number 2 US hit (UK Top 10) hit, while that same year her collaboration with Dolly Parton and Emmylou Harris, *Trio*, and a selection of mariachi songs, *Canciones De Mi Padre*, showed an artist determined to challenge preconceptions. Her 1989 set, *Cry Like A Rainstorm*, revealed a crafted approach to mainstream recording and included 'Don't Know Much', a haunting duet with Aaron Neville, which gave Linda Ronstadt another number 2 hit in the USA (and the UK). The highly acclaimed *Winter Light* was produced by herself and George Massenburg, and came across as a personal and highly emotional album. Ronstadt, while hugely popular and successful, has never been truly recognized by the cognoscenti. Her change in styles may have been a contributing factor. She has courted (with great success) country rock, country, rock 'n' roll, Latin, standards, opera, light opera, AOR and white soul. In 1996 she was firmly in the middle of the road with *Dedicated To The One I Love*, an album of lullabies and love songs.

● ALBUMS: *Hand Sown, Home Grown* (Capitol 1969)★★, *Silk Purse* (Capitol 1970)★★, *Linda Ronstadt* (Capitol 1971)★★, *Don't Cry Now* (Asylum 1973)★★★, *Heart Like A Wheel* (Capitol 1974)★★★★, *Prisoner In Disguise* (Asylum 1975)★★★, *Hasten Down The Wind* (Asylum 1976)★★★, *Simple Dreams* (Asylum 1977)★★★, *Living In The USA* (Asylum 1978)★★, *Mad Love* (Asylum 1980)★★, with Kevin Kline, Estelle Parsons, Rex Smith *Pirates Of Penzance* (1981)★★, *Get Closer* (Asylum 1982)★★, *What's New* (Asylum 1983)★★★, *Lush Life* (Asylum 1984)★★★, *For Sentimental Reasons* (Asylum 1986)★★★, with Emmylou Harris, Dolly Parton *Trio* (Warners 1987)★★★★, *Canciones De Mi Padre* (Elektra 1987)★★★, *Cry Like A Rainstorm - Howl Like The Wind* (Elektra 1989)★★★, *Mas Canciones*

(Elektra 1991)★★★, *Frenesi* (Elektra 1992)★★★, *Winter Light* (Elektra 1993)★★★★, *Feels Like Home* (Warners 1995)★★★, *Dedicated To The One I Love* (Elektra 1996)★★.
● COMPILATIONS: *Different Drum* includes five Stone Poney tracks (Capitol 1974)★★, *Greatest Hits: Linda Ronstadt* (Asylum 1976)★★★★, *A Retrospective* (Capitol 1977)★★★, *Greatest Hits: Linda Ronstadt Volume 2* (Asylum 1980)★★★.
● FURTHER READING: *Linda Ronstadt: A Portrait*, Richard Kanakaris. *The Linda Ronstadt Scrapbook*, Mary Ellen Moore. *Linda Ronstadt*, Vivian Claire. *Linda Ronstadt: An Illustrated Biography*, Connie Berman. *Linda Ronstadt: It's So Easy*, Mark Bego.

ROSE, FRED

b. 24 August 1897, Evansville, Indiana, USA, d. 1 December 1954, Nashville, Tennessee, USA. Rose was an important and influential figure in country music during the 40s and early 50s, and was known as a composer, singer, pianist, music publisher and record producer. He grew up in St. Louis, and at the age of 15 played piano in Chicago honky tonks. He recorded for Brunswick Records in the early 20s as a singer-pianist. After working for a short time with Paul Whiteman, he teamed with whistler Elmo Tanner on Chicago radio, and later had his own show. His early songs in the 20s included 'Doo Dah Blues', 'Honest And Truly', 'Charlestonette', 'Deep Henderson' and 'Deed I Do'. The latter, written with lyricist Walter Hirsch, was a hit for Ruth Etting. During the 30s Rose worked in Chicago, New York, and Nashville, before moving to Hollywood and collaborating with the enormously popular cowboy star Gene Autry. One of their songs, 'Be Honest With Me', from the movie *Ridin' On A Rainbow*, was nominated for an Academy Award in 1941, only to be beaten by Jerome Kern and Oscar Hammerstein II's 'The Last Time I Saw Paris'. Having stumbled into the area of country music virtually by accident, previously not particularly caring for the genre, Rose formed the first all-country music publishing company, Acuff-Rose Music, in 1942, with singer-fiddler-bandleader Roy Acuff, who was known as 'The King Of Country Music'. In 1946 the company signed Hank Williams to a writer's contract, although Williams could neither read or write music. All of Williams' hit records were produced by Rose, and he co-wrote several of them, including 'A Mansion On The Hill', 'Crazy Heart', 'Settin' The Woods On Fire', 'Kaw-Liga' and 'Take These Chains From My Heart'. The latter was subsequently given an agonized reading by Ray Charles in 1963. Rose's background was ideally suited to promote country hits across into the more popular field. His major successes included Pee Wee King's compositions, such as 'Slow Poke', a hit for Ralph Flanagan, Helen O'Connell and King himself; 'Bonaparte's Retreat', successful for Kay Starr and Gene Krupa; 'You Belong To Me', a US and UK number 1 hit for Jo Stafford; and 'Tennessee Waltz', recorded by several artists and a number 1 for Patti Page in 1950. Other big Acuff-Rose crossover hits included 'Your Cheatin' Heart' (Joni James), 'Hey, Good Lookin' (Frankie Laine and Jo Stafford) and 'Jambalaya' (the Carpenters). Rose's own compositions included 'Tears On My Pillow', 'I'm Trusting In You', 'You Waited Too Long', 'Blue Eyes Crying In The Rain', 'Sweet Kind Of Love', 'Texarkana Baby', 'Pins And Needles', 'Fire Ball Mail', No One Will Ever Know', 'We Live In Two Different Worlds', 'Home In San Antonio', 'Roly Poly', 'You'll Be Sorry When I'm Gone', and many more. His collaborators included Steve Nelson, Ed G. Nelson, and Hy Heath. After Fred Rose's death in 1954, his son Wesley took over his interest in Acuff-Rose.

● FURTHER READING: *Fred Rose And The Development Of The Nashville Music Industry, 1942-1954*, John Woodruff Rumble.

ROSE, JUDY

b. 1938, Chicago, USA, d. 25 November 1990, California, USA. The youngest daughter of Patsy Montana, she naturally followed in her mother's country music footsteps. She made her first public appearance at the age of four, when she sang 'Danny Boy' on the *National Barn Dance* on WLS Chicago. Eventually, she joined her elder sister Beverley (b. 1935, New York) and mother, who were then singing on WLS, and the three sang as a trio, until Beverley quit the music business (Patsy and Beverley were probably the first mother-daughter duo to sing on national radio). Judy also retired for a time but returned to work with her mother during the 60s, singing modern country songs as opposed to Patsy's old-time numbers. They played extensively in the USA and Judy also built herself a reputation as a solo artist, making appearances on the *Grand Ole Opry*. In the 70s and early 80s, she and Patsy made trips to Europe, during which they proved a popular act on several tours around the British country music clubs. In 1977, they even recorded an album together for Look Records in England. A September 1988 tour to Europe had to be cancelled, when Judy was found to be suffering with cancer. It seemed that the disease had successfully responded to treatment, when sadly, a recurrence resulted in her death in November 1990.

● ALBUMS: with Patsy Montana *Mum And Me* (Look 1977)★★★, *A Girl Nobody Knows* (Westwood 1978)★★★.

ROSE, WESLEY

b. 11 February 1918, Chicago, Illinois, USA, d. 26 April 1990, Nashville, Tennessee, USA. The son of Fred Rose, he lived with his mother when his parents divorced and after completing college, worked as an accountant in the Chicago offices of Standard Life. (He married Margaret Erdelyan on 16 November 1940 and they had one daughter, Scarlett.) In April 1945, while visiting an aunt in St. Louis, he was persuaded to call on his father. They had not seen each other since 1933 and he did not recognize Fred, nor, apparently, did the short-sighted Fred recognize his son. After this first reunion, Fred saw Wesley on his regular business trips to Chicago and tried to persuade him to work for the mighty Acuff-Rose publishing company, established by himself and Roy Acuff on 13 October 1942 as Nashville's first publishing house. At the time, Wesley Rose had no interest at all in country music and certainly no desire to live in Nashville. After considerable discussions and much hesitation on Wesley's part, he finally accepted his father's offer of the post of general manager with responsibility for all business decisions. From December 1945, Wesley Rose became a most important part of the family business and his undoubted business skills and accountancy training freed his father to concentrate more on handling the music side of the business - not least of all the emerging talent of Hank Williams. Although Wesley had no love for country music in his early days, he had no hesitation in believing that a good country song such as those written by Hank could be a hit

in popular music. He soon proved his point and made the initial breakthrough when, under his careful guidance, 'Cold Cold Heart' became a million-seller for Tony Bennett in 1951. Other crossover hits followed, including 'Jambalaya' for Jo Stafford and 'Hey Good Lookin'' for Frankie Laine. When Fred Rose died in 1954, Roy Acuff immediately recognized Wesley as the natural successor and placed him in full charge of all the company's business. Under his guidance the successes are too numerous to mention, but the company's list of talented songwriters included the Everly Brothers (whom he also managed for seven years), Don Gibson, Marty Robbins, the Louvin Brothers and Roy Orbison. In spite of his work as the head of the organization, Rose still became very active in record production of artists, including Bob Luman and others, on the company's Hickory Label, which he had founded. Exactly when Rose's opinion of country music changed is not clear, but in later years, he was certainly a staunch supporter of traditional country singers such as Boxcar Willie and, while he had no objections or qualms about using a country song for a crossover hit, he had a considerable abhorrence for rock 'n' roll. Several journalists have related the story of his statement that radio stations should not play a particular Elvis Presley recording because he always maintained that Presley was not a country singer. It was a dedicated belief, particularly when one takes into consideration that Acuff-Rose would have benefited by Presley's record sales, since the song concerned was on their own roster. Over the years, some of his dealings caused animosity and problems. In September 1982, Roy Orbison filed a $50 million suit accusing Wesley Rose of mismanagement and fraud; Rose had been his manager since 1958. It was settled out of court for around $3 million and then the law firm sued Orbison for non-payment of fees. The Everlys also had a disagreement with him. In the early 60s, they began to record songs that were not Acuff-Rose and dropped Rose as manager. He sued them for lack of earnings and refused to let Felice and Boudleaux Bryant give them any more songs. Don Everly took to writing songs under a pseudonym so that Rose could not seize them. Over the years, Rose became connected with many aspects of the industry and also served on various boards, including the Nashville Chamber Of Commerce, Vanderbilt Medical Centre, First American National Bank and Boy Scouts Of America. He was the first southern publisher elected to the board of ASCAP and also served as National President of NARAS. He was a founder-member of the Country Music Association, being chairman of the organization on three different occasions, and he also served on the board of Country Music Foundation. In 1986, he was elected to the Country Music Hall Of Fame, thus joining his father, who had been one of the first three entrants (with Jimmie Rodgers and Hank Williams) when the award was first created in 1961. He remained active with Acuff-Rose until the company was sold to Opryland USA in 1985. Wesley Rose, who was once the most powerful man in Nashville's music industry, died in 1990 in the Edgefield Hospital, Nashville. Mrs. Margaret Rose died in Nashville in late December 1990.

ROUNDER RECORDS

The label was founded in 1970 by Ken Irwin, Marian Leighton Levy and Bill Nowlin, three Boston-area college students, merely to further their common interest in traditional music and its contemporary offshoots. They released only two albums in their first year, 0001 George Pegram (a North Carolina banjoist) and 0002 Spark Gap Wonder Boys (a Cambridge old-time String Band). Initially, with financial support from other employment, they operated mainly as a home-based mail-order outlet, and by investing any profits they raised from selling their releases at festivals, they slowly built up the company. By the third year there were 19 releases. Now, with their ventures into varying types of music, the annual average is around 100. In the 70s, they became noted for releases of folk, blues and bluegrass music by such artists as Norman Blake and Del McCoury and achieved a major success with the first album by J.D. Crowe And The New South featuring Ricky Skaggs. In the late 70s, the label was boosted by sales of over 500,000 for two albums by blues guitarist George Thorogood. During the 80s, Rounder acquired the Philo label, which led to recordings by Nanci Griffith and Iris Dement, and in 1982, they founded their Heartbeat label as an outlet for reggae. By the mid-80s, their Modern New Orleans Masters series had been launched and the label has now become one of the most active labels to record Cajun and Zydeco music by such exponents as D.L Menard, Jo-El Sonnier and Buckwheat Zydeco. Their Bullseye label deals with white blues music. Bluegrass has always been an important genre and Rounder have released material by such leading exponents as Alison Krauss and the Johnson Mountain Boys. Releases of important early-day country artists include series of recordings of the Carter Family, Jimmie Rodgers and the Louvin Brothers. Their current catalogue exceeds 1,500 and they additionally represent 19 other labels on exclusive national and, in many cases, worldwide distribution. Their other business interests include Rounder Music (ASCAP), Happy Valley Music (BMI) (music publishing companies) and Roundup Records (mail-order retailer). There are over 20 independent distributors representing the Rounder group in countries around the world. In 1995 Rounder acquired Flying Fish Records, whose late founder Bruce Kaplan had originally worked with Rounder's founding trio. That year also brought Rounder multi-platinum awards for their work with Alison Krauss. The family feelgood factor and original spirit is still present after more than 25 years. The original three founders are equal shareholders in a company that now has an annual turnover in excess of $20 million, employs over 100 people and operates from three adjacent warehouses in Cambridge, Massachusetts.

● ALBUMS: *25 Years Of Rounder Records* 8-CD box set (Rounder 1995)★★★★.

● VIDEOS: *The Musical Family Of Rounder Records* (BMG 1995).

ROWAN BROTHERS

Chris and Lorin Rowan (both guitar, vocals) began working together as a duo in San Francisco, California, USA, during the early 70s. They were helped by Grateful Dead guitarist Jerry Garcia who occasionally played with them live. Their debut was a pleasant, if uninspired, collection. In 1975 the Rowans re-emerged as a trio with the addition of elder brother Peter Rowan, formerly of Earth Opera and Sea Train and a respected bluegrass musician. *The Rowan Brothers* was enhanced by his distinctive voice and skilled songwriting, as were their next two albums. Peter Rowan resumed his solo

career 18 months later, after which his younger brothers were dropped by their record label. In 1981 an Italian specialist outlet issued *Livin' The Life*, recorded in 1971 with the aid of Jerry Garcia, David Grisman and Grateful Dead drummer Bill Kreutzmann.

● ALBUMS: *The Rowan Brothers* (Columbia 1973)★★★★, *The Rowan Brothers* (Asylum 1975)★★★, *Sibling Rivalry* (Asylum 1976)★★★, *Jubilation* (Asylum 1977)★★★, *Livin' The Life* (Apoloosa 1981)★★★★.

ROWAN, PETER

b. 4 July 1942, Boston, Massachusetts, USA. Rowan's long career began as a member of the Cupids, a college band that developed his interest in an amalgam of Tex-Mex and roots music. After he graduated he played mandolin with the Mother Bay State Entertainers and later on joined two influential groups, the Charles River Valley Boys and Bill Monroe's Bluegrass Boys. For two years he led the critically acclaimed progressive rock band Earth Opera with fellow traditional acolyte David Grisman, before joining Sea Train in 1970. Although both units were rock-based, Rowan maintained his bluegrass roots as a member of Muleskinner, Old And In The Way, which also featured Jerry Garcia, and the Free Mexican Airforce. His subsequent solo work has placed the performer firmly within America's folk heritage. A prolific and engaging artist and now established as one of the leaders in his field of music, his recordings have embraced Tex-Mex, country, folk, acid rock and ethnic material, each of which has been performed with empathy and purpose. His vast catalogue also includes albums with his siblings, the Rowan Brothers.

● ALBUMS: *Peter Rowan* (Flying Fish 1979)★★★, *Medicine Trail* (Flying Fish 1980)★★★, *Peter Rowan* (Flying Fish 1980)★★★, *Hiroshima Mon Amour* (1980)★★★, *Peter Rowan, Richard Green And The Red Hot Pickers* (1980)★★★★, *Texican Badman* (Appaloosa 1981)★★★, *The Walls Of Time* (Sugar Hill 1981)★★★, *The Usual Suspect* (1982)★★, *Peter Rowan And The Wild Stallions* (Apaloosa 1983)★★★, *Peter Rowan And The Red Hot Pickers* (Sugar Hill 1984)★★★★, *Revelry* (Waterfront 1984)★★★, *Festival Tapes* (1985)★★★, *T Is For Texas* (Waterfront 1985)★★★, *The First Whipoorwill* (Sugar Hill 1985)★★★, with David Grisman, Keith, Greene And White *Muleskinner* (1987)★★★★, *New Moon Rising* (Special Delivery 1988)★★★, *Dust Bowl Children* (Sugar Hill 1989)★★★, *All On A Rising Day* (Special Delivery 1991)★★★, *Awake Me In The New World* (1993)★★★, as the Rowan Brothers *Tree On A Hill* (Sugar Hill 1994)★★★, *Bluegrass Boy* (Sugar Hill 1996)★★★, with Jerry Douglas *Yonder* (Sugar Hill 1996)★★★★, *Bluegrass Boy* (Sugar Hill 1997)★★★.

● VIDEOS: *Muleskinner - Live The Video* (1991).

ROYAL, BILLY JOE

b. 3 April 1942, Valdosta, Georgia, USA. Raised in Marietta, Georgia, Royal's father owned a truck-driving company and the family moved to Atlanta when Royal was aged 10. At school he entertained in school concerts, and after graduation, worked for two years in a nightclub in Savannah, Georgia. Starting in 1962, Royal made several unsuccessful singles, but then teamed with a local songwriter/producer, Joe South. In 1965 they made the US Top 20 with 'Down In The Boondocks' and 'I Knew You When', the latter of which in theme and vocal delivery was similar to Gene Pitney's hits. Royal's subsequent records were not as successful, but he failed to appreciate the potential of 'Rose Garden', as it later became a hit for Lynn Anderson. In 1969, he returned to the US Top 20 with 'Cherry Hill Park' and worked for several years in Las Vegas. Royal, whose early influences came from country musicians, turned to country music and his 1987 *Looking Ahead* spent a year on the US country albums chart. His US country hits include 'Burned Like A Rocket', 'I'll Pin A Note On Your Pillow', 'I Miss You Already' and a duet with Donna Fargo, 'Members Only'. He has also revived Aaron Neville's 'Tell It Like It Is' and Johnny Tillotson's 'It Keeps Right On A-Hurtin''. He continues to make successful singles and regularly appears in the US country chart.

● ALBUMS: *Down In The Boondocks* (Columbia 1965)★★★, *Billy Joe Royal* (Columbia 1965)★★★, *Hush* (Columbia 1967)★★★, *Cherry Hill Park* (Columbia 1969)★★★, *Looking Ahead* (Atlantic 1987)★★★★, *The Royal Treatment* (Atlantic 1987)★★★, *Tell It Like It Is* (Atlantic 1989)★★★, *Out Of The Shadows* (Atlantic 1990)★★★.

● COMPILATIONS: *Greatest Hits* (Columbia 1989)★★★, *Greatest Hits* (Atlantic 1991)★★★★, *The Best Of Billy Joe Royal* (Sony 1995)★★★★.

RUN C&W

Run C&W are country music's equivalent to the Travelin' Wilburys. Here, four key musicians pretend to be a bluegrass band who know nothing of modern life and perform 60s soul standards as though they are traditional tunes. You can hear a herd of cows in Ray Charles' 'What'd I Say' and country stars are substituted for the soul brothers in 'Sweet Soul Music'. The group consists of Russell Smith (Rug Burns) together with ex-Eagles and Flying Burrito Brothers Bernie Leadon (Crashen Burns), Vince Melamed (Wash Burns) and Jim Photoglo (Side Burns), collectively known as the Burns Brothers. With backgrounds such as the Eagles and the Amazing Rhythm Aces, the playing is immaculate and the results are often hilarious. The second album, dispensing with the dialogue from the first set, includes guest appearances from George Jones (Possum Burns) and Vince Gill (Sun Burns) on Joe Tex's 'Hold What You Got'. It was inevitable that the band would split and Russell Smith re-formed the Amazing Rhythm Aces. Their two albums of rhythm and bluegrass deserve to remain in catalogue.

● ALBUMS: *Into The Twangy-First Century* (MCA 1993)★★★, *Row Vs Wade* (MCA 1994)★★★.

RUSSELL, JOHNNY

b. John Bright Russell, 23 January 1940, Sunflower County, Mississippi, USA. Russell's family moved to Fresno, California, when he was 12 years old and his ambitions were centred around country music. He wrote his own songs and performed as a singer/guitarist. Jim Reeves heard his first record, 'In A Mansion Stands My Love' (for Radio Records when he was 18), and recorded the song as the b-side of 'He'll Have To Go'. Other early Russell compositions include Loretta Lynn's 'Two Mules Pull This Wagon' and the Wilburn Brothers' 'Hurt Her Once For Me'. Russell was working on a song about Hollywood but a chance remark, 'They're gonna put me in the movies', enabled him to complete it as 'Act Naturally'. Russell's co-writer, Vonnie Morrison, placed the song with Buck Owens and it became a number 1 US

country hit. 'Act Naturally' was recorded by the Beatles with Ringo Starr on lead vocals for their *Help!* album, and was also the b-side of their US number 1, 'Yesterday'. Russell, who had recorded as a sideline for MGM and ABC-Paramount, took his own career seriously when he signed with Chet Atkins for RCA in 1971. He had US country hits with 'Catfish John', 'The Baptism Of Jesse Taylor', 'She's In Love With A Rodeo Man' and, most significantly, 'Rednecks, White Socks And Blue Ribbon Beer', which became an anthem in the south. 'I was appearing on Charley Pride's road show,' says Russell, 'and he wouldn't let me sing the song 'cause he thought it was racial.' Strangely, Russell did not write his biggest RCA singles. He explains, 'I like singing people songs and as I tend to write hurting love songs, I never wrote the kind of songs that were right for me.' Russell's 1977 single 'Obscene Phone Call' was banned by several US radio stations. In 1978 he moved to Mercury and his singles included 'While The Choir Sang The Hymn, I Thought Of Her', 'You'll Be Back Every Night In My Dreams' and 'Song Of The South'. Russell married his second wife, Beverly Heckel, in 1977 when she was 17. She had her own chart success with 'Bluer Than Blue' and she joined his stage show. George Strait had a US country number 1 in 1984 with Russell's 'Let's Fall To Pieces Together' and Gene Watson did well with 'I Got No Reason Now For Going Home'. Although Johnny Russell's name was known only to die-hard fans in the UK, he was a show-stopper at the 1985 Wembley country music festival with his Burl Ives-styled personality and humour (Ives did, in fact, record a Russell song, 'Mean Mean Man'). Russell weighs 25 stone and his opening remark, 'Can you all see me at the back?', was a winner; a successful UK tour with Boxcar Willie followed. A heart attack put Russell out of action for some time but he is now back on the road and still remains one of Nashville's leading songwriters. As he says, 'I carry a lot of weight in this town.'

● ALBUMS: *Mr. And Mrs. Untrue* (1971)★★★, *Catfish John/Chained* (RCA Victor 1972)★★★, *Rednecks, White Socks And Blue-Ribbon Beer* (RCA Victor 1973)★★, *She's In Love With A Rodeo Man* (RCA Victor 1974)★★★, *Here Comes Johnny Russell* (RCA Victor 1975)★★★, *Something Old Something New* (1991)★★.

RUSSELL, TOM

b. 5 March 1950, Arizona, USA. The 90s country singer Tom Russell grew up on a ranch in Santa Monica and had twin influences of cowboys and country music. He says, 'Southern California was very rich in country music, not only with Merle Haggard and Buck Owens, but also the Hollywood cowboy scene. My brother became a full-on cowboy. It's in the blood.' In the 60s, Russell became immersed in folk and blues music, and he became very interested in Ian And Sylvia (Tyson). After playing numerous small-scale gigs, he struck lucky in 1974 when a song about the end of the Indian culture in Canada, 'End Of The Trail', won an award at an American song festival and was recorded by the Hagers. Tom then worked with the pianist Patricia Hardin as a folk duo, Hardin And Russell, strongly influenced by Ian And Sylvia. They recorded two excellent albums, *Ring Of Bone* and *Wax Museum*. Russell moved to New York in 1980 and after trying to establish contacts, he was offered work at a circus in Puerto Rico. 'I was drinking a lot and my marriage was breaking up. I learnt all the time that there are lower depths to hell because the carnival was a major fiasco and there was a lot of violence. I had to sing "Folsom Prison Blues" with a French-Canadian disco band, who couldn't speak much English and hated country music, to a Puerto Rican audience, who couldn't speak English and also hated country music. It was a real life Fellini movie and I wrote about it in "Road To Bayoman". Russell started driving a cab in New York City and met up with Andrew Hardin, the guitarist who has since been his long-time musical partner. One of his passengers, Robert Hunter, the lyricist for the Grateful Dead, encouraged him to return to music by having him open for that band. 'Gallo Del Cielo', a brilliant song about cock-fighting, was recorded by Ian Tyson, leading to a songwriting and performing relationship, including 'Navajo Rug', which was recorded by Jerry Jeff Walker. Russell has also written with, and produced albums for, Tyson's ex-wife Sylvia Tyson, and one of their joint songs is 'Chocolate Cigarettes' about Edith Piaf. Russell has also written songs about Little Willie John ('Blue Wing'), Bill Haley ('Haley's Comet') and Mitch Ryder ('The Extra Mile'). He wrote 'Walking On The Moon' with Katy Moffatt, 'Outbound Plane' with Nanci Griffith and 'Angel Of Lyon' with Steve Young. He has also produced the R&B musician Barrence Whitfield singing folk and country songs, and occasionally, Andrew Hardin, Russell and Whitfield work as the Hillbilly Voodoo Trio. He has also played with Dave Alvin - they co-wrote 'Haley's Comet' and also co-produced a tribute album to Merle Haggard, *Tulare Dust*. Russell is both a superb and a prolific writer, a latter-day John Stewart, possessing his integrity and also chronicling the life of blue-collar America. Many of the songs reflect incidents in his own life and he relives his worst gig in one - 'We were just outside Toronto during Halloween week and these people were so ugly that they came to the party dressed as AIDS patients. You couldn't find a decent bite to eat and our car was hit head on by some drunk kid. It was in the dead of winter in Canada, 20 below zero, and there were fights all the time. It's all in that song, "Northern Towns".

● ALBUMS: *Heart On A Sleeve* (Bear Family 1984)★★★, *Box Of Visions* (Round Tower 1993)★★★, with Barrence Whitfield *Hillbilly Voodoo* (Round Tower 1993)★★★, with Whitfield *Cowboy Mambo* (Round Tower 1994)★★★, *The Rose Of The San Joaquin* (Round Tower 1995)★★★★. As Hardin And Russell *Ring Of Bone* (Dark Angel 1976)★★★★, *Wax Museum* (Dark Angel 1978)★★★, *Road To Bayamon* (Rounder 1987)★★★★, *Poor Man's Dream* (Round Tower 1989)★★★, *Hurricane Season* (Round Tower 1991)★★★, *Cowboy Real* (Munich 1991)★★★, *Out Of California* mini-album (Round Tower 1996)★★★, *Song Of The West* (Hightone 1997)★★★.

● COMPILATIONS: *Beyond St Olav's Gate, 1979-1992* (Round Tower 1992)★★★, with Hardin *The Early Years 1975-79* (Edsel 1996)★★★★, *The Long Way Around: The Acoustic Collection* (Hightone 1997)★★★★.

● FURTHER READING: *And Then I Wrote*, Tom Russell and Sylvia Tyson.

SAHM, DOUG

b. 6 November 1941, San Antonio, Texas, USA. Born of Lebanese-American extraction, Sahm is a highly knowledgeable and superbly competent performer of Texan musical styles, whether they be blues, country, rock 'n' roll, western swing, Cajun or polkas. He made his recording debut in 1955 with 'A Real American Joe' under the name of Little Doug Sahm, and within three years was fronting the Pharoahs, the first of several rough-hewn backing groups. Sahm recorded a succession of singles for local labels, including his Little Richard pastiche 'Crazy Daisy' (1959), plus 'Sapphire' (1961) and 'If You Ever Need Me' (1964). For several years, Sahm had been pestering producer Huey P. Meaux to record him. Meaux, having success with Barbara Lynn and Dale And Grace, was not interested. However, the producer found himself without a market when Beatlemania hit America, and shut himself away in a hotel with the Beatles' records, determined to discover what made them sell. He then called Sahm, told him to grow his hair, form a group and write a tune with a Cajun two-step beat. Accordingly, Sahm assembled his friends, Augie Meyers (keyboards), Frank Morin (saxophone), Harvey Kagan (bass) and Johnny Perez (drums). Meaux gave them an English-sounding name, the Sir Douglas Quintet, and subsequently scored an international hit in 1965 with the catchy 'She's About A Mover'. The group also had success in the US charts with 'The Rains Came', but after being arrested for possession of drugs, the group disbanded and Sahm moved to California to avoid a heavy fine. He formed the Honkey Blues Band, but had difficulty in getting it on the road. He then gathered the rest of the Quintet in California for another classic single, 'Mendocino', its spoken introduction being characteristic of the hippie era. The album, also called *Mendocino*, is a forerunner of country rock. The Sir Douglas Quintet toured Europe and made the successful *Together After Five*, while Sahm made an excellent country single under the name of Wayne Douglas, 'Be Real'. He moved to Prunedale in northern California and befriended a Chicano band, Louie And The Lovers, producing their *Rise*. Sahm, having resolved his problems with the authorities, went back to Texas and released *The Return Of Doug Saldaña*, the name reflecting his affection for Chicanos. The album, co-produced with Meaux, included an affectionate tribute to Freddy Fender, 'Wasted Days And Wasted Nights', which prompted Meaux to resurrect Fender's career and turn him into a country superstar. Sahm appeared with Kris Kristofferson in the film *Cisco Pike*, and told his record company that a song he performed, 'Michoacan', was about a state in Mexico. Disc jockeys, however, realized that he was actually praising marijuana and air play was restricted. Atlantic Records' key producer, Jerry Wexler, decided that progressive country was becoming fashionable and signed both Willie Nelson and Doug Sahm. Sahm's high-spirited *Doug Sahm And Band*, was made in New York with Bob Dylan, Dr. John and accordionist Flaco Jiminez, and Sahm achieved minor success with 'Is Anybody Going To San Antone?'. The Sir Douglas Quintet was resurrected intermittently which resulted in two fine live albums, *Wanted Very Much Alive* and *Back To The 'Dillo*. Although it might seem strange that the band should tour with the new wave band the Pretenders, Sahm's voice and style were arguably an influence on Elvis Costello. Sahm himself says, 'I'm a part of Willie Nelson's world and at the same time I'm a part of the Grateful Dead's. I don't ever stay in one bag'. Among Sahm's finest albums are *Hell Of A Spell*, a blues album dedicated to Guitar Slim, and *The Return Of The Formerly Brothers*, with guitarist Amos Garrett and pianist 'Gene Taylor. In 1990 Sahm formed the Texas Tornados with Meyers, Jiminez and Fender. The debut album, which included Sahm's witty 'Who Were You Thinkin' Of?, showed that he had lost none of his powers, and subsequent Tornados releases were equally popular. In the UK, the Sir Douglas Quintet may be regarded as one-hit-wonders, but in reality Sahm has recorded a remarkable catalogue of Texas music. *Day Dreaming At Midnight* was a prime example; it was produced by ex-Creedence Clearwater Revival member Doug Clifford and was a rousing collection, notable for 'Too Little Too Late' and the blistering Bob Dylan pastiche 'Dylan Come Lately'.

● ALBUMS: *Doug Sahm And Band* (Atlantic 1973)★★, *Rough Edges* (Mercury 1973)★★, *Texas Tornado* (Atlantic 1973)★★★, *Groovers Paradise* (Warners 1974)★★★, *Texas Rock For Country Rollers* (ABC/Dot 1976)★★★, *Live Love* (1977)★★, *Hell Of A Spell* (Takoma 1979)★★★, *Texas Road Runner* (Moonshine 1986)★★★, *Live Doug Sahm* (Topline 1987)★★★, *Back To The 'Dillo* (Sonet 1988)★★★★, with Amos Garrett, Gene Taylor *The Return Of The Formerly Brothers* (Stony Plain 1988)★★★, *Juke Box Music* (Antone's 1989)★★★★, *Day Dreaming At Midnight* (Elektra 1994)★★★★, *The Last Real Texas Blues Band* (Antone's 1995)★★★.

● COMPILATIONS: *Sir Douglas - Way Back When He Was Just Doug Sahm* (1979)★★★, *Sir Douglas - His First Recordings* (1981)★★★, *Sir Doug's Recording Trip* (Edsel 1989)★★★, *The Best Of Doug Sahm And The Sir Douglas Quintet* (Rhino 1991)★★★★.

SAMPLES, JUNIOR

b. Alvin Samples, 10 August 1926, Cumming, Georgia, USA, d. 13 November 1983, Cumming, Georgia, USA. Samples had worked for most of his life in a sawmill, when he became an unexpected star. Weighing in at well over 20 stone, he revelled in being called the 'world's biggest liar' - a title he acquired from relating what some termed 'hilarious' tales. One such story brought him to the attention of Chart Records and he scored a minor country hit in 1967 with 'World's Biggest Whopper'. He subsequently recorded a solo album and one with fellow comedian Archie Campbell. This record success saw him become a member of *Hee Haw* even though, in the words of Bill C. Malone, 'he was at the time a natural but semi-literate rural comedian with virtually no professional experience'. Samples died suddenly following a heart attack at his home in 1983.

● ALBUMS: *The World Of Junior Samples* (Chart 1967)★★, with Archie Campbell *Bull Session At Bull's Gap* (Chart 1968)★★, *That's A Hee Haw* (Chart 1970)★★.

● COMPILATIONS: *The Best Of Junior Samples* (Chart 1971)★★★.

SANDERS, ED

A veteran of New York's bohemian enclave, poet Sanders co-founded the Peace Eye Bookstore and edited the publication *Fuck You - A Magazine Of The Arts*, before joining Tuli Kupferberg and Ken Weaver in the Fugs. Sanders wrote many of this irreverent group's best-known songs, including 'Frenzy', 'Wet Dream' and 'Ramses II Is Dead, My Love'. He embarked on a solo career following the Fugs' disintegration, completing two country-influenced albums, which, if not commercially successful, did at least inspire a cult following. However, Sanders is better known for his literary work, in particular his book *The Family* (1971), a widely acclaimed investigative account of the Charles Manson and Sharon Tate murder case. During the 80s Sanders collaborated with Shockabilly on *Nicaragua*, and reconvened the Fugs for a series of fascinating releases. In 1987 his poetry was anthologized in *Thirsting For Peace In A Raging Century*.

● ALBUMS: *Sanders' Truckstop* (Reprise 1969)★★★, *Beer Cans On The Moon* (1973)★★.

SANDERS, MARK D.

b. Mark Daniel Sanders, Southern California, USA. Sanders obtained a degree in literature - he later write a song using the name of the US author, Bobbie Ann Mason, for Rick Trevino - and worked as a teacher. This work did not satisfy him and he moved to Nashville with the idea of becoming a successful songwriter. He drove a tour bus around Twitty City and gradually his songs were accepted - first by Vince Gill ('Oh Carolina') and then by Judy Rodman, who had a hit with 'Girls Ride Horses, Too'. His publishing company is called Starstruck and his successes include 'Money In The Bank' (Jon Anderson), 'Mirror, Mirror' (Diamond Rio), 'Runnin' Behind' (Tracy Lawrence), 'Victim Of The Game' (Garth Brooks) and 'The Heart Is A Lonely Hunter' (Reba McEntire). He had an extraordinary year in 1996 with 10 considerable country hits including 'It Matters To Me' (Faith Hill), 'Blue Clear Sky' (George Strait), 'No News' (Lonestar), 'Daddy's Money' (Ricochet) and 'Don't Get Me Started' (Rhett Atkins), all of which were number 1 country singles. His best song is the irresistible 'Heads Carolina, Tails California', a country number 2 for Jo Dee Messina, in which he applied Bruce Springsteen's trademarks to country music. He includes more wry humour in his songs than most Nashville songwriters. Sanders has been so successful that he has featured in business magazines. He says, 'I write about 80 songs a year but I write better when I work at that pace.'

SATHERLEY, ART

b. Arthur Edward Satherley, 19 October 1889, Bristol, England, d. 1986. Known as 'Uncle Art', Satherley was a pioneer in the US recording industry during the 20s and 30s. As a talent scout, producer and A&R representative, he was credited with providing the American Recording Company with one of the strongest country music catalogues in the USA. After travelling to America in 1913, he worked for the Wisconsin Chair Company, which also made phonograph cabinets. He soon moved into the recording business, promoting blues artists such as Ma Rainey, Blind Blake and Blind Lemon Jefferson for the Paramount label. In 1929, he joined the newly formed ARC, and toured the USA in search of new talent in the areas of country, hillbilly, blues and 'race' music, and was at the forefront in promoting new markets. During the 30s he recorded artists such as Hank Penny, Roy Acuff, Bob Wills, Big Bill Broonzy, Bill and Cliff Carlisle, Blind Boy Fuller and Gene Autry. The latter had enormous hits with 'Silver Haired Mother Of Mine', 'Yellow Rose Of Texas' and 'Tumbling Tumbleweeds'. When ARC became Columbia in 1938, Satherley stayed with the company as an A&R executive until his retirement in 1952. Among the artists whose careers he guided and influenced were Marty Robbins, Lefty Frizzell, Bill Monroe, Carl Smith, Spade Cooley, Al Dexter and Little Jimmy Dickens. Satherley's assistant for many years, David Law, eventually became a leading producer, and was responsible for the early recordings of David Frizzell, younger brother of the legendary Lefty. Satherley was elected to the Country Music Hall Of Fame in 1971 for his pioneering work in the genre.

● COMPILATIONS: *Uncle Art Satherley: Country Music's Father* (Columbia 1991)★★★★.

SAUNDERS, JANE

b. 1966, Windsor, New South Wales, Australia. The family of 90s country singer Jane Saunders moved to the Blue Mountains when she was young, and she describes the area as 'pretty, picturesque with not many neighbours'. She met her husband, David Saunders, in 1985 and he backed her on guitar. A track from her promotional tape was used on a compilation, *The Best Of Australia*, and she was subsequently signed to ABC Records. She wrote several songs on her debut album, *Stranger To Your Heart*, and the others were carefully chosen. 'Life In A Small Town' was nominated for Song Of The Year in the Australian Country Music Awards. Her producer is John Kane of the Flying Emus and she has worked with John's wife, Genni, and Shanley Del as Saunders, Kane and Del, a country harmony group that owes much to the *Trio* album by Dolly Parton, Emmylou Harris and Linda Ronstadt. The key track is a gorgeous version of the Beatles' 'Here Comes The Sun'. She is also featured on 'I Am A Child', a single by Rod McCormack and Mick Albeck. Saunders' voice, choice of material and acoustic music are all extremely impressive.

● ALBUMS: *Stranger To Your Heart* (ABC Australia 1994)★★★, as Saunders, Kane And Del *Tea For Three* (ABC Australia 1995)★★★.

SAWYER BROWN

The members of the band Sawyer Brown come from different parts of the USA: Mark Miller (b. Dayton, Ohio, USA; vocals) and Gregg Hubbard (keyboards) were schoolfriends in Apopka, Florida; Bobby Randall (b. Midland, Michigan, USA, guitar), Jim Scholten (b. Michigan, USA; bass) and Joe Smyth (drums) were part of the Maine Symphony Orchestra. They all came to Nashville around 1980 and took varying roles in singer Don King's band. In 1983 they decided to work together without King, first as Savanna and then as Sawyer Brown, taking their name from a street in Nashville. In 1983, they took part in a US television talent show, *Star Search*. They won the first prize of $100,000 and a

recording contract. Their first single, 'Leona', was a US country hit and they toured with Kenny Rogers and Dolly Parton. Miller wrote their second single, a country number 1 hit, 'Step That Step' (1985), about the perseverance needed in the music business. They established themselves as a goodtime country band and had further country hits with 'Used To Blue', 'Betty's Bein' Bad', 'This Missin' You Heart Of Mine' and a remake of George Jones' 'The Race Is On'. 'My Baby's Gone' made number 11 on the country charts in 1988 and, despite losing some of their impetus, they returned with two Top 5 hits from 1992's successful *The Dirt Road*. Having consistently produced Top 10 hits since then, they went on to win the Vocal Group Award at the 32nd Academy Of Country Music Awards.

● ALBUMS: *Sawyer Brown* (Capitol/Curb 1985)★★★, *Shakin'* (Capitol/Curb 1985)★★★, *Out Goin' Cattin'* (Capitol/Curb 1986)★★★, *Somewhere In The Night* (Capitol/Curb 1987)★★★, *Wide Open* (Capitol/Curb 1988)★★★, *The Boys Are Back* (Capitol/Curb 1989)★★★, *Buick* (Curb 1991)★★★, *The Dirt Road* (Curb 1992)★★★, *Cafe On The Corner* (Curb 1992)★★★, *Outskirts Of Town* (Curb 1993)★★, *This Thing Called Wantin' And Havin' It All* (Curb 1995)★★, *Six Days On The Road* (Curb 1997)★★★.

● COMPILATIONS: *Greatest Hits* (Curb 1990)★★★, *Greatest Hits 1990-1995* (Curb 1995)★★★★.

● VIDEOS: *Greatest Video Hits: Vol. 2* (1993), *This Time* (Curb 1994), *Outskirts Of Town* (High Five 1994), *I Don't Believe In Goodbye* (Curb 1995).

SCHNEIDER, JOHN

b. 8 April 1954, Mount Kisco, Westchester County, New York, USA. Schneider, a gifted musician and actor, has appeared in musicals from the age of 14. He played Bo Duke in the long-running US television series about a disaster-prone hillbilly family, *The Dukes Of Hazzard*, from 1979-85. He is featured on the 1982 cast album of the same name. In 1981 he had his first US hit (pop chart number 14, country number 4) with a revival of Elvis Presley's 'It's Now Or Never', and proved himself to be one television star who could sing. However, despite other successes on the US country chart, he was not accepted as a bona fide artist by country disc jockeys. In 1984, the disc jockeys were given unmarked copies of 'I've Been Around Enough To Know', and many of them played the record believing it to be by George Strait. Schneider's identity was revealed and the single topped the US country chart. He had further number 1s with 'Country Girls', 'What's A Memory Like You (Doing In A Love Like This)?' and 'You're The Last Thing I Needed Tonight'. Schneider, however, unlike most country stars, did not care for touring and his final US Top 10 country hit was in 1987 with 'Love, You Ain't Seen The Last Of Me', at a time when he was planning just that. He returned to acting and was in a successful series, *Grand Slam*, in 1990.

● ALBUMS: *Now Or Never* (Scotti Bros 1981)★★★, *White Christmas* (Scotti Bros 1981)★★, *Dukes Of Hazzard* television cast (Scotti Bros 1982)★★, *Quiet Man* (1982)★★, with Jill Michaels *If You Believe* (1983)★★, *Too Good To Stop Now* (MCA 1984)★★★, *Trying To Outrun The Wind* (MCA 1985)★★★, *A Memory Like You* (MCA 1986)★★★, *Take The Long Way Home* (MCA 1986)★★★, *You Ain't Seen The Last Of Me!* (MCA 1987)★★★.

● COMPILATIONS: *Greatest Hits* (MCA 1987)★★★.

SCHNEIDER, MARY

b. c.1933, Rockampton, Queensland, Australia. From a German family, she grew up in Brisbane and began performing with elder sister Rita (b. c.1928) after being influenced by radio broadcasts of Carson Jay Robison And His Pioneers. They played local venues and entertained troops before finally establishing themselves with an appearance on Australia's Amateur Hour in 1945. Their act, which contained singing, yodelling and comedy, eventually included their 'schneiderphone' - a one-man band contraption that consisted of a washboard with horns, bells, cymbals and various other noise-making gadgets attached. They recorded eight sides for Regal-Zonophone in 1950 and during the 50s and 60s, they toured extensively throughout Australia, New Zealand, Asia and the Far East. They appeared on countless television programmes and even recorded an EP of rock 'n' roll music called Rockin' With The Schneider Sisters for Magnasound. In 1970, they did a major tour of American bases in the Far East that, at one stage, saw them play no less than 170 shows (including 20 in 12 days), during a four and a half-month period that comprised only part of the tour. In 1972, after further tours, they decided amicably to stop performing as a duo. Rita (who later recorded an EP, Country Fun, for Hadley) had developed an interest in writing and began working within the television industry, while Mary went on to develop her solo act. She even experimented with jazz and blues but soon began to place more and more emphasis on her yodelling and quickly became very proficient in varying styles of the art. She had been initially attracted to yodelling after hearing recordings of Harry Torrani and the Austrian yodeller Minna Reverelli, as well as her natural interest in such country yodellers as Elton Britt. Her busy schedules seemingly left little time for recording, in spite of many requests for her to do so from her fans. Surprisingly, with many rating her as one of the finest yodellers, she herself at one stage modestly doubted her own abilities and for a time, seemed reluctant to make recordings. Always in demand, she toured for almost 10 years before she eventually decided to record some yodel numbers. When record companies told her 'there is no demand for yodelling', she ignored them and financed her own Magic Of Yodelling. Initially released on the Bluebell label, it received extensive air play on 2KY Sydney and after being taken over by KTel, it soon went platinum. In 1984, she recorded a double album, Can't Stop Yodelling, which did well until the record company ran into difficulties. Two years later, it was reissued on Colstal and after television exposure, it also became a big seller. In 1994, after working with Rita to produce lyrics for popular classics such as 'The Skater's Waltz', 'In A Monastery Garden' and 'Tritsch Tratsch Polka', she demonstrated her amazing abilities by recording what knowledgeable experts of the art have described as 'a yodelling masterpiece'. She is constantly in demand for live appearances and tours extensively, usually accompanied by her talented daughter Melinda, a modern performer in her own right. Her much talked-about version of Toranni's 'Mockingbird Yodel' was released in the UK on Yodelling Crazy by EMI in 1992. The early duet recordings and the Magnasound EP (for which it is reported they never received payment) are now collector's items.

● ALBUMS: Magic Of Yodelling (Bluebell/K-Tel 1981)★★★, Can't Stop Yodelling (K-Tel 1984, reissued Colstal 1986)★★★, Sound Of Yodelling (Paganini 1991)★★, Yodelling The Classics (Dino 1994)★★.

SCOTTSVILLE SQUIRREL BARKERS

This historically important bluegrass band - also known as the Kentucky Mountain Boys - was formed in 1958 by patrons of a San Diego club, the Blue Guitar. Its proprietor, Ed Douglas, played bass in the founding line-up alongside Larry Murray (guitar, vocals), Kenny Wertz (guitar, banjo), Gary Carr (guitar) and Chris Hillman (mandolin, vocals). They remained active for four years, during which time Bernie Leadon replaced Wertz. This version of the Barkers was featured on Bluegrass Favourites, which was distributed solely in local supermarkets. The quintet broke up soon after its release. Hillman teamed with Rex and Vern Godsin in the Hillmen, before rejoining Murray in the Green Grass Group. He later became a founder-member of the Byrds, while Murray and Leadon were reunited in Hearts And Flowers. Wertz, meanwhile, resurfaced in Country Gazette.

● ALBUMS: Bluegrass Favourites (Crown 1962)★★★.

SCRUGGS, EARL

b. 6 January 1924, Cleveland County, North Carolina, USA. Scruggs was raised in the Appalachian Mountains, and learned to play banjo from the age of five. In 1944, he joined Bill Monroe's Bluegrass Boys, where he perfected his three-finger banjo technique. He later left with fellow member Lester Flatt, to form the Foggy Mountain Boys in 1948. They enjoyed a long career spanning 20 years, and were reportedly only outsold during the 60s, on CBS Records, by Johnny Cash. The duo became synonymous with their recordings of 'Foggy Mountain Breakdown', which was used in the film Bonnie And Clyde and 'The Ballad Of Jed Clampett', which was the theme tune for the television series The Beverly Hillbillies. In 1969, after Flatt and Scruggs parted company, the Earl Scruggs Revue was formed featuring Earl (banjo, vocals), and his sons, Randy (lead guitar, slide guitar, bass, vocals), Gary (bass, harmonica, vocals), Steve (guitar), plus Josh Graves (dobro, guitar, vocals) and Jody Maphis (drums, vocals). His Family And Friends, which comes from a 1971 National Educational Television Soundtrack, included guest appearances by Bob Dylan, Joan Baez and the Byrds. Anniversary Special, Volume 1 included a broad line-up from the music scene, including Roger McGuinn and Dan Fogelberg. Graves left the group during the mid-70s to pursue a solo career. Scruggs' innovation in taking traditional fiddle tunes and transposing them for playing on banjo helped push back the boundaries of bluegrass, and paved the way for the later 'Newgrass' revival.

● ALBUMS: Earl Scruggs, 5-String Instructional Album (Peer International 1967)★★★, Nashville's Rock (1970)★★★, Where Lillies Bloom (1970)★★★, Earl Scruggs Performing With His Family And Friends (1972)★★★, I Saw The Light With Some Help From My Friends (1972)★★★, Live At Kansas State (Columbia 1972)★★★, Duelling Banjos (Columbia 1973)★★★★, The Earl Scruggs Revue (Columbia 1973)★★★★, Rockin' 'Cross The Country (Columbia 1974)★★★, Anniversary Special, Volume 1 (1975)★★★★, The Earl Scruggs Revue, Volume 2 (1976)★★★★, Family Portrait (1976)★★★, Live From Austin City Limits (1977)★★★, Strike Anywhere (1977)★★★, Bold And New (1978)★★★, Today And Forever (1979)★★★, with Tom T.

Hall *The Storyteller And The Banjoman* (1982)★★★★, *Top Of The World* (1983)★★★.
● FURTHER READING: *Earl Scruggs And The 5-String Banjo*, Earl Scruggs

SEALS, DAN

b. 8 February 1948, McCamey, Texas, USA. Leaving successful pop duo England Dan And John Ford Coley was, at first, a disastrous career move for Dan Seals. His management left him with unpaid tax bills and mounting debts and he lost his house, his van and his money. He says, 'I was bankrupt, separated and living at friends' places. My kids were with friends. It was a real bad time'. Furthermore, the two albums that he made for Atlantic Records as a solo artist, *Stones* and *Harbinger*, had little impact. However, Kyle Lehning, who produced his hits with England Dan And John Ford Coley, never lost faith and helped to establish him on the US country charts with 'Everybody's Dream Girl' in 1983. Further country hits followed and he had a US number 1 hit with 'Meet Me In Montana', a duet with Marie Osmond, in 1985. Seals then had an extraordinary run of nine consecutive US number 1 country singles: the dancing 'Bop', the rodeo story 'Everything That Glitters (Is Not Gold)', 'You Still Move Me', 'I Will Be There', 'Three Time Loser', the wedding song 'One Friend', 'Addicted' and 'Big Wheels In The Moonlight', many of which he wrote himself. Two further number 1 hits in 1990 included a reworking of soul singer Sam Cooke's 'Good Times'. *Won't Be Blue Anymore* sold half a million copies in the USA, while another big-selling record, *On The Front Line*, included an exquisite duet with Emmylou Harris, 'Lullaby'. Seals signed to Warner Brothers Records in 1991, but *Walking The Wire* was a commercial failure and he has since concentrated on touring. *In A Quiet Room* features acoustic versions of Seals' best-known songs.
● ALBUMS: *Stones* (Atlantic 1980)★★, *Harbinger* (Atlantic 1982)★★, *Rebel Heart* (Liberty 1983)★★, *San Antone* (EMI America 1984)★★, *Won't Be Blue Anymore* (EMI America 1985)★★, *On The Front Line* (EMI America 1986)★★, *Rage On* (Capitol 1988)★★, *On Arrival* (Capitol 1990)★★, *Walking The Wire* (Warners 1992)★★, *In A Quiet Room* (Intersound 1995)★★.
● COMPILATIONS: *The Best Of Dan Seals* (Capitol 1987)★★★, *Early Dan Seals* (Liberty 1991)★★★, *Greatest Hits* (Liberty 1991)★★★.

SEALS, TROY

b. 16 November 1938, Big Hill, Kentucky, USA. Seals, a cousin of Dan Seals, began playing guitar in his teens and formed his own rock 'n' roll band. In 1960, he was working in a club in Ohio with Lonnie Mack and Denny Rice, where he befriended a visiting performer, Conway Twitty. Twitty introduced him to Jo Ann Campbell, who had had a few successes on the US pop charts. Seals married Campbell and they worked as a duo, making the US R&B charts with 'I Found A Love, Oh What A Love' in 1964. After some time spent as a construction worker, Seals moved to Nashville to sell his songs. 'There's A Honky Tonk Angel (Who'll Take Me Back In)', written by Seals and Rice, was a US country number 1 for Conway Twitty, while Cliff Richard's version for the UK market was withdrawn when he discovered what honky tonk angels were (!). Elvis Presley also recorded the song, along with Seals' 'Pieces Of My Life'. Seals' most

recorded song is 'We Had It All', written with Donnie Fritts, which has been recorded by Rita Coolidge, Waylon Jennings, Brenda Lee, Stu Stevens and Scott Walker. His songwriting partners include Don Goodman and Will Jennings, a university professor in English literature, and together they all wrote 'Feelins'', a US country number 1 for Conway Twitty and Loretta Lynn; he also wrote with Mentor Williams 'When We Make Love', a US country number 1 for Alabama, and with Max D. Barnes 'Don't Take It Away' (another US country number 1 for Conway Twitty) and 'Storms Of Life' (Randy Travis). One of his best songs is the mysterious 'Seven Spanish Angels', written with Eddie Setser, a US country number 1 for Willie Nelson and Ray Charles. Seals has done much session work as a guitarist and has had a few minor country hits himself.
● ALBUMS: *Now Presenting Troy Seals* (Atlantic 1973)★★, *Troy Seals* (Columbia 1976)★★.

SEELY, JEANNIE

b. Marilyn Jeanne Seely, 6 July 1940, Titusville, Pennsylvania, USA. Seely had studied banking but she had been singing in public from the age of 11. She gained valuable experience by working as a secretary in Los Angeles for Liberty Records. In 1965, with encouragement from the man she later married, Hank Cochran, she went to Nashville. She worked for Ernest Tubb and then for Porter Wagoner. In 1966, she reached number 2 on the US country charts with Cochran's 'Don't Touch Me', and won a Grammy as the Best Country Female Vocalist. She had success with more of Cochran's songs, notably 'I'll Love You More', 'Welcome Home To Nothing' and 'Just Enough To Start Me Dreaming', and dedicated an album to him, *Thanks, Hank*. Being a small blonde in a miniskirt, she was a distinctive partner for the six-foot Jack Greene, and they had a succession of US country hits, including a number 2, 'I Wish I Didn't Have To Miss You'. Seely wrote 'It Just Takes Practice' (Dottie West), 'Senses' (Willie Nelson and Connie Smith) and 'Leavin' And Sayin' Goodbye' (Jack Greene, Faron Young and Norma Jean). In 1973 she had success with 'Can I Sleep In Your Arms Tonight, Mister?', a parody by Hank Cochran of the old-time 'May I Sleep In Your Barn Tonight, Mister?'. She also made a bid for the outlaw country market with a song addressed to Jessi Colter, 'We're Still Hangin' In There, Ain't We, Jessi?'.
● ALBUMS: *The Seely Style* (Monument 1966)★★★★, *Thanks, Hank!* (Monument 1967)★★★★, *I'll Love You More* (Monument 1968)★★★★, *Little Things* (Monument 1968)★★★, *Jeannie Seely* (1969)★★★, *Please Be My New Love* (1970)★★★, *Make The World Go Away* (1972)★★★★, *Can I Sleep In Your Arms?* (MCA 1973)★★★; with Jack Greene *I Wish I Didn't Have To Miss You* (Decca 1969)★★★, *Jack Greene And Jeannie Seely* (Decca 1970)★★★, *Two For The Show* (Decca 1971)★★, *Live At The Grand Ole Opry* (1978)★★★.
● COMPILATIONS: *Greatest Hits On Monument* (Monument 1993)★★★★.

SELDOM SCENE

Formed in late 1971, as a Washington DC-based semi-professional newgrass bluegrass band. A fellow musician, most probably Charlie Waller of the Country Gentlemen, was responsible for the name, when he suggested that since the

members had to fit their musical appearances around their daily employment, they would be seldom seen playing in the area. The founder-members were John Duffey (b. 4 March 1934, Washington DC, USA, d. 10 December 1996, Arlington, Virginia, USA; mandolin, guitar, vocals) and Tom Gray (b. c.1946, Chicago, Illinois, USA; string bass, guitar, mandolin, vocals), who had both previously played with Waller in the Country Gentlemen, Mike Auldridge (b. 1938, Washington DC, USA; dobro, vocals), Ben Eldridge (banjo, guitar, vocals) and John Starling (guitar, lead vocals). All had daily work outside the music industry, although Duffey actually repaired musical instruments through an Arlington, Virginia music store. Gray worked for the National Geographic magazine as a cartographer, Eldridge was a mathematician, while Starling was a US Army surgeon, then working at a local hospital. Auldridge, now one of country music's finest dobro players, having played on countless recordings as a session musician, as well as recording solo albums, was working as a commercial artist. (Auldridge's uncle, Ellsworth T. Cozens, a talented multi-instrumentalist, had played steel guitar, mandolin and banjo on Jimmie Rodgers' recordings in 1928.) Seldom Scene first played a residency at the Red Fox Inn, Bethesda, in January 1972. This soon led to festival and concert appearances and by 1974, their fine harmonies and musicianship had seen them achieve a popularity almost equal to that of the long-established Country Gentlemen. They recorded a series of albums for Rebel in 1972, before moving to Sugar Hill in 1980. There were no personnel changes until 1977, when Phil Rosenthal, who had already written material for the band, including their popular 'Willie Boy' and 'Muddy Water', replaced Starling (Starling, an exceptional bluegrass vocalist and songwriter, subsequently become a popular artist in his own right, recording several very successful albums for Sugar Hill). In 1986, Rosenthal (who also recorded solo albums) left and was replaced by Lou Reid (fiddle, guitar, dobro, mandolin, lead vocals), who had previously worked with Ricky Skaggs and Doyle Lawson. Tom Gray finally left the group soon afterwards, his place being taken by T. Michael Coleman, who had played previously with Doc Watson. This change also saw an instrumental variation, since Coleman played an electric bass guitar instead of the acoustic stand up bass that Gray had always used. The band played a special concert, on 10 November 1986, at Washington's John F. Kennedy Center For The Performing Arts, to commemorate their 15 years in the music business, which was recorded as a double album and included several guest appearances by artists such as Emmylou Harris, Linda Ronstadt, John Starling, Jonathan Edwards and Charlie Waller. The album even contained a liner note from President Ronald Reagan. Five years later, all the eight artists who had been members over the years played together to record another live album, this time at Birchmere, to commemorate the 20th anniversary of Seldom Scene's formation. Auldridge, Klein and Coleman left in 1995 to form Chesapeake, and were replaced by Dudley Connell (ex-Johnson Mountain Boys) and Ronnie Simkins and Fred Travers. Duffey died of a heart attack in December 1996 prior to the release of a new album.
● ALBUMS: Seldom Scene-Act 1 (Rebel 1972)★★★, Seldom Scene-Act 2 (Rebel 1973)★★★, Seldom Scene-Act 3 (Rebel 1974)★★★, Old Train (Rebel 1974)★★★, Live At The Cellar

Door (Rebel 1976)★★, The New Seldom Scene Album (Rebel 1977)★★★★, Baptizing (Rebel 1978)★★★, Seldom Scene-Act 4 (Sugar Hill 1980)★★★★, After Midnight (Sugar Hill 1981)★★★, At The Scene (Sugar Hill 1984)★★, with Jonathan Edwards Blue Ridge (Sugar Hill 1985)★★★, 15th Anniversary Celebration (Sugar Hill 19887)★★★, A Change Of Scenery (Sugar Hill 1988)★★★, Scenic Roots (Sugar Hill 1991)★★★, Scene 20: 20th Anniversary Concert (Sugar Hill 1992)★★, Dream Scene (Sugar Hill 1997)★★★.
● COMPILATIONS: Best Of Seldom Scene, Volume 1 (Rebel 1987)★★★★.

SESSIONS, RONNIE

b. 7 December 1948, Henrietta, Oklahoma, USA. Sessions grew up in Bakersfield, California. His first record, in 1957, was a novelty version of Little Richard's 'Keep A-Knockin'' made with Richard's band. Through a schoolboy friend he knew Herb Henson, the host of a television series, Trading Post, and he became a regular performer. He studied to be a vet but he also recorded for local labels and, joining Gene Autry's Republic label in 1968, he had regional hits with 'The Life Of Riley' and 'More Than Satisfied'. He moved to Nashville and his songwriting talent was recognized by Hank Cochran. However, his first country hits were with revivals of pop songs, 'Never Been To Spain' and 'Tossin' And Turnin''. Over at MCA, he had major country hits in 1977 with 'Wiggle, Wiggle' and Bobby Goldsboro's 'Me And Millie (Stompin' Grapes And Gettin' Silly)'. He failed to consolidate his success and, after being dropped by MCA in 1980, he has hardly recorded since. His last US country chart entry was in 1986 with 'I Bought The Shoes That Just Walked Out On Me'.
● ALBUMS: Ronnie Sessions (MCA 1977)★★.

SHAMBLIN, ELDON

b. 24 April 1916, Weatherford, Oklahoma, USA. He learned to play guitar in his early teens and at 17, was playing in Oklahoma City honky tonks. In 1935, he moved to Tulsa with a western swing band, the Alabama Boys, but soon left them to become the staff guitarist playing swing music on KTUL. In November 1937, Bob Wills persuaded Shamblin to join his Texas Playboys. His rhythm guitar work and previous experience of swing groups quickly became a prime factor of Wills' music. Shamblin not only reorganized the rhythm section but also became the band's arranger and made his first recordings with Wills in 1938. Early in 1940, Shamblin took to playing electric lead guitar and his clever abilities to blend with steel guitarist Leon McAuliffe, set standards that future musicians have tried to emulate. They recorded their noted 'Twin Guitar Special' in February 1941. He stayed with Wills until called up for military service in World War II, which saw him attain the rank of captain. In 1947, he rejoined a much changed Wills band in Texas and acted as manager as well as playing rhythm and occasional lead guitar until 1954. In 1954, he left to join Hoyle Nix's western swing band, but in 1956, Shamblin went back to Wills. In 1957, he returned to Tulsa and though playing locally, he worked as a piano tuner and electric organ repairer. In 1970, Merle Haggard persuaded him and former Texas Playboys to play on his tribute album to Wills, A Tribute To The Best Damn Fiddle Player In The World. Following this, he and nine other old Playboys made further recordings at Haggard's home. The experience rekindled his interest and between 1975 and 1981, he played as a member of Haggard's band, the Strangers, until he retired to Tulsa. Shamblin's earlier work may be heard on many Wills recordings, particularly Columbia's Special Products and Historical Series, while some post-war recordings are captured on the first three volumes of the Kaleidoscope label's *Tiffany Transcriptions*. In the late 70s, he also recorded on the *Reunion* album made by a western swing band led by Johnnie Lee Wills. Shamblin made few solo recordings but he did also record a highly acclaimed album of country jazz for Flying Fish with the legendary jazz violinist Joe Venuti, Curly Chalker, a leading country jazz and western swing steel guitarist, and mandolin expert Jethro Burns, who for years had been one half of the comedy duo Homer And Jethro. In 1993, Shambling played with Asleep At The Wheel on their Grammy winner 'Red Wing'. Shambling has been rated by many experts as the world's best and most influential rhythm guitarist.

● ALBUMS: with Joe Venuti, Curly Chalker, Jethro Burns *S'Wonderful (4 Giants Of Swing)* (Flying Fish 1977)★★★, *Guitar Genius* (Delta 1980)★★★.

SHAPIRO, TOM

b. Kansas City, Missouri, USA. Shapiro studied music at the University of Boston and co-founded a music school. He moved to Los Angeles and played in a jazz trio. His first songs were recorded by George Benson, Sister Sledge and Smokey Robinson. Frank Sinatra recorded 'Nobody Has A Better Dream Than Me', but the track has not been released. Since concentrating on country music Shapiro has written 28 Top 10 singles. His country hits include 'I'm Not Through Loving You Yet' (Conway Twitty), 'In A New York Minute' and 'Love Talks' (Ronnie McDowell), 'Only When I Love' (Holly Dunn), 'Touch And Go Crazy' (Lee Greenwood) and 'Your Heart's Not In It' (Janie Fricke). He has recently co-written 'Take That' (Lisa Brokop), 'Watch Me' (Lorrie Morgan) and 'Wink' (Neal McCoy). Kathy Mattea's 'Walkin' Away A Winner' has become a feminist statement, but Shapiro wrote it after seeing the film *Rocky*: 'I thought that was real cool - he lost, but he won.' He also produced Dusty Springfield's 1995 album, *A Very Fine Love*.

SHARP, KEVIN

b. 10 December 1970, California, USA. Although born in California, Sharp lived many of his early years in Weiser, Idaho. His father, Glen, owned a restaurant and every year he was taken with the contestants for the Old Times Fiddlers Contest who performed there. Sharp was a keen sportsman but he intended to become a professional light-opera singer. On finishing high school, he began his professional career with Sacramento's Music Circus. When 18 years old, he developed bone cancer and, for a time, it was feared that his leg would be amputated. When his condition deteriorated, the Make-A-Wish foundation arranged for him to meet someone he admired - David Foster, producer of Barbra Streisand and Whitney Houston. A long course of chemotherapy was successful. He then sang at a California theme park and set up a singing telegram business. He self-financed an album, *You Can Count On Me*, and appeared in a Biblical musical about Joshua. Through David Foster's help, he was signed to Asylum Records with Chris Farren as

producer. To the label's surprise and perhaps engendered by his remarkable resilience, *Measure Of A Man* became a best-selling album, and early in 1997, Sharp had a US number 1 country hit with 'Nobody Knows', which was a revival of a pop hit by the Tony Rich Project. A six-month tour with Sawyer Brown followed plus the release of 'She's Sure Taking It Well', and plans were made for a television movie of his life. He says, 'Today I appreciate everything in life so much more than ever. Even the smallest things are beautiful to me. I think I'm a better person, a better Christian, because of what I've been through. Music has made a difference every day of my life. Whenever I needed strength, there was always a song.'

● ALBUMS: *You Can Count On Me* (North Star 1994)★★★, *Measure Of A Man* (Asylum 1996)★★★★.

SHAVER, BILLY JOE

b. 15 September 1941, Corsicana, Texas, USA. Shaver was raised in Waco, Texas, and lost two fingers in a sawmill accident. In typically contradictory fashion, he took up bronc-busting as a safer job and started to learn guitar. An early song, 'Two Bits Worth Of Nothing', was written about his wife - a lady he has both married and divorced three times! Shaver spent some years in Nashville before Bobby Bare discovered him. He and Bare co-wrote his first single, 'Chicken On The Ground', for Mercury Records in 1970. Bare hit the US country charts with the simple, gutsy philosophy of 'Ride Me Down Easy' in 1973. Johnny Rodriguez did well with 'I Couldn't Be Me Without You', while Tom T. Hall favoured 'Old Five And Dimers' and a song about Willie Nelson, 'Willy The Wandering Gypsy And Me'. Waylon Jennings' important album *Honky Tonk Heroes* contained nine Shaver songs, including their co-written 'You Ask Me To', which was subsequently recorded by Elvis Presley. Shaver's first album, produced by Kris Kristofferson, contained his gruff-voiced versions of many excellent songs including his first country hit, 'I Been To Georgia On A Fast Train'. His Texan influences (blues, jazz, Mexican) and his themes (life on the road, brief encounters, how it used to be) fitted in with outlaw country music. His best song, 'Black Rose', tells of his love for a black girl and contains the dubious line, 'The Devil made me do it the first time, The second time I done it on my own.' Shaver hated live performances and he fell prey to ulcers, alcoholism and drug-addiction, so much so that an album for MGM Records was never made. Other songwriters wrote about him, including Kris Kristofferson's 'The Fighter' and Tom T. Hall's 'Joe, Don't Let The Music Kill You'. In 1976, Shaver released his second album and followed it with a glittering line-up (Willie Nelson, Ricky Skaggs, Emmylou Harris) for 'Gypsy Boy'. He turned to religion and 'I'm Just An Old Chunk Of Coal (But I'm Gonna Be A Diamond Someday)' was recorded by both Johnny Cash and John Anderson. Perhaps there were too many outlaw singers and Shaver, with his lack of product, was overlooked. His output up to 1990 of six studio albums in 17 years, with several songs repeated, was astonishingly low, particularly for a country singer. He now records as Shaver, with his guitar-playing son Eddy, releasing three studio albums in the 90s.

● ALBUMS: *Old Five And Dimers Like Me* (Monument 1973)★★★, *When I Get My Wings* (Capricorn 1976)★★★, *Gypsy Boy* (Capricorn 1977)★★★★, *I'm Just An Old Chunk Of Coal* (Columbia 1981)★★★, *Billy Joe Shaver* (Columbia

1982)★★★★, *Salt Of The Earth* (Columbia 1987)★★★, *Live In Australia* (1989)★★, as Shaver *Tramp On Your Street* (Zoo/Praxis 1993)★★★, *Honky Tonk Heroes* (Bear Family 1994)★★★★, as Shaver *Unshaven: Live At Smith's Olde Bar* (Zoo Entertainment 1995)★★, as Shaver *Highway Of Life* (Justice 1996)★★★.
● COMPILATIONS: *Restless Wind: The Legendary Billy Joe Shaver 1973-1987* (Razoe & Tie 1995)★★★★.

SHAW, VICTORIA

b. USA. Having first established herself as a hugely successful Music Row songwriter, Victoria Shaw achieved a long-held ambition by releasing her major label debut album in 1995. Earlier, she had formed her first band at the age of 12 and become a professional singer by 18. She was prompted by her musical mother, who found fame in her own right by starting the magazine *Big Beautiful Women*. However, her daughter's success as a songwriter took some time to come to fruition. For 10 years she commuted between New York and Nashville, earning a meagre existence in the piano bars of the former to subsidise her trips to the country music capital. Her hard work eventually paid off after eight years, when she was offered a publishing contract. It was another two years before she enjoyed a substantial hit, though when she did, it was for no lesser artist than Garth Brooks. He took 'The River' to the top of the country charts, and also recorded Shaw's 'She's Every Woman'. Other artists then formed a queue for her services, including Doug Stone ('Too Busy Being In Love') and John Michael Montgomery ('I Love The Way You Love Me'). Eventually she was able to launch her own solo career, doing so with 1995's *In Full View*. Among the many notable tracks on this were '(A Day In The Life Of) A Single Mother', which embodied Shaw's ability to write slice-of-life narratives without compromising either her viewpoints or country music's traditional values. The self-titled follow-up was a solid if rather unadventurous collection.
● ALBUMS: *In Full View* (Reprise 1995)★★★★, *Victoria Shaw* (Reprise 1997)★★.

SHAY, DOROTHY

b. Dorothy Sims, 1923, Jacksonville, Florida, USA, d. 22 October 1978. A popular country-style comedienne, she became known as the Park Avenue Hillbilly and regularly appeared on the Spike Jones radio series in 1947. She appeared in the 1951 film *Comin' 'Round The Mountain* and later made appearances on *The Waltons* television series. She recorded for Columbia Records and is perhaps best remembered for her 1947 recording of 'Feudin' And Fightin'' (from the Broadway musical *Laffing Room Only*), which became a number 4 hit in both the country and pop charts. She died in 1978 following a heart attack.

SHELTON BROTHERS

A very popular harmony duo of the 30s, which comprised Bob (b. Robert Attlesey, 4 July 1909, Reilly Springs, Hopkins County, Texas, USA, d. 1983; guitar, fiddle, vocals) and his brother Joe (b. Joseph Attlesey, 27 January 1911, Reilly Springs, Hopkins County, Texas, USA, d. 26 December 1980; guitar, mandolin, vocals). They grew up with a great interest in old-time music, after listening to early radio programmes and recordings of Jimmie Rodgers. They first entertained

locally in the late 20s and, together with vocalist Leon Chappelear, they began singing on KWKH Shreveport in 1930. The trio recorded for Bluebird Records as the Lone Star Cowboys in 1933, and also recorded as backing musicians for Jimmie Davis, with whom they were close friends. The brothers then worked with fiddler Curly Fox at WSB Atlanta and WWL New Orleans. The Attleseys joined Decca Records and made their first recordings for the label in Chicago, on 22/23 February 1935. With their popularity increasing, Decca suggested a change of name and the brothers therefore adopted Shelton, which was their mother's maiden name. At further sessions that year, they were joined by Fox and the material varied widely from their very popular 'Just Because' to the humorous 'Coupon Song' and plaintive ballads such as 'Will There Be Any Cowboys In Heaven'. Between 1937 and 1941, they recorded around 120 more sides in 14 more Decca sessions, which arguably makes them the most recorded brother duo of the period. In 1937, they added other musicians to their show, who at times included fiddler Leon Hall and Gene Sullivan (he later worked with Wiley Walker as Wiley And Gene). After leaving New Orleans, they fluctuated between KWKH Shreveport and several stations in the Dallas and Fort Worth area. In 1944, their long-time friendship with Jimmie Davis saw them work with him on his successful run for State Governor of Louisiana. They made their last recordings for King in 1947, which almost marked the end of their career as a duo. Bob worked solo for some years as a comedian in the Fort Worth area before finally retiring. Joe died on 26 December 1980 and although the date of Bob's death seems unclear, it is believed to have been in 1983. They were an important act in the development of country music and should not be confused with Jack and Curly Shelton, who were no relation. Their noted 'Just Because' has appeared on one or two compilation albums, including the Smithsonian Institution's *Collection Of Classic Country*, but in recent years, it has seemingly been left to a German company and Old Homestead to reissue albums of their work.
● ALBUMS: *The Shelton Brothers/The Carlisle Brothers* one side only (MCA 1976)★★.
● COMPILATIONS: *Just Because* (CowgirlBoy 1992)★★★, *Those Dusty Roads* (CowgirlBoy 1992)★★★, *The Shelton Brothers: Bob & Joe* (Old Homestead 1993)★★★.

SHELTON, RICKY VAN

b. 12 January 1952, Danville, near Lynchburg, Virginia, USA. Shelton was raised in a church-going family and he learned to love gospel music. His brother worked as a musician and through travelling with him, he also acquired a taste for country music. He worked as a pipefitter but his fiancée Bettye realized his singing potential, and in 1984, suggested that they went to Nashville where she had secured a personnel job. In 1986 he impressed producer Steve Buckingham during a club performance, and his first recording session yielded a US Top 30 country hit in 'Wild-Eyed Dream'. He then made the country Top 10 with one of his best records, the dramatic story-song 'Crimes Of Passion'. In 1987 he had a US country number 1 by reviving a song from a Conway Twitty album, 'Somebody Lied'. In 1988 he had another number 1 with Harlan Howard's 'Life Turned Her That Way', which, unlike Merle Tillis, he performed in its original 4/4 tempo. His revival of an obscure Roger Miller song, 'Don't We All Have The Right', also went to number 1, giving him five country hits from his first album. Since then, he has had US country number 1s with revivals of 'I'll Leave This World Loving You', Ned Miller's 'From A Jack To A King' and a new song, 'Living Proof'. Although Shelton has much in common with his hard-nosed contemporaries, he succumbed to a middle-of-the-road album of familiar Christmas songs. He recorded a duet of 'Sweet Memories' with Brenda Lee, while 'Rockin' Years' with Dolly Parton was a number 1 country single in 1991. To help his career, Shelton's wife has been studying law, while he knows that he must conquer his fear of flying. In 1992, Shelton recorded an album of semi-spiritual material, *Don't Overlook Salvation*, as a gift to his parents, before enjoying more hits with the new recordings included on *Greatest Hits Plus*. From then on, Shelton has lost ground, unable to achieve country hits with the same regularity. He recorded an ironic song, 'Still Got A Couple Of Good Years Left', which became a US country Top 50 hit in 1993. In 1997 he returned with the independently released *Making Plans*.

● ALBUMS: *Wild-Eyed Dream* (Columbia 1987)★★★, *Loving Proof* (Columbia 1988)★★★, *Ricky Van Shelton Sings Christmas* (Columbia 1989)★★, *RVS III* (Columbia 1990)★★★, *Backroads* (Columbia 1991)★★★, *Don't Overlook Salvation* (Columbia 1992)★★★, *A Bridge I Didn't Burn* (Columbia 1993)★★★, *Love And Honor* (Columbia 1994)★★★, *Making Plans* (RVS 1997)★★★.

● COMPILATIONS: *Greatest Hits Plus* (Columbia 1992)★★★, *Super Hits* (Columbia 1995)★★★.

● VIDEOS: *Where Was I* (1993), *Live* (1993), *To Be Continued...* (1993).

SHENANDOAH

The founding members of Shenandoah, formed in Muscle Shoals, Alabama, USA, in the mid-80s were Marty Raybon (b. 26 June 1953, Greenville, Alabama, USA; lead vocals), who started out as a bricklayer before joining American Bluegrass Express, where he stayed for 9 years before leaving to join Heartbreak Mountain, Jim Seales (b. 20 March 1954, Hamilton, Alabama, USA; guitar), Ralph Ezell (b. 26 June 1953, Union, Mississippi, USA; bass), Stan Thorn (b. 3 March 1959, Kenosha, Wisconsin, USA; keyboards) and Mike McGuire (b. 28 December 1958, Hamilton, Alabama, USA; drums). They were first known as the MGM Band, but after the songwriter Robert Byrne recommended them to the producer Rick Hall (of Fame Studios) and they signed with Columbia Records, they were renamed Shenandoah. Their self-titled 1987 debut included the Top 10 hit 'She Doesn't Cry Anymore', the first recording to introduce Raybon's powerful singing voice to a wider audience. They made their major commercial breakthrough in the mid-90s. Much of this success was due to their collaboration with bluegrass artist Alison Krauss, 'Somewhere In The Vicinity Of The Heart', which helped make Krauss a major country star. It was included on their Don Cook-produced debut for Capitol Records' Nashville division, *In The Vicinity Of The Heart*, which saw them receive several nominations from the Country Music Association Awards committee. Previously the group had suffered numerous trials and tribulations, including bankruptcy (caused by a 1989 law suit over the use of their name), record label changes and the loss of long-standing member Stan Thorn. They filed for

bankruptcy but re-emerged with RCA in 1992 with two strong albums, *Long Time Comin'* and *Under The Kudzu*, which spawned a number of hits, notably 'Rock My Baby', 'Hey Mister (I Need This Job)', 'Leavin's Been A Long Time Comin'', 'Janie Baker's Love Slave' and 'I Want To be Loved Like That'. Thorn left to pursue a career in jazz and in 1994 they topped the country chart with 'If Bubba Can Dance (I Can Too)'. Following the release of the successful *In The Vicinity Of The Heart*, the group disintegrated further. Ezell was replaced by Rocky Thacker, and Raybon released a solo album for gospel label Sparrow Records before joining up with his brother Tim for *The Raybon Brothers*, released by MCA in 1997. *Now And Then* included lacklustre new recordings of their Columbia material.

● ALBUMS: *Shenandoah* (Columbia 1987)★★★, *The Road Not Taken* (Columbia 1989)★★★, *Extra Mile* (Columbia 1990)★★★, *Long Time Comin'* (RCA 1992)★★★, *Under The Kudzu* (RCA 1993)★★★, *In The Vicinity Of The Heart* (Liberty 1995)★★★, *Now And Then* (Capitol 1996)★★, *Shenandoah Christmas* (Capitol 1996)★★★.
Solo: Marty Raybon *Marty Raybon* (Sparrow 1995)★★★.

● COMPILATIONS: *Greatest Hits* (Columbia 1992)★★★★.

SHENANDOAH CUT-UPS

This popular bluegrass band were initially the Blue Grass Cut-Ups of Reno And Smiley. They underwent the name change early in 1969, when a change in management, at WDBJ-TV Roanoke, ended the station's *Top Of The Morning Show*, on which the band had appeared for a considerable time. Smiley's ill health saw him withdraw and three of the band members re-formed under their new name. The three were fiddler Tater Tate, Billy Edwards (b. William Gene Edwards, 26 September 1936, Tazewell County, Virginia, USA; banjo, bass, vocals) and John Palmer (b. 28 May 1927, Union, South Carolina, USA, d. 26 December 1993; bass, guitar). They were joined by Herschel Sizemore (b. 6 August 1935, Sheffield, Alabama, USA; mandolin). Initially, they worked with vocalist Jim Eanes, with whom they made their first recordings as the Shenandoah Valley Quartet, but Edwards, who sang lead on most of the numbers, became the band's accepted vocalist when Eanes resumed his solo career. In the early 70s, sometimes reinforced by guitarist Wesley Golding, they worked numerous venues and recorded for Revonah. Around 1973, Edwards retired, being replaced by Tom McKinney, and with a more modernized sound, the new line-up recorded for Rebel. Soon afterwards, Tate and Palmer's unhappiness with the new sound saw Golding, McKinney and Sizemore leave to form their own band, County Grass. Edwards rejoined Tate and Palmer and with new members Gene Burrows (b. 12 September 1928, Bedford County, Virginia, USA, d. 14 September 1992; mandolin, guitar, vocals) and Udell McPeak (guitar), the Cut-Ups continued until 1977 without further changes (Burrows and McPeak had previously both played with Red Smiley). They recorded for Revonah, played numerous festivals and worked with Mac Wiseman. In 1977, Edwards retired (Larry Hall replaced him), while Tate, who had always acted as the band's leader, joined Lester Flatt. Bobby Hicks played fiddle in his place and Palmer became band leader. Sizemore also returned to play on occasions. By 1980, the Cut-Ups mainly played local venues but made further recordings on Grassound, Palmer's own label. They finally disappeared around 1988, as members retired or moved on to other careers. Burrows died in Roanoke in 1992 and Palmer the following year from cancer.

● ALBUMS: with Jim Eanes *Shenandoah Valley Quartet* (County 1970)★★★★, with Curly Seckler *Sings Again* (County 1971)★★★, *Shenandoah Cut-Ups Plant Grass In Your Ear* (Major 1971)★★★, *Bluegrass Autumn* (Revonah 1972)★★★★, *Shenandoah Cut-Ups* (Rebel 1973)★★★, *Shenandoah Cut-Ups Sing Gospel* (Revonah 1973)★★, *Traditional Bluegrass* (Revonah 1974)★★★, *A Tribute To The Louvin Brothers* (Revonah 1975)★★★, *Bluegrass Spring* (Revonah 1976)★★★, with Mac Wiseman *New Traditions Volume 1* (Vetco 1976)★★★, with Wiseman *New Traditions Volume 2* (Vetco 1977)★★★, *Keep It Bluegrass* (Grassound 1980)★★★★, *Bluegrass Blaze Of Glory* one side only (Grassound 1982)★★.

SHEPARD, JEAN

b. Imogene Shepard, 21 November 1933, Pauls Valley, Oklahoma, USA. Shepard was one of 11 children in her family, who moved to Visalia, California, in 1946. Shepard learned to sing by listening to Jimmie Rodgers records on a wind-up Victrola. She joined the Melody Ranch Girls, in which she played string bass and sang, and recorded for Capitol while still at school. The record was not successful but she subsequently played on the same bill as Hank Thompson, who assured Capitol of her talent. In 1953 a single for the Korean war, 'Dear John Letter', with a narration from Ferlin Husky, topped the US country charts for 23 weeks. However, because she was under 21, she could not legally leave the state on her own to tour to promote the song. Shepard followed 'Dear John' with 'Forgive Me, John,' while the original was satirized by Stan Freberg. Shepard had further country hits with 'Satisfied Mind' and 'Beautiful Lies' and she has been a regular member of the *Grand Ole Opry* since 1955. She worked with Red Foley from 1955-57 on his television show *Ozark Jubilee*. Her 1956 *Songs Of A Love Affair* was a concept album, one side from the single woman's view, the other from the wife's. She was married to Hawkshaw Hawkins, who was killed in 1963 in the plane crash that also took the lives of Patsy Cline and Cowboy Copas. At the time, Shepard was eight months pregnant with their second child. She returned to country music in 1964 with 'Second Fiddle To An Old Guitar' and she named her road band The Second Fiddles. She also had success with 'Happy Hangovers To You', 'If Teardrops Were Silver', and two duets with Ray Pillow, 'I'll Take The Dog' and 'Mr. Do-It-Yourself.' Shepard was one of the first artists to be produced by crossover producer Larry Butler. In the 70s, she did well on the US country charts with Bill Anderson's songs 'Slippin' Away', 'At The Time', 'The Tips Of My Fingers' and 'Mercy', and recorded an album of his songs, *Poor Sweet Baby*. In 1975 she recorded a tribute to Hawkshaw Hawkins, 'Two Little Boys', which was written by their sons. Shepard was one of the objectors to Olivia Newton-John's award from the Country Music Association and she helped to found the Association Of Country Music Entertainers to 'keep it country'. To the public, it looked like sour grapes, especially as she had recorded 'Let Me Be There' and several pop hits. In recent years, Shepard has recorded duets with Gerry Ford, and plays live accompanied by her guitarist/husband, Benny Birchfield.

● ALBUMS: *Songs Of A Love Affair* (Capitol 1956)★★, *Lonesome Love* (Capitol 1959)★★★, *This Is Jean Shepard* (Capitol 1959)★★★, *Got You On My Mind* (Capitol 1961)★★★★, *Heartaches And Tears* (Capitol 1962)★★★, *Lighthearted And Blue* (Capitol 1964)★★★, *It's A Man Every Time* (Capitol 1965)★★★, *Many Happy Hangovers* (Capitol 1966)★★★, with Ray Pillow *I'll Take The Dog* (Capitol 1966)★★, *Hello Old Broken Heart* (Capitol 1967)★★★, *Heart, We Did All That We Could* (Capitol 1967)★★★, *Your Forevers Don't Last Very Long* (Capitol 1967)★★★, *A Real Good Woman* (Capitol 1968)★★★, *Heart To Heart* (Capitol 1968)★★★, *Seven Lonely Days* (Capitol 1969)★★★, *I'll Fly Away* (Capitol 1969)★★★, *A Woman's Hand* (Capitol 1970)★★★, *Declassified Jean Shepard* (Mercury 1971)★★, *Here And Now* (Capitol 1971)★★★, *Just As Soon As I Get Over Loving You* (Capitol 1972)★★★, *Just Like Walking In The Sunshine* (Capitol 1972)★★, *Slippin' Away* (United Artists 1973)★★★, *Poor Sweet Baby And Ten More Bill Anderson Songs* (United Artists 1975)★★★, *For The Good Times* (United Artists 1975)★★, *I'm A Believer* (United Artists 1975)★★★, *Mercy, Ain't Love Good* (United Artists 1976)★★★, *I'll Do Anything It Takes* (Scorpion 1978)★★★.
● COMPILATIONS: *The Best Of Jean Shepard* (Capitol 1963)★★★, *Greatest Hits* (United Artists 1976)★★★, *Honky Tonk Heroine: Classic Capitol Recordings, 1952-1962* (CMF 1995)★★★★, *The Melody Ranch Girl* 5-CD box set (Bear Family 1997)★★★★.

SHEPPARD, T.G.

b. William Neal Browder, 20 July 1944, Humboldt, Tennessee, USA. Sheppard is a nephew of old-time country performer Rod Brasfield, and his mother was a piano teacher who gave him lessons. Sheppard began his professional musical career in Memphis in the early 60s, working as a backing vocalist for Travis Wammack and then performing as Brian Stacey, having a regional hit with 'High School Days'. After his marriage in 1965, Sheppard became a record promoter for Stax and RCA. In 1974, he was signed by Motown's country arm, Melodyland, and had two number 1 country records with 'The Devil In The Bottle' and 'Trying To Beat The Morning Home'. He took his stage name from German shepherd dogs, although many have thought his name represents The Good Shepherd. Sheppard merged his Memphis soul background with country music, which included revivals of the Four Tops' 'I Can't Help Myself' and Neil Diamond's 'Solitary Man'. Over at Warners, Sheppard had a US country number 1 with 'Last Cheater's Waltz'. In 1981 Sheppard made the US Top 40 with 'I Loved 'Em Every One'. His duets include 'Faking Love' with Karen Brooks, 'Home Again' with Judy Collins and 'Make My Day' with Clint Eastwood. The hits continued after Sheppard signed to Columbia Records, but with the advent of new country stars such as George Strait and Dwight Yoakam his style rapidly went out of date and he was dropped from the label in 1990. Apart from a brief resurgence on Curb Records he remained without a record contract throughout the 90s.

● ALBUMS: *T.G.Sheppard* (Melodyland 1975)★★, *Motels And Memories* (Melodyland 1976)★★★ *Solitary Man* (Hitsville 1976)★★★★, *T.G.* (Warner/Curb 1978)★★, *Daylight* (1978)★★★, *Three-Quarters Lonely* (Warner/Curb 1979)★★★, *Smooth Sailin'* (Warner/Curb 1980)★★★, *I Love 'Em All* (Warner/Curb 1981)★★, *Finally!* (Warner/Curb 1982)★★★,

Perfect Stranger (Warner/Curb 1982)★★★, *Slow Burn* (Warner/Curb 1983)★★★, *One Owner Heart* (Warner/Curb 1984)★★, *Livin' On The Edge* (Columbia 1985)★★★, *It Still Rains In Memphis* (Columbia 1986)★★★, *1ne 4 The $* (Columbia 1987)★★★, *Crossroads* (Columbia 1988)★★★.
● COMPILATIONS: *T.G. Sheppard's Greatest Hits* (Warner/Curb 1983)★★★★, *Biggest Hits* (Columbia 1988)★★★.

SHERRILL, BILLY

b. Philip Campbell, 5 November 1936, Winston, Alabama, USA. Sherrill's father was a travelling evangelist - he is shown on horseback on the cover of Charlie Rich's album *Silver Linings* - and Sherrill played piano at his meetings. He also played saxophone in a local rock 'n' roll band, Benny Cagle and the Rhythm Swingsters. In 1956 he left to work with Rick Hall in the R&B-styled Fairlanes. His 1958 Mercury single, 'Like Making Love', was covered for the UK market by Marty Wilde, and he had some success in Alabama with an instrumental, 'Tipsy', in 1960. He worked for Sun Records' new Nashville studios from 1961 to 1964; in particular, he brought out Charlie Rich's talent as a blues singer. He and Rick Hall then established the Fame studios in Nashville. In 1964 he started working for Columbia Records and he produced R&B records by Ted Taylor and the Staple Singers, as well as an album by Elvis Presley's guitarist, Scotty Moore, *The Guitar That Changed The World*. He co-wrote and produced David Houston's US number 1 country hit, 'Almost Persuaded', and his subsequent hits with Houston include a duet with Tammy Wynette, 'My Elusive Dreams'. It was Sherrill who discovered Wynette and in 1968 they wrote 'Stand By Your Man' in half an hour and recorded it immediately. Although Sherrill's records crossed over to the pop market, he did not avoid country music instruments such as the steel guitar, although he did favour lavish orchestrations. He also discovered Tanya Tucker, Janie Frickie and Lacy J. Dalton, and has made successful records with Charlie Rich ('Behind Closed Doors', 'The Most Beautiful Girl'), George Jones, Marty Robbins and Barbara Mandrell. He became a freelance producer in 1980 but continued to work with many of the same artists. He has produced over 10 albums apiece for David Allan Coe, George Jones and Tammy Wynette; other credits include *The Baron* for Johnny Cash and the soundtrack for the film *Take This Job And Shove It*. His best works include two all-star country albums, *My Very Special Guests* with George Jones, and *Friendship* with Ray Charles. The friction between him and Elvis Costello while making the album *Almost Blue* was shown on a UK television documentary, but the album did very well and yielded a Top 10 hit, 'A Good Year For The Roses'.
● ALBUMS: *Classical Country* (Epic 1967)★★.

SHOLES, STEVE

b. Stephen Henry Sholes, 12 February 1911, Washington DC, USA, d. 22 April 1968, Nashville, Tennessee, USA. Sholes' father worked in the music industry and in 1920, he moved the family to Merchantville, New Jersey, in order that he could work for Victor at their Camden recording studio. The boy inherited his father's love of music and learned to play clarinet and saxophone, and after graduating, he worked for a time as a professional musician. In 1935, realizing he

would never reached the heights towards which he aimed as a musician, he gained employment with Victor. In 1939, he was appointed A&R man dealing with popular, jazz and big band music. He soon proved successful in this post and in the early 40s, he was allotted the task of overseeing all of RCA's country and R&B recordings. This work led to his making regular visits to Nashville, where he quickly spotted the potential recording talents of Eddy Arnold. His career was interrupted for army service in World War II, but on his discharge in 1945, he concentrated more and more on recording artists in Nashville. It was through Sholes' careful guidance that RCA became the first major label to have permanent recording facilities in Music City. He was subsequently responsible for managing the recording careers of several major stars, including Hank Snow, Jim Reeves, Skeeter Davis and Chet Atkins. In 1955, he signed Elvis Presley from Sun Records. He also groomed Atkins in the business side of the industry, appointing him as his assistant in 1952 and in 1957, he named Atkins the chief of RCA's country music operations in Nashville. In the early 60s, Sholes was one of the prominent members of the country music world who worked hard to see the foundation of Nashville's Country Music Hall Of Fame. In 1967, he was himself honoured with membership of that institution. The plaque erected on his induction stated: 'Record Company executive and giant influence toward making country music an integral part of cultural America'. Sholes died following a heart attack in 1968.

SHOOTERS

The Shooters comprised Walt Aldridge (guitar, vocals), Gary Baker (bass), Barry Billings (guitar), Chalmers Davis (keyboards) and Michael Dillon (drums). They had US country hits with 'They Only Come Out At Night', 'Tell It To Your Teddy Bear' and 'Borderline', among others, in the late 80s. Their albums combined various forms of music, with *Solid As A Rock* being recorded in Muscle Shoals, where Aldridge worked as a sessionman, producer and songwriter.
● ALBUMS: *Shooters* (Epic 1987)★★, *Solid As A Rock* (Epic 1989)★★★.

SIEBEL, PAUL

b. c.1945, Buffalo, New York, USA. For many years Paul Siebel was a popular performer in Greenwich Village clubs. His blend of country and folk music predated its more widespread appeal following the release of Bob Dylan's *Nashville Skyline* album. Although actively pursuing a musical career throughout most of the 60s, it was not until the following decade that the singer made his recording debut. *Woodsmoke And Oranges* was a critically acclaimed collection and featured 'Louise', Siebel's original composition, which was later covered by several acts, including Linda Ronstadt and Iain Matthews. The artist's *Jack-Knife Gypsy* was equally meritorious and an excellent supporting group, including Richard Greene (fiddle) and David Grisman (mandolin), enhanced Siebel's evocative delivery. Public indifference sadly undermined his development, although he has remained a popular live attraction.
● ALBUMS: *Woodsmoke And Oranges* (Elektra 1970)★★★★, *Jack-Knife Gypsy* (Elektra 1971)★★★★, *Paul Siebel Live At McCabes* (Rag Baby 1981)★★.
● COMPILATIONS: *Paul Siebel* (Philo 1996)★★★★.

SILVERSTEIN, SHEL

b. Shelby Silverstein, 1932, Chicago, Illinois, USA. A former artist with *Stars And Stripes* magazine, Silverstein joined the staff of *Playboy* at its inception during the early 50s and for almost two decades his cartoons were a regular feature of the publication. He later became a successful illustrator and author of children's books, including *Uncle Shelby's ABZ Book*, *Uncle Shelby's Zoo* and *Giraffe And A Half*. Silverstein was also drawn to the folk scene emanating from Chicago's Gate Of Horn and New York's Bitter End, latterly becoming a respected composer and performer of the genre. Early 60s collaborations with Bob Gibson were particularly memorable and in 1961 Silverstein completed *Inside Folk Songs*, which included the original versions of 'The Unicorn' and '25 Minutes To Go', later popularized, respectively, by the Irish Rovers and Brothers Four. Silverstein provided 'novelty' hits for Johnny Cash ('A Boy Named Sue') and Loretta Lynn ('One's On The Way'), but an association with Dr. Hook proved to be the most fruitful. A series of successful singles ensued, notably 'Sylvia's Mother' and 'The Cover Of *Rolling Stone*', and a grateful group reciprocated by supplying the backing on *Freakin' At The Freaker's Ball*. This ribald set included many of Silverstein's best-known compositions from this period, including 'Polly In A Porny', 'I Got Stoned And I Missed It' and 'Don't Give A Dose To The One You Love Most', the last of which was adopted in several anti-venereal disease campaigns. *The Great Conch Robbery*, released on the traditional music outlet Flying Fish Records, was less scatological in tone, and since that release, Silverstein has adopted a less public profile.

● ALBUMS: *Hairy Jazz* (Elektra 1959)★★★, *Inside Folk Songs* (Atlantic 1961)★★★, *I'm So Good I Don't Have To Brag* (Cadet 1965)★★★, *Drain My Brain* (Cadet 1966)★★★, *A Boy Named Sue* (RCA Victor 1968)★★★, *Freakin' At The Freaker's Ball* (Columbia 1969)★★★, *Songs And Stories* (1972)★★, *The Great Conch Train Robbery* (Flying Fish 1979)★★.

SINGING STOCKMEN

Norm Scott III (b. 1 January 1907, Sydney, New South Wales, Australia) and brother Arthur (b. 1903, Sydney, New South Wales, Australia, d. 1968) were the eldest of nine Scott children. A pioneer duo of Australian country music, Norm played guitar and banjo-mandolin and was singing professionally in 1924. In the late 20s, after hearing recordings of Jimmie Rodgers, he was probably the first Australian singer to perform in the style of Rodgers. Around 1928, he opened his Hawaiian Club, where he built up a business that saw him teach five guitar classes, including hillbilly, to over 100 pupils every week (the business eventually extended to other cities and towns, later employing 32 teachers and at one time having over 4,000 students in Sydney alone). He also formed his Hawaiian Club Band, which commenced a series of broadcasts on 2GB, lasting until the mid-50s. During the early days several later famous artists including Buddy Williams played at the club, while Tim McNamara and the McKean Sisters had guitar lessons there. After noting the success of Tex Morton's early recordings, Norm and Arthur began performing as the Singing Stockmen and cut two sides, 'Night Time In Nevada' and 'Hillbilly Valley', for Regal-Zonophone in October 1938, followed by six further recordings on 12 May 1939. Realizing that the Hawaiian Band, who were used on the recordings, were unsuitable for

country music work, Norm formed a hillbilly band. It included Dick Carr (b. 1911, Melbourne, Australia), a steel guitarist who later had solo success before becoming the leader of EMI's noted studio band. Carr and his band the Bushlanders provided the backing for Slim Dusty's 1957 hit 'The Pub With No Beer'. The new band also included George Raymond (a fiddler who later forged a solo career as a novelty instrumentalist) and Hal Carter (an accordionist and later the leader of a popular old-time dance band). Scott's hopes for further recordings with his new band floundered when Carr and Raymond left to join Tex Morton's Roughriders. The Singing Stockmen never recorded again and Arthur, who had first sung successfully as a boy soprano around 1913, retired from the music scene. Norm Scott continued in the business until he finally sold his interest in the Hawaiian Club in the 50s and nominally retired from music.

SINGLETARY, DARYLE

b. Georgia, USA. With his roots in the farming communities of rural Georgia, Singletary's first musical influence came from his parents and grandparents who all performed in a gospel quartet. However, he was converted to the cause of country music by the voice of George Jones on local radio, and by the late 80s he elected to pursue a professional career as a honky tonk singer. He travelled to Nashville in 1990 where he performed in numerous talent shows and open microphone events attempting to gain attention. However, his big break actually came as the result of attending a Randy Travis show in Louisville, Kentucky, where Travis's wife and manager, Lib Hatcher, was also in attendance. They were impressed enough by the demo tape he submitted to pass it on to a management company, through which Singletary signed with Giant Records in 1994. His self-titled debut album for the label, promoted with tours in support of Travis, included the three country chart hits 'I Let Her Lie', 'Too Much Fun' and 'I'm Living Up To Her Low Expectations'. Singletary's second album, released in 1996, established him as one of country music's better new-traditionalist artists.

● ALBUMS: *Daryle Singletary* (Giant 1995)★★★, *All Because Of You* (Giant 1996)★★★.

SIZEMORE, ASHER, AND LITTLE JIMMY

Asher Sizemore (b. 6 June 1906, Manchester, Kentucky, USA, d. c.1973) and his eldest son Jimmy (b. 29 January 1928, Paintsville, Kentucky, USA). Sizemore initially worked as a bookkeeper for a mining company in Pike County but aspired to be a singer. In 1931, singing old-time and cowboy songs, he appeared on radio in Huntington, West Virginia, before moving to WCKY Cincinnati and then WHAS Louisville, where he was first joined on air by his five-year-old son. In 1933, the duo were hired by the *Grand Ole Opry*, where they remained a popular act for about 10 years. Jimmy, at the age of five, allegedly had a repertoire of over 200 songs and understandably because of his extreme youth, his *Opry* and radio performances gained him a considerable following. He sang duets with his father but is remembered for his youthful renditions of such numbers as 'Chewing Gum' and 'The Booger Bear'. In 1934, he achieved recording success with a maudlin rendition of 'Little Jimmy's Goodbye To Jimmie Rodgers'. The Sizemores toured regularly but to augment their income, Asher established a very successful mail-order service for their annual books of *Health & Home Songs* and they also made transcription disc recordings that Asher syndicated to stations throughout the south and Midwest. By the late 30s, the act also included Jimmy's younger brother Buddy. Drawing mainly on sentimental numbers that contained regular references to mother, home, death, heaven and righteousness, with some interruption for part of World War II, they maintained a successful career throughout the 40s, mainly in the Midwest. In 1950, now joined by daughter Nancy Louise, Asher returned to WKLO Louisville. Jimmy and Buddy both served in the US Forces in Korea, Buddy being killed in action in November 1950. Asher and Jimmy later moved to Arkansas where they both worked on radio. Asher died in the 70s but Jimmy was still working on radio in an executive capacity into the 80s.

● ALBUMS: *Mountain Ballads & Old Hymns* (Decca 1966)★★★★, *Songs Of The Soil* (1984)★★★.

SKAGGS, RICKY

b. Ricky Lee Skaggs, 18 July 1954, Brushey Creek, near Cordell, Kentucky, USA. His father, Hobert, was a welder, who enjoyed playing the guitar and singing gospel songs with Skaggs' mother, Dorothy. Skaggs later recorded one of her songs, 'All I Ever Loved Was You'. Hobert returned from a welding job in Ohio with a mandolin for the five-year-old Skaggs, but had to go back before he could show him how to play it; within two weeks, Skaggs had worked it out for himself. In 1959 he was taken on stage during one of Bill Monroe's concerts and played 'Ruby' on Monroe's mandolin to rapturous applause. At the age of seven, he played mandolin on Flatt And Scruggs' television show, and then learnt guitar and fiddle. While working at a square dance with his father, he met Keith Whitley; they were to form a trio with Whitley's banjo-playing brother, Dwight, recording bluegrass and gospel shows for local radio. In 1970 they opened for Ralph Stanley, formerly of the Stanley Brothers, who was so impressed that he invited them to join his band, the Clinch Mountain Boys. They both made their recording debuts on Stanley's *Cry From The Cross*. The youngsters made two albums together, but Skaggs soon left in 1972, discouraged by the long hours and low pay. Skaggs married Stanley's cousin and worked in a boiler room in Washington DC. However, he returned to music by joining the Country Gentlemen, principally on fiddle. Then, from 1974-75, he played in the modern bluegrass band, J.D. Crowe And The New South. He later recorded a duet album with another member of the band, Tony Rice. Skaggs' first solo album, *That's It*, included contributions from his own parents. He formed his own band, Boone Creek, and recorded bluegrass albums, although they also touched on western swing and honky tonk. He was then offered a job in Emmylou Harris's Hot Band: 'Emmy tried to get me to join three times before I went. I wanted to stay in bluegrass and learn as much about the music as I could, but when Rodney Crowell left, I had an incentive to join her because I knew I'd be able to sing a lot.' From 1977-80, Skaggs encouraged Harris's forays into traditional country music via her *Blue Kentucky Girl*, *Light Of The Stable* and, especially, *Roses In The Snow*. Although Skaggs had rarely been a lead vocalist, his clear, high tenor was featured on an acoustic-based solo album, *Sweet Temptation*, for the North Carolina label Sugar Hill. Emmylou Harris and Albert Lee were among the guest musicians. While he was

working on another Sugar Hill album, *Don't Cheat In Our Hometown*, Epic Records took an interest in him. He switched to Epic and made his debut on the US country charts with a revival of Flatt And Scruggs' 'Don't Get Above Your Raising', which he later re-recorded in concert with Elvis Costello. *Rolling Stone* likened Skaggs' first Epic release, *Waitin' For The Sun To Shine*, to Gram Parsons' *Grievous Angel*, stating that they both represented turning points in country music. Skaggs was putting the country back into country music by making fresh-sounding records that related to the music's heritage. As if to prove the point, he had US number 1 country hits by reviving Flatt And Scruggs' 'Crying My Heart Out Over You' and Webb Pierce's 'I Don't Care'. He was the Country Music Association Male Vocalist of the Year for 1982, and became the sixty-first - and youngest - member of the *Grand Ole Opry*. Despite the old-time feeling, he also appealed to rock fans, performing a sell-out concert at London's Dominion Theatre; it was later released on a live album. Skaggs had played on Guy Clark's original version of 'Heartbroken' and his own recording of the song gave him another country chart-topper. He also completed his *Don't Cheat In Our Hometown*, which was released, after much negotiation, by Epic. Skaggs is a principled performer who leaves drinking or cheating songs to others, but he justified the title track, originally recorded by The Stanley Brothers, by calling it a 'don't cheat' song. Skaggs played on Albert Lee's first-class solo *Hiding*, and he had another number 1 with his own version of Lee's 'Country Boy', although the whimsical lyric must have baffled American listeners. With a revival of Bill Monroe's 'Uncle Pen', Skaggs is credited as being the first performer to top the country charts with a bluegrass song since Flatt And Scruggs in 1963, although he says, '"Uncle Pen" would not be a bluegrass single according to law of Monroe because there are drums and electric instruments on it.' Skaggs won a Grammy for the best country instrumental, 'Wheel Hoss', which was used as the theme music for his BBC Radio 2 series, *Hit It, Boys*. In 1981 Skaggs, now divorced, married Sharon White of the Whites. They won the Vocal Duo of the Year award for their 1987 duet, 'Love Can't Ever Get Better Than This'. He also recorded a playful duet of 'Friendship' with Ray Charles, and says, 'The people who call me Picky Ricky can't have met Ray Charles. He irons out every wrinkle. I would sing my lead part and he'd say, "Aw, honey, that's good but convince me now: sing to your ol' daddy."' Skaggs has worked on albums by the Bellamy Brothers, Rodney Crowell, Exile and Jesse Winchester. Johnny Cash had never previously used a fiddle player until Skaggs worked on *Silver*. Skaggs' busy career suffered a setback when his son Andrew was shot in the mouth by a drug-crazed truck-driver, but returned in 1989 with two fine albums in the traditional mould: *White Limozeen*, which he produced for Dolly Parton, and his own *Kentucky Thunder*. *My Father's Son* in 1991 was his most consistent album in years, but its poor sales led Columbia Records to drop him from their roster in 1992. He resurfaced on Atlantic Records for whom he has released two solid albums. Skaggs is modest about his achievements, feeling that he is simply God's instrument. He has rekindled an interest in country music's heritage, and many musicians have followed his lead.

● ALBUMS: with Keith Whitley *Tribute To The Stanley*

Brothers (Jalyn 1971)★★★, with Whitley *Second Generation Bluegrass* (1972)★★★, *That's It* (1975)★★★, as Boone Creek *Boone Creek* (Rounder 1977)★★★, as Boone Creek *One Way Track* (Sugar Hill 1978)★★★, with Tony Rice *Take Me Home Tonight In A Song* (Sugar Hill 1978)★★★, *Sweet Temptation* (Sugar Hill 1979)★★★★, with Rice *Skaggs And Rice* (Sugar Hill 1980)★★★, *Waitin' For The Sun To Shine* (Epic 1981)★★★, *Family And Friends* (Rounder 1982)★★★, *Highways And Heartaches* (Epic 1982)★★★, *Don't Cheat In Our Hometown* (Epic 1983)★★★★, *Country Boy* (Epic 1984)★★★, *Favorite Country Songs* (Epic 1985)★★★★, *Live In London* (Epic 1985)★★★, *Love's Gonna Get Ya!* (Epic 1986)★★★, *Comin' Home To Stay* (Epic 1988)★★★, *Kentucky Thunder* (Epic 1989)★★★, *My Father's Son* (Columbia 1991)★★★★, *Solid Ground* (Atlantic 1996)★★★, *Life Is A Journey* (Atlantic 1997)★★★.

● COMPILATIONS: *Super Hits* (Epic 1993)★★★★.

SKB

(see SKO)

SKILLET LICKERS

The original members were James Gideon Tanner (b. 6 June 1885, near Monroe, Georgia, USA, d. 1962, Winder, Georgia, USA; fiddle, vocals), Riley Puckett, Clayton McMichen (b. 26 January 1900, Allatoona, Georgia, USA, d. 3 January 1970, Battletown, Kentucky, USA; fiddle, vocals) and Fate Norris (banjo, harmonica, vocals). The members had been performing in various combinations around Atlanta before 1924, but it was in that year that Tanner (a fiddle-playing chicken farmer) and the blind guitarist Puckett recorded to become Columbia Records' first hillbilly talent. In 1926 with McMichen and Norris, they recorded for the first time as Gid Tanner And The Skillet Lickers. Over the years there were line-up variations and other important members included Lowe Stokes, Bert Layne (both outstanding fiddlers), Hoke Rice (guitar), Gid's brother Arthur (banjo, guitar) and teenage son Gordon (fiddle). By 1931, in some combination or other, they had cut 88 sides for Columbia - all but six being released. Their material included fiddle tunes, traditional ballads and pop songs, plus little comedy skits such as their noted 'A Corn Licker Still In Georgia'. In 1934, Gid Tanner And The Skillet Lickers were credited with a million-selling record for their recording of 'Down Yonder' (Gordon Tanner was the featured fiddler on the recording). (In 1959 pianist Del Wood also sold a million with her version of this tune.) After the Skillet Lickers disbanded in the 30s, Tanner returned to chicken farming until his death in 1962. McMichen went on to a successful career with his own band the Georgia Wildcats (which at one time included Puckett) and held the title of National Fiddling Champion from 1934-49. Gordon Tanner, who later led the Junior Skillet-Lickers, died following a heart attack on 26 July 1982. Bill C. Malone suggests that 'much of the band's popularity can be attributed to the energetic personality and showmanship of Tanner who whooped, sang in falsetto and in general played the part of the rustic fool'. McMichen is reputed to have suggested that 'Tanner's fiddle playing was just as unrestricted and tended to detract from the overall quality of the band'. In the 80s, Tanner's grandson, Phil, led a band known as the Skillet Lickers II.

● COMPILATIONS: *Gid Tanner* (70s)★★★, *Gid Tanner & His Skillet Lickers* (1973)★★★★, *Gid Tanner & His Skillet Lickers, Volume 2* (1975)★★★, *Kickapoo Medicine Show* (1977)★★, *A Day At The County Fair* (1981)★★★, *A Corn Licker Still In Georgia* (80s)★★★, *Skillet Lickers* (County 1996)★★★★.

SKINNER, JIMMIE

b. 29 April 1909, Blue Lick, near Berea, Kentucky, USA, d. 27 October 1979. Skinner relocated with the family to Hamilton, near Cincinnati, Ohio, in 1926, where he found work in a factory. In 1928, he heard recordings by Jimmie Rodgers that impressed him so much that he bought a guitar and set out to be a singer. He first broadcast on WCKY Covington and in the early 30s with his brother Esmer, he recorded two instrumentals for Gennett, though neither was released. Skinner began to write songs and continued to perform in his local area. In 1941, he was signed by RCA, but again due to wartime material shortages he had no releases. During the next few years, he played regularly on several stations including WHPD Mt. Orab, Ohio, and WHTN Huntingdon, West Virginia. He finally had record releases after recording for Red Barn Records, although he had to handle distribution himself. His recording of 'Will You Be Satisfied That Way' was popular enough in Knoxville to win him a regular spot over WROL. In the late 40s, he and a partner took over the Cincinnati Radio Artist label and he issued several of his recordings including 'Don't Give Your Heart To A Rambler' (revived by Travis Tritt in 1991) and 'Doin' My Time'. The same year Ernest Tubb had major US country chart success with Skinner's song 'Let's Say Goodbye Like We Said Hello'. In 1949, Skinner achieved his first chart hit with 'Tennessee Border'. In 1951, he was working both as a disc jockey on WNOP Covington and as an entertainer. He decided that there should be a specialized shop for country music followers and accordingly, with Lou Epstein, he opened *The Jimmie Skinner Music Center* in Cincinnati. The shop, which sold records, instruction manuals, songbooks and magazines by mail order, proved a tremendous success. He publicized the shop in trade publications and even presented live radio programmes from it. Other artists quickly realized its value and contributed adverts for their own records. He also later formed his own Vetco record label. The resultant publicity saw Skinner become a nationally known artist, although he had no major chart success during several years with Capitol and Decca. He joined Mercury in 1956 and the following year had a Top 10 country hit with 'I Found My Girl In The U.S.A.'. He had written the song as his answer to the Bobby Helms hit 'Fraulein'. Skinner then wrote an answer called 'I'm The Girl In The U.S.A', which was recorded by fellow Mercury artist Connie Hill. Between 1958 and 1960, he had 8 further country hits including 'What Makes A Man Wander', 'Dark Hollow' and 'Reasons To Live'. Skinner never became a major star but he was always busily connected with the industry through his music store and his radio and touring work. In 1974, he decided to move to Nashville; he thought it more suited to his songwriting ideas, but he still continued to tour his beloved Kentucky and Ohio. It was on such an occasion that, following a show near Louisville, he complained of pains in his arm and immediately headed for his Henderson, Nashville home, where he died on 27 October 1979, presumably as the result of an heart attack. Noted writer John Morthland described his style as 'Unusually elo-

quent. He was probably the most underrated of those who sought to follow in the footsteps of Jimmie Rodgers and always less maudlin than most white country blues singers'.
● ALBUMS: *Songs That Make The Jukebox Play* (Mercury 1957)★★★★, *Country Singer* (Decca 1961)★★★★, *Jimmie Skinner Sings Jimmie Rodgers* (Mercury 1962)★★★, *Jimmy Skinner (The Kentucky Colonel)* (Starday 1963)★★★, *Country Blues* (Mercury 1964)★★★★, *Jimmie Skinner's Number One Bluegrass* (1966)★★★, *Sings Bluegrass* (1968)★★★, *Have You Said Hello To Jesus Today* (1969)★★, *Bluegrass Volume 2* (1976)★★★, with Joe Clark *Old Joe Clark* (1976)★★★, *Jimmie Skinner And His Country Music Friends* (1976)★★★, *Number 1 Bluegrass* (1977)★★★★, *Requestfully Yours* (1977)★★, *Another Saturday Night* (1988)★★.

SKO

In 1986 three top Nashville songwriters, Thom Schuyler, Fred Knobloch and Paul Overstreet formed the group SKO. They were signed to Mary Tyler Moore's MTM label and had US country hits with 'You Can't Stop Love' and 'Baby's Got A New Baby', which was a number 1. Overstreet went solo the following year and Schuyler and Knobloch recruited Craig Bickhardt, but SKB only released one album in 1987, *No Easy Horses*, before they disbanded, their most successful singles being 'No Easy Horses' and 'Givers And Takers'.
● ALBUMS: *SKO* (MTM 1986)★★. As SKB *No Easy Horses* (MTM 1987)★★.

SLEDD, PATSY

b. Patsy Randolph, 29 January 1944, Falcon, Missouri, USA. One of 10 children, she began to play the guitar and sing at the age of 10. She entertained locally by the time she was 15, performing as the Randolph Sisters with one of her sisters, but soon followed a solo career. She was featured on the *Ozark Opry* and worked with a band on Austin's *Nashville Opry* before moving to Nashville in 1965. She joined Roy Acuff and toured with him all over the USA, the Caribbean and Vietnam. Her performances led to solo spots on *Hee-Haw* and the *Mid-Western Hayride*. In 1961, she recorded for United Artists and in 1971 for Epic but failed to chart on either label. She moved to Mega in 1972 and gained her first US country chart hit with 'Nothing Can Stop My Loving You'. Her biggest chart hit, 'Chip Chip', came in 1974, the year she made her British debut at London's Wembley Festival as a support member of the George Jones-Tammy Wynette Show. When Jones's mother died suddenly and the two stars returned to the USA without appearing at the festival, she found herself the star rather than the support, and gained respect from the crowd for her fine performance with the Jones Boys. Surprisingly, very little seems to have been heard from her since that time. After a minor hit with 'The Cowboy And The Lady' in 1976, her name was missing from the charts until 1987 when, recording on Showtime Records, she briefly charted with 'Don't Stay If You Don't Love Me' - apparently, it was Sledd who ultimately did not stay.
● ALBUMS: *Yours Sincerely* (Mega 1973)★★★, *Chip Chip* (Mega 1974)★★★.

SMILEY, RED

b. Arthur Lee Smiley, 17 May 1925, Asheville, North Carolina, USA, d. 2 January 1972; guitar, vocals. During World War II, Smiley served in the US Army and was seri-

ously wounded in action in Sicily. He underwent major surgery, losing one lung and was hospitalized for almost two years. The majority of Smiley's input to bluegrass music came as one half of the famed Reno And Smiley partnership. However, at the end of 1964, diabetes and the worsening effects of the wounds received during wartime service forced Smiley to give up the travelling with Don Reno, although he still made some appearances with him on the *Wheeling Jamboree*. He continued to appear on a Roanoke television show and recorded in his own name with the Bluegrass Cut-Ups. In 1968, the Roanoke show ended, when the station changed hands and Smiley partially retired. He rejoined Reno for some appearances in 1970 and recorded with Bill Harrell the following year. The long-time Reno And Smiley partnership finally ended with Smiley's death in 1972. After his death, a Japanese company released recordings made during a tour there and some other recordings were issued by Old Homestead.
● ALBUMS: as Red Smiley And The Bluegrass Cut-ups *Where No Cabins Fall* reissued by Rimrock as *18 Most Requested Gospel Songs* (Smiley 1966)★★★★, with Tater Tate *Town & Country* (Smiley 1967)★★★, *Red Smiley & The Bluegrass Cut-Ups Volume 1* (Rural Rhythm 1967)★★★★, *Red Smiley & The Bluegrass Cut-Ups Volume 2* (Rural Rhythm 1967)★★★, *Red Smiley & The Bluegrass Cut-Ups Volume 3* (Rural Rhythm 1968)★★★, *J.E. Mainer & Red Smiley & The Bluegrass Cut-ups* (Rural Rhythm 1968)★★★★, *Red Smiley And The Bluegrass Cut-ups With Jim Eanes* (Rural Rhythm 1969)★★★★, *Live* (Seven Seas 1974, Japan)★★, *Most Requested Sacred Songs* (Old Homestead 1978)★★. With Don Reno And Bill Harrell *Letter Edged In Black* reissued by Rebel as *Songs From Yesterday* (Wango 1971)★★★, *Together Again* (Rome 1971)★★, *Live At The Lone Star Festival* (Atteiram 1977)★★.

SMITH BROTHERS

A popular brother act comprising Tennessee Smith (b. John Onvia Smith, 15 August 1918, Oneida, Tennessee, USA; mandolin, fiddle, vocals) and his brother Smitty Smith (b. Aubrey Lee Smith, 13 March 1916, Oneida, Tennessee, USA; guitar, vocals). In 1938, with guitarist Milton Richman, they played on WCPO Cincinnati, before joining the Georgia Crackers on WKRC Columbus. In 1940, the three moved to WCHS Charleston, where they sang as the Red River Rangers. They relocated to Atlanta and worked with Eddie Wallace as a quartet called the Sunshine Boys with a repertoire that ranged from gospel to western swing. They also made film appearances in B-westerns with popular silver screen cowboys, including Lash LaRue, Charles Starrett and Eddie Dean. In 1949, Wallace and Richman relocated to Wheeling to continue their careers as the Sunshine Boys. The Smiths then occasionally worked with steel guitarist Boots Woodhall but usually as a duo. In the late 40s, they based themselves in Atlanta, where they first worked on radio and for almost seven years, as part of the TV Wranglers, they presented the daily *TV Ranch*, a 75-minute programme that proved extremely popular with WAGA viewers. They also presented a gospel programme, *Camp Meeting*, which led them to move more and more towards performing gospel music. Their recording career was minimal compared to some of their contemporaries but they recorded with the Sunshine Boys for Decca Records in the late 40s, and in 1951, they made their first recording as a duo for Mercury Records. In 1953, further recordings made for Capitol Records were almost all gospel numbers, such as their popular 'Child Of The King'. They worked with Slim Bryant's band on KDKA-TV, Pittsburgh, in 1960 and also made appearances on the *Wheeling Jamboree*. Between 1963 and 1965, they played regularly on television in Macon before they retired.

● ALBUMS: with the Sunshine Boys *That's My Jesus* (Sing 1964)★★★.

SMITH, ARTHUR

b. 1 April 1921, Clinton, South Carolina, USA. After the Smith family moved to Kershaw when Arthur was four years old, his father ran the town band and his son played trumpet with it. A few years later, by now playing guitar, mandolin and banjo, he formed a country band with two of his brothers. He graduated with honours in the late 30s but turned down lucrative employment, deciding instead to form a Dixieland Jazz Band, the Crackerjacks, which played on WSPA Spartanburg. After his brothers were drafted, he worked on WBT Charlotte before joining the navy in 1944. He played in the navy band, wrote songs and on his return to civilian life, organized variety shows featuring country and gospel music on WBT and WBT-TV; in 1947, he also gave bible classes. In 1948, he achieved Top 10 US country chart success with his MGM recordings of 'Guitar Boogie' and 'Banjo Boogie', with the former crossing over to the US pop chart, introducing many people to the potential of the electric guitar (in 1959, 'Guitar Boogie' was a US and UK pop hit for the Virtues and the same year became British guitarist Bert Weedon's first UK pop hit, although both recorded it as 'Guitar Boogie Shuffle') - *Billboard* initially seemed unsure in which chart to place the recording. Fender began to produce his 'Broadcaster' model, soon changing the name to 'Telecaster', the beginning of that instrument's popularity. The following year 'Boomerang', another guitar instrumental, became a country hit. *The Arthur Smith Show* on television started in the 50s and became so popular that by the mid-70s, it was still networked to most of the USA; artists from all fields were eager guests. Smith and the Crackerjacks (no longer a jazz band) recorded regularly over the years for various labels, with gospel music always prominent. Smith later became a deacon in a Baptist church. By the 70s, he had extended his business interests to include record, show and commercial productions and was also a director of a large insurance company. For a time in the mid-70s, he even ran a chain of supermarkets and formed the Arthur Smith Inns Corporation. In 1973, he and banjoist Don Reno instigated legal action against Warner Brothers over the use of 'Duellin' Banjos' as the theme music for the film *Deliverance*. They claimed that the music was based on a tune called 'Feudin' Banjos', written by Smith and recorded by them in 1955. After approximately two years of legal wrangling they won the case, received damages and legal rulings about future royalties. 'Duellin' Banjos' was named 'Best Country Music Song Of The Year' in 1973. The following year George Hamilton IV recorded his *Bluegrass Gospel* album at Smith's recording studio in Charlotte, North Carolina. Smith has copyrighted more than 500 songs, only one of which, 'Our Pilot Knows The Sea', is co-authored. In 1991, he published his first book, *Apply It To Life*. It includes the words and music to 10 of his best-known hymns, which have also been released as an album with vocals by Johnny Cash, George Beverly Shea, George Hamilton IV and Smith himself with the Crossroads Quartet. This artist should not be confused with Fiddlin' Arthur Smith or with Arthur Q. Smith (real name James A. Pritchett), a Knoxville songwriter, who sometimes co-wrote songs with Jim Eanes.

● ALBUMS: *Foolish Questions* 10-inch album (MGM 1955)★★★, *Specials* (MGM 1955)★★★, *Fingers On Fire* (MGM 1957)★★★★, *Mr Guitar* (Starday 1962)★★★, *Arthur Smith And The Crossroads Quartet* (Starday 1962)★★★, *Arthur 'Guitar Boogie' Smith Goes To Town* (Starday 1963)★★★, *In Person* (Starday 1963)★★★, *The Arthur Smith Show* (Hamilton 1964)★★, *Original Guitar Boogie* (Dot 1964)★★★★, *Down Home With Arthur 'Guitar Boogie' Smith* (Starday 1964)★★★, *Great Country & Western Hits* (Dot 1965)★★★, *Arthur Smith & Son* (1966)★★★, *Presents A Tribute To Jim Reeves* (Dot 1966)★★★, *Arthur 'Guitar' Smith And Voices* (ABC-Paramount 1968)★★, *Guitar Boogie* (Nashville 1968)★★★, *The Guitars Of Arthur 'Guitar Boogie' Smith* (Starday 1968)★★★, *Arthur Smith* (1970)★★★, *Battling Banjos* (Monument 1973)★★★★, with George Hamilton IV *Singing On The Mountain* (1973)★★, *Guitars Galore* (1975)★★★, with Don Reno *Feudin' Again* (1979)★★★, *Jumpin' Guitar* (1987)★★★, with Johnny Cash, George Beverly Shea and George Hamilton IV *Apply It To Life* (1991)★★★.

● FURTHER READING: *Apply It To Life*, Arthur Smith.

SMITH, ARTHUR 'FIDDLIN''

b. 1898, Bold Springs, Humphreys County, Tennessee, USA, d. 1973. One of the 14 children of an old-time fiddle player, he started to play the fiddle at the age of four, and later the banjo, began playing locally in his teens. He seriously thought of a musical career around 1925, when he worked as a lineman for the railroad. Several of his siblings also played instruments and around 1929, he first played on the *Grand Ole Opry* with his guitar playing brother, Homer. In 1930, he teamed with brothers Sam and Kirk McGee and played the *Opry* as the Dixieliners, soon after giving up his railroad work and becoming a full-time professional musician. His excellent playing, coupled with the McGees' guitar and banjo, soon made the Dixieliners one of the most influential of the *Opry* bands, who even through the Depression were in great demand. Surprisingly they did not record together until reunited in the 60s. Smith recorded under his own name and was accompanied by the Delmores, probably because the record company initially thought that their name would attract even more attention.

He first recorded fiddle tunes for Bluebird Records in 1935, including his now famous 'Mocking Bird'. At the time they were not successful and to keep his contract, his next recordings featured vocals, with 'More Pretty Girls Than One' being very successful. He left both the *Opry* and the McGees in 1938 and relocated to Hollywood, where he appeared in B-westerns and toured with Jimmy Wakely and the Sons Of The Pioneers. In the early 50s 'Beautiful Brown Eyes', co-written by Smith and Alton Delmore, was a US country and pop hit for Jimmy Wakely and also for pop singer Rosemary Clooney. He eventually returned to Nashville in the late 50s, where he rejoined his old friends the McGees. This time they did record together and played numerous folk festivals and other concert appearances. Noted authority Charles K.

Wolfe in *The Grand Ole Opry, The Early Years 1925-35* comments that 'Arthur Smith's fiddling style was more influential in the South than that of any other fiddler except possibly, Clayton McMichen'. This artist should not be confused with Arthur 'Guitar Boogie' Smith or Arthur Q. Smith (real name James A. Pritchett), a Knoxville songwriter, who sometimes co-wrote songs with Jim Eanes.
● ALBUMS: with Sam & Kirk McGee *Fiddlin'* (1961)★★★ *Arthur Smith & His Dixieliners* (1962)★★★, with Sam & Kirk McGee *Rare Old Fiddle Tunes (Fiddlin' Arthur Smith & His Dixieliners)* (Folkways 1962)★★★, with Sam & Kirk McGee *Old Timers Of The Grand Ole Opry* (1964)★★★, with Sam & Kirk McGee *Milk 'Em In The Evening Blues* (1965)★★★.
● COMPILATIONS: *Fiddlin' Arthur Smith, Volume 1 & 2* (1978)★★★★.

SMITH, CAL

b. Calvin Grant Shofner, 7 April 1932, Gans, Oklahoma, USA. The Shofner family moved to California, where Calvin met the rodeo-rider Todd Mason, becoming his stooge for knife and bullwhip tricks. Mason taught him how to play the guitar and at the age of 15 he was a vocalist with the San Francisco country band Kitty Dibble And Her Dude Ranch Wranglers. After military service, he played bass for Bill Drake, whose brother Jack was a prominent member of Ernest Tubb's Texas Troubadours. This led to him becoming master of ceremonies under the name of Grant Shofner, for Ernest Tubb and the Texas Troubadours from 1962-68. His first appearance on one of Tubb's recordings was 'The Great Speckled Bird' in 1963. Tubb arranged a record contract with Kapp and Smith's first record on the US country charts was 'The Only Thing I Want' in 1967. Two years with Decca followed and he finally broke through with 'I've Found Someone Of My Own' and a chart-topping Bill Anderson song, 'The Lord Knows I'm Drinking'. He joined MCA in 1973 and had further chart-toppers with the Don Wayne songs 'Country Bumpkin' and 'It's Time To Pay The Fiddler'. A 1974 hit, also written by Bill Anderson, was called 'Between Lust And Watching TV' and he recorded a popular 'mother' song, 'Mama's Face'. His last Top 20 hit on the US country charts was 'I Just Came Home To Count The Memories' in 1977. Although Smith has a good voice, he was often presented with mediocre material and subsequently left the business for several years. He joined Ernest Tubb on his double album *The Legend And The Legacy*.
● ALBUMS: *All The World Is Lonely Now* (Kapp 1966)★★★, *Goin' To Cal's Place* (Kapp 1967)★★★, *Travellin' Man* (Kapp 1968)★★★, *At Home With Cal* (Kapp 1968)★★, *Drinking Champagne* (Kapp 1969)★★, *It Takes Me All Night Long* (Kapp 1969)★★, *Country Hit Parade* (1970)★★★, *I've Found Someone Of My Own* (Decca 1972)★★★, *Swinging Doors* (MCA 1973)★★★, *Country Bumpkin* (MCA 1974)★★, *It's Time To Pay The Fiddler* (MCA 1975)★★★, *My Kind Of Country* (MCA 1975)★★, *Jason's Farm* (MCA 1976)★★, *I Just Came Home To Count The Memories* (MCA 1977)★★, *Stories Of Life* (1986)★★★.
● COMPILATIONS: *The Best Of Cal Smith* (Kapp 1971)★★★.

SMITH, CARL

b. 15 March 1927, Maynardsville, Tennessee, USA. The legendary Roy Acuff also came from Maynardsville and was Smith's hero. Smith sold seeds to pay for his first guitar and then cut grass to pay for lessons. He became a regular on a Knoxville country radio station, served in the navy in World War II, and was discovered by the 40s country singer Molly O'Day, which led to a recording contract with Columbia Records. In 1951 he made his US country chart debut with 'Let's Live A Little', had a double-sided success with 'If Teardrops Were Pennies'/'Mr. Moon' and followed it with a number 1, 'Let Old Mother Nature Have Her Way'. His impressive tally of 41 chart records during the 50s included four more chart-toppers, 'Don't Just Stand There', 'Are You Teasing Me?' (both 1952), 'Hey, Joe' (1953) and 'Loose Talk' (1955) as well as having success with 'This Orchid Means Goodbye', 'Cut Across Shorty' and 'Ten Thousand Drums'. Smith was a ballad singer with a rich, mature voice and, as he preferred steel guitars and fiddles to modern instrumentation, he did not cross over to the pop market. Known as the Tall Gentleman, he was a natural for television and for several years he hosted a highly successful country series in Canada, *Carl Smith's Country Music Hall*. He also appeared in the westerns *The Badge Of Marshal Brennan* (1957) and *Buffalo Gun* (1961), the latter with Webb Pierce and Marty Robbins. Smith had a tempestuous marriage to June Carter from the Carter Family; their daughter, Carlene Carter, is also a recording artist. After their divorce, in 1957 Smith married Goldie Hill, who had had her own number 1 country single with 'I Let The Stars Get In My Eyes' (1953). Although Smith rarely made the US country Top 10 after the 50s, he had hits until well into the 70s and his total of 93 has rarely been surpassed. In the 80s, Carl re-recorded his hits for new albums, but it was only a half-hearted comeback. His main interest is in his prize-winning quarter-horses, which he raises on a 500-acre ranch outside Nashville.
● ALBUMS: *Carl Smith* 10-inch album (Columbia 1956)★★★★, with the Carter Sisters *Softly And Tenderly* 10-inch album (Columbia 1956)★★★★, *Sentimental Songs* 10-inch album (Columbia 1956)★★★, *Smith's The Name* (Columbia 1957)★★★, *Sunday Down South* (Columbia 1957)★★★★, *Let's Live A Little* (Columbia 1958)★★★★, *The Carl Smith Touch* (Columbia 1960)★★★, *Easy To Please* (Columbia 1962), *The Tall, Tall Gentleman* (Columbia 1963)★★★, *There Stands The Glass* (Columbia 1964)★★, *I Want To Live And Love* (Columbia 1965)★★★, *Kisses Don't Lie* (Columbia 1965)★★★ *Man With A Plan* (Columbia 1966)★★★, *Satisfaction Guaranteed* (Harmony 1967)★★★, *The Country Gentleman* (Columbia 1967)★★★, *The Country Gentleman Sings His Favourites* (Columbia 1967)★★★, *Country On My Mind* (Columbia 1968)★★★, *Deep Water* (Columbia 1968)★★★, *Gentleman In Love* (Harmony 1968)★★★, *Take It Like A Man* (Harmony 1969)★★, *Carl Smith Sings A Tribute To Roy Acuff* (Columbia 1969)★★, *Faded Love And Winter Roses* (Columbia 1969)★★★, *Carl Smith And The Tunesmiths* (Columbia 1970)★★★, *I Love You Because* (Columbia 1970)★★★, *Knee Deep In The Blues* (Columbia 1971)★★, *Carl Smith Sings Bluegrass* (Columbia 1971)★★★, *Don't Say You're Mine* (Columbia 1972)★★★, *The Great Speckled Bird* (Columbia 1972)★★★★, *If This Is Goodbye* (Columbia 1972)★★★, *The Girl I Love* (1975)★★, *The Way I Lose My Mind* (Hickory/MGM 1975)★★★, *This Lady Loving Me* (1977)★★, *Silver Tongued Cowboy* (1978)★★, *Greatest Hits, Volume 1* (1980)★★★, *Legendary* (1981)★★, *Old Lonesome Times* (Rounder 1988)★★.
● COMPILATIONS: *Carl Smith's Greatest Hits* (Columbia

1962)★★★, *Carl Smith's Greatest Hits, Volume 2* (Columbia 1969)★★★, *The Carl Smith Anniversary Album/20 Years Of Hits* (Columbia 1970)★★★, *The Essential Carl Smith (1950-1956)* (Columbia/ Legacy 1991)★★★★, *Satisfaction Guaranteed* 5-CD set (Bear Family 1996)★★★.

SMITH, CONNIE

b. Constance June Meadows, 14 August 1941, Elkhart, Indiana, USA. Raised in West Virginia and Ohio as one of 14 children, Meadows longed to be a country singer and taught herself to play the guitar while in hospital recovering from a leg injury, caused by an accident with a lawnmower. She sang at local events as a teenager and appeared on several radio and television shows. She married and for a time led the life of a housewife, but after the birth of her first child, she again took to singing. Her break came in 1963, when she was booked to sing at the Frontier Ranch, a park near Columbus. Headlining the show was Bill Anderson, who was so impressed with her performance that he invited her to Nashville to appear on the *Ernest Tubb Record Shop* live show. Two months later, she returned to make demo recordings, which won her an RCA contract. In 1964, her recording of Anderson's song 'Once A Day' became her first hit, spending eight weeks at number 1 and 28 weeks in the US country charts. She became an overnight success and in the next five years added more Top 10 hits, including 'If I Talk To Him', 'The Hurtin's All Over', 'Cincinnati, Ohio' and 'Baby's Back Again'. She later recorded an album of Anderson's songs, although she did not work with him. She became a member of the *Grand Ole Opry* in 1965, was much in demand for tours and concert appearances and appeared in such films as *Road To Nashville, Las Vegas Hillbillies* and *Second Fiddle To An Old Guitar.* In the early 70s, further Top 10 hits included 'I Never Once Stopped Loving You', 'Just One Time' and 'Just For What I Am' and tours included Europe, Australia and the Far East. She moved to Columbia in 1973, where her first hit came with a recording of her own song 'You've Got Me Right Where You Want Me' and in 1977 to Monument, where her biggest hit was a country version of 'I Just Want To Be Your Everything' (a pop number 1 for Andy Gibb). From 1979-85, she abandoned active participation in music, apart from some *Opry* appearances, as she devoted her time to raising her family. A born-again Christian (her eldest son Darren is a missionary), she has performed gospel music on the *Opry* and recorded an album of Hank Williams' gospel songs. She regularly plays the *Opry*, network radio and television shows, and delighted her British fans with her appearance in the UK in 1990.

● ALBUMS: *The Other Side Of Connie Smith* (RCA Victor 1965)★★★, *Cute 'N' Country* (RCA Victor 1965)★★★★, *Miss Smith Goes To Nashville* (RCA Victor 1966)★★★, *Connie Smith Sings Great Sacred Songs* (RCA Victor 1966)★★, *Born To Sing* (RCA Victor 1966)★★★★, *Connie In The Country* (Camden 1967)★★★★, *Downtown Country* (RCA Victor 1967)★★★, *Connie Smith Sings Bill Anderson* (RCA Victor 1967)★★★, *Soul Of Country Music* (RCA Victor 1968)★★★, *I Love Charley Brown* (RCA Victor 1968)★★★, *Sunshine And Rain* (RCA Victor 1968)★★★, *Connie's Country* (RCA Victor 1969)★★★, with Nat Stuckey *Young Love* (RCA Victor 1969)★★★★, *Back In Baby's Arms* (RCA Victor 1969)★★★, *I Never Once Stopped Loving You* (RCA Victor 1970)★★★, *Sunday Morning With Nat Stuckey And Connie Smith* (RCA Victor 1970)★★★, *Where Is My Castle* (RCA Victor 1971)★★★, *Just One Time* (RCA Victor 1971)★★★, *Come Along And Walk With Me* (1971)★★, *My Heart Has A Mind Of Its Own* (1971)★★★, *Ain't We Havin' Us A Good Time'* (RCA Victor 1972)★★★, *If It Ain't Love (And Other Great Dallas Frazier Songs)* (RCA Victor 1972)★★★, *City Lights-Country Favorites* (1972)★★★, *Love Is The Look You're Looking For* (RCA Victor 1973)★★★, *A Lady Named Smith* (Columbia 1973)★★★, *Dream Painter* (RCA Victor 1973)★★★, *God Is Abundant* (Columbia 1973)★★★, with Nat Stuckey *Even The Bad Times Are Good* (RCA Victor 1973)★★★, *That's The Way Love Goes* (Columbia 1974)★★, *Connie Smith Now* (RCA Victor 1974)★★★, *I Never Knew (What That Song Meant Before)* (Columbia 1974)★★, *Collections* (1974)★★★, *Connie Smith Sings Hank Williams Gospel* (Columbia 1975)★★, *Joy To The World* (1975)★★, *I Got A Lot Of Hurtin' Done Today* (1975)★★★, *The Song We Fell In Love To* (Columbia 1976)★★★, *I Don't Want To Talk It Over Anymore* (Columbia 1976)★★★, *Pure Connie Smith* (1977)★★, *New Horizons* (Monument 1978)★★★, *Live In Branson, MO, USA* (1993)★★.

● COMPILATIONS: *The Best Of Connie Smith* (RCA Victor 1967)★★★★, *The Best Of Connie Smith, Volume 2* (RCA Victor 1970)★★★, *The Essential Connie Smith* (RCA 1997)★★★★.

SMITH, DARDEN

b. 11 March 1962, Brenham, Texas, USA. Smith is among a clutch of singer-songwriters to emerge from Texas during the 90s. Smith wrote his first songs at the age of 10, but began to take music seriously once his family moved to Houston when he was 13. His influences ranged from Guy Clark to Townes Van Zandt and Bob Dylan, or as he has said, 'Anyone who can tell a story.' He changed his name to Darden, after a local rodeo star, at the start of his career in the mid-80s. The Texas independent Redmix Records released his first album, *Native Soil*, in 1986, which included his most notable early composition - 'Two Dollar Novels', featuring Nanci Griffith on guest vocals. This led to a move to Epic Records, where his self-titled second album, produced by Ray Benson of Asleep At The Wheel, included another version of that song. However, the rest of the album saw him move away from the folk/country style that had dominated his debut, as Smith reached instead into new musical territory. Perhaps as a result of this, Smith was released from his contract with the Nashville-based Epic label to join the main CBS label in New York. Before this happened, however, Smith had partnered UK singer Boo Hewerdine on a jointly billed album for Ensign Records. Hewerdine also guested on Smith's debut for CBS, *Trouble No More*. Arguably his best album, it again caused a mixed reaction due to the sustained move away from his country roots. By now he was refusing to play older material (notably the perennially popular 'Two Dollar Novels') live on stage and 1994's *Little Victories* was essentially a rock album. That it was also a very good one passed by many critics, confused by the direction of this talented but idiosyncratic artist.

● ALBUMS: *Native Soil* (Redmix 1986)★★★, *Darden Smith* (Epic 1988)★★★★, with Boo Hewerdine *Evidence* (Ensign 1989)★★★, *Trouble No More* (Columbia 1990)★★★★, *Little Victories* (Chaos 1994)★★★, *Deep Fantastic Blue* (Demon 1997)★★★★.

SMITH, MARGO

b. Betty Lou Miller, 9 April 1942, Dayton, Ohio, USA. Smith began her singing career while still at school as a member of the Apple Sisters vocal group. She trained as a teacher but also had aspirations towards a singing career. She wrote songs in her spare time and eventually made some unsuccessful recordings for Chart Records. In 1975, after changing labels to 20th Century, she made her US country chart debut with her own song, 'There I've Said It', and quit her job as a teacher. She moved to Warner Brothers Records the following year and immediately had two Top 10 country hits with 'Save Your Kisses For Me' and 'Take My Breath Away'. By 1981, she had 20 chart entries including two number 1s, 'Don't Break The Heart That Loves You' and 'It Only Hurts For A Little While'. Several others such as 'If I Give My Heart To You' and 'My Guy' were versions of songs that had already been pop chart successes for other singers. She also duetted with Norro Wilson ('So Close Again') and Rex Allen Jnr. ('Cup Of Tea'). Smith was dropped by Warners in 1981 but managed a few minor hits on independent labels (the last being 'Echo Me' on Playback in 1988), but recorded an album for Dot/MCA in 1986. Traditionalists would rate much of her work as country pop, but she is a brilliant yodeler and usually features this now unusual talent for lady vocalists in her stage show.

● ALBUMS: *Margo Smith* (20th Century 1975)★★★, *Song Bird* (Warners 1976)★★★, *Happiness* (Warners 1977)★★★, *Don't Break The Heart That Loves You* (Warners 1978)★★★, *Just Margo* (Warners 1979)★★, *A Woman* (Warners 1979)★★, *Diamonds And Chills* (Warners 1980)★★, *Margo Smith* (Dot 1986)★★★, *The Best Yet* (1988)★★★.

SMITH, SAMMI

b. Jewel Fay Smith, 5 August 1943, Orange, California, USA. As her father was a serviceman, the family moved around, and when aged only 11, she was singing pop standards in nightclubs. She was discovered in 1967 by Johnny Cash's bass player, Marshall Grant. Minor US country hits followed with 'So Long, Charlie Brown' and 'Brownsville Lumberyard'. She toured with Waylon Jennings and befriended a janitor at Columbia Records, Kris Kristofferson. Her warm, husky version of his song 'Help Me Make It Through The Night' sold two million copies and was voted the Country Music Association's Single of the Year for 1971. Ironically, her record label, Mega, had been formed as a tax write-off and the last thing the owner wanted was a hit record. Smith had further country hits with 'Then You Walk In', 'For The Kids', 'I've Got To Have You', 'The Rainbow In Daddy's Eyes' and 'Today I Started Loving You Again', but she never topped 'Help Me Make It Through The Night', because, as she says, 'It was like following a Rembrandt with a kindergarten sketch'. Smith wrote 'Sand-Covered Angels', recorded by Conway Twitty, and 'Cedartown, Georgia' by Waylon Jennings. At Elektra Records, she recorded 'As Long As There's A Sunday' and 'Loving Arms', but in the 80s she had only limited US country chart success. Smith's former husband is Willie Nelson's guitarist Jody Payne and, being part Apache herself, she has adopted two Apache children and has an all American Indian band, Apache Spirit. In 1978 she set up the Sammi Smith Scholarship for Apache Advance Education, the aim being to increase the number of Apache lawyers and doctors.

● ALBUMS: *He's Everywhere* (1970)★★, *Help Me Make It Through The Night* (Mega 1970)★★★, *The World Of Sammi Smith* (1971)★★★, *Lonesome* (Mega 1971)★★★★, *Something Old, Something New, Something Blue* (Mega 1972)★★★, *The Toast Of '45* (Mega 1973)★★★, *Rainbow In Daddy's Eyes* (1974)★★★, *Sunshine* (1975)★★★, *Today I Started Loving You Again* (Mega 1975)★★★, *As Long As There's A Sunday* (Elektra 1976)★★★, *Her Way* (Zodiac 1976)★★★, *Mixed Emotions* (Elektra 1977)★★, *New Winds, All Quadrants* (Elektra 1978)★★, *Girl Hero* (Cyclone 1979)★★, *Better Than Ever* (1986)★★, *Here Comes That Rainbow Again* (1990)★★.

● COMPILATIONS: *The Best Of Sammi Smith* (Mega 1973)★★★★, *The Very Best Of Sammi Smith* (Mega 1975)★★★, *The Best Of ...* (Varese Sarabande 1997)★★★.

SNOW, HANK

b. Clarence Eugene Snow, 9 May 1914, Brooklyn, near Liverpool, Nova Scotia, Canada. After his parents divorced when he was eight years old, Snow spent four unhappy years with his grandmother, finally running away to rejoin his mother when she remarried. However, he was cruelly mistreated by his stepfather, which prompted him to abscond again. Though only 12 years old, he went to sea and spent the next four years working on fishing boats in the Atlantic where, on several occasions, he almost lost his life. An early interest in music, gained from his mother who had been a pianist for silent films, led him to sing for fellow crew members. On his return home, he worked wherever he could but at the same time seeking a singing career. He gained great inspiration listening to his mother's recordings of Jimmie Rodgers, and, acquiring a cheap guitar, he practised Rodgers' blue yodel, guitar playing and delivery, and set out to emulate his idol. He began to sing locally and eventually, through the help of Cecil Landry, the station announcer and chief engineer, he obtained a weekly unpaid spot on CHNS Halifax on a programme called *Down On The Farm*, where he became known as 'Clarence Snow and his Guitar' and 'The Cowboy Blue Yodeller'. It was Landry who, in 1934, first suggested the name of Hank, since he thought the boy needed a good western name. Snow became a talented guitarist and in the following years always played lead guitar for his own recordings. He met and married his wife Minnie in 1936 and the couple struggled to overcome financial hardship; eventually through sponsorship, he was given a programme on the network *Canadian Farm Hour*. In October 1936, by now known as 'Hank the Yodelling Ranger', he persuaded Hugh Joseph of RCA Victor, Montreal, to allow him to record two of his own songs, 'Lonesome Blue Yodel' and 'The Prisoned Cowboy'. This marked the start of a recording career destined to become the longest that any one country artist ever spent with the same record company. Rodgers' influence remained with him and when Snow's only son was born in 1937, he was named Jimmie Rodgers Snow. In 1944, after further recordings and regular work in Canada, and having become 'Hank The Singing Ranger' (due to the fact that as his voice deepened he found he could no longer yodel), he extended his career to the USA. He played various venues, including the *Wheeling Jamboree*, and worked in Hollywood, usually appearing with his performing horse, Shawnee. However, the anticipated breakthrough did not materialize; RCA, New York informed him that they could not record him until he was known in

America, but eventually they relented and in 1949 his recording of 'Brand On My Heart' brought him success in Texas. In December 1949, he achieved his first minor country chart hit with 'Marriage Vow'. At the recommendation of fellow Jimmie Rodgers devotee Ernest Tubb, he made his debut on the *Grand Ole Opry* in January 1950; he did not make a great impression and seriously considered abandoning thoughts of a career in the USA. This idea was forgotten when his self-penned million-seller, 'I'm Moving On', established him for all time. It spent 44 weeks on the US country charts, 21 at number 1 and even reached number 27 on the US pop charts. In the late 40s, Snow worked on tours with Hank Williams, later stating, 'I found Hank to be a fine person but the stories about him have been blown completely out of proportion. Take it from me, Hank Williams was okay'. Williams can be heard introducing Snow on the 1977 *A Tribute To Hank Williams*. Snow formed a booking agency with Colonel Tom Parker and in 1954, they were responsible for Elvis Presley's only *Opry* performance. Presley sang 'Blue Moon Of Kentucky', but failed to make any impression with the audience that night. Parker, to Snow's chagrin, took over Presley's management, but Presley recorded material associated with Snow, including 'A Fool Such As I', 'Old Shep' and later, 'I'm Movin' On'. 'I don't mean to brag but Elvis was a big fan of mine and he was always sitting around singing my songs', says Snow. After his initial breakthrough, Snow became an internationally famous star whose records sold in their millions, and between 1950 and 1980, he amassed 85 country chart hits. Further number 1 records were 'The Golden Rocket', 'I Don't Hurt Anymore', 'Let Me Go, Lover', 'Hello Love' and the tongue-twisting 'I've Been Everywhere'. The last, which gave him his second million-seller, was an Australian song originally naming Australian towns, but Snow requested that the writer change it to appeal to Americans. He was later proud to state he recorded it on the sixth take, in spite of the fact that there were 93 place names to memorize. Hank Snow's penchant for wearing a toupee that does not always appear to fit correctly has at times caused mirth, and many people believe he deliberately emphasizes it. Legend has it that, as a joke for the audience, one night on stage his fiddler player removed it with his bow and, understandably, received instant dismissal from his boss. Some album sleeves clearly show the toupee; others, such as *My Nova Scotia Home*, are most beautiful designs, while the noose on *Songs Of Tragedy* easily makes it one of the most remembered. It is generally assumed that the character played by Henry Gibson in Robert Altman's controversial 1975 film *Nashville* was modelled on Snow. Over the years his melodic voice, perfect diction and distinctive guitar playing make his recordings immediately identifiable, and his band, the Rainbow Ranch Boys, has always contained some of country music's finest musicians. His songwriting gained him election to the Nashville Songwriters' International Hall Of Fame in 1978 and the following year he was inducted to the Country Music Hall Of Fame, the plaque rightly proclaiming him as one of country music's most influential entertainers. In 1981, after a 45-year association, he parted company from RCA, stating it was 'because I would not record the type of things that are going today'. Snow has not recorded since, feeling that 'I have done everything in the recording line that was possible'. He resisted over-commercializing country

music during his long career and says of the modern scene that '80% of today's would be country music is a joke and not fit to listen to - suggestive material and a lot of it you can't even understand the words, just a lot of loud music'. Snow has played in many countries all over the world, being a particular favourite in the UK. An ability to handle all types of material has led to him being classed as one of the most versatile country artists in the music's history. In memory of his own unhappy childhood, he set up a foundation in Nashville to help abused children. He rarely tours now but maintains his regular *Opry* appearances and is still readily recognizable by his flamboyant stage costumes.

● ALBUMS: *Hank Snow Sings* 10-inch album (RCA Victor 1952)★★★★, *Country Classics* 10-inch album (RCA Victor 1952)★★★★, *Hank Snow Salutes Jimmie Rodgers* 10-inch album (RCA Victor 1953)★★★★, *Country Guitar* 10-inch album (RCA Victor 1954)★★★, *Just Keep A-Moving* (RCA Victor 1955)★★★★, *Old Doc Brown & Other Narrations* (RCA Victor 1955)★★★, *Country & Western Jamboree* (RCA Victor 1957)★★★, *Hank Snow Sings Sacred Songs* (RCA Victor 1958)★★, *The Hank Snow E-Z Method of Spanish Guitar* (School Of Music 1958)★, *When Tragedy Struck* (RCA Victor 1958)★★★, *Hank Snow Sings Jimmie Rodgers Songs* (RCA Victor 1959)★★★★, *The Singing Ranger* (RCA Victor 1959)★★★, *Hank Snow's Souvenirs* (RCA Victor 1961)★★★, *Big Country Hits (Songs I Hadn't Recorded Till Now)* (RCA Victor 1961)★★★, *The Southern Cannonball* (RCA Victor 1961)★★★★, *One & Only Hank Snow* (Camden 1962)★★★, with Anita Carter *Together Again* (RCA Victor 1962)★★★, *Railroad Man* (RCA Victor 1963)★★★★, *I've Been Everywhere* (RCA Victor 1963)★★★★, *The Last Ride* (Camden 1963)★★★, *More Hank Snow Souvenirs* (RCA Victor 1964)★★★, *Old & Great Songs by Hank Snow* (Camden 1964)★★★, *Songs Of Tragedy* (RCA Victor 1964)★★★, with Chet Atkins *Reminiscing* (RCA Victor 1964)★★★, *Gloryland March* (RCA Victor 1965)★★★, *Heartbreak Trail - A Tribute To The Sons Of The Pioneers* (RCA Victor 1965)★★★, *The Highest Bidder And Other Favorites* (Camden 1965)★★★, *Your Favorite Country Hits* (RCA Victor 1965)★★★, *Gospel Train* (RCA Victor 1966)★★★, *The Guitar Stylings Of Hank Snow* (RCA Victor 1966)★★, *This Is My Story* (RCA Victor 1966)★★★, *Gospel Stylings* (RCA Victor 1966)★★, *Travelin' Blues* (Camden 1966)★★★, *Spanish Fireball* (RCA Victor 1967)★★, *My Early Country Favorites* (Camden 1967)★★★★, *Snow In Hawaii* (RCA Victor 1967)★★★, *Christmas With Hank Snow* (RCA Victor 1967)★★★, *My Nova Scotia Home* i (RCA Victor 1967)★★★, *My Nova Scotia Home* ii (RCA Victor 1968)★★★, *Lonely And Heartsick* (RCA Victor 1968)★★★, *Somewhere Along Life's Highway* (RCA Victor 1968)★★★, *Tales of The Yukon* (RCA Victor 1968)★★★, *I Went To Your Wedding* (RCA Victor 1969)★★★, *Snow In All Seasons* (RCA Victor 1969)★★★, *Hits Covered By Snow* (RCA Victor 1969)★★★, *Cure For The Blues* (RCA Victor 1970)★★★, *Hank Snow Sings In Memory Of Jimmie Rodgers* (RCA Victor 1970)★★★★, *Memories Are Made Of This* (RCA Victor 1970)★★★, with Chet Atkins *C.B. Atkins & C.E. Snow By Special Request* (RCA Victor 1970)★★★, *Wreck Of The Old 97* (Camden 1971)★★★, *Award Winners* (RCA Victor 1971)★★★, *Tracks & Trains* (RCA Victor 1971)★★★, *Lonesome Whistle* (RCA Victor 1972)★★★, *The Jimmie Rodgers Story* (RCA Victor 1972)★★★★, *Legend Of Old Doc Brown* (RCA Victor 1972)★★★, *Snowbird* (RCA Victor

1973)★★★, *When My Blue Moon Turns To Gold Again* (RCA Victor 1973)★★★, *Grand Ole Opry Favorites* (RCA Victor 1973)★★★, *Hello Love* (RCA Victor 1974)★★★, *I'm Moving On* (RCA Victor 1974)★★★, *Now Is The Hour - For Me To Sing To My Friends In New Zealand* (RCA Victor 1974)★★★, *That's You And Me* (RCA Victor 1974)★★★, *You're Easy To Love* (RCA Victor 1975)★★★, *All About Trains* one side Jimmie Rodgers (RCA Victor 1975)★★★★, with Rodgers *Live From Evangel Temple* (1976)★★★, *#104 - Still Movin' On* (RCA Victor 1977)★★★, *Living Legend* (RCA Victor 1978)★★★, *Mysterious Lady* (RCA Victor 1979)★★★, *Instrumentally Yours* (RCA Victor 1979)★★★, with Kelly Foxton *Lovingly Yours* (1980)★★★, *By Request* (RCA Victor 1981)★★★, with Foxton *Win Some, Lose Some, Lonesome* (1981)★★★, with Willie Nelson *Brand On My Heart* (Columbia 1985)★★★.
● COMPILATIONS: *The Best Of Hank Snow* (RCA Victor 1966)★★★, *Hits, Hits & More Hits* (RCA Victor 1968)★★★★, *Hank Snow, The Singing Ranger Volume 1 (1949-1953)* (Bear Family 1989)★★★★, *Hank Snow, The Singing Ranger Volume 2 (1953-1958)* 4-CD box set (Bear Family 1990)★★★★, *Hank Snow, The Thesaurus Transcriptions (1950-1956)* 5-CD box set (Bear Family 1991)★★★★, *Hank Snow, The Singing Ranger Volume 3 (1958-1969)* 12-CD box set (Bear Family 1992)★★★★, *The Yodelling Ranger 1936-47* 5-CD box set (Bear Family 1993)★★★★, *The Singing Ranger Volume 4* 9-CD box set (Bear Family 1994)★★★★, *My Early Country Favorites* (RCA Camden 1996)★★★, *The Essential Hank Snow* (RCA 1997)★★★★.
● FURTHER READING: *The Hank Snow Story*, Hank Snow with Jack Ownby and Bob Burris.

SONNIER, JO·EL

b. 2 October 1946, Rayne, Louisiana, USA. The son of share-croppers, Sonnier (pronounced Sawn-ya) was working in cottonfields from the age of five. He began singing and playing accordion, worked on local radio and recorded his first single, 'Tes Yeaux Bleus' (Your Blue Eyes) when aged 13. He recorded his 'white roots Cajun music' for the Swallow and Goldband labels, and when 26 years old, moved to California and then to Nashville in search of national success. In 1976 he recorded Lefty Frizzell's 'Always Late (With Your Kisses)' for Mercury and then formed a band called Friends, which included Albert Lee, David Lindley and Garth Hudson. His session work has included 'Cajun Born' for Johnny Cash and 'America Without Tears' for Elvis Costello. In 1987 Sonnier was signed to RCA and Steve Winwood guested on 'Rainin' In My Heart', a track on *Come On Joe*. He had a country hit with a frenzied version of Richard Thompson's 'Tear-Stained Letter'. He has toured the USA with Alabama and the Charlie Daniels Band and, by all accounts, his UK debut at the Mean Fiddler in 1989 was electrifying. He was once known as the 'Cajun Valentino'. He signed to Capitol-Nashville in 1991, but found commercial success hard to achieve. The album with Eddy Raven was a welcome return to recording.
● ALBUMS: *Cajun Life* (Rounder 1984)★★★, *Come On Joe* (RCA Victor 1988)★★★★, *Have A Little Faith* (RCA 1989)★★★, *Tears Of Joy* (Liberty 1991)★★★, *Hello Happiness Again* (Liberty 1992)★★★, with Eddy Raven *Cookin' Cajun* (K-Tel 1997)★★★.
● COMPILATIONS: *The Complete Mercury Sessions* (Mercury 1992)★★★★, *Cajun Roots* (Rounder 1994)★★★★.

SONS OF THE PIONEERS

The Sons Of The Pioneers was founded in 1933 by Leonard Slye (aka Roy Rogers), when he recruited two friends - Bob Nolan (b. Robert Clarence Nobles, 1 April 1908, New Brunswick, Canada) and Tim Spencer (b. Vernon Spencer, 13 July 1908, Webb City, Missouri, USA) - to re-form a singing trio, known originally as the O-Bar-O Cowboys, and undergo a name change to the Pioneer Trio. When they found regular radio work in Los Angeles, they added fiddle player Hugh Farr (b. 6 December 1903, Llano, Texas, USA). Someone suggested that they looked too young to be pioneers so they became the Sons Of The Pioneers. They were signed to US Decca Records in 1935, and Hugh's brother Karl (b. Karl Marx Farr, 25 April 1909, Rochelle, Texas, USA) joined as a guitarist. The Sons Of The Pioneers sang in numerous Western films and when Rogers was groomed as a singing cowboy in 1937, he was replaced as lead singer by Lloyd Perryman (b. Lloyd Wilson Perryman, 29 January 1917, Ruth, Arkansas, USA). Their bestselling records include 'Cool Water' and 'Tumbling Tumbleweeds', both written by Nolan. Spencer wrote the country standards 'Cigarettes, Whisky And Wild, Wild Woman' and 'Room Full Of Roses'. Owing to throat problems, Tim Spencer retired from performing in 1949 but managed the group for some years. He died on 26 April 1974. Lloyd Perryman, who became the leader of the group when Spencer and Nolan left in 1949, died on 31 May 1977. On 20 September 1961, Karl Farr collapsed and died on stage after being agitated when a guitar-string broke, while his brother survived until 17 April 1980. Nolan died on 16 June 1980, requesting that his ashes be scattered across the Nevada desert. Other members of The Sons Of The Pioneers included Pat Brady, Ken Carson, Ken Curtis, Tommy Doss and Shug Fisher. Many critics rate the Perryman, Curtis and Doss recordings, which include the 1949 versions of 'Riders In The Sky' and 'Room Full Of Roses', as the best. Despite personnel changes, The Sons Of The Pioneers' recordings reflect a love of God, the hard-working life of a cowboy, and an admiration for a 'home on the range'. The legacy of the Hollywood cowboys is still with us in the work of Ian Tyson, but his songs paint a less romantic picture. They were elected to the Country Music Hall Of Fame in 1980.
● ALBUMS: *Cowboy Classics* 10-inch album (RCA Victor 1952)★★★★, *Cowboy Hymns And Spirituals* 10-inch album (RCA Victor 1952)★★★★, *Western Classics* 10-inch album (RCA Victor 1953)★★★★, *25 Favourite Cowboy Songs* (RCA Victor 1955)★★★★, *How Great Thou Art* (RCA Victor 1957)★★★, *One Man's Songs* (RCA Victor 1957)★★★, *Cool Water (And 17 Timeless Favourites)* (RCA Victor 1959)★★★, *Lure Of The West* (RCA Victor 1961)★★★★, *Tumbleweed Trails* (RCA Victor 1962)★★★★, *Our Men Out West* (RCA Victor 1963)★★★, *Hymns Of The Cowboy* (RCA Victor 1963)★★★, *Good Old Country Music* (Camden 1963)★★★, *Trail Dust* (RCA Victor 1963)★★★, *Country Fare* (RCA Victor 1964)★★★, *Down Memory Trail* (RCA Victor 1964)★★★, *Legends Of The West* (RCA Victor 1965)★★★, *The Sons Of The Pioneers Sing The Songs Of Bob Nolan* (RCA Victor 1966)★★★, *The Sons Of The Pioneers Sing Campfire Favorites* (RCA Victor 1967)★★★, *San Antonio Rose And Other Country Favorites* (Camden 1968)★★★★, *South Of The Border* (RCA Victor 1968)★★★, *The Sons Of The Pioneers Visit The South Seas* (RCA Victor 1969)★★★, *A Country And*

Western Songbook (RCA Victor 1977)★★★, Let's Go West Again (1981)★★★.

● COMPILATIONS: Wagons West (Camden 1958)★★★, Room Full Of Roses (Camden 1960)★★★, Westward Ho! (RCA Victor 1961)★★★, Sons Of The Pioneers Best (Harmony 1964)★★★, Tumbleweed Trails (Vocalion 1964)★★★, Best Of The Sons Of The Pioneers (RCA Victor 1966)★★★, Riders In The Sky (Camden 1973)★★★★, The Sons Of The Pioneers - Columbia Historic Edition (Columbia 1982)★★★★, 20 Of The Best (RCA 1985)★★★, Radio Transcriptions - Volumes 1 & 2 (Outlaw 1987)★★★, Cool Water, Vol. 1 (1945-46) (Bear Family 1987)★★★★, Teardrops In My Heart, Vol. 2 (1946-47) (Bear Family 1987)★★★★, A Hundred And Sixty Acres, Vol. 3 (1946-47) (Bear Family 1987)★★★★, Riders In The Sky, Vol. 4 (1947-49) (Bear Family 1987)★★★★, Land Beyond The Sun, Vol. 5 (1949-50) (Bear Family 1987)★★★★, And Friends, Vol. 6 (1950-1951) (Bear Family 1987)★★★★, There's A Goldmine, Vol. 7 (1951-1952) (Bear Family 1987)★★★★, Country Music Hall Of Fame (MCA 1991)★★★★, Wagons West 4-CD boxed set (Bear Family 1993)★★★★.

● FURTHER READING: Hear My Song: The Story Of The Celebrated Sons Of The Pioneers, Ken Griffis.

SONS OF THE SAN JOAQUIN

A western vocal trio formed in the San Joaquin Valley of California, comprising brothers Joe Hannah (b. 1 February 1931, Marshfield, Missouri, USA; bass, vocals) and Jack Hannah (b. 25 October 1933, Marshfield, Missouri, USA; guitar, vocals), and Joe's son, Lon Hannah (b. 10 April 1956, Pasadena, California, USA; lead guitar, vocals). The brothers had always been attracted by the singing of the Sons Of The Pioneers, but it was Lon, at the time singing as a solo artist, who convinced them in 1987, that they should form a trio. At the time, the brothers worked as teachers and on occasions even worked cattle on local ranches. They made their performing debut at the major Clovis Rodeo and in 1989 appeared at the Cowboy Poetry Gathering in Elko, Nevada, where they proved an immediate hit and have become a regular act ever since. Michael Martin Murphey, present at the event, took them to Nashville to provide harmony vocals for Cowboy Songs, his noted western revival album. The Sons Of The San Joaquin went on to tour in their own right, soon building up a reputation for their close harmonies and authentic western sounds. Along with Texas singer Don Edwards and cowboy poet Waddie Mitchell, they were the first artists signed by the new Warner Western label. They began to write much of their own material, which portrayed the western lifestyle, and with Riders In The Sky, they do much to popularize the sounds started many years ago by the Sons Of The Pioneers. They toured to Saudi Arabia and Pakistan in 1993 as goodwill ambassadors for the United States Information Service. The following year, they proved very successful when they performed with the Fresno Philharmonic Symphony Orchestra. The show consisted of selections from their recordings arranged in symphony setting, and was accompanied by a video screen that showed scenes from some classic westerns while they performed. They became associated with Edwards and Mitchell, forming The Cowboy Jubilee, a travelling show of western music and verse.

● ALBUMS: Bound For The Rio Grande (1989)★★★, Great American Cowboy (1991)★★★, A Cowboy Has To Sing (Warner Western 1992)★★★, Songs Of The Silver Screen (Warner Western 1993)★★, From Whence Came The Cowboy (Warner Western 1995)★★★.

SOUTHERN PACIFIC

When the Doobie Brothers broke up in 1982, guitarist/fiddler John McFee and drummer Keith Knudsen went into session work. Both of them are featured on Emmylou Harris's White Shoes, and McFee is particularly known for his contribution, playing both lead and steel guitar, on Elvis Costello's Almost Blue. With vocalist Tim Goodman from New Grass Revival and two of Elvis Presley's musicians, Jerry Scheff and Glen D. Hardin, they made some demos and were signed to Warner Brothers Records by Jim Ed Norman. They originally thought of calling themselves the Tex Pistols but decided on Southern Pacific. Their first album was a continuation of the soft rock and country that was pioneered by the Eagles. For touring purposes, Scheff and Hardin were replaced by Stu Cook from Creedence Clearwater Revival and session musician Kurt Howell. Emmylou Harris sang on an early hit, 'Thing About You', in 1985, and, by way of thanks, they recorded 'A Girl Like Emmylou'. In 1988, Tim Goodman was replaced by David Jenkins, the former lead singer from Pablo Cruise, and they sang 'Any Ole Wind That Blows' on the soundtrack of the Clint Eastwood film Pink Cadillac. The permanence of the group was put into question when the Doobie Brothers decided to re-form, but a final album was made in 1990. It included a revival of 'GTO' with the Beach Boys.

● ALBUMS: Southern Pacific (Warners 1985)★★★, Killbilly Hill (Warners 1986)★★★, Zuma (Warners 1988)★★, Country Line (Warner 1990)★★.

● COMPILATIONS: Greatest Hits (Warners 1991)★★★.

SOVINE, RED

b. Woodrow Wilson Sovine, 17 July 1918, Charleston, West Virginia, USA, d. 4 April 1980, Nashville, Tennessee, USA. Sovine was taught the guitar by his mother and was working professionally by the time he was 17 on WCHS Charleston with Johnny Bailes, and then as part of Jim Pike And His Carolina Tarheels. In 1948 Sovine formed his own band, The Echo Valley Boys, and became a regular on Louisiana Hayride. Sovine acquired the nickname of 'The Old Syrup Sopper' following the sponsorship by Johnny Fair Syrup of some radio shows, and the title is apt for such narrations as 'Daddy's Girl'. Sovine recorded for US Decca Records and first made the country charts with 'Are You Mine?', a duet with Goldie Hill. Later that year, a further duet, this time with Webb Pierce, 'Why Baby Why', made number 1 on the US country charts. They followed this with the tear-jerking narration 'Little Rosa', which became a mainstay of Sovine's act. From 1954 Sovine was a regular at the Grand Ole Opry and, in all, he had 31 US country chart entries. He was particularly successful with maudlin narrations about truck-drivers and his hits include 'Giddyup Go' (a US country number 1 about a truck-driver being reunited with his son), 'Phantom 309' (a truck-driving ghost story!) and his million-selling saga of a crippled boy and his CB radio, 'Teddy Bear' (1976). Sequels and parodies of 'Teddy Bear' abound; Sovine refused to record 'Teddy Bear's Last Ride', which became a US country hit for Diana Williams. He retaliated with 'Little Joe' to indicate that Teddy Bear was not dead after all.

Among his own compositions are 'I Didn't Jump The Fence' and 'Missing You', which was a UK hit for Jim Reeves. Sovine recorded 'The Hero' as a tribute to John Wayne, and his son, Roger Wayne Sovine, was named in his honour. The young Sovine was briefly a country singer, making the lower end of the US country charts with 'Culman, Alabam' and 'Little Bitty Nitty Gritty Dirt Town'. Red Sovine's country music owed nothing to contemporary trends but his sentimentality was popular in UK clubs. He had no big-time image and, while touring the UK, he made a point of visiting specialist country music shops. In 1980 Sovine died of a heart attack at the wheel of his car in Nashville. The following year, as CB radio hit the UK, a reissue of 'Teddy Bear' reached number 5, his first UK chart entry.

● ALBUMS: *Red Sovine* (MGM 1957)★★★★, *The One And Only Red Sovine* (Starday 1961)★★★★, *Golden Country Ballads Of The 60's* (Somerset 1962)★★★, *Red Sovine* (Decca 1964)★★★★, *Red Sovine - Fine* (1964)★★★, *Little Rosa* (1965)★★★, *Town And Country Action* (Starday 1965)★★★, *Country Music Time* (Decca 1966)★★★, *Giddyup Go* (Starday 1966)★★★, *I Didn't Jump The Fence* (Starday 1967)★★★, *Farewell So Long Goodbye* (Metro 1967)★★★, *The Nashville Sound Of Red Sovine* (Starday 1967)★★★, *Phantom 309* (Starday 1967)★★★, *Sunday With Sovine* (Starday 1968)★★★, *Tell Maude I Slipped* (Starday 1968)★★★, *The Country Way* (Vocalion 1968)★★★, *Classic Narrations* (1969)★★, *Closing Time 'Til Dawn* (1969)★★★, *Who Am I?* (Starday 1969)★★, *I Know You're Married* (1970)★★★, *Ruby, Don't Take Your Love To Town* (1970)★★★, *The Greatest Grand Ole Opry* (Chart 1972)★★★, *It'll Come Back* (Chart 1974)★★★, *Teddy Bear* (Starday 1976)★★★, *Woodrow Wilson Sovine* (Gusto/Starday 1977)★★★, *16 New Gospel Songs* (1980)★★.

● COMPILATIONS: *Red Sovine's 16 Greatest Hits* (Gusto/Starday 1977)★★★★.

SPARKS, LARRY

b. 15 September 1947, Lebanon, Ohio, USA. After learning to play guitar in his early teens, he first played with local bluegrass and country bands. He made his professional debut at 16, and in the mid-60s, he made some appearances with the Stanley Brothers. In February 1967, following Carter Stanley's death, he joined Ralph Stanley's Clinch Mountain Boys. His singing resembled that of Carter Stanley and he sang the popular Stanley Brothers duets with Ralph, while his talented guitarwork saw him often playing lead during his time with the group. He recorded five albums with Stanley and worked with him until 1970, when he formed his own Lonesome Ramblers, which on occasions featured his sister, Bernice, playing rhythm guitar. Throughout the 70s and 80s, Sparks built a considerable reputation. Although, at times, he varied his music from old-time traditional to more contemporary bluegrass, he has never been afraid to use country material; in fact, one of his popular 70s albums was a collection of the songs of Hank Williams. He made his first recordings for Pine Tree but later recorded for several others, including his own Lesco label. He has written many songs, sometimes with Bernice, including 'Memories And Dreams', 'Goodbye Little Darling' and 'Just Loving You'. Wendy Miller (mandolin), Mike Kelly (banjo) and Art Wydner (bass) have played on many of his recordings and there have also been appearances by Ricky Skaggs. Known

affectionately by followers of the bluegrass genre as 'The Most Soulful Voice In Bluegrass', he continued to play into the 90s and although resident in Richmond, Virginia, he appears at most major bluegrass festivals.

● ALBUMS: *Ramblin' Guitar* (Pine Tree 1970)★★★★, *New Gospel Songs* (Pine Tree 1971, reissued by Old Homestead as *Green Pastures In The Sky* 1982)★★★★, *Pickin' And Singin'* (Pine Tree 1975, reissued by Old Homestead as *Where The Dim Lights Are Dimmest* 1982)★★★, *Ramblin' Bluegrass* (Starday 1972)★★★★, *Bluegrass Old & New* (Old Homestead 1972, reissued as *Early & Essential Vol. 1* 1980)★★★★, *Where The Sweet Waters Flow* (Old Homestead 1973)★★★, *The Lonesome Sounds* (Old Homestead 1974)★★★, *The Footsteps Of Tradition* (King Bluegrass 1974)★★★, *Sparkling Bluegrass* (King Bluegrass 1975)★★★, *Thank You Lord* (Old Homestead 1976)★★, *You Could Have Called* (King Bluegrass 1976)★★★, *Christmas In The Hills* (King Bluegrass 1976)★★★, *Larry Sparks Sings Hank Williams* (County 1977)★★, *Kind'a Lonesome* (Lesco 1979)★★★, *Early & Essential Vol. 2* (Old Homestead 1980)★★★, *John Deere Tractor* (Rebel 1980)★★★, *It's Never Too Late* (June Appal 1980)★★★, *Ramblin' Letters* (Acoustic Revival 1981)★★★, *Dark Hollow* (Rebel 1982)★★★, *The Testing Times* (Rebel 1983)★★★, *Blue Sparks* (Rebel 1984)★★★, *Lonesome Guitar* (Rebel 1985)★★★★, *A Face In The Crowd* (Old Homestead 1985)★★★, *Live In Concert* (Rebel 1985)★★, *Gonna Be Moving* (Rebel 1986)★★★, *Silver Reflections* (Rebel 1988)★★★, *The Rock I Stand On* (Rebel 1994)★★★.

● COMPILATIONS: *The Best Of Larry Sparks* (Rebel 1983)★★★★, *Classic Bluegrass* (Rebel 1989)★★★★.

● FURTHER READING: *Larry Sparks - A Discography*, Henning Peterson.

SPEARS, BILLIE JO

b. 14 January 1937, Beaumont, Texas, USA. Discovered by songwriter Jack Rhodes, Spears' first record, as Billie Jo Moore, 'Too Old For Toys, Too Young For Boys', earned her $4,200 at the age of 15. Despite appearances on *Louisiana Hayride*, she did not record regularly until she signed with United Artists in 1964. Following her producer, Kelso Herston, to Capitol Records, she had country hits with 'He's Got More Love In His Little Finger' and 'Mr. Walker, It's All Over'. After time off following the removal of a nodule on her vocal cords, she recorded briefly for Brite Star and Cutlass. In 1974, Spears returned to United Artists where producer Larry Butler was developing a successful country roster. Her transatlantic smash, 'Blanket On The Ground', was controversial in America. 'It sounded like a cheating song,' says Spears, 'and the public don't think girls should sing cheating songs!' In actuality, it was about adding romance to a marriage and its success prompted other records with a similar theme and tempo - 'What I've Got In Mind' (which had originally been a rhumba) and ''57 Chevrolet'. The traditional 'Sing Me An Old-Fashioned Song' sold well in the UK, while her cover version of Dorothy Moore's ballad 'Misty Blue' was successful in the USA. She is also known for her cover version of Gloria Gaynor's 'I Will Survive'. She maintains, 'It is still a country record. I am country. I could never go pop with my mouthful of firecrackers.' A duet album with Del Reeves, *By Request*, and a tribute to her producer, *Larry Butler And Friends* with Crystal Gayle and Dottie West, were not released in the UK. A single of her blues-soaked cover version of 'Heartbreak Hotel' was cancelled in 1977 because she did not want to exploit Elvis Presley's death. Billie Jo Spears has performed prolifically, including over 300 concerts in the UK and her ambition is to make a live album at the Pavillion, Glasgow. Among her UK recordings are a duet with Carey Duncan of 'I Can Hear Kentucky Calling Me' and an album *B.J. - Billie Jo Spears Today* with her stage band, Owlkatraz. More recently, she recorded husky-voiced versions of familiar songs for mass-marketed albums. A true ambassador of country music, she signs autographs and talks to fans after every appearance. She buys all her stage clothes in the UK and refuses to wear anything casual; 'If I didn't wear gowns,' she says, 'they'd throw rotten tomatoes.' Spears made a welcome return to recording in 1996 with the co-produced *Outlaw Woman*.

● ALBUMS: *The Voice Of Billie Jo Spears* (Capitol 1968)★★★, *Mr.Walker, It's All Over!* (Capitol 1969)★★★, *Miss Sincerity* (Capitol 1969)★★★, *With Love* (Capitol 1970)★★★, *Country Girl* (Capitol 1970)★★★, *Just Singin'* (Capitol 1972)★★★, *Blanket On The Ground* (United Artists 1974)★★★, *Billie Jo* (United Artists 1975)★★★, *What I've Got In Mind* (United Artists 1976)★★★, with Del Reeves *By Request* (United Artists 1976)★★, *I'm Not Easy* (United Artists 1976)★★★, *Everytime I Sing A Love Song* (United Artists 1977)★★★, *Lonely Hearts Club* (United Artists 1977)★★★, *If You Want Me* (United Artists 1977)★★★, *Love Ain't Gonna Wait For Us* (United Artists 1978)★★★, *I Will Survive* (United Artists 1979)★★★, *Standing Tall* (United Artists 1980)★★★, *Special Songs* (Liberty 1981)★★★, with Reeves *Del And Billie Jo* (1982)★★, *B.J. - Billie Jo Spears Today* (Ritz 1983)★★★, *We Just Came Apart At The Dreams* (Parliament 1984)★★, *Misty Blue* (1992)★★, *Unmistakably* (1992)★★, *Outlaw Woman* (Country Skyline 1996)★★★.

● COMPILATIONS: *Singles - Billie Jo Spears* (United Artists 1979)★★★, *17 Golden Pieces Of Billie Jo Spears* (Bulldog 1983)★★★, *20 Country Greats* (Warwick 1986)★★★, *Best Of Billie Jo Spears* (CEMA 1992)★★★, *50 Original Tracks* (1993)★★★, *The Queen Of Country Music* (MFP 1994)★★★.

● VIDEOS: *Country Girl Live At The Peterborough International Country Music Festival* (Magnum Video 1997).

SPENCER, TIM

b. Vernon Spencer, 13 July 1908, Webb City, Missouri, USA, d. 26 April 1974, Apple Valley, California, USA. An important member of the Sons Of The Pioneers. The large Spencer family relocated as homesteaders to New Mexico in 1913, which initiated his love for the Old West. In 1921, an argument with his father, regarding the purchase of a banjo ukulele on credit without permission, saw the 13-year-old leave home and find work in Texas until his father fetched him home to finish his education. After leaving school, he worked in the mines until an accident left him hospitalized with a cracked vertebra. Unable to return to the mines, he began singing in local venues. A yearning to be in western films saw him relocate to his brother Glenn's home in Los Angeles, where he took a daytime job in Safeway's warehouse and sought musical work in the evenings. He sang and yodelled with Leonard Slye (Roy Rogers) and Bob Nicholls as a replacement for Bob Nolan in the Rocky Mountaineers and later in the International Cowboys. In 1934, he and Slye were rejoined by Nolan to become the Pioneer Trio, which eventually became the Sons Of The

Pioneers. Spencer, who had not written songs previously, soon began to contribute many of the group's most successful numbers. His own songs include 'The Everlasting Hills Of Oklahoma', 'Gold Star Mother With Silvery Hair', 'Room Full Of Roses' and the comedy standard 'Cigareetes, Whuskey And Wild Women'. He also co-wrote with brother Glenn and with Nolan. In late 1936, he left after a difference of opinion but returned in 1938, by which time Rogers had been replaced by Lloyd Perryman. Owing to voice problems, he retired from performing in 1949 (finding his own replacement, Ken Curtis), but acted as the group's manager for several years. After finally leaving the Pioneers, he ran his own gospel publishing company, Manna Music, until illness forced him to hand over to his son Hal.

SPRAGUE, CARL T.

b. 1895, near Houston, Texas, USA, d. 1978, Bryan, Texas, USA. Sprague, one of the first of the singing cowboys, was born on a ranch where he learned western songs around the camp fire. Although he attended college to study ranching, he accepted a coaching post in the college's athletic department. In 1925, impressed by Vernon Dalhart's success, he wrote to Victor Records and suggested that they record his cowboy songs. 'When The Work's All Done This Fall', a story of a cowboy killed in a night stampede, sold nearly a million copies. Despite its success, he was unwilling to give up his college post, but he continued to make records, sometimes accompanied by two fiddle players from the college band. Among his recordings are 'Following The Cow Trail', 'The Girl I Loved In Sunny Tennessee', 'Rounded Up In Glory' and 'Roll On Little Dogies', as well as such familiar cowboy songs as 'Home On The Range' and 'Red River Valley'. In 1937 he left his coaching post and ran a general store before being recalled to the army. During World War II, he was involved with recruitment in the Houston and Dallas areas and became a Major. After selling insurance and undertaking various other jobs, he retired to Bryan, Texas, but during the 60s he donned a working cowboy's clothes for television appearances and university lectures. Between 1972 and 1974, he recorded 29 tracks, which have been released by Bear Family. Sprague's singing was a hobby but his knowledge has been an invaluable guideline for all students of western music.

● ALBUMS: *The First Popular Singing Cowboy* (Bear Family 1973)★★★★, *Cowboy Songs From Texas* (Bear Family 1975)★★★.

STAFFORD, JIM

b. 16 January 1944, Eloise, Florida, USA. Stafford had a series of novelty hits in the mid-70s, but his career began as a member of the Legends, which also included Gram Parsons and Lobo (Kent Lavoie). Working with Miami producer Phil Gernhard, Stafford signed to MGM as a solo singer, releasing 'Swamp Witch' in 1973. A minor hit, it was followed by the million-selling 'Spiders And Snakes', which used a swamp-rock sound reminiscent of Tony Joe White to tell a humorous tale. The song was composed by David Bellamy of the Bellamy Brothers. In 1974, Stafford tried a soft ballad with a twist, 'My Girl Bill' (his biggest UK hit) and another zany number, 'Wildwood Weed', which reached the US Top 10. Both were co-produced by Lobo. The same strand of humour ran through Stafford's 1975 singles 'Your Bulldog

Drinks Champagne' and 'I Got Drunk And Missed It'. By now a minor celebrity, Stafford hosted a networked summer variety show from Los Angeles, where he met and married Bobbie Gentry. Such later records as 'Jasper' (Polydor 1976), co-written with Dave Loggins, and 'Turns Loose Of My Leg' (Curb/Warner Brothers Records 1977) were only minor hits, but Stafford continued to record into the 80s for labels such as Elektra, Town House and CBS.
● ALBUMS: *Jim Stafford* (MGM 1974)★★, *Spiders And Snakes* (MGM 1974)★★, *Not Just Another Pretty Fool* (MGM 1975)★★.

STAMPLEY, JOE

b. 6 June 1943, Springhill, Louisiana, USA. Stampley met Hank Williams when he was 7 years old, who gave him the advice to 'just be yourself and act like yourself and maybe later on it will pay off for you'. When he was 15, he became friends with local disc jockey Merle Kilgore, and they began to write songs together. In 1958, Kilgore secured for him the chance to record for Imperial. This led to the release of a single, 'Glenda', which sold well in his own locale but failed elsewhere. In 1961 a further recording on Chess Records, 'Teenage Picnic', also failed. He later recorded a tribute to his labelmate Chuck Berry, 'The Sheik Of Chicago'. Stampley, influenced in his early days by artists such as Jerry Lee Lewis, chose the piano as his instrument and in his high school years turned his interests to rock music. In the mid-60s, he was the lead singer of a pop group, the Cut-Ups, who soon became the Uniques. In 1966, they had minor local successes with 'Not Too Long Ago' (a Kilgore/Stampley song), 'Will You Love Me Tomorrow' and 'All These Things', but in 1969 the Uniques disbanded. In the early 70s, he decided to return to country music and moved to Nashville, where initially he worked as a staff writer for Gallico Music. He signed with Dot Records and achieved minor chart success in 1971 with 'Take Time To Know Her'. The following year he gained his first US country number 1 with his own 'Soul Song' (it also became his only US pop chart success, peaking at number 37). This proved the start of a very successful period for him as a recording artist. By 1979, he had taken his total of country chart entries to 32, including two more number 1 hits with 'Roll On Big Mama' (1975) and a solo version of the song that he had recorded ten years previously in the rock band, 'All These Things' (1976). Other Top 5 hits included 'I'm Still Loving You', 'Take Me Home To Somewhere' and 'Do You Ever Fool Around'. He moved to Epic in 1975, working with Norro Wilson as his producer until 1978, when Billy Sherrill took over. It was during 1979, as a result of touring together in Europe, that Stampley joined forces with Moe Bandy, and the single release of 'Just Good Ol' Boys' became a number 1 country hit and led to a continuation of the partnership over the following years. The idea of Moe and Joe came to them in the Hard Rock Cafe, London, during their appearance at the Wembley Festival. It was perhaps not too surprising that they proved a successful double act; they sounded somewhat similar when they sang and on stage they looked alike. Between 1979 and 1985 their further hits were to include 'Holding The Bag', 'Tell Ol' I Ain't Here', 'Hey Joe (Hey Moe)'. In 1984, they ran into copyright problems with their parody about pop singer Boy George called 'Where's The Dress', when they used the intro of Culture Club's hit 'Karma

Chameleon'. Quite apart from their single successes they recorded several albums together. During the 80s, Stampley continued to make solo *Billboard* chart entries but many critics, perhaps unfairly, suggested they came because of the publicity achieved by his association with Bandy. Recordings with Bandy apart, his only Top 10 hits in the 80s were 'I'm Gonna Love You Back To Loving Me Again' and 'Double Shot Of My Baby's Love'. He also had a minor hit with a duet recording with Jessica Boucher of 'Memory Lane'. His overall total of 57 US *Billboard* country chart entries is impressive but few traditional country fans would be too enthusiastic with some of his recordings. Perhaps his contributions were accurately summed up by the critic who wrote: 'Joe Stampley and Billy 'Crash' Craddock led a field of country rockers, who in the 70s, injected a 50s flavour into their songs'. During his career Stampley claims to have played every state in the union and many other countries too. He played the *Grand Ole Opry* in the 70s, in the days when it was centred at the Ryman Auditorium, but has never been a regular member. He once stated that his regret was that he had never had a million-selling record.
● ALBUMS: *If You Touch Me (You've Got To Love Me)* (Dot 1972)★★, *Soul Song* (Dot 1973)★★★, *I'm Still Loving You* (Dot 1974)★★★, *Take Me Home To Somewhere* (ABC/Dot 1974)★★★, *Joe Stampley* (Epic 1975)★★★★, *Billy, Get Me A Woman* (Epic 1975)★★★, *The Sheik Of Chicago* (Epic 1976)★★, *All These Things* (ABC/Dot 1976)★★★, *Ten Songs About Her* (Epic 1976)★★★, *Saturday Nite Dance* (Epic 1977)★★★, *Red Wine And Blue Memories* (Epic 1978)★★★, *I Don't Lie* (Epic 1979)★★★, with Moe Bandy *Just Good Ol' Boys* (Columbia 1979)★★★, *After Hours* (Epic 1980)★★★, with Bandy *Hey Joe!, Hey Moe!* (Columbia 1981)★★, *I'm Gonna Love You Back To Loving Me Again* (Epic 1981)★★★, *Encores* (1981)★★★, *I'm Goin' Hurtin'* (Epic 1982)★★★, *Backslidin'* (Epic 1982)★★★, *Memory Lane* (Epic 1983)★★★, with Bandy *The Good Ol' Boys Alive And Well* (Columbia 1984)★★, with Bandy *Live From Bad Bob's In Memphis* (Columbia 1985)★★, *I'll Still Be Loving You* (Epic 1985)★★★.
● COMPILATIONS: with Bandy *Greatest Hits* (Columbia 1982)★★★, *The Best Of Joe Stampley* (Varèse Sarabande 1995)★★★★, *Good Ol' Boy* (Razor & Tie 1995)★★★.

STANLEY BROTHERS

Carter Glen Stanley (b. 27 August 1925, McClure, Dickenson County, Virginia, USA) and his brother Ralph Edmond Stanley (b. 25 February 1927, Big Spraddle Creek, near Stratton, Dickenson County, Virginia, USA). Their father Lee Stanley was a noted singer and their mother played banjo. They learned many old-time songs as children and soon began to sing at church and family functions. In 1941, with two schoolfriends, they formed the Lazy Ramblers and played some local venues. In 1942, with Carter playing guitar and Ralph the banjo, they appeared as a duo on WJHL Johnson City, Tennessee. After graduation, Ralph spent eighteen months in the army, mainly serving in Germany. In 1946, after a brief spell with Roy Sykes' Blue Ridge Mountain Boys, they formed their own Clinch Mountain Boys and began playing on WNVA Norton. Soon afterwards they moved to WCYB Bristol, Tennessee, to appear regularly on *Farm And Fun Time*. Their intricate harmony vocal work (Carter sang lead to Ralph's tenor harmony) and their variety of music, with styles varying from the old-time to bluegrass, then being popularized by Bill Monroe, proved a great success. In 1947, they made their first recordings for the Rich-R-Tone label and later moved to WPTF Raleigh, North Carolina. With their standard five instrument line-up, they became one of the most renowned bluegrass bands and were much in demand for concert appearances.

Between 1949 and 1952 they made some recordings for Columbia which are now rated as classic bluegrass. These included many of Carter's own compositions, such as 'The White Dove', 'Too Late To Cry', 'We'll Be Sweethearts In Heaven' and 'The Fields Have Turned Brown'. They disbanded for a short time in 1951. Ralph briefly played banjo with Bill Monroe before being injured in a car crash. During this time, Carter played guitar and recorded with Bill Monroe. However, they soon re-formed their band and returned to *Farm And Fun Time* on WCYB. After leaving Columbia, they first recorded a great many sides for Mercury. The material included more self-penned numbers, honky-tonk songs, instrumentals and numerous gospel songs recorded with quartet vocal harmonies. Ralph Stanley has always maintained that this period produced their best recordings and experts have rated the mid-50s as the Stanley Brothers' 'Golden Era'. Later recordings were issued on Starday, King, Wango, Rimrock and Cabin Creek. (Over the years Copper Creek records have released a series taken from radio shows, which at the time of writing already totals 10 albums.) Their only US country chart success came in 1960; a Top 20 hit for 'How Far To Little Rock'.

Through the 50s and up to the mid-60s, they played at venues and festivals all over the USA and made overseas tours. It was during a European tour in March 1966 that they appeared in concert in London. The hectic schedules caused Carter to develop a drink problem; his health was badly affected and he died in hospital in Bristol, Virginia, on 1 December 1966. After his brother's death, Ralph Stanley re-formed the Clinch Mountain Boys and continued to play and record bluegrass music. In 1970, he started the annual Bluegrass Festival (named after his brother), an event that attracted large numbers of musicians and bluegrass fans. Over the years, his style of banjo playing has been copied by many young musicians and he has become respected (like Monroe) as one of the most important artists in the popularization of bluegrass music. During the 70s and 80s, the Clinch Mountain Boys have included within their ranks such country artists as Ricky Skaggs, Keith Whitley and Larry Sparks, and others, including John Conlee and Emmylou Harris, have recorded Stanley Brothers songs. British bluegrass followers were delighted to see Ralph Stanley live at the 1991 Edale Festival.

● ALBUMS: by the Stanley Brothers *Country Pickin' & Singin'* (Mercury 1958)★★★★, *The Stanley Brothers* (King 1959)★★★★, *Mountain Song Favorites* (Starday 1959)★★★★, *Sing Everybody's Country Favorites* (King 1959)★★★, *Hymns & Sacred Songs* (King 1959)★★, *Sacred Songs Of The Hills* (Starday 1960)★★★, *For The Good People* (King 1960)★★★, *Old Time Camp Meeting* (King 1961)★★★★, *The Stanley Brothers* (Harmony 1961)★★★, *The Stanleys In Person* (King 1961)★★, *The Stanley Brothers And The Clinch Mountain Boys Sing The Songs They Like The Best* (King 1961)★★★, *Stanley Brothers Live At Antioch College-1960* (Vintage 1961)★★, *Award Winners At The Folk Song Festival* (King 1962)★★, *The Mountain Music Sound* (Starday 1962)★★★, *Good Old Camp Meeting Songs* (King 1962)★★★★, *Five String Banjo Hootenanny* (1963)★★★, *The World's Finest Five String Banjo* (King 1963)★★★, *Just Because (Folk Concert)* (King 1963)★★, *Hard Times* (Mercury 1963)★★★★, *Country-Folk Music Spotlight* (King 1963)★★★, *Old Country Church* (1963)★★★, *Sing Bluegrass Songs For You* (King 1964)★★★, *Hymns Of The Cross* (King 1964)★★, *The Stanley Brothers - Their Original Recordings* (1965)★★★, *The Angels Are Singing* (Harmony 1966)★★★, *Jacob's Vision* (Starday 1966)★★★, *Bluegrass Gospel Favorites* (Cabin Creek 1966)★★, *The Greatest Country & Western Show On Earth* (King 1966)★★, *A Collection Of Original Gospel & Sacred Songs* (1966)★★★, *The Stanley Brothers Go To Europe* (1966)★★, *An Empty Mansion* (1967)★★★, *Memorial Album* (1967)★★★★, *The Best Loved Songs Of The Carter Family* (King 1967)★★★, *The Legendary Stanley Brothers Recorded Live, Volume 1* (1968)★★★, *The Legendary Stanley Brothers Recorded Live, Volume 2* (1969)★★, *On Stage* (1969)★★, *How Far To Little Rock* (1969)★★★, *Deluxe Album* (1970)★★★, *Together For The Last Time* (1971)★★★, *Rank Strangers* (1973)★★★, *The Stanley Brothers* (1974)★★★, *The Stanley Brothers On The Air* (1976)★★★★, *A Beautiful Life* (1978)★★★, *I Saw The Light* (1980)★★★, *Stanley Brothers On Radio, Volume 1* (1984)★★★★, *Stanley Brothers On Radio, Volume 2* (1984)★★★★, *The Starday Sessions* (1984)★★★★, *On WCYB Bristol Farm & Fun Time* (1988)★★★, *Gospel Songs From Cabin Creek* (1990)★★★. By Ralph Stanley: *The Bluegrass Sound* (Jalyn 1968)★★★★, *Brand New Country Songs By Ralph Stanley* (King 1968)★★★, *Over The Sunset Hill* (King 1968)★★★, *Old Time Music* (1969)★★★★, *Hills Of Home* (King 1970)★★★, *Cry From The Cross* (1971)★★★, *Ralph Stanley Live In Japan* (1971)★★, *Sings Michegan Bluegrass* (1971)★★★, *Something Old Something New* (1972)★★★, *Plays Requests* (1973)★★★, *I Want To Preach The Gospel* (1973)★★★, *The Stanley Sound Around The World* (1973)★★★, *Gospel Echoes Of The Stanley Brothers* (1973)★★★, *A Man And His Music* (1975)★★★, *Let Me Rest On A Peaceful Mountain* (1975)★★, *Live at McClure* (Rebel 1976)★★★, *Old Home Place* (1977)★★★, *Clinch Mountain Gospel* (1978)★★★, *Down Where The River Bends* (1979)★★★, *I'll Wear A White Robe* (1980)★★, *Hymn Time* (1980)★★★, with Jimmy Martin *First Time Together* (1980)★★★, *The Stanley Sound Today* (1981)★★★, *The Memory Of Your Smile* (1982)★★★, *Child Of The King* (1983)★★★, *Bluegrass* (1983)★★★, *Sings Traditional Bluegrass And Gospel* (1983)★★★, *Live At The Old Home Place* (1983)★★, *Snow Covered Mound* (1984)★★★, *Singing Sixteen Years* (1984)★★★, *Shadows Of The Past* (1984)★★★, *I Can Tell You The Time* (1985)★★★, *Live In Japan* (1986)★★★, *Lonesome & Blue* (1986)★★★, *I'll Answer The Call* (1988)★★★, *Ralph Stanley & Raymond Fairchild* (Rebel 1989)★★★, *(Clawhammer) The Way My Mama Taught Me* (1990)★★★, *Like Father Like Son* (1990)★★★, *Pray For The Boys* (1991)★★★, *Back To The Cross* (Freeland 1992)★★★, *Saturday Night And Sunday Morning* (Freeland 1993)★★★.

● COMPILATIONS: *The Columbia Sessions, Volume 1* (Rounder 1981)★★★★, *Shadows Of The Past* (1981)★★★, *The Columbia Sessions, Volume 2* (Rounder 1982)★★★★, *The Stanley Series* 11-volume set (Copper Creek 80s)★★★★, *Early Years 1958-1961* 4-CD box set (King 1994)★★★★, *The Stanley Brothers And The Clinch Mountain Boys* (Bear Family 1994)★★★★, *Angel Band: The Classic Mercury Recordings* (Mercury Nashville 1995)★★★★, *Complete Columbia*

Recordings (Columbia/Legacy 1996)★★★.
Albums issued on Wango in early 60s as John's Gospel Quartet: *John's Gospel Quartet* (reissued 1973 as *The Stanley Brothers of Virginia Volume.1*)★★★, *John's Country Quartet* (reissued 1973 as *The Long Journey Home*)★★★, *John's Gospel Quartet Volume 2* (reissued 1973 as *The Stanley Brothers Volume 4*)★★★, *John's Gospel Quartet Songs Of Mother & Home* (reissued 1973 as *The Little Old Country Church House*)★★★.

STANLEY, JAMES LEE

b. Philadelphia, Pennsylvania, USA. Stanley recorded for LeGrand Records when aged only 14. He gained a degree in music and served in the US air force as a Chinese linguist. Working as a singer-songwriter, he opened shows for Bonnie Raitt, Robin Williams, Bill Cosby and, for three years, Steven Wright. The warmth and humour of his stage act can be heard in *Live*, which was nominated for a Grammy. *Simpatico*, a Latin-American experiment, was also nominated for a Grammy. He loved Tom Robbins' novel *Even Cowgirls Get The Blues*, and wrote a series of songs about the characters. Robbins endorsed the album and contributed to the title cut. Rodney Crowell has since written a song of the same title and the film's score was by k.d. lang. Stanley often tours as a duo with Peter Tork of the Monkees and produced Tork's album *Stranger Things Have Happened*.
● ALBUMS: *Midnight Radio* (Regency 1980)★★★, *The Envoy* (Beachwood 1992)★★★, *Even Cowgirls Get The Blues* (Beachwood 1993)★★, with Peter Tork *Two Man Band* (Beachwood 1996)★★, *Domino Harvest* (Beachwood 1997)★★★.

STAPP, JACK

b. 8 December 1912, Nashville, Tennessee, USA, d. 20 December 1980. The family relocated to Atlanta in 1921, where Stapp was educated. He attended Georgia Tech, who had their own radio station, and became Programme Controller when WGST went commercial. He then relocated to New York, where he became a senior CBS executive and a friend of Phil Carlin, the Production Manager of NBC. Stapp's abilities came to the attention of WSM in Nashville and in 1939, they appointed him Programme Manager. He created new shows on WSM and he used his friendship with Carlin to gain some of the programmes, including the *Prince Albert* segment of the *Grand Ole Opry*, network exposure. He has also been credited for ending the predominance of string bands on the *Opry*, by promoting Roy Acuff and later Pee Wee King and Ernest Tubb. During World War II, Stapp was involved with the study of psychological warfare in New York but spent some time working on the preparation of propaganda in London. He returned to WSM and although he had no initial interest in country music, he was appointed manager of the *Opry* and in that capacity instigated many continuing WSM events such as the annual DJ Convention. In 1951, with his partner providing the money and Stapp providing the know-how, he and Lou Cowan launched Tree Publishing. He hired Buddy Killen to review songs and, in 1954, the first Tree-published song, 'By The Law of My Heart', was recorded by Benny Martin. In 1955, two of Tree's writers, Mae Boren Axton and Tommy Durden (with the assistance of Elvis Presley), came up with 'Heartbreak Hotel', which firmly established the company when

Presley's recording topped the US country and pop charts. In 1957, Stapp left WSM to become head of WKDA, a rock station and when Cowan left Tree, Killen was made a partner. In 1964, when Stapp left WKDA to devote all his time to Tree, he made Killen his vice-president. In 1975, Stapp became chairman of the Tree Board. A founder-member of the Country Music Association, he also held top posts in other organizations, including NARAS. He died in 1980, but in 1989, he received acknowledgment of his services to country music by his induction to the Country Music Hall Of Fame. Tree Publishing, now part of the Japanese Sony company, has been rated by *Billboard* as the most successful publishing company in country music.

STARCHER, BUDDY

b. Oby Edgar Starcher, 16 March 1906, Kentuck, Jackson County, West Virginia, USA. Starcher first learned to play banjo but later became an outstanding guitarist. In 1928, he was probably the first hillbilly artist to appear on radio in the Baltimore area. Between 1930 and 1960, he continually moved around, not only playing venues in his home state, Virginia and Kentucky (especially Charleston and Fairmont), but further afield to Miami, Iowa and Philadelphia. In 1946, he recorded in Chicago for Four Star, including his best-known song 'I'll Still Write Your Name In The Sand'. Now a much recorded bluegrass standard, it reached number 8 in the country charts. Later he recorded for other labels including Columbia, Starday, Decca, Bluebonnet and Bear Family. In 1960, his television show in Charleston had higher local ratings than NBC's *Today*. In 1966, he had a number 2 country and number 39 pop hit with 'History Repeats Itself' - his cleverly written narration detailing the many similarities between the assassinations of Presidents Lincoln and Kennedy. In the late 60s, he returned to radio and for some years managed radio stations, being usually brought in as a troubleshooter to pick up ailing stations - once they were running successfully, he moved on to the next challenge. He has written many fine songs including 'Song Of The Water Wheel' (a hit for Slim Whitman) and also some prose. In the late 30s, he married fellow artist Mary Ann (Vasas), who in 1941 took over from Patsy Montana on WLS Chicago.
● ALBUMS: *Buddy Starcher & His Mountain Guitar* (Starday 1962)★★★, *History Repeats Itself* i (Decca 1966)★★★, *History Repeats Itself* ii (Starday 1966)★★★, *Buddy Starcher Volume 1* (Bluebonnet 1967)★★★, *Country Soul & Inspiration* (c.60s)★★★, *Country Love Songs* (Bear Family 1980)★★, *The Boy From Down Home* (1984)★★, *Pride Of The West Virginia Hills* (1984)★★, *Me And My Guitar* (1986)★★★.
● FURTHER READING: *Buddy Starcher - Biography*, Robert H. Cagle.

STARR, KENNY

b. Kenneth Trebbe, 21 September 1953, Topeka, Kansas, USA. Starr grew up in Burlingame, Kansas, and, according to publicity, was fronting his own band, the Rockin' Rebels, from the age of nine. As a teenager, he played clubs as part of a pop act, Kenny and the Imperials. Starr switched to country music in 1969 and won a talent contest in Wichita. A promoter invited him to appear on a forthcoming show with Loretta Lynn and Conway Twitty, where he won a standing ovation. Lynn suggested he move to Nashville and gave him

a job with her roadshow. With her support, he recorded for MCA from 1973-78 and had a US country Top 10 hit with 'The Blind Man In The Bleachers'. He had further success with 'Tonight I Face The Man Who Made It Happen', 'Hold Tight', 'Slow Drivin'' and 'Me And The Elephant', but he was soon forgotten.
● ALBUMS: *The Blind Man In The Bleachers* (MCA 1975)★★★.

STATLER BROTHERS

The Statler Brothers hail from Staunton, a town on the edge of Shenandoah Valley, Virginia, USA. In 1955 Harold W. Reid (b. 21 August 1939, Augusta County, Virginia, USA; bass), Philip E. Balsley (b. 8 August 1939, Augusta County, Virginia, USA; baritone), Lew C. DeWitt (b. 8 March 1938, Roanoke County, Virginia, USA, d. 15 August 1990; tenor) and Joe McDorman formed a gospel quartet. Although McDorman never became a Statler, he has worked with them occasionally. In 1960 he was replaced by Harold's brother, Donald S. Reid (b. 5 June 1945, Staunton, Virginia, USA), who is now the group's lead singer. Originally the quartet was called The Kingsmen, but they changed it to avoid confusion with a US pop group. The Statler Brothers was chosen from the manufacturer's name on a box of tissues, and the group point out that they might have been the Kleenex Brothers. In 1963, they auditioned for Johnny Cash, who invited them to be part of his roadshow. He also secured a record contract with Columbia, but the label was disappointed with the poor sales of their first records. Having been refused further studio time, they recorded Lew DeWitt's song 'Flowers On The Wall', during a break in one of Johnny Cash's sessions. The infectious novelty made number 4 on the US pop charts (number 2 country) and, despite the American references, also entered the UK Top 40. The Statler Brothers continued with Cash's roadshow and recorded both with him ('Daddy Sang Bass') and on their own ('Ruthless', 'You Can't Have Your Kate And Edith Too'). Dissatisfied by the promotion of their records and by the lukewarm material they were given, they switched to Mercury Records in 1970 and their records have been produced by Jerry Kennedy since then. With such US country hits as 'Bed Of Roses', 'Do You Remember These?', 'I'll Go To My Grave Loving You' and the number 1 'Do You Know You Are My Sunshine?', they established themselves as the number 1 country vocal group. They left Cash's roadshow in 1972, but they recorded a tribute to him, 'We Got Paid By Cash', as well as tributes to their favourite gospel group ('The Blackwood Brothers By The Statler Brothers') and their favourite guitarist ('Chet Atkins' Hand'). DeWitt was incapacitated through Crohn's disease and left in 1982. He released the solo *On My Own* in 1985, but he died in Waynesboro, Virginia, on 15 August 1990. Many of their songs relate to their love of the cinema - 'The Movies', 'Whatever Happened To Randolph Scott?' and 'Elizabeth', a country number 1 inspired by watching the film *Giant*, and written by Jimmy Fortune, who replaced DeWitt. Fortune also wrote two other number 1 US country records for them, 'My Only Love' and 'Too Much On My Heart'. They also had considerable success with a spirited revival of 'Hello Mary Lou', which was praised by its composer, Gene Pitney. Their stage act includes the homespun humour of their alter egos, Lester 'Roadhog' Moran And The Cadillac Cowboys, and they gave themselves a plywood disc when the first 1,250

copies of the resulting album were sold. On the other hand, The Statler Brothers' Old-Fashioned Fourth Of July Celebration in Staunton attracts 70,000 a year. The Statler Brothers are managed from office buildings that used to be the school attended by Dewitt and the Reids.
● ALBUMS: *Flowers On The Wall* (Columbia 1966)★★★, *Big Hits* (Columbia 1967)★★★, *Oh Happy Day* (Columbia 1969)★★, *Bed Of Roses* (Mercury 1971)★★★, *Pictures Of Moments To Remember* (Mercury 1971)★★★, *Innerview* (Mercury 1972)★★, *Country Music Then And Now* (Mercury 1972)★★★, *The Statler Brothers Sing Country Symphonies In E Major* (Mercury 1973)★★, *Carry Me Back* (Mercury 1973)★★★, *Thank You World* (Mercury 1974)★★★, as Lester 'Roadhog' Moran And His Cadillac Cowboys *Alive At The Johnny Mack Brown High School* (Mercury 1974)★★★, *Sons Of The Motherland* (Mercury 1975)★★★, *The Holy Bible - Old Testament* (Mercury 1975)★★, *The Holy Bible - New Testament* (Mercury 1975)★★, *Harold, Lew, Phil And Don* (Mercury 1976)★★★, *The Country America Loves* (Mercury 1977)★★★, *Short Stories* (Mercury 1977)★★★, *Entertainers ... On And Off The Record* (Mercury 1978)★★★, *The Statler Brothers Christmas Card* (Mercury 1979)★★, *The Originals* (Mercury 1979)★★★, *Tenth Anniversary* (Mercury 1980)★★★, *Years Ago* (Mercury 1981)★★★, *The Legend Goes On* (Mercury 1982)★★★, *Country Gospel* (Mercury 1982)★★★, *Today* (Mercury 1983)★★★, *Atlanta Blue* (Mercury 1984)★★★, *Pardners In Rhyme* (Mercury 1985)★★★, *Christmas Present* (Mercury 1985)★★, *Four For The Show* (Mercury 1986)★★★, *Radio Gospel Favourites* (Mercury 1986)★★★, *Maple Street Memories* (Mercury 1987)★★★, *The Statler Brothers Live - Sold Out* (Mercury 1989)★★★, *Music, Memories And You* (Mercury 1990)★★★, *All American Country* (Mercury 1991)★★★, *Words And Music* (Mercury 1992)★★★, *Home* (Mercury 1993)★★★, *Today's Gospel Favorites* (Mercury 1993)★★★.
● COMPILATIONS: *The Best Of The Statler Bros.* (Mercury 1975)★★★, *The Best Of The Statler Bros. Ride Again Volume 2* (Mercury 1980)★★★, *The Statlers Greatest Hits* (Mercury 1988)★★★★, *30th Anniversary Celebration* 3-CD box set (Mercury 1995)★★★, *Flowers On The Wall: The Essential Statler Brothers* (Columbia/Legacy 1996)★★★★.
● VIDEOS: *Brothers In Song* (Polygram 1986).

STEAGALL, RED

b. Russell Steagall, 22 December 1937, Gainesville, Texas, USA. In 1954, he contracted polio, which badly affected the use of his left hand and arm. Realizing his prospective football career was no longer a possibility, he turned his attention to music. During his convalescence, as part of the therapeutic treatment, he first began to play the mandolin and then, as his fingers strengthened, the guitar. By playing local dances and clubs, he financed his course at West Texas State University, where he gained a degree in Agriculture and Animal Science and then for five years worked for Sand Mark Oil as a soil analyst. He moved to California in 1965, sang locally and for a year worked as a salesman of industrial chemicals. Working first with his friend Don Lanier, he began to develop his songwriting and in 1966, Ray Charles recorded their song 'Here We Go Again'. He concentrated on his writing, later claiming that by 1969 sixty of his songs had been recorded by other artists. In 1969, Ray Sanders had a hit with his song 'Beer Drinkin' Music' and Steagall himself made his first recordings on Dot. In 1971, Del Reeves had a hit with 'A Dozen Pairs Of Boots' and the following year, having moved to Nashville and joined Capitol, Steagall gained his own first country chart hit with 'Party Dolls And Wine'. During the 70s, later recording for ABC/Dot and Elektra and with his continued strong leaning towards Western-swing and honky tonk songs, Steagall charted a steady succession of country chart entries, though none made the Top 10. His biggest came with 'Lone Star Beer And Bob Wills Music' - a number 11 in 1976. His love for Bob Wills' music also saw him chart a tribute song, 'Bob's Got A Swing Band In Heaven'. For years, with his band the Coleman County Cowboys, he played dancehalls and rodeos all over the West. Steagall became a genuine singing cowboy with his own Texas ranch, and his keen interest in things Western saw him become one of the top entertainers on the US rodeo circuit, playing some 250 dates a year for many years. In 1974, he was instrumental in Reba McEntire becoming a star, after hearing her sing the national anthem at the National Rodeo Finals. In the 80s, he cut down touring drastically but remained active in various ventures, including his publishing house. He also cut out most of his songwriting to concentrate on writing poetry about the West and breeding quarter-horses on his ranch. In 1987, he made his debut as an actor in a children's film called *Benji, The Hunted*. Somewhat surprisingly, his last chart entry was 'Hard Hat Days And Honky Tonk Nights' back in 1980. He has released an excellent series of albums in the 90s.

● ALBUMS: *Party Dolls And Wine* (Capitol 1972)★★★, *Somewhere My Love* (Capitol 1973)★★★, *If You've Got The Time I've Got The Song* (Capitol 1973)★★★, *The Finer Things In Life* (Capitol 1974)★★★, *Lone Star Beer And Bob Wills Music* (ABC/Dot 1976)★★★★, *Texas Red* (ABC/Dot 1976)★★★, *For All Our Cowboy Friends* (ABC 1977)★★★, *Hang On Feelin'* (ABC 1978)★★★, *It's Our Life* (1980)★★★, *Cowboy Favorites* (1985)★★★, *Red Steagall* (1986)★★★, *Born To This Land* (Warner Western 1993)★★★, *Faith And Values* (Warner Western 1995)★★★★, *Dear Mama, Now I'm A Cowboy* (Warner Western 1997)★★★★.

STEGALL, KEITH

b. 1 November 1954, Wichita Falls, Texas, USA. Keith is the son of Bob Stegall, who played steel guitar for Johnny Horton. He made his stage debut when only eight years old and performed in a variety of folk and country groups during his adolescence. He formed his own band, the Pacesetters, when only 12 and toured overseas with the folk group the Cheerful Givers. He moved to Nashville and became a staff writer for CBASS. He wrote 'Sexy Eyes' (Dr Hook), 'We're In This Love Together' (Al Jarreau) and 'Hurricane' (Leon Everette). He had a few minor US country hits with Capitol Records but had more success with Epic, making the Top 10 with 'Pretty Lady' and a further hit with 'California'. Stegall co-produced all of Alan Jackson's albums including the landmark *Here In The Real World*, and also sang harmony vocals on it. He has produced many other albums including those for Tracy Byrd, Terri Clark, Shenandoah, Randy Travis and Aaron Neville. He writes with Alan and Roger Murrah and their songs have included 'Blue Blooded Woman', 'Dallas' (Alan Jackson) and 'If I Could Make A Living' (Clay Walker). Additionally he became vice-president of A&R with Mercury Records. He returned to singing on his own projects again in 1995 after deciding the new songs suited his own voice better than others.

● ALBUMS: *Keith Stegall* (Epic 1985)★★★, *Passages* (Mercury 1996)★★★.

STEVENS, RAY

b. Ray Ragsdale, 24 January 1941, Clarksdale, Georgia, USA. A prolific country-pop writer and performer, Stevens' novelty hits of the 70s and 80s illustrate the history of the fads and crazes of the era. He became a disc jockey on a local station at 15 and the following year recorded 'Five More Steps' on the Prep label. Stevens' first nonsense song, 'Chickie Chickie Wah Wah', was written in 1958 but it was not until 1961, with Mercury Records that he had a Top 40 hit with the tongue-twisting 'Jeremiah Peabody's Poly Unsaturated Quick Dissolving Fast Acting Pleasant Tasting Green And Purple Pills'. This was followed by 'Ahab The Arab' (1962) and 'Harry The Hairy Ape' (1963). Stevens also had a penchant for social comment which emerged in songs such as 'Mr Businessman' (1968), 'America Communicate With Me' and the first recording of Kris Kristofferson's 'Sunday Morning Coming Down'. However, the zany songs were the most successful and in 1969 he sold a million copies of 'Gitarzan' and followed with a version of Leiber And Stoller's Coasters hit 'Along Came Jones' and 'Bridget The Midget (The Queen Of The Blues)'. His first number 1 was the simple melodic ballad 'Everything Is Beautiful' in 1970. All of these, however, were outsold by 'The Streak', which topped the charts on both sides of the Atlantic in 1974. Stevens' softer side was evident in his version of Erroll Garner's 'Misty' which won a Grammy in 1976 for its bluegrass-styled arrangement. Later novelty efforts, aimed principally at country audiences, included 'Shriner's Convention' (1980), 'It's Me Again Margaret' (1985), 'I Saw Elvis In A UFO' (1989) and 'Power Tools'. He has made several videos in the 90s, and released two studio albums in 1997.

● ALBUMS: *1,837 Seconds Of Humor* (Mercury 1962)★★★, *Ahab The Arab* (1962)★★, *This Is Ray Stevens* (Mercury 1963)★★★, *Even Stevens* (Monument 1968)★★★, *Gitarzan* (Monument 1969)★★★, *Have A Little Talk With Myself* (Monument 1969)★★, *Unreal!!!* (Barnaby 1970)★★★, *Everything Is Beautiful* (Barnaby 1970)★★★, *Turn Your Radio On* (Barnaby 1972)★★★, *Boogity Boogity* (Barnaby 1974)★★★, *Misty* (Barnaby 1975)★★★, *Just For The Record* (Warners 1975)★★★, *Feel The Music* (Warners 1976)★★★, *Shriner's Convention* (RCA 1980)★★★, *Don't Laugh Now* (1982)★★★, *Me* (1983)★★★, *He Thinks He's Ray Stevens* (RCA 1984)★★★, *I Have Returned* (MCA 1985)★★★, *Surely You Joust* (MCA 1986)★★, *Crackin' Up!* (MCA 1987)★★★, *I Never Made A Record I Didn't Like* (MCA 1988)★★★, *Beside Myself* (MCA 1989)★★★, *#1 With A Bullet* (Curb/Capitol 1991)★★★, *Hum It* (MCA 1997)★★★, *Through A Different Window* (MCA 1997)★★★.

● COMPILATIONS: *Ray Stevens' Greatest Hits* (Barnaby 1974)★★★, *The Very Best Of Ray Stevens* (Barnaby 1975)★★★, *Greatest Hits* (RCA 1983)★★★, *Greatest Hits* (MCA 1987)★★★, *Greatest Hits Volume 2* (MCA 1987)★★★, *His All Time Greatest Comic Hits* (Capitol 1990)★★★, *The Best Of Ray Stevens* (More Music 1995)★★★, *Everything Is Beautiful* (Rhino 1996)★★★.

● VIDEOS: *Comedy Video Classics* (1993), *Live* (Club Video 1994), *Get Serious* (MCA Music Video 1996).

STEVENS, STU

b. Wilfrid Pierce, 25 September c.1937, Annesley Woodhouse, Kirkby-In-Ashfield, Nottinghamshire, England. He drove tractors on the farm at the age of eight, but his ambition to be a farmer was never fully realized. When he was about 13 years old, his father, a miner, died, and Wilfrid left school to work in the mines. His first singing experience came after his brother entered him in a local talent show around 1965. He won, and his deep, powerful voice found him a regular paid singing spot at the club. He bought himself a guitar (and later learned piano) and began to put together a repertoire of songs. In the late 60s, as Stuart Stevens, he made his first recordings for EMI, including the release of a single ('Soft Is The Night'/'Tender Hearted'). He also appeared on the Lonnie Donegan television show. In March 1970, he was booked to entertain at a reception for the American country stars of the Wembley Festival. Performing as Willard Pierce, he created such an impression that it led to him appearing at the Festival itself the following day - seemingly the first British artist to do so. He made a noteworthy appearance on *Opportunity Knocks* in 1972 (unfortunately falling foul of the 'never work with children or animals' adage, losing by three votes to a child drummer). He recorded for the Youngblood label in 1972, with the subsequent album, *Stories In Song*, selling some 12,000 copies. In 1973, he performed at a disc jockey convention in Nashville, subsequently appearing at many major venues, including the *Grand Ole Opry* and on network television. He was signed by Cliffie Stone to the US Granite label in 1974, who released his Youngblood album in the USA and in Europe. His recording of 'My Woman My Woman My Wife' became popular on both sides of the Atlantic, even drawing praise from the song's writer, Marty Robbins. Further trips to the USA followed until, sadly for him, both Granite and Youngblood ceased record production, leaving him without a label in either country. He had continued to play the British clubs, first with his band Silver Mist, then with Pat and Roger Johns, before eventually appearing with his two sons Stuart (bass guitar) and Steven (keyboards). He also opened his own recording studios and worked on production with other artists. He formed his own Major Oak, Eagle and Ash labels and released albums that proved popular with his British fans. Twelve out of 28 unissued Youngblood tracks later appeared on his album *The Loner*. In 1979, he almost made the British Top 40 with 'The Man From Outer Space', which, after initially being released on his own Eagle label, was picked up by MCA Records and received air play and jocularity from Terry Wogan on BBC Radio. Further singles followed, including 'If I Heard You Call My Name', 'One Red Rose' and 'Hello Pretty Lady', which sold well for country records, but not well enough for a major label seeking pop record sales. This resulted in him parting company with MCA. Stevens' national popularity increased and he regularly played the theatre and concert hall circuit, always doing it his way and always refusing to perform anything he did not wish to sing. Many think, no doubt correctly, that had he become a 'yes' man and allowed himself to be typecast, he would undoubtedly have become a major star. In 1984, Stu and his wife were devastated by the death, from a rare heart disease, of their youngest son. Steven (19), a keyboard player of very outstanding abilities, had appeared on stage from the age of seven. Although Stu Stevens played out his immediate special bookings, he soon tended to withdraw from active participation in the music scene. In recent years, he has made infrequent appearances, but in the main, 'The Voice', as he was affectionately known to his fans, has been silent - a great, if understandable, loss to British country music.

● ALBUMS: *Stories In Song* (Youngblood 1973)★★★, *Command Performance* (1976)★★, *Together Again* (1977)★★★, *Stu Stevens - Country Music Volume 7* cassette only (1977)★★, *Stories In Song Volume 2 - The Loner* (1978)★★★, *The Man From Outer Space* (1979)★★★, *Stu* (1979)★★★, *Emma And I* (1980)★★, *Old Rugged Cross* cassette only (1981)★★, *Songs That Made Stu Stevens* (1981)★★★, *The Voice - Live* cassette only (1982)★★★, *In Memory Of Steven (Live)* cassette only (1986)★★★, *The Man And His Music* cassette only (1986)★★★.

STEVENSON, B.W.

b. Louis C. Stevenson, 5 October 1949, Dallas, Texas, USA, d. 28 April 1988, USA. B.W. Stevenson (the initials stood for Buckwheat) is now best remembered for his 1973 *Billboard* Top 10 single 'My Maria'. Stevenson performed with many local Texas rock bands as a teenager, before attending college and then joining the US Air Force. Upon being discharged from the Air Force, Stevenson returned to the thriving club scene, particularly in the burgeoning Austin, Texas area. Although he considered himself a blues and rock singer, he was signed to RCA Records as a country artist and released 'Shambala', a song that charted but did not fare as well as the version by rockers Three Dog Night. Stevenson and Daniel Moore's 'My Maria' became a number 9 pop hit (oddly missing the country charts), and the album of the same title reached number 45, also in 1973. Stevenson continued to record, placing two further singles on the charts in the 70s (the latter, 'Down To The Station', for Warner Brothers Records). He also recorded for MCA Records. Stevenson died following heart surgery in April 1988.

● ALBUMS: *B.W. Stevenson* (RCA 1972)★★★, *Lead Free* (RCA 1972)★★, *My Maria* (RCA 1973)★★, *Calabasas* (RCA 1974)★★★, *Lost Feeling* (Warners 1977), *Lifeline* (1980)★★.

STEWART, GARY

b. 28 May 1945, Jenkins, Kentucky, USA. Stewart's family moved to Florida when he was 12, where he made his first record for the local Cory label and played in a beat group called the Amps. Teaming up with a policeman, Bill Eldridge, he wrote Stonewall Jackson's 1965 US country hit, 'Poor Red Georgia Dirt'. Several songwriting successes followed including chart entries for Billy Walker ('She Goes Walking Through My Mind', 'When A Man Loves A Woman (The Way I Love You)', 'Traces Of A Woman', 'It's Time To Love Her'), Cal Smith ('You Can't Housebreak A Tomcat', 'It Takes Me All Night Long') and Nat Stuckey ('Sweet Thang And Cisco'). Stewart recorded an album for Kapp, *You're Not The Woman You Used To Be*, and then moved to RCA. He had his first US country hit with a country version of the Allman Brothers' 'Ramblin' Man' and then made the Top 10 with 'Drinkin' Thing'. For some years Stewart worked as the pianist in Charley Pride's road band and he can be heard on Pride's *In Concert* double album. He established himself as a hard-driving, honky-tonk performer with *Out Of Hand* and a US country number 1, 'She's Actin' Single (I'm Drinkin'

Doubles)', although his vibrato annoyed some. His 1977 *Your Place Or Mine* included guest appearances from Nicolette Larson, Emmylou Harris and Rodney Crowell. His two albums with songwriter Dean Dillon were not commercial successes, and Stewart returned to working in honky-tonk clubs. However, drug addiction got the better of him and his life collapsed when his wife left him and his son committed suicide. In the late 80s, he returned to performing, carrying on in the same musical style as before with albums such as *Brand New* and *I'm A Texan*.

● ALBUMS: *You're Not The Woman You Used To Be* (MCA 1973)★★, *Out Of Hand* (RCA 1975)★★★★, *Steppin' Out* (RCA 1976)★★, *Your Place Or Mine* (RCA 1977)★★★, *Little Junior* (RCA 1978)★★★, *Gary* (RCA 1979)★★★, *Cactus And Rose* (RCA 1980)★★, with Dean Dillon *Brotherly Love* (RCA 1982)★★★, with Dillon *Those Were The Days* (RCA 1983)★★, *Brand New* (Hightone 1988)★★, *Battleground* (Hightone 1990)★★★, *I'm A Texan* (Hightone 1993)★★.

● COMPILATIONS: *Greatest Hits* (RCA 1981)★★★, *Gary's Greatest* (Hightone 1992)★★★★, *Essential Gary Stewart* (RCA 1997)★★★.

STEWART, JOHN

b. 5 September 1939, San Diego, California, USA. Stewart's musical career began in the 50s when, as frontman of the Furies, he recorded 'Rocking Anna' for a tiny independent label. Having discovered folk music, Stewart began performing with college friend John Montgomery, but achieved wider success as a songwriter when several of his compositions, including 'Molly Dee' and 'Green Grasses', were recorded by the Kingston Trio. Indeed, the artist joined this prestigious group in 1961, following his spell in the similar-sounding Cumberland Three. Stewart left the Kingston trio in 1967. His reputation was enhanced when a new composition, 'Daydream Believer', became a number 1 hit for the Monkees, and this dalliance with pop continued when the artist contributed 'Never Goin' Back' to a disintegrating Lovin' Spoonful on their final album. In 1968 Stewart was joined by singer Buffy Ford, whom he would marry in 1975. Together they completed *Signals Through The Glass*, before the former resumed his solo path with the excellent *California Bloodlines*. This country-inspired collection established Stewart's sonorous delivery and displayed a view of America which, if sometimes sentimental, was both optimistic and refreshing. It was a style the performer would continue over a series of albums which, despite critical approval, achieved only moderate success. Stewart's fortunes were upturned in 1979 when a duet with Stevie Nicks, 'Gold', became a US hit. The attendant *Bombs Away Dream Babies*, featured assistance from Fleetwood Mac guitarist Lindsay Buckingham and, although markedly different in tone to its predecessors, the set augured well for the future. However, despite contributions from Linda Ronstadt and Phil Everly, the follow-up, *Dream Babies Go To Hollywood*, proved an anti-climax. Stewart subsequently turned from commercial pursuits and resumed a more specialist direction with a series of low-key recordings for independent companies.

● ALBUMS: *Signals Through The Glass* (1968)★★, *California Bloodlines* (Capitol 1969)★★★, *Willard* (Capitol 1970)★★, *The Lonesome Picker Rides Again* (Warners 1972)★★★, *Sunstorm* (1972)★★★, *Cannons In The Rain* (RCA 1973)★★,

The Phoenix Concerts - Live (RCA 1974)★★★, *Wingless Angels* (RCA 1975)★★, *Fire In The Wind* (RSO 1977)★★, *Bombs Away Dream Babies* (RSO 1979)★★★★, *Dream Babies Go Hollywood* (RSO 1980)★★, *Blondes* (1982)★★, *Trancas* (Sunstorm 1984)★★, *Centennial* (1984)★★, *The Last Campaign* (Homecoming 1985)★★, *Secret Tapes '86* (Homecoming 1986)★★★, *Secret Tapes 2* (Homecoming 1986)★★, *Punch The Big Guy* (Cypress 1987)★★★, *Neon Beach* (Line 1991)★★★, *Bullets In The Hour Glass* (1993)★★★, *Greetings From John Stewart* (1993)★★, *Airdream Believer* (Shanachie 1995)★★.

● COMPILATIONS: *Forgotten Songs Of Some Old Yesterday* (RCA 1980)★★★, *California Bloodlines Plus...* (See For Miles 1987)★★★, *Turning Love Into Gold: The Best Of John Stewart* (Polydor 1995)★★★★.

STEWART, REDD

b. Henry Redd Stewart, 21 May 1921, Ashland City, Tennessee, USA. After the family relocated to Kentucky, Stewart learned piano, fiddle and guitar while still at school and by the mid-30s, was performing in the Louisville area. He joined Pee Wee King's Golden West Cowboys on WHAS in 1937, first as a musician but also became featured vocalist when Eddy Arnold left to pursue his solo career. Stewart moved with King to the *Grand Ole Opry* until he was called up for military service, during which he wrote 'A Soldier's Last Letter', which became a hit for Ernest Tubb. He rejoined King after the war and from 1947-57, they appeared on a popular weekly radio and television show on WAUE Louisville and toured extensively. The two were to enjoy some 30 years of successful songwriting collaboration. Their successes included 'Tennessee Waltz' (Stewart added lyrics to King's signature tune the 'No Name Waltz'), the song becoming a hit for both King and Cowboy Copas in 1948, a million-seller for Patti Page in 1950 and charted again by Lacy J. Dalton in 1980. Other million-sellers were 'Slowpoke', a 1951 hit for King, and 'You Belong To Me' for Jo Stafford in 1952. Stewart also wrote the Jim Reeves hit, 'That's A Sad Affair'. He sang on all of King's hits but never charted with his solo recordings, although he recorded for several labels. After King retired in 1969, Stewart continued to be active in the music world.

● ALBUMS: *Sings Favorite Old Time Songs* (Audio Lab 1959)★★★, *I Remember* (1974)★★★. (See also album listing for Pee Wee King).

STEWART, WYNN

b. Wynnford Lindsey Stewart, 7 June 1934, on a farm near Morrisville, Missouri, USA, d. 17 July 1985, Hendersonville, Tennessee, USA. Stewart's uncle was a major league pitcher, which inspired hopes of a baseball career, until he was told that he would never be big enough. He became interested in songwriting, learned to play the guitar, and at the age of 13, he appeared regularly on KWTO Springfield. A year later the family moved to California, where Stewart became friendly and for a time ran a band with Ralph Mooney, the now legendary steel guitarist. Stewart first recorded for Intro in 1954 and local success with his own song, 'Strolling', led to him signing for Capitol. In 1956, his recording of 'Waltz Of The Angels' became his first hit, further minor ones followed but it was not until 1959, after he moved to the Challenge label, that he achieved major success with 'Wishful Thinking' and also recorded with Jan Howard. In the late 50s, he moved to Las Vegas, where he opened the Nashville Nevada Club and hosted his own television series on KTOO. In 1959, Miki And Griff had a UK pop chart hit with Stewart's song 'Hold Back Tomorrow'. Competition for places in his band was fierce and in 1962, Stewart gave Merle Haggard the job of playing bass and singing the odd song during his own breaks. A year later he provided Haggard with 'Sing A Sad Song', which became his first chart hit. He returned to California in the mid-60s, toured with his band the Tourists and also rejoined Capitol, where between 1965 and 1971, he had 17 country chart hits, including 'It's Such A Pretty World Today', his only number 1. He moved to RCA in 1972, but achieved his next Top 20 hits in 1976 with 'After The Storm' and his own version of 'Sing A Sad Song', after moving to Playboy Records. Stewart's reputation became somewhat marred by problems; his private life suffered (he was married three times) and at times drinking caused him to miss bookings. He eventually moved to Nashville, where he believed he could achieve another breakthrough with a special come-back tour. At 6 pm on 17 July 1985, the evening the tour was due to start, he suffered a heart attack and died. Stewart was a fine singer, who should have been a bigger star, for, as John Morthland later wrote, 'He may not have been as consistent as Haggard or Buck Owens but at his best, he was their equal as a writer'.

● ALBUMS: with Jan Howard *Sweethearts Of Country Music* (Challenge 1961)★★★, *Wynn Stewart* (Wrangler 1962)★★★, *The Songs Of Wynn Stewart* (Capitol 1965)★★★, *Above And Beyond* (1967)★★★, *It's Such A Pretty World Today* (Capitol 1967)★★★, with Howard *Wynn Stewart And Jan Howard Sing Their Hits* (Starday 1968)★★★★, *In Love* (Capitol 1968)★★★, *Love's Gonna Happen To Me* (Capitol 1968)★★★, *Something Pretty* (Capitol 1968)★★★, *Let The Whole World Sing With Me* (Capitol 1969)★★, *Yours Forever* (Capitol 1969)★★★, *You Don't Care What Happens To Me* (Capitol 1970)★★★, *It's A Beautiful Day* (Capitol 1970)★★★, *Baby It's Yours* (Capitol 1971)★★★, *After The Storm* (Playboy 1976)★★★.

● COMPILATIONS: *Wishful Thinking (The Challenge Years 1958-1963)* (1988)★★★★, *California Country: The Best Of The Challenge Masters* (AVI 1995)★★★.

STOCKARD, OCIE

b. Ocie Blanton Stockard, 11 May 1909, Crafton, Texas, USA, d. 23 April 1988, Fort Worth, Texas, USA. A talented musician and stalwart of western swing music, he learned guitar from his sister's boyfriend, fiddle breakdowns from his father and played at dances at the age of 10. He later learned to read music, and improved his fiddle playing as well as becoming an accomplished banjo and tenor guitar player. While working as a barber in Fort Worth, he began to play on KTAT. In 1930, often alternating instruments, he played in a band known as the High Fliers and also at dances with Milton and Derwood Brown, Bob Wills and Herman Arnspiger. When Milton Brown formed his Musical Brownies, Stockard became a regular band member, playing banjo on their first recordings in April 1934. Throughout his time with Brown, he played different instruments as the occasion demanded and also added harmony vocals. After Milton Brown's death, he continued with the band under Derwood Brown's leadership making Decca recordings (including vocals) in

February 1937. Soon afterwards, Stockard formed his own band, the Wanderers and made recordings for Bluebird. It proved a popular Texas band until it folded in the late 40s, when Stockard relocated to California and for some years played with Bob Wills' Texas Playboys. He also played with Tommy Duncan's Western All Stars in Los Angeles, until he finally tired of the business and returned to Fort Worth. He ran a bar until his retirement and subsequently died in a nursing home in April 1988.

STONE, CLIFFIE

b. Clifford Gilpin Snyder, 1 March 1917, Burbank, California, USA. In the early 30s Stone played bass and trombone in dance bands before becoming a country music compere and disc jockey in 1935. During the 40s he was bandleader and host of the CBS network *Hollywood Barn Dance* and from 1943-47 he compered almost 30 other country radio shows weekly. He joined Capitol Records in 1946, working on production as well as recording and had chart hits in 1947-48, including 'Peepin' Through The Keyhole' and 'When My Blue Moon Turns To Gold Again'. In 1949, he hosted the famed *Hometown Jamboree* and, from 1953 to its closure in 1960, the radio and television show *Town Hall Party*. These shows did much to popularize country music over a wide area and many artists benefited from their appearances on them. One prominent regular on *Hometown Jamboree* was Stone's father, a banjo-playing comedian who performed as Herman The Hermit. Stone discovered Tennessee Ernie Ford in 1949 and was his manager for many years; he also worked with many other artists including Spade Cooley, Lefty Frizzell, Hank Thompson and Molly Bee. During the 60s he cut back on his own performing, concentrating on management, a booking agency and several music publishing firms including Central Songs, which he sold to Capitol in 1969. Throughout the 60s and 70s he was involved in production, formed Granite records, and did committee work for the Country Music Association and ATV Music before retiring in the late 70s. Over the years he wrote many songs and worked with Merle Travis on such classics as 'Divorce Me C.O.D', 'So Round So Firm So Fully Packed' and 'No Vacancy'. Stone, who rarely left his native California during his illustrious career, was elected to Nashville's Country Music Hall Of Fame in 1989 for his services to music in the non-performer category.

● ALBUMS: *Square Dances* 10-inch album (Capitol 1955)★★★★, *The Party's On Me* (Capitol 1958)★★★★, *Cool Cowboy* (Capitol 1959)★★★★, *Square Dance Promenade* (Capitol 1960)★★★, *Original Cowboy Sing-a-long* (Capitol 1961)★★★, *Together Again* (Capitol 1967)★★★.

STONE, DOUG

b. Douglas Brooks 19 June 1956, Newnan, Georgia, USA. Stone, the product of a broken home, was encouraged to become a musician by his mother. She taught him to play guitar and had put him onstage by the age of 7. Stone, in addition to possessing a rich country voice, plays guitar, keyboards, fiddle and drums. He worked as part of a trio around Georgia for several years without finding commercial success, but his determination to become a success never faltered. Even when he was forced to take a job as a mechanic with his father he would still spend every evening either playing or making demos in his home-made recording studio. He then auditioned for the top producer Bob Montgomery after being recommended by Phyllis Bennett in 1988, who immediately signed him to Epic Records. There was much angst in Stone's work at this time and in 1990, he had his first US country hit with the self-pitying 'I'd Be Better Off In A Pine Box'. Like many other 'new country' singers, he was a throwback to the honky tonk tradition of George Jones and Merle Haggard and in particular Gene Watson. His other major successes have included 'In A Different Light', another angst-ridden lyric 'I Thought It Was You', 'A Jukebox With A Country Song', 'Come In Out Of The Pain', 'Too Busy Being In Love', 'Why Didn't I Think Of That', 'I Never Knew Love' and one of the slickest country songs of recent years, 'Warning Labels'. *From The Heart* was an unfortunate choice of title as shortly before its release in 1992, his career suffered a major setback when he had quadruple heart bypass surgery, but he recovered while the hits kept being released (such was the quality of his stockpile of strong album tracks). *More Love* featured songs from the film *Gordy*, while *Faith In Me, Faith In You* contained the prophetic 'You Won't Outlive Me'. Further disaster came in December 1995 when he suffered another heart attack. He says, 'I wasn't scared. I figured if I'm going to die now, there's nothing I can do about it.' He returned to touring again in early 1996.

● ALBUMS: *Doug Stone* (Epic 1990)★★★, *I Thought It Was You* (Epic 1991)★★★, *From The Heart* (Epic 1992)★★★, *The First Christmas* (Epic 1992)★★, *More Love* (Epic 1993)★★, *Faith In Me, Faith In You* (Columbia 1995)★★.

● COMPILATIONS: *Greatest Hits, Volume 1* (Epic 1994)★★★.

● VIDEOS: *I Never Knew Love* (1993).

STONEMAN FAMILY

The Stoneman Family originated with Ernest V. 'Pop' Stoneman (b. 25 May 1893, in a log cabin near Monarat, Carroll County, Virginia, USA, d. 14 June 1968, Nashville, Tennessee, USA), who learned to play guitar, autoharp, banjo and harmonica and showed a talent for quickly learning songs that he either heard or read in early songbooks. He worked in cotton mills, coalmines and as a carpenter in various parts of the area. It was while working as the last at Bluefield, West Virginia, that he heard the first recordings of fellow Virginian Henry Whitter. Stoneman was unimpressed by Whitter's singing and like others, believed that he could do better. He travelled to New York where, providing his own autoharp and harmonica backings, he auditioned for Columbia and OKeh. The former showed no interest, but he made his first recordings for OKeh in September 1924, including his million-seller, 'The Sinking Of The Titanic'. It proved to be one of the biggest hits of the 20s and has since been recorded by many artists, including Roy Acuff. The records sold well enough and further sessions soon followed; on one he was accompanied by Emmett Lundy, a noted Virginian fiddler, and on occasions, he recorded with his fiddle-playing wife Hattie Stoneman (b.1900, d. 22 July 1976, Murfreesboro, Tennessee, USA). In 1926, he recorded for RCA-Victor with his first band the Dixie Mountaineers and later with the Blue Ridge Cornshuckers. In the following years many recordings were made, which saw release on various labels, some under pseudonyms such as Slim Harris, Ernest Johnson, Uncle Ben Hawkins and Jim Seaney. In July 1927, he recorded at the noted sessions at Bristol,

Tennessee, where Ralph Peer also recorded the Carter Family and Jimmie Rodgers. Due to the Depression, he did not record between 1929 and 1933, but even so he had proved so popular that between 1925 and 1934, he had still recorded over two hundred songs. Some recordings were with other musicians, including his banjoist cousin George Stoneman (1883-1966), fiddlers Alex 'Uncle Eck' Dunford (c.1978-1953) and Kahle Brewer (b.1904) and on his last pre-World War II session in 1934, he was accompanied by his eldest son Eddie (b. 1920), who played banjo and took some vocals. In 1931, financially insecure in spite of the earnings from record sales, he moved to Washington DC, where, to support his family (he and his wife had 23 children in all), he worked as a carpenter in a naval gun factory. Some of the children learned to play instruments during childhood and when, after the war, he gradually began to return to entertaining, his band was made up of his wife and their own children.

A winning appearance on a television quiz show in 1956 led him to reactivate his career. With his wife and five of his children, he recorded again (on Folkways) in 1957. After adding some contemporary country and bluegrass music to the old-time and folk songs that he had always performed, the Stoneman Family became a popular touring act. They played on the *Grand Ole Opry* in 1962 and even appeared at *Fillmore West* in San Francisco, America's first psychedelic ballroom. In 1964, they moved their home to California, where they became active on the west coast folk scene and appeared at the prestigious Monterey Folk Festival. They also played on various network television shows in the 60s, including that of Jimmy Dean, and between 1966 and 1968, they hosted their own series. At this time, the group consisted of Pop (autoharp, guitar), Calvin 'Scotty' Scott (fiddle), Van Haden (b. 1941, d. 3 June 1995; guitar), Donna (mandolin), Roni (Veronica) (banjo) and Jim (bass). They had five minor hits with recordings on MGM in the late 60s but later recorded for other labels including Starday and RCA. In 1967, the CMA voted the Stoneman Family the Vocal Group Of The Year. Ernest Stoneman made his last recordings on 11 April 1968, and continued to perform with the group almost up to his death. He was in all probability the first person ever to record using an autoharp and he is well remembered by exponents for his ability to play the melody line, instead of merely playing chords, the standard method of playing the instrument, even by its inventor (this ability is demonstrated on some of his recordings, including 'Stoney's Waltz'). He is also accepted as being the only country musician to record on both Edison cylinders and modern stereo albums and he was also the leading performer of string-band music in the Galax area of Virginia. After 'Pop' Stoneman's death, Patti (autoharp) gave up her solo career to join with Donna, Roni, Van and Jim and as the Stoneman Family, they continued to play his music and toured all over the USA and Europe. In 1972, they recorded a live album, *Meet The Stonemans*, at London's Wembley Festival. Scotty Stoneman who also worked with the Blue Grass Champs and the Kentucky Colonels, won many fiddle competitions, including the national contest on several occasions and at the time of his death, in 1973, he was rated one of the world's finest bluegrass fiddle players. Hattie Stoneman, who first recorded in 1925, died in hospital aged 75. In later years, Donna left to concentrate on gospel music, and Roni became a featured star of the television show *Hee-Haw*. Patti, Jim and Van continued to play as the Stoneman Family. Twin brothers Gene and Dean (b. 1931) performed for a time in the Maryland area as the Stoneman Brothers, until Dean formed his Vintage Bluegrass band. In 1981, several members of the family reunited to record a special album. Dean Stoneman died of a lung complaint in Lanham, Maryland, on 28 February 1989.

● ALBUMS: *American Banjo Tunes & Songs* (Folkways 1957)★★★★, *Old Time Tunes Of The South* (Folkways 1957)★★★★, *Bluegrass Champs* (Starday 1963)★★★★, *Big Ball In Monterey* (World Pacific 1964)★★★, *White Lightning* (Starday 1965)★★★, *Those Singin', Swingin', Stompin', Sensational Stonemans* (MGM 1966)★★★★, with the Tracy Schwarz Band *Down Home* (Folkways 1966)★★★★, with the Tracy Schwarz Band *The Stoneman Family* (Folkways 1966)★★★, *All In The Family* (MGM 1967)★★★, *Stoneman's Country* (MGM 1967)★★★, *The Great Stonemans* (MGM 1968)★★★, *A Stoneman Christmas* (MGM 1968)★★, *The Stoneman Family Live* (Sunset 1968)★★★, *Tribute To Pop Stoneman* (MGM 1969)★★★, *In All Honesty* (RCA Victor 1970)★★★, *Dawn Of The Stoneman's Age* (RCA Victor 1970)★★★, *The Stonemans* (MGM 1970)★★★, *California Blues* (RCA Victor 1971)★★★★, *Live At Wembley* UK only (NAL 1972)★★, *Meet The Stonemans* (1972)★★★, *Cuttin' The Grass* (CMH 1976)★★★, *On The Road* (CMH 1977)★★, *Country Hospitality* (Meteor 1977)★★★, *Hot And Gettin' Hotter* cassette only (Stonehouse c.80s)★★, *Live At The Roy Acuff Theater* cassette only (Stonehouse c.80s)★★, *The Stoneman Family Volume 1; Live From Their T.V. Shows* cassette only (Stonehouse c.80s)★★, *First Family Of Country Music* (CMH 1981)★★, *Family Bible* (Rutabaga 1988)★★★, *For God And Country* (Old Homestead 1990)★★★.

Solo: Ernest V. Stoneman *Cool Cowboy* (Capitol 1958)★★★, *Ernest V. Stoneman & His Dixie Mountaineers (1927-1928)* (Historical 1968)★★★★, *The Pop Stoneman Memorial Album* (MGM 1969)★★★, *Ernest V. Stoneman & the Blue Ridge Corn Shuckers* (Rounder 1975)★★★★, *Round The Heart Of Old Galax* (County 1976)★★★, *Ernest V. Stoneman Volume 1* (Old Homestead 1986)★★★★, *Ernest V. Stoneman Volume 2* (Old Homestead 1986)★★★, *Ernest V. Stoneman Volume 3* (Old Homestead 1988)★★★, *A Rare Find* covers early 60s (Stonehouse c.80s)★★★. Scotty Stoneman: *Mr Country Fiddler* (Design 1967)★★★★, with the Kentucky Colonels *1965 Live In L.A.* (Sierra-Briar 1978)★★★, with Bill Emerson *20 Fiddlin' Banjo Hits* (Country Music Legends 1980)★★★. Donna Stoneman: *I'll Fly Away* (Temple c.70s)★★★, *Donna Stoneman And Family - Gospel* cassette only (No Label c.80s)★★★, *Donna Stoneman And Family - Old Rugged Cross* cassette only (No Label c.80s)★★★. Roni Stoneman: *First Lady Of Banjo* cassette only (Stone Ray 1989)★★★, *Pure And Country* cassette only (Stone Ray 1989)★★★.

● FURTHER READING: *The Stonemans*, Ivan M. Tribe.

STORY, CARL

b. 29 May 1916, Lenoir, Caldwell County, North Carolina, USA, d. 30 March 1995. Story followed his musical father by playing the fiddle and he was fronting his own band when only 19 years old. He played fiddle with Bill Monroe in 1942-43, but was then enlisted for the war. After demobilization, he turned to guitar and re-formed his own band, the Rambling Mountaineers, becoming popular on several radio

stations. His records for Mercury were a mixture of mainstream country and bluegrass, and his many excellent musicians include Clarence 'Tater' Tate (fiddle), Bobby Thompson (banjo) and the brothers Bud and Willie Brewster (mandolin and banjo, respectively). Story's own bass-baritone was not the most natural voice for bluegrass music but he developed a counter-tenor that was ideally suited to the music. He co-wrote 'I Overlooked An Orchid', later a country hit for Mickey Gilley, as well as many gospel songs - 'Lights At The River', 'My Lord Keeps A Record' and 'Are You Afraid To Die?'. Many of Story's early recordings have been reissued by the German Cattle label.

● ALBUMS: *Gospel Quartet Favorites* (Mercury 1958)★★★★, *America's Favorite Country Gospel Artist* (Starday 1959)★★★, *Preachin', Prayin', Shoutin' and Singin'* (Starday 1959)★★★, *All Day Singing With Dinner On The Ground* (Starday 1961)★★★, *Everybody Will Be Happy* (1961)★★★★, *Get Religion* (Starday 1961)★★★, *Gospel Revival* (1961)★★★, *Mighty Close To Heaven* (Starday 1963)★★★, *Good Ole Mountain Gospel Music* (Wing 1964)★★★, *There's Nothing On Earth That Heaven Can't Cure* (Starday 1965)★★★, *Sacred Songs Of Life And The Hereafter* (Starday 1965)★★★, *Glory Hallelujah* (1966)★★, *Songs For Our Saviour* (Sims 1966)★★, *From The Altar To Vietnam* (1966)★★★, *Carl Story Sings The Gospel Songs You Asked For* (1966)★★★, *The Best Of Country Music* (1967)★★★★, *My Lord Keeps A Record* (1968)★★★, *Daddy Sang Bass* (1969)★★★, *Precious Memories* (1969)★★★, *'Neath The Tree Of Life* (1971)★★, *Precious Memories* (1971)★★★, *Light At The River* (1974)★★★, *Mother's Last Word* (1975)★★★, *Mountain Music* (1976)★★★, *The Bluegrass Gospel Collection* (1976)★★★, *Live At Bill Grant's Bluegrass Festival* (1977)★★, with the Brewster Brothers *Just A Rose Will Do* (1977)★★★, *Lonesome Wail From The Hills* (1977)★★★, *Songs From The Blue Ridge Mountains* (1979)★★★, *Bluegrass Sound In Stereo* (1980)★★★, *The Early Days* (1980)★★★★, *It's A Mighty Hard Road To Travel* (1980)★★★, *Bluegrass Time* (1980)★★★, *A Beautiful City* (1982)★★★, *Country And Bluegrass Classics* (1983)★★★.

STRAIT, GEORGE

b. 18 May 1952, Poteet, Texas, USA. Strait, the second son of a schoolteacher, was raised in Pearsall, Texas. When his father took over the family ranch, he developed an interest in farming. Strait heard country music throughout his youth but the record that cemented his love was Merle Haggard's *A Tribute To The Best Damn Fiddle Player In The World (Or, My Salute To Bob Wills)*. Strait dropped out of college to elope with his girlfriend, Norma, and then enlisted in the US Army. While there, he began playing country music. While at university studying agriculture, he founded the Ace In The Hole band (his 1989 US country number 1, 'Ace In The Hole', was not about his band, nor did it feature them). In 1976, he briefly recorded for Pappy Daily's D Records in Houston, one title being 'That Don't Change The Way I Feel About You'. Starting in 1977, Strait made trips to Nashville, but he was too shy to do himself justice. Disillusioned, he considered a return to Texas but his wife urged him to persevere. A club owner he had worked for, Erv Woolsey, was working for MCA Records; he signed him to the label and then became his manager. In 1981, Strait's first single, 'Unwound', made number 6 in the US country charts. After two further hits, 'Fool Hearted Memory', from *The Soldier*, a film in which he had a cameo role, went to number 1. Strait was unsure about the recitation on 'You Look So Good In Love', but it was another chart-topper and led to him calling a racehorse Looks Good In Love. Strait's run of 18 US country number 1 hits also included 'Does Fort Worth Ever Cross Your Mind?' (1985), 'Nobody In His Right Mind Would've Left Her' (1986), 'Am I Blue' (1987), 'Famous Last Words Of A Fool' (1988) and 'Baby's Gotten Good At Goodbye' (1989). Strait was a throwback to the 50s honky-tonk sound of country music. He used twin fiddles and steel guitar and his strong, warm delivery was similar to that of Haggard and Lefty Frizzell. He made no secret of his influences, recording a fine tribute to Frizzell, 'Lefty's Gone'. Strait suffered a personal tragedy when his daughter, Jennifer, died in a car accident in 1986. Managing to compose himself, *Ocean Front Property* became the first album to enter *Billboard*'s country music chart at number 1, and it included another classic single, 'All My Ex's Live In Texas', which also demonstrated his love of western swing. The white-stetsoned Strait, who also manages to run a large farm, became one of the USA's top concert attractions, winning many awards from the Country Music Association, but it was only in 1989 that he became their Entertainer of the Year. After the impressive *Chill Of An Early Fall*, Strait enjoyed a major commercial success with a starring role in the film *Pure Country*.The magnificent box set *Strait Out Of The Box* demonstrates how consistent he has been over the years. Among the previously unissued tracks is a bizarre duet of 'Fly Me To The Moon', featuring that well-known honky tonk singer Frank Sinatra. A box-set retrospective often indicates that a career is nearing its end, but *Lead On* in 1994 and *Clear Blue Sky* in 1996 are as as good as anything he has recorded, the latter making its debut at number 1 on the *Billboard* country chart. The title track also became his 26th US country number 1. *Carrying Your Love With Me*, another excellent collection, probably ranks Strait as the leading male country artist of the 90s - even though the creases on his jeans are dangerously straight. His status was confirmed when he picked up awards for best male artist and best album at the 1997 CMA Awards.

● ALBUMS: *Strait Country* (MCA 1981)★★★★, *Strait From The Heart* (MCA 1982)★★★, *Right Or Wrong* (MCA 1983)★★★, *Does Fort Worth Ever Cross Your Mind?* (MCA 1984)★★★★, *Something Special* (MCA 1985)★★, *No. 7* (MCA 1986)★★★, *Merry Christmas Strait To You!* (MCA 1986)★★★, *Ocean Front Property* (MCA 1987)★★★★, *If You Ain't Lovin' (You Ain't Livin')* (MCA 1988)★★★, *Beyond The Blue Neon* (MCA 1989)★★★, *Livin' It Up* (MCA 1990)★★, *Chill Of An Early Fall* (MCA 1991)★★★★, *Holding My Own* (MCA 1992)★★★, *Pure Country* film soundtrack (MCA 1992)★★★, *Easy Come, Easy Go* (MCA 1993)★★★, *Lead On* (MCA 1994)★★★★, *Clear Blue Sky* (MCA 1996)★★★★, *Carrying Your Love With Me* (MCA 1997)★★★★.

● COMPILATIONS: *Greatest Hits* (MCA 1985)★★★★, *Greatest Hits, Volume 2* (MCA 1987)★★★★, *Strait Out Of The Box* 4-CD box set (MCA 1995)★★★★.

● VIDEOS: *The Man In Love With You* (1994), *Pure Country* (1995).

● FURTHER READING: *George Strait: The Story Of Country's Living Legend*, Mark Bego.

STREET, MEL

b. King Malachi Street, 21 October 1933, near Grundy, West Virginia, USA, d. 21 October 1978, Hendersonville, Tennessee, USA. Street performed on local radio in the 50s and then he moved to Niagara Falls and New York, making his living on building sites. He later wrote and recorded the song 'The High Line Man', about working on radio station masts. He returned to West Virginia and worked in car repairs. He also played clubs and honky tonks, and he recorded his song 'Borrowed Angel' in 1970. Two years later it was reissued and became a US country hit. He had further hits with 'Lovin' On Back Streets' and 'I Met A Friend Of Yours Today'. Street became an alcoholic and, beset by personal problems, he shot himself on his 45th birthday in Hendersonville, Tennessee. His US single at the time was 'Just Hangin' On'. George Jones sang 'Amazing Grace' at his funeral. Since his death, he has had country hits with 'The One Thing My Lady Never Puts In Words', and a duet with Sandy Powell, 'Slip Away'. In 1981, his television-advertised *Mel Street's Greatest Hits* sold a remarkable 400,000 copies.

● ALBUMS: *Borrowed Angel* (Metromedia 1972)★★★, *Mel Street* (Metromedia 1973)★★★, *Two Way Street* (GRT 1974)★★★, *Smokey Mountain Memories* (GRT 1975)★★★, *Country Colours* (1976)★★★, *Mel Street* (Polydor 1977)★★, *Country Soul* (Polydor 1978)★★.

● COMPILATIONS: *Greatest Hits* (GRT 1976)★★★, *The Many Moods Of Mel Street* (Sunbird 1980)★★★, *Mel Street's Greatest Hits* (Highland 1996)★★★.

STRICKLIN, AL

b. Alton Meeks Stricklin, 29 January 1908, Antioch, Johnson County, Texas, USA, d. 15 October 1986, Cleburne, Texas, USA. He started to play piano at the age of five so that he could accompany his fiddle-playing father. By the age of 12, he was a competent pianist. He worked his way through college by playing for functions and giving piano lessons. He left college to help with the family finances during the Depression. He found employment as staff pianist with KFJZ Fort Worth, and met Bob Wills for the first time when he auditioned Wills and Milton Brown for the station. In 1933, he lost his job at KFJZ and for a time worked as a teacher, but in 1935, he returned to the station playing on a daily programme with the High Flyers. Soon afterwards, when Bob Wills formed his Texas Playboys, he asked Stricklin to play piano for him. He stayed with Wills for seven years. In the late 40s, he worked with several bands even, on occasions, rejoining Wills. He played on the session made at Merle Haggard's home in 1971 and on the famous last recordings made by Wills in December 1973. In the late 70s, when Leon McAuliffe fronted a line-up of ex-Texas Playboys, Stricklin played and recorded with them. He recorded a solo album and also left a graphic account of his years with Wills in a book. Stricklin was undoubtedly a founder of western swing piano playing and is highly respected by experts on the genre.

● FURTHER READING: *My Years With Bob Wills*, Al Stricklin.

STRINGBEAN

b. David Akeman, 17 June 1914, Annville, Jackson County, Kentucky, USA, d. 10 November 1973. Akeman was raised on a farm and received his first banjo by trading a pair of his prized bantams. Between 1935 and 1939 he worked with several bands including that of local celebrity Asa Martin, who, because of his gangling appearance, first gave him the nickname of String Beans. Akeman's baseball pitching attracted the attention of Bill Monroe, who signed him for his private team, not knowing that he was also a banjo player. During his time with Monroe, Akeman also worked with Willie Egbert Westbrooks as String Beans and Cousin Wilbur. In 1945 he left Monroe, being replaced by Earl Scruggs and for three years worked with Lew Childre, the two becoming a popular *Grand Ole Opry* act. Akemen, now known as Stringbean, also adopted a strange stage attire, probably based on an outfit worn by old-time comedian Slim Miller, which gave the effect of a tall man with very short legs. He married Estelle Stanfill in 1945, who shared his love of the outdoor life and acted as his chauffeur (Akemen had two cars but never learned to drive). In 1946, he formed a lasting friendship with Grandpa Jones and by 1950 was an established solo star of the *Opry*, which he remained to his death. Akeman recorded for Starday in the 60s, achieving success with songs such as 'Chewing Gum', 'I Wonder Where Wanda Went' and 'I'm Going To The Grand Ole Opry And Make Myself A Name'. In 1969, along with Jones, he also became a regular on the network television show *Hee-Haw*. His love of the quiet country life and his distrust of banks had fatal consequences when, on returning to their farm at Goodlettsville after his *Opry* performance on 10 November 1973, the Akemans surprised two intruders. Stringbean was shot on entering the house and his wife, then parking the car, was pursued and shot down on the lawn. The killers fled with $250 leaving the bodies to be discovered early next morning by Grandpa Jones. John and Douglas Brown were arrested, charged with murder and in spite of the public outcry for the death penalty, were sentenced to life imprisonment.

● ALBUMS: *Old Time Pickin' & Singin' With Stringbean* (Starday 1961)★★★, *Stringbean* (Starday 1962)★★★★, *Kentucky Wonder* (1962)★★★, *A Salute To Uncle Dave Macon* (Starday 1963)★★★, *Old Time Banjo Picking And Singing* (1964)★★★, *Way Back In The Hills Of Old Kentucky* (Starday 1964)★★★, *Hee-Haw Cornshucker* (Nashville 1971)★★★, *Me & Old Crow (Got A Good Thing Goin')* (Nugget 1972)★★★, *Stringbean Goin' To The Grand Ole Opry* (Ovation 1977)★★.

STROUD, JAMES

The country producer James Stroud played drums for the 80s country rock group the Snakes. They cut 'Pay Bo Diddley' with Bo Diddley himself - sample lyric: 'You all may laugh but it just ain't funny, Whatever happened to Bo Diddley's money?'. Stroud produced US country number 1 hits for S-K-O ('Baby's Got A New Baby') and the Forester Sisters ('You Again'). In 1989 he produced Clint Black's album *Killin' Time*, and he has remained with Black since then. He owns Giant Records and one of his artists is Clay Walker. In 1996 he produced US country hits for Tim McGraw, Doug Stone, John Anderson and Lorrie Morgan.

STRUNK, JUD

b. Justin Strunk, Jnr., 11 June 1936, Jamestown, New York, USA, d. 15 October 1981. Strunk was a story-telling banjo player who was popular in both the country and pop markets at the time he died in a plane crash. He was raised in Farmington, Maine, and was entertaining locals even as a child. He performed as a one-man show for the US Armed Forces and appeared in an off-Broadway musical production titled *Beautiful Dreamer*. He relocated to California in the early 70s and appeared on television with his story-songs. In 1973 he signed to MGM Records and released 'Daisy A Day', a song that appeared on both the pop and country charts. He returned to the country charts three more times, with other humorous tales such as 'Next Door Neighbor's Kid' and 'The Biggest Parakeets In Town'.

● ALBUMS: *Jud Strunk's Downeast Viewpoint* (1970)★★★, *Daisy A Day* (MGM 1973)★★.

STRUTT, NICK

b. Nicholas Charles Strutt, 8 October 1946, Upminster, Essex, England. A talented British country musician, who first played banjo at the age of 15 and then mastered guitar, autoharp, mandolin and bass. In 1965, he relocated to Leeds and graduated from Leeds University in 1970. Between 1966 and 1969, he played in a duo with Roger Knowles, which featured regularly on various radio broadcasts, including the BBC *Country Meets Folk*, where they sometimes played with Brian Golbey and Pete Stanley as a four-piece unit. Strutt and Knowles played as support for Hank Snow and Willie Nelson on UK appearances, before their influences saw them turn more to seminal country rock. In 1970 Strutt turned fully professional but between 1969 and 1971, he and Knowles played with Natchez Trace. In 1972, they parted amicably with Knowles opting for more traditional music and Strutt favouring the contemporary. He joined Bob and Carole Pegg in the folk rock band Mr. Fox and recorded two albums with Pegg for Transatlantic. When folk rock waned, he returned to country music, playing regularly around the northern country club scene. In the late 70s, he worked on production and played as a session musician for the now defunct Look label. Here he worked with many artists, especially with Mel Hague but also produced albums for folk singer Alex Campbell and country star Tommy Collins. In the early 80s, he turned more to old-time music again and often worked and recorded with Brian Golbey. He commented that 'with the advent of New Country, line dancing and blander performances, our picking and grinning style was regarded as a novelty.' During the mid-80s, he played part-time with various units, including a swing quartet, but returned to full-time professionalism in 1990. He began teaching guitar, mandolin and bass and appeared regularly with Mel Hague's band. He also played old-time music at regular venues with banjoist Tim Howard of the Muldoon Brothers. In 1994, he began working with a trio called Finnegan's Wake. Over the years, Strutt has refused to be pigeonholed and his mandolin playing is unique. He acknowledges the influence of Bill Monroe and John Duffey but confesses: 'I was never any good at stealing licks accurately, so I made up my own; copying any instrument I liked be it trumpet, dobro, clarinet or trombone.' He runs jam sessions in Leeds, which often feature 20 musicians on numerous different instruments. Asked to pinpoint his musical contribution in retrospect, he replied, 'It is quite hard but probably organizing musicians into good economically viable units where you walk that narrow line twixt creativity, money and satisfaction.'

● ALBUMS: with Natchez Trace *From Natchez To Nashville*

(Philips 1971)★★★, with Trace *Last Time Together* (Avenue 1972)★★★, with Bob Pegg *Bob Pegg & Nick Strutt* (Transatlantic 1972)★★★★, with Pegg *The Shipbuilder* (Transatlantic 1972)★★★, with Brian Golbey *Last Train South* (Waterfront 1983)★★★.

STUART, MARTY

b. 30 September 1958, Philadelphia, Mississippi, USA. Stuart learned the mandolin as a young child and played with the Sullivan Family Gospel Singers, and went on the road with Lester Flatt when only 13 years old. After Flatt's death in 1979, Stuart became part of Johnny Cash's band. He married Cash's daughter, Cindy, although in keeping with most of the Cash's musical marriages they were soon divorced. Cash was among the guests on his excellent Sugar Hill recording *Busy Bee Cafe*. Stuart had a US country hit with 'Arlene' in 1985. When his first album for US Columbia, *Marty Stuart*, did not sell, they shelved plans to release a second, *Let There Be Country*, which featured Emmylou Harris and Mark O'Connor. He has appeared on many albums, including all-star gatherings such as *Will The Circle Be Unbroken, Vol. 2*, *Class Of '55* and *Highwaymen*. In 1988 he returned to playing mandolin for Jerry Sullivan's gospel group and he subsequently produced their highly acclaimed album, *A Joyful Noise*. He revitalized his own career with a powerful mixture of country and rockabilly called *Hillbilly Rock* for MCA. His duets with Travis Tritt, 'The Whiskey Ain't Workin' and 'This One's Gonna Hurt You For A Long Long Time', were both US country hits and they worked together on the hugely lucrative 'No Hats' tour. He was part of Mark O'Connor's influential 1991 album, *The Nashville Cats*. Stuart collects rhinestone suits, owns one of Hank Williams' guitars, tours in Ernest Tubb's bus and follows his dictum of 'Hillbilly rules, OK?'. He performed 'Don't Be Cruel' with the Jordanaires on *It's Now Or Never - The Tribute To Elvis* and in addition to the duets with Tritt he also duetted with his former father-in-law Johnny Cash on 'Doin' My Time' and with Pam Tillis on 'High On A Mountain'. He hosted the 1995 *Great British Country Music Awards*. His trademark rhinestone Nudie suits are a wonderful throwback to the days of Porter Wagoner and in 'Me And Hank And Jumpin' Jack Flash' he describes how he received Hank Williams' blessing in a dream. The title of his 1996 album best describes Stuart's role in new country.

● ALBUMS: *Busy Bee Cafe* (Sugar Hill 1982)★★★, *Marty Stuart* (Columbia 1985)★★★, *Hillbilly Rock* (MCA 1989)★★★★, *Tempted* (MCA 1991)★★★, *This One's Gonna Hurt You* (MCA 1992)★★★, *Love And Luck* (MCA 1994)★★★, *Honky Tonkin's What I Do Best* (MCA 1996)★★★.

● COMPILATIONS: *The Marty Party Hit Pack* (MCA 1995)★★★★.

● VIDEOS: *Hillbilly Rock* (1994), *Kiss Me, I'm Gone* (Scene Three) (1994).

STUCKEY, NAT

b. Nathan Wright Stuckey II, 17 December c.mid-30s, Cass County, Texas, USA (his date of birth has been variously given as 1933, 1934, 1937 or 1938), d. 24 August 1988. After studying for and obtaining a degree in radio and television, he worked as a disc jockey, first on KALT Atlanta, Texas, and then moving to KWKH Shreveport, Louisiana. He began to entertain and between 1958 and 1959, fronting his own band

the Cornhuskers, he played the local clubs until his performances won him a spot on KWKH's *Louisiana Hayride*, which he played from 1962-66. After first recording for Sim, he joined the Paula label and in 1966, 'Sweet Thang', which reached number 4, gave him his first US country chart entry. He named his band after the song and during the late 60s, he registered further hits on Paula before moving in 1968 to RCA, when he also relocated to Nashville. His Top 20 hits included 'Oh Woman', 'My Can Do Can't Keep Up With My Want To', 'Plastic Saddle', 'Joe And Mabel's 12th Street Bar And Grill', 'Cut Across Shorty', 'Sweet Thang And Cisco' and a duet with Connie Smith of the Sonny James' 1957 country and pop number 1 'Young Love'. (Gary Stewart played piano in Stuckey's band for some time). He recorded three albums with Connie Smith, including in 1970, an all-gospel album with one track, 'If God Is Dead (Who's That Living In My Soul)', making the *Billboard* charts. During the 60s, he also had success as a songwriter with his songs becoming hits for other artists, such as 'Waitin' In Your Welfare Line' (a country number 1 for Buck Owens) and 'Pop A Top' (a country number 3 for Jim Ed Brown). His name continued to appear in the charts in the 70s and he had major success with 'She Wakes Me With A Kiss Every Morning' and 'I Used It All On You'. In 1976, he moved to MCA but by the end of the decade his career had begun to fade and his name had disappeared from the charts, the last entry being 'The Days Of Sand And Shovels' in 1978. He continued to tour but could not maintain his earlier successes and was reduced to playing minor venues. In his later years, he was even working as a jingle singer and doing commercials. In 1985, he made a final trip to Europe (he had toured several times previously), when he appeared in London at the Wembley Festival. He formed his own publishing company in Nashville but died of lung cancer in August 1988.

● ALBUMS: *Nat Stuckey Really Sings* (Paula 1966)★★★, *All My Tomorrows* (Paula 1967)★★★, *Country Favorites* (Paula 1967)★★★★, *Nat Stuckey Sings* (RCA Victor 1968)★★★, *Keep 'Em Country* (RCA Victor 1969)★★★, with Connie Smith *Young Love* (RCA Victor 1969)★★★★, *New Country Roads* (RCA Victor 1969)★★★, *Old Man Willis* (RCA Victor 1970)★★★, with Smith *Sunday Morning With Nat Stuckey And Connie Smith* (RCA Victor 1970)★★, *Country Fever* (RCA Victor 1970)★★★, *Only A Woman Like You* (RCA Victor 1971)★★★, *She Wakes Me With A Kiss Every Morning* (RCA Victor 1971)★★★, *Forgive Me For Calling You Darling* (RCA Victor 1972)★★, *Is It Any Wonder That I Love You* (RCA Victor 1972)★★, *Take Time To Love Her/Used It All On You* (RCA Victor 1973)★★★, *Nat Stuckey* (RCA Victor 1973)★★★, with Smith *Even The Bad Times Are Good* (RCA Victor 1973)★★★, *In The Ghetto* (RCA Victor 1974)★★★, *Independence* (MCA 1976)★★★.

● COMPILATIONS *The Best Of Nat Stuckey* (RCA Victor 1974)★★★★.

STURR, JIMMY

b. Florida, USA. An underrated but prolific Nashville recording artist, Jimmy Sturr is one of the leading lights in the renaissance of polka music. By the mid-90s he was at last seeing some reward for several decades of live work and recording, with his collaboration with Willie Nelson, *Polka! All Night Long*, winning a Grammy. Despite the higher profile this brought him, Sturr insisted it was the music itself

and its traditions he was promoting: 'Polka has the stigma that it's only for older people or only for ethnic people, sung in a native language. But we've Americanized the polka (so) all the singing is done in English.' Part of the new audience opening up for polka came in the shape of traditional country music fans, who lapped up performances by Sturr's band at the *Grand Ole Opry*. He followed up the break-through success of *Polka! All Night Long* with 1997's *Living On Polka Time*, which this time saw him collaborate with Bill Anderson ('Loving Arms') and Flaco Jiminez ('Hey Baby').
● ALBUMS: *Polka! All Night Long* (Rounder 1996)★★★★, *Living On Polka Time* (Rounder 1997)★★.

SUGAR HILL RECORDS

An independent label founded in 1978 by Barry Poss, who had previously worked with County Records, Sugar Hill spe-cializes mainly in bluegrass music, but has also done much to popularize recordings of acoustic music. In the 60s, some independent labels including King and Starday released bluegrass material by such artists as the Stanley Brothers, but when these labels folded, bluegrass music tended to become a neglected genre. The major labels rarely covered the music (Bill Monroe's work on Decca, later MCA, excepted) and it was left to labels like County to provide the recordings of acoustic music. In the 70s, Rounder Records appeared and later Rebel became a noted bluegrass label. When Sugar Hill was launched, they neatly bridged the gap between labels such as Rounder and the major labels.

Their first release was *One Way Track* by Boone Creek, a short-lived five-piece bluegrass band, whose members included Ricky Skaggs and Jerry Douglas. It was also Skaggs who gave the label its first real boost with *Sweet Temptation* (SH3706). It was an album that drew glowing praise from the critics, both for the artist and the label, for the clever way it combined bluegrass and country. It also sent Skaggs on the way to major stardom, albeit not with Sugar Hill, although he did make further recordings for the label. From that point Sugar Hill moved on and using their 3000 series, they have built an enviable reputation with recordings by artists including Seldom Scene, Country Gentlemen, Doyle Lawson, John Starling, Doc Watson, Peter Rowan and the excellent Nashville Bluegrass Band. Later the label launched other series such as the 1000, which issued recordings by artists ranging from Texas singer-songwriters Townes Van Zandt and Guy Clark to the more folk country songs of Robin And Linda Williams. Gospel music fans may find some excellent examples on the 9100 series. Over the years, the label's production staff have built a reputation for their excellent sound reproduction. Their catalogue is perhaps smaller than some independent labels but they have never allowed attempts at quick sales to deter them from pro-ducing the highest possible standard of recordings, an approach justified by the many Grammy awards their recordings have won.

SUN, JOE

b. James J. Paulson, 25 September 1943, Rochester, Minnesota, USA. Sun says, 'I grew up on a farm and, like almost everyone else in the middle of nowhere, listened to the radio.' Sun listened to country and blues stations, hence the strong blues edge to his country music. In the early 70s, he moved to Chicago for a job in computers but he attended folk clubs along Wells Street and was further influenced by John Prine and Steve Goodman. He built up the confidence to become a performer himself, first working as Jack Daniels and then with a group, the Branded Men. During a stint as a disc jockey in Minneapolis, he was mesmerized by Mickey Newbury's 'Are My Thoughts With You?' and decided to move to Nashville. He arrived in 1972 and formed his own graphics company, The Sun Shop, and then used his disc jockey experience to become a record-plugger. He helped to re-establish Bill Black's Combo. In 1977 he worked for the newly formed country division of Ovation Records, defiantly promoting a b-side, the Kendalls' 'Heaven's Just A Sin Away', which went to number 1 in the US country chart. Ovation invited him make his own recordings and he quickly went to number 14 in the US country charts with Hugh Moffatt's song, 'Old Flames (Can't Hold A Candle To You)'. He had fur-ther hits with 'High And Dry', 'I Came On Business For The King' and, with Sheila Andrews, 'What I Had With You'. 'Shotgun Rider' also made the US pop charts, while his cover version of 'The Long Black Veil' includes an introduction from its writers, Danny Dill and Marijohn Wilkin. After Ovation went bankrupt, he moved to Elektra but his hard-rocking country style was poorly promoted. With his group, the Solar System, he took to touring Europe two or three times a year. His album, *Hank Bogart Still Lives*, is a tribute to his heroes.
● ALBUMS: *Old Flames (Can't Hold A Candle To You)* (Ovation 1978)★★★, *Out Of Your Mind* (Ovation 1979)★★★, *Livin' On Honky Tonk Time* (1980)★★★, *Storms Of Life* (1981)★★★, *I Ain't Honky Tonkin' No More* (Elektra 1982)★★, *The Sun Never Sets* (Sonet 1984)★★, *Twilight Zone* (Dixie Frog 1987)★★, *Hank Bogart Still Lives* (Dixie Frog 1989)★★, *Dixie And Me* (1992)★★★, *Some Old Memories 1988-1993* (Crazy Music 1994)★★★.

SUNDOWNERS

Eric Tutin (b. *c.*1914, near Childers, Queensland, Australia; piano, accordion, vocals) and Joan Martin (b. 1924, Queensland, Australia; guitar, vocals). An early Australian country music duo, formed in Toowoomba in 1939, they worked locally before moving first to 4BK Brisbane and then to Sydney. They made their only recordings for Regal-Zonophone on 30 June 1942, being joined by fiddler Ted McMinn as they recorded six original songs, which proved very popular. In 1944, Martin decided without warning to quit the business to marry. She reputedly moved to America but in the 60s, she was rumoured to be living in Victoria. Tutin first played piano with a dance band, before forming a country quartet, which included Aphra Lorraine, whom he married. Between 1946 and 1950, they toured extensively with Lester's Follies, before forming their own touring show, the Vanities. In 1952, they gave up touring to run a music shop in Gympie, Queensland, from where they established a popular radio country show on 4GY called *Tutin's Tune Time*, which proved so popular it ran for many years. They even-tually retired to Toowoomba.

SUNNYSIDERS

Freddy Morgan (b. 7 November 1910, New York City, New York, USA, d. 1970), formed the Sunnysiders in the mid-50s with Margie Rayburn, Norman Milkin and Jad Paul. Morgan was a banjoist and songwriter and a member of Spike

Jones's City Slickers between 1947 and 1958. The group signed with Kapp Records and their first single, 'Hey, Mr. Banjo', penned by Morgan and Milkin, reached number 12 in the USA. They followed it up with other banjo-related songs, including 'The Lonesome Banjo' and 'Banjo Picker's Ball', but were unable to return to the charts. Rayburn (who married Milkin) did have her own US Top 10 single in 1957 with 'I'm Available'.

● COMPILATIONS: *Motor City Bluegrass* (1970)★★★.

SUPERNAW, DOUG

b. 26 September 1960, Houston, Texas, USA. It surprises many to find that Supernaw, which he claims is of French/Native American extraction, is his real name. His mother was a coalminer's daughter and a fanatical country music fan, while his father was a scientist who only liked classical music. He learned to play guitar and grew up heavily influenced by fellow Texans George Jones, Gene Watson and Joe Ely. Supernaw briefly attended college on a golf scholarship but dropped out in 1979. He worked on an oilrig before playing with a local band and acting as a local theatre promoter booking country acts. In 1987, he relocated to Nashville, where he worked as a songwriter for four years, before tiring of Music City and returning to Texas. He formed his own band, Texas Steel, and built a reputation playing a residency in Tyler. In 1993, a scout for RCA Records was impressed and sent him back to Nashville, where RCA assigned him to their BNA label. Three singles from his debut, *Red And Rio Grande*, provided the breakthrough that he needed. After 'Honky Tonkin' Fool' charted at number 50, 'Reno' (a number 4) quickly followed, before the catchy 'I Don't Call Him Daddy' gave him his first number 1. The album's title track also charted but during this time, Supernaw encountered more than his fair share of bad luck. At the time of his chart success, he first suffered a broken neck surfing, followed by being involved in a head-on car crash. Soon afterwards, all his band's instruments and equipment were stolen from the tour bus. Finally, he suffered a very severe case of food poisoning, which saw him rushed to hospital after collapsing in the street in Richmond. When his follow-up album failed to live up to the high standards of his first, he moved label to Giant, still with Richard Landis as his producer. By January 1996, 'Not Enough Hours In The Night', taken from his debut Giant album, had re-established Supernaw and there is little doubt that, providing fate treats him more kindly in the future, he is destined to become one of the most successful of the modern era of country singers.

● ALBUMS: *Red And Rio Grande* (BNA 1993)★★, *Deep Thoughts From A Shallow Mind* (BNA 1994)★★★, *You've Still Got Me* (Giant 1995)★★★★.

● VIDEOS: *She Never Looks Back* (Giant 1996).

SWAN, BILLY

b. Billy Lance Swan, 12 May 1942, in Cape Giradeau, Missouri, USA. Swan grew up listening to country stars such as Hank Williams and Lefty Frizzell and then fell under the spell of 50s rock 'n' rollers. At the age of 16, he wrote 'Lover Please', which was recorded by a local plumber who also had an early morning television show (!), *Mirt Mirley And The Rhythm Steppers*. Elvis Presley's bass player, Bill Black, approved and recorded it with his Combo in 1960 before

passing it to Clyde McPhatter. McPhatter's version went to number 7 on the US charts, but was overshadowed in the UK by the Vernons Girls, whose version made number 16. Swan, who had insurance money as a result of losing an eye in an accident, moved to Memphis, primarily to write for Bill Black's Combo. He befriended Elvis Presley's uncle, Travis Smith, who was a gate guard at Graceland. Soon, Swan was also minding the gate and attending Elvis's late-night visits to cinemas and funfairs. Swan decided that he would be more likely to find work as a musician in Nashville, but the only employment he found was as a janitor at Columbia's studios. He quit while Bob Dylan was recording *Blonde On Blonde*, offering his job to Kris Kristofferson who had entered the building looking for work. Billy swanned around for some time, mainly working as a roadie for Mel Tillis, before meeting Tony Joe White and producing demos of his 'swamp rock'. Swan was invited to produce White officially and their work included *Black And White*, with its million-selling single, 'Polk Salad Annie'. By now Kristofferson had his own record contract and he invited Swan to play bass with his band. After accompanying Kristofferson at his unpopular appearance at the Isle of Wight Festival in 1970, Swan joined Kinky Friedman in his band the Texas Jewboys; he appears on his albums and Friedman recorded 'Lover Please'. Kristofferson invited him to join his band again and producer Chip Young invited him to record for Monument. The first single was a revival of Hank Williams' 'Wedding Bells'. Swan was given an electric organ as a wedding present by Kristofferson and Rita Coolidge. He was fooling around and the chords to 'I Can Help' appeared. Within a few minutes, he also had the lyrics. On the record, Chip Young's guitar effectively balances Swan's swirling organ and, with its heavy echo, the production was very 50s. The tune was so infectious that it topped the US charts for two weeks and made number 6 in the UK. The subsequent album was a cheerful, goodtime affair, almost as though Sun Records had decided to modernize their sound. Swan had a similar song prepared for the follow-up single, 'Everything's The Same (Ain't Nothin' Changed)', but Monument preferred to take something from the album to promote its sales. 'I'm Her Fool', with its humorous barking ending was released but it was banned by several radio stations because of the line, 'She pets me when I bury my bone'. A slow version of 'Don't Be Cruel' made number 42 in the UK. Elvis Presley recorded a full-blooded version of 'I Can Help' in 1975, which became a UK Top 30 hit in 1983. Apparently, Presley was amused by the line, 'If your child needs a daddy, I can help', and he sent Swan the socks he wore on the session as a souvenir. Elvis died before he could record Swan's 'No Way Around It (It's Love)'. One of the many asides on Jerry Lee Lewis' version of 'I Can Help' is 'Think about it, Elvis'. Billy Swan released three more albums for Monument and then one each for A&M and Epic, but he failed to recapture the overall quality of his first. Among his guest musicians were Carl Perkins, who joined him on remakes of 'Blue Suede Shoes' and 'Your True Love' and an unreleased 'Matchbox', and Scotty Moore and Otis Blackwell. The Kristoffersons recorded 'Lover Please', also a song by Swan and his wife, Marlu, 'Number One'. Swan and Kristofferson co-wrote 'Nobody Loves Anybody Anymore' on Kristofferson's *To The Bone*. Swan has also played on albums by Barefoot Jerry, Harry Chapin, Fred Frith and Dennis Linde. He has worked with T-Bone

Burnett on several of his albums and they co-wrote 'Drivin' Wheel' (later recorded by Emmylou Harris), 'The Bird That I Held In My Hand'. Swan briefly worked with Randy Meisner of the Eagles in a country rock band, Black Tie, who released *When The Night Falls* in 1986. Since then, Swan has preferred the security of touring with Kris Kristofferson.

● ALBUMS: *I Can Help* (Monument 1974)★★★★, *Rock 'N' Roll Moon* (Monument 1975)★★★, *Billy Swan* (Monument 1976)★★★★, *Billy Swan - Four* (Monument 1977)★★★, *You're OK, I'm OK* (A&M 1978)★★, *I'm Into Lovin' You* (Epic 1981)★★, *Bop To Be* (Elite 1995)★★★.

● COMPILATIONS: *Billy Swan At His Best* (Monument 1978)★★★.

SWEETHEARTS OF THE RODEO

Sisters Janis and Kristine Oliver grew up in California and spent much time harmonizing. In 1973 they started working as an acoustic duo, taking their name from a Byrds album. Although they mostly performed contemporary country rock songs, they also had some traditional country leanings. They both married, becoming Janis Gill and Kristine Arnold. Janis went to Nashville with her husband, Vince Gill, who became one of the first of the 'new country' singers. Janis invited her sister to Nashville, where they won a major talent contest. In 1986, they recorded their first album, *Sweethearts Of The Rodeo*, which yielded five US country singles including 'Hey Doll Baby'. By and large, Kristine is the lead singer and Janis the songwriter, although their wide repertoire includes 'I Feel Fine' and 'So Sad (To Watch Good Love Go Bad)'. The long delay before Columbia Records released *Sisters* led to rumours that the duo's time at the label was drawing to a close. This was confirmed by a move to Sugar Hill Records, for whom the sisters have so far released two albums characterized by their beautiful harmony singing.

● ALBUMS: *Sweethearts Of The Rodeo* (Columbia 1986)★★★, *One Time One Night* (Columbia 1988)★★★, *Buffalo Zone* (Columbia 1990)★★★, *Sisters* (Columbia 1992)★★★, *Rodeo Waltz* (Sugar Hill 1993)★★★, *Beautiful Lies* (Sugar Hill 1996)★★★.

SYLVIA

b. Sylvia Kirby Allen, 9 December 1956, Kokomo, Indiana, USA. Sylvia was singing in a church choir from a young age and always wanted to be a professional singer. She took a secretarial job for producer Tom Collins in Nashville in 1976 and he was soon using her on songwriting demos. She worked as a backing vocalist on sessions for Ronnie Milsap and Barbara Mandrell and went on the road with Janie Frickie. She was signed to RCA and worked as an opening act for Charley Pride. She had US country hits with 'Tumbleweed', 'Drifter' (a number 1), 'The Matador' and 'Heart On The Mend', which all came from her first album. In 1982 she had her second US country number 1 and a Top 20 pop hit with 'Nobody', which had only been completed hours before the session. She did not develop her style of merging country music with a disco beat as, in 1985, she took time out to write more personal material. Her duet with Michael Johnson, 'I Love You By Heart', was on the US country chart for 25 weeks, but her most unusual success was with James Galway on a revival of 'The Wayward Wind'. She was dropped by RCA in 1987 and, following a lengthy absence from the music scene, resumed live dates in 1992.

● ALBUMS: *Drifter* (RCA Victor 1981)★★★★, *Just Sylvia* (RCA Victor 1982)★★★, *Snapshot* (RCA Victor 1983)★★★, *Surprise* (RCA Victor 1984)★★, *One Step Closer* (RCA Victor 1985)★★.

● COMPILATIONS: *Greatest Hits* (RCA 1987)★★★.

TALLEY, JAMES

The US country singer James Talley was raised in New Mexico and his album *The Road To Torreon* is a serious project about poverty in the area. It is typical of Talley's work, which is usually serious material examining the world around him. The first album, *Got No Bread ...* , was self-produced and self-financed, and had a spoken intimacy about it as well as a feel for the country bands. His second was more upbeat and included his well-known 'Are They Going To Make Us Outlaws Again'. His best-known album, *Blackjack Choir*, includes a guest appearance from B.B. King, who recorded 'Bluesman', and 'When The Fiddler Packs His Case'. Although Talley is no longer a full-time performer, the German label, Bear Family Records, has reissued his albums and new material as well. *Live* comes from the Lone Star Cafe, New York City, in 1979.

● ALBUMS: *Got No Bread, No Milk, No Money, But We Sure Got A Lot Of Love* (Capitol 1975)★★★, *Tryin' Like The Devil* (Capitol 1976)★★★, *Blackjack Choir* (Capitol 1977)★★★, *Ain't It Somethin'* (Capitol 1978)★★★, *American Originals* (Bear Family 1985)★★★★, *Lovesongs And The Blues* (Bear Family 1989)★★★★, *The Road To Torreon* (Bear Family 1993)★★★★, with Cavalliere Ketchum *Live* (Bear Family 1994)★★★.

TANNER, GID
(see Skillet Lickers)

TARLETON, JIMMIE
(see Darby And Tarleton)

TATE, TATER

b. Clarence E. Tate, 4 February 1931, Gate City, Virginia, USA. The youngest of a family of nine, he displayed an amazing ability to play stringed instruments as a child and made his radio debut playing guitar in 1940. He played on radio in Elizabethton during World War II but in 1946, he became a member of Jim Smith's Ridge Runners at WKPT Kingsport, Tennessee, during which time he turned his attention more to the fiddle (he also played bass, banjo and mandolin). In the late 40s, he played in Knoxville, as a regular on both WNOX's *Mid-Day Merry Go Round* and on WROL's *Cas Walker Show* (it was Walker who gave him his nickname in 1950). In the early 50s, he played with both the Sauceman and Bailey Brothers, before spending two years in military service. When discharged, he worked with Bill Monroe, but after a time, the excessive travelling caused him migraine problems and he returned to Knoxville. He alternated between appearances on the *Cas Walker Show* and working with various artists, including the Baileys, Hylo Brown and Carl Story. During these years, he recorded with almost every artist with whom he worked. In 1965, he relocated to Roanoke, where he became a member of Red Smiley's Bluegrass Cut-Ups. Apart from their own recordings, the band backed several other artists, including Jim Eanes and Lee Moore, but Tate also recorded his first solo albums. Early in 1969, a change in management at WDBJ-TV saw the *Top Of The Morning Show* dropped. Ill health saw Smiley withdraw but Tate (who acted as the band's leader) and fellow Cut-Ups, Billy Edwards and John Palmer, recruited Herschel Sizemore and they recorded numerous albums as the Shenandoah Cut-Ups. In 1977, Tate left to work with Lester Flatt's Nashville Grass, with whom he also recorded. He later worked with Wilma Lee Cooper before rejoining Bill Monroe around 1985. During his long career, there can be few major artists with whom he has not worked and recorded. In later years, he has often played bass fiddle but Tate must be rated one of the best all-round fiddlers ever to have played in bluegrass music, even though he has not been afforded the full credit his input has deserved.

● ALBUMS: with Billy Edwards *Fiddle & Banjo Instrumentals* (Rimrock 1966)★★★★, with Red Smiley *Town & Country* (Smiley 1967)★★★, *All Time Fiddle Favorites* (Smiley 1966)★★, *Fiddle Favorites Of The USA And Canada* (Rural Rhythm 1967)★★, *Beautiful Waltz Melodies* (Rural Rhythm 1967)★★★, *Country Favorite Waltzes* (Rural Rhythm 1968)★★★, *More Favorite Waltzes* (Rural Rhythm 1969)★★★, *The Fiddle And His Lady* (Revonah 1981)★★★★.

TAYLOR, CARMOL

b. Carmol Lee Taylor, 5 September 1931, Brilliant, Alabama, USA, d. 5 December 1986, Brilliant, Alabama, USA. Taylor worked local shows and square dances from the age of 15. In 1954, he formed his Country Pals, with whom he played various radio stations for many years and from 1962-71, a regular television show in Columbus, Mississippi. Through his friendship with Billy Sherrill, he was signed to Al Gallico music as a songwriter and in 1965, Charlie Walker gave him a number 8 hit with his recording of 'Wild As A Wild Cat'. He then began writing with Sherrill, George Richey and Norro Wilson and the partnership produced a string of hit songs. They included number 1s for Tammy Wynette ('He Loves Me All The Way' and 'My Man') and George Jones ('The Grand Tour'). He also wrote the Jones/Wynette hits 'Let's Build A World Together' and 'We Loved It Away'. Taylor, a competent vocalist, first recorded in 1955, but his only chart entries came with eight mostly minor hits in the mid-70s and it is for his writing that he is usually remembered. His first chart entry was a version of the Chuck Berry pop hit 'Back In The USA', which just made the Top 50 in 1975. His highest chart placing came with 'I Really Had A Ball Last Night' (number 23) and 'Play The Saddest Song On The Jukebox' (number 35), both in 1976. In 1977, he charted a minor duet hit with Stella Parton, 'Neon Women'. He formed his own publishing company (Taylor & Watts Music) and in 1985, 'Size Seven Round (Made Of Gold)', co-written with Gary Lumpkin, was a Top 20 hit for George Jones and Lacy J. Dalton. Other Top 20 hits included '1959' (John Anderson) and 'Drinking And Driving' (Johnny Paycheck). Taylor died of lung cancer in 1986 but in 1993, fans were reminded of his songwriting when Aaron Neville achieved US country and pop success with his recording of 'The Grand Tour'.

● ALBUMS: *Song Writer* (Elektra 1976)★★, with the Country Line Band *Honky Tonk Two Steppin' Beer Drinking Saturday Nite* UK release (Password 1987)★★★.

TAYLOR, EARL

b. 17 June 1929, Rose Hill, Lee County, Virginia, USA, d. 28 January 1984. In the late 30s, Taylor was attracted to the music of the Monroe Brothers and learned to play mandolin (on which he later specialized), guitar and harmonica. In 1946, he relocated to Michigan where he played with the Mountaineers, before forming his own Stoney Mountain Boys. In 1948, broke and disenchanted, he disbanded his group and returned to Virginia before moving to Maryland, where he worked outside of music until 1953. He became friendly with teenagers Charlie Waller (later of Country Gentlemen fame), Sam Hutchins and Louie Profitt and the quartet began playing bluegrass music. With some changes, they played their local area until 1955, when Taylor joined Jimmy Martin in Detroit. He also recorded with Martin, before returning to Maryland in 1957, where he formed a new version of the Stoney Mountain Boys and worked the club circuit in the Baltimore area. In April 1959, Taylor and his group had the distinction of being the first bluegrass band to play in Carnegie Hall. Soon afterwards, he relocated to Cincinnati and played various venues and did television and radio work until 1965. During this time, he recorded for Rebel, United Artists and Capitol Records. He disbanded to work with Jimmy Martin until 1966, when he spent 18 months touring and recording with Flatt And Scruggs. He later returned to Cincinnati and, after re-forming his band, he not only worked the local area but also spent some time in California. In the early 70s, he continued to play the Cincinnati and Columbus area with bands that saw various personnel changes, and made further recordings for Rural Rhythm (listed as Earl Taylor And Jim McCall) and Vetco. In 1975, his own ill health and the tragic death of his young son saw him withdraw from public appearances for some time. He returned in the early 80s, before declining health severely limited his playing and finally led to his death in 1984. Experts on the genre maintain that over the years, Taylor's various line-ups of Stoney Mountain Boys played some of the finest bluegrass music, but writers on the music have neglected to afford him the credit he deserved.

● ALBUMS: *Folk Songs From The Bluegrass* (United Artists 1959)★★★, *Bluegrass Taylor-Made* UK reissue by Stetson 1988 (Capitol 1963)★★★, *Bluegrass Favorites* (Rural Rhythm 1968)★★★★, *Bluegrass Favorites Volume 2* (Rural Rhythm 1971)★★★, *Bluegrass Favorites Volume 3* (Rural Rhythm 1971)★★★, *The Bluegrass Touch* covers 1969 (Vetco 1974)★★★, *Body & Soul* (Vetco 1976)★★★.

TENNEVA RAMBLERS

Formed in 1924, they comprised Claude Grant (b. 1906, d. 1976; guitar, vocals), his brother Jack (b. 1903, d. 1968; mandolin), both from Bristol, Tennessee, USA, and Jack Pierce (b. 1908; fiddle) of Smyth County, Virginia, USA, but they were sometimes joined by Smokey Davis (a blackface comedian) and on recordings by Claude Slagle (banjo). In 1927, Jimmie Rodgers offered them work as his backing group. After initially refusing, they changed their name to the Jimmie Rodgers Entertainers and made some appearances with him. They were scheduled to back Rodgers on his first recordings but just prior to the session, they left him and reverted to their old name to pursue a recording career of their own. They remained active on various radio stations until 1954, sometimes being known as the Grant Brothers. They are remembered for their recording of 'The Longest Train'.
● COMPILATIONS: *The Tenneva Ramblers* (c.70s)★★.

TEXAS RUBY

(see Fox, Curly, And Texas Ruby)

TEXAS TORNADOS

Following the success of the Highwaymen (Johnny Cash, Waylon Jennings, Kris Kristofferson, Willie Nelson), four lesser-known Tex-Mex musicians formed the Texas Tornados and secured a contract with a major label, Reprise/WEA. Doug Sahm and organist Augie Meyers, who had been part of the Sir Douglas Quintet and had frequently worked together, were joined by accordionist Flaco Jiminez and one-time country star Freddy Fender. Their enthusiastic debut, *Texas Tornados*, was both a commercial success and a Grammy winner. In the event, Fender and Jiminez were absent from several tracks and the album, with its mixture of country, blues and Mexican music, was similar to what Sahm and Meyers had been playing for years. Subsequent albums also sound like the Sir Douglas Quintet with friends; their excellent music has included an English/Spanish version of Bob Dylan's 'To Ramona', Butch Hancock's 'She Never Spoke Spanish To Me' and Sahm's standards, 'Who Were You Thinkin' Of' and 'Is Anybody Goin' To San Antone?'.
● ALBUMS: *Texas Tornados* (Reprise 1990)★★★★, *Zone Of Our Own* (Reprise 1991)★★, *Hangin' On By A Thread* (Reprise 1992)★★, *4 Aces* (Reprise 1996)★★.
● COMPILATIONS: *The Best Of Texas Tornados* (Reprise 1994)★★★★.

THOMAS, B.J.

b. Billy Joe Thomas, 7 August 1942, Hugo, Oklahoma, USA. B.J. Thomas maintained a sturdy career in the USA in both the pop and country fields from the mid-60s into the late 80s. After getting experience by singing in church during his youth, Thomas joined the Triumphs in Houston, Texas, who released a number of unsuccessful singles on small labels. Collaborating with songwriter Mark Charron, a member of the Triumphs, the group recorded an original song, 'Billy And Sue', and released it on the Bragg label without national success (it was re-released on Warner Brothers Records in 1964 but again failed to take off). Thomas then recorded a cover version of Hank Williams' 'I'm So Lonesome I Could Cry' for Texas producer Huey P. Meaux. It was released on

Scepter Records, a New York company and vaulted to number 8 on the national singles chart in the USA. Thomas enjoyed further Top 40 hits with 'Mama' (also recorded successfully by Dave Berry), 'Billy And Sue' and 'The Eyes Of A Woman'. In 1968, Thomas returned to the US Top 10 with the soft-rock 'Hooked On A Feeling', written by Mark James, who also penned 'Suspicious Minds' and 'Always On My Mind' for Elvis Presley. In late 1969, Thomas reached number 1 in the USA with 'Raindrops Keep Falling On My Head', a song by Burt Bacharach and Hal David that was featured in the hit film *Butch Cassidy And The Sundance Kid*. 1970 ended with another Top 10 success, 'I Just Can't Help Believing', written by Barry Mann and Cynthia Weil. Thomas's last significant single for Scepter was 1972's 'Rock And Roll Lullaby', another Mann and Weil composition, which reached number 15 and featured Duane Eddy on guitar and the Blossoms on backing vocals. After that, the company folded, and it was not until 1975, now signed to ABC Records (after a brief, unproductive stint at Paramount), that Thomas enjoyed another hit. '(Hey Won't You Play) Another Somebody Done Somebody Wrong Song' provided his second number 1 and also topped the country charts. That record provided a second career for Thomas as a country star. Although he switched record company affiliations frequently, moving from ABC to MCA in 1978, to Cleveland International in 1983, and to Columbia Records in 1985, Thomas maintained his status in that field until the late 80s. Featuring gospel material in his act as well as straight country, he drew a new audience and continued to sell records. Thomas enjoyed a particularly strong string of country singles in 1983-84, beginning with two number 1 records, 'Whatever Happened To Old Fashioned Love' and 'New Looks From An Old Lover'. 'Two Car Garage' and 'The Whole World's In Love When You're Lonely' also made the Top 10, while a duet with Ray Charles, 'Rock And Roll Shoes', reached number 15. Simultaneous with his country career, Thomas recorded a number of gospel-inspired albums for the Myrrh label. He was firmly seen as a Christian artist in the 90s.
● ALBUMS: *I'm So Lonesome I Could Cry* (1966)★★, *Tomorrow Never Comes* (1966)★★, *Songs For Lovers And Losers* (1967)★★★, *On My Way* (1968)★★★, *Young And In Love* (1969)★★★, *Raindrops Keep Fallin' On My Head* (1969)★★★★, *Everybody's Out Of Town* (1970)★★★, *Most Of All* (1970)★★★, *Billy Joe Thomas* (1972)★★★, *B.J. Thomas Country* (1972)★★★★, *Songs* (1973)★★★, *Longhorn And London Bridges* (1974)★★, *Reunion* (ABC 1975)★★, *Help Me Make It (To My Rockin' Chair)* (ABC 1975)★★, *B.J. Thomas* (MCA 1977)★★★, *Home Where I Belong* (MCA 1977)★★★, *Everybody Loves* (MCA 1978)★★, *Happy Man* (MCA 1979)★★★, *New Looks* (Cleveland International 1983)★★★★, *The Great American Dream* (Cleveland International 1983)★★★, *Shining* (Columbia 1984)★★★, *Throwin' Rocks At The Moon* (Columbia 1985)★★★★, *Precious Memories* (Warner Resound 1996)★★★, *I Believe* (Warner Resound 1997)★★★.
● COMPILATIONS: *Greatest Hits, Vol. 1* (1969)★★★★, *Greatest Hits, Vol. 2* (1971)★★★, *The ABC Collection* (ABC 1976)★★★, *16 Greatest Hits* (Trip 1986)★★★, *Greatest Hits* (Rhino 1990)★★★★, *More Greatest Hits* (Varèse Sarabande 1995)★★★★.

THOMPSON, HANK

b. Henry William Thompson, 3 September 1925, Waco, Texas, USA. Thompson, as a young boy, was fond of records by Jimmie Rodgers and the Carter Family. He first learned the harmonica and then his parents gave him a guitar for his tenth birthday. He also played Hawaiian guitar, learned conjuring tricks and had a ventriloquist's doll. With his range of talents, he was a popular performer at Saturday morning stage shows in Waco. In 1942, he began his own local radio series, *Hank - The Hired Hand*. From 1943 Thompson served three years in the US Navy. He worked as an electrical engineer and, in his spare time, he entertained his shipmates. He says, 'The navy enhanced my career as it gave the opportunity to perform all the time. When I was overseas, I knew the guys were getting tired of hearing the same songs and so I started writing.' In 1946, he returned to Waco, formed the Brazos Valley Boys (named after the river running through Waco), and began performing at dances throughout Texas. His own song, 'Whoa Sailor', was a regional hit on Globe Records. It was followed by 'A Lonely Heart Knows' on Bluebonnet. Country star Tex Ritter heard Thompson and recommended him to his label, Capitol Records. Almost immediately, Thompson had a number 2 country hit with '(I've Got A) Humpty Dumpty Heart'. In 1949 he had another country hit with a re-recorded 'Whoa Sailor'. Thompson was a tall, upright performer with a resonant voice not unlike Ritter's, who dressed himself and his band in expensive Nudie suits. Applying his engineering knowledge, he gave the band a powerful live sound and lighting, and soon had the most successful western swing band in the USA. In 1951 Thompson began a 13-year partnership with the Hollywood record producer Ken Nelson and recorded his most successful single, 'The Wild Side Of Life', in one take (ironically 'Crying In The Deep Blue Sea' was the original a-side). 'The Wild Side Of Life' stayed at the top of the US country charts for 15 weeks and won Thompson a gold record. Kitty Wells recorded an answer version, 'It Wasn't God Who Made Honky Tonk Angels', while Thompson himself answered 'Goodnight, Irene' with 'Wake Up, Irene'. Defying convention, Thompson was permitted to repeat its snare drum sound on the *Grand Ole Opry*. Thompson had further country hits with 'Waiting In The Lobby Of Your Heart', 'Rub-A-Dub-Dub', 'Breakin' The Rules', 'Honky Tonk Girl', 'The Blackboard Of My Heart', and 'Breakin' In Another Heart', which was co-written with his wife Dorothy. In 1957 Thompson parodied rock 'n' roll in 'Rockin' In The Congo' and became a successful performer in Las Vegas. He heard 'Squaws Along The Yukon' on a hunting trip in Alaska with Merle Travis and together they arranged and updated the song. In 1959 he became the first country artist to record in stereo via the bestselling *Songs For Rounders*, and the first to record an 'in concert' album, *Live At The Golden Nugget*. He heard a band in a club in Holbrook, Arizona, and was most impressed with their original song, 'A Six Pack To Go'. Thompson turned the song into a country standard, later reviving it in duet with George Strait, and had further country hits with 'She's Just A Whole Lot Like You' and 'Oklahoma Hills'. Since Thompson left Capitol in 1964, he has recorded for several labels and his country hits have included 'Smokey The Bar', 'Where Is The Circus?', 'The Older The Violin, The Sweeter The Music' and, appropriately, 'Mr. Honky Tonk, The King Of Western Swing'. He has recorded tribute albums to the Mills Brothers (*Cab Driver*) and Nat 'King' Cole. In 1973 Thompson opened a school of country music in Claremore, Oklahoma, where he taught. He was elected to the Country Music Hall Of Fame in 1989, and still tours throughout the world, wearing his sequinned jackets: 'The public is entitled to something that is colourful and flashy. We're in showbusiness and there's nothing colourful about a T-shirt and ragged jeans.' His excellent 1997 album included duets with Tanya Tucker, Kitty Wells and Junior Brown.

● ALBUMS: *Songs Of The Brazos Valley* (Capitol 1953/1956)★★★, *North Of The Rio Grande* (Capitol 1953/1956)★★★★, *New Recordings Of Hank's All Time Hits* (Capitol 1953/1956)★★★, *Hank Thompson Favorites* (Capitol 1953/1957)★★★, *Hank!* (Capitol 1957)★★★★, *Hank Thompson's Dance Ranch* (Capitol 1958)★★★, *Favorite Waltzes By Hank Thompson* (Capitol 1959)★★★, *Songs For Rounders* (Capitol 1959)★★★★, *Most Of All* (Capitol 1960)★★★, *This Broken Heart Of Mine* (Capitol 1960)★★★, *An Old Love Affair* (Capitol 1961)★★★, *At The Golden Nugget* (Capitol 1961)★★★★, *The No. 1 Country And Western Band* (Capitol 1962)★★★, *Live At The Cherokee Frontier Days Rodeo In Wyoming* (Capitol 1962)★★★, *Live At The State Fair Of Texas* (Capitol 1963)★★★, *It's Christmas Time With Hank* (Capitol 1964)★★, *Breakin' In Another Heart* (Capitol 1965)★★★, *The Luckiest Heartache In Town* (Capitol 1965)★★★, *A Six Pack To Go* (Capitol 1966)★★★★, *Breakin' The Rules* (Capitol 1966)★★★, *Just An Old Flame* (Capitol 1967)★★★, *The Countropolitan Sound Of Hank's Brazos Boys* (Warners 1967)★★★, *Country Blues* (Tower 1968)★★★, *On Tap, In The Can Or In The Bottle* (Dot 1968)★★★, *Smokey The Bar* (Dot 1969)★★★, *Hank Thompson Salutes Oklahoma* (Dot 1969)★★★, *The Instrumental Sound Of Hank Thompson's Brazos Valley Boys* (1970)★★★, *Next Time I Fall In Love (I Won't)* (Dot 1971)★★★, *Cab Driver - A Salute To The Mills Brothers* (Dot 1972)★★★, *1000 And One Nighters* (1973)★★★, *Kindly Keep It Country* (Dot 1973)★★★, *Movin' On* (ABC 1974)★★★, *Hank Thompson Sings The Hits Of Nat 'King' Cole* (Dot 1975)★★★, *Back In The Swing Of Things* (ABC/Dot 1976)★★★, *The Thompson Touch* (ABC 1977)★★★, with Roy Clark, Freddy Fender, Don Williams *Country Comes To Carnegie Hall* (ABC/Dot 1977)★★★★, *Doin' My Thing* (1977)★★★, *Brand New Hank* (1978)★★★, *Take Me Back To Texas* (1980)★★★, *Here's To Country Music* (1988)★★★, *Hank Thompson and Friends* (Curb 1997)★★★★.

● COMPILATIONS: *The Best Of Hank Thompson* (Capitol 1963)★★★, *Golden Country Hits* (Capitol 1964)★★★★, *Where Is The Circus (And Other Heart Breakin' Hits)* (Warners 1966)★★★★, *The Best Of Hank Thompson, Volume 2* (Capitol 1967)★★★, *The Gold Standard Collection Of Hank Thompson* (Warners 1967)★★★★, *Hank Thompson's 25th Anniversary Album* (Dot 1971)★★★★, *Hank Thompson's Greatest Hits, Volume 1* (Dot 1973)★★★, *Best Of The Best Of Hank Thompson* (Gusto 1980)★★★, *Hank Thompson* (MCA 1987)★★★, *Capitol Collector's Series* (Capitol 1989)★★★★, *All-Time Greatest Hits* (Curb 1990)★★★, *Country Music Hall Of Fame Series* (MCA 1992)★★★, *Vintage* (Capitol 1996)★★★★, *Hank Thompson And His Brazos Valley Boys (1946-1964)* 12-CD box set (Bear Family 1996)★★★★, *The Best Of Hank Thompson 1966-1979* (Varèse Sarabande 1997)★★★★.

THOMPSON, SUE

b. Eva Sue McKee, 19 July 1926, Nevada, Missouri, USA. Thompson's earliest ambition was to be a singing cowgirl, and she sang at many local functions. She continued performing when the family moved to California and she appeared regularly on Dude Martin's country television show in San Francisco. A single with Martin, 'If You Want Some Lovin'', led to a solo contract with Mercury Records. In 1960, she sang on Red Foley's portion of the *Grand Ole Opry* and she signed with the country label Hickory. John D. Loudermilk wrote 'Sad Movies (Make Me Cry)' and 'Norman', which went to numbers 5 and 3, respectively, on the US pop charts and both became million-sellers. Boudleaux and Felice Bryant wrote another US hit, 'Have A Good Time', and Loudermilk returned with the novelties 'James (Hold The Ladder Steady)' and 'Paper Tiger'. Despite her American success, Thompson only had two minor Top 50 entries in the UK, but she was unlucky, as Carol Deene covered all three Loudermilk songs. Through her novelty songs she became known as 'the girl with the itty bitty voice', and she subsequently turned to more mature material. In the 70s she was teamed with Don Gibson, the two registering nine US country successes including 'The Two Of Us Together' and 'Oh How Love Changes'. Her last significant country success was with 'Big Mabel Murphy' in 1975. She married singer Hank Penny.

● ALBUMS: *Meet Sue Thompson* (Hickory 1962)★★★, *Two Of A Kind* (Hickory 1962)★★★, *The Country Side Of Sue Thompson* (Wing 1964)★★★, *Paper Tiger* (Hickory 1965)★★★★, *Sue Thompson With Strings Attached* (Hickory 1966)★★★★, *This Is Sue Thompson* (Hickory 1969)★★★, *... And Love Me* (Hickory 1974)★★★, *Sweet Memories* (Hickory 1974)★★★, *Big Mabel Murphy* (1975)★★. With Don Gibson: *The Two Of Us Together* (Hickory 1973)★★★, *Warm Love* (Hickory 1973)★★★, *Oh How Love Changes* (Hickory 1975)★★★.

● COMPILATIONS: *Sue Thompson's Golden Hits* (Hickory 1963)★★★★.

THOMPSON, UNCLE JIMMIE

b. James Donald Thompson, 1848, near Baxter, Smith County, Tennessee, USA, d. 17 February 1931, Laguardo, Tennessee. Little is known of his early life except that the family moved to Texas just before the Civil War, and by 1860 Thompson was already a capable fiddle player using a style described as the long bow technique, common to the state. He learned tunes from Civil War veterans and other sources and though generally described as a farmer, he travelled extensively. He returned to Smith County, Tennessee, probably in the early 1880s, where he married a local girl. Around 1902 Thompson and his family returned to Texas. By this time he was playing more public performances and in 1907 he won an eight-day fiddling contest in Dallas. Around 1912, he once more returned to Tennessee and bought a farm near Henderson. His wife died soon afterwards but in 1916 he remarried and moved to Laguardo, Wilson County. He acquired an old truck, which he adapted as a mobile caravan and began to tour the state playing his fiddle at fairs or wherever he could make a dollar. He was always a hard-drinking man and stubborn in his ways. About 1923 he drove all the way back to Texas just to take part in a fiddling contest. At the age of 77 his wish to broadcast came true when George D. Hay made him the first artist on his new *WSM Barn Dance* programme, which later became the *Grand Ole Opry*. He boasted that he could play a thousand tunes and was deeply upset when he found that his niece Eva made him have his trousers pressed for the occasion. His comment was, 'Hey, thar, who ironed them damn wrinkles im my britches? I like my britches smooth and round to fit my kneecaps.' Following his broadcast, Uncle Jimmie became somewhat of a celebrity, with his eccentricity endearing him to many people. Some of his habits did not endear him to George D. Hay, particularly his liking for a jug of local moonshine, 'just to lubricate his arm', nor his seeming inability to play to his allotted time without considerably overrunning. By 1927, with the emergence of many new artists, his *Opry* appearances were very limited. He first recorded in Atlanta for Columbia in 1926 and later in 1930 recorded in Knoxville for Brunswick/Vocalion. Experts comment that he was still a player of great ability when he made his last recordings. He died from pneumonia at his home in Laguardo, Tennessee, in 1931. Eva Thompson Jones was the only member of the *Opry* cast to attend his funeral. He once stayed at Eva's house in Nashville and, when later asked how he liked it, replied, 'I wouldn't have it, there ain't nowhere for to spit when I chew my tobacco'. Examples of his recorded work may be found on various compilation albums of early string band and country music.

● FURTHER READING: *The Grand Ole Opry (The Early Years 1925-35)*, Charles K. Wolfe.

THOMS, SHIRLEY

b. 12 January 1925, Toowoomba, Queensland, Australia. Thoms grew up on a farm and by her early teens, she was singing and yodelling the songs of Buddy Williams and Tex Morton that she heard on the radio. In 1940, she won a radio talent competition with her version of Harry Torrani's 'Mocking Bird Yodel'. This success led to her first six recordings for Regal-Zonophone, made in Sydney on 27 May 1941. She wrote her own material and the songs included 'Where The Golden Wattle Blooms'. They soon proved popular and six more recordings quickly followed, including her version of 'Mother's Old Red Shawl'. She toured with various shows, including Sole Bros Circus, and during World War II, she was also very popular as a member of an army entertainment unit. Between 1942 and 1946, she recorded 20 more sides, including her weepy 'The Faithful Old Dog' for the same label. She married John Sole in 1950 and nominally retired, although she recorded six sides for the Rodeo label in 1952. Her son Peter was born in 1956 but in 1958 her husband died. She later married a veterinary surgeon and although the marriage failed, she developed an interest in veterinary science. She has also written on philosophy and designed and built herself a palatial home in Sydney. In 1970, she was persuaded to appear at the Tamworth Festival. She also returned to the recording studios, this time for Hadley, where she quickly proved that her voice had lost none of its appeal, nor had she lost her ability to yodel with the best (her Austrian-born grandfather had always stoutly maintained her ability to yodel was hereditary). Although her recorded output was not large, she has the unique distinction of being the first female Australian country singer to make solo recordings, as well as being the first Queenslander to make a record. She sang with a plaintiveness similar to Kitty Wells and her original 78 recordings are still highly sought after by collectors. However, during the 70s, all her original Regal-Zonophone recordings were reissued (in recording order) on three albums. In 1980, she became the fifth artist but the first female performer to be elected to the Country Music Roll Of Renown (Australia's equivalent to Nashville's Country Music Hall Of Fame).

● ALBUMS: *Australia's Yodelling Sweetheart* (Hadley 1970)★★★, *Shirley Thoms* (Hadley 1972)★★★, *The Complete Shirley Thoms Collection Volumes 1-3* 1941-46 recordings (Hadley 70s)★★★★.

THRASHER SHIVER

Country music duo Thrasher Shiver were the subject of an unusual promotional campaign by their record label, Asylum Records, in 1996. Asylum launched the group's self-titled debut album as 'an election campaign', with campaign badges and banners mirroring the approach of the ongoing presidential electioneers. The subjects of their optimism, Neil Thrasher and Kelly Shiver, met as aspiring songwriters at a publishing company in 1992. Thrasher's father was previously a member of MCA Records' recording artists the Thrasher Brothers. Prior to the duo he had enjoyed success writing for artists such as Kenny Chesney, Ricky Lynn Gregg and Diamond Rio (the hit single 'That's What I Get For Loving You'). Shiver had formerly been a member of County Line, in Savannah, Tennessee. He too has written for other artists, including Lari White, Keith Stegall and Larry Stewart. Discovering a shared affection for mainstream, emotive country ballads, they started writing and recording demos together. That bond was strengthened when they realized their tenor voices blended together melodically. This has informed the approach of their songs ever since, with both singers following the lead rather than the melody line. Their debut album for Asylum was co-produced with Justin Niebank, and promoted by the single 'Goin' Goin' Gone'.

● ALBUMS: *Thrasher Shiver* (Asylum 1996)★★★.

TILLIS, MEL

b. Lonnie Melvin Tillis, 8 August 1932, Tampa, Florida, USA. The family relocated to Dover, 18 miles east of Tampa, when Tillis was only eight months old. He contracted malaria when aged only three, and was left with a permanent stutter. During his school days, various treatments failed to cure this speech problem and though originally embarrassed by it, he managed in later years to turn it into a trademark. He learned to play guitar (and later the fiddle) during his early teens and at high school was a football player and also played drums in a band. In the early 50s, devoid of any real career ideas, he enlisted in the Air Force. He was discharged in 1955 when for a short time he attended the University of Florida. Bored, he dropped out and worked at various tasks including strawberry picking and truck-driving. In 1956 he wrote a song called 'I'm Tired', which was recorded by and became a big hit for Webb Pierce. This enabled Tillis, as he said later, 'to get the hell out of the strawberry patch in a hurry'. He found that the stutter never appeared when he sang and gradually his confidence grew and he moved to Nashville. During 1956 and 1957 he began to perform and made his first recording, only to be told he needed original material, which prompted him to concentrate more on writing. He signed with Columbia and had his first US

country chart success with his co-written song 'The Violet And The Rose' in 1958. In the next few years several of his songs proved hits for other artists including Webb Pierce ('Tupelo County Jail' and 'I Ain't Never'), Johnny And Jack ('Lonely Island Pearl'), Ray Price ('Heart Over Mind') and Carl Smith ('Ten Thousand Drums'). His status received a further boost in 1963 when Bobby Bare had major country and pop hits with 'Detroit City', which he had co-written with Danny Dill. Three years later 'The Snakes Crawl At Night' launched the recording career of Charley Pride. In the mid-60s Tillis moved to Kapp Records, and in 1967 achieved his biggest hit up to that time with the Harlan Howard song 'Life Turned Her That Way', which made both pop and country charts (the song later became a standard and a US country number 1 in 1988 for Ricky Van Shelton). In 1967 Johnny Darrell had a number 9 US country hit with 'Ruby, Don't Take Your Love To Town', a song that two years later became a million-selling US pop hit for Kenny Rogers And The First Edition (it also reached number 2 in the UK pop charts the same year). By the late 60s Tillis had established a reputation as both a writer and a performer and with his band the Statesiders, named after his 1966 hit 'Stateside', he toured extensively.The same pattern continued throughout the 70s, when he averaged 250 concerts annually and was also much in demand for appearances on network television shows. He achieved his first country Top 10 hit in 1969 with 'These Lonely Hands Of Mine'. During the 70s, recording for MGM and MCA, he had 33 country hits, of which 24 were Top 10 records, including five number 1s with 'I Ain't Never', 'Good Woman Blues', 'Heart Healer', 'I Believe In You' and 'Coca Cola Cowboy' (the last, like his number 2 hit 'Send Me Down To Tucson', featured in the Clint Eastwood film *Every Which Way But Loose*). In 1970 he recorded an album with Bob Wills and during the 70s he also made several hit recordings with Sherry Bryce, including 'Take My Hand', which achieved crossover success. He recorded for Elektra in the early 80s, charting seven successive Top 10 hits, including a further number 1 with 'Southern Rains'. In 1983, he returned to MCA and the next year made number 10 with his recording of Tommy Collins' 'New Patches'. He later recorded for RCA and Mercury. Duet recordings in the 80s were with Glen Campbell and Nancy Sinatra. In the 80s, his daughter Pam Tillis began to forge a flourishing career as a songwriter, graduating to a successful recording career in the 90s.

He has appeared in several films including *W.W. And The Dixie Dance Kings, Smokey And The Bandit 2, Murder In Music City* and in 1986 he co-starred with Roy Clark in a comedy western called *Uphill All The Way*, which they both also produced. He became a very successful businessman and at one time owned several publishing companies including Sawgrass and Cedarwood. His recordings have generally balanced out between honky tonk and the accepted Nashville Sound. Around 1980, he went to play what he thought was a car convention in Tulsa; the 'limousine' in question turned out to be an exotic breed of cattle. He developed an interest by buying a 2,200 pound bull which he named 'Stutterin' Boy'. It was only one of 50 such bulls in the USA and he had a party to introduce it to the media! Tillis has been buying adjacent smallholdings outside Nashville and he himself owns a 400-acre farm. He said, 'A lot of people invest their money in tax shelters, but I feel I am doing something to benefit the country . . . this bull is going to breed more and better cattle, and that's no b-b-b-bull.' During his career, he has won many awards, including being named as CMA Entertainer Of The Year in 1976 and, as one of country music's most prolific songwriters, he was inducted into the Nashville Songwriters' International Hall Of Fame the same year. The stutter still exists when he speaks but he always jokes and uses it to his advantage, regularly opening his show with comments such as 'I'm here to d-d-dispel those rumours going round that M-M-Mel T-Tillis has quit st-st-st-stuttering. That's not true I'm still st-st-stuttering and making a pretty good living at it t-t-too'.

● ALBUMS: *Heart Over Mind* (Columbia 1962)★★★, *Stateside* (Kapp 1966)★★★★, *The Great Mel Tillis* (1966)★★★, *Life Turned Her That Way* (Kapp 1967)★★★, *Mr Mel* (Kapp 1967)★★★★, *Let Me Talk To You* (Kapp 1968)★★★, *Something Special* (Kapp 1968)★★★, *Who's Julie?* (Kapp 1969)★★★, *Mel Tillis Sings Ole Faithful* (Kapp 1969)★★★, *One More Time* (MGM 1970)★★★, *She'll Be Hanging 'Round Somewhere* (Kapp 1970)★★★, *Big 'N' Country* (Vocalion 1970)★★★, *Walking On New Grass* (Vocalion 1970)★★★, *The Arms Of A Fool/Commercial Affection* (MGM 1971)★★★, *Recorded Live At The Sam Houston Coliseum, Houston, Texas* (MGM 1971)★★, with Sherry Bryce *Living & Learning/Take My Hand* (MGM 1971)★★, *Would You Want The World To End* (MGM 1972)★★★, *I Ain't Never/Neon Rose* (MGM 1972)★★★, *Mel Tillis* (Harmony 1972)★★★, *Mel Tillis & The Statesiders On Stage Live In Birmingham* (MGM 1973)★★, *Sawmill* (MGM 1973)★★★, with Bryce *Let's Go All The Way Tonight* (MGM 1974)★★★, *Midnight, Me And The Blues/Stomp Them Grapes* (MGM 1974)★★★, *Mel Tillis & The Statesiders* (MGM 1974)★★★, *M-M-Mel* (MGM 1975)★★★, *Love Revival* (MCA 1976)★★★, *Welcome To Mel Tillis Country* (MGM 1976)★★★★, *Heart Healer* (MCA 1977)★★★, *Love's Troubled Waters* (MCA 1977)★★★, *I Believe In You* (MCA 1978)★★★, *Are You Sincere* (MCA 1979)★★★, *Mr Entertainer* (MCA 1979)★★★, *Me And Pepper* (Elektra 1979)★★★, *The Great Mel Tillis* (1979)★★★★, *M-M-Mel Live* (MCA 1980)★★★, *Your Body Is An Outlaw* (Elektra 1980)★★★, *Southern Rain* (Elektra 1980)★★★, with Nancy Sinatra *Mel And Nancy* (Elektra 1981)★★, *It's A Long Way To Daytona* (Elektra 1982)★★★, *After All This Time* (MCA 1983)★★★, *New Patches* (MCA 1984)★★★, with Jerry Lee Lewis, Webb Pierce, Faron Young *Four Legends* (1985)★★★, *California Road* (1985)★★★.

● COMPILATIONS: *Mel Tillis' Greatest Hits* (Kapp 1969)★★★★, *Mel Tillis' Greatest Hits Volume 2* (Kapp 1971)★★★, *The Very Best Of Mel Tillis And The Statesiders* (MGM 1972)★★★, *Mel Tillis' Greatest Hits* (MGM 1974)★★★, *The Best Of Mel Tillis And The Statesiders* (MGM 1976)★★★, *24 Great Hits* (MGM 1977)★★★, *Mel Tillis' Greatest Hits* (Elektra 1982)★★★, *The Very Best Of Mel Tillis* (MCA 1986)★★★★, *American Originals* (Columbia 1989)★★★, *Greatest Hits* (Curb 1991)★★★, *The Memory Maker* (Mercury 1995)★★★.

● FURTHER READING: *Stutterin' Boy, The Autobiography Of Mel Tillis*, Mel Tillis with Walter Wager.

TILLIS, PAM

b. 24 July 1957, Plant City, Florida, USA. The eldest of the five children of country singer Mel Tillis, Pam did not have the happiest childhood. Mel spent much of his time touring, her parents eventually parted and she grew up often looking after her siblings. Initially, she had no wish to follow in her father's country footsteps, although she had ambitions to sing and write songs. After her education at the University of Tennessee, she relocated to San Francisco where, for a time, she worked on a show with a jazz group. She married Rick Mason, moved back to Nashville and worked as a writer with Sawgrass Publishing. Around 1974, a few weeks after the birth of her son, Ben, she and Mason parted. She gradually became more active in music and sang and wrote in styles that varied from jazz and rock, to R&B and pop, without achieving any major success in any genre. In the early 80s, she spent some time in Britain but on her return to Nashville, moving more towards new country, she spent most of her time singing demos and advertising jingles. After joining Warner Brothers Records, for whom she recorded what has often been described as a pop album, she gained her first country chart success in 1984, with 'Goodbye Highway'. In 1986/7, she managed four more minor hits, including 'Those Memories Of You', but later described the late 80s as 'years of languishing in obscurity', although she did attract attention in 1986, when she performed a mock-country show she called *Twang Night*. In 1990, still seeking to establish her own identity and reluctant to be known as 'Mel Tillis's daughter', she joined Arista Records. Her first single for the label, 'Don't Tell Me What To Do', became a Top 5 country hit and finally launched her career. 'One Of Those Things', originally released five years earlier on Warner, quickly followed and peaked at number 6. During the next two years, further Top 5 hits followed with 'Maybe It Was Memphis', 'Shake The Sugar Tree' and 'Let The Pony Run'. Her own compositions accounted for more than half of the songs on her first two Arista albums and included the autobiographical 'Melancholy Child' and 'Homeward Looking Angel', which she co-wrote with new husband Bob DiPiero. Her rocking number 11 hit, 'Cleopatra, Queen Of Denial', also proved a popular video. In 1994, she registered further hits that included 'Spilled Perfume', her version of Jackie DeShannon's 'When You Walk In The Room' and her own 1995 number 1, 'Mi Vida Loca' (My Crazy Life). She has never been afraid to dress in an unusual manner and has appeared in hats that could have come from Minnie Pearl's wardrobe. An American magazine once described her as 'a failed punk rocker, one-time hell on wheels, reincarnated as a drop-dead country singer'. Her powerful vocal styling may not suit everybody; one reviewer commenting on an album wrote 'if strident-voiced females are your thing, this should suit you nicely'. Her songs are recorded by other artists but it still remains to be seen whether she can really establish herself with the hardline country traditionalists. She still has a long way to go to equal her father's tally of chart hits, but she has made a promising start.

● ALBUMS: *Above & Beyond The Call Of Cutey* (Warners 1983)★★★, *Put Yourself In My Place* (Arista 1991)★★★★, *Homeward Looking Angel* (Arista 1992)★★★★, *Sweetheart's Dance* (Arista 1994)★★★, *All Of This Love* (Arista 1995)★★★.

● COMPILATIONS: *Pam Tillis Collection* (Warners 1994)★★★, *Greatest Hits* (Arista 1997)★★★.

● VIDEOS: *When You Walk In The Room* (Arista 1994).

TILLMAN, FLOYD

b. 8 December 1914, Ryan, Oklahoma, USA. Tillman was the youngest of 11 children of a sharecropping family who moved to Post, Texas, when he was a few months old. He first learned to play mandolin and banjo but later changed to guitar, performing with Adolph Hofner's band, even singing a few songs, though later admitting he wished to be a songwriter since he could not sing. He moved to Mack Clark's dance band in Houston, leaving to join the Blue Ridge Playboys of Leon Selph, when Clark's band professed his song 'It Makes No Difference Now' was too hillbilly (the song later became a hit for both Gene Autry and Bing Crosby and established Tillman as a songwriter, in spite of the fact that he once sold it to Jimmie Davis for $200 but managed to obtain joint ownership in 1966, when the copyright came up for renewal). The Blue Ridge Playboys, who included Moon Mullican, Bob Dunn and Cliff Bruner, became noted as specialists of honky tonk music. During World War II he served in the Army Air Corps but returned to songwriting and playing with his band around the honky tonks of the Houston area on his discharge. He first recorded for Decca in 1939 but had his own solo chart successes in the 40s. He had a number 1 US country hit with 'They Took The Stars Out Of Heaven' in 1944 and followed with other Top 10 hits, including 'G.I. Blues', 'Drivin' Nails In My Coffin', 'I Love You So Much It Hurts', 'I Gotta Have My Baby Back', 'Slippin' Around' and the follow-up, 'I'll Never Slip Around Again' (the last two songs have led to suggestions that Tillman was one of the first artists to write and record songs about cheating and infidelity). His songs proved even more successful when recorded by other artists. In 1949 'Slippin' Around' was a million-selling number 1 US country and pop hit for Margaret Whiting and Jimmy Wakely and a country number 1 and pop number 17 for Ernest Tubb. The song has charted for others since, including Texas Jim Robertson (1950), Marion Worth and George Morgan (1964), Roy Drusky and Priscilla Mitchell (1965) and Mack Abernathy (1988) (the Whiting and Wakely combination also registered Top 10 country and pop chart success with the follow-up song later the same year). In the early 50s, Tillman gave up his band and inclined towards semi-retirement. The last track he recorded with the band, 'I Don't Care Anymore', possibly summed up his feelings. He gained his last chart entry in 1960 with 'It Just Tears Me Up', but he made further recordings on minor labels, including an album of his songs with various friends such as Merle Haggard and Willie Nelson, both of whom were influenced by his style. Tillman was one of the first to champion the use of the electric guitar in country music and also one of the first country artists to travel by aeroplane to get to his bookings. At times his growling raucous vocals made Ernest Tubb seem gentle and completely in tune, but his songwriting alone gained him admission to the Nashville Songwriters Association International Hall Of Fame in 1970 and saw him inducted into the Country Music Hall Of Fame in 1984.

● ALBUMS: *Let's Make Memories* (Cimarron 1962)★★★, *Floyd Tillman Sings His Great Hits Of Lovin'* (Hilltop 1965)★★★, *Floyd Tillman's Country* (Musicor 1967)★★★, *Dream On* (Musicor 1968)★★★, *I'll Still Be Loving You* (Harmony 1969)★★, *Floyd Tillman & Friends* (Gilley's 1982)★★.

● COMPILATIONS: *Floyd Tillman's Greatest* (RCA Victor 1958)★★★, *Floyd Tillman's Best* (Harmony 1964)★★★, *Portraits Of Floyd Tillman* (1971)★★★, *Golden Hits* (1975)★★★, *Country Music Hall Of Fame* (MCA 1991)★★★.

TILLOTSON, JOHNNY

b. 20 April 1939, Jacksonville, Florida, USA. Tillotson's father was a country music disc jockey and Tillotson himself was appearing on local radio from the age of nine. His parents encouraged his talent by giving him first a ukulele and then a guitar, and he was influenced by the singing cowboys (Gene Autry, Roy Rogers) and country singer Hank Williams. He appeared regularly on Tom Dowdy's television show, from which he was recommended to Archie Bleyer, the owner of Cadence Records. His first single in 1958 combined the teen ballad 'Dreamy Eyes' with the up-tempo 'Well, I'm Your Man'. Although his roots were in country music, he was encouraged to revive the R&B ballads 'Never Let Me Go', 'Pledging My Love' and 'Earth Angel'. In 1960 he released the classic teen-ballad 'Poetry In Motion', which went to number 2 in the USA and number 1 in the UK. The b-side, 'Princess, Princess', was popular in its own right and the equal of many of his later hits. Tillotson's follow-up, 'Jimmy's Girl', was less successful but he went to number 3 in the USA with 'It Keeps Right On A-Hurtin'', a self-penned country ballad. The song has been recorded by over 100 performers including Elvis Presley. Tillotson's baby-face and slight frame made him an ideal teen-idol for the early 60s, but his musical preference was country music. He had further success by reviving the country songs 'Send Me The Pillow That You Dream On' and 'I Can't Help It (If I'm Still In Love With You)'. In the film *Just For Fun* he sang 'Judy, Judy, Judy', which he wrote with Doc Pomus and Mort Shuman. His ballad 'You Can Never Stop Me Loving You' was a US Top 20 hit, but Kenny Lynch's version was preferred by UK record-buyers. A spell in the US Army prevented Tillotson from capitalizing on his success, but when he signed with MGM Records he was determined to become a country performer. 'Talk Back Trembling Lips' was a US Top 10 hit, but his subsequent records - 'Worried Guy', 'I Rise, I Fall', 'She Understands Me', 'Heartaches By The Number' - only reached the Top 40. He also appeared in Las Vegas, hence a single of 'Cabaret'. Tillotson is popular on US army bases in Europe and he has had several hits in Japan, following successful appearances there. The 30-track compilation *All The Early Hits - And More!!!*, which was released in the UK by Ace Records in 1990, is the best introduction to his work and includes an early version of 'Poetry In Motion'.

● ALBUMS: *Tillotson's Best* (Cadence 1961)★★★, *It Keeps Right On A-Hurtin'* (Cadence 1962)★★★, *You Can Never Stop Me Loving You* (Cadence 1963)★★★, *Judy, Judy, Judy* (1963)★★★, *Alone With You* (1963)★★★, *Johnny Tillotson* (1964)★★★, *Talk Back Trembling Lips* (MGM 1964)★★★, *The Tillotson Touch* (MGM 1964)★★★, *She Understands Me* (MGM 1964)★★, *That's My Style* (MGM 1965)★★★, *Our World* (MGM 1966)★★★, *Tillotson Sings Tillotson, Volume 1* (1966)★★★, *No Love At All* (MGM 1966)★★★, *The Christmas Touch* (MGM 1966)★★, *Here I Am* (MGM 1967)★★★, *Tears On My Pillow* (1970)★★★, *Johnny Tillotson* (1971)★★★, *Johnny Tillotson* (1977)★★.

● COMPILATIONS: *Scrapbook* (Bear Family 1984)★★★, *All The Early Hits - And More!!!* (Ace 1990)★★★★, *Poetry In Motion* (Varèse Sarabande 1996)★★★★.

TIPPIN, AARON

b. 3 July 1958, Pensacola, Florida, USA. Tippin was raised in South Carolina and was granted a pilot's licence when he was 15. At that time he wanted to be an airline pilot but circumstances changed when he lost his job in the aircraft industry, and when he was 28 he found himself working in Nashville as a songwriter. Charley Pride recorded 'Whole Lotta Love On The Line' and he secured a contract with RCA Records. Comedian Bob Hope was impressed with his debut, 'You've Got To Stand For Something', and he invited Tippin to come and sing this patriotic anthem to the troops involved in the Gulf War. This was a major boost for his career. He wrote all the tracks on his debut album, *You've Got To Stand For Something Else*, which he recorded with a crack studio band including Mark O'Connor, Larrie Londin, and Emory Gordy Jnr., who also produced. The album was both modern and a throwback to the country music of the 40s, and its title track was a favourite of American soldiers during the Gulf War. Many of his songs are about the American working man and he has acquired a strong female following with such macho songs as 'I Wouldn't Have It Any Other Way'. On *Lookin' Back At Myself* he parodies the Blues Brothers in 'Mission From Hank', while 'Country Boy's Tool Box' features the dubious lyric, 'you just don't fool with a country boy's tool'.

● ALBUMS: *You've Got To Stand For Something* (RCA 1990)★★★, *Read Between The Lines* (RCA 1992)★★, *Call Of The Wild* (RCA 1993)★★★, *Lookin' Back At Myself* (RCA 1994)★★★★, *Tool Box* (RCA 1995)★★★.
● COMPILATIONS: *Greatest Hits . . . And Then Some* (RCA 1997)★★★★.
● VIDEOS: *Call Of The Wild* (1994).

TOMPALL AND THE GLASER BROTHERS

The three youngest of the six children of Louis and Marie Glaser, namely, Tompall (b.Thomas Paul Glaser, 3 September 1933), Chuck (b. Charles Vernon Glaser, 27 February 1936) and Jim (b. James Wilson Glaser, 16 December 1937), were born in Spalding, Nebraska, USA. They were raised in a farming community and, from the time Tompall was 14, he was singing in a trio with Chuck and Jim. Their break into professional showbusiness came in 1957 when they won *Arthur Godfrey's Talent Show* on television. Other on-screen appearances followed and they joined Marty Robbins' roadshow and moved to Nashville in 1958. Their first singles included a cover version of the Coasters' 'Yakety Yak', and in 1959, they were signed to US Decca Records, primarily as folk-singers, but they soon switched to country. They sang on several of Robbins' records, including 'She Was Only Seventeen' and 'El Paso' and Jim and Tompall wrote 'Running Gun'. They also toured with Johnny Cash and can be heard on his 1962 *The Sound Of Johnny Cash* as well as his transatlantic success, 'Ring Of Fire'. Among their sessions are Roy Orbison's 'Leah' and Claude King's 'The Comancheros' and others for Patsy Cline, George Jones and Hank Snow, who also recorded Chuck's song 'Where Has All The Love Gone?'. Jim wrote a transatlantic pop hit for Gary Puckett And The Union Gap, 'Woman Woman', while Tompall (with Harlan Howard) wrote an archetypal country song in 'Streets Of Baltimore', recorded by Bobby Bare, Charley Pride and Gram Parsons. In 1965 they recorded a folk EP as the Charleston Trio for Bravo

Records. In 1966 the brothers moved to MGM and created some of the best harmony singing in country music. Among their successes on the US country charts were 'Rings', 'Gone, On The Other Hand', 'The Moods Of Mary' and 'Faded Love'. In 1971 they launched the Glaser Sound Studios in Nashville and continued to work there after disbanding in 1973.

Tompall found success as a solo artist after being part of the highly successful *Wanted! The Outlaws* project with Waylon Jennings and Willie Nelson (the 1996 Anniversary reissue added nine tracks, plus the brand new Steve Earle song 'Nowhere Road', sung by Nelson and Jennings). Many Nashville outlaws recorded at the studios, notably Kinky Friedman. In 1975 Chuck Glaser, who had discovered John Hartford and Dick Feller, had a stroke that paralyzed his vocal cords, but with enormous resilience he regained his abilities. He produced Hank Snow's *The Mysterious Lady* and the story-album of *Christopher The Christmas Tree*. Jim Glaser's solo career floundered when he failed to have solo hits and could no longer support a band. In 1979 the brothers re-formed and, with Tompall gruffer than ever, had success with 'Lovin' Her Was Easier' and 'Weight Of My Chains'. In 1983 Jim was replaced by Sherrill Nielsen (also known as Shaun Nielsen), who had sung alongside Elvis Presley's narration of 'Softly, As I Leave You' and released the improbably titled *The Songs I Sang For Elvis*. Jim had US country hits with 'The Man In The Mirror', 'When You're Not A Lady', 'You Got Me Running' and 'You're Gettin' To Me Again', a US country number 1. His song 'Who Were You Thinking Of (When We Were Making Love Last Night)?', was a US pop hit for Dandy and the Doolittle Band. Tompall has also worked as a solo artist and his albums include love ballads from World War II. An album tribute to Bob Wills remains unreleased. He recorded 'Ugly Women And Pick-Up Trucks' with Jimmy Payne and he produced the 1986 *Mac Wiseman*, and Ethel And The Shameless Hussies' *Born To Burn*.

● ALBUMS: by Tompall And The Glaser Brothers *This Land Folk Songs* (Decca 1960)★★★★, *Country Folks* (Vocalion 1967)★★★★, *Tompall And The Glaser Brothers* (MGM 1967)★★★★, *Through The Eyes Of Love* (MGM 1968)★★★, *The Wonderful World Of Tompall And The Glaser Brothers* (MGM 1968)★★★, *Now Country* (MGM 1969)★★★, *Tick Tick Tick* (MGM 1970)★★★, *The Award Winners* (MGM 1971)★★★, *Rings And Things* (MGM 1972)★★★, *Tompall And The Glaser Brothers Sing Great Hits From Two Decades* (1973)★★, *Busted* (Elektra 1981)★★★, *Lovin' Her Was Easier* (Elektra 1981)★★★, *After All These Years* (Elektra 1982)★★★.

Solo: Jim Glaser *Just Looking For A Home* (as Jim Glaser and the Americana Folk Trio) (Starday 1961)★★★★, *The Man In The Mirror* (Noble Vision 1983)★★★, *Past The Point Of No Return* (MCA 1985)★★★, *Everyone Knows I'm Yours* (MCA 1986). Tompall Glaser *Tompall Glaser Sings The Ballad Of Namu The Killer Whale And Other Ballads Of Adventure* (United Artists 1966)★★★★, *Charlie* (MGM 1973)★★★, *Take The Singer With The Song* (1974)★★★, *Tompall (Sings The Songs Of Shel Silverstein)* (MGM 1974)★★★, with Waylon Jennings, Willie Nelson, Jessi Colter *Wanted! The Outlaws* (RCA 1976)★★★★, *The Great Tompall And His Outlaw Band* (MGM 1976)★★★★, *Tompall Glaser And His Outlaw Band* (ABC 1977)★★★, *The Wonder Of It All* (ABC 1977)★★★, *Nights On The Borderline* (MCA 1986)★★★, *A Collection Of*

Love Ballads From World War II (1987)★★★, with Waylon Jennings, Willie Nelson, Jessi Colter *Wanted! The Outlaws (1976-1996, 20th Anniversary)* (RCA 1996)★★★★.
● COMPILATIONS: *The Rogue* (Bear Family 1992)★★★.

TOROK, MITCHELL

b. 28 October 1929, Houston, Texas, USA. A singer and songwriter, Torok played guitar at the age of 12. In 1953, while Torok was still at college, he saw Jim Reeves' Abbott recording of a song he had written, called 'Mexican Joe', become a smash hit number 1 on all charts (Torok, who at the time did not know anything about Jim Reeves, had hoped that Hank Snow would be given the song - his wish came true the following year when his song 'My Arabian Baby' appeared as the b-side of Snow's hit 'I Don't Hurt Anymore'). Torok was himself signed to the Abbott label and later that year, he had a number 1 in both the *Billboard* country and juke-box charts with his song 'Caribbean'. The song, which remained in the country charts for 24 weeks, also became a Top 5 hit in both the Best Sellers and Jockey charts. He became a member of the *Louisiana Hayride* on KWKH Shreveport. In 1954, Torok gained a number 9 country hit with the ridiculous-sounding 'Hootchy Kootchy Henry (From Hawaii)', and in 1956/7, he even had success in the UK pop charts with his songs 'When Mexico Gave Up The Rhumba' and 'Red Light, Green Light'. This success led to him touring in the UK in 1957. Torok made further recordings for Mercury, RCA, and Starday, and his last US chart entry was 'Instant Love', for the Reprise label in 1967. He continued to write songs, usually working in partnership with his wife (she has used both Gayle Jones and Ramona Redd as pseudonyms), and some have been recorded by top artists including Skeeter Davis, Kitty Wells, Glen Campbell and even Dean Martin. Hank Snow recorded 'The Mysterious Lady From Martinique' on one of his last RCA albums and 'Redneck' was a Top 20 hit for Vernon Oxford in 1976. Torok joined Cedarwood Music in the late 70s and worked on a recording project telling the history of Nashville from 1780 to 1980. He is also a talented painter and painted a mural on display in the Elvis Presley Museum in Nashville.
● ALBUMS: *Caribbean* (Guyden 1960)★★★, *Guitar Course (Instant Fun)* (Reprise 1966)★.
● COMPILATIONS: *Mexican Joe In The Caribbean* 4-CD box set (Bear Family 1996)★★★★.

TOWN HALL PARTY

This popular programme first began in 1951 as a Barn Dance on KFI Compton, California, USA. In 1953, as a one-hour show, it was moved to KFI television and networked by NBC, and filmed for use overseas by the Armed Forces Network television service. The show had its regular stars, which included performers such as Rex Allen, Johnny Bond (who usually wrote the show), Eddie Dean, Wayne Raney, Tex Ritter, Merle Travis, Tex Williams and special guest stars that once included Lefty Frizzell. It also helped to start the careers of Freddie Hart and Buck Owens. The show, which included comedy and even non-country performers at times, was directed by Wesley Tuttle and ran until 1960, when it was dropped by the station. During its existence, Screen Gems filmed 39 half-hour segments, which were syndicated to stations all over the world, in some areas being shown long after the show had ended.

TRACTORS

The 90s country group the Tractors were formed in Tulsa, Oklahoma, USA, and are led by Steve Ripley (b. 1950) who started playing in Oklahoma honky tonks while still in his teens. He has worked with Leon Russell and J.J. Cale and was Bob Dylan's lead guitarist on *Shot Of Love* in 1981. He has also invented a guitar that can be recorded in stereo and which has been used by J.J. Cale, Eddie Van Halen and Ry Cooder. Before the band was formed the other members had also had strong musical backgrounds. Walt Richmond (keyboards, co-producer) had toured with Bonnie Raitt, Ron Getman (electric and steel guitar) had played with Janis Ian and Leonard Cohen, Casey Van Beek (bass) had toured with the Righteous Brothers and Linda Ronstadt, and Jamie Oldaker (drums) had played with Eric Clapton. *The Tractors*, which was recorded (as was their second album) at Leon Russell's Church Studios in Tulsa, featured Ry Cooder and James Burton, and sold two million copies in the USA. They reworked the single 'Baby Likes To Rock It' as 'Santa Claus Is Comin' (In A Boogie Woogie Choo Choo Train)' for their Christmas album. Steve Ripley has said of their approach to music: 'We're doing music the way people did it before it was so specifically categorized - rock 'n' roll, rockabilly, country, country-rock. Back then no-one knew what it was - they just did what they felt.'
● ALBUMS: *The Tractors* (Arista 1994)★★★, *Have Yourself A Tractors Christmas* (Arista 1995)★★.

TRASK, DIANA

b. 23 June 1940, Warburton, Victoria, Australia. In 1959, after success as a singer of popular music in Australia, she sought success in the USA. After two years (still singing pop), she eventually gained a recording contract with Columbia. In the mid-60s, after a brief retirement in Australia, she moved to Nashville where she hoped for success in country music. Her first country chart entry was 'Lock Stock And Teardrops' for the Dial label in 1968. She moved to Dot, where she recorded several albums and by 1975, she had registered 15 further hits, 'Lean It All On Me', which peaked at number 13 in 1974, being the biggest. Others included her versions of Patsy Cline's 'I Fall To Pieces' and the Joe Simon pop hit 'The Choking Kind'. She played various television shows and in the late 60s, she toured for a time with Hank Williams Jnr. The fact that her style never strayed too far from her pop roots meant that she was probably far more comfortable singing with an orchestra in Las Vegas night spots, than she was in country venues. She returned to Australia in 1975, where her recording of 'Oh Boy' proved popular and eventually led to recordings for RCA (1977) and Polydor (1980). Her two final US country chart entries came in 1981 on the small Kari label. The highest was 'This Must Be My Ship' (a number 62), but it would seem the ship never completed the voyage as she appears to have drifted into country obscurity.
● ALBUMS: *Diana Trask* (Columbia 1961)★★★★, *Diana Trask On TV* (Columbia 1961)★★★, *Miss Country Soul* (Dot 1969)★★★, *From The Heart* (Dot 1969)★★★, *Diana's Country* (Dot 1971)★★★, *Sings About Loving* (Dot 1972)★★★, *It's A Man's World* (Dot 1973)★★★, *Lean It All On Me* (Dot 1974)★★★, *The Mood I'm In* (ABC/Dot 1975)★★★, *Believe Me Now Or Believe Me Later* (ABC/Dot 1976)★★★.
● COMPILATIONS: *Diana Trask's Greatest Hits* (ABC/Dot 1974)★★★, *The ABC Collection* (ABC/Dot 1977)★★★★.

TRAVIS, MERLE

b. Merle Robert Travis, 29 November 1917, Rosewood, Kentucky, USA, d. 20 October 1983, Tahlequah, Oklahoma, USA. He was the son of a tobacco farmer but by the time Travis was four years old, the family had moved to Ebenezer, Kentucky, and his father was working down the mines. Travis's father often remarked, 'Another day older and deeper in debt', a phrase his son used in 'Sixteen Tons'. His father played the banjo, but Travis preferred the guitar. He befriended two coalminers, Mose Reger and Ike Everly, the father of the Everly Brothers, who demonstrated how to use the thumb for the bass strings while playing the melody on treble strings. Travis hitched around the country, busking where he could, and in 1935, he joined the Tennessee Tomcats and from there to a better-known country group, Clayton McMichen's Georgia Wildcats. In 1937 he became a member of the Drifting Pioneers, who performed on WLW Cincinnati. In 1943 he recorded for the local King label, recording a solo as Bob McCarthy and a duet with Grandpa Jones as the Shepherd Brothers. He and Jones did many radio shows together and many years later, recreated that atmosphere for an album. Travis, Jones and the Delmore Brothers also worked as a gospel quartet, the Browns Ferry Four. After war service in the marines, he settled in California and worked with artists such as Tex Ritter. Travis's arrangement of 'Muskrat' for Ritter was later developed into a hit single for the Everly Brothers.

He played with several bands, becoming one of the first to appreciate that a guitar could be a lead instrument, and he had success as a solo artist for the newly formed Capitol Records with 'Cincinnati Lou', 'No Vacancy', 'Divorce Me C.O.D.', 'Missouri' and a US country number 1, 'So Round, So Firm, So Fully Packed'. He co-wrote Capitol's first million-seller, 'Smoke, Smoke, Smoke That Cigarette' with Tex Williams, who recorded it. Burl Ives and Josh White were spearheading a craze for folk music, so Capitol producer, Lee Gillette, asked Travis for a 78 rpm album set of Kentucky folk songs. 'I don't know any' said Travis. 'Then write some' was the reply. His eight-song *Folk Songs Of Our Hills*, included 'Nine Pound Hammer' (a rewritten folk song), 'Dark As A Dungeon' and 'Sixteen Tons', with spoken introductions about the coalmining locale. Although Travis maintained that 'Sixteen Tons' was a 'fun song', it dealt with the exploitation of miners in the company store. It won a gold record for Tennessee Ernie Ford in 1955 and was parodied by Spike Jones as 'Sixteen Tacos' and by Max Bygraves as 'Seventeen Tons'. Travis himself was also enjoying a country hit with a revival of 'Wildwood Flower' with Hank Thompson, and he won acclaim for his portrayal of a young GI in the 1954 film *From Here To Eternity*, in which he sang 'Re-enlistment Blues'. Travis's *Walkin' The Strings* was a highly-regarded album of acoustic guitar solos. His style influenced Doc Watson, who named his son after him, and Chet Atkins, who did the same with his daughter.

In 1948 he devised a solid-body electric guitar, which was built for him by Paul Bigsby and developed by Leo Fender. 'I got the idea from a steel guitar,' he said, 'I wanted the same sustainability of notes, and I came up with a solid-body electric guitar with the keys all on one side.' Travis had an entertaining stage act in which he would mimic animals on his guitars. He was a good cartoonist and he worked as a scriptwriter on Johnny Cash's television shows. He took part in the Nitty Gritty Dirt Band's tribute to country music, *Will The Circle Be Unbroken?*, and was one of the Texas Playboys in the Clint Eastwood film *Honkytonk Man*. Travis was elected to the Country Music Hall Of Fame in 1977 but his drug addiction and alcoholism made him unreliable and wrecked his private life. Says Tennessee Ernie Ford, 'Merle Travis was one of the most talented men I ever met. He could write songs that would knock your hat off, but he was a chronic alcoholic and when those binges would come, there was nothing we could do about it.' Travis died in October 1983. A posthumous album of blues songs played on 12-string guitar, *Rough, Rowdy And Blue*, included a tune from his mentor, Mose Reger, 'Merry Christmas, Pretty Baby'. His friend and fellow guitarist Joe Maphis wrote a tribute 'Me And Ol' Merle', which concluded, 'We liked good whiskey and we loved the pretty girls, And we loved them guitars - Me and Ol' Merle.'

● ALBUMS: *Folk Songs Of The Hills* 10-inch album (Capitol 1947)★★★, *The Merle Travis Guitar* (Capitol 1956)★★★, *Back Home* expanded reissue of *Folk Songs Of The Hills* (Capitol 1957)★★★, *Walkin' The Strings* (Capitol 1960)★★★★, *Travis!* (Capitol 1962)★★★, *Songs Of The Coal Mines* (Capitol 1963)★★★, with Joe Maphis *Two Guitar Greats* (Capitol 1964)★★★, with Johnny Bond *Great Songs Of The Delmore Brothers* (Capitol 1969)★★★, *Strictly Guitar* (Capitol 1969)★★★★, with Chet Atkins *The Atkins-Travis Traveling Show* (RCA Victor 1975)★★★, with Maphis *Country Guitar Giants* (CHM 1979)★★★, *Light Singin' And Heavy Pickin'* (1980)★★★, *Guitar Standards* (1980)★★★, *Travis Pickin'* (CMH 1981)★★★, with Mac Wiseman *The Clayton McMichen Story* (CHM 1982)★★★, with Grandpa Jones *Merle And Grandpa's Farm And Home Hour* (1985)★★★, *Rough, Rowdy And Blue* (CMH 1985)★★★.
● COMPILATIONS: *The Best Of Merle Travis* (Capitol 1967)★★★, *The Merle Travis Story* (CMH 1979)★★★★, *The Best Of Merle Travis* (Rhino 1990)★★★, *The Radio Shows 1944-1949* (Country Routes 1991)★★★, *Capitol Country Music Classics* (Capitol 1993)★★★.
● FURTHER READING: *In Search Of My Father*, Pat Travis Eatherly.

TRAVIS, RANDY

b. Randy Bruce Traywick, 4 May 1959, Marshville, North Carolina, USA. The second of the six children of Harold and Bobbie Rose Traywick, this singer-songwriter shows in his style and delivery the heavy influence of Lefty Frizzell and Merle Haggard. His father, a builder, was a country music fanatic who even built a music room complete with stage onto the Travis's house just so that the family could perform for friends. Although not a working musician, he played guitar, wrote songs, on occasions performed in public and had once recorded two of his songs, 'A Lonely Shadow' and 'The Reason I Came'. He is also reputed to have had problems with drink and later acquired a reputation for his drinking, fighting, shooting and generally frightening people around the Marshville area. In 1982, he lost his home and everything else, after a venture into turkey-farming went wrong (he managed to regain his home in 1985). Through his father's insistence, Randy learned guitar and began performing publicly with his elder brother Ricky, a more accomplished guitarist, when he was nine. The two were later joined by bass-playing brother David and with their father arranging the bookings, they played local clubs over a wide area. Over the years they were frequently in trouble with the law for varying offences such as drunkenness, theft, drugs and driving offences, including being clocked by the police at 135 miles an hour. While on probation in 1977, Travis appeared at the *Country City USA*, a Charlotte nightclub managed and co-owned by Lib Hatcher (Mary Elizabeth Robertson). Impressed by his vocals, she found him regular work at the club and also provided him with a home, although the association soon saw her divorced from husband Frank Hatcher. Under her guidance (in spite of objections from his father, whom she eventually banned from the club) and with variations made to his probation orders, Travis began to develop his musical career. She financed his first recordings (as Randy Traywick), made on the Paula label under Joe Stampley's production in Nashville, which resulted in 'She's My Woman' making a brief US country chart appearance in 1979. In 1981 Travis and Hatcher moved to Nashville. The following year she became manager of the Nashville Palace nightclub and hired Travis (under the name of Randy Ray) as the resident singer, who also assisted as a dishwasher and cook. In November 1982, he recorded his first album, *Randy Ray Live At The Nashville Palace*, and gradually, through Hatcher's shrewd management, he began to establish himself around Nashville. Late in 1984, he came to the attention of Martha Sharp, an A&R director of Warner Brothers, who was looking for a young and preferably sexy-looking singer to record following the successes at CBS by Ricky Skaggs and at MCA by George Strait. With another name change, this time to Randy Travis (at the suggestion of Sharp) and under the production of Kyle Lehning, he cut four tracks on 30 January 1985. 'Prairie Rose' was used on the soundtrack album for the Patrick Wayne (son of John) film *Rustler's Rhapsody*. 'On The Other Hand' made number 67 on the US country charts. Two weeks later Travis officially signed a contract with Warner Brothers. Soon afterwards, he scored his first Top 10 hit with '1982'. The year 1986 was an important one for him with reissues of 'On The Other Hand' and 'Diggin' Up Bones' both making number 1 and 'No Place Like Home' peaking at number 2. His first Warner album, *Storms Of Life*, became the first country debut album to sell a million within a year of issue, he won a Grammy as Best Country Newcomer and he joined the *Grand Ole Opry*. In 1987-88, he registered six more successive number 1s with 'Forever And Ever, Amen', 'I Won't Need You Anymore (Always And Forever)', 'Too Gone Too Long', 'I Told You So' (a self-penned song), 'Honky Tonk Moon' and 'Deeper Than The Holler'. The majority of the songs were composed by noted songwriters, including Don Schlitz, Paul Overstreet, Troy Seals and Max D. Barnes. By 1988, Travis was a superstar and had collected a great many awards along the way, including that of Male Vocalist of the Year by the Country Music Association. In 1989, he survived a car crash and registered further number 1s with 'Is It Still Over' and 'It's Just A Matter Of Time' (the latter song was co-written by Brook Benton, and recorded under the production of famed producer Richard Perry, who used the recording as the only country number on his noted *Rock Rhythm And Blues* compilation album). An attempt at more varied material with 'Promises', cut with only an acoustic guitar, failed by his standards when it peaked at number 17. In 1990, *Heroes And Friends* drew glowing reviews and found

him duetting with a number of stars including Merle Haggard, George Jones, Loretta Lynn, Dolly Parton, Tammy Wynette and non-country notables such as B.B. King and Clint Eastwood; 'Happy Trails' was recorded with singing cowboy legend Roy Rogers. In 1990-91, Travis faced strong competition from Ricky Van Shelton, Clint Black and Garth Brooks, but he registered further number 1 hits with 'Hard Rock Bottom Of Your Heart' and 'Forever Together'. In 1991, it was revealed that he had married Lib Hatcher, putting an end to a long period of speculation about his private life and the nature of their relationship. Pundits reckoned the affair would harm his career, but the simultaneous release of two greatest hits collections in 1992 confirmed his continued popularity, and produced another number 1 hit, 'Look Heart, No Hands'. Also in 1992, Travis made a television documentary about western music, *Wind In The Water*, together with an album of the same name. He returned to a more conventional format with *This Is Me* and the songs were as strong as ever. *Full Circle* was another consistent album and featured the Mark Knopfler penned 'Are We In Trouble Now'. Travis does much charity work for Operation Smile, an organization to help children with facial deformities. He was the first modern performer to demonstrate that country music could appeal to a wider public, and perhaps Garth Brooks owes him a debt. Travis left Warners in 1997.

● ALBUMS: *Randy Ray Live At The Nashville Palace* (No Label 1982)★★, *Storms Of Life* (Warners 1986)★★★★, *Always And Forever* (Warners 1987)★★★★, *Old 8 x 10* (Warners 1988)★★★, *No Holdin' Back* (Warners 1989)★★★, *An Old Time Christmas* (Warners 1989)★★★, *Heroes And Friends* (Warners 1990)★★★, *High Lonesome* (Warners 1991)★★★, *Wind In The Wire* (Warners 1993)★★, *This Is Me* (Warners 1994)★★★★, *Full Circle* (Warners 1996)★★★.
● COMPILATIONS: *Greatest Hits Volume 1* (Warners 1992)★★★, *Greatest Hits Volume 2* (Warners 1992)★★★, *Forever And Ever... The Best Of Randy Travis* (Warners 1995)★★★★.
● VIDEOS: *Forever & Ever* (Warner Music Video 1992), *Wind In The Wire* (1993).
● FURTHER READING: *Randy Travis; The King Of The New Country Traditionalists*, Don Cusic.

TRENT, BUCK

b. Charles Wilburn Trent, 17 February 1938, Spartanburg, South Carolina, USA. A multi-talented instrumentalist, he played steel guitar by the time he was seven and was playing on local radio at 10. In 1955, playing banjo, he became a regular on television in Asheville, North Carolina, followed by venues in California and Texas, before joining Bill Carlisle on the *Grand Ole Opry* in Nashville. In 1962, after joining Porter Wagoner, he began to play an electric banjo, which he invented and which was built for him by steel guitarist Shot Jackson. The instrument was constructed in a similar manner to a steel guitar and had a movable bridge that altered its pitch. He stayed with Wagoner's band until 1973, when he joined Roy Clark, with whom he developed his own act, while working as the opener on Clark's shows. He also appeared in his own right on *Hee Haw*. In 1975 and 1976, he was voted Instrumentalist Of The Year and he and Clark were voted Instrumental Group Of The Year in the CMA's annual awards. He remained with Clark's show until 1980, when he began to operate mainly as a solo artist. He has made numerous solo overseas tours, as well as touring with Clark and Wagoner. In 1962, he made his first recordings for Smash Records, with two albums being released as Charles Trent. Over the years, he has recorded for several other labels, including recording with both Wagoner and Clark. In 1984, he released a 'live' album on his own label. He became a regular performer at Nashville's, Music City USA, before relocating to Branson, Missouri. In 1992, an increasing medical problem saw him hospitalized for a triple heart bypass operation. Trent, affectionately known as Mr Banjo, also played mandolin, dobro, bass and guitar, and was an amazingly versatile country music instrumentalist.

● ALBUMS: *The Sound Of A Bluegrass Banjo* (Smash 1962)★★★, *The Sound Of A Five String Banjo* (Smash 1962)★★★, *Give Me Five* (Boone 1967)★★★, *Five String General* (Boone 1967)★★, *Sounds Of Now & Beyond* (RCA Victor 1972)★★★, with Roy Clark *A Pair Of Fives (Banjos That Is)* (Dot 1975)★★★★, *Bionic Banjo* (ABC/Dot 1976)★★★, with Clark *Banjo Bandits* (ABC 1978)★★★★, *Live From The Hee Haw Theatre* (Buck Trent 1984)★★, *Buck Trent* (MCA 1986)★★★.

TREVINO, RICK

b. 16 May 1971, Austin, Texas, USA. The 90s country artist Rick Trevino is a Mexican-American who sings in both English and Spanish. His first single was released in English as 'Just Enough Rope' and in Spanish as 'Bastante Cordon', with a bilingual version also available. Similarly, his first album, *Just Enough Rope*, was also available in Spanish as *Dos Mundos*. He moved to Columbia Records where the producer Steve Buckingham encouraged him into the mainstream of 90s country music with a strong element of 60s honky tonk. The second album included the catchy 'Bobbie Ann Mason', a US country hit single. He always includes Spanish material in his act and has said: 'People love it as Spanish is such a romantic language.' *Learning As You Go* was his major commercial breakthrough in 1996.

● ALBUMS: *Just Enough Rope* aka *Dos Mundos* (Sony Discos 1993)★★★, *Rick Trevino* (Columbia 1994)★★★, *Looking For The Light* aka *Un Rayo De Luz* (Columbia 1995)★★★, *Learning As You Go* (Columbia 1996)★★★★.

TRISCHKA, TONY

b. Anthony Cattel Trischka, 16 January 1949, Syracuse, New York, USA. Although competent on several instruments, Trischka is one of the most influential of modern banjoists. His work is to be found in several forms of bluegrass music, particularly the 70s' more progressive styling with occasional excursions into jazz. In 1970, he graduated from Syracuse University, by which time he had been playing with the Down City Ramblers for five years. From 1971-75, he played with both Country Granola and Country Cooking, before becoming a member of Breakfast Special. Between 1976 and 1978, he led the musical backing (and toured with) the Broadway show *The Robber Bridegroom*, as well as playing with the band Monroe Doctrine. In the late 70s, he toured to Japan with Peter Rowan and Richard Greene and to Australia with Stacy Phillips. In 1981, he formed his own band, Skyline and during the 80s, he made numerous European trips, both with his band and as a solo artist. In 1989, he appeared on the BBC's television documentary *History Of The Banjo*. In 1991, after Skyline broke up, he

formed Big Dogs and released his noted *Live At The Birchmere* and also appeared in Korea with the Korean National Radio Orchestra. He continues to be in great demand in the 90s, and has appeared in numerous countries and composed music for many film and television productions. His recorded output, which began in 1971, has been very extensive, incorporating both solo albums and recordings with groups and/or other musicians. He has also written many highly respected tuition books, compiled video and audio tapes on the banjo, run workshops and gives private tuition for aspiring musicians on the instrument. He still makes concert appearances, narrating the history of the instrument and playing material that varies from early-day and traditional banjo pieces to his own contemporary numbers.

● ALBUMS: *Bluegrass Light* (Rounder 1974)★★★★, *Heartlands* (Rounder 1975)★★★★, *Banjoland* (Rounder 1977)★★★★, with Bill Keith, Bela Fleck *Fiddle Tunes For Banjo* (Rounder 1981)★★★★, *Robot Plane Flies Over Arkansas* (Rounder 1983)★★★, *Hill Country* (Rounder 1985)★★★★, *Dust On The Needle* (Rounder 1988)★★★, *Rounder Banjo Extravaganza* (Rounder 1992)★★★, with Beppe Gambetta *Alone & Together* (Brambus 1992)★★★, with Fleck *Solo Banjo Works* (Rounder 1993)★★★★, with Van Dyke Parks, Dudley Connell, Alison Krauss *World Turning* (Rounder 1993)★★★★, *Glory Shone Around: A Christmas Collection* (Rounder 1995). With Country Cooking *15 Bluegrass Instrumentals* (Rounder 1971)★★★, *Frank Wakefield With Country Cooking* (Rounder 1972)★★★, *Barrel Of Fun* (Rounder 1974)★★★, *Country Cooking* (Rounder 1989). With Skyline *Late To Work* (Flying Fish 1983)★★★★, *Stranded In The Moonlight* (Flying Fish 1984)★★★, *Skyline Drive* (Flying Fish 1986)★★★, *Just Stayin' Around* (SBGE 1987)★★★. With Big Dogs *Live At The Birchmere* (Strictly Country 1991)★★.

TRITT, TRAVIS

b. 8 February 1963, Marietta, Georgia, USA. He started writing songs and playing honky tonks and beer joints when he was about 14 years old. One of Tritt's songs is called 'Son Of The New South', and his US country hit 'Put Some Drive Into Your Country' includes the lines, 'I made myself a promise when I was just a kid/I'd mix Southern rock and country and that's just what I did.' In other words, Tritt is where Merle Haggard meets Lynyrd Skynyrd. Although the title track of his debut album presented him as a honky tonk revivalist, Tritt's music reflects his childhood love for the classic country of George Jones and the southern rock of the Allman Brothers. He reached superstar status in 1991 with the first single from *It's All About To Change* - a wonderful bar-room ballad of love betrayed, 'Here's A Quarter (Call Someone Who Cares)'. The follow-up, 'Anymore', proved his credentials as a balladeer, while his acting in the award-winning video clip for the song won him several offers of film work. After two magnificent albums, *T-R-O-U-B-L-E* was something of a holding operation, though it contained at least one classic, the traditional-sounding 'Lord Have Mercy On The Working Man'. Tritt further extended the boundaries of modern country with a nine-minute workout on Buddy Guy's blues standard, 'Leave My Woman Alone'. He combined with Marty Stuart for two hit singles and a series of concerts playfully titled The No-Hats Tour in honour of the duo's full heads of hair. Only some outspoken criticism of Billy Ray Cyrus in the summer of 1992, and the decision to issue a sentimental album of Christmas favourites later in the year, threatened his relentless progress to the top. He is well on his way to becoming an American icon, having given a half-time performance at the 1993 Super Bowl in Atlanta's Georgiadome. *Ten Foot Tall And Bulletproof* is as much southern rock as it is country and included guest appearances from Waylon Jennings and Hank Williams Jnr. The power-charged title track was helped by a fine video and Tritt's incredible rise continued with the hugely successful *Greatest Hits*, which contained an astonishing 10 country number 1 singles. He contributed Jackson Browne's 'Take It Easy' to *Common Thread: The Songs Of The Eagles*, and 'Lawdy Miss Clawdy' to *It's Now Or Never - The Tribute To Elvis*. In 1996 he sang the main song, a revival of the Platters' 'Only You (And You Alone)', for the Steve Martin film *Sgt. Bilko*. *The Restless Kind*, produced by Don Was, was a pure honky-tonk country album, with no rock drum timings or hard guitar. An accomplished songwriter and performer, with one of the most distinctive voices in country music, he is potentially a gigantic talent who is set to encompass every branch of country music.

● ALBUMS: *Country Club* (Warners 1990)★★★, *It's All About To Change* (Warners 1991)★★★, *T-R-O-U-B-L-E* (Warners 1992)★★★, *A Travis Tritt Christmas - Loving Time Of The Year* (Warners 1992)★★, *Ten Feet Tall And Bullet Proof* (Warners 1994)★★★, *The Restless Kind* (Warners 1996)★★★.
● COMPILATIONS: *Greatest Hits, From The Beginning* (Warners 1995)★★★★.
● VIDEOS: *A Celebration* (1993), *Ten Feet Tall And Bulletproof* (Warner Reprise 1994), *It's All About To Change* (Warner Reprise 1994), *From The Beginning* (Warner 1995).

TUBB, ERNEST

b. Ernest Dale Tubb, 9 February 1914, near Crisp, Ellis County, Texas, USA, d. 6 September 1984, Nashville, Tennessee, USA. Ernest was the youngest of five children of Calvin Tubb, the foreman of a 300-acre cotton farm, and his wife Sarah. In 1920 the family relocated to Benjamin, and then moved again, to Kemp, in 1925. The following year, his parents divorced and initially he stayed with his mother when she moved to her brother's farm near Lively. His mother, a very religious woman who was one-quarter Cherokee, played the piano and organ and sang hymns around the farms and at the local church. Ernest's education suffered and he later related that he only went to school when he could not find work. In 1928 he heard a recording of Jimmie Rodgers singing one of his blue yodels. He was immediately fascinated and quickly decided that he wanted to be a singer; he began to learn Rodgers' songs and whenever he had the money, he bought his records. In 1930 after his mother remarried, he travelled around, working on various tasks and living at different times with married siblings or his remarried father. Early in 1933, while working on the roads near Benjamin, he became friendly with a young guitarist called Merwyn 'Buff' Buffington, who liked Tubb's singing but suggested he should learn to play guitar. He bought his first guitar from a pawnshop in Abilene and Buffington taught him his first chords. In May 1933 Tubb was greatly distressed by the death of Rodgers, although the event served to strengthen his resolve to emulate his idol.

He moved to San Antonio, where he lived with his brother Calvin Jnr. He also renewed his acquaintance with Buffington, who at the time was playing guitar with the Castleman Brothers (Joe and Jim) on Radio KONO. He persuaded Tubb to make some appearances as guest vocalist with them, which led to him being offered his own twice-weekly early morning show. On 26 May 1934 he married Lois Elaine Cook. Still very much the Rodgers imitator, he decided to contact Jimmie Rodgers' widow; Carrie Rodgers was impressed with Tubb and not only gave him a picture, but also showed him many of her late husband's possessions and agreed to listen to his radio show. She also offered to help him with his career, and in 1936 she loaned him one of Jimmie's C.F. Martin guitars. In October of that year, mainly due to her influence with her late husband's label, Tubb made his first recordings for RCA (she later gave him the guitar, which, after using it for many years, Tubb eventually donated to the Country Music Hall Of Fame Museum). The first two of the six songs recorded were tribute songs written by Elsie McWilliams, Rodgers' sister-in-law; the others were self-penned numbers. RCA released the first two but sales were poor. A further session in March 1937 saw another single released but again sales were poor. These two singles are so scarce that they represent the most collectable recordings of Tubb's entire career (the other RCA tracks were not released until 1942, by which time Tubb was a known artist). He played countless small venues and appeared on various radio stations as he struggled to keep his family, which by now comprised Justin (b. 1935) and Violet Elaine (b. 1939). (His son Roger Dale (b. 1938) had died in a car crash when only seven weeks old.) In spite of Carrie Rodgers' help, it was not until April 1940 that Tubb recorded again, this time for Decca. By now his style and sound had changed, due to the fact that late in 1939 his tonsils had been removed, taking with them his ability to yodel. This effectively stopped him being a Rodgers clone and he began to develop his own identity (in later years, he recalled the event with his song 'He Took 50 Dollars And My Yodel, When He Took My Tonsils Out'). Decca were impressed enough to record further sessions. He was sponsored by a flour company and began touring and appearing on KGKO Fort Worth as the Gold Chain Troubadour.

He continued to write songs and in April 1941, this time using a backing that included the electric guitar of KGKO's staff guitarist Fay 'Smitty Smith', he recorded six more numbers. After some argument with Decca over which song to release first, Tubb's choice of 'Walking The Floor Over You' was accepted. In the first year it sold 400,000 copies and went on to become a million-selling record and Tubb's greatest hit. In 1941 he sang it and three more songs in the Charles Starrett film *Fighting Buckeroos*, and in 1942 he appeared with Starrett again in *Ridin' West*. That same year, his popularity secured him a release from his Gold Chain contract and he moved to Nashville. By January 1943 the *Grand Ole Opry* had a new honky-tonk singer who dared to use an electric lead guitar on that sacred stage. When a union strike stopped recordings in 1942 and 1943, he toured extensively on various shows, including tours with Pee Wee King, but he was soon fronting his own band, the Texas Troubadours. In 1944 he appeared in the film *Jamboree* and the same year, making his first recordings with his own band, he gained his first US country chart number 1 and a pop chart number 16 with 'Soldier's Last Letter'. In February 1946 he was probably only the second modern country artist ever to record in Nashville, Decca having recorded Red Foley the previous year. In 1947, he opened the now world-famous Ernest Tubb Record Shop in Nashville and started his *Midnight Jamboree*, initially on the *Opry*, but before long the show was being broadcast direct from the actual record shop itself. He also headlined the first ever country music show held in New York's Carnegie Hall, telling the audience: 'This place could sure hold a lot of hay'. He continued to tour and record and by the end of 1948 he had amassed 16 country Top 5s, including two more number 1s with 'It's Been So Long Darling' and 'Rainbow At Midnight', and four songs had made the pop charts. His popularity was increased even further in 1949, when he tallied 12 chart entries (11 Top 10 hits) including number 1 hits with 'Slippin' Around' and 'Blue Christmas'. He also had number 2 hits with duet recordings with Red Foley ('Tennessee Border #2') and with the Andrews Sisters ('I'm Biting My Fingernails And Thinkin' Of You'). Bing Crosby even asked to record with him but the session never materialized (Bing did record 'I'm Walking The Floor Over You' and in 1960 it also became a UK pop hit for Pat Boone). In 1948 Tubb's first marriage ended in divorce but in June 1949, he married Olene Adams Carter (this marriage lasted 26 years and produced five children). Tubb was always ready to offer a helping hand and in 1950 he helped fellow Rodgers admirer Hank Snow to appear on the *Opry*. He had befriended Hank Williams when he first broke into country music and in 1953, he sang 'Beyond The Sunset' at Williams' funeral. During the 50s he maintained a rigorous touring and recording schedule. By the end of the decade, although only achieving one number 1 with his duet with Red Foley of 'Goodnight Irene', he totalled 34 hits, the majority being Top 10s. Major hits included 'I Love You Because', 'Driftwood On The River' and 'Missing In Action'. In 1953 he and Hank Snow, Danny Dill and Lew Childre were the first country acts to tour a live war zone when they played about 40 shows in Korea, many in the open air and within range of enemy guns. Tubb had been advised not to go - on his return his health suffered and for a time he was unable to perform. By the mid-50s, his eldest son Justin Tubb, then establishing himself as an artist and songwriter, became involved with the business organization. The hits slowed in the 60s but Tubb's popularity did not, and in spite of his health problems, he kept up a rigorous touring schedule and hosted his network television show. His hits at this time included 'Thanks A Lot', 'Pass The Booze', his nostalgic 'Waltz Across Texas' and a duet with Loretta Lynn titled 'Mr & Mrs Used To Be'. In 1965, in recognition of his important contribution to the music, he became the sixth member of the Country Music Hall Of Fame. The many songs that he had written and successfully recorded also led to him being one of the first writers elected to the Nashville Songwriters' International Hall Of Fame when it was founded in 1970. During the 70s he played the *Opry*, hosted the *Midnight Jamboree* and in spite of the worsening effects of the emphysema that had first developed in 1965, he still kept up a touring schedule that would have taxed younger men.

He finally parted company with Decca and in 1979, to mark his 65th birthday, Pete Drake masterminded a tribute on First Generation Records called *The Legend And The Legacy*, on which various stars overdubbed vocal contributions on Tubb's recordings (Tubb was not informed until the project was completed). The album became a bestseller and singles of a Tubb and Willie Nelson duet of 'Waltz Across Texas' and a joint Merle Haggard, Chet Atkins, Charlie Daniels and Tubb version of 'Walking The Floor Over You' both charted. It was initially released as a double album but ran foul of various claims of conflicting contractual details or unauthorized performances. It was subsequently withdrawn and copies supposedly destroyed. Record One of the original issue soon reappeared as a single album on Cachet, minus only a single track - the Nelson/Tubb duet. By 1982 his failing health forced him to retire. In the last year of touring, he had to rest on his bed in his customized touring bus and take oxygen between and during shows (ironically similar to the latter days of the career of his idol, Jimmie Rodgers, almost 50 years earlier). He made one of his last recordings in 1982, when he spoke a line on the Waylon Jennings and Hank Williams Jnr. song 'Leave Them Boys Alone'.

Ernest Tubb died in September 1984 of emphysema and related complications in Nashville's Baptist Hospital. He was buried on 10 September in Nashville's Hermitage Memorial Gardens. Over the years the Texas Troubadours included some of country music's finest musicians, such as Jimmie Short, Leon Rhodes, Billy Byrd, Jerry Byrd and Red Herron. Two others, Jack Greene and Cal Smith, went on to successful solo careers. Ernest Tubb registered in total 91 country chart hits, of which only 17 failed to reach the Top 20. His distinctive growling vocals, in a voice that deepened but softened as the years went by, usually began somewhat off-key, and by some unique means, he managed to use this flatness to emphasize and convey the songs, whether they were happy or sad. After starting out as a blatant imitator, no one could deny that he became a completely original and unique artist.

● ALBUMS: *Ernest Tubb Favorites* 10-inch album (Decca 1951)★★★★, *Jimmie Rodgers Songs Sung By Ernest Tubb* 10-inch album (Decca 1951)★★★, *Old Rugged Cross* 10-inch album (Decca 1951)★★★, *Sing A Song Of Christmas* 10-inch album (Decca 1952)★★★, *Ernest Tubb Favourites* (Decca 1956)★★★★, *The Daddy Of 'Em All* (Decca 1956)★★★, with the Wilburn Brothers *Ernest Tubb & The Wilburn Brothers* (Decca 1959)★★★★, *The Importance Of Being Ernest* (Decca 1959)★★★★, *Ernest Tubb & His Texas Troubadours* (Vocalion 1960)★★★★, *Ernest Tubb Record Shop* (Decca 1960)★★★★, with guests *Midnight Jamboree* (Decca 1960)★★★, *All Time Hits* (Decca 1961)★★★, *On Tour* (Decca 1962)★★, *Just Call Me Lonesome* (Decca 1963)★★★, *The Family Bible* (Decca 1963)★★★, *Presents The Texas Troubadours* (Decca 1964)★★★★, *Thanks A Lot* (Decca 1964)★★★, *Blue Christmas* (Decca 1964)★★★, *My Pick Of The Hits* (Decca 1965)★★★, *Country Dance Time* (Decca 1965)★★★★, *Hittin' The Road* (Decca 1965)★★★, with Loretta Lynn *Mr & Mrs Used To Be* (Decca 1965)★★★★, *Ernest Tubb's Fabulous Texas Troubadours* (Decca 1966)★★★★, *By Request* (Decca 1966)★★★, *Country Hits Old & New* (Decca 1967)★★★, *Another Story* (Decca 1967)★★★, *Stand By Me* (Vocalion 1967)★★★, with Lynn *Ernest Tubb & Loretta Lynn Singin' Again* (Decca 1967)★★★★, *The Terrific Texas Troubadours* (Decca 1968)★★★, *Country Hit Time* (Decca 1968)★★★, *Ernest Tubb Sings Hank Williams* (Decca 1968)★★★, with Lynn *If We Put Our Heads Together* (Decca 1969)★★★★, *Let's Turn Back The Years* (Decca 1969)★★★, *Saturday Satan,*

Sunday Saint (Decca 1969)★★★, *Great Country* (Vocalion 1969)★★★, *A Good Year For The Wine* (Decca 1970)★★★, *One Sweet Hello* (Decca 1971)★★★, *Baby, It's So Hard To Be Good* (Decca 1972)★★★, *Say Something Nice To Sarah* (Decca 1972)★★★, *I've Got All The Heartaches I Can Handle* (Decca 1973)★★★, *Ernest Tubb* (MCA 1975)★★★, *Living Legend* (1977)★★★, *Ernest Tubb & His Texas Troubadours* (1983)★★★, *Rare Recordings* (1983)★★★★, *Live, 1965* (Rhino 1990)★★★★.
● COMPILATIONS: *The Ernest Tubb Story* contains re-recorded material (Decca 1958)★★★★, *Ernest Tubb's Golden Favorites* (Decca 1961)★★★, *Ernest Tubb's Greatest Hits* contains re-recorded material (Decca 1968)★★, *Ernest Tubb's Greatest Hits Volume 2* contains re-recorded material(Decca 1970)★★★, with Loretta Lynn *The Ernest Tubb/Loretta Lynn Story* (MCA 1973)★★★★, *Ernest Tubb: Country Music Hall Of Fame* (Coral 1979)★★★, with various artists *The Legend & The Legacy* (First Generation/Cachet 1979)★★★★, *Honky Tonk Classics* (Rounder 1982)★★★, *Country Music Hall Of Fame* (MCA 1987)★★★★, with various artists *The Ernest Tubb Collection Parts 1 & 2* (1990)★★★★, *Let's Say Goodbye Like We Say Hello* 5-CD box set (Bear Family 1991)★★★★, *Yellow Rose Of Texas* 5-CD box set (Bear Family 1993)★★★★, *Walking The Floor Over You* 8-CD box set (Bear Family 1996)★★★★, *Best Of Ernest Tubb* (Curb 1996)★★★★, *The Legend And The Legacy* (Edsel 1997)★★★, *The Very Best Of Ernest Tubb* (Half Moon 1997)★★★★.
● FURTHER READING: *Ernest Tubb:The Original E.T.*, Norma Barthel. *The Texas Troubadour*, Ronnie Pugh.

TUBB, JUSTIN

b. Justin Wayne Tubb, 20 August 1935, San Antonio, Texas, USA. The eldest son of country music legend Ernest Tubb, he attended Castle Heights Military School, Lebanon, from 1944-48. He was naturally attracted to his father's music and when school holidays permitted, he toured with his father and regularly appeared on his WSM radio programme. He made his debut on the *Grand Ole Opry* at the age of nine. He began to write songs and by the time he left Brackenridge High School, San Antonio, he was an accomplished guitarist and singer. In 1952, tiring of being told he was going to be just like his father, he entered the University of Texas at Austin with thoughts of a career in journalism. The following year he wrote a tribute song to Hank Williams that his father recorded. He left university when he was offered a job as a disc jockey on WHIN Gallatin. This gave him the chance to sing some of his own songs to his listeners and also led to a Decca contract. He gained his first US country chart hit in 1954 when 'Looking Back To See', a duet with Goldie Hill, reached number 4. In 1955 he became the youngest ever regular member of the *Opry*. He always resisted any attempt to capitalize on his father's name and for some time he deliberately avoided appearing on the same shows. In the 60s when Ernest's health worsened, he began to combine his career with assisting his father in his business ventures and later became manager of the *Ernest Tubb Midnight Jamboree* radio show and record shops, as well as forming his own publishing company. He had solo Top 10s with 'I Gotta Go Get My Baby' and 'Take A Letter Miss Gray', and further duet successes with Lorene Mann with 'Hurry, Mr Peters' (the answer song to the Roy Drusky-Priscilla Mitchell hit 'Yes, Mr Peters') and 'We've Gone Too

Far Again'. Many of his songs became hits for others, including 'Keeping Up With The Joneses' (Faron Young-Margie Singleton), 'Love Is No Excuse' (Jim Reeves-Dottie West) and 'Lonesome 7-7203' (Hawkshaw Hawkins). Over the years, he has recorded for several labels, including Starday, Challenge and RCA. He has toured all over the USA, Canada, Europe, even to Vietnam, and he has also appeared on most major US television shows. Like his father, Tubb is a strict traditionalist, and during the 70s his career faltered. He registered his personal feelings about attempts to change country music in his song 'What's Wrong With The Way That We're Doing It Now', which won him five standing ovations for encores on the first occasion that he sang it on the *Opry*. He still makes *Opry* appearances and is regularly expected to sing that song and his tribute to his late father, 'Thanks Troubadour, Thanks'.
● ALBUMS: *Country Boy In Love* (Decca 1957)★★★, *The Modern Country Sound Of Justin Tubb* (Starday 1962)★★★, *Star Of The Grand Ole Opry* (Starday 1962)★★★, *Justin Tubb* (Vocalion 1965)★★★, *Where You're Concerned* (RCA Victor 1965)★★★, with Lorene Mann *Together And Alone* (RCA Victor 1966)★★★, *That Country Style* (1967)★★★, *Things I Still Remember Very Well* (Dot 1969)★★★, *New Country Heard From* (1974)★★★, *Justin Tubb* (1979)★★.
● COMPILATIONS: *The Best Of Justin Tubb* (Starday 1965)★★★.

TUCKER, TANYA

b. Tanya Denise Tucker, 10 October 1958, Seminole, Texas, USA. Tucker's father, Beau, a construction worker, and her mother, Juanita, encouraged her fledgling musical talents. Her early years were spent in Wilcox, Arizona, before moving to Phoenix in 1967. Her father booked her to perform with visiting country stars on stage at local fairs. Never one to consider that some songs might be too old for her, she was singing 'You Ain't Woman Enough To Take My Man' before she was 13. The family moved to St. George, Utah, and her mother impressed the producer of the Robert Redford film *Jeremiah Johnson*, which led to Tucker (and her horse!) being featured. To further their daughter's career, they moved to Las Vegas, where Beau financed a demo tape. In 1972 Tucker was signed to Columbia Records in Nashville by producer Billy Sherrill, although she disliked his choice of song - 'The Happiest Girl In The Whole USA', later a hit for Donna Fargo. Subsequently, she made the US country Top 10 with Alex Harvey's 'Delta Dawn', and did equally well with the double-sided 'Jamestown Ferry'/'Love's The Answer', and then had a US country number 1 with 'What's Your Mama's Name?', a story song with a twist in its last line. 'Blood Red And Goin' Down', the title referring to a Georgia sunset, was about a daughter watching her father kill her cheating mother, while 'Would You Lay With Me (In A Field Of Stone)?' was an adult love song, written by David Allen Coe for his brother's wedding. The young Tucker became a country star, was featured on the cover of *Rolling Stone*, and, through 200 appearances a year, developed a powerful, if precocious, stage presence. Moving to MCA on her 16th birthday, she was determined to make records that were in keeping with the sophisticated country rock of the Eagles, and she topped the country charts with 'Lizzie And The Rainman' (also US Top 40), which was based on the Burt Lancaster film *The Rainmaker*, 'San Antonio Stroll' and

'Here's Some Love'. In 1978 she wrote and recorded 'Save Me', an ecologically inspired single about seal culls on Canada's Magdalen Islands. The provocative cover picture of *TNT* caused controversy, but it certainly represented a different approach for a country star. She was booed on the *Grand Ole Opry* for performing raucous rock 'n' roll. *Tear Me Apart* was made with the producer-of-the-moment, Mike Chapman, and included a hoarse segue of 'San Francisco' with 'I Left My Heart In San Francisco'. Neither album sold as well as expected, but Tucker found herself in gossip columns as a result of her stormy relationship with Glen Campbell. She commented: 'Men are supposed to slow down after 40, but it's the opposite with Glen', and their duets included a revival of Bobby Darin's 'Dream Lover'. The dream was over when Campbell knocked out her front teeth. Hardly surprisingly, she kept her mouth shut for the glum cover of her next album, *Changes*. As fate would have it, they were to find themselves on the same label, Capitol, and Tucker's career was revitalized with *Girls Like Me*, an album that spawned four Top 10 country singles. In 1988 she had three number 1 country singles - 'I Won't Take Less Than Your Love' (with Paul Davis and Paul Overstreet), 'If It Don't Come Easy' and 'Strong Enough To Bend' - but it was also the year in which she entered the Betty Ford clinic for cocaine and alcohol addiction. Tucker has only written sporadically, but she co-wrote Hank Williams Jnr.'s 'Leave Them Boys Alone'. After many years in country music her contributions were finally rewarded by the Country Music Association when they voted her Female Vocalist Of The Year in 1991, although she had to miss attending the event, having just had her second child. Her country chart successes included two number 2s with 'Down To My Last Teardrop' and '(Without You) What Do I Do About Me'. In 1992 further hits included 'Some Kind Of Trouble', but more awards were not forthcoming, although she did receive a nomination for *What Do I Do About Me* as Album Of The Year. The title track of her 1995 release *Fire To Fire* was a duet with Willie Nelson, but the album was marred by weak song selection. In 1996 her autobiography was published; among the contents were details of her volatile relationship with Glen Campbell. She returned to form in 1997 with *Complicated*.

● ALBUMS: *Delta Dawn* (Columbia 1972)★★★, *What's Your Mama's Name?* (Columbia 1973)★★★, *Would You Lay With Me* (Columbia 1974)★★★, *Tanya Tucker* (MCA 1975)★★★, *Lovin' And Learnin'* (MCA 1975)★★★, *Here's Some Love* (MCA 1976)★★★, *You Are So Beautiful* (Columbia 1977)★★★, *Ridin' Rainbows* (MCA 1977)★★★, *You Are So Beautiful* (Columbia 1977)★★★, *TNT* (MCA 1978)★★★★, *Tear Me Apart* (MCA 1979)★★, *Dreamlovers* (MCA 1980)★★★, *Should I Do It?* (MCA 1981)★★, *Live* (MCA 1982)★★★, *Changes* (Arista 1983)★★★, *Girls Like Me* (Capitol 1986)★★, *Love Me Like You Used To* (Capitol 1987)★★★, *Strong Enough To Bend* (Capitol 1988)★★★, *Tennessee Woman* (Capitol 1990)★★★, *What Do I Do With Me* (Capitol 1991)★★★★, *Lizzie And The Rainman* (Cottage 1992)★★★, *Can't Run From Yourself* (Liberty 1992)★★★★, *Soon* (Liberty 1993)★★, *Fire To Fire* (Liberty 1995)★★, *Complicated* (Capitol 1997)★★★.

● COMPILATIONS: *Greatest Hits* (Columbia 1975)★★★★, *Tanya Tucker's Greatest Hits* (MCA 1978)★★★★, *The Best Of Tanya Tucker* (MCA 1988)★★★★, *Greatest Hits* (Capitol 1989)★★★★, *Greatest Hits - Encore* (Capitol 1990)★★★, *Greatest Hits 1990-1992* (Liberty 1993)★★★★, *Love Songs* (Capitol 1996)★★★.

● FURTHER READING: *Nickel Dreams - My Life*, Tanya Tucker with Patsi Bale Cox.

TURNER, GRANT

b. Jesse Granderson Turner, 17 May 1912, Abilene, Texas, USA, d. 19 October 1991. Turner grew up with a passionate interest in radio and broadcasting and developed an early love of country music, encouraged by actually seeing Jimmie Rodgers, when the singer visited a local radio station. He first studied journalism and on graduation, he worked on some local papers before getting a job with *The Dallas Morning News*. Eventually the desire to work in radio saw him gain announcer's work on KFYO Abilene, KRRV Sherman and KFRO Longview but in 1942, after answering an advert for an early morning disc jockey, he left Texas to work on WBIR Knoxville, Tennessee. Turner was physically unfit for military service during World War II but he worked hard to establish his radio reputation. He auditioned for WSM and on 6 June 1944, when the Allied forces were making the D-Day landings, Turner moved to Nashville. He became a station announcer and his friendship with George D. Hay soon saw him at first assigned to announce the segment of the *Grand Ole Opry* sponsored by Crazy Water Crystals, before quickly becoming the regular announcer for the whole *Opry*. Turner announced many major events in the *Opry*'s history, including Hank Williams' debut on the show, while it also fell to him to make some sad statements, including the deaths of artists, especially the murder of Stringbean. Although he did not aspire to sing, write songs or play any instrument, he surprisingly made a one-week country chart appearance at number 48 with a recording of 'The Bible In Her Hand' on the Chart label. Turner became a very respected member of the *Opry* organization, so much so that the management decided that, in his case, the rule that all employees retire at 65 would not apply. In 1981, his dedication, hard work and the help that he had given to others in the industry saw him inducted into the Country Music Hall Of Fame. Known affectionately as The Dean of the Opry Announcers, he was, to millions of people, the Voice of the Opry. Although, in later years, Turner retired from the majority of his commitments, he continued to fulfil his weekend *Opry* duties. After working the customary Friday evening show, he died suddenly on Saturday 19 October 1991.

TUTTLE, WESLEY

b. 30 December 1917, Lamar, Colorado, USA. When Tuttle was aged four the family relocated to the San Fernando Valley and his professional career began when he was 15. He subsequently worked with such popular west coast luminaries as Stuart Hamblen and the Beverley Hillbilies and appeared on regular radio shows on various stations including WLW Cincinnati and KMTR Hollywood. In the early 40s, he also sang in a trio with Merle Travis and Eddie Dean's brother Jimmy (not he of 'Big Bad John' fame), in a programme that was broadcast three times a week on CBS radio. Tuttle became a respected left-handed rhythm guitarist, who seemingly overcame the problem of having certain fingers missing. He was the second country artist (after

Tex Ritter) to record for Capitol and in October 1944, he and Merle Travis (with fiddler Charles Linville's accompaniment) recorded eight tracks for the label in Hollywood. The material included their co-written numbers 'I Dreamed That My Daddy Came Home', 'It May Be Too Late' and 'I Know It's Wrong'. Some of the recordings were actually released as Wesley Tuttle And The Coon Hunters. A recording of 'Give Me Your Hand' was unissued by Capitol but finally appeared on Bear Family's 1994 boxed set of Merle Travis recordings. In 1945, Tuttle had a solo country number 1 with his recording of 'With Tears In My Eyes'. In 1946, he registered Top 5 country hits with 'Detour', 'I Wish I Had Never Met Sunshine' and 'Tho' I Tried I Can't Forget You'. Tuttle briefly left Capitol in 1949 and made a few recordings for Coral before returning to Capitol where he stayed until 1957. He also recorded duets with his wife Marilyn (a former member of the Sunshine Girls, a western singing group who appeared in some Shirley Temple films and also B-movie westerns), and in 1954, they had a Top 15 country hit with 'Never'. He was a popular artist on the Saturday night west coast *Town Hall Party*, broadcast on KFI radio and KTTV-TV, and in the 50s, he and Marilyn were regular members of the B-K Ranch Gang that appeared on the *Ranch Party* television series. He appeared in several B-westerns with various stars including Jimmy Wakely's *Song Of The Sierras* (1946) and *Rainbow Over The Rockies* (1947). In the late 50s Tuttle retired from the music scene to become a minister and he and Marilyn recorded some gospel tracks for the Sacred label. Various recordings by Tuttle may be found on compilation albums but his seeming desire for a peaceful life and his usual avoidance of publicity means that little information about him is now available.
● COMPILATIONS: *Tennessee Rose* (Provincia 80s)★★★, *More Days Of The Yodeling Cowboys Volume 1* (Cowgirl Boy 80s)★★★.

TWAIN, SHANIA

b. 28 August 1965, Timmins, Ontario, Canada. This glamorous Canadian country star (her Christian name is pronounced 'Shu-nye-ah') is descended from the Ojibway tribe. Before her musical career began she planted trees with her father as part of a forest crew. Poor even by rural Canadian standards, her family made great sacrifices to support her embryonic career. She took a job at the Deerhurst resort in northern Ontario as the headline vocalist in a variety of musical productions. Afterwards she concentrated on country music, employing her friend and former performer Mary Bailey as her manager. Bailey put her in contact with attorney Dick Frank in 1991, leading to a demo tape recorded in Nashville with songwriter and producer Norro Wilson and Buddy Cannon, Mercury Records' A&R manager. Both the tragedy of her parents' death and their musical legacy were explored on her debut, with songs written by Mike Reid and Kent Robbins. The album's best song, 'God Ain't Gonna Get You For That', was the only one part-composed by the artist, pointing the way to future artistic growth. Elsewhere the single 'Dance With The One That Brought You', a staple of Country MTV, directed by Sean Penn, provoked comparisons with Trisha Yearwood. The follow-up album saw a rare non-rock outing for her producer, songwriting partner and husband Robert Mutt Lange, who spent much of 1994 working on sessions with Twain in

Nashville. *The Woman In Me* was an extraordinary success in the USA, not only when it was first released, but over a year later, when it went back to the top of the album charts for another six months. Sales of this album topped 9 million by 1997. During that eventful year she won most of the country music awards, including the Entertainer Of The Year trophy.
● ALBUMS: *Shania Twain* (Mercury 1993)★★★, *The Woman In Me* (Mercury 1995)★★★★, *Come On Over* (Mercury 1997)★★★.
● VIDEOS: *Any Man Of Mine* (Mercury 1995), *The Complete Woman In Me* (Polygram 1996).

TWISTER ALLEY

The 90s country group Twister Alley come from Arkansas, USA, and are named after the tornadoes that sometimes hit the area. The group consists of Shellee Morris (vocals), Amy Hitt, Lance Blythe and Steve Goins (guitars), Randy Lloyd (bass) and Kevin King (drums). They started playing traditional country at Gilley's but it soon developed into more high-energy country. Their techno-country single, the furiously paced 'Dance', was too outlandish for country radio, so they compromised with a revival of 'Young Love'. Shellee Morris has said: 'There isn't anything else that sounds like what we're doing. We want to take country music one step farther.'
● ALBUMS: *Twister Alley* (Mercury 1994)★★★.

TWITTY, CONWAY

b. Harold Lloyd Jenkins, 1 September 1933, Friars Point, Mississippi, USA, d. 5 June 1993, Springfield, Missouri, USA. His father, a riverboat pilot, named him after a silent-film comedian and gave him a guitar when he was five years old. The family moved to Helena, Arkansas, and Twitty's schoolboy friends - Jack Nance, Joe E. Lewis and John Hughey - have since played in his professional bands. In 1946, he recorded a demo, 'Cry Baby Heart', at a local radio station, although he was convinced that his real calling was to be a preacher. He was drafted into the US Army in 1954 and worked the Far East service bases with a country band, the Cimarrons. He hoped for a baseball career, but when he returned to the USA in 1956 and heard Elvis Presley's 'Mystery Train', he opted for a career in music. Like Presley, he was signed by Sam Phillips to Sun Records, although his only significant contribution was writing 'Rockhouse', a minor US hit for Roy Orbison. His various Sun demos are included, along with later recordings for Mercury and MGM, in the eight-album, Bear Family set, *Conway Twitty - The Rock 'n' Roll Years*. In 1957, while touring with a rockabilly package, he and his manager stuck pins in a map and the pairing of a town in Arkansas with another in Texas led to 'Conway Twitty', a name as memorable as Elvis Presley. Twitty then moved to Mercury where 'I Need Your Lovin'' made number 93 in the US pop charts. He had written 'It's Only Make Believe' with his drummer Jack Nance in-between sets at the Flamingo Lounge, Toronto, and he recorded it for MGM with the Jordanaires. Memorable for its croaky vocal and huge crescendo, the record became a transatlantic number 1, and subsequent UK Top 10 versions of 'It's Only Make Believe' appeared by Billy Fury (1964), Glen Campbell (1970) and Child (1978). Twitty's record sounded much like an Elvis Presley parody, so it was ironic that Peter Sellers should lampoon him as Twit Conway and that he became the model for Conrad Birdie in the musical *Bye Bye Birdie*. Twitty, unwisely but understandably, followed 'It's Only Make Believe' with more of the same in 'The Story Of My Love', while the b-side, the harsh and sexy 'Make Me Know You're Mine', remains one of the 'great unknowns'. His debut, *Conway Twitty Sings*, includes a beat treatment of 'You'll Never Walk Alone', which was undoubtedly heard by Gerry And The Pacemakers. Twitty came to the UK for ITV's pioneering *Oh Boy!* and his presence eased his rock 'n' roll version of Nat 'King' Cole's 'Mona Lisa' into the Top 10. His US Top 10 recording of 'Lonely Blue Boy', a song that had been left out of Elvis Presley's film *King Creole*, led to him naming his band the Lonely Blue Boys, although they subsequently became the Twitty Birds. Another US hit, 'Danny Boy', could not be released in the UK because the lyric was still in copyright; however, this did not apply to its melody, 'The Londonderry Air', and so Twitty recorded a revised version, 'Rosaleena'. While at MGM, he appeared in such unremarkable movies as *Platinum High School* and *Sex Kittens Go To College*, which also featured Brigitte Bardot's sister. Twitty continued croaking his way through 'What Am I Living For?' and 'Is A Bluebird Blue?', but was also recording such country favourites as 'Faded Love' and 'You Win Again'. After being dropped by MGM and having a brief spell with ABC-Paramount, Twitty concentrated on placing his country songs with other artists, including 'Walk Me To The Door' for Ray Price. He began recording his own country records for producer Owen Bradley and US Decca Records in Nashville, saying, 'After nine years in rock 'n' roll, I had been cheated and hurt enough to sing country and mean it.' In March 1966 Twitty appeared in the US country charts for the first time with 'Guess My Eyes Were Bigger Than My Heart'. His first US country number 1 was with 'Next In Line' in 1968 and this was followed by 'I Love You More Today' and 'To See An Angel Cry'. He became the most consistent country chartmaker of all time, although none of his country records made the UK charts. His most successful country record on the US pop charts is 'You've Never Been This Far Before', which made number 22 in 1973. 'Hello Darlin'' was heard around the world when he recorded a Russian version for the astronauts on a USA/USSR space venture in 1975. His records, often middle-of-the-road ballads, include 'I See The Want To In Your Eyes', 'I'll Never Make It Home Tonight', 'I Can't Believe She Gives It All To Me', 'I'd Love To Lay You Down' and 'You Were Named Co-Respondent'. He has recorded several successful duet albums with Loretta Lynn, and also recorded with Dean Martin and his own daughter, Joni Lee ('Don't Cry, Joni'). His son, who began recording as Conway Twitty Jnr., changed his name to Mike Twitty, while another daughter, Kathy Twitty, had minor country hits both as herself ('Green Eyes') and as Jesseca James ('Johnny One Time'). Through the 70s, Twitty expanded into property, banking and fast food, although his Twittyburgers came to a greasy end. His wife Mickey, whom he married and divorced twice, published *What's Cooking At Twitty City?*, in 1985, and his tacky museum and theme park, Twitty City, was up for sale. Despite new successes, the focal point of his stage act was still 'It's Only Make Believe', right up until his death in June 1993, by which time his tally of chart-toppers stood at 41 - higher than any other artist in any genre.

● ALBUMS: *Conway Twitty Sings* (MGM 1959)★★★, *Saturday Night With Conway Twitty* (MGM 1959)★★★, *Lonely Blue Boy* (MGM 1960)★★★, *The Rock 'N' Roll Story* (MGM 1961)★★★, *The Conway Twitty Touch* (MGM 1961)★★★, *Conway Twitty Sings 'Portrait Of A Fool' And Others* (MGM 1962)★★★, *R&B '63* (MGM 1963)★★★, *Hit The Road* (MGM 1964)★★★, *It's Only Make Believe* (Metro 1965)★★★, *Conway Twitty Sings* (Decca 1966)★★★, *Look Into My Teardrops* (Decca 1966)★★★, *Conway Twitty Country* (Decca 1967)★★★, *Here's Conway Twitty And His Lonely Blue Boys* (Decca 1968)★★★, *Next In Line* (Decca 1968)★★★, *Darling, You Know I Wouldn't Lie* (Decca 1969)★★★, *I Love You More Today* (Decca 1969)★★★, *You Can't Take The Country Out Of Conway* (MGM 1969)★★★, *To See My Angel Cry* (Decca 1970)★★★, *Hello Darlin'* (Decca 1970)★★★, *Fifteen Years Ago* (Decca 1970)★★★, with Loretta Lynn *We Only Make Believe* (Decca 1971)★★★★, *How Much More Can She Stand?* (Decca 1971)★★★, *I Wonder What She'll Think About Me Leaving* (Decca 1971)★★★, with Lynn *Lead Me On* (Decca 1971)★★★, *Conway Twitty* (MGM 1971)★★★, *I Can't See Me Without You* (Decca 1972)★★★, *Conway Twitty Sings The Blues* (MGM 1972)★★★, *Shake It Up* (Pickwick 1972)★★★, *I Can't Stop Loving You* (Decca 1972)★★★, *She Needs Someone To Hold Her (When She Cries)* (MCA 1973)★★★, with Lynn *Louisiana Woman, Mississippi Man* (MCA 1973)★★★, *You've Never Been This Far Before/Baby's Gone* (MCA 1973)★★★, *Clinging To A Saving Hand/Steal Away* (MCA 1973)★★★, *Conway Twitty's Honky Tonk Angel* (MCA 1974)★★★, with Lynn *Country Partners* (MCA 1974)★★★, *I'm Not Through Loving You Yet* (MCA 1974)★★★, *Linda On My Mind* (MCA 1975)★★★, with Lynn *Feelin's* (MCA 1975)★★★, *The High Priest Of Country Music* (MCA 1975)★★★, *Twitty* (MCA 1975)★★★, *Now And Then* (MCA 1976)★★★, with Lynn *United Talent* (MCA 1976)★★★, *Play, Guitar, Play* (MCA 1977)★★★, with Lynn *Dynamic Duo* (MCA 1977)★★★, *I've Already Loved You In My Mind* (MCA 1977)★★★, *Georgia Keeps Pulling On My Ring* (MCA 1978)★★★, *Conway* (MCA 1978)★★★, with Lynn *Honky Tonk Heroes* (MCA 1978)★★★, *Cross Winds* (MCA 1979)★★★, *Country-Rock* (MCA 1979)★★★, *Boogie Grass Band* (MCA 1979)★★★, with Lynn *Diamond Duet* (MCA 1979)★★★, *Heart And Soul* (MCA 1980)★★★, *Rest Your Love On Me* (MCA 1980)★★★, with Lynn *Two's A Party* (MCA 1981)★★★, *Mr.T.* (MCA 1981)★★★, *Southern Comfort* (Elektra 1982)★★★, *Dream Maker* (Elektra 1982)★★★, *Classic Conway* (MCA 1983)★★★, *Shake It Up Baby* 1956-57 recordings (Bulldog 1983)★★★, *Lost In The Feeling* (Warners 1983)★★★, *Merry Twismas From Conway Twitty And His Little Friends* (Warners 1983)★★★, *By Heart* (Warners 1984)★★★, *Don't Call Him A Cowboy* (Warners 1985)★★★, *Chasin' Rainbows* (Warners 1985)★★★, *Fallin' For You For Years* (Warners 1986)★★★, *Live At Castaway Lounge* (Demand 1987)★★★, *Borderline* (MCA 1987)★★★, *Still In Your Dreams* (MCA 1988)★★★, with Lynn *Making Believe* (MCA 1988)★★★, *House On Old Lonesome Road* (MCA 1989)★★★, *Crazy In Love* (MCA 1990)★★★, *Even Now* (MCA 1991)★★★, *Final Touches* (MCA 1993)★★★.

● COMPILATIONS: *Conway Twitty's Greatest Hits* (MGM 1960)★★★, *Conway Twitty's Greatest Hits, Volume 1* (Decca 1972)★★★★, *Conway Twitty's Greatest Hits, Volume 2* (MCA 1976)★★★★, *The Very Best Of Conway Twitty* (MCA 1978)★★★★, with Loretta Lynn *The Very Best Of Conway And Loretta* (MCA 1979)★★★★, *Number Ones* (MCA

1982)★★★★, *Conway's #1 Classics Volume 1* (Elektra 1982)★★★★, *Conway's #1 Classics Volume 2* (Elektra 1982)★★★★, *Conway's Latest Greatest Hits - Volume 1* (Warners 1984)★★★, *The Rock 'N' Roll Years* 8-LP box set (Bear Family 1985)★★★★, *The Beat Goes On 1958-1962* recordings (Charly 1986)★★★★, *20 Greatest Hits* (MCA 1987)★★★★, *Number Ones: The Warner Brothers Years* (Warners 1988)★★★, *Greatest Hits, Volume 3* (MCA 1990)★★★, *Silver Anniversary Collection* (MCA 1990)★★★★, *The Best Of Conway Twitty, Vol. 1: The Rockin' Years* (Polygram 1991)★★★★, *Rockin' Conway: The MGM Years* (Mercury 1993)★★★, *The Conway Twitty Collection* 4-CD box set (MCA 1994)★★★★, *Super Hits* (Epic 1995)★★★, *The Final Recordings Of His Greatest Hits* (Pickwick 1995)★★★, *Country Classics* (Critique 1996)★★★, *Conway Twitty - The High Priest Of Country Music* (Edsel 1997)★★★★.
● VIDEOS: *Golden Country Greats* (1993).
● FURTHER READING: *The Conway Twitty Story - An Authorised Biography*, Wilbur Cross and Michael Kosser.
● FILMS: *College Confidential* (1959).

TYLER, T. TEXAS

b. David Luke Myrick, 20 June 1916, Mena, Arkansas, USA, d. 28 January 1972, Springfield, Missouri, USA. Tyler spent his early childhood in Texas but was educated in Philadelphia. He learned guitar in his teens and appeared on local radio in the early 30s. He worked with Slim Clere as Slim And Tex in Charleston between 1939 and 1942, before adopting a solo career at Shreveport, Fairmont and Indianapolis. Tyler saw military service from 1944-46 and then moved to Los Angeles where he formed his own band, and his television series *Range Round Up* gained an award as Best Country Music Show of 1950. In 1946 he recorded for 4 Star Records, having initial success with 'Filipino Baby', but he established himself in 1948 when his recitation 'Deck Of Cards' made number 2 in the US country and number 21 in the US pop charts. A version by Tex Ritter also became a Top 10 US country chart hit the same year (the narration later became a million-seller for Wink Martindale in 1959 and a UK pop hit in 1973 for comedian Max Bygraves). The number may be medieval and it was certainly used as a church sermon long before Tyler was born. Over the years it has appeared in many different forms and it is possible that it was a version entitled 'The Gentleman Soldier's Prayer Book' that Tyler first read in the late 30s. He may well also have known a poem about Wild Bill Hickok's card playing written by Captain Jack Crawford, the 'Poet Scout'.

Tyler had further Top 10 successes with the tear-jerking narration 'Dad Gave My Dog Away', 'Memories Of France', 'My Bucket's Got A Hole in It', 'Bumming Around' and finally in 1954 with 'Courtin' In The Rain'. He also recorded for Starday and Capitol, appeared in several western films and was one of the first country stars to appear at Carnegie Hall. He perhaps favoured western swing, but performed all types of country music in a growl. His many *Grand Ole Opry* and touring appearances and theme song 'Remember Me' won him the nickname of 'The Man With A Million Friends'. In 1957, after some alcohol problems, Tyler became an ordained church minister and gospel singer at Springfield, Missouri, where he died of cancer in January 1972.
● ALBUMS: *Deck Of Cards* (Sound 1958)★★★, *T. Texas Tyler* (King 1959)★★★, *The Great Texan* (King 1960)★★★,

Songs Along The Way (King 1961)★★★, *Salvation* (Capitol 1962)★★, *Ten Songs He Made Famous* (Design 1962)★★★, *The Hits Of T. Texas Tyler* (Capitol 1965)★★, *The Man With A Million Friends* (Starday 1966)★★★.
● COMPILATIONS: *Great Hits* (Hilltop 1967)★★★.

TYSON, IAN

b. Ian Dawson Tyson, 25 September 1933, British Columbia, Canada. After the professional and personal break-up of Ian And Sylvia Tyson in the early 70s, Ian Tyson worked on his ranch in Longview, Alberta, Canada. His tributes to working cowboys, *Old Corrals And Sagebrush* and *Ian Tyson*, were made with a similar simplicity to those by the Sons Of The Pioneers. *Cowboyography* then sold 50,000 copies in Canada alone. Tyson had a hit with 'Navajo Rug' which he wrote with his protégé Tom Russell and it has since been recorded by Jerry Jeff Walker. His songs show compassion and understanding for the cowboy's life, and when they are not his own compositions, they are usually well-chosen cover versions, for example 'Night Rider's Lament' and 'Gallo Del Cielo'. He also sings 'Navajo Rug' and 'Gallo Del Cielo' on Tom Russell's 1992 album *Cowboy Real*. Tyson has said of his subject matter: 'As the song says, my heroes have always been cowboys and still are it seems.'
● ALBUMS: *Ol' Eon* (A&M 1974)★★★, *One Jump Ahead Of The Devil* (Boot 1978)★★★★, *Old Corrals And Sagebrush* (Columbia 1983)★★★★ *Ian Tyson* (Columbia 1984)★★★★, *Cowboyography* (Stony Plain 1987)★★, *I Outgrew The Wagon* (Stony Plain 1989)★★★, *And Stood There Amazed* (Stony Plain 1991)★★★, *Eighteen Inches Of Rain* (Stony Plain 1994)★★★, *All The Good 'Uns* (Stony Plain 1996)★★★.

TYSON, IAN AND SYLVIA

b. Ian Dawson Tyson, 25 September 1933, British Columbia, Canada. His father went to Canada in 1906 with dreams of being a cowboy and passed on his aspirations to his son, who worked on a farm, entered amateur rodeos and worked as a lumberjack. He says, 'I'm always grateful for my logging and rodeo days because that's where the songs come from.' While recovering from a rodeo injury, Tyson taught himself guitar and then played 'rockabilly in the chop-suey bars of Vancouver'. He says, 'I couldn't play very well as I only knew A, D and E. That's when I wrote "Summer Wages".' In 1959, he met Sylvia Fricker (b. 19 September 1940, Chatham, Ontario, Canada) at the Village Corner, a Toronto club. She was the daughter of a music teacher. They formed a folk duo, Ian and Sylvia, and were married in 1964. They moved to Greenwich Village and were signed by Bob Dylan's manager, Albert Grossman. Ian says, 'I could never match Dylan's output. For every good song I wrote, he wrote eight.' Their debut album, *Ian And Sylvia*, showed a debt to traditional stylings, but a second collection, *Four Strong Winds*, saw them embrace a more contemporary direction. This release not only featured Tyson's evocative title song, which quickly became a standard, but also contained an early reading of Bob Dylan's 'Tomorrow Is A Long Time'. *Northern Journey*, released in 1964, opened with 'You Were On My Mind', a much-covered Fricker song which became a folk-rock hit in the hands of We Five and Crispian St. Peters. Ian And Sylvia, meanwhile, began using session musicians on their recordings. Rick Turner, later of Autosalvage, and bassist Felix Pappalardi helped to define the duo's new direction, while a trip to Nashville in 1968 resulted in their embracing country music. Their folk-based albums popularized the songs of fellow Canadian Gordon Lightfoot, including 'Early Morning Rain' and 'For Lovin' Me'. Ian wrote about migrant workers in 'Four Strong Winds', later recorded by Neil Young, and about a rodeo from a girl's point of view in 'Someday Soon', beautifully recorded by Judy Collins. Fricker wrote 'You Were On My Mind', a US hit for We Five and a UK one for Crispian St Peters. By the end of the 60s, they went electric and formed a folk/rock group, the Great Speckled Bird, and the album of the same name was produced by Todd Rundgren. They then veered towards country music, and Sylvia wrote Crystal Gayle's US country hit, 'River Road'. They split up professionally in 1974 and were divorced in 1975, although Ian produced Sylvia's *Woman's World*. She was featured on the Canadian Live Aid single, 'Tears Are Not Enough' by Northern Lights. Ian bought a 160-acre ranch in Longview, Alberta, Canada, and reared cutting horses with his second wife, Twylla, while embarking on a solo career.

● ALBUMS: *Ian And Sylvia* (Vanguard 1962)★★★, *Northern Journey* (Vanguard 1964)★★★★, *Four Strong Winds* (Vanguard 1964)★★★★, *Early Morning Rain* (Vanguard 1965)★★★, *Play One More* (Vanguard 1966)★★★, *So Much For Dreaming* (Vanguard 1967)★★★, *Lovin' Sound* (Vanguard 1967)★★★, *Nashville* (Vanguard 1968)★★, *Full Circle* (Vanguard 1968), *Great Speckled Bird* (1969)★★★, *Ian And Sylvia* (Columbia 1971)★★, *You Were On My Mind* (Columbia 1972)★★.

● COMPILATIONS: *The Best Of Ian & Sylvia* (Vanguard 1968)★★★, *Greatest Hits, Volume 1* (Vanguard 1970)★★★, *Greatest Hits, Volume 2* (Vanguard 1971)★★★, *The Best Of Ian & Sylvia* (Columbia 1973)★★.

● FURTHER READING: *Never Sold My Saddle*, Ian Tyson and Colin Escott.

TYSON, SYLVIA

b. 19 September 1940, Chatham, Ontario, Canada. 'I didn't feel particularly bitter,' says Sylvia Tyson, looking back on the break-up of her marriage and musical partnership with Ian Tyson. 'I wanted to get on with my own life and make sure that people knew what I did.' *Woman's World* was regarded as a feminist album, but she continues, 'It may have been a feminist album for its day, but it's very tame in terms of what's coming out now. The title song talks about having babies and keeping house.' Based in Toronto, Sylvia has continued to make her mark, often as a television host. She was featured on the Canadian equivalent of Band Aid, singing the track 'Tears Are Not Enough' by Northern Lights. With the help of singer-songwriter Tom Russell she revived her musical career with *You Were On My Mind*. She chronicles small-town Canadian life in such songs as 'The Night The Chinese Restaurant Burned Down' and wrote a sensitive song about Edith Piaf, 'Chocolate Cigarettes'. They also compiled a book of quotes and anecdotes about songwriting, *And Then I Wrote*. Tyson has subsequently recorded with the acoustic-based Quartette alongside Colleen Peterson (d. 9 October 1996), Cindy Church and Caitlin Hanford; the group have released two albums to date.

● ALBUMS: *Woman's World* (Capitol 1975)★★★, *Cool Wind From The North* (Capitol 1976)★★★, *Satin On Stone* (Salt 1978)★★, *Sugar For Sugar - Salt For Salt* (Salt 1979)★★, *Big*

Spotlight (Stony Plain 1986)★★, *You Were On My Mind* (Stony Plain 1990)★★★★, *Gypsy Cadillac* (Sony 1992)★★★. With Quartette *Quartette* (Round Tower 1993)★★★, *Work Of The Heart* (Demon 1996)★★★.

● FURTHER READING: *And Then I Wrote*, Sylvia Tyson with Tom Russell.

VAGABONDS

A vocal harmony trio of minister's sons comprising Dean Upson (who had first formed a trio at WLS Chicago in 1925), Curt Poulton (who joined Upson in 1928) and Herald Goodman, who joined them on KMOX St. Louis in 1930. All were trained musicians (though only Poulton played guitar) who read and arranged music. In 1931, their performances attracted the attention of Harry Stone, who signed them to the *Grand Ole Opry* in Nashville. Their appointment represented a turning point for the *Opry* and Stone's action was against *Opry* founder George D. Hay's usual policy of using only what he termed 'down home folk' and his preference for string bands. The Vagabonds were the first really true professional entertainers to play the *Opry* and proved so popular that they also appeared regularly on WSM's other shows. They made many recordings and are reputed to have formed Nashville's first country music publishing house Old Cabin Music on their arrival in 1931. Equally accomplished with gospel, pop or country music, they are remembered for their reflective ballad 'When It's Lamp Lighting Time In The Valley', which they recorded in 1933 and which has been recorded by many artists since including Tex Ritter and Hylo Brown. They remained a popular act for many years although there were naturally some personnel changes. In the late 30s, Goodman left to front his own band, Upson eventually worked for WSM and later became the commercial manager at KWKH Shreveport. Poulton became involved with promotional work. (They should not be confused with Dunn's Vagabonds, a Houston-based band of the late 30s).

VAN DYKE, LEROY

b. Leroy Frank Van Dyke, 4 October 1929, Spring Fork, Missouri, USA. Besides working on the family farm, he learnt the guitar and sang country songs. He gained a degree in agriculture from the University of Missouri. He then worked as a farm reporter and also trained as an auctioneer. He worked for army intelligence during the Korean War and because he entertained the troops so successfully, he was determined to be a professional entertainer. He wrote a tongue-twisting song based on his experience as an auctioneer, and, following television appearances, 'The Auctioneer' made the US Top 20 in 1956 and remains one of the classic novelty records. Although he had no further hits with Dot Records, 'Honky Tonk Song', 'Heartbreak Cannonball' and 'Leather Jacket' are highly rated by rockabilly fans, and they include Al Casey and Joe Maphis among the studio musicians. Moving to Mercury, he recorded a sophisticated cheating song, 'Walk On By', which topped the US country charts and was also a transatlantic pop hit (UK number 5, USA number 5). He followed it with 'If A Woman Answers (Hang Up the Phone)', 'Black Cloud', and his only other UK success, 'Big Man In A Big House'. Two of his best records, 'I Sat Back And Let It Happen' and a cover version of Bob Dylan's 'It's All Over Now, Baby Blue', have been overlooked, and his last US country hit of any significance was 'Texas Tea' in 1977. He also put his auctioneering skills to advantage in the 1967 film *What Am I Bid*, but despite looking like James Garner, he never became a movie star.

● ALBUMS: *At The Trade Winds* (1962)★★, *Walk On By* (Mercury 1962)★★★★, *Movin' Van Dyke* (Mercury 1963)★★★, *Songs For Mom & Dad* (Mercury 1964)★★★, *Out Of Love* (Warners 1965)★★★, *The Leroy Van Dyke Show* (Warners 1965)★★, *Country Hits* (Warners 1966)★★★, *Lonesome Is* (Kapp 1968)★★★, *I've Never Been Loved* (Kapp 1969)★★, *Just A Closer Walk With Thee* (1969)★★, *World's Most Famous Auctioneer* (1974)★★★, *Gospel Greats* (1977)★★, *Rock Relics* (1979)★★, *Leroy Van Dyke* (1982)★★.

● COMPILATIONS: *Greatest Hits* (Mercury 1963)★★★, *Leroy Van Dyke's Greatest Hits* (Kapp 1969)★★★, *The Auctioneer* (Ace 1984)★★★, *Leroy Van Dyke: The Original Auctioneer* (Bear Family 1988)★★★, *Hits And Misses* (Bear Family 1994)★★★.

VAN ZANDT, TOWNES

b. 7 March 1944, Fort Worth, Texas, USA, d. 1 January 1997, Mount Juliet, Tennessee, USA. A country and folk-blues singer and guitarist, Van Zandt was a native Texan and great-grandson of one of the original settlers who founded Fort Worth in the mid-nineteenth century. The son of a prominent oil family, Van Zandt turned his back on financial security to pursue the beatnik life in Houston. First thumbing his way through cover versions, his acoustic sets later graced the Jester Lounge and other venues where his 'bawdy barroom ballads' were first performed. Although little known outside of a cult country rock following, many of his songs are better publicized by the cover versions afforded them by Merle Haggard, Emmylou Harris, Don Gibson and Willie Nelson. This gave songs such as 'Pancho And Lefty' and 'If I Needed You' the chance to rise to the top of the country charts. Much of Van Zandt's material was not released in the UK until the late 70s, though his recording career actually began with *For The Sake Of A Song*, released in the US in 1968. His media awareness belied the debt many artists, including the Cowboy Junkies and Go-Betweens, profess to owing him. Steve Earle went further: 'Townes Van Zandt is the best songwriter in the whole world, and I'll stand on Bob Dylan's coffee table in my cowboy boots and say that'. Interest is still alive as the recent reissue of *Live And Obscure* (albeit retitled *Pancho And Lefty*) on Edsel proves. Van Zandt

continued to live a reclusive life in a cabin in Tennessee up to his untimely death, recording occasionally purely for the chance to 'get the songs down for posterity'.

● ALBUMS: *For The Sake Of A Song* (Poppy 1968)★★★, *Our Mother The Mountain* (Tomato 1969)★★★★, *Townes Van Zandt* (Tomato 1969)★★★, *Delta Momma Blues* (Tomato 1971)★★★, *High And Low And In Between* (Tomato 1972)★★★, *The Late Great Townes Van Zandt* (Tomato 1972)★★★, *Live At The Old Quarter (Houston, Texas)* (Tomato 1977)★★★, *Flyin' Shoes* (Tomato 1978)★★★, *At My Window* (Sugar Hill 1987)★★★, *Live And Obscure* recorded 1985 (Sugar Hill 1989)★★★, *Rain On A Conga Drum* recorded 1990 (Exile 1991)★★★, *Pancho And Lefty* reissue of *Live And Obscure* (Edsel 1992)★★★, *The Nashville Sessions* unreleased Poppy material (Tomato 1993)★★★, *Rear View Mirror* (Sundown 1993)★★★, *Roadsongs* (Sugar Hill 1994)★★★, *No Deeper Blue* (Sugar Hill 1995)★★★, *The Highway Kind* (Sugar Hill 1997)★★★.

VANWARMER, RANDY

b. Randall Van Wormer, 30 March 1955, Indian Hills, Colorado, USA. Randy Vanwarmer is best remembered for his 1979 US Top 5/UK Top 10 single 'Just When I Needed You Most'. Vanwarmer and his mother moved to England when Randy was 12, following the death of his father in a car accident. He began singing and making demo tapes and in 1979 moved back to the USA, settling in Woodstock, New York. He signed with Bearsville Records, based in Woodstock, and recorded his own composition, 'Just When I Needed You Most', that same year. The easy-listening hit was followed by two more minor chart singles and a low-charting album, *Warmer*, also in 1979. Vanwarmer never returned to the pop scene but in 1988 he made the country charts with two singles, 'I Will Hold You' and 'Where The Rocky Mountains Touch The Morning Sun', on 16th Avenue Records. He also recorded an album for that company, *I Am*, which was not a success. Another of his songs, 'I Guess It Never Hurts To Hurt Sometime', was sung at Ernest Tubb's funeral.

● ALBUMS: *Warmer* (Bearsville 1979)★★, *Terraform* (1980)★★★ *Beat Of Love* (1981)★★★, *Thing That You Dream* (1983)★★, *I Am* (16th Avenue 1988)★★, *The Vital Spark* (Alias 1994)★★, *The Third Child* (Demon 1995)★★★.

VIRGINIA SQUIRES

This modern US bluegrass group comprised Rickie Simpkins (fiddle, mandolin, vocals), Ronnie Simpkins (bass, vocals), Sammy Shelor (guitar, banjo, vocals) and Mark Newton (guitar, vocals). The Simpkins Brothers originate from a musical family from the hills just south-west of Roanoke, Virginia. They played together in a family group but eventually formed Upland Express, a bluegrass band that had an album release on Leather Records in the 70s. They separated in the early 80s, when Rickie worked with the McPeak Brothers and Ronnie became a member of the Bluegrass Cardinals. In 1982 they reunited, in a band called the Heights Of Grass, but early in 1983, with Mark Newton (previously a member of Knoxville Grass) and Sammy Shelor (one-time member of the Country Boys), they became the Virginia Squires. Playing a variety of bluegrass, rock, old-time and country, they became a very popular band in their native state and recorded for the Rebel label.

● ALBUMS: *Bluegrass With A Touch Of Class* (Rebel

1984)★★★, *Mountains And Memories* (Rebel 1985)★★★, *I'm Working My Way* (Rebel 1986)★★★, *Hard Times And Heartaches* (1987), *Variations* (1988)★★★.

VOKES, HOWARD

b. 13 June 1931, Clearfield, Pennsylvania, USA. One of the 13 children of a coalminer, Vokes owned his first guitar by the time he was eight. At the age of 15, influenced by the recordings he heard of Roy Acuff and Jimmie Rodgers and by radio broadcasts of the *Grand Ole Opry*, he played on local radio and at rowdy venues in nearby mining towns. Two years later, he was shot in the ankle in a hunting accident and during his long convalescence, he took to writing songs. When he recovered, he formed the Country Boys and toured with and managed other artists, including Hank King and Denver Duke and Jeffrey Null (the latter duo found success with two Hank Williams tribute songs that Vokes had written). His first recording success came with his version of Doc Williams' 'Willie Roy, The Crippled Boy'. Vokes also had success with his recordings of 'Mountain Guitar' and 'A Plastic Heart', both of which were also recorded by Roy Acuff. Other artists have recorded Vokes' songs, including Wanda Jackson, who enjoyed great success with her recording of 'Tears At The Grand Ole Opry'. Vokes visited Nashville and recorded an album of downbeat songs for Starday. Apart from his own appearances, Vokes, a staunch traditionalist whose own recordings have been released in many countries, has worked tirelessly over the years promoting traditional country music and working to help young artists in his native state. In 1995, still very active in the business, Vokes was honoured for his services to country music by the Governor of Kentucky, who commissioned him a 'Kentucky Colonel'. Highly respected in the country music world, and having started his career with the nickname of 'Cowboy', Vokes is now known internationally as 'Pennsylvania's King Of Country Music'.
● ALBUMS: *Tragedy & Disaster In Country Songs* (Starday 1963)★★★, *Sings The Songs Of Broken Love Affairs* (1977)★★★, *Tears At The Grand Ole Opry* (1979)★★★.

WADE, NORMAN

b. Columbus, Georgia, USA. Little is known of Wade's early years, except that he developed an interest in country music as a child and was particularly attracted to the music of Hank Williams. In 1959, after learning guitar and singing in local clubs, he relocated to Nashville. Marty Robbins, who became Wade's biggest influence, offered him a job that led to his working for the star for the next 15 years, including appearances with him on the *Grand Ole Opry* (Robbins later even played dobro on some tracks on Wade's *Pure Country*). Wade first recorded in 1959, but it was in 1978 that he achieved minor success with 'Close Every Honky Tonk'. Although he continued to record and achieved some local chart successes, his only *Billboard* entry was a 1979 recording of Hank Williams' 'I'm A Long Gone Daddy'. Wade has written many songs and excels at recording honky tonk numbers. He has played the *Opry* in his own right and in 1984, he was honoured with lifetime membership of the Jimmie Rodgers Memorial Festival in Meridian, Mississippi. He remains active but, like Vernon Oxford, his ability to sing in the style of Hank Williams and his love for the downhome country sound of fiddle and steel guitar mean that he was probably born 10 years too late to gain the proper acclaim his ability merits.
● ALBUMS: *Back To The Country* (CMI 80s)★★★, *Wadin' Deep In The Country* (CMI 80s)★★★, *Pure Country* (Ritason 1985)★★★, *Remember Country* (NCR 1986)★★★, *Tennessee Eyes* (CD Grady 1993)★★★, *For A Minute There* (Associated Artists 1997)★★★.

WAGONER, PORTER

b. 12 August 1930, on a farm near West Plains, Missouri, USA. Wagoner grew up listening to country music on the radio, particularly the weekly *Grand Ole Opry* broadcasts. He learned to play the guitar at the age of 10 and owing to his father's illness, his education was curtailed in order that he could help with the farm work. He made his first singing performances at the age of 17, in the grocery store where he also worked. The store owner was so impressed that he sponsored an early-morning show on the local radio in West Plains. In 1951, his singing attracted the attention of the programme director of KWTO Springfield, who offered him work on that station. Soon afterwards, Red Foley, who was then organizing his new television series the *Ozark Jubilee*, heard him and promptly added him to the cast. Although he was relatively unknown, the television and radio exposure gained him a recording contract with RCA Records and he made his debut in the US country charts in 1954 with 'Company's Comin''. The following year, 'A Satisfied Mind' gave him his first major country chart hit, spending four of the 33 weeks that it was charted at number 1. This marked the start of a recording career that, between 1955 and 1983, scarcely saw a year when his name did not appear at least once in the country charts. He began to write songs and also adopted the Nudie Cohen suits and coloured boots that were to remain his trademark. Wagoner's glittering and twinkling outfits, and blonde hair in a D.A. style, once led someone to remark that it was the first time they were aware that a Christmas tree could sing (he and Hank Snow were two of the few artists to retain this type of dress, when most others were adopting more conservative styles - although it should be stressed that Snow had more dress sense). When RCA suggested that he record some rock 'n' roll tracks to keep abreast of the current trend, he refused, stating, 'It just didn't suit my personality. I couldn't sing the songs'. Following further Top 10 country hits with 'Eat Drink And Be Merry' and the semi-narration 'What Would You Do (If Jesus Came To Your House)?', he became a regular member of the *Opry* in 1957. He also turned down the opportunity to record 'Bye Bye Love', which became a country and pop hit for both the Everly Brothers and Webb Pierce that year. In 1960, Wagoner was given a television series sponsored by the Chattanooga Medicine Company. Whatever their reason for choosing the lanky Wagoner (he had become known as the Thin Man From West Plains) to host the show is not clear, but it was certainly a wise choice. Initially carried by 18 stations, it became so popular that by the end of the 60s, it was networked to 86 and, soon afterwards, to over 100 stations. The show, which featured Wagoner and his band The Wagonmasters, also acted as a shop window for new and established stars. His musicians included Buck Trent (who first used his electric banjo on the show), fiddler Mack Magaha and bass-playing comedian Speck Rhodes, who was one of the last of the rustic country comedians. Norma Jean was the show's female singer for several years until she retired to get married in 1967 and was replaced by a young newcomer called Dolly Parton.

Between 1957 and 1964, Wagoner had further Top 10 country hits with 'Your Old Love Letters', 'I've Enjoyed As Much Of This As I Can Stand' and 'Sorrow On The Rocks', plus another number 1 with 'Misery Loves Company'. In 1965, he had a major hit in the USA with the original version of 'Green Green Grass Of Home'. The following year Tom Jones's recording became a UK pop number 1 and in 1975, Elvis Presley also achieved minor UK pop success with the song. The late 60s also saw Wagoner have number 2 US country hits with 'The Cold Hard Facts Of Life' and 'The Carroll County Accident', the latter even attaining US pop chart status; both songs have now become country standards. In 1967, Wagoner began his association with Dolly Parton, which during the next seven years produced a great many Top 10 country hits, such as 'The Last Thing On My Mind', 'Just Someone I Used To Know', 'Daddy Was An Old Time Preacher Man', 'If Teardrops Were Pennies' and 'Please Don't Stop Loving Me' (their only number 1). Together they won many awards, including the CMA Vocal Group of the Year in 1968 and Vocal Duo of the Year in both 1970 and 1971. However, the partnership ended acrimoniously in 1974, when Dolly Parton left to pursue her solo career. Most authorities believe that, having already become a star in her own right, she should have moved on earlier. Wagoner was naturally upset to lose so obvious an asset; lawsuits followed and it was several years before they renewed their friend-

ship. After the split with Parton, his career began to slow down, and before the late 70s, he was classed as 'the last of the hillbillies' by the modern producers. During the 70s, when many of RCA's main artists were recording material of a crossover nature, Wagoner continued rigidly with his strict country music. He still managed some chart solo hits, albeit of a more minor nature, such as the wistful 'Charlie's Picture' (also a minor US pop hit), 'Carolina Moonshiner' (penned by Dolly Parton) and 'Ole Slew Foot'. In 1981, RCA dropped his records from their catalogue and he left the label. He joined Warner Brothers and had minor hits with 'Turn The Pencil Over', a beautiful country ballad that he sang on the soundtrack of the Clint Eastwood film *Honkytonk Man*, and 'This Cowboy's Hat'. When the latter charted in 1983, it took his country chart hits to 81. He also re-recorded some of his earlier hits on *Viva*, including 'Green Green Grass Of Home', and demonstrated that he was still very much a solid country artist. Over the years he became a wealthy man and in recent times has devoted more time to various business interests, as well as working in record production. He is still active as a performer, at one time appearing regularly with his All-Girls Band and still wearing his rhinestones. During his career he kept up a punishing schedule of touring, playing over 200 concerts a year, while still maintaining his network television show and *Opry* appearances. The quality of his duets with Dolly Parton are arguably the finest by any duo in country music and his own solo vocal abilities ranged from toe-tapping material to soleful country ballads. He was also probably the next best exponent to Hank Williams in performing heartfelt monologues, such as 'Men With Broken Hearts', in a convincing and genuine manner.

● ALBUMS: *A Satisfied Mind* (RCA Victor 1956)★★★, *Porter Wagoner And Skeeter Davis Sing Duets* (RCA Victor 1962)★★, *A Slice Of Life - Songs Happy And Sad* (RCA Victor 1963)★★★, with Norma Jean and Curly Harris *The Porter Wagoner Show* (RCA Victor 1963)★★★, *Y'All Come* (RCA Victor 1963)★★★, with Norma Jean *Porter Wagoner In Person* (RCA Victor 1964)★★★, *The Bluegrass Story* (RCA Victor 1965)★★★, *The Thin Man From West Plains* (RCA Victor 1965)★★★, *Old Log Cabin For Sale* (Camden 1965)★★★, with the Blackwood Brothers *Grand Old Gospel* (RCA Victor 1966)★★★, with Norma Jean *Live - On The Road* (RCA Victor 1966)★★★, *Confessions Of A Broken Man* (RCA Victor 1966)★★★, *I'm Day Dreamin' Tonight* (RCA Victor 1966)★★★, *Your Old Love Letters* (Camden 1966)★★★, *Soul Of A Convict And Other Great Prison Songs* (RCA Victor 1967)★★★, *The Cold Hard Facts Of Life* (RCA Victor 1967)★★★, with the Blackwood Brothers *More Grand Old Gospel* (RCA Victor 1967)★★★, *Sings Ballads Of Heart & Soul* (Camden 1967)★★★, with Dolly Parton *Just Between You And Me* (RCA Victor 1968)★★★, *The Bottom Of The Bottle* (RCA Victor 1968)★★★, *Gospel Country* (RCA Victor 1968)★★, with Parton *Just The Two Of Us* (RCA Victor 1968)★★★, *Green Green Grass Of Home* (Camden 1968)★★★, *The Carroll County Accident* (RCA Victor 1969)★★★, *Me And My Boys* (RCA Victor 1969)★★★, with Parton *Always, Always* (RCA Victor 1969)★★★, *Country Feeling* (Camden 1969)★★★, *You Got-ta Have A License* (RCA Victor 1970)★★★, with Parton *Porter Wayne And Dolly Rebecca* (RCA Victor 1970)★★★, *Skid Row Joe/Down In The Alley* (RCA Victor 1970)★★, with Parton *Once More*

(RCA Victor 1970)★★★, *Howdy Neighbor, Howdy* (Camden 1970)★★★, *Sings His Own* (1971)★★★, with Parton *Two Of A Kind* (RCA Victor 1971)★★★, *Porter Wagoner Country* (Camden 1971)★★★, *Blue Moon Of Kentucky* (Camden 1971)★★★, *The Silent Kind* (Camden 1971)★★★, *Simple As I Am* (1971)★★★, with Parton *The Right Combination* (RCA Victor 1972)★★★, with Parton *Together Always* (RCA Victor 1972)★★★, *What Ain't To Be Just Might Happen* (1972)★★★, *Experience* (1972)★★★, *Ballads Of Love* (1972)★★★, with Parton *Love And Music* (RCA Victor 1973)★★★, *The Farmer* (1973)★★★, with Parton *We Found It* (RCA Victor 1973)★★★, *I'll Keep On Loving You* (1973)★★★, *Highway Headed South* (1974)★★, with Parton *Porter 'N' Dolly* (RCA 1974)★★★, *Tore Down* (1974)★★★, *Sings Some Love Songs* (1975)★★★, with Parton *Say Forever You'll Be Mine* (RCA 1975)★★★, *Porter* (1977)★★★, *Today* (RCA 1979)★★★, with Parton *Porter Wagoner & Dolly Parton* (RCA 1980)★★★, *Down Home Country* (1982)★★★, *Natural Wonder* (1982)★★★, *Viva* (1983)★★★, *One For The Road* (1983)★★★, *Porter Wagoner* (MCA 1986)★★★, with Parton *Sweet Harmony* (1993)★★.

● COMPILATIONS: *The Best Of Porter Wagoner* (RCA Victor 1966)★★★★, *The Best Of Porter Wagoner Volume 2* (RCA Victor 1970)★★★, with Parton *The Best Of Porter Wagoner And Dolly Parton* (RCA Victor 1971)★★★★, with Parton *Hits Of Dolly Parton And Porter Wagoner* (RCA 1977)★★★★, *Hits Of Porter Wagoner* (RCA 1978)★★★, *20 Of The Best: Porter Wagoner* (RCA 1982)★★★, *Country Memories* cassette only (K-Tel 1984)★★★, *The Thin Man From West Plains* (Stetson 1989)★★★, *The Bluegrass Story* (Stetson 1989)★★★, *Pure Gold* (RCA 1991)★★★, with Parton *The Essential Porter & Dolly* (RCA 1996)★★★★.

WAKEFIELD, FRANK

b. Franklin Delano Wakefield, 26 June 1934, Emory Gap, Tennessee, USA. A bluegrass multi-instrumentalist, he played harmonica, guitar and bass by the time he was 12. In 1950, after relocating to Dayton, Ohio, he specialized in mandolin and, in 1951, he and his guitarist brother Ralph were featured on local radio as the Wakefield Brothers. In 1952, he worked for a time with a travelling evangelist's show before joining Red Allen to form the Kentuckians and start a partnership that, with a few separations, lasted until 1972. In 1953, he added banjo to his instruments and soon afterwards, the dobro, autoharp and fiddle. In the late 50s, he was turned down for military service due to his illiteracy (he eventually learned to read and write in the early 60s). He recorded with Allen and also played with Jimmy Martin and, in 1960, he moved his sphere of operations to Washington DC, where he also worked with the Stoneman Family and Bill Keith and tutored future mandolin great David Grisman. Between 1965 and 1970, he worked with the Greenbriar Boys, before leaving to form Country Classics and the Good Old Boys. In 1971, he recorded for Rounder Records and three years later recorded *Pistol Packin' Mama* with Don Reno, Dave Nelson, Chubby Wise and Jerry Garcia for United Artists Records. Legal problems arose and it was withdrawn, but the album surfaced in 1993 on the Grateful Dead label. In the mid-70s, he formed his Frank Wakefield Band with which he recorded. In the early 90s, he was teaching young musicians, although after playing twin mandolins with Bill Monroe on one occasion, he said that he was also teaching Monroe. He has actually played Beethoven with the New York Symphony Orchestra at Carnegie Hall and is rated one of the greatest mandolin players of all time. He also on occasion angers some and amuses others with his 'reverse' talking - one example being his telephone answering technique, when he would be inclined to say: 'Goodbye. You're glad I phoned me'. He has written several songs over the years, two of the best-known being 'New Camptown Races' and 'Leave Well Enough Alone'.

● ALBUMS: *Red Allen, Frank Wakefield & The Kentuckians* (Folkways 1964)★★★, *Frank Wakefield With Country Cooking* (Rounder 1972)★★★★, *The Frank Wakefield Band* (Rounder 1974)★★★, *The Good Old Boys Featuring David Nelson And Frank Wakefield Pistol Packin' Mama* (Round 1976)★★, *Frank Wakefield & The Good Old Boys* (Flying Fish 1978)★★★, *Blues Stay Away From Me* (Takoma 1980)★★★, *End Of The Rainbow* (Bay 1980)★★★, *Frank Wakefield & Dave Nelson & The Good Old Boys* (Grateful Dead 1993)★★★.

● COMPILATIONS: *She's No Angel* (Relic 1993)★★★.

WAKELY, JIMMY

b. Clarence Wakely, 16 February 1914, near Mineola, Arkansas, USA, d. 25 September 1982, Mission Hills, California, USA. Wakely's family relocated to Oklahoma when he was child, moving several times as they struggled to make a living, usually by sharecropping. He gave himself the name of Jimmy and attended High School at Cowden, Oklahoma, where he learned to play the guitar and piano and worked on various projects, until, after winning a local radio talent contest, he became a musician. In 1937, he married and moved to Oklahoma City, where he first worked as the pianist with a local band and appeared in a medicine show, before he was given a spot on WKY with Jack Cheney and Scotty Harrel as the Bell Boys (Cheney was soon replaced by Johnny Bond). In 1940, as the Jimmy Wakely Trio, they were hired by Gene Autry to appear on his CBS *Melody Ranch* radio show in Hollywood. He worked with Autry for two years, at one time being known as the Melody Kid, before leaving to form his own band, which at times included Merle Travis, Cliffie Stone and Spade Cooley. Wakely made his film debut in 1939, in the Roy Rogers B-movie western *Saga Of Death Valley*, and went on to appear in support roles (sometimes with his trio) in many films and with many other cowboy stars. In 1944, he starred in *Song Of The Range* and between then and 1949, when he made *Lawless Code*, he starred in almost 30 Monogram films. He became so popular as a cowboy actor that, in 1948, he was voted the number 4 cowboy star after Rogers, Autry and Charles Starrett. He made his first appearance in the US country charts in 1944 with his Decca recording of 'I'm Sending You Red Roses'. In 1948, recording for Capitol, he charted two country number 1 hits - 'One Has My Name, The Other Has My Heart' (which held the top spot for 11 weeks and remained in the country charts for 32, as well as being a national US Top 10 hit) and 'I Love You So Much It Hurts'. In 1949, he had even more success with solo hits including 'I Wish I Had A Nickel' and 'Someday You'll Call My Name', plus several duet hits with Margaret Whiting, including their million-selling recording of Floyd Tillman's song 'Slipping Around', which was a country and pop number 1. At this time, Wakely's popularity was such that, in *Billboard*'s nationwide poll, he was voted America's third most popular singer behind Perry Como and Frankie Laine - edging Bing Crosby into fourth place. Wakely and Whiting followed it with several more Top 10 country and pop hits, including 'I'll Never Slip Around Again' and 'A Bushel And A Peck'. Strangely, after his 1951 solo Top 10 hits 'My Heart Cries For You' (a UK pop hit for Guy Mitchell), 'Beautiful Brown Eyes' and a further duet with Margaret Whiting, entitled 'I Don't Want To Be Free', Wakely never made the country charts again. During the late 40s and the 50s, he toured extensively throughout the USA, the Pacific, the Far East, Korea and Alaska, sometimes appearing with Bob Hope. Musical tastes changed with the advent of Hank Williams and other country singers, and the cowboy song and image lost much of its appeal. Wakely, however, hosted his own network radio show from 1952-58 and in 1961 he co-hosted a network television series with another silver-screen cowboy, Tex Ritter. During the 60s and throughout much of the 70s, he was still a popular entertainer, mainly performing on the west coast (he made his home in Los Angeles) or playing the club circuits of Las Vegas and Reno with his family show, which featured his children Johnny and Linda. He had formed his own Shasta label in the late 50s and in the 70s, he recorded a great deal of material on that label. In 1971, he was elected to the Nashville Songwriters' Association International Hall Of Fame.

● ALBUMS: *Songs Of The West* (Capitol 1954)★★★★, *Christmas On The Range* (Capitol 1954)★★, *Santa Fe Trail* (Decca 1956)★★★★, *Enter And Rest And Pray* (Decca 1957)★★★, *Country Million Sellers* (Shasta 1959)★★★, *Merry Christmas* (Shasta 1959)★★, *Jimmy Wakely Sings* (Shasta 1960)★★★, *Slipping Around* (Dot 1966)★★★, *Christmas With Jimmy Wakely* (Dot 1966)★★, with Margaret Whiting *I'll Never Slip Around Again* (Hilltop 1967)★★★, *Show Me The Way* (1968)★★★, *Heartaches* (Decca 1969)★★★, *Here's Jimmy Wakely* (Vocalion 1969)★★★, *Lonesome Guitar Man* (60s)★★★, *Big Country Songs* (Vocalion 1970)★★★, *Now And Then* (Decca 1970)★★★, *Jimmy Wakely Country* (1971)★★★, *Blue Shadows* (Shasta 1973)★★★, *Family Show* (Shasta 1973)★★, *The Wakely Way With Country Hits* (Shasta 1974)★★★, *Jimmy Wakely* (Shasta 1974)★★★, *On Stage Volume 1* (1974)★★, *Western Swing And Pretty Things* (Shasta 1975)★★★, *The Gentle Touch* (Shasta 1975)★★★, *The Jimmy Wakely CBS Radio Show* (1975)★★★, *Jimmy Wakely Country* (Shasta 1975)★★★, *Singing Cowboy* (Shasta 1975)★★★, *An Old Fashioned Christmas* (Shasta 1976)★★, *A Tribute To Bob Wills* (Shasta 1976)★★★, *Precious Memories* (Shasta 1976)★★★, *Moments To Remember* (Shasta 1977)★★★, *Reflections* (Shasta 1977)★★★, *Great Hillbilly & Western Swing Rarities* (Bronco Buster 1997)★★★.

● COMPILATIONS: *Vintage Collection* (Capitol 1996)★★★★.

● FURTHER READING: *See Ya Up There, Baby - A Biography*, Linda Lee Wakely.

WALKER, BILLY

b. Billy Marvin Walker, 14 January 1929, Ralls, Texas, USA. Walker was born on a farm but was raised in an orphanage after his mother's death. When he was 11 years old, he returned to live with his father, who had remarried. Walker learned the guitar from his father, and after seeing a Gene Autry film, he was determined to become a singer. He appeared on radio in Clovis when aged 15 and two years later appeared as 'The Travelling Texan' on the Big D

Jamboree radio show on KRLD Dallas. Walker recorded for Capitol Records from 1949-51, but he did not make the US country charts until he recorded 'Thank You For Calling' for Columbia in 1954. He dispensed with his mask and joined both *Louisiana Hayride* and *Ozark Jubilee*. Since 1960, Walker has been a regular performer at the *Grand Ole Opry*. Walker was the first to record Willie Nelson's 'Funny How Time Slips Away' and he passed another of another Nelson's songs, 'Crazy', to Patsy Cline. In 1962 Walker had his first US country number 1 with 'Charlie's Shoes' and subsequent successes included 'Cross The Brazos At Waco', 'A Million To One', 'Sundown Mary', 'She Goes Walking Through My Mind' and 'Sing Me A Love Song To Baby', followed by a succession of minor chart successes for a variety of companies, including his own Tall Texan label. By the end of 1988, he had placed 65 records in the US country charts, including duets with Barbara Fairchild, 'The Answer Game' and 'Let Me Be The One'. Among his own songs is a tribute to Marty Robbins, 'He Sang The Songs About El Paso'. Walker, who is a born-again Christian, has built up a UK following with appearances at Wembley festivals and country clubs. In 1986, Walker said, 'Current crossover trends are like mixing chocolate, strawberry and vanilla in the same bowl. Not only is it an ugly colour but it leaves a bad taste in one's mouth.'

● ALBUMS: *Everybody's Hits But Mine* (Columbia 1961)★★★★, *Thank You For Calling* (Columbia 1964)★★★, *Anything Your Heart Desires* (Harmony 1964)★★★, *The Gun, The Gold And The Girl* (1965)★★★, *A Million And One* (Monument 1966)★★★, *The Walker Way* (Monument 1967)★★★, *I Taught Her Everything She Knows* (Monument 1968)★★★, *Billy Walker Salutes The Hall Of Fame* (Monument 1968)★★, *How Big Is God* (Monument 1969)★★, *Portrait Of Billy* (Monument 1969)★★★, *Country Christmas* (Monument 1969)★★, *Charlie's Shoes* (Monument 1970)★★★, *Darling Days* (Monument 1970)★★★, *When A Man Loves A Woman* (MGM 1970)★★★, *I'm Gonna Keep On Lovin' You* (MGM 1971)★★★, *Billy Walker Live* (MGM 1972)★★, *There May Be No Tomorrow* (MGM 1972)★★★, *The Billy Walker Show* (MGM 1972)★★, *The Hand Of Love* (MGM 1973)★★★, *Too Many Memories* (MGM 1973)★★★, *Fine As Wine* (MGM 1974)★★★, *Lovin' And Losin'* (RCA 1975)★★★, *Alone Again* (RCA 1976)★★★, *The Tall Texan Sings His Songs* (1978)★★★, *Star Of The Grand Ole Opry* (1979)★★, *Lovin' Things* (Caprice 1979)★★★, with Barbara Fairchild *The Answer Game* reissued as *It Takes Two* (Paid 1979)★★★, *Soap And Water* (1980)★★★, *Don't Ever Leave Me In Texas* (1980)★★★, *Circumstances* (1980)★★★, *Waking Up To Sunshine* (1980)★★★, *How Great Thou Art* (1981)★★★, *Are You Sincere?* (1982)★★★, *Life Is A Song* (1983)★★★, *The Tall Texan* (Tall Texan 1985)★★★, *Precious Memories* (Word 1985)★★★, *Billy Walker* (1986)★★★, *For My Friends* (Bulldog 1987)★★★, *Wild Texas Rose* (Tall Texan 1988)★★★.

● COMPILATIONS: *Billy Walker's Greatest Hits* (Columbia 1963)★★★★, *Big Country Hits* (Harmony 1967)★★★★, *All Time Greatest Hits* (1973)★★★, *Best Of The Best Of Billy Walker* (Gusto 1988)★★★, *Cross The Brazos At Waco* 6-CD set (Bear Family 1994)★★★★.

WALKER, CHARLIE

b. 2 November 1926, Copeville, Collins County, Texas, USA. A talented musician, Walker joined Bill Boyd's Cowboy Ramblers in 1943 and worked as a disc jockey for the Armed

Forces Radio Network during World War II. By the early 50s, he was voted one of country music's Top 10 DJs and his vocal talent saw him join Decca. His first chart hit was 'Only You, Only You', but after moving to Columbia in 1958, he enjoyed a number 2 hit with Harlan Howard's song 'Pick Me Up On Your Way Down', which established him as a major artist. Between 1960 and 1974, Walker achieved 23 more country hits, having Top 10 success with 'Wild As A Wild Cat' and 'Don't Squeeze My Sharmon'. He later recorded for Epic, RCA, Capitol and Plantation. Many of his most popular recordings are honky tonk songs such as 'Close All The Honky Tonks', 'Honky Tonk Season' and 'Honky Tonk Women' (a number 1 British pop hit for the Rolling Stones). He joined the *Grand Ole Opry* in 1967 (having first guested in 1954) and still makes appearances. Walker is also noted for his ability as a compere and in that capacity, he has appeared at such prestigious venues as Las Vegas's *Golden Nugget*. A fine golfer, he also regularly broadcasts on major golfing events. He appeared in the film *Country Music* and is still active, although mainly as a broadcaster. His last chart hit was 'Odds And Ends (Bits And Pieces)'.

● ALBUMS: *Close All The Honky Tonks* (Epic 1965)★★★, *Born To Lose* (Epic 1965)★★★, *Wine Women And Walker* (Epic 1966)★★★, *Country Style* (1967)★★★, *Don't Squeeze* (Epic 1967)★★★ *He Is My Everything* (1968)★★★, *Live In Dallas* (Epic 1969)★★, *Honky Tonkin'* (1971)★★, *Charlie Walker* (1972)★★, *Break Out The Bottle (Bring On The Music)* (1973)★★.

● COMPILATIONS: *Greatest Hits* (Columbia 1961)★★★, *Golden Hits* (1978)★★★, *Texas Gold* (1979)★★★, *Greatest Hits* (1981)★★★.

WALKER, CINDY

Often described as the greatest living songwriter of country music, Walker's achievements were finally honoured when she was inducted into the Country Music Hall Of Fame in September 1997. The writer of hundreds of classic country hits from the 40s onwards, her successes have included 'Dream Baby' (Roy Orbison), 'Distant Drums' (Jim Reeves), 'Bubbles In My Beer' (Bob Wills), 'I Don't Care' (Webb Pierce, Ricky Skaggs), 'Blue Canadian Rockies' (Gene Autry) and 'You Don't Know Me' (Eddy Arnold, Ray Charles).

Walker (b. Mart, Texas, USA) was brought up in a musical family. Her mother Oree was a gifted piano player who accompanied her daughter up until her death in 1991, and her grandfather, F.L. Eiland, was renowned as a composer of hymns. Walker performed in local shows and achieved her first taste of success when a tune she composed for the Texas Centennial, 'Casa De Manana', was later adopted by the Paul Whiteman Orchestra. Later, on a family trip to Los Angeles, Walker visited the Crosby Building on Sunset Boulevard. By the time she came out she had convinced Larry Crosby that Bing Crosby should record her 'Lone Star Trail', and the song became Walker's first songwriting hit. She also recorded for Decca Records as a solo artist until 1947, reaching number 5 in the country charts in April 1944 with her cover version of the standard 'When My Blue Moon Turns To Gold Again'. She also appeared as a cowgirl in several films. Country legend Bob Wills was an early champion of Walker's songwriting, recording five of her songs ('Dusty Skies', 'Cherokee Maiden', 'Blue Bonnet Lane', 'It's All Your Fault' and 'Don't Count Your Chickens') in 1941, and then commissioning her

to write 39 more for the eight movies he was contracted to make in 1942. Their partnership produced three hit singles in 'You're From Texas', 'Sugar Moon' and 'Bubbles In My Beer', while Walker penned other hits for Autry ('Silver Spurs'), Ernest Tubb ('Red Wine'), George Morgan ('I Love Everything About You'), Johnny Bond ('Oklahoma Waltz') and Eddy Arnold ('Take Me In Your Arms And Hold Me'). Despite moving back to Texas in 1954, she continued to pour out hits, including two country classics, 'I Don't Care' and 'You Don't Know Me', the latter proving most successful when Ray Charles included it on his ground-breaking 1962 album *Modern Sounds In Country & Western Music*. A number of other artists have covered the track successfully, including Mickey Gilley, Elvis Presley and Roy Orbison. Further hits during the 60s included 'Heaven Says Hello' (Sonny James), 'You Are My Treasure' (Jack Greene) and Jim Reeves' posthumous number 1 in 1966 with 'Distant Drums'. The run of hits has slowed down since then, although Merle Haggard successfully revived 'Cherokee Maiden' in 1976, and Ricky Skaggs topped the charts with his cover version of 'I Don't Care' in 1981. Her Hall Of Fame induction proved to be a fitting tribute to her reputation in country music.

WALKER, CLAY

b. 19 August 1969, Beaumont, Texas, USA. From the same city and similar strand of country music as Tracy Byrd and Mark Chesnutt, the 90s US country singer Clay Walker owes much of his vocal style to George Strait. He was taught guitar by his father at a young age and started to write songs as soon as he knew enough chords. Walker was no overnight success, and toured throughout the USA and Canada, playing bars and small clubs, building a reputation and desperately trying to attract attention. He finally secured a contract with Giant Records in Nashville. His debut single in 1993, 'What's It To You', was a US country number 1. The debut album, *Clay Walker*, did well on the US country charts and the single 'Live Until I Die' reached number 3 in the country singles chart. Other singles that have been hits include 'If I Could Make A Living', 'Who Needs You Baby', 'This Woman And This Man' 'Hypnotize The Moon' and another number 1 in 1997 with 'Rumor Has It'. Walker was reported to be suffering from multiple sclerosis the same year.

● ALBUMS: *Clay Walker* (Giant 1993)★★★, *If I Could Make A Living* (Giant 1994)★★★★, *Hypnotize The Moon* (Giant 1995)★★★, *Rumor Has It* (Giant 1997)★★★★.

● VIDEOS: *If I Could Make A Living* (1994).

WALKER, JERRY JEFF

b. 16 March 1942, Oneonta, New York, USA. Although Walker initially pursued a career as a folk-singer in New York's Greenwich Village, he first forged his reputation as a member of Circus Maximus. He left this promising group following their debut album, when a jazz-based initiative proved incompatible with his own ambitions. Having moved to Key West in Florida, Walker resumed work as a solo artist with *Drifting Way Of Life*, before signing with the Atco label when his former outlet showed little interest in his country/folk material. He enjoyed a minor hit with 'Mr. Bojangles', a tale of a street dancer Walker reputedly met while drunk. Although the singer's own rendition stalled in the chart's lower reaches, it became a US Top 10 hit for the Nitty Gritty Dirt Band and has since been the subject of numerous cover versions, including a lethargic one by Bob Dylan. By the early 70s Walker was based in Austin, Texas, where he became a kindred spirit to the city's 'outlaw' fraternity, including Willie Nelson and Waylon Jennings. He also built one of the region's most accomplished backing groups, later to pursue its own career as the Lost Gonzo Band. A low-key approach denied the artist equivalent commercial success, but Walker has enjoyed the approbation of colleagues and a committed cult following.

● ALBUMS: *Mr. Bojangles* (Atco 1968)★★★, *Drifting Way Of Life* (Vanguard 1969)★★★, *Five Years Gone* (Atco 1969)★★★, *Bein' Free* (1970)★★★, *Jerry Jeff Walker* (MCA 1972)★★★, *Viva Terlingua!* (MCA 1973)★★★, *Walker's Collectables* (MCA 1975), *Ridin' High* (MCA 1975)★★★, *It's A Good Night For Singin'* (MCA 1976)★★★★, *A Man Must Carry On* (MCA 1977)★★★, *Contrary To Ordinary* (MCA 1978)★★★, *Jerry Jeff* (Elektra 1978)★★★, *Too Old To Change* (Elektra 1979)★★, *Reunion* (South Coast 1981)★★, *Cowjazz* (MCA 1982)★★, *Gypsy Songman* (Temple Music 1985)★★, *Navajo Rug* (Rykodisc 1987)★★, *Live At Guene Hall* (Rykodisc 1989)★★★, *Hill Country Rain* (Rykodisc 1992)★★, *Viva Luckenbach!* (Rykodisc 1994)★★, *Christmas Gonzo Style* (Rykodisc 1994)★, *Night After Night* (Tried And True 1995)★★, *Scamp* (Tried And True 1997)★★★.

● COMPILATIONS: *The Best Of Jerry Jeff Walker* (MCA 1980)★★★★, *Great Gonzos* (MCA 1991)★★★★.

WALL, CHRIS

b. Los Angeles, California, USA. Wall grew up in southern California but spent his summers on his uncle's ranch in Montana. After gaining a degree in history, he decided on a career in music, working as a bartender in Jackson while he established himself. He jammed with Pinto Bennett and the Famous Motel Cowboys and he and Bennett later wrote 'No Sweat'. Wall's talent was recognized by Jerry Jeff Walker, who suggested he move to Austin to further his career. He was signed to Walker's own Tried And True label and he wrote and played skilfully worded but danceable honky-tonk music. He penned 'I Feel Like Hank Williams Tonight' for Walker, who also made the US country charts with a cover of 'Trashy Woman'. The song went on to become a substantial hit for Confederate Railroad. Wall's debut album is full of wry, cynical material, such as 'I Wish John Stetson Made A Heart' ('Mine's been stomped and stole and stepped on and damn near tore apart/Lord, I wish John Stetson made a heart'), 'Entourage' ('I want an entourage/I got a big old ego and I need to get that sucker massaged'), and 'Something To Shoot' ('We got deer, we got elk, we got old owls that hoot/And when I killed them all, there are yankees to shoot'). Wall tours with his band the Rhythm Wranglers.

● ALBUMS: *Honky Tonk Heart* (Tried And True/Rykodisc 1989)★★★★, *No Sweat* (Tried And True/Rykodisc 1991)★★★, *Cowboy Nation* (Cold Spring 1994)★★★, *Any Saturday Night In Texas* (Cold Spring 1997)★★★.

WALLACE, JERRY

b. 15 December 1928, Guildford, Missouri, USA. A pop-country singer and guitarist who made his initial recordings for Allied in 1951, but achieved his first chart success when his 1958 Challenge recording of 'How The Time Flies' reached number 11 in the US pop charts. After further pop successes, including his recording of film star Audie Murphy's song 'Shutters And Boards', he first appeared in the country charts with his 1965 Mercury recording of 'Life's Gone And Slipped Away'. Between then and 1979, he went on to register 32 more country hits, including a number 1 with 'If You Leave Me Tonight I'll Cry' (also a minor pop hit) and a number 2 with 'Do You Know What It's Like To Be Lonesome'. His later recordings were on many different labels including Liberty and MCA, and his last chart entry was 'If I Could Set My Love To Music' on the Door Knob label in 1980. A talented actor and narrator, he has done voice-overs for commercials and appeared in many top television plays and shows such as *Night Gallery* and *Hec Ramsey*.

● ALBUMS: *Just Jerry* (Challenge 1959)★★, *There She Goes* (Challenge 1960)★★★, *Shutters And Boards* (Challenge 1962)★★, *In The Misty Moonlight* (Challenge 1964)★★, *Another Time, Another Place, Another World* (Liberty 1968)★★★★, *This One's On The House* (Liberty 1968)★★★, *Sweet Child Of Sunshine* (Liberty 1968)★★★, *Bitter Sweet* (Liberty 1969)★★★, *This Is Jerry Wallace* (Decca 1971)★★★, *Jerry Wallace* (Decca 1972)★★★, *Do You Know What It's Like To Be Lonesome* (Decca 1973)★★, *Primrose Lane* (MCA 1973)★★★, *To Get To You* (MCA 1973)★★★, *I Wonder Whose Baby/Make Hay While The Sun Shines* (MCA 1974)★★★, *Coming Home To You* (MGM 1975)★★★, *Jerry Wallace* (MGM 1975)★★★, *All I Want Is You* (MGM 1975)★★★, *I Miss You Already* (BMA 1977)★★★.

● COMPILATIONS: *The Best Of Jerry Wallace* (Mercury 1966)★★★, *Greatest Hits* (1969)★★★.

WALTERS, HANK

b. William Ralph Walters, 2 August 1933, Liverpool, England. Walters acquired the name 'Hank' while working on the Liverpool docks, in reference to his love of country music. As a schoolboy, Walters learned accordion and acquired a passion for Jimmie Rodgers' and Hank Williams' music. In 1946 he formed Spike Walters And His Hillbillies, one of the UK's first country groups. Conscripted in 1951, he and some other soldiers were billed as the Dusty Road Ramblers for a show in Khartoum, Sudan. Back home, Walters used the name for his own country group and they appeared regularly at the Cavern club as well as having a residency at the Black Cat Club. Most of the early Merseybeat groups saw him perform and Walters recalls, 'John Lennon said to me, "I don't go much on your music, but give us your hat." I told him that I didn't think his group would get anywhere unless they got with it and played country.' By 1962 the Cavern favoured beat groups, but Walters was still able to secure bookings with his country music and Scouse humour. He turned down an offer from Polydor to record a cover version of 'Twenty Four Hours From Tulsa', but he was featured on the Decca album *Liverpool Goes Country*. Hank Walters and the Dusty Road Ramblers continue as one of the most popular acts on Merseyside and he also fronts the Hank Walters Family. The hillbilly docker has performed at national country music festivals, but the group has been reluctant to travel because of day jobs, although Walters has now retired from the docks. Walters' 'Progress', 'Sweet Liverpool', 'Rollin' Home' and 'The Dosser' are well-known songs in Liverpool. The mainstays of his repertoire are 'I Could Never Be Ashamed Of You', 'Are You Teasing Me?', 'Close To The

Edge', 'I Saw The Light' and, surprisingly, 'The Ugly Bug Ball'. He says, 'New country is just young voices singing old songs. I've been doing them for years.'

● ALBUMS: *Hank Walters* (1973)★★★, *Progress* (1979)★★★, *Live From Radio Merseyside* (1993)★★★.

WANGFORD, HANK

b. Samuel Hutt, 15 November 1940, Wangford, Suffolk, England. Wangford's father, Allen Hutt, was chief sub-editor of the communist newspaper *The Daily Worker* and president of the National Union of Journalists. His mother taught English to Russian students. Wangford studied medicine at Cambridge University and later became a doctor. He was converted to country music by Gram Parsons who attended him for treatment in 1971. After a period in the USA, Wangford became gradually more involved in country music and, despite the demands of his professional work, yearned to be a performer. When his girlfriend married his best friend, he consoled himself in a pub near the Wangford bypass in Suffolk. Here he devised the character of Hank Wangford, who would sing songs from the Wangford Hall of Pain. Starting in 1976, Wangford built a reputation on the London pub-rock circuit. His persona was both a glorification of country music and an affectionate parody of its excesses. He formed Sincere Management (motto: 'It's in the post.') and Sincere Products ('Brought to you with no regard for quality'). Wangford generated publicity as a gynaecologist-cum-country singer, often being photographed with a Harley Street sign. His media image, however, has proved more sustainable than the lightweight music which, in fairness, is highly successful in the pub/club environment. 'Chicken Rhythm' is derived from Ray Stevens' quirky 'In The Mood', and 'Cowboys Stay On Longer' is a close cousin to David Allan Coe's 'Divers Do It Deeper'. Wangford has always been able to surround himself with musically talented band members, notably Andy Roberts (Brad Breath) and Melanie Harrold (Irma Cetas). His fiddler and co-singer, ex-Fabulous Poodles and Clark Gable lookalike, Bobby Valentino, later embarked on a solo career. Wangford, with his ponytail, stubble and gap-toothed features is an engaging entertainer, creating a stage show, 'Radio Wang', and presenting two country music series for Channel 4 Television. He also works as the senior medical officer at a family planning clinic in London, and he says, 'I have had letters of referral from doctors which start "Dear Dr. Wangford", so the transmogrification is complete.'

● ALBUMS: *Live: Hank Wangford* (Cow Pie 1982)★★, *Hank Wangford* (Cow Pie 1985)★★★, *Rodeo Radio* (Situation 2 1985)★★, *Stormy Horizons* (New Routes 1990)★★, *Hard Shoulder To Cry On* (1993)★★, *Wake Up Dead* (Way Out West 1997)★★★.

● FURTHER READING: *Hank Wangford, Vol. III The Middle Years*, Sam Hutt. *Lost Cowboys: From Patagonia To The Alamo*, Hank Wangford.

WARD, CHRIS

b. c.1960, South Bronx, New York, USA. Chris Ward had all the right credentials to enter the machismo world of the honky-tonk singer in the mid-90s - his former professions included being a rodeo bull rider, a Marine sergeant and a SWAT team member in a Californian police department. During these spells, Ward had always been a practising

musician, having taken up drums during his itinerant childhood, caused by his father's executive career with IBM. It was while employed as a bull-rider in Spokane, Washington, that Ward first had the chance to test his musical talents. Fellow rider Deb Copenhaver encouraged him to join the stage when country act Bonnie Guitar was playing a local nightclub. Guitar was sufficiently impressed to offer him a full-time job as her drummer and horse trainer. There then followed a spell in the Marine Corps then the San Diego police, while maintaining links with the band he formed in the army, Christopher John And The Wheels. After becoming a SWAT sniper, he would often take the stage wearing his police pager. In 1984 he went to Nashville to record demos, but the venture went nowhere. Discouraged, he returned to Los Angeles club work. He was employed as a detective until selling up in 1994 and moving to Nashville permanently, initially to work as a demo singer. He finally secured a contract with Giant Records, and recorded his debut album, *One Step Beyond*.

● ALBUMS: *One Step Beyond* (Giant 1996)★★★.

WARD, FIELDS

b. Fields Mac Ward, 23 January 1911, Buck Mountains, Virginia, USA, d. 26 October 1987, Bel Air, Maryland, USA. Ward came from a musical family, his father being old-time fiddler Crockett Ward, his mother a singer, and four siblings played various instruments. He learned to play guitar from local fiddler Uncle Eck Dunford and by listening to the recordings of Riley Puckett. He made his first recordings for OKeh Records in 1927, with his father and two brothers Current and Sampson. In 1929, together with Sampson, Dunford and Ernest V. Stoneman, he recorded as the Grayson County Railsplitters for Gennett (the label withheld release for some reason and they remained unissued until the 60s, when they appeared on Historical Records). During the 30s, he worked with his uncle Wade Ward in the Buck Mountain String Band and with the family band, the Bogtrotters, who won awards at the Galax convention in 1935. Later, with non-family members participating, they proved popular at various folk festivals, and between 1937 and 1942, they recorded for the Library of Congress with Alan Lomax at Galax and Washington DC. Offered the chance by John Lair to go solo on the *Renfro Valley Barn Dance*, Ward refused to leave the band. World War II finally saw the end of the Bogtrotters and Ward relocated north to settle first near Baltimore, but later to Bel Air, Maryland. He mainly worked as a painter until his retirement. In the 60s, the Folk revival saw him persuaded to play again and he recorded albums for Biograph and Rounder Records. He also had material released without his knowledge on Folkways Records, which greatly angered him. Ill health caused by emphysema, arthritis, ulcers and diabetes gave him major problems during his latter years, but he maintained a performing schedule almost up to his death in October 1987. He wrote several songs including 'Those Cruel Slavery Days' and 'Way Down In North Carolina'.

● ALBUMS: *Fields Ward & The Buck Mountain Band* (Historical 70s)★★★, *Fields & Wade Ward Recorded In Galax, Virginia* (Biograph 70s)★★★, *Bury Me Not On The Prairie* (Rounder 1974)★★★.

WARDEN, MONTE

Guitarist Brent Wilson (b. USA) and drummer Tom Lewis (b. USA) had both toured with the vintage rock 'n' roller Sleepy LaBeef. In the late 80s they teamed up with singer-songwriter Monte Warden and bass player Craig Pettigrew to form the neo-rockabilly band, the Wagoneers. *Stout And High* included a guest appearance from Herb Alpert (owner of A&M who released the album) and they had moderately successful singles with 'I Want To Know Her Again' and 'Every Step Of The Way'. The Wagoneers never fulfilled their potential and a third album was shelved, largely because of disagreements between Lewis and Warden. Since then, Warden has formed Monte Warden And The Lone Sharks, working with the drummer and producer Mas Palermo.
● ALBUMS: as the Wagoneers *Stout And High* (A&M 1988)★★, *Good Fortune* (A&M 1989)★★, as Monte Warden And The Lone Sharks *Monte Warden* (Watermelon 1993)★★★, *Here I Am* (Watermelon 1995)★★.

WARINER, STEVE

b. 25 December 1954, Noblesville, Indiana, USA. Wariner played in his father's country group from the age of 10. One night he had a residency at a club near Indianapolis and the starring attraction, Dottie West, went on stage to harmonize with him. He then played bass for West and after that, for Bob Luman. Luman recorded several of Wariner's songs, while Wariner revived Luman's success, 'Lonely Women Make Good Lovers'. He played for Chet Atkins, who took him to RCA Records as a solo performer. Wariner was offered, and rejected, 'You Needed Me', but in 1978 he had a minor US country hit with his own song, 'I'm Already Taken', which was subsequently recorded by Conway Twitty. After several other chart records (including 'Your Memory' and 'By Now'), he had his first country number 1 in 1981 with 'All Roads Lead To You', but his follow-ups, 'Kansas City Lights', 'Midnight Fire' and 'What I Didn't Do', were only moderately successful. Keen to make records with a stronger country element, he moved to MCA Records in 1985 and had further country number 1 hits with 'Some Fools Never Learn', 'You Can Dream On Me' (which he wrote with John Hall of Orleans), 'Life's Highway', 'Small Town Girl', 'Lynda' (a tribute to actress Lynda Carter who played 'Wonder Woman'), 'The Weekend', 'Where Did I Go Wrong' and 'I Got Dreams'. He has recorded duets with Nicolette Larson ('That's How You Know When Love's Right') and Glen Campbell ('The Hand That Rocks The Cradle'); the latter is one of the strongest influences on his work. After winning a CMA Vocal Event award for his contribution to Mark O'Connor's 'Restless' in 1991, Wariner adopted a tougher image and sound for the highly successful *I Am Ready*. The follow-up *Drive* found similar chart success, although he had stated that he was never comfortable being a country star. Not merely content with being viewed as a star singer-songwriter, after a long gap he made an album that showcased his virtuosity on his Takamine guitar. *No More Mr Nice Guy* featured guest appearances from Chet Atkins, Sam Bush, Vince Gill and Mark O'Connor.
● ALBUMS: *Steve Wariner* (RCA 1982)★★★, *Midnight Fire* (1983)★★★, *One Good Night Deserves Another* (MCA 1985)★★, *Life's Highway* (MCA 1985)★★★, *Down In Tennessee* (MCA 1986)★★★ *It's A Crazy World* (MCA 1987)★★★, *I Should Be With You* (MCA 1988)★★★, *I Got*

Dreams (MCA 1989)★★★, *Laredo* (MCA 1990)★★, *I Am Ready* (Arista 1991)★★★★, *Drive* (Arista 1993)★★★★, *No More Mr Nice Guy* (Arista 1996).★★★
● COMPILATIONS: *Greatest Hits* (RCA Victor 1985)★★★, *Greatest Hits* (MCA 1987)★★★★, *Greatest Hits Volume II* (MCA 1991)★★.

WARMACK, PAUL, AND THE GULLY JUMPERS

One of the *Grand Ole Opry*'s first string bands, it comprised Paul Warmack (mandolin, guitar, vocals), Charlie Arrington (fiddle), Roy Hardison (banjo) and Burt Hutcherson (guitar). Warmack ran his own car repair business, Hardison was a garage foremen, Arrington a farmer and Hutcherson a woodworker. Hardison occasionally played with other groups and prior to joining Warmack and Hutcherson had previously played with Dr. Humphrey Bate's Possum Hunters. Apart from their Saturday night spot, Warmack and Hutcherson also broadcast an early-morning WSM show as the Early Birds. In October 1928, when the Victor Company decided to record some of the early *Opry* acts, the Gully Jumpers became one of the first bands to record in Nashville (Victor actually recorded 69 sides but only 36 were issued). The first record issued by Victor, which therefore had the distinction of being the first commercially released Nashville recording by a major label, was Paul Warmack And The Gully Jumpers' 'Tennessee Waltz' (not the popular Pee Wee King/Redd Stewart composition) and 'The Little Red Caboose Behind The Train' (Victor V-40067). The band also recorded four instrumentals but only two, 'Robertson County' and 'Stone Rag', were released and they made no further recordings. The Gully Jumpers remained with the *Opry* for 20 years until, following the death of some members of various *Opry* bands, the management effected mergers of the remaining musicians. Hutcherson taught guitar in Nashville for many years.

WARREN, DALE

b. Dale Henry Warren, 1 June 1925, Summerville, Kentucky, USA. A member of the Sons Of The Pioneers. It was not unexpected that Warren should pursue a career in entertainment; his father, Henry Green Warren, was the 'Uncle Henry' of Uncle Henry's Kentucky Mountaineers (later the Original Kentucky Mountaineers) and his piano-playing mother, Wava, performed with the group as Sally the Mountain Gal. In the early 30s, the group played various stations, before becoming popular with their *Early Morning Jamboree* on WHAS Louisville. It was here, as young Jimmy Dale, that Warren made his debut with his father, singing the occasional solo and standing on a box to play bass fiddle. They moved to WJJD Chicago's *Supper Time Frolics* in 1936 and stayed until the group disbanded in June 1947. During World War II, Warren served with the US Air Force but returned to the group on discharge. Late in 1947, Henry, Wava and Dale, with backing musicians, recorded for Capitol, after which Henry retired. Dale and Wava toured the Midwest being joined by Margie DeVere (Fiddling Kate), whom Dale later married. He formed the Jimmy Dale Quartet, but in 1949, he and Margie moved to California. He first played on the *Hometown Jamboree* with Cliffie Stone before spending a year with Foy Willing's Riders Of The Purple Sage, with whom he recorded and made film appearances. When the Sons Of The Pioneers were seeking a replacement for Ken Curtis, Warren was recommended and joined the group in December 1952, although Curtis remained a part of the radio trio for a further six weeks. Dale Warren, Lloyd Perryman and Tommy Doss made trio recordings for Decca in 1954 and from 1958-67, he appeared on their RCA recordings. When Perryman died in 1977, Warren became the leader of the group. He introduced changes into the group's activities by cutting down on touring and having the group perform a more nostalgic kind of show at large major venues.

WARREN, FIDDLIN' KATE

b. Margie Ann DeVere, 19 January 1922, Grand Junction, Ohio, USA. She made her radio debut with Stuart Hamblen in 1937, while she was studying music at the Hollywood Conservatory. In 1940, Warren continued her studies at Hartnell College, Salinas, California, graduating in 1942. She first played on the *Country Barn Dance* and then, in 1943, she worked as a member of Jimmy Wakely's band. She formed her own band in 1944 but she also played on occasions as a member of Paul Warren's band on the WLS *Barn Dance*. She fronted her own band on the *Renfro Valley Barn Dance* and played on the *Grand Ole Opry* during 1948. Also in the late 40s, she worked with and for a time, was married to Dale Warren. They worked together in the Jimmy Dale Quartet and, on relocating to California, on Cliffie Stone's *Hometown Jamboree*. Between 1952 and 1960, she played the *Ranch Party* with Merle Travis and made show appearances with Joe Maphis and later with Tex Ritter and, in her own right, on *Town Hall Party*. She made her first recordings for King in 1943, later recording solo material for Capitol, Windsor and Columbia Records. She also recorded as a studio musician with various artists, including Rose Lee Maphis. Little seems known of her later years but after her retirement from full-time performing, she apparently continued to make some appearances at special events. Her composition 'Kate Warren Breakdown' is a noted fiddle tune.
● ALBUMS: *Fire On The Strings* (Columbia 1958)★★★★.

WARREN, PAUL

b. Dorris Paul Warren, 17 May 1918, Lyles, Hickman County, Tennessee, USA, d. 12 January 1978. He acquired his interest in the fiddle from his father, who also played banjo, and drew his main inspiration from Fiddlin' Arthur Smith, whom he heard on the *Grand Ole Opry* broadcasts. In 1938, after playing at local dances, he became fiddle player with Johnnie Wright on WSIX Nashville, playing with the Tennessee Mountain Boys at various venues, until he was drafted in September 1942. While serving in the US Army in North Africa, he was captured and spent over two years in a German prisoner-of-war camp. He eventually returned to play with Johnnie And Jack on the *Louisiana Hayride* at Shreveport and on the *Opry*. He played not only on all their recordings made between 1947 and 1953, but also on all those made by Kitty Wells, including her hit 'It Wasn't God Who Made Honky Tonk Angels'. In February 1954, for some reason, he and fiddler Benny Martin exchanged bands and Warren began to play with Flatt And Scruggs. When the duo split in 1969, he continued to play with Flatt in the Nashville Grass until 1977. During those years, he played on hundreds of recordings, appeared on countless radio shows and made

many personal appearances. Ill health caused his retirement and he died in 1978. Although he was undoubtedly one of country and bluegrass music's best fiddlers, he never made any solo studio recordings. This was partly due to the fact that Flatt was not inclined to allow any members of his band to record as solo artists. However, examples of Warren's fiddle playing, taken from live appearances or from radio shows, were later released on a tribute album.
● ALBUMS: *America's Greatest Breakdown Fiddle Player* (CMH 1979)★★★.

WATSON, DALE

b. 7 October 1962, Birmingham, Alabama. An old-fashioned honky tonk performer of the traditional variety, Dale Watson made a major impact in 1995 with the release of his *Cheatin' Heart Attack* debut set for Hightone Records. Growing up in Alabama, he had been introduced to country music by his marine father who ran a small band. His father even released a single, 'Poor Baby', in the late 60s for Chaparral Records. When the family relocated to Pasadena, Texas, Watson began to learn ukulele, then guitar. Together with brothers Jim, who taught him the guitar, and Donny, he formed the Classic Country Band. They worked together for a year before Dale elected to set out on his own. However, he soon tired of playing other artists' material and moved once again to Los Angeles in 1988. There he met John Jorgenson of the Desert Rose Band, who helped to secure Watson a record contract with Curb Records. He released two singles for Curb, 'One Tear At A Time' and 'You Pour It Out, I'll Pour It Down', before the contract collapsed. Watson's problems were then exacerbated by his involvement in a serious car crash. However, after leaving Curb he was offered a publishing agreement with Gary Morris in Nashville. When that too proved an abortive venture, he returned to Los Angeles and appeared alongside River Phoenix in the film *The Thing Called Love*. A promising acting career was foiled by Phoenix's subsequent death, and the ever itinerant Watson moved to Austin. There, he finally managed to secure a contract with Hightone, who released his debut album. Watson's subsequent releases have shown him to be a reliable performer of high-quality honky tonk.
● ALBUMS: *Cheatin' Heart Attack* (Hightone 1995)★★★, *Blessed Or Damned* (Hightone 1996)★★★, *I Hate These Songs* (Hightone 1997)★★★.

WATSON, DOC

b. Arthel L. Watson, 3 March 1923, Stony Fork, near Deep Gap, Watauga County, North Carolina, USA. One of nine children in a farming family, he grew up in a musical environment; his mother, Annie, had a vast knowledge of folk songs and his father, General Dixon, played banjo and led his family in nightly hymn singing. He contracted a serious eye defect as a baby and was blind by the age of two. Owing to family poverty and his blindness, he received no formal schooling until he was 10, when he attended the State School for the Blind at Raleigh. Disliking the treatment he received at the school, he left after only a year and gained much of his later education from talking books and Braille. During his life, Watson has never surrendered to his disability and he attributed his determination to the training he received from his father, who encouraged him to work on the farm and attempt various tasks that at first appeared impossible for a blind person. He played harmonica as a child until, at the age of 11, his father gave him a home-made banjo, reputedly with the head covered by the skin of the recently departed family cat. A year later he obtained his first guitar and quickly mastered the instrument by accompanying recordings by artists such as the Carter Family, Riley Puckett and the Carolina Tar Heels that were played on the family's Victrola and on radio broadcasts from the *Grand Ole Opry*. Soon afterwards, he and his guitar-playing elder brother Linney began playing on street corners. He soon became very proficient in a fingerpicking style of guitar playing, and in 1940, he played at a major fiddlers' convention at Boone. A year later he became a member of a band playing on a radio station in Lenoir, North Carolina, and there acquired the nickname of 'Doc' when an announcer proclaimed that Arthel was far too awkward for radio use (Watson has many times denied an often repeated story that the nickname referred to the Dr. Watson of the Sherlock Holmes stories). In 1947, Watson married Rosa Lee Carlton, the daughter of a noted old-time fiddler, Gaither Carlton, and from his father-in-law he began to amass a considerable repertoire of old-time mountain ballads and tunes. He continued to play with a band but also worked as a piano tuner to assist the family finances. In 1953, at the age of 30, he eventually became a professional musician, when,prompted by his friend, pianist Jack Williams, he changed to an electrified instrument and played lead guitar in a country and western swing band. He stayed with the band for almost eight years, including touring and playing for square dances where, since the band had no fiddler, he played electric guitar lead for the fiddle tunes. During this time he never lost contact with his folk and old-time music roots, and, when commitments permitted, he often played acoustic music with his family and his friend Clarence Tom Ashley, an original member of the Carolina Tar Heels. In the early 60s, the emerging interest in folk music led to Ralph Rinzler recording Ashley; Watson subsequently played banjo and guitar on the sessions. In 1961, Watson, accompanied by Ashley, Clint Howard and Fred Price, played a concert for Friends Of Old Time Music in New York. Watson's performance led to him making his solo debut at Gerde's Folk City, Greenwich Village, the following year, when he also played in Los Angeles with Ashley. In 1963, he made a major impression at the Newport Folk Festival and after his appearance with Bill Monroe at a New York concert, Watson, at the age of 40, found himself a star and in great demand for public appearances. In 1964, his son Merle (b. Eddy Merle Watson, 8 February 1949, d. 23 October 1985) became his rhythm guitarist, chauffeur and road manager (Watson named him after two of his heroes, Eddy Arnold and Merle Travis). In 1964, with Gaither Carlton and other Watson family members, they played the Newport Festival. Watson toured the UK with Rinzler in 1966 (he and Merle also played in London in 1977). In 1968, Doc and Merle toured African countries as part of the State Department's cultural exchange programme. In 1972, Doc made an outstanding contribution to the triple album project *Will The Circle Be Unbroken*, organized by the Nitty Gritty Dirt Band. Watson received Grammy awards in 1973 and 1974 for *Then And Now* and *Two Days In November*. When the interest in folk music declined, Doc, unlike many other artists, found that his popularity was unaffected, and from the mid-70s, he and

Merle, usually accompanied by bass guitarist Michael T. Coleman, continued their hectic touring schedules, flying to many venues in their private aircraft (they were in such great demand that they sometimes played as many as 300 concerts a year). Although content to play as accompanist to his father, Merle was in his own right an excellent flatpicker and slide guitarist and banjo player, and was instrumental in helping his father to become popular with both folk and country audiences. In the early 80s, Merle split his time equally between touring with his father and working as a record producer and session musician. In 1984 he produced his father's *Down South* on Sugar Hill Records. Despite serious hip joint damage (the result of childhood polio), Merle had always managed to keep pace with his father's driving output; however, in 1985 he was killed in an accident, when a tractor overturned on him on the family farm. For a time, Doc cut down on his appearances, but, gradually coming to terms with his loss, he and Coleman resumed touring, with Jack Lawrence taking Merle's place. Doc Watson has become a living legend and a man who, like Ronnie Milsap, has never let his blindness deter him. Fans have even offered him cornea transplants, and when asked what he would have done had he not been blind, he commented that he would probably have been an electrician, although it should be noted that he did once successfully rewire his own house. In 1986, *Doc And Merle*, a film biography, was released and Doc won another Grammy for Best Traditional Folk Recording for *Riding The Midnight Train*. In 1990, he repeated his success with *On Praying Ground*. He has often announced his retirement but in the mid-90s he still records and makes some personal appearances. Over the years, he has recorded numerous solo albums, albums with Merle, and with other artists, including Chet Atkins and Flatt And Scruggs, for various labels. In 1996, a 4-CD compilation set of Watson's Vanguard Records releases, complete with a booklet containing biographical material, was issued, the fourth disc being devoted to previously unissued live festival recordings with Merle.

● ALBUMS: with Clarence Tom Ashley *Old Time Music At Tom Ashley's Volume 1* (Folkways 1961)★★★, with Ashley *Old Time Music At Tom Ashley's Volume 2* (Folkways 1963)★★★, *Doc Watson & Family* (Folkways 1963)★★★, with Jean Ritchie *Jean & Doc At Folk City* (Folkways 1963)★★★, with Roger Sprung *Progressive Bluegrass And Other Instrumentals* (Folkways 1963)★★★, *Doc Watson* (Vanguard 1964)★★★, *Doc Watson & Son* (Vanguard 1965)★★★, *Southbound* (Vanguard 1966)★★★, *Home Again* (Vanguard 1967)★★★, with Flatt And Scruggs *Strictly Instrumental* (Columbia 1967)★★, *Good Deal - Doc Watson In Nashville* (Vanguard 1968)★★★, featuring Merle Watson *Doc Watson On Stage* (Vanguard 1970)★★★, *Ballads From Deep Gap* (Vanguard 1971)★★★, *The Elementary Doc Watson* (Poppy 1972)★★★, *Then And Now* (Poppy 1973)★★★, *The Essential Doc Watson* (Vanguard 1973)★★★, *Two Days In November* (Poppy 1974)★★★, *Doc Watson - Memories* (United Artists 1975)★★★, bootleg of live recordings with Bill Monroe *Bill & Doc Sing Country Songs* (FBN 1975)★★★, *Doc & The Boys* (United Artists 1976)★★★, *Lonesome Road* (United Artists 1977)★★★, *Old Timey Concert* (Vanguard 1977)★★★, *The Watson Family Tradition* (Topic 1977)★★★, *Look Away* (United Artists 1978)★★★, *Live And Pickin'* (United Artists 1979)★★★, with Chet Atkins *Reflections* (RCA 1980)★★★,

The Watson Family Tradition reissue (Rounder 1980)★★★, *Red Rocking Chair* (Flying Fish 1981)★★★, *Favorites* (Liberty 1983)★★★, *Doc & Merle Watson Guitar Album* (Flying Fish 1983)★★★, with Sam Bush, Michael T. Coleman *Down South* (Sugar Hill 1984)★★★, *Pickin' The Blues* (Flying Fish 1985)★★★, *In The Pines* (Sundown 1985)★★★, *Riding The Midnight Train* (Sugar Hill 1986)★★★, *Portrait* (Sugar Hill 1987)★★★, *On Praying Ground* (Sugar Hill 1990)★★★, *Doc Watson Sings Songs For Little Pickers* (Sugar Hill 1990)★★★, *My Dear Old Southern Home* (Sugar Hill 1991)★★★, *Remembering Merle* (Sugar Hill 1992)★★★, *Elementary Doctor Watson* (Sugar Hill 1993)★★★, *Docabilly* (Sugar Hill 1995)★★★, as Doc Watson Family *Tradition* (Rounder 1995).
● COMPILATIONS: *The Best Of Doc Watson* (Vanguard 1973)★★★★, *The Essential Doc Watson* (Vanguard 1986)★★★★, *Then And Now/Two Days In November* CD reissue of United Artists material (Sugar Hill 1994)★★★, *Original Folkways Recordings* (Smithsonian/ Folkways 1994)★★★, *The Vanguard Years* 4-CD box set (Vanguard 1996)★★★★.
● VIDEOS: *Rare Performances 1982-1993* (Vestapol 1995), *Rare Performances 1963-1981* (Vestapol 1995).
● FURTHER READING: *The Songs Of Doc Watson*, Doc Watson.

WATSON, GENE

b. Gary Gene Watson, 11 October 1943, Palestine, Texas, USA. Raised in Paris, Texas, in a musical family, he first worked as a professional at the age of 13. In 1963, he moved to Houston, where he found daytime employment in car engine and bodywork repairs. During the evenings, his vocal style, with its slight nasal sound in the best country tradition, made him a very popular honky-tonk singer around the local clubs, such as the Dynasty, where he was resident for several years. He recorded for several labels including Reeder (whose owner Russ Reeder went on to become his manager and producer), Wide World and Stoneway before gaining his first country chart entry with 'Bad Water' on the Resco label in 1975. The same year, he moved to Capitol Records and had a US Top 10 country hit with the suggestive 'Love In The Hot Afternoon'. Further Top 10 hits followed, including 'Paper Rosie', 'One Sided Conversation', 'Farewell Party', 'Should I Come Home?' and 'Nothing Sure Looked Good On You'. In 1981, after moving to MCA Records, his recording of 'Fourteen Carat Mind' gave him his first US country number 1. He moved to Epic in 1985, gaining a number 5 hit with 'Memories To Burn', but changed to Warner Brothers Records in 1988, where he immediately repeated the success with 'Don't Waste It On The Blues'. Although he charted regularly throughout the 80s, he failed to find another number 1. In 1987, he recorded 'Tempted' with Tammy Wynette, which appears on her *Higher Ground* album. In 1989, Watson enjoyed three chart hits, namely 'Back In The Fire' (number 20), 'The Jukebox Played Along' (number 24) and 'The Great Divide' (number 41). In 1991, *At Last* showed that he had lost none of his ability to render honky tonk songs, with the title track and 'You Can't Take It With You When You Go' attaining Top 70 chart placings. In 1992, he recorded for the Canadian Broadland label, before joining Step One the following year, where he quickly registered a Top 75, with 'One And One And One'. Watson is at his best with sad ballads and with his band, the Farewell Party,

he has become a favourite of George Jones and George Strait. The decision by Lib Hatcher, Randy Travis's manager, to handle Watson's career in the late 80s sparked hopes of a commercial renaissance, but the liaison ended in rancour and talk of litigation. Watson has since released strong albums on the independent label Step One.
● ALBUMS: *Gene Watson* (Stoneway 1971)★★★, *Love In The Hot Afternoon* (Capitol 1975)★★★, *Because You Believed In Me* (Capitol 1976)★★★, *Paper Rosie* (Capitol 1977)★★★, *Beautiful Country* (Capitol 1977)★★★, *Reflections* (Capitol 1978)★★★, *Should I Come Home (Or Should I Go Crazy)* (Capitol 1979)★★★, *No One Will Ever Know* (Capitol 1980)★★★, *Between This Time And Next Time* (MCA 1981)★★★, *Old Loves Never Die* (MCA 1981)★★★, *This Dreams On Me* (MCA 1982)★★★, *Sometimes I Get Lucky* (MCA 1983)★★★, *Little By Little* (MCA 1984)★★★, *Heartaches, Love And Stuff* (MCA 1985)★★★, *Memories To Burn* (Epic 1985)★★★, *Starting New Memories* (Epic 1986)★★★, *Honky Tonk Crazy* (Epic 1987)★★★, *Back In The Fire* (Warners 1989)★★★★, *At Last* (Warners 1991)★★★, *In Other Words* (Mercury/Canada 1992)★★★, *Uncharted Mind* (Step One 1993)★★★, *The Good Ole Days* (Step One 1997)★★★★, *A Way To Survive* (Step One 1998)★★★.
● COMPILATIONS: *Greatest Hits* (MCA 1986)★★★★, *Greatest Hits* (Curb 1990)★★★★.

WELCH, GILLIAN

b. 1968, California, USA. Welch's debut album drew strong acclaim for its revival of Appalachian musical styles and the lyrical evocation of Depression-era rural America. The daughter of Hollywood television composers, Welch attended the Berklee College Of Music in Boston, where she met her musical and songwriting partner David Rawlings. They began playing bluegrass clubs as a duo, gradually incorporating original material into a set consisting of traditional country songs. Moving to Nashville in 1993, they gained a writing contract at Almo-Irving, before Welch signed as a solo artist to Almo Sounds (the new label started by Herb Alpert and Jerry Moss after they sold A&M Records). Produced by T. Bone Burnett, *Revival* (marketed under Welch's name, but essentially a duo album with Rawlings) featured a stellar list of session men including James Burton, Roy Huskey Jnr., Buddy Harmon and Jim Keltner. Beautifully melodic and brutally moral, the songs ranged from the dirty, rockabilly groove of 'Pass You By' to the sparse gospel of 'By The Mark', a surprise favourite on American alternative radio. Though they are often seen as part of the 'alternative country' scene, Welch and Rawlings have supported more mainstream artists such as Mark Knopfler and Emmylou Harris. The latter had provided Welch with her first success when she covered 'Orphan Girl' on her acclaimed *Wrecking Ball* album.
● ALBUMS: *Revival* (Almo 1996)★★★★.

WELCH, KEVIN

b. 17 August 1955, Long Beach, California, USA, although he was raised in Oklahoma. Welch worked as a jobbing songwriter for many years after he moved to Nashville as a teenager. His songs include 'Let It Be You' (Ricky Skaggs), 'Plain Brown Wrapper' (Gary Morris), 'Those Shoes' (Joy Lynn White), 'Time's Up' (Carlene Carter with Southern Pacific), 'Too Old To Die Young' (Moe Bandy) and 'Velvet

Chains' (Gary Morris). After building up a reputation as a good club act, he has recorded his own albums of tough, hard-hitting songs with his band, the Overtones. They were signed to Warner/Reprise in 1988 although it took a further two years for his debut to be released. There is no compromise for radio play with his rough-edged, acoustic-based music, and the nearest comparison is with Steve Earle. Warner/Reprise were uncomfortable with *Western Beat* and would have rather had an album in the Garth Brooks mould. Welch left the label and while touring in Norway with Kieran Kane they hatched a plan to start their own record label, Dead Reckoning. Although Welch is a popular performer, it is as an outstanding songwriter that his reputation must grow, as the cream of contemporary country artists queue up to record his songs.

● ALBUMS: *Kevin Welch* (Reprise 1990)★★, *Western Beat* (Reprise 1992)★★, *Life Down Here On Earth* (Dead Reckoning 1995)★★★.

WELL OILED SISTERS

This five-piece Scottish, lesbian country band was formed in Edinburgh around lead singer, Lucy Edwards. The token heterosexual in the band, Alison Jones, is among the best UK country fiddlers. They appeared in the 1991 film *Blonde Fist*, and their mixture of traditional country with punk haircuts, nose rings and blatant lesbianism goes down well in gay clubs, but such songs as 'Dirty Cowgirls' and 'It Ain't Hard Being Easy' are not suited to the more conservative world of UK country clubs. They walked naked into a Swedish press conference and have also been mistaken for terrorists in Northern Ireland. They more recently appeared with transvestite Lily Savage in a West End stage musical, *Prisoner - Cell Block H*, a camp version of the Australian television series.

● ALBUMS: *Alcohol And Tears* (Cycle 1994)★★★.

WELLER, FREDDY

b. 9 September 1947, Atlanta, Georgia, USA. Weller played guitar and sang at school and was in a group, the Believers, with Joe South. One of his first sessions was for Billy Joe Royal's hit single, 'Down In The Boondocks'. Weller replaced the lead guitarist in the successful 60s pop band Paul Revere And The Raiders. He wrote several songs with Tommy Roe, including his transatlantic number 1, 'Dizzy'. His opportunity to go solo came when a recording session for the Raiders was cancelled and producer Mark Lindsay offered to record Weller on his own. They cut 'Games People Play', which became a US number 2 country hit. Weller had further country hits with 'These Are Not My People', 'Down In The Boondocks' and 'The Promised Land', eventually leaving the Raiders in 1971. His sensual songs were sometimes seen as controversial, notably his song for Bob Luman, 'Lonely Women Make Good Lovers'. His last country hit, a minor one in 1980 called 'Lost In Austin', might explain his absence from the charts.

● ALBUMS: *Games People Play/These Are Not My People* (Columbia 1969)★★★, *Listen To The Young Folks* (Columbia 1970)★★, *The Promised Land* (Columbia 1971)★★★, *Country Collection* (1972)★★★, *Roadmaster* (1972)★★, *Too Much Monkey Business* (1973)★★★, *Sexy Lady* (1974)★★, *Freddy Weller* (ABC 1975)★★★, *Liquor, Love And Life* (1976)★★★, *One Man Show* (1977)★★, *Love Got In The Way*

(Columbia 1978)★★★, *Go For The Night* (Columbia 1980)★★★, *Ramblin' Man* (1982)v.

● COMPILATIONS: *Freddy Weller's Greatest Hits* (RCA 1975)★★★★.

WELLS, HOUSTON, AND THE MARKSMEN

Houston Wells (b. Andrew Smith, 1938, Northumberland, England) left school at 14 years of age and worked in a timber mill. He then became a tree-feller for the Forestry Commission and, after a spell in the merchant navy, worked in a pulp mill in Vancouver, Canada. On returning to England, he and his family moved to Wickford, Essex. In nearby Southend, Pete Willsher (lead guitar, lap steel guitar) had formed a country band, the Coasters, which comprised Brian Gill (bass), Norman Hull (guitar) and Peter Nye (drums). When Wells joined them in 1959, they became Andy Smith And The Coasters. Because of the American group of the same name, the Coasters changed to the Marksmen, while Parlophone Records decided that 'Smith' was too plain, and renamed him Houston Wells. Record producer Joe Meek was impressed with their sound and their first two singles were 'This Song Is Just For You' and 'Shutters And Boards', which was backed by Meek's 'North Wind'. Their third single, 'Only The Heartaches', made the UK Top 30 in August 1963. They recorded further singles, an EP, *Ramona*, and *Western Style*, for Meek. They were particularly popular in Ireland where 'Only The Heartaches' made the Top 10. However, the Marksmen felt that they were being exploited by Wells and his management, and on a trip to Ireland, they tore up Wells' return ticket home in his presence. Wells continued to record using another group, the Outlaws, as the Marksmen. Meek was fascinated by dead performers and so his resident songwriter, Geoff Goddard, wrote a tribute to Jim Reeves, 'We'll Remember You', for Wells. However, Goddard and Meek became embroiled in an argument regarding the credits for 'Have I The Right?', and the song remained unreleased until 1964 when the Honeycombs took the song to the UK number 1 spot and the US Top 5. Wells continued with his Irish success and had a number 6 single in 1966 with 'Above And Beyond'; he also revived 'Hello Mary Lou'. Of the Marksmen, Pete Willsher has become one of the UK's top country steel guitarists. The 28 released tracks that Houston Wells recorded with Joe Meek have never been reissued, largely because of problems with Meek's estate. Once this is resolved, listeners will be able to hear one of the UK's first professional country bands. As it stands, their records are more collectable than many of their American counterparts.

● ALBUMS: *Western Style* (Parlophone 1963)★★.

WELLS, KITTY

b. Muriel Ellen Deason, 30 August 1919, Nashville, Tennessee, USA. The family relocated to Humphries County but returned to Nashville in 1928, where Deason's father, who played guitar and sang for local dances, worked as a brakeman for the Tennessee Central Railroad. She grew up singing in the church choir, learned to play guitar and in 1934, she dropped out of school to work in a local shirt factory. The following year, she teamed with her sisters Mabel and Willie Mae and their cousin, Bessie Choate, to form the singing Deason Sisters. In 1936, they appeared on WSIX Nashville singing 'Jealous Hearted Me', and were cut off in mid-song by the station, who for some reason believed the song to be too risqué for their listeners. The audience disagreed and the girls were given a regular early-morning programme. In 1937, Muriel met aspiring country singer Johnnie Wright and on 30 October that year, the two were married. Soon afterwards, the newlyweds and Wright's sister Louise began appearing on radio station WSIX as Johnnie Wright And The Harmony Girls. In 1939, Wright and Muriel teamed up with Jack Anglin (their future brother-in-law), first appearing as Johnnie Wright And The Happy Roving Cowboys with Jack Anglin, later becoming Johnnie And Jack And The Tennessee Hillbillies, then the Tennessee Mountain Boys. In 1943, Muriel first became known as Kitty Wells. Wright chose the name from an old song popularized on the *Grand Ole Opry* by the Pickard Family and the Vagabonds. Over these years, Wells did not always sing on a regular basis with Wright, due to the fact that, by this time, she had two children, Ruby Wright and Bobby Wright, to look after; a second daughter, Carol Sue Wright, followed. Wells made her first solo recordings for RCA-Victor in 1949, one song being 'Gathering Flowers For The Master's Bouquet', now generally rated to be the first recording, on a major label, of a song that has become a country gospel standard. A further session the next year failed to produce a hit and she left the label. In December 1951, she moved back to Nashville and with Johnnie And Jack becoming members of the *Opry* in January 1952, she decided to retire. However, for the session fee, she had been persuaded by Wright and Paul Cohen of Decca to record a demo of a female answer song to Hank Thompson's then current US country number 1, 'The Wild Side Of Life'. On 3 May 1952, under the production of Owen Bradley, she recorded 'It Wasn't God Who Made Honky Tonk Angels'. Two months later, unaware that it had been released, Kitty Wells found she had recorded a future million-seller. By 8 August, it was beginning a six-week stay at number 1 in the country charts and had become a Top 30 pop hit. The publishers of 'Wild Side Of Life' sued on the grounds that their song's melody had been used. Since both songs had used the tune of the old song 'I'm Thinking Tonight Of My Blue Eyes' and 'The Great Speckled Bird', the case was thrown out of court. The song was the first woman's song in country music and the recording made Kitty Wells country music's first female singing star in her own right, giving her the distinction of becoming the first female country singer to have a number 1 record (initially the *Opry* management felt the lyrics were unsuitable, but an intervention by the influential Roy Acuff saw them relent). Inevitably, Kitty Wells' retirement was shelved and by the end of the 50s, she had registered 35 successive Top 20 country hits, 24 making the Top 10. There were further answer songs in 'Paying For That Back Street Affair', 'Hey Joe' and 'I'll Always Be Your Fraulein', and a less successful one called 'My Cold Cold Heart Is Melted Now'. During this time, as one of several duet hits with Red Foley, 'One By One' became a country number 1 in 1954. She also had Top 10 duets with Webb Pierce, including 'Oh, So Many Years' and 'Finally'. She also recorded with Roy Acuff.

In 1959, Decca took the unusual step of signing her to a lifetime contract. During the 60s, her list of chart hits extended to almost 70 and although only 'Heartbreak USA' (1961) made number 1, there were 11 more that made the Top 10. These included 'Left To Right' and 'Unloved Unwanted'. The

hits slowed down during the 70s, the last two coming in 1979 and taking her total to 81 in all. From the 50s through to the end of the 70s, she toured extensively, making personal appearances not only in the USA and Canada but all over the world. After Jack Anglin's death in 1963, Johnny Wright toured with his wife and family as the Kitty Wells And Johnny Wright Family Show. In 1969, they hosted a syndicated television show that ran for many years. In the early 70s, she severed her connections with Decca (by then MCA Records) and signed with Capricorn where, backed by some of the Allman Brothers Band, she recorded *Forever Young* (the title track was a Bob Dylan song - a daring move for a traditional country singer at the time). She made her first appearance in Britain at the 1974 Wembley Festival. She also continued to record for several minor labels, including in 1989, two albums for Step One with Owen Bradley, the man who had produced her million-seller at Decca 37 years previously. Over the years she has won many awards, including being voted *Billboard*'s Female Country Artiste from 1953 to 1965, but her greatest award came in 1976, when she was elected to the Country Music Hall Of Fame in Nashville. The plaque noted: 'In true country tradition her sincere vocal stylings convey the real feeling of the songs, be they happy or sad'. Many of her hits were country weepies such as 'Mommy For A Day', 'I Gave My Wedding Dress Away', 'This White Circle On My Finger' and 'I Hope My Divorce Is Never Granted'. There is little doubt that her successes opened the way for many subsequent female country music singers. In 1952, Kitty Wells was named the Queen Of Country Music by Fred Rose and in the opinions of country traditionalists, she still holds her title with dignity and sincerity. She has, as country historian Bill C. Malone noted, 'preserved an image of wholesomeness and domesticity that was far removed from the world she often sang about'.

● ALBUMS: *Country Hit Parade* (Decca 1956)★★★, *Winner Of Your Heart* (Decca 1956)★★★★, *Dust On The Bible* (Decca 1959)★★★, *After Dark* (Decca 1959)★★★, *Kitty's Choice* (Decca 1960)★★★★, with Red Foley *Kitty Wells & Red Foley's Greatest Hits* (Decca 1961)★★★, *Heartbreak USA* (Decca 1961)★★★★, *Queen Of Country Music* (Decca 1962)★★★, *Singing On Sunday* (Decca 1962)★★★, *Christmas With Kitty Wells* (Decca 1962)★★, *Especially For You* (Decca 1964)★★★★, *Country Music Time* (Decca 1964)★★★, *Burning Memories* (Decca 1965)★★★, *Lonesome, Sad & Blue* (Decca 1965)★★★★, *Kitty Wells Family Gospel Sing* (Decca 1965)★★, *Lonely Street* (Decca 1966)★★★★, *Songs Made Famous By Jim Reeves* (Decca 1966)★★★, *Country All The Way* (Decca 1966)★★★, *The Kitty Wells' Show* (Decca 1966)★★, *Kitty Wells* (Vocalion 1966)★★★, *Love Makes The World Go Round* (Decca 1967)★★★★, with Foley *Together Again* (Decca 1967)★★★, *Queen Of Honky Tonk Street* (Decca 1967)★★★, *Kitty Wells' Showcase* (Decca 1968)★★★, with Johnnie Wright *We'll Stick Together* (Decca 1968)★★★, *Country Heart* (Vocalion 1969)★★★★, *Singing 'Em Country* (Decca 1970)★★★, *Your Love Is The Way* (Decca 1970)★★★, *Pledging My Love* (Decca 1971)★★★, *They're Stepping All Over My Heart* (Decca 1971)★★★, *I've Got Yesterday* (Decca 1972)★★★, *Sincerely* (Decca 1972)★★★, with Wright *Heartwarming Gospel Songs* (Decca 1972)★★★, *Yours Truly* (1973)★★★, *Forever Young* (1974)★★★.

● COMPILATIONS: *Kitty Wells' Golden Favourites* (Decca 1961)★★★, *The Kitty Wells Story* (Decca 1963)★★★, *Cream*

Of Country Hits (Decca 1968)★★★, *Bouquet Of Country Hits* (Decca 1969)★★★★, *Hall Of Fame, Volume 1* (1979)★★★, *Early Classics* (1981)★★★, *The Kitty Wells Story* (MCA 1986)★★★, *The Golden Years 1949-1957* 5-album box set (Bear Family 1987)★★★★, *Greatest Hits Volume 1* (Step One 1989)★★★★, *Greatest Hits Volume 2* (Step One 1989)★★★★, *Country Music Hall Of Fame Series* (MCA 1991)★★★★, *The Queen Of Country Music* 4-CD box set (Bear Family 1993)★★★★, *Kitty Wells Duets* (Pair 1996)★★★.
● FURTHER READING: *Queen Of Country Music: The Life Story Of Kitty Wells*, A.C. Dunkleburger. *Kitty Wells: The Golden Years*, Pinson, Weize & Wolfe. *The Honky Tonk Angels: A Dual Biography*, Walt Trott.

WERNER, SUSAN

b. Manchester, Iowa, USA. One of the more eclectic of contemporary country music's rising stars, Susan Werner conversely boasts outstanding honky tonk credentials - she was born and raised on a hog farm, though her surname derived from her father's German background. By the age of 11 she had begun playing saxophone, later appearing in jazz and marching bands during high school. She took a degree in voice before moving to Philadelphia in 1987 to study for an MA. However, her original intention to pursue a professional career as an opera singer was abandoned after she attended a Nanci Griffith concert at the end of the decade. With new resolve, Werner began to perform as a solo act on the local coffee bar circuit, her set initially comprising cabaret standards. She soon began writing her own compositions, inspired increasingly by folk and country music, eventually making a breakthrough appearance at the Philadelphia Folk Festival in 1992. She independently financed her debut album, *Midwestern Saturday Night*, the following year, which brought together nine of her own compositions and one cover version, Greg Simon's 'The Great Out There'. Among the more astute lyrics was 'Born A Little Late', a pastiche on the baby-boom generation - 'they sit around the campfire singing the Beatles and the Byrds, and they laugh at me 'cause I don't know the words.' 'Rubber Glove Blues', meanwhile, addressed safe sex - hardly a standard subject for a country artist, even in the 90s. It was followed by a live set recorded at the Tin Angel in Philadelphia over three nights, which featured a 15-song repertoire. Subsequently featured on compilations issued by New York's *Fast Folk Magazine* and the *Martha's Vineyard Singer/Songwriters Retreat*, her profile rose steadily. Eventually, this resulted in a move to Private Music for March 1995's *Last Of The Good Straight Girls*. Produced by Fernando Saunders, guest musicians included Marshall Crenshaw and k.d. lang, and Dave Alvin associate Greg Liesz on mandolin and pedal steel guitar.
● ALBUMS: *Midwestern Saturday Night* (Golden Guru 1993)★★★, *Live At Tin Angel* (Golden Guru 1993)★★, *Last Of The Good Straight Girls* (Private Music 1995).

WEST, DOTTIE

b. Dorothy Marie Marsh, 11 October 1932, McMinnville, Tennessee, USA, d. 4 September 1991. The eldest of 10 children, West worked the cotton and sugar cane crops on the family farm as well as looking after her younger siblings. Country music was popular with her parents and she first learned to play guitar from her father. She completed a college education and graduated with a music degree. During her college days she sang at various events and met and married Bill West, an electronics engineering student, who later became a noted country steel guitarist and her manager (the marriage produced four children, including country singer Shelly West, and lasted until 1969). They moved to Cleveland in the mid-50s, where they both appeared regularly on the *Landmark Jubilee* television show. They moved to Nashville in 1959, where Dottie was befriended by Patsy Cline and briefly joined Starday and Atlantic Records. In 1962, at the recommendation of Jim Reeves, Chet Atkins signed her to RCA Records. Her first US country chart hit, 'Let Me Off At The Corner', was in 1963, the same year that the first song she wrote, 'Is This Me', became a number 3 country hit for Jim Reeves. The following year a duet with Reeves, 'Love Is No Excuse', was a country Top 10 hit as well as a minor pop chart entry. A country Top 10 solo hit of her own song, 'Here Comes My Baby', followed, which so successfully launched her career that between 1964-84, she charted a further 60 US country hits. The following year, she was the first female country singer to win a Grammy. In the late 60s, she had country hits with 'Would You Hold It Against Me', 'Paper Mansions', 'Country Girl' (which became a successful Coca-Cola advert), 'Reno' and duet recordings with Don Gibson, including a number 2 country hit with 'Rings Of Gold'. Her ability to sing country tear-jerkers was adequately shown with such numbers as 'Mommy, Can I Still Call Him Daddy' (which even featured her four-year-old son Dale). She recorded with Jimmy Dean in the early 70s, and in 1973 she had further major success with commercials for Coca-Cola, which featured her own award-winning song 'Country Sunshine' and led to her nickname of the 'Country Sunshine Girl'.

She left RCA in 1976 and in 1980 she had number 1 country hits with 'A Lesson In Leavin'' and 'Are You Happy?' on the United Artists label. In the mid-70s, she married her band's drummer Byron Metcalf, but they later divorced in 1980. Between 1979 and 1981 she registered three country number 1 duet recordings alongside Kenny Rogers with 'Every Time Two Fools Collide', 'All I Ever Need Is You' and 'What Are We Doin' In Love?'. She won many solo awards and in 1978 and 1979 she and Rogers were voted the Country Music Association Vocal Duo of the Year. She appeared in two films, *Second Fiddle To An Old Guitar* and *There's A Still On The Hill*, and has played the *Grand Ole Opry* regularly since first becoming a member in 1964. Between 1981 and 1985, she registered some minor hits on Liberty and Permian but only 'It's High Time' and 'Together Again' (another duet with Kenny Rogers) made the US country Top 20. In 1991, she was declared bankrupt and many of her possessions were auctioned off to pay an Inland Revenue Service debt of almost $1 million. On Friday 30 August 1991, due to problems with her own car, she asked an 81-year-old neighbour to drive her to the *Opry* for her scheduled appearance. His car crashed at speed when it left the ramp to the *Opry* car park, vaulted in the air and hit the central division. Both occupants were rushed to the Vanderbilt Medical Centre in a critical condition. Dottie West suffered a severe rupture of the liver and, in spite of several operations, surgeons could not control the bleeding. Although fully aware of the extent of her injuries, she was unable to speak and sadly died a few days later on 4 September. During her career she toured extensively, played all the major network television shows and was popular in Europe where she appeared on several occasions.

● ALBUMS: *Country Girl Singing Sensation* (Starday 1964)★★★, *Here Comes My Baby* (RCA Victor 1965)★★★, shared with Melba Montgomery *Queens Of Country Music* (Starday 1965)★★★, *Dottie West Sings* (RCA Victor 1966)★★★, *Suffer Time* (RCA Victor 1966)★★★★, *I'll Help You Forget Her* (RCA Victor 1967)★★★, *Sings Sacred Ballads* (RCA Victor 1967)★★★, *The Sound Of Country Music* (RCA Victor 1967)★★★, *With All My Heart And Soul* (RCA Victor 1967)★★★, *Country Girl* (RCA Victor 1968)★★★, *What I'm Cut Out To Be* (RCA Victor 1968)★★★, *I Fall To Pieces* (RCA Victor 1969)★★★, *Sings Eddy Arnold* (RCA Victor 1969)★★★, with Don Gibson *Dottie & Don* (RCA Victor 1969)★★★, *Feminine Fancy* (RCA Victor 1969)★★★, *Making Memories* (RCA Victor 1970)★★★, *Making Believe* (RCA Victor 1970)★★★, *Forever Yours* (RCA Victor 1970)★★, *Country And West* (RCA Victor 1970)★★★, with Jimmy Dean *Country Boy And Country Girl* (RCA Victor 1970)★★, *A Legend In My Time* (RCA Victor 1971)★★★, *Have You Heard* (RCA Victor 1971)★★★, *Careless Hands* (RCA Victor 1971)★★★, *I'm Only A Woman* (RCA Victor 1972)★★★, *Country Sunshine* (RCA Victor 1973)★★★★, *Would You Hold It Against Me* (RCA Victor 1973)★★★, *Dottie* (RCA Victor 1973)★★★, *Dottie West* (RCA Victor 1973)★★★, *House Of Love* (RCA Victor 1974)★★★, *If It's All Right With You/Just What I've Been Looking For* (RCA Victor 1974)★★★, *Loving You* (RCA Victor 1974)★★★, *Carolina Cousins* (RCA Victor 1975)★★, *When It's Just You And Me* (1977)★★, with Kenny Rogers *Every Time Two Fools Collide* (United Artists 1978)★★★★, with Rogers *Classics* (United Artists 1979)★★, *Special Delivery* (United Artists 1979)★★★, *Go For The Night* (United Artists 1980)★★★, *Wild West* (Liberty 1981)★★★, *Once You Were Mine* (Liberty 1981)★★★, *High Times* (Liberty 1981)★★★, *Full Circle* (Liberty 1982)★★★, *New Horizons* (Liberty 1983)★★, with Rogers *Duets* (Liberty 1984)★★★, *Just Dottie* (1984)★★.

● COMPILATIONS: *The Best Of Dottie West* (1973)★★★★, *Twenty Of The Best* (1986)★★★★, *Essential Dottie West* (RCA 1996)★★★★.

● FURTHER READING: *Country Sunshine - The Dottie West Story*, Judy Berryhill and Frances Meeker.

WEST, SHELLY

b. 23 May 1958, Cleveland, Ohio, but raised in Nashville, Tennessee, USA. The daughter of country singer Dottie West, it seemed natural that she should follow her mother into showbusiness. After completing her high school education in 1975, she sang backing harmonies for her mother. In 1977, she married Allen Frizzell (Lefty and David Frizzell's youngest brother), who was her mother's bandleader. They moved to California, where they joined David Frizzell and played the club circuits over several states. She began to sing with David and in 1981 charted a US country number 1 with 'You're The Reason God Made Oklahoma', which featured in the Clint Eastwood film *Any Which Way You Can*. Further country Top 10 hits followed, including 'A Texas State Of Mind' and 'I Just Came Here To Dance'. In 1982, their duet 'Please Surrender' was used by Eastwood in his film *Honky Tonk Man*. In 1983, she had a solo US country number 1 with 'Jose Cuervo' and further solo hits with 'Flight 309 To

Tennessee' and 'Another Motel Memory'. A further Top 20 duet hit, 'It's A Be Together Night' with David Frizzell, followed in 1984. She was divorced in 1985 and her career seems to have slowed down, with no chart hits since 1986.

● ALBUMS: *Red Hot* (Viva 1983)★★★, *West By West* (Warners/Viva 1983)★★★, *Don't Make Me Wait On The Moon* (Warners/Viva 1985)★★★; with David Frizzell *Carrying On The Family Names* (Warners 1981)★★★, *Our Best To You* (Viva 1982)★★★, *In Session* (Viva 1983)★★★, *Golden Duets* (Viva 1984)★★★★.

WHEELER, BILLY EDD

b. 9 December 1932, Whitesville, West Virginia, USA. He grew up in coalmining camps and his song 'Coal Tattoo', which was recorded by Judy Collins, is based on what he saw around him. He collected folk songs himself and elements of both folk and country music can be heard in his songwriting. He performed with his guitar at school and college events, was in the US navy from 1957-58 and then became a schoolteacher. In 1958 his rock 'n' roll version of 'The Boll Weevil Song', which he called 'Rock Boll Weevil', was recorded by Pat Boone. He performed folk songs with the Lexington Symphony Orchestra in 1961, and then became a full-time professional performer. 'Rev. Mr Black', a narrative song about a travelling preacher, made the US Top 10 for the Kingston Trio in 1963, and they followed it with the story of 'Desert Pete'. Wheeler himself had a solo US hit with a song about an outside toilet, 'Ode To The Little Brown Shack Out Back'. His 1967 composition, 'Jackson', was successful for the duos Johnny Cash and June Carter, and Nancy Sinatra and Lee Hazlewood. Other compositions include 'Blistered' (Johnny Cash), 'Blue Roses' and 'The Man Who Robbed The Bank At Santa Fe' (both Hank Snow). His *Nashville Zodiac* album was made with Doug Kershaw and includes three Kershaw compositions. Wheeler continues to perform and says, 'I can't bear to think how empty my life would have been without my guitar.' His biggest success has proved to be co-writing Kenny Rogers 1980 hit single 'Coward Of The County'. He is also an acclaimed poet and playwright.

● ALBUMS: *Billy Edd: USA* (Monitor 1961)★★★, with the Bluegrass Singers and the Berea Three *Billy Edd And Bluegrass Too* (Monitor 1962)★★★, *New Bag Of Songs* (Kapp 1964)★★★, *Memories Of America/Ode To The Little Brown Shack Out Back* (Kapp 1965)★★★★, *The Wheeler Man* (Kapp 1965)★★★, *Goin' Town And Country* (Kapp 1966)★★★, *Paper Birds* (Kapp 1967)★★★, *I Ain't The Worrying Kind* (Kapp 1968)★★★, *Nashville Zodiac* (1969)★★★, with Shelly Manne *Young Billy Young* film soundtrack (1969)★★, *Billy Edd Wheeler - Love* (1971)★★★, *The Music Of Billy Edd Wheeler* (1973)★★★, *Wild Mountain Flowers* (Flying Fish 1979)★★.

WHEELER, CHERYL

b. 10 July 1951, Baltimore, Maryland, USA. Wheeler was raised in Timonium, Maryland, and has been playing guitar since she was 10 years old. One of her first jobs was singing in a restaurant and working as a waitress - at the same time. In the late 70s, she was a familiar figure in the Newport folk clubs. Her first album was produced by singer-songwriter Jonathan Edwards and she played bass and sang harmony in his road band. That album also features the Saddle Sores, a vocal group led by Mary-Chapin Carpenter. Wheeler's sister told her about her love life ('I'm addicted to a bad thing'), which prompted the song 'Addicted', a US country number 1 for Dan Seals. Since then, Juice Newton has recorded 'I'm Only Walking', Maura O'Connell 'Summer Fly', Suzy Bogguss both 'Aces' (another US country hit) and 'Don't Wanna', and Christine Lavin both 'On A Winter's Night' and 'When Fall Comes To New England'. Wheeler is a witty concert performer and her songs include the zany 'TV' and the grim humour of 'Estate Sale', which shows the poignancy of her work. She appeared in the UK at the 1991 Cambridge Folk Festival. Usually she writes alone but 'Orbiting Jupiter' on *Driving Home* was written with Janis Ian.

● ALBUMS: *Cheryl Wheeler* (North Star 1986)★★, *Half A Book* (Cypress 1990)★★★, *Circles And Arrows* (Capitol 1991)★★★, *Driving Home* (Philo 1993)★★★, *Mrs. Pinocci's Guitar* (Philo 1995)★★★.

WHEELER, ONIE

b. Onie Daniel Wheeler, 10 November 1921, Senath, Missouri, USA, d. 26 May 1984. Wheeler was a country singer whose career lasted for nearly 40 years, although only one single charted in the USA. Wheeler won a talent contest while serving in the armed forces during World War II and, upon leaving the service in 1945, he chose to pursue a singing career. He performed on a number of southern radio stations in Missouri, Arkansas and Kentucky, and moved to Michigan in 1948, where he made his first recordings for the tiny Agana label. Wheeler and his singing partner and wife Betty Jean went back to Missouri in 1952 and performed a stint on radio station KSIM in addition to performing in clubs. Continuing to move from one location to another, Wheeler was finally signed to OKeh Records in 1953 and released numerous singles for that label and then its parent, Columbia Records, fusing honky-tonk country and gospel styles. Although he did not quite perform in the rockabilly style, his up-tempo bop found him sharing billings with artists such as Elvis Presley and Jerry Lee Lewis. At the end of his Columbia contract in 1957, Wheeler recorded a number of tracks at the Sun Records studios in Memphis, which were not released for another two years. Further moves saw him relocate to California and back to St. Louis, Missouri, where he recorded for small labels into the early 60s. A 1962 session for Epic Records featured a duet between Wheeler and his daughter Karen. Working as a member of George Jones's roadshow, Wheeler recorded for United Artists Records and Musicor Records in 1964-65, after which he left Jones to join Roy Acuff's show. Wheeler gained his only placement on the country charts, 'John's Been Shucking My Corn', in 1971, on Royal American Records. After that, the recordings dwindled and Wheeler repaired guitars at home, although he continued to tour sporadically in Europe and Asia. He underwent an operation on an aneurysm in January 1984 and died onstage at the *Grand Ole Opry* in May 1984.

● ALBUMS: *John's Been Shucking My Corn* (Onie 1971)★★★, *Something New And Something Old* (1975)★★.

● COMPILATIONS: *Onie's Bop* (Bear Family 1991)★★★.

WHEELING JAMBOREE, THE

One of country music's oldest and most popular radio shows, it was instrumental in popularizing country music to many listeners, especially those in the north-eastern part of the USA and eastern Canada. It was first broadcast, live at midnight, from the Capitol theatre, Wheeling, West Virginia, by WWVA, on 7 January 1933. WWVA, created in 1926, began to promote country music presented by local artists in the studio, and the *Jamboree* was the result of listeners' demand for the music. Early stars included Cowboy Loye, Cap, Andy And Flip, Hugh And Shug's Radio Pals (Hugh Cross and Shug Fisher) and, in May 1937, arguably the best-known and longest-serving members of the cast, Doc Williams and his wife Chickie arrived. WWVA's output increased to 50,000 Watts, in October 1942, which meant the signals were then heard over a larger area. In January 1943, because of World War II, the live show was discontinued and a studio-based *Jamboree* substituted until the end of the war. The live shows, broadcast this time from the Virginia theatre, resumed in June 1946 and proved such a major attraction that, within six months, a million people had paid to see the show. Like the *Grand Ole Opry* and the *Louisiana Hayride*, the *Jamboree* organized tours for its artists to advertise the show. Major stars still included the Williams, Big Slim, the Lone Cowboy and Wilma Lee And Stoney Cooper, but there was also a regular turnover of other artists, many using the station as a stepping stone to the *Opry*. From around 1955, CBS networked a part of the show every third week. In 1962, the Virginia theatre was demolished and the show moved to the Rex theatre, where it remained until 1966; it was then relocated at the Wheeling Island Exhibition Centre, and featured stars that included Jim Eanes, Red Smiley, Dick Curless and the Williams. The programme was renamed *Jamboree USA* and moved again in 1969, this time back to the Capitol theatre, where it had started 36 years earlier. In 1983, the show reached its fiftieth birthday and although, in its present form, it mainly features guest artists rather than producing its own stars, it is still going strong.

WHITE, BRYAN

b. 17 February 1974, Whitesville, West Virginia, USA. One of the most successful new country acts of the 90s, four of White's first eight singles topped the US country charts. A major factor in his breakthrough was the songwriting of Skip Ewing, who provided the hits 'Rebecca Lynn', 'I'm Not Supposed To Love You Anymore' and 'Someone Else's Star' for White. Although both White's first two albums sold well, more interesting was his third effort, *The Right Place*. This saw him attempt to develop his own vision, rather than rely on a team of writers to frame his points of reference and image. As he told *Billboard* magazine in 1997, 'Obviously, I sang every song on the album, but I also got to do a lot of percussive and background vocal stuff that I've never had time to do.' Although Ewing was on hand to co-compose 'Leave My Heart Out Of This' and 'Tree Of Hearts', new collaborators, including friend and guitarist Derek George, also provided material ('A Bad Day To Let You Go' and 'Never Get Around To It'). Steve Wariner, a long-time idol of White's, also provided one of the songs, 'One Small Miracle'. With Asylum Records launching the biggest marketing campaign in the company's history to help push sales, *The Right Place* looked set to take White into the first rank of Nashville stars.

●ALBUMS: *Bryan White* (Asylum 1995)★★★, *Between Now And Forever* (Asylum 1996)★★★★, *The Right Place* (Asylum 1997)★★★★.

WHITE, BUCK

b. 13 December 1930, Oklahoma, USA. H.C. White grew up in Wichita Falls, Texas. He named himself Buck because of his love of the cowboy film star Buck Jones. He had roots in western swing music and played piano on the original recording of Slim Willet's 'Don't Let The Stars Get In Your Eyes' in 1952. He played piano in various western swing bands and as a sideman to visiting country stars in the Wichita Falls area, where his daughters, Sharon (b. 17 December 1953) and Cheryl (b. 27 January 1955), were born. In 1962 the family settled in Greenwood, Arkansas, and White became involved in bluegrass music for the first time, forming the Down Home Folks with his wife and their friends, Arnold and Peggy Johnston. The children of the two families worked together as the Down Home Kids. In 1967, working as Buck White And The Down Home Folks, the family group consisted of Buck, his wife Pat and their daughters Cheryl and Sharon. Following a successful impromptu performance at Bill Monroe's Beanblossom Festival in 1971, they moved to Nashville to further their career. Pat retired from the group in 1973 and they developed a clean-cut sound around Cheryl and Sharon's distinctive harmonies, Buck's mandolin playing and Jerry Douglas's dobro. A short-lived contract with Capitol Records in 1982 led to a single on the US country charts as the Whites, 'Send Me The Pillow That You Dream On', and they had their first US country Top 10 entry with 'You Put The Blue In Me'. Emmylou Harris invited them to be the opening act for the tour to support *Blue Kentucky Girl*, which featured Cheryl and Sharon's harmonies. Ricky Skaggs, who married Sharon in 1981, produced *Whole New World*, and Buck White played piano on Skaggs' number 1 country hit 'Crying My Heart Out Over You'. The Whites have appeared on numerous sessions, but their own US country hits include 'Hangin' Around', 'I Wonder Who's Holding My Baby Tonight', 'Pins And Needles', 'If It Ain't Love (Let's Leave It Alone)' and 'Hometown Gossip'.

● ALBUMS: As Buck White And The Down Home Folks *Buck White And The Down Home Folks* (County 1972)★★★, *Live At The Old Time Pickin' Parlour* (1975)★★, *That Down Home Feeling* (Ridge Runner 1975)★★★★, *Poor Folks Pleasure* (1978)★★★. Buck White solo *More Pretty Girls Than One* (Sugar Hill 1979)★★★★. As the Whites *Old Familiar Feeling* (1983)★★★, *Forever You* (MCA/Curb 1984)★★★, *Whole New World* (1986)★★★, *Doing It By The Book* (Canaan 1989)★★.

● COMPILATIONS: *Greatest Hits* (Curb 1987)★★★★.

WHITE, CLARENCE

b. 7 June 1944, Lewiston, Maine, USA, d. 14 July 1973. White started playing acoustic guitar and singing in a bluegrass group with his brothers when only 10 years old, and the group materialized into the Kentucky Colonels in 1961. After leaving the Kentucky Colonels, he switched to electric guitar and became a session musician, playing on albums by Randy Newman and Linda Ronstadt. He joined Nashville West in 1968, and then the Byrds, whose line-up was Roger McGuinn, Gene Parsons, and John York, who was subsequently replaced by Skip Battin. White is featured on the (untitled) album and on the hit single 'Chestnut Mare'. He still worked on sessions, including the Everly Brothers' superb 'I'm On My Way Home Again'. The Byrds flew the coop in 1973 and White re-formed the Kentucky Colonels to play Los Angeles clubs and also to tour Europe. He worked on albums by Maria Muldaur and Gene Parsons and also began his solo album, although only four tracks were recorded. He was knocked down and killed while loading equipment after a show on 14 July 1973. What there is of his solo album was included on the compilation on Sierra Briar Records, *Silver Meteor*.

● VIDEOS: *Muleskinner - Live The Video* (1991).

WHITE, JOHN I.

b. John Irwin White, 1902, Washington DC, USA, d. 1992. After spending a holiday on an Arizona ranch, White developed a love of things Western. He abandoned his clarinet, learned the guitar and took to singing cowboy songs. He relocated to New York and in 1926, he was offered an unpaid spot on WEAF, but soon moved to a paid one on WOR. He supported himself by working for General Drafting Company, a map-making concern, with whom he stayed for almost 40 years. His singing was what he termed 'a moonlighting operation'. He sang with a quartet as the Lone Star Rangers but soon went solo to become the Lonesome Cowboy. In 1929, he published a songbook, *The Lonesome Cowboy: Songs Of Plains And Hills*. In 1930, he became a singer and narrator for the network radio show *Death Valley Days*, which was sponsored by Pacific Coast Borax Company. The show ran until 1941, but because of his day-time work, White left in 1936 (it was later revived as a television show in 1951). A further songbook, *Cowboy Songs As Sung By John White, 'The Lonesome Cowboy' In Death Valley Days*, appeared in 1934. (The west coast's time difference also meant that the show was broadcast in San Francisco, using the same script but different actors, and with Charles Marshall billed as the Lonesome Cowboy.) White became very popular and although some critics commented that 'he was neither lonesome nor is he a cowboy', or 'instead of spurs he wears spats', their reviews were mostly very favourable. He finally retired from the map company in September 1965, to become a freelance writer of magazine articles on songs of the west, and he also returned to singing. White had made his first recordings for ARC in 1931 but in 1973, he recorded 17 songs that were released on cassette. White died in 1992 but his vast collection of material, gathered during his many years of research, is available for examination at the Utah State University in Logan. While his actual recordings may be hard to find, White left an informative and interesting collection of articles about the song makers in his book *Git Along, Little Dogies: Songs And Songmakers Of The American West*, which was published by the University of Illinois Press in 1975.

● ALBUMS: *Songs Of The American West* cassette only (1973)★★★.

WHITE, JOY LYNN

b. Turrell, Arkansas, USA, but raised in Mishawaka, Indiana. Her parents were amateur musicians and encouraged Joy, who knew Dolly Parton songs before she could read, in her love of music. Taking Linda Ronstadt as a role model, White was in local bands as a teenager and she recorded jingles and beer store commercials. She moved to Nashville when only 19 years old with $200 and a dilapidated car. She recorded a demo for songwriter Mike Henderson, and 'Mr Man In The Moon' became a country hit for Patty Loveless.

Henderson wrote several tracks on White's debut, *Between Midnight And Hindsight*, issued by Columbia as Joy White. It was impressive but none of the singles, 'Little Texas', 'True Confessions' (written by Marty Stuart and featuring his guitar) and 'Cold Day In July', were big US country singles. Her second album includes backing vocals from Hal Ketchum and Nanci Griffith. Highway 101 have recorded her song 'Big City Bound'. *The Lucky Few*, produced by Pete Anderson, was a disappointing collection.

● ALBUMS: *Between Midnight And Hindsight* (Columbia 1992)★★★, *Wild Love* (Columbia 1994)★★★, *The Lucky Few* (Little Dog/Mercury 1997)★★.

WHITE, TONY JOE

b. 23 July 1943, Oak Grove, Louisiana, USA. A country singer and songwriter, White was also tagged with the label 'swamp rock', a musical genre he helped to create. Originally he was a member of Tony And The Mojos before defecting to Texas to start Tony And The Twilights. He started recording in 1968 and many people presumed he was black after hearing his layered vocals. He had his first hit single on Monument with 'Polk Salad Annie' in 1969, later covered by Elvis Presley. Also contained on his debut *Black And White* was 'Willie And Laura Mae Jones', which was covered by Dusty Springfield. After succeeding once more with 'Groupie Girl', he wrote 'Rainy Night In Georgia', which became a standard. His first three albums were produced by Billy Swan, and Cozy Powell drummed for him at the 1970 Isle Of Wight festival. He moved to Warner Brothers Records in 1971 and had a hit in 1979 with 'Mamas Don't Let Your Cowboys Grow Up To Be Babies', an answer record to Ed Bruce's country chart-topper of the previous year, 'Mamas Don't Let Your Babies Grow Up To Be Cowboys'. White co-wrote 'Steamy Windows' with Tina Turner, which gave her a Top 20 UK hit in 1990. White is an artist who refuses to compromise; however, his most recent albums (*Decent Groove* and *Lake Placid Blues*) indicate a man totally at peace with himself.

● ALBUMS: *Black And White* (Monument 1969)★★★, *Continued* (Monument 1969)★★★, *Tony Joe* (Monument 1970)★★★★, *Tony Joe White* (Warners 1971)★★★★, *The Train I'm On* (Warners 1972)★★★, *Home Made Ice Cream* (Warners 1973)★★★, *Eyes* (20th Century 1977)★★, *Real Thing* (Casablanca 1980)★★, *Dangerous* (Columbia 1983)★★★, *Roosevelt And Ira Lee* (Astan 1984)★★★, *Live!* (Dixie Frog 1990)★★★, *Closer To The Truth* (Swamp 1992)★★★, *The Path Of A Decent Groove* (1993)★★★, *Lake Placid Blues* (Remark 1995)★★★.

● COMPILATIONS: *The Best Of Tony Joe White* (Warners 1979)★★★★, *Polk Salad Annie: The Best Of Tony Joe White* (Warner Archive 1994)★★★★.

● FILMS: *Catch My Soul* (1974).

WHITES

(see White, Buck)

WHITLEY, KEITH

b. 1 July 1955, Sandy Hook, Kentucky, USA, d. 8 May 1989, Goodlettsville, Tennessee, USA. Whitley, who grew up in a musical family, learned to play the guitar from the age of six and was on the radio with Buddy Starcher in Charleston, West Virginia, aged eight. He joined Ralph Stanley And His Clinch Mountain Boys when he was 15, and both he and his

friend Ricky Skaggs made their recording debut on the same record, *Cry From The Cross*. At the age of 17, he survived a 120 mph car crash that killed a friend, and at 19, he drove a car off a cliff into a river. Whitley joined J.D. Crowe And The New South and his lead vocals on *Somewhere Between* were appreciated in Nashville. In 1983 he signed with RCA Records, recorded a mini-album, *A Hard Act To Follow*, and had his first US country success with 'Turn Me To Love' in 1984. He had further successes with 'I've Got The Heart For You' and 'Miami, My Amy'. Whitley's excessive drinking made him unreliable, but it did give him a hardened, honky-tonk voice, and he then only needed the right song. Unfortunately, his version of 'Does Fort Worth Ever Cross Your Mind?' was never released and 'On The Other Hand' was only an album track. He found what he needed in 'Don't Close Your Eyes', which was a number 1 US country single in 1988, with the resulting album selling over half a million copies. The song was inspired by the film *California Suite*. Whitley had another country number 1 with 'When You Say Nothing At All', and his version of Lefty Frizzell's 'I Never Go Around Mirrors' includes an additional verse by its co-writer, Whitey Shaffer, and harmonies from Frizzell's brother Allen. In 1986 he married Lorrie Morgan, the daughter of country singer George Morgan, and a performer in her own right. Whitley recovered from his alcoholism and the couple started a family. In 1989 he had a US country number 1 with a Sonny Curtis song, 'I'm No Stranger To The Rain', but he subsequently returned to drinking, which resulted in his death at his home in Goodlettsville, Tennessee, in 1989. He had a posthumous number 1 with 'I Wonder Do You Think Of Me?'. *Kentucky Bluebird* collected together out-takes and broadcast material from throughout his career and spawned a posthumous hit single, 'Brotherly Love', a duet with Earl Thoams Conley. *Wherever You Are Tonight* was a collection of demos given a professional arrangement. Lorrie Morgan organized *Keith Whitley - A Tribute Album* in 1994, which featured Alan Jackson, Joe Diffie and Alison Krauss.

● ALBUMS: with Ricky Skaggs *Tribute To The Stanley Brothers* (Jalyn 1971)★★★, with Skaggs *Second Generation Bluegrass* (1972)★★★, *A Hard Act To Follow* (RCA 1984)★★★, *L.A. To Miami* (RCA 1985), *Don't Close Your Eyes* (RCA 1988)★★★★, *I Wonder Do You Think Of Me?* (RCA 1989)★★★★, *Kentucky Bluebird* (RCA 1992)★★, *Wherever You Are Tonight* (BNA 1995)★★★.

● COMPILATIONS: *Greatest Hits* (RCA 1990)★★★★, *The Essential Keith Whitley* (RCA 1996)★★★★.

WHITLEY, RAY

b. Raymond Otis Whitley, 5 December 1901, Atlanta, Georgia, USA, d. 21 February 1979. He began his singing and acting career in New York in 1930, when, while working on the building of the Empire State Building, he formed his Range Ramblers and began to broadcast on WMCA. In 1932, he worked and travelled with the World Championship Rodeo organization, renaming his band the Six Bar Cowboys. By 1938, he was with RKO Pictures; having received an early-morning call from the studio on the day of recording, informing him that an extra song was required for the film *Border G-Man*, he returned to his bedroom to dress, telling his wife, 'I'm back in the saddle again'. She suggested this would make a good title for a song and, sitting on the edge of the bed, he wrote the first verse of 'Back In The Saddle

Again'. Later that day he sang it for the film and on 26 October 1938, he recorded it for Decca. In 1939, he and his friend Gene Autry revised the song and Autry sang it in his film *Rollin' Tumbleweeds*, later adopting it as his theme song for his CBS *Melody Ranch* show. Between 1936 and 1954, Whitley appeared in 54 films and recorded for several other labels including OKeh and Apollo. He also co-wrote several songs with Fred Rose and later in his career he managed both the Sons Of The Pioneers and Jimmy Wakely. He also worked with Gibson on the production of their J-200 guitar, which has been used by many country singers. In the late 70s, he was a popular figure at Western festivals where he entertained with songs and his talents with a heavy bull-whip. Whitley died while on a fishing trip to Mexico in 1979.

WHITMAN, SLIM

b. Otis Dewey Whitman Jnr., 20 January 1924, Tampa, Florida, USA. As a child, Whitman's stutter was ridiculed by other children and consequently, he left school as soon as he could. Even though his stutter is now cured, he has never cared for public speaking and says little during his stage act. Several members of his family were musical and he became interested in Jimmie Rodgers' recordings when he discovered that he too could yodel. After leaving school, he worked in a meat-packing plant where he lost part of a finger, which, several years later, led to him turning a guitar tutor upside down and learning to play left-handed. He later remarked, 'Paul McCartney saw me in Liverpool and realized that he too could play the guitar left-handed.' Whitman sang at his family's local church, the Church of the Brethren, and it was here, in 1938, that he met the new minister's daughter, Geraldine Crisp. After borrowing $10 from his mother for the license, he married her in 1941. Whitman regards his long-standing marriage as a major ingredient in his success, and he wrote and dedicated a song to her, 'Jerry'. During World War II, he worked as a fitter in a shipyard and then saw action in the US Navy. While on board, he soon realized his talents for entertaining his fellow crew members, but in his first concert, he tempted fate by singing 'When I'm Gone You'll Soon Forget Me'. However, his singing became so popular that the captain blocked his transfer to another ship - fortunately for Whitman, as the other ship was sunk with all hands lost.

After his discharge, he had some success in baseball, but he preferred singing, choosing the name Slim Whitman as a tribute to Wilf Carter (Montana Slim), and often working on radio. He first recorded for RCA Victor at the suggestion of Tom Parker, in 1949. After moderate successes with 'I'm Casting My Lasso Towards The Sky' and 'Birmingham Jail', he moved to Shreveport, Louisiana, so that he could appear each week on the radio show *Louisiana Hayride*. His wife embroidered black shirts for Whitman and the band, which has led him to claim he was the original 'Man In Black'. His steel player, Hoot Rains, developed an identifiable sound, but it came about by accident: when Rains overshot a note on 'Love Song Of The Waterfall', Whitman decided to retain it as a trademark. Whitman maintained a level-headed attitude towards his career and was working as a postman while his first single for Imperial Records, 'Love Song Of The Waterfall', was selling half a million copies. 'You don't quit on one record,' he says, 'then I had "Indian Love Call" and I decided to go. I was told that if I ever wanted my job back, I

could have it'. 'Indian Love Call' came from Rudolph Friml's operetta *Rose Marie*, and in 1955, the song gave Slim Whitman 11 consecutive weeks at the top of the UK charts. 'All I did was throw in a few yodels for good measure,' says Slim, 'and the folks seemed to go for it.' The b-side of 'Indian Love Call', 'China Doll', was a UK hit in its own right, and his other chart records include 'Cattle Call', 'Tumbling Tumbleweeds', 'Serenade' and 'I'll Take You Home Again, Kathleen', although, astonishingly, he has never topped the US country charts. He says, 'A lot of people think of me as a cowboy because I've sung "Cattle Call" and one or two others. The truth is, I've never been on a horse in my life.' In 1955, Whitman moved back to Florida, which restricted his appearances on the *Grand Ole Opry* because he found the trips too time-consuming. In 1956 Whitman became the first country star to top the bill at the London Palladium. Despite being a light-voiced country balladeer, he was featured in the 1957 rock 'n' roll film *Disc Jockey Jamboree*. He has always taken a moral stance on what he records, refusing, for example, to record 'Almost Persuaded'. He says, 'I'm not a saint. It's just that I've no interest in singing songs about cheating or the boozer'. His popularity in Britain was such that his *25th Anniversary Concert* album was recorded at the Empire Theatre, Liverpool, in March 1973. He had a UK hit in 1974 with 'Happy Anniversary', but United Artists executive Alan Warner decided that his US country albums were unsuitable for the UK market, and that he should record albums of pop standards that could be marketed on television. His 1976 album, *The Very Best Of Slim Whitman*, entered the UK album charts at number 1, and was followed by *Red River Valley* (number 1) and *Home On The Range* (number 2). Whitman then repeated his role as a purveyor of love songs for the middle-aged in the USA. Since 1977, Whitman has toured with his son Byron (b. 1957) who, he says, is matching him 'yodel for yodel', and they have pioneered the double yodel. Of his continued success, constantly playing to full houses, he says, 'I don't know the secret. I guess it's the songs I sing and my friendly attitude. When I say hello, I mean it'. In 1996, Whitman's name was made known to younger audiences in the film *Mars Attacks!* - after failing to destroy the evil, marauding Martian invaders with nuclear strikes, it is discovered that their brains explode upon hearing any Slim Whitman recording.

● ALBUMS: *Slim Whitman Sings And Yodels* (RCA Victor 1954)★★★, *America's Favorite Folk Artist* (Imperial 1954)★★★, *Slim Whitman Favorites* (Imperial 1956)★★★, *Slim Whitman Sings* (Imperial 1957)★★★★, *Slim Whitman Sings* (Imperial 1958)★★★★, *Slim Whitman Sings* (Imperial 1959)★★★★, *Slim Whitman Sings Annie Laurie* (Imperial 1959)★★★, *I'll Walk With God* (Imperial 1960)★★, *First Visit To Britain* (Imperial 1960)★★, *Just Call Me Lonesome* (Imperial 1961)★★★, *Once In A Lifetime* (Imperial 1961)★★★, *Heart Songs And Love Songs* (Imperial 1961)★★★, *I'm A Lonely Wanderer* (Imperial 1962)★★★, *Yodeling* (Imperial 1963)★★★, *Irish Songs - The Slim Whitman Way* (Imperial 1963)★★, *Love Song Of The Waterfall* (Imperial 1964)★★★★, *Reminiscing* (Imperial 1964)★★★, *More Than Yesterday* (Imperial 1965)★★★, *Forever* (Imperial 1966)★★★, *God's Hand In Mine* (Imperial 1966)★★, *A Travellin' Man* (Imperial 1966)★★★, *A Time For Love* (Imperial 1966)★★★, *A Lonesome Heart* (Sunset 1967)★★★, *Country Memories* (Imperial 1967)★★★, *In Love, The*

Whitman Way (Imperial 1968)★★★, *Unchain Your Heart* (Sunset 1968)★★★, *Happy Street* (Imperial 1969)★★★, *Slim!* (Imperial 1969)★★★, *The Slim Whitman Christmas Album* (Imperial 1969)★★, *Ramblin' Rose* (1970)★★★, *Tomorrow Never Comes* (Liberty 1970)★★★, *It's A Sin To Tell A Lie* (1971)★★★, *Guess Who* aka *Snowbird* (1971)★★★, *I'll See You When* (1973)★★★, *25th Anniversary Concert* (1973)★★★, *Happy Anniversary* (1974)★★★, *Everything Leads Back To You* (1975)★★★, *Home On The Range* (United Artists 1977)★★★, *Red River Valley* (United Artists 1977)★★★, *Ghost Riders In The Sky* (United Artists 1978)★★★, *Till We Meet Again* (United Artists 1980)★★★, *Just For You* (Suffolk 1980)★★★, *Songs I Love To Sing* (1980)★★★, *Christmas With Slim Whitman* (1980)★★, *Mr. Songman* (Liberty 1981)★★★, *I'll Be Home For Christmas* (1981)★★, *Country Songs, City Hits* (1982)★★★, *Angeline* (Epic 1984)★★★, *A Dream Come True - The Rarities Album* (1987)★★★, with Byron Whitman *Magic Moments* (1990)★★★.

● COMPILATIONS: *Country Hits Volume 1* (Imperial 1960)★★★, *All Time Favourites* (Imperial 1964)★★★, *Birmingham Jail* (Camden 1966)★★★, *Fifteenth Anniversary* (Imperial 1967)★★★, *The Very Best Of Slim Whitman* (United Artists 1976)★★★, *All My Best* (Suffolk 1979)★★★, *Slim Whitman's 20 Greatest Love Songs* (MFP 1981)★★★, *The Best Of Slim Whitman (1952-1972)* (Rhino 1990)★★★, *20 Golden Greats* (1992)★★★, *EMI Country Masters: 50 Orginal Tracks* (EMI 1993)★★★, *Love Songs* (Music For Pleasure 1994)★★★, *Rose Marie: Slim Whitman 1949-1959* 6-CD box set (Bear Family 1996)★★★, *50th Anniversary Collection* (EMI 1997)★★★.

● FURTHER READING: *Mr. Songman - The Slim Whitman Story*, Kenneth L. Gibble.

● FILMS: *Jamboree* aka *Disc Jockey Jamboree* (1957).

WHITSTEIN BROTHERS

Robert (Bob) and Charles Whitstein were both born in the mid-40s, on the family farm at Colfax, Louisiana, USA. They were the eldest of the nine children of R.C. Whitstein, who, apart from farming, was a skilled guitarist, fiddler and vocalist, and who presented a weekly programme of country music on the local radio station. Under their father's guidance, the boys first appeared in their pre-teens on a local television talent show. Their close-harmony singing to their own accompaniment, Bob playing guitar and Charles on mandolin, soon attracted attention and they made their debut recording for a small Texas label, J-Bo. Around 1963, they moved to Hopkinsville, Kentucky, and while working as part-time carpenters and bricklayers, they began to play and sing around Nashville. They appeared on the *Grand Ole Opry* and toured with Faron Young as the Whitt Brothers. They were both drafted for military service, with Robert serving in Vietnam. In the early 70s, finding no success in Nashville, they settled in Louisiana, performing only locally while following other occupations. In 1984, after making some demo recordings and receiving some assistance from Tillman Franks and Jesse McReynolds (of Jim And Jesse), they recorded their first album for Rounder Records. Their biggest influence of all the earlier brother harmony acts was the Louvin Brothers, and Charlie Louvin stated that the Whitsteins were the nearest that he had ever heard to the sound of the Louvins. The Whitsteins are not full-time musicians and in 1988, when Robert was unable to take time off

work to tour the UK, his place was taken by Charlie Louvin. The brothers toured in the UK in 1990 and are a popular act, particularly at bluegrass festivals both in Europe and in the USA. Charles Whitstein recorded with Charlie Louvin following a temporary split, but by 1994 the brothers had reunited and were recording again.

● ALBUMS: *Rose Of My Heart* (Rounder 1984)★★★, *Trouble Ain't Nothing But The Blues'* (Rounder 1987)★★★, *Old Time Duets* (Rounder 1989)★★★★, *Sing Gospel Songs Of The Louvins* 1969 recording (Rounder 1995)★★★, *Sweet Harmony* (Rounder 1996)★★★★. Charles Whitstein and Charlie Louvin *Hoping That You're Hoping* (Copper Creek 1992)★★★.

WHITTER, HENRY

b. William Henry Whitter, 6 April 1892, near Fries, Grayson County, Virginia, USA, d. 10 November 1941, Morganton, North Carolina, USA. Whitter first entertained fellow workers at a cotton mill in Fries but, in March 1923, bored with the work, he travelled to New York. Using his own guitar and harmonica, he auditioned for OKeh Records. OKeh were unsure about his raw, nasal singing, but the increasing interest in hillbilly records encouraged them to release a song about the crash of a mail train, 'The Wreck Of The Old '97'. Vernon Dalhart realized the song's potential and recorded a better version, which became a million-seller. In 1924 Whitter formed a successful string band, the Virginia Breakdowners, with James Sutpin (fiddle) and John Rector (banjo). In 1927 Whitter started performing with a blind fiddler, G.B. Grayson. Their work included the first recorded version of 'Tom Dooley'. After Grayson died in a car crash in 1930, Whitter lost interest in his music and made few recordings. He died of complications from diabetes in 1941.

● COMPILATIONS: *Grayson And Whitter, 1927-1930* (1976)★★★, *Going Down Lee Highway* (1976)★★★.

WHYTON, WALLY

b. 23 September 1929, London, England, d. 22 January 1997, London, England. Broadcaster and singer Wally Whyton enjoyed a fascinating and varied professional career after initially training as a commercial artist. However, after socializing with Lionel Bart and his first exposure to the jazz records of Louis Armstrong and Bessie Smith, Whyton soon developed ambitions to become a singer. He subsequently formed a skiffle band, the Vipers, with himself on vocals and fellow members Johnny Martyn, Jean Van den Bosch, Tony Tolhurst and John Pilgrim. They established a residency at the 21s Coffee Bar in New Compton Street, Soho, in 1956. A record contract with Parlophone Records ensued, and the group's second single, 'Don't You Rock Me Daddy-O', entered the UK Top 10 later that year. Their other chart successes were 'Cumberland Gap' and 'Streamline Train' (a version of 'Maggie May' was banned by the BBC), but the skiffle boom quickly faded, although the Vipers remained active until the end of the 50s. During that period several musicians passed through the group's ranks, including future Shadows Hank Marvin, Jet Harris and Tony Meehan. Hoping to concentrate on a career as a folk-singer, Whyton was then diverted into television entertainment when a one-off appearance on a Rolf Harris show led to a permanent spot. Eventually, he hosted his own children's series, *The Five O'Clock Show*, for

Rediffusion. Here he introduced the hugely popular glove puppet Pussycat Willum, followed by other creations including Ollie Beak, Joe Crow and Spike McPike. Whyton recorded a series of successful children's albums, but also remained active on the folk scene. Recording for Argo and Phillips Records, he became a regular on BBC Radio, presenting *Folk Room*, *Strings 'n' Things* and *Junior Choice*. He was then approached to host *Country Meet Folk*, a series where the two complementary musical styles were to be combined. It ran for over six years after originally being conceived of as potentially a six-week series. He was a natural choice as host when the BBC launched *The Country Club* show in the mid-70s. With his regular visits to Nashville and reports on the Silk Cut Country Music Festival at Wembley, Whyton effectively became 'the voice of country music' in Britain throughout the 70s and 80s. He was still presenting a show for the BBC World Service until a month before his death in January 1997.

WIGGINS, JOHN AND AUDREY

Johnny Wiggins, father of the 90s US country singers John and Audrey Wiggins, went to Nashville in 1960 in the hope of becoming a country star, but he ended up driving Ernest Tubb's coach and opening his concerts as 'The Singing Bus Driver'. When he was only 12, Audrey Wiggins was introduced by Ernest Tubb at the *Grand Ole Opry* and sang 'Lovesick Blues'. In 1981 John and Audrey, along with Clinton Gregory, became the house band at the Stompin' Ground in Maggie Valley, North Carolina. They moved to Nashville with little success, although they were eventually signed by Mercury Records. Their father was killed in a car accident just before their debut album was made. Audrey generally takes the lead vocals and they have had US country chart success with 'Fallin' Out Of Love' and 'Has Anybody Seen Amy'. Following a long absence from the recording scene, the more up-tempo and commercial *The Dream* was released in 1997.
● ALBUMS: *John And Audrey Wiggins* (Mercury 1994)★★★, *The Dream* (Mercury 1997)★★★.
● VIDEOS: *Has Anybody Seen Amy (Think Pictures)* (1994).

WIGGINS, LITTLE ROY

b. Ivan Leroy Wiggins, 27 June 1926, Nashville, Tennessee, USA. As a child, he was fascinated by the Hawaiian guitar-playing of Bert Hutcherson on the *Grand Ole Opry* and immediately decided to learn to play the steel guitar. Wiggins proved a very adroit learner; at the age of 14, he was playing the instrument on the *Opry* as a member of Paul Howard's band, in a style that was reminiscent of the earlier melodic Hawaiian styles. He called himself Roy and purely because of his age, his fellow musicians added the Little. He later worked the *Opry* for a year with Pee Wee King's Golden West Cowboys, but in 1943, he became Eddy Arnold's steel guitarist. He remained with Arnold until 1968 and during those years, he was responsible for the effective and immediately recognizable steel guitar playing that became an accepted part of Arnold's hits, such as 'Bouquet Of Roses' and 'Anytime'. He made no solo recordings until the early 60s, since Arnold, like several top stars, frowned on his musicians recording in their own right. In the late 60s, Wiggins played with George Morgan, where again he added the distinctive steel sound to recordings such as 'Hey Mr

Ting-A-Ling Steel Guitar Man' and Morgan's smash hit 'Candy Kisses'. After Morgan's death in 1975, Wiggins worked partly as a session musician but also played with several *Opry* artists, including Ernie Ashworth and the Willis Brothers. In the late 80s, he relocated to the tourist centre of Pigeon Forge, Tennessee, where, until 1993, he played the local *Smoky Mountain Hayride* and also, for a time, managed Ernest Tubb's local record shop. In 1992, he opened his own musical instrument shop and eventually, with the exception of several special concert appearances, he devoted his attention to running his business. Wiggins is a member of the Steel Guitar Hall Of Fame. In recent years he has recorded some cassettes, which he markets from his shop.
● ALBUMS: *Mister Steel Guitar* (Starday 1962)★★★ *18 All Time Hits* (Starday 1966)★★, *Songs I Played For Eddy Arnold* (Diplomat 1969)★★★★, *Memory Time* (Power Pak 1974)★★★.

WILBURN BROTHERS

Brothers Virgil Doyle Wilburn (b. 7 July 1930, Hardy, Arkansas, USA, d. 16 October 1982) and Thurman Theodore 'Teddy' Wilburn (b. 30 November 1931, Hardy, Arkansas, USA). They started their careers as children singing with their siblings as the Wilburn Family. This featured two elder brothers, Lester (b. 19 May 1924), Leslie (b. 13 October 1925) and sister Vinita Geraldine (b. 5 June 1927), all born in Hardy, Arkansas. Their father, Benjamin Wilburn, a disabled World War I veteran, whose ill health prevented him doing normal work, thought that a career for his children in entertainment might help the family budget. He bought a mandolin, guitar and fiddle from the Sears, Roebuck catalogue and in 1937, after his tuition, the Family were singing on the streets of Thayer, 18 miles over the state line in Missouri. They went on to play local radio stations and in 1940, after a reference from Roy Acuff, who saw them singing at Birmingham, Alabama, they were invited to join the *Grand Ole Opry*. They immediately became very popular and attracted large amounts of mail but after six months, beset with problems concerning child labour laws, the *Opry* management asked them to leave. They returned home and continued to entertain, although the onset of World War II affected their careers. Between 1948 and 1951, the Wilburn Family worked on KWKH Shreveport, where the four brothers regularly appeared on the *Louisiana Hayride* (Geraldine left the group in 1948 to marry). In 1951, because of the Korean War, both Teddy and Doyle were drafted for US Army service. In 1953, after discharge, they began to work as a duo, touring and working with several major acts, including Webb Pierce, Faron Young and Ernest Tubb, and they played on the *Opry*, becoming full cast members in 1956. They recorded for Decca, first charting in 1955 with 'I Wanna Wanna Wanna', but the following year they had Top 10 country hits with 'I'm So In Love With You' and 'Go Away With Me'. Further chart successes followed, including two Top 10 duets with Ernest Tubb ('Mister Love' and 'Hey, Mr Bluebird'). In the late 50s, they joined with Leslie and Lester to found the publishing company Sure-Fire Music, which handled their own and other artists' songs. During the 60s, they toured extensively and frequently made the country charts with their recordings. Their Top 5 hits included 'Trouble's Back In Town' (1962), 'Roll Muddy River' (1963), 'It's Another World' (1965) and 'Hurt Her Once For Me'

(1967). They hosted their own network television show, on which they featured the young Loretta Lynn (they also obtained a Decca recording contract for her), and also appeared in a series on Australian television. They extended their business interests to include Wil-Helm Talent, which became one of Nashville's top booking agencies and handled many of the major stars. Although they had no chart successes after 'Arkansas' in 1972, they maintained their popularity and still appeared on the *Opry* throughout the 70s. Doyle Wilburn died in Nashville in 1982 as the result of cancer. Teddy maintained the family tradition and continued to appear on the *Opry*, often accompanied by brothers Lester and Leslie.

● ALBUMS: *The Wilburn Brothers* (Decca 1957)★★★, *Side By Side* (Decca 1958)★★★★, *Living In God's Country* (Decca 1959)★★★, with Ernest Tubb *Ernest Tubb & The Wilburn Brothers* (Decca 1959)★★★★, *The Big Heartbreak* (Decca 1960)★★★, *City Limits* (Decca 1961)★★★, *The Wilburn Brothers Sing* (Decca 1961)★★★, *The Wonderful Wilburn Brothers* (King 1961)★★★, *Folk Songs* (Decca 1962)★★★, *Carefree Moments* (Vocalion 1962)★★★, *Trouble's Back In Town* (Decca 1963)★★★, *Take Up Thy Cross* (Decca 1964)★★★, *Never Alone* (Decca 1964)★★★, *I'm Gonna Tie One On Tonight* (Decca 1965)★★★, with Ernest Tubb and Loretta Lynn *The Wilburn Brothers Show* (Decca 1966)★★★★, *Let's Go Country* (Decca 1966)★★★★, *Two For The Show* (Decca 1967)★★★★, *Cool Country* (Decca 1967)★★★★, *Its Another World* (Decca 1968)★★★, *I Walk The Line* (Vocalion 1968)★★★, *We Need A Lot More Happiness* (Decca 1969)★★★, *It Looks Like The Sun's Gonna Shine* (Decca 1969)★★★, *Little Johnny From Down The Street* (Decca 1970)★★★, *Sing Your Heart Out Country Boy* (Decca 1970)★★★, *That Country Feeling* (Decca 1970)★★★, *That She's Leaving Feeling* (Decca 1971)★★★, *A Portrait* (Decca 1973)★★★, *Sing Hinson And Gaither* (1978)★★★, *Stars Of The Grand Ole Opry* (1979)★★★.

● COMPILATIONS: *Country Gold* reissued 1985 (Decca 1965)★★★★, *The Wilburn Brothers' Greatest Hits* (Decca 1968)★★★★.

WILEY AND GENE

This duo are best remembered as the writers of the country standard 'When My Blue Moon Turns To Gold Again', although both had solo careers before their successful partnership started in 1939. Wiley (b. Wiley Walker, 17 November 1911, Laurel Hill, Florida, USA, d. 17 May 1966; songwriter, vocals, fiddle, dancer) learned to play fiddle and buck and wing dance as a child, and began his career as an entertainer on touring tent shows in 1925. In 1932, he began working with Lew Childre in New Orleans (and later Birmingham) as the Alabama Boys. In 1937, they parted and Walker played briefly with the Swift Jewel Cowboys, before moving to Shreveport. Here, while working with the Shelton Brothers, he met Gene Sullivan (b. 16 November 1914, Carbon Hill, Alabama, USA, d. 24 October 1984; songwriter, vocals, instrumentalist). Sullivan was a professional boxer, but in 1932, he turned to country music. After learning guitar, he worked for a time with the Tune Wranglers, before joining the Lone Star Cowboys on KWKH Shreveport. When the Shelton Brothers left the Cowboys to form their own act, Sullivan went with them and first met and worked with Walker as musicians and comedians for the Sheltons. They

eventually formed a duo in 1939 and worked radio stations in Fort Worth, Lubbock, and finally ended their careers in Oklahoma City. In 1941, they recorded 'When My Blue Moon Turns To Gold Again'/'Live And Let Live' for Columbia Records. Their version achieved some local success but it would be the 1956 pop version by Elvis Presley that finally launched the song, which, in later years, has been recorded by numerous artists. In 1946, the duo registered their only chart entry, 'Make Room In Your Heart For A Friend', which became a number 2 US country hit. In the late 40s, they were regulars on Oklahoma City television but their careers ended in the early 50s. Sullivan enjoyed a solo Top 10 success in 1957 with his comedy number 'Please Pass The Biscuits'. He had originally recorded it as a demo for Little Jimmie Dickens, but Columbia released his version in preference. Sullivan subsequently retired to run an Oklahoma City music store, but he made a few appearances with Walker until the early 60s. Walker died in 1966 but Sullivan, in later years, made a few solo appearances, outlasting his old partner until 1984. Some of their recordings were issued in album form after his death, by Old Homestead.

● COMPILATIONS: *Wiley Walker & Gene Sullivan Volume 1* (Old Homestead 1987)★★★.

WILLIAMS, BUDDY

b. Harry Taylor, 5 September 1918, Newtown suburb, Sydney, New South Wales, Australia, d. 1986. A major pioneer of Australian country music, as a child Williams never knew his parents and was placed in an orphanage, where he soon became a nuisance to the authorities by his attempts to escape. Fostered out to a farming couple in Dorrigo, he found he was treated more as an unpaid worker than as an adopted son. He heard recordings of Jimmie Rodgers when visiting neighbours and was immediately captivated by the music. When 15 years old, he ran away and did a series of labouring jobs. He had learned to play guitar and, while working in a quarry at Coffs Harbour, was dared to sing on the streets and was amazed at the amount of money he received. In 1936, he made a successful appearance at the Jacaranda Festival and as Buddy Williams, he continued to earn his living busking around the country, spending some time at Newcastle, before heading for Sydney. When, on 7 September 1939, singing six of his own songs, he made his first historic recordings for Regal-Zonophone (who later became EMI), he became the first Australian-born solo country recording artist (Tex Morton recorded in 1936 but he was a New Zealander). Later stating that he gained inspiration from Goebel Reeves and Jimmie Rodgers, he continued busking but soon gained radio exposure, where he built a reputation with his ballads and yodels. He made further recordings on 14 May 1940, including his well-known 'Australian Bushman's Yodel' and 'Happy Jackeroo'. He ran a sawmill in Walcha, supplying hardwood to the army, before enlisting for military service himself. He served as a Bren gunner and in spite of his army commitments, he recorded 30 sides during his period of war service. In 1941, he made two recordings with first wife Bernie Burnett (they were later divorced) and two more in 1943, including 'Stockmen In Uniform'. In March 1945, he recorded five songs including 'Where The Lazy Murray River Rolls Along' with Lenore Miller, who later achieved success as folk-singer Lenore Somerset in the 60s. A few weeks before the end of the war in 1945, he was seriously wounded while serving in Borneo, and defied medical predictions by recovering.

In 1946, he recorded his noted 'The Overlander Trail' and made a film appearance. He married Grace Maidman in Brisbane on 31 January 1947, and the two formed and ran rodeo tent shows, which featured a variety of acts, including noted rodeo performers, clowns and magicians. Williams naturally sang and also did trick shooting and showed his skill with a bullwhip (sadly, in 1949, their first child Donita, then aged 21 months, tragically died in Tasmania, when she was accidentally run over by a truck driven by one of the rodeo riders in Williams' show). From the late 40s throughout the 50s, he continued to tour with his show and to record regularly. The rodeo side of the show was eventually dropped and it became a Country and Western Variety Show. His recordings were generally of Australian songs, many of his own writing, but some cover versions of American hits were made, including his very successful 1953 recording of 'Missing In Action'. Between 1958 and 1964, he recorded almost 60 sides and he was one of the last Australian artists to forsake just a solo guitar and use a backing group. In 1965, he changed labels to RCA. It was around this time that he was joined both on his recordings and on stage by his son Harold George (b. 23 June 1948, Rylstone, New South Wales, Australia) and daughter Kaye Elizabeth (b. 31 January 1950, Ivanoe, Victoria, Australia). Together they recorded a series of albums. In 1972, youngest daughter Karen Anne (b. 20 May 1957, Brisbane, Queensland, Australia) also became part of the Williams Family Show. In 1972, he toured in company with another pioneer, Tex Morton. In 1977 and 1978, Williams suffered heart attacks, which forced him to stop touring personally, but the Williams show continued. In 1977, he became the second artist (after Morton) to be elected to the newly created Country Music Roll Of Renown (Australia's equivalent to Nashville's Country Music Hall of Fame). In 1979, RCA presented him with a gold-plated map of Australia to celebrate his 40 years of recording country music - one of the many awards that he has received. He has written many songs and three of them, namely 'Where The White Faced Cattle Roam', 'Heading For The Warwick Rodeo' and 'Music In My Pony's Feet', are included in Australia's 50 most popular country songs. In 1979, Williams featured in a documentary called *The Last Fair Dinkum Aussie Outback Entertainer*. There is little doubt that he has been a major inspiration for many Australian artists, and experts on the genre rate some of the recordings that he made between 1942 and 1946 among the best examples of Australian country. Harold Williams went on to record in his own right, even recording the album *Buddy Williams Jnr Sings*. He later did solo work and in 1982, with Lindsay Butler, also formed the Tamworth Country Show Band. Kaye Williams also recorded in her own right, being joined by her father for two tracks on her album *Just Between The Two Of Us*.

● ALBUMS: *Sings Jimmie Rodgers* (EMI 1962)★★★, *Buddy Williams Remembers Vol. 1* (EMI 1965)★★★★, *Buddy Williams Remembers Vol. 2* (EMI 1966)★★★, with Harold and Kaye Williams *Family Album* (EMI 1966)★★, *Country Style* (RCA 1966)★★★★, *The Williams Family* (RCA 1966)★★★, *Songs Of The Australian Outback* (Readers Digest 60s)★★★, *Buddy Sings Hank* (RCA 60s)★★★, *Family Affair* (RCA 60s)★★★, *Cowboy's Life Is Good Enough For Me*

(RCA 60s)★★★, *Sentimental Buddy* (RCA 60s)★★★, *Buddy And Shorty* (RCA 1969)★★★, *Hard Times* (RCA 1970)★★★, *Along The Outback Tracks* (RCA 1971)★★★, *Aussie On My Mind* (RCA 1972)★★★, *Bushland Of My Dreams* (EMI 1979)★★★, *Wonder Valley* (RCA 1980)★★, *An Old Hillbilly From Way Back* (RCA 1981)★★★, *Big Country Muster* (RCA 1983)★★, *Blazing The Trail* (EMI 1983)★★★, *Reflections* (RCA 1987)★★★.

WILLIAMS, CURLEY

b. Doc Williams, 1913, Southern Georgia, USA, d. 5 September 1970. He was christened Doc because family legend maintained that the seventh child would be a doctor. Little is known of Williams' early life, but in the early 40s, instead of being a doctor, he was the fiddle-playing leader of a western swing band on WALD Albany, Georgia. In December 1942, with his Sante Fe Riders, he arrived at the *Grand Ole Opry* in Nashville, where George D. Hay saw fit to change both his and his band's name to avoid confusion with Doc Williams And His Border Riders, who were then an established act on WWVA's *Wheeling Jamboree*. Williams' hair provided one simple suggestion and, being a native of Georgia (the Peach State), he became Curley Williams And His Georgia Peach Pickers. They began playing networked *Opry* shows in September 1943, and made their first recordings for Columbia Records in 1945 (the delay was caused by the recording ban operating at that time). Between 1945 and 1948, they relocated to play the dancehall circuits on the west coast and even appeared in a Charles Starrett B-western, *Riders Of The Lone Star*, in 1947. In the late 40s, they also starred on the *Louisiana Hayride*. Williams wrote 'Half As Much', which he recorded in 1951, at his band's last Columbia session and in 1952, Hank Williams took the song to number 2 in the US country charts. There has been confusion over the years, with many assuming Hank Williams, who was in fact no relation but was a friend of Curley's, to be the writer of the song (the song became a million-seller for Rosemary Clooney, and was also recorded successfully in the UK by Alma Cogan and Lita Rosa). During his years with Columbia, Williams also provided backing on various other artists' recordings, including on one occasion, Fred Rose, who at the time was recording for the label as the Rambling Rogue. In the early 50s, Williams and his band played regularly on the *Smoky Mountain Jamboree* in Georgia and for a time did sponsored shows on WSFA Montgomery, Alabama, until, in 1954, Williams tired of the showbusiness life and retired.

● COMPILATIONS: *Curley Williams - The Original Half As Much* (CowgirlBoy 1990)★★★.

WILLIAMS, DOC

b. Andrew J. Smik Jnr., 26 June 1914, Cleveland, Ohio, USA. A noted traditionalist who, except for short spells at Memphis (1939) and Frederick (1945), was associated with the *Wheeling Jamboree* at WWVA Wheeling, West Virginia, for over 40 years, after first appearing with his band the Border Riders in 1937. He married Chickie (b. Jessie Wanda Crupe, 13 February 1919, Bethany, West Virginia, USA) in 1939 and she sang regularly with the band (in later years they were sometimes joined by their three daughters, Barbara, Madeline and Karen). Their family show also featured brother Cy Williams (fiddle) and Marion Martin (chordovox).

Doc regularly played hundreds of shows a year in the north-eastern states, the New England area and in eastern Canada. He has also made several trips to Britain, where he proved immensely popular around the country clubs. He has made many recordings for his own Wheeling label and though he never achieved any chart entries, he is associated with such songs as 'Wheeling Back To Wheeling', 'My Old Brown Coat And Me' and the tear-jerkers 'Daddy's Little Angel' and 'He Said He Had A Friend'. It has also been claimed that Chickie recorded the original version of 'Beyond The Sunset'.

● ALBUMS: *Sings Country & Western* (Wheeling *c*.50s-*c*.70s), *25th Anniversary Album* (Wheeling *c*.50s-*c*.70s), *Wheeling Back To Wheeling* (Wheeling *c*.50s-*c*.70s), *Williams Family Sacred Album* (Wheeling *c*.50s-*c*.70s), *Doc Williams Show* (Wheeling *c*.50s-*c*.70s), *Collector's Series Volumes 1 & 2* (Wheeling *c*.50s-*c*.70s), *Daddy's Little Angel* (Wheeling *c*.50s-*c*.70s), *From Out Of The Beautiful Hills Of West Virginia* (Wheeling *c*.50s-*c*.70s), *Doc & Chickie Together* (Wheeling *c*.50s-*c*.70s), *Favorites Old And New* (Wheeling *c*.50s-*c*.70s), *Reminiscing* (Wheeling *c*.50s-*c*.70s), with Karen Williams *The Three Of Us* (Wheeling *c*.50s-*c*.70s), *We've Come A Long Way Together* (*c*.50s-*c*.70s).

WILLIAMS, DON

b. 27 May 1939, Floydada, Texas, USA. Williams' father was a mechanic whose job took him to other regions and much of his childhood was spent in Corpus Christi, Texas. Williams' mother played guitar and he grew up listening to country music. He and Lofton Kline formed a semi-professional folk group called the Strangers Two, and then, with the addition of Susan Taylor, they became the Pozo-Seco Singers, the phrase being a geological term to denote a dry well. Handled by Bob Dylan's manager Albert Grossman, they had US pop hits with 'Time', 'I Can Make It With You' and 'Look What You've Done'. Following Lofton Kline's departure, they employed several replacements, resulting in a lack of direction, and they were as likely to record 'Green Green Grass Of Home' as 'Strawberry Fields Forever'. After Williams had failed to turn the trio towards country music, they disbanded in 1971. He then worked for his father-in-law but also wrote for Susan Taylor's solo album via Jack Clement's music publishing company. Clement asked Williams to record albums of his company's best songs, mainly with a view to attracting other performers. In 1973 *Don Williams, Volume 1* was released on the fledgling JMI label and included such memorable songs as Bob McDill's apologia for growing old, 'Amanda', and Williams' own 'The Shelter Of Your Eyes'. Both became US country hits and JMI could hardly complain when Tommy Cash and then Waylon Jennings released 'I Recall A Gypsy Woman', thus depriving Williams of a certain winner (in the UK, Williams' version made number 13, his biggest success). Williams' work was reissued by ABC/Dot and *Don Williams, Volume 2* included 'Atta Way To Go' and 'We Should Be Together'. Williams then had a country number 1 with Wayland Holyfield's 'You're My Best Friend', which has become a standard and is the perennial singalong anthem at his concerts. By now, the Williams style had developed: gently paced love songs with straightforward arrangements, lyrics and sentiments. Williams was mining the same vein as Jim Reeves but he eschewed Reeves' smartness by dressing like a ranch-hand. At concerts, he would put his hand to his battered stetson and say,

'You want me to remove my what?'. Besides having a huge contingent of female fans, Williams counted Eric Clapton and Pete Townshend among his admirers. Clapton recorded his country hit 'Tulsa Time', written by Danny Flowers from Williams' Scratch Band. The Scratch Band released their own album, produced by Williams, in 1982. Williams played a band member himself in the Burt Reynolds film *W.W. And The Dixie Dancekings* and also appeared in *Smokey And The Bandit 2*. Williams' other successes include 'Till The Rivers All Run Dry', 'Some Broken Hearts Never Mend', 'Lay Down Beside Me' and his only US Top 30 pop hit, 'I Believe In You'. Unlike most established country artists, he has not sought duet partners, although he and Emmylou Harris found success with an easy-paced version of Townes Van Zandt's 'If I Needed You'. Williams' best record is with Bob McDill's homage to his southern roots, 'Good Ol' Boys Like Me'. Moving to Capitol Records in the mid-80s, Williams released such singles as 'Heartbeat In The Darkness' and 'Senorita', but the material was not as impressive. He took a sabbatical in 1988 but subsequent RCA recordings, which include 'I've Been Loved By The Best', showed that nothing had changed. Williams' most recent album, the more sombre *Flatlands*, was released on the Carlton label. He continues to be a major concert attraction, maintaining his stress-free style. When interviewed, Williams gives the impression of being a contented man who takes life as he finds it. He is a rare being - a country star who is free of controversy.

● ALBUMS: with the Pozo-Seco Singers *Time* (Columbia 1966)★★★, with the Pozo-Seco Singers *I Can Make It With You* (Columbia 1967)★★★, with the Pozo-Seco Singers *Shades Of Time* (Columbia 1968)★★★, *Don Williams, Volume 1* (JMI 1973)★★★★, *Don Williams, Volume 2* (JMI 1974)★★★, *Don Williams, Volume 3* (ABC 1974)★★★, *You're My Best Friend* (ABC 1975)★★★★, *Harmony* (ABC 1976)★★★★, *Visions* (ABC 1977)★★★★, *Country Boy* (ABC 1977)★★★, with Roy Clark, Freddy Fender, Hank Thompson *Country Comes To Carnegie Hall* (ABC/Dot 1977)★★★★, *Expressions* (ABC 1978)★★★★, *Portrait* (1979)★★★, *I Believe In You* (MCA 1980)★★★★, *Especially For You* (MCA 1981)★★★★, *Listen To The Radio* (MCA 1982)★★★★, *Yellow Moon* (MCA 1983)★★★, *Cafe Carolina* (MCA 1984)★★★★, *New Moves* (Capitol 1986)★★, *Traces* (Capitol 1987)★★, *One Good Well* (RCA 1989)★★★, *As Long As I Have You* (RCA 1989)★★★, *True Love* (RCA 1990)★★★, *Currents* (RCA 1992)★★★, *Borrowed Tales* (Carlton/American Harvest 1995)★★★, *Flatlands* (Carlton 1996)★★★.

● COMPILATIONS: *Greatest Hits, Volume 1* (MCA 1975)★★★★, *Greatest Country Hits* (Curb 1976)★★★, *Best Of Don Williams, Volume 2* (MCA 1979)★★★★, *Prime Cuts* (Capitol 1981)★★★, *Best Of Don Williams, Volume 3* (MCA 1984)★★★, *Best Of Don Williams, Volume 4* (MCA 1985)★★★, *20 Greatest Hits* (MCA 1987)★★★★, *The Very Best Of Don Williams* (Half Moon 1997)★★★★.

● VIDEOS: *Live, The Greatest Hits Collection, Volume One* (Prism 1996).

WILLIAMS, HANK

b. Hiram (misspelt on birth certificate as Hiriam) Williams, 17 September 1923, Georgiana, Alabama, USA, d. 1 January 1953, Virginia, USA. Misspelling notwithstanding, Williams disliked the name and took to calling himself Hank. He was born with a spine defect that troubled him throughout his life, and which was further aggravated after being thrown from a horse when he was 17 years old. Initially, his parents, Lon and Lilly, ran a general store, but Lon later entered a veterans' hospital following a delayed reaction to the horrors he had experienced during World War I. The young Williams was raised by his imposing, resourceful mother, who gave him a cheap guitar when he was seven. He learned chords from an elderly black musician, Teetot (Rufe Payne). Williams later said, 'All the musical training I ever had came from him.' It also explains the strong blues thread that runs through his work. In 1937, Lilly opened a boarding house in Montgomery, Alabama. Williams won a talent contest and formed his own band, the Drifting Cowboys. As clubs were tough, Hank hired a wrestler, Cannonball Nichols, as a bass player, more for protection than musical ability, but he could not be protected from his mother, who handled his bookings and earnings (in truth, Williams was not particularly interested in the money he made). While working for a medicine show, he met Audrey Sheppard and married her in December 1944. Although rivals, both his wife and his mother would thump the pale, lanky singer for his lack of co-operation. Williams was a local celebrity, but on 14 September 1946, he and Audrey went to Nashville, impressing Fred Rose and his son Wesley at the relatively new Acuff-Rose publishing. On 11 December 1946 Williams made his first recordings for the small Sterling label. They included 'Callin' You' and 'When God Comes And Gathers His Jewels'. Fred Rose secured a contract with the more prestigious MGM Records, and he acted as his manager, record producer and, occasionally, co-writer ('Mansion On The Hill', 'Kaw-liga'). Williams' first MGM release, 'Move It On Over', sold several thousand copies. He then joined the prestigious radio show *Louisiana Hayride* in 1948 and was featured on its concert tours. Fred Rose opposed him reviving 'Lovesick Blues', originally recorded by Emmett Miller in 1925, and later a success for Rex Griffin in 1939; nevertheless, he recorded the song, following Miller's and Griffin's playful yodels. 'Lovesick Blues' topped the US country charts for 16 weeks and remained in the listings for almost a year. The *Grand Ole Opry*, although wary of his hard-drinking reputation, invited him to perform 'Lovesick Blues', which led to an unprecedented six encores. He and the Drifting Cowboys became regulars and the publicity enabled them to command $1,000 for concert appearances; they even upstaged comedian and film star Bob Hope. 'Wedding Bells' made number 2, as did a contender for the greatest country single ever released, the poignant 'I'm So Lonesome I Could Cry', backed with the old blues song, 'My Bucket's Got A Hole In It'; the *Opry* sponsors, disapproving of the word 'beer' in the latter song, had Williams sing 'milk' instead. In 1950, he had three country number 1 hits, 'Long Gone Lonesome Blues', 'Why Don't You Love Me?' and 'Moanin' The Blues'. The following year, he had two further chart-toppers with 'Cold, Cold Heart' and 'Hey, Good Lookin''. Another superb double-sided hit, 'Howlin' At The Moon'/'I Can't Help It (If I'm Still In Love With You)', made number 2.

In 1952, Williams went to number 1 with his praise of Cajun food in 'Jambalaya', while 'Half As Much' made number 2. Another well-balanced double-sided hit, 'Settin' The Woods On Fire'/'You Win Again', made number 2. Williams was a

showman, often wearing a flashy suit embroidered with sequins and decorated with musical notes. Although MGM studios thought about making films with him, nothing materialized. It is arguable that, with his thinning hair, he looked too old, or it may have been that he was just too awkward. His lifestyle was akin to the later spirit of rock 'n' roll; he drank too much, took drugs (admittedly, excessive numbers of painkillers for his back), played with guns, destroyed hotel rooms, threw money out of windows and permanently lived in conflict. His son, Hank Williams Jnr., said, 'I get sick of hearing people tell me how much they loved my daddy. They hated him in Nashville.' Williams' songs articulated the lives and loves of his listeners and he went a stage further by recording melodramatic monologues as Luke The Drifter. They included 'Beyond The Sunset', 'Pictures From Life's Other Side', 'Too Many Parties And Too Many Pals' and 'Men With Broken Hearts'. Although Luke the Drifter's appeal was limited, Fred Rose saw how Williams' other songs could have wide appeal. Country songs had been recorded by pop performers before Williams, but Rose aggressively sought cover versions. Soon Tony Bennett ('Cold, Cold Heart'), Jo Stafford ('Jambalaya') and Joni James ('Your Cheatin' Heart') had gold records. Williams' wife, 'Miss Audrey', also made solo records, but Williams knew her talent was limited. She was frustrated by her own lack of success and many of Williams' songs stemmed from their quarrels. They were divorced on 29 May 1952 and, as Williams regarded possessions as unimportant, she was awarded their house and one half of all his future royalties. He did, however, have the sadness of losing custody of his son.

Like any professional show, the *Opry* preferred sober nondescripts to drunk superstars, and on 11 August 1952, Williams was fired and told that he could return when he was sober. However, Williams did not admit to his problem, joking about missing shows and falling off stage. He lost Fred Rose's support, the Drifting Cowboys turned to Ray Price, and, although the *Louisiana Hayride* tolerated his wayward lifestyle, his earnings fell and he was reduced to playing small clubs with pick-up bands. When Williams met the 19-year-old daughter of a policeman, Billie Jean Jones, he said, 'If you ain't married, ol' Hank's gonna marry you.' On 19 October 1952 he did just that - three times. First, before a Justice of the Peace in Minden, Louisiana, and then at two concerts at the New Orleans Municipal Auditorium before several thousand paying guests. The newlyweds spent Christmas with relations in Georgiana, Alabama. His biggest booking for some time was on New Year's Day, 1953 with Hawkshaw Hawkins and Homer And Jethro in Canton, Ohio, but because of a blizzard, Williams' plane was cancelled. An 18-year-old taxi driver, Charles Carr, was hired to drive Williams' Cadillac. They set off, Williams having a bottle of whiskey for company. He sank into a deep sleep. A policeman who stopped the car for ignoring speed restrictions remarked, 'That guy looks dead'. Five hours later, Carr discovered that his passenger was indeed dead. Death was officially due to 'severe heart attack with haemorrhage', but alcohol and pills played their part. At the concert that night, the performers sang Williams' 'I Saw The Light' in tribute. An atmospheric stage play, *Hank Williams: The Show He Never Gave*, by Maynard Collins, filmed with Sneezy Waters in the title role, showed what might have happened had Williams arrived that night. Some commentators took

Williams' then-current number 1, 'I'll Never Get Out Of This World Alive', as an indication that he knew he had little time left. Chet Atkins, who played 'dead string rhythm' on the record, disagreed: 'All young men of 28 or 29 feel immortal and although he wrote a lot about death, he thought it was something that would happen when he got old.' 20,000 saw Williams' body as it lay in state in an embroidered Nudie suit (designed by Miss Audrey) at the Montgomery Municipal Auditorium. His shrine in Montgomery Oakwood Cemetery is the subject of Steve Young's song, 'Montgomery In The Rain'.

1953 was a remarkable year for his records. 'Kaw-Liga', inspired by a visit to South Alabama and backed by 'Your Cheatin' Heart', went to the top of the chart, and his third consecutive posthumous number 1 was with Hy Heath and Fred Rose's 'Take These Chains From My Heart'. MGM, desperate for fresh material, overdubbed a backing onto demos for 'Weary Blues From Waitin'' and 'Roly Poly' - Hank Williams was the first deceased star to have his recordings altered. Albums of Hank Williams with strings and duets with his son followed. In 1969, Hank Jnr. completed some of his father's scribblings for an album, 'Songs My Father Left Me', the most successful being 'Cajun Baby'. In recent years, Williams and Willie Nelson proved a popular duo with 'I Told A Lie To My Heart', while a battered demo of 'There's A Tear In My Beer', which had been given by Williams to Big Bill Lister to perform, was magically restored with the addition of Hank Williams Jnr.'s voice and, accompanied by an even more ingenious video, sold 250,000 copies.

Hank Williams recorded around 170 different songs between 1946 and 1952, and there are over 230 and around 130 'Tribute to Hank Williams' albums that have also been recorded, not only by country artists, but by artists including Spike Jones, Del Shannon and Hardrock Gunter. The first was 'The Death Of Hank Williams' by disc jockey Jack Cardwell. Other contemporary ones included 'Hank, It Will Never Be The Same Without You' by Ernest Tubb, 'Hank Williams Will Live Forever' by Johnnie And Jack, 'The Life Of Hank Williams' by Hawkshaw Hawkins and 'Hank Williams Meets Jimmie Rodgers' by Virginia Rounders. Most tributes lack inspiration, are too morbid and too reverent, and are recorded by artists who would usually never enter a recording studio. The most pertinent tributes are Moe Bandy's reflective 'Hank Williams, You Wrote My Life', Johnny Cash's jaunty 'The Night Hank Williams Came To Town', Tim Hardin's plaintive 'Tribute To Hank Williams', Kris Kristofferson's rousing 'If You Don't Like Hank Williams' and Emmylou Harris's isolated 'Rollin' And Ramblin''. Hank Williams is the Phantom of the Opry; his influence on Moe Bandy, George Jones, Vernon Oxford and Boxcar Willie is especially marked. They have all recorded albums of his songs, as have Roy Acuff, Glen Campbell, Floyd Cramer, Don Gibson, Ronnie Hawkins, Roy Orbison, Charley Pride, Jack Scott, Del Shannon and Ernest Tubb. Johnny Cash, Jerry Lee Lewis, Little Richard, Elvis Presley, Linda Ronstadt and Richard Thompson have also appropriated his repertoire. Major UK chart hits include 'Lovesick Blues' by Frank Ifield, 'Take These Chains From My Heart' by Ray Charles, and 'Jambalaya' by the Carpenters. Before Williams was laid to rest, Lilly, Audrey and Billie Jean were squabbling for the rights to Williams' estate. Audrey's name is on his tombstone, and the inaccurate 1964 biopic Your

Cheatin' Heart, which starred George Hamilton as Hank Williams, miming to Hank Williams Jnr.'s recordings, did not even mention Billie Jean. Both wives performed as Mrs. Hank Williams, and Billie Jean was widowed a second time when Johnny Horton died in 1960. A more recent development has been the claims of Jett Williams, the illegitimate daughter of Williams and country singer Bobbie Jett, who was born three days after his death. The pressures Williams suffered in his life appear to have sharpened his awareness and heightened his creative powers. His compact, aching songs flow seamlessly and few have improved upon his own emotional performances. Hank Williams is the greatest country singer and songwriter who ever lived. His plaque in the Country Music Hall Of Fame states: 'The simple beautiful melodies and straightforward plaintive stories in his lyrics of life as he knew it will never die.'

● ALBUMS: Hank Williams Sings (MGM 1951)★★★★, Moanin' The Blues (MGM 1952)★★★★, Memorial Album (MGM 1953)★★★★, Hank Williams As Luke The Drifter (MGM 1953)★★★, Honky Tonkin' (1954)★★★, I Saw The Light (MGM 1954)★★★, Ramblin' Man (MGM 1955)★★★, Hank Williams as Luke The Drifter overdubbed as Beyond The Sunset MGM 1963 (MGM 1955)★★★, Sing Me A Blue Song (MGM 1957)★★★, The Immortal Hank Williams overdubbed as First Last And Always MGM 1969 (MGM 1958)★★★, The Unforgettable Hank Williams overdubbed MGM 1968 (MGM 1959)★★★, Lonesome Sound Of Hank Williams (MGM 1960)★★★, Wait For The Light To Shine overdubbed MGM 1968 (MGM 1960)★★★, Let Me Sing A Blue Song overdubbed 1968 (MGM 1961)★★★, Wanderin' Around overdubbed 1968 (MGM 1961)★★★, I'm Blue Inside overdubbed MGM 1968 (MGM 1961)★★★, The Spirit Of Hank Williams overdubbed MGM 1969 (MGM 1961)★★★, On Stage-Live Volume 1 (MGM 1962)★★★, On Stage Volume II (MGM 1963)★★★, Lost Highways & Other Folk Ballads (MGM 1964)★★★, Father And Son, overdubbed (MGM 1965)★★★, Kawliga And Other Humerous Songs some overdubbed (MGM 1965)★★★, Hank Williams With Strings overdubbed (MGM 1966)★★★, Hank Williams, Hank Williams Jr. Again (MGM 1966)★★★, Movin' On - Luke The Drifter overdubbed (MGM 1966)★★★, Mr & Mrs Hank Williams (With Audrey) (Metro 1966)★★★, More Hank Williams And Strings (MGM 1967)★★★, I Won't Be Home No More overdubs (MGM 1967)★★★, Hank Williams And Strings, Volume III (MGM 1968)★★★, In The Beginning (MGM 1968)★★★, Life To Legend Hank Williams (MGM 1970)★★★, The Last Picture Show Film Soundtrack (MGM 1971)★★★, Hank Williams/Hank Williams Jr. Legend In Story And Song (MGM 1973)★★★, Hank Williams/Hank Williams Jr. Insights In Story And Song (MGM 1974)★★★, A Home In Heaven (MGM 1975)★★★, Live At The Grand Ole Opry (MGM 1976)★★★★, Hank Williams And The Drifting Cowboys On Radio (Golden Country 1982)★★★★, Early Country Live Volume 1 (Hank Williams On Radio Shows Plus Others) (ACM 1983)★★★★, Rare Takes And Radio Cuts (Polydor 1984)★★★, Early Country Live Volume 2 (Hank Williams On Radio Shows) (ACM 1984)★★★★, Early Country Music Live Volume 3 (Hank Williams On Radio Shows (ACM 1985)★★★★, Just Me And My Guitar (CMF 1985)★★★, Hank Williams - The First Recordings (CMF 1985)★★★★, Hank Williams - On The Air (Polydor 1985)★★★, Hank Williams: I Ain't Got Nothin' But Time December 1946-August 1947 (Polydor 1985)★★★★, Hank Williams: Lovesick Blues - August

1947-December 1948 (Polydor 1985)★★★, *Hank Williams: Lost Highway - December 1948-March 1949* (Polydor 1986)★★★, *Hank Williams: I'm So Lonesome I Could Cry - March 1949-August 1949* (Polydor 1986)★★★, *Hank Williams: Long Gone Lonesome Blues - August 1949-December 1950* (Polydor 1987)★★★, *Hank Williams: Hey, Good Lookin' - December 1950-July 1951* (Polydor 1987)★★★, *Hank Williams: Let's Turn Back The Years, July 1951-June 1952* (Polydor 1987)★★★, *Hank Williams: I Won't Be Home No More, June 1952-September 1952* (Polydor 1987)★★★, *There's Nothing As Sweet As My Baby* (Mount Olive 1988)★★★, *Hank Williams - Jambalaya* (Creative Sounds 1992)★★★, *Health And Happiness Shows* (Mercury 1993)★★★, *Alone And Forsaken* (Mercury 1995)★★★, *Three Hanks, Men With Broken Hearts* (Curb 1996)★★★.
● COMPILATIONS: *Greatest Hits* (Polydor 1963)★★★, *The Very Best Of Hank Williams* (Polydor 1963)★★★, *24 Of Hank Williams' Greatest Hits* (MGM 1970)★★★, *24 Greatest Hits, Volume 2* (Polydor 1976)★★, *40 Greatest Hits* (Polydor 1978)★★★, *The Collectors' Edition* 8-LP box set of Polydor albums listed above (Polydor 1987)★★★★★, *Rare Demos: First To Last* (CMF 1990)★★★, *The Original Singles Collection Plus* 3-CD box set (Polydor 1990)★★★★★, *Low Down Blues* (Polygram 1996)★★★.
● VIDEOS: *The Hank Williams Story* (1994).
● FURTHER READING: *Sing A Sad Song: The Life Of Hank Williams*, Roger M. Williams. *Hank Williams: From Life To Legend*, Jerry Rivers. *I Saw The Light: The Gospel Life Of Hank Williams*, Al Bock. *Hank Williams: Country Music's Tragic King*, Jay Caress. *The First Outlaw: Hank Williams*, Jim Arp. *Your Cheating Heart, A Biography Of Hank Williams*, Chet Flippo. *Hank Williams: A Bio-Bibliography*, George William Koon. *Still In Love With You: The Story Of Hank And Audrey Williams*, Lycrecia Williams and Dale Vinicur. *Ain't Nothin' As Sweet As My Baby: The Story Of Hank Williams' Lost Daughter*, Jett Williams. *Hank Williams: The Complete Lyrics*, Don Cusic. *The Life And Times Of Hank Williams*, Arnold Rogers and Bruce Gidoll. *Hank Williams: The Biography*, Colin Escott.

WILLIAMS, HANK, JNR.

b. Randall Hank Williams Jnr., 26 May 1949, Shreveport, Louisiana, USA. The son of the most famous man in country music, Hank Williams, he was nicknamed Bocephus after a puppet on the *Grand Ole Opry*. Being the son of a country legend has brought financial security, but it was difficult for him to firmly establish his own individuality. His mother, Audrey, was determined that he would follow in his father's footsteps. When only eight years old, he was touring, performing with his father's songs, and even appeared on the *Grand Ole Opry*. He also had a high school band, Rockin' Randall And The Rockets. He signed for the same label as his father, MGM Records, as soon as his voice broke. In the 60s, Williams had country hits with 'Long Gone Lonesome Blues', 'Cajun Baby', a revival of 'Endless Sleep', and the only version of 'Nobody's Child' ever to make the country charts. He also recorded an embarrassing narration about his relationship with his father, 'Standing In The Shadows'. Even worse was his maudlin dialogue as Luke the Drifter Jnr., 'I Was With Red Foley (The Night He Passed Away)'. He copied his father's style for the soundtrack of the film biography of his father, *Your Cheatin' Heart* (1964), and starred in

the inferior *A Time To Sing*. He was just 15 years old and Connie Francis was 26 when they released a duet about adultery, 'Walk On By'.
In 1974, Williams Jnr. moved to Alabama where he recorded a hard-hitting album, *Hank Williams Jnr. And Friends*, with Charlie Daniels and other top-class southern country rockers. Like his father, he has had arguments with Audrey, gone through an unhappy marriage and overindulged in alcohol and drugs. 'Getting Over You' relates to his life, and in another song, he explains that it's the 'Family Tradition'. On 8 August 1975, Hank Williams Jnr. fell 500 feet down a Montana mountain face. Although close to death, he made a remarkable recovery, needing extensive medical and cosmetic surgery. Half of his face was reconstructed and he had to learn to speak (and sing) all over again. It was two years before he could perform once more. Since 1977, Williams Jnr., who is managed by his opening act Merle Kilgore, has been associated with the 'outlaw country music' genre. Waylon Jennings, for example, wrote Williams Jnr.'s country hit 'Are You Sure Hank Done It This Way?' and produced his album *The New South*. In 1983, he had eight albums on the US country charts simultaneously, yet was not chosen as Entertainer of the Year in the Country Music Awards. In 1985, Williams released his fiftieth album, *Five-O*. Williams' songs often lack distinctive melodies, while the lyrics concentrate on his macho, defiant persona. His best compositions include 'Montana Cafe', 'OD'd In Denver', the jazzy 'Women I've Never Had' and his tale of a visit to a gay disco, 'Dinosaur'. 'If The South Woulda Won' was criticized for being racist but, possibly, he was being sardonic. However, there was no mistaking of his tone towards Saddam Hussein in 'Don't Give Us A Reason'. Among his other successes are 'I Fought The Law', 'Tennessee Stud', 'Ain't Misbehavin'' and his *cri de coeur*, 'If Heaven Ain't A Lot Like Dixie'. Although Williams has shown a determination to move away from his father's shadow, he still sings about him. Many tribute songs by others - 'If You Don't Like Hank Williams' and 'Are You Sure Hank Done It This Way?' - gain an extra dimension through his interpretations. Williams himself was the subject of a tribute from David Allan Coe, who insisted that a man of six feet four inches and 15 stone should not be called 'Jnr'. Williams' rowdy image did not fit in well with the clean-cut 'hat acts' of the early 90s, and his record sales and air play faltered. He remains a sell-out concert draw, although a well-publicized incident during 1992 where he arrived onstage drunk, and spent most of the 20-minute performance insulting his audience, did little for his status in the Nashville community, although his father would have been mighty proud.
● ALBUMS: *Hank Williams Jnr. Sings The Songs Of Hank Williams* (MGM 1963)★★★, *Connie Francis And Hank Williams Jnr. Sing Great Country Favorites* (MGM 1964)★★★, *Your Cheatin' Heart* film soundtrack (MGM 1964)★★, *Ballad Of The Hills And Plains* (MGM 1965)★★★, *Father And Son - Hank Williams Sr And Hank Williams Jnr. Again* (MGM 1965)★★★, *Blue's My Name* (MGM 1966)★★★, *Country Shadows* (MGM 1966)★★★, *In My Own Way* (MGM 1967)★★★, *My Songs* (MGM 1968)★★★, *A Time To Sing* film soundtrack (MGM 1968)★★, *Luke The Drifter Jnr.* (MGM 1969)★★★, *Songs My Father Left Me* (MGM 1969)★★★, *Live At Cobo Hall, Detroit* (MGM 1969)★★★★, *Luke The Drifter Jnr., Volume 2* (MGM 1969)★★★, *Sunday*

Morning (MGM 1970)★★★, *Singing My Songs* (MGM 1970)★★★, *Luke The Drifter Jnr., Volume 3* (MGM 1970)★★★, with Louis Johnson *Removing The Shadow* (MGM 1970)★★, *All For The Love Of Sunshine* (MGM 1970)★★★, *I've Got A Right To Cry/They All Used To Belong To Me* (MGM 1971), *Sweet Dreams* (MGM 1971)★★★, *Eleven Roses* (MGM 1972)★★, with Johnson *Send Me Some Lovin'/Whole Lotta Lovin'* (MGM 1972)★★★, *After You/Pride's Not Hard To Swallow* (MGM 1973)★★★, *Hank Williams/Hank Williams Jr: The Legend In Story And Song* a double album in which Hank Jnr. narrates his father's life (MGM 1973)★★★, *Just Pickin' - No Singing* (MGM 1973)★★★, *The Last Love Song* (MGM 1973)★★★, *Hank Williams/Hank Williams Jr. Insights In Story And Song* (MGM 1974)★★★, *Bocephus* (MGM 1975)★★, *Hank Williams Jnr. And Friends* (MGM 1975)★★★★, *One Night Stands* (Warners/Curb 1977)★★★, *The New South* (Warners 1978)★★★★, *Family Tradition* (Elektra/Curb 1979)★★★★, *Whiskey Bent And Hell Bound* (Elektra/Curb 1979)★★★★, *Habits Old And New* (Elektra/Curb 1980)★★★, *Rowdy* (Elektra/Curb 1981)★★★★, *The Pressure Is On* (Elektra/Curb 1981)★★★★, *High Notes* (Elektra/Curb 1982)★★★, *Strong Stuff* (Elektra/Curb 1983)★★★, *Man Of Steel* (Warners/Curb 1983)★★★★, *Major Moves* (Warners/Curb 1984)★★★★, *Five-O* (Warners/Curb 1985)★★★★, *Montana Cafe* (Warners/Curb 1986)★★★★, *Hank Live* (Warners/Curb 1987)★★★, *Born To Boogie* (Warners/Curb 1987)★★★★, *Wild Streak* (Warners/Curb 1988)★★★★, *Lone Wolf* (Warners/Curb 1990)★★, *America - The Way I See It* (Warners/Curb 1990)★, *Pure Hank* (Warners/Curb 1991)★★★, *Maverick* (Curb/Capricorn 1992)★★★★, *Out Of Left Field* (Curb/Capricorn 1993)★★★, *Chronicles - Health And Happiness* (1993)★★★, *Hog Wild* (MCG/Curb 1995)★★★, *AKA Wham Bam Sam* (MCG/Curb 1996)★★, *Three Hanks, Men With Broken Hearts* (MCG/Curb 1996)★★★.
● COMPILATIONS: *The Best Of Hank Williams Jnr.* (MGM 1967)★★★, *Living Proof: The MGM Recordings 1963 - 1975* (Mercury 1974)★★★★, *14 Greatest Hits* (Polydor 1976)★★★, *Hank Williams Jnr.'s Greatest Hits* (Warners/Curb 1982)★★★, *Greatest Hits Volume Two* (Warners/Curb 1985)★★★★, *The Early Years 1976-1978* (Warners/Curb 1986)★★★, *The Magic Guitar Of Hank Williams Jnr.* (1986)★★★, *Country Store* (Country Store 1988)★★★, *Standing In The Shadows* (Polydor 1988)★★★★, *Greatest Hits Volume 3* (Warners/Curb 1989)★★★★, *The Bocephus Box: Hank Williams Jnr. Collection '79 - 92* (Capricorn 1992)★★★, *The Best Of, Volume 1: Roots And Branches* (Mercury 1992)★★★, *Hank Williams Jnr.'s Greatest Hits* (Curb 1994)★★★.
● VIDEOS: *Live In Concert* (1993).
● FURTHER READING: *Living Proof*, Hank Williams Jnr. with Michael Bane.

WILLIAMS, LEONA

b. Leona Belle Helton, 7 January 1943, Vienna, Missouri, USA. One of the 12 children of musical parents (all played instruments), Leona worked with the family group as a child. In 1958, she had her own show on KWOS Jefferson City. She married drummer Ron Williams in 1959 and with Leona playing bass, both worked with Loretta Lynn. In 1968, she signed for Hickory with whom she achieved three minor hits, including 'Once More', before moving to MCA. In 1975,

she joined Merle Haggard's show, initially as a backing vocalist. However, when Haggard divorced Bonnie Owens, she not only became the featured vocalist but on 7 October 1978, she also became the third Mrs Haggard. They combined to write several songs and recorded an album together but the marriage soon proved turbulent. In 1978, they had a number 8 US country hit with 'The Bull And The Beaver' but in 1983, when the marriage ended, they appeared in the charts with the appropriately named 'We're Strangers Again'. She later married songwriter and guitarist Dave Kirby. She also made solo recordings for Elektra and Mercury and her songs have been recorded by other stars including Tammy Wynette, but she has so far failed to achieve a big solo hit. Williams does hold the distinction of being the first female country singer to record a live album in a prison.
● ALBUMS: *That Williams Girl* (Hickory 1970)★★, *San Quentin's First Lady* (MCA 1976)★★★, *A Woman Walked Away* (MCA 1977)★★★, with Merle Haggard *Heart To Heart* (Mercury 1983)★★★★, *Someday When Things Are Good* (1984)★★★.

WILLIAMS, LUCINDA

b. 26 January 1953, Lake Charles, Louisiana, USA. Her father, Miller Williams, is a professor of literature and a professional poet, but it was her mother, a music graduate, who influenced Lucinda the most. She played folk clubs in Texas in the mid-70s and made her first albums for Folkways Records. Her career failed to take off until she moved to Los Angeles some years later, but she was further stymied by an abortive development contract with CBS Records in the mid-80s. She describes songwriting as 'like writing a journal but I don't want it to sound self-indulgent.' Her self-titled album for Rough Trade Records in 1989 finally re-established her with its attendant strong press. *Sweet Old World* provided darker subject matter than most folk-country albums; the title song is about suicide and 'Pineola' similarly concerns a poet who shot himself. It included a cover version of Nick Drake's 'Which Will', with musical backing by Benmont Tench, Bryce Berline and Doug Atwell. She has also performed on the tribute albums to Merle Haggard (*Tulare Dust*) and Victoria Williams (*Sweet Relief*). In the 90s Mary-Chapin Carpenter earned a major US country hit with her 'Passionate Kisses'. Williams is now signed to American Recordings.
● ALBUMS: *Ramblin' On My Mind* (Folkways 1979)★★★, *Happy Woman Blues* (Folkways 1980)★★★★, *Lucinda Williams* (Rough Trade 1988)★★★, *Sweet Old World* (Chameleon 1992)★★★.

WILLIAMS, TEX

b. Sollie Paul Williams, 23 August 1917, Ramsey, Fayette County, Illinois, USA, d. 11 October 1985, Newhall, California, USA. His father was a keen fiddler, and by the time he was 13 years old, Williams had a local radio programme as a one-boy band. He toured with the Reno Racketeers but he soon turned to Hollywood. In 1940 he appeared alongside Tex Ritter in Rollin' Home To Texas and then made a long chain of westerns, many of them Saturday morning serials. He managed to overcome his limp, a legacy of childhood polio, and he became known as 'Tex', as, presumably, Illinois Williams did not have the same ring. Williams also played bass and sang with Spade Cooley's western swing band, establishing himself as a vocalist on Cooley's 1945 country hit, 'Shame On You'. In 1947, Capitol Records had their first million-selling record with Williams' fast-talking, deep-voiced monologue, 'Smoke! Smoke! Smoke!', which he wrote with Merle Travis. As his songs often praised smoking, he became known as 'The Man Who Sings Tobacco Best', but this was before the link between cigarettes and cancer was known. In 1948, Williams had success with another narration, 'Life Gits Tee-jus, Don't It?', but the composer Carson J. Robison took the main honours. Williams' other successes included 'That's What I Like About The West', 'Never Trust A Woman', 'Don't Telephone, Don't Telegraph, Tell A Woman', 'Suspicion' and 'Talking Boogie'. He and his band played dancehalls all over the USA and he promoted Nudie's stage suits, helping Nudie become the tailor to country stars. His 1963 album, *Tex Williams In Las Vegas*, was recorded at the Mint Club in 1963, featuring Glen Campbell and produced by one of the Crickets, Tommy Allsup. His subsequent singles included 'Too Many Tigers', 'Bottom Of The Mountain', 'The Night Miss Nancy Ann's Hotel For Single Girls Burned Down' and 'Smoke! Smoke! Smoke! '68' with Merle Travis. The smoke, smoke, smoke caught up with him and he died of lung cancer in 1985 at his home in Newhall, California.

● ALBUMS: *Dance-O-Rama-Tex Williams* (Decca 1955)★★★★, *Tex Williams Best* (Camden 1958)★★★, *Smoke! Smoke! Smoke!* (Capitol 1960)★★★, *Country Music Time* (Decca 1962)★★★ *Tex Williams In Las Vegas* (Liberty 1963)★★★, *Tex Williams* (Sunset 1966)★★★, *Two Sides Of Tex Williams* (Boone 1966)★★★★, *The Voice Of Authority* (Imperial 1966)★★★, *A Man Called Tex* (1971)★★★★, *Those Lazy, Hazy Days* (1974)★★★, *Tex Williams And California Express* (1981)★★★.

● COMPILATIONS: *14 All-Time Country Hits* (1978)★★★★, *Vintage Collection Series* (Capitol 1996)★★★★.

WILLING, FOY

b. Foy Willingham, 1915, Bosque County, Texas, USA, d. 24 July 1978. After first singing on local radio while still at school, he moved to New York where he appeared on radio for Crazy Water Crystals in 1933. He returned to radio work in Texas in 1935 but two years later, he moved to California, where he formed the Riders Of the Purple Sage. Initially, it comprised himself, Jimmy Dean and Al Sloey, but over the years there were many others, including Scotty Herrell, Billy Leibert, Paul Sellers and Johnny Paul. Using an instrumental line-up that included accordion, fiddle and guitar and closely resembling the Sons Of The Pioneers, they became very popular on several radio shows including the *Hollywood Barn Dance*. They also appeared in numerous Republic pictures with either Roy Rogers or Monte Hale. Their popularity saw them record for several labels and they are best remembered for their recordings of 'Ghost Riders In The Sky' (Capitol) and 'No One To Cry To' (Majestic). They formally disbanded in 1952 but later made nostalgic appearances at festivals, some further recordings and in 1959, they toured with Gene Autry. Foy Willing continued to appear at Western events until his death in 1978. (This group should not be confused with the New Riders Of The Purple Sage, a country rock band of the 70s.)

● ALBUMS: *Cowboy* (1958)★★★, *New Sound Of American Folk* (1962)★★★.

WILLIS BROTHERS

Guy (b. James Willis, 5 July 1915, Alex, Arkansas, USA, d. 13 April 1981, Nashville, Tennessee, USA; guitar, vocals), Skeeter (b. Charles Willis, 20 December 1917, Coalton, Oklahoma, USA, d. March 1976; fiddle, vocals) and Vic (b. Richard Willis, 31 May 1922, Schulter, Oklahoma, USA; accordion, piano, vocals). Using clever combinations that saw any brother able to sing lead or harmony, they first appeared on KGEF Shawnee in 1932 as the Oklahoma Wranglers. In 1942, they moved to the Brush Creek Follies on KMBC Kansas City, Missouri, but their careers were interrupted by military service. In 1946, they backed Hank Williams when he made his first Sterling recordings in December that year. They also joined the *Grand Ole Opry* and began a long association with Eddy Arnold. They left the *Opry* in 1949 and during the 50s, were popular on various shows including the *Ozark Jubilee* and the *Midwestern Hayride*. They rejoined the *Opry* in 1960 and during the decade found country chart success on Starday including a Top 10 hit with 'Give Me Forty Acres'. During their career they recorded for several other labels, even worked as session musicians and toured extensively including overseas trips. They appeared in several films including *Feudin' Rhythm* and *Hoe Down*, and also hold the distinction of being the first country act to perform at the Constitution Hall in Washington. Guy retired after Skeeter died of cancer in 1976 and Vic formed the Vic Willis Trio and continued to perform.

● ALBUMS: *In Action* (Starday 1962)★★★, *Code Of The West* (Starday 1963)★★★★, *Let's Hit The Road* (Starday 1965)★★, *The Sensational Willis Brothers* (Hilltop 1965)★★★, *Give Me Forty Acres* (Starday 1965)★★★★, *Road Stop-Jukebox Hits* (Starday 1965)★★★, *The Wild Side Of Life* (Starday 1966)★★★, *The Willis Brothers Goin' To Town* (Starday 1966)★★, *Bob* (Starday 1967)★★★, *Hey, Mister Truck Driver* (Starday 1968)★★★, *Bummin' Around* (Starday 1969)★★★, *Truck Driver Hits* (Nashville 1969)★★★, *Y'All* (Nashville 1969)★★★, *For The Good Times* (Starday 1971)★★★.

● COMPILATIONS: *Country Hits* (Alshire 1969)★★★★, *The Best Of The Willis Brothers* (Starday 1970)★★★★.

WILLIS, KELLY

b. 1 October 1968, Annandale, Virginia, USA. Willis formed her first band when aged 16, and when she moved to Austin, Nanci Griffith arranged an audition for her at MCA. Willis has been compared to another MCA artist, Brenda Lee, because her records suggest the same blend of rockabilly, rock 'n' roll and ballads, updated for the 90s. The title track of *Bang Bang*, for example, is an obscure title from rock 'n' roller Janis Martin. The songwriting credits on her albums are always interesting and 'Sincerely' was written by Steve Earle and Robert Earl Keen. Don Was produced her third album, which included songs she had written with John Leventhal and Paul Kennerley. She also duets with Kevin Welch on 'That'll Be Me' and took time out to add background harmonies to Chris Wall's *Cowboy Nation*. She sings the Paul Kennerley song 'I Don't Want To Love You (But I Do)' on the soundtrack of *Thelma And Louise* (1991) and she appeared as Clarissa Flan in *Bob Roberts* (1992). She returned to recording with 1996's *Fading Fast EP*.

● ALBUMS: *Well Travelled Love* (MCA 1990)★★★, *Bang Bang* (MCA 1991)★★★★, *Kelly Willis* (MCA 1993)★★★.

WILLS, BILLY JACK

b. 1926, on a farm near Memphis, Hall County, Texas, USA. Billy Jack was the youngest brother of Bob Wills and the ninth of the Wills family's children. He naturally grew up influenced by his brother Bob's music and joined the Texas Playboys in 1945. He initially played bass but, after 1949, he usually played drums and also took some vocals. He added the lyrics to the old fiddle tune called 'Faded Love' that had been written by Bob and his father John Wills. He shared the vocal when it was first recorded in 1950 and the song reached number 8 in the US country charts. It went on to become a country standard and was later a hit for Patsy Cline (1963), Leon McAuliffe (1963), Tompall And The Glaser Brothers (1971) and Willie Nelson and Ray Price (1980). In the mid-50s, he formed his own band and recorded for Four Star.

● COMPILATIONSS: *Billy Jack Wills & His Western Swing Band* (Western 1983)★★★, *Crazy Man Crazy* (Western 1985)★★★.

WILLS, BOB

b. James Robert Wills, 6 March 1905, on a farm near Kosse, Limestone County, Texas, USA, d. 13 May 1975, Fort Worth, Texas, USA. The eldest of the ten children of John Thompkins Wills and Emmaline (Foley), Bob was a sickly child and there were fears that he would not survive his early years. His father, known locally as Uncle John, was a skilled fiddler, and later taught his son Bob to play the mandolin so that he could accompany his father's playing; however, initially Bob showed no great interest in music. In 1913, the Wills family relocated to Memphis, Texas. Bob rode his donkey behind the family wagon and the 500-mile journey took over two months. John and Bob played for farm dances along the way to raise money for food and it was at one of these dances that Bob first became interested in music played by black families, featuring trumpet and guitar. When he was 10 years old, much to his father's relief, he took up the fiddle and made his first solo public appearance. On one occasion, his father failed to appear to play at a dance, and in spite of knowing only six fiddle tunes for dancing, he kept playing alone (his father eventually arrived at 2 am, too drunk to play). John Wills was successful as a farmer and by 1921, he had moved to a 600-acre ranch/farm near Oxbow Crossing, which remained their home until 1931. The family continued to play for local functions; it was suggested that the Wills family, which by 1926 included nine children, produced more music than cotton. Realizing the farm could not sustain them all, in 1924, Bob moved to Amarillo where, by working on building sites and as a shoeshine boy, he made enough money to buy himself a fiddle. He then found work playing for dances on Saturday nights and made his first radio broadcasts on Amarillo's two radio stations, KGRS and WDAG. A year later, he returned home driving a Model T Ford, which enabled him to travel around playing. In 1926, he married for the first time and leased a farm, but after a crop failure in 1927, he and his wife moved to Amarillo and he gave up farming for good. He moved to Fort Worth where, sometimes in blackface, he found work in a Medicine Show. Here he met guitarist Herman Arnspiger and the two men began to appear as the Wills Family Band. They played for dances, did comedy routines and in November 1929, they recorded for Brunswick in

Dallas, although the two songs were not released. In 1930, the duo became a quartet when Milton Brown and his brother Durwood joined as vocalist and guitarist, respectively, although Durwood was at the time still at school (Milton Brown later became famous with his own band, the Musical Brownies). They found regular work playing for dances, at times adding banjoist Frank Barnes, and played on KTAT and KFJZ where the assistant programme director of the latter station, Alton Strickland, would five years later became Wills' pianist. In 1930, Wills' band were sponsored on WBAP by the Aladdin Lamp Company (they appeared as the Aladdin Laddies), and also gained a residency at the Crystal Springs dancehall in Fort Worth. In January 1931, through the sponsorship of the Burrus Mill and Elevator Company and billed as the Light Crust Doughboys, he and the band began to advertise Light Crust Flour on KFJZ. After two weeks, in spite of their popularity with the listeners, the President of Burrus Mill, Mr. Wilbert Lee O'Daniel (later a US Senator and Governor of Texas) sacked them, because he considered their music was too hillbilly. KFJZ kept them on air without a sponsor and Wills succeeded in getting O'Daniel to resume sponsorship and pay the band as well, although for a time all members had to work a 40-hour week in the mill. Their popularity grew and soon the programme was being heard over all the south-west, even reaching as far as Oklahoma City. The band recorded for RCA Victor in 1932, the only recordings made by Wills with the Light Crust Doughboys. The same year, vocalist Thomas Elmer Duncan replaced Milton Brown. In 1933, after differences of opinion and occasional drinking sprees that saw him miss shows, Wills was sacked by O'Daniel. He moved to Waco, assembled a band that included his brother, Johnnie Lee Wills, and Duncan, and for the first time, he called his band the Playboys; he also added 'formerly the Light Crust Doughboys' (he found himself in lawsuits from O'Daniel for using the name, but eventually the courts found in his favour). He then moved to Oklahoma City, where he began to call his band the Texas Playboys, but O'Daniel stopped his programme by promising the radio station he would put on the *Burrus Mill Show* in Oklahoma if they did not broadcast Wills' band. Wills moved to KVOO Tulsa, where in February 1934, Bob Wills And The Texas Playboys finally began to broadcast and this time O'Daniel's attempts to stop them failed.

In 1935, the group made their first historic studio recordings. The band consisted of twelve musicians, namely Bob Wills (fiddle), Tommy Duncan (vocals, piano), Johnnie Lee Wills (tenor banjo), Son Lansford (bass), Herman Arnspiger (guitar), Sleepy Johnson (guitar), Jesse Ashlock (fiddle), Art Baines (fiddle, trombone), Smokey Dacus (drums), Robert McNally (saxophone), Al Stricklin (piano) and Leon McAuliffe (steel guitar). Wills stayed in Tulsa and during the late 30s, he continued to shape his band; changes in personnel saw the arrival of guitarist Eldon Shamblin and saxophonist Joe Ferguson. In 1936, Leon McAuliffe first recorded his 'Steel Guitar Rag'. Wills made further recording sessions in Chicago (1936) and Dallas (1937 and 1938). When he recorded in Saginaw, Texas, in April 1940, his band numbered 18 musicians - more than the big bands of the period such as Glenn Miller, Benny Goodman and the Dorseys were using. It was at this session that he recorded his million-selling version of 'New San Antonio Rose', the (Tommy

Duncan) vocal version of his 1935 fiddle tune, previously known as 'Spanish Two Step'. This version differed from his original fiddle one in that it featured only reeds and brass and was played in the swing style as used by the big bands of the time (over the years the song has usually been referred to as simply 'San Antonio Rose'). Wills was by this time one of the top-selling recording artists in the USA. In 1939, the demand was such that Wills decided for the first time to run a second band, which was led by his brother Johnnie Lee and also included his younger brother Luke Wills. Although successful with his music, Bob Wills was far from successful in marriage. He had troubles at times with excessive drinking and a fondness for the ladies. He was divorced in 1935 and married and divorced a second time in 1936. In 1938, he married again but once more was divorced within the year, and though he persuaded this wife to remarry him, they were divorced for the second time in 1939. He married again in July 1939, only to be divorced (yet again!) in June 1941.

In 1940, he appeared with Tex Ritter in the film *Take Me Back To Oklahoma*, even duetting with Ritter on the title track, and the following year, with his full band, he featured in the film *Go West Young Man*. In 1942, Duncan left for military service (he rejoined on discharge) but Wills maintained a band containing 15 instruments, although only four were stringed. He recorded in Hollywood and made eight B-movie westerns with Russell Hayden. He was also married that year to Betty Anderson, a girl 18 years his junior and this time, in spite of his drinking, the marriage would last until his death. After the filming was completed, more band members left for the US Army and Wills moved to Tulsa, finally disbanding the group in December 1942. He enlisted himself but was discharged in July 1943. He moved to California, re-formed a band and returned to the film studios. Wills never liked Hollywood but he loved the cowboy image. He spent lavishly on horses, harnesses and dress for himself and was a popular figure on his favourite stallion, Punkin, around the California rodeo circuit. He bought a ranch in the San Joaquin Valley and stocked it with horses and a dairy herd 'just to keep my father busy'. At one stage in 1944, his band consisted of 22 instruments and 2 vocalists, but he never recorded with this unit. Duncan left in 1947 to form his own band, probably because he had tired of having to take responsibility for fronting the band when Wills failed to appear through drinking sprees. During 1944-45, Wills had US country and pop chart hits with 'New San Antonio Rose', 'We Might As Well Forget It' and 'You're From Texas'. He also had country number 1 hits with such war songs as 'Smoke On The Water', 'Stars And Stripes At Iwo Jima', 'Silver Dew On The Blue Grass Tonight' and 'White Cross At Okinawa'. In 1946, his 'New Spanish Two-Step' topped the country charts for 16 weeks as well as having Top 20 pop success. Wills left Columbia Records in 1947 to record for MGM Records and in 1950, he recorded his classic 'Faded Love' - a composition that he and his father wrote with some words added by brother Billy Jack Wills. He toured extensively and relocated to Dallas, where he invested heavily in a dancehall that he called Bob Wills' Ranch House. Due to unscrupulous advisers and accountants, he soon found himself heavily in debt. Faced with jail, he sold his Bob Wills Music Company and accidentally with it the ownership of 'San Antonio Rose'. For two years, he struggled to raise funds; he ran two bands

- one played at the Ranch House and he toured with the other. In January 1952, he finally sold the Ranch House to a Jack Ruby - a name then unknown outside Dallas, but later internationally known following the assassination of Lee Harvey Oswald (in turn, killer of President John F. Kennedy). Throughout the 50s, he recorded and toured extensively and several times moved his base of operations. Wills continued to experiment but the influence of television began to affect the dancehalls; tastes had changed and he never recaptured the earlier successes. He recorded in Nashville for the first time in 1955, and again in 1956, but most of his recordings were made in California. In 1959, he appeared at the Golden Nugget in Las Vegas but still missed a few shows through his drinking. He was reunited with Tommy Duncan, and during the period of 1960/1 they recorded over 40 sides for Liberty Records. In 1962, he suffered a heart attack but in 1963, he was back, even though he had sold his band to Carl Johnson. He suffered a further heart attack in 1964 and when he recovered sufficiently to work again, he always acted as a frontman for other bands. Between 1963 and 1969, he recorded almost 100 sides for either Liberty, Longhorn or Kapp Records. He was elected to the Country Music Hall Of Fame in 1968.

After an appearance on 30 May 1969, he suffered a stroke and was rushed to hospital where he underwent two major operations. The stroke left him paralyzed on his right side and hospitalized for months. In 1970, he moved to Tulsa and in 1971 underwent surgery for a kidney complaint, but suffered a stroke on the left side a few hours after the operation. Months later, he recovered sufficiently to talk and to use his left arm, even telling people that he would play again. Country star Merle Haggard admired Wills and in 1970, he recorded his album *Tribute To The Best Damn Fiddle Player In The World (Or My Salute To Bob Wills)*, which actually featured some of the Texas Playboys. Wills was unable to attend the recordings but in 1971, he was reunited with 10 of his old Texas Playboys at Haggard's house, near Bakersfield, and watched and listened as recordings were made. In 1973, he made a few appearances, at one even holding his fiddle while Hoyle Nix used the bow. He travelled to Dallas to attend a recording session of the Texas Playboys and on 3 December even included a few of his famous yells and 'hollers' as the band recorded some of his hits. During the night, he suffered a further stroke and remained unconscious for almost 18 months until his death from pneumonia on 13 May 1975. He was buried in Memorial Park, Tulsa, a city that saw most of the glory days of Bob Wills' western swing music. It could never be said that he copied any other style - he devised his own, as the words of his song said, 'Deep within my heart lies a melody'. His long-time friend, steel guitarist Leon McAuliffe, who, though 12 years younger than Wills, had retired from the music scene, summed things up when he said, 'My desire wore out before my body, Bob never did wear out at this. His body wore out before his desire did'. There have been other bands that played the music but none that ever matched the instrumental integration or the wide variation in the styles and music of Bob Wills. His habit of uttering spasmodic high-pitched shouts during the playing of numbers, such as his famed 'Ah haaa', originated from the days when, as a young boy, he performed with his father at ranch dances in Texas. His father (and the cowboys) used similar loud cries at points when the music or the whiskey moved them to feel that something was special. As Waylon Jennings sang, 'When you're down in Austin, Bob Wills is still the King'.

● ALBUMS: *Bob Wills Round-Up* 10-inch album (Columbia 1949)★★★, *Ranch House Favorites* 10-inch album (MGM 1951)★★★★, *Old Time Favorites By Bob Wills & His Texas Playboys 1* (Antone's 1953)★★★, *Old Time Favorites By Bob Wills & His Texas Playboys 2* (Antone's 1953)★★★, *Dance-O-Rama No: 2* (Decca 1955)★★★, *Ranch House Favorites ii* (MGM 1956)★★★, *Bob Wills Special* (Harmony 1957)★★★★, *Bob Wills & His Texas Playboys* (Decca 1957)★★★★, *Western Swing In Hi-Fi* (1957)★★★★, with Tommy Duncan *Together Again* (Liberty 1960)★★★, with Tommy Duncan *Bob Wills & Tommy Duncan* (Liberty 1961)★★★, *Living Legend - Bob Wills & His Texas Playboys* (Liberty 1961)★★★, *Mr Words & Mr Music* (Liberty 1961)★★★, *Bob Wills Sings And Plays* (Liberty 1963)★★★, *Best Of Bob Wills & His Texas Playboys - Original Recordings* (Harmony 1963)★★★★, *My Keepsake Album* (Longhorn 1965)★★★, *The Great Bob Wills* (Harmony 1965)★★★, *San Antonio Rose/Steel Guitar Rag* (Starday 1965)★★★, *Western Swing Band* (Vocalion 1965)★★★, with Leon Rausch *From The Heart Of Texas* (Kapp 1966)★★★, *King Of Western Swing* (Kapp 1967)★★★, *Bob Wills* (Metro 1967)★★★, *Here's That Man Again* (Kapp 1968)★★★★, *Plays The Greatest String Band Hits* (Kapp 1969)★★★, *A Country Walk* (Sunset 1969)★★★, *Time Changes Everything* (Kapp 1969)★★★, *The Living Legend* (Kapp 1969)★★★, *Bob Wills Special* (Harmony 1969)★★★, *The Bob Wills Story* (Starday 1970)★★★, *Bob Wills In Person* (Kapp 1970)★★★, *A Tribute To Bob Wills* (MGM 1971)★★★, *The History Of Bob Wills & The Texas Playboys* (MGM 1973)★★★, *The Best Of Bob Wills* (MCA 1973), *For The Last Time* (United Artists 1974)★★★★, *Bob Wills & His Texas Playboys In Concert* (Capitol 1976)★★★, *I Love People* (1976)★★★, *Lonestar Rag* (1979)★★★, *Faded Love* (1981)★★★, *31st Street Blues* (1981)★★★, *The San Antonio Rose Story* (1982)★★★, *Texas Fiddle & Milk Cow Blues* (1982)★★★, *Heaven, Hell Or Houston* (1983)★★★, *Swing Hi! Swing Lo!* (1993)★★★.

● COMPILATIONS: with Tommy Duncan *Legendary Masters - Bob Wills & Tommy Duncan* (United Artists 1971)★★★★, *The Bob Wills Anthology* (Columbia 1973)★★★★, *The Legendary Bob Wills* (Columbia 1975)★★★, *The Tiffany Transcriptions 1945-1948* (Lariat 1977)★★★, *The Tiffany Transcriptions* (Tishomingo 1978)★★★, *The Rare Presto Transcriptions Volumes 1 - 5* German releases (Outlaw 1981-1985)★★★, *Columbia Historic Edition* (Columbia 1982)★★★, *The Tiffany Transcriptions Volumes 1 - 9* (Kaleidoscope 1983-1988, reissued by Rhino in the 1990s)★★★, *The Golden Era* (Columbia 1987)★★★, *Fiddle* (CMF 1987)★★★, *Anthology 1935-1973* (Rhino 1991)★★★★, *Country Music Hall Of Fame Series* (MCA 1992)★★★★, *The Essential Bob Wills And His Texas Playboys 1935-47* (Columbia 1992)★★★★, *The Longhorn Recordings* (Bear Family 1993)★★★, *Classic Western Swing* (Rhino 1994)★★★, *Encore* 3-CD box set (Liberty 1994)★★★★.

● FURTHER READING: *San Antonio Rose, The Life and Music of Bob Wills*, Charles R.Townsend. *The Life Of Bob Wills, The King Of Western Swing*, Jimmy Latham. *My Years With Bob Wills*, Al Stricklin. *Hubbin' It, The Life Of Bob Wills*, Ruth Sheldon.

WILLS, JOHNNIE LEE

b. 2 September 1912, on a farm near Kosse, Limestone County, Texas, USA, d. 25 October 1984. Younger brother of Bob Wills and the fourth of the Wills family's children. He learned to play the guitar as a child but later played tenor banjo and fiddle. He made his musical debut in 1933, when he became one of brother Bob's second band, working as Johnnie Lee Wills and His Rhythmaires. He appeared with Bob in the 1940 Tex Ritter film *Take Me Back To Oklahoma*. In early 1941, he recorded for Decca, having success with 'Milk Cow Blues'. Throughout the 40s and 50s, he led western swing bands, working in conjunction with brother Bob. He played the south-west dance circuits but was mainly centred in Oklahoma City or Tulsa where, until 1964, he played a residency at *Cain's Dancing Academy*. In 1950, recording on Bullet, he achieved Top 10 US country and pop chart success with 'Rag Mop' (a number he co-wrote with Deacon Anderson that was also a pop hit for the Ames Brothers) and a country number 7 with 'Peter Cottontail'. He also made further recordings for Decca, MGM and RCA-Victor, as well as over 200 15-minute transcription discs for use on KVOO Tulsa and other stations. In 1964, he left Cain's, ran his western wear store in Tulsa and organized the Tulsa Annual Stampede rodeo. He returned to leading a band in the 70s and with some of the old Playboys, he recorded for the Flying Fish and Delta labels. In 1971, he played banjo on the Bob Wills tribute recordings made at Merle Haggard's home in Bakersfield, and later made some appearances at Playboy Reunion Shows, but did not appear on the 1973 recording session in Dallas, Texas. He modestly never rated himself as a good enough solo banjo or fiddle player for people to listen to, but he was highly respected as a bandleader. He died in Tulsa in October 1984.

● ALBUMS: *Where There's A Wills There's A Way* (Sims 1962)★★★, *At The Tulsa Stampede* (Sims 1963)★★★, *Reunion* (Flying Fish 1978)★★★, *Dance All Night* (Delta 1980)★★.

● COMPILATIONS: *Best Of Johnnie Lee Wills* (Crown 1975)★★★, *Tulsa Swing* (Rounder 1978)★★★, *Rompin' Stompin' Singin' Swingin'* (Bear Family 1984)★★★★.

WILLS, LUKE

b. Luther J. Wills, 10 September 1920, on a farm near Memphis, Hall County, Texas, USA. Younger brother of Bob Wills and the seventh of the Wills family's children. He was rated so differently from the rest of the family that it became a family joke that his mother had picked up the wrong baby, after one of the many social dances held in the area. He learned to play stand-up bass as a child and made his musical debut in 1939 in the second Wills band, led by elder brother Johnnie Lee Wills, called the Rhythmaires. He appeared in B-movie westerns in the early 40s with Bob but in 1943, he joined the US Navy. After service, he led Bob's second band and covered the dance circuit of northern and central California, appearing first as Luke Wills And The Texas Playboys Number 2, but to avoid confusion this soon became Luke Wills' Rhythm Busters. He recorded for King and RCA-Victor, adopting a similar style of comments and interjections as Bob, though not in a high-pitched voice. In 1948, the Rhythm Busters were disbanded and he worked with Bob until 1950, when he re-formed his own band and took over in Oklahoma City, when Bob returned to Texas to his new dancehall. He rejoined Bob in 1952 and played and sang with the Playboys, often fronting the band in Bob's absence, until they disbanded in 1964. He then worked outside of the music industry in Las Vegas. In 1971, he played bass on the Bob Wills tribute recordings made at Merle Haggard's home in Bakersfield and later made some appearances at Playboy Reunion Shows, but did not appear on the 1973 recording session in Dallas. Although contributing in no small way to his eldest brother's legend, he was not elected to the Country Music Hall Of Fame. In the late 70s, he left the music business and retired to Las Vegas.

● COMPILATIONS: *Luke Wills' Rhythm Busters - High Voltage Gal* (1988)★★★.

WILLS, MARK

b. 8 August 1973, Cleveland, Tennessee, USA. Wills is produced by the highly acclaimed Keith Stegall. His debut album on sold well and indicated a star in the making. Among the tracks is a country version of the Who's 'Squeeze Box'.

● ALBUMS: *Mark Wills* (Mercury 1996)★★.

WISE, CHUBBY

b. Robert Russell Wise, 2 October 1915, Lake City, Florida, USA, d. 6 January 1996. His father was an old-time fiddler but Robert first played banjo and guitar, before changing to fiddle at the age of 12, greatly influenced by Curly Fox and Clayton McMichen. In 1936, Wise drove taxis in Jacksonville and played fiddle in bars in his spare time, but in 1938, he became a full-time musician. After playing for a time with the Jubilee Hillbillies, he joined Bill Monroe on the *Grand Ole Opry* in 1942. He remained with Monroe until 1948, in a line-up that included Flatt And Scruggs and played on most of the band's best-known recordings. In 1947, he co-wrote 'Shenandoah Waltz' with Clyde Moody and it has also been suggested that, in 1938, he may well have worked with Ervin Rouse on the writing of the fiddle classic 'Orange Blossom Special'. He returned to Monroe briefly and in the early 50s, he played with several acts including Flatt And Scruggs until 1954, when he became a member of Hank Snow's Rainbow Ranch Boys. Except for a spell in 1964, he played on the *Opry*, toured extensively and recorded with Snow until March 1970. He played with Snow's band when, in 1955, they dubbed on new instrumentation to several of Jimmie Rodgers' classic recordings (Snow devotes almost a chapter of his autobiography to memories of the days when Wise played with him). During that time, he also recorded with Mac Wiseman, Hylo Brown and Red Allen. He cut a solo album for Starday in 1961 and in 1969, he began to record for Stoneway. He relocated to Livingstone, Texas, where throughout the 70s into the early 80s, he recorded a series of albums for the label, made personal appearances and also recorded as a session musician or guest with various artists and bluegrass groups, including Charlie Moore, Mac Wiseman, Frank Wakefield and the Boys From Indiana and cut twin fiddle albums with Howdy Forrester. In 1984, he moved to Florida and although he cut down his workload drastically, he still made numerous festival appearances and recorded with the Bass Mountain Boys. He continued to remain active into the 90s, recorded a twin fiddle album with Raymond Fairchild and late in 1995, he recorded what turned out to be his final album for Pinecastle. In December 1995, he and his wife were visiting relatives in Maryland for Christmas, when he was hospitalized with pneumonia. Soon after being released from hospital, he suffered a fatal heart seizure and died in Washington DC on 6 January 1996. Wise was one of country music's greatest fiddlers and also noted for his humour. Once asked why he took up playing the fiddle, he replied, 'The fiddle bow fit my hand a lot better than them plough handles did'.

● ALBUMS: *Chubby Wise & The Rainbow Ranch Boys* (Starday 1961)★★★, *Chubby Wise & His Fiddle* (Stoneway 1969)★★★, *Chubby Fiddles Around* (Stoneway 1970)★★★, *Chubby Plays Uptown* (Stoneway 1970)★★★, *Chubby Plays, W.C. Averitt Sings Bluegrass* (Stoneway 1970)★★★, *Hoedown* (Stoneway 1970)★★★, *Chubby Wise Plays Bob Wills* (Stoneway 1970)★★★★, *Precious Memories* (Stoneway 1971)★★★, *Thru The Years With Chubby Wise* (Stoneway 1971)★★★, *Chubby Plays Polkas* (Stoneway 1971)★★★, *Waltzes* (Stoneway 1972)★★★, *At His Best* (Stoneway 1972)★★★, *Hoedown #2* (Stoneway 1973)★★★, *Page 13* (Stoneway 1973)★★★, with Howdy Forrester *Sincerely Yours* (Stoneway 1974)★★★, with Forrester *Fiddle Favorites* (Stoneway 1975)★★★, *Grassy Fiddle* (Stoneway 1975)★★★, *The Golden Rocket* (Stoneway 1975)★★★, *The Million Dollar Fiddle* (Stoneway 1976)★★★★, *Sweet Milk And Peaches* (Stoneway 1977)★★★, *Chubby Wise Plays Hank Williams* (Stoneway 1977)★★★, *Moody Fiddle Sound* (Stoneway 1978)★★★, with Mac Wiseman *Give Me My Smokies & The Tennessee Waltz* (Gilley's 1982)★★★, *The Nashville Sound* (Guest Star 80s)★★★, with Boys From Indiana *Live At Gilley's* (Gilley's 1988)★★, with Raymond Fairchild *Cherokee Tunes & Seminole Swing* (Rebel 1990)★★★, *In Nashville* (1993)★★★, *An American Original* (Pinecastle 1993)★★★.

WISEMAN, MAC

b. Malcolm B. Wiseman, 23 May 1925, Crimora, Virginia, USA. Wiseman attended the Conservatory of Music at Dayton, Virginia, and developed a great knowledge of the folk music of his native Shenandoah Valley. He first worked as a disc jockey on WSVA Harrisburg but was soon playing such shows as the *Tennessee Barn Dance* on WLOX Knoxville, where he also worked with Molly O'Day. During the 40s, his talent with bluegrass music saw him play and record with the bands of Bill Monroe and Flatt And Scruggs. He made his first solo recordings for Dot in 1951 and from 1957-61, he was the label's A&R man. After recording for Capitol, he returned to Dot but in the early 70s, he later recorded with Lester Flatt for RCA. Over the years Wiseman has worked on a variety of radio stations, played all the major US country venues and travelled extensively, including several tours to Britain, where he is always a popular artist. A prolific recording artist on various labels, his most popular recordings include 'Tis Sweet To Be Remembered'. His few actual chart hits include Top 10 successes with 'The Ballad Of Davy Crockett' and 'Jimmy Brown The Newsboy', and a minor hit with his humorous 'Johnny's Cash And Charley's Pride'. In 1979, he even charted with 'My Blue Heaven' as Mac Wiseman & Friend (the friend being Woody Herman). In 1993 he was inducted into the Bluegrass Hall Of Fame.

● ALBUMS: *I Hear You Knocking* (1955)★★★, *Songs From The Hills* (1956)★★★★, *Tis Sweet To Be Remembered* (Dot 1958)★★★, *Beside The Still Waters* (Dot 1959)★★★★, *Great Folk Ballads* (Dot 1959)★★★★, *Mac Wiseman Sings 12 Great Hits* (Dot 1960)★★★, *Keep On The Sunny Side* (Dot

1960)★★★, *Fireball Mail* (Dot 1961)★★★, *Best Loved Gospel Hymns* (1961)★★★, *Bluegrass Favorites* (Capitol 1962)★★★, *Sincerely* (Hamilton 1964)★★★, *A Master At Work* (Dot 1966)★★★, *This Is Mac Wiseman* (Dot 1966)★★★, *Songs Of The Dear Old Days* (Hamilton 1966)★★★, *20 Old Time Country Favorites* (1966)★★★, *Mac Wiseman i* (1967)★★★, *Sings Johnny's Cash & Charley's Pride* (1970)★★★, with Lester Flatt *Lester 'N' Mac* (RCA Victor 1971)★★★, with Flatt *On The Southbound* (RCA Victor 1972)★★★, with Flatt *Over The Hills To The Poorhouse* (RCA Victor 1973)★★★, *Concert Favorites* (1973)★★★, *Country Music Memories* (CMH 1976)★★★, with Shenandoah Cut-Ups *New Traditions Volume 1* (Vetco 1976)★★★, with Shenandoah Cut-Ups *New Traditions Volume 2* (Vetco 1977)★★★, *Sings Gordon Lightfoot* (CMH 1977)★★★, *Mac Wiseman ii* (1977)★★★, with Osborne Brothers *Essential Bluegrass Album* (CMH 1979)★★★★, *Songs That Made The Jukebox Play* (CMH 1980)★★★, with Chubby Wise *Give Me My Smokies & The Tennessee Waltz* (Gilley's 1982)★★★, with Merle Travis *The Clayton McMichen Story* (CHM 1982)★★★, *Bluegrass Gold* (1982)★★★, *Live In Concert* (1982)★★, *If Teardrops Were Pennies* (1984)★★★, *Mac Wiseman iii* (1986)★★★, *Grassroots To Bluegrass* (CMH 1990)★★★★, *Teenage Hangout* (1993)★★★.
● COMPILATIONS: *Golden Hits Of Mac Wiseman* (Dot 1968)★★★, *16 Great Performances* (1974)★★★, *The Mac Wiseman Story* (CMH 1976)★★★★, *Golden Classics* (Gusto 1979), *Early Dot Recordings Volume 1* (County 1985)★★★★, *Early Dot Recordings Volume 2* (County 1985)★★★★, *Greatest Bluegrass Hits* (CMH 1989)★★★★, *Early Dot Recordings Volume 3* (County 1992)★★★, *Rare Singles And Radio Transcriptions* (Cowgirlboy 1992)★★★.

WITHERS, TEX

b. *c*.1933. No one knows when and where Tex Withers was born, his real name or his parents. The deformed baby was abandoned in the USA, and his rise in British country music showed remarkable resilience: he was four feet tall and a hunchback with a painful history of severe spinal problems and tuberculosis. Withers wore western dress throughout the day as he longed to be an American Indian - his wife, known as White Fawn, dressed as his squaw and smoked a clay pipe. A good-natured man who laughed at his handicaps, Withers was the long-standing compere at West London's Nashville Room and won several awards as the Top UK country singer, his show-stoppers being 'These Hands' and a narration about a Red Indian's difficulties in coming to terms with society, 'The Ballad Of Ira Hayes'. *Tex Withers Sings Country Style* sold 135,000 copies, while his 1973 album, *The Grand Ole Opry's Newest Star* was recorded mainly in Nashville, Tennessee. He was championed by Hank Snow, but his professional career was cut short by throat illness. Withers became bankrupt and his illiteracy made work difficult. His last years were spent as a cleaner at Gatwick Airport and Haywards Heath railway station. He found his happy hunting ground on 29 December 1986, probably aged 53, and merited an obituary in *The Times*.
● ALBUMS: *Tex Withers Sings Country Style* (1970)★★★, *The Grand Ole Opry's Newest Star* (1973)★★★, *Tex Withers* (RCA 1976)★★.
● COMPILATIONS: *Blue Ribbon Country* (Homespun 1984)★★★.

WOOD, DEL

b. Adelaide Hazlewood, 22 February 1920, Nashville, Tennessee, USA, d. 3 October 1989. Wood's parents gave her a piano for her fifth birthday with the hope that she would become a classical pianist. She had different ideas and aimed for a career at the *Grand Ole Opry*. She developed a thumping ragtime style that, in 1951, saw her record her version of 'Down Yonder', a tune that had proved a million-seller for Gid Tanner and the Skillet Lickers in 1934. Wood's version on the Tennessee label reached number 5 in the US country charts and also became a million-seller. After guesting on the *Opry* in 1952 and refusing the chance of playing with Bob Crosby, she joined the roster in 1953. Her playing proved so popular that she toured with *Opry* shows, even to Japan. She recorded for several labels, making popular versions of such numbers as 'Johnson Rag' and 'Piano Roll Blues'. She had no more chart entries, but she won herself the nickname of 'Queen Of The Ragtime Pianists'. She remained a member of the *Opry* until her death in the Baptist Hospital, Nashville, on 3 October 1989, following a stroke on 22 September, the day she was scheduled to appear on the *Legendary Ladies Of Country Music Show*.
● ALBUMS: *Down Yonder* (RCA Victor 1955)★★★, *Hot Happy & Honky* (1957)★★★, *Mississippi Showboat* (1959)★★★, *Buggies, Bustles & Barrellhouse* (1960)★★★, *Flivvers, Flappers & Fox Trots* (1960)★★★, *Ragtime Goes International* (1961)★★★, *Ragtime Goes South Of The Border* (1962)★★★, *Honky Tonk Piano* (1962)★★★, *Piano Roll Blues* (1963)★★★, *It's Honky Tonk Time* (1964)★★★, *Roll Out The Piano* (1964)★★★, *Uptight, Lowdown & Honky Tonk* (1966)★★★, *There's A Tavern In The Town* (60s)★★, *Del Wood Favorites, Encore-Del Wood, Ragtime Favorites, Plays Berlin & Cohen Volumes, Ragtime Glory Special* (all 70s).

WOODRUFF, BOB

b. 14 March 1961, USA. Bob Woodruff, a Nashville, Tennessee, USA-based singer-songwriter, received a generally favourable critical response on the release of his 1994 debut, *Dreams & Saturday Nights*. However, further progress was impeded by what he later described as 'philosophical differences' with his label, Asylum Records. He re-emerged in 1997 with *Desire Road*, released on Imprint Records, a new Nashville label. As he told *Billboard* magazine on its release: 'The major difference with *Desire Road* is the label move from Asylum to Imprint. I was one of the first artists signed to Asylum when it opened in Nashville, and based on an artist roster including singer/songwriters like Guy Clark and Emmylou Harris, I felt like it was the perfect home for me. But towards the end of my record's promotion, I felt their philosophy changed, and after an amicable split, I and my manager, Jim Della Croce, met with Roy (Wunsch) and felt that he was starting up a label similar to Asylum, at the beginning, that would be the right place for me to make records.' Co-produced with Roy Kennedy, who occasionally adds guitar to Woodruff's live performances, this second collection added a rockier edge to many of Woodruff's compositions. *Desire Road* featured nine originals, as well as cover versions of John Fogerty's 'Almost Saturday Night' and two Arthur Alexander songs, 'Every Day I Have To Cry Some' and 'If It's Really Got To Be This Way'.
● ALBUMS: *Dreams & Saturday Nights* (Asylum 1994)★★★, *Desire Road* (Imprint 1997)★★★★.

WOOLEY, SHEB

b. Shelby F. Wooley, 10 April 1921, near Erick, Oklahoma, USA. Wooley, who is part Cherokee Indian, grew up on the family farm, learned to ride as a child and rode in rodeos as a teenager. His father swopped a shotgun to get him his first guitar and while still at high school, he formed a country band that played at dances and on local radio. After leaving school, he found work in an oilfield as a welder, but soon tired of this work and moved to Nashville. He appeared on the WLAC and WSM radio stations and recorded for the Bullet label. In 1946, he relocated to Fort Worth, where until 1949, he became the frontman for a major show on WBAP, sponsored by Calumet Baking Powder. He then moved to Los Angeles, where he signed with MGM Records and with thoughts of a film career, he also attended the Jack Koslyn School of Acting. In 1949, he had his first screen role (as a heavy) in the Errol Flynn film *Rocky Mountain*. In 1952, he made a memorable appearance as Ben Miller, the killer plotting to gun down Gary Cooper in the classic western *High Noon*. During the 50s, he appeared in several other films including *Little Big Horn* (1951), *Distant Drums* (1951), *Man Without A Star* (1955), *Giant* (1956) and *Rio Bravo* (1959). He is also well remembered for his performances as Pete Nolan in the television series *Rawhide*, which ran from 1958-65 (he also wrote some scripts for the series). During his career, he appeared in over 40 films.

Other artists began to record songs he had written and in 1953, Hank Snow had a big hit with 'When Mexican Joe Met Jole Blon' - a parody of two hit songs. In 1958, his novelty number, 'Purple People Eater', became a million-seller and even reached number 12 in the UK pop charts. He based the song on a schoolboy joke that he had heard from Don Robertson's son and initially, MGM did not consider it to be worth releasing. Further US pop successes included 'Sweet Chile'. He first appeared in the US country charts in 1962, when another novelty number, 'That's My Pa', became a number 1. It was intended that Wooley should record 'Don't Go Near The Indians' but due to film commitments Rex Allen's version was released before he could record it. Wooley jokingly told MGM that he would write a sequel and came up with the comedy parody 'Don't Go Near The Eskimos'. He developed an alter-ego drunken character, whom he called Ben Colder, and in this guise, he recorded and charted it and other humorous parodies of pop/country hits, including 'Almost Persuaded No. 2', 'Harper Valley PTA (Later That Same Day)' and 'Fifteen Beers (Years) Ago'. (The name Ben Colder was the selection made by MGM from the three alternatives that Wooley offered. The other two were Ben Freezin and Klon Dyke.) He had some further minor hits with serious recordings, including 'Blue Guitar' and 'Tie A Tiger Down'. In 1969, he joined the CBS network *Hee Haw* country show, remaining with it for several years, and also wrote the theme music. Throughout the 60s and 70s, he maintained a busy touring schedule, appearing all over the USA and overseas. In 1968, Ben Colder was voted Comedian of the Year by the Country Music Association. He cut back his work during the 80s and although he has remained a popular entertainer, he has had no chart entries since 1971. Over the years, the parodies by the drunken Ben Colder have proved more popular than his serious recordings and have certainly accounted for the majority of his record sales.

● ALBUMS: as Sheb Wooley *Sheb Wooley* (MGM 1956)★★★, *Songs From The Days Of Rawhide* (MGM 1961)★★★, *That's My Pa & That's My Ma* (MGM 1962)★★★★, *Tales Of How The West Was Won* (MGM 1963)★★★★, *It's A Big Land* (MGM 1965)★★★, *Warm & Wooley* (MGM 1969)★★★. As Ben Colder *Spoofing The Big Ones* (MGM 1962)★★★, *Ben Colder* (MGM 1963)★★★, *Big Ben Strikes Again* (MGM 1966)★★★★, *Wine Women & Song* (MGM 1967)★★★, *Harper Valley PTA & Other Parodies Of Top Ten Hits* (MGM 1968)★★★, *Have One On Ben Colder* (1969)★★, *Big Ben Colder Wild Again* (1970)★★★, *Ben Colder* (1970)★★★, *Live & Loaded At Sam Houston Coliseum* (1971)★★★, *Wacky World Of Ben Colder* (1973)★★★.

● COMPILATIONS: as Sheb Wooley *The Very Best Of Sheb Wooley* (MGM 1965)★★★★, *Country Boogie Wild And Wooley (1948-55)* (1984)★★★, *Blue Guitar* (Bear Family 1985)★★★; as Ben Colder *Golden Hits* (Gusto 1979)★★★.

WORTH, MARION

b. Mary Ann Ward, 4 July 1930, Birmingham, Alabama, USA. She learned to play piano as a child (later adding guitar) and after initially starting nursing training, she decided to pursue a singing career. She first sang with her sister, before appearing on local radio and television in Birmingham. In 1957, she gained a number 12 US country hit with her self-penned 'Are You Willing, Willie', recorded on the tiny Cherokee label. In 1960, another self-penned song, 'That's My Kind Of Love', recorded on Happy Wilson's Guyden label, reached number 5, which resulted in her joining Columbia Records (she also married Wilson). She became a regular on WSM's *Friday Night Frolics*. In 1961, her first Columbia hit, 'I Think I Know', made the Top 10, with the follow-up, 'There'll Always Be Sadness', peaking at number 21. Between 1963 and 1968, she achieved eight more *Billboard* chart entries, with 'Shake Me I Rattle' and 'Crazy Arms' both making the Top 20. She also gained Top 25 status with 'Slippin' Around', a duet with George Morgan. In 1967, she moved to Decca Records but after the self-penned 'Mama Sez', in 1968, she failed to make the charts again. Her ability to change from sultry ballads to lively barn dance-type numbers made her a popular performer on the *Grand Ole Opry*, where she was rated a singer's singer, and she was one of the first country stars to play Carnegie Hall in New York. She continued to tour in the USA and Canada and, in later years, she became a popular performer in various Las Vegas venues.

● ALBUMS: with George Morgan *Slippin' Around* (Columbia 1964)★★★★, *Marion Worth Sings Marty Robbins* (Columbia 1964)★★★, *A Woman Needs Love* (Columbia 1967)★★★.

● COMPILATIONS: *Marion Worth's Greatest Hits* (Columbia 1963)★★★.

WRIGHT, BOBBY

b. 30 March 1942, Charleston, West Virginia, USA. The son of Kitty Wells and Johnnie Wright, he appeared with his parents on the *Louisiana Hayride* at the age of eight, and three years later made his first recordings. After the family relocated to Nashville, he learned to play guitar but initially he had more interest in sports and drama. In 1962, he went to California and successfully auditioned for the role of a young guitar-playing southern boy in a proposed drama. The show did not materialize, but his performance won him the role of Willie the radio operator in a new comedy television

series called *McHale's Navy*. He stayed as a regular until the series ended in 1966. He recorded for Decca (his parent's label) and in 1967, he gained his first US country chart hit with 'Lay Some Happiness On Me'. A few more minor hits followed and after further acting roles, his dislike of Hollywood saw him return to Nashville, where he began to appear with his parents. He had by this time also learned to play bass, trumpet and drums and he soon became an important part of the family show. In the early 70s, he appeared on their syndicated television series and toured extensively with them. Over the years, he has also been a popular artist on other syndicated television shows. In 1971, he had a Top 15 country hit with 'Here I Go Again'. He recorded country cover versions of some pop hits and in 1974, he had Top 30 country success with his ABC recording of Terry Jacks' pop number 1, 'Seasons In The Sun'. He later recorded for United Artists, registering his last solo success, 'I'm Turning You Loose', on that label in 1979. He appeared in the UK with his parents at the 1974 Wembley Festival and received praise for his performance with the family at the 1988 Peterborough Festival. A talented all-round entertainer, he continues to be an important part of the family show and has not made any further attempts to pursue a solo career.
● ALBUMS: *Here I Go Again* (Decca 1971)★★★, *Seasons Of Love* (ABC 1974)★★★.

WRIGHT, CAROL SUE

b. 1945, Nashville, Tennessee, USA. The youngest of the three children of Kitty Wells and Johnnie Wright, she began to sing with her parents from an early age. In December 1955, standing on a chair to reach the microphone, Wright duetted with her mother when she recorded their well-known version of 'How Far Is Heaven?'. In the late 50s, she sang with her sister, Ruby Wright, as the Wright Sisters, recording under the production of Chet Atkins for the Cadence label, who saw them as the female version of the label's popular Everly Brothers. She toured for a time with the family show but eventually, with no desire to pursue a singing career, she restricted her appearances and devoted her time to raising her own family. In the 80s, she and sister Ruby ran the family Museum and Tourist attraction in Nashville.

WRIGHT, CHELY

b. 1971, Wellesville, Kansas, USA. As a child the 90s country singer Chely Wright wanted to be a star and aged 11 she had her first band. When she was 18 she was working at Opryland USA in Nashville where she met songwriters and musicians. When times were tough, she would say, 'This will be great when they do the movie of my life.' She pestered producer Harold Shedd until he signed her and, with another producer Barry Beckett, she made the modern honky-tonk album *Woman In The Moon* and charted with a revival of Harlan Howard's 'He's A Good Ol' Boy'. This album brought her immediate plaudits, including the Academy Of Country Music's Best New Female Vocalist award. Despite this, the album's sales were modest. She subsequently spent a year and a half on the road, playing with Alan Jackson, Confederate Railroad, Tim McGraw and Alabama. These experiences were condensed into the performances for her second album, *In The Middle Of It*, on which she changed producers, employing Ed Seay. As she told *Billboard* maga-

zine prior to its release, 'Instead of finding songs that were country and trying to make great records out of them, we tried to find great songs.' The album was accompanied by a heavily promoted attendant single, 'Listen To The Radio'. 'The Last Supper' finds a wife cooking the last meal for her cheating husband: 'He'll break the bread and drink his wine alone.' Wright disciplines herself to write in an office on Music Row and she says, 'I'm not a great singer or a great poet, but I write some good songs.'
● ALBUMS: *Woman In The Moon* (A&M 1994)★★, *Right In The Middle Of It* (A&M 1996)★★★★, *Let Me In* (MCA 1997)★★★.

WRIGHT, JOHNNIE

b. John Robert Wright, 13 May 1914, on a farm near Mt. Juliet, Wilson County, Tennessee, USA. His grandfather was a champion old-time fiddler, his father a banjo player and while still at school, Wright learned to play these instruments, as well as the guitar, and began to sing locally. He relocated to Nashville in 1933, where he worked daily as a cabinetmaker and entertained at local venues. In 1936, he began to appear on radio WSIX Nashville and the following year, he met Kitty Wells who, as Muriel Deason, was appearing on the station as part of the singing Deason Sisters. On 30 October 1937, they were married and with Wright's sister, Louise, the trio began to play WSIX as Johnnie Wright And The Harmony Girls. In 1939, they teamed up with their brother-in-law Jack Anglin, first appearing as Johnny Wright and the Happy Roving Cowboys with Jack Anglin, but by 1940, Wright and Anglin had become Johnnie And Jack. After Anglin's untimely death in 1963, Wright reorganized their band, the Tennessee Mountain Boys, and recorded for Decca as a solo artist. He made his US country chart debut in 1964 with the strangely titled 'Walkin', Talkin', Cryin', Barely Beatin' Broken Heart'. In 1965, he enjoyed a number 1 country hit with Tom T. Hall's song 'Hello Vietnam'. He followed with further minor hits including 'I'm Doing This For Daddy', 'Mama's Little Jewel' and 'American Power'. During this time, he toured and worked in conjunction with Kitty Wells and in 1968, they charted with their duet 'We'll Stick Together'. After this, their careers fully merged and with their children Ruby, Bobby and Carol Sue Wright, they become the Kitty Wells-Johnny Wright Family Show.
● ALBUMS: *Hello Vietnam* (Decca 1965)★★★★, *Country Music Special* (Decca 1966)★★★, *Country The Wright Way* (Decca 1967)★★★, *Johnny Wright Sings Country Favorites* (Decca 1968)★★★, with Kitty Wells *We'll Stick Together* (Decca 1968)★★★, with Wells *Heartwarming Gospel Songs* (Decca 1972)★★.

WRIGHT, MARK

Wright wrote 'Paradise Tonight', a US country number 1 for Charly McClain and Mickey Gilley in 1983, but he has since established himself as a record producer. He was the co-producer with James Stroud of Clint Black's 1989 success *Killin' Time*, and his current artists include Rhett Atkins.

WRIGHT, MICHELLE

b. 1 July 1957, Chatham, Ontario, Canada. Wright grew up in a farming community in Merlin, Ontario, and her parents were both country music performers. With her distinctive low and husky voice, she became one of Canada's most popular country singers and several songs from her first album, *Do Right By Me*, were recorded for the US market by Reba McEntire. Wright moved to Nashville but her progress was impaired by a drink problem, which she has now overcome. Her second American album, *Now And Then*, led to 12 industry awards in one year and sales in the USA alone of over 500,000. Her powerful, husky voice was heard to good effect on 'Take It Like A Man' and she topped the Canadian charts with a touching song about adoption, 'He Would Be Sixteen'. Her more raucous performances, such as 'One Good Man', are closer to Bonnie Tyler than country music. Her 'good man', Joel Kane, is also her manager and bass player. She can be seen reading Patsy Cline's letters on the video *Remembering Patsy* (1993). After a four-year gap in the USA, she released an album in 1996, although some momentum had been lost in her career when her record company failed to release the excellent *The Reasons Why* in 1994; the reason why, nobody really knows, but the Arista president took full responsibility for this error.

● ALBUMS: *Do Right By Me* (Savannah 1988)★★★, *Michelle Wright* (Arista 1990)★★★, *Now And Then* (Arista 1992)★★★, *The Reasons Why* (Arista 1994)★★★★, *For Me It's You* (Arista 1996)★★★.

● VIDEOS: *One Good Man* (1994).

WRIGHT, RUBY

b. 27 October 1939, Nashville, Tennessee, USA. The eldest of the three children of Kitty Wells and Johnnie Wright, she sang with her parents from an early age. At the age of 13, she was signed by RCA Records and under the production of Chet Atkins, she had single releases as Ruby Wells (there was a pop singer called Ruby Wright, but no doubt RCA believed it would help to use her mother's stage name). In the mid-50s, she was a member of a close-harmony female singing trio, Nita, Rita and Ruby (Nita was Anita Carter and Rita was Rita Robbins, the sister of Marty Robbins' guitarist and yodeler, Don Winters). Working with Atkins, they leaned heavily towards a pop presentation but were backed by country studio musicians, and they had minor success with numbers such as 'Rock Love' and 'Hi De Ank Tum'. They were basically only a recording act, since family touring made live appearances difficult for Nita and Ruby. Rita never conquered her stage fright; the trio broke up and she retired. Ruby began to sing with her sister, Carol Sue Wright, as the Wright Sisters, recording (again with Atkins) for Cadence, who saw them as a female version of the label's popular Everly Brothers. In 1964, she had a Top 15 solo US country and minor pop hit with 'Dern Ya', a female answer song to Roger Miller's 'Dang Me'. In the late 60s, she made the country chart with her Epic label recordings of 'A New Place To Hang Your Hat' and 'A Better Deal Than This'. During the 1970s, she recorded for several small labels including Plantation and Scorpion and had some success with 'Yester-me, Yester-you, Yesterday'. She continued to appear with her parents' show but in the 1980s, along with her sister Carol Sue, took to running the family Museum and Tourist attraction in Nashville.

● ALBUMS: *Dern Ya* (Kapp 1966)★★★, as Nita, Rita & Ruby *Rock Love* (1985)★★★.

WYNETTE, TAMMY

b. Virginia Wynette Pugh, 5 May 1942, Itawamba County, near Tupelo, Mississippi, USA. Wynette is primarily known for two songs, 'Stand By Your Man' and 'D.I.V.O.R.C.E.', but her huge catalogue includes 20 US country number 1 hits, mostly about standing by your man or getting divorced. After her father died when she was 10 months old, she was raised by her mother and grandparents and picked cotton from an early age. When aged 17, she married construction worker Euple Byrd, and trained as a hairdresser. She subsequently made an album with their third child, Tina - *George, Tammy And Tina* - in 1975. Byrd did not share her ambition of being a country singer, so she left and moved to Nashville. She impressed producer Billy Sherrill and had her first success in 1966 with a Johnny Paycheck song, 'Apartment No. 9'. She almost topped the US country charts with 'I Don't Want To Play House', in which a child shuns his friends' game because he senses his parents' unhappiness. It was the template for numerous songs, including 'Bedtime Story', in which Wynette attempts to explain divorce to a three-year-old, and 'D.I.V.O.R.C.E.' in which she does not.

Her own marriage to guitarist Don Chapel disintegrated after he traded nude photographs of her and, after witnessing an argument, country star George Jones eloped with her. Unaware of the turmoil in Wynette's own life, American feminists in 1968 condemned Wynette for supporting her husband, right or wrong, in 'Stand By Your Man', but she maintains, 'Sherrill and I didn't have women's lib in mind. All we wanted to do was to write a pretty love song'. The way Wynette chokes on 'After all, he's just a man' indicates pity rather than than support. Having previously recorded a country chart-topper with David Houston ('My Elusive Dreams'), an artistic collaboration with George Jones was inevitable. Their albums scaled new heights in over-the-top romantic duets, particularly 'The Ceremony', which narrates the marriage vows set to music. In an effort to separate Jones from alcohol, she confiscated his car-keys, only to find him riding their electric lawnmower to the nearest bar. 'The Bottle' was aimed at Jones as accurately as the real thing. 'Stand By Your Man' was used to good effect in *Five Easy Pieces* (which starred Jack Nicholson), and the record became a UK number 1 on its sixth reissue in 1975. It was followed by a UK Top 20 placing for 'D.I.V.O.R.C.E.', but it was Billy Connolly's parody about his 'D.O.G.' that went to the UK number 1 slot.

Wynette also had two bestselling compilations in the UK album charts. By now her marriage to Jones was over and 'Dear Daughters' explains the position to them. Jones, in more dramatic fashion, retaliated with 'The Battle'. Even more difficult to explain to her daughters was her 44-day marriage to estate agent Michael Tomlin. After torrid affairs with Rudy Gatlin (of Larry Gatlin And The Gatlin Brothers) and Burt Reynolds (she saved the actor's life when he passed out in the bath), she married record producer George Richey, whose own stormy marriage had just ended. In 1978, she was kidnapped outside a Nashville car-park and was subjected to a brutal beating. She has also experienced many health problems, including several stomach operations. Throughout the traumas, she continued to record songs about married life, 'That's The Way It Could Have Been', 'Til I Can Make It On My Own', '(You Make Me Want To Be) A Mother' and 'Love Doesn't Always Come (On The

Night That It's Needed)'. None of these songs have found acceptance outside the country market, but 'Stand By Your Man' has become a standard, with versions ranging from Loretta Lynn (who also took an opposing view in 'The Pill'), Billie Jo Spears and Tina Turner, to two male performers, David Allan Coe and Lyle Lovett. Her autobiography was made into a television movie in 1981. In 1986, Wynette entered the Betty Ford clinic for drug dependency and, true to form, followed it with a single, 'Alive And Well'. She played in a daytime soap, *Capital*, in 1987, although its drama was light relief when compared to her own life. Her stage show includes a lengthy walkabout to sing 'Stand By Your Man' to individual members of the audience. Her standing in the rock world increased when she was co-opted by the KLF to appear on 'Justified And Ancient', which became a Top 3 UK hit in 1991. Her duet album, *Higher Ground*, is more imaginatively produced than her other recent albums and, although she undoubtedly has many more dramas to come, she says, 'All I really want to do is stay country and keep going 'til I'm older than Roy Acuff.'

Wynette's turbulent time with Jones has been well documented, so much so that they were the most famous couple in the history of country music. The announcement that they were working together again came as a pleasant surprise to their many followers. Their previous reconciliation at the end of 1979 had merely been an attempt to help Jones save his washed-up career. *One*, released in 1995, is felt by many to be the best of their career; the good feeling that is conveyed by tracks such as 'Solid As A Rock' is the result of their having chosen to sing together for purely musical reasons. There is no longer any emotional baggage, nor any resurrection needed - perhaps for the first time in their lives, they were motivated purely by the enjoyment of making music together.

● ALBUMS: *Your Good Girl's Gonna Go Bad* (Epic 1967)★★★★, *Take Me To Your World* (Epic 1967)★★★★, *D.I.V.O.R.C.E.* (Epic 1967)★★★★, *Stand By Your Man* (Epic 1968)★★★★, *Inspiration* (Epic 1969)★★, *The Ways To Love A Man* (Epic 1969)★★★★, *Run Angel Run* (Epic 1969)★★★, *Tammy's Touch* (Epic 1970)★★★★, *The First Lady* (Epic 1970)★★★★, *Christmas With Tammy Wynette* (Epic 1970)★★, *We Sure Can Love Each Other* (Epic 1971)★★★★, with George Jones *We Go Together* (Epic 1971)★★★★, *Bedtime Story* (Epic 1972)★★★, with Jones *Me And The First Lady* (Epic 1972)★★★★, *My Man* (Epic 1972)★★★, with Jones *We Love To Sing About Jesus* (Epic 1972)★★, *Kids Say The Darndest Things* (Epic 1973)★★★★, with Jones *Let's Build A World Together* (Epic 1973)★★★, with Jones *We're Gonna Hold On* (Epic 1973)★★★★, *Another Lonely Song* (Epic 1974)★★★, *Woman To Woman* (Epic 1974)★★, *George, Tammy And Tina* (Epic 1975)★★, *I Still Believe In Fairy Tales* (Epic 1975)★★, *Til I Can Make It On My Own* (Epic 1976)★★★, with Jones *Golden Ring* (Epic 1976)★★★★, *You And Me* (Epic 1976)★★★★, *Let's Get Together* (Epic 1977)★★, *One Of A Kind* (Epic 1977)★★★, *Womanhood* (Epic 1978)★★★, *Just Tammy* (Epic 1979)★★, *Only Lonely Sometimes* (Epic 1980)★★, with Jones *Together Again* (Epic 1980)★★★, *You Brought Me Back* (Epic 1981)★★★, *Good Love And Heartbreak* (Epic 1982)★★★, *Soft Touch* (Epic 1982)★★★, *Even The Strong Get Lonely* (Epic 1983)★★★, *Sometimes When We Touch* (Epic 1985)★★★, *Higher Ground* (Epic 1987)★★★, *Next To You* (Epic 1989)★★, *Heart Over Mind* (Epic 1990)★★★, with Dolly Parton, Loretta Lynn *Honky Tonk Angels* (Columbia 1993)★★★, *Without Walls* (Epic 1994)★★★, with Jones *One* (MCA 1995)★★★.

● COMPILATIONS: *Tammy's Greatest Hits* (Epic 1969)★★★★, *The World Of Tammy Wynette* (Epic 1970)★★★, *Tammy's Greatest Hits, Volume II* (Epic 1971)★★★★, *Tammy's Greatest Hits, Volume III* (Epic 1975)★★★, with Jones *Greatest Hits* (Epic 1977)★★★★, *Tammy's Greatest Hits, Volume IV* (Epic 1978)★★★, with Jones *Encore: George Jones & Tammy Wynette* (Epic 1981)★★★★, *Classic Collection* (Epic 1982)★★★, *Biggest Hits* (Epic 1983)★★★★, with Jones *Super Hits* (Epic 1987)★★★, *Anniversary: 20 Years Of Hits* (Epic 1988)★★★★, *Tears Of Fire - The 25th Anniversary Collection* 3-CD set (Epic 1992)★★★★, *Encore* (1993)★★★, *Super Hits* (Epic 1996)★★★.

● VIDEOS: *Live In Nashville*, *Tammy Wynette In Concert* (Vestron Music 1987), with George Jones, *Country Stars Live* (Platinum Music 1990), *First Lady Of Country Music* (Prism Leisure 1991), *25th Anniversary Collection* (1991).

● FURTHER READING: *Stand By Your Man*, Tammy Wynette.

WYNONNA

b. Christina Ciminella, 30 May 1964, Ashland, Kentucky, USA. The mother-and-daughter duo the Judds was one of the most successful country acts of the 80s. After contracting chronic hepatitis, Naomi Judd decided to retire owing to ill health but, having announced this, they undertook a farewell world tour of 100 concerts. With her lead vocals and rhythm guitar, Wynonna had become the dominant part of the Judds and, indeed, their final album, *Love Can Build A Bridge*, is virtually Wynonna's solo debut. The Judds played their final concert in December 1991 and the following month Wynonna performed on her own at the American music awards in Los Angeles with, as it happens, her mother in the audience. Her solo album, *Wynonna*, led to three US country number 1s, 'She Is His Only Need', 'I Saw The Light' and 'No One Else On Earth' (which, with its synthesizer effects, was far removed from traditional country music). The album touched many musical bases and Wynonna's role model was Bonnie Raitt. By the mid-90s the sales had topped four million. *Tell Me Why* was an equally assured album; opening with the breezy title track, written by Karla Bonoff, there was rarely a dull moment. Songs by Jesse Winchester, Sheryl Crow and Mary-Chapin Carpenter enabled Wynonna to cross over into the AOR market. After contributing an excellent version of 'Freebird' for the *Skynyrd Friends* album, she came off the road when she became pregnant with her son Elijah. At that emotional time she also broke up with her manager and discovered the real identity of her father. She said that making *Revelations* kept her sane, and during the recording she married Nashville businessman Arch Kelley III (Elijah's father). This album and the following year's *The Other Side* provided a further indication of her move away from country, with strong rock and blues influences. Wynonna's position is now far removed from the cosy American family unit of the Reagan era, one that the Judds espoused.

● ALBUMS: *Wynonna* (Curb 1992)★★★, *Tell Me Why* (Curb 1994)★★★★, *Revelations* (Curb 1996)★★★★, *The Other Side* (Curb 1997)★★★.

● COMPILATIONS: *Collection* (Curb 1997)★★★★.

Y

YEARWOOD, TRISHA

b. 19 September 1964, Monticello, Georgia, USA. In 1985, Yearwood started working as a session singer in Nashville. She was discovered by Garth Brooks and sang backing vocals on his album *No Fences*. She was the opening act on his 1991 tour and became the first female singer to top the US country charts with her sparkling debut single, 'She's In Love With The Boy'. Further singles such as 'Like We Never Had A Broken Heart', 'That's What I Like About You', 'The Woman Before Me' and 'Wrong Side Of Memphis' quickly established her as a major new talent in contemporary country music. By 1994 she had accomplished major headlining tours, placed albums in the national charts and published her (ghosted) autobiography. Yearwood is at the vanguard of a wave of highly creative female country singers, including Suzy Bogguss, Kathy Mattea and Mary-Chapin Carpenter. Together they have breathed exciting new life into an old formula. Her mid-90s album *Thinkin' Bout You* contained irresistible light rockers such as the Berg/Randall composition 'XXX's And OOO's' (with apologies to Richard Thompson's 'I Feel So Good'). Her choice of material is one of her great strengths; her use of contemporary songwriters, and her country-tinged interpretations of their songs, is inspiring. Melissa Etheridge's 'You Can Sleep While I Drive' benefited greatly from the Yearwood treatment, as did James Taylor's 'Bartender Blues'. Married to the Mavericks' bassist Robert Reynolds in 1995, she is at present riding a peak of popularity and won the CMA award in September 1997 for best female artist.
● ALBUMS: *Trisha Yearwood* (MCA 1991)★★★, *Hearts In Armor* (MCA 1992)★★★, *The Song Remembers When* (MCA 1993)★★★★, *The Sweetest Gift* (MCA 1994)★★★, *Thinkin' Bout You* (MCA 1995)★★★★, *Everybody Knows* (MCA 1996)★★★.
● COMPILATIONS: *Songbook: A Collection Of Hits* (MCA 1997)★★★★.
● FURTHER READING: *Get Hot Or Go Home: The Making Of A Nashville Star*, Lisa Rebecca Gubernick.

YOAKAM, DWIGHT

b. 23 October 1956, Pikeville, Kentucky, USA. Yoakam, the eldest of three children, moved with his family to Columbus, Ohio, when he was two. A singer-songwriter with an early love of the honky-tonk country music of Buck Owens and Lefty Frizzell, he has always shown a distinct antipathy towards the Nashville pop/country scene. After an abortive spell studying philosophy and history at Ohio State University, he briefly sought Nashville success in the mid-70s, but his music was rated too country even for the *Grand Ole Opry*. He relocated to Los Angeles in 1978 and worked the clubs, playing with various bands including Los Lobos,

but for several years he worked as a truck driver. In 1984, the release of a self-financed mini-album on the Enigma label led to him signing for Warner/Reprise Records. Two years later, following the release of his excellent debut *Guitars Cadillacs Etc*, he registered Top 5 US country chart hits with Johnny Horton's 'Honky Tonk Man' and his own 'Guitars, Cadillacs'. His driving honky-tonk music made him a popular visitor to Britain and brought him some success in the USA, but his outspoken views denied him wider fame. In 1987 he had success with his version of the old Elvis Presley pop hit 'Little Sister'. He followed it in 1988 with a US country number 9 hit with his idol Lefty Frizzell's classic 'Always Late (With Your Kisses)', and a number 1 with his self-penned 'I Sang Dixie'. He would also make the top of the country charts with 'The Streets Of Bakersfield', duetting with veteran 60s superstar Buck Owens. Yoakam played several concerts with Owens, after being instrumental in persuading him to come out of retirement and record again for Capitol Records. Like Don Williams and others, he retains the traditional stetson hat. There seems little doubt that Yoakam's songwriting talents and singing style will ensure further major success and much of his hip honky-tonk music has paved the way for rock audiences accepting country music of the 90s, much in the way that Garth Brooks has done. His straight country style is his most effective work, even though he attempted to cross over into the mainstream rock market with *La Croix D'Amour*. Although by nature shy of publicity, he earned notoriety by the bucket-load when he arrived at the 1992 Academy Awards with Sharon Stone on his arm. She went public on the affair when their relationship ended, although Yoakam maintained a dignified silence. He has also recently turned his hand to acting, appearing in a Los Angeles stage production, *Southern Rapture*, directed by Peter Fonda. He came back in 1993 with the hardcore country of *This Time*. The album included the number 1 country hit 'Ain't That Lonely Yet', which won a Grammy award for Best Country Vocal Performance, while 'A Thousand Miles From Nowhere' was accompanied by an excellent video. *Dwight Live*, recorded at San Francisco's Warfield Theatre, captured the fervour of his concert performances. He wrote all the tracks on *Gone* and to quote *Rolling Stone*, 'Neither safe nor tame, Yoakam has adopted Elvis' devastating hip swagger, Hank Williams' crazy-ass stare and Merle Haggard's brooding solitude into one lethal package. Yoakam is a cowgirl's secret darkest dream.' After more than a decade of commercial success, Yoakam has established beyond all doubts his staying power as one of the leading artists of the new era of country music.
● ALBUMS: *Guitars, Cadillacs, Etc., Etc.* (Reprise 1986)★★★★, *Hillbilly DeLuxe* (Reprise 1987)★★★★, *Buenas Noches From A Lonely Room* (Reprise 1988)★★★★, *If There Was A Way* (Reprise 1990)★★★★, *La Croix D'Amour* (Reprise 1992)★★★, *This Time* (Reprise 1993)★★★★, *Dwight Live* (Reprise 1995)★★, *Gone* (Reprise 1995)★★★★, *Under The Covers* (Reprise 1997)★★, *Come On Christmas* (Reprise 1997)★★.
● COMPILATIONS: *Just Lookin' For A Hit* (Reprise 1989)★★★★.
● VIDEOS: *Dwight Yoakam, Just Lookin' For A Hit* (1989), *Fast As You* (1993), *Pieces Of Time* (1994), *Live On Stage* (Magnum Video 1997).

YORK BROTHERS

A popular harmony duo comprising George York (b. 17 February 1910, Louisa, Lawrence County, Kentucky, USA, d. July 1974; guitar, harmonica, vocals) and Leslie York (b. 23 August 1917, Louisa, Lawrence County, Kentucky, USA, d. 21 February 1984; guitar, vocals). George first worked in the coalmines before moving to Denver, where he played on local radio. In the late 30s, somewhat influenced by the Delmores, the brothers began their career in Portsmouth, Ohio, and made their first recordings for the Universal label in 1939. Their version of 'Little White Washed Chimney' (recorded as 'Going Home') sold well enough to gain them a contract with Decca Records. After recording for that label in 1941, and at a time when their popularity was spreading nationally, America's involvement in World War II saw both brothers drafted for service with the US Navy. After their discharge, they settled in Nashville where, until 1950, they played the *Grand Ole Opry*. They then relocated to Detroit until 1953, when they moved to Dallas, becoming regulars on the *Big D Jamboree* and the *Saturday Night Shindig*. Between 1947 and 1956, they recorded for King, and later for their own label. In the latter half of their career, their music changed from the old-time style of the usual brother harmony acts to anticipate the popular mix of nostalgia and sentimental ballads later popularized by such artists as Red Foley, even introducing a piano to add a honky tonk effect on some numbers. Leslie sang solo on some of their later recordings, due to the fact that George at times suffered throat problems. They eventually retired from the music but remained in Dallas where George owned a nightclub.
● ALBUMS: *The York Brothers Volume 1* (King 1958)★★★, *The York Brothers Volume 2* (King 1958)★★★, *16 Great Country Songs* (King 1963)★★★★.
● COMPILATIONS: *Early Favorites* (Old Homestead 1987)★★★

YOUNG, FARON

b. 25 February 1932, Shreveport, Louisiana, USA, d. 10 December 1996, Nashville, Tennessee. Young was raised on the farm his father bought just outside Shreveport and learned to play the guitar and sing country songs as a boy. Greatly influenced by Hank Williams (in his early days he was something of a soundalike) and while still at school, he formed a country band and began to establish a local reputation as an entertainer. In 1950, he gave up his college studies to accept an offer of a professional career and joined radio station KWKH, where he soon became a member of the prestigious *Louisiana Hayride* show and found other work in the nightclubs and honky tonks. He became friends with Webb Pierce and for a time toured with him as a vocalist with Pierce's band. In 1951, he made his first recordings for the Gotham label with Tillman Franks and his band, and achieved minor success with 'Have I Waited Too Long' and 'Tattle Tale Eyes' before he joined Capitol Records. In the summer of 1952, Faron was dating a girl called Billie Jean Jones, when she attracted the attention of Hank Williams. He persuaded Faron to arrange a double date, which resulted in Williams threatening him with a pistol and claiming Jones for his own. Young backed off and Billie Jean became the second Mrs. Hank Williams. In 1953, Young formed his own band, moved to Nashville, where he became a member of the *Grand Ole Opry* and gained his first US

country chart hit with a self-penned song called 'Goin' Steady'. His career was interrupted when, because of the Korean War, he was drafted into the army. Although interrupted by this, his career certainly benefited from the exposure he received after winning an army talent competition. This led to him touring the world entertaining US forces, as well as appearing on recruiting shows that were networked to hundreds of radio stations. Young returned to Nashville in November 1954 and resumed his career, gaining his first US country number 1 the following year with 'Live Fast, Love Hard, Die Young'.This established him beyond any doubt as a major recording star, and between 1955 and 1969 he amassed a total of 63 US country chart hits of which 46 made the Top 20. He developed the knack of picking the best material by other writers and had a number 2 hit with Don Gibson's 'Sweet Dreams' and further number 1s with Roy Drusky's songs 'Alone With You' and 'Country Girl'. In 1961, he recorded 'Hello Walls', thereby making the song one of the first Willie Nelson compositions to be recorded by a major artist. It reached number 1 in the US country charts, also became a Top 20 US pop hit and was Young's first million-seller.

In 1956, his popularity as a singer earned him a role in the film *Hidden Guns*. This led to his own nickname of The Young Sheriff and his band being called the Country Deputies (at one time Roger Miller was a member of the band). In later years he became the Singing Sheriff before, as he once suggested, someone queried his age and started asking 'What's he trying to prove?' After the initial success with this easily forgettable B-movie western, he made further film appearances over the years including *Daniel Boone, Stampede, Raiders Of Old California, Country Music Holiday, A Gun And A Gavel, Road To Nashville* and *That's Country*. He left Capitol for Mercury in 1962, immediately charting with 'The Yellow Bandanna', 'You'll Drive Me Back' and a fine duet recording with Margie Singleton of 'Keeping Up With The Joneses'. In 1965, he had a US country Top 10 hit with 'Walk Tall', a song that had been a UK pop hit for Val Doonican the previous year. Young quit the *Opry* in the mid-60s, finding, like several other artists, that it was not only difficult keeping up the expected number of Saturday night appearances but also that he lost many other lucrative bookings. After the success of 'Hello Walls', he perhaps unintentionally tended to look for further pop chart hits, and in consequence his recordings, at times, became less country in their arrangements. He soon returned to his country roots, usually choosing his favourite twin fiddle backings. Young easily maintained his popularity throughout the 60s and 70s and toured extensively in the USA and made several visits to Europe, where he performed in the UK, France and Germany. He appeared on all the major network television shows but seemed to have little interest in having his own regular series. At times he has not endeared himself to some of his fellow performers with his imitations of their acts. In the 70s he was still a major star with a series of Top 10 US country hits, including 'Step Aside', 'Leavin' And Saying Goodbye', 'This Little Girl Of Mine' and 'Just What I Had In Mind'. 'It's Four In The Morning', another country number 1, had crossover success and also gave him a second million-seller. It also became his only UK pop chart success, peaking at number 3 during a 23-week chart run. He left Mercury Records in 1979 and briefly joined MCA. In 1988, he joined

Step One Records and 'Stop And Take The Time', a minor hit, became country chart entry number 85. Over the years, he became involved in several business interests and, with the exception of heavy losses in the 60s (in respect of investments to convert an old baseball stadium into a stock-car racing track in Nashville), he was very successful. Young became involved in publishing companies, a recording studio, and a booking agency, plus co-ownership of *Music City News* newspaper. He was always noted for very plain speaking and has incurred the wrath of the establishment on several occasions for his outspoken views. A suggested association with Patsy Cline led to various stories of his dalliances and whether correct or not, it may well be that he revelled in the publicity they caused. In September 1972, he gained unwanted publicity by his reaction to an incident at a show. At a time when 'This Little Girl Of Mine' was a hit for him, he invited six-year-old Nora Jo Catlett to join him on stage in Clarksville, West Virginia. She refused, whereupon Young swore at the audience, stormed off stage, grabbed the child and spanked her repeatedly (the child collected autographs and had been told by her mother not to approach the stage but to wait near the front until Young finished his act). The child's father swore out a warrant for his arrest and after pleading guilty to a charge of assault, he was fined $35. The following year a civil action claiming $200,000 was filed. In his defence, Young claimed the child spat in his face. Eventually, almost two years later, the Catlett family were awarded only $3400. He has been involved in various actions, once stating, 'I am not an alcoholic, I'm a drunk', and on one occasion, he shot out the light fittings of a Nashville bar. He is reputed to have had affairs with many women while supposedly remaining happily married. In 1987, after 34 years of marriage, his wife finally obtained a divorce on the grounds of physical abuse. She claimed that he had also threatened her and their 16-year-old daughter with a gun and often shot holes in the kitchen ceiling. It may perhaps be more accurate to describe him as the singing outlaw rather than the singing sheriff! A fair and concise summary was offered in 1980 by Bob Allen, who parodied Young's hit song in his article entitled 'Live Fast, Love Hard And Keep On Cussin'. Faron Young is one of country music's greatest legends, while remaining relatively unknown to many. Paddy MacAloon of Prefab Sprout paid tribute to him when he wrote the beautiful 'Faron Young' on the group's *Steve McQueen* album. Until his death in 1996 he was semi-retired but still made concert performances as well as guest appearances on the *Opry*.

● ALBUMS: *Sweethearts Or Strangers* (Capitol 1957)★★★, *The Object Of My Affection* (Capitol 1958)★★★, *My Garden Of Prayer* (Capitol 1959)★★, *This Is Faron Young* (Capitol 1959)★★★★, *Talk About Hits* (Capitol 1959)★★★, *Sings The Best Of Faron Young* (Capitol 1960)★★★, *Hello Walls* (Capitol 1961)★★★, *The Young Approach* (Capitol 1961)★★★, *This Is Faron* (Mercury 1963)★★★★, *Faron Young Aims At The West* (Mercury 1963)★★★, *Country Dance Favorites* (Mercury 1964)★★★★, *Story Songs For Country Folks* (Mercury 1964)★★★★, *Story Songs Of Mountains And Valleys* (Mercury 1964)★★★★, *Memory Lane* (Capitol 1965)★★★, *Falling In Love* (Capitol 1965)★★★, *Pen And Paper* (Mercury 1965)★★★, *Faron Young* (Hilltop 1966)★★★, *Faron Young Sings The Best Of Jim Reeves* (Mercury 1966)★★★, *If You Ain' t Lovin', You Ain't Livin'* (Capitol 1966)★★★, *It's A Great Life* (Tower 1966)★★★, *Unmitigated Gall* (Mercury 1967)★★★, *Here's Faron Young* (Mercury 1968)★★★, *I'll Be Yours* (Hilltop 1968)★★★★, *This Is Faron Young* (Mercury 1968)★★★, *Just Out Of Reach* (Mercury 1968)★★★, *The World Of Faron Young* (Mercury 1968)★★★★, *I've Got Precious Memories* (Mercury 1969)★★★, *Wine Me Up* (Mercury 1969)★★★★, *20 Hits Over The Years* (Mercury 1969)★★★★, *Occasional Wife/If I Ever Fall In Love With A Honky Tonk Girl* (Mercury 1970)★★★, *Leavin' And Sayin' Goodbye* (Mercury 1971)★★★, *Step Aside* (Mercury 1971)★★★, *It's Four In The Morning* (Mercury 1972)★★★, *This Little Girl Of Mine* (Mercury 1972)★★★, *This Time The Hurtin's On Me* (Mercury 1973)★★★, *Just What I Had In Mind* (Mercury 1973)★★★, *Some Kind Of Woman* (Mercury 1974)★★★, *A Man And His Music* (Mercury 1975)★★★★, *I'd Just Be Fool Enough* (Mercury 1976)★★★, *That Young Feelin'* (Mercury 1977)★★★, *Chapter Two* (1979)★★★, *Free And Easy* (MCA 1980)★★★, *The Young Sheriff (1955-1956 Radio Broadcasts)* (1981)★★★★, *The Sheriff* (Allegiance 1984)★★, with Jerry Lee Lewis, Webb Pierce, Mel Tillis *Four Legends* (1985)★★★, *Here's To You* (Step One 1988)★★★, *Country Christmas* (1990)★★, with Ray Price *Memories That Last* (1992)★★★.

● COMPILATIONS: *All-Time Great Hits* (Capitol 1963)★★★★, *Capitol Country Classics* (Capitol 1980)★★★, *Greatest Hits Volumes 1, 2 & 3* (1988)★★★★, *All Time Greatest Hits* (Curb 1990)★★★, *The Capitol Years 1952 - 1962* 5-CD set (Bear Family 1992)★★★★, *Live Fast, Love Hard: Original Capitol Recordings, 1952-1962* (CMF 1995)★★★★, *All American Country* (Spectrum 1997)★★★★.

YOUNG, STEVE

b. 12 July 1942, Noonan, Georgia, USA. Young has claimed to be the reincarnation of a cavalry officer in the American Civil War, and has written songs about reincarnation, including 'In The Ways Of The Indian'. He was raised in Alabama and his superb 'Montgomery In The Rain' is about congregating around Hank Williams' grave. Young played folk music in New York and various southern towns before moving to Los Angeles. In 1968 he recorded as part of the group Stone Country for RCA. Then in 1969, he made his first album, *Rock, Salt And Nails*, for A&M Records, with sessionmen including James Burton, Gene Clark and Gram Parsons. It included a song written while he was homesick, the pastoral and mystical 'Seven Bridges Road', which has been recorded by Rita Coolidge and Joan Baez and, with commercial success, by the Eagles. Young's albums often repeat songs but sometimes for good reason: 'I originally did "Lonesome, On'ry And Mean" as a bluesy bluegrass song in 3/4, but Waylon Jennings turned it into a rocker in 4/4. I got intrigued by that and so I did it that way too.' He dedicated the autobiographical 'Renegade Picker' to Jerry Lee Lewis because 'he refuses to play it safe'. *No Place To Fall* was delayed because RCA were too busy pressing Elvis Presley albums following his death and Young's career lost momentum. He also had to combat drug and alcohol addiction: 'Every waking moment I was drinking and I just didn't care. I don't do drink or drugs anymore, but I am into Zen meditation, which certainly helps my creativity.' Although Young is better known as a songwriter, his only US country success is with Willie Nelson's 'It's Not Supposed To Be That

Way'. He has made several engaging UK appearances, often in country clubs and with a sense of humour that belies his grim material: 'I don't think of myself as a country singer or a folk singer. What I do comes from Southern roots, American roots, and I just let it go where it goes.' *Solo, Live*, recorded at Houston's Anderson Fair in 1990, is an effective career overview.

● ALBUMS: *Rock, Salt And Nails* (A&M 1969)★★★, *Seven Bridges Road* (Blue Canyon 1972)★★★, *Honky Tonk Man* (Rounder 1975)★★★★, *Renegade Picker* (RCA 1976)★★★★, *No Place To Fall* (RCA 1977)★★★, *To Satisfy You* (Rounder 1981)★★★, *Look Homeward Angel* (Mill 1986)★★★, *Long Time Rider* (Voodoo 1990)★★★, *Solo, Live* (Watermelon 1991)★★★★, *Switchblades Of Love* (Watermelon 1993)★★★.

INDEX